Learning and Memory

From Brain to Behavior

THIRD EDITION

Mark A. Gluck

Rutgers University–Newark

Eduardo Mercado

University at Buffalo, The State University of New York

Catherine E. Myers

Department of Veterans Affairs, VA New Jersey Health Care System,
and Rutgers University–New Jersey Medical School

worth publishers
Macmillan Learning

New York

Publisher, Psychology and Sociology: Rachel Losh
Senior Acquisitions Editor: Daniel DeBonis
Development Editor: Moira Lerner Nelson
Assistant Editor: Katie Pachnos
Executive Marketing Manager: Katherine Nurre
Executive Media Editor: Rachel Comerford
Assistant Media Editor: Nicole Padinha
Director, Content Management Enhancement: Tracey Kuehn
Managing Editor, Sciences and Social Sciences: Lisa Kinne
Project Editor: Kayci Wyatt
Media Producer: Elizabeth Dougherty
Senior Photo Editor: Christine Buese
Photo Researcher: Jacqui Wong
Senior Production Supervisor: Paul Rohloff
Director of Design, Content Management: Diana Blume
Design Manager: Vicki Tomaselli
Cover and Interior Design: Kevin Kall
Art Manager: Matthew McAdams
Illustrations: Todd Buck, Eli Ensor, Matthew Holt, Christy Krames, and Hans Neuhart
Composition: MPS North America LLC
Printing and Binding: RR Donnelley
Cover Photo: *Man Ray Contemplating the Bust of Man Ray*, 1978
                    William Wegman
                    Silver Gelatin Print
                    8×8 Inches

Library of Congress Control Number: 2015960602

ISBN-13: 978-1-4641-0593-7
ISBN-10: 1-4641-0593-6

Printed in the United States of America

First printing

The views expressed in this book are those of the authors and do not necessarily reflect those of the Federal Government, or any other institution with which the authors are affiliated.

Worth Publishers
One New York Plaza, Suite 4500
New York, New York 10004-1562
www.macmillanlearning.com

To my nifty nieces, Mandy (19) and Kamila (16):
Over the course of three editions you have grown—both in real life
and as the fictional characters herein—from darling little girls
to delightful young ladies.

M. A. G.

To my son, Iam.

E. M. III

To the memory of dear friends lost to cancer this year,
and in honor of the brave friends who continue their battles.
You teach me the true meaning of courage and commitment.

C. E. M.

ABOUT THE AUTHORS

Mark A. Gluck is a Professor of Neuroscience at Rutgers University–Newark, Director of the Memory Disorders Project at Rutgers University, and Co-Director of the African-American Brain Health Initiative. His research focuses on the cognitive, computational, and neural bases of learning and memory, and the consequences of memory loss due to aging, trauma, and disease. He is co-author of *Gateway to Memory: An Introduction to Neural Network Modeling of the Hippocampus and Learning* (MIT Press, 2001) and co-editor of three other books. In 1996, he was awarded an NSF Presidential Early Career Award for Scientists and Engineers by President Bill Clinton. That same year, he received the American Psychological Association (APA) Distinguish Scientific Award for Early Career Contribution to Psychology. More on his research and career at www.gluck.edu.

Eduardo Mercado is a Professor of Psychology and of Ecology, Evolution, and Behavior at the University at Buffalo, The State University of New York. His research focuses on how different brain systems interact to develop representations of experienced events, and how these representations can be changed over time through training, especially as these processes relate to neural and cognitive plasticity. He is a Fellow of the Center for Advanced Studies in the Behavioral Sciences at Stanford, and an investigator in the multi-institutional Temporal Dynamics of Learning Center.

Catherine E. Myers is a Research Scientist with the Department of Veterans Affairs, New Jersey Health Care System, and a Professor in the Department of Pharmacology, Physiology, and Neuroscience at the New Jersey Medical School, Rutgers University. Her research includes both computational neuroscience and experimental psychology, and focuses on human learning and memory, especially in clinical disorders such as amnesia and post-traumatic stress disorder (PTSD). She is co-author of *Gateway to Memory: An Introduction to Neural Network Modeling of the Hippocampus and Learning* (MIT Press, 2001) and author of *Delay Learning in Artificial Neural Networks* (Chapman and Hall, 1992).

BRIEF CONTENTS

CONTENTS

PREFACE

This is the third edition of *Learning and Memory: From Brain to Behavior*, following the success of our first two editions published in 2008 and 2014. The new edition continues our approach of presenting a comprehensive, accessible, and engaging introduction to the scientific study of learning and memory. The modular table of contents unique to this textbook allows the course to be taught in any of at least four different ways: (1) Learning first, then Memory; (2) Memory first, then Learning; (3) Memory only; or (4) Learning only. As described in greater detail below, the chapters are grouped into four modules: an Introductory Module, a Learning Module, a Memory Module, and an Integrative Topics Module. Adding to the convenience of this organizational scheme, the topics within all the core chapters are grouped into the same three major subsections: Behavioral Processes, Brain Substrates, and Clinical Perspectives. This innovative organization has been acclaimed by users of the second edition. It provides a highly flexible curriculum suited to the many different ways that teachers prefer to teach this material.

Notable changes in our new edition include:

- *Increased use of real-world examples*, concrete applications, and clinically relevant perspectives.

- *Expansion of integrated and end-of-chapter pedagogy* to help students assess their own progress and understanding. By integrating pedagogy into the body of each chapter, we provide students with immediate practice and feedback, help them organize and prioritize information, and generally assist them in using the book more effectively. A new end-of-chapter quiz tests recall of key information after reading of the chapter is completed.

- *Stronger and more extensive teacher support* through supplemental materials and a complete, ready-to-use package of PowerPoint slides for each section of each chapter.

- *Even more integration of topics across chapters*, highlighting connections between themes and concepts that arise repeatedly in different parts of the book.

In addition to the flexible modular structure and solid pedagogy, *Learning and Memory: From Brain to Behavior*, Third Edition, is notable among textbooks in its field for its strong neuroscience focus, integrative coverage of animal learning and human memory, engaging writing style, extensive four-color art program, and emphasis on showing students how basic research has direct implications for everyday life and clinical practice.

Flexible Modular Table of Contents

There are at least four different ways in which teachers can choose to teach this material:

1. **Learning only.** Focusing on animal conditioning and behaviorist approaches; teachers may or may not include neuroscience perspectives.

2. **Memory only.** Focusing primarily on human memory and cognition; teachers include varying degrees of cognitive neuroscience perspectives.

3. **Learning, then memory.** Starting with basic learning phenomena such as habituation, sensitization, and associative conditioning—phenomena most extensively studied in animals—and progressing to the more complex facets of human memory. Neuroscience coverage, when included, begins with the most elemental building blocks of neurons and circuits and works up to the larger anatomical perspectives required by the human memory studies.

4. **Memory, then learning.** Here, teachers start with the most engaging and familiar material on human memory, including its many failings and idiosyncrasies, topics that students usually find especially relevant and appealing. As the course progresses, teachers present material on how human memory is built up from basic processes that can be studied in greater precision in animal models. Neuroscience coverage begins with the most accessible and easily understood big-picture view of anatomical regions and their functional relevance and then works toward presenting the greater detail and neuronal focus of studies that can be done invasively in animal preparations, especially studies of conditioning and other forms of associative learning.

Does the field really need four different types of textbooks to support the diversity of approaches to teaching this material? In the past, the answer was, unfortunately, "yes": every textbook followed one of these approaches, and instructors had to find the book whose orientation, organization, and coverage best matched their own plans for the course. However, with *Learning and Memory: From Brain to Behavior*, Third Edition, there is now available a single textbook that is sufficiently modular in its overall structure and in the execution of individual chapters to accommodate all four approaches to teaching this material.

How can one textbook suit every teaching approach?

To accomplish this feat, we have divided the book into four multichapter modules:

- The **Introductory Module** is the natural starting point for all courses; teachers can assign either or both of two introductory chapters, one a conceptual and historical overview of the study of psychology and behavior, the other an introduction to the neuroscience of learning and memory.

- The heart of the book consists of two "parallel" modules, the **Learning Module** and the **Memory Module**. These can be covered singly (for those teachers who wish to teach only learning or only memory) or in either order, allowing for a learning-then-memory syllabus or a memory-then-learning syllabus. Each of these modules is a self-contained collection of chapters, neither of which assumes that the student has read the other module. The Learning Module has four chapters, covering basic exposure-driven learning mechanisms; classical conditioning; operant conditioning; and, finally, generalization, discrimination, and similarity. The Memory Module has three chapters, covering episodic and semantic memory, skill memory, and working memory and cognitive control.

- The final module of the book, the **Integrative Topics Module**, consists of three optional stand-alone chapters (so that any subset of the three can be assigned), covering emotional learning and memory, social learning and memory, and lifespan changes in learning and memory, from prenatal development to old age.

Given the book's flexible, modifiable, and modular structure, we believe we have written the first textbook for every instructor in the fields of learning and/or memory, reflecting and respecting the heterogeneity and diversity of the many different approaches to teaching this material.

Can this book be used for a Principles of Learning and Behavior course?

Indeed it can. Although more and more colleges are offering courses that integrate animal learning and human memory and include ever-increasing amounts of neuroscience, there are still a large number of teachers who prefer to focus primarily on animal learning and conditioning, along with modest coverage of related studies of human associative learning, all presented primarily from a behavioral perspective.

For such a course, we recommend starting with Chapter 1, "The Psychology of Learning and Memory," then covering the four chapters of the Learning Module (Chapters 3 through 6), and concluding with Chapter 10, "Emotional Influences on Learning and Memory," which examines key topics in fear conditioning. Together these six chapters present a lucid, compelling, accessible, and engaging introduction to the principles of learning and behavior. We recognize, of course, that six chapters cannot provide as much detailed coverage as a single-approach textbook with 12 or more chapters on these topics. For this reason, we have included extensive additional materials on learning and behavior in the teacher's supplemental materials for the Learning Module chapters. These materials provide the additional flexibility and content to support spending two weeks, rather than one week, on each of the four Learning Module chapters. This combination of textbook and supplemental materials serves well the teacher who wishes to spend 10 or more weeks on principles of learning and behavior with a primary focus on animal learning and conditioning.

Specialized learning and behavior textbooks are often dry and unappealing to most students. By adopting our book, instructors who prefer the learning and behavior approach will be providing their students with a text that has a uniquely engaging writing style, helpful integrated pedagogy, extensive four-color art, and a strong focus on showing students how basic research has direct implications for everyday life and clinical practice.

Neuroscience Focus

Neuroscience has altered the landscape for behavioral research, shifting priorities and changing our ideas about the brain mechanisms of behavior. *Learning and Memory: From Brain to Behavior* integrates neuroscience research into each chapter, emphasizing how new findings from neuroscience have allowed psychologists to consider the functional and physiological mechanisms that underlie the behavioral processes of learning and memory. Chapter 2, "The Neuroscience of Learning and Memory," offers an accessible introduction to neuroscience for students unfamiliar with the basics of brain structure and function. Thereafter, the "Brain Substrates" section of each of the book's core chapters (3 through 12) presents the neuroscience perspectives relevant to the chapter topic, to be assigned or not as the teacher wishes (omitted by those teachers who prefer to present only a behavioral perspective).

Integrated Presentation of Learning and Memory Research across Species

The field of learning and memory has undergone enormous changes over the last decade, primarily as a result of new developments in neuroscience. As we have gained a greater understanding of the neurobiological bases of behavior, the strict conceptual boundary between the biological approach and the psychological approach to the study of learning and memory has begun to disappear. Moreover, after several decades during which learning by humans was studied and described in one field of science and learning by animals was studied in another, the discovery of basic biological mechanisms common to all species has launched a unified approach to behavioral studies. Although our book takes a modular approach to teaching this course, distinguishing the chapters that focus primarily on learning from those that focus primarily on memory, the story that emerges from covering both sets of chapters is, we believe, the strongest and most up-to-date representation of the field as a whole.

Clinical Perspectives

In addition to examining and explaining new research in learning and memory, *Learning and Memory: From Brain to Behavior*, Third Edition, traces how these findings have spurred the development of new diagnoses and treatments for a variety of neurological and psychiatric disorders. Recent advances in neuroscience have produced dramatic changes in clinical practices over the last decade, greatly affecting how neurologists, psychiatrists, clinical psychologists, nurses, and rehabilitation specialists diagnose and treat the clinical disorders of learning and memory. Alzheimer's disease, autism, schizophrenia, Parkinson's disease, dyslexia, anxiety disorders, ADHD, and stroke are just a few of the disorders for which new treatment options have been developed as a result of basic behavioral and cognitive neuroscience studies of learning and memory. To reflect this broader impact of the field of learning and memory, each of the core chapters (Chapters 3 through 12) includes a "Clinical Perspectives" section that shows how knowledge of behavioral processes and brain substrates is being applied to understand clinical disorders that lead to disruptions of learning and memory. These sections are one way in which the book emphasizes the influence of learning and memory research in the real world and shows how neuropsychological research informs our understanding of memory mechanisms.

Student Friendliness

- **No Prerequisites.** We understand that students may come to this course from different backgrounds, even different disciplines, so we do not assume any previous level of familiarity with basic psychology or neuroscience concepts. The first two chapters of the text offer a complete overview of the field of the psychology of learning and memory and the neuroscience foundations of behavior. Later chapters explain all new concepts clearly with emphasis on real-life examples and teaching-oriented illustrations.

- **Engaging Narrative.** Our aim has been to create a lively, clear, and example-rich narrative, a colorful conversation between authors and readers that communicates our vision of an exciting field in transition and captures the interest of students by igniting their curiosity.

- **Full-Color Art Program.** The full-color art program consists of original anatomical art, state-of-the-art brain scans, and color-coded figures to help students visualize the processes involved in learning and memory. Photos offer a link to the real world, as well as a look back in time; cartoons provide occasional comical commentary (and often additional insights) alongside the main narrative.

- **Real-World Implications.** *Learning and Memory: From Brain to Behavior* is noted for a strong focus on applications and on the relevance of learning and memory concepts to everyday life. In addition to the "Clinical Perspectives" section at the end of every core chapter, we have included throughout each chapter many concrete, real-world examples of learning and memory that help students grasp the implications of what they are studying and its relevance in their own lives.

- **Consistent Organization.** The integration of both neuroscience and relevant clinical issues throughout the text is made more accessible to the student by the book's consistent tripartite division of each chapter into the sections "Behavioral Processes," "Brain Substrates," and "Clinical Perspectives." As described above, this also allows teachers to selectively omit the discussions of brain substrates or clinical perspectives from some or all of the reading assignments if that better suits a teacher's syllabus. In addition, each chapter ends with a "Synthesis" discussion that recaps and integrates selected key issues in the chapter.

Extensive Pedagogy

- **Test Your Knowledge** exercises introduced at intervals throughout each chapter give students the opportunity to check their comprehension and retention of more challenging topics immediately after having read about them. Suggested answers are provided.

- **Learning and Memory in Everyday Life** boxes in each chapter illustrate the practical implications of research, especially those that are relevant and interesting to undergraduate students.

- **Interim Summaries** follow each chapter subsection to help students review major concepts presented in the pages they have just finished reading.

- **Quiz Yourself** fill-in-the blank exercises at the end of each chapter test recall of key topics and concepts. Page numbers where the information was presented are provided with each exercise, and answers are given at the end of the book.

- **Concept Checks** at the end of each chapter ask critical-thinking questions that require an understanding and synthesis of the key material in the chapter. These exercises ask students to apply the knowledge they've gained to a real-life situation. Suggested answers are provided at the end of the book.

- **Key Terms** are defined in the text margins for emphasis and easy reference and then are listed at the end of each chapter, with page numbers, to help students review chapter terminology. All key terms with their definitions are also included in an end-of-text glossary.

Media and Supplements

All of the supplementary materials can be downloaded from the Macmillan Learning catalog site at www.macmillanlearning.com.

Book-Specific Lecture and Art PowerPoint Slides

To ease your transition to *Learning and Memory*, a prepared set of lecture and art slides, in easy-to-adopt PowerPoint format, is available to download from the catalog site. The book-specific PowerPoint Lecture Slides include a variety of in-class activities and are authored by Robert Calin-Jageman of Dominican University and Chrysalis Wright of the University of Central Florida.

Instructor's Resource Manual

The Instructor's Resource Manual, authored by Chrysalis Wright of the University of Central Florida, includes extensive chapter-by-chapter suggestions for in-class presentations, projects, and assignments, as well as tips for integrating multimedia into your course. It also provides more comprehensive material on animal learning for instructors who allocate more of their courses to the classic studies of animal learning.

Diploma Computerized Test Bank

The Test Bank, written by Anjolii Diaz of Ball State University, features approximately 100 questions per chapter as well as an assortment of short-answer and essay questions. The Diploma software allows instructors to add an unlimited number of questions, edit questions, format a test, scramble questions, and include pictures, equations, or multimedia links. With the accompanying Gradebook, instructors can record students' grades throughout a course, sort student records and view detailed analyses of test items, curve tests, generate reports, add weights to grades, and more.

Course Management Aids

As a service for adopters who use course management systems, the various resources for this textbook are available in the appropriate format to be downloaded into their campus CMS. The files can be customized to fit specific course needs or they can be used as is. Course outlines, pre-built quizzes, links, and activities are included, eliminating hours of work for instructors.

Acknowledgments, to Our Colleagues

This book has benefited from the wisdom of expert reviewers and instructors from laboratories and classrooms around the country. From the earliest stages of the development process, we solicited feedback and advice from the leading voices in the field of learning and memory to ensure that the book expresses the most current and accurate understanding of the topics in each chapter. Over the course of the book's development, we have relied on these experts' criticism, corrections, encouragement, and thoughtful contributions. We thank them for lending us their insight, giving us their time, and above all for sharing in our commitment to creating a new textbook and a new curriculum that reflect a contemporary perspective on the field.

Michael Todd Allen
University of Northern Colorado

John Anderson
Carnegie Mellon University

Hal Arkes
Ohio State University

Larissa Arnold
Iowa State University

Amy Arnsten
Yale University

Ed Awh
University of Oregon

Padmini Banerjee
Delaware State University

Deanna Barch
Washington University, St. Louis

Carol Barnes
University of Arizona

Mark Basham
Metropolitan State College of Denver

Mark Baxter
Oxford University

Kevin Beck
VA New Jersey Health Care System and New Jersey Medical School

Matthew Bell
Santa Clara University

April Benasich
Rutgers University–Newark

Anjan Bhattacharyya
New Jersey City University

Evelyn Blanch-Payne
Georgia Gwinnett College

Monica Bolton
University of Nevada, Las Vegas

Gordon Bower
Stanford University

Jennifer Breneiser
Valdosta State University

György Buzsáki
New York University

John Byrnes
University of Massachusetts

Larry Cahill
University of California, Irvine

Robert Calin-Jageman
Dominican University

Thomas Carew
University of California, Irvine

Leyre Castro Ruiz
The University of Iowa

KinHo Chan
Hartwick College

Henry Chase
Cambridge University

Arlo Clark-Foos
University of Michigan-Dearborn

Jennifer Coleman
Western New Mexico University

Roshan Cools
Cambridge University

James Corter
Columbia University

Stephen Crowley
Indiana University

Clayton Curtis
New York University

Carrie Cuttler
Washington State University

Irene Daum
Ruhr University Bochum Germany

Nathaniel Daw
New York University

Mauricio Delgado
Rutgers University–Newark

Dennis Delprato
Eastern Michigan University

Mark D'Esposito
University of California, Berkeley

David Diamond
University of South Florida

Michael Domjan
University of Texas, Austin

Howard Eichenbaum
Boston University

Michael Emond
Laurentian University

William Estes
Indiana University

Marianne Fallon
Central Connecticut State University

Robert Ferguson
Buena Vista University

Julia Fisher
Coker College

John Forgas
University of South Wales

April Fugett
Marshall University

Aubyn Fulton
Pacific Union College

Joaquin Fuster
*University of California,
Los Angeles*

Sherry Ginn
Wingate University

Robert Goldstone
Indiana University

John Green
University of Vermont

Robert Greene
Case Western Reserve University

Pauline Guerin
*Pennsylvania State University,
Brandywine*

Martin Guthrie
Bordeaux University

Lisa Haber-Chalom
Rutgers University–Newark

Karl Haberlandt
Trinity College

Frank Hammonds
Troy University

Stephen Hanson
Rutgers University–Newark

Kent Harber
Rutgers University–Newark

Michael Hasselmo
Boston University

Robert Hawkins
Columbia University

Mohammad Herzallah
Rutgers University—Newark

Kathleen Hipp
Daniel Webster University

Kurt Hoffman
Virginia Tech University

Donald Homa
Arizona State University

Merritt Hoover
University of California—Santa Cruz

Ramona Hopkins
Brigham Young University

Steven Horowitz
Central Connecticut State University

James Hunsicker
*Southwestern Oklahoma State
University*

Dharmananda Jairam
*Pennsylvania State University Erie,
The Behrend College*

Sterling Johnson
University of Wisconsin

Stephen Joy
Albertus Magnus College

Jennifer Joy-Gaba
Virginia Commonwealth University

Lee Jussim
Rutgers University–New Brunswick

Daniel Kahneman
Princeton University

Narinder Kapur
London Memory Clinic

E. James Kehoe
University of South Wales

Szabolcs Kéri
University of Szeged, Hungary

Alan Kersten
Florida Atlantic University

Kristopher Kimbler
Florida Gulf Coast University

Brock Kirwan
Brigham Young University

Alan Kluger
Lehman College, CUNY

Stephen Kosslyn
Harvard University

John Kruschke
Indiana University

Joseph LeDoux
New York University

Dorothea Lerman
University of Houston-Clear Lake

Derick Lindquist
Ohio State University

Elizabeth Loftus
University of California, Irvine

Robert Lubow
Tel-Aviv University

Elliot Ludvig
University of Alberta

Gail Mauner
University at Buffalo, SUNY

James McClelland
Stanford University

Daniel McConnell
University of Central Florida

James McGaugh
University of California, Irvine

Martijn Meeter
Vrije Universiteit Amsterdam, Netherlands

Barbara Mellers
University of California, Berkeley

Earl Miller
Massachusetts Institute of Technology

George Miller
Princeton University

Mortimer Mishkin
National Institutes of Mental Health

John Moore
University of Massachusetts

Lynn Nadel
University of Arizona

Danielle Nadorff
Mississippi State University

Michelle Nicolle
Wake Forest University School of Medicine

Ken Norman
Princeton University

Robert Nosofsky
Indiana University

Laura O'Sullivan
Florida Gulf Coast University

Linda Oliva
University of Maryland, Baltimore County

Ken Paller
Northwestern University

Mauricio Papini
Texas Christian University

Denis Paré
Rutgers University–Newark

Vinay Parikh
Temple University

Nikole Patson
Ohio State University

Marsha Penner
The University of North Carolina at Chapel Hill

Michael Petrides
McGill University

Elizabeth Phelps
New York University

Raymond Phinney
Wheaton College

Steven Pinker
Harvard University

Russell Poldrack
University of California, Los Angeles

Michaela Porubanova
Farmingdale State College, SUNY

Sarah Queller
Indiana University

Sheila Quinn
Salve Regina University

Gabriel Radvansky
University of Notre Dame

Arthur Reber
Brooklyn College, Graduate Center CUNY

Celinda Reese-Melancon
Oklahoma State University

Lisa Rezi
University of Georgia

Trevor Robbins
University of Cambridge

Herbert Roitblat
OrcaTec

Carolyn Rovee-Collier
Rutgers University—New Brunswick

Jerry Rudy
University of Colorado

Linda Rueckert
Northeastern Illinois University

Michelle Ryder
Daniel Webster University

Jeffery Sables
University of Memphis

Sharleen Sakai
Michigan State University

Richard Schiffrin
Indiana University

Ana Schwartz
University of Texas at El Paso

Richard Servatius
VA New Jersey Health Care System and New Jersey Medical School

David Shanks
University College London

Sonya Sheffert
Central Michigan University

Art Shimamura
University of California, Berkeley

Zachary Shipstead
Arizona State University

Daphna Shohamy
Columbia University

Shepard Siegel
McMaster University

Julia Sluzenski
Drexel University

Edward Smith
Columbia University

Patrick Smith
Florida Southern College

Paul Smolensky
Johns Hopkins University

Larry Squire
University of California, School of Medicine, San Diego

Mark Stanton
University of Delaware

Joseph Steinmetz
Indiana University

Greg Stone
Arizona State University

Helen Sullivan
Rider University

Nanthia Suthana
University of California, Los Angeles

Lauren Taglialatela
Kennesaw State University

Paula Tallal
Rutgers University—Newark

Herbert Terrace
Columbia University

Philip Tetlock
University of California, Berkeley

Frederic Theunissen
University of California, Berkeley

Richard Thompson
University of Southern California

Lucy Troup
Colorado State University

Endel Tulving
University of Toronto

Barbara Tversky
Stanford University

Nehal Vadhan
Columbia University Medical School

Anthony Wagner
Stanford University

Jonathon Wallis
University of California, Berkeley

Xiao Wang
University of South Dakota

Mary Waterstreet
Saint Ambrose University

Sheree Watson
University of Southern Mississippi

Daniel Weinberger
National Institutes of Health

Norman Weinberger
University of California, Irvine

J. W. Whitlow, Jr.
Rutgers University—Camden

Andreas Wilke
Clarkson University

James Woodson
University of Tampa

Bonnie Wright
Gardner-Webb University

Diana Younger
University of Texas of the Permian Basin

Laszlo Zaborszky
Rutgers University–Newark

Susan Zelinski
Rutgers University—Newark

Thomas Zentall
University of Kentucky

Acknowledgments, to the Team at Worth Publishers

Textbooks share much in common with Hollywood movies or Broadway shows: the people you see onstage or whose names are on the marquee (or book cover) are only the tip of the proverbial iceberg. Behind them stands a much larger supporting team that is essential to putting on the show. In our case, the two people most central to this book's production and quality are **Daniel DeBonis**, our editor, who served as the effective executive producer of the entire project, managing the various people and components and keeping everyone and everything on track and oriented toward a common vision (and deadline); and **Moira Lerner**, our developmental editor, who functioned like a shadow (but mostly uncredited) fourth author, revising our drafts, identifying problematic gaps in logic and pedagogy, and generally raising the level of coherence, consistency, and communication in the book far beyond what any of the three authors would have been capable of on our own. Special thanks also go to executive marketing manager Kate Nurre for her hard work promoting our book and assistant editor Katie Pachnos for her tremendous attention to detail and help keeping the book on schedule.

Many other people at Worth Publishers provided important contributions to various facets of the book, including Diana Blume, Christine Buese, Rachel Comerford, Lisa Kinne, Tracey Kuehn, Charles Linsmeier, Rachel Losh, Nicole Padinha, Paul Rohloff, Vicki Tomaselli, Catherine Woods, and Kayci Wyatt.

Learning and Memory

The Psychology of Learning and Memory

A T AGE 46, CLIVE WEARING HAD IT ALL. He was a well-known, highly regarded symphony conductor; he was handsome, charming, and witty; and he was deeply in love with his wife, Deborah. Then his memory was stripped from him. Clive had developed a rare condition in which a virus, which usually causes nothing more serious than cold sores, invaded his brain. His brain tissue swelled, crushing against the confines of his skull. Although most patients die when this happens, Clive survived, but his brain remained significantly damaged.

When Clive awoke in the hospital, he had lost most of his past. He could recognize Deborah but couldn't remember their wedding. He knew he had children but couldn't remember their names or what they looked like. He could speak and understand words, but there were huge gaps in his knowledge. On one test, when shown a picture of a scarecrow, he replied: "A worshipping point for certain cultures." Asked to name famous musicians, he could produce four names: Mozart, Beethoven, Bach, and Haydn. Conspicuously absent from this list was the sixteenth-century composer Lassus: Clive had been the world expert on this composer (Wilson & Wearing, 1995).

But Clive Wearing hadn't just lost the past: he'd also lost the present. Now he would remain conscious for only a few seconds of whatever he happened to be experiencing, and then the information would melt away without forming even a temporary memory. During his stay in the hospital, he had no idea where he was or why he was surrounded by strangers. Whenever he caught sight of Deborah—even if she'd only left the room for a few minutes—he'd run to her and kiss her joyously, as if she'd been absent for years.

A few minutes later, he'd catch sight of her again and stage another passionate reunion. Clive now lived "in the moment," caught in an endless loop of reawakening. His numerous journals

Jiri Rezac/Polaris

Clive Wearing with his wife, Deborah.

show his desperate efforts to make sense of what he was experiencing: "7:09 a.m.: Awake. 7:34 a.m.: Actually finally awake. 7:44 a.m.: Really perfectly awake . . . 10:08 a.m.: Now I am superlatively awake. First time aware for years. 10:13 a.m.: Now I am overwhelmingly awake. . . . 10:28 a.m.: Actually I am now first time awake for years. . . ." Each time he added a new entry, he might go back and scratch out the previous line, angry that a stranger had written misleading entries in his journal.

Yet even when Clive knew nothing else, he knew that he loved his wife. Emotional memory— love—survived when almost everything else was gone. And he could still play the piano and conduct an orchestra so competently that a nonmusician wouldn't suspect anything was wrong with Clive's mind. Those specialized skill memories survived, along with more mundane skills, such as making coffee or playing card games. And although Clive was unable to consciously learn any new facts, he could acquire some new habits through repeated practice. After moving to a nursing home, he eventually learned the route from the dining hall to his room, and when prompted to put on his coat for his daily walk past the local pond, he would ask if it was time to go feed the ducks (Wilson & Wearing, 1995). Clive's memory was more like an imperfectly erased blackboard than a blank slate.

Clive Wearing's case is tragic but makes two important points. The first is the unrivaled importance of learning and memory to our lives. Most of the time, we take for granted our memories of who we are and what we know. When these are stripped away, life becomes a series of unrelated moments, isolated from past and future, like those fuzzy moments we all experience when we've just awakened and are disoriented.

The second point is that speaking of memory as if it were a single, cohesive process is misleading. In fact, there are many different kinds of memory, and as with Clive's, some can be damaged while others are spared. Normally, these different kinds of memory function together seamlessly, and we aren't aware of whether a given instance of learning has been preserved as a fact, habit, skill, or emotion. But this cohesion is in many ways an illusion. By confronting the limits of this illusion, we can begin to understand how memory works, both in healthy people and in individuals whose memory has broken down. You will read more about amnesic patients like Clive Wearing in Chapter 7, "Episodic and Semantic Memory: Memory for Facts and Events."

learning. The process by which changes in behavior arise as a result of experiences interacting with the world.

memory. The record of past experiences acquired through learning.

This book is about **learning**, the process by which changes in behavior arise as a result of experience interacting with the world, and **memory**, the record of our past experiences, which are acquired through learning. The study of learning and memory began far back in human history and continues today. Some of humanity's greatest minds have struggled with the question of how we learn and remember. As you read this chapter, you will see why the questions that fascinated philosophers and psychologists of long ago are still relevant today. (For an immediate appreciation of the relevance to your own life, see

"Learning and Memory in Everyday Life" below.) Five themes emerge that have reappeared in different guises across the centuries:

1. How do sensations or ideas become linked in the mind?
2. How are memories built from the components of experience?
3. To what extent are behaviors and abilities determined by biological inheritance (nature) and to what extent by life experiences (nurture)?
4. In what ways are human learning and memory similar to learning and memory in other animals, and in what ways do they differ?
5. Can the psychological study of the mind be rigorously scientific, uncovering universal principles of learning and memory that can be described by mathematical equations and considered fundamental laws?

LEARNING AND MEMORY IN EVERYDAY LIFE

Top Ten Tips for a Better Memory

1. *Pay attention.* Often when we "forget" something, it's not that we've somehow lost the memory of it but that we didn't learn the thing properly in the first place. If you pay full attention to what you are trying to learn, you'll be more likely to remember it later.

2. *Create associations.* Associate what you're trying to learn with other information you already know. For example, it will be easier to remember that Ag is the chemical symbol for silver if you know it is short for *argentum*, the Latin word for "silver." It might also help if you know that Argentina got its name from early European explorers who mistakenly thought the region was rich in silver.

3. *A picture is worth a thousand words.* Names and dates and such are more memorable if you can link them to an image. The effort you expend generating an image strengthens the memory. For example, in an art history course, you might have to remember that Manet specialized in painting figures and his contemporary, Monet, is famous for paintings of haystacks and water lilies. Picture the human figures lined up acrobat-style to form a letter "A" for Manet and the water lilies arranged in a daisy chain to form the letter "O" for Monet.

4. *Practice makes perfect.* There's a reason to drill kindergarteners on their ABCs and make third graders repeatedly recite their multiplication tables. Memories for facts are strengthened by repetition. The same principle holds for memories for skills, such as bike riding and juggling: they are improved by practice.

5. *Use multiple senses.* Instead of just reading information silently, read it aloud. You will encode the information aurally as well as visually. You can also try writing it out; the act of writing activates sensory systems and also forces you to think about the words you're copying.

6. *Reduce overload.* Use memory aids such as Post-it Notes, calendars, or electronic schedulers to remember appointments, due dates, and other obligations, freeing you to focus on remembering items that must be called to mind without written aids—say, during an exam!

7. *Time travel.* Remembering information for facts doesn't depend on remembering the exact time and place where you acquired it. Nevertheless, if you can't remember a fact, try to remember where you first heard it. If you can remember your high school history teacher lecturing on Napoleon, perhaps what she said about the causes of the Napoleonic Wars will also come to mind.

8. *Get some sleep.* Two-thirds of Americans don't get enough sleep. Consequently, they are less able to concentrate during the day, which makes it harder for them to encode new memories and retrieve old ones (see Tip 1). Sleep is also important for helping the brain organize and store memories.

9. *Try a rhyme.* Do you have to remember a long string of random information? Create a poem (or better yet, a song) that includes the information. Remember the old standards "'I' before 'E' except after 'C' or sounded as 'A,' as in 'neighbor' or 'weigh'"? This ditty uses rhythm and rhyme to make it easier to remember a rule of English spelling.

10. *Relax.* Sometimes trying hard to remember is less effective than turning your attention to something else; often, the missing information will pop into your awareness later. If you are stumped by a question on a test, skip that one and come back to it later, when perhaps the missing information won't be so hard to retrieve.

1.1 From Philosophy and Natural History to Psychology

Today, learning and memory researchers consider themselves scientists. They develop new theories and test those theories with carefully designed experiments, just like researchers in any other branch of science. However, this wasn't always the case. In fact, for most of human history, the study of learning and memory was a branch of *philosophy*, the abstract study of principles that govern the universe, including human conduct. Philosophers gain insight not through scientific experiments but through a process of reasoned thought and logical argument. These insights may be no less important than those gained through modern science; some are so profound that people continue talking about them centuries after they were first disseminated.

The Empiricism and Associationism of Aristotle

Aristotle (384–322 BC), a Greek philosopher and teacher, was one of the earliest thinkers to write about memory. Like many wealthy young men of his day, Aristotle was educated in Athens, the preeminent intellectual center of the western world at that time. There, he studied under Plato (c. 427–347 BC), perhaps the greatest of the Greek philosophers. Years later, Aristotle himself became a mentor to many students, including the young prince later known as Alexander the Great, who went on to conquer much of the world.

data. Facts and figures from which conclusions can be inferred.

A keen observer of the natural world, Aristotle loved **data**, the facts and figures from which he could infer conclusions. He collected plants and animals from around the world and made careful notes about their structure and behavior. From such data, Aristotle attempted to formulate **theories**, sets of statements devised to explain a collection of facts. His data-oriented approach to understanding the world stood in marked contrast to the methods of his intellectual forebears, including Plato and Plato's teacher, Socrates, both of whom relied primarily on intuition and logic rather than natural observation.

theory. A set of statements devised to explain a group of facts.

associationism. The principle that memory depends on the formation of linkages ("associations") between pairs of events, sensations, and ideas, such that recalling or experiencing one member of the pair elicits a memory or anticipation of the other.

One of Aristotle's key interests was memory. His theory about it, called **associationism**, argued that memory depends on the formation of linkages ("associations") between pairs of events, sensations, or ideas, so that recalling or experiencing one member of the pair elicits a memory or anticipation of the other. Imagine someone reading a list of words and for each word asking you to say the first word that comes to mind. If he says "hot," you might say "cold"; if he says "chair," you might say "table," and so on. The words "hot" and "cold" are linked, or associated, in most people's minds, as are "table" and "chair." How do these associations come about?

contiguity. Nearness in time (temporal contiguity) or space (spatial contiguity).

Aristotle described such linkages as reflecting three principles of association. The first principle is **contiguity**, or nearness in time and space: events experienced at the same time (temporal contiguity) or place (spatial contiguity) tend to be associated. The ideas of "chair" and "table" are linked because we often see chairs and tables together at the same time and in the same place. The second principle is *frequency*: the more often we experience events that are contiguous, the more strongly we associate them. Thus, the more often we see tables and chairs together, the stronger the table–chair link grows. Modern behavioral and neurobiological studies of the interaction between contiguity and frequency in learning will be discussed further in Chapter 4, "Classical Conditioning: Learning to Predict Significant Events."

Aristotle's third principle is *similarity*: if two things are similar, the thought or sensation of one will tend to trigger a thought of the other. Chairs and tables are similar in that both are often made of wood, both are found in kitchens, and both have a function associated with eating meals. This similarity strengthens the association between them. In Chapter 6, "Generalization, Discrimination Learning, and Concept Formation," you will see why similarity has continued to be a core focus of research on learning. Together, Aristotle concluded, these three principles of association—contiguity, frequency, and similarity—are the basic ways humans organize sensations and ideas.

Aristotle's ideas, refined in the ensuing two millennia, have provided the foundation for modern theories of learning in both psychology and neuroscience. Aristotle's view was that knowledge emerges from experience. This idea identifies him with a philosophical school of thought known as **empiricism**, which holds that all the ideas we have are the result of experience. (The Greek word *empiricus* means "experience.") To Aristotle, the mind of a newborn child is like a blank slate, not yet written on.

In this regard, Aristotle differed sharply from his teacher Plato, who believed staunchly in **nativism**, which holds that the bulk of our knowledge is inborn (or native). Plato's most influential book, *The Republic*, described an idealized society in which people's innate differences in skills, abilities, and talents form the basis for their fixed roles in life: some rule while others serve. The tension between empiricism and nativism has continued through the centuries, although today it is more often called the "nature versus nurture" debate: researchers argue about whether our "nature," including genes, or our "nurture," including upbringing and environment, has the greater influence on our learning and memory abilities. Table 1.1 shows some of the major philosophers and scientists who have contributed to this debate over the millennia and which side of the debate they espoused; the names and ideas in the table will be revisited throughout the book.

Western philosophy and science have deep roots in the ideas and writings of the ancient Greeks, whose philosophy and science continued to flourish under the Roman Empire. By the fifth century AD, however, the empire had collapsed, and Europe plunged into the Dark Ages, overrun by successive waves of warring tribes who seemed to care little for philosophy or learning. (Meanwhile, in China, India, Persia, and the Arabian Peninsula, flourishing civilizations achieved major advances in science, mathematics, medicine, and astronomy—but that's another story.) It was not until the middle of the fifteenth century that European science flourished once again. This was the Renaissance, the era that brought forth the art of Leonardo da Vinci, the plays of William Shakespeare, and the astronomy of Nicolaus Copernicus and Galileo Galilei. This cultural and scientific revival set the stage for the emergence of new ideas about the nature of mind and memory.

Scala/Art Resource, NY

Aristotle (right) and his teacher, **Plato**

empiricism. A philosophical school of thought that holds that all the ideas we have are the result of experience.

nativism. A philosophical school of thought that holds that the bulk of knowledge is inborn (or native).

Descartes and Dualism

René Descartes (1596–1650) grew up in France as the son of a provincial noble family. His family inheritance gave him the freedom to spend his life studying,

Table 1.1 Nativism and empiricism: The role of nature and nurture in learning and memory

Nativism: Knowledge is inborn	Empiricism: Knowledge is acquired through experience
Plato (c. 427–347 BC) Most of our knowledge is innate.	**Aristotle (384–322 BC)** Memory depends on the formation of associations, for which there are three principles: contiguity, frequency, and similarity.
René Descartes (1596–1650) The mind and the body are distinct entities, governed by different laws. The body functions as a machine with innate and fixed responses to stimuli.	**John Locke (1632–1704)** A newborn's mind is a blank slate (a *tabula rasa*) that is written on by experience. Education and experience (learning) allow common people to transcend their class.
Gottfried Leibniz (1646–1716) Three quarters of human knowledge is learned, but one quarter is inborn.	**William James (1842–1910)** Habits are built up from inborn reflexes through learning; memory is built up through networks of associations.
Charles Darwin (1809–1882) Natural selection: species evolve when they possess a trait that is inheritable, varies across individuals, and increases the chances of survival and reproduction.	**Ivan Pavlov (1849–1936)** In classical (Pavlovian) conditioning, animals learn through experience to predict future events.
	Edward Thorndike (1874–1949) The law of effect (instrumental conditioning): an animal's behaviors increase or decrease depending on the consequences that follow the response.

Musée des Augustins, Toulouse, France/The Bridgeman Art Library

| **René Descartes**

thinking, and writing, most of which he did in bed (he hated to get up before noon). Although raised as a Roman Catholic and trained by the Jesuits, Descartes harbored deep doubts about the existence of everything. Despairing of being able to know anything for certain, he concluded that the only evidence that he himself even existed was his ability to think: "*Cogito ergo sum*," or "I think, therefore I am" (Descartes, 1637).

Where does Descartes' *cogito*—the ability to think—come from? Descartes was a firm believer in **dualism**, the principle that the mind and body exist as separate entities, each with different characteristics, governed by its own laws (Descartes, 1662). The body, Descartes reasoned, functions like a self-regulating machine, much like the clockwork statues and fountains that were so fashionable during the Renaissance. A person strolling through the royal gardens of Saint-Germain-en-Laye, just outside Paris, would step on a hidden trigger, releasing water into pipes that caused a gargoyle to nod its head, a statue of the god Neptune to shake its trident, and the goddess Diana to modestly retreat. The body, Descartes reasoned, works through a similar system of hydraulics and switches. The process begins when a **stimulus**, a sensory event from the outside world, enters the system; for example, light reflected off a bird enters the eye as a visual stimulus. Like the trigger switch in the gardens, this stimulus causes fluids (Descartes called them "spirits") to flow through hollow tubes from the eyes to the brain and then to be "reflected" back as an outgoing motor

response, the behavioral consequence of perception of the stimulus, as illustrated by Descartes' sketch in Figure 1.1 (Descartes, 1662). Such a pathway from sensory stimulus to motor response is called a **reflex arc**.

Descartes got many of the details of reflexes wrong. There are no spirits that flow through the body to produce movement hydraulically as he described. Nevertheless, Descartes was the first to show how the body might be understood through the same mechanical principles that underlie physical machinery. This mechanistic view of the processes that give rise to behavior returned in full force many centuries later in the mathematical and computer models of the brain and behavior described in several of the chapters in this book.

In contrast to Aristotle, who believed knowledge was attained through experience, Descartes was strongly in the nativist camp with Plato. Descartes had no interest in theories of learning. He acknowledged that people do derive some information from experience, but he believed that much of what we know is innate. The nature–nurture debate continues today to inform our efforts at understanding how and to what degree we are able to change and evolve within the span of our own lifetimes, a topic covered in Chapter 12, "Development and Aging: Learning and Memory across the Lifespan."

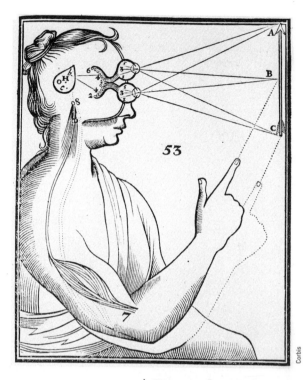

Figure 1.1 Descartes' reflex A mechanism for producing an automatic reaction in response to external events, as illustrated in Descartes' *De Homine* (1662). The diagram shows the flow of information from the outside world, through the eyes, to the brain, and then through the muscles of the arm, creating a physical response in which the arm moves to point to an object in the external world.

John Locke and His Reliance on Empiricism

By the late 1600s, England (along with the rest of Europe) had undergone the conflicts of the Reformation, a religious and political movement that weakened the political power of the Roman Catholic Church and placed new emphasis on individual rights and responsibilities. This was a period when science flourished. Famous scientists were the celebrities of their day; people attended lectures on philosophy and natural sciences the way they now go to movies and rock concerts. One especially renowned scientist, Isaac Newton, demonstrated that white light can be refracted into component colors by a prism lens and then recombined by another lens to produce white light again.

Inspired by Newton's work, John Locke (1632–1704) hoped to show that the mind, too, could be broken down into elements that when combined produced the whole of consciousness. Locke, like Descartes before him, borrowed methods from the physical sciences that would help him better understand the mind and the processes of learning and memory. This practice of philosophers and psychologists of borrowing from other, more established and rigorous domains of science continues to this day.

To describe the way elementary associations might account for the more complex ideas and concepts that make up our memories and knowledge, Locke drew from the work of his former Oxford medical instructor, Robert Boyle, who 30 years before had demonstrated that chemical compounds are composed of elementary parts (what we now know to be molecules and atoms). Locke reasoned that complex ideas are similarly formed from the combination of more elementary ideas that we passively acquire through our senses (Locke, 1690). For example, simple ideas such as "red" and "sweet" are acquired automatically by our senses of sight and taste, and more complex ideas such as "cherry" are acquired by combining these simpler components.

dualism. The principle that the mind and body exist as separate entities.

stimulus. A sensory event that provides information about the outside world.

response. The behavioral consequence of perception of a stimulus.

reflex arc. An automatic pathway from a sensory stimulus to a motor response.

INTERFOTO/Alamy

| **John Locke**

Perhaps Locke's most lasting idea is that all knowledge is derived from experience. Borrowing Aristotle's analogy of a tablet on which nothing is yet written, Locke suggested that children arrive in the world as a blank slate or tablet (in Latin, a *tabula rasa*) just waiting to be written on.

Locke's view of the power of experience to shape our capabilities through a lifetime of learning had great appeal to reformers of the eighteenth century, who were challenging the aristocratic system of government, in which kings ruled by right of birth. Locke's ideas meant that a man's worth was not determined at birth. All men are born equal, he believed, with the same potential for knowledge, success, and leadership. Common people, through striving and learning, could transcend the limits and barriers of class. Therefore, Locke argued, access to a good education should be available to all children regardless of their class or family wealth (Locke, 1693). These ideas heavily influenced Thomas Jefferson as he drafted the Declaration of Independence, which in 1776 proclaimed the American colonies' independence from Great Britain and asserted that "all men are created equal," with the same innate rights to "life, liberty, and the pursuit of happiness"—words taken almost verbatim from Locke's writings.

Although Locke's writings were influential throughout European philosophical and scientific circles, he was not without his critics. One of Locke's contemporaries, German mathematician Gottfried Wilhelm Leibniz (1646–1716), conceded to Locke that three quarters of knowledge might be acquired but claimed that the other quarter is inborn and innate, including habits, predispositions, and potentials for success or failure (Leibniz, 1704). In many ways, Leibniz's more moderate position echoes that adopted by many modern researchers, who believe that human ability is not due solely to nature (nativism) or solely to nurture (empiricism) but is a combination of both: nature (as encoded in our genes) provides a background of native ability and predispositions that is modified by a lifetime of experience and learning (nurture).

William James and Associationism

Born to a wealthy and prominent New York family, William James (1842–1910) spent his early years traveling around the world, living in fine hotels, and meeting many of the great writers and philosophers of his time. After receiving his medical degree in 1869, James accepted a position as an instructor of physiology and anatomy at Harvard, where he offered an introductory course in **psychology**, the study of mind and behavior. It was the first course on psychology ever given at Harvard or at any college in America. He once joked that the first psychology lecture he heard was his own.

James's introductory psychology course soon became one of the most popular courses at Harvard, and he signed a contract with a publisher, promising to deliver within two years a book based on his acclaimed lectures. In the end, it took him 12 years to finish the book. James's two-volume *Principles of Psychology* (1890) was an immediate scientific, commercial, and popular success. Translated into many languages, it was for decades the standard psychology text around the world.

psychology. The study of mind and behavior.

James was especially interested in how we learn new habits and acquire new memories. He enjoyed telling the story of a practical joker who, seeing a recently discharged army veteran walking down the street carrying a load of groceries, shouted, "Attention!" The former soldier instantly and instinctively brought his hands to his side and stood ramrod straight as his mutton and potatoes rolled into the gutter. The soldier's response to this command was so deeply ingrained as a reflex that, even after he had left the army, it was all but impossible to suppress. James believed that most abilities and habits were similarly formed by our experiences, especially early in life. He proposed that a central goal of psychology should be to understand the principles that govern the formation and maintenance of new skills and memories, including how and why old learning may block or facilitate the formation of new learning (James, 1890); indeed, this tension between old memories and new learning has been an ongoing focus of experimental psychology in the last century, as reviewed in many of the chapters to follow, especially Chapter 7, "Episodic and Semantic Memory: Memory for Facts and Events," and Chapter 8, "Skill Memory: Learning by Doing."

James was a strong proponent of associationism, and his theories elaborated on the work of Aristotle and Locke. The act of remembering an event, such as a dinner party, he wrote, would involve multiple connections between the components of the evening. These might include memories for the taste of the food, the feel of his stiff dinner jacket, and the smell of the perfume of the lady seated next to him (Figure 1.2). Activation of the memory for the dinner party, with all of its components, could in turn activate the memory for a second

| William James

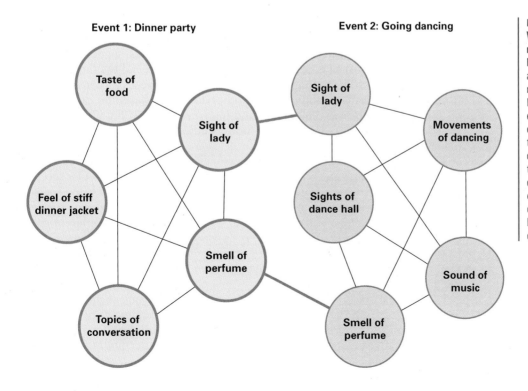

Event 1: Dinner party

- Taste of food
- Sight of lady
- Feel of stiff dinner jacket
- Smell of perfume
- Topics of conversation

Event 2: Going dancing

- Sight of lady
- Movements of dancing
- Sights of dance hall
- Sound of music
- Smell of perfume

Figure 1.2
William James's memory model
Memory of an event, such as a dinner party, has multiple components all linked together. Another event, such as going dancing with a lady from the dinner party, also has component parts linked together. A mental association between the two events in turn consists of multiple connections between the underlying components.

event that shared some related elements—such as a visit to a dance hall with the same lady on the next night. This second event would be composed of its own parts: the sights of the dance hall, the movements of dancing, the smell of his partner's perfume, and so on. The two events (dinner party and dancing) would be associated by a linkage between their common or related components (the sight of the lady and the smell of her perfume).

This model, or simplified description, of memory was one of James's many seminal contributions to psychology. James took his model literally, believing that the associations it described would eventually be mapped directly onto physical connections in the brain (James, 1890). With this idea, James was far ahead of his time: linking brain processes to learned behaviors didn't attract much interest for many decades. Today, most modern theories of memory draw on James's idea of learning as a process of forming associations between the elements of an experience, as you will see in many chapters to come, including Chapter 4, "Classical Conditioning: Learning to Predict Significant Events," and Chapter 7, "Episodic and Semantic Memory: Memory for Facts and Events."

Charles Darwin and the Theory of Natural Selection

How unique are humans within the animal kingdom? Plato and other early Greek philosophers took one extreme view: they believed that humans are unique among living things because they possess an everlasting soul. Aristotle, in contrast, argued that humans exist in a continuum with other animals and that the ability to reason is their sole distinguishing feature. Renaissance philosophers tended to side with Plato, bolstered by the Church-sponsored view that mankind was created in God's image. For example, Descartes believed that humans and animals are fundamentally different, just as he believed that mind and body are separate.

But by the early 1800s, this view of humans as being fundamentally different from animals was beginning to meet serious challenge. European naturalists had begun to collect and study a wide variety of plants and animals from around the world. The geological study of rock formations that are shaped by eons of water movement, along with fossils found embedded in these rocks, suggested a world millions of years old. The facts these scientists uncovered and the theories they developed upended many long-held beliefs about who we are, where we come from, and how similar we might be to other animals. These new perspectives on the relationship between animals and humans would profoundly affect the study of natural history, as well as all future studies of the psychology of learning and memory.

evolution. The theory that species change over time, with new traits or characteristics passed from one generation to the next; natural selection is one mechanism by which evolution occurs.

Erasmus Darwin (1731–1802), the personal doctor to King George III of England, was an early and vocal proponent of **evolution**, the theory that species change over time, with new traits or characteristics emerging and being passed from one generation to the next. With sufficient time, he argued, one species could evolve so far that it would come to constitute an entirely different species from its ancestor (E. Darwin, 1794). It was many years later, however, that Erasmus's grandson Charles developed a theory of how this evolutionary process might take place and in doing so made the term "evolution" synonymous with the name Darwin.

natural selection. A proposed mechanism for evolution, also known as "survival of the fittest," which holds that species evolve when there is some trait that varies naturally across individuals, is inheritable, and increases an individual's "fitness," or chance of survival and reproductive success.

Charles Darwin (1809–1882) was the son of a prosperous doctor, while his mother hailed from the wealthy Wedgwood family of ceramic ware fame. His family's financial position meant that he didn't have to work for a living. Instead, what Darwin most enjoyed was to walk through the English countryside collecting and cataloging animals.

In 1831, at age 22, with no career direction other than his amateur interest in natural history, Charles Darwin accepted an offer to accompany the captain of the HMS *Beagle* on an expedition to chart the coast of South America. In South America, Darwin encountered an abundance of previously unknown species, many on the Galápagos Islands, an isolated archipelago off the coast of Ecuador. Of particular interest to Darwin were the many species of birds he observed, especially the finches—of which he identified at least 14 varieties, each on a different island (Figure 1.3). On one island that had plentiful nuts and seeds, the finches had strong, thick beaks that they used to crack open nuts. On another island, with few nuts but plenty of insects, the finches had long, narrow beaks, perfect for grabbing insects from the crevices of tree bark. Each isolated island in the archipelago was populated by a different kind of finch, with a beak ideally suited to that island's distinct habitat. In his account of the trip, Darwin wrote that "one might really fancy that from an original paucity of birds in this archipelago, one species had been taken and modified for different ends" (C. Darwin, 1845). Charles Darwin, like his grandfather Erasmus, was convinced that life on earth was evolving and was not immutably fixed.

Darwin's most important legacy was his theory of **natural selection**, which proposed a mechanism for how evolution occurs (C. Darwin, 1859). He argued that species evolve when they possess a trait that meets three conditions (Table 1.2). First, the trait must be *inheritable*, meaning it can be passed from parent to offspring. (Keep in mind that genes—the carriers of inherited traits—had not yet been discovered in Darwin's time.) Second, the trait must *vary*, having a range of forms among the individual members of the species. Third, the trait must make the individual more "*fit*," meaning that it must increase reproductive success—that is, increase the chance that the individual will survive, mate, and reproduce, passing on the trait to its offspring. This, in turn, will make the offspring more fit, increasing their chances of surviving and passing on the trait. Over time, natural selection (sometimes called "survival of the fittest") means that the trait will spread through the population. This, Darwin argued, was the underlying mechanism by which species evolve.

Darwin tinkered with his ideas for 20 years. Finally, in 1859, he published *On the Origin of Species by Means of Natural Selection, or the Preservation of Favoured Races in the Struggle for Life*, more commonly known by its abbreviated title, *The Origin of Species*. Darwin's book became a best seller, was translated into many languages, and ignited a major public controversy that resulted in thousands of reviews, articles, and satires. Why the uproar? Darwin's view of natural selection upset many people's view that there is an important distinction between "man and beast." Theologians were alarmed because the idea

| **Charles Darwin**

Figure 1.3 Finches of the Galápagos Islands Note the strong, heavy beak of the bird at the upper left (good for cracking nuts) and the long, narrow beak of the bird at the lower right (good for grabbing insects from cracks in bark).

Table 1.2 Darwin's three criteria for traits to evolve through natural selection

Criterion	Finches
1. Inheritable trait	Beak shape
2. Natural variability	Thin or thick
3. Relevance to survival	Correct shape improves access to insects (thinner beak) or ability to crack nuts (thicker beak)

evolutionary psychology. A branch of psychology that studies how behavior evolves through natural selection.

Darwin was the subject of many personal attacks. What inspired this caricature published in *Hornet* magazine on March 22, 1871?

GraphicaArts/Getty Images

that humans and apes evolved from a common ancestor seemed to challenge the biblical doctrine that people were created by the hand of God, in God's own image. *The Origin of Species* is among the most controversial scientific books ever written.

What are the implications of Darwin's work for the psychology of learning and memory? Darwin argued that behavioral traits could evolve through the same process of natural selection as do physical traits (C. Darwin, 1872). Today, the study of how behavior evolves through natural selection is known as **evolutionary psychology**. The basic premise of evolutionary psychology is that learning has enormous value for survival, allowing organisms to adapt to a changing and variable world. Organisms with more capacity for learning and memory are more fit—better able to survive and more likely to breed and pass their inherited capacities on to offspring. Notice that the content of what is learned is not passed on: learned knowledge is an acquired trait, which cannot be inherited. What can be inherited is the capacity or ability for learning and memory. Further discussion of evolutionary theory, and the revolution in genetics that it spawned, will be covered in Chapter 12, "Development and Aging: Learning and Memory across the Lifespan."

Interim Summary

- Early philosophers interested in learning and memory wrestled with many key issues that are still central to modern theories.

- Aristotle was an associationist, believing that the effects of experiences can be understood as associations formed between sensations or ideas. He described three key principles of associative learning: contiguity (in space and time), frequency, and similarity. A later associationist, William James, proposed an early and influential memory model built on similar principles.

- John Locke, like Aristotle and James, was an empiricist: he believed that we are all born equal, as blank slates, to be shaped by our experiences. In contrast, René Descartes was a nativist, arguing that we are shaped primarily by our inherited nature. He viewed the body as a machine that works through mechanical (especially hydraulic) principles; as a dualist, he believed that the mind was a separate entity from the body.

- Modern researchers are less likely to be strict nativists or strict empiricists and are more likely to accept that both nature (genes) and nurture (experience) play a role in human learning and memory.

- Charles Darwin's theory of natural selection proposed a mechanism for evolution: survival of the fittest. According to this theory, evolution occurs when one variation of a naturally occurring and inheritable trait gives an organism a survival advantage, making the organism more fit—more likely to survive and reproduce and pass this trait on to its offspring.

1.2 The Birth of Experimental Psychology

Most of the scientists and philosophers described to this point in the chapter observed the natural world and derived general principles to explain what they saw. In the late 1800s, an important change took place. Instead of merely observing the world, scientists interested in psychology began to follow the lead of scientists making strides in the physical sciences by conducting systematic **experiments**, specific tests to examine the validity of a hypothesis by actively manipulating the variables being investigated. The testing of psychological theories by experimentation rather than merely by observation of natural occurrences is called **experimental psychology**.

experiment. A test made to examine the validity of a hypothesis, usually by actively manipulating the variable(s) being investigated and measuring the effect on a behavior.

Hermann Ebbinghaus and Human Memory Experiments

Hermann Ebbinghaus (1850–1909), a contemporary of William James, conducted the first rigorous experimental studies of human memory. After earning his PhD, Ebbinghaus lived an itinerant life, traveling, attending occasional seminars, and working for short periods as a teacher and private tutor. One day, browsing at a bookstall, he came across a book by a German physicist, Gustav Fechner (1801–1887), that described the science of human perception. Fechner showed that there are highly predictable regularities in how people perceive variations in physical stimuli, such as changes in the brightness of a light or the weight of a ball. The book showed how a simple mathematical equation could describe the relationship between the physical world and the psychological world. Captivated by these ideas, Ebbinghaus proposed that the psychology of memory could also become a rigorous natural science, defined by precise mathematical laws.

Unlike many of the scientists discussed in this chapter, Ebbinghaus was not a wealthy man. Unable to afford to pay anyone to participate in his research, he did his studies using himself as the only participant. Despite this limitation, his work laid the foundation for all future experimental studies of human memory; in fact, Ebbinghaus is often considered to be the father of modern memory research.

Ebbinghaus sought mathematical equations to explain how memories are acquired and how they fade. Early on, he realized that if he studied lists of real words, his data would be strongly affected by the fact that he was more familiar with some words

| Hermann Ebbinghaus

Bettmann/Corbis

forgetting. The loss or deterioration of memory over time.

retention curve. A graph showing forgetting or relearning as a function of time since initial learning.

independent variable. The factor that is manipulated in an experiment, such as the factor that differentiates the control group and experimental group.

dependent variable. In an experiment, the factor whose change is measured as an effect of changes in the independent variable.

subject bias. The degree to which a subject's prior knowledge or expectations concerning an experiment can (consciously or unconsciously) influence the outcome.

blind design. An experimental design in which the participants do not know the hypothesis being tested or whether they are part of the experimental group or the control group.

Figure 1.4 Ebbinghaus's retention curve These experimental data show the percentage savings in time for relearning a list of words as a function of the delay between learning and relearning. Ebbinghaus's early study demonstrated that retention drops quickly in the first few days (up to about 100 hours for the task shown here) and then tapers off more slowly with increasing delays.

Data from Ebbinghaus, 1885/1913.

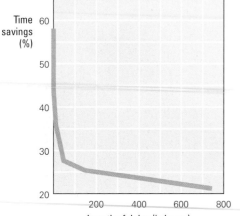

than others. To avoid this problem, he used three-letter nonsense words, such as BAP, KEP, and DAK, which would be unfamiliar to him. Ebbinghaus's use of simple, unfamiliar nonsense words was a critical advance in the methodology for studying principles of human memory. In one of his experiments, Ebbinghaus read a list of 20 words out loud to himself, put away the list for a while, then tried to remember as many words as possible. Afterward, he checked which words he missed, reviewed the list, and tried again. He repeated this process until he could remember all 20 words from the original list. This experiment contains the four key stages of a memory experiment—*learning, delay, test, relearning*—that represented the basic methodology for human memory experiments for years to follow. Further examples of these kinds of studies will be discussed in Chapter 7, "Episodic and Semantic Memory: Memory for Facts and Events."

Ebbinghaus was especially interested in **forgetting**, that is, in how memory deteriorates over time. He measured forgetting by examining how long it took him to relearn a previously learned list. If it initially took him 10 minutes to learn the list and later took only 6 minutes to relearn the same list, Ebbinghaus recorded a "time savings" of 4 minutes, or 40% of the original learning time. By testing himself at various intervals after learning, Ebbinghaus was able to plot a **retention curve**, which measures how much information is retained at each point in time following learning. Figure 1.4 shows an example of this, graphing the percentage savings in time for relearning the list at various delays between the initial learning and relearning (Ebbinghaus, 1885/1913).

As you can see in Figure 1.4, there is a strong time savings (nearly 100%) if the delay between learning and relearning is short. But as the delay grows longer, to about 100 hours (approximately 4 days), the savings declines to 25%. The retention curve also illustrates that most forgetting occurs early on: if a memory can survive the first few hours after learning, there is little additional forgetting. Thus, Ebbinghaus showed a savings of 25% after 150 hours, and this dropped only to 20% after 750 hours. In other studies, Ebbinghaus showed that shorter lists were easier to remember than longer lists. He also demonstrated that increasing the amount of initial practice improved later recall.

Ebbinghaus designed and conducted experiments in which one variable factor, called the **independent variable**, was carefully manipulated (for example, the length of the delay between learning and relearning), and its effect on the factor under observation, the **dependent variable** (in his experiments, usually memory retention), was carefully measured. Through this design, Ebbinghaus was able to show how changes in the independent variable (e.g., delay length) determine changes in the dependent variable (e.g., memory retention).

The major limitation of Ebbinghaus's studies was that they were conducted with just one participant, Ebbinghaus himself. There are several reasons why such self-experimentation is problematic and would not meet modern scientific standards for research. First, what if Ebbinghaus's memory was different from most other people's? If so, the results of his experiments would tell us a lot about Ebbinghaus but would not be applicable to other people. For this reason, modern research on memory usually involves testing a large number of people.

A second problem is that, because he was the experimenter as well as the participant, Ebbinghaus knew which variables were being manipulated. If, for example, he believed that longer lists were harder to learn, then this belief might subtly influence him to take longer to learn those lists. This problem is sometimes called **subject bias**. To avoid such problems, modern studies of memory employ a **blind design**, which means that the participant does not know the hypothesis being tested or the variables being manipulated. There is also a corresponding problem of **experimenter bias**, which means that even a well-meaning experimenter might influence the outcome (for example, by implicitly encouraging the participant to respond in an expected manner). Experimenter bias can be avoided by use of a **double-blind design**, in which neither the participant nor the experimenter knows the hypothesis being tested. A common modern example of the double-blind strategy is its use to test experimental medications. Patients receive either the test drug or a **placebo** (an inactive pill that looks just like the real drug), and neither the patients nor the doctors know who is receiving which kind of pill; only the people analyzing the results (who never interact directly with the research participants) know which is which.

Despite the imperfections in his experimental designs, Ebbinghaus led the way in the use of scientific experimentation to study learning and memory. There are few studies of human memory conducted today that don't owe their methodology to the early and influential work of Hermann Ebbinghaus.

Ivan Pavlov's Conditioning Studies

While Ebbinghaus was revolutionizing the study of human memory, the Russian physiologist Ivan Pavlov (1849–1936) was developing methods for studying animal learning that are still in widespread use today. As a young man, Pavlov trained to be a Russian Orthodox priest, like his father and grandfather. In addition to his religious readings, he read Darwin's recently published *Origin of Species*. Inspired by Darwin's accomplishments, Pavlov abandoned his plan to become a priest and enrolled in the school of natural sciences at the University of St. Petersburg. For the rest of his life, Pavlov would acknowledge the enormous impact of Darwin's writings on his own career and thinking.

Although remembered today for his seminal contributions to the psychology of learning, Pavlov's 1904 Nobel Prize in Physiology or Medicine was awarded for his research on the physiology of salivation and digestion in dogs (see Figure 1.5a). As described in more detail in Chapter 4, "Classical Conditioning: Learning to Predict Significant Events," Pavlov conducted a systematic study of the factors that influence how an animal learns. Pavlov inserted surgical tubes into the mouths of dogs to collect saliva and could then measure salivation in response to various cues. In one study, he began by training a dog to expect that the sound of a doorbell always preceded delivery of food; over many trials in which the sound of the doorbell was paired with food, the dog developed a stronger and stronger salivation response to the sound of the bell. This form of learning, in which an animal learns that one stimulus (in this case, a doorbell) predicts an upcoming important event (in this case, delivery of food), is known today as **classical conditioning** (or Pavlovian conditioning). Modern studies of classical conditioning usually report the results as a **learning curve**, like that shown in Figure 1.5b, which plots the number of training trials (the independent variable, plotted on the horizontal axis) against the animal's response (the dependent variable, plotted on the vertical axis).

Pavlov's view of how an animal learns a new behavioral response was based on an analogy to what at the time was a new technology that had recently been introduced in Russia: the

experimenter bias. The degree to which an experimenter's prior knowledge or expectations can (consciously or unconsciously) influence the outcome of an experiment.

double-blind design. An experimental design in which neither the experimenters nor the subjects know group assignment.

placebo. An inactive substance, such as a sugar pill, that is administered to the control subjects in an experiment to compare against the effects of an active substance, such as a drug.

classical conditioning. A type of learning in which the organism learns to respond with a conditioned response (CR) to a previously neutral stimulus (the CS) that has been repeatedly presented along with an unconditioned stimulus (US); also called Pavlovian conditioning.

learning curve. A graph showing learning performance (the dependent variable, usually plotted along the vertical axis) as a function of training time (the independent variable, usually plotted along the horizontal axis).

| Ivan Pavlov

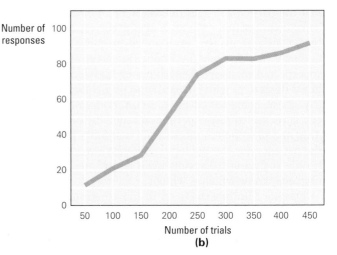

(a)

(b)

The Granger Collection, New York

Figure 1.5 Pavlov and learning experiments (a) Pavlov (with white beard) and his assistants in the laboratory, along with one of the dogs they used in their studies of the salivary response. (b) A learning curve from a modern study of classical conditioning. The curve plots the number of training trials (the independent variable) against the animal's conditioned response (the dependent variable).

extinction. The process of reducing a learned response to a stimulus by ceasing to pair that stimulus with a reward or punishment.

generalization. The transfer of past learning to novel events and problems.

telephone. As Pavlov explained it, he could call his lab from home via a *direct* private line, which was a fixed connection, much like the fixed connection between food and salivation in a dog's brain. Alternatively, he could call his lab by going through an *indirect* pathway, via a switchboard operator, creating a modifiable connection, much like the newly learned connection between the bell and the dog's salivation (Pavlov, 1927).

In other studies, Pavlov and his assistants showed that they could also *weaken* an animal's trained response to the bell. This was done by first pairing the bell with food, until the animal had learned to salivate to the bell, and then pairing the bell with the absence of food. Pavlov called this process **extinction:** the salivation to the bell gradually decreased as the animal learned that the bell no longer predicted food.

Pavlov also demonstrated that an animal will transfer what it has learned about one stimulus to similar stimuli. For example, he observed that once an animal learned to respond to a metronome ticking at 90 beats per minute, it also responded to similar sounds, such as a metronome ticking at 80 beats per minute or 100 beats per minute. However, the more dissimilar the new stimulus was to the original stimulus, the less intense was the dog's salivation response. These graded responses to stimuli of varying dissimilarity to the original training stimulus are an example of **generalization**, the ability to transfer past learning to novel events and problems. In Chapter 6, "Generalization, Discrimination Learning, and Concept Formation," you will see that generalization occurs in many different forms of learning and memory.

Ivan Pavlov lived through the Russian Revolution of 1917, developing a deep animosity toward the new Communist regime (especially after it stole his Nobel Prize money). Nevertheless, when Pavlov died, in 1936, he was given an elaborate funeral with full honors as a hero of the Soviet state.

Edward Thorndike and the Law of Effect

Meanwhile, over in the United States, Edward Thorndike (1874–1949), a student of William James, was studying how animals learn the relationship or connection between a stimulus and a behavioral response that leads to a desirable outcome. Some of Thorndike's most influential studies involved how cats learn to escape from puzzle boxes—cages secured with complex locking (and unlocking) devices. Thorndike called this kind of training, in which organisms learn to make responses in order to obtain or avoid important consequences, **instrumental conditioning**, because the organism's behavior is instrumental in determining whether the consequences occur. This is in contrast, for example, to the learned response (salivation) of Pavlov's dogs, in which the dogs received their food reward regardless of whether or not they made the learned response. Instrumental conditioning, now more commonly referred to as **operant conditioning**, is the focus of Chapter 5, "Operant Conditioning: Learning the Outcome of Behaviors."

In his studies, Thorndike observed that the probability of a particular behavioral response increased or decreased depending on the consequences that followed. He called this the **law of effect** (Thorndike, 1911). If a particular response led to a desirable consequence, such as access to food, then the probability of the animal making that response in the future *increased*. On the other hand, if the response led to an undesirable consequence (say, an electric shock), then the probability of the animal making that response in the future *decreased*. Fascinated, Thorndike began to methodically investigate the factors that influence how an animal learns new behaviors to maximize its chances of obtaining desirable consequences and avoiding undesirable ones.

| Edward Thorndike

Like many psychologists of his era, Thorndike was strongly influenced by Charles Darwin's theory of natural selection. The basic idea of Thorndike's law of effect has much in common with Darwin's principle of survival of the fittest. In Darwin's theory of evolution, variability in traits was key: animals possessing an inherited trait that increases the likelihood of survival pass it on to future generations. Thorndike's law of effect applied the same principle to explain how behaviors evolve during an animal's lifetime. According to the law of effect, an animal has a range of behaviors: those behaviors that lead to positive consequences for the animal tend to persist; those that do not tend to die out. Starting from this basic principle, Thorndike argued that the psychology of learning should center on the search for the rules describing how, when, and to what degree connections among stimuli and responses are increased or decreased through experience (Thorndike, 1932, 1949).

In 1917, Thorndike became the first psychologist elected to the prestigious U.S. National Academy of Sciences, and in the early 1920s he was often identified as one of the most influential scientists in the United States. He died in 1949, the last of the pioneers in experimental psychology of learning and memory. Thorndike's work set the stage for the next major movement in learning research: the behaviorists of the mid-twentieth century.

Interim Summary

- With the emergence of experimental psychology in the late 1800s, the study of learning and memory, as well as other branches of psychology, began to employ experiments designed to test specific hypotheses. Many of the central figures in this movement were strongly influenced by Charles Darwin's recent work on evolution and natural selection.

instrumental conditioning. The process whereby organisms learn to make responses in order to obtain or avoid important consequences.

operant conditioning. The process whereby organisms learn to make responses in order to obtain or avoid important consequences.

law of effect. The observation, made by Thorndike, that the probability of a particular behavioral response increases or decreases depending on the consequences that have followed that response in the past.

- Hermann Ebbinghaus conducted the first rigorous experimental studies of human memory. He introduced the technique of studying lists of short nonsense words and collected data on how information is retained and forgotten.

- Ivan Pavlov discovered a basic method for training animals to associate a previously neutral stimulus, such as a bell, with a naturally significant stimulus, such as food.

- Edward Thorndike showed that the probability of an animal making a behavioral response increases or decreases depending on the consequences that follow. He called this principle the law of effect. It was analogous to Darwin's idea of survival of the fittest: those responses that produce the most beneficial effects survive, while others die out.

Test Your Knowledge

Who's Who in the History of Learning and Memory?

Below is a (slightly tongue-in-cheek) review of the major researchers and ideas covered in the first two sections of this chapter. See if you can fill in the blanks with the names of the researchers. (Answers appear in the back of the book.)

1. Old _____ was a Greek
   Who thought about association.
   _____, the dualist, liked to speak
   Of mind-and-body separation.

2. To _____, a baby's mind was blank,
   As all empiricists have said.
   Nativists called him a crank,
   Believing knowledge is inbred.

3. _____'s models of the mind
   Had features linked together,
   Updating Greeks from ancient times
   And going them one better.

4. _____ learned nonsense words;
   Dogs learned to drool for _____ .
   _____ studied food rewards
   (And coined "effect, the law of").

1.3 The Reign of Behaviorism

In the 1920s, an American approach to learning emerged that was called **behaviorism**. Building on the work of Pavlov and Thorndike, it argued that psychology should restrict itself to the study of observable behaviors (such as lever presses, salivation, and other measurable physical actions) and avoid reference to unobservable, and often ill-defined, internal mental events (such as consciousness, intent, and thought). Proponents of this approach, who were called *behaviorists*, wanted to distance themselves from philosophers and psychologists who explored the inner workings of the mind through personal introspection and anecdotal observation. Behaviorists wanted psychology to be taken seriously as a rigorous branch of natural science, no less solid than biology or chemistry.

behaviorism. A school of thought that argues that psychology should restrict itself to the study of observable behaviors (such as lever presses, salivation, and other measurable actions) and not seek to infer unobservable mental processes.

John Watson's Behaviorism

Brash, ambitious, and self-made, John Watson (1878–1958) is considered the founder of behaviorism. He was born in Greenville, South Carolina, to a ne'er-do-well father who abandoned the family when Watson was 13 years old. Although a poor student as a child, Watson not only finished college but went on to graduate school, where he conducted research on how rats learn. In these studies, Watson placed a rat at the entrance to a maze and rewarded it with food if it found its way through the corridors to the exit.

Initially, a "naive" (i.e., untrained) rat might spend half an hour wandering randomly through the maze until it reached the exit. After 30 training trials, however, the rat could traverse the maze in less than 10 seconds. To find out what drove the rat's performance, Watson systematically eliminated various possibilities. First, he trained rats to run through the maze under normal conditions. Then he surgically blinded the rats, or rendered them deaf, or removed their whiskers (which rats use like fingertips to feel their way). None of these treatments impaired the rats' performance. Thinking the rats might be using olfactory cues to find their way, Watson boiled the mazes to eliminate all odors. The rats still found their way through. Only when the maze was rotated or when the corridors were made shorter or longer did the rats show a significant loss in their ability to navigate the maze. From these studies, Watson argued that the rats had learned an automatic set of motor habits for moving through the maze and that these motor habits were largely independent of any external sensory cues (Watson, 1907). Such learned motor habits, or skills, are discussed further in Chapter 8, "Skill Memory: Learning by Doing."

According to Watson, psychology should be viewed as a "purely objective experimental branch of natural science. Its theoretical goal is the prediction and control of behavior" (Watson, 1913). Watson was a strong empiricist, sharing Locke's belief in the overwhelming influence of experience (nurture) versus heredity (nature) in determining our behaviors and capabilities. In a rousing affirmation of Aristotle's principle of the blank slate, Watson wrote: "Give me a dozen healthy infants, well-formed, and my own specified world to bring them up in, and I'll guarantee to take any one at random and train him to become any type of specialist I might select—doctor, lawyer, artist, merchant, chief, and yes even beggarman and thief, regardless of the talents, penchants, tendencies, abilities, vocations, and race of his ancestors" (Watson, 1924, p. 82). In the years following World War I, many people hoped for a new dawn of equal opportunity and freedom from class-based constraints on social progress. Watson's bold claims had a strong appeal for scientists and the wider public. By the early 1920s, behaviorism had become the predominant approach to the psychology of learning, especially in the United States.

Watson's career as an academic researcher came to a sudden end when he became involved in a relationship with his research assistant, Rosalie Rayner. Given Watson's fame as a scientist, his status as a married man, and Rayner's socially prominent family, the affair received intense media scrutiny. In the end, the scandal grew so great that Johns Hopkins University gave Watson a choice between ending his affair or resigning from his position at the university. Choosing to stay with Rayner, Watson resigned from Johns Hopkins and started a successful career in advertising, where he applied the same strict scientific principles to marketing research as to his earlier experiments. In spite of this controversy, the American Psychological Association honored him, soon before his death in 1958, with a gold medal for lifetime contributions to the field of psychology.

| John Watson

Underwood & Underwood/Corbis

| Clark Hull

Clark Hull and Mathematical Models of Learning

Born on a farm near Akron, Ohio, Clark Hull (1884–1952) devoted his career to developing mathematical equations to describe the relationships among the factors that influence learning. Hull's early life was marked by life-threatening illness. He survived an attack of typhoid fever but sustained lasting brain damage, which caused memory difficulties that plagued him for the rest of his life. He also survived a bout of polio that left him paralyzed in one leg and dependent on crutches to walk.

In Hull's day, the new doctrine of behaviorism claimed that all behavior could be understood as a set of connections between stimuli and responses. When Pavlov's dogs heard the doorbell, they salivated (doorbell→salivation); when Watson's rats entered the maze, they made a series of motor-habit responses (maze entry→turn left, turn right, and so on). Such learning is often called *stimulus–response learning*, abbreviated as $S \rightarrow R$ *learning*. Of course, the behaviorists acknowledged that the real world is complicated and that other factors might affect the response. For example, Pavlov's dogs might salivate to the doorbell only if they were hungry. Still, the behaviorists believed that if you could specify all the existing factors, you ought to be able to predict exactly whether and when a stimulus would provoke an animal to make a response.

Hull set himself the goal of developing a comprehensive mathematical model of animal learning that would predict exactly what an animal will learn in any given situation. Much as Einstein had recently shown that a single equation, $E = mc^2$, could explain the complex relationship between energy (E), mass (m), and the speed of light (c), Hull hoped to find a similarly powerful equation to relate all the key factors contributing to a learning experience. The variables that Hull entered into his equations included the number of learning trials, the frequency of reward, the spacing between trials, the intensity of the stimulus cues, the animal's motivation for reward, and the incentive value (desirability) of the reward (Hull, 1943). Hull conducted an intensive program of research on learning in animals and humans, seeking to test and refine his mathematical models. One measure of a model's value is its ability to serve as a basis for experimental research; in this regard, Hull's model was a great success. By the 1940s, Hull's work was cited in 70% of all scientific papers on learning published in the major journals (Spence, 1952).

Although Hull's equations were influential in their time, their specifics are no longer considered relevant today. Hull's models have been abandoned because modern psychologists have despaired of ever being able to reduce all the factors governing learning into a single equation, as Hull had hoped to do. Nevertheless, Hull's many students and followers (often called neo-Hullians) carried on toward a smaller goal: to develop mathematical equations to describe basic kinds or components of learning. (You will read in Chapter 4, "Classical Conditioning: Learning to Predict Significant Events," about one of the most enduring neo-Hullian learning theories: the Rescorla–Wagner rule, which describes some factors governing classical "Pavlovian" conditioning). Neo-Hullian researchers showed that learning indeed follows reliable, predictable patterns and pointed the way toward an understanding of how the same basic patterns govern learning in humans as in other animals.

B. F. Skinner's Radical Behaviorism

Burrhus Frederic Skinner (1904–1990), born in rural Pennsylvania, became the most famous—and perhaps most infamous—behaviorist of the twentieth century. Although his original goal was to be a writer, Skinner instead went to graduate school in psychology. He placed himself squarely in the behaviorist camp, believing that psychologists should limit themselves to the study of observable behaviors and not try to speculate about what is going on in the mind of an animal while it learns.

In research that extended and refined the techniques Thorndike had developed to study how animals learn new responses, Skinner developed an automated learning apparatus that was widely adopted by others, who dubbed it the "Skinner box" (you'll read more about this and Skinner's other innovations in Chapter 5, "Operant Conditioning: Learning the Outcome of Behaviors"). He also made many important contributions to our understanding of how animals learn the relationship between responses and consequences. One of the most important happened by accident.

In the early 1940s, Skinner was in his laboratory on a Friday afternoon, setting up some studies in which he taught rats to perform a response in order to obtain food pellets. He realized he didn't have enough food pellets to get him through all the experiments planned for that weekend. Rather than cancel the experiments or go out and get more rat food, Skinner decided to save pellets by providing food only after the rats made two or three correct responses in a row. This led Skinner to one of his greatest discoveries: when trained with intermittent reinforcements, rats learn to respond as quickly and as frequently as when they are rewarded on every trial—in fact, sometimes even more so. Skinner and his students began a massive new program of research on how learning is affected by the reliability with which an organism's responses result in consequences (such as obtaining a food pellet).

Today, B. F. Skinner's name is far better known than Watson's or Thorndike's because his influence extended beyond the laboratory. Fulfilling his early ambition of becoming a writer, Skinner wrote several popular books, including *Walden Two* (1948), which described a highly regulated utopian society in which socially desirable behaviors would be maintained through the same kind of training regimens Skinner applied to his pigeons and rats (other ways of transmitting socially desirable behaviors are discussed in Chapter 11, "Social Learning and Memory: Observing, Interacting, and Reenacting"). In another best-selling book, *Beyond Freedom and Dignity* (1971), Skinner advocated an extreme form of behaviorism, often called **radical behaviorism**, in which he asserted that consciousness and free will are illusions. Humans, like all other animals, he argued, function by blindly producing pre-programmed (learned) responses to environmental stimuli. By the middle of the twentieth century, Skinner was the most famous psychologist in the world. Skinner continued promoting radical behaviorism right up until the night of his death in 1990, which he spent working on a talk for an upcoming convention. The talk was to be titled "Can Psychology Be a Science of the Mind?" (His answer, of course, was a resounding no!) But by that time, mainstream psychology had

© Bettmann/CORBIS

| B. F. Skinner

radical behaviorism. An extreme form of behaviorism, championed by B. F. Skinner, holding that consciousness and free will are illusions and that even so-called higher cognitive functions (e.g., human language) are merely complex sets of stimulus response associations.

| Edward Tolman

cognitive map. An internal psychological representation of the spatial layout of the external world.

moved past the strict confines of behaviorism to focus on the very mental events that Skinner and his fellow behaviorists had fought so hard to discredit.

The Neo-Behaviorism of Edward Tolman

As a college student at the Massachusetts Institute of Technology (MIT), Edward Tolman (1886–1959) originally planned to pursue a career in chemistry. However, during his senior year he read William James's *Principles of Psychology* and was so inspired that he decided instead to pursue a graduate degree in psychology.

Tolman began building a series of rat mazes for the study of learning, much as Thorndike and Watson had done before him. In contrast to Watson, who had argued for a purely mechanical approach that described rat learning as the formation of connections between stimuli and responses, Tolman was convinced his rats were learning something more. He believed they had goals and intentions, such as the goal of finding the exit and seeking food. Rats, he argued, are intrinsically motivated to learn the general layout of mazes by forming what he called a **cognitive map**, an internal psychological representation of the spatial layout of the external world (Tolman, 1948). "Behavior reeks of purpose" was Tolman's well-known and oft-repeated maxim (Tolman, 1932).

In one series of studies, Tolman showed the value of cognitive maps for understanding how rats can apply what they have learned in novel situations. Rats, he showed, are able to find food in mazes by using alternative routes if their preferred route is blocked, as shown in Figure 1.6 (Tolman, 1948). They can also find their way to the goal if they are started from a novel position in

Figure 1.6 Cognitive maps in rats Tolman believed that rats form cognitive maps, internal representations of the layout of the world. (a) In one experiment, rats placed in a maze (at "Start") learned to run directly to a box ("Goal box") where food was provided; the purple line shows the rats' route. (b) If the preferred route was blocked, rats could easily find an effective alternative route (orange line); this indicates that they had information about the spatial layout of the maze.

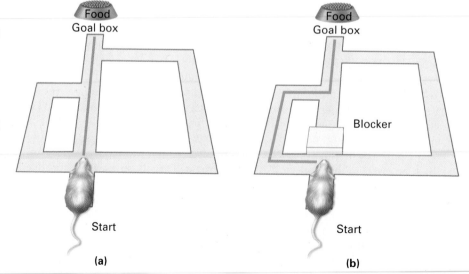

the maze rather than the usual starting point. None of this could be explained by the learning of simple stimulus–response connections.

Tolman even showed that rats can form cognitive maps in the absence of any explicit reward (such as food). He allowed some rats to freely explore a maze (like the one in Figure 1.6), with no food in it, for several days. Later, when he placed these rats in the maze with a food reward at one location ("Goal box"), the rats learned to find the food much faster than rats not previously exposed to the maze and almost as fast as rats that had been explicitly trained to find the food in the goal box. These studies are described in more detail in Chapter 3, "Habituation, Sensitization, and Familiarization: Learning about Repeated Events" (see especially Figure 3.6). This, Tolman argued, showed that during their free exploration, the rats were learning a cognitive map that they could exploit later. He called this **latent learning**, meaning learning that takes place even when there is no specific motivation to obtain or avoid a specific consequence, such as food or shock (Tolman, 1932). Tolman argued that such latent learning is a natural part of our everyday life. The idea of latent learning challenged a strict behaviorist assumption that all learning reflects stimulus–response associations. Further discussion of the latent learning that results from exposure to places or events can be found in Chapter 3. The effects of latent learning are discussed both in Chapter 3 and in Chapter 6, "Generalization, Discrimination Learning, and Concept Formation."

At a time when Clark Hull and other theorists were seeking to discover fundamental principles of behavior that avoided any mention of unobservable mental events, Tolman took a different approach. Emphasizing the importance of internal representations of the environment and utilizing concepts such as purpose and intent that are not directly observable, only inferred, Tolman broke away from the stricter confines of behaviorist dogma, all the while satisfying the behaviorists' high standards of experimental control and methodological rigor. For this reason, Tolman is often referred to as a *neo-behaviorist*. His influential theoretical and experimental research—though at odds with many of his behaviorist contemporaries—laid the foundation for cognitive studies of animal and human learning.

latent learning. Learning that is undetected (latent) until explicitly demonstrated at a later stage.

Interim Summary

- Behaviorists argue that psychologists should study only observable events and should not attempt to speculate about what's going on inside an organism. Behaviorism doesn't deny that internal mental processes exist, just that they are unnecessary and inappropriate subjects for the scientific study of behavior.

- John Watson, the father of behaviorism, proposed that psychology should be a purely experimental branch of natural science whose goal is the prediction and control of behavior in both animals and humans.

- The comprehensive mathematical theories of animal and human learning developed by Clark Hull could be rigorously tested in experimental studies.

- B. F. Skinner conducted detailed studies of the factors that control behavior while at the same time taking the behaviorists' message to the broader public through widely read and controversial books.

- Edward Tolman, a neo-behaviorist, combined the scientific rigor of the behaviorist methodology with consideration of internal mental events such as goals and cognitive maps of the environment.

1.4 The Cognitive Approach

The behaviorist approach to learning had great appeal. It was rigorous, precise, and amenable to mathematical specification. By avoiding vague and unverifiable suppositions, it offered the promise that psychology would rise in the twentieth century to the status of a serious branch of science, alongside chemistry and physics. However, by the mid-1950s, there was a growing consensus that behaviorism could not, ultimately, deliver a full account of the complexities of human behavior (and probably was insufficient to understand all of animal behavior as well). As you have just read, it failed to account for Tolman's studies of rats and their cognitive maps. It also failed to explain language, perception, reasoning, and memory, the fundamental components of higher-level human cognition.

Skinner, the radical behaviorist, had argued that language and language acquisition could be explained with behaviorist principles, as a (complex) series of stimulus–response associations (B. F. Skinner, 1957). To counter these claims, linguist Noam Chomsky wrote what may be the most influential book review ever published in the sciences: a critique of Skinner's book, demonstrating how and why behaviorist principles alone could not explain how children acquire complex aspects of language such as grammar and syntax (Chomsky, 1959). By the early 1960s, many psychologists interested in human cognition began to turn away from behaviorism, with its focus on animal research and the idea that all learning could be reduced to a series of stimulus–response associations. The stage was set for the rise of **cognitive psychology**, a new subfield of psychology that focused on human abilities such as thinking, language, and reasoning—the abilities not easily explained by a strictly behaviorist approach.

W. K. Estes and Mathematical Psychology

William K. Estes (1919–2011) had a long and productive career that encompassed the science of learning and memory from behaviorism to **cognitive science**, the interdisciplinary study of thought, reasoning, and other higher mental functions. Estes, born in 1919, began his graduate studies under the tutelage of Skinner during the early 1940s. As you will read in Chapter 4, "Classical Conditioning: Learning to Predict Significant Events," Estes and Skinner developed a new method for studying classical "Pavlovian" conditioning of fear in rats. Within a few years, their method became one of the most widely used techniques for studying animal conditioning, and it is still in use today. In Chapter 10, "Emotional Influences on Learning and Memory," you will read that learning about emotions, such as fear, has become an important subfield of learning and memory research.

As soon as he completed his PhD, Estes was called into military service. He was stationed in the Philippines as the commandant of a prisoner-of-war camp—an undemanding job that gave him lots of free time to read the mathematics books his wife sent from home. When the war ended, Estes returned to the United States and to the study of psychology. Much to Skinner's dismay, Estes soon began to stray from his mentor's strict behaviorism. He began to use mathematics to describe mental events that could only be inferred indirectly from behavioral data, an approach quite unacceptable to behaviorists. Years later, in his autobiography, Skinner bemoaned the loss of Estes as a once-promising behaviorist, speculating that Estes's preoccupation with mathematical models of unobservable mental events was a war-related injury, resulting perhaps from too much time in the hot Pacific sun (Skinner, 1979).

cognitive psychology. A subfield of psychology that focuses on human abilities—such as thinking, language, and reasoning—that are not easily explained by a strictly behaviorist approach.

cognitive science. The interdisciplinary study of thought, reasoning, and other higher mental functions.

| W. K. Estes

Estes built on Hull's mathematical modeling approach to develop new methods for interpreting a wide variety of learning behaviors (Estes, 1950). Most learning theorists of that era, including Hull, assumed that learning should be viewed as the development of associations between a stimulus and a response. For example, suppose that a pigeon is trained to peck whenever it sees a yellow light, in order to obtain a bit of food. Hull assumed that this training caused the formation of a direct link between the stimulus and the response, so that later presentations of the yellow light evoked the peck-for-food response (Figure 1.7a).

Estes, however, suggested that what seems to be a single stimulus, say a yellow light, is really a collection of many different possible elements making up the yellow light, where each element is some small simple feature or component of a feature associated with yellow light. According to Estes, only a random subset of these elements are noticed (or "sampled," in Estes's terminology) on any given training trial (Figure 1.7b). Only those elements sampled on the current trial are associated with the food. On a different trial, a different subset is sampled (Figure 1.7c), and those elements are now associated with the food. Over time, after many

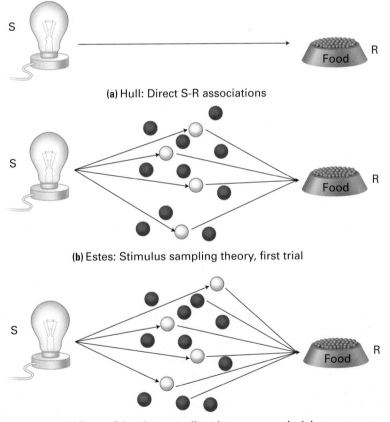

(a) Hull: Direct S-R associations

(b) Estes: Stimulus sampling theory, first trial

(c) Estes: Stimulus sampling theory, second trial

Figure 1.7 Stimulus-response models How does a stimulus (S) become associated with a response (R)? (a) Hull assumed that a direct link was formed between a stimulus (such as a yellow light) and a learned response (such as, in pigeons, pecking for food). (b) Estes proposed an intervening stage, in which a stimulus activates a random sample of feature elements encoding "yellow"; the activated elements are then associated with the response. (c) On a different trial, a different random subset of elements are activated by the stimulus and associated with the response. Over time, with many such random samples, most elements that could potentially be activated by the stimulus become associated with the response. At this point, when a random sample of elements are activated by presentation of the light, most of them are already linked with the response.

such random samples, most of the elements of the stimulus become associated with the correct response. At this point, any presentation of the light activates a random sample of elements, most of which are already linked with the response.

Estes called his idea *stimulus sampling theory*. A key principle is that random variation ("sampling") is essential for learning, much as it is essential for the adaptation of species in Charles Darwin's theory of evolution through natural selection (Estes, 1950). Estes's approach gave a much better account than other theories (such as Hull's) of the variability seen in both animal and human learning, and it helped to explain why even highly trained individuals don't always make the same response perfectly every time: on any given trial, it's always possible that (through sheer randomness) a subset of elements will be activated that are not yet linked to the response. In Chapter 6, "Generalization, Discrimination Learning, and Concept Formation," you will see how Estes's stimulus sampling theory also explains how animals generalize their learning from one stimulus (e.g., a yellow light) to other, physically similar stimuli (e.g., an orange light), as Pavlov had demonstrated back in the 1920s.

mathematical psychology. A subfield of psychology that uses mathematical equations to describe the laws of learning and memory.

Estes's work marked the resurgence of mathematical methods in psychology, reviving the spirit of Hull's earlier efforts. Estes and his colleagues established a new subdiscipline of psychology, **mathematical psychology**, which used mathematical equations to describe the laws of learning and memory. From his early work in animal conditioning, through his founding role in mathematical psychology, to his later contributions to cognitive psychology, Estes continued to be a vigorous proponent of mathematical models to inform our understanding of learning and memory. He died in 2011, following a long struggle with Parkinson's disease, a neurological disorder that destroys the brain cells required to learn new habits, and severely impairs movement (see Chapters 5 and 8).

Gordon Bower: Learning by Insight

Gordon Bower was born in 1932 in Scio, Ohio, a small town struggling to survive the Great Depression. After playing varsity baseball in college, he had two career choices: professional baseball or graduate school in psychology. Although tempted by the former, Bower figured he had a better chance of long-term success in psychology than in baseball. In graduate school at Yale, Bower got caught up in the heady excitement of mathematical psychology and the efforts of Estes and other mathematical psychologists to describe behavior through mathematical equations.

The dominant psychological learning theories of the time assumed that human learning, like animal learning, proceeded gradually through incremental changes either in association strengths (the Hull approach) or in the probability of choosing the correct response (the Estes approach), both of which predicted gradual transitions in learning performance. In contrast, Bower proposed a new "one-step" model of some human learning. If you've ever solved a difficult puzzle or word game, you may have experienced an "aha" moment of insight: Initially, you don't know the answer; then, all of a sudden, you do know it. Unlike the smooth, incremental learning curves seen in classical conditioning, some learning is experienced as a transition from ignorance to knowledge in a single trial.

Although behaviorists had largely avoided talking about learning by insight, Bower thought it could be explained by a simple mathematical model (Bower, 1961; Bower & Trabasso, 1968). Suppose a person is assigned some task, such as figuring out the sequence in which to press four buttons to open a combination lock. In the beginning, he has no knowledge of the correct answer, but on each trial he will probably try out a different sequence. Odds are that it will take a few trials before he happens to try

Gordon Bower (seated) and his graduate adviser **Neal Miller** conduct a rat learning experiment at Yale University in the 1950s.

Courtesy of Gordon Bower

the correct order. But once he does, and he opens the lock—aha!—he knows the answer. Thereafter, he will press the correct sequence on all subsequent trials. Unlike the smooth learning curve shown in Figure 1.5b, this person's learning curve would look like the one in Figure 1.8a: a long period of 0% correct responses that transitions all at once into a period of 100% correct responses.

The problem, however, is that most psychologists report *average* learning curves for a group of people, summarizing the data from many participants in the same experiment. Bower's important insight was that if every participant solves the task in one insightful moment, the trial on which this occurs will vary from one person to another. One participant might learn on the fifth trial, another might get lucky and guess the correct answer on the first or second trial, and someone else might not guess the correct answer until the 15th trial. If a large number of participants are tested, the data will show that almost no one responds correctly on the first or second trial, a few respond correctly on the third or fourth trial, a few more respond correctly on the trials after that, and so on, until, by the end of the experiment, almost everyone is giving the correct response. If we graph the percentage of subjects who give the correct response on each trial of the combination-lock task, the result will look very much like a standard learning curve that moves incrementally from 0 to 100% in the course of the experiment (Figure 1.8b), even though no *individual* participant ever showed incremental learning! By studying such phenomena, Bower showed that to understand learning, it is necessary to consider individual performance, not just averages across a large group of participants. Some other studies that show similar one-trial learning of skills are discussed in Chapter 8, "Skill Memory: Learning by Doing."

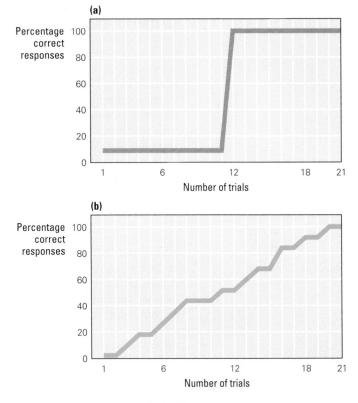

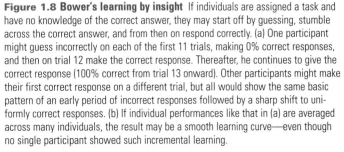

Figure 1.8 Bower's learning by insight If individuals are assigned a task and have no knowledge of the correct answer, they may start off by guessing, stumble across the correct answer, and from then on respond correctly. (a) One participant might guess incorrectly on each of the first 11 trials, making 0% correct responses, and then on trial 12 make the correct response. Thereafter, he continues to give the correct response (100% correct from trial 13 onward). Other participants might make their first correct response on a different trial, but all would show the same basic pattern of an early period of incorrect responses followed by a sharp shift to uniformly correct responses. (b) If individual performances like that in (a) are averaged across many individuals, the result may be a smooth learning curve—even though no single participant showed such incremental learning.

Bower's influence on the field of memory research stems not only from his own research but also from his role as a prolific educator and mentor to young psychologists, many of whom went on to play major roles in the growing field of cognitive psychology.

George Miller and Information Theory

Estes and Bower were not the only investigators becoming disillusioned with the strict confines of the behaviorist approach. Other psychologists too began to seek explanations for observations that could not be explained by the assumption of an incrementally learned association between stimulus and response. One of these was George Miller (1920–2012), another child of the Depression, who grew up in Charleston, West Virginia.

During World War II, many of Harvard's faculty worked on problems for the military. As a graduate student at Harvard, Miller was given the task of designing a jamming signal to disrupt German radio communications. This wartime research on spoken communications led Miller to study other questions of speech perception, such as how context affects communication. For example, if a man floundering in the sea shouts, "Help, I'm drowning!" you might understand the message easily, even if the speech is garbled or indistinct—given the context, it's obvious what the man is trying to communicate. On the other hand, if you meet a man on the street, with no prior expectation of what he might be trying to communicate, his speech would need to be much clearer for you to understand his message: is he greeting you, asking for directions, telling you your shoelaces are untied, or soliciting money?

While puzzling over this, Miller read a paper by mathematician and electrical engineer Claude Shannon that described *information theory*, a mathematical theory of communication that provides a precise measure of how much information is contained in a message, based not only on the message itself but also on the listener's prior knowledge (Shannon, 1948). For example, if a friend tells you that Chris, a student in his psychology class, is male, how much information is in the message? That depends on what you already know. If you already know that all the students in his class are male, then the message contains no new information. If, however, you know that the class is co-ed, information theory would say that your friend's message contains 1 *bit* of information, where a bit is a "binary digit," 1 or 0, that can represent two alternative states (such as 1 = female, 0 = male). If you ask your friend about Chris's gender, all he has to do is reply "1" (female) or "0" (male)—a message composed of a single bit of information is all the answer you need.

Miller's goal was to adapt information theory to psychology. Specifically, could information theory help us understand how people make judgments about the magnitude of various stimuli? How bright is it? How loud? How high in pitch? Miller discovered that people's capacity to make judgments concerning magnitude across a range was limited to about seven alternative values (this is why many rating scales ask you to rate your opinions on a scale of 1 to 7, such as a survey that asks you your opinion of a new product, ranging from 1, not satisfied, to 7, totally satisfied).

At the same time, Miller was conducting a seemingly unrelated project to measure the capacity of people's short-term memory for digits: he would read aloud strings of numbers and ask people to repeat the numbers from memory. Most people, Miller found, could accurately repeat strings of up to 5 to 9 numbers, but almost no one could remember strings of 10 or more digits. The average memory capacity for numbers (sometimes called a *digit span*) seemed to be about 7 digits, plus or minus 2.

Noting that a capacity of seven appeared in both projects—magnitude rating and digit span—Miller used this seemingly superficial connection as the humorous title of a paper that summarized both projects: "The Magical Number Seven, Plus or Minus Two" (Miller, 1956). The paper became one of the most influential and oft-cited papers in cognitive psychology and spurred later research that showed similar limits on the capacity of human working memory for other kinds of information: the "magic number seven" applied not just to digits but to words, pictures, and even complex ideas. Miller's central message was that the human mind is limited in capacity, that information theory provides a way to measure this capacity, and that these limits apply to a diverse range of human

| **George Miller**

capabilities. Our working memory capacity and capabilities are the focus of Chapter 9, "Working Memory and Cognitive Control."

Test Your Knowledge

Borrowing from the Physical and Natural Sciences to Explain the Mind

Throughout the history of learning and memory, many (if not most) of the scientists who contributed important theoretical advances did so by liberally borrowing from (and sometimes aping) the methods and concepts of the physical and natural sciences. In the table below we list many of these scientists (or philosophers) and the source from which they borrowed. Tell us what they used these borrowed concepts to help explain in the psychology of learning and memory. (Answers appear in the back of the book.)

Who . . .	Borrowed from . . .	To explain what?
1. René Descartes	Hydraulic engineering	
2. John Locke	Physics (Newton), chemistry (Boyle)	
3. Hermann Ebbinghaus	Laws of perception (Fechner and Weber)	
4. Ivan Pavlov	Telephone exchanges	
5. Edward Thorndike	Evolution by natural selection (Darwin)	
6. Clark Hull	Theory of relativity (Einstein)	
7. George Miller	Information theory (Shannon)	

---

connectionist models. Networks of uniform and unlabeled connections between simple processing units called nodes.

distributed representation. A representation in which information is coded as a pattern of activation distributed across many different nodes.

The Connectionist Models of David Rumelhart

| David Rumelhart

David Rumelhart (1942–2011), born in rural South Dakota, was the first of his family to graduate from college. As a graduate student working under Estes, Rumelhart acquired a firm grounding in both psychology and mathematics. He began to apply the tools of mathematics to a wide range of problems in cognition and perception, hoping to improve on the cognitive models in vogue at the time. By the late 1970s, Rumelhart and his colleague James McClelland shared a growing belief that cognition was best understood as networks of connections between simple processing units that in their theory were called *nodes*. Borrowing a term from Thorndike (who had thought much the same), Rumelhart and McClelland called such networks **connectionist models** (Rumelhart & McClelland, 1986).

In connectionist models, ideas and concepts in the external world are not represented as distinct and discrete symbols but rather as patterns of activity over populations of many nodes. In a connectionist model, a golden retriever might be represented by a pattern of activation across a set of nodes (the orange circles in Figure 1.9a). A cocker spaniel might be represented by a different pattern of nodes (blue circles in Figure 1.9b). Such a representation is known as a **distributed representation**, because the information consists of the activation of many different nodes—that is, it is "distributed" across many nodes rather than represented by only

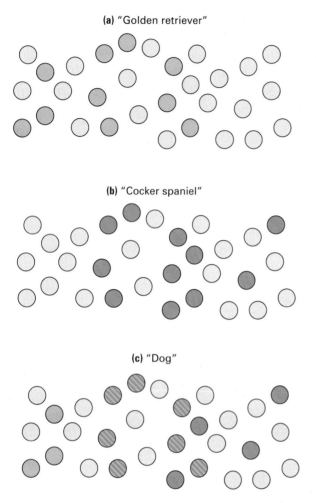

(a) "Golden retriever"

(b) "Cocker spaniel"

(c) "Dog"

Figure 1.9 Distributed representations (a) The representation of "golden retriever" activates one subset of nodes, shown in orange. (b) "Cocker spaniel" activates a different subset, shown in blue. (c) The similarity between them—both are dogs—emerges naturally as a function of the overlap between representations, shown by the orange-and-blue-striped nodes.

one—in a process similar to what Estes had proposed in his stimulus sampling theory. In a connectionist model, the similarity of spaniels to retrievers emerges because they activate common elements—the "dog" elements coded as orange-and-blue-striped circles in Figure 1.9c. The importance of distributed representations and shared elements is discussed in more detail in Chapter 6, "Generalization, Discrimination Learning, and Concept Formation."

Connectionist models were inspired in part by ideas about how the brain is organized (see Chapter 2, "The Neuroscience of Learning and Memory"). Part of the expectation held for connectionist models was that they would fulfill William James's hope for a psychology that links brain physiology to behavior. Connectionist models laid the groundwork for a more complete integration of neuroscience with psychology, a goal that is also a core theme of this book.

After many productive years helping psychologists understand the computational power of networks of brain connections, David Rumelhart's own brain networks began to fail him. In 1998, at the age of 56, he was diagnosed with Pick's disease, an illness (similar to Alzheimer's disease) that causes degeneration of the brain. For the last years of his life, until he died in 2011, he was no longer able to speak or recognize old friends and colleagues. Like Clive Wearing, David Rumelhart lost the vital memories that defined who he was.

And . . . what next? In the past few decades there has been a revolution in the field of learning and memory. As you will see in the next chapter, our growing ability to measure and manipulate brain function has fundamentally altered how we look at learning and memory. One consequence of this recent progress has been a fusion of neuroscience and psychology into the integrated study of learning and memory in animals and humans. Despite these recent changes, most current research in the field of learning and memory can be understood as building on the challenges, issues, and questions that have been evolving in philosophy and psychology over the centuries.

Interim Summary

- W. K. Estes built on Hull's mathematical modeling approach to develop new mathematical models for interpreting a wide variety of learning behaviors.

- Gordon Bower developed a simple model of one-trial insight learning that illustrated how individual performance can look quite different from averaged group performance during learning.

- George Miller used information theory to understand memory's limits and mechanisms.

- David Rumelhart played a key role in showing how connectionist network models could link brain processes to the complexities of human memory and cognition.

Synthesis

At the start of this chapter summarizing the history of the psychology of learning and memory, we urged you to notice five themes, or basic questions, interwoven throughout.

1. *How do sensations or ideas become linked in the mind?* Aristotle identified the basic requirements for association more than 2,000 years ago: contiguity, frequency, and similarity. Pavlov showed how we can study and measure learning about associations that exist in the world. Thorndike showed how reward and punishment govern which associations we learn to make. Both Hull and Skinner built on the work of Thorndike, with Hull focusing on mathematical models to explain the factors that influence learning and Skinner expanding the experimental analyses of reward and punishment and applying his research to society. Today, most psychologists take for granted the idea that memory involves forming associations among ideas or sensations, although there are still arguments about exactly how these associations are formed and how they are used.

2. *How are memories built from the components of experience?* Early philosophers and psychologists sought to describe how elements of our experiences could be combined into the whole of consciousness (Locke) or into networks of associations that describe our memories and knowledge (James). Estes's model of memory as distributed patterns of selected elements was updated by Rumelhart and others into connectionist network models that drew inspiration from brain circuits as well as from James's early models of memory.

3. *To what extent are behaviors and abilities determined by biological inheritance (nature) and to what extent by life experiences (nurture)?* Aristotle and Locke firmly believed that we enter the world as blank slates, with our experiences the sole factor influencing our behavior and capabilities. This position, empiricism, carried over into the behaviorism of Watson and Skinner. At the other extreme, Descartes was more strongly allied with the nature (or nativist) camp and believed that we inherit our talents and abilities. Today, most researchers take the middle road: acknowledging the profound influence of genes (nature) on learning and memory, while noting that a lifetime of experience (nurture) modifies these influences.

4. *In what ways are human learning and memory similar to learning and memory in other animals, and in what ways do they differ?* Most early philosophers assumed that humans were quite distinct from and innately superior to animals, but the proponents of evolution, such as Erasmus and Charles Darwin, showed how similar we are. Behaviorists also emphasized the similarities between animal and human learning. In contrast, the early cognitive psychologists chose to focus on computer-based models of language and abstract reasoning—cognitive behaviors that are not easily studied in nonhuman animals. More recent efforts to reconcile the associationist theories of animal learning and the higher capabilities of human cognition are seen in the connectionist models of Rumelhart, McClelland, and their intellectual descendants. Today, many researchers think of cognition as a continuum, with some animals (e.g., rats and pigeons) perhaps possessing only limited capability for abstract reasoning, but others (e.g., dolphins and chimpanzees) capable of a degree of communication, reasoning, and use of symbol representation approaching that of humans.

5. *Can the psychological study of the mind be rigorously scientific, uncovering universal principles of learning and memory that can be described by mathematical equations and considered fundamental laws?* Throughout the history of studies on learning and memory, philosophers and psychologists have borrowed methods and metaphors from physics, chemistry, and other scientific fields to enhance their understanding. Ebbinghaus was among the first to show that psychology could indeed be the subject of careful experimentation. Hull attempted to devise mathematical equations to describe learning, and the tradition was continued by Estes and others working in mathematical and cognitive approaches. In current research, most psychologists hold themselves to the same rigorous principles of experimental methodology adhered to by scientists in other disciplines; if psychologists want their work to be taken seriously, they have to pay close attention to experimental design and analysis.

KNOW YOUR KEY TERMS

associationism, *p. 4*
behaviorism, *p. 18*
blind design, *p. 14*
classical conditioning, *p. 15*
cognitive map, *p. 22*
cognitive psychology, *p. 24*
cognitive science, *p. 24*
connectionist models, *p. 29*
contiguity, *p. 4*
data, *p. 4*
dependent variable, *p. 14*
distributed representation, *p. 29*
double-blind design, *p. 15*
dualism, *p. 7*
empiricism, *p. 5*

evolution, *p. 10*
evolutionary psychology, *p. 12*
experiment, *p. 13*
experimental psychology, *p. 13*
experimenter bias, *p. 15*
extinction, *p. 16*
forgetting, *p. 14*
generalization, *p. 16*
independent variable, *p. 14*
instrumental conditioning, *p. 17*
latent learning, *p. 23*
law of effect, *p. 17*
learning, *p. 2*
learning curve, *p. 15*

mathematical psychology, *p. 26*
memory, *p. 2*
nativism, *p. 5*
natural selection, *p. 10*
operant conditioning, *p. 17*
placebo, *p. 15*
psychology, *p. 8*
radical behaviorism, *p. 21*
reflex arc, *p. 7*
response, *p. 7*
retention curve, *p. 14*
stimulus, *p. 7*
subject bias, *p. 14*
theory, *p. 4*

QUIZ YOURSELF

1. Philosophers utilized both _____ and _____ to gain insight into the abstract principles that govern the universe, as opposed to relying on the _____ that is characteristic of today's research. (p. 4)

2. According to Aristotle's principle of _____, we form a strong association between peanut butter and jelly because they appear together very often. (p. 4)

3. Plato was a proponent of _____, which holds that the bulk of our knowledge is ingrained from birth. His student Aristotle was identified with a school of thought known as _____, which claims that our ideas stem from experience. (p. 5)

4. The belief that the mind and body exist as separate entities is known as _____. A believer in this principle, _____, reasoned that a sensory stimulus and motor response follow a pathway known as the _____. (p. 6–7)

5. According to Darwin, a trait can evolve through _____ if it is inheritable, variable, and _____. (p. 10)

6. The late 1800s saw the birth of _____, as scientists interested in psychology began to conduct systematic experiments examining the validity of a hypothesis through manipulation of variables. (p. 13)

7. A contemporary of William James, _____, proposed that the psychology of memory can be

defined precisely through mathematical laws as a rigorous natural science. (p. 13)

8. How memory deteriorates over time is known as _____. Measuring how much information is retained at each point in time following learning, Ebbinghaus was able to plot a _____. (p. 14)

9. Thorndike referred to the training in which organisms learn to make certain responses in order to obtain or avoid important consequences as _____, which is now also known commonly as _____. (p. 17)

10. In Pavlov's classic conditioning, an animal or person learns to associate the _____ with a(n) _____ so as to produce a(n) _____ (p. 15)

11. Emerging in the 1920s, the American approach to learning known as _____ centered around the argument that psychology should exclusively study observable behaviors. (p. 18)

12. Although the work of _____ is no longer considered relevant today, his students and followers carried on toward developing mathematical equations to explain learning. (p. 20)

13. In _____'s law of _____, behaviors that lead to desirable consequences are _____ likely to happen again in the future. (p. 17)

14. Edward Tolman, a neo-behaviorist, argued that his rats, intrinsically motivated to learn the general layout of mazes, had formed _____, internal psychological representations of the external world. (p. 22)

15. Learning that takes place even in the absence of any specific motivation to obtain or avoid important consequences is called _____. (p. 23)

16. An increasing focus on human abilities such as language, reasoning, and thinking led to the rise of _____ psychology. These abilities are not readily explained by a strict _____ approach. (p. 24)

17. The trial-by-trial variability in the elements we attend to when experiencing a stimulus is captured in the _____ of _____ . (p. 26)

18. The number of digits in a standard phone number (not including area code) is relevant to the work of _____. (p. 28)

19. The importance of looking at individual subjects' performance, not just group averages, was illustrated by the work of _____ on _____. (p. 27)

20. The _____ models of cognition suggest that ideas and concepts in the external world are not represented as distinct symbols but as patterns of activity over populations of many nodes. In these models, a _____ representation consists of the activation of many different nodes as opposed to only one. (p. 29)

Answers appear in the back of the book.

CONCEPT CHECK

1. Categorize the following thinkers as taking either the empiricism approach or nativism approach: Aristotle, Plato, Descartes, Locke, James. Describe how each was influenced by the others.

2. Several studies have shown what seems to be a genetic influence on some kinds of memory ability: parents with high memory ability are likely to have children who also have high memory ability. How would an empiricist account for such findings?

3. How did Tolman's latent learning studies challenge behaviorism? Could you develop an alternative interpretation of his studies that are consistent with behaviorism?

4. Give an example of a piece of information that consists of 3 bits, and explain how you came up with it.

Answers appear in the back of the book.

CHAPTER 2

The Neuroscience of Learning and Memory

I N THE MIDST OF A NEIGHBORHOOD BASEBALL GAME, a ball hit Orlando Serrell in the head so hard that it knocked him to the ground. At the time, he was only 10 years old, and like most boys who take a hit while playing with peers, he walked it off and eventually went back to the game. This seemingly innocuous incident proved anything but typical, however. Sometime after the hit, Orlando discovered an amazing ability to remember the day of the week on which any date fell that occurred after the fateful game, as well as what the weather was like on most of those days, without making any conscious effort to memorize this information or perform calculations with dates. Orlando's case is not unique but is an instance of a rare condition called *acquired savant syndrome* (Treffert, 2009). Chapter 1 described Clive Wearing, who lost many of his memory abilities after part of his brain was destroyed. Unlike Clive, individuals with acquired savant syndrome actually gain prodigious memory capacities as the result of brain injury. The startling implication of this phenomenon is that at least some human brains (and perhaps all) appear to have a much greater capacity for storing and recalling memories than people typically exhibit. If humans have hidden learning and memory capacities, might other animals also possess capacities of which we are currently unaware? If brains have such capacities, then why can't all individuals take full advantage of them? Might it be possible to develop neural technologies that enable a person to better encode and recall specific information or to erase memories of episodes one would prefer to forget?

The story of how scientists explore such questions, and identify the biological factors that determine what an individual remembers or forgets, is the story of the neuroscience of learning and memory. Although scientists still have a long way to go in understanding how nervous systems work, they are compiling

---

Top Five Tips for Faster Forgetting

Chapter 1 provided 10 tips for how you can change your behavior to improve your memory. In case you are more interested in erasing memories than retaining them (wasting time is fun!), you can also modify your brain function to improve your forgetting. Here's what you do.

1. *Don't sleep.* People who don't get enough sleep are less able to concentrate during the day, which makes it harder for them to encode new memories and retrieve old ones. Sleepy brains work worse.

2. *Stress out.* Stress generally interferes with recall. So, if you want to make retrieving information particularly troublesome, just keep fixating on trying to remember things you can't, until frustration overcomes you.

3. *Overextend yourself.* The more things you try to keep in mind simultaneously, the greater the chance you'll forget a bunch of them. So put aside all your note-taking devices—your pens, pads, computers, and iPhones—if you really want to maximize your loss.

4. *Deprive your senses.* The more impoverished your sensory inputs, the less likely you will encode facts, events, and skills well enough to recall them later. Wear headphones, shades, and oven mitts. Minimize the brain activity.

5. *Be apathetic.* Nothing is more forgettable than something you couldn't care less about. Just keep chanting inside your head, "Whatever . . . Whatever . . . Whatever," and you can easily avoid the kinds of emotionally triggered brain states that make memories stick.

---

fascinating information about the brain's structure and functioning and the ways it contributes to learning and memory. New imaging and sensing technologies allow researchers to observe healthy human brains as they form and retrieve memories, while new techniques for animal research allow researchers to measure and manipulate neural changes during learning. Insights into the neural mechanisms of learning and memory can help you to understand how your actions may impact your own attempts to learn, remember, and in some cases forget the materials you study (for some ideas, see "Learning and Memory in Everyday Life," on this page).

2.1 Structural Properties of Nervous Systems

neuroscience. The study of the brain and the rest of the nervous system.

Researchers in the field of **neuroscience**—the study of the brain and the rest of the nervous system—overwhelmingly believe that the brain is the seat of learning and memory. This was not always the prevailing opinion. When ancient Egyptians mummified a body, they first removed the organs they considered important, preserving them in special airtight jars—but they discarded the brain. Many centuries later, Aristotle, one of the most empirically oriented philosophers in history, argued that the brain served primarily to cool the blood. However, observations over the centuries since Aristotle's time have convinced scientists that brain activity controls behavior and, by extension, the changes in behavior associated with learning and memory.

Historically, most early studies of learning and memory focused on observable behavior rather than on the brain and how it functions (Chapter 1). This is not because early learning and memory researchers were oblivious to the importance of the brain. Ivan Pavlov designed all of his behavioral experiments to answer questions about how the brain works. John Watson, the originator of behaviorism, started out studying how developmental changes in neural structures correlate with developmental changes in learning abilities. B. F. Skinner, perhaps the most famous behaviorist of the twentieth century, began his career as a physiologist. Why, then, did these researchers place so much emphasis on behavior and so little emphasis on the role of the brain?

Part of the answer is that brains are among the most complex structures in nature. Even as recently as 50 years ago, the complexity of the neural functions required for most learning tasks seemed incomprehensible. As new technologies became available, however, the study of brain function became more manageable. Today, aspects of brain function that previously were inaccessible are being measured daily in laboratories and medical institutions around the world. These new technologies have dramatically increased the number and productivity of studies exploring the neural substrates of learning and memory.

What Brains Are Like

The brain is just one—albeit very important—component of a collection of body organs called the **nervous system**, the organ system devoted to the distribution and processing of signals that affect biological functions throughout the body. The tissues that are specialized for accomplishing these tasks include cells called **neurons**, which collect incoming signals from the sensory organs of the system (leading to sight, taste, smell, touch, and sound) and from the rest of the body (indicating such conditions as hunger and sleepiness), process these signals, and react to them by coordinating the body's responses (such as muscle movement and activity of internal organs).

In vertebrates, the nervous system can be divided into two parts: the central nervous system and the peripheral nervous system. As its name suggests, the **central nervous system (CNS)** is where many of the events responsible for learning and memory take place: the CNS is made up of the brain and the spinal cord (Figure 2.1). The **peripheral nervous system (PNS)** consists of nerve fibers that connect sensory receptors (for example, visual receptors in the eye or touch receptors in the skin) to the CNS and of other fibers that carry signals from the CNS back out to the muscles and organs. Most of these fibers pass through the spinal cord, but a few—such as those from the light receptors in your eyes and those that activate the muscles controlling eye movements—travel directly to the brain without first making connections in the spinal cord.

Although all vertebrates possess a CNS and PNS, there are big differences between the nervous systems of different species. Let's start with the vertebrate you're probably most familiar with: the human.

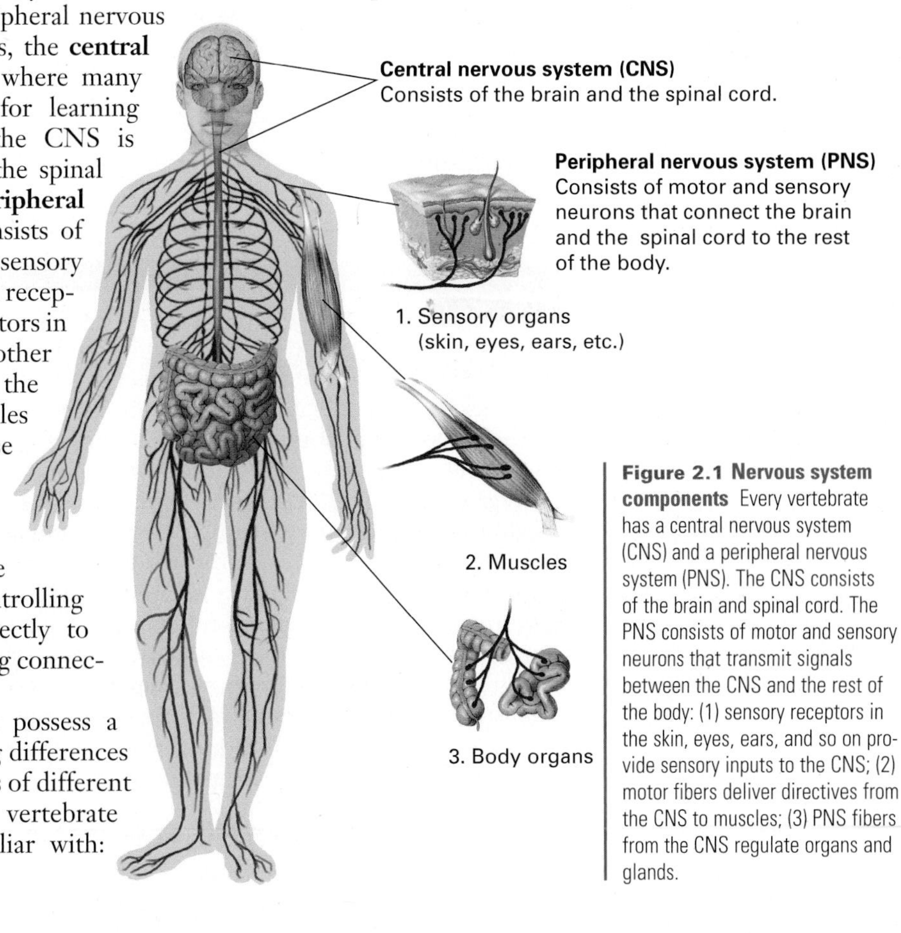

nervous system. An organism's system of tissues specialized for distributing and processing information.

neuron. A type of cell that is specialized for information processing.

central nervous system (CNS). The part of the vertebrate nervous system consisting of the brain and spinal cord.

peripheral nervous system (PNS). The part of the nervous system that carries information from sensory receptors to the central nervous system and carries commands from the CNS to muscles.

Central nervous system (CNS)
Consists of the brain and the spinal cord.

Peripheral nervous system (PNS)
Consists of motor and sensory neurons that connect the brain and the spinal cord to the rest of the body.

1. Sensory organs (skin, eyes, ears, etc.)

2. Muscles

3. Body organs

Figure 2.1 Nervous system components Every vertebrate has a central nervous system (CNS) and a peripheral nervous system (PNS). The CNS consists of the brain and spinal cord. The PNS consists of motor and sensory neurons that transmit signals between the CNS and the rest of the body: (1) sensory receptors in the skin, eyes, ears, and so on provide sensory inputs to the CNS; (2) motor fibers deliver directives from the CNS to muscles; (3) PNS fibers from the CNS regulate organs and glands.

Figure 2.2 The visible surface of a human brain (a) A photograph of a human brain. (b) In each brain hemisphere, the visible cerebral cortex is divided into four principal areas: frontal lobe, parietal lobe, occipital lobe, and temporal lobe. Below the cerebral cortex are the cerebellum and brainstem. The brainstem connects the brain to the spinal cord.

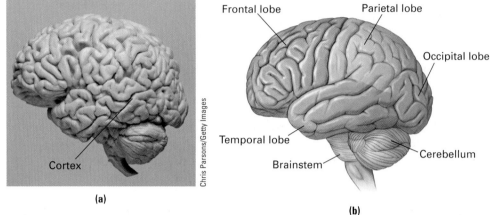

(a)

(b)

Chris Parsons/Getty Images

cerebral cortex. The brain tissue covering the top and sides of the brain in most vertebrates; involved in storage and processing of sensory inputs and motor outputs.

frontal lobe. The part of the cerebral cortex lying at the front of the human brain; enables a person to plan and perform actions.

parietal lobe. The part of the cerebral cortex lying at the top of the human brain; important for processing somatosensory (touch) information.

temporal lobe. The part of the cerebral cortex lying at the sides of the human brain; important for language and auditory processing and for learning new facts and forming new memories of events.

occipital lobe. The part of the cerebral cortex lying at the rear of the human brain; important for visual processing.

cerebellum. A brain region lying below the cerebral cortex in the back of the head. It is responsible for the regulation and coordination of complex voluntary muscular movement, including classical conditioning of motor-reflex responses.

brainstem. A group of structures that connects the rest of the brain to the spinal cord and plays key roles in regulating automatic functions such as breathing and body temperature.

The Human Brain

The **cerebral cortex**, the tissue covering the top and sides of the brain in most vertebrates, is by far the largest structure of the human brain (Figure 2.2a). The word *cortex* is Latin for "bark" or "rind," reflecting that the cortex, although about the size of the front page of a newspaper if spread out flat, is only about 2 millimeters thick. To fit inside the skull, the cerebral cortex is extensively folded, much like a piece of paper crumpled into a ball. In humans, as in all vertebrates, the brain consists of two sides, or *hemispheres*, that are roughly mirror images of each other, so brain scientists talk about the cortex in the "left hemisphere" or the "right hemisphere." In each hemisphere, the cortex is divided further into the **frontal lobe** at the front of the head, the **parietal lobe** at the top of the head, the **temporal lobe** at the side of the head, and the **occipital lobe** at the back of the head (Figure 2.2b). The term *lobe* refers to the fact that these regions are anatomically distinct. The individual lobes got their somewhat odd names from the names of the skull bones that cover them. If you have trouble memorizing these four terms, remember: "*F*rontal is *F*ront, *P*arietal is at the *P*eak, *T*emporal is behind the *T*emples, and the *O*ccipital lobe is *O*ut back." Subregions within each lobe are associated with a wide variety of perceptual and cognitive processes. For example, your frontal lobe helps you to plan and perform actions, your occipital lobe allows you to see and recognize the world, your parietal lobe enables you to feel the differences between silk and sandpaper, and your temporal lobe makes it possible for you to hear and to remember what you've done. We will discuss the functional roles of cortical subregions in greater detail throughout this book, and knowing the names and locations of the different lobes will help you to keep track of what is happening where in your brain.

Sitting behind and slightly below the cerebral cortex is the **cerebellum** (Figure 2.2b). The cerebellum contributes to the coordination of sensation and movements and is thus especially important for learning that involves physical action. At the base of the brain is the aptly named **brainstem** (Figure 2.2b). The brainstem is a collection of structures connecting the brain to the spinal cord and playing key roles in the regulation of automatic functions, such as breathing and the regulation of body temperature.

Other brain structures, buried under the cerebral cortex, are not visible in photographs such as that shown in Figure 2.2a. You'll learn about many of these structures later in the book; for now, we'll just introduce a few that are especially important for learning and memory (Figure 2.3).

First, near the center of the brain lies the *thalamus*, a structure that receives various sensory signals (associated with sight, sound, touch, and so forth) and that connects to many cortical and subcortical regions. You can think of the thalamus as a gateway through which almost all sensory signals can affect brain activity. Sitting near the thalamus are the *basal ganglia*, a group of structures important for planning and producing skilled movements such as throwing a football or juggling. The *hippocampus* lies a little farther away, inside the temporal lobe; it is thought to be important for learning new facts (say, the capital of France) or remembering autobiographical events (what you did last summer). Sitting at the tip of the hippocampus is a group of cells called the *amygdala*; this little brain region is important for emotional memories. If you remember the happiest—or saddest—day of your life, it is probably because your amygdala was particularly active at the time, adding emotional strength to those memories. Because you have two hemispheres, you actually have duplicates of each of these structures. For example, you have a left hippocampus and a right hippocampus, and a left amygdala and a right amygdala.

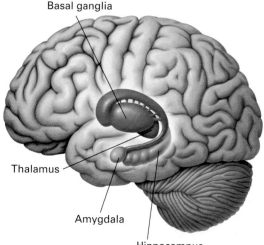

Basal ganglia

Thalamus

Amygdala

Hippocampus

Figure 2.3 Brain regions known to contribute to learning and memory Lying near the center of the human brain, the basal ganglia, thalamus, hippocampus, and amygdala all contribute to learning and memory in different ways.

Scientists are only beginning to understand what these brain areas do and how they relate to learning and memory, but it is becoming increasingly clear that it's a mistake to think of the brain as a single organ, like a liver or a kidney. Instead, the brain is a society of "experts," with each region making its own specialized contribution to what we do and what we think.

Comparative Neuroanatomy

In spite of the wide differences in nervous systems from species to species, much of what is known about the neural bases of learning and memory comes from studies of animals other than humans. Many aspects of a rat brain, a monkey brain, or even an insect brain are similar enough to a human brain to have made this possible (as predicted by Darwin's theory of natural selection, described in Chapter 1). The study of similarities and differences between organisms' brains is called *comparative neuroanatomy*. Comparative neuroanatomical studies provide a foundation for understanding how brain structure and function relate to learning and memory abilities.

The brains of vertebrate species are similar in that all have a cerebral cortex, a cerebellum, and a brainstem; all vertebrate brains are also similarly organized into two hemispheres. Figure 2.4 shows the brains of some representative vertebrate species. In general, bigger animals have bigger brains. It might seem that increasing brain size should go hand in hand with increased capacity:

Figure 2.4 Comparative anatomy of the brains of several vertebrate species All vertebrate brains have two hemispheres and a recognizable cortex, cerebellum, and brainstem, but species differ in the relative volumes of these areas. In mammals (such as the human) and birds, the cortex is much larger than the cerebellum; in fish and amphibians (such as the frog), the cortex and cerebellum are closer in size.

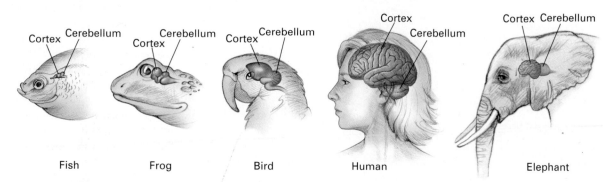

Cortex Cerebellum

Cortex Cerebellum

Cortex Cerebellum

Cortex Cerebellum

Cortex Cerebellum

Fish

Frog

Bird

Human

Elephant

human brains are bigger than frog brains, and humans seem to be able to learn things frogs can't. But elephant brains are larger than human brains, and elephants can't learn to read and write, build cities, or study calculus. So, just as birds with larger wings are not necessarily better at flying than smaller birds, animals with larger brains are not necessarily better learners than other animals. In general, scientists don't yet fully understand the relationship between brain size and functional capacity. Studies of intelligence in humans suggest that differences in the size of certain subregions in the frontal and parietal lobes do predict differences in performance on intelligence tests (Jung & Haier, 2007), indicating that it is not overall brain size that matters but how different brain parts are structured (Mercado, 2008).

Aside from differences in overall brain volume, different species have different proportions of cerebral cortex. In humans, the cerebral cortex takes up a much larger percentage of total brain volume than it does in, say, frogs. Whereas the large human cortex has to be folded up to fit inside the human skull, the frog cortex can fit quite comfortably in its skull without wrinkling. The relative size of the human cortex is intriguing because the cerebral cortex is associated with functions such as language and complex thought—the very things that seem to distinguish humans from other animals. And in fact, other species with a relatively large cortex—including chimpanzees, dolphins, and, yes, elephants—are often those that we associate with greater ability for abstract thought, problem solving, and remembering the details of past events.

Only vertebrates have both a CNS and a PNS. Some invertebrates—the octopus and the bee, for example—have a recognizable brain, but these brains are organized very differently from vertebrate brains. Much of the octopus "brain" is distributed in various parts of its body, particularly inside its rubbery legs. Yet the octopus is a remarkably capable learner: it can learn to find its way through a maze and to open a jar to get at the food inside. It even shows signs of social learning, that is, learning from watching another octopus's behavior. In one study, researchers trained some octopuses to grab the white ball when presented with a choice between a white and a red one. Other, untrained octopuses were then allowed to watch the trained octopuses make their selection. Later, when the observer octopuses were offered the two balls, they promptly grabbed the white one—just as they had seen the trained octopuses doing (Fiorito, Agnisola, d'Addio, Valanzano, & Calamandrei, 1998). Such social learning was once believed to be exclusive to "higher" animals, such as humans, dolphins, and chimpanzees. But we now know that an octopus, with a decentralized brain, can learn from observing others, too.

Other invertebrates, such as worms and jellyfish, have no recognizable brains at all. These animals have neurons that are remarkably similar to vertebrate neurons, but the neurons are few in number and are not organized into a centralized structure like a brain. For example, microscopic worms known as nematodes (including the species that infects pigs and then humans who eat the pigs, causing trichinosis) have 302 individual neurons, compared with a few hundred million in the octopus and about 100 billion in the human. Nematode neurons are organized into a "nerve net" that is similar to a vertebrate PNS but with no central processing area. Yet these little organisms can learn to approach tastes or odors that predict food and to avoid tastes and odors that predict the absence of food (Rankin, 2004). Not bad for a creature without a brain.

When an invertebrate such as the octopus learns about a novel object, is the learning happening in its head, or is it happening in one or more of its legs?

Mauro Fermariello/Science Source

Studies of invertebrate nervous systems have been particularly rewarding because of their very simplicity. For example, because a nematode has such a small number of neurons, scientists are able to map out the entire set of connections in its nervous system in a way not yet possible for a human brain or even a rat brain. Many of the important insights into human brains and human learning have come from studying how invertebrates learn and remember.

Neurons

Neurons are the building blocks of the nervous system. Some act as sensory receptors (such as those in the eyes, ears, and tongue that respond to visual, auditory, and taste stimuli), and some transmit signals from the spinal cord to the muscles. In vertebrates, many neurons are centralized in the brain. Neurons are capable of changing their function and modifying the way they respond to incoming signals. These changes, some of which we examine in Section 2.3, are thought to be the basis of learning in the brain.

The prototypical neuron has three main components: (1) **dendrites**, which are input areas that receive signals from other neurons; (2) the **cell body**, or **soma**, which integrates signals from the dendrites; and (3) one or more **axons**, which transmit signals to other neurons (Figure 2.5). For the most part, neural activity flows in one direction, from dendrites to axons.

It is convenient to talk about a "prototypical neuron," but in reality neurons, like brains, come in a wide array of shapes and sizes. For example, *pyramidal cells* are neurons with pyramid-shaped cell bodies (shown in Figure 2.5a); *stellate cells* have star-shaped cell bodies. Some neurons have a single main axon, some have two, and some have many. Neurons known as *interneurons*, which connect two or more neurons, have short axons or no axons at all. The neurons that carry signals from the spinal cord to the feet have axons that stretch a meter or more in humans. The various shapes and sizes of different neurons undoubtedly contribute to their function. But, in many cases, neuroscientists do not know the specific advantages that a particular shape or size provides.

dendrite. Extension of a neuron that is specialized to receive signals from other neurons.

cell body. The central part of the neuron that contains the nucleus and integrates signals from all the dendrites; also known as the soma.

soma. The central part of the neuron that contains the nucleus and integrates signals from all the dendrites; also known as the cell body.

axon. The output extension of a neuron, specialized for transmitting information to other neurons or to muscles.

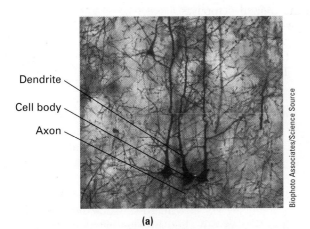

Dendrite

Cell body

Axon

Biophoto Associates/Science Source

(a)

Figure 2.5 Neurons, the building blocks of brains
(a) Brain tissue, stained to make neurons evident and photographed through a powerful microscope. The pyramid-shaped cell bodies and interconnecting branches of several neurons are visible. (b) The prototypical neuron has three main components: dendrites for monitoring the activity of other neurons, a cell body (soma) that integrates incoming signals, and one or more axons that transmit signals to other neurons. Neural activity flows mainly from dendrites to axon(s).

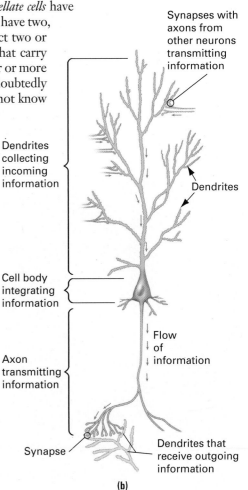

Synapses with axons from other neurons transmitting information

Dendrites

Dendrites collecting incoming information

Cell body integrating information

Axon transmitting information

Flow of information

Synapse

Dendrites that receive outgoing information

(b)

glia. A type of cell that provides functional or structural support to neurons.

Neurons are not the only kind of cell in the brain; they are far outnumbered by **glia**, cells that provide functional and structural support to neurons. *Astrocytes* are glia that line the outer surface of blood vessels in the brain and may help in the transfer of oxygen and nutrients from the blood to neurons. Glia called *oligodendrocytes* wrap the axons of nearby neurons in *myelin*, a fatty substance that insulates electrical signals transmitted by neurons, speeding the transmission of signals down the axon. Glia are as important as neurons for normal brain (and overall central nervous system) function. For example, multiple sclerosis is a disease in which the myelin coating of axons degenerates; this interferes with neural function, leading to jerky muscle movements and impaired coordination, as well as problems with vision and speech. Glia may also directly contribute to certain learning mechanisms. Even so, most neuroscientists who study the neural bases of learning and memory focus their efforts on understanding neurons: how they control behavior, and how they change during learning.

Observing Learning-Related Changes in Brain Structure

In the late 1800s, Franz Joseph Gall (1758–1828), a German anatomist and physiologist, pioneered the idea that different areas of the brain are responsible for different behaviors and capabilities. In addition, he reasoned that differences in character or ability should be reflected in differences in the size of the corresponding parts of the brain: people with a special skill for learning language must have a larger-than-average part of the brain associated with speech; people with better memories must have an overgrown memory area in the brain. Gall assumed that these differences in brain areas would be reflected in the shape of the skull, and he concluded that it should be possible to tell which areas of a person's brain were enlarged—and, thus, what abilities and personality traits that person would display—by examining bumps in the person's skull. Gall and his colleagues pursued a systematic study they called **phrenology**, in which they carefully measured the size and shape of many individuals' skulls and compared those measurements with the individuals' personalities and abilities (Gall & Spurzheim, 1810).

phrenology. A field of study that attempted to determine mental abilities by measuring head shape and size.

Phrenology maps attributed various aspects of cognition, personality, and memory abilities to variations in the sizes of different regions of a person's brain as indicated by bumps on the person's skull. How is the fundamental flaw of phrenology reflected in this image?

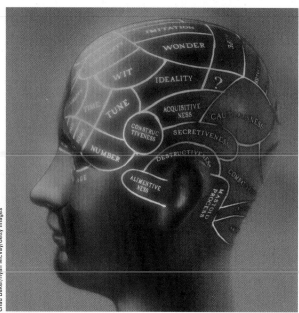

Chad Baker/Ryan McVay/Getty Images

Phrenology captured the public imagination. The approach was quickly taken over by quacks, who found various ways of making the idea pay. There was another, even more serious problem than the enthusiastic overuse of phrenology, however. It was that Gall's fundamental premise was wrong. Bumps on the skull do not imply bulges in the underlying brain. Gall did not discover this flaw because he had no way to examine the brain of a living person. It would be nearly 200 years before technology advanced to the point where scientists could see inside the skull of a healthy, living person and begin to identify brain structures that determine what individuals can learn and remember.

Structural Neuroimaging in Humans

Today, several technologies are available that allow physicians to see a living person's brain without causing damage or malfunction. Collectively, these modern techniques for creating pictures of anatomical structures within the brain are called

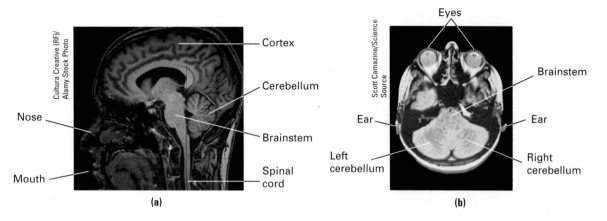

(a) **(b)**

structural neuroimaging, brain imaging, or "brain scanning." The brain scans produced by these methods show the size and shape of brain areas and also brain **lesions**, areas of damage caused by injury or illness.

Currently, brain images are most often collected from people through **magnetic resonance imaging (MRI)**, in which changes in magnetic fields are used to generate images of internal structure. MRI employs an extremely powerful magnet, usually constructed like a giant tube. The person lies on a pallet that slides into the tube, and magnetic changes are induced in the brain tissues, which are then allowed to return to normal. During this latter phase, a computer collects the different signals emitted by different tissues and uses them to generate images that look like photographs of a sliced brain. For example, Figure 2.6a shows an image comparable to what you would see if someone's head were sliced in half (minus the spewing blood), revealing a cross section of cerebral cortex, cerebellum, and brainstem, as well as some facial structures. An image measured at the level of the eyeballs, as in Figure 2.6b, shows a different cross section.

Recently, a new type of MRI called **diffusion tensor imaging (DTI)** was developed that can measure the diffusion of water in brain tissue, permitting bundles of axons throughout the brain—the so-called white matter—to be imaged. DTI is better than conventional MRI at visualization of groups of axons, so it's particularly useful for physicians trying to assess diffuse brain injury, as well as diseases such as multiple sclerosis that specifically target axons. Researchers also use DTI to study how different regions in the brain interact, by studying the pathways between them.

Structural neuroimaging provides a way not only to directly observe physical properties of a live person's brain but also *to track changes in those properties over time*. These include changes that might occur as a function of aging, injury, or disease, as well as gross structural changes produced by learning experiences. In Chapter 7, on skill memories, we discuss recent structural neuroimaging work showing that learning to juggle leads to changes in the amount of cortical tissue. Structural images of human brains are also critical for analyzing and interpreting changes in brain *function* that occur with learning, a topic we discuss in greater detail below.

It is easy to confuse structural neuroimaging, which shows what brains are physically like, with a different kind of imaging known as *functional neuroimaging*, which is presented in Section 2.2 and shows what brains are *doing* at the time of imaging. Both types of neuroimaging can reveal changes associated with learning, and we will present examples of both throughout the following chapters. Whenever you see an image in which patches of color are superimposed on a picture of a brain, the first thing you should ask yourself is, are these colored regions showing me changes in structure, or do they show changes in brain activity?

Figure 2.6 MRI images (a) This brain image measured near the center of the head shows a cross section through cortex, cerebellum, brainstem, and an upper portion of spinal cord, as well as nose and mouth cavities. (b) An image measured at the level of the eyeballs (visible at the top of the image) contains little cortex (since the position is so far down in the person's head) but captures the low-hanging cerebellum.

structural neuroimaging. Techniques (such as MRI) for creating images of anatomical structures within the living brain.

lesion. Damage caused by injury or illness.

magnetic resonance imaging (MRI). A method of structural neuroimaging based on recording changes in magnetic fields.

diffusion tensor imaging (DTI). A type of MRI that measures the diffusion of water in brain tissue, permitting bundles of axons throughout the brain to be imaged.

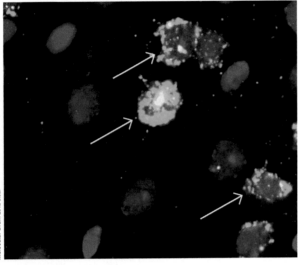

Sakaguchi and Hayashi: Catching the engram: strategies to examine the memory trace. Molecular Brain 2012 5:32.

Techniques for imaging neurons in brains make it possible to visualize structural changes that occur during learning. Do you think the changes shown here in green occurred in the dendrites, soma, or axons of these neurons?

enriched environment. An environment that provides sensory stimulation and opportunities to explore and learn; for a rat, this may mean housing in a large cage with many toys to play with and other rats to socialize with.

Effects of Learning

Experimental studies with animals permit even more detailed measures of learning-related structural changes. Chemicals have been developed that essentially dye neurons that have recently undergone structural changes, making it possible to map out the number and distribution of neurons that have changed as a function of specific learning experiences. For some imaging techniques, the brain tissue has to be bathed in the chemicals, and the dyed neurons are only visible through a microscope, so the brain must be removed from the animal soon after the learning occurs. For other techniques, however, it is possible to collect images of single neurons and even individual dendrites in living animals. These methods are most often employed in studies of learning that use rodents, small birds, or small invertebrates as subjects.

Early studies of brain structure in rats found that simply providing young rats with more opportunities for learning could lead to visible changes in their neurons. Researchers housed one group of rats in an **enriched environment**, meaning an environment where there was plenty of sensory stimulation and opportunity to explore and learn. For the rats, this meant a large cage filled with toys to play with and other rats with whom to socialize. A second group of rats lived in standard laboratory housing, each rat isolated in a small chamber that contained nothing but a drinking spout and food cup. The results? The rats housed in the enriched environment showed better maze learning than the rats kept in standard laboratory housing (Rosenzweig, 1984; Renner & Rosenzweig, 1987).

These increased learning capacities are associated with structural changes in neurons. Rats raised in an enriched environment have cortical neurons with more and longer dendrites than their experience-impoverished counterparts (Figure 2.7). The dendrites of rats in the enriched environment also have more connections with other neurons (Globus, Rosenzweig, Bennet, & Diamond, 1973; Greenough, West, & DeVoogd, 1978). These neural changes occur quickly: as few as 60 days of housing in an enriched environment can result in a 7% to 10% increase in brain weight of young rats and a 20% increase in the number of connections in the visual cortex. Similar changes are seen in the brains of monkeys and cats raised in enriched environments. Even the brains of fruit flies housed in large communal cages with visual and odor cues show similar changes, compared with flies housed alone in small plastic vials (Technau, 1984).

Do similar effects occur in humans? Preschool children placed in "high-quality" day care (with lots of toys, educational experiences, and teacher interaction) often fare better in elementary school than children whose day care offers fewer opportunities for learning (Peisner-Feinberg, Burchinal, & Clifford, 2001). There isn't yet definitive evidence that human brains undergo enlargement similar to that of rats after environmental enrichment, because the current structural neuroimaging approaches used on children do not have the resolution necessary to detect change in individual neurons. However, suggestive data come from a study of London taxi drivers.

London is a sprawling city with hundreds of small, crooked streets. To receive an official license, London taxi drivers must study for up to three years and pass a grueling exam that requires them, for example, to indicate the shortest path between random London addresses. This means that licensed London taxi drivers are a group of people sharing an extensive fund of spatial knowledge.

Researcher Eleanor Maguire and her colleagues used MRI to compare brain volumes in a group of London taxi drivers with those of age-matched Londoners who had not studied the geography of their city so extensively (Maguire et al., 2000). The only part of the brain that differed significantly between the groups was the hippocampus: the taxi drivers had slightly larger hippocampal volumes than non–taxi drivers. Further, the size of the hippocampus differed even among individual taxi drivers: those who had been driving for more than a decade had a larger volume than those who had been driving for only a few years. One possible interpretation of these volume differences is that the intensive spatial learning in taxi drivers causes an increase in dendritic branching in hippocampal neurons—making those neurons take up more room, just like the rat neurons shown in Figure 2.7.

Interim Summary

- The brain and spinal cord make up the vertebrate central nervous system (CNS). The brain controls behavior through connections with the peripheral nervous system (PNS), which consists of sensory neurons coming from sensory receptors and motor neurons going to body muscles.

- The vertebrate brain is made up of several different regions that contribute to learning and memory, including the cerebral cortex, cerebellum, hippocampus, basal ganglia, and amygdala.

- Neurons, the building blocks of the nervous system, are capable of changing their function and modifying the way they process information.

- Modern structural brain-imaging techniques (including MRI and DTI) provide ways to measure variations in the brain structure of living humans without causing harm.

- Techniques for imaging neural structures in non-humans make it possible to collect detailed information about neural changes that occur during learning.

- Enriched environment studies show that learning experiences can have a profound impact on brain structure and on an individual's learning and memory abilities.

2.2 Functional Properties of Learning and Memory Systems

Modern brain scientists assume that brains are composed of multiple systems that specialize in collecting, processing, and storing particular kinds of information. But there is no one-to-one relationship, as phrenologists supposed, in which each individual function or ability is performed in a dedicated corner of the brain. Instead, one brain area may play a role in many functions, and one function may rely on contributions from many brain areas.

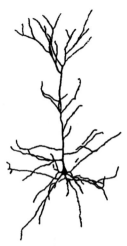

(a) Standard laboratory housing

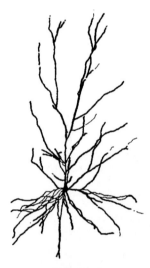

(b) Enriched laboratory environment

Figure 2.7 Deprived environment vs. enriched environment Representations of neurons from the cortex of (a) a rat raised in standard laboratory housing and (b) a rat raised in an enriched laboratory environment. Neurons from rats raised in enriched environments typically have more and longer dendrites than their experience-impoverished counterparts.

What determines how brain regions contribute to learning and memory processes? Two major factors are the kinds of *input* a region receives and the kinds of *output* it produces. These inputs and outputs are closely related to the stimuli and responses that behaviorists emphasized in their theories of learning (reviewed in Chapter 1).

What Brains Do

Chapter 1 defined learning as a process by which changes in behavior arise as a result of experience. Thus, when Pavlov's dogs began to salivate after hearing a sound that predicted food, this change in behavior—salivation in response to a sound—provided evidence that the dogs learned about the relationship between the sound and the food. But even before Pavlov began using the dogs in his experiments, they would salivate in response to food. Salivation during eating is a reflexive behavior that dogs (and other mammals) develop early in life; it helps the digestive system get ready to process incoming food.

reflex. An involuntary and automatic (unlearned) response.

A **reflex** is an involuntary and automatic response "hardwired" into an organism; in other words, it is present in all normal members of a given species and does not have to be learned. Just like Pavlov's dogs, humans salivate when eating food. This is only one of several reflexes that humans are biologically prepared to perform: newborns suck when they encounter a nipple (sucking reflex), hold their breath when submerged underwater (the diving reflex), and grasp a finger so tightly that they can support their own weight by hanging on to it (the palmar grasp reflex). Adults have reflexes, too, such as the knee-jerk reflex when the doctor hits your knee with a rubber mallet and an eyeblink reflex when someone blows air at your eye.

Recall from Chapter 1 that Descartes explained reflexes as hydraulic movements caused by spirits flowing from the brain into the muscles. For many years, scientists accepted this explanation, assuming that there must be some kind of fluid carrying instructions from the brain to the muscles. It wasn't until the early twentieth century that researchers discovered, first, that there is no such fluid and, second, that the brain isn't in absolute control of the muscles at all.

Instead of a hydraulic fluid, there are two distinct types of nerve fibers (axons) connecting the muscles to the spinal cord: one set of fibers carrying sensory signals from the peripheral nervous system into the spinal cord, and a second set carrying motor signals back from the spinal cord to the muscles (Bell, 1811; Magendie, 1822). If a pinprick or other painful stimulus is applied to a dog's leg, its leg jerks reflexively (just as you'd pull your leg away if someone pricked you). If the sensory fibers are cut, the dog's sensation of pain disappears and the reflex fails to occur, although the dog can still move its leg normally. On the other hand, if the motor fibers are cut, the animal can still feel pain but, again, does not make reflexive leg movements. In the spinal cord, sensory fibers are separate from motor fibers. They run in two parallel nerve pathways, one devoted to sensing and the other to responding. This finding, called the *Bell–Magendie law of neural specialization*, represents the historical first step toward understanding the neural mechanisms of learning. Specifically, it shed light on how the nervous system responds to stimuli, and how it controls responses evoked by those stimuli.

I Why isn't this infant drowning?

Elli Thor Magnusson/Getty Images

Following up on the discovery of neural specialization, English physiologist Charles Sherrington (1857–1952) conducted many studies on dogs whose spinal cord had been surgically disconnected from their brain, so that the spinal cord no longer received any brain signals. Such surgically altered dogs show many basic reflexes, such as jerking their leg away from a painful stimulus. Because the brain cannot contribute to these reflexes, they must be generated by the spinal cord alone. In fact, we now know that sensory inputs can activate motor fibers traveling out of the spinal cord, without waiting for signals from the brain. (The sensory pathways in the spinal cord are largely separate from the motor pathways there, yet at the same time, sensory and motor neurons are closely interconnected, throughout the nervous system.) If you've ever stuck your hand into dangerously hot or cold water and jerked it away almost before realizing what you've done, or watched your knee jerk in response to the doctor's rubber mallet, then you've experienced your spinal cord responding without receiving any help from your brain.

Sherrington concluded that such simple "spinal reflexes" could be combined into complex sequences of movements and that these reflexes were the building blocks of all behavior (Sherrington, 1906). Sherrington's description of reflexes differed from that of Descartes in assuming that spinal reflexes did not depend on the brain and did not involve the pumping of spirits or fluids into the muscles. Sherrington received a Nobel Prize in 1932 for his work in this area, and he is now considered to be one of the founding fathers of neuroscience. His ideas provided the groundwork and motivation for Pavlov's early investigations of reflex conditioning in dogs (Pavlov, 1927) and have continued to influence learning and memory researchers ever since.

If the spinal cord controls reflexes and if complex actions can be described as combinations of these reflexes, then where does the brain come in? Sensory fibers enter the spinal cord and connect to motor fibers there, but some fibers also travel up to the brain. The brain processes these inputs and produces its own outputs, some of which may travel back down the spinal cord and out to the muscles. The parallel sensory and motor pathways traveling up and down the spinal cord, to and from the brain, are similar to the parallel sensory and motor pathways that were identified traveling into and out of the spinal cord.

Figure 2.8 Cortical regions for processing inputs and outputs Specific regions of cerebral cortex are specialized for processing light (primary visual cortex), sound (primary auditory cortex), and sensation produced by physical movement (primary somatosensory cortex). Other regions are specialized for generating coordinated movements (primary motor cortex).

Incoming Stimuli: Sensory Pathways into the Brain

Let's focus first on the sensory pathways that provide inputs to the brain. As noted earlier in this chapter, most sensory inputs enter the brain through the thalamus. The thalamus in turn distributes these inputs to cortical regions specialized for processing particular sensory stimuli, such as the primary auditory cortex (A1), for sound; the primary somatosensory cortex (S1), for sensations from skin and internal organs; and the primary visual cortex (V1), for sight. A1 is located in the temporal lobe, S1 in the parietal lobe, and V1 in the occipital lobe (Figure 2.8). Such areas are collectively called *primary sensory cortices*, as they are the first stage of cortical processing for each type of sensory information. Each primary sensory cortex can then transmit outputs to surrounding cortical regions for further processing. For example, the primary visual cortex may start the processing of stimuli from the eye by extracting simple features—say, lines and shading—from a visual scene; later stages of cortical processing

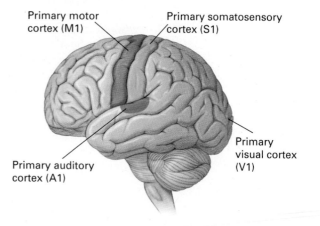

Primary motor cortex (M1)

Primary somatosensory cortex (S1)

Primary auditory cortex (A1)

Primary visual cortex (V1)

elaborate by detecting motion or shape in the scene and, finally, by responding to features of individual objects and their meaning. Damage to primary sensory cortices can eliminate particular perceptual abilities. For instance, people with damage to V1 can become blind, even though their eyes are in perfect working order, and damage to A1 can cause deafness.

Outgoing Responses: Motor Control

Just as various brain regions are specialized for processing sensory inputs, other brain regions are specialized for processing the outputs that control movements. Chief of these is the primary motor cortex (M1), which generates coordinated movements. M1 is located in the frontal lobe, adjacent to S1 in the parietal lobe (Figure 2.8), and it sends output to the brainstem, which in turn sends instructions down the spinal cord to activate motor fibers that control the muscles.

M1 gets much of its input from the frontal lobes, which are responsible for making high-level plans based on the present situation, past experience, and future goals. (Should you pick up that hot coffee cup? Should you try to catch that ball with one hand or two?) Other important inputs come from the basal ganglia and cerebellum, which help to translate the high-level plans into concrete sets of movements. All these inputs help determine the outputs that M1 sends to the brainstem. Other motor areas—including the cerebellum, basal ganglia, frontal cortex, and the brainstem itself—also produce their own outputs, all of which converge on the spinal cord and travel from there to the muscles. Complex motor movements—such as picking up a hot coffee cup without spilling the liquid or burning your hand, or picking up an egg without crushing it, or dancing without stepping on your partner's toes—require exquisitely choreographed interactions between all of these brain structures and the muscles they control.

Let's consider one of these examples in greater detail: you see a cup of coffee and pick it up (Figure 2.9). The process begins with visual input from your eyes traveling to your visual cortex (V1), which helps you find and identify the cup. Regions in your frontal lobes coordinate the necessary plans for grasping the cup, which your motor cortex (M1) then directs by means of outputs through the brainstem, down sets of fibers in the spinal cord, and out to the muscles of the arm and fingers. As you reach for the cup, your basal ganglia and cerebellum continually track the movement, making tiny adjustments as necessary. These brain regions enable you to exert just the right amount of pressure on the cup: enough to lift it against gravity, but not so much that you yank it off the table and spill the contents. As you pick up the cup, sensory information from touch, heat, and pressure receptors in your fingers travels back up your arms, through sensory fibers in the spinal cord, and to the somatosensory cortex (S1), providing evidence that the cup is firmly in your hand. If the handle of the cup is hotter than expected, it could produce a reflexive withdrawal of the hand. This response is the kind of spinal reflex studied by Charles Sherrington; the short path from the hand to the spinal cord and back is sometimes called a *reflex arc*.

All that input and output just to pick up a cup—before you've even taken your first sip! Infants of many vertebrate species, including humans, are born fairly clumsy and spend a large part of their infancy and childhood learning how to walk or fly or swim gracefully, reach accurately, move throat and tongue muscles to produce coherent sounds, and so on. This relatively long period spent learning coordinated motor control reflects both the complexity of the operations and the many brain structures that have to interact with one another and with the outside world to perform them.

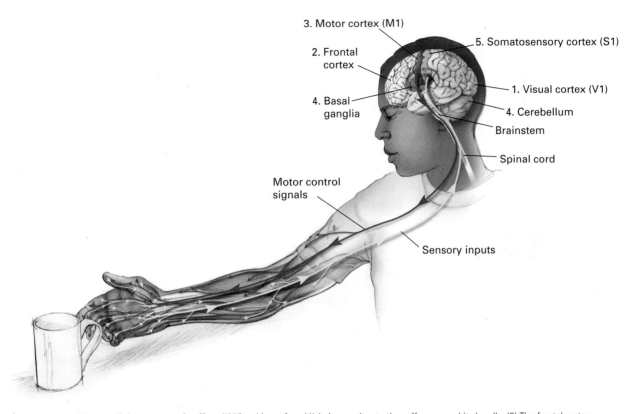

Figure 2.9 How to pick up a cup of coffee (1) Visual input from V1 helps you locate the coffee cup and its handle. (2) The frontal cortex helps you plan the movement. (3) Outputs from the motor cortex (M1) travel through the brainstem and down sets of fibers in the spinal cord to the muscles in the arm, causing you to reach out your hand. (4) The basal ganglia and cerebellum continuously monitor whether your hand is on track, making tiny adjustments to ensure that your hand reaches the correct target. (5) Sensory signals travel back up the arm and spinal cord, through a second set of fibers, to somatosensory cortex (S1), confirming that the cup has been grasped.

The Synapse: Where Neurons Connect

So far, we've been describing the transmission of signals into and out of the brain as if these signals flowed from one place to another in the nervous system like water through a pipe (similar to the way Descartes described the mechanisms of behavior). What really happens is that neurons throughout the nervous system are continually communicating with one another in vast networks that are similar in some ways to social networking systems such as Twitter or Facebook. It is this communication between neurons that makes learning and memory possible.

Generally, neurons that communicate with each other are not actually physically connected. Rather, communicating neurons are separated by a narrow gap of about 20 nanometers (1 nanometer is one-billionth of a meter), called a **synapse**, across which the neurons pass chemicals (Figure 2.10a). Most synapses are formed between the axon of the **presynaptic**, or sending, neuron and a dendrite of the **postsynaptic**, or receiving, neuron, but synapses can also be formed between an axon and a cell body, between an axon and another axon, and even between dendrites.

Neurons contain **neurotransmitters**, chemical substances that can cross a synapse to affect the activity of a postsynaptic neuron. Neurotransmitters are kept conveniently on hand at the end of the presynaptic axon, in packets known as *vesicles*. To transmit a signal, one or more vesicles of the presynaptic

synapse. A narrow gap between two neurons across which chemical messages can be transmitted.

presynaptic. On the sending side of a synapse.

postsynaptic. On the receiving side of a synapse.

neurotransmitter. One of several classes of molecule released by neurons to carry chemical messages to other neurons.

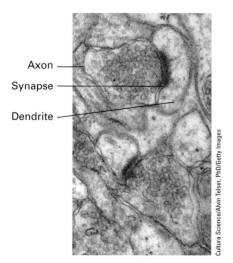

Axon

Synapse

Dendrite

Cultura Science/Alvin Telser, PhD/Getty Images

(a)

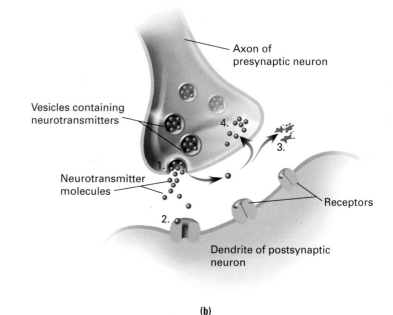

Axon of
presynaptic neuron

Vesicles containing
neurotransmitters

Neurotransmitter
molecules

Receptors

Dendrite of postsynaptic
neuron

(b)

Figure 2.10 Transmission across a synapse (a) This photo (taken through an electron microscope) shows the tiny gaps, or synapses, between neurons. Vesicles filled with neurotransmitters, ready for release into the synapse, are visible as circular packets inside the presynaptic neuron. (b) A signal is transmitted between neurons when (1) the presynaptic neuron releases neurotransmitter into the synapse and (2) the neurotransmitter molecules dock at receptors on the surface of the postsynaptic neuron. This may activate the receiving neuron. Leftover neurotransmitter in the synapse is either (3) broken down or (4) reabsorbed into the presynaptic neuron.

receptor. A specialized molecule, located on the surface of a neuron, to which one or more particular neurotransmitters can bind; when a neurotransmitter activates a receptor, effects may be initiated in the neuron.

axon release neurotransmitters into the synapse (Figure 2.10b). Several different chemicals act as neurotransmitters. Major ones include *glutamate, gamma-aminobutyric acid (GABA), acetylcholine, dopamine, norepinephrine, epinephrine, and serotonin*. Once neurotransmitters have been released into the synapse, the next step is for the postsynaptic neuron to collect them. **Receptors** are molecules embedded in the surface of the postsynaptic neuron that are specialized to bind with and respond to particular kinds of neurotransmitters.

The effect of a particular neurotransmitter depends on what its corresponding postsynaptic receptors do when activated. Some receptors open a channel for the flow of electrically charged molecules into or out of the cell, thus changing the charge characteristics in a small area of the neuron. Similar electrical changes may be occurring simultaneously in other locations on the neuron as other receptors on other dendrites become active. The neuron's cell body integrates this cocktail of electrical signals; if the total electrical charge exceeds a threshold, the neuron "fires," propagating an electrical charge, called an *action potential*, down its axon. This propagation is an all-or-nothing event: either the neuron fires or it doesn't; there is no in-between stage. When a neuron fires, sending an electrical charge to the end of the axon, it causes the release of neurotransmitters there.

Some neurotransmitters—glutamate, for example—are *excitatory*, activating receptors that tend to increase the likelihood of the postsynaptic neuron firing. Other neurotransmitters—such as GABA—are *inhibitory*, activating receptors that tend to decrease the likelihood of the postsynaptic neuron firing. Usually, a given neuron produces and releases only one kind of neurotransmitter. But that neuron may be able to respond to signals from many different presynaptic neurons, each releasing a different kind of neurotransmitter.

After a neuron fires, there is a brief period, called a *refractory period*, during which it can't fire again, no matter how much input it receives. Once this refractory period has passed, the neuron is again open for business. If the neuron is still receiving a lot of input from its neighbors, it may fire again and again in rapid succession, interrupted only by the refractory period after each action potential. If the excitatory inputs are less frequent or less strong or if there is a lot of inhibitory input, some time may pass before the neuron fires again.

In the meantime, neurotransmitters have to be cleared out of the synapse so that the synapse can receive future signals. In some cases, this consists of breaking the neurotransmitter molecules down into their constituent parts in a process called *inactivation*. In other cases, they are brought back into the presynaptic neuron and recycled for future use, a process called *reuptake*. When cleanup is complete, the synapse and receptors are ready to receive new transmissions.

Several areas in the brainstem contain neurons that send axons widely throughout the brain; when these neurons fire, they release neurotransmitters called **neuromodulators** that can affect activity in entire brain regions, rather than just at a single synapse. Neuromodulators alter, or modulate, how neurons transmit and receive signals, although they themselves are not part of the signal. For example, acetylcholine often functions as a neuromodulator, and one of its effects is to temporarily alter the number of receptors that have to be active before a postsynaptic neuron can fire. If you think of synaptic transmission as a message, then acetylcholine levels help determine whether the message is heard as a whisper or a shout. Many human diseases that affect learning and memory seem to involve a global decline in neuromodulators. Examples include Alzheimer's disease, which is associated with a reduction in acetylcholine (Francis, Palmer, Snape, & Wilcock, 1999), and Parkinson's disease, which is characterized by a reduction in dopamine (Evans & Lees, 2004).

The 5th Wave   By Rich Tennant

@RICHTENNANT

THE BRAIN

"Information is moved via neurotransmitters from neuron to neuron via the synapses into the brain where it is then retrieved by the memory via a slap on the back of the head."

neuromodulator. A neurotransmitter that acts to modulate activity in a large number of neurons rather than in a single synapse.

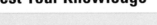

Test Your Knowledge

Synaptic Transmission

Several complex processes that occur at the synapse allow neurons to communicate. Which, if any, of the statements below do not describe one of these processes? (Answers appear in the back of the book.)

1. Neurotransmitters are reabsorbed by the axon that released them.
2. Neurotransmitters are broken down while they remain in the synapse.
3. Neurotransmitters bind to the dendrite of the postsynaptic neuron.
4. Neurotransmitters are released from vesicles and enter the synapse.

Observing Learning-Related Changes in Brain Function

Given that learning is a process that can lead to changes in behavior, and that brains control behavior through changes in neural activity, it is clear that learning must be associated with new patterns of activity in the brain. However, knowing that your brain is doing something different after years of practicing or after experiencing a traumatic event is a far cry from knowing what it is doing differently or why. Even if structural imaging techniques reveal that experience has led to physical changes in parts of neurons or to increases in the volume of a brain region, understanding how these changes contribute to performance is not straightforward. Neuroscientists are attempting to gain a clearer understanding of how experiences change brain function by monitoring specific changes in activity that occur within the central nervous system before, during, and after such experiences.

Functional Neuroimaging and Electroencephalography

As noted above, structural neuroimaging methods (such as MRI) allow researchers to look at the *structure* of a living human brain, whereas **functional neuroimaging** allows them to look at the *activity*, or function, of a living brain. For example, when a brain structure becomes active, it requires more oxygen. Within 4 to 6 seconds, blood flow (with its cargo of oxygen) increases to that region. On the other hand, when a brain structure becomes less active, it requires less oxygen, and blood flow decreases. By tracking local changes in blood flow, researchers can discover which brain regions are active or inactive.

functional neuroimaging. Techniques (such as fMRI or PET) for observing the activity or function of a living brain.

Rather than focusing on where blood flow is heavier in the brain, functional neuroimaging studies typically examine how blood flow in a particular brain region *changes* depending on what the person is doing or thinking. To see such changes in blood flow, researchers may first scan the brain while the person is relaxed—not doing anything. The resulting image is called a *baseline* image. Even though the person isn't performing any task, the brain is still active. Next, the researchers scan the brain again while the person is performing a task, such as looking at pictures or reading a story. (The pictures or words are projected on the inside ceiling of the scanner so that the person can see them while lying on his or her back.) During the task, some areas of the brain should become more active than they were at baseline. Others might decrease in activity. From each point (or pixel) in the image, researchers then subtract the activity at that identical point in the baseline image. The result, called a **difference image**, shows how activity at each point in the image has increased or decreased in the task condition compared with the baseline condition (Figure 2.11a).

difference image. An image of differences in brain activity obtained by taking an fMRI or PET image of a person performing a particular task, then subtracting the image of the same individual at baseline (not performing a task).

Usually, the difference image is color coded, with white, red, or yellow indicating areas where blood flow *increased* most during the task relative to the baseline. Colors such as blue and green may indicate where blood flow *decreased* most during the task. Uncolored areas indicate regions where no significant change took place. For example, the difference image in Figure 2.11a shows the parts of the brain that become significantly more active when a person is viewing pictures, confirming the current understanding that areas of the cerebral cortex in the occipital lobe are important for visual processing. When used in studies of learning and memory, functional neuroimaging methods can reveal differences in brain activity that are associated with performing different kinds of memory tasks (for instance recognizing faces versus recalling what happened at a recent party), differences associated with successful recall versus forgotten facts, and differences in memory function associated with particular disorders (for example, by comparing activity in people with and without schizophrenia as they perform a memory task).

Typically, researchers do not rely on measurements from a single person to decide which brain regions are most likely to show changes in activity levels during performance of a particular task. Instead, they usually collect data from multiple individuals and then calculate a mean difference image for a group (Figure 2.11b). One consequence of this approach is that the results of functional neuroimaging studies emphasize differences in activity that are prevalent

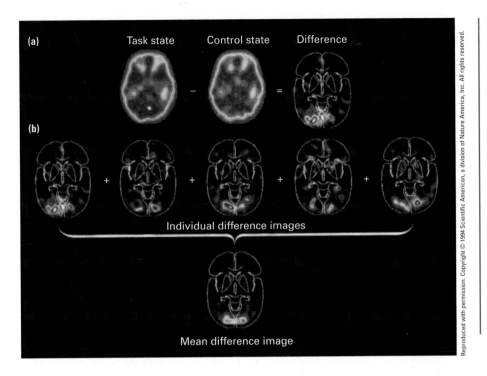

(a)

Task state — Control state = Difference

(b)

Individual difference images

Mean difference image

Figure 2.11 Creating a difference image with functional neuroimaging (a) A PET scan detecting blood flow as the brain performs a certain task (in this case, viewing pictures projected on the inside of the scanner). A baseline image taken while the participant is not performing the task is subtracted from an image collected during performance of a task to create a difference image, color coded to show areas where blood flow significantly increased (or decreased) in the task condition compared with the baseline condition. The white lines are a standard drawing of the same cross section as the PET images to clarify which brain regions correspond to the colored areas. (b) Difference images from multiple individuals are combined to calculate an average difference image.

across many participants, but do not necessarily reveal the full suite of changes in activity that occur within any particular individual.

Two commonly used functional neuroimaging technologies are **positron emission tomography (PET)** and **functional magnetic resonance imaging (fMRI)**. PET measures brain activity by detecting radiation from the emission of subatomic particles called positrons, associated with the brain's use of glucose from the blood. fMRI makes use of the same MRI technologies employed for structural imaging described above. Researchers can take an MRI at baseline and a second one while the person is performing a task. Oxygenated blood produces slightly different signals than deoxygenated blood, so there are fluctuations in the signal received from areas of the brain that undergo a change in activity level during the task.

Although PET and fMRI are powerful tools for observing the brain in action, they are only indirect measures of brain activity; respectively, they measure glucose utilization and blood oxygenation in a brain region rather than directly measuring the activity of neurons. Also, because functional neuroimaging studies typically focus on differences in activity under different conditions (through difference images), they tend to emphasize associations between specific brain regions and particular functions (much like phrenology), as opposed to revealing the full range of brain activity that contributes to mental and physical functioning. Finally, current functional neuroimaging techniques are comparatively slow: fMRI allows images to be taken every few seconds, while PET images can be taken only every few minutes, but changes in the brain occur much more rapidly than that. To track changes in real time, other techniques, such as electroencephalography, are needed.

Electroencephalography (EEG) is a technique for measuring electrical activity in the brain, using the same type of recording electrodes that are used in electrocardiograms. (The Greek word *enkephalos* means "brain," and so "electro-encephalo-graphy" means drawing or graphing the electrical activity

positron emission tomography (PET). A method of functional neuroimaging based on detecting radiation from the emission of subatomic particles called positrons, associated with the brain's use of glucose from the blood.

functional magnetic resonance imaging (fMRI). A method of functional neuroimaging based on comparing an MRI of the brain during performance of a task with an MRI of the brain at rest.

electroencephalography (EEG). A method for measuring electrical activity in the brain by means of electrodes placed on the scalp; the resulting image is an electroencephalogram (also EEG).

of the brain.) The electrodes simply record changes in electrical activity. When such electrodes are placed on a person's chest, they measure electrical activity resulting from heart contractions. When the electrodes are placed on the scalp, they measure the combined tiny electrical charges of large numbers of neurons in the brain, especially those near the location on the skull where the electrodes are placed. The resulting picture is called an *electroencephalogram* (also abbreviated as EEG).

Just as blood is always flowing through the brain, so electrical activity is always occurring in the brain, reflecting the firing patterns of neurons. The exact pattern of activation changes depending on what the brain is doing. For example, when a tone sounds, sensory receptors in the ear become active, and signals travel to the primary auditory cortex (A1), affecting electrical activity there. But detecting this particular electrical change in an EEG is difficult because lots of other neurons in other brain areas that are not involved in hearing may also be active—those responding to whatever visual stimuli happen to be in front of you, for instance, or those activated as you wiggle your fingers and think about what you want to have for lunch.

To detect an electrical change associated with hearing a stimulus, such as a tone, researchers typically present the same stimulus hundreds of times and then average the EEGs produced throughout those repetitions in a given individual. The principle is that activity in other brain areas will come and go, but only the neurons responding to the specific sensory stimulus will be consistently activated each time the stimulus is repeated—and so only their activity patterns will survive the averaging process. EEGs averaged across many repetitions of the same event are called **event-related potentials (ERPs)**. Just as functional neuroimaging shows how the brain changes while performing a task, so ERPs can be used to show different brain states at different stages of learning, such as how a person's brain responds to different sounds as the person gradually learns to make subtle distinctions between them (discussed in Chapters 3 and 6).

Compared with fMRI and PET, EEG recording is a simple and cheap way to monitor changes in brain activity during learning and memory tasks. In addition, EEG can detect rapid changes in the brain with more precision than fMRI or PET. Yet what EEG gains in temporal precision it often sacrifices in spatial precision. Whereas fMRI and PET can localize activation to within a few millimeters, EEG signals show activity over a wide swath of the brain. Some memory researchers are combining functional neuroimaging and EEG methods to generate images that show precisely when and where neural activity occurs during memory storage and recall by humans.

event-related potential (ERP). Electroencephalograms (EEGs) from a single individual averaged over multiple repetitions of an event (such as a repeated stimulus presentation).

To record neural activity from humans as they perform tasks, researchers attach multiple electrodes to a person's scalp. Traditionally, signals from electrodes are collected from wires attached to the electrodes (as shown here for the infant), but recent wireless technologies make it possible to record neural activity in any setting. How might EEG be used to measure functional brain changes that have occurred in the adult model as a result of her modeling experiences?

Aaron MCcoy/Getty Images

www.emotiv.com

Recording from Neurons

In the brain, memory functions are affected not only by *which* neurons fire but also by *how often* they fire. Neuroimaging and EEG studies can reveal the contributions of large areas of the brain to learning and memory, but they don't reveal much about which individual neurons are firing or how often. To gather this information, researchers have to record neural activity directly. **Neurophysiology** is the study of the activity and function of neurons.

One technique scientists use to measure the firing patterns of individual neurons is **single-cell recording** (the single cell in this case is a neuron). The microelectrodes that are used in this method function somewhat like EEG electrodes, but they are shaped like extremely thin needles and can penetrate brain tissue with a minimum of damage. A microelectrode can be inserted in brain tissue until its tip is very close to, or sometimes even inside, a target neuron. In some cases, researchers anesthetize an animal and surgically implant one or more microelectrodes in the brain areas they wish to study. Then, when the animal wakes, the researchers can record from the neuron(s) as the animal goes about its daily business. (Most animals don't seem to be much bothered by, or even aware of, the wires connected to their heads.) Such experiments allow researchers to determine what role a given neuron or network of neurons might play in the animal's behavior. Alternatively, if the researcher is interested in looking more closely at how individual neurons interact, it is possible to remove pieces (or "slices") of a brain, keep the neurons alive in a bath of nutrients, and record their activity in the slices.

Single-cell recordings have provided some of the most dramatic evidence to date of how neural firing relates to behavior. For example, Apostolos Georgopoulos and colleagues recorded spike patterns from the motor cortex of a monkey while the monkey moved a joystick in different directions (Figure 2.12a; Georgopoulos, Taira, & Lukashin, 1993). Some neurons fired most strongly when the monkey pushed the lever in a particular direction. Figure 2.12b shows recordings from one such neuron as the monkey moved the lever toward different compass points. Each vertical line in the recording represents one action potential, sometimes referred to as a *spike*. When the monkey moved its arm toward the point labeled 6 in Figure 2.12a, the neuron initially produced several spikes, then fell silent. When the monkey moved its

neurophysiology. The study of the activity and function of neurons.

single-cell recording. Use of an implanted electrode to detect electrical activity (spiking) in a single cell (such as a neuron).

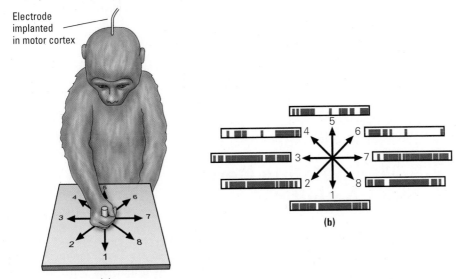

(a)

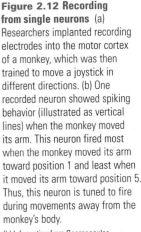

Figure 2.12 Recording from single neurons (a) Researchers implanted recording electrodes into the motor cortex of a monkey, which was then trained to move a joystick in different directions. (b) One recorded neuron showed spiking behavior (illustrated as vertical lines) when the monkey moved its arm. This neuron fired most when the monkey moved its arm toward position 1 and least when it moved its arm toward position 5. Thus, this neuron is tuned to fire during movements away from the monkey's body.

(b) Information from Georgopoulos et al., 1993.

arm to a slightly different position, point 7, the neuron produced a more sustained burst of activity, continuing to spike for the duration of the movement. But when the monkey moved its arm directly away from its body, toward point 1, the neuron really went into action, spiking as fast and frequently as it could. By contrast, when the monkey moved its arm in the opposite direction, toward its body (point 5), the neuron was much less active. Thus, this neuron's firing patterns are correlated with arm movements, and neuroscientists would say it is specialized, or "tuned," to fire maximally during movements in a particular direction: away from the body. Georgopoulos and colleagues found that other neurons in the motor cortex were tuned to fire during arm movements in other directions. Given what we know about the motor cortex from functional imaging studies, it is reasonable to assume that these neurons may be playing a direct role in issuing the commands that cause the monkey's arm to move. Because monkeys generally must be trained to move a joystick in different directions in laboratory experiments, such recordings can potentially reveal how the firing patterns of neurons change as monkeys learn to perform such tasks. In fact, such research has led to new technologies that enable both monkeys and humans to learn to control the movements of robotic arms simply by thinking about where they want the arm to move (discussed in Chapter 8).

Interim Summary

- Reflexes are natural, automatic responses to stimuli. Sherrington and other early neuroscientists believed that all complex learning involved combining simple spinal reflexes.

- In the brain, sensory signals (produced by stimuli) are initially processed in cortical regions specialized for processing such signals, and ultimately lead to activity in other cortical regions, such as the motor cortex, that are specialized for coordinating movements (responses).

- The neural transmission that enables stimuli to generate responses takes place across tiny gaps, or synapses: the presynaptic, or sending, neuron releases neurotransmitters into the synapse; these chemicals cross the synapse to activate receptors on the postsynaptic, or receiving, neuron.

- Functional neuroimaging methods (such as fMRI and PET) allow researchers to track brain activity during the performance of memory tasks by measuring increases and decreases in glucose utilization and blood oxygenation in different brain regions.

- Electroencephalographic recordings make it possible to track the activity of large populations of neurons over time, as well as monitor how such activity changes as learning progresses.

- Single-cell recordings allow researchers to directly monitor and record the electrical activity (or "firing") of single neurons and changes in their firing patterns that occur during learning or the recall of memories.

2.3 Manipulating Nervous System Activity

Imagine that a Martian scientist comes to Earth and encounters an automobile, a method of transportation unknown on Mars, powered by an energy source also unknown to Martians. Since the Martian speaks no Earth languages and can't simply ask a mechanic for an explanation, how might she learn how the car works? One way would be to look under the hood and examine the many components there. But studying the car's "structure" would only get her so far; to learn about the car's function, she'd have to take it for a test drive and see how it behaves normally. However, simply seeing cars in action cannot reveal what makes them go.

One approach the Martian might use to better understand cars would be to investigate what the different parts do. For instance, she could try disconnecting or removing parts, one at a time, noting the consequences in each case. If she removed the axle, she'd learn that the motor would work but couldn't transfer energy to make the wheels turn. If she removed the radiator, she'd learn that the car would run but would quickly overheat. In the end, by discovering the function of each of the car parts, the Martian could probably develop a pretty good idea of how the car works.

Taking a Hand in Brain Function

Neuroscientists trying to understand how nervous systems make it possible for organisms to learn and remember face a challenge similar to the Martian's. No surprise then that one of the earliest approaches researchers took was something like the Martian's: to examine people with one or more pieces of their brains damaged or missing to see how such losses affect performance. Although no scientist would disassemble the brain of a living human the way the Martian might disassemble a car, humans regularly suffer damage to one or more brain areas, through accident, injury, or disease, making it possible to explore the effects of missing or damaged brain regions on learning and memory abilities. Neuroscientists also have developed techniques for controlling or changing the firing patterns of neurons by triggering their electrical activity or by introducing foreign chemicals into the brain. How each of these different approaches to intervening in brain function can be used to better understand the neural substrates of learning and memory is described in the following pages.

neuropsychology. The branch of psychology that deals with the relation between brain function and behavior.

Brain injuries can lead to the loss of large portions of brain tissue. In this MRI image, missing cerebral cortex appears as a dark region on the right side of the image. Is this lesion more likely to be in the temporal lobe or the occipital lobe?

Effects of Brain Injuries

Neuropsychology is the branch of psychology that deals with the relation between brain function and behavior, usually by examining the functioning of patients with specific types of brain damage. These individuals volunteer their time and effort in experiments that test their learning and memory abilities, as well as other kinds of cognitive function—language, attention, intelligence, and so on. The test results can potentially be used to guide a patient's rehabilitation, but they also serve a research purpose. By recognizing patterns in the impaired and spared abilities of a group of patients who have experienced damage to a similar region of the brain, researchers hope to build a better picture of that brain region's normal function—just like the Martian trying to understand what a radiator does by watching what happens to a car that doesn't have one.

Animal researchers have conducted parallel studies by removing or deactivating specific brain regions to create animal "models" of humans with brain damage. Because human brain damage is almost always caused by accident, injury, or illness, every

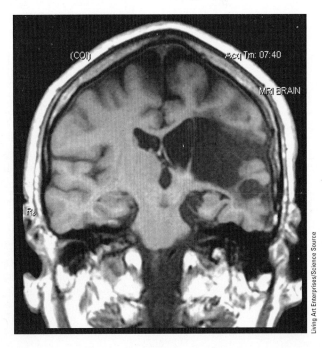

Living Art Enterprises/Science Source

engram. A physical change in the brain that forms the basis of a memory.

patient's damage—and disability—is slightly different. By contrast, in animal models, researchers can remove or disable specific brain regions with great precision, making it much easier to compare results across individuals. Instances in which the experimental results from human patients and animal models converge give the clearest picture of how the brain works normally and how it functions after damage.

Some of the most famous experimental brain lesion studies of learning and memory were conducted by Karl Lashley (1890–1958), an American psychologist who was looking for the location of the **engram**—the supposed physical change in the brain that forms the basis of a memory (also referred to as a *memory trace*). Lashley would train a group of rats to navigate a maze, and then he'd systematically remove a different small area (covering, say, 10%) of the cortex in each rat. He reasoned that once he'd found the lesion that erased the animal's memories of how to run through the maze, he would have located the site of the engram (Lashley, 1929).

Alas, the results were not quite so straightforward. No matter what small part of the cortex Lashley lesioned, the rats kept performing the task. Bigger lesions would cause increasingly large disruptions in performance, but no one cortical area seemed to be more important than any other. Hence, Lashley couldn't find the engrams for memories formed during maze learning. Finally, in mock despair, he confessed that he might be forced to conclude that learning "simply is not possible" (Lashley, 1929).

theory of equipotentiality. The theory that memories are stored globally, by the brain as a whole, rather than in one particular brain area.

Eventually, Lashley settled on a different explanation. He endorsed the **theory of equipotentiality**, which states that memories are not stored in one area of the brain; rather, the brain operates as a whole to store memories. Although Lashley is often credited with formulating this theory, it was actually first proposed in the 1800s as an alternative to phrenology (Flourens, 1824). In the theory of equipotentiality, memories are spread over many cortical areas; damage to one or two of these areas won't completely destroy the memory, and over time the surviving cortical areas may be able to compensate for what's been lost.

Lashley's work, and his endorsement of the theory of equipotentiality, were milestones in the neuroscience of memory because researchers could no longer take for granted the compartmentalized structure–function mapping that phrenologists had proposed. But, like the phrenologists before him, Lashley was only partly right. The phrenologists were in fact on the right track when they proposed that different brain areas have different specialties; the specialization just wasn't as extreme as they thought. Lashley was also on the right track when he proposed that engrams aren't localized to specific areas of the cortex, but we now know that the cortex isn't quite as undifferentiated as he came to believe. The truth is somewhere in the middle. Moreover, as you will discover in subsequent chapters, part of the reason Lashley's experiments did not work out the way he expected was because of his assumption that memories formed during maze learning were stored only in cerebral cortex. If Lashley had instead made his lesions beneath the cortex, he might have discovered that other brain regions (such as the hippocampus) more strongly affect spatial learning and memory (the role of the hippocampus in spatial learning is discussed in Chapters 3 and 7).

Useful as brain lesion experiments are, they are limited in what they can reveal. Suppose a researcher lesions part of a rat's cortex and then finds, as Lashley did, that the rat can still learn how to get around in a maze. Would that prove that the lesioned cortical area is not involved in spatial memory? Not necessarily; the rat may now be learning the maze in a different way. This would be analogous to your being able to find your way around a house with the lights out, even though you use visual input when it's available. Data from lesion studies are strongest when supplemented by data from other techniques showing that a brain region normally participates in a given behavior, or that artificial stimulation of that region affects performance in related tasks.

Test Your Knowledge

Equipotentiality versus Phrenology

What are the main differences between the explanations of brain function proposed by Franz Joseph Gall and those ultimately proposed by Karl Lashley? What evidence did each use to support his viewpoint? (Answers appear in the back of the book.)

Electromagnetic Control of Neurons

In addition to using microelectrodes to observe neural activity, researchers can also use electrodes to stimulate neural activity by delivering tiny amounts of electrical current into the brain. As you read above, when neurons fire, an action potential sweeps down the axon, triggering the release of neurotransmitters into the synapse. A stimulating electrode can cause spiking activity to happen where and when the researcher is ready to observe and record it.

Electrical stimulation of neurons was used as early as the 1800s, to prove that neural activity in the motor cortex produces motor behavior. Pavlov, for instance, was able to produce a wide range of movement patterns in an anesthetized dog by electrically stimulating its motor cortex (Pavlov, 1927). Similar techniques can be used in primates to map which parts of the motor cortex are responsible for generating movements in particular body parts. For example, electrical stimulation delivered to certain neurons in M1 in the right hemisphere, near the top of the brain, cause a monkey's lips to twitch. A little farther down and an arm might twitch. Still lower and movements occur in the legs. By painstakingly testing the effects of stimulating each point in M1, scientists can draw a map—called a *homunculus* (or "little man")—on the surface of M1, showing which parts of the body each subsection of M1 controls. The homunculus for M1 in humans (Figure 2.13a) has been worked out with the assistance of patients who were candidates for brain surgery (for example, to remove a tumor). Before removing any brain tissue, neurosurgeons do preliminary testing, which often involves cutting away a piece of the skull to expose the brain underneath and then carefully stimulating different areas. The idea is to determine whether the brain tissue can be cut away without leaving the patient in worse shape than before. To remove a tumor, for example, it may be reasonable to risk damaging the part of M1 that controls movements in one leg, but risk to other parts—say, the areas that control the tongue and allow swallowing and speaking—may call for extra caution.

Looking at the homunculus of Figure 2.13a, you'll notice that some body areas (the lips and hands, for example) seem grossly enlarged, while others (the arms and legs) seem shrunken. In other words, the physical size of a body area doesn't directly correspond to its relative size in the cortical map. In fact, if the homunculus were assembled into a figurine, it would look something like Figure 2.13b. The distortions aren't random. The parts of the body that are exaggerated on the homunculus are precisely those parts in which humans have the highest degree of fine motor control: fingers that are able to type, knit, and

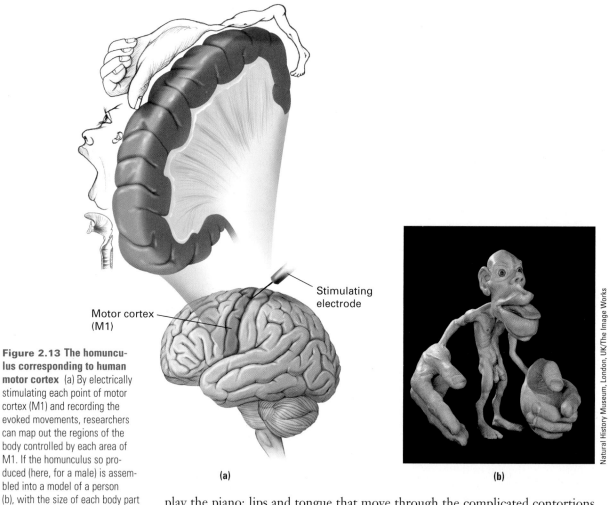

Figure 2.13 The homunculus corresponding to human motor cortex (a) By electrically stimulating each point of motor cortex (M1) and recording the evoked movements, researchers can map out the regions of the body controlled by each area of M1. If the homunculus so produced (here, for a male) is assembled into a model of a person (b), with the size of each body part determined by the relative amount of cortex devoted to it, the result is a figure with enlarged lips and hands—areas where human motor control is particularly precise.

Motor cortex (M1)

Stimulating electrode

Natural History Museum, London, UK/The Image Works

(a)

(b)

play the piano; lips and tongue that move through the complicated contortions of speech; and facial muscles that display emotion. Other areas of the body that are physically larger, like the arms and legs, have proportionately less fine motor control, and so proportionately less area of motor cortex is devoted to them.

Electrical stimulation can be used not only to generate movements in individuals, but also to generate visual, auditory, and somatosensory sensations (by stimulating neurons in sensory cortices). It is also possible to evoke feelings of *déjà vu*, the illusion of feeling that a novel experience has happened before, by stimulating neurons within the temporal lobe. It is even possible to classically condition animals (as described in Chapter 1) by using one electrode to generate neural firing patterns that would occur during the sensation of a sound and pairing that with stimulation from a second electrode that provokes a reflexive motor response. This kind of "virtual reality" training is described in greater detail in Chapter 4.

Neural stimulation studies in patients and animal models have greatly increased our understanding of how neural activity is translated into behavior. The relatively new methods of *transcranial magnetic stimulation (TMS)* and *transcranial direct-current stimulation (tDCS)* now allow researchers to extend these kinds of studies to humans not undergoing brain surgery. TMS changes activity in cerebral cortex by generating strong magnetic pulses over the skull (Figure 2.14), and tDCS delivers low-level electrical current through electrodes placed on the scalp. Both approaches activate large cortical networks rather than individual neurons. Depending on the level of stimulation, transcranial stimulation can either facilitate neural functions or disrupt them. Some recent work suggests that both TMS and TDCS can improve function in patients with memory disorders (Floel, 2014; Reis et al., 2008). Data from transcranial stimulation studies may be most useful when combined with results from other studies of neural stimulation in animals and from functional neuroimaging studies in humans to help build the most complete picture possible of which parts of the brain give rise to which kinds of behavioral changes.

Chemical Control of Brain States

In addition to electrical and magnetic stimulation, a third method for manipulating neural activity is the use of **drugs**, chemical substances that alter the biochemical functioning of the body. For example, memory researchers have used the drug scopolamine to temporarily impair memory abilities by disrupting the actions of acetylcholine in the brain. Researchers may not always have a clear idea of why specific drugs enhance or hinder behavior, but it is clear that drugs can change neural activity, so it is no surprise that they can alter learning and memory processes.

Drugs that work on the brain generally do so by altering synaptic transmission. The effects of the drug on behavior depend on which neurotransmitters are involved and whether their ability to carry messages across the synapse is enhanced or impaired.

Drugs can affect any of the four major processes of synaptic transmission described in Section 2.2—neurotransmitter release, activation of postsynaptic receptors, neurotransmitter inactivation, and neurotransmitter reuptake (depicted in Figure 2.10b):

1. Drugs can increase or decrease the ability of the presynaptic neuron to produce or release neurotransmitter. For example, amphetamines alter the function of neurons that produce the neurotransmitter dopamine, causing the neurons to release greater than normal quantities of dopamine. This means that post-synaptic neurons receive stronger and more frequent messages than normal. Because the dopamine system is involved in the processing of reward in the brain, the result may be feelings of pleasurable anticipation or excitement. (You will learn more about dopamine in Chapter 5, on operant conditioning.)

2. Drugs can increase or decrease the ability of postsynaptic receptors to receive the chemical message. For example, heroin and morphine are chemically very similar to a class of naturally occurring neurotransmitters called endogenous opioids. When heroin or morphine is released into the brain, molecules of the drug can activate the receptors normally activated by the endogenous opioids. In effect, the drugs "fool" the postsynaptic neuron into thinking that strong signals are being received from many presynaptic neurons. As a result, weak chemical messages that would not normally cause firing in postsynaptic neurons instead cause lots of neurons to fire. The endogenous opioids seem to be important in

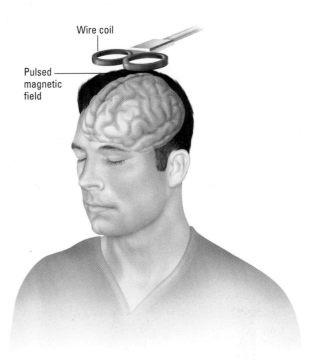

Wire coil

Pulsed magnetic field

Figure 2.14 Using TMS to modulate cortical activity This technique enables researchers (1) to disrupt cortical activity in volunteers to temporarily simulate cortical lesions or, conversely, (2) to temporarily increase the probability that cortical neurons respond to inputs, thereby enhancing some cortical functions.

drug. A chemical substance that alters the biochemical functioning of the body and in many cases affects the brain.

Drugs that work on the brain generally do so by altering what?

how the brain processes and signals pleasure, most likely explaining why drugs that mimic endogenous opioids often cause intense feelings of pleasure (also discussed further in Chapter 5).

3. and 4. Drugs can alter the mechanisms for clearing neurotransmitter molecules out of the synapse. Some antidepressant medications (including the selective serotonin reuptake inhibitors, or SSRIs) work by reducing the rate at which serotonin is cleared from synapses. Thus, each time a presynaptic neuron releases serotonin molecules into the synapse, the molecules remain in the synapse longer, increasing their chance of activating a receptor and eliciting a reaction in the postsynaptic cell.

This list is just the beginning of the ways in which drugs can affect brain function. In addition, a drug can have more than one effect, and it can affect more than one neurotransmitter system. Some of the most commonly used drugs, including alcohol and nicotine, have been intensively studied. Yet although their effects on behavior are well documented, their effects on neurons and synaptic transmission are so varied that the precise mechanisms by which these drugs affect the neural substrates of learning and memory are not yet entirely clear.

Few pharmaceutical drugs have been developed specifically to affect learning and memory abilities (see "Learning and Memory in Everyday Life" on page 63 for efforts in this direction). More commonly, a drug's positive or negative effects on these abilities are considered side effects. For example, some types of general anesthesia administered to ease the pain of childbirth can also inadvertently "erase" a mother's memory of her baby being born.

Causing Changes in Neural Connections

Any physical change in neurons, or in the systems that support them such as glia and blood vessels, can affect how they communicate and how brain systems interact. Nevertheless, learning and memory researchers have focused almost exclusively on understanding the role of **synaptic plasticity**, the ability of synapses to change as a result of experience. The idea that connections between neurons change during learning was first popularized by Santiago Ramón y Cajal (1852–1934), a famous Spanish physiologist and anatomist. Specifically, Cajal theorized that learning involves strengthening or weakening connections between individual neurons (Ramón y Cajal, 1990 [1894]). This same basic idea was also proposed by William James, who as you may recall from Chapter 1, believed that changes in physical connections within the brain determined how memories were linked together.

But how exactly can the right connections between neurons be weakened or strengthened by learning experiences? One of neuroscience's most enduring insights regarding the neural substrates of learning came from Donald Hebb, a Canadian neuroscientist who studied under Karl Lashley. In one of the most often quoted passages in neuroscience, Hebb wrote: "When an axon of cell A is near enough to excite a cell B and repeatedly or persistently takes part in firing it, some growth process or metabolic change takes place such that A's efficiency, as one of the cells firing B, is increased" (Hebb, 1949). In other words, if two neurons that meet at a synapse—we'll call them neuron A and

synaptic plasticity. The ability of synapses to change as a result of experience.

Can a Pill Improve Your Memory?

If you've ever studied for a difficult exam, you've probably wished for a pill that could make your brain function like a copy machine. Instead of reading, reviewing, and rehearsing, you could swallow the pill, read the material once, and have it encoded in your brain forever (or at least until the exam is over). Sounds like science fiction, right?

In fact, several companies, ranging from pharmaceutical giants to smaller biotech firms, are looking for a drug to improve memory in healthy people (Lynch, Palmer, & Gall, 2011; Monti & Contestabile, 2009). Some possible candidates are currently being tested on laboratory rats, and a few are even being tested in small groups of human volunteers. It remains to be seen which, if any, of these new drugs will be safe and effective.

Until a new generation of memory-boosting drugs becomes available, researchers continue to examine existing drugs, many already approved for the treatment of other illnesses, to see whether any might provide a memory boost in normal, healthy people. For example, several drugs used in treating Alzheimer's disease—including donepezil (Aricept)—increase brain levels of the neurotransmitter acetylcholine, which is abnormally low in people with Alzheimer's. These drugs can produce modest, temporary memory improvements in Alzheimer's patients, raising the possibility that they might also improve memory in healthy (or mildly impaired) adults (Whitehead et al., 2004). However, there is little evidence so far to suggest that the drugs can boost memory in otherwise healthy people (Beglinger et al., 2004; Stern & Alberini, 2013).

Another approach to finding memory-enhancing drugs is based on the fact that attention and concentration can increase the storage and retention of new information. Perhaps drugs that improve attention will also improve memory. Such attention-boosting drugs include modafinil (Provigil), which is used to treat sleep disorders, and methylphenidate (Ritalin), used to treat attention deficit hyperactivity disorder (ADHD). Many college students already pop Ritalin in an effort to boost studying or exam performance. But it's not clear that boosting attention beyond normal levels is necessarily good for memory. The jury is still out on whether these drugs improve memory in healthy humans (Mehta et al., 2000; Turner et al., 2003). The bottom line is that, so far, no pill can substitute for the hard work of learning. Instead of spending money on "brain-boosting" drugs of questionable efficacy and safety, healthy people are best advised to do their learning the old-fashioned way: by devoting the necessary time to study.

---

neuron B—often fire at nearly the same time, then the synapses between them should be strengthened, "wiring" the two neurons together. This would increase the probability that whenever neuron A became active, it would cause neuron B to become active, too. A shorthand version of this "rule" that neuroscientists often use is *neurons that fire together, wire together*.

Hebbian Learning

Learning that involves strengthening connections between neurons that work together is called **Hebbian learning**. Figure 2.15 shows a simple model of Hebbian learning. Eight hypothetical cortical neurons are shown, each with weak connections to surrounding neurons (Figure 2.15a). Now let's assume that some sensory stimulus evokes activation in a subset of these neurons that are tuned to features of this stimulus (solid circles in Figure 2.15a). As those neurons become active, they produce outputs that are transmitted to other nearby neurons. According to Hebb's rule—neurons that fire together, wire together—the connections between coactive neurons are strengthened as a result. Repeated coactivity of the same subset of neurons, in response to the same stimulus, has a cumulative effect, resulting in the strong connections (heavy lines) shown in Figure 2.15b. Thus, repeated exposure to a stimulus can strengthen connections within a distinctive subset of cortical neurons, and this subset can then provide an increasingly reliable basis for identifying the stimulus that is activating them. Changing the connections between cortical neurons creates a pattern that makes a repeated stimulus more likely to be recognized and distinguished from other stimuli.

Hebbian learning. The principle that learning involves strengthening the connections of coactive neurons; often stated as, "Neurons that fire together, wire together."

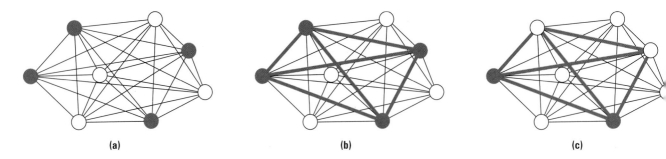

Figure 2.15 A simple model of Hebbian learning Circles correspond to cortical neurons, and lines denote connections between them. (a) Stimulus inputs activate a subset of the neurons (solid circles). (b) Connections between coactive neurons are strengthened (heavy lines). (c) After connections between coactive neurons have been established, an incomplete version of a familiar stimulus may activate just some of the neurons (solid circles) in the subset that represents the stimulus. Activation flows along the strengthened connections and ultimately retrieves the complete stimulus, resulting in the representation shown in (b).

Hebbian learning can also explain how repeated experiences can enhance the ability to recognize familiar stimuli (discussed further in Chapter 3). Suppose that once connections have been established between cortical neurons, the organism encounters an incomplete version of a familiar stimulus (Figure 2.15c). Only some of the subset of neurons that represents that familiar stimulus are activated at first (solid circles in Figure 2.15c), but the connections already established through repeated experiences will produce outputs that complete the familiar pattern, reconstructing Figure 2.15b. Similarly, recognition of distorted versions of a familiar stimulus, such as might occur when you meet an old friend who has dyed her hair, could also be facilitated by stored patterns encoded as connections between neurons that on previous occasions were simultaneously active.

According to Hebb, learning-related changes in synaptic connections between neurons are an automatic result of the neurons' mutual activity. We now know that Hebb was on the right track. But it was several more decades before technology advanced to the point where researchers gained the ability to directly control such experience-related changes in neural activity.

Long-Term Potentiation and Long-Term Depression

In the late 1960s, Terje Lømo was pursuing his doctoral degree in the lab of Per Andersen at the University of Oslo in Norway. Part of Lømo's research consisted of electrically stimulating the axons of presynaptic neurons that provided inputs to the hippocampus of a rabbit. He simultaneously recorded electrical activity produced by postsynaptic neurons within the hippocampus (Figure 2.16a). Normally, a certain amount of stimulation produced a certain level of response: a single weak stimulation would produce a low response in hippocampal neurons, and a strong burst of high-frequency stimulation (say, 100 stimulations in a second) would produce a more robust response. But to Lømo's surprise, the high-frequency stimulation also caused a lasting change in responding, so that hippocampal neurons would over-respond to subsequent weak stimulation (Figure 2.16b). This change could last for hours (Bliss & Gardner-Medwin, 1973; Bliss & Lømo, 1973; Lømo, 1966).

Imagine you have a brother who constantly torments you with his snide comments. Most of the time, you don't react. But one day he says something that's really over the top, and you respond with some strong language of your own. A few minutes later, before you've had a chance to calm down, he makes another little snide comment. Ordinarily, you might not have bothered to respond. But this time you haven't yet cooled down from the earlier explosion, so you lose

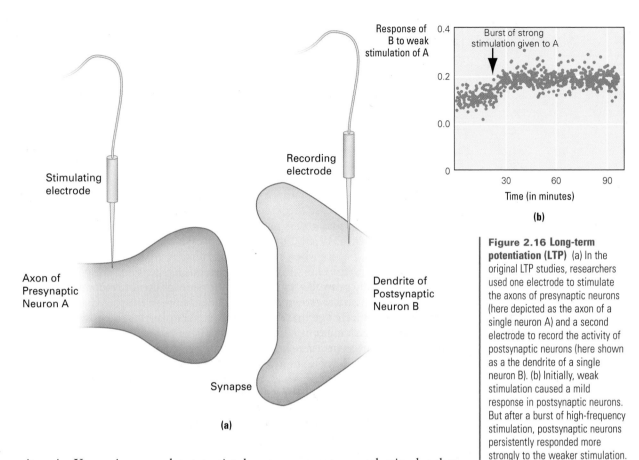

(a)

Figure 2.16 Long-term potentiation (LTP) (a) In the original LTP studies, researchers used one electrode to stimulate the axons of presynaptic neurons (here depicted as the axon of a single neuron A) and a second electrode to record the activity of postsynaptic neurons (here shown as a the dendrite of a single neuron B). (b) Initially, weak stimulation caused a mild response in postsynaptic neurons. But after a burst of high-frequency stimulation, postsynaptic neurons persistently responded more strongly to the weaker stimulation.

it again. Your prior anger has *potentiated* your response to a weak stimulus that normally wouldn't have evoked such a strong reaction.

Potentiation of a neuron by a strong stimulus is similar (except that the "irritation" can last much longer), making the neuron more likely to respond to any subsequent stimulus. This effect, in which synaptic transmission becomes more effective as a result of recent activity, came to be called **long-term potentiation (LTP)**. The reports by Lømo and his coworkers demonstrated that electrical stimulation could not only be used to cause neurons to change their activity but that these changes could last for hours or even days (Bliss & Gardner-Medwin, 1973; Bliss & Lømo, 1973). Since that time, LTP has become one of the most extensively investigated phenomena in the neuroscience of memory.

Despite intensive study of LTP in the decades since it was initially reported, many questions remain about exactly what changes occur to produce it, and how it relates to learning in more natural contexts. Perhaps postsynaptic neurons change to become more responsive to subsequent inputs. This would mean that when presynaptic neurons release neurotransmitters after strong stimulation, the postsynaptic neurons will have a heightened sensitivity to that neurotransmitter, producing the enhanced response seen in Figure 2.16b.

LTP may also involve changes to presynaptic neurons. This idea is controversial, because it isn't clear exactly how signals could travel backward across the synapse. But perhaps some kind of chemical—a *retrograde messenger*—could be released by postsynaptic neurons and diffuse across the synapse, causing an increase in the amount of neurotransmitter the presynaptic neurons release in the future. These changes might occur within a few minutes and last several hours. In addition, however, most researchers currently believe there are

long-term potentiation (LTP). A process in which synaptic transmission becomes more effective as a result of recent activity; with long-term depression, widely believed to represent a form of synaptic plasticity that could be the neural mechanism for learning.

components of LTP that take place over several hours and can last a lifetime. This would involve changes such as strengthening of existing synapses or even the building of new ones (Chen, Rex, Casale, Gall, & Lynch, 2007).

As excited as researchers were about the possibilities of LTP as a mechanism for learning and memory, they were aware of a significant remaining question. LTP represents a way to strengthen neural connections, but this alone isn't much use. If you think of the activity patterns of a neuron as being like an audio signal, then LTP corresponds to pumping up the volume of particular input patterns. But imagine an orchestra conductor who can only make the musicians play louder. Every symphony would be deafening by the time it ended! There has to be a way to turn the volume down as well as up. For LTP to be effective as a way to increase the strength of useful synapses, there would also have to be a process that can decrease the strength of less useful synapses.

Soon after Lømo and others' original reports, such a process was discovered (Dunwiddie & Lynch, 1978). **Long-term depression (LTD)**, also referred to as *synaptic depression*, occurs when synaptic transmission becomes *less* effective as a result of recent activity. One situation in which this happens is if presynaptic neurons are repeatedly active but the postsynaptic neurons do not respond. Neurons that fire together wire together, but connections between neurons that don't fire together weaken, a change that is believed to reflect a weakening in synapses. As with the synaptic changes in LTP, researchers have various ideas about how the weakening might occur: there may be a decrease in the responsiveness of postsynaptic neurons, a decrease in neurotransmitter release by presynaptic neurons, or long-term structural changes in the neurons and synapses. As with LTP, many of the details of LTD remain to be worked out. Scientists still have a long way to go to understand synaptic plasticity and its relation to learning and memory.

long-term depression (LTD).
A process in which synaptic transmission becomes less effective as a result of recent activity; with long-term potentiation, widely believed to represent a form of synaptic plasticity that could be the neural mechanism for learning.

Test Your Knowledge

Synaptic Plasticity

Synaptic plasticity is one of the most researched phenomena in the field of neuroscience, yet many of its features remain poorly understood. Identify which of the following statements accurately describe what is known about synaptic plasticity. (Answers appear in the back of the book.)

1. Synaptic change can be produced through electrical stimulation.
2. Whenever firing patterns change in a neural circuit, synaptic change has occurred somewhere in the circuit.
3. Synaptic plasticity can weaken or strengthen connections between neurons.
4. Synaptic plasticity can be measured in humans with fMRI.
5. LTP is observed only in animals that have recently been learning.

Interim Summary

- Accidental brain lesions in humans have revealed much about how different brain regions function. Intentional brain lesions in animal models have similarly provided insights into how different regions contribute to learning and memory.

- Researchers can also use implanted electrodes to stimulate neurons into activity so that the sensations or responses that they evoke can be observed. Just as lesions can degrade memory abilities, stimulation can sometimes enhance memory.

- Drugs are chemicals that alter the biochemical functioning of the body. Drugs that affect the brain generally change neural activity by interfering with synaptic transmission.

- The ability of synapses to change with experience is called synaptic plasticity. Strengthening or weakening the connections between neurons can influence when they fire. Such changes in connections are thought to be a primary mechanism of memory formation.

- Long-term potentiation (LTP) occurs when synaptic transmission becomes more effective as a result of strong electrical stimulation of neurons.

- An opponent process to LTP, called long-term depression (LTD), occurs when synaptic transmission becomes less effective after neurons do not fire together.

Synthesis

We've covered a lot of ground in this chapter. We started with the basic geography of nervous systems, moved on to some key principles of how the various brain regions process different kinds of inputs and outputs, and ended by looking at how synapses can change over time.

If you get the feeling that, for all this information, there are still a frustrating number of unresolved questions about the neural substrates of learning and memory, you're absolutely correct. But this is also a time when neuroscientists have access to an unprecedented selection of techniques: neuroimaging and recording methods that allow visualization of brain activity at multiple scales in living organisms; advanced microscopes that make synapses, dendrites, and neurotransmitter-containing vesicles visible; and systems capable of recording single-cell activity from hundreds of neurons simultaneously. These tools, now in fairly routine use, didn't even exist a few decades ago.

In the following chapters, we dig deeper into the mechanisms that make learning and memory possible. The involvement of the hippocampus in these processes has been widely studied in humans and other animals. Consequently, this brain region is discussed in more chapters than any other part of the brain. Chapter 3 describes links between the hippocampus and spatial memories, Chapter 4 describes hippocampal contributions to eyeblink conditioning, and Chapter 7 describes the dramatic impacts of hippocampal damage on memories for facts and events. Hippocampal processing also contributes to generalization of learning (Chapter 6), emotional learning (Chapter 10), and the social transfer of information (Chapter 11). Intriguingly, the hippocampus is also one of the few regions in the mammalian brain where new neurons are born throughout adulthood, a process that may contribute to our ability to keep learning new information across a lifetime (Chapter 12).

Several regions of the cerebral cortex have also been shown to underlie various learning and memory capacities, and so discussion of cortical processing is likewise spread across multiple chapters. Changes in sensory and motor cortices associated with learning are described in Chapters 3, 6, and 8, while the roles of frontal and association cortex in memory formation and retrieval are reviewed in Chapter 7. Frontal cortex also is discussed extensively in Chapter 9, where it is related to the ability to juggle thoughts and memories and to voluntarily manipulate how memories are used.

Three other brain regions emphasized in the following discussions are the cerebellum, the basal ganglia, and the amygdala. The cerebellum has been studied extensively as a site of memory storage and processing in classical conditioning research (Chapter 4) and in relation to skill learning (Chapter 8). The basal

Figure 2.17 Overview of brain regions discussed in subsequent chapters The hippocampus, cortex, cerebellum, basal ganglia, and amygdala all contribute to learning and memory in different ways. Their roles are described in further detail in the chapters indicated.

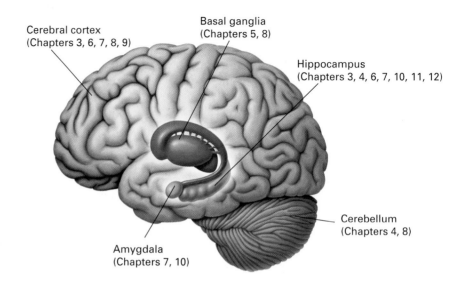

Cerebral cortex
(Chapters 3, 6, 7, 8, 9)

Basal ganglia
(Chapters 5, 8)

Hippocampus
(Chapters 3, 4, 6, 7, 10, 11, 12)

Cerebellum
(Chapters 4, 8)

Amygdala
(Chapters 7, 10)

ganglia are also implicated in skill learning, particularly when learning involves reinforcement (Chapter 5) and sensory-guided actions (Chapter 8). Finally, the amygdala is central to emotional learning, affecting how rapidly memories are formed (Chapter 10) and how long they last (Chapter 7). Figure 2.17 summarizes where each of these brain regions is discussed in the book.

We hope that the following chapters will engage all of these brain regions and more, enabling you to better encode and organize your own knowledge about learning and memory phenomena.

KNOW YOUR KEY TERMS

axon, *p. 41*
brainstem, *p. 38*
cell body, *p. 41*
central nervous system (CNS), *p. 37*
cerebellum, *p. 38*
cerebral cortex, *p. 38*
dendrite, *p. 41*
difference image, *p. 52*
diffusion tensor imaging (DTI), *p. 43*
drug, *p. 61*
electroencephalography (EEG), *p. 53*
engram, *p. 58*
enriched environment, *p. 44*
event-related potential (ERP), *p. 54*
frontal lobe, *p. 38*

functional magnetic resonance imaging(fMRI), *p. 53*
functional neuroimaging, *p. 52*
glia, *p. 42*
Hebbian learning, *p. 63*
lesion, *p. 43*
long-term depression (LTD), *p. 66*
long-term potentiation (LTP), *p. 65*
magnetic resonance imaging (MRI), *p. 43*
nervous system, *p. 37*
neuromodulator, *p. 51*
neuron, *p. 37*
neurophysiology, *p. 55*
neuropsychology, *p. 57*
neuroscience, *p. 36*
neurotransmitter, *p. 49*

occipital lobe, *p. 38*
parietal lobe, *p. 38*
peripheral nervous system (PNS), *p. 37*
phrenology, *p. 42*
positron emission tomography (PET), *p. 53*
postsynaptic, *p. 49*
presynaptic, *p. 49*
receptor, *p. 50*
reflex, *p. 46*
single-cell recording, *p. 55*
soma, *p. 41*
structural neuroimaging, *p. 43*
synapse, *p. 49*
synaptic plasticity, *p. 62*
temporal lobe, *p. 38*
theory of equipotentiality, *p. 58*

QUIZ YOURSELF

1. The brain and spinal cord together make up the _____. (p. 37)

2. Sensory receptors within your fingers and toes are part of your_____. (p. 37)

3. The temporal lobe, parietal lobe, occipital lobe, and frontal lobe are all subdivisions of the _____. (p. 38)

4. The _____ looks like a smaller brain hiding underneath the cerebral cortex. (p. 38)

5. _____ collect neurotransmitters released from a presynaptic neuron. (p. 49)

6. Cells other than neurons that are found throughout the brain include _____. (p. 42)

7. A major technique currently used to collect structural images of human brains is _____. (p. 43)

8. The fact that by nature babies placed underwater do not inhale water is an example of a(n) _____. (p. 46)

9. Neurons in the _____ play an important role in the generation and control of motor responses in humans. (p. 38–39)

10. The prototypical connections between neurons are between _____ and _____. (p. 41)

11. A(n) _____ is a hypothetical physical change in neurons that forms the basis of a memory. (p. 58)

12. _____ are a technique for identifying specific brain regions that are more or less active during the performance of particular memory tasks. (p. 52)

13. If electrodes are attached to a person's head, it is probably because _____ recordings are being collected. (p. 53)

14. One method for activating neurons in the cerebral cortex of humans without requiring surgery is _____. (p. 60)

15. Chemical substances that when brought into the body can change how long neurotransmitters can activate receptors in a synapse are called _____. (p. 61)

16. When connected neurons are firing at the same time, _____ can result. (p. 62–66)

Answers appear in the back of the book.

CONCEPT CHECK

1. In addition to learning to salivate whenever they heard a bell, some of Pavlov's dogs learned to salivate whenever Pavlov walked into the room. Use the concepts of synaptic plasticity and Hebbian learning to explain why this might have occurred. What region(s) of a dog's cortex might have changed as a result of this learning?

2. Neuroimages of different individuals performing the same task often differ greatly in the brain regions shown to be activated. Does this mean that the brains of these individuals function differently? If not, why not?

3. Drugs that block LTP in the hippocampus impair learning in some tasks but facilitate learning in other tasks. Similarly, some researchers have correlated LTP-like effects with learning in a variety of tasks, whereas others have observed learning in the absence of these LTP effects. What does this tell us about the relationship between LTP and learning?

4. Carbon monoxide poisoning can damage many different parts of the brain, resulting in many different kinds of deficits—for example, severe impairments in language or an inability to recognize objects. Describe one way a neuropsychologist could determine what part(s) of the brain might have been damaged.

5. Lashley's findings from lesion experiments in rats suggest that the brain can function when only part of the cerebral cortex is available. Additionally, invertebrates have been learning successfully for millions of years with less than 1% of the total neurons mammals have. What does this information imply about the role of the cerebral cortex in learning and memory?

Answers appear in the back of the book.

CHAPTER 3

Habituation, Sensitization, and Familiarization

Learning about Repeated Events

J EFFREY'S GRANDMOTHER WAS FED UP. It was two o'clock in the morning, and once again her grandson was banging around in the basement. She couldn't remember how many times she had told him to stop making such a racket. It had taken her a couple of years to get used to the neighbor's dogs barking all night. They almost never woke her up now. But Jeffrey's noisiness was another matter altogether. Every time he started up with the sawing, banging, and yelling, it seemed worse than the last time. Eventually, she forced Jeffrey to move out of the house. If she had known what he was doing to raise such a din, it would have disturbed her a lot more.

At first Jeffrey Dahmer was annoyed at being kicked out of his grandmother's house, but he soon got used to the convenience of having his own apartment. He took to cruising around the Pink Flamingo and other bars that were popular among young gay men, his potential victims. Dahmer had learned to recognize which of the customers were most likely to take his bait and follow him home. He couldn't say what it was about them that let him know they were susceptible, but he was confident that he could discriminate the "maybes" from the "probably nots."

During this same period, reports began to appear in the news media of young men going missing from the neighborhood. But disappearances were all too common in Milwaukee; for most people this was just more of the same. When one of Dahmer's victims—a 14-year-old Laotian who spoke no English—escaped to run naked through the streets, police picked him up and returned him to Dahmer's apartment. Dahmer convinced them that the boy was his lover and an adult, and that they were just having a lover's tiff. The police noticed a terrible stench in the apartment, but noxious smells weren't uncommon in that part of the city. The officers left, and the boy was not seen alive again.

Behavioral Processes

Recognizing and Responding to Repetition

Learning and Memory in Everyday Life: Sex on the Beach

The What and Where of Exposure-Based Learning

Learning and Memory in Everyday Life: Unconscious Racial Bias

Brain Substrates

An Invertebrate Model System

Perceptual Learning and Cortical Plasticity

Temporal Lobe Involvement in Spatial Learning and Familiarity

Clinical Perspectives

Rehabilitation after Stroke: Habituation Gone Awry

Sensitization to Stress in Anxiety and Depression

Human–Machine Interfaces: Regaining Sensory Modalities through Perceptual Learning

J Meul-Van Cauteren/age fotostock

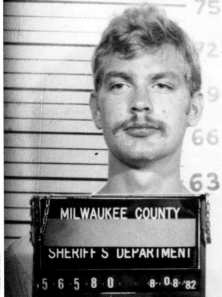

AP Photo/Handout

In what ways did habituation help Jeffrey Dahmer to kill 17 people before being captured?

It wasn't until another victim escaped and flagged down a squad car that police returned to Dahmer's apartment. This time, they noticed some photos of dismembered bodies in the bedroom. That got the officers' attention, and when they investigated further, they found a human head in the refrigerator. The public, initially blasé about the news of one more captured criminal, paid considerably more attention when they learned that Dahmer was not only killing his victims but also eating them. The Jeffrey Dahmer case quickly became the biggest news story of its day.

When an individual experiences the same event many times, the brain accumulates memories of those experiences. Sometimes the memories lead a person to ignore additional repetitions of the events. Dahmer's grandmother heard the neighbor's dogs barking many times and eventually got used to them; the Milwaukee police had experienced many smelly apartments and consequently did not investigate the source of the putrid smell in Dahmer's apartment; the public was used to news reports of disappearances and so did not think too much about what might be causing them. None of these occurrences elicited much of a reaction until new and more alarming aspects came to light.

Such loss of responding to repeated experiences is called *habituation*, and it's one of the most widespread forms of learning. All organisms ever tested—even those without a brain, such as protozoa—show habituation. It is just one example of how experiencing an event over and over can lead to learning about that event. Through habituation, a person learns to disregard an event, but in other instances, repetition can increase attention to the event. Jeffrey's grandmother became *sensitized* to the sounds she repeatedly heard coming from her basement, and eventually they annoyed her so much that she kicked Jeffrey out. Repeated experiences can also lead to *perceptual learning*, which enabled Jeffrey Dahmer to recognize suitable victims. This chapter focuses on the contrasting ways people and other organisms respond to repeated events and looks at how memories for repeated events are acquired.

3.1 Behavioral Processes

Recall from Chapter 1 that learning is a process by which experiences can lead to changes in behavior. Such changes in behavior are not always immediately obvious, however. For example, *latent learning*, described in the Chapter 1 discussion of Edward Tolman, takes place without any initial indications of changes in behavior. As a student reading this chapter, you are actively attempting to understand and remember the information it contains. At the same time, you are automatically forming memories of your reading experiences. As a student reading this chapter, you are actively attempting to understand and remember the information it contains. Did that last sentence seem familiar? Although you are probably not attempting to memorize every word of every sentence in this book, it is still relatively easy for you to recognize a sentence you have just read. To an outside observer, however, you are simply a person staring at words. There is no direct evidence that you understand the words you are looking at, much less that you have detected any repetition within the sentences. Your learning and recognition are effectively hidden from the world.

As a student reading this chapter, you are easily able to detect that repetition is occurring. As a student reading this chapter, you should be curious about how it is that you and other organisms do this. As a student reading this chapter, you should recognize that these are exactly the kinds of repetitions that might lead to habituation, if not for the variation in the way each repetition ends. As a student reading this chapter, you might also be aware of how this sort of persistent repetition can easily become aggravating (if so, you are beginning to understand what sensitization is like). As a student reading this chapter, you have just directly experienced some of the phenomena associated with latent learning about repeated events.

Section 3.1 will introduce you to learning processes that occur when you respond reflexively to repeated events, as when you habituate, and also to learning processes that occur when you repeatedly encounter similar stimuli while actively exploring the world around you, as when you recognize a celebrity in a magazine.

Recognizing and Responding to Repetition

Suppose a man who was born and raised on the Caribbean island of Jamaica has never seen snow. If he moves to Buffalo, New York, he will probably be excited and fascinated by his first snowfall. But a man of the same age who has grown up in Buffalo will react to the same snowfall very differently. For him, snow is recognizable, common, nothing to write home about—something he accepts and lives with on a daily basis.

Everything is novel the first time it happens to you. Even the most ordinary events only become mundane after repeated exposures. Through repetition, you may learn not to respond to a particular event, even if—like the Jamaican in the snow—you originally responded with great excitement. This kind of learning, **habituation**, is formally defined as a decrease in the strength or occurrence of a behavior after repeated exposure to the stimulus that produces the behavior. Habituation is sometimes described as the simplest or most basic kind of learning. Nevertheless, experimental studies conducted over the last 100 years have yet to reveal exactly how habituation works (Rankin et al., 2009; Thompson, 2009). In the following discussions, we describe some of what researchers have discovered about habituation and its underlying mechanisms.

habituation. A decrease in the strength or occurrence of a behavior after repeated exposure to the stimulus that produces that behavior.

The Process of Habituation

You've experienced habituation if you've ever moved to a new home. Possibly, the first night or two, you had trouble getting to sleep because of the strange noises outside your window (whether wailing police sirens or chirping crickets). But after a few nights, you probably were no longer awakened by the noises and slept until morning.

In the laboratory, researchers examine simpler examples of habituation that they can describe in terms of a single easily controlled stimulus and a single easily measurable response. One such response is the **acoustic startle reflex**, which is a defensive response to a loud, unexpected noise. When a rat in an experimental chamber is startled by a loud noise, it jumps, much as you might jump if someone sneaked up behind you and yelled in your ear. If the same noise is presented over and over again, every minute or so, the rat's startle response declines (Figure 3.1a), just as your responsiveness to noises would decrease after moving into a new home; if the process goes on long enough, the rat may cease to startle altogether. At this point, the rat's startle response has habituated to the loud noise.

acoustic startle reflex. A defensive response (such as jumping or freezing) to a startling stimulus (such as a loud noise).

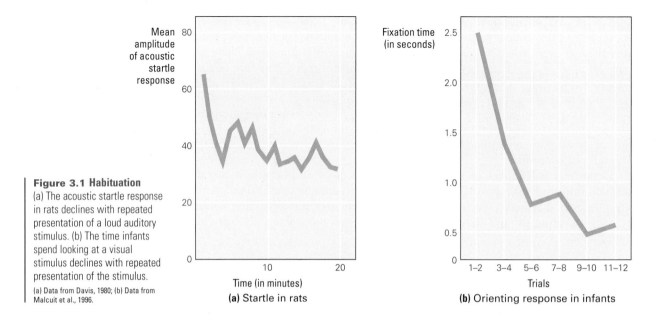

Figure 3.1 Habituation
(a) The acoustic startle response in rats declines with repeated presentation of a loud auditory stimulus. (b) The time infants spend looking at a visual stimulus declines with repeated presentation of the stimulus.

(a) Data from Davis, 1980; (b) Data from Malcuit et al., 1996.

orienting response. An organism's innate reaction to a novel stimulus.

Another common way to study habituation uses the **orienting response**, an organism's natural reaction to sensing a novel stimulus or an important event. For example, if a checkerboard pattern (or any other unfamiliar visual stimulus) is presented to an infant, the infant's orienting response is to turn her head and look at it for a few seconds before shifting her gaze elsewhere. If the checkerboard is removed for 10 seconds and then redisplayed, the infant will respond again—but for a shorter time than on the first presentation (Figure 3.1b). The duration of staring, called *fixation time*, decreases with repeated presentations of the stimulus, in a manner very much like the habituation of a rat's startle response (Malcuit, Bastien, & Pomerleau, 1996).

Normally, habituation is advantageous for an organism. Through habituation to familiar stimuli, the individual avoids wasting time and energy on unnecessary responses to each repeated event. But habituation carries risks. A deer that has gotten used to the sound of gunshots is a deer whose head may end up as a hunter's trophy. A poker player whose responses become habituated to the excitement of winning a small pot may start to play for larger and larger stakes, putting his finances at risk. The dangers of habituation are immortalized in the story of the boy who cried wolf. In this folk tale, the boy plays practical jokes on his neighbors, calling them to come save him from an imaginary wolf; eventually the villagers learn there is no reason to respond when he calls. Later, a real wolf attacks, but the villagers ignore the boy's cries, and no one comes to save him.

This might seem like a case in which the villagers just learned that the boy was unreliable. Think, however, about situations in which you have heard a fire or car alarm go off repeatedly for no apparent reason. Each time the alarm goes off, you will become more skeptical, and at the same time your orienting or startle response will likely decrease. Anytime your response decreases with repeated experiences, there is a good chance that habituation is occurring. Of course, it is also possible that you are simply falling asleep, especially if the alarm is going off at night. One way researchers are able to distinguish habituation from fatigue and other causes of decreased behavioral responding to repetition is by disrupting the repetition of experienced events, as described below.

Stimulus Specificity and Dishabituation

An important feature of habituation is that habituation to one event doesn't cause habituation to every other stimulus in the same sensory modality. In other words, habituation is *stimulus specific* (Thompson & Spencer, 1966). After a baby's orienting response to one visual stimulus (say, a donut shape) has decreased after several repetitions, the baby will still show a strong orienting response to a new visual stimulus (say, a cross shape). This renewal of responding provides evidence of habituation to the first visual stimulus, because if the baby was simply falling asleep, it should not matter what visual stimulus appears. Interestingly, a baby's fixation time when shown a "new" image depends on how similar that image is to the one that was repeatedly experienced. The more similar the image, the less the fixation time will increase. This phenomenon, called *stimulus generalization*, is observed in all forms of learning; we discuss generalization in greater detail in Chapter 6.

In some cases, presenting a novel stimulus after multiple presentations have caused habituation to an earlier stimulus can actually lead to recovery of the response to the familiar stimulus. For example, a baby shown a donut shape many times may show little interest the twentieth time it is presented. If, however, the baby is briefly shown a live kitten after the nineteenth repetition of the donut, the baby is likely to respond to the twentieth presentation of a donut shape as if it were a novel image, showing a much longer fixation time than in the kitten-free scenario. This renewal of responding after a new stimulus has been presented is called **dishabituation**. Dishabituation often occurs when an arousing stimulus (like a kitten) is introduced into a sequence of otherwise monotonous repetitions, but it can also accompany less eventful changes. Simply adding motion to a familiar stimulus can lead to dishabituation, as demonstrated when adults start waving toys around in front of an infant who seems uninterested. Dishabituation provides another useful way of demonstrating that the absence of responding to a repeated stimulus is indeed the result of habituation and not some other factor like fatigue.

All organisms that show habituation also show dishabituation. In the laboratory, a male rat will mate with an unfamiliar female many times over a period of a few hours but eventually reaches a point at which the mating stops. If the now-familiar female is replaced with a new female, however, the male rat will rush to mate some more. This dishabituation of the mating response shows that habituation occurred with the first partner rather than the rat's merely running out of energy or interest in sex (Dewsbury, 1981; Fisher, 1962). The dishabituation of sexual responding is sometimes referred to as the *Coolidge effect*, after an anecdote involving President Coolidge. While touring a poultry farm, the story goes, the president and his wife were informed that a single rooster could mate dozens of times in a single day. "Ha," said Mrs. Coolidge. "Tell that to Mr. Coolidge." The president then asked the tour guide whether the rooster was always required to mate with the same female. Told that it was not, the president reportedly remarked, "Ha—tell that to Mrs. Coolidge." (See "Learning and Memory in Everyday Life" on page 77 for information on habituation and dishabituation of human sexual responses.)

"May the habituation commence."

Andrew Evans/CartoonStock

Is habituation an inevitable consequence of long-term relationships? Read on...

dishabituation. A renewal of a response, previously habituated, that occurs when the organism is presented with a novel stimulus.

Factors Influencing the Rate and Duration of Habituation

How rapidly a response habituates and how long the decrease in responding lasts depend on several factors, including how startling the stimulus is, the number of times it is experienced, and the length of time between repeated exposures. It is relatively easy to get used to the feeling of the tag in the back of your shirt—most people can learn to ignore this stimulus relatively quickly. In fact, at this point you probably would have to make an effort to notice that the tag is even there. It would probably take you longer to get used to the feeling of a spider crawling on the back of your neck—or you might never get used to that at all, even after many repeated experiences. In general, the less arousing an event is, the more rapidly a response to that event will habituate. Whenever habituation does occur, larger decreases in responding are seen after earlier repetitions than after later exposures (see Figure 3.1). In other words, the biggest changes in responding are seen when one is first becoming familiar with a stimulus. This pattern is seen for many kinds of learning and will be discussed in greater detail in Chapters 4 and 8.

Animals given sessions of multiple exposures to stimuli in which the exposures are separated by short intervals will typically show habituation after fewer exposures than animals given sessions in which the same number of exposures are more spread out over time (Rankin & Broster, 1992; Thompson & Spencer, 1966): more rapid repetition of a stimulus generally leads to more rapid habituation. Exposures that are repeated close together in time are called *massed*, whereas exposures that are spread out over time are called *spaced*. If your goal is to habituate your response to some repeated stimulus as rapidly as possible, your best bet is to find a way to make that stimulus as nonarousing as possible, to expose yourself to closely spaced repetitions of that stimulus, and to repeat the process frequently (as you do when you wear shirts with tags in the back).

The effects of habituation may last for a few minutes or several hours and under some circumstances may last a day or more. But they generally do not last forever and are especially likely to dissipate if the stimulus is absent for a while. Habituation that goes away in seconds or minutes is called *short-term habituation*; habituation that lasts longer is called *long-term habituation* (Rankin et al., 2009). If a rat has gotten used to a loud noise and then goes through a period of an hour or so in which the noise does not occur, the rat is likely to startle anew when the noise is played again, a process called **spontaneous recovery** (referred to in the box on page 77). In spontaneous recovery, a stimulus-evoked response that has been weakened by habituation increases in strength or reappears after a period of no stimulus presentation. The factors that determine how quickly an individual's response habituates also affect how long the effects of habituation last. Animals that experience massed exposures to a stimulus learn to ignore that stimulus faster than animals given spaced exposures, but if they are retested after a relatively long break, the animals given massed exposures are also more likely to show spontaneous recovery. When exposures are spaced in time, it takes longer for responding to habituate, but once habituation occurs, it lasts for a longer time (Gatchel, 1975; Pedreira, Romano, Tomsic, Lozada, & Maldonado, 1998).

This finding makes intuitive sense, because animals that have gotten used to the intermittent occurrence of a stimulus should find the recurrence of the stimulus after a long interval to be familiar. As a student reading this chapter, you are easily able to detect that repetition is occurring, even when that repetition occurs after moderately long intervals. If your repeated experiences are spread out over time, the likelihood is greater that you will continue to recognize repeating events farther into the future. So, if you want habituation to last for

spontaneous recovery.
Reappearance (or increase in strength) of a previously habituated response after a short period of no stimulus presentation.

as long as possible, your best bet is to repeatedly expose yourself to the relevant stimulus after longer and longer stretches of time.

Although spontaneous recovery might seem to suggest that habituation is a temporary effect, habituation effects accumulate over time. So, if an infant is shown a donut shape 20 times during a single session, her orienting response to that image will likely habituate. If a day or two later the infant is shown the donut shape again, spontaneous recovery will probably have occurred, and the infant's fixation time will be as long as if the image were completely novel. However, this time it may only take eight trials before the infant's orienting response becomes habituated: the effects of repeated experiences have been potentiated by the prior repetitions. This shows that the effects of earlier repeated experiences have not simply faded away. Furthermore, the mechanisms underlying habituation continue to change with repeated exposures, even when behavioral responses are no longer changing. For instance, a rat exposed to a loud sound many times might stop showing any indication that it even hears the sound—its response has decreased to the point at which there no longer is a response. Nevertheless, if the sound continues to be repeated many times after this point, the amount of time required before spontaneous recovery occurs will increase. In this case, the learning associated with repeated exposures is latent, because there are no observable changes in the rat's behavior associated with the increased number of repetitions. The additional effects of repeated exposures after behavioral responding to a stimulus has ceased are only evident when subsequent tests show delayed spontaneous recovery (Thompson & Spencer, 1966).

LEARNING AND MEMORY IN EVERYDAY LIFE

Sex on the Beach

Advertisements for travel to exotic locales with long, sandy beaches often show happy couples falling in love all over again, rediscovering the romance that may have drained out of their everyday existence back home. Can two people really reignite their old flame simply by taking it to a new location? The answer is probably—and the reason is *dishabituation*.

It's easier to study dishabituation of sexual responding in rats than in humans. Most human research has instead focused on sexual arousal in male undergraduate volunteers during the viewing of sexually explicit photos. Such studies have shown that if the same arousing photos are presented repeatedly, human males respond less strongly, just like other animals (Koukounas & Over, 2001; Plaud, Gaither, Henderson, & Devitt, 1997).

Relatively few studies of habituation of sexual arousal have been conducted in women. One problem is that women usually do not become as aroused as their male counterparts when viewing sexually explicit photos. Obviously, it is hard for researchers to measure decreases in an arousal response if they can't reliably elicit arousal to begin with. But in studies that have managed to solve this problem, habituation to sexual arousal seems to occur to a lesser degree in female undergraduates than in male undergraduates (Laan & Everaerd, 1995; Youn, 2006).

An interesting aspect of sexual habituation is that it seems to happen without conscious awareness. For example, male students in a sexual habituation experiment often show habituation within a single session, responding less and less to the same sexually explicit photo as the session goes on—but they also show habituation across sessions, responding less and less each day of a multi-day experiment (Plaud et al., 1997). Under these circumstances, participants often report that they were aware that their arousal was decreasing within a single session, but they seemed to be unaware that their arousal also decreased across sessions. Such continuous but imperceptible decreases in arousal might be a factor in promiscuity and infidelity, which not only threaten stable relationships but may contribute to the spread of sexually transmitted diseases (Plaud et al., 1997).

How can someone in a long-term relationship deal with the scourge of sexual habituation? Prolonged abstinence could lead to *spontaneous recovery* of interest. Another option is to introduce novel stimuli to bring about dishabituation—for example, staging romantic interludes or trying a different technique. So the next time you're feeling bored with an old relationship, a trip to Tahiti might be just what the doctor ordered!

The Process of Sensitization

Several times a year, news reports appear of a celebrity attacking a member of the paparazzi. The actor Sean Penn was charged with attempted murder after he grabbed a photographer by the ankles and held him over a ninth-floor balcony. Rapper Kanye West was arrested for attacking a reporter at Los Angeles International Airport and destroying his camera. Given that celebrities have lots of photos taken of them by lots of people on a daily basis, you might expect that they would eventually become used to all the attention and take no notice of photographers. What causes some celebrities to become so aggressive when confronted with paparazzi? Is it just a case of bad tempers?

One possible explanation is that celebrities have had negative experiences involving photographers in the past that are affecting their responses to new interactions with random members of the paparazzi. **Sensitization** is a phenomenon in which experiences with an arousing stimulus lead to stronger responses to a later stimulus. In some cases, a single, very intense stimulus can produce sensitization, whereas in others, repeated exposures are required. In some ways, sensitization seems to be almost the opposite of habituation. Whereas in habituation repeated experiences can attenuate a rat's acoustic startle reflex, in sensitization repeated experiences can heighten it. As described above, when rats are subjected to a loud noise over and over again, their startle response often habituates (Figure 3.2, green line). But if some of these rats are given an electric shock (Figure 3.2, red line) and then the loud noise is played again, their startle response will be much greater than that of the rats who did not receive a shock (Davis, 1989). In other words, the strong electric shock sensitizes the rats, increasing their startle response to a subsequent loud noise stimulus. Such sensitization is usually short-lived, however. It may persist for 10 or 15 minutes after the shock, but beyond that, the startle response drops back to normal levels. You may notice that the effect of shock in this experiment is very similar to dishabituation. In fact, some researchers have argued that dishabituation is the result of introducing a sensitizing stimulus (Thompson & Spencer, 1966).

Like habituation, sensitization is seen in a wide range of species, including bullfrogs, sea slugs, and humans (Bee, 2001; Eisenstein, Eisenstein, & Bonheim, 1991; Marcus, Nolen, Rankin, & Carew, 1988). Also like habituation, sensitization can rapidly dissipate in some situations and can lead to longer-lasting learning in others (Borszcz, Cranney, & Leaton, 1989; Davis, 1972, 1980; Poon & Young, 2006). However, fewer exposures are typically necessary to produce sensitization than to produce habituation, and whereas habituation is stimulus specific, sensitization is not. For example, an animal's startle response may habituate to one loud tone that is repeated over and over; but if a different loud noise is presented, the startle response reappears in full force—habituation doesn't transfer to the new sound. By contrast, exposure to a sensitizing stimulus (such as an electric shock) can amplify the startle response to any stimulus that comes later: tone, loud noise, butterfly, or anything else. Similarly, a celebrity who catches a photographer peering into his house might be responding not just to that particular photographer but, as an aftereffect, to other even more annoying photographers that he has previously encountered.

One way that researchers study sensitization experimentally in humans is using the **skin conductance response (SCR)**. The SCR is a rapid change in the skin's electrical conductivity that is caused by the nervous system and associated with

sensitization. A phenomenon in which a salient stimulus (such as an electric shock) temporarily increases the strength of responses to other stimuli.

skin conductance response (SCR). A change in the skin's electrical conductivity associated with emotions such as anxiety, fear, or surprise.

Figure 3.2 Sensitization of the rat acoustic startle reflex When a startle-provoking noise is presented repeatedly over a 20-minute period, rats' startle reflex habituates (green line). If a foot shock is then administered to a subset of the rats (at minute 21, red line), the amplitude of their startle reflex to a subsequent noise (at minute 22) is then greater than in the unshocked rats.
Data from Davis, 1989.

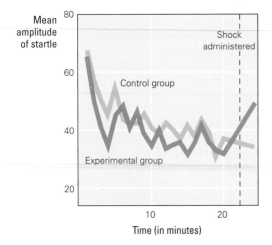

anxiety, fear, or surprise. In the laboratory, researchers record SCRs with electrodes similar to those used for recording electroencephalograms (EEG; see Chapter 2 for details). Exposure to an unexpected loud noise (say, an explosion or a yell) causes a pronounced startle response in humans, accompanied by a sharp SCR. A neutral musical tone may cause a mild orienting response as well as a small SCR. If the loud noise is played before presentation of the tone, the participant's SCRs to the tone are stronger than they would be without the loud noise (Lang, Davis, & Ohman, 2000). Portable sensors are now commercially available that make it possible for you to record your SCRs 24-7 (Figure 3.3a). In principle, you could use such sensors to track and monitor events in your life that are leading to sensitization (Figure 3.3b; Poh, Swenson, & Picard, 2010). Access to such information might make it easier to avoid or mitigate some psychological disorders (discussed in more detail in the Clinical Perspectives section).

Loud noises can sensitize a person's response to tones, just as electric shock sensitizes the startle response in rats. Surprisingly, if the order of stimuli is reversed, then the effects on responding can also reverse. Specifically, if a relatively quiet tone is presented just before a much louder and more startling noise, then the startle response to the louder noise may be reduced relative to the response that would have occurred if only the startling sound had been heard. This effect is called *prepulse inhibition*. Prepulse inhibition is similar to habituation in that some stimuli are "tuned out" based on past experience, leading to reduced responses. However, it is also similar to sensitization in that (1) the initial weak stimulus can affect responding to a wide range of subsequent stimuli, including stimuli in other modalities; and (2) a single presentation of the weak stimulus can produce the effect (Braff, Geyer, & Swerdlow, 2001). These properties have led some researchers to describe prepulse inhibition as a case of *desensitization*, in which past experiences reduce responses to a wide range of stimuli (Poon & Young, 2006; Poon, 2012). You are probably familiar with the idea of people becoming "desensitized" to violence or to events that are unpleasant (like changing dirty diapers). It is difficult to distinguish desensitization from habituation in these natural contexts, because both involve decreased responses to specific kinds of stimuli. Laboratory studies of the neural processes engaged by habituation and desensitization provide new ways of disentangling these two closely related phenomena (discussed further, below, in the Brain Substrates section).

Interestingly, the nature of repeated events and their distribution in time are not the only factors that determine whether they will lead to habituation, desensitization, or sensitization. A series of events that might normally lead to habituation can, in a sick animal, lead to sensitization (Domjan, 1977). In other words, the state of the observer can play a large role in what he or she learns about repeated events. So, a celebrity who repeatedly encounters paparazzi while being sleep deprived, hung over, or ill may be more likely to become sensitized to annoying intrusions of privacy and therefore more likely to strike back.

Figure 3.3 Continuous recording of skin conductance responses (a) Wrist-worn sensors make it possible to record measurements of nervous system activity throughout the day and night. (b) Skin conductance responses (here shown as vertical deflections) can provide indications of how repeated experiences lead to increases or decreases in physiological responses.
(b) Data from Poh, Swenson, & Picard, 2010.

(a)

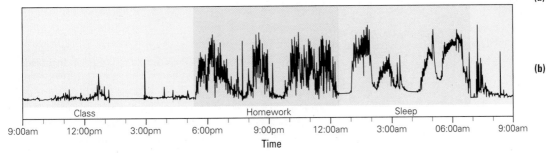

(b)

Dual Process Theory

dual process theory. The theory that habituation and sensitization are independent of each other but operate in parallel.

If repeated events can potentially lead to *either* habituation or sensitization, how can anyone predict what an organism will learn from repeated exposures? Novel stimuli are often arousing, but what is it that determines whether an event will generate increasing arousal with repetition as opposed to becoming boring? One popular theory, called **dual process theory,** suggests that, in fact, repeated events *always lead to the processes underlying both sensitization and habituation* (Groves & Thompson, 1970; Thompson, 2009). Here's how it works. Imagine that when a stimulus S is presented, it evokes a chain of neural responses that (1) eventually leads to activation of a motor response R and (2) also activates a *state system* that signals detection of a stimulus (Figure 3.4a). Habituation after repeated exposures to the stimulus (let's say 10 repetitions) can then be modeled as a weakening of the connection between S and R (Figure 3.4b), combined with only mild arousal of the state system. The weaker connection decreases the likelihood of activity within motor neurons, making the response to S weaker or less likely to occur. If the stimulus is not very arousing, then the weakened connection essentially determines responding. Sensitization can be modeled as an increase in the effect of the state system on sensory-evoked responses (Figure 3.4c), such that even harmless stimuli may be able to produce strong responses.

Figure 3.4 The dual process theory of habituation Dual process theory suggests that both habituation and sensitization processes occur in parallel during every presentation of a stimulus and that the final response after repeated presentations results from the combination of both processes. (a) Initially, a stimulus such as S activates sensory neurons that lead to a motor response R and also activate a separate state system signaling detection of the stimulus. (b) In habituation, repeated presentations of S can weaken the connections between neurons (thinner arrow), thus reducing the strength of R or the likelihood that S leads to R. (c) In sensitization, exposure to an arousing stimulus increases the likelihood that subsequent presentations of S lead to R.

(a) Information from Groves and Thompson, 1970.

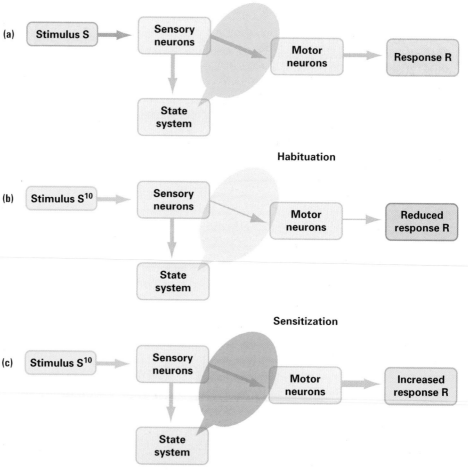

In dual process theory, both sensitization and habituation processes occur in response to every stimulus presentation, and it is the summed combination of these two independent processes that determines the strength of responding (Groves & Thompson, 1970). The actual outcome—the strength of the response to S on a given presentation—depends on such factors as how often S has been repeated and the intensity and recency of highly arousing events. It can also depend on whether other stimuli have activated the state system. For stimuli that lead to little arousal, decreases in connection strengths associated with processes of habituation will be the main determinants of how an organism's responses change over time, leading to the behavioral phenomenon that researchers call habituation. When stimuli are highly arousing, global effects of sensitization will be more evident in responses, leading to the behavioral phenomenon known as sensitization. In dual process theory, both sensitization and habituation processes change over time such that the largest effects of repetition always occur in early exposures.

Opponent Process Theory

Studies of emotional responses to extreme events—to a roller-coaster ride, for example—suggest that there are multiple phases of emotional responding. An initial phase that is scary is followed by a rebound effect of exhilaration. After repeated experiences, the initial fear responses may become weaker, whereas the rebound responses grow stronger (such that what was once scary can become fun). One model of this process, called *opponent process theory*, explains this effect as a way that organisms maintain emotional stability.

Opponent process theory is similar to dual process theory in that it assumes that an experienced event leads to two independent processes—in this case, two emotional processes, one that is pleasurable and one that is less pleasant. The overall emotion that one experiences in response to an event is the combined result of these two independent processes. Repeated experiences have different effects on the initial reaction versus the "rebound" reaction, such that over time, the initial response habituates faster than its counterpart. Thus, your first time bungee jumping may not be nearly as much fun as your fifth time. Both dual process theory and opponent process theory suggest that the learning resulting from repeated experiences is not as simple as might at first appear. A "simple" decrease or increase in responding to an increasingly familiar event may reflect multiple learning processes occurring in parallel. Additionally, repeated experiences can change not only how an individual reflexively responds to familiar events but also how the person perceives and interprets those events, as described in the following section.

Test Your Knowledge

Maximizing Habituation

In some cases, such as in romantic relationships, it makes sense to try and minimize habituation. In contrast, if you discover that the shirt you are wearing is itchy, you'd be better off if you could maximize habituation and avoid sensitization. So what can you do (aside from wearing a different shirt)? Try to come up with at least three strategies that could help you to maximize your habituation to the repeated tactile stimulation produced by the shirt. (Answers appear in the back of the book.)

The What and Where of Exposure-Based Learning

Habituation and sensitization generally do not require much physical or mental effort or initiative. For example, a couch potato may quickly learn to loathe certain annoying commercials simply by repeatedly sitting through them, without ever paying attention. Similarly, rats and babies can habituate to a tone in a laboratory simply by being there. In many situations, however, individuals exert more control over the kinds of stimuli they repeatedly experience. Animals rarely just sit around waiting for something to happen. Instead, they spend much of their time traveling, searching, and exploring the world around them. These actions play a decisive role in determining the kinds of stimuli they are repeatedly exposed to as well as the frequency of exposure. This in turn affects what the individuals learn about, what they remember, and how long the memories last.

Much of what is known about the learning and memory processes that occur when organisms inspect their surroundings comes from studies of object recognition and spatial navigation. Exposure to objects and places often does not initially lead to obvious changes in behavior; latent learning is the norm. Appropriately designed tests can, however, reveal the short- and long-term effects of repeated exposures.

Novel Object Recognition

Earlier we noted that when a novel stimulus appears after repeated presentations of a familiar stimulus, babies show a strong orienting response to the new stimulus (because habituation is stimulus-specific). A similar phenomenon can be seen in exploratory behavior. In the **novel object recognition** task, people, monkeys, or rodents are first acclimated to the *context* of the experiment (the room or box where the tests will be given) by being allowed to freely explore it. Next, two identical objects or pictures are briefly presented within the experimental setting (Figure 3.5a). After a variable delay, one of these stimuli is presented again, but this time paired with a new object or picture (Figure 3.5b). Generally, individuals will spend about twice as much time examining the novel object as they will inspecting the familiar one. From this difference, researchers can infer that the individual recognizes the previously experienced object as one it has investigated before—that is, the repeated stimulus is perceived as familiar.

Not all animals are so eager to investigate novel objects, however. Some actively avoid them, a phenomenon known as *neophobia*. For example, when dolphin trainers want to teach a dolphin to use an object, they often spend several sessions rewarding the dolphin for simply not bolting when the new object is brought near them (many dolphins are neophobic). In this case, the dolphin's fear response provides evidence that an object is not familiar.

novel object recognition. An organism's detection of and response to unfamiliar objects during exploratory behavior.

Figure 3.5 Novel objection recognition (a) Subjects are first exposed to objects and allowed to explore and become familiar with them. (b) Later, subjects are given another opportunity to explore, but with a novel object in place of one of the familiar objects. Typically, subjects show more interest in the novel object, showing that they recognize the familiar object.

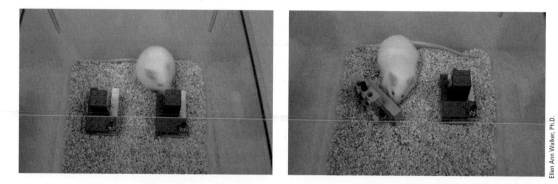

(a)   (b)

Ellen Ann Walker, Ph.D.

Psychologists have used variants of the novel object recognition task to determine what kinds of information individuals remember about objects and places they have inspected in the past, such as an object's position, observable properties, and the circumstances under which it was observed. This task is also useful for investigating the resilience of memories formed through observations or exploration. The perception of *familiarity* is a fundamental component of memory. William James (1890) described memory in general as *"the knowledge of an event, or fact,* of which meantime we have not been thinking, *with the additional consciousness that we have thought or experienced it before"* [italicized as in James, 1890]. **Familiarity** can be defined as the perception of similarity that occurs when an event is repeated—it is, in James's words, a "sense of sameness."

Although it is difficult to know what this feeling of sameness is like for a rat or monkey, we can conclude from tasks such as the novel object recognition task that rats and monkeys discriminate different levels of familiarity, just as they distinguish different frequencies of tones or wavelengths of light (discussed in more detail in Chapter 6 on generalization, discrimination learning, and concept formation). In the past decade, memory researchers have intensively investigated how individuals judge familiarity, how this capacity relates to other memory abilities, and what brain mechanisms contribute to familiarity judgments (Eichenbaum, Yonelinas, & Ranganath, 2007). Consequently, novel object recognition, which scientists once used mainly to distinguish habituation from fatigue, has transformed into a cornerstone of modern memory research.

familiarity. The perception of similarity that occurs when an event is repeated.

Priming

Prior exposure to a stimulus can lead to a sense of familiarity the next time that stimulus is observed. Even when it does not lead to a sense of familiarity, it can affect the individual's response to a repeated stimulus (or related stimuli); this latter effect is called **priming**. For example, priming in humans is often studied using a **word-stem completion task**, in which a person is given a list of word stems (MOT__, SUP__, and such) and asked to fill in the blank with the first word that comes to mind. People generally fill in the blanks to form common English words (MOTEL or MOTOR, SUPPOSE or SUPPER). But if the people were previously exposed to a list of words containing those stems (MOTH, SUPREME, and so on), then they are much more likely to fill in the blanks to form words that were present in that list, even if they don't consciously remember having previously seen the words on the list (Graf, Squire, & Mandler, 1984). When they complete the word stem with a previously experienced word, they do not recognize the word as one they recently saw, and yet the prior experience clearly affects their word choice. Such effects are consistent with the findings from sexual habituation studies, described in "Learning and Memory in Everyday Life" on page 77, that repeated exposures can affect a person's behavior and perception even if the person is not aware that this is happening.

Nonhuman animals show priming, too. For example, blue jays like to eat moths, and moths have evolved coloration patterns that help them blend into the background where they alight. Therefore, blue jays have to be very good at detecting subtle differences in visual patterns that distinguish a tasty meal from a patch of tree bark. Researchers studied this detection ability by training blue jays to look at pictures on a screen (Figure 3.6a) and to peck at the screen to signal "there's a moth here" or at a key to signal "no moth" (Figure 3.6b). The birds did very well, but they were quicker and more accurate at detecting a particular species of moth if they had recently detected other members of that species, as shown in Figure 3.6c (Bond & Kamil, 1999). In other words, recent observations of one kind of moth *primed* the jays' abilities to recognize similar moths later.

priming. A phenomenon in which prior exposure to a stimulus can improve the ability to recognize that stimulus later.

word-stem completion task. A task in which participants are asked to fill in the blanks in a list of word stems (e.g., MOT___) to produce the first word that comes to mind; in a priming experiment, participants are more likely to produce a particular word (e.g., MOTEL) if they have been exposed to that word previously.

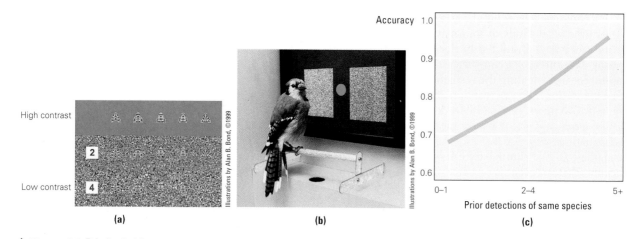

High contrast

Low contrast

(a)

Illustrations by Alan B. Bond, ©1999

(b)

Illustrations by Alan B. Bond, ©1999

Accuracy

Prior detections of same species

(c)

Figure 3.6 Priming in blue jays (a) Virtual moths on a gray background are more easily detectable than the same images of moths on speckled backgrounds. Higher numbers at left indicate more cryptic backgrounds. (b) Blue jays learn to peck on screens when they detect a virtual moth and to peck on a green key when they detect no moths. (c) The blue jays are better able to detect a moth if it is similar to a recently detected one, suggesting that prior exposure facilitates detection. In other words, priming has occurred. Data and images from Bond and Kamil, 1999.

perceptual learning. Learning in which experience with a set of stimuli makes it easier to distinguish those stimuli.

As noted above, priming can occur even in the absence of any feelings of familiarity or recognition that a stimulus was previously experienced. Additionally, priming effects may persist much longer than recognition of past encounters (Tulving, Schacter, & Stark, 1982). These findings led some researchers to propose that priming and recognition involve independent processes (Tulving & Schachter, 1990). More recent behavioral studies indicate, however, that a single memory process might be able to account for both priming and recognition-related effects of repetition (Berry, Shanks, Speekenbrink, & Henson, 2011).

Questions about the number of different processes that are required to explain different phenomena have loomed large in experimental and theoretical studies of learning and memory. Even in "simple" cases where you repeatedly experience an object or word, a currently unknown number of learning and memory processes may be engaged. These so-called simple scenarios are further complicated by the fact that repeatedly experiencing a stimulus can change how you perceive the stimulus, a phenomenon known as *perceptual learning*.

Perceptual Learning

Perceptual learning is learning in which repeated experiences with a set of stimuli makes those stimuli easier to distinguish. Let's consider a couple of examples. Commercial poultry farmers like to sort male from female chicks as soon after hatching as possible to save the cost of feeding male chicks (males don't lay eggs, and they produce lower-quality meat than females). By the time a chick is 5 or 6 weeks old, its sex is clearly revealed by its feather patterns. But highly trained individuals, called chicken sexers, can distinguish whether a day-old chick is male or female just by glancing at the chick's rear end. Accomplished chicken sexers can make this distinction with high accuracy at a viewing rate of one chick per half second, even though the male and female chicks look identical to the untrained eye (Biederman & Shiffrar, 1987). Some chicken sexers can't even verbalize the subtle cues they use to make the distinction; they have seen so many examples of male and female chicks that they "just know which is which." Medical diagnosticians have similar sensitivities to subtle differences in symptoms. All rashes may look alike to an inexperienced medical student, but an experienced dermatologist can glance at a rash and tell immediately, and with high accuracy, whether a patient has contact dermatitis, ringworm, or some other condition.

Although you might not personally be an expert at distinguishing chicken genitals or rashes, you probably have become a connoisseur in other areas. Perhaps you can easily distinguish Coke from Pepsi or McDonald's french fries

racism?

from those of any other fast-food restaurant. Maybe for you, the sound of a Fender electric guitar is very different from the sound of a Gibson. Whatever your specialty, you likely developed your capacities to detect subtle differences through repeated exposures to those stimuli. This is the essence of perceptual learning.

Chicken sexers gain expertise not by accident but through extensive, deliberate practice. This falls into the category of perceptual skill learning, which is discussed more extensively in Chapter 8. Sometimes, however, perceptual learning does happen through mere exposure to stimuli, without any conscious effort by the individual, a situation similar to what occurs during habituation, sensitization, and priming. For example, Eleanor Gibson and colleagues exposed one group of rats to large triangular and circular shapes mounted on the walls of their home cages for about a month (E. Gibson & Walk, 1956). The researchers then trained this group and a control group of rats to approach one of the shapes but not the other. Rats familiar with the shapes learned to discriminate between them faster than rats that had never seen the shapes before. During the initial exposure phase, nothing was done to teach the rats in the experimental group about the shapes, and the shapes were irrelevant to the rats' daily activities. Nevertheless, experience viewing the shapes facilitated later learning about them. Because the perceptual learning in such experiments happens without explicit training, it is sometimes called **mere exposure learning**. This learning process is a type of latent learning (which we discussed at the chapter's beginning), because before the rats begin training with the shapes, there is no behavioral evidence that they learned anything about the shapes that were present in their home cages. This initial learning only became evident when the rats were explicitly trained to respond in different ways to the two different shapes.

People show mere exposure learning too. In one study, volunteer participants learned to discriminate between complex line drawings—the scribbles seen in Figure 3.7. First, each participant was asked to look briefly at a card containing a target scribble. Then the participant was shown a series of individual cards that each contained a scribble and was told that some of the cards contained the same scribble seen on the first card. As each card was presented, the participant was asked to tell the experimenter whether it matched the target scribble. The experimenter gave no feedback—no indication of whether a participant's answer was correct or not—but at

Getty Images

Through extensive experience, gem assessors become attuned to subtle visual differences in stones. In what ways could mere exposure learning assist in this endeavor, and in what ways might it be insufficient?

✗ racism

mere exposure learning. Learning through mere exposure to stimuli, without any explicit prompting and without any outward responding.

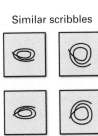

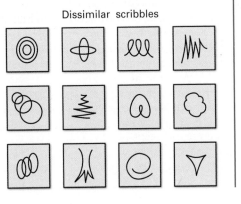

Target scribble

Similar scribbles

Dissimilar scribbles

Figure 3.7 Mere exposure learning in humans A person repeatedly views a particular scribble (target), then tries to identify cards with the same scribble when they are mixed into a deck of cards with other scribbles varying in similarity to the target scribble. The ability to identify the target scribble gradually improves, even without feedback about performance.

Images from J. J. Gibson and Gibson, "Perceptual Learning and Differentiation or Enrichment?" Vol. 62, No. 1, 32-41, 1955, APA. Adapted with permission.

the end of the process, the same steps (beginning with the scrutiny of the target card) were repeated all over again, after which they were run through a third time. Initially, participants were pretty accurate at identifying repetitions of the target scribble, as well as correctly rejecting as unfamiliar the novel scribbles that were very unlike the target ("dissimilar scribbles"). Early in the experiment, however, participants would also incorrectly "recognize" many scribbles that were similar to the target scribble. But with more and more exposure to scribbles, the participants began to distinguish the target scribble from very similar but novel stimuli (J. J. Gibson & Gibson, 1955). This is an example of perceptual learning through mere exposure to scribbles.

Your ability to distinguish among individuals may have developed similarly. In general, you will be better at distinguishing individuals belonging to racial groups that you have frequently encountered throughout your life than individuals of racial groups you don't interact with much (for further discussion of this topic see "Learning and Memory in Everyday Life" below).

Perceptual learning is similar to priming in that repeatedly experienced stimuli are processed more effectively after learning. Additionally, as we have seen, perceptual learning can happen even if the learner is not aware that her sensitivities to perceptual differences are increasing. One way in which perceptual learning differs from priming is that perceptual learning is associated with an increased ability to tell similar stimuli apart (discussed further in Chapter 6). Priming is more often associated with changes in the detection and recognition of stimuli caused by recent experiences with similar stimuli.

LEARNING AND MEMORY IN EVERYDAY LIFE

Unconscious Racial Bias

People typically judge the faces of people from another racial group to be more similar to one another than are the faces of unfamiliar people from their own race (Malpass & Kravitz, 1969). This bias is called the "other-race effect." Current psychological theories suggest that the other-race effect results from a person's having more experience with faces from certain racial groups than from others. Consistent with this idea, non-Caucasian children who are adopted by Caucasian families show better discrimination of Caucasian faces than of faces from members of their own racial group (Meissner & Brigham, 2001).

You may like to think that you treat all strangers equally, without taking appearance or speech patterns into account. But laboratory experiments suggest that this is unlikely. Despite people's stated ideals, they also often show racial biases in situations other than the distinguishing of faces. For example, people often show evidence of unconscious negative associations when answering questions about racial groups other than their own (Greenwald, McGhee, & Schwartz, 1998). These biases are not predictable from their self-reports. You can try some of these unconscious racial bias experiments yourself online at https://implicit.harvard.edu/implicit/ if you are curious to see how you fare. Recent research suggests that people's insensitivity to facial differences among members of other races can actually contribute to unconscious racial biases (Lebrecht, Pierce, Tarr, & Tanaka, 2009). The explanation offered for this is that the less able a person is to reliably differentiate individuals of a certain racial classification, the more likely it is that they will unconsciously apply generic racial stereotypes to all individuals of that group.

If the ability to distinguish faces is a consequence of the frequency with which different types of faces are encountered, then the other-race effect is essentially a side effect of visual perceptual learning. In that case, you might expect that if you trained an individual to distinguish faces of racial groups they are not familiar with, you might be able to reduce that person's other-race effect. Furthermore, if the other-race effect contributes to unconscious racial biases, such training might reduce those biases, as well. This prediction has recently been confirmed in laboratory experiments. Caucasian participants who were extensively trained to distinguish between faces of African American individuals showed both a reduction in the other-race effect and a reduction in unconscious racial biases (Lebrecht et al., 2009). Apparently, learning to recognize individuals of other racial groups can reduce overgeneralization of racial stereotypes, even when that learning involves no social interactions that might counteract the stereotypes (see Chapter 6 for further discussion of the origins of differential processing of race-related stimuli).

Habituation, sensitization, and perceptual learning might seem at first glance to be very different kinds of learning. However, current theories suggest that these seemingly different phenomena depend on similar (or identical) learning mechanisms. For example, the *dual process theory* of habituation, introduced earlier in the chapter, explains perceptual learning as resulting from a combination of habituation and sensitization processes (Hall, 2009). Consider again the experiment on mere exposure learning in which rats lived in a cage with triangles and circles on

---

Test Your Knowledge

Perceptual Learning versus Habituation

Both habituation and perceptual learning can result from repeated exposures to stimuli. Although the experiences that lead to these phenomena can be similar, the kinds of responses that provide evidence of these two forms of learning are notably different. For each of the following photographs, identify what kind or kinds of learning might have contributed to the scene depicted. (Answers appear in the back of the book.)

Sheer Photo, Inc/Getty Images

Sheer Photo, Inc/Getty Images

Ian Shaw/Stone/Getty Images

the walls (E. Gibson & Walk, 1956). The triangles and circles shared some features: both shapes were constructed of the same material, both were located on the walls (but never, for example, on the floor of the cage), and so on. They also differed in some features: for example, the triangles had straight sides and the circles had round sides. According to dual process theory, when the rat viewed a triangle on the wall, its orienting responses and responses to novelty (like neophobia) habituated to all of the features it experienced. Similarly, its responses also habituated to all visual aspects of the circle on the wall. Notice that the shared features of the shapes were experienced every time the rat viewed either shape but that distinguishing features were experienced only when the rat viewed one shape or the other. Since the shared features were repeatedly experienced twice as often, the effects on responding to viewing the shared features would have been greater—there would be twice as much habituation of responses to the shared features as to the unshared features. The end result would be that distinctive features (such as straight versus round edges) would be more likely to provoke orienting responses than shared features would. In other words, for rats that lived with the shapes, the features that distinguished the two shapes became more noticeable than the shared features. Thus, rats that lived with the shapes would be expected to learn to distinguish the shapes faster than rats that had never seen them before, because the experienced rats should pay less attention to the shared features of the shapes.

Spatial Learning

When animals explore, they learn more than just what objects look, smell, and sound like. They also learn how to get from one place to another and what to expect when visiting particular places. **Spatial learning**—the acquisition of information about one's surroundings—can be accomplished in different ways. In one of the earliest laboratory studies of exploratory spatial learning, Edward Tolman, working with C. H. Honzik, placed rats in a complex maze (Figure 3.8a) and trained them to make their way to a particular location in it—the food box—to be rewarded with a bit of food (Tolman & Honzik, 1930). These trained rats learned to run to the food box with fewer and fewer errors (wrong turns) as the days went by (Figure 3.8b). Rats in a second group were simply placed in the maze for the

spatial learning. The acquisition of information about one's surroundings.

Figure 3.8 Learning by exploration in rats (a) Tolman placed rats in the start box of a complex maze. (b) Rats rewarded with food every time they reached the food box ("trained rats") learned gradually to run to the food box. Other rats ("exploration-first rats") were simply placed in the maze and allowed to explore, with no food reward. On the 11th day, these rats began receiving rewards and immediately learned to run to the box for food.

(a) Information from Elliot, 1928; (b) Data from Tolman and Honzik, 1930.

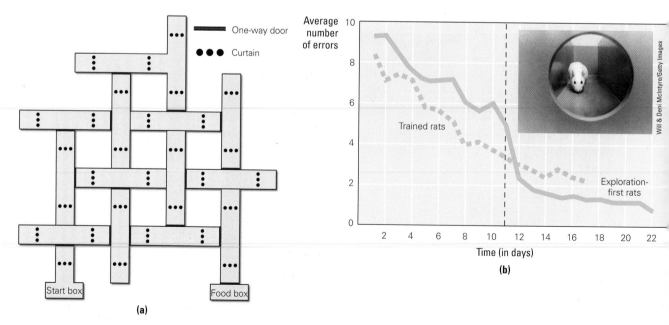

(a)

(b)

first 10 days of the study and allowed to explore. If they happened into the food box, they received no food but were removed from the maze. On the eleventh day, these rats started getting food every time they entered the food box. As Figure 3.8b shows, these exploration-first rats also learned to run to the food box to get their food—and they learned this task so well that their performance quickly surpassed that of the rats who'd been training on the task all along! Tolman and Honzik concluded that both groups of rats had learned about the location of the food box. One group had learned how to get to the food box through explicit training and the other group learned the spatial layout of the maze simply by exploring it. This is yet another example of latent learning, because until food was placed in the food box, there was little evidence that the explorer rats knew how to get there quickly.

What were the rats learning? Perhaps they were learning a sequence of turns that they could perform to get to certain spots: turn right from the start box, then left, and so on. Such learning does occur, but it isn't enough to account for everything the rats did in the maze, because a rat could be placed in a new start position and still find its way to the goal. Rats also appear to use visual cues to determine their location in such mazes. For example, a rat in a laboratory maze may use the sight of a window or a wall decoration visible over the edges of the maze to orient itself. As long as these cues are in sight, the rat may learn to navigate from any starting point in the maze, although if the cues are then moved around, the rat may get temporarily confused (we describe such an experiment later in the chapter). In fact, rats can learn many things while exploring a maze; as a result, spatial tasks have played a major role in studies of many different kinds of learning and memory, including studies of operant conditioning (Chapter 5), memories for events (Chapter 7), skill memories (Chapter 8), and working memory (Chapter 9). Exploration is important in these tasks because a rat that refuses to explore a maze will learn very little about its spatial organization.

Many kinds of animals in the wild also navigate based on visual cues they have learned through exploration. In a classic study, Niko Tinbergen examined wasps' ability to locate their home nest. Before leaving their hives or burrows to look for food, certain species of wasps and bees engage in orientation flights during which they circle their home base. In one experiment, Tinbergen and William Kruyt laid a circle of pinecones around a wasp burrow while the wasp was inside (Tinbergen & Kruyt, 1972). The experimenters left the pinecone circle intact for several orientation flights—long enough for the wasp to learn to recognize these landmarks (Figure 3.9a). Then, while the wasp was away on a foraging trip, the experimenters moved the circle of pinecones away from the burrow (Figure 3.9b). When the wasp returned, it repeatedly searched for its burrow within the ring of pinecones.

Tinbergen and Kruyt concluded that when wasps leave home to forage, they use the orientation flight to collect visual information about landmarks that will later help them locate the burrow. If these landmarks are repositioned while the wasp is away, the wasp will search for the burrow based on the landmarks, revealing that it has learned about the spatial relationship between the burrow and surrounding landmarks. Just like Tolman's rats, the wasps learn about the spatial properties of their environments through exploration.

As illustrated in Figure 3.9, wasps often make several passes over the nest before departing. After multiple trips, a wasp will have repeatedly experienced the visual cues surrounding its nest. Such repeated events could lead to habituation, sensitization, perceptual learning, or other forms of learning. In this sort of naturalistic experiment, there is no way to know exactly what a wasp is learning from its experiences. After exploring the neurological bases of habituation and sensitization, the following section describes more-controlled studies that are helping researchers get a better handle on what individuals learn from repeated exposures to stimuli during exploration.

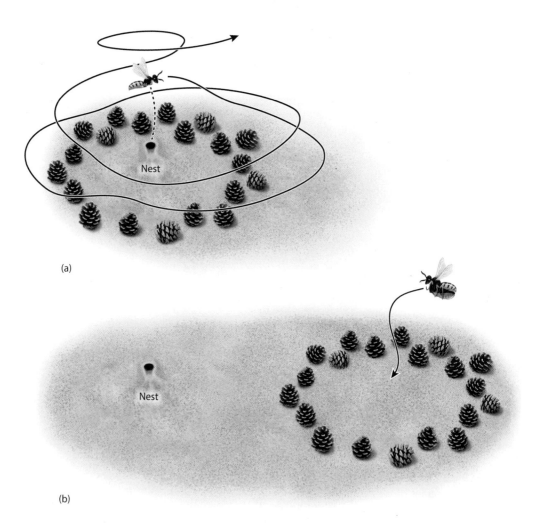

(a)

(b)

Figure 3.9 Use of landmarks by wasps (a) Tinbergen and Kruyt placed pinecones around a wasp's burrow (an underground nest) to provide visual information about the burrow's location. When leaving home, wasps take orientation flights, during which they seem to note local landmarks (such as the pinecones) that will help them return. (b) When the circle of pinecones was moved to flat ground near the nest, the returning wasp searched for the burrow inside the circle of pinecones.

Information from Tinbergen, 1951.

Interim Summary

- Habituation is a process in which repeated exposure to a stimulus leads to a decrease in the strength or frequency of the responses evoked by that stimulus.

- In sensitization, exposure to an arousing stimulus causes a heightened response to stimuli that follow.

- Dual process theory proposes that behavioral changes caused by repeated exposures to a stimulus reflect the combined effects of habituation and sensitization processes.

- In novel object recognition tasks, an organism typically responds more to a novel stimulus than to a stimulus it was previously exposed to, providing evidence of familiarity.

- Priming is a phenomenon in which exposure to a stimulus, even without a conscious memory of that exposure, affects the organism's response to the stimulus later.

- Perceptual learning occurs when repeated experiences with a set of stimuli improve the organism's ability to distinguish those stimuli.

- Spatial learning often involves latent learning about features of the environment (including encountered objects) through exploration.

3.2 Brain Substrates

The discussion above considered several ways in which repeated exposures to stimuli can lead to learning. In some cases, gradual changes in behavior revealed this learning, but in others the learning was latent until the right test was given. Even in the "simple" case of habituation, learning seems to involve multiple parallel processes that can sometimes operate without any associated changes in behavior. As a consequence, it is extremely difficult to understand how and what organisms learn from repeated events on the basis of behavioral evidence alone.

Because researchers recognized this dilemma early on, there is a long history of neurophysiological studies of habituation (Thompson, 2009), starting in the early 1900s with Charles Sherrington's studies of the spinal reflex (discussed in Chapter 2). More recently, neuroimaging and electrophysiological studies have begun to shed new light on the processes underlying perceptual learning and object recognition. The ability to observe how brain function and structure changes as an individual learns about repeated events has provided many new clues about the nature of these phenomena, as the following discussions will illustrate.

Dogs and cats are natural antagonists, as any dog or cat owner knows. Some of the earliest brain studies on habituation, using dogs and cats as subjects, seemed to bear out the view that these animals are fundamentally antithetical. Ivan Pavlov, for example, found that when a dog's cortex was removed, the dog no longer showed habituation to auditory stimuli: the dog would instead continue to show orienting responses to the sounds, even after many exposures (Pavlov, 1927). Such findings led researchers to suggest that the cortex was critical for habituation and that it actively suppressed reflexive orienting responses to stimuli perceived as familiar (Sokolov, 1963). The data from cats, however, seemed completely contradictory. Cats that had their brain disconnected from their spinal cord, called *spinal cats*, still showed habituation to tactile stimulation (Thompson & Spencer, 1966). This seemed to prove that the spinal cord by itself contained all the neural machinery necessary for habituation; the cortex—and indeed the rest of the brain—wasn't needed. The cat data were consistent with the finding that many other organisms known to habituate, including roaches, protozoa, and numerous other invertebrates, don't have any cortex.

How to reconcile the dog data and the cat data? For one thing, the animals in these early studies were learning about different kinds of stimuli. Whether cortical processing is involved in habituation likely depends on the kinds of stimuli that are being repeated, where they are normally processed, and where memories of the stimuli are formed. One way to avoid these complications is to study habituation not with mammals, such as cats and dogs, but with smaller-brained animals such as everyone's favorite—the sea slug.

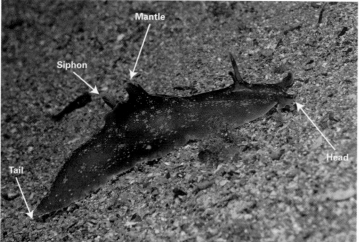

Figure 3.10 *Aplysia californica*, the sea hare This marine invertebrate, a shell-less mollusk, has a relatively simple nervous system, useful for studying the neural bases of learning. If the siphon is touched lightly, both siphon and gill are protectively withdrawn (the gill-withdrawal reflex). With repeated light touches, the gill-withdrawal reflex habituates. In this photo, the gill is underneath the mantle.

Information from Squire and Kandel, 2000.

An Invertebrate Model System

Much work on the neural substrates of habituation has been conducted on a group of marine invertebrates called *Aplysia*, the sea slugs (or sea hares), such as the species *Aplysia californica* shown in Figure 3.10. Like many marine animals, *Aplysia* breathes through gills, which extend upward from between the two wings of the mantle, the animal's outer covering. A structure called the siphon works like a tube to blow aerated water over the gills to assist respiration. The gills are delicate and easily damaged. When danger threatens, the sea hare tends to retract them under the safety of the mantle. This is called a gill-withdrawal reflex.

One advantage of studying learning in *Aplysia* is that they have a relatively simple nervous system—only about 20,000 neurons, compared with the tens of billions in a cat or human. Plus, some of the neurons are very big. A few are large enough to be seen with the naked eye. Best of all, the pattern of neurons in *Aplysia* seems to be "hardwired," meaning that researchers can identify a particular neuron in one sea hare (say, motor neuron L7G) and find the same neuron in the same place in another member of the species. This type of nervous system makes things much easier for a neuroscientist trying to understand how the brain encodes new memories.

Neuroscientists have documented each of the neurons involved in *Aplysia*'s gill-withdrawal reflex. The siphon contains 24 sensory neurons that are directly connected to 6 motor neurons that innervate the gill. Figure 3.11a shows a simplified scheme of this system of neurons, consisting of three sensory neurons S, T, and U and one motor neuron M. When the siphon is touched, sensory neuron S fires, releasing a neurotransmitter, *glutamate*, into the synapse (Figure 3.11b). Molecules of glutamate diffuse across the synapse to activate receptors in motor neuron M. If enough receptors are activated, neuron M fires, causing the muscles to retract the gill for a few seconds.

As simple as sea hares are, they are still capable of adapting their behavior in response to experience. *Aplysia* show habituation, sensitization, and several other forms of learning, just as rats and humans do. In *Aplysia*, however, scientists can actually watch the nervous system in action as these learning processes occur. Nobel prize winner Eric Kandel pioneered the use of sea hare reflexive responses as a way of exploring how repeated experiences change the neural circuits that generate those responses, especially in situations where animals become habituated or sensitized to tactile stimuli.

Habituation in Sea Hares

An initial, light touch on a sea hare's siphon will activate the gill-withdrawal response, but if the touch is repeated, the gill-withdrawal reflex gradually becomes weaker, or habituates. The amount of habituation is proportional to the intensity of the stimulus and the repetition rate. If a sufficiently light touch is delivered every minute, the withdrawal response habituates after 10 or 12 touches, and the habituation can last for 10 to 15 minutes (Pinsker, Kupfermann, Castellucci, & Kandel, 1970).

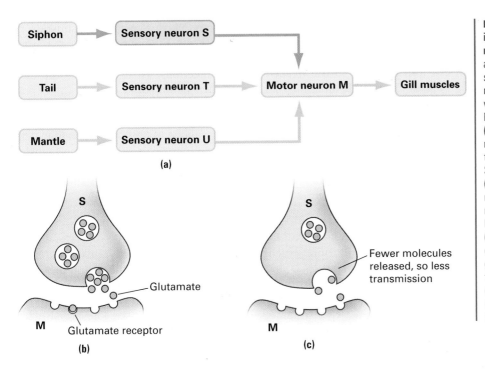

(a)

S

Glutamate

M

Glutamate receptor

(b)

S

Fewer molecules
released, so less
transmission

M

(c)

Figure 3.11 Neural circuits in *Aplysia* gill-withdrawal reflex (a) Sensory neurons S, T, and U respond to a touch on the siphon, tail, and upper mantle, respectively. These neurons converge on motor neurons such as M, which contract the gill muscles. (b) When sensory neuron S fires, it releases the neurotransmitter glutamate into the synapse between S and M. The glutamate molecules (shown in yellow) may dock at receptors on neuron M. If enough receptors are activated, neuron M will fire, retracting the gill. (c) If neuron S is activated repeatedly, it gradually releases less glutamate each time, decreasing the response of M. This synaptic depression underlies habituation of the gill-withdrawal response in sea hares.

In sea hares, we can see exactly what is causing this habituation. Refer back to the schematic diagram in Figure 3.11a. Recall that touching the siphon excites sensory neuron S, which releases the neurotransmitter glutamate, which in turn excites motor neuron M, which drives the withdrawal response (Figure 3.11b). With repeated stimulation, however, neuron S releases less glutamate (Figure 3.11c), decreasing the chance that neuron M will be excited enough to fire (Castellucci & Kandel, 1974). The reduction in glutamate release is evident even after a single touch and lasts for up to 10 minutes. This decrease in neurotransmitter release is associated with a decrease in the number of glutamate-containing vesicles positioned at release sites. Thus, in *Aplysia*, habituation can be explained as a form of **synaptic depression**, a reduction in synaptic transmission. This is exactly the sort of weakening of connections that is proposed by the dual process theory of habituation (see Figure 3.4b) and that is thought to contribute to the long-term depression of neural connections described in Chapter 2.

An important feature of habituation in sea hares is that it is **homosynaptic**, which means it involves only those synapses that were activated during the habituating event: changes in neuron S will not affect other sensory neurons, such as T or U in Figure 3.11a. In other words, a light touch to the tail or upper mantle still elicits the defensive gill withdrawal, even though a touch to the siphon is ignored. The responsiveness of the motor neuron M is not changed. In this case, habituation in the short term affects only how much neurotransmitter neuron S releases.

Long-term habituation in sea hares can often last much longer than 10 minutes, especially when exposures are spaced over several days (Cohen, Kaplan, Kandel, & Hawkins, 1997). How are the animals storing information about past exposures for such a long time? When a sea hare is repeatedly exposed to the same stimulus over several days, the actual number of connections between the affected sensory neurons and motor neurons decreases. Specifically, the number of presynaptic terminals in the sensory neurons of animals that have been

synaptic depression. A reduction in synaptic transmission; a possible neural mechanism underlying habituation.

homosynaptic. Occurring in one synapse without affecting nearby synapses.

repeatedly exposed to the same stimulus is reduced. Synaptic transmission in *Aplysia* can thus be depressed not only by decreases in neurotransmitter release but also by the elimination of synapses. This suggests that repeated experiences can lead not only to the weakening of connections, as suggested by the dual process theory of habituation, but also to their elimination.

Do the mechanisms of habituation in sea hares tell us anything about habituation in larger-brained animals? It is currently impossible to trace the entire neuronal circuit of habituation through the billions of neurons in a mammalian brain. However, neuroscientists have good reason to believe that the mechanisms of habituation documented in *Aplysia* occur in other species too. In fact, repeated stimulation of sensory neurons in other species, including crayfish and cats, also causes a reduction in neurotransmitter release. This suggests that at least some of the biological mechanisms of habituation are constant across species.

Sensitization in Sea Hares

What about sensitization, which, in contrast to habituation, causes increased responding to stimuli? *Aplysia* also provide a way to study the neural processes involved in this kind of learning. Suppose, instead of a light touch to the siphon, the researcher applies a more unpleasant stimulus: a mild electric shock to the tail that causes a large, sustained gill-withdrawal response. The aversive tail shock sensitizes subsequent responding, so that a weak touch to the siphon now produces a strengthened gill withdrawal.

To understand how this occurs, let's take the simplified circuit diagram from Figure 3.11a and add one more level of neural detail, as shown in Figure 3.12a. The tail shock activates sensory neuron T, which activates motor neuron M, causing the gill-withdrawal response. But because of the arousing nature of shocks, neuron T also activates modulatory interneurons, such as I_N. An *interneuron*, as its name suggests, is a neuron that neither directly receives sensory inputs nor produces motor outputs but instead carries a message between two

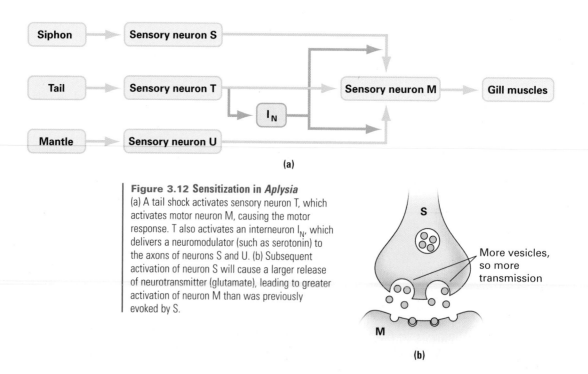

(a)

Figure 3.12 Sensitization in *Aplysia*
(a) A tail shock activates sensory neuron T, which activates motor neuron M, causing the motor response. T also activates an interneuron I_N, which delivers a neuromodulator (such as serotonin) to the axons of neurons S and U. (b) Subsequent activation of neuron S will cause a larger release of neurotransmitter (glutamate), leading to greater activation of neuron M than was previously evoked by S.

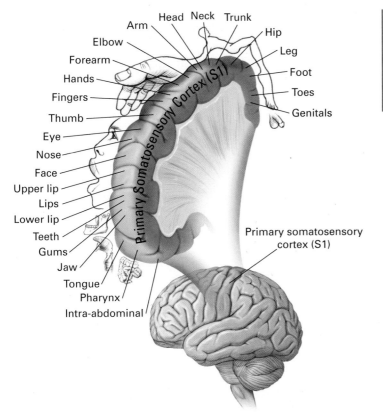

Figure 3.13 The homunculus corresponding to human somatosensory cortex Different regions of somatosensory cortex respond most strongly to touches of specific body parts. These regions are organized such that body parts close together activate adjacent regions of somatosensory cortex.

The range of stimuli that cause a particular cortical neuron to fire is called the neuron's **receptive field**. Figure 3.14 shows the receptive field for one neuron in the auditory cortex of a guinea pig that was measured using single-cell recording techniques. This neuron fired when the guinea pig heard tones pitched between 0.7 and 3 kilohertz (kHz); this range of pitches is the neuron's receptive field. The neuron fired most when the guinea pig heard tones pitched near 0.9 kHz. Neuroscientists would say that this cortical neuron is *tuned* to 0.9 kHz, meaning that this pitch causes the most firing. In somatosensory cortex, the receptive field of a neuron is defined as the patch of skin or other tissue that when stimulated causes the neuron to fire. In general, the more neurons that are tuned to a particular type, source, or strength of stimulus (or any other feature of a stimulus), the better the organism will be able to make fine distinctions related to that stimulus. So, for example, in the body map shown in Figure 3.13, the region sensitive to touches on the thumb is larger than the region sensitive to touches on the neck; a larger region in the cortex means more neurons, with the result that the skin on the thumb is able to detect finer distinctions than the skin on the neck is.

The spatial organization (body map) of somatosensory cortex shown in Figure 3.13 reflects the fact that neurons with similar receptive fields are often found clustered together in sensory cortices. In like manner, visual and auditory cortices also contain clusters of similarly tuned neurons. When these clusters are organized in predictable ways, the pattern of cortical organization is described as a *topographic map*, which simply means that cortical neurons that are physically close together are tuned to similar stimulus features. In topographic maps, neighboring cortical neurons have overlapping receptive fields. For example, if you collected recordings across the surface of a guinea pig's auditory cortex, you would find that adjacent neurons respond to gradually increasing or decreasing sound

receptive field. The range (or "field") of physical stimuli that activates a single neuron.

Figure 3.14 Receptive field of a neuron in the auditory cortex of a guinea pig Receptive fields are identified by measuring the amount of neural activity produced in response to different stimuli—in this case, to sounds ranging from 0.1 to 100 kilohertz (kHz). This neuron responds most to 0.9 kHz, but it also responds to a narrow range of similarly pitched sounds, and this range constitutes the neuron's receptive field.

Data from Weinberger, 2004.

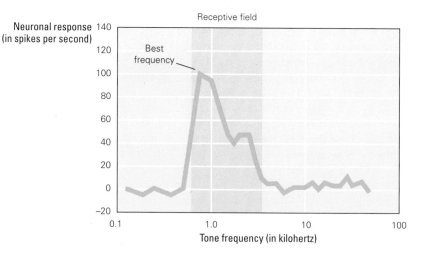

cortical plasticity. The capacity to change cortical organization as a result of experience.

frequencies—neurons tuned to 0.9 kHz will be surrounded by neurons tuned to 0.8, 0.9, or 1.0 kHz. If you sat at a piano and played the keys one at a time from left to right up the keyboard, activity in your auditory cortex would gradually shift in a pattern that corresponds to the movement of your hand across the keyboard.

For most of the history of neuroscience, it was thought that neurons in sensory cortices responded to sensations in ways that were directly analogous to how piano strings respond to the pressing of piano keys. It was thought that every time a specific set of sensory receptors detected a stimulus, a particular set of cortical neurons became active. You may recall from Chapter 1 that René Descartes proposed that sensations cause this type of reflexive chain reaction. Neuroscientists were surprised to discover that in fact the receptive fields of neurons in sensory cortices change during early development and also after various injuries and as a result of repeated experiences. In other words, the topographic maps in your sensory cortices right now are not the same ones that were in your brain 10 years ago (although they are probably quite similar). The capacity for cortical receptive fields and cortical spatial organization to change as a result of experience is called **cortical plasticity**.

If what you perceive depends on how neurons in your sensory cortices are tuned and if the tuning of your sensory cortices changes over time, then what does this suggest about your perception? It suggests that your perception may also change over time—which is exactly what studies of perceptual learning show. The clearest evidence that repeated experiences can change perception by changing sensory cortices comes not from learning studies, however, but from studies of perceptual development.

Cortical Plasticity during Development

Normally, as young organisms develop, their ability to perceive differences in visual stimuli increases. Neurophysiological studies of neurons within the visual cortex of kittens show that their tuning becomes more selective over time and that topographic maps within their visual cortex become more organized. If, however, a kitten's eye is sewn shut during development or if vision in an infant's eye is occluded by a cataract for several years, then even if vision in that eye is later restored, the acuity of that eye will be permanently degraded. Similarly, if young animals are experimentally deprived of vision in one eye, their cortical neurons will show less tuning to that eye than is seen in animals that grew up with both eyes functional. These findings suggest that normal development of visual cortical maps in mammals requires neural activity from both eyes. In other words, repeated visual experiences shape the organization of the visual cortex during development, which in turn determines an organism's perception of the visual world (Morishita & Hensch, 2008).

If perceptual experiences change how sensory cortices respond to stimuli, what happens if stimulation from both eyes is cut off, such as when a person is born blind or loses her sight soon after birth? Neuroimaging studies show that the areas of visual cortex that normally respond to visual stimuli in sighted people will, in blind people, respond to sounds and tactile stimulation. For example, activity in the visual cortex is seen to increase in blind individuals during Braille reading and other tactile tasks but decreases in sighted individuals performing these same tasks (Lewis, Saenz, & Fine, 2010; Sadato et al., 1998).

Cortical plasticity produced by early blindness has been studied experimentally in developing opossums (Kahn & Krubitzer, 2002; Karlen, Kahn, & Krubitzer, 2006). Researchers blinded half of the animals at birth and then, when the animals reached adulthood, exposed both the blinded and sighted opossums to visual, auditory, and somatosensory inputs to measure between-group differences in cortical structure and receptive fields. Sighted opossums possessed distinct cortical regions tuned exclusively either to visual, auditory, or somatosensory inputs. At the same time, receptive fields in other regions of the cortex were *multimodal*, meaning that neurons in those areas responded to inputs from more than one sensory modality—for example, visual *and* auditory stimuli. A different pattern was seen in opossums that had grown up blind. The cortical areas that were tuned exclusively to visual stimuli in sighted opossums had shrunk, and *within* those areas, some neurons now responded to auditory or somatosensory stimuli or both. In addition, the auditory and somatosensory areas of the cortex had increased beyond normal size. Most striking of all, the blinded opossums possessed a new cortical region with unique anatomical and physiological characteristics that didn't exist in any sighted opossum's brain.

Clearly, developmental experiences can have a huge effect on how neurons within sensory cortices respond to stimuli, influencing both the perception of sensory events and the development of responses to perceived events. In the case of opossums that developed without sight, the absence of vision radically changed the sensory experiences to which cortical neurons were exposed and the opossums' brains changed accordingly. In all animals, not just those that have been blinded (or similarly injured) at birth, experience modifies sensory cortical maps. Your own cortical maps changed drastically during your infancy, and they will continue to change throughout your life, although you won't perceive that this is happening. In the Clinical Perspectives section, we describe how perceptual learning during development makes it possible for individuals to overcome sensory deficits such as blindness and deafness using new technologies.

Studies with opossums have revealed that the development of cortical structure and function depends on repeated experiences. How might sensory cortices in an opossum born both deaf and blind differ from those born with all sensory modalities intact?

Cortical Changes in Adults after Exposure

During development, the arrival of inputs from different sensory receptors determines how cortical neurons become tuned, as well as the proportion of available neurons that respond to a particular class of input. Someone born without vision is likely to have proportionately more neurons available to respond to tactile stimuli, and someone born deaf typically will come to have larger cortical regions sensitive to visual stimuli. Granted, these are extreme cases of depriving a brain of a particular class of input. What might happen in more subtle cases—for example, in a person who chooses to listen only to rap music, or to classical music, or to country music? Might the topographic map in the auditory cortex reflect the kinds of songs the person listens to the most? How much exposure is required for the cortical neurons to become retuned?

Neuroimaging studies suggest that it is relatively easy to retune neurons within the sensory cortices of adults and that it can be done in less than a day. For example, simply touching a person's fingertip repeatedly with tiny pins was shown to improve the person's ability to distinguish subtle differences in the pins' positions. Initially, people were able to discriminate two simultaneous touches on the tip of their index finger as long as the touches were spaced at least 1.1 mm apart (Figure 3.15a). After receiving 2 hours of exposure consisting of repeated simultaneous stimulation of two closely spaced points (0.25–3 mm apart) on the tip of their right index finger, participants' ability to discriminate touches improved (Dinse, Ragert, Pleger, Schwenkreis, & Tegenthoff, 2003; Hodzic, Veit, Karim, Erb, & Godde, 2004; Pilz, Veit, Braun, & Godde, 2004).

Like the experiment with squiggles described earlier (Figure 3.7), this study shows that humans can learn to make fine distinctions through mere repeated exposures. What's going on in the brain when this happens? Before repeated exposures, fMRI difference images showed that touching the right index finger resulted in localized activation within the somatosensory cortex (Figure 3.15b). After this finger was stimulated repeatedly for 2 hours, subsequent instances of stimulation activated a larger region of the somatosensory cortex than was observed before exposure (Figure 3.15c; Hodzic et al., 2004). Thus, repeated touching of the fingertip led to both perceptual learning and cortical reorganization. The increase in the size of the region of somatosensory cortex that was selectively activated during stimulation of the tip of the right index finger was likely associated with an increase in the number of cortical neurons tuned to touches of the fingertip.

Figure 3.15 Cortical reorganization in humans after exposure (a) Participants improved their ability to distinguish two separate touch points on their right index finger (Right IF) after 2 hours of passive exposure to stimulation of closely spaced points on that finger. (b) fMRI showing cortical activation patterns in somatosensory cortex during tactile stimulation of the right index finger before exposure. (c) After 2 hours of stimulation to the right index finger, activation in the left hemisphere (where the right finger is represented) has increased.

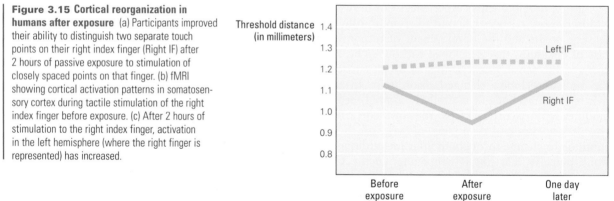

(a)

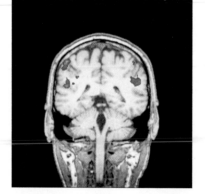

(b)

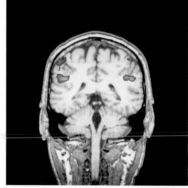

(c)

This same phenomenon has also been examined using magnetoencephalographic (MEG) recordings of neural activity in somatosensory cortex. MEGs are similar to EEGs in that both reflect the activity of groups of neurons (unlike fMRI, which only measures blood oxygenation in the brain). The main difference between MEGs and EEGs is that MEGs measure small changes in magnetic fields rather than changes in electrical fields. MEG recordings showed that larger changes in somatosensory-cortex activity in response to tactile stimulation predicted larger improvements in discrimination abilities (Godde, Ehrhardt, & Braun, 2003). Together, these neuroimaging, neurophysiological, and behavioral results suggest that perceptual learning and cortical changes occur in parallel and that both can occur after repeated exposures to inconsequential stimuli.

Many neuroscientists now believe that all forms of perceptual learning in mammals depend on cortical plasticity (Dinse & Merzenich, 2002; Kujala & Naatanen, 2010). In fact, almost every type of learning discussed in the subsequent chapters of this book has been shown to lead to retuning of cortical receptive fields (Hoffman & Logothetis, 2009; Weinberger, 2007). The role of cortical plasticity in learning and memory is further discussed in Chapter 6, on generalization, discrimination, and concept formation.

Temporal Lobe Involvement in Spatial Learning and Familiarity

As mammals experience repetitions of sensory events, neurons in their sensory cortices gradually become tuned to specific features of those events. Might similar processes explain the kinds of latent learning observed when individuals actively explore the world around them? One way that researchers have tried to answer this question is by measuring and manipulating brain activity in rodents performing spatial tasks. Initially, the emphasis was on discovering where memories of mazes were stored in the cortex. Karl Lashley's failed attempt to locate cortical *engrams* for maze learning in rats (described in Chapter 2) represents one of the earliest efforts. Later neurophysiological studies of rats navigating through mazes revealed that spatial learning actually depends much more on activity in the hippocampus than on cortical engrams.

The hippocampus is one of the most extensively studied brain regions in the field of learning and memory. In humans and other primates, it is a relatively small structure lying just beneath each temporal lobe (see Figure 2.3 and Figure 3.16a). In rodents, however, the hippocampus makes up a much larger proportion of the brain (Figure 3.16b). Many other vertebrates, including birds and reptiles, also possess a hippocampus. Although the hippocampus in birds is proportionately smaller than in rodents (Figure 3.16c), the size of a bird's hippocampus is known to be important for spatial memory. Specifically, bird species that store their food in many different locations for use in the winter have a hippocampus that is bigger than in related bird species that

Figure 3.16 The hippocampus in several types of animals Cross sections showing the hippocampus in a monkey, rat, and bird.

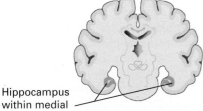

(a) Monkey

Hippocampus within medial temporal lobes

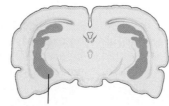

(b) Rat

Hippocampus

(c) Bird

Hippocampus

do not need to keep track of hidden food (Sherry & Hoshooley, 2010). Generalizing across species, you might expect that given the size of their hippocampus, rats should be quite adept at spatial learning. This prediction is borne out by the success with which rats learned to traverse thousands of different mazes during the early history of psychological research.

Identifying Places

As a first step toward understanding the role of the hippocampus in spatial learning, English neuroscientist John O'Keefe implanted electrodes in rats' hippocampal regions to record neuronal activity under various conditions (O'Keefe & Dostrovsky, 1971). When the rats were placed in an environment and allowed to explore freely, the investigators made a surprising discovery. Some hippocampal neurons seemed to fire only when a rat wandered into particular locations, and other hippocampal neurons fired only when the rat was in other locations. O'Keefe coined the term **place cells** to refer to neurons with such spatially tuned firing patterns. Each of these neurons had a certain preferred location to which it responded with maximal activity, and this location was termed the *place field* for that neuron (analogous to the receptive fields of sensory cortical neurons described above). The activity of these cells was so reliable that a blindfolded researcher could tell when a rat entered a particular region of the maze just by hearing the corresponding place cell begin to fire. O'Keefe suggested that place cells might form the basis for spatial learning and navigation. In 2014, O'Keefe received a Nobel Prize for his contributions to this groundbreaking field of research.

How might place cells help with spatial navigation? If a certain neuron fires only when an individual is in a particular place, then that neuron might serve as an identifier for that place (much like road signs at street corners or mile markers along the highway). When the neuron fires, the brain would then "know" that the body is in a particular location. You could figure out where you are just by noting which place cell is firing. Of course, if you were to begin life with enough place cells to code for every possible location you might ever visit, you would require an incredibly large number of place cells. Such a method, in which cells are kept on reserve to encode locations that you haven't yet visited, would be extremely wasteful. Instead, it would be smarter to create place cells as you need them. In other words, place fields should form during learning, as an animal explores its environment. This turns out to be the case.

An explanation of how place cells work must begin with a discussion of what defines a place. Put another way, what exactly determines whether a place cell will respond? Part of what leads a place cell to respond seems to be the animal's inner sense of its location in space: a rat's place cells often continue to respond in an orderly fashion even when the rat is running through a maze with the lights out. But place cell responses also depend heavily on visual inputs. For example, suppose a rat is allowed to explore a maze like the one shown in Figure 3.17a. This maze has three identical arms (labeled 1, 2, and 3 in the figure) differentiated by one salient visual cue: a card placed outside the maze between arms 2 and 3. After the initial exploration, various place cells in the rat's hippocampus will have place fields corresponding to parts of this maze. One hippocampal neuron, for example, had the place field shown in Figure 3.17b (darker areas indicate maximal firing; lighter areas, lesser firing). In other words, this place cell responded preferentially when the rat was in the southwest corner of the maze (as oriented in Figure 3.17a), at the outer edge of arm 2, on the side nearest the card (Lenck-Santini, Save, & Poucet, 2001).

Now suppose the experimenter takes the rat out of the maze and rotates the maze and card 120 degrees clockwise. What do you think will happen when the rat is put back in the maze (Figure 3.17c)? Will the place cell continue to

place cell. A neuron that fires maximally when the organism enters a particular location within an environment.

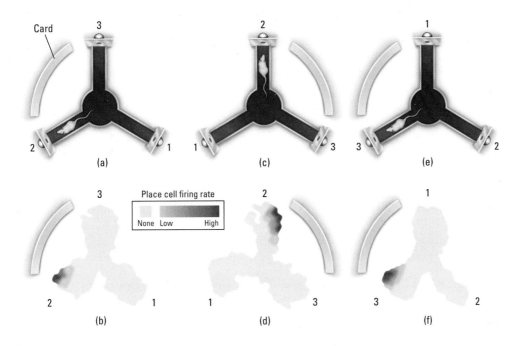

Figure 3.17 Effects of a visual landmark on a rat's place field Upper images show the rat's environment: a three-armed maze and a visual cue (a card, location marked in dark purple). Lower images show how a representative place cell fires in this environment: dark areas are regions that evoke heavy firing; lighter areas, regions that evoke lesser firing. (a, b) When the maze is in its initial position, this place cell fires maximally when the rat is in arm 2. (c, d) When maze and cue card are rotated 120 degrees clockwise, the place field is determined by visual cues; maximal firing still occurs in arm 2. (e, f) If the maze is rotated another 120 degrees but the card is returned to its original location, the place cell fires when the rat is in the southwest corner, even though this is now arm 3. In other words, place cell firing seems to depend on the rat's location relative to the visual landmark.
Data from Lenck-Santini et al., 2001.

fire when the rat is in the southwest corner of the maze? Or will it fire when the rat is at the end of arm 2, even though that is now the north-most corner of the maze? The answer is shown in Figure 3.17d: the place cell's preferred location has rotated along with the maze. In this particular case, since the three arms all look, smell, and feel pretty similar, the rat probably used the visual cue as a landmark. When the maze was rotated again, another 120 degrees clockwise, but the card was returned to its original place, to the west (Figure 3.17e), then the place cell again fired in the southwest corner of the maze, even though this was now arm 3 (Figure 3.17f). These findings illustrate the importance of visual landmarks (such as the card) in determining when a hippocampal place cell will fire. In addition to landmarks, some place cells in rats seem to be sensitive to other variables, such as the speed or direction in which a rat is moving. Thus, place cells respond like sensory cortical neurons with multimodal receptive fields.

Some place cells have place fields that are stable for months: if the rat is returned to the maze in Figure 3.17 after a long absence, the same place cell may still fire when the rat is in the same location as before. Research also shows that when place fields are unstable, spatial navigation is disrupted. The stability of place fields and their selectivity in terms of particular visual scenes are consistent with the idea that place cells provide the basis for a "cognitive map" that rats use to navigate through the world. But how, exactly, do place cells become tuned to a particular place?

One factor affecting the creation of place fields is experience. When rats repeatedly experience an environment, their place cells become increasingly tuned to locations within that environment (Lever, Wills, Cacucci, Burgess, & O'Keefe, 2002). Imagine the size of the dark place field in Figure 3.17 (b, d, and f) getting smaller and smaller, providing an increasingly precise and reliable report of where in the maze the rat is. This place-field shrinkage seems to correlate with rats' spatial navigation abilities in a maze; experiments in which rats' place-field shrinkage is disrupted (for example, by blocking inputs from the thalamus) show that the rats' spatial learning abilities decline (Cooper & Mizumori, 2001; Mizumori, Miya, & Ward, 1994; Rotenberg, Abel, Hawkins, Kandel, & Muller, 2000).

Place cells are not the only neurons in the temporal lobes tuned to spatial features. Other neurons located in cortical regions surrounding the hippocampus show selectivity when an animal is headed in a particular direction (*head direction cells*), or when animals cross through equal distances within an environment (called *grid cells*). Although these neurons likely contribute to an individual's ability to learn about locations in ways that are similar to place cells, there is little evidence that the firing properties of head direction cells or grid cells are affected by repeated experiences with particular environments (Gupta, Beer, Keller, & Hasselmo, 2014). This lack of evidence may mean that grid cells and head direction cells are less affected by learning experiences than are place cells, or that they are affected in different ways that haven't yet been detected experimentally.

The findings presented above suggest that spatial learning that occurs during exploration is correlated with changes in the stability and selectivity of hippocampal neurons (Rosenzweig, Redish, McNaughton, & Barnes, 2003). This phenomenon may explain the latent learning by which Tolman's rats came to know the layout of a complex maze even without associating specific locations with food rewards. Perhaps as the nonrewarded rats explored the maze, their place fields shrunk as much as (or more than) those of the rewarded rats, providing them with a precise representation of various locations within the maze that they could later take advantage of when the researchers initiated training with food.

Recognizing Familiar Objects

In order to use visual landmarks to navigate within a maze, rats must be able to recognize those landmarks. This suggests that as rats explore an environment, they not only learn how to navigate through that environment, but they also learn the properties of objects within and around the paths they are traveling. Recall that some of the earliest evidence of visual perceptual learning came from studies in which triangles and circles were mounted in the home cages of rats. If neurons within the temporal lobes are sensitive to visual landmarks within a maze, might they also contribute to a rat's ability to recognize novel objects and distinguish them from familiar landmarks?

Several studies have examined this possibility in rats performing the novel object recognition task described earlier, as well as in monkeys performing shape recognition tasks. In early experiments, researchers lesioned the hippocampus of rats after the rats repeatedly explored fixed configurations of objects. Rats with hippocampal damage showed impaired object recognition memory, exploring objects that they had experienced many times as if they had not seen them before. Later studies found, however, that such lesions disrupted object recognition in certain situations only (Langston & Wood, 2010)—specifically, those in which memories of the position of the object and the context in which it was experienced were integrated. Studies in cortical regions surrounding the hippocampus found neurons that fired differently when visual inputs were novel versus familiar (Xiang & Brown, 1998): those neurons responded less when familiar stimuli were presented.

Related findings are reported in humans. Neuropsychological studies of patients with lesions to the hippocampus and surrounding cortical regions found impaired recognition of familiar objects (Squire, Wixted, & Clark, 2007). Neuroimaging studies, too, implicate regions in the temporal lobes in the detection of familiarity and novelty, although there is debate about the specific roles that the hippocampus and cortical regions play. Intriguingly, electrical stimulation in cortical regions within the temporal lobes can produce feelings of *deja vu* in human patients, further implicating these regions in the detection of familiarity (Bartolomei et al., 2012).

Overall, past findings suggest that neurons in the hippocampus and surrounding cortical regions contribute to exploratory learning in ways that go beyond simply constructing spatial maps or identifying familiar objects. These brain regions likely contribute to the encoding and retrieval of memories in numerous ways, some of which you will discover as you study further in this book. In addition, recent work suggests that other brain regions, including sensory cortices, may also play a pivotal role in mechanisms of novel object recognition and familiarity. For example, researchers studying mice have linked changes in the responses of neurons in primary visual cortex (V1) to both long-term habituation after repeated presentations of visual images and to the detection of novel images (Cooke, Komorowski, Kaplan, Gavornik, & Bear, 2015). Local application of drugs that interfered with cortical plasticity in V1 blocked the behavioral changes associated with repeated exposures to images and also those produced by novel stimuli, showing that these behavioral changes were dependent on cortical plasticity in V1.

The new findings suggest that the processes underlying habituation, perceptual learning, and novel object recognition may be more closely linked than researchers previously thought. As you will see in the following section, discoveries such as these not only can provide new insights into the processes underlying various forms of learning, but can also lead to new approaches to correcting such processes when they are disrupted by brain disorders.

Interim Summary

- In *Aplysia*, habituation is the result of synaptic depression in circuits that link sensory neurons to motor neurons. Long-term habituation involves physical changes in the connections between these neurons.

- Sensitization in *Aplysia* reflects heterosynaptic increases in synaptic transmission caused by the activation of interneurons.

- During perceptual learning, cortical neurons refine their responses to sensory inputs as discrimination abilities improve.

- Hippocampal place cells are neurons that become most active when an animal is at a particular location. These neurons and other spatially sensitive cells in surrounding cortical regions may help animals identify and navigate through familiar environments.

- Neurons in the hippocampus and surrounding cortical regions also contribute to the recognition of novel objects, giving rise to a sense of familiarity.

3.3 Clinical Perspectives

Even though you are probably not consciously aware of it, habituation, sensitization, and perceptual learning influence every experience you have. From your ability to understand speech to your ability to find your way to school or work, everything you perceive is influenced by the memories you've acquired through repeatedly experiencing similar stimuli. When neural circuits that process sensory information are damaged or when highly aversive events are experienced, the result can be a fundamental change in how stimuli are perceived, processed, and learned about, which in turn can affect one's mental health and quality of life.

Rehabilitation after Stroke: Habituation Gone Awry

stroke. When blood flow to some region of the brain stops or when an artery ruptures, causing neurons in the affected region to die.

The leading cause of brain damage in the United States is stroke. A **stroke** occurs when blood flow to some region of the brain stops or when an artery ruptures. Lack of blood causes neurons in the affected region to die, effectively creating a brain lesion. Immediately after a stroke, a patient often experiences large losses in perceptual function. For example, a patient may lose all sensation in one of his arms. Subsequently, although nothing may be wrong with the motor control of that arm, the patient may begin to ignore the numb arm and make greater use of the arm he can still feel. Over time, he may stop trying to use the numb arm altogether, a phenomenon called *learned non-use*. Effectively, the patient gets used to the lack of feeling in the dysfunctional arm and stops attempting to use it. In short, the patient's repeated experiences with the dysfunctional arm lead to the decrease in use.

Monkeys show similar patterns of learned non-use when they lose sensation in a limb. For example, if somatosensory information from a monkey's left arm is blocked so that it cannot feel the arm, the monkey will stop using that arm and start using the right arm exclusively. If the right arm is bound so that the monkey can no longer use it, however, the monkey may begin using the numb left arm, even after not using it for several years. Once the monkey has become accustomed to using the left arm again, release of the right arm typically leads to the monkey's using both arms, showing that it can overcome the learned non-use of the dysfunctional arm (Knapp, Taub, & Berman, 1963). One interpretation of this functional recovery is that binding the right arm created a new situation that dishabituated the monkey's responses to numbness in the left arm.

Techniques like those employed with the monkey are sometimes used in therapy for human stroke patients. For example, a patient who has lost the use of his left arm might consent to have his preferred right arm immobilized in a sling so that he is forced to try to use his left arm for eating, dressing, and other daily activities. As Figure 3.18 shows, patients receiving this kind of therapy, called

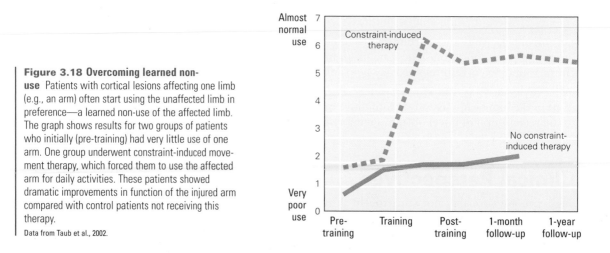

Figure 3.18 Overcoming learned non-use Patients with cortical lesions affecting one limb (e.g., an arm) often start using the unaffected limb in preference—a learned non-use of the affected limb. The graph shows results for two groups of patients who initially (pre-training) had very little use of one arm. One group underwent constraint-induced movement therapy, which forced them to use the affected arm for daily activities. These patients showed dramatic improvements in function of the injured arm compared with control patients not receiving this therapy.
Data from Taub et al., 2002.

constraint-induced movement therapy, often recover much more function in their affected arm than patients who are simply told to try to use their affected arm as often as possible (Taub, Uswatte, & Elbert, 2002; Wolf et al., 2010).

The idea behind constraint-induced movement therapy is to force the patient to use the affected arm as often as possible to encourage changes in cortex that compensate for stroke-related damage. This rehabilitation strategy is similar in some ways to the method used to reorganize cortical processing in opossums during development, as described above. Recall that the new-born opossums were blinded so that cortical areas normally devoted to visual processing were instead reallocated to other sensory modalities. In stroke patients, constraint-induced movement therapy may help undamaged cortical areas take up some of the work that damaged areas once performed. Recent neuroimaging studies show that this therapy is associated with increases in the blood flowing to the sensory and motor cortex (Wittenberg & Schaechter, 2009). After constraint-induced movement therapy, structural changes are seen in these cortical regions that are not seen after other rehabilitation techniques (Gauthier et al., 2008). The beneficial effects of this therapy are thought to involve perceptual learning in which, through repeated efforts, patients acquire the ability to make distinctions between sensations that are initially quite faint (and therefore difficult to discriminate). Recall that weak inputs facilitate habituation, and in the case of learned non-use, processes of habituation increase the difficulties patients face in overcoming physical limitations. Conversely, perceptual learning processes may help patients to counteract reduced responses to weak stimuli by reorganizing the cortical regions that process those stimuli.

Sensitization to Stress in Anxiety and Depression

At repeated intervals in horror movies, directors use techniques intended to increase the viewers' arousal, thereby increasing the likelihood and amplitude of startle responses evoked by scary and even not-so-scary stimuli (such as jumpy cats). In research laboratories and movie theaters, sensitization is relatively innocuous, because the stimuli that lead to sensitization are purposefully controlled so as not to be too arousing. In some situations, however, arousal can be extreme and have much more dire consequences. In the most severe cases, a single highly emotional event can lead to life-long amplification of emotional responses to a wide range of stimuli, as occurs in *post traumatic stress disorder* (discussed in Chapter 10). Recent studies suggest that even in cases where highly arousing events are not traumatic, they can still potentially increase a person's susceptibility to certain mental illnesses (Harkness, Hayden, & Lopez-Duran, 2015).

Early evidence that repetition of arousing events could lead to problematic behavioral states came from studies showing that rodents repeatedly exposed to relatively low doses of amphetamines (a stimulant drug) exhibited gradual increases in bizarre, stereotyped behaviors that persisted months after drug exposure ended (Robinson & Becker, 1986). Repeated exposures to low doses apparently sensitized the animals to the effects of the drug, because the behaviors were the same as those seen in non-sensitized rodents given higher doses of the drug.

The amphetamine-related sensitization seen in these studies attracted researchers' interest because patients diagnosed with *schizophrenia* (discussed in Chapter 6) who were being treated with amphetamines sometimes showed similar behavioral problems. As in rodents, sensitization to amphetamines in humans can have negative effects on behavior years after the drugs are no longer used.

constraint-induced movement therapy. A motor rehabilitation technique in which unaffected limbs are restrained to increase usage of dysfunctional limbs.

The fact that repeated drug-induced arousal led to long-lasting sensitization in presumably non-schizophrenic rats led researchers to consider the possibility that repeated natural arousal might have similar effects in humans without mental disorders. Evidence consistent with this possibility was first described in the early nineties (Post, 1992).

Robert Post (1992) found that after an initial stressful event triggered a disorder such as depression, increasingly minor stressful events could trigger additional bouts of depression later on. He proposed that this tendency occurred because some individuals become sensitized to stress and its associated physiological states, much in the way that the rats given amphetamines became sensitized to the stimulating effects of the drug. Recent studies show that depressed individuals show stronger responses to minor stressors than do healthy individuals (Wichers et al., 2009). Additionally, depression promotes repetitive thoughts about symptoms and negative events (Ruscio et al., 2015), potentially further sensitizing individuals to low-level stressors.

These findings might seem to imply that people should avoid stressful events as much as possible, to minimize the opportunities for sensitization to stress to take hold. However, animal research suggests that low rates of exposure to stressful events may actually lead to greater sensitivity to future stressors (Liu, 2015), and that experience with moderate stress over time may increase an individual's resilience when faced with a high-stress event. If similar effects occur in humans, then this would suggest that overprotective parents who do everything in their power to prevent their children from suffering could in some cases be increasing the risk that their children will be more adversely affected whenever those children do encounter a highly stressful event. At the other end of the spectrum, parents that repeatedly expose their children to highly stressful events may also be gradually increasing their children's risks for mental illnesses later in life (Laurent et al., 2015).

Sensitization to stress not only can contribute to depression but also is thought to be a factor in anxiety disorders (Mclaughlin, Conron, Koenen, & Gilman, 2010; Rosen & Schulkin, 1998). Repeated exposures to high stress levels during development, for example, can increase chances for depression later in life and also puts children at risk of developing anxiety disorders, such as *obsessive compulsive disorder*. Just as depressed individuals tend to dwell on the factors that they perceive as contributing to their depressed state, individuals with obsessive compulsive disorder tend to repeatedly focus on certain thoughts that lead them to repeat certain actions many times. Again, such repetition may facilitate further sensitization, exacerbating the problem.

Pathological anxiety can be viewed as an exaggerated response to potentially scary stimuli, resulting when sensitization to stress associated with fear-inducing situations amplifies a person's emotional responses to lower-level stimulation (the role of learning in fear responses is discussed in detail in Chapter 10). Understanding the mechanisms that lead to sensitization is key to developing new techniques for preventing such disorders and for treating them effectively when they arise.

Human–Machine Interfaces: Regaining Sensory Modalities through Perceptual Learning

If training can lead to cortical change that helps people recover motor functions after a brain injury, might it also enable people to develop perceptual abilities they don't have? For example, could perceptual learning help someone who is deaf learn to hear or someone who is blind learn to see? This is indeed possible

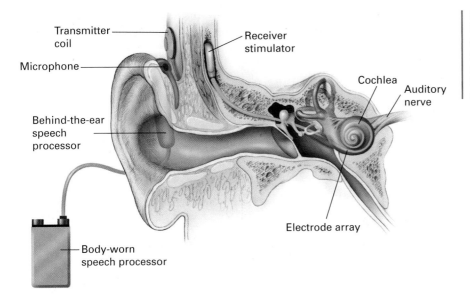

Transmitter coil

Microphone

Behind-the-ear speech processor

Body-worn speech processor

Receiver stimulator

Cochlea

Auditory nerve

Electrode array

Figure 3.19 Cochlear implant Cochlear implants use electricity to stimulate neurons in the auditory system, thereby creating virtual speech sounds in the brain. Information from Clarke, 2002.

and has in fact already been accomplished with sensory prostheses. **Sensory prostheses** are electromechanical devices that interface with neural circuits that normally process sensory information.

To date, the most extensively developed and successful sensory prosthetic technology is the **cochlear implant** (Figure 3.19). This device electrically stimulates auditory nerves to produce hearing sensations in profoundly deaf individuals, primarily to assist them in processing speech. Multiple electrodes implanted in the cochlea (the part of the ear that converts sounds into neural firing patterns) modify responses in the auditory nerve in ways that roughly simulate the neural activity normally produced by sounds. This technology is most effective in young children and in adults who have only recently lost their hearing. Conventional hearing aids amplify external sounds, but cochlear implants re-create the effects of sounds within the brain, generating "virtual sounds" from information about environmental sound that has been electronically detected and processed.

The virtual speech sounds generated by cochlear implants are quite different from normal speech, so people using the implants must learn to discriminate between the new sounds before they can begin to understand what they hear, an example of perceptual learning. Speech perception by individuals with cochlear implants shows initial rapid improvement in the early months of use, followed by more gradual improvement over years (Clarke, 2002; Tajudeen, Waltzman, Jethanamest, & Svirsky, 2010). Although cochlear implants make it possible for a deaf person to understand speech, they do not totally restore hearing. For instance, music is dramatically distorted by cochlear implants because they filter out many of the pitches that make music melodic.

It is likely that changes in speech-processing abilities after installation of a cochlear implant are the result of cortical plasticity, but this has yet to be experimentally demonstrated in humans. Neural activity generated by the implant may lead to changes in many areas of cortex, because the implant provides the brain with access not only to new sounds but also to a range of other experiences that require the ability to hear (such as the opportunity to engage in spoken conversations). Researchers have found that cochlear implants in deaf

sensory prosthesis. A mechanical device designed to supplement or substitute for a faulty sensory modality such as vision or hearing; the device's sensory detectors interface with brain areas that normally process those sensory inputs.

cochlear implant. A sensory prosthesis that directly stimulates auditory nerves to produce hearing sensations in deaf individuals.

Researchers at Duke University have developed retinal implants that are providing blind users with virtual sight. If these sensory prosthetics were used on an opossum blinded at birth, do you think its sensory cortices would reorganize to be more like those of animals that had never been blind?

cats lead to massive changes in auditory cortex (Klinke, Kral, Heid, Tillein, & Hartmann, 1999). After implantation, auditory cortex becomes organized differently from what is seen in deaf cats without implants and also from what is seen in hearing cats, suggesting that the virtual sounds these cats hear are driving the observed changes in cortex.

Most current sensory prostheses are designed to replace lost abilities, but in principle, it should also be possible to use such devices to enhance existing capabilities or create new sensory abilities. In fact, researchers have already achieved this in rats, giving them night vision by sending signals generated by head-mounted infrared sensors directly to their somatosensory cortex (Thompson, Carra, & Nicolelis, 2013). No one knows how well cortical neurons in humans would be able to process inputs from sensors detecting stimuli such as infrared light or ultrasonic sounds that humans are normally unable to perceive. Given how easily deaf people have learned to process novel inputs from cochlear implants, however, it seems likely that the human brain could accommodate a wide range of machine-provided inputs through perceptual learning.

Interim Summary

- Learned non-use of a limb, which may be due to habituation, can be overcome by constraint-induced movement therapy, which forces the individual to use the limb.

- Repeated exposure to stressful events may sensitize a person to stress, which can increase the likelihood of developing depression or anxiety disorders later in life.

- Sensory prostheses provide deaf or blind individuals with new sensory-processing capabilities. Use of these devices leads to perceptual learning that improves the user's ability to recognize sensory events.

Synthesis

Habituation, perceptual learning, and other learning processes driven by repeated exposures to stimuli are often described as the simplest forms of learning. This is partly because even the most primitive animals show habituation (even amoebas!). Moreover, none of these forms of learning demands much if any obvious effort from the learner. The processes involved in learning about repeated events can, however, be highly complex, drawing on the combined activities of multiple brain regions interacting in many different ways. A good example is the learning of landmarks for spatial navigation. Spatial learning can happen independent of observable changes in responses, which means it is difficult for an observer to determine what another individual is learning about any particular set of landmarks. If you see someone staring out of a car window as they ride along, you'd be hard pressed to tell if they are storing information about certain landmarks that might help them find their way back to that location later. Even so, complex combinations of events, including percepts both of visual patterns and of specific movements, determine how neurons in the hippocampus and surrounding cortical regions respond, which in turn controls the nature and qualities of the memories that are formed (a topic we return to in Chapters 7 and 11).

Repeated experiences can slow down your ability to learn (in the case of habituation) or speed it up (in the case of priming and perceptual learning). They can also affect your responses to other, seemingly unrelated, stimuli (as in the case of sensitization). For example, reading about the cannibalistic murderer Jeffrey Dahmer in the beginning of this chapter was probably novel in your experiences of reading psychology textbooks. If you have gotten used to experiencing the relatively predictable material within college textbooks (in other words, if you get bored reading textbooks), then this disturbing example may have caused your learned response to textbooks to dishabituate, which may have in turn increased your capacity to encode and remember the subsequent material, despite the fact that this material may have little to do with psychopathic killers. How is it that repeated exposures to stimuli can generate such a wide range of learning phenomena? Part of the answer, at least in humans and other mammals, is the contribution made by the cerebral cortex, one of the most complex structures in the brain. Experience-dependent changes in how cortical neurons respond to repeated events constitute one of several powerful mechanisms that seem to contribute to perceptual learning, object recognition, spatial learning, and habituation.

Changes in behavior stemming from memories of repeated events have important implications for our daily lives, especially when the brain is not processing information the way it should. Understanding the mechanisms by which brains learn from repeated experiences can help clinicians interpret the effects of cortical damage and take steps to alleviate sensory deficits. The ability of brains to adapt in the ways described in this chapter may be the key to overcoming many mental disorders for which there are currently no cures. Thus, although the learning processes engaged by repetition can sometimes lead to negative outcomes (as in the circumstances surrounding Jeffrey Dahmer and in learned non-use), these processes also point to ways of rehabilitating patients and expanding people's perceptual abilities.

As you read through the following chapters, you will discover that the situations and mechanisms that contribute to learning from exposure also play a role in other learning phenomena. For example, in classical conditioning (discussed in Chapter 4), repeated exposure to a sequence of two events gradually increases an organism's sensitivity to the first of the two events, and many of the circuits that contribute to habituation and sensitization in *Aplysia* are involved. As another example, the learning that results from repeatedly pairing events with rewards or punishment (discussed in Chapter 5) depends on active exploration by the individual doing the learning. How such learning generalizes to novel situations (described in Chapter 6) depends on how well an individual can discriminate those novel events from more familiar stimuli. Understanding the relationships between different learning processes is one of the main goals of learning and memory research.

KNOW YOUR KEY TERMS

acoustic startle reflex, *p. 73*

cochlear implant, *p. 109*

constraint-induced movement therapy, *p. 107*

cortical plasticity, *p. 98*

dishabituation, *p. 75*

dual process theory, *p. 80*

familiarity, *p. 83*

habituation, *p. 73*

heterosynaptic, *p. 95*

homosynaptic, *p. 93*

mere exposure learning, *p. 85*

novel object recognition, *p. 82*

orienting response, *p. 74*

perceptual learning, *p. 84*

place cell, *p. 102*

priming, *p. 83*

receptive field, *p. 97*

sensitization, *p. 78*

sensory prosthesis, *p. 109*

skin conductance response (SCR), *p. 78*

spatial learning, *p. 88*

spontaneous recovery, *p. 76*

stroke, *p. 106*

synaptic depression, *p. 93*

word-stem completion task, *p. 83*

QUIZ YOURSELF

1. If you are nervous about driving in the rain because you once slid off the road when it was raining, you may have become _____ to driving in the rain. (p. 78)

2. If you don't mind getting fillings at the dentist because you've had so much dental work in the past, you probably are _____ to dental drills. (p. 73)

3. If you've become habituated to the beeping of a fire alarm with a low battery near your bedroom, then having a crow attack you in your bedroom may _____ your responses to the beeping. (p. 75)

4. Researchers can tell when a baby perceives an object as novel by monitoring the duration of its _____. (p. 74)

5. Repetition of _____ stimuli leads to faster habituation. (p. 81)

6. Long-term habituation is more likely to occur after _____ exposure than after _____ exposure. (p. 77)

7. A physiological response that researchers sometimes use to monitor the effects of habituation and sensitization is the _____. (p. 78)

8. The suggestion that sensitization and habituation are independent processes is a major feature of _____. (p. 80)

9. When an organism learns but does not provide observable evidence that learning has occurred, this is referred to as _____. (p. 72)

10. The _____ task makes it possible to determine when a rat is familiar with a particular object. (p. 82)

11. Sensitization of the gill-withdrawal reflex in *Aplysia* is associated with increased release of _____ by _____. (p. 95)

12. Learning-related changes in the receptive fields of cortical neurons provide evidence of _____. (p. 98)

13. Blinding an opossum at birth can increase the number of cortical neurons with _____ receptive fields. (p. 99)

14. Neurons in the hippocampus that respond strongly in particular locations are called _____. (p. 102)

15. Repeated exposures to stressful events during development can lead to _____. (p. 78)

16. Devices called _____, created to facilitate sensory processing in patients who have lost some sensory function, work better over time because of _____. (p. 84, 109)

Answers appear in the back of the book.

CONCEPT CHECK

1. A weight lifter repeatedly lifts a barbell. After several repetitions, he begins lifting it more slowly, until eventually he stops. Would you say this is habituation? Why or why not?

2. A common example of sensitization is the experience of walking down a dark alleyway at night. The setting may produce feelings of nervousness, which lead to heightened arousal: you'll jump if you hear a noise behind you. Can you think of any situations (other than movies) in which people are intentionally sensitized?

3. After reading this chapter, you'll be familiar with at least some of the information it contains. If you read the chapter again, you may learn even more. Is this an example of learning from repeated events?

4. Chapter 2 described a study in which structural MRIs of London taxi drivers were compared with those of control participants who did not drive taxis (Maguire et al., 2000). In that study, researchers discovered that the size of the hippocampus in the taxi drivers was correlated with the number of years they had been driving a taxi. Why might that be?

Answers appear in the back of the book.

Classical Conditioning

Learning to Predict Significant Events

W HAT DO THE FOLLOWING FOUR people have in common? Four-year-old Moira, who screams with delighted anticipation for ice cream when she hears the jingle of the vendor's truck in the distance; Dan, who starts feeling anxious about the carpeting in his home when he sees rain clouds on the horizon and realizes that he left the windows open this morning; Nathalie, a former cigarette smoker, who always feels the urge to light up after sex; Sharon, who broke up with her ex-boyfriend years ago but still finds the sound of his voice arousing. It's not immediately apparent, but a little investigation will show that the link connecting Moira, Dan, Nathalie, and Sharon's reactions is Ivan Pavlov—or to be more precise, Ivan Pavlov's principle of classical conditioning. They have all had their behaviors altered by classical (or "Pavlovian") conditioning.

Most people, even if they never took a psychology course, are vaguely aware of the story of Ivan Pavlov (1849–1936) and how he trained, or "conditioned," his dogs to salivate to cues such as bells or tones that predicted the impending delivery of food; references to "Pavlov's dogs" can be found throughout popular culture, including in movies, TV shows, and many cartoons, as shown here and later in this chapter. Chapter 1 briefly introduced you to Pavlov and his training method; this chapter will explain why his work was so important and influential and why it continues to be relevant to experimental and clinical studies today.

Like many advances in science, Pavlov's discovery of classical conditioning was largely accidental. He was originally studying digestion, and he noticed that his dogs often started salivating even before they received their daily meat rations—when they saw the bowl that usually contained their food or when they heard the footsteps of the laboratory assistant who fed them (Pavlov, 1927). Initially, Pavlov viewed the premature salivation as a nuisance that interfered with his efforts to understand how the digestive system responds to food. Soon, however, Pavlov realized that he had stumbled on a way of studying how associations are formed in the brain of a dog.

Behavioral Processes
Basic Concepts of Classical Conditioning

Refining the Basic Principles

Error Correction and the Modulation of US Processing

Stimulus Attention and the Modulation of CS Processing

Other Determinants of Conditioning

Brain Substrates
Mammalian Conditioning of Motor Reflexes

Invertebrates and the Cellular Basis of Learning

Clinical Perspectives
Classical Conditioning and Drug Addiction Tolerance

Learning and Memory in Everyday Life: Extinguishing a Drug Habit

Reducing Medication through Classical Conditioning

wim claes/Shutterstock

Tom Prisk via CartoonStock

Why might a visitor ringing the doorbell interfere with Pavlov's experiments?

Pavlov and his assistants began a systematic study of factors that influence how an animal learns. By keeping the dogs in restraints and collecting saliva through a tube surgically inserted into their mouths (Figure 4.1), Pavlov could measure salivation in response to various cues. He began one study by first training a dog that a doorbell always preceded delivery of food; over many paired doorbell–food trials, the dog developed a stronger and stronger salivation response to the sound of the doorbell. This form of learning, in which an animal learns that one stimulus (such as a doorbell) predicts an upcoming important event (such as delivery of food), is known today as **classical conditioning** or **Pavlovian conditioning**.

There is much more to classical conditioning than dogs and saliva, however. This chapter will show why an understanding of classical "Pavlovian" conditioning (despite its seeming simplicity) is indispensable for building a behavioral and biological understanding of learning and memory. Moreover, classical conditioning is one of the few forms of learning for which the brain substrates have been worked out in precise detail, for every step, from the initial sensory input to the commands that drive the resulting motor responses. For these reasons, classical conditioning is avidly studied today by psychologists, neuroscientists, and clinical neuropsychologists, with implications far beyond what Pavlov could have anticipated when he made his accidental discovery almost one hundred years ago.

Figure 4.1 Pavlov's apparatus for studying learning
A restrained dog has a surgical tube inserted into its mouth to collect and measure salivation in response to meat placed in front of it or to a cue, such as a doorbell, that predicts delivery of the food.

4.1 Behavioral Processes

Classical Pavlovian conditioning is a way of learning about one's environment. As a child, Moira learned that the distant sound of a certain jingle predicts the imminent arrival of an ice cream truck. Since she loves ice cream, she can exploit her foreknowledge of the truck's arrival by asking her mother for money now, so she can be ready at the curb when the truck approaches. This is an example of learning to anticipate a positive event so as to take maximal advantage of it. Being able to anticipate negative events is also useful. If Dan is surprised by a sudden rainstorm in midday, he must rush home from work to close all the windows to keep rain from blowing in and soaking his carpets. Had he anticipated the rainstorm earlier, Dan could have closed the windows before he left for work.

This section begins by introducing the basic concepts and terminology of classical conditioning and then explores subsequent research into this type of learning. It describes an elegant and simple theory of conditioning, developed in the early 1970s, that helps explain a wide range of learning phenomena, and it discusses how conditioning behaviors seen in the simplest of animals help us understand the more complex cognitive behaviors observed in human learning. It ends by discussing several other facets of classical conditioning, including how attention can affect what is learned, how timing is important, and to what degree we may be biologically prepared to learn some things more easily than others.

Basic Concepts of Classical Conditioning

A dog will naturally salivate when it sees or smells food. No learning is needed for it to make this response. For this reason, psychologists call the food an **unconditioned stimulus**, or **US**, meaning a stimulus that naturally—that is, without conditioning—evokes some response. An unconditioned stimulus, such as food, evokes a natural response, such as salivation, which psychologists call the **unconditioned response**, or **UR**; their relationship does not depend on learning. Similarly, Moira's craving for ice cream and Dan's dismay at wet carpets in his house are natural—that is, unconditioned—responses to good and bad things in their lives. They both occur unconditionally without prior training. In contrast, a neutral stimulus, such as a bell that the dog has not heard before, evokes no such salivation by the dog (Figure 4.2a).

unconditioned stimulus (US). A cue that has some biological significance and in the absence of prior training naturally evokes a response.

unconditioned response (UR). The naturally occurring response to an unconditioned stimulus (US).

How Pavlov Conditioned Dogs to Salivate

After Pavlov put his dogs into the apparatus shown in Figure 4.1, he repeatedly paired the bell with food: each time the bell was rung, an assistant promptly delivered food to the dog. This resulted in the formerly neutral stimulus, the bell, becoming a **conditioned stimulus**, or **CS**, as illustrated in Figure 4.2b. After repeated presentations of the bell CS and the food US, the two became linked in the dog's mind. This training—or conditioning, as Pavlov called it—resulted in the dog learning something new: the bell predicts the food. We can evaluate the degree to which the dog learned this prediction—that is, how strongly it expects the food when it hears the bell—by measuring how much the dog salivates to the bell alone. This is shown in Figure 4.2c, in which the bell alone, the conditioned stimulus (CS), now evokes an anticipatory response, called the **conditioned response**, or **CR**, even in the absence of the food.

conditioned stimulus (CS). A cue that is paired with an unconditioned stimulus (US) and comes to elicit a conditioned response (CR).

For Moira, the truck jingle is a conditioned stimulus (CS), which, after being repeatedly paired with the arrival of the ice cream truck, evokes an anticipatory conditioned response (CR) consisting of Moira asking her mother for money and running to the street corner. When this response has been fully learned, Moira will be waiting at the street corner, money in hand, when the unconditioned stimulus (US)—the ice cream truck—arrives at her house. For

conditioned response (CR). The trained response to a conditioned stimulus (CS) in anticipation of the unconditioned stimulus (US) that it predicts.

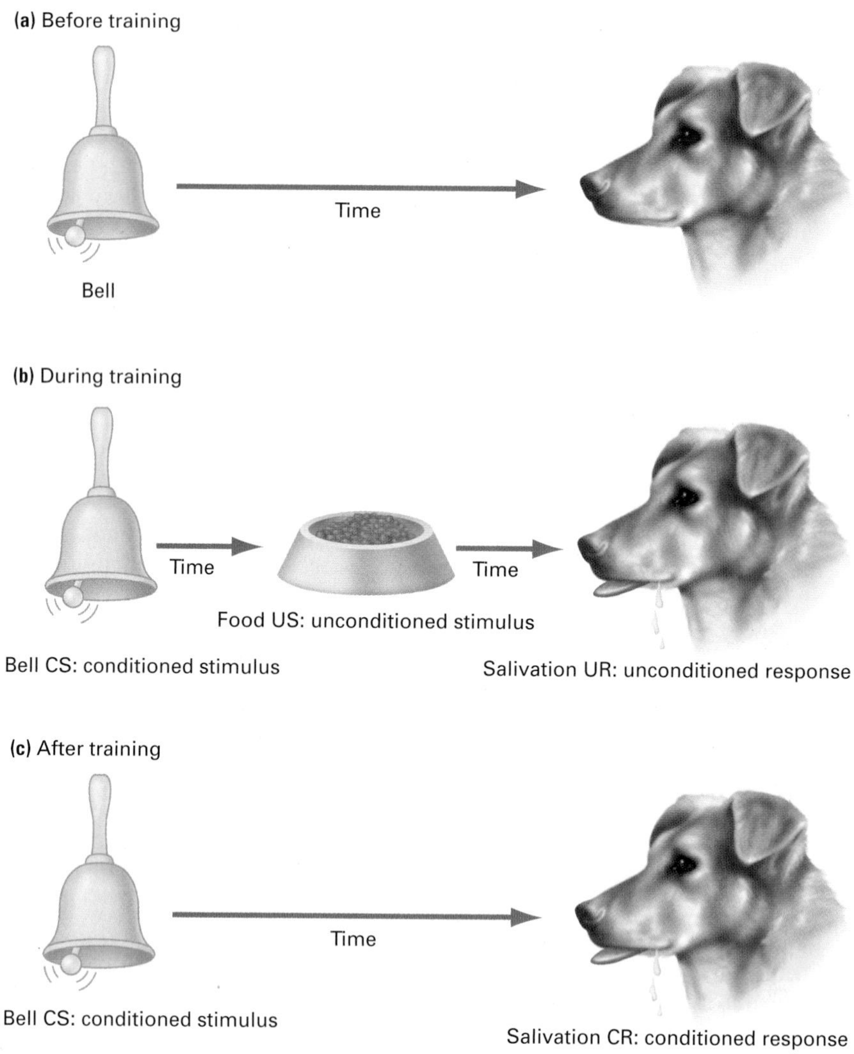

Figure 4.2 Schematic illustration of Pavlov's experiment (a) Before training, a neutral stimulus, such as a bell, evokes no response from a dog. In contrast, the presence of food, an unconditioned stimulus (US) would naturally evoke an unconditioned response (UR), salivation. (b) During training, the bell, formerly a neutral stimulus, becomes a conditioned stimulus (CS) when it is repeatedly paired with the food US to evoke a salivation UR. (c) After training, the bell, now a conditioned stimulus (CS), evokes a learned response, the conditioned response (CR) of salivation.

(a) Before training

Time

Bell

(b) During training

Time — Time

Food US: unconditioned stimulus

Bell CS: conditioned stimulus

Salivation UR: unconditioned response

(c) After training

Time

Bell CS: conditioned stimulus

Salivation CR: conditioned response

Dan, the dark clouds in the sky are an ominous conditioned stimulus (CS), which have become associated with subsequent heavy rains through his past experiences. These experiences have taught him a *preparatory conditioned response* (CR): to close all the windows in his house before the arrival of the rain, the unconditioned stimulus (US). In all three examples—Pavlov's dog, Moira, and Dan—a learned association between a CS and subsequent US generates a CR that follows the CS. Table 4.1 reviews these terms and their relation

Table 4.1 Terminology of Pavlovian conditioning, with examples

	Unconditioned stimulus, US	Unconditioned response, UR	Conditioned stimulus, CS	Conditioned response, CR
Pavlov's dog	Food	Salivation	Bell	Salivation
Moira	Ice cream truck	Appetite for ice cream	Truck jingle	Get money from Mom, run to corner before truck arrives
Dan	Rain	Closing windows while carpets get wet	Dark clouds	Closing windows before the rain starts

to the three examples. We will continue to use all four terms—US, UR, CS, CR—throughout this chapter as well as the rest of this book, so it's a good idea to be sure you are comfortable with all four before moving on.

Test Your Knowledge

Pavlov's Experiment

Table 4.1 describes Pavlov's experiment from the perspective of the experimenter, Pavlov. From the dog's perspective, however, the scenario seems quite different. Using the cartoon here, identify Pavlov's CS and CR as viewed by the dog. (Answers appear in the back of the book.)

Appetitive Conditioning

When the US is a positive event (such as food delivery for Pavlov's dog or ice cream for Moira), the conditioning is called **appetitive conditioning**. In general, appetitive conditioning consists of learning to predict something that satisfies a desire or appetite. Food and sex are among the most powerful of appetitive USs. Recall Sharon, one of the four people described at the chapter's beginning; she was conditioned to the sound of her ex-boyfriend's voice by its past association to her having sex with him. Michael Domjan and colleagues have studied a similar form of conditioning using male domesticated Japanese quail, who will copulate readily with a sexually receptive female (Figure 4.3). When an arbitrary stimulus, such as a light CS, is paired repeatedly with access to a sexually receptive female (the US), the male quail exhibits a CR of approaching and remaining near the light (Domjan, Lyons, North, & Bruell, 1986).

appetitive conditioning. Conditioning in which the US is a positive event (such as food delivery).

Aversive Conditioning

Dan's learning that clouds predict rain damage to his home (if the windows are not shut) is an example of **aversive conditioning**, learning to avoid or minimize the consequence of an expected aversive event. Many of the procedures used for the experimental study of conditioning are examples of aversive conditioning.

In Chapter 1 you read about both B. F. Skinner, the father of behaviorist approaches to the science of learning, and W. K. Estes, a founder of mathematical psychology and learning theory. In the early 1940s, Estes was a graduate

aversive conditioning. Conditioning in which the US is a negative event (such as a shock or an airpuff to the eye).

Figure 4.3 Sexual conditioning in male Japanese quail Michael Domjan and colleagues conditioned male domesticated Japanese quail to approach and remain near a light (the CS) that is associated with access through a door to a sexually receptive female (the US).

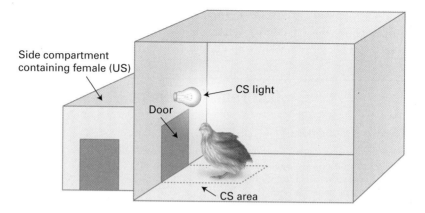

student of Skinner's. At that time, the United States had not yet entered World War II. The Germans were using a new technology—rockets—to bomb England. As Londoners heard the whine of the rocket engines approaching, they stopped whatever they were doing—eating, walking, talking—and waited for the explosions. After the rockets dropped elsewhere and people realized they were safe, they resumed their interrupted activities.

Intrigued by these stories from London, Estes and Skinner developed a new conditioning procedure for rats that was similar, in some respects, to what they imagined Londoners were experiencing. This procedure, which they called the "Conditioned Emotional Response" (CER), was a technique for studying learned fear (Estes & Skinner, 1941). Estes and Skinner placed hungry rats in a cage that delivered food pellets whenever the rats pressed a lever. The cage also had a metal grid floor wired to deliver a mild shock to the rats' feet. Normally, the hungry rats busily pressed the lever to obtain food, but if the experimenters trained the rats to learn that a tone (the conditioned stimulus, or CS) predicted an upcoming shock (the unconditioned stimulus, or US), the rats would freeze (their conditioned response, CR) when they heard the tone, interrupting their lever presses and waiting for the shock. Measuring this freezing behavior allowed Estes to quantify trial-by-trial changes in the learned response. Within a few years, this conditioned emotional response procedure became one of the most widely used techniques for studying animal conditioning, and it is still in use today. (In Chapter 10 you can read more about fear conditioning and how emotions, such as fear, influence learning and memory.)

In 1928, Cole Porter wrote "Birds do it, bees do it, even educated fleas do it," for the Broadway show *Paris*. Porter was, of course, referring to falling in love, but he could just as well have been writing about learning by classical conditioning. Even insects such as fleas and flies can be trained using classical conditioning methods. In fact, studies of classical conditioning of the fruit fly *Drosophila* have been enormously important for understanding the biology of learning (we'll see an example of such a study later in this chapter).

Figure 4.4 illustrates the behavioral procedure used in studies of fly conditioning (Dudai, Jan, Byers, Quinn, & Benzer, 1976). First the flies are placed in a container that contains one odor, designated odor 1 (Figure 4.4a), and nothing happens. Then the flies are exposed to another odor, odor 2, and in the presence of that odor (the CS), they are given a mild but aversive shock (the US). Later, the flies are placed in the middle of a container that has odor 1 at one end and odor 2 at the other end (Figure 4.4b). As the flies explore the container, they avoid the side where they smell odor 2 (which has been associated with shock) and gravitate toward the side where they smell odor 1 (which was not paired

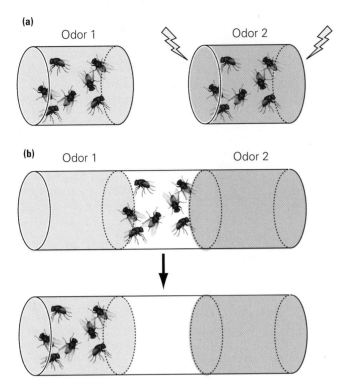

Figure 4.4 Odor conditioning in flies (a) Flies are placed sequentially in two different containers, first in one with odor 1, where they are not shocked, and then in another with odor 2, where they are shocked. (b) Later, they are placed in the middle of a container that has odor 1 at one end and odor 2 at the other end. The flies move toward odor 1, which was not associated with shock, indicating that they have learned the odor 2–shock association from their previous training.

with shock). Like Dan's keeping out the rain, the rats' and flies' avoidance of shocks are examples of aversive conditioning to predictors of a significant negative event.

Understanding the Conditioned Response

So far, we have introduced four different procedures for experimenting with classical conditioning. Two of these are appetitive conditioning procedures: Pavlov's original study with dogs and food, and Domjan's studies of quails and sex. The other two are aversive conditioning procedures: the conditioned emotional response in which rats freeze when they hear a tone that predicts a shock (Estes & Skinner, 1941), and the fly shock preparation shown in Figure 4.4.

In each of these four cases, we can ask, why does the animal exhibit the conditioned response? In all four, the conditioned response can be understood as an anticipatory response that prepares the animal for the expected US, in much the same way that Moira prepares for the arrival of an anticipated ice cream truck, or Dan prepares for a predicted rainstorm. By moving away from the odor associated with shock, the fly is more likely to avoid being shocked. By salivating in anticipation of food, the dog is better prepared to efficiently digest the food. By freezing in anticipation of a shock, the rat is better prepared to ward off danger and also avoids having ongoing motor behaviors (such as eating) disrupted by the shock. By moving toward the light, the quail is all the sooner able to mount and copulate with the female.

Mammalian Conditioning of Motor Reflexes: Eyeblink Conditioning

Another widely studied form of aversive conditioning—one that induces an anticipatory defensive response much like Dan's shutting his windows—is **eyeblink conditioning**, perhaps the most thoroughly studied form of motor reflex

eyeblink conditioning. A classical conditioning procedure in which the US is an airpuff to the eye and the conditioned and unconditioned responses are eyeblinks.

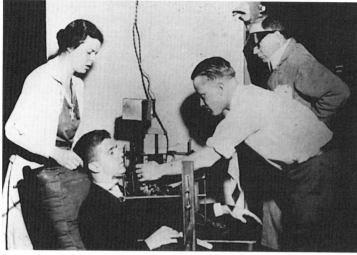

Figure 4.5 Face-slap eyeblink conditioning in the 1920s Clark Hull (standing with visor) and his young graduate student Ernest Hilgard (seated) in an early study of classical eyeblink conditioning at Yale University. Hull trained Hilgard to blink in anticipation of a slap to the face.

Figure 4.6 Eyeblink conditioning in humans and rabbits (a) In human eyeblink conditioning, a tone CS is delivered through headphones. The US is a puff of air delivered through the rubber tube. The eyeblink CR is recorded by EMG electrodes placed above and below the eye. (b) In rabbit eyeblink conditioning, a similar rubber tube delivers the airpuff US to the rabbit in the restraining acrylic glass case; a photobeam measures the CR and UR.

conditioning in mammals (Gormezano, Kehoe, & Marshall, 1983). You may recall Clark Hull of Yale from Chapter 1, one of the fathers of mathematical learning. He used (and perhaps abused) his graduate students by teaching them to blink in anticipation of a slap to the face, as shown in Figure 4.5. The subject in this photo is Ernest "Jack" Hilgard, who later went on to become a pioneer in the study of the psychology of hypnosis and the author of a leading textbook on memory.

Hull arranged for a tone (CS) to play just prior to each face slap (US). After many repeated presentations of the CS followed by the US, poor Jack began to blink (the CR) every time he heard a tone, whether or not it was followed by a slap.

For practical as well as ethical reasons, researchers no longer use the face slap as a US in human eyeblink conditioning. Instead, they often use an airpuff to the eye. This is not painful, but it does cause a reflexive—that is, unconditioned—eyeblink UR (if you don't believe this, ask a friend to blow lightly in your eye). The blink UR in human eyeblink conditioning can be measured in several different ways, one of which is through the use of electromyography (EMG) detectors of electrical activity of muscles, placed above and below the eye as shown in Figure 4.6a. The CS is a tone, typically delivered through headphones so that the volume can be regulated (and outside noises masked). With repeated pairings of the tone CS and airpuff US, subjects develop a CR: in this case, an anticipatory blink that occurs before US arrival, so that the eye is partially shut and partially protected when the airpuff occurs.

What is most important about eyeblink conditioning is the similarity of its appearance in many different species, so that the results found in one species can reasonably be expected to apply to others. Eyeblink conditioning has been shown in mice, rats, and monkeys, but one of the most common animals for the study of eyeblink conditioning has been the rabbit, because of its propensity to sit still for long periods and to blink very little except when something bothers its

(a)

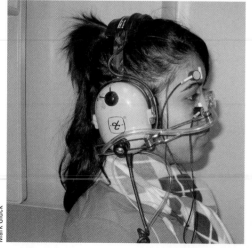

(b)

eyes. Figure 4.6b shows a rabbit in a restraining acrylic glass case within which eyeblink conditioning is often conducted. The tube at the rabbit's left eye delivers the airpuff US while the eyeblink CR and UR are measured by photo beams.

With rabbits, just as with humans, the airpuff is the US, and the reflexive blink is the UR, as shown in Figure 4.7. Before training, the tone does not cause the rabbit to blink because it is a neutral stimulus, as shown in Figure 4.7a. However, if the airpuff US is repeatedly preceded by a tone, then the animal learns that the tone predicts the airpuff US and is a warning signal to get ready, as shown in Figure 4.7b. Eventually, the animal will blink as a response to the tone alone, as shown in Figure 4.7c. At this point, the tone has become a CS, and the anticipatory eyeblink is the CR.

To the uninformed observer, the learned conditioned response, the eyeblink CR, is identical to the automatic unconditioned response, the eyeblink UR. However, the learned CR takes place during the warning period provided by the CS (analogous to a weather report predicting rain) in advance of the US and

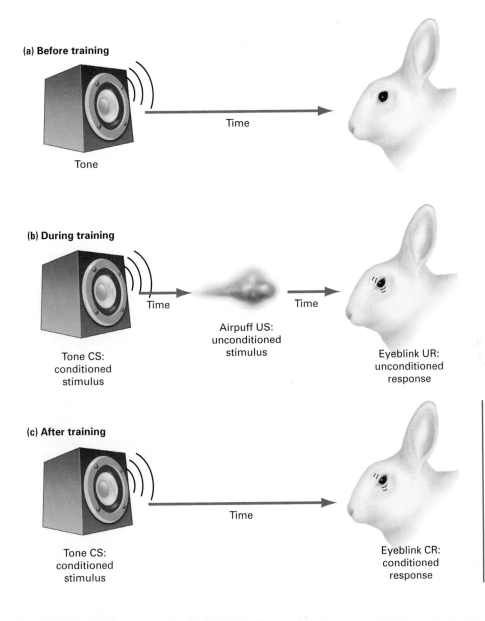

(a) Before training

Tone

Time

(b) During training

Tone CS:
conditioned
stimulus

Time

Airpuff US:
unconditioned
stimulus

Time

Eyeblink UR:
unconditioned
response

(c) After training

Tone CS:
conditioned
stimulus

Time

Eyeblink CR:
conditioned
response

Figure 4.7 Learning progression in rabbit eyeblink conditioning (a) Before training, the tone is a neutral stimulus that has no relevance to the rabbit. (b) The tone CS followed by airpuff US causes an eyeblink UR in a naive rabbit. (c) The tone CS is followed by a blink CR in a rabbit that has undergone eyeblink conditioning. Compare these diagrams to Figure 4.2, showing analogous stages of Pavlov's conditioning procedure.

Table 4.2 Widely used classical conditioning procedures

	Unconditioned stimulus, US	Unconditioned response, UR	Conditioned stimulus, CS	Conditioned response, CR
Appetitive conditioning				
Pavlov's dog	Food	Salivation	Bell	Salivation
Quail sex	Sexually available female	Approach, mounting, and copulation	Light	Approach
Aversive conditioning				
Fly shock	Shock	Attempt to escape	Odor	Attempt to escape
Conditioned emotional response	Shock	Freezing	Tone	Freezing
Eyeblink conditioning	Airpuff	Blink	Tone	Blink

UR, adaptively protecting the eye from the onset of the airpuff. The same is true for Pavlov's original salivation study, in which the learned CR, salivation, is the same as the dog's natural unconditioned response to food, but it takes place *before* the food is presented, at the sound of the doorbell that predicts the food.

You have now been introduced to five different formats that are used for experiments in classical conditioning: two appetitive preparations and three aversive preparations. These are all reviewed in Table 4.2. To see if you really understand this material and can tell your USs, URs, CSs, and CRs apart, try to identify each in the real-world examples given in the accompanying Test Your Knowledge box.

Real life example

Test Your Knowledge

Classical Conditioning in Everyday Life

Are you sure you can tell the US, UR, CS, and CR apart? Test yourself by identifying each of them in the real-world situations described below. For each, indicate if it is an example of appetitive or aversive conditioning. (Answers appear in the back of the book.)

1. Advertisements for a new sports car show a sexy female model draped over the car's hood.
2. Mark loves pizza. When he was a boy, his parents frequently had it delivered to their home. Because the pizzas often arrived only lukewarm, his parents would put the pizza, still inside the box, into the oven to heat up. This caused the box to give off a smell of burning cardboard. Now, years later, whenever Mark smells cardboard burning, he gets hungry for pizza.

Learning a New Association

How, exactly, does learning progress in eyeblink conditioning or other classical conditioning procedures? Figure 4.8 shows an eyeblink CR becoming stronger over several days of training in a rabbit eyeblink-conditioning study.

Each day, the animal received 80 training trials, each of which presented a tone followed shortly thereafter by an airpuff to the eye. The graphs (green lines) in Figure 4.8 show the extent to which the rabbit's eyelid lowers at the start of different days during the experiment; the higher the curve, the farther the eyelid has shut. Note that on the beginning of day 1, the only response is the eyeblink UR that occurs *after* the onset of the airpuff US. However, with training, an eyeblink CR emerges: By day 3, there is movement of the eyelid before the US arrives. This anticipatory blink in response to the CS is the beginning of a CR. With further training, by about day 5, a strong anticipatory eyeblink CR occurs, timed so that the eyelid is safely closed before the airpuff US occurs.

In both rabbits and humans, eyeblink conditioning is a gradual process, occurring over many trials. Figure 4.9 shows trial-by-trial changes in the percentage of human participants and rabbits giving conditioned eyeblink responses in a study of tone–airpuff conditioning in both species. Although the graphs in the figure are not identical (humans learn faster), they are quite similar. Most important to note is that in both humans and rabbits, the percentage rises over time until most trials elicit an appropriately timed predictive eyeblink CR.

Refining the Basic Principles

Studies of classical conditioning have led to a broad range of insights into the subtle factors that influence animal and human learning. In this section we explore four of these topics, looking more closely at variations in the USs that develop, the constraints on what makes a cue a CS or a US, how old associations are extinguished when no longer applicable, and what happens when two cues, rather than one, are presented during learning.

Conditioned Compensatory Responses

Remember Dan who learned (from past bad experiences) to notice signs of impending rain and close his windows in advance of it to protect his carpets? Dan also has a swimming pool out back. If he were expecting heavy rains for several days, he might worry about the pool overflowing and damaging his lawn and house. Given the weather forecast, he might think it prudent to partially drain his pool, lowering the level a few inches before the rain arrives. When the rain does come, it will return the water level to the point it was at before he drained it, lessening the likelihood of an overflow. In this way, Dan's preparatory response (preemptively lowering the water level in the pool) compensates for the expected rise in water level and ensures that the pool never gets too full.

An analogous conditioned *compensatory response* was demonstrated by two of Pavlov's colleagues more than 60 years ago (Subkov & Zilov, 1937). These researchers injected dogs on several occasions with adrenaline (also known as epinephrine), a chemical normally produced by the adrenal glands in response to stress or anxiety. The usual effect of adrenaline is an increase in heart rate. However, the dogs' heart rate increased less and less with each subsequent injection. Such a decrease in reaction to a drug, so that larger doses are required to achieve the original effect, is known as **tolerance.** What causes tolerance to develop?

To explore this question, the researchers placed their dogs on injection stands, where the dogs normally received the drug injection, but they

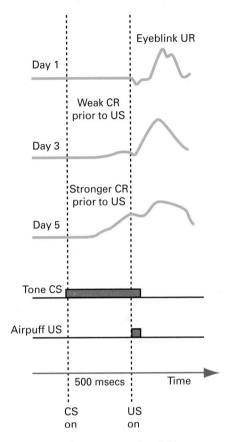

Figure 4.8 Acquisition of eyeblink-conditioning response Development of a conditioned response as measured at the beginning of day 1, day 3, and day 5 of training, using a standard tone–airpuff trial sequence. On day 1, only a UR to the eyepuff is observed, but by day 3, an anticipatory eyeblink starts to emerge. By day 5, this anticipatory CR is strong and occurs reliably before the airpuff US.

tolerance. A decrease in reaction to a drug so that larger doses are required to achieve the same effect.

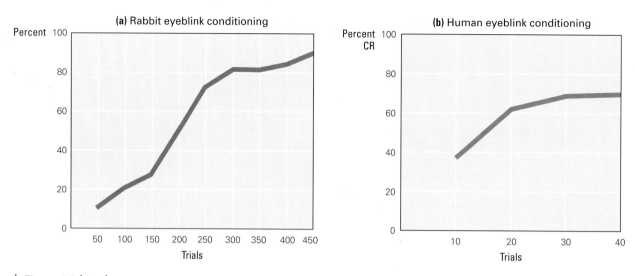

Figure 4.9 Learning curves for rabbit and human eyeblink conditioning (a) A learning curve showing the percent CRs in rabbits across blocks of training trials. (b) Analogous learning curve for human eyeblink conditioning. Although these curves are qualitatively similar, they reflect different training regimes, since the rabbits are usually trained in blocks of 1-hour trial sessions on successive days, while humans are trained in a single hour-long session.

(a) Data from Allen, Chelius, & Gluck, 2002; (b) Data from Allen, Padilla, Myers, & Gluck, 2002.

homeostasis. The tendency of the body (including the brain) to gravitate toward a state of equilibrium or balance.

administered a neutral inert substance rather than the adrenaline. The researchers observed that this caused the dogs' heart rate to *decrease*. Apparently, the various cues (the stand, the injection) that predicted the adrenaline injection triggered a conditioned compensatory response that lowered the dogs' heart rate in anticipation of the adrenaline causing an increase in heart rate. Such automatic compensatory responses occur primarily in body systems that have a mechanism for **homeostasis,** the tendency of the body (including the brain) to gravitate toward a state of equilibrium or balance.

Much like the homeowner who acts to prevent the pool from overflowing during a storm, the dogs in these studies unconsciously used advance information about the forthcoming adrenaline injection to compensate for the drug's effect. The learned anticipatory decrease in heart rate combined with the increase produced by the drug resulted in a lower total increase in heart rate than was experienced on the first (unexpected) administration of adrenaline. Since the dogs had been conditioned to expect adrenaline after seeing cues such as the stand or the syringe, their bodies compensated by lowering their heart rates to maintain a constant level. The same compensatory mechanisms at work in certain aspects of drug addiction will be discussed in Section 4.3.

What Cues Can Be CSs or USs?

The USs in a conditioning experiment are by definition events that are biologically significant, either because they are inherently positive (such as food or sex) or because they are inherently negative (such as shock or an airpuff to the eye). In contrast, a CS can be any cue in the environment, even a US. Thus, an airpuff to the eye, which is a US in the eyeblink-conditioning paradigm, can serve as the CS in another experiment, where for example an animal might learn that an airpuff predicts food delivery (the new US). Thus, stimulus cues are not inherently CSs or USs; rather, those terms define the roles the cues play in a particular learning situation.

Remember the description of Nathalie at the beginning of this chapter. She is a former smoker who gets an urge for a cigarette after sex. In Nathalie's case, sex is the CS that has become associated with cigarette smoking, the US, as shown in Table 4.3. After a person gets into the regular habit of having a cigarette after sex, the craving for and expectation of cigarettes becomes the CR. (You'll read more about addiction and conditioning later on in this chapter.) In contrast, for Sharon, who becomes aroused at the sound of her ex-boyfriend's voice, his voice

Table 4.3 Sex as a CS and a US

	Unconditioned stimulus, US	Unconditioned response, UR	Conditioned stimulus, CS	Conditioned response, CR
Nathalie	Smoking a cigarette	Reduced craving for cigarette	Sex	Desire for a cigarette
Sharon	Sex	Sexual gratification	Ex-boyfriend's voice	Sexual arousal

is now the CS and her sexual arousal is her CR. Thus, for Nathalie sex can be a CS that predicts cigarette smoking, while for Sharon, it is the US that previously followed hearing her boyfriend's voice. It all depends on the individual's unique experiences.

Extinguishing an Old Association

What do you think would happen if Moira moved to a new neighborhood where jingling trucks sold not ice cream, which she loves, but broccoli, which she hates? If each time she heard the jingle, she got broccoli (rather than ice cream), you might expect that her excited reaction to the jingle would eventually disappear. In this case, a previously acquired association would become diminished through repeated presentation of the CS (jingle) in the absence of the US (ice cream), a process known as **extinction**, which was first described in the early studies of Pavlov (1927), as noted in Chapter 1.

Once it is acquired, eyeblink conditioning can also undergo extinction if the former CS (tone) is presented repeatedly without an airpuff. Eventually, the rabbit (or person) that was formerly conditioned to blink to the tone begins to learn that the world has changed and the tone no longer predicts the US. Figure 4.10 shows what happens if, after 70 trials of eyeblink-conditioning acquisition training, rabbits are given 20 trials of tone-alone extinction training (Moore & Gormezano, 1961).

It is tempting to think of the extinction in Figure 4.10 as simply the unraveling of acquisition. However, in recent years a consensus has been building in support of the idea that extinction is not just unlearning but rather a combination of unlearning and the learning of a new, opposing response to the CS. Specifically, it appears that during extinction, the CS acquires a second "don't respond" meaning that competes with the originally acquired "do respond" association. This suggests that even though the animal (or person) is no longer responding to the CS at the end of extinction training (as seen in Figure 4.10), the learned response is not gone, just unexpressed.

Some of the most compelling evidence for this view of extinction comes from studies that show the original learned response can reappear if the extinction was accompanied by a change in context (such as another room or testing chamber). In one example from the laboratory of Mark Bouton, a CS is paired with a shock in one context (context X) and then extinguished in another context (context Y); then the CS is again presented in context X, and the response is renewed (Bouton & King, 1983). As noted above, the most parsimonious explanation seems to be that there are two associations: CS–US and CS–no US; the context determines which response is retrieved (Bouton, 1991). During initial training, a CS–US association is created in context X

extinction. The process of reducing a learned response to a stimulus by ceasing to pair that stimulus with a reward or punishment.

Figure 4.10 Acquisition and extinction of eyeblink conditioning Percent of rabbits exhibiting conditioned eyeblinks during 70 trials of acquisition and 20 trials of extinction.

Data from Moore & Gormezano, 1961.

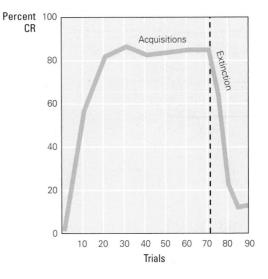

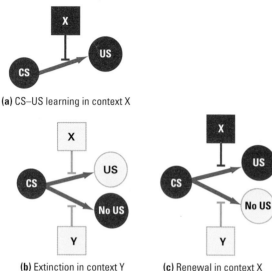

(a) CS–US learning in context X

(b) Extinction in context Y

(c) Renewal in context X

Figure 4.11 An account of extinction and renewal that involves context (a) CS–US learning in context X. (b) Extinction in context Y. (c) Renewal in context X

Information from Bouton, 1991.

(Figure 4.11a); then, in context Y, a CS–no US association is created. At this point, the CS–US association learned in X has not disappeared, even though there is no responding to the CS in context Y (Figure 4.11b). When the animal is returned to context X, the original CS–US association is retrieved, and the response "spontaneously" reappears (Figure 4.11c).

Another way in which extinction can be undone is if a long time passes before the animal is retested with a presentation of the CS. The return of a CR after such a delay is another example of spontaneous recovery (which you previously encountered in Chapter 3, in our discussion of habituation) and was first reported by Pavlov (1927). These findings (seen in almost all forms of classical conditioning) suggest that an association that became dormant following extinction training is not entirely lost.

Further evidence that extinction does not involve the total loss of what was previously learned comes from studies of rapid reacquisition, where a previously extinguished CS is learned more rapidly than a novel CS. Rapid reacquisition suggests that the learned association between a CS and a US is saved during extinction even if the behavioral CR is no longer evident following extinction trials.

Compound Conditioning and Overshadowing

When Robi was a young mother, her two children, Roberta and Mark, would often talk to her (or more often, shout at her) at the same time, competing for their mother's attention. As you can imagine, it was hard for Robi to pay full attention to both kids. The same competition can occur when two cues, such as a tone and light, appear together in a conditioning experiment, a paradigm known as **compound conditioning**. When an animal or person is trained in a tone + light → US compound conditioning paradigm, learning of the compound stimulus usually proceeds much like learning of a simple single-cue stimulus. However, when one of the stimuli, such as the tone, is later tested alone, it becomes apparent that something different has happened. Many studies have shown that the tone will have less association with the US if it is trained in compound than if it had been trained alone in a tone → US procedure. This suggests that two cues, like the two young children, Roberta and Mark, are competing against each other, and neither produces as much learning as it would have had it been trained alone.

However, imagine if Roberta had a soft, quiet voice but Mark was prone to shouting out loud. As much as their mother might want to listen to both equally, it is likely that Mark would be the one more easily heard. Again, this can be analogous to compound conditioning studies: if one of the two stimuli, say the light, is very dim and hard to see, while the tone is loud and salient, the tone is said to overshadow the light during learning. In classical conditioning,

off the mark.com   by Mark Parisi

BELL RINGS, I GET A TREAT... BELL RINGS, I GET A TREAT... IT WENT ON THAT WAY FOR DAYS. THEN, OUT OF THE BLUE ... BELL RINGS, I GET **NOTHING AT ALL!!** NADA! I MEAN, CAN YOU SERIOUSLY CALL MY ATTACK UNPROVOKED?

THE DARK TRUTH ABOUT PAVLOV'S DOG.

Identify the conditioning paradigm illustrated here.

overshadowing occurs when a more salient cue within a compound acquires far more of the share of attention and learning than the less salient cue. For example, the learning that accrues to a loud tone in a loud tone + dim light US compound training paradigm will be far more than to the dim light, because the loud tone is far more salient than the dim light. In contrast, if the tone was very soft and the light very bright, the opposite pattern would be seen, with the bright light overshadowing the soft tone and accruing more learning. Even so, both the cues, when tested individually, command less attention than they would have if they were trained alone and not in a compound.

Dissecting the interactions between cues that co-occur during learning led to fascinating insights into what and how animals are learning during conditioning experiments. From what you read previously in this section, it might appear that animals and people in conditioning studies are only passively responding to which cues do (or do not) go together. However, as you will see in the discussions to follow, conditioning involves a much more subtle form of learning than was previously appreciated, and the subtlety emerges most clearly when two or more cues are present during learning.

Error Correction and the Modulation of US Processing

Chapter 1 introduced Aristotle's argument that contiguity—closeness in time and space—is necessary for a new association, such as that between a CS and US, to be learned. For most of the first half of the twentieth century, psychologists believed that contiguity was both necessary and sufficient: so long as a potential CS and a US occurred with little separation in time and space, animals and people were expected to form an association between them (Hull, 1943). But would it really make sense for animals or people to learn associations between all the simultaneously occurring stimuli that they perceive? Would it even be possible?

The Informational Value of Cues

Imagine you are a struggling stock investor whose livelihood depends on correctly predicting whether the stock market will go up or down the next day. One morning Doris, an eager new stock analyst, walks into your office and says that if you hire her, she will tell you each day which way the next day's market will go. You agree, and during her first week of work, you are amazed to see that she is 100% accurate, correctly predicting each day whether the market will rise or fall. The next week, Herman comes to visit and offers you his services as a stock analyst to predict the market's movements. Would you hire him? Probably not, because he is redundant if you already have Doris; that is, Herman offers no value beyond what you are already getting from Doris. You might say that Doris's early success at predicting the stock market has blocked you from valuing Herman's similar, but redundant, ability to do the same, as summarized in Table 4.4.

A similar situation can occur in medical diagnosis. Consider a young physician who treated a patient, Janae, who came into the emergency room on several occasions in January, each time with a bad stomach ache. She reviews what Janae ate the day before each outbreak. It turns out that each time Janae got a stomach ache, she had eaten the same kind of chocolate that very morning. The physician suspects this may be the cause of the stomach ache, a bad reaction to the chocolate. The next month, Janae comes back to the emergency room, once again with a stomach ache. Again the physician asks her to list everything she ate the day of the outbreak. This time, she notices that Janae ate both chocolate

Table 4.4 Informational redundancy blocks learning

Group	Phase 1	Phase 2	Phase 3 (test)
Stock Prediction	Doris → stock market	Doris & Herman → stock market	*Hire Herman?* "No way; don't need him."
Medical Diagnosis	Janae eats chocolate → stomach ache	Janae eats chocolate & licorice → stomach ache	*Could the licorice be causing the stomach ache?* "Unlikely; Janae should enjoy licorice but avoid chocolate."
Bower & Trabasso (1965). See p. 136 and Figure 4.13	Circle → A Triangle B	Circle + top dot → A Triangle + bottom dot → B	Rectangle + top dot → ? Rectangle + bottom dot → ? "Participants have no idea which is A or B"

and red licorice just prior to her stomach ache. Although it's possible that the licorice caused the stomach ache, the physician dismisses this as unlikely, since she already believes that the chocolate is causing the stomach ache and this theory is sufficient to explain the new occurrence. As schematized in Table 4.4, the physician's recommendation to Janae, given her history of eating candy and getting stomach aches, is to avoid the chocolate but enjoy the licorice.

In both of these examples, new information—or evidence—can be viewed in terms of its informational value, how much new predictive value it gives us relative to what we already know or believe. For the stock investor, Herman offers no additional aid in predicting the market beyond what Doris already tells him. For the emergency room physician, the presence of licorice offers no new explanatory value in understanding the cause of Janae's stomach aches, given that she can already explain the problem as being caused by the chocolate. Research on learning has shown that humans and other animals are similarly sensitive to the informational value of cues in determining which associations they do or do not learn.

Kamin's Blocking Effect

Compare the story of Doris and Herman to the earlier story of siblings Mark and Roberta. In both cases there was competition going on. Mark beat out Roberta for their mother's attention because he shouted louder and was thus the more salient of the two children. In contrast, Doris beat out Herman for the stock-picking job not because she was louder, or even necessarily any better than Herman at the job, but because she got there sooner. From these stories we see that there are two ways to win a competition—by being more salient (i.e., louder) and by getting there sooner. These two situations mimic the two types of cue competition seen in conditioning paradigms. Competition based on salience is, as noted earlier, akin to what happens when overshadowing occurs in compound conditioning. But, a form of overshadowing can also occur between two cues when the associative or predictive value of one of the cues is learned earlier than the other, as suggested by the story of Doris and Herman (and by the chocolate and licorice example, as well). This kind of overshadowing due to temporal priority reflects a sensitivity to the informational value of one cue relative to another, co-occurring cue for making a prediction.

In the late 1960s, several studies of classical conditioning in animals made a similar point: for a potential CS to become associated with a US, the CS must provide valuable new information that helps an animal predict the future. Moreover, even if a given cue does predict a US, it may not become associated with that US if its usefulness has been preempted (blocked) by a co-occurring cue that has a longer history of predicting the US. Much as Doris's predictive value blocked the hiring of Herman, and Janae's prior history of chocolate causing a stomach ache blocked the physician from believing that licorice was the cause, a prior-trained CS can block learning about another, redundant CS that is added later in training (Kamin, 1969).

In a classic study by Leon Kamin, rats were first trained that a light predicts a shock and later trained that a compound stimulus of a light and tone also predicts the shock (Kamin, 1969). Kamin found that, with this training, the rat will learn very little about the tone because the tone does not improve the rat's ability to predict the shock. This phenomenon is now formally known as **blocking**; it demonstrates that classical conditioning occurs only when a cue is both a useful and a nonredundant predictor of the future (Table 4.5).

Kamin's 1969 blocking study is worth describing in detail because of its influence on subsequent theories of learning. In this study, one group of rats (the control group) was trained with a compound cue consisting of a light and a tone; this cue was reliably followed by a shock (see Table 4.5, control group, phase 2). The light and tone constituted a compound CS that the rats learned to associate with the shock US. Later, these rats would give a medium-strong CR to either the tone alone or the light alone, though not as strong a response as to both the light and tone together.

Consider, however, the behavior of Kamin's second group of rats, identified as the experimental, or pre-trained, group in Table 4.5. These rats first received pre-training in which the light by itself predicted a shock (phase 1). From this training, they learned an association between the light CS and the shock US. Next (phase 2), they were given training that paired the light-and-tone compound cue and the shock, just like the control group animals had received. However, unlike the control rats, rats in the pre-trained group were already responding strongly to the light CS when they began the phase 2 compound training. For these rats, the additional presence of the tone provided no new information for predicting the US.

Phase 3 was a testing phase. When the pre-trained rats were tested with the light alone, they continued to exhibit a strong CR to the light, much as they had at the end of phase 1. However, in phase 3, if they were tested with the tone alone, they would give almost no response at all. This suggests that they learned almost nothing about the relationship between the tone and the US, despite the compound training received in phase 2, in which the tone (combined with light) was repeatedly followed by the US (Kamin, 1969). In contrast, rats in the control group, which did not receive phase 1 pre-training, exhibited significant (albeit medium-strength) CRs to both the light by itself and the tone by itself in phase 3. Thus, the blocking phenomenon, exhibited by the pre-trained rats, can

blocking. A two-phase training paradigm in which prior training to one cue (CS1 → US) blocks later learning of a second cue when the two are paired together in the second phase of the training (CS1 + CS2 → US).

Table 4.5 **Kamin's blocking paradigm**			
Group	**Phase 1**	**Phase 2**	**Phase 3 (test)**
Control group	Rat sits in chamber; no training	Tone CS combined with light CS → shock US	Tone CS or light CS: medium CR
Experimental "pre-trained" group	Light CS → shock US	Tone CS combined with light CS → shock US	Tone CS: little or no CR (learning is "blocked")

be summarized as follows: prior training of the light → shock association during phase 1 blocks learning of the tone → shock association during compound (light + tone) training in phase 2. This is very similar to what happened with the emergency room physician. Having previously deduced that chocolate candies lead to a stomach ache, Janae's doctor failed to credit the licorice with any stomach-ache–inducing properties when she later encountered both chocolate and licorice preceding the next tummy ache. For this physician, learning the chocolate → tummy ache association blocked learning of the redundant licorice → tummy ache association (refer again to Table 4.4).

The Rescorla–Wagner Model of Conditioning

The blocking effect posed a challenge for simple theories of classical conditioning. It suggested that cues do not acquire strength solely on the basis of their individual relationships with the US; rather, *cues appear to compete with one another for associative strength*. Thus, in phase 2 of the blocking experiment in Table 4.5, the tone competes with the light, and in the case of the pre-trained group, the tone loses: Since the light already accurately predicts the US, the tone provides no additional predictive information (much as Herman provides no additional value over Doris in predicting stocks, or as knowing that Janae ate licorice presents no additional value for predicting her stomach ache if we already know that she ate chocolate; see Table 4.4).

The blocking paradigm demonstrated that contiguity between a cue and a US is not enough to elicit a CR, contrary to what Aristotle expected. For a stimulus to become associated with a US, it must impart reliable, useful, and nonredundant information (Kamin, 1969; Rescorla, 1968; Wagner, 1969). Apparently, "simple" Pavlovian conditioning is not as simple as psychologists once thought! In fact, rats (and other animals, including humans) appear to be very sophisticated statisticians. But how does one learn which are the most useful and informative cues to remember?

In the early 1970s, two psychologists at Yale, Robert Rescorla and Allan Wagner, were independently trying to understand Kamin's blocking effect and other related conditioning phenomena. Although the two researchers worked at the same university, they didn't realize that they were using the same approach to solve the same problem until they happened to take a train together to a conference and began chatting about their research. To their surprise, they realized that they had each come up with the same idea, and they decided to join forces (Rescorla & Wagner, 1972).

Rescorla and Wagner sought to understand how animals become aware of the informational value of stimuli, and they developed an elegantly simple way to formalize their approach. The key idea behind the Rescorla–Wagner model is that changes in CS–US associations on a trial are driven by the discrepancy (or error) between the animal's expectation (or prediction) of the US and whether or not the US actually occurred. This error is sometimes referred to as the **prediction error**, and how one can learn using these errors is described in the next section.

prediction error. The difference between what was predicted and what actually occurred.

Error-Correction Learning

"I have not failed," said Thomas Edison, "I've just found 10,000 ways that won't work." Like Edison, we can, and do, learn from our failures. Consider Herman, who we saw earlier didn't have much of a future as a stock analyst. His real passion is tennis, and he hopes to become a professional. He practices hours each day, focusing especially on his serve. His goal is to put the ball as far back in the serving zone as possible, but not so far that it goes over the line and is considered a fault. On his first serve of the day, he puts the ball into the middle of the serving zone (where his opponent could easily return it). To serve the next ball better, he adjusts his stance a little, throws the ball higher, and swings harder. This time the ball goes closer to the end of the zone. On the third serve, he throws the ball a little higher still and hits it just a bit harder. This time, however, the ball goes too far; it is a fault. In response to this error, Herman again adjusts his serve. He throws the ball a little less high and hits it a little softer than the last time. This results in a perfect serve. After several tries, correcting his serve each time on the basis of how well he did previously, Herman has learned to hit a ball at just the right height and strength to make it land at the outer end of the service zone: not too close, and not too far.

Herman has learned through a process of trial and error, using a method called **error-correction learning**, in which the errors on each trial lead to small changes in performance that seek to reduce the error on the next trial. Error-correction learning can be summarized by describing three situations representing three types of errors Herman experienced: (1) when Herman hits the ball too close, he changes his next serve to hit the ball harder, so that it will land a little farther; (2) when Herman hits a perfect serve, he tries to do exactly the same thing the next time; and (3) when Herman hits the ball too far, he changes his next serve to hit the ball a little lighter so it lands a little closer next time.

Rescorla and Wagner proposed that there are three key situations to consider in interpreting a prediction error, as summarized in Table 4.6, and they are very similar to the three ways Herman learned from past errors to improve his tennis serve. One is a situation in which either no CS or a novel CS is presented followed by a US, so that the US will be unexpected; this is considered a positive prediction error because there is more US than expected. The Rescorla–Wagner theory expects that the CS → US association should increase proportional to the degree that the US is surprising; that is, the larger the error, the greater the learning. This makes sense because if you failed to predict the US, you want to increase (move in a positive direction) your likelihood of predicting it in the future (given the

Every time Herman serves too far outside the box, he learns to correct his swing, so that next time he hits the ball not so far, exhibiting what kind of learning?

error-correction learning. A mathematical specification of the conditions for learning that holds that the degree to which an outcome is surprising modulates the amount of learning that takes place.

Table 4.6 Error correction and response in the Rescorla–Wagner model and tennis

Conditioning error	R–W model response	Tennis error	Herman's response
Positive error: CS predicts nothing or too little, but US unexpectedly occurs or is unexpectedly strong	Increase association	Ball falls short	Increase strength of serve
No error: CS predicts US, and predicted US occurs	No new learning	Ball lands perfectly	Do same thing next time
Negative error: CS predicts US, but no US occurs	Decrease association	Ball goes too far	Decrease strength of serve

same CS). It is similar to what Herman does when his serve is too short and he positively increases the strength of his serve to send it farther next time.

If, however, a well-trained CS is followed by the expected US, there is no error in prediction (the US was fully predicted by prior presentation of the CS), and thus no new learning is expected. This is similar to what happens when Herman makes a perfect serve; he doesn't want to change a thing from what he did last time. Finally, if the CS predicts a US and the US does not occur, the prediction error is considered negative, and Rescorla and Wagner expect it to be followed by a decrease in the CS → US association. This is similar to what happens when Herman hits the ball too far and he has to reduce the strength of his serve next time.

Associative Weights and Compound Conditioning

associative weight. In the Rescorla–Wagner model of conditioning, a value representing the strength of association between a conditioned stimulus (CS) and an unconditioned stimulus (US).

The Rescorla–Wagner model assumes that each CS has an **associative weight**, which is a value representing the strength of association between that cue and the US. In the blocking experiment described above and in Table 4.5, there would be two cue weights, one for light and one for tone. Think of these weights as numbers that indicate how strongly the CS predicts the US. Before any training takes place, all associative weights are 0.0, meaning that when a potential CS first appears, there is no expectation that any US will follow. These associative weights change through learning as the animal discovers which stimuli predict the US and therefore which should have strong weights.

A critical property of the Rescorla–Wagner model is that the weights associated with one cue can indirectly influence the weights accruing to other co-occurring cues. That is, if a tone and a light are both present on a trial, they will compete for associative strength (much like Doris and Herman compete for the stock analyst job). This competitive property of the Rescorla–Wagner model allows it to account for many important conditioning phenomena, especially those with complex stimuli involving the presentation of multiple stimulus elements (such as tones and lights paired together). Most importantly, this cue-competition property of the Rescorla–Wagner model allows it to account for Kamin's blocking effect as described next.

Using the Rescorla-Wagner Model to Explain Blocking

Consider the simple network model of eyeblink conditioning in Figure 4.12. For every aspect of the real world that the model represents, the model contains a node—a small element that is activated, or "turned on," when the network believes that a certain aspect of the world is or will be present. You can think of these nodes as being something like abstract neurons, or collections of neurons, which process information in a manner analogous to how activation flows through the brain. In the network model of Figure 4.12 there is an input node for each CS (tone and light), an "actual output" node for the eyeblink CR, and a "teaching node" that shows whether or not the US (airpuff) actually occurred and a CR blink would have been appropriate (that is, the "desired output").

Figure 4.12a represents the state of affairs after phase 1 training in which a tone predicts the airpuff US: the tone has acquired an association weight of 1.0 and the light has a weight of 0.0. Now, at the start of phase 2, the light and tone are presented together (Figure 4.12b). The actual output node receives activation equal to the sum of the association weights of all the active (present) cues, which in this case is 1.0 for the tone plus 0.0 for the light, for a total of 1.0. This is the output node's activation in Figure 4.12b. Since the airpuff US is also administered in this trial, the response is correct—and the error is 0.0. Since weight change is determined by the error and the error is 0.0, there is no learning on this trial—or, indeed, on any other phase 2 trial. By the end of

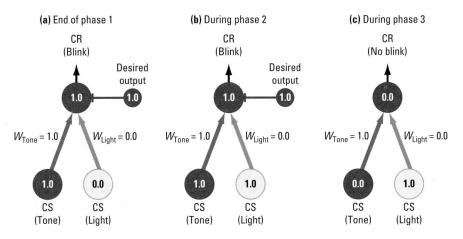

(a) End of phase 1   **(b)** During phase 2   **(c)** During phase 3

Figure 4.12 Blocking in the Rescorla–Wagner model (a) Phase 1 involves repeated pairing of the tone CS with an airpuff US. At the end of this phase, there is a strong weight for the tone input node, which in turn can activate the output node. (b) Phase 2 involves presentation of both tone and light CSs, paired with the US. Since the tone already perfectly predicts the US, causing the output node to be fully activated, there is no output error and no learning occurs. Hence, the weight from the light input node remains at 0.0. (c) Finally, in phase 3, the network is tested with presentations of light alone. Since the weight of the light node was never changed from 0.0, there is no activation of the output node, and no behavioral response occurs. Hence, the Rescorla–Wagner model correctly shows blocking.

phase 2, the network weights will still be the same as they were at the beginning of phase 2: the tone is strongly weighted, and the light is not. A subsequent test presentation of the light alone in phase 3 is shown in Figure 4.12c: There is no association weight on the light input node, so there is no activation of the output node—and therefore there is no response to the light alone. Thus this simple graphical network model representation of the Rescorla–Wagner model shows Kamin's blocking effect, just like the pre-trained animals in Table 4.5.

As compared to the experimental pre-trained animals, the control rabbits (Table 4.5) get no training at all in phase 1, so the expected US starts at 0.0 and remains at 0.0 from start to end of phase 1. In phase 2, where the tone-and-light compound cue is paired with the US, there is a big error (1.0) on the first trial when the US appears totally unexpectedly. Over the course of the training trials in phase 2, the association weights for both the tone and light CSs will rise together until both are equally (but only mildly) associated with the US—but their sum will be enough together to predict the US, leading to an expected US of 1.0 by the end of phase 2 and an error that has been brought down over the course of phase 2 from 1.0 to 0.0. In a subsequent testing phase (phase 3), a medium-strong response is given to either the tone or the light if they are presented individually, because the association weights for both tone and light alone are only at half the strength required to predict the US (since they have always been presented together as a pair, with their associations combined and summed during phase 2).

Influence of the Rescorla–Wagner Model

More than four decades after its publication, the Rescorla–Wagner model is generally acknowledged as the most influential formal model of learning. Its broad acceptance is due to its elegant simplicity and to the fact that it explains a wide range of previously puzzling empirical results. One hallmark of a successful model is that it reveals underlying connections between a series of observations that initially seemed unrelated or even contradictory.

The Rescorla–Wagner model also made surprising predictions about how animals would behave in *new* experimental procedures, and experimenters rushed to test those predictions. This is another feature of a successful model: it should allow scientists to make predictions that could not otherwise be foreseen without the model. Ideally, modeling and empirical work should constitute a cycle in which the model makes predictions that, when tested, provide new empirical data. If the data match the predictions, the model is supported. If not, then the model must be revised. The revised model then generates new predictions, and the cycle continues.

Owing to its simplicity, the Rescorla–Wagner model cannot account for every kind of learning, and should not be expected to. However, many researchers have devoted their careers to showing how one or another addition to the model would allow it to explain a wider range of phenomena. With so many additions, the model may be in danger of losing some of its clarity and appeal. Nevertheless, the Rescorla–Wagner model has been the starting point from which many other promising models have been built, including the models of human learning discussed below.

Error Correction in Human Category Learning

Do concepts such as blocking and models such as the Rescorla–Wagner model apply only to classical conditioning, or might they also provide insights into higher forms of human cognition and behavior, especially those that involve prediction or categorization?

Early research evidence for blocking-like effects in humans came from work by Gordon Bower and Tom Trabasso, who used error-correction–type methods to train college students to categorize objects according to certain predefined rules (Bower & Trabasso, 1964). The students were presented with geometric figures varying in five dimensions: color, shape, number of internal lines, position of a dot, and position of a gap (non-colored examples are shown in Figure 4.13). Phase 1 of the experiment consisted of training the participants by asking them to guess whether each figure belonged to class A or class B; each time, they were told whether they had guessed correctly or not. For example, some participants were trained that all circular shapes belong in class A, while all triangular shapes belong in class B (and all other features are irrelevant), as illustrated by the two

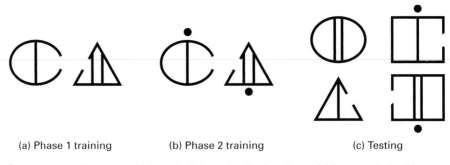

(a) Phase 1 training   (b) Phase 2 training   (c) Testing

Figure 4.13 Human sensitivity to the informational value of cues (a) Examples of stimuli from phase 1 training of the Bower and Trabasso experiment, in which all circular shapes belong in class A and all triangular shapes belong in class B. (b) Examples of stimuli from phase 2. Participants are shown only circles and triangles, and the same circle → A/triangle → B rule still applies. However, now there is also a dot on the top of all class A items and a dot on the bottom of all class B items. (c) A final testing phase. Participants are given novel stimuli to see if they have learned that the dot-top → A/dot-bottom → B rule by itself can predict class membership.

Research from Bower & Trabasso, 1964.

sample stimuli shown in Figure 4.13a, and schematized in Table 4.4. Given enough trials with different stimuli, participants would deduce the rule: circle → A/triangle → B.

Once this lesson was mastered, the experimenter showed participants a slightly different set of figures: now all figures that were circular and thus belonged to class A had a dot on top, while all figures that were triangular and thus belonged to class B had a dot on the bottom (Figure 4.13b). This addition of a redundant cue in phase 2 (position of the dot) parallels the addition of the licorice stimulus in the second month of the physician trying to figure out what caused her patient's stomach ache. Participants in the Bower and Trabasso study continued to perform well by using their old rule of sorting on the basis of shape; the question was whether they would also learn that the dot position by itself predicted class membership.

To test this, the experimenters used new figures, shown in Figure 4.13c. Given a figure with no dot, all participants continued to sort the circles into class A and the triangles into class B. However, when given a figure with a new shape (rectangle), none of the participants correctly sorted on the basis of dot position. Thus, these humans performed much like the physician (who dismissed the possibility that licorice could be causing her patient's discomfort), in that they displayed little or no response to the redundant cue added in phase 2. In effect, prior learning that the shape predicted class membership appears to have *blocked* subsequent learning that the dot position also predicted class membership. More recent studies have verified that this tendency to "tune out" information that is redundant with regard to previously learned cues is pervasive in many forms of human learning (Kruschke, Kappenman, & Hetrick, 2005).

Although the fields of animal and human learning were originally closely intertwined, they became largely divorced from each other in the late 1960s and early 1970s. Animal learning at that time remained primarily concerned with elementary associative learning, while human learning studies focused more on memory abilities, characterized in terms of information processing and rule-based symbol manipulation, approaches borrowed from the emerging field of artificial intelligence. Ironically, this schism occurred just as animal learning theory was being reinvigorated by the new Rescorla–Wagner model in the early 1970s.

In the late 1980s, the expanding impact of computer simulations of network models of human learning (also called connectionist models) revived interest in relating human cognition to elementary associative learning processes. Some of this work was discussed in Chapter 1, when we reviewed David Rumelhart's contributions to the field. Because of the growing influence of these connectionist network models in cognitive psychology, the people working on simpler associative processes, such as classical conditioning, were motivated to re-explore the Rescorla–Wagner model. The connectionist network models adapted their association weights using a generalized (and more powerful) variation on the Rescorla–Wagner model to show how numerous complex human abilities (including speech recognition, motor control, and category learning) might emerge from configurations of elementary associations similar to those studied in conditioning experiments.

An example of one such linking of conditioning and cognition is a simple neural network model developed by Mark Gluck and Gordon Bower to model how people learn to form categories (Gluck & Bower, 1988). In this study, college students were asked to learn how to diagnose patients suffering from one of two nasty-sounding (but fictitious) diseases—midosis or burlosis. The students reviewed medical records of fictitious patients, who were each suffering from one or more of the following symptoms: bloody nose, stomach cramps, puffy

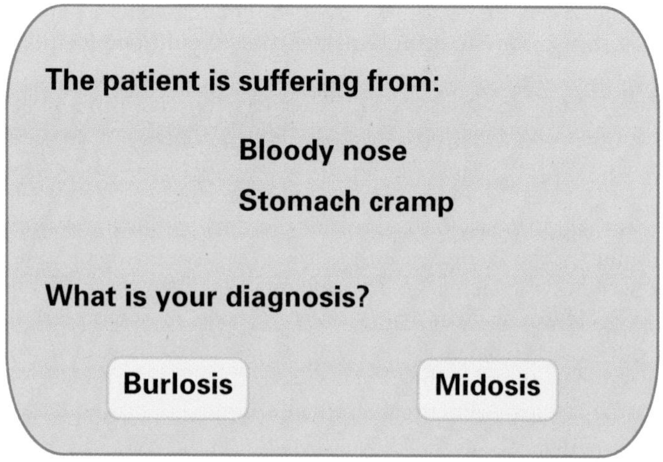

Figure 4.14 A sample training trial in Gluck and Bower's probabilistic categorization task On a particular learning trial, a research subject would see some symptoms (e.g., bloody nose and stomach cramp) and make a diagnosis, and then be given feedback as to whether or not the diagnosis was correct.

> **The patient is suffering from:**
>
> **Bloody nose**
>
> **Stomach cramp**
>
> **What is your diagnosis?**
>
> **Burlosis**   **Midosis**

eyes, discolored gums. During the study, each student reviewed several hundred medical charts, proposed a diagnosis for each patient, and then was told the correct diagnosis (Figure 4.14). The students initially had to guess, but with practice they were able to diagnose the fictitious patients quite accurately. The fact that the different symptoms were differentially diagnostic of the two diseases helped them improve. Bloody noses were very common in burlosis patients but rare in midosis, while discolored gums were common in midosis patients but rare in burlosis.

This kind of learning can be modeled using the network in Figure 4.15. The four symptoms are represented by four input nodes at the bottom of the network, and the two disease categories correspond to the two output nodes at the top of the network. As learning progresses, the weights of the arrows leading from the symptoms to the diseases are updated according to the learning rule from the Rescorla–Wagner model, much as if the symptoms were CSs and the diseases were alternate USs.

Learning and performance in the model works as follows. As the subject learns the correct associations, the connections between nodes and diseases acquire weights that capture the true diagnosticity of each cue for each disease. For example, presentation to a research subject of the chart of a patient with the symptoms "bloody nose" and "stomach cramp" (as in Figure 4.14) is modeled in Figure 4.15 by turning "on" the corresponding input nodes. Activating

Figure 4.15 Gluck and Bower's network model of category learning The arrows from bloody nose and stomach cramp to burlosis and from puffy eyes and discolored gums to midosis are thick, indicating highly diagnostic relationships (that is, heavily weighted cues). The other cues are of only moderate diagnosticity. This figure shows a trial in which a patient presents with two symptoms, bloody nose and stomach cramp; thus, these two input nodes are active (dark red). The other two input nodes represent symptoms that are not present (puffy eyes and discolored gums), and these nodes are inactive (gray). Relative activation levels (dark red and light red) of the two "expected" category nodes are based only on the weight of the input (the current associative weights of these cues) flowing up the arrows from the active and present symptoms (bloody nose and stomach cramp).

Information from Gluck & Bower, 1988.

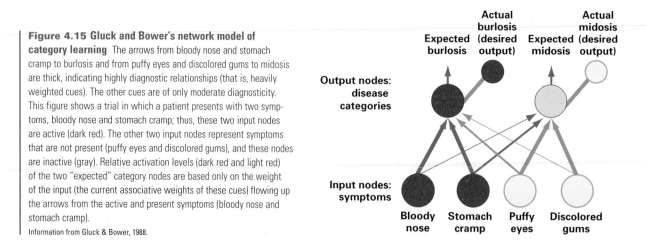

these two input nodes causes simulated neural activity to travel up four weighted connections, shown as arrows: two to burlosis and two to midosis (Figure 4.15). On this trial, burlosis is the correct label, indicated by the very dark "actual burlosis" node. The model is more likely to diagnose the patient as having the disease with the higher activation, namely, burlosis, which in fact is the correct diagnosis.

By analogy with the Rescorla–Wagner model, these output-node activations are equivalent to the network's *expectation* of one disease versus another. After a student guesses at a diagnosis and is told the correct answer, learning in that student is modeled by modification of the network's weights so as to reduce future error, in accordance with the Rescorla–Wagner model's error-correction learning rule. The network model shown in Figure 4.15 incorporates nothing more than the learning principle of the Rescorla–Wagner conditioning model, yet this "animal conditioning" model of human cognition accounts for variations in how the participants classified different patient charts. The model correctly predicted the percent of participants who would classify each of the 14 possible symptom charts as being midosis versus burlosis and also predicted how well the participants were later able to make judgments about the probabilities of the two diseases when they only knew one of the symptoms.

Cue–Outcome Contingency and Judgments of Causality

Another area in which classical conditioning and cognitive studies of category learning have converged is the study of cues that are only partially valid predictors of category membership. Consider, for example, what would happen if Doris, the stock analyst you recently hired, was a good but not perfect stock predictor. Suppose her predictions are correct on 3 out of every 5 days. That rate is not bad, but you yourself may already be able to make accurate predictions about the stock market 3 out of 5 days just from reading the *Wall Street Journal*. In that case, you might decide that Doris doesn't provide you with any additional useful information. If your ability to invest wisely is the same regardless of whether or not Doris is helping you, you probably wouldn't view her as a great asset to your business.

Rescorla showed a similar phenomenon in an animal conditioning experiment that provided additional support for the Rescorla–Wagner model (Rescorla, 1968). His experiment demonstrated that conditioning to a tone stimulus depends not only on the frequency of tone–US pairings but also on the frequency of the US in the absence of the tone. If the US occurs just as often without the tone as it does in the presence of the tone, then little or no conditioning will accrue to the tone. These results suggest that animals are sensitive to the *contingency* of (or degree of correlation between) the potential CS and the US. The Rescorla–Wagner model explains this effect by viewing the experimental chamber itself as a cue presented in combination with (compounded with) the experimentally manipulated tone. The experimental chamber can be thought of as the *context*, that is, the background stimuli that are relatively constant on all trials (rather than being manipulated by the experimenter), both when there is a US and when there is not; these stimuli include the sound, smell, and feel of the conditioning chamber. In the stock investor example, the context includes all the generally available information for investors, such as the stock analyses in the daily *Wall Street Journal*; the potential CSs are the extra tips occasionally provided by Doris.

In the Rescorla–Wagner model, the animal actually experiences the trials in which the tone occurs alone as trials in which a compound cue is present, a cue consisting of the tone CS in combination with the context. The Rescorla–Wagner model expects that the context will, in effect, compete with the tone for the credit of predicting the US. If the US occurs as frequently on context-alone trials as on context-and-tone trials, the context is a more reliable cue, and thus it wins the credit and, hence, the bulk of the associative weight. Therefore, according to the Rescorla–Wagner model, the degree to which the US is contingent on the CS depends on a competition between the CS and the co-occurring background context.

Similar sensitivity to cue–outcome contingencies has also been found in studies of human causal inference. These are studies of how people deduce cause and effect in their environment. In typical experiments, people might be asked to judge which risk factors (smoking, lack of exercise, weight gain) are more or less responsible for some observable outcome, such as heart disease. These studies have shown that increasing the frequency of the outcome in the absence of the risk factor (say, the frequency of lung cancer in the absence of smoking) decreases people's estimates of the causal influence on the outcome—in much the same way that the presence of the US in the context alone decreased conditioning to the potential CS as described above. What are the implications of this finding? For one thing, it suggests that if there is a spike in the frequency of a disease (like lung cancer) but no similar increase in a risk factor (like smoking), people will come to view smoking as less harmful than they did previously. In effect, if you're going to get lung cancer anyway, why not smoke?

Stimulus Attention and the Modulation of CS Processing

Despite the many successes of the Gluck and Bower model in predicting human cognitive data, several limitations of the model became evident in further studies of human category learning. In particular, as a model of category learning, it fails to account for people's ability to actively focus their attention on one or another symptom (such as bloody nose *or* stomach cramp) or to shift or refocus this attention during learning. These limitations echo similar problems of the Rescorla–Wagner model (on which the Gluck and Bower model is based), specifically its inability to account for how attention to stimuli is modulated during learning, especially when animals or people are repeatedly exposed to stimuli that have no consequence.

To better understand where and how the Rescorla–Wagner model (and by analogy the Gluck and Bower model) falls short in accounting for attentional changes, let's consider the example of Moira, the little girl at the beginning of the chapter who learned to run to the corner with money each time she heard the ice cream truck jingle in the distance. What do you think would have happened if, soon after she arrived in the neighborhood, she continued to hear the jingle off in the distance each day, but the ice cream truck never arrived? If weeks later the truck did begin to appear again after the jingle was heard, do you think Moira would so quickly learn to associate the jingle in the distance with the forthcoming arrival of the ice cream truck? Prior exposure to the cue's having been irrelevant (like the jingle without the ice cream truck appearing) retards our ability to learn later that the cue has acquired some new predictive or associative relevance.

This learning about a cue's irrelevance through exposure to the cue alone (with no associated significant event) is quantified by a measure known as **latent inhibition**, a reduction in learning about a stimulus (CS) to which there has been prior exposure without any consequence (that is, no US). The name refers to the fact that the exposure latently (that is, implicitly) appears to inhibit later learning about the cue. This phenomenon was first described in the animal conditioning literature by Robert Lubow and Ulrich Moore (Lubow &

latent inhibition. A conditioning paradigm in which prior exposure to a CS retards later learning of the CS–US association during acquisition training.

Moore, 1959). Lubow and Moore's study was conducted using sheep and goats; however, for consistency with the rest of this chapter (and to facilitate comparison with other studies previously discussed), we will describe their latent inhibition paradigm using rabbit eyeblink conditioning, which has reliably produced the same results.

Table 4.7 **The latent inhibition paradigm**		
Group	Phase 1	Phase 2
Control group	Animal sits in chamber	Tone CS →→ shock US
Experimental "pre-trained" group	Tone CS presented (but not US)	

Latent inhibition studies use two groups of subjects: the first group, the control group, receives no pre-training, and the second group does receive pre-exposure training, as summarized in Table 4.7. Control animals simply sit in their chambers until they are ready for the critical phase 2, in which they are trained to associate a tone CS with an airpuff-in-the-eye US. In contrast, animals in the pre-exposed group are repeatedly exposed to a tone with no US in phase 1 before they undergo the same tone training in phase 2 as the control animals do. Thus, the only difference between the two groups is that one group is pre-exposed to the tone in phase 1.

As illustrated in Figure 4.16, rabbits in the pre-exposed group learn to associate the tone with a puff of air much more slowly in phase 2 than do rabbits in the control group (Shohamy, Allen, & Gluck, 2000). The same kind of slow learning following CS pre-exposure is seen in a variety of species; for example, it is seen in human eyeblink conditioning as well (Lubow, 1973).

Latent inhibition—that is, impaired learning following cue pre-exposure—is problematic for the Rescorla–Wagner model: there is no surprise during the first phase of tone-alone exposure and thus no prediction error. Therefore, the Rescorla–Wagner model expects no learning to occur in phase 1. As a consequence, the Rescorla–Wagner model makes the incorrect prediction that the pre-exposed group should be no different from the control group at the start of phase 2, a prediction clearly disconfirmed by Lubow's studies, as well as by the data in Figure 4.16.

Latent inhibition and similar paradigms that involve learning during mere exposure to apparently neutral cues suggest that there is more going on during conditioning than the error-driven learning characterized by the Rescorla–Wagner model. Chapter 3 introduced some of these non-associative mechanisms, such as habituation and sensitization. To account for latent inhibition and other phenomena beyond the scope of the Rescorla–Wagner model, several alternative theories of conditioning have been proposed, and these are described next.

US modulation theory. Any of the theories of conditioning that say the stimulus that enters into an association is determined by a change in how the US is processed.

Figure 4.16 Latent inhibition in rabbit eyeblink conditioning This graph shows the percent of trials producing CRs in each block of 50 trials during the common phase 2 tone–airpuff training of the rabbits in the study. The rabbits in the control group (dotted line) learned rapidly. In contrast, the rabbits in the pre-exposed group (solid line), who had previously experienced 850 trials of tone-alone presentations in phase 1, learned much more slowly.

Data from Shohamy et al., 2000.

An Attentional Approach to Stimulus Selection

The Rescorla–Wagner model is often called a **US modulation theory** of learning because it proposes that the manner in which the US is processed determines what stimuli become associated with that US. Thus, in the Rescorla–Wagner model, the ability of the US to promote learning is modulated by how unexpected the US is, given the potential CS that precedes it. The error-correction principle of learning described above—the core idea behind the Rescorla–Wagner

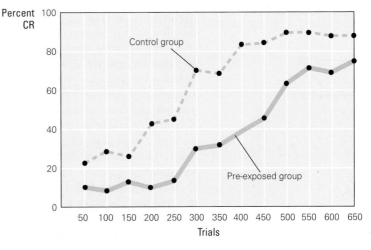

model—is that error modulates the ability of a US to promote learning about the CSs that preceded it.

An alternative class of learning theories focuses instead on the CSs, suggesting various mechanisms that modulate (either increase or reduce) the ease with which potential CSs can be incorporated into an association. For this reason, they are referred to as **CS modulation theories:** they propose that the way attention to different CSs is modulated determines which of them become associated with the US. One such theory, presented by Nicholas Mackintosh in the early 1970s, is based on the observation that people and animals have a limited capacity for processing incoming information (Mackintosh, 1975). This limited capacity means that paying attention to one stimulus diminishes (and hence modulates) our ability to attend to other stimuli.

Remember the blocking analogy in which Doris was the first to establish herself as a reliable predictor of the stock market so that later, when Herman showed up, you gave him little credit for making equally successful predictions? (See also Table 4.4.) The Rescorla–Wagner model argues that this outcome is due to the stock market (the US) already being well predicted by Doris (the first CS), so that no additional value (no learning) is attached to Herman (a potential second CS). However, Mackintosh's view of blocking is quite different. He argues that you come to devote all of your attention to Doris because she has a long history of predicting the stock market, and therefore you have no attention left to pay to Herman. The core idea of the Mackintosh theory is that a previously conditioned stimulus derives its salience from its past success as a predictor of important events (Mackintosh, 1975), and this happens at the expense of other co-occurring cues that don't get access to your limited pool of attention. In essence, Rescorla and Wagner's model lets Herman come in for an interview but doesn't consider him valuable for predicting the market, while Mackintosh's model never lets Herman in the door.

In addition to Mackintosh, several other learning theorists, most notably John Pearce and Geoffrey Hall, have proposed alternative hypotheses of how CS salience is modulated during training (Pearce & Hall, 1980). All of these models share the basic underlying idea that the changes in weighting of the CS are due to modulations of the CS, not of the US. We turn next to review one of the situations in which the CS-modulation theory of Mackintosh does a better job than the US-modulation theory of Rescorla and Wagner in explaining some aspects of learning phenomena.

An Attentional Explanation of Latent Inhibition

Recall that the Rescorla–Wagner model cannot explain cue–pre-exposure phenomena such as latent inhibition because, as a US modulation theory of learning, it only explains learning that takes place when a US is present or when previously trained cues predict the US. Thus, the Rescorla–Wagner model suggests incorrectly that no learning takes place when a neutral (previously untrained) cue is presented. In contrast, Mackintosh's model predicts that the salience of a tone as a potential CS will decrease when the tone is presented without any US because the tone develops a history of predicting nothing. According to Mackintosh, the animal treats these tone-alone trials as if they were the little boy who cried wolf. Eventually the tones (like the boy) are ignored because they don't reliably predict that anything bad or good is about to happen.

Although these CS modulation models have had many successes, especially in explaining behavioral phenomena that are not explained by the Rescorla–Wagner model, they have had less of an impact on the field of learning and memory, in part because they are more complex than the Rescorla–Wagner

CS modulation theory. Any of the theories of conditioning holding that the stimulus that enters into an association is determined by a change in how the CS is processed.

model and because they don't explain as broad a range of behaviors. Moreover, as discussed earlier in this chapter, the Rescorla–Wagner model has been especially influential because it works on the same fundamental principle as the learning algorithms employed in the connectionist network models of human memory used by cognitive psychologists, including both the models of David Rumelhart and colleagues described in Chapter 1 (Rumelhart & McClelland, 1986) and the category learning model of Gluck and Bower (1988) discussed above.

Which view is correct, the CS modulation or the US modulation approach to conditioning? For many years the two camps were viewed as being in direct conflict, with each entrenched on a different side of the Atlantic Ocean: the US modulation view predominated in the United States (where Rescorla and Wagner worked), while the CS modulation view predominated in the United Kingdom (where Mackintosh, Pearce, and Hall worked). However, behavioral and biological studies of conditioning now suggest that *both* views are probably correct; that is, there are likely to be both CS modulation and US modulation mechanisms engaged in learning. As you will see in Section 4.2, part of what has helped resolve this debate is new data from neuroscience that have identified differential neural substrates for these two types of learning processes. This is one more example of the many areas where new forms of data from neuroscience have informed and helped resolve long-standing questions in psychology.

Test Your Knowledge

Contrasting the Rescorla–Wagner and Mackintosh Models

1. Fill in the blanks: The Rescorla–Wagner model explains conditioning as modulation of the effectiveness of the _____ for learning, while the Mackintosh model explains conditioning through modulation of attention to the _____.

2. From the examples below, which of these explanations of Connie's behavior would be best explained by the Rescorla–Wagner model? Which would be better explained by the Mackintosh model?

   a. Connie loved the oatmeal raisin cookies so much, she devoted all of her attention to them. She didn't even bother tasting the chocolate chip cookies.

   b. Connie was happy eating only the oatmeal raisin cookies, and she didn't feel any need to begin eating a new type of cookie.

(Answers appear in the back of the book.)

Other Determinants of Conditioning

Both the US-modulation model of Rescorla and Wagner and the CS-modulation model of Mackintosh have been influential in enhancing our understanding of associative learning (Rescorla & Wagner, 1972; Mackintosh, 1975). They are powerful models precisely because they reduce the behavioral process of learning to its essential elements so that we can see the underlying, fundamental principles at work. However, as a result of such simplification, these models necessarily ignore many of the more subtle facets of conditioning, such as the role of timing in conditioning and the importance of innate biases for associating different stimulus cues.

Timing

The Rescorla–Wagner model and the Mackintosh model both treat classical conditioning as if it were always composed of a series of discrete trials that occur one after the other. Moreover, these **trial-level models** treat each trial as a single event, resulting in a single change in learning. In reality, conditioning is more complex, and a trial consists of many events that can vary in different ways from trial to trial. For example, these models don't describe the timing of the animal's response within a given trial: does the CR occur right after the CS begins, or is it delayed until just before the US occurs? This information is lost in a trial-level model that only describes the aggregate effect of a training trial in terms of an overall association strength. Thus, one cost of having a simple and powerful model is that it can't account for every detail of the animal's behavior.

One important aspect of many conditioning studies is the temporal relationship between the CS and the US. Figure 4.17a illustrates eyeblink conditioning that is conducted using an approach known as **delay conditioning**, in which the tone CS continues throughout the trial and only ends once the US has occurred (this is, in fact, how all of the animals were trained in the rabbit eyeblink-conditioning studies reported so far in this chapter). The term "delay" refers to the delay from time of onset of the CS to the onset of the US (as opposed to them occurring simultaneously). Another form of conditioning also includes a delay, but here the CS is first turned off before the US begins. This training procedure is called **trace conditioning** and is represented in Figure 4.17b; it uses a shorter CS that terminates some time before the onset of the US, requiring the animal to maintain a memory "trace" of the CS to associate with the subsequently arriving US. Although many trial-level learning models treat these types of conditioning as if they were equivalent, many studies have shown that learning behaviors, and the neural substrates associated with them, can be quite different for trace and delay-training procedures.

Even within a simple delay-training procedure such as that shown in Figure 4.17a, variations in the **interstimulus interval (ISI)**, the temporal gap between the onset of the CS and the onset of the US, can have significant effects. For eyeblink conditioning in the rabbit, the optimal ISI for fastest learning is about one-quarter of a second (250 msec), as shown in Figure 4.17c.

trial-level model. A theory of learning in which all of the cues that occur during a trial and all of the changes that result are considered a single event.

delay conditioning. A conditioning procedure in which there is no temporal gap between the end of the CS and the beginning of the US, and in which the CS co-terminates with the US.

trace conditioning. A conditioning procedure in which there is a temporal gap between the end of the CS and the beginning of the US.

interstimulus interval (ISI). The temporal gap between the onset of the CS and the onset of the US.

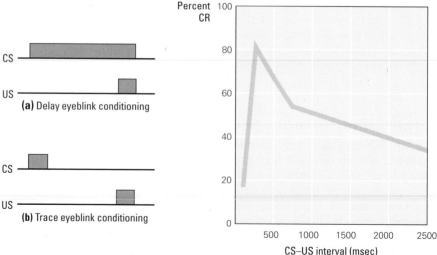

Figure 4.17 Delay and trace forms of eyeblink conditioning (a) In delay conditioning, the CS continues throughout the training trial and only terminates when the US terminates. (b) In trace conditioning, a short CS is followed by a gap before the US occurs. (c) The percentage of conditioned eyeblinks as a function of the length of the interval between the onset of CS and the US in a delay-conditioning experiment. Data from McAllister, 1953.

Shorter or longer intervals make learning more difficult for the animal and necessitate additional training trials. One of the remarkable aspects of rabbit eyeblink conditioning is that the timing of the CR corresponds exactly to the ISI (see Figure 4.8), so that the eyelid is maximally closed at precisely the moment the onset of the US is expected.

Researchers have begun to integrate both US- and CS-modulation learning theories into unified learning theories that also accommodate some of the subtle temporal aspects of learning. One notable early example is the work of Allan Wagner, who proposed a model called SOP (for sometimes opponent process) that allows both for error-correction learning (US modulation) and for changes in the salience of CS cues (CS modulation), with these events occurring at different times through different processes (Wagner, 1981). Other researchers, too, have argued that a full understanding of classical conditioning must involve closer attention to the subtle timing interactions that occur during and between trials (Gallistel & Gibbon, 2000). The need for a better understanding of the role of timing in learning is one of the challenges at the forefront of current learning research.

Associative Bias and Ecological Constraints

The formal learning models described above imply that any arbitrary cue (such as a tone or a light) can be associated with any outcome, be it a shock or food. But is that really true? Consider Mandy, who came down with a strange illness soon after eating escargot (snails) at dinner. The same evening that she ate the snails, she also went to the movies with her date and saw a romantic comedy. Later that night, she woke up with a fever and a terrible case of hives. Both eating the escargot and watching the romantic comedy were events that preceded the illness. But whereas Mandy hasn't been able to eat escargot since that evening, she has not stopped going to see romantic comedies. What this suggests is that not all cues are equally likely to be associated with every outcome. Rather, it appears that there is an associative bias whereby some cues (such as food) are more likely to be associated with some outcomes (such as illness).

This was strikingly demonstrated in a study of **conditioned taste aversion**, conditioning in which subjects learn to avoid specific tastes (Garcia & Koelling, 1966). John Garcia and R. A. Koelling trained rats with compound stimuli consisting of an unfamiliar taste and an unfamiliar tone (a rat's version of watching a romantic comedy while eating snails). One group of rats were then injected with a poison that made them ill. A second group of rats were given an electric shock instead (Table 4.8). Which cue would the rats in each group "blame" for their illness or shock, the taste or the tone stimulus? To see which cues were most readily associated with which outcomes, the experimenters subsequently tested the rats with each of the cues independently: on some test trials the rats were given food with the same novel taste but no tone, while on other test trials, the rats were presented with the tone but no food.

What the researchers found was that the rats in the poison group were far more likely to associate the taste stimulus with their illness than to associate the tone with their illness (much as Mandy would be more likely to blame snails rather than romantic comedies for her illness). In contrast, the rats in the shock group were more fearful in the presence of the tone stimulus than when they encountered the taste stimulus. Garcia and his colleagues concluded that taste is a more effective

conditioned taste aversion. A conditioning preparation in which a subject learns to avoid a taste that has been paired with an aversive outcome, usually nausea.

If Mandy gets sick next morning, will she blame the escargot or the movie she saw? What does that illustrate?

Mark Gluck

Table 4.8 **The Garcia–Koelling taste-aversion study**		
Group	**Phase 1**	**Phase 2**
Poison group	Tone + taste → poisoning	Tone → ?
Shock group	Tone + taste → shock	Taste → ?

stimulus for learning to predict illness but that an audio cue is more effective for learning to predict a shock. Clearly, rats, like people, have prior biases about what should predict what. This isn't to say that you couldn't be trained to throw up at romantic comedy movies, but it would be much harder (and require more training) than Mandy learning to avoid the taste of escargot.

Remember the quail that were trained to associate a light with sex? Although the quail were able to learn this association following many trials of training, Domjan and colleagues found that quail could be conditioned much faster and more robustly if the CS, rather than being an arbitrary cue like a light, were something that is naturally associated in the wild with available females. These cues included the sight of a female at a distance or the sight of a female's head when the rest of her body is hidden in the underbrush (Cusato & Domjan, 1998).

Why are both Mandy and Garcia's rats more likely to associate food, rather than other cues, with getting sick? The answer may have to do with the potential *causal* relationship between eating food and getting sick that is a very real part of a person's or other animal's natural environment. In contrast, there is unlikely to be a natural causal relationship between watching a movie (good or bad) or hearing a tone and getting sick. Perhaps a sensitivity to the likely causal relationships is what guides and biases associative learning in animals. The best predictors of future events are the causes of those events, or at least their detectable indicators (Dickinson, 1980). Thus, it would make evolutionary sense for humans and other animals to be biased toward learning associations that correspond to causal relationships in the ecological niches in which the animals live and evolve.

Interim Summary

- Classical conditioning involves learning about the predictive nature of stimuli in the environment, that is, what cues predict desirable or undesirable events. If an unconditioned stimulus, US, is repeatedly and reliably preceded by a neutral stimulus, such as a bell, that neutral stimulus can become a conditioned stimulus, or CS, that evokes an anticipatory response, called the conditioned response, or CR. Conditioned responses are anticipatory responses that prepare an animal for the expected US.

- The pairing of a potential CS with a US is not sufficient for conditioning to occur. Rather, for a CS to become associated with a US, it must provide valuable new information that helps an animal predict the future. Even if a given cue is predictive of a US, it may not become associated with that US if its usefulness has been preempted ("blocked") by a co-occurring cue that has a longer history of predicting the US.

- Rescorla and Wagner (1972) argue that learning should occur in proportion to the degree to which the US is unexpected when it is experienced. A key assumption in the Rescorla–Wagner model is that when there are multiple CS cues present, the expectation (or prediction) of the US is calculated as the sum of the association weights of all of the cues present on that trial.

Although all animals show classical conditioning, this cartoon reminds us that not all animals will condition equally well to the same CSs and USs. If Pavlov had used cats rather than dogs, what CSs and US might he have used instead of bells and meat?

Bradford Veley/www.CartoonStock.com

- CS-modulation theories of learning (like Mackintosh's model) presume that limits in attentional capacity cause attention to one stimulus to decrease our ability to attend to other stimuli. In contrast, the Rescorla–Wagner model is a US-modulation theory of learning because it describes the learning of associations as depending on how accurately the US is predicted based on all available information. Current behavioral and biological studies of conditioning now suggest that both CS-modulation and US-modulation mechanisms are likely to be involved in learning.

- Taste is more effective than an audiovisual stimulus for learning to predict illness, while an audiovisual cue is more effective for learning to predict a shock. One interpretation of this difference is the potential causal relationship between eating food and getting sick that is part of the animal's natural ecological environment.

4.2 Brain Substrates

Pavlov was a physiologist. When he discovered associative learning in his dogs in the early 1900s, he was naturally interested in understanding the brain mechanisms responsible for it. He even conducted a few experiments examining how cortical lesions affect conditioning. However, at the beginning of the last century, the technology for observing the brain's inner workings was not highly developed. Only in recent years have scientists gained knowledge and techniques that allow detailed study of the neural circuits for conditioning. We review here two neural systems, one in mammals and the other in invertebrates, that illustrate how studies of the neural bases of conditioning have yielded insights into the circuits, cells, molecules, and genes controlling the formation of new memories.

Mammalian Conditioning of Motor Reflexes

As you saw in Figure 2.4, the **cerebellum** sits just behind and slightly below the rest of the brain and looks like a miniature brain itself. In fact, the name *cerebellum* is Latin for "little brain."

In the early 1980s, Richard Thompson and his coworkers made a startling discovery: small lesions in the cerebellum of rabbits permanently prevented the acquisition of new classically conditioned eyeblink responses and abolished retention of previously learned responses (Thompson, 1986). Thompson and his colleagues have studied the cerebellum and its role in motor-reflex conditioning for more than 25 years. Their work provides an instructive example of how support for a theory can be strengthened by converging evidence from a variety of scientific methods, such as electrophysiological recordings, brain stimulation, experimental lesions, temporary inactivation of brain structures, and genetically mutated animals (Thompson & Steinmetz, 2009).

The cerebellum has two main regions, as diagrammed in Figure 4.18. Lying along its top surface is the *cerebellar cortex*, which contains certain large, drop-shaped, densely branching neurons called **Purkinje cells**. Beneath the cerebellar cortex lies a collection of cells called the *cerebellar deep nuclei*, one of which is the **interpositus nucleus**. There are two major sensory-input pathways to the cerebellum: the CS input pathway and the US input pathway. The CS input pathway is shown in purple in Figure 4.18. (Not all the cells in the cerebellum are shown here, only the cells and pathways critical for understanding the cerebellar circuits for motor-reflex conditioning.) CS pathways from elsewhere in

Purkinje cell. A type of large, drop-shaped, and densely branching neuron in the cerebellar cortex.

interpositus nucleus. One of the cerebellar deep nuclei.

Figure 4.18 Cerebellar circuits for motor-reflex conditioning in mammals A schematic diagram of the cerebellar circuits for conditioning. The CS input pathway is purple, the CR output pathway is red, and the US input pathway is green. Excitatory synapses are shown as arrows, and inhibitory synapses terminate with a rectangle.

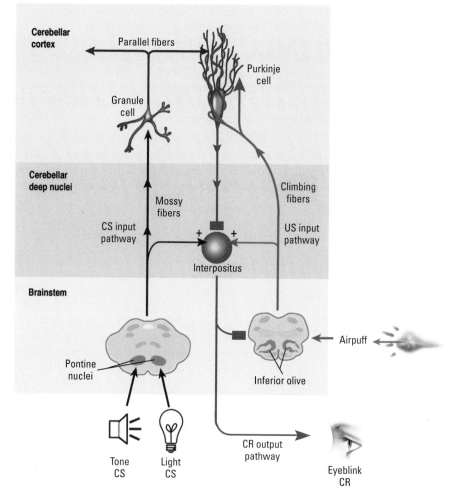

inferior olive. A nucleus of cells with connections to the thalamus, cerebellum, and spinal cord.

the brain project first to an area in the brainstem called the pontine nuclei. The pontine nuclei have different subregions for each kind of sensory stimulation. Thus, a tone CS would travel to one area of the pontine nuclei and a light CS to another. This CS information then travels up to the deep nuclei of the cerebellum along axon tracts called the mossy fibers, which branch in two directions. One branch makes contact with the interpositus nucleus. The other branch projects up toward the cerebellar cortex (by way of the granule cells and other cells not shown) and across the parallel fibers, and connects to the dendrites of the Purkinje cells.

The second sensory-input pathway, shown in green, is the US pathway. An airpuff US to the eye activates neurons in the **inferior olive**—a structure in the lower part of the brainstem—which in turn activates the interpositus nucleus. In addition, a second branch of the pathway from the inferior olive projects up to the cerebellar cortex by means of the climbing fibers (Figure 4.18). Each climbing fiber extends to and wraps around a Purkinje cell. The climbing fibers have a very strong excitatory effect on the Purkinje cells, indicated in Figure 4.18 by the large arrowhead at this synaptic junction.

Complementing these two converging input pathways is a single output pathway for the CR, shown in red, which starts from the Purkinje cells. The Purkinje cells project down from the cerebellar cortex into the deep nuclei, where they form an inhibitory synapse (shown as a red rectangle) with the interpositus nucleus. To produce an eyeblink response, output from the interpositus nucleus travels (via several other intermediary cells) to the muscles in the eye to generate the eyeblink CR. You may notice that Figure 4.18 also includes an inhibitory pathway from the interpositus to the inferior olive, but we will postpone discussion of this pathway until later in the chapter. The unconditioned response (UR) pathway is not shown in Figure 4.18 because that is an innate response; it is not learned and does not originate in, or require, the cerebellum. Instead, it is a reflex circuit, similar in principle to the spinal reflexes you read about in Chapter 2.

The most important thing to note about this circuit (as diagrammed in Figure 4.18) is that there are two sites in the cerebellum where CS and US information converge and, thus, where information about the CS–US association might be stored: (1) the Purkinje cells in the cerebellar cortex and (2) the interpositus nucleus. These two sites of convergence are intimately interconnected in the output pathway: the Purkinje cells project down to the interpositus nucleus with strong inhibitory synapses.

Electrophysiological Recording in the Cerebellum

When an electrode is inserted into the interpositus nucleus (one of the two sites where CS and US information converge and the final exit point of CR information from the cerebellum), the recordings of spiking neurons during conditioned eyeblink responses display a pattern that corresponds very closely to the pattern of the eyeblinks themselves, as seen in Figure 4.19a, taken from a rabbit after one day of tone CS–US training (McCormick & Thompson, 1984). The main difference between the two patterns is that the neural activity occurs just a few milliseconds before the actual behavior. The upper blue line shows the eyeblink behavior (the extent of eyelid closure over time), while the lower graph shows

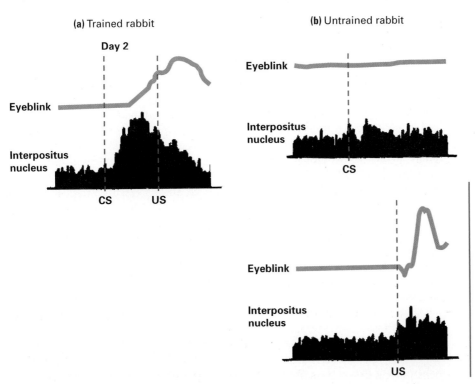

(a) Trained rabbit

Day 2

Eyeblink

Interpositus nucleus

CS   US

(b) Untrained rabbit

Eyeblink

Interpositus nucleus

CS

Eyeblink

Interpositus nucleus

US

Figure 4.19 Electrophysiological recordings in the rabbit cerebellum during classical conditioning (a) Response of a trained rabbit to the CS. (b) Response of an untrained, naive rabbit to the CS alone (top) and to the US alone (bottom). The blue lines show the eyeblink behavior (the extent of eyelid closure over time), while the graphs below them show the frequency of neuronal firing in the interpositus nucleus.
Data from McCormick and Thompson, 1984.

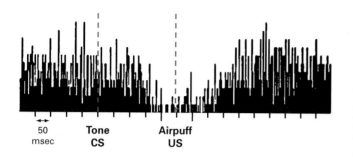

Figure 4.20 Purkinje cell activity in a well-trained rabbit The Purkinje cell's normal high rate of firing is halted in response to the CS and resumes after the US has occurred.

Data from R. F. Thompson.

the frequency of neuron firing in the interpositus nucleus, averaged over several rabbits and several trials.

Researchers have also recorded unpaired CS- or US-alone trials in naive rabbits. In both cases, where there is no CR (eyeblink), there is no activity in the interpositus nucleus, as seen in Figure 4.19b. The lack of substantial interpositus activity in a US-alone trial (despite a strong eyeblink UR) confirms that the cerebellum is responsible for conditioned eyeblink CRs only and not for the unconditioned eyeblink URs.

Figure 4.20 shows the firing rates recorded for a single Purkinje cell in a well-trained rabbit, with the time of the CS onset and the US indicated below. Purkinje cells spontaneously fire all the time, even when nothing is happening. However, in a well-trained animal, many of these cells *decrease* their firing in response to the tone CS, as shown in Figure 4.20. Why would the Purkinje cells turn off in response to a CS? Looking back at the diagram of cerebellar circuitry in Figure 4.18, note that Purkinje cells *inhibit* the interpositus nucleus, the major output pathway driving the conditioned motor response. Shutting off the Purkinje cells removes inhibition from the interpositus, freeing the interpositus to fire (as in Figure 4.19a).

Brain Stimulation as a Substitute for Behavioral Training

What if we knew exactly which pathways in your brain would change as a result of reading the words on this page? If so, we might be able to put electrodes in your brain and electrically stimulate those pathways in just the right pattern, at just the right time, to mimic the effect of reading this text. If that were possible, you wouldn't have to bother reading this book any further or studying for the final exam. Instead, you could stimulate a few neural pathways, create a little synaptic change, and then take the final exam and score an A+, even if you had never opened the textbook or sat through your professor's lectures! Science fiction, right? Unfortunately, it is still a fantasy because we don't yet know exactly where or in what way complex learning is stored in the brain. However, for simpler forms of learning, like eyeblink conditioning, this scenario is not only possible, it's been done.

Through electrical brain stimulation of the CS and US pathways shown in Figure 4.18, an experimenter can create conditioned eyeblink responses in the rabbit that are indistinguishable from those arising from behavioral training.

Recall that different parts of the pontine nuclei respond to different kinds of sensory input, such as auditory tones or visual signals, as illustrated in Figure 4.18. It is even possible to find a specific region in the pontine nuclei that responds to a *particular* tone. As a result, it is possible to condition rabbits merely by pairing electrical stimulation of the pontine nuclei (CS) with electrical stimulation of the inferior olive (US), that is, without presenting any external stimuli (airpuff or tone). After training with this type of brain stimulation, rabbits give precisely timed, reliable eyeblink responses the very first time they hear an actual tone corresponding to the pontine nuclear region that was stimulated, just as if they had been trained all along with tones and airpuffs (Steinmetz et al., 1989).

In these studies, direct stimulation of the inferior olive causes the rabbit to blink and can be substituted for an airpuff US, as shown in Figure 4.21. Similar conditioning over 4 days of training is seen whether an airpuff US (dashed line)

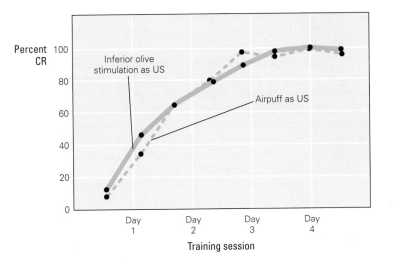

Figure 4.21 Substituting stimulation of the inferior olive for a US Four days of training using stimulation of the inferior olive as the US (solid line) produces the same amount of conditioned eyeblink response as four days of training with an airpuff US (dotted line).
Data from Steinmetz et al., 1989.

or a stimulation of the inferior olive (solid line) is used (Steinmetz, Lavond, & Thompson, 1989).

Thus, rabbits that have had their inferior olives and pontine nuclei electrically stimulated will "pass the eyeblink test" much as if they had gone through days of tone–airpuff training. Like the science fiction fantasy alluded to earlier, stimulating the correct pathways creates learning that seems indistinguishable from conditioning in a rabbit that has gone through the usual training with tones and airpuffs.

Impaired Conditioning Following Cerebellar Damage

Another experimental approach for investigating the neural bases of classical conditioning is to introduce brain lesions—that is, to selectively remove small areas of the brain—and observe the consequences. Recall that the interpositus nucleus (see Figure 4.18) projects information about the CR out of the cerebellum. Thus, without the interpositus nucleus, you would expect that there could be no CR. This is exactly what Thompson and colleagues found: removing even 1 cubic millimeter of tissue from the interpositus nucleus completely and permanently abolished all previously learned conditioned responses and prevented all future eyeblink learning.

In contrast to lesions of the interpositus, which totally abolish learned eyeblink CRs, lesions of the cerebellar cortex (including the Purkinje cells) disrupt, but do not eliminate, eyeblink conditioning. Animals with lesions of the cerebellar cortex show small, poorly timed conditioned CRs (Perret, Ruiz, & Mauk, 1993). Recently, researchers have developed mutant mice with a genetic variation that causes selective degeneration of Purkinje cells. These mutant mice are slow at learning eyeblink conditioning, much like animals that have their cerebellar cortex physically removed (Chen, Bao, Lockard, Kim, & Thompson, 1996). Together, these lesion and mutant studies provide strong converging evidence that the interpositus nucleus is involved in the formation and execution of the conditioned response, while the cerebellar cortex is involved in response timing.

Given the critical role of the cerebellum in motor-reflex conditioning, it is not surprising that patients with cerebellar damage display significant deficits in acquiring the eyeblink conditioning. Such patients are slower to learn the CR and show low overall frequency and abnormal timing of CRs (Daum et al., 1993). Interestingly, patients who have undergone surgery that spares the deep nuclei are able to acquire a little conditioning, while patients with more extensive cerebellar damage show no conditioning at all. It is important to note that cerebellar damage does not impair all forms of associative learning. For example, cerebellar patients perform within the normal range on learning verbal associations, such as matching names with faces, which suggests that other areas of the brain play a role in these more abstract tasks (Daum et al., 1993). There is also a clear lateralization of cerebellar involvement in eyeblink conditioning: damage to the left cerebellum interferes only with conditioning to the left eye, while damage to the right cerebellum interferes only with conditioning to the right eye; this is true in both rabbits and humans (Thompson & Krupa, 1994; Woodruff-Pak & Lemieux, 2001).

Genetics offers additional insights into human eyeblink conditioning. Irene Daum and colleagues have studied several groups of patients in whom chromosomal irregularities cause abnormalities and degeneration in either the cortical Purkinje cells or the deep nuclei (Daum et al., 1993). They found that patients with genetic abnormalities of the deep nuclei are severely impaired at acquiring the eyeblink CRs, while those with abnormalities in the Purkinje cells show more mixed results. These genetic studies provide additional evidence that the deep cerebellar nuclei are essential for learning the CR, while the Purkinje cells in the cerebellar cortex exert some modulating but nonessential influence on this learning.

Error Correction through Inhibitory Feedback

As described in Chapter 2, long-term potentiation (LTP) of a synapse occurs when simultaneous activity in two adjoining neurons leads to a strengthening of the connecting synapse. LTP is a mechanism for synaptic change that occurs whenever two adjoining neurons fire at the same time and is thus much simpler than the error-correcting rule of the Rescorla–Wagner model, in which associative changes depend on many inputs (such as all the CSs present on a trial). Given its complexity, the Rescorla–Wagner model of learning probably does not describe what takes place in a learning brain at the cellular level, but the error-correction mechanisms the model predicts do appear to emerge from brain circuits.

If you look again at the cerebellar network in Figure 4.18, you will see an additional pathway within the cerebellum we have not yet discussed. This inhibitory feedback pathway projects from the interpositus nucleus to the inferior olive. In a well-trained animal, the production of a CR, through activation of the interpositus nucleus, will in turn inhibit the inferior olive from sending US information to the Purkinje cells in the cerebellar cortex (Sears & Steinmetz, 1991). This means that activity in the inferior olive will reflect the actual US minus (due to inhibition) the expected US, where the expected US is measured by the interpositus activity that drives the CR. Actual US minus expected US: sound familiar? It should. This is the same difference (actual US minus expected US) that the Rescorla–Wagner model uses to calculate the prediction error on a trial, which is then used to determine how much weight should accrue to the CS association.

If the inferior olive is where the brain codes the prediction error during conditioning, then we should be able to predict changes in the firing of the inferior olive based on the Rescorla–Wagner model (Gluck, Reifsnider, & Thompson, 1990; Gluck, Allen, Myers, & Thompson, 2001). During CS–US acquisition training, the prediction error diminishes on each successive learning trial. Thus, we should expect to see inferior olive activity in response to the US diminish the more the US is predicted by the trained CS. Eventually, when the CR is well learned, there should be very little activity in the inferior olive (that is, when error in the Rescorla–Wagner model is close to zero). What happens matches the predictions exactly: inferior olive activity starts off high early in training and then gradually diminishes as the conditioned response is acquired (Sears & Steinmetz, 1991).

This interpretation of how the cerebellar circuits compute the changes in association weight called for in the Rescorla–Wagner model implies that Kamin's blocking effect (the clearest experimental evidence for error-correction learning) should depend on the inhibitory pathway from the interpositus to the inferior olive. This prediction was confirmed in a study by Thompson and colleagues. The researchers first trained rabbits to give reliable eyeblink responses to a tone CS and then injected a drug into the interpositus that temporarily disabled the inhibitory connection from the interpositus to the inferior olive. With this pathway disabled, they predicted, the inferior olive's activity would reflect the presence of the actual US and no longer the expected US.

The rabbits were then given phase 2 blocking training, in which a compound tone-and-light CS was paired with the US. The rabbits showed high inferior olive activity whenever the US was presented, whether or not a conditioned response was generated. As a result, in phase 3, the rabbits gave a strong response to the light CS. In other words, by disabling that one inhibitory pathway which is essential for the actual US minus expected US computation, Thompson and colleagues were able to "*block*" blocking" (Kim, Krupa, & Thompson, 1998). These and related results suggest that the cerebellar–inferior olive circuit plays a role in the execution of Rescorla and Wagner's error-correction rule.

Test Your Knowledge

The Cerebellum in Motor Reflex Conditioning

1. What is the role of the Purkinje cells in the cerebellar cortex? Discuss the evidence that suggests this.
2. What are the two main cerebellar regions and the major sensory-input pathways to the cerebellum? Where do these two pathways in the cerebellum converge?
3. How do electrophysiological recordings in the rabbit cerebellum during classical conditioning demonstrate that the cerebellum is responsible for conditioned responses and not for unconditioned responses?

(Answers appear in the back of the book.)

The Hippocampus in CS Modulation

Error correction as explained by the Rescorla–Wagner model is only one mechanism at work in classical conditioning. Another, CS modulation, was suggested, as noted above, by the theories of Mackintosh and of Pearce and Hall. Here we briefly discuss some of the brain systems that appear to govern these mechanisms for modulating the processing of CS cues.

As you learned in Chapter 2, the hippocampus is a string-bean–shaped structure that lies, in humans, just inward from the ears. Figure 4.22 shows the hippocampus in various species.

The hippocampus is not necessary for learning new conditioned responses. For example, animals or humans with hippocampal damage are able to learn a basic conditioned eyeblink response quite normally. Nevertheless, electrophysiological recordings of animals show that the hippocampus is very active during conditioning, especially early in training. What role does the hippocampus

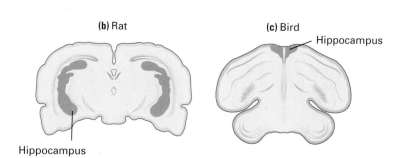

(a) Human

Hippocampus with medial temporal lobes

Figure 4.22 The hippocampus in different species of animals, including humans The medial (inner) part of the temporal lobes contains the hippocampus, the amygdala, and several nearby cortical areas.

play in conditioning? One way to find possible clues to its role is to look at more complex conditioning paradigms, such as latent inhibition (described in Table 4.7). As you learned in Section 4.1, latent inhibition is demonstrated when, before training, an organism is exposed to a cue unassociated with a US; later, during conditioning, the organism is then slow to learn that the cue does predict a US.

As you also learned, the Rescorla–Wagner model is *not* able to explain the phenomenon of latent inhibition. If the Rescorla–Wagner model's error-correction process cannot explain latent inhibition and if the cerebellum implements the error-correction principle, then perhaps other brain regions involved in classical conditioning besides the cerebellum are responsible for latent inhibition. Might the hippocampus be such a region? If so, then the animal learning theories that capture behavioral phenomena other than error-correction learning might provide us with some ideas of what the hippocampus may do during classical conditioning.

The CS modulation theories of Mackintosh and of Pearce and Hall, discussed earlier in this chapter, suggest that to find the system responsible for latent inhibition and related phenomena, we should look for a system involved in determining the salience of sensory cues. If the hippocampus is needed for CS modulation effects in classical conditioning, then an animal *without* a hippocampus should *not* exhibit CS modulation effects such as latent inhibition. In fact, this is exactly what researchers have found: removing the hippocampus (and associated cortical input regions) eliminates the latent inhibition effect in classical conditioning of the rabbit eyeblink reflex (Solomon & Moore, 1975; Shohamy, Allen, & Gluck, 2000).

Many other behavioral phenomena that cannot be explained by the Rescorla–Wagner model are also found to disappear in animals that have lesions to the hippocampus and surrounding brain regions. This suggests that the Rescorla–Wagner model may be better described as a model of the cerebellar contributions to motor-reflex conditioning in hippocampal-lesioned animals than as a model of conditioning in healthy, intact animals. That is to say, the model applies best to the brain regions responsible for error-correction learning, such as the cerebellum, but does not explain the additional contributions of the hippocampus.

What functional role, then, does the hippocampus play in classical conditioning of motor reflexes such as the eyeblink response? If the hippocampus is necessary for latent inhibition and other forms of CS modulation, we might infer that the hippocampus plays a role in determining how sensory cues are processed before they are used by the cerebellum to form long-term memory traces.

Further discussion of the role of the hippocampus in processing sensory relationships while remembering new facts and events will be discussed in Chapter 6. Later, in Chapter 9, we describe some specific theories about how the hippocampus modulates sensory processing in various forms of learning and memory.

Invertebrates and the Cellular Basis of Learning

Chapter 3 introduced you to the sea snail *Aplysia* and studies by Eric Kandel and colleagues on the neural substrates of two forms of non-associative learning: habituation and sensitization. To briefly recap, habituation occurs when *Aplysia's* siphon (see Figure 3.9) is repeatedly but lightly touched. Initially this results in a gill-withdrawal reflex. However, each subsequent stimulation of the siphon elicits a progressively smaller response. The circuit for this learned response includes a sensory neuron (activated by touching the siphon) that makes an excitatory synapse with a motor neuron that controls the gill withdrawal (see Figure 3.10). The neural mechanism for habituation is thought to be a progressive decrease in the number of neurotransmitter (in this case, glutamate) vesicles available in the sensory neuron's axon for each successive stimulation of the siphon. In contrast, sensitization is a global increase in responding to all or most stimuli following an unpleasant stimulus, such as an electric shock to *Aplysia's* tail. The tail shock activates modulatory interneurons that release serotonin onto the axon terminals of all the sensory neurons that project to the gill-withdrawal motor neuron. Serotonin increases the number of glutamate vesicles released when the sensory neuron is stimulated. This results in the generalized (non–stimulus-specific) increase in gill withdrawal elicited by all future stimuli, including touches on either the siphon or the mantle. The top two entries in Table 4.9 summarize the key differences between these two forms of non-associative learning.

What do you think would happen if both kinds of stimuli—touching the siphon and shocking the tail—were repeatedly paired? Tom Carew, in collaboration with Kandel and other colleagues, showed that *Aplysia's* siphon-withdrawal reflex can be classically conditioned, as illustrated in Figure 4.23a. When touching the siphon (a potential CS) is repeatedly paired with shocking the tail (the US), an enhanced siphon withdrawal (CR) results in response to subsequent touches of the siphon (Carew, Hawkins, & Kandel, 1983). The enhanced siphon-withdrawal response to the siphon-touch CS following paired training is considerably greater than the generalized sensitization that occurs from presentation of the tail shock alone. Moreover, this classically conditioned

Table 4.9 **Varieties of learning in *Aplysia***

Type of learning	Associative	Stimulus specific	Mechanism(s)	Locus of effect
Habituation	No	Yes	Decrease in glutamate	Cellular process
Sensitization	No	No	Serotonin-induced increase in glutamate	Cellular process
Classical conditioning	Yes	Yes	1. Presynaptic activity–dependent enhancement of glutamate release from sensory neuron	Cellular process
			2. Postsynaptic change in receptors of motor neuron	Structural change
			3. A cascade of intracellular molecular events that activate genes in the neuron's nucleus, causing an increase in the number of sensory-motor synapses	Structural change

(a)

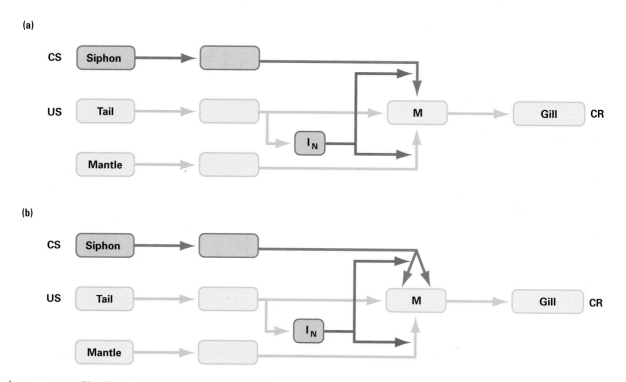

(b)

Figure 4.23 Classical conditioning in *Aplysia* (a) As with habituation and sensitization, classical conditioning (a CR) in *Aplysia* results when three sensory pathways—the siphon (CS), the tail (US), and the mantle—converge on the gill-withdrawal motor neuron (M). The tail pathway includes a secondary pathway through an interneuron (I_N), and this releases serotonin onto the other sensory synapses when the tail is shocked. (b) Long-lasting forms of classical conditioning require the formation of new synapses (the dark green arrow heads) between the sensory neurons of the siphon and the motor neuron. The new synapses are created through a molecular cascade set in motion by the serotonin released by the interneuron.

siphon-withdrawal CR is also specific to the siphon and does not generalize to other stimuli, such as a touch on the mantle.

What happens inside the nervous system of *Aplysia* when these two stimuli are paired? Kandel and colleagues demonstrated that paired training produces an increase in the glutamate vesicles that are released in the siphon's synapse on the motor neuron, much like an exaggerated form of the mechanism for sensitization described in Chapter 3 (Hawkins, Abrams, Carew, & Kandel, 1983). This implies that a cellular mechanism for classical conditioning can be understood as an elaboration of the same cellular mechanism used for sensitization.

The pairing-specific enhancement of glutamate release in the sensory neuron synapse is called an **activity-dependent enhancement** because it depends on activation of the sensory neuron prior to the administration of the US. Earlier in this chapter, we discussed how classical conditioning of the rabbit eyeblink response is sensitive to the order and timing of the tone CS and the airpuff US. The same holds true for conditioning of *Aplysia's* siphon withdrawal: conditioning occurs only if the siphon-touch CS is presented about half a second before the tail-shock US. If the US occurs much later (more than 2 seconds after the CS) or before the CS, nothing other than nonspecific sensitization will occur. Thus, after sensory stimulation, whatever process occurs within the neuron to prime the neuron for an increase in glutamate release has a time course of about a half a second.

To summarize, Kandel and colleagues demonstrated that activation of *Aplysia's* sensory neuron has at least three consequences. First, it causes the motor neuron to fire, by the release of the neurotransmitter glutamate into

activity-dependent enhancement. Paired training of CS and US that produces an increase in the glutamate vesicles released from sensory to motor neurons.

the synapse. Second, it causes a decrease in glutamate vesicles available for any subsequent stimulation of the sensory neuron, resulting in habituation. Third, it primes the synapse, through a series of intracellular events lasting about half a second, so that a subsequent presentation of the neurotransmitter serotonin (released following activation of an aversive tail shock) creates an increase in future glutamate release—resulting in a classically conditioned increase in gill withdrawal following pairing of the sensory stimulus (the CS) and the tail shock (the US).

Presynaptic versus Postsynaptic Changes during Learning

This activity-dependent enhancement of the sensory neuron's release of glutamate onto the motor neuron is a presynaptic form of synaptic plasticity, because like the mechanism for sensitization discussed in Chapter 3, it involves a change in the sensory neuron. However, the story is actually more complicated. Later studies demonstrated that there is also a postsynaptic mechanism for conditioning that involves changes in neurotransmitter receptors on the motor neuron (Bao, Kandel, & Hawkins, 1998). Thus, the mechanisms for classical conditioning in *Aplysia* involve both presynaptic and postsynaptic changes in the circuits connecting the CS and the CR, as summarized in Table 4.9.

One advantage of *Aplysia* as a model system for studying the intracellular molecular pathways of learning is that it is possible to identify key neurons (such as entire memory-trace circuits), remove them from the animals, and keep those neurons functioning in a culture dish. By isolating the key circuits for learning and studying them outside the animal, Kandel and colleagues were able to explore the question, What long-term changes in *Aplysia* circuitry could account for long-lasting forms of classical conditioning? The search for the answer to this question took scientists back to the very origins of who we are—our genes—and has given rise to an important new field, the molecular genetics of memory (and also won Kandel the Nobel Prize for Physiology or Medicine in 2001). As we review in more detail in Chapter 12, genes are stretches of DNA molecules (deoxyribonucleic acid), found in the nucleus of every cell, that encode information needed to produce protein molecules. Most people are aware of the role that genes play in determining how our bodies and brains develop during gestation in the uterus. However, our genes don't stop working after birth; rather, they play a critical role throughout our lives, continuing to maintain and guide further growth and development of our bodies and brains, including the changes that result in long-lasting forms of memory.

Long-Term Structural Changes and the Creation of New Synapses

Using recent advances in molecular biology techniques, Kandel and colleagues were able to show that the serotonin released by *Aplysia's* interneurons following a tail-shock US does more than cause a short-term increase in the sensory neuron's release of glutamate; it also launches a cascade of intracellular molecular events that set the stage for long-term structural changes in the neuron. Following multiple pairings of the CS and US, protein molecules in the sensory neuron's synapse travel back up the axon of the sensory neuron all the way to the cell body. There they switch on genes inside the nucleus of the neuron that in turn set in motion the growth of new synapses (Figure 4.23b).

More recent work by Kandel and others has identified two proteins that are found inside neurons and that play critical regulatory roles in this synapse-creation process. The first protein, CREB-1, activates genes in the neuron's nucleus that initiate the growth of new synapses. The second protein, CREB-2, plays an opponent role, inhibiting the actions of CREB-1. The creation of new synapses during learning requires a cascade of processes inside the cell that activate CREB-1 and suppress CREB-2.

What do you think would happen if functioning of the CREB-1 protein was impaired? Kandel and colleagues demonstrated that if CREB-1 is rendered inactive by injection of molecules into the neuron that compete with CREB-1's ability to activate genes for new synapses, the circuits subsequently fail to show long-lasting forms of associative learning (Dash, Hochner, & Kandel, 1990). Most important, the inactivation of CREB-1 does not affect the short-lasting forms of learning that depend only on increased glutamate release. This study provided critical evidence for a dissociation between short-lasting forms of learning, which do not require the CREB-1 protein, and long-lasting forms, which do.

In a related study, Kandel and colleagues showed that removing the influence of the opponent protein, CREB-2, had the opposite effect: with the CREB-2 inactivated, long-lasting learning occurs rapidly at the sensory neurons, after even a single exposure to serotonin (Bartsch et al., 1995). The role of CREB molecules in modulating long-lasting forms of memory is not limited to *Aplysia*; increasing CREB-1 in fruit flies (*Drosophila*) allows them to learn much more rapidly than usual, while increasing their CREB-2 blocks the formation of long-term memories, such as those produced in the odor-conditioning task described earlier in this chapter (Yin et al., 1994). The CREB molecules also play a critical role in mammals' learning; studies in mice have shown that activity of CREB-1 in the hippocampus is critical to long-lasting but not short-term increases in neuron-to-neuron associations based on LTP (Bourtchuladze et al., 1994).

Studies of classical conditioning in *Aplysia* have demonstrated that anatomical changes in neural circuits, including the growth or deletion of synapses, are characteristic of long-lasting forms of memory. In contrast, short-term, labile forms of memory are associated with temporary intracellular changes within existing anatomical pathways, including shifts in the location, size, or number of neurotransmitter vesicles, which alter synaptic transmission efficacy. Thus, as was also discussed in Chapter 3, the transition from short-term to long-term learning may be characterized as a shift from transmission-process–based changes within the neuron to structural changes within the neural circuits (see Table 4.9).

Interim Summary

- There are two sites in the cerebellum where CS and US information converges and that might potentially be locations for the storage of the CS–US association: (1) the Purkinje cells in the cerebellar cortex and (2) the interpositus nucleus. The interpositus nucleus is the only output pathway from the cerebellum; it is the route through which the learned response travels to the motor systems that control behavior, such as an eyeblink CR.

- The inferior olive is believed to compute the degree to which a US is unexpected, providing the information necessary to implement Rescorla and Wagner's principle of error-correction learning in the cerebellum.

- The hippocampus is a structure underlying some of the CS-modulation effects in conditioning. This is consistent with data showing that an animal without a hippocampus does not exhibit CS-modulation effects such as latent inhibition.

- Kandel and colleagues demonstrated that activation of *Aplysia*'s sensory neuron by an external stimulation (such as presentation of a stimulus cue) primes the synapse, through a series of intracellular events lasting about half a second, so that a subsequent presentation of serotonin (released following activation of an aversive tail shock) creates an increase in future glutamate release, resulting in a classically conditioned increase in gill withdrawal.

- After multiple pairings of the CS and US in *Aplysia*, protein molecules in the sensory neuron's synapse travel back up the axon of the sensory neuron all the way to the cell body. There they activate genes inside the nucleus of the neuron that in turn set in motion the growth of new synapses.

4.3 Clinical Perspectives

In this final section of the chapter, we focus on two clinical applications of classical conditioning. The first involves recognition of the ways drug addiction and drug abuse are intimately linked to classical conditioning, the other harnesses classical conditioning to reduce the amount of medication needed for treating a chronic disease.

Classical Conditioning in Tolerance to Addictive Drugs

The role of learning and memory in drug addiction is a fascinating topic that we consider from several viewpoints in this textbook. In Chapter 5, we explore the neural mechanisms of reward that are impaired by most drugs of abuse. Chapter 8 discusses the role of the frontal lobes as the brain's executive controller, their importance in inhibiting inappropriate behaviors, and how this role is compromised in drug addicts. In the following discussion of drug tolerance, we see how the behavioral and biological mechanisms of classical conditioning influence another aspect of drug addiction and abuse.

Early in this chapter, we discussed how automatic compensatory responses occur in body systems that have a mechanism for **homeostasis**, the tendency of the body (including the brain) to gravitate toward a state of equilibrium or balance. An addict's tolerance to drugs of abuse such as alcohol, cocaine, or ecstasy develops in the same way. As the addict's body adjusts to the drug effects (through expectation of the forthcoming "high"), larger and larger doses are required to produce the same high the addict experienced on first taking the drug. One way this happens is through conditioning: environmental cues that accompany drug use can classically condition the user to expect to receive the drug. In other words, the environmental cues (people, places, and so on) act like CSs associated with the drug (the US). The intense craving an addict feels in response to these cues is the CR and results from the body's conditioned compensatory response of lowering the levels of the brain chemicals enhanced by the drug in anticipation of the drug's arrival (more on the role of conditioning in drug addiction in Chapter 5).

A potential consequence of such conditioned tolerance is that victims of heroin who overdose are rarely novice users (Siegel, 2001). Rather, they tend to be long-time heroin addicts who have developed a high degree of tolerance to the drug but make the mistake of taking their usual dose in an unusual setting. For example, the situational cues that result in conditioned drug tolerance can include the room in which the drug is usually taken. You may recall reports of rock stars and others dying of heroin overdoses in hotel bathrooms, which were most likely far different from the settings in which they were used to taking their drug. What might have happened is that they overdosed on what was

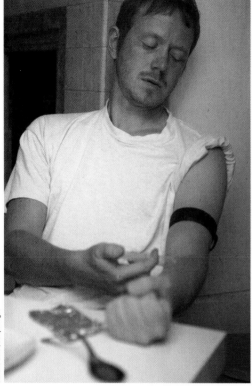

Banana Stock/Getty Images

Why would an addict be more likely to die of an overdose in a hotel room rather than at home?

otherwise their normal dosage of drug because, in this novel setting, their body was not prepared for the large influx of drug that occurred.

Different methods of drug injection are another form of environmental cue that can become associated with drug expectation. One longtime heroin addict is reported to have died of an overdose when, looking for an accessible blood vein, he injected himself in his penis for the first time (Winek, Wahaba, & Rozin, 1999). Without the compensatory response to customary cues, the net effect of his usual dose was far greater than he was used to and resulted in his death (for reports of similar real-life cases, see Siegel, 2001; Siegel & Ellsworth, 1986).

An unusual taste to a beverage can serve as a novel situational cue influencing the effects of alcohol on the brain. This was demonstrated in a study in which college students showed greater cognitive and motor impairments when they consumed a given amount of alcohol in an unusual drink (in this case, a blue, peppermint-flavored beverage) than when they had the same amount of alcohol in a familiar drink, such as beer (Remington, Roberts, & Glauthier, 1977). Perhaps this is yet another reason why people get wilder at holiday parties, when they are drinking alcohol in sweet and bubbly holiday punches.

Research has demonstrated conditioned tolerance in a wide variety of animal species. For example, Shepard Siegel and colleagues examined the effect of cues when heroin is administered to rats (Siegel, Hinson, Krank, & McCully, 1982). Siegel gave three groups of rats a fairly large (for their body weight) dose of heroin. The first group of rats had previously received a lower dose of heroin, administered in the same cage and room where they were later tested with the larger dose (the "same-tested" group in Figure 4.24). The second group of rats had also previously received the lower dose of heroin, but in a different cage and room (the "different-tested" group). Finally, the "first-time tested" group of rats were receiving heroin for the first time.

As shown in Figure 4.24, Siegel and colleagues found that the large dose of heroin almost always (96% of the time) resulted in a fatal overdose in the "first-time tested" rats. In contrast, the "different-tested" group showed some evidence of tolerance; only 64% of these rats suffered a fatal overdose. But the "same-tested" rats, who were tested in the same environment in which

Figure 4.24 A study of drug tolerance Rats in the "first-time tested" group, which had received no prior heroin, showed the highest percentage of fatal overdose. Of those rats that had received a smaller prior dose, the ones tested in the same cage as previously ("same-tested") showed the lowest level of overdoses, while the ones tested in a different cage ("different-tested") showed an intermediate level of overdosing. Data from Siegel et al., 1982.

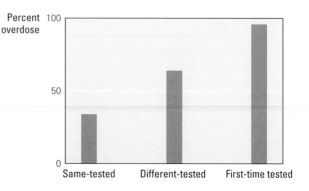

they had previously been administered low doses of heroin, had a mortality rate of only 32%. Thus, these rats were protected from overdose by the conditioned tolerance that they learned during the administration of lower doses of heroin in the same setting.

If drug tolerance is a form of classical conditioning, you might expect that the same rules and principles would apply to it as to eyeblink and other forms of conditioning. This appears to be the case. Recall the paradigm of latent inhibition discussed earlier and shown in Table 4.7: pre-exposure to a CS delays subsequent learning of a CS–US association. If this latent inhibition effect applies to drug tolerance, then pre-exposing an animal to the cues that predict drug delivery should slow down development of learned tolerance to the drug. To test latent inhibition in the context of drug use, researchers have given animals an injection of an inert placebo to pre-expose them to the contextual cues (the sound and feel of getting an injection) of drug use. This pre-exposure does prove to slow down, by latent inhibition, the development of a cue–drug association where the cue is the CS and the drug is the US. In fact, this is exactly what Siegel and colleagues found in studies of morphine tolerance in rats (Siegel, 1983).

Such results provide compelling evidence for the applicability of Pavlovian analyses to learned drug tolerance. They suggest that drug tolerance and the loss of drug tolerance in novel drug-taking environments are mediated by basic processes of classical Pavlovian conditioning.

As you recall from Section 4.1, an extinction paradigm should eliminate (or at least reduce) the association between conditioned cues and conditioned response when the cues are repeatedly presented alone and not paired with the prior US. If drug craving is viewed as a conditioned response, then the same principle of extinction should also apply, and indeed it does. In carefully controlled laboratory studies, rats that became addicted to alcohol showed significant extinction of this addiction through repeated nonreinforced exposure to experimentally manipulated cues that had previously been paired with administration of alcohol (Krank & Wall, 1990). In real life, however, it is very hard to both identify and extinguish all the cues that have become associated with drug use.

Eventually, these and other studies, by deepening scientists' understanding of the role of classical conditioning in drug addiction, may provide new tools to help drug addicts overcome their addiction. For example, perhaps further research on the extinction of conditioned responses will shed light on why addicts so often relapse when they are trying to kick their drug habit. You can read more about this mechanism in "Learning and Memory in Everyday Life: Extinguishing a Drug Habit" on the next page.

Reducing Medication through Classical Conditioning

Classical conditioning—specifically, the pairing of a neutral stimulus with a powerful medication—offers a way of training the body to cope with a disease without continued use of a medication that may have unfortunate side effects. In one example, an 11-year old girl suffering from the autoimmune disease lupus was able to benefit from this approach (Olness & Adler, 1992; Giang et al., 1996). The standard treatment for lupus requires suppressing a person's immune system in order to protect their tissues and organs from being targeted by their own white blood cells. The chemotherapeutic drug the girl would have had to take orally, however, had many severe and disabling side effects.

Extinguishing a Drug Habit

Even in a well-controlled laboratory, extinguishing a cue and keeping it extinguished turns out to be extremely difficult. Mark Bouton and colleagues, studying the extinction of conditioned responses in rats, demonstrated that manipulations such as changing the context, or just waiting a specific period, often result in the extinguished cues reacquiring their conditioned associative properties (Bouton, 2000). Is it any surprise, then, that efforts to adapt extinction methods to therapy for drug addiction have yielded only mixed results at best (Carroll, 1999; Siegel & Ramos, 2002)? The fact that the addict remains susceptible to the first drink or smoke suggests that to extinguish the drug associations, we would have to include small doses of the drugs during cue-exposure therapy to better reproduce and extinguish the cravings. Clearly, such a procedure would result in many practical and legal difficulties. Nevertheless, Bouton's work suggests three principles that can help guide anyone trying to extinguish a habit or association:

1. Since extinction effects are highly context-sensitive, cue-exposure therapy should be conducted in as many different contexts as possible, including those that are part of the patient's everyday life. This will prevent the extinction of drug craving from becoming dependent on any one context (such as a drug rehab center).

2. The extinction training should be spread out over time rather than conducted all at once, because time serves as a powerful context. A 2-week stint in a rehab clinic may not be enough to make a long-term difference. Multiple therapy sessions at different times and in different contexts are more effective.

3. Whenever possible, the cue-exposure therapy should take place in the same contexts in which the original drug habits were acquired. Thus, it is better to go through the cue-exposure therapy at home rather than in a very unfamiliar setting, such as a drug rehabilitation center.

To minimize her need to take the drug for an extended time, her doctors used classical conditioning methods in which she was initially given the drug in a liquid that tasted of cod liver oil and smelled of roses. Following that initial treatment, the doctors continued to give her the same rose-smelling cod liver oil every month but in only half of the months did they include the chemotherapeutic drug. By cutting back her total medication by half, they significantly reduced her suffering from side effects of the drug. At the same time, her body appeared to learn to suppress its own immune system in response to the compound cue of cod liver taste and rose smell, and after several years following this treatment she was still in remission from the disease.

Interim Summary

- The situational cues that result in conditioned drug tolerance can be any sensory cues associated with drug use, including the feel of the needle and the method of injection.

- Rats are protected from heroin overdose by the conditioned tolerance that they learned during the administration of lower doses in the same setting.

- Addiction can be partially reduced through Pavlovian extinction: rats who became addicted to alcohol showed significant extinction of this addiction through repeated non-reinforced exposure to experimentally manipulated cues that had previously been paired with administration of alcohol.

■ Classical conditioning methods can be used to train people to suppress their own immune responses by pairing an immune-suppressing drug with a previously neutral odor and taste.

Synthesis

Classical conditioning is far more than just another behavioral process or tool for investigating brain systems: it is the mother of all memory systems. Evidence of classical "Pavlovian" conditioning surrounds us every day. Like Moira, who runs to the curb when she hears the musical jingle of an ice cream truck, and like Mandy, who has sworn off snails after a bout of illness, everyone has been conditioned by cues in the environment to predict what might follow next.

In recent years, classical conditioning experiments have moved to the forefront of research into the physiological bases of learning because of the exquisite control they afford over what stimuli are presented as cues and because of the highly refined behavioral analyses and models that have been developed as a result. Building on these analyses and models, biological research has shown how different forms of classical conditioning are mediated by different brain systems, leading to fundamental insights into the neurobiology of learning and often providing tools that help us understand various clinical brain disorders.

Thus, influenced and guided by the error-correcting model of Rescorla and Wagner, along with other elegant mathematical theories, researchers are uncovering the neural bases of conditioning in a broad range of brain systems, including the cerebellum, the amygdala (to be discussed in the context of fear conditioning in Chapter 10), and the role of dopamine in reward prediction (see Chapter 5). Links between conditioning and complex forms of cognition, such as category learning, help us see how mechanisms for learning studied in simple animal circuits can provide insights into the behavioral and neural bases of human cognition. The studies in animals also illustrate the general biological principle that evolution does not work like an engineer, creating new specialized systems for each new function. Rather, evolution works more like a tinkerer, using preexisting components, in slightly modified form, to perform new functions. The behavioral and biological processes for classical conditioning are the basic building blocks, the biological alphabet, from which more complex forms of learning emerge in all species, including humans.

KNOW YOUR KEY TERMS

activity-dependent enhancement, *p. 156*	CS modulation theory, *p. 142*	overshadowing, *p. 129*
appetitive conditioning, *p. 119*	delay conditioning, *p. 144*	Pavlovian conditioning, *p. 116*
associative weight, *p. 134*	error-correction learning, *p. 133*	prediction error, *p. 132*
aversive conditioning, *p. 119*	extinction, *p. 127*	Purkinje cells, *p. 147*
blocking, *p. 131*	eyeblink conditioning, *p. 121*	tolerance, *p. 125*
classical conditioning, *p. 116*	homeostasis, *p. 126*	trace conditioning, *p. 144*
compound conditioning, *p. 128*	inferior olive, *p. 148*	trial-level model, *p. 144*
conditioned response (CR), *p. 117*	interpositus nucleus, *p. 147*	unconditioned response (UR), *p. 117*
conditioned stimulus (CS), *p. 117*	interstimulus interval (ISI), *p. 144*	unconditioned stimulus (US), *p. 117*
conditioned taste aversion, *p. 145*	latent inhibition, *p. 140*	US modulation theory, *p. 141*

QUIZ YOURSELF

1. The relationship between a US and a UR <u>does/does not</u> involve learning. (p. 117)

2. A CR that precedes the US is often a _____ response. (p. 117–118)

3. In eyeblink conditioning, the blink is both a _____ and a _____, although they differ in their _____. (p. 121–122)

4. In most conditioning paradigms, extinction is <u>faster/slower</u> than the original acquisition of the conditioned response. (p. 127)

5. _____ conditioned responses in the body are most often the result of a biological mechanism called _____. (p. 126)

6. Evidence that extinction is more than just unlearning, comes primarily from studies that look at shifts in _____ between learning and testing. (p. 127)

7. When two cues compete to predict a US or other outcome, the one that is most strongly learned is usually the cue that is learned _____, as revealed in studies of blocking. (p. 131)

8. The principle of cue competition in learning arises in the Rescorla–Wagner model, where the association weights of two cues are _____ to generate a prediction of the US. (p. 134)

9. The Rescorla–Wagner model's account of contingency learning depends on viewing the _____ as a conditionable CS. (p. 139)

10. Latent inhibition cannot be explained by the Rescorla–Wagner model because during preexposure there is no _____. (p. 141)

11. Beneath the _____ cells of the cerebellar cortex lie the cerebellar deep nuclei, including the _____ nucleus. (p. 147)

12. CS information travels up to the deep nuclei of the cerebellum along axon tracts called the _____. (p. 148)

13. An airpuff US to the eye activates neurons in the _____, a structure in the lower part of the brainstem. (p. 148)

14. Purkinje cells <u>inhibit/excite</u> the interpositus nucleus, the major output pathway driving the conditioned motor response. (p. 147)

15. Animals with lesions to the cerebellum show CRs, but they are _____. (p. 151)

16. Latent inhibition and other expressions of CS modulation are impaired or eliminated by lesions to the _____. (p. 154)

17. The neural mechanism for habituation is thought to be a progressive decrease in the number of _____ neurotransmitter vesicles available in the sensory neuron's axon. (p. 156–157)

18. The _____ of the sensory neuron's release of glutamate onto the motor neuron is a presynaptic form of _____. (p. 156)

19. Two proteins found inside neurons play critical regulatory roles in the synapse-creation process. The first protein, CREB-1, activates genes in the neuron's nucleus that _____ the growth of new synapses. The second protein, CREB-2, _____ the actions of CREB-1. (p. 157–158)

20. Rats can be protected from overdose by the _____ that they learned during the administration of lower doses of heroin in the same setting. (p. 160)

21. Appealing due to its simplicity, the _____ model has proven itself to be a starting point for many promising models of learning. (p. 132)

22. The learning that takes place in order to avoid or minimize the consequences of expected aversive events is known as _____. (p. 119)

23. Rescorla demonstrated that conditioning to a tone stimulus depends not only on the frequency of tone–US pairings but also on the frequency of the US in the _____ of the tone. The results of his experiment imply that animals are sensitive to _____: the degree of correlation between a potential CS and US. (p. 139)

Answers appear in the back of the book.

CONCEPT CHECK

1. Returning to our stock analysts Doris and Herman, consider what would happen if Doris showed up every day to work but Herman only came in every now and then. On the days that Doris works alone, she does a great job of predicting the stock market. But on the days that Herman shows up, the pair of them do a lousy job. What would you think about Herman? You'd probably conclude that he is no great asset. In fact, worse than being a do-nothing, he seems to interfere with Doris's ability to perform. You might even say that Herman *inhibits* Doris's predictive value. This is similar to what occurs in conditioning procedures where a tone cue is always followed by the US except when the tone appears as part of a compound tone-and-light stimulus. On these compound trials, no US occurs. What does the Rescorla–Wagner model predict will happen to the associations during this training?

2. A recovering drug addict attends therapy sessions in which cue-exposure therapy is used. The addict is exposed to drug-related stimuli (e.g., photos of common drug-taking environments, drug paraphernalia, etc.) in the therapy center several times a week for an extended period of time. Why might this treatment fail?

Answers appear in the back of the book.

Operant Conditioning

Learning the Outcome of Behaviors

OST CHILDREN ARE TOILET TRAINED AS TODDLERS. A few lucky kids seem to grasp the idea almost intuitively; others are prone to wetting accidents during the early school years. But, for most children, learning occurs over a span of days or weeks.

Consider toddler Annie. After she has had a drink, and her bladder is likely to be full, her parents put her on a toddler-sized potty seat and wait for nature to run its course. When Annie successfully uses the potty, her parents provide verbal praise ("What a good girl you are, Annie!"), a gold sticker, or even a small toy. When a wetting accident occurs, her parents may admonish her ("Mommy is very disappointed in you, Annie"). Gradually, the toddler learns that using the potty will result in parental approval, and failing to do so will result in parental disapproval. Eventually, the behavior becomes automatic enough that Annie continues to use the potty seat, and eventually the toilet, even though she no longer receives an explicit reward for doing so.

This kind of learning is an example of **operant conditioning**: the process whereby organisms learn to make or refrain from making certain responses in order to obtain or avoid certain outcomes. The learning is called "operant" because the organism "operates" on the environment in a way that causes an outcome to occur. Operant conditioning is sometimes also called *instrumental conditioning*, meaning that the organism's behavior is "instrumental" in producing the outcome.

Operant conditioning is a deceptively simple-sounding process, but it can be used to train fantastically complex behaviors. A famous animal act from the 1950s, "Priscilla the Fastidious Pig," featured a pig whose routine included turning on the radio, eating breakfast at a table, putting dirty clothes in a hamper,

Behavioral Processes

The "Discovery" of Operant Conditioning

Components of the Learned Association

Learning and Memory in Everyday Life: Bomb-Detecting Dogs

Learning and Memory in Everyday Life: The Problem with Punishment

Putting It All Together: Building the $S^D{\rightarrow}R{\rightarrow}O$ Association

Choice Behavior

Brain Substrates

The Dorsal Striatum and Stimulus–Response ($S^D{\rightarrow}R$) Learning

The Orbitofrontal Cortex and Learning to Predict Outcomes

Mechanisms of Reinforcement Signaling in the Brain

Punishment Signaling in the Brain

Clinical Perspectives

Drug Addiction

Behavioral Addiction

Learning and Memory in Everyday Life: Addicted to Love?

Treatments for Addiction

operant conditioning. The process whereby organisms learn to make responses in order to obtain or avoid certain outcomes; compare *classical conditioning*.

running the vacuum cleaner, and—of course—picking out her favorite brand of pig chow (Breland & Breland, 1951). By the end of this chapter, you should have a pretty good idea of how to train your own pig to do the same.

5.1 Behavioral Processes

Humans have been using the principles of operant conditioning as long as there have been sheep to herd, horses to ride, and toddlers to toilet-train. But it wasn't until the end of the nineteenth century (about the same time that Ivan Pavlov was "discovering" classical conditioning) that Edward Thorndike first tried to systematically explore how animals learn new behaviors.

The "Discovery" of Operant Conditioning

In Chapter 1, you read about Edward Thorndike and his studies of how cats learned to escape from puzzle boxes, such as the one shown in Figure 5.1a. The puzzle boxes were made from fruit crates, each with a door that could be opened from the inside if the animal executed the correct sequence of pressing levers, pulling ropes, and stepping on pedals (Thorndike, 1898, 1911, 1932). When Thorndike would put a cat in such a box for the first time, the animal would hiss, claw at the walls, and generally try to fight its way free. Eventually, the cat would accidentally perform the movements needed to open the door and get out. Thorndike recorded how long it took the animal to escape, and then returned the cat to the box to try again. After a few experiences in the box, a cat typically learned the sequence of moves that allowed it to escape. Figure 5.1b shows the data from one cat; after a dozen or so trials in the box, the cat was able to get out almost immediately.

Figure 5.1 Thorndike's studies of animal learning (a) One of Thorndike's puzzle boxes. (b) Data from one cat that learned to escape from the puzzle box efficiently after a few experiences. Data source: Thorndike, 1911.

Thorndike concluded that when an animal's response was followed by a satisfying outcome (such as escaping from a puzzle box or obtaining food), then the probability of that response occurring again in the future would increase.

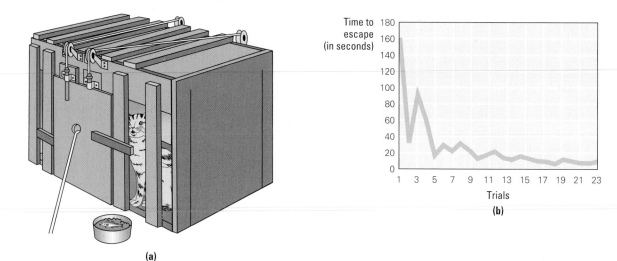

(a)

(b)

Thorndike formalized this idea in his *law of effect*, which you read about in Chapter 1. Specifically, in the presence of a particular stimulus, called the **discriminative stimulus**, or S^D, a particular response (R) may lead to a particular outcome (O). S^D is called a "discriminative stimulus" to emphasize that it helps the organism "discriminate" the conditions under which R will lead to O. The law of effect, as originally formulated, states that if O is desirable or pleasant, R will tend to increase in frequency, strengthening the $S^D \rightarrow R$ association and making it more likely that S^D will evoke the same R in future. This process of providing an outcome for a behavior that increases the probability of that behavior is called **reinforcement**.

But as you also read in Chapter 1, Tolman argued that the $S^D \rightarrow R$ framework was too limiting; Tolman believed that animals make responses because they (in some sense) understand that response R leads to a specific, predicted outcome O. More recent studies have supported many of Tolman's ideas, and have even identified places in the brain where $S^D \rightarrow R$ associations may be stored and where expected outcomes O are processed (more on that in the Brain Substrates section, below). For now, we'll formalize operant conditioning as a three-way association:

Discriminative Stimulus S^D $\rightarrow$ Response R $\rightarrow$ Outcome O

In the case of a puzzle box, S^D is the box, R is the sequence of movements needed to open the door, and O is escape. The $S^D \rightarrow R$ association is strengthened when R is followed by a desirable outcome O.

Classical versus Operant Conditioning

A few decades after Thorndike published his original account of operant conditioning, B. F. Skinner read it, along with Pavlov's work on classical conditioning, and concluded that these two types of learning were fundamentally different (Skinner, 1938). In classical conditioning, organisms experience an outcome (the unconditioned stimulus, or US) whether or not they perform the conditioned response (CR). In operant conditioning, by contrast, the outcome O depends on whether the organism performs the response R.

For example, in classical conditioning of the eyeblink response, a rabbit may hear a tone (the conditioned stimulus, or CS) that is reliably followed by an airpuff US, and the rabbit may learn to make an eyeblink CR to the tone. The airpuff follows the tone whether or not the CR occurs—so this paradigm is classical conditioning. By contrast, a cat placed in a puzzle box (S^D) must learn to make a series of responses (R) in order to escape and obtain food (O). If the responses R are not made, the outcome O doesn't occur. Therefore, this paradigm is operant conditioning. Whenever you have to decide whether a paradigm is operant or classical, focus on the outcome. If the outcome occurs regardless of responding, then the paradigm is classical; if it is contingent on a response, then the paradigm is operant.

Differences aside, operant and classical conditioning share many characteristics, including a negatively accelerated learning curve: Figure 5.1b shows that the time to escape from a puzzle box decreases rapidly in the first few trials and then levels off; similar learning curves occur in classical conditioning (as you saw back in Figure 4.7). Both operant and classical conditioning also show extinction: a tendency for learned responses to extinguish if no longer paired with an outcome. Researchers who want to investigate phenomena such as extinction or latent inhibition are generally free to use either classical or operant conditioning, depending on which is more convenient and what specific hypothesis they are testing.

discriminative stimulus (S^D). A stimulus that signals whether a particular response will lead to a particular outcome.

reinforcement. The process of providing outcomes for a behavior that increase the probability of that behavior occurring again in the future.

Test Your Knowledge

Is It Classical or Operant?

In classical conditioning, the outcome (US) follows the stimulus (CS) whether or not a learned response (CR) is made. In operant conditioning, the outcome (O) only follows the discriminative stimulus (S^D) if a particular response (R) is made. Analyze the following scenarios to check whether you understand the difference. (Answers appear in the back of the book.)

1. Since retiring, Jim spends a lot of time sitting on his back porch, watching the birds and whistling. One day, he scatters crumbs, and birds come and eat them. The next day, he sits and whistles and strews crumbs, and the birds return. After a few days, as soon as Jim sits outside and starts whistling, the birds arrive.

2. Shevonne's dog Snoopy is afraid of thunder. Snoopy has learned that lightning always precedes thunder, so whenever Snoopy sees lightning, he runs and hides under the bed.

3. Michael takes a new job close to home, and now he can walk to work. On the first morning, there are clouds in the sky. It starts to rain while Michael is walking to work, and he gets very wet. On the next morning, there are again clouds in the sky. Michael brings his umbrella along, just in case. When it rains, he stays dry. After that, Michael carries his umbrella to work anytime the sky looks cloudy.

4. In Carlos's apartment building, whenever someone flushes the toilet, the shower water becomes scalding hot, causing him to flinch. Now, whenever he's in the shower and hears the noise of flushing, he automatically flinches, knowing he's about to feel the hot water.

Free-Operant Learning

Chapter 1 introduced B. F. Skinner as the "radical behaviorist." Skinner was attracted to Thorndike's work, with its promise of animal responses that could be measured and evaluated without requiring speculation about the animal's mental states. But Skinner thought he could refine Thorndike's techniques. Thorndike's procedures were characterized by *discrete trials*, meaning that the experimenter defined the beginning and end of each trial. For example, on one trial with the puzzle box, the experimenter would pick up a cat, put it in the box, shut the door, and record how long it took the cat to escape. He would then pick up the cat and return it to the box to start the next trial. Similarly, when testing rats in a maze, the experimenter would place a rat at the start of the maze and record how long it took the rat to reach the goal. He would then pick up the rat and return it to the start to begin the next trial. Each trial is separate, or discrete, and the experimenter decides when and how often to begin a new trial.

Skinner developed a maze with a return ramp, so that the animal could finish one trial in the maze, collect the food, and then run back to the beginning of the maze by itself to start the next trial—and obtain the next piece of food. Part of Skinner's intention was to automate data collection, so that the experimenter no longer had to intervene at the end of each trial by returning the rat to the starting position for the next trial. But a side effect was that the animal—not the experimenter—now controlled its own rate of responding, by how quickly or slowly it ran around to start the next trial. This type of set-up is often referred to as a **free-operant paradigm**, meaning that the animal could operate the apparatus freely, whenever it chose – as distinct from the **discrete trials paradigm**, where trials were controlled by the experimenter.

free-operant paradigm. An operant conditioning paradigm in which the animal can operate the experimental apparatus "freely," responding to obtain reinforcement (or avoid punishment) when it chooses.

discrete trials paradigm. An operant conditioning paradigm in which the experimenter defines the beginning and end points.

To measure behavior more directly, Skinner also devised a cage—now commonly called a **Skinner box**—with a trough in one wall through which food could be delivered automatically (Figure 5.2a). The box contained a mechanism, such as a lever or a pressure-sensitive disk, that controlled the delivery of food. When the animal pressed the lever or tapped the disk, food dropped into the trough. As the animal explored its cage, eventually it would accidentally manipulate the lever or disk and receive the food. Over time, as animals learned the relationship between the response R (pressing the lever or disk) and the outcome O (obtaining food), they would dramatically increase their rate of responding. The experiment can be made a bit more elaborate by adding a discriminative stimulus S^D, such as a light on the cage wall, that signals whether response R will be reinforced: for example, pressing the lever while the light is

Skinner box. A conditioning chamber in which reinforcement or punishment is delivered automatically whenever an animal makes (or ceases making) a particular response (such as pressing a lever).

Figure 5.2 Operant conditioning (a) A Skinner box, in which lever press responses are reinforced by delivery of food into a food cup. (b) Hypothetical data illustrating learning by a rat in a Skinner box, shown as the mean response rate during a 26-minute experiment. During the first 13 minutes (acquisition phase), lever presses are reinforced by food delivery, so the rate of responses per minute increases. During the last 13 minutes (extinction phase), lever presses are no longer reinforced by food delivery, so the rate of responding decreases. (c) A cumulative recorder provides another way to display the data from (b). (d) In the cumulative record, the steep upward slope in the first half of the experiment reflects the increased rate of responding (acquisition); the flattened slope in the second half shows the rate of responding is petering out (extinction).

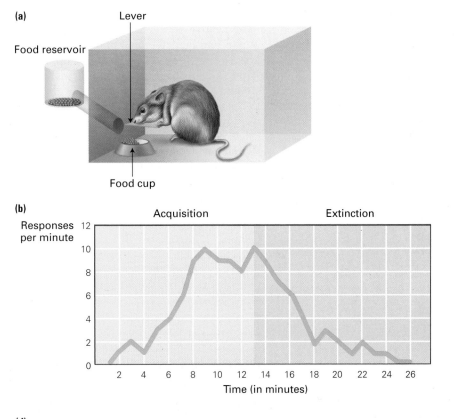

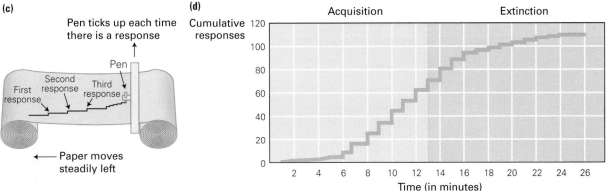

on will trigger food delivery (outcome O), whereas lever presses while the light is off will not. Over time, the animal learns that, in the presence of the light (S^D), lever presses (R) will result in food (O), and the frequency of R when S^D is present will increase.

Figure 5.2b shows an example of the data that might be obtained from a free-operant experiment in which lever presses in the presence of the light are reinforced by food delivery for the first 13 minutes of the experiment; during this period, the number of lever presses per minute increases rapidly with time, as the animal learns the $S^D \rightarrow R \rightarrow O$ association. Finally, minutes 14 to 26 of the experiment illustrated in Figure 5.2b show that the response extinguishes if it no longer produces reinforcement: as the animal learns the new association $S^D \rightarrow R \rightarrow$ no O, frequency of R in the presence of S^D decreases.

Skinner next invented a means of recording responses automatically. Back before the advent of modern computers, mechanical devices such as the one shown in Figure 5.2c recorded data on a long piece of paper rolling steadily underneath a pen. (Until fairly recently, such devices were also used for seismographs and lie detectors.) Skinner hooked up one of these devices to a Skinner box, so that the pen would move up slightly each time the animal responded. If the animal made no responses, the pen did not move, thus drawing a long straight line as the paper scrolled by. But whenever the animal made a response, the pen ticked up, and the resulting line sloped up more steeply as responses were made faster and faster (Figure 5.2d). The device shown in Figure 5.2c is called a **cumulative recorder**, because the height of the line at any given time represents the total number of responses that have been made in the entire experiment (cumulatively) up to that time.

One modern example of a cumulative recorder is the odometer in a car. The odometer ticks off miles driven, and the ticks occur faster if you drive faster. When you park the car for the night and then start it up the next morning, the new mileage is added right on top of the old, for a cumulative record of total miles driven so far.

Although pen-and-paper cumulative recorders aren't in general use anymore, data from operant conditioning experiments are still sometimes reported as cumulative responses (as in Figure 5.2d) instead of as response rates (as in Figure 5.2b). The label on the *y*-axis will tell you which kind of data you're looking at. The actual behavior being recorded is the same, whichever type of graph is used.

Components of the Learned Association

We've now defined operant conditioning as a three-way association between S^D, R, and O. But, in fact, each of these components (S^D, R, and O) can independently influence what's learned. Let's consider each of these components separately, starting with the discriminative stimulus, S^D.

Discriminative Stimuli

At a swim meet, swimmers line up at the edge of the pool before a race. At the sound of the starting whistle, they dive in as quickly as possible, to get a good start in the race. But any swimmer who dives in too early (before the starting whistle) may be penalized or even disqualified. The outcome varies, depending on whether the dive occurs before or after the whistle.

Discriminative stimuli are stimuli that signal whether a particular response will lead to a particular outcome. In other words, they help the learner discriminate or distinguish the conditions where a response will be followed by a particular outcome. For the swimmers, the starting whistle is

cumulative recorder. A device that records behavioral responses; the height of the line drawn represents the number of responses that have been made (cumulatively) up to the present time.

a discriminative stimulus signaling that dive responses will now result in a favorable outcome:

S^D **(starting whistle) → R (dive) → O (good start in the race)**

In a Skinner box, a light may be used as a discriminative stimulus: lever-press responses while the light is on result in the outcome of food delivery, and lever presses while the light is off do not:

S^D **(light on) → R (press lever) → O (get food)**

S^D **(light off) → R (press lever) → O (no food)**

As the $S^D \rightarrow R \rightarrow O$ notation suggests, the discriminative stimulus is the first part of the chain that triggers the response and leads to the outcome. Sometimes, the $S^D \rightarrow R$ association is so strong that the discriminative stimulus S^D seems to evoke the learned response R automatically, no matter what other options are available. In one striking example, well-trained rats in a familiar maze ran right through a pile of food on their way to the goal box (Stoltz & Lott, 1964). Apparently, the discriminative stimulus of the maze environment S^D was so strongly associated with the maze-running response R that unexpected food encountered along the way couldn't disrupt the $S^D \rightarrow R$ association. Such behavior is sometimes called a *habit slip*. People exhibit habit slips all the time, particularly when drowsy or distracted. Perhaps you've started driving to a friend's house only to find that your attention lapsed and the car is now heading along the more frequently traveled route to school, or perhaps you've awoken late one morning and started hurriedly dressing for class, only to realize it's a weekend and you can stay in bed. If so, you've experienced the effects of a strong $S^D \rightarrow R$ association.

Responses

In operant conditioning, the organism learns to make a specific response R that produces a particular outcome O. A response is defined not by a particular pattern of motor actions, however, but instead by the outcome it produces. For example, a rat in a Skinner box may receive access to food when it presses a lever:

S^D **(lever in box) → R (press lever) → O (get food)**

If the lever is pressed, the food arrives—whether the rat presses the lever with its left front paw, its right front paw, or even its nose—anything that depresses the lever sufficiently to trigger the food delivery device. Back in Chapter 1, you read about Karl Lashley and his experiments with rats in mazes. In one experiment, Lashley trained rats to run through shallow water in a maze, making a correct series of turns to reach the goal; later, he raised the water level so that the animals had to swim. The rats continued to navigate to the goal, even though swimming involved a new set of motor responses that the rats had never executed in this environment (Lashley, 1924). Similarly, Annie's parents may reinforce neatness in their older daughter, Becky, by providing an allowance if Becky cleans her room; the precise sequence of movements by which Becky accomplishes this is unimportant, as long as the clothes come off the floor and the toys are put away.

But in cases this complex, how do Becky and the animals learn which responses lead to particular outcomes in the first place? Consider Priscilla the Fastidious Pig. If it took Thorndike's cats several hours to stumble across the response that opened a puzzle box door, one can only imagine how long it might have taken Priscilla to accidentally run a vacuum cleaner and discover that her trainers would reinforce this behavior.

As you may have guessed, researchers and animal trainers who want to train complex behaviors rarely rely on accidents. Instead, they use a process called **shaping**, in which successive approximations to the desired response are

shaping. An operant conditioning technique in which successive approximations to a desired response are reinforced.

reinforced. For example, when a rat is first placed in a Skinner box, it may perform any of its natural behaviors: grooming, exploring, or just sitting quietly. When the rat happens to wander near the food tray, the experimenter drops in a piece of food. The rat eats the food, and starts to learn an association between the tray and food. After a few such trials, the rat starts spending all its time near the food tray. The experimenter then changes the rules so that being near the food tray isn't enough: now, the rat must also be near the lever before food is dropped. Soon, the rat learns to loiter in the vicinity of the lever. Once the rat has learned this, the rules change again: food is dropped only if the animal is actually touching the lever, then only if the animal is rearing up and touching the lever, then only if the animal is pressing down on the lever. Gradually, by a series of successive approximations, the desired response is learned: the rat presses the lever to obtain food.

If you think this sounds like a difficult and time-consuming process, you're right. Shaping requires considerable skill on the part of the experimenter, who must decide how fast to proceed, how hard to make each new stage, and even whether to back up a few steps if the animal appears to be getting confused. Some researchers have proposed standardized methods and criteria that can help optimize shaping techniques (e.g., Galbicka, 1994). Still, the difficulties of shaping are one reason that people often pay professional animal trainers to housebreak puppies.

Annie's parents use a similar shaping procedure when first introducing the potty seat. When they think Annie might be ready to use the potty seat, they put her on it; if she does use the potty seat successfully, they reinforce this behavior with praise. Gradually, through a series of progressive approximations, Annie learns to approach the potty and perform the response on her own.

The utility of shaping in humans is not limited to toilet training. Physical therapists use shaping to help patients recover the use of limbs—for example, requiring a patient first to open and close the hands, then progressively working up to the fine motor control needed to grasp and use a spoon. Shaping has been used to teach autistic children to speak, by first reinforcing any vocalizations, then reinforcing only vocalizations that sound like words, and eventually reinforcing actual word production (Lovaas, 1987). Shaping is also used to train service animals, including guide dogs for the blind and sniffer dogs that detect explosives or contraband at airports and border crossings (see "Learning and Memory in Everyday Life," on the next page, for more on how sniffer dogs are trained).

A related technique is **chaining,** in which organisms are gradually trained to execute complicated sequences of discrete responses. Skinner once trained a rat to pull a string that released a marble, then to pick up the marble with its forepaws, carry it over to a tube, and drop the marble inside the tube (Skinner, 1938). Skinner couldn't have trained such a complex sequence of responses all at once. Instead, he added "links" to the chain of learned responses one at a time: he first trained the rat to pull the string, then trained it to pull the string and pick up the marble, and so on. Sometimes, it is more effective to train the steps in reverse order, in a process called *backward chaining:* first train the rat to drop the marble in the tube, then train the rat to carry the marble to the tube and drop it in, and so on. At each stage, the rat must perform a progressively longer sequence of responses to gain its food.

Chaining is a useful technique for training humans, too. Workers learning to manufacture items

chaining. An operant conditioning technique in which organisms are gradually trained to execute complicated sequences of discrete responses.

Twiggy is a squirrel who water-skis behind a miniature remote-controlled speedboat at a water park in Florida. How do you think she was trained to do this trick?

Bomb-Detecting Dogs

If you've traveled by air in the last few years, then your luggage has probably been inspected by specially trained sniffer dogs, now commonly used at airports and border crossings to help authorities detect smuggled drugs, explosives, and other illegal substances. The sniffer dogs can search baggage in a fraction of the time it would take a human. And the dogs aren't only fast, they're sensitive; they can detect faint odors even if the target substance is sealed inside plastic or smeared with chocolate to disguise the scent.

So how are sniffer dogs taught their jobs? By the basic principles of operant conditioning. Training usually starts with positive reinforcement, in which a puppy learns to fetch a toy to obtain a reward such as playtime with the trainer, which most dogs find highly enjoyable. Then, the toy is doused with the scent of explosives or drugs—whatever the dog will be trained to detect. Each time the dog retrieves the toy and gets a rewarding bout of playtime, the association between odor, retrieval, and reward is strengthened. As training continues, the dog may be required to sniff out other objects doused with the same odor, so that the dog learns to retrieve any object with the target scent. Still later, a verbal command may be added ("Go find!") to indicate that the dog is to begin searching. At this point, the verbal command acts as a discriminative stimulus:

S^D ("Go find!") → R (find an object with target scent) → O (playtime)

As training continues, a new response may be shaped, so that instead of retrieving the scented object, the dog simply sits when the odor is detected. This allows the dog to discreetly signal to the handler, who can then take appropriate action without unnecessarily alerting passersby.

The canine sense of smell has proven useful in other fields too. The military uses dogs on the battlefield, to sniff out explosives and landmines. Pest control companies employ dogs to sniff out bedbugs. Medical labs are experimenting with dogs' ability to detect odorant molecules that may signal prostate cancer in urine samples (Cornu, Cancel-Tassin, Ondet, Girardet & Cussenot, 2011) or lung cancer in breath samples (Boedeker, Friedel & Walles, 2012). And after the terrorist attacks of September 11, 2001, sniffer dogs were used to help comb the wreckage of the Twin Towers site in search of survivors buried under the rubble.

However, there is controversy here too. Some question the dogs' accuracy. In one controlled study, where handlers were led to believe that the target odor was hidden in a location marked by a piece of red paper, the dogs sniffed significantly more in that location, even though no odor was present, suggesting that the animals were responding to subtle (possibly unconscious) cues from their handlers (Lit, Schweitzer & Oberbauer, 2011). And a report by the *Chicago Tribune* claimed that, when police used drug-sniffing dogs to check cars pulled over during traffic stops, the dogs generated more false alarms than correct responses (Hinkel & Mahr, 2011). Such false alarms can have serious economic consequences, as when an airport is shut down for several hours after a bomb-detecting dog identifies a suspicious object that is later determined to be harmless.

Other critics say it is unethical to send dogs into situations, such as minefields and building collapses, deemed "too dangerous" for humans, and suggest that robotic olfactory sensors (already in use at some U.S. airports) may be the most cost-effective sniffers of all.

---

are often taught the process one step at a time (Walls, Zane & Ellis, 1981), and trainee pilots may master landing sequences by practicing progressively longer sequences on a flight simulator (Wightman & Sistrunk, 1987).

Reinforcers

So far we've discussed outcomes fairly loosely, but now let's get to a formal definition. A **reinforcer** is a consequence of behavior that leads to increased likelihood of that behavior in the future. For example, food is a reinforcer to a hungry animal, and the animal will repeat behaviors that result in access to food. Food, water, sleep, the need to maintain a comfortable temperature, and sex are all examples of **primary reinforcers**, meaning that they are of biological value to the organism, and therefore organisms will tend to repeat behaviors that provide access to these things. Psychologist Clark Hull's **drive reduction theory** proposed that all learning reflects the innate, biological need to obtain primary reinforcers (Hull, 1943, 1952). This motivation to obtain primary reinforcers

reinforcer. A consequence of behavior that leads to increased likelihood of that behavior occurring again in future.

primary reinforcer. A stimulus, such as food, water, sex, or sleep, that has innate biological value to the organism and can function as a reinforcer.

drive reduction theory. The theory that organisms have innate drives to obtain primary reinforcers and that learning is driven by the biological need to reduce those drives.

was a key variable in Hull's equations with which, as you read in Chapter 1, he hoped to explain all learning.

One complication is that primary reinforcers are not always reinforcing. Thirsty animals will work to obtain access to water, a primary reinforcer; but once they've drunk to satiation, further water is not reinforcing. In addition, primary reinforcers are not all created equal. Hungry animals will work to obtain food, but they will work even harder for food they like. For example, rats will run a maze faster for bread and milk (which they find especially tasty) than for sunflower seeds, even though the seeds satiate hunger just as effectively (Simmons, 1924).

secondary reinforcer. A stimulus (such as money or tokens) that has no intrinsic biological value but that has been paired with primary reinforcers or that provides access to primary reinforcers.

In addition to primary reinforcers, learning can also be driven by **secondary reinforcers**, which are reinforcers that initially have no biological value, but that have been paired with (or predict the arrival of) primary reinforcers (Shahan, 2010). The best example of a secondary reinforcer is money. Money itself has no biologically reinforcing properties, but it can be exchanged for any number of primary reinforcers, including food, shelter, and even sex (millionaires tend to attract potential mates much more easily than paupers do). People may work for food only so long as they are hungry, but they will work indefinitely for secondary reinforcers; as Donald Trump and Bill Gates demonstrate, you can never have too much money. For a student, grades can function as secondary reinforcers: an "A" won't feed you if you're hungry or warm you if you're cold, but good grades can (eventually) be exchanged for a degree, which in turn can be exchanged for a good job, resulting in money, which in turn can be exchanged for primary reinforcers.

token economy. An environment (such as a prison or schoolroom) in which tokens function the same way as money does in the outside world.

Secondary reinforcement is often used in prisons, psychiatric hospitals, and other institutions where the staff has to motivate inmates or patients to behave well and to perform chores such as making beds or taking medications. Each desired behavior is reinforced with a token, and tokens can then be exchanged for privileges (say, access to the telephone or group activities). Such arrangements are called **token economies**, since the tokens function in the same way as money does in the outside world (Hackenberg, 2009). Token economies have also been used with some success to modify behavior in children with intellectual disability or with autism (Matson & Boisjoli, 2009); even non-verbal children may be able to learn that certain responses result in acquisition of tokens, which in turn can be exchanged for candy or toys.

African pouched rats have been trained to sniff out buried landmines left over from the civil war in coastal Mozambique. Guided by little harnesses, the rats scamper around the minefield without detonating the mines and give a decisive scratch with both forepaws when they smell an explosive. Pieces of banana function effectively as reinforcers for these animals. Knowing this, and given that you yourself would not want to cross the minefield to provide banana reinforcement each time the rat identifies a buried explosive, how might you go about training one of these rats to do its job?

Animals, too, will work for secondary reinforcers. For example, trainers can use secondary reinforcement to teach dolphins to do tricks. The trainer first pairs a whistle sound with food reinforcement until the dolphin has learned an association between whistle and food; at this point, the whistle has become a secondary reinforcer, and it can be used to maintain the behavior (Pryor, Haag & O'Reilly, 1969). Horse trainers often use a similar technique, pairing a clicking noise with oats and then eventually using the clicking noise alone (Skinner, 1951). In both cases, as long as the secondary reinforcer is occasionally followed by food, the behavior is maintained.

Reuters/Howard Burditt/Landov

Secondary reinforcers are particularly useful in animal training because the animal trainer can deliver clicker reinforcement immediately, without waiting till the trick is finished; the more quickly the response is followed by reinforcement, the more effective the reinforcement is. Another benefit of secondary reinforcers is that, although animals will not work for food unless they're hungry, they—like money-seeking humans—may continue to work indefinitely for secondary reinforcers.

The standard explanation of secondary reinforcement is that, by virtue of being paired with a primary reinforcer (such as food), secondary reinforcers (such as the clicker) became reinforcers themselves, which the organism will work to obtain. Some evidence supports this view. However, other research suggests that animals aren't "fooled" into thinking that the secondary reinforcers are worth working to obtain; rather, the secondary reinforcers provide informational feedback or "signposts" that behavior is on the right track for obtaining the primary reinforcer: "Keep executing this response, and you'll eventually get food" (Shahan, 2010). This is similar to a prison inmate who completes chores not because he is particularly motivated to obtain tokens *per se*, but because he knows that the acquisition of tokens is a way to obtain things that he does like.

The story doesn't end with primary and secondary reinforcers. As you'll read below, later experiments showed that the definition of reinforcer must be extended to activities and experiences that seem to have no connection to primary reinforcers: for example, when Becky's parents tell her, "You can watch TV after you've finished your homework," the opportunity to watch TV becomes a reinforcer for the behavior of completing homework.

Although many things can function as reinforcers, the identity of the reinforcer does matter. The organism learns that response R results not just in any random outcome but in a particular outcome O. A switch in the outcome may produce a change in responding. For example, hungry deer will eat food pellets strongly flavored with tannin, a bitter taste that they normally dislike; but deer that first eat from a bowl of weakly flavored pellets and are then switched to a bowl with the strongly flavored pellets eat less from the second bowl than deer that had been given the strongly flavored pellets all along (Bergvall, Rautio, Luotola & Leimar, 2007). Similarly, while rats can be trained to make lever press responses to obtain either food pellets or water sweetened with sucrose, they tend to prefer the latter. If the sweetened water is used as the reinforcer during the first half of each training session, and food pellets as the reinforcer during the second half of each session, rats typically make many more responses during the first half of the session (Weatherly, Plumm, Smith, & Roberts, 2002). These phenomena are examples of **negative contrast**: organisms given a less-preferred reinforcer in place of an expected and preferred reinforcer will respond less strongly for the less-preferred reinforcer than if they had been given that less-preferred reinforcer all along (Flaherty, 1982).

Negative contrast can be observed in humans, too. In one classic study, infants would suck a nipple providing either plain water or sweetened water, but the sweetened water (Figure 5.3, dark green line) evoked a higher rate of responding than plain water (light green line). Thus, sweetened water was the preferred reinforcer. If infants were started on sweetened water for the first session, then switched to plain water in session 2, the sucking response plummeted (red line)—meaning that those infants sucked less plain water in session 2 than the infants who received plain water all along (Kobre & Lipsitt, 1972). Similar negative contrast effects can be observed in children who go trick-or-treating expecting candy and instead get pennies (which they would usually appreciate), and in game-show contestants who hope to win the $1,000,000 grand prize and instead dejectedly settle for a consolation prize such as a new car or a free vacation.

Punishers

Reinforcers are not the only kind of outcome. There are also **punishers**, or negative outcomes. Common punishers for animals include pain, confinement, and exposure to predators (or even the scent of predators). Common punishers for humans are monetary fines, social disapproval, and jail time. Formally, **punishment** is the process of providing outcomes

negative contrast. Situation in which an organism will respond less strongly to a less-preferred reinforcer that is provided in place of an expected preferred reinforcer than it would have if the less-preferred reinforcer had been provided all along.

punisher. A consequence of behavior that leads to decreased likelihood of that behavior occurring again in the future.

punishment. In operant conditioning, the process of providing outcomes for a behavior that decrease the probability of that behavior occurring again in the future.

Figure 5.3 The negative contrast effect A normally acceptable reinforcer evokes less responding if a preferred reinforcer is expected: Human infants will suck at a higher rate for sucrose-sweetened water (dark green) than for plain water (light green), indicating that sweetened water is a preferred reinforcer. But infants who receive sweetened water in session 1 and are then switched to plain water in session 2 (red line) will suck less vigorously in session 2 than the infants who received plain water all along.
Data source: Kobre and Lipsitt, 1972.

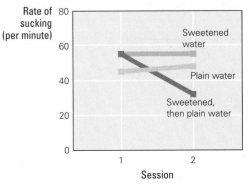

for a behavior that decrease the probability of that behavior. A rat will learn to stop pressing a lever if it receives an electric shock for doing so; Becky will learn to stop teasing her younger sister, Annie, if the teasing is always punished by parental scolding.

As you read in Chapter 1, Thorndike (1911) originally assumed that punishers were simply the inverse of reinforcers: whereas reinforcement increases the probability that a response will occur again in future, punishment decreases that probability. Later, both Thorndike (1932) and Skinner (1938, 1953) concluded that punishment was not nearly as effective as reinforcement at controlling behavior. In the end, Thorndike dropped the idea of punishment from his law of effect: concluding that while reinforcement does indeed increase the probability that a response will be repeated in future, the effects of punishment are erratic and unreliable, and can even at times result in paradoxical increases in the punished behavior (Thorndike, 1943; Postman 1962).

However, many modern researchers argue that punishment can indeed be very effective in modifying behavior (see Staddon, 1995, for a review). The problem is that there are several factors that determine how effective the punishment will be. We describe four of the most important factors here.

1. Punishment leads to more variable behavior. According to the law of effect, reinforcement of a particular response R increases the probability that the same response R will occur in the future. In contrast, punishment of R decreases the probability that R will occur in the future. But this does not tell us what response will occur instead of R. In fact, punishment tends to produce variation in behavior, as the organism explores other possible responses. That's okay if the primary goal is simply to eliminate an undesired response (such as training a child not to go near a hot stove). But it's not a particularly good way to train desired behaviors. If the goal of conditioning is to shape behavior in a predetermined way, then reinforcing the desired response generally produces much faster learning than simply punishing alternate, undesired responses.

2. Discriminative stimuli for punishment can encourage cheating. Remember how discriminative stimuli can signal to an organism whether an operant response will be reinforced? Discriminative stimuli can also signal whether a response will be punished. For a speeding driver, the sight of a police car is a discriminative stimulus for punishment: speeding in the presence of this stimulus will probably be punished. But speeding in the absence of a police car will probably not be punished. In this case, punishment doesn't train the driver not to speed—it only teaches him to suppress speeding in the presence of police cars. When no police car is visible, speeding may resume. Similarly, the dominant male in a group of chimpanzees may punish females for mating with any other males—but when his back is turned, the females often sneak off into the bushes with lower-ranking males. And rats that have been trained to eat no more than four pellets at a time will happily eat all the food in sight if no human is watching (Davis, 1989).

3. Concurrent reinforcement can undermine the punishment. The effects of punishment can be counteracted if reinforcement occurs along with the punishment. Suppose a rat first learns to press a lever for food but later learns that lever presses are punished by shock. Unless the rat has another way to obtain food, it is likely to keep pressing the lever to obtain food reinforcement, in spite of the punishing effects of shock. Similarly, a child who is reprimanded for talking in class will suppress this behavior much less if the behavior is simultaneously reinforced by approval from classmates. And although a speeding driver risks a hefty ticket, the effects of this punisher may be counteracted by the reinforcing fun of driving fast.

4. Initial intensity matters. Punishment is most effective if a strong punisher is used from the outset. In one study, rats received a shock as they ran through a maze to the goal box (Brown, 1969). The shock was initially delivered at the lowest intensities (1 or 2 volts) and had little effect on behavior. Gradually, across several days, shock intensity increased to 40 volts. Behavior was essentially unaffected, even though naive rats given a 40-volt shock would stop running immediately. Apparently, early weak shocks made rats insensitive to later, stronger ones. The effectiveness of the strong shock was completely undermined by starting weak and working up from there.

Unfortunately, the principle of intense punishment for a first offense often conflicts with our sense of what is appropriate and fair. Instead, humans have a tendency to start with a mild punisher and work up to more intense punishments for repeated offenses. A child who misbehaves in class may first receive a warning, then a scolding, then detention, then expulsion. The expulsion, when it comes, may be much less effective at deterring future misbehavior because of the prior, milder punishments. Similarly, a speeding driver may not be deterred much by a hefty $500 ticket if he is already accustomed to paying lesser fines. In each case, the prior weak punishers may undermine the effectiveness of the severe punisher, when it finally comes. (See "Learning and Memory in Everyday Life" on p. 180 for more discussion of the problems with punishment.)

Given the problems with punishment, many prefer using the carrot rather than the stick. Rather than delivering punishment each time the unwanted behavior is exhibited, it's possible to reward preferred, alternate behaviors—a process known as **differential reinforcement of alternative behaviors** (abbreviated **DRA**). For example, some children with autism or developmental disorders show persistent habits of self-injurious behavior, such as repeatedly banging their head against the wall or biting their own hand. Rather than punishing the child for each instance of the unwanted behavior, parents or therapists can reward instances of desired behavior, such as compliance with instructions to complete a task or eat a nourishing meal (Petscher, Rey & Bailey, 2009). DRA can work particularly well if the rewarded behavior is incompatible with the unwanted behavior. For example, as long as she is sitting in a chair to complete homework or eat a meal, the child is physically unable to bang her head against the wall.

In 2011, the movie theater chain Cinemark introduced a mobile phone application that allows customers to check movie listings and buy tickets. It also tried a new tactic to combat a pernicious feature of the modern cinema experience: fellow moviegoers who text during the performance (the light from the phone screen can be distracting to those seated nearby). Warnings at the start of the film to put away cell phones, threats to eject the disobedient, and even social disapproval all having failed, Cinemark turned to reinforcement of an alternate behavior: users activate the phone app at the start of the movie, and if they don't use the phone again for the rest of the movie, they earn coupons—secondary reinforcers that can be exchanged for rewards like free popcorn and soda. The jury is still out on whether this attempt at DRA has actually reduced texting-while-viewing, compared with more traditional punishment-based approaches.

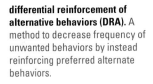

differential reinforcement of alternative behaviors (DRA). A method to decrease frequency of unwanted behaviors by instead reinforcing preferred alternate behaviors.

What types of social cues can serve as punishers for unwanted public behavior?

The Problem with Punishment

In the United States, 94% of parents of toddlers report that they use spanking or other forms of physical punishment to discourage unwanted behaviors (Kazdin & Benjet, 2003). There is no question that physical punishment is an effective technique for reducing the frequency of an unwanted response. Spanking is a form of punishment that even a very young child can understand, and it can effectively modify behavior.

But physical punishment is controversial. Many people believe that hitting a child is never justifiable. Some studies have suggested that children who are spanked can develop emotional problems, including aggression and stress (Gershoff, 2002), although other studies have found that occasional mild spanking does not cause any lasting harm (Baumrind, 2002; Larzelere, 2000).

Parents who want to avoid spanking have other options. Punishment does not have to cause physical pain to be effective. Scolding is a form of punishment that does not cause physical harm; other methods are time-out, grounding, and withholding of allowance.

But there is still the problem that punishment is hard to apply effectively. Let's take a hypothetical example. Shawn has two busy working parents, and he has to compete with his older siblings for their attention. When Shawn is well-behaved, his siblings tend to get most of the parental attention; but when Shawn breaks china, fights with his brothers, or causes trouble at school, the parental spotlight shines on him. Although they may think they are punishing Shawn, his parents are actually reinforcing his bad behavior by giving him attention when he misbehaves.

What's to be done? For one thing, Shawn's parents should punish unwanted behavior with a minimum of fuss, so that the offender gets less attention—and less reinforcement—for it. They can also reduce unwanted behavior by differential reinforcement of alternative behaviors, praising Shawn on the days when he does not misbehave. This means that Shawn's parents have to commit the extra time and effort to pay more attention to their youngest child, not just punishing him when he's bad, but acknowledging him when he's good. The payoff may be a well-behaved child and a happier family, while avoiding many of the problems of punishment.

Putting It All Together: Building the $S^D{\rightarrow}R{\rightarrow}O$ Association

Now that you've learned about discriminative stimulus, response, and outcome in some detail, let's explore the ways in which they can be arranged, and to what effect. An experimenter can vary several factors: the temporal spacing between S^D and R and O, whether the outcome is added or subtracted following the response, and even the regularity with which the outcome follows the response. The rules determining when outcomes are delivered in an experiment are called **reinforcement schedules**.

reinforcement schedule. A schedule determining how often reinforcement is delivered in an operant conditioning paradigm.

Timing Affects Learning

In most of the operant conditioning examples presented so far, the outcome (reinforcer or punisher) has immediately followed the response. For example, as soon as the rat presses a lever, food drops into the Skinner box; as soon as a dolphin executes a trick, the trainer provides whistle reinforcement; as soon as Becky teases her sister, her parents scold her.

Normally, immediate outcomes produce the fastest learning. This principle—that operant conditioning is faster if the $R{\rightarrow}O$ interval is short—is similar to the principle of temporal contiguity in classical conditioning, which you read about in Chapter 4. In classical conditioning, learning is fastest when the CS and US are closely related in time. Similar effects occur in operant conditioning. If there is no delay between response and reinforcement, then the odds are good that the most recent behavior will be identified as the response that caused the outcome, and the frequency of that response will increase. But if there is a long delay, it is more likely that other behaviors have crept in during the interval; now these are more likely to be associated with the outcome. To illustrate this idea, Figure 5.4 shows that rats learn a lever-pressing task quickly when the delay between response and food delivery is 0 seconds, but are slower to learn the association if the delay is 4 seconds; if the delay is lengthened to 10 seconds, there seems to be little learning at all (Schlinger & Blakely, 1994).

Temporal contiguity of response and outcome has a similar impact on the effectiveness of punishment. Unfortunately, human society often employs delayed punishment. Criminals may not come to trial—much less serve their sentence—until months or years after committing the crime. A middle school student who misbehaves in the morning and receives detention after school experiences a delay of several hours between response and outcome. These delays undermine the punishment's effectiveness, and may weaken learning.

The time lag between response and outcome is an important factor in **self-control,** an organism's willingness to forego a small immediate reward in favor of a larger future reward. For example, suppose a pigeon can choose to peck at one key for a small, immediate food reinforcement or at a second key for a larger food reinforcement that arrives 6 seconds later. Under these circumstances, pigeons almost always choose the small, immediate reinforcement—even though, overall, they obtain less food this way (Green, Fischer, Perlow, & Sherman, 1981).

The same trade-off occurs in humans: it is easy to convince a student to study if a test is coming up tomorrow; it is harder if the exam is not for 5 weeks. The delay between response (studying) and reinforcement (good grade) makes the reinforcement less effective in evoking the response. Similarly, one reason a weight-loss diet is difficult to maintain is that, at each meal, the dieter has to choose between the immediate reward of a dessert and the delayed reward of future weight loss.

The ability to wait for a delayed reinforcement differs across individuals and across the age span. When asked, "Would you rather receive $500 today or $1,000 in one year?" adults in their sixties are likely to choose the larger, delayed reward; college students are somewhat less likely to choose the delayed reward; and 12-year-olds almost never choose the delayed reward—preferring immediate gratification (Green, Fry, & Myerson, 1994).

One way of improving an individual's ability to wait for a reward is to induce the person to make a *precommitment,* that is, to make a choice that is difficult to change later. So, for example, a student may be more likely to study early in the semester if he joins a weekly study group, in which case he will experience peer pressure to attend the group and to study a little each week. A dieter may be less likely to cheat on her diet if she first empties the kitchen of chips and ice cream, so that when the cravings hit, it will be difficult for her to sneak some junk food. These precommitments do not make it impossible to get the immediate reward (the student can skip a study meeting, and the dieter can drive to the supermarket to buy ice cream), but they do make it harder to get the immediate reward, and the individual is consequently more likely to stick by an earlier decision to wait for the later, larger reward.

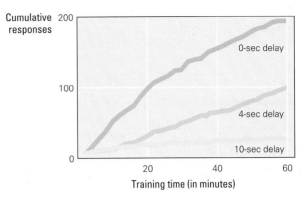

Figure 5.4 The delay between response and outcome affects speed of learning Rats were trained to lever-press, with food reinforcement delivered immediately or after a short delay. Rats learned more quickly with no delay than with 4-second delays, and rats with 10-second delays hardly ever pressed the lever, as indicated by a nearly flat cumulative response curve.

Information from Schlinger & Blakely, 1994.

self-control. An organism's willingness to forego a small immediate reinforcement in favor of a large future reinforcement.

Outcomes Can Be Added or Subtracted

Toddler Annie learns that, in the presence of the potty seat (S^D), emptying her bladder (R) will result in the reinforcement of parental praise (O); when S^D is absent, the same response R will result in the punishment of parental disapproval (O). Note that in both these examples, the outcome is something "added" to Annie's environment:

S^D (potty present) → R (emptying bladder) → O (praise)

S^D (potty absent) → R (emptying bladder) → O (disapproval)

Added to environment

positive reinforcement. A type of operant conditioning in which the response causes a reinforcer to be "added" to the environment; over time, the response becomes more frequent.

positive punishment. A type of operant conditioning in which the response causes a punisher to be "added" to the environment; over time, the response becomes less frequent.

negative reinforcement. A type of operant conditioning in which the response causes a punisher to be taken away, or "subtracted from," the environment; over time, the response becomes more frequent.

For that reason, these paradigms are technically called **positive reinforcement** and **positive punishment**. Note that here the word *positive* doesn't mean *good*; instead it means *added* in the mathematical sense (like a positive number). In positive reinforcement, the desired response causes the reinforcer to be added to the environment; in positive punishment, an undesired response causes a punisher to be added to the environment.

But there are also learning situations in which the outcome is taken away from or "subtracted" from the environment. In **negative reinforcement,** behavior is encouraged (reinforced) because it causes something to be subtracted from the environment. Thus, if you have a headache, you can take aspirin to make the headache go away:

S^D (headache) → R (take aspirin) → O (no more headache)

taken away from environment

The net result is that you are more likely to take aspirin again next time you have a headache, so this scenario is an example of reinforcement. The outcome, though, is not something added but something subtracted: the headache is taken away. Similarly, a rat can be placed in a chamber with an electrified floor grid from which it receives electric shocks. The rat can escape these shocks by climbing onto a wooden platform. In this case, the response is climbing, and the outcome is escape from shock—shock has been subtracted (negative) from the rat's immediate environment:

S^D (shock) → R (climb) → O (no more shock)

The net result is that the rat is more likely to climb the platform in the future. In other words, the climbing response has been reinforced. Because the outcome involves a subtraction (shock is taken away), this is an example of negative reinforcement. Negative reinforcement is sometimes called *escape* or *avoidance* training, because the response causes an escape from, or avoidance of, something aversive (such as headache or shock).

negative punishment. A type of operant conditioning in which the response causes a reinforcer to be taken away, or "subtracted from," the environment; over time, the response becomes less frequent.

Just as behavior can be reinforced by taking bad things away, so behavior can be punished by taking good things away. This kind of paradigm is called **negative punishment,** because something is subtracted (negative) from the environment, and this subtraction punishes the behavior. Again, as with negative reinforcement, the word *negative* does not mean "bad"; it means "subtraction" in a mathematical sense. (Negative punishment is also sometimes called *omission training* because the response R results in something being "omitted from" the environment.) For example, if Becky displays aggressive behavior toward other children during recess, the teacher may make Becky sit by herself while the other children play:

S^D (recess) → R (aggressive behavior) → O (loss of playtime)

The net effect is that Becky may be less likely to display aggressive behavior in the future. This kind of negative punishment is sometimes called a time-out: Becky is punished by time away from a normally reinforcing activity. Time-outs work only if the activity being restricted is something reinforcing. A time-out from an activity the child doesn't like may actually serve to reinforce, rather than reduce, the bad behavior that earned the time-out!

Negative punishment is widely applied in human society: teenagers may be grounded for staying out too late, drivers may have their licenses suspended for

Table 5.1 Operant conditioning paradigms

	Response increases (reinforcement)	Response decreases (punishment)
Outcome is added (positive)	Positive reinforcement *Example: Clean room → get weekly allowance*	Positive punishment *Example: Tease little sister → receive parental scolding*
Outcome is removed (negative)	Negative reinforcement (escape/avoidance training) *Example: Take aspirin → headache goes away*	Negative punishment (omission training) *Example: Fight with other children → time-out from play*

speeding, and people who don't pay their credit card bills on time may have their credit rating reduced, decreasing their ability to get credit in the future. In each case, an undesirable behavior is punished by revoking privileges, in the hope of decreasing the likelihood that such behavior will occur again in the future.

Table 5.1 summarizes the four types of training. Keep in mind that the terms *reinforcement* and *punishment* describe whether the response increases (reinforcement) or decreases (punishment) as a result of training. The terms *positive* and *negative* describe whether the outcome is added (positive) or taken away (negative).

Laboratory experiments often fit neatly into the grid shown in Table 5.1, but real life is more complicated. Sometimes it is difficult to determine whether an individual is learning based on reinforcement or punishment or both. For example, when students study for an exam, are they working to obtain a good grade (positive reinforcement) or to avoid flunking (negative reinforcement)? It could be either—or both. Similarly, a child who misbehaves may receive both a scolding (positive punishment) and a time-out (negative punishment), and both considerations may motivate her to keep bad behavior to a minimum.

Test Your Knowledge

Reinforcement vs. Punishment

It's easy to confuse the ideas of negative reinforcement, positive punishment, and so on, since we often use the words *positive* and *negative* to mean "good" and "bad." Don't fall into this trap! You can determine what kind of paradigm you're dealing with by asking yourself whether the outcome is added to (positive) or subtracted from (negative) the environment, and whether the outcome causes a behavior to increase (reinforcement) or decrease (punishment).

Try your hand at the following scenarios, and see if you can tell whether each is an example of positive reinforcement, negative reinforcement, positive punishment, or negative punishment. For each scenario, ask yourself: (a) Who does the learning? (b) What is the response (the behavior that is being altered)? (c) What is the outcome? (d) What is the discriminative stimulus that determines whether the response will produce that outcome? (e) Is the outcome something added or taken away? (f) Does the response increase or decrease as a result of learning? (Answers appear in the back of the book.)

1. At the grocery store, 2-year-old Lucy sees candy and wants it. Her mother says no, and Lucy starts to cry. The situation quickly escalates into a full-blown temper tantrum. Eventually, Lucy's mother relents and buys Lucy some candy. The next time they go shopping, Lucy sees candy and immediately throws another tantrum. This time, she obtains the candy quickly.

2. An interesting aspect of conditioning is that sometimes more than one person is doing the learning. Scenario 1 is presented from Lucy's point of view. But consider the same story from the mother's point of view: Susan takes her toddler on a shopping trip. The child sees candy, wants it, and throws a tantrum. Overtired and in a rush, Susan gives the child some candy, and the tantrum stops. On the next trip, as soon as the child starts a preliminary wail, Susan quickly hands over some candy, to stop the screaming.

3. Shevonne installs an electric fence system around the perimeter of her yard, and gives her dog Snoopy a collar that makes a high-pitched noise whenever he gets too close to the boundary. The first time Snoopy strays out of bounds while wearing the collar, the noise plays and distresses him. Soon, Snoopy learns to avoid the noise by staying inside the yard.

4. Miguel's football team has a no-alcohol policy: players sign pledges not to drink alcohol during the football season. One night, Miguel goes out with some friends and has a few beers. The coach finds out and revokes Miguel's playing privileges for a week. When allowed to rejoin the team, Miguel is careful to stay away from alcohol for the rest of the season.

5. Rachel is a ten-year-old who hates gym class. One day, after eating the school lunch, she gets a stomachache. She tells the school nurse she is feeling sick, and the nurse gives her a pass to skip gym class that afternoon. Now Rachel frequently feels sick after eating lunch at school.

Reinforcement Need Not Follow Every Response

In addition to controlling whether a response results in reinforcement or punishment being added or taken away, and whether the outcome ensues immediately or after a delay, an experimenter can also control the frequency with which these outcomes are delivered. So far, almost all of the examples in this chapter have been ones in which the outcome reliably follows the response. For example, whenever the rat presses a lever, it gets food; whenever Annie uses the potty, she gets praise; and so on. These examples illustrate **continuous reinforcement schedules,** meaning that each response R is always followed by the outcome O.

But in some situations, a response must be repeated multiple times before resulting in the expected outcome. For example, Becky has to clean her room seven days in a row to obtain her weekly allowance (seven responses for one reinforcement), and a baseball player is allowed to swing and miss three times before he strikes out (three responses for one punishment). In the laboratory, an experimenter can devise a schedule defining exactly when outcomes are delivered. Patterns in which an outcome follows a response less then 100 percent of the time are called **partial reinforcement schedules** (or *intermittent reinforcement schedules*). The term *reinforcement schedule* is used for simplicity, but these schedules can be applied either to reinforcement (Becky's weekly allowance) or to punishment (three strikes and you're out). There are four basic types of partial reinforcement schedule.

continuous reinforcement schedule. A reinforcement schedule in which every instance of the response is followed by the consequence.

partial reinforcement schedule. A reinforcement schedule in which only some responses are reinforced.

What kind of learning is going on here?

© King Features Syndicate, Inc.

1. Fixed-ratio (FR) schedule. In an FR schedule, some fixed number of responses must be made before a reinforcer is delivered. For example, if a rat must press a lever five times to obtain one food pellet, the ratio of responses to reinforcers is 5:1; this is often called an FR 5 schedule. Using this same notation, continuous reinforcement can be expressed as an FR 1 schedule: every (one) response results in reinforcement. Ratios can gradually be increased—for example, by starting with an FR 1 schedule and working up through an FR 5 schedule to an FR 50 schedule, and so on. In fact, animals can be trained to make several hundred responses for each reinforcement on an FR schedule.

Rats on an FR schedule show a characteristic pattern of steady responding leading up to the reinforcement, followed by a few seconds with no responding. This short break in responding after a reinforcement is called the **postreinforcement pause**. This pattern of responding under an FR schedule is most easily seen using a graph of cumulative responding (the type introduced in Figure 5.2c), which is one reason why some researchers continue to display data in this format. Figure 5.5a shows the hypothetical behavior of a rat trained to respond on an FR 5 schedule: steady response rates leading up to each reinforcement, followed by a brief pause before another round of responding begins in order to obtain a new reinforcement.

During the postreinforcement pause, it seems almost as if the animal is pausing to take a rest before its next bout of responding. And in fact, the length of the postreinforcement pause is related to the number of responses required to obtain the next reinforcement: thus, the postreinforcement pause when an animal is on an FR 50 schedule is longer than when the animal is on an FR 5 schedule. In effect, the rat is behaving like a human teenager who does a short chore (say, taking out the trash) the first time his mother asks, but procrastinates for hours before starting a really time-consuming chore (mowing the lawn).

Examples of fixed-ratio schedules in human life include factory workers who get paid a flat fee for every 100 pieces they turn out, and migrant farm workers who get paid a fixed amount for every bushel of apples picked. In fact, such workers tend to show behavior similar to that of rats on an FR schedule—steady

fixed-ratio (FR) schedule. In operant conditioning, a reinforcement schedule in which a specific number of responses are required before a reinforcer is delivered; for example, FR 5 means that reinforcement arrives after every fifth response.

postreinforcement pause. In operant conditioning with a fixed-ratio (FR) schedule of reinforcement, a brief pause following a period of fast responding leading to reinforcement.

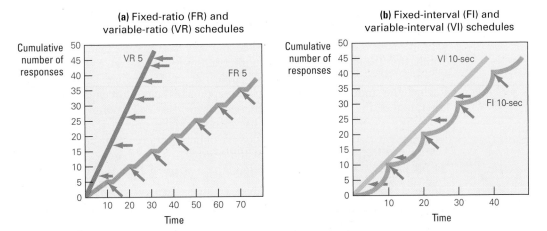

Figure 5.5 Reinforcement schedules In each figure, data show cumulative responding by a hypothetical rat; arrows indicate food delivery (reinforcement). (a) An FR 5 schedule (reinforcement after every fifth response) produces a pattern of steady responding leading up to each reinforcement, with a short postreinforcement pause (flat line) following each delivery of food. A VR 5 schedule (reinforcement after every fifth response, on average) produces fast and steady responding, with little or no postreinforcement pause— because the next response could produce another reinforcement. (b) An FI 10-sec schedule (reinforcement for the first response after a 10-second interval) produces a scalloped curve. After each postreinforcement pause, the response rate gradually increases until the next reinforcement arrives. A VI 10-sec schedule (reinforcement for the first response after a 10-second interval, on average) produces steady responding, with no postreinforcement pause, as the rat keeps checking to see whether a new reinforcement is available yet.

bursts of responding followed by postreinforcement pauses: the workers complete a batch, take a few minutes for a coffee break, and then start in again. A similar phenomenon occurs in readers: they may complete a chapter or a fixed number of pages before putting the book aside. Novelists often try to combat this "postreinforcement pause" by ending each chapter with an exciting cliffhanger, so that readers will keep turning pages to see what happens next.

2. Fixed-interval (FI) schedule. Whereas an FR schedule provides reinforcement after a fixed *number* of responses, an FI schedule reinforces the first response after a fixed *amount of time*. For example, on an FI 10-sec schedule, the rat is reinforced for the first response it makes after an interval of 10 seconds since the last reinforcement. Importantly, the reinforcement is not automatically obtained after the fixed interval, it merely becomes available to be earned—the organism must still respond in order to actually receive that reinforcement. Once the interval has elapsed, the reinforcement remains available until the response occurs and the reinforcement is obtained. At that point, the clock starts ticking on the next fixed interval until the next reinforcement becomes available.

Under these circumstances, the most efficient strategy on the rat's part would be to wait exactly 10 seconds after each reinforcement, then respond once to obtain the next reinforcement. Earlier responses (before the 10 seconds have elapsed) are wasted effort. However, Figure 5.5b shows how an animal on an FI schedule actually behaves: each reinforcement is followed by a period of few or no responses, but the animal's rate of responding gradually increases as the end of the interval nears. Presumably, animals (including humans) cannot judge time intervals perfectly, so they estimate as best they can how much time has passed and err a little on the side of wishful thinking by responding too soon. The result is a characteristic "scalloped" cumulative response curve, as illustrated in Figure 5.5b.

An example of fixed-interval reinforcement would be a high school student who is sentenced to detention from 3 p.m. to 4 p.m. After he arrives, there is little point in checking his watch for the first 15 or 20 minutes. But it might be worth checking after he estimates 30 to 40 minutes have passed, just in case time is flying by faster than he thinks. As the elapsed time gets closer and closer to an hour, he might check his watch more and more frequently, not wanting to stay a moment longer than necessary. In this example, the response is checking the time, the reinforcement is escape from detention, and only the response that occurs immediately after the end of the detention interval is reinforced—the rest are "wasted" responses. Notice that this is an FI schedule, not an FR schedule, because the rate at which the student checks his watch doesn't make the reinforcement appear any faster. Rather, the reinforcement arrives following the first response after the time interval has elapsed. Here, once 4 p.m. arrives, the student doesn't obtain reinforcement until he checks his watch and realizes he's free to go.

3. Variable-ratio (VR) schedule. A VR schedule provides reinforcement after a certain average number of responses. For example, whereas an FR 5 schedule produces reinforcement after every fifth response, a VR 5 schedule produces reinforcement after every 5 responses, *on average*. Thus, the responder never knows exactly when a reinforcement is coming. As a result, there is a steady, high rate of responding even immediately after a reinforcement is delivered, because the very next response just might result in another reinforcement (Figure 5.5a). Thus,

fixed-interval (FI) schedule. In operant conditioning, a reinforcement schedule in which the first response after a fixed amount of time is reinforced; thus, FI 1-m means that reinforcement arrives for the first response made after a one-minute interval since the last reinforcement.

variable-ratio (VR) schedule. In operant conditioning, a reinforcement schedule in which a certain number of responses, on average, are required before a reinforcer is delivered; thus, VR 5 means that, on average, every fifth response is reinforced.

Some restaurants and stores provide "customer reward" cards ("Buy 10—get the 11th one free!"), to modify customer behavior by increasing brand loyalty. Which type of reinforcement schedule does this represent?

Ronnie Kaufman/Getty Images

the VR schedule eliminates (or greatly reduces) the postreinforcement pause observed under FR schedules.

A real-life example of a VR schedule could be a slot machine. Even if you know that, on average, the slot machine pays off on every 10th game (in a generous casino), you don't know exactly which games will pay off. Even if you have just won a game, the very next game might be a winner too, so there is a strong incentive to keep playing.

4. Variable-interval (VI) schedule. Whereas an FI schedule reinforces the first response after a particular time interval, a VI schedule reinforces the first response after an interval that averages a particular length of time. So, for example, a VI 10-sec schedule reinforces the first response after an interval that is 10 seconds *on average*—but the actual interval might be longer or shorter on any particular trial.

In the VI schedule, as in the VR schedule, the responder never knows exactly when the next reinforcement is coming: a response a few seconds after the previous reinforcement just might be reinforced too. Thus, the response rate of animals under a VI schedule is usually steadier than under an FI schedule, as the animals check periodically to see whether reinforcement is available (Figure 5.5b).

An everyday example of the effect of a VI schedule is demonstrated by Tom, a college student whose girlfriend is studying abroad for a semester. She's promised to keep in touch through daily online posts, but sometimes she posts in the morning, sometimes in the evening—and sometimes more than once a day. Tom loves her and wants to read her posts as soon as they arrive, but he also doesn't want to spend 24 hours a day mooning in front of the computer waiting for the next post to come. A sensible compromise is for Tom to check online every few hours. This minimizes the time unread posts will sit waiting for him, while leaving him free to go pursue other interests in the meantime. Notice that this is a VI schedule, not a VR schedule, because the rate at which Tom checks online doesn't make the posts appear any faster. Once a new post does appear, it sits there waiting until Tom logs in; his next response is rewarded, as he gets to read the note.

Just as VR schedules tend to produce higher rates of responding than FR schedules, so VI schedules tend to produce higher rates of responding than FI schedules. For example, if Tom's girlfriend posts every day at the fixed time of 2 p.m., Tom will tend to check online once every day at about that time; if she posts at variable times, he is likely to check much more often, just in case a new post is waiting.

variable-interval (VI) schedule. In operant conditioning, a reinforcement schedule in which the first response after a fixed amount of time, on average, is reinforced; thus, VI 1-m means that the first response after one minute, on average, is reinforced.

Test Your Knowledge

Reinforcement Schedules

Operant conditioning is common in human behavior. Try your hand at identifying whether each of the examples below is an example of an FR, FI, VR, or VI schedule. (Answers appear in the back of the book.)

1. A first-grade teacher gives each student a gold star if the child completes that day's math worksheet; at the end of the week, five gold stars can be exchanged for a toy.

2. A good telemarketer scores an average of two sales for every 20 phone calls he makes, so he earns the most profit if he makes a lot of calls.

3. A couple go to their favorite restaurant on a Saturday night and are told that seating will be available in about 30 minutes. They wait in the bar and periodically return to the reception area to check whether a table is free.

4. Maria donates blood regularly at the local hospital; they pay her for her donation, and it makes her feel good to know she's helping people in need. However, due to hospital policy, donors must wait at least 2 weeks between donations.

5. A surfer spends all available afternoons at his favorite beach, where he is sure of at least a couple of big waves every hour or so. After catching a big wave, he immediately paddles back out to await the next big one.

6. A man who likes to eat spicy foods for lunch always carries a pack of spearmint chewing gum so he can freshen his breath before returning to work in the afternoon.

7. The U.S. president gives a video address on Saturday mornings. He and his staff plan the central ideas of the address early each week, but revisions are made right up until the actual delivery of the speech if world events occur that need to be included.

8. A woman likes to play bingo at her local church. The game is set up so that one in every 100 cards will be a winner, but it's impossible to know in advance which specific cards will win. To increase her chances of winning, the woman buys 10 cards each time she plays.

Choice Behavior

concurrent reinforcement schedule. A reinforcement schedule in which the organism can make any of several possible responses, each of which may lead to a different outcome reinforced according to a different reinforcement schedule.

In addition to continuous and partial reinforcement schedules, there are also **concurrent reinforcement schedules**, in which the organism can make any of several possible responses, each leading to a different outcome. These allow researchers to examine how organisms choose to divide their time and efforts among different options. For example, suppose a pigeon is placed in a chamber with two keys, key A and key B. Pecking on key A is reinforced on a VI 1-m schedule (1-m = 1 minute), and pecking on key B is reinforced on a VI 2-m schedule. In other words, the pigeon can obtain food by pecking on A at 1-minute intervals or by pecking on B at 2-minute intervals. What should the pigeon do?

Within a 2-minute interval, the pigeon can get two food pellets for pecking on A but only one for pecking on B. So, you might think that the pigeon would concentrate on A and ignore B. On the other hand, if the experiment goes on for longer than 2 minutes, there is a food pellet waiting to be delivered as soon as the pigeon pecks at B—and this pellet will never be obtained if the pigeon ignores B completely. Therefore, the optimal behavior is some strategy that allows the pigeon to maximize the amount of food it can get from both keys, probably by spending the most effort on A but occasionally switching over to B, just to check. In fact, this is more or less what animals do. This behavior is analogous to channel surfing in humans: confronted with several possibly entertaining television programs, a typical response is to watch the preferred program but switch over to other choices during the commercials, just in case something interesting is going on.

Variable-Interval Schedules and the Matching Law

Let's look more closely at the pigeon given a choice between key A on a VI 1-m schedule and key B on a VI 2-m schedule. Can we be more precise about the pigeon's allocation of time? One way to discover the pigeon's strategy is simply to let the pigeon peck away for a few minutes, according to its own preference, and then calculate the proportion of time it spent on key A versus key B. In fact, such calculations show that a pigeon will spend about 67% of its time pecking on A and about 33% of its time pecking on B—or about twice the time on A as on B (Herrnstein, 1961). Note that this 2:1 ratio is identical to the relative rate of reinforcement on the two keys, since A is reinforced twice as often as B. On the other hand, if A and B are reinforced equally often (say, both on a VI 1-m schedule), the pigeon will divide its time approximately equally between the two keys. This idea, that an organism's response patterns will closely mimic the relative rates of reinforcement for each possible response, is called the **matching law of choice behavior.**

Of course, even within a lab experiment, a rat or pigeon has more options than just pecking one of two keys: it will spend some of its time eating the food it earns, and it can even take a break and spend some of its time grooming, exploring, or napping. Nevertheless, the matching law is a fairly good description of how the animal will allot its time and effort among a set of possible operant responses.

Behavioral Economics and the Bliss Point

A pigeon confronted with two keys is the simplest possible example of a choice situation. Outside the laboratory, choices are far more complicated. A college student has to divide her allotted studying time among different classes according to how that studying is likely to pay off best, and she has to divide her total time among studying, sleeping, eating, socializing, and so forth. A dieter who is allowed a fixed number of calories per day must decide whether to eat several low-calorie meals or splurge on a bowl of ice cream (and then survive on water and lettuce for the rest of the day).

Behavioral economics is the study of how organisms allocate their time and resources among possible options. For example, a worker who makes $3,000 a month after taxes can distribute this income on rent, food, new clothes, savings, and so on. If she lives in a very expensive apartment, there is less money available for fancy food and new clothes; if she rents a less expensive apartment, she has more money to spend on other things. How does she choose?

Economic theory predicts that each consumer will allocate resources in a way that maximizes her "subjective value," or relative satisfaction. (In microeconomics, the word *utility* is used instead of *subjective value*.) The value is subjective because it differs from person to person: one individual may find much subjective value in an expensive apartment, but another may find more subjective value in having extra money to buy clothes and food. The particular allocation of resources that provides maximal subjective value to an individual is called the **bliss point** (Allison, 1983; Timberlake, 1980). We determine an individual's bliss point simply by recording what that individual chooses to do. For example, suppose Jamie, a college student, has a part-time job and takes home about $100 a week. Assuming that Jamie has no other expenses, he can spend this money on his hobby of collecting new music (downloading albums at, say, $10 apiece from an online store) or going out to dinner with his friends (say, $20 at a local restaurant). Each week, he can spend the full $100 on 10 albums, or he can eat out five times—or any other combination that adds up to $100.

Figure 5.6a shows Jamie's possible options. So, given these options, what does Jamie actually do? Most weeks, he eats out twice and downloads six albums. This point (shown in Figure 5.6a) is Jamie's bliss point—the distribution of expenditures that (apparently) results in maximum subjective value for this individual: he gets plenty of new music and also gets to eat out frequently. Of course, both the curve and the bliss point can shift if economic conditions change: if the restaurant raises its prices ($50 for dinner), then Jamie may shift to one dinner out and five albums per week—resulting in the new bliss point shown in Figure 5.6b.

Humans aren't the only animals that have to choose how to allocate their time and energy among competing options. College student Jamie has a bliss point that reflects the monetary cost of his different options. Animals—who don't use money—also allocate their behaviors in a way that reflects the "cost"

matching law of choice behavior. The principle that an organism, given a choice between multiple responses, will make a particular response at a rate proportional to how often that response is reinforced relative to the other choices.

behavioral economics. The study of how organisms allocate their time and resources among possible options.

bliss point. In behavioral economics, the allocation of resources that maximizes subjective value or satisfaction.

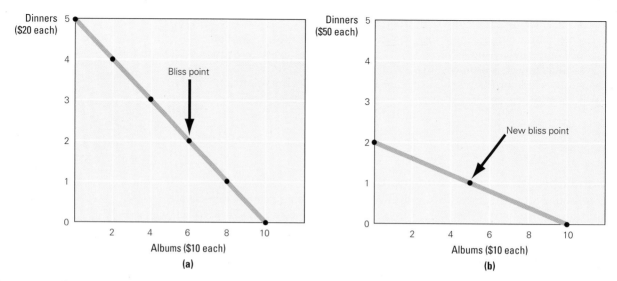

Figure 5.6 Behavioral economics (a) A student with $100 income per week may choose to distribute it between downloading new albums ($10 apiece) and eating out ($20 per meal); any point on the line will satisfy the budgetary constraints. The bliss point is the point at which this particular individual gets maximum subjective value for his money. (b) The bliss point may shift as conditions change—for example, if the cost of eating out increases to $50.

of each option. For example, predators such as sunfish must decide whether to invest energy chasing down a small prey animal like a guppie or wait for a larger one to come along—which could result in a bigger meal for the same energy expenditure. How to choose? One factor is the density of prey. If prey are rare, then the predator should probably chase any meal it sees, small or large. If prey are plentiful, then the predator might as well skip the guppies and wait for a larger victim. And this is just what the sunfish does. In a laboratory tank where large and small fish are plentiful, a sunfish generally only bothers to chase large prey. But when there are only a few fish in the tank, the sunfish will go after both large and small prey, whatever it can find (Warner & Hall, 1974). The sunfish's bliss point—the allocation of its resources among different classes of prey—changes when environmental conditions change, just as Jamie's bliss point shifts when economic conditions change.

Similarly, a naive rat in a Skinner box will spend some amount of time grooming, exploring, sitting quietly—and a very small amount of time pressing the lever. However, after the rat learns that lever pressing results in food (and assuming that the animal is hungry), it will begin to spend more of its time on lever pressing (and eating) and proportionately less on other activities, because the subjective value of pressing the lever has been increased. From the behavioral economics perspective, then, operant conditioning is not so much training an organism to execute a specific novel behavior as causing the organism to shift its allocation of time and energy among existing behaviors (Baum, 2002, 2004).

The Premack Principle: Responses as Reinforcers

There is one final complication in the study of choice behavior: although organisms do spend a lot of time and effort on responses that result in reinforcers, they also spend a lot of time and effort on behavior that does not produce obvious reinforcement. For example, pet gerbils often run enthusiastically in an exercise wheel, dogs happily chase their own tails, and humans spend hours reading novels, watching television, listening to music, and engaging in hobbies. In none of these cases does the behavior result in a primary reinforcer, such as food, or even an obvious secondary reinforcer, such as money. And yet organisms devote considerable resources to these behaviors, at the expense of doing other things such as eating and sleeping. Why?

This question was explored by David Premack, a student of B. F. Skinner (Premack, 1959, 1961, 1962). Premack gave a group of rats free access to drinking

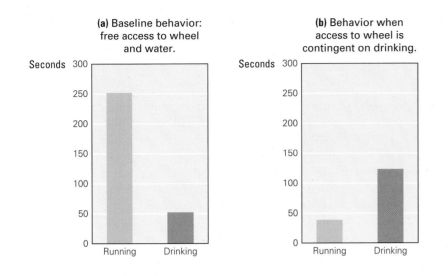

(a) Baseline behavior: free access to wheel and water.

(b) Behavior when access to wheel is contingent on drinking.

Figure 5.7 The Premack principle (a) At baseline, a rat may spend more time running on an exercise wheel than drinking water. Thus, running is the preferred activity and drinking is the less-preferred activity. (b) When running is restricted, and the rat must drink to gain access to the wheel, then the amount of drinking increases. Thus, the opportunity to perform the preferred activity (running) has reinforced the less-preferred activity of drinking. Data from Premack, 1962.

water and a running wheel (Premack, 1959). Each rat spent some time drinking and some time running, but on average rats spent more time running than drinking (Figure 5.7a). Then, Premack restricted the rats' access to the wheel: they were allowed to run only after they had drunk a certain amount of water. The rats soon learned the R→O association and started drinking water (R) in order to gain access to the wheel (O). Unsurprisingly, the total amount of running decreased, because the rats now had to work to obtain access to the wheel. But the total amount of drinking increased, as the rats now performed this behavior more often in order to gain access to the wheel (Figure 5.7b). In effect, the activity of running was acting as a reinforcer, and it was increasing the probability of an otherwise infrequent behavior, drinking.

Premack also showed a similar pattern in human children (Premack, 1959). He put the children in a room that contained a pinball machine and a bowl of candy, and he recorded how much time each child spent playing pinball and eating candy. Some of the children spent more time playing pinball. Premack then restricted access to the pinball machine, allowing these children to play (O) only after they had eaten some candy (R). Candy eating increased, showing that access to the preferred activity (pinball) could reinforce the less-preferred activity (candy eating).

Thus, in both rats and children, the opportunity to perform a highly frequent behavior can reinforce a less-frequent behavior. This idea came to be known as the **Premack principle**. Examples of the Premack principle abound in human life. For example, left to their own devices, most children will spend more time watching television than doing their homework. Thus, watching television is a preferred activity, and it can be used to reinforce the less-preferred activity of homework. The parent restricts television time, making it contingent on homework. As a consequence, the child spends more time doing homework than he would have if television had not been restricted.

A later extension of the Premack principle, the **response deprivation hypothesis**, suggests that the critical variable is not which response is normally more frequent but merely which response has been restricted: by restricting the ability to execute almost any response, you can make the opportunity to perform that response reinforcing (Allison, 1993; Timberlake & Allison, 1974). For example, perhaps you have a chore, such as cleaning your room or doing laundry, that you normally detest. But if access to this activity is restricted, it

Premack principle. The theory that the opportunity to perform a highly frequent behavior can reinforce a less frequent behavior; later refined as the *response deprivation hypothesis*.

response deprivation hypothesis. A refinement of the Premack principle stating that the opportunity to perform any behavior can be reinforcing if access to that behavior is restricted.

can become reinforcing. If you have been studying for several hours straight, the idea of "taking a break" to clean your room or do the laundry can begin to look downright attractive. If so, you've experienced the Premack principle at work.

Interim Summary

- In operant conditioning, organisms learn to make responses under particular conditions in order to obtain or avoid outcomes: Discriminative stimulus $S^D \rightarrow$ Response R $\rightarrow$ Outcome O.

- In operant conditioning, the outcome (reinforcement or punishment) occurs only if the organism makes the response. In classical conditioning, by contrast, the unconditioned stimulus (US) occurs whether or not the organism makes a conditioned response (CR).

- Discriminative stimuli signal to the organism whether a particular response will result in a particular outcome.

- An outcome that an organism will work to obtain is called a reinforcer; an outcome that an organism will work to avoid is called a punisher. While punishment can be effective in eliminating an undesired response, it leads to more varied behavior and can be undermined by discriminative stimuli that encourage cheating, by concurrent reinforcement, or by weakness of the initial punisher. Another approach to eliminating unwanted behavior is differential reinforcement of alternative behaviors (DRA).

- Complex responses can be trained via shaping, in which progressive approximations to the desired response are reinforced, and chaining, in which organisms are gradually trained to execute a sequence of responses.

- The four basic types of operant paradigm are positive reinforcement, negative reinforcement, positive punishment, and negative punishment. The words positive and negative denote whether the outcome is added or subtracted; *reinforcement* and *punishment* denote whether the response increases or decreases as a result of learning.

- Schedules of reinforcement define whether the outcome O follows every response R, is available after some (fixed or variable) number of responses, or is available only after some (fixed or variable) time interval.

- When multiple responses are reinforced under a VI schedule, the matching law predicts that organisms will allocate time among those responses based on the relative rates of reinforcement for each response.

- Behavioral economics is the study of how organisms choose to allocate their time and resources among various responses that result in different outcomes. The bliss point is the particular allocation of resources that provides maximal subjective value to an individual.

- The Premack principle states that the opportunity to perform a highly frequent behavior can reinforce performance of a less-frequent behavior. The response deprivation hypothesis states that any behavior can be reinforcing if the opportunity to perform that behavior is restricted.

5.2 Brain Substrates

The previous section defined operant conditioning as learning an association between a discriminative stimulus S^D, a response R, and an outcome O. In studying such associations, neuroscientists are discovering that the parts of the brain that link stimuli with responses ($S^D \rightarrow R$ learning) are different from the parts of the brain that learn about the expected outcomes (O) of those responses. While many brain areas play a role in these processes, two key areas are the dorsal striatum, which appears to be particularly important for $S^D \rightarrow R$ learning, and the orbitofrontal cortex, which appears important for learning about expected outcomes. Different brain areas may help us evaluate whether those outcomes are reinforcers or punishers.

The Dorsal Striatum and Stimulus–Response ($S^D \rightarrow R$) Learning

Voluntary motor responses occur when neurons in the motor cortex send messages to motor neurons in the muscles that control movements. The motor cortex receives its primary inputs from cortical areas that process sensory information, such as the visual cortex (V1) and the somatosensory cortex (S1), which you saw back in Figure 2.7, and also from the frontal cortex. Thus, when you see a book, this visual stimulus is registered by your visual cortex. If you decide to pick up the book, this "decision" is made in your frontal cortex, and signals from both the visual cortex and the frontal cortex travel to motor cortex, which integrates these signals and produces the appropriate instructions, resulting in your picking up the book.

Information from the sensory cortex to the motor cortex can also travel via an indirect route, through the **basal ganglia** (colored purple in Figure 5.8). The basal ganglia are a collection of *ganglia* (clusters of neurons) that lie at the base of the forebrain. One part of the basal ganglia is the **dorsal striatum** (Figure 5.8), which can be further subdivided into the *caudate nucleus* and the *putamen*. The dorsal striatum receives highly processed stimulus information from sensory cortical areas and projects to the motor cortex, which produces a behavioral response.

The dorsal striatum plays a critical role in operant conditioning, particularly if discriminative stimuli are involved. Rats with lesions of the dorsal striatum can learn operant responses (e.g., when placed in a Skinner box, lever-press R to obtain food O). But if discriminative stimuli are added (e.g., lever-press R is reinforced only in the presence of a light S^D), then the lesioned rats are markedly impaired (Featherstone & McDonald, 2004). In humans, too, individuals with damage or disruption to the striatum due to Parkinson's disease or Huntington's disease show deficits in the ability to associate a discriminative stimulus with a correct response (Ashby & Waldron, 2000; Robbins, 1996). In short, the dorsal striatum appears necessary for learning $S^D \rightarrow R$ associations based on feedback about reinforcement and punishment (McDonald & White, 1994; O'Doherty et al., 2004).

$S^D \rightarrow R$ associations that depend on the dorsal striatum tend to be relatively automatic or habitual (Balleine, Daw, & O'Doherty, 2008). Remember the well-trained rats, discussed earlier in this chapter, who would run right through a pile of food on their way to a goal box in the maze? That behavior probably reflects $S^D \rightarrow R$ learning in the striatum, making the maze-running automatic even when other behaviors (such as pausing to eat) would have resulted in reward. In this case, running is based on a history of learning in which that response resulted in desirable outcomes; but after a long period of training, the response is performed even though the outcome is no longer contingent on that action.

basal ganglia. A brain region that lies at the base of the forebrain and includes the dorsal striatum.

dorsal striatum. A region of the basal ganglia that is important for stimulus–response learning.

Figure 5.8 Some brain substrates of operant conditioning During operant conditioning, the dorsal striatum may help create links between the sensory cortex and the motor cortex so that stimuli can evoke appropriate motor responses ($S^D \rightarrow R$ learning). Parts of the frontal cortex, including the orbitofrontal cortex, may play a role in learning that specific responses lead to particular outcomes.

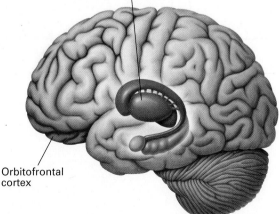

Dorsal striatum

Orbitofrontal cortex

The Orbitofrontal Cortex and Learning to Predict Outcomes

$S^D \rightarrow R$ learning is, of course, only half the picture in operant conditioning. Organisms learn to predict that particular responses R (in the presence of S^D) will result in particular outcomes O. For example, you read about the negative contrast effect in the Behavioral Processes section above: monkeys may shriek in annoyance if their response earns them a less-preferred food than the one they expected, and trick-or-treaters may feel cheated if they receive pennies rather than the expected candy. Such results show that organisms don't make responses blindly but make them in anticipation of particular outcomes.

orbitofrontal cortex. An area of the prefrontal cortex that is important for learning to predict the outcomes of particular responses.

Several brain areas appear to be involved in learning to predict the outcomes of behavior. Among these are parts of the *prefrontal cortex*, including the **orbitofrontal cortex**, which lies at the underside of the front of the brain in primates (Figure 5.8), and which appears to contribute to goal-directed behavior by representing predicted outcomes (Schoenbaum, Roesch, Stalnaker, & Takahashi, 2009; Tanaka, Balleine, & O'Doherty, 2008). The orbitofrontal cortex receives inputs conveying the full range of sensory modalities (sight, touch, sound, etc.) and also visceral sensations (including hunger and thirst), allowing this brain area to integrate many types of information; outputs from the orbitofrontal cortex travel to the striatum, where they can help determine which motor responses are executed.

Evidence that the orbitofrontal cortex plays a role in predicting the outcome of responses comes from neuronal recordings. For example, thirsty rats can be trained on a discrimination task in where the discriminative stimuli are two odors, the response R is to poke the nose into a nearby water cup, and the two possible outcomes are a tasty sucrose solution or a bitter quinine solution:

Odor 1 → R → (delay) → sucrose (reward)

Odor 2 → R → (delay) → quinine (punisher)

Here, a short delay (typically less than a second) is introduced between the response and the outcome, during which period the animal is "expecting" the outcome. During this delay, some neurons in orbitofrontal cortex fire differently, depending on whether a reward or punisher is expected (Schoenbaum, Chiba, & Gallagher, 1998). Figure 5.9a shows an example of the firing patterns of one neuron

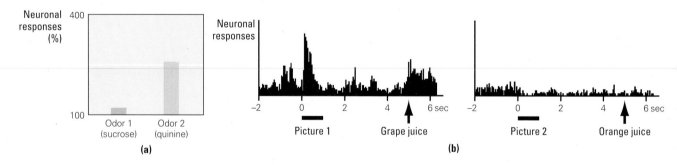

Figure 5.9 Orbitofrontal neurons code expected outcomes (a) Responses of a single neuron in orbitofrontal cortex of a rat learning that responding to odor 1 produces sucrose while responding to odor 2 produces quinine. Responses are shown during the delay between response and outcome. This neuron shows very little increase above baseline (100%) after the rat has responded to odor 1, but a strong increase after the rat has (mistakenly) responded to odor 2. Thus this neuron appears to code for expectation of quinine. (b) A single neuron in orbitofrontal cortex of a monkey trained that some pictures (e.g., Picture 1) predict that a response will be reinforced by grape juice but other pictures (e.g. Picture 2) predict that the response will be rewarded by orange juice. Each picture is presented for 1 second, with juice delivered 4 seconds later. This neuron responds strongly (height of bars indicate neuronal activity) when Picture 1 (which predicts grape juice) appears, and again when grape juice is delivered, but the same neuron does not fire to Picture 2 (which predicts orange juice) nor when orange juice is delivered. Thus, this neuron codes not only expectation of reward but also expectation of a specific outcome: grape juice.

(a) Data from Schoenbaum et al., 1998, Figure 3a. (b) Information from Tremblay & Schultz, 1999, Figure 3b.

in the orbitofrontal cortex of a rat learning such a task. This particular neuron fires strongly if the rat has just made a (mistaken) response to odor 2 and is expecting quinine, but less strongly if the rat has just made a response to odor 1 and is expecting sucrose. Thus, this neuron appears to code expectation of the punisher rather than the reward. If the contingencies are reversed, so that odor 1 now predicts quinine and odor 2 now predicts sucrose, such neurons often alter their responses to reflect the new contingencies (Stalnaker, Franz, Singh, & Schoenbaum, 2007).

Neurons in orbitofrontal cortex don't only learn whether to expect reinforcement or punishment; they even appear to code the actual identity of the expected outcome. Thus, monkeys can be trained with a set of pictures that predict whether the upcoming reward will be grape juice or orange juice. Figure 5.9b shows the responses of a single neuron that became active whenever a stimulus that predicted grape juice was presented, but not when pictures predicting orange juice were presented (Tremblay & Schultz, 1999). This same neuron also fired during the actual delivery of grape juice, but not orange juice.

Given their ability to encode specific predicted outcomes, orbitofrontal cortex neurons play an important role in helping us select between potential actions based on their expected consequences. When monkeys are trained to choose between two responses that result in different outcomes (say, water vs. Kool-Aid), most individual monkeys have a preference for one beverage over another. Given a choice between licking to obtain water or Kool-Aid, a particular monkey will alter his responses based on the amount of each he will get. If response R1 produces 1 cc of water and response R2 produces 1 cc of Kool-Aid, he may choose to lick to obtain the sugary Kool-Aid. But if R1 produces 6 cc of water, he may choose that option instead. In fact, the likelihood that the monkey will make response R1 depends on the trade-off between his individual preference of beverage and the relative amount of each he would obtain, resulting in choice behavior very much like the pigeon allocating pecks between key A and key B. Neurons in the monkey's orbitofrontal cortex respond with a strength proportional to the perceived value of each choice (Padoa-Schioppa & Assad, 2006).

Remember college student Jamie, who could spend his weekly income by distributing it among choices such as music purchases and restaurant dinners? Possibly, neurons in Jamie's orbitofrontal cortex were helping him to evaluate the potential outcomes of his actions, and to choose between them. When dinners were cheap, certain of these neurons may have responded strongly, indicating that dinners were the preferred choice. But when the cost of dining out rose, the same neurons may have responded more weakly, leading Jamie to prefer the opposite alternative for spending his money.

Mechanisms of Reinforcement Signaling in the Brain

The previous section suggested that neurons in the orbitofrontal cortex code not only the identity of an outcome (e.g., grape juice vs. orange juice) but also whether that outcome is reinforcing or not (e.g., water flavored with sucrose vs. quinine). This distinction is critical: if an outcome is reinforcing, the $S^D \rightarrow R$ association should be strengthened, increasing the likelihood that S^D evokes R in the future; if it is a punisher, the association should be weakened, decreasing the likelihood of R. How does the brain determine whether an outcome is a reinforcer or a punisher?

"Wanting" and "Liking" in the Brain

In 1954, James Olds was experimenting with delivering electrical stimulation to the rat brain. He inserted an electrode into an area that researchers now believe to have been the lateral hypothalamus. Olds waited until the rat wandered into one corner of the experimental chamber, and then he applied a brief electrical current. After a few minutes of wandering around the chamber, the rat

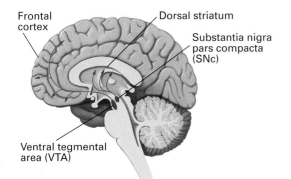

Frontal cortex

Dorsal striatum

Substantia nigra pars compacta (SNc)

Ventral tegmental area (VTA)

Figure 5.10 The ventral tegmental area (VTA) and substantia nigra pars compacta (SNc) The VTA (part of the midbrain) and the SNc (a part of the basal ganglia) are small regions containing neurons that project dopamine to many brain areas, including the dorsal striatum and frontal cortex.

ventral tegmental area (VTA). A region in the midbrain that contains dopamine-producing neurons which project to the frontal cortex and other brain areas.

hedonic value. The subjective "goodness" or value of a reinforcer.

motivational value of a stimulus. The degree to which an organism is willing to work to obtain access to that stimulus.

substantia nigra pars compacta (SNc). A part of the basal ganglia that contains dopamine-producing neurons which project to the striatum.

came back to the same corner, where Olds gave it a second stimulation. The rat caught on quickly, and began to loiter in that corner of the chamber, apparently hoping for more electrical stimulation (Olds, 1955). Thus, electrical stimulation to this area of the brain seemed to be acting much like a reinforcer: increasing the probability of certain responses (in this case, hanging around the correct location).

Olds was intrigued, to say the least. He rigged a Skinner box so that the rats could press a lever to turn on the electrical stimulation. The rats were soon lever-pressing at a furious rate: as many as 700 times an hour (Olds, 1958). If allowed, rats would press the lever continuously for up to 48 hours, until they collapsed from physical exhaustion! Given a choice between electrical stimulation and food, the rats would literally starve themselves, preferring the stimulation (Routtenberg & Lindy, 1965).

Later studies identified that rats would work for electrical stimulation in several brain areas, including the **ventral tegmental area (VTA),** a small region in the midbrain of rats, humans, and other mammals (Figure 5.10). The electrodes in Olds's original studies were probably stimulating hypothalamic neurons that project to the VTA, so that the electrical current was indirectly activating this area. Because VTA stimulation was such a powerful reinforcer, some researchers inferred that the rats "liked" the stimulation, and the VTA and other areas of the brain where electrical stimulation was effective became informally known as "pleasure centers."

However, the idea of "pleasure centers" is something of an oversimplification. For one thing, rats lever pressing for electrical brain stimulation don't tend to act as if they're enjoying it; they tend to become agitated and may bite the lever instead of simply pressing it, or even scratch the walls or show other behaviors such as eating, fighting, or shredding of nesting material. This is more like the behavior of an excited animal than one who is enjoying food. Skinner, of course, would caution that we can't infer what an animal might be feeling just by watching its behaviors. Nevertheless, some researchers have suggested that electrical brain stimulation causes not pleasure but rather excitement or anticipation of reinforcement—much like the anticipation we experience when expecting a good meal or a big present (Flynn, 1972).

Currently, many researchers believe that we have separate brain systems for signaling **hedonic value**—meaning the subjective "goodness" of a reinforcer, or how much we "like" it—that are distinct from those signaling **motivational value**—meaning how much we "want" a reinforcer and how hard we are willing to work to obtain it. No matter how much we may "like" chocolate cake, most of us will not be very motivated to obtain more if we have just eaten three slices; similarly, Olds's rats doubtless still "liked" food and rest, but they were more motivated to obtain electric brain stimulation, even when starving and exhausted. In these examples, provision of a "liked" reinforcer isn't enough to evoke responding. Only when "wanting" and "liking" signals are both present will the arrival of the reinforcer evoke responding and strengthen the $S^D \rightarrow R$ association.

Dopamine: How the Brain Signals "Wanting"?

The neurotransmitter dopamine is produced by neurons in several areas of the brain, including the ventral tegmental area (VTA), which projects to the frontal cortex (among other places), and also including the nearby **substantia nigra pars compacta** (SNc), which is a part of the basal ganglia that projects to the striatum (Figure 5.10). As you read above, the dorsal striatum is an important site of $S^D \rightarrow R$ association, and the orbitofrontal cortex (and other frontal areas) is important for learning about predicted outcomes, so dopaminergic neurons in the VTA/SNc are a good place to start looking at how the brain signals motivational value.

In rats, dopamine release from the VTA/SNc is triggered by encounters with food, sex, drugs of abuse, and secondary reinforcers. In humans, PET and fMRI studies have shown that presentation of juice, cocaine, money, humor, and even video games causes heightened activity in dopamine target sites such as the striatum (Berridge & Robinson, 1998; Knutson, Fong, Adams, Varner, & Hommre, 2001; Mobbs, Greicius, Abdel-Azim, Menon, & Reiss, 2003). Even in invertebrates, such as the sea slug *Aplysia*, dopamine is released in conjunction with positive reinforcement during operant conditioning (Brembs, 2003; Nargeot, Baxter, Patterson, & Byrne, 1999).

Most researchers believe that dopamine does not simply signal hedonic value or "liking." For example, Parkinson's disease damages dopamine-producing neurons that project to the striatum. But when patients with Parkinson's disease are asked to rate the perceived pleasantness of sweet and salty tastes, their ratings are the same as those of healthy people. Apparently, the dopamine reduction in these patients causes no loss of the ability to "like" pleasurable stimuli (Travers et al., 1993).

Similar results are obtained from non-human animals. Researchers can't simply ask rats to rate the perceived pleasantness of different tastes. But researchers can infer degree of liking by watching the animals' reactions. When a sweet substance is placed in a rat's mouth, the animal shows a recognizable cluster of responses that include rhythmic movements of the mouth and protrusion of the tongue. This is sometimes called the hedonic or "yum" reaction. A bitter taste produces a different cluster of responses: gapes, shakes of the head, and wiping of the face with paws (the aversive or "ugh" reaction). Rats given injections of a drug that destroys dopaminergic neurons exhibit hedonic and aversive responses that are just as strong as or stronger than those of control rats (Berridge & Robinson, 1998). This suggests that rats with damaged dopamine systems continue to "like" and "dislike" food just as much as control rats do. What seems to change is their willingness to work for it.

The **incentive salience hypothesis** of dopamine function states that the role of dopamine in operant conditioning is to signal how much the animal "wants" a particular outcome—how motivated it is to work for it. According to this hypothesis, the incentive salience of food and other reinforcers—their ability to attract attention and motivate responding—is reduced in dopamine-depleted animals (Berridge, 1996, 2007; Berridge & Robinson, 1998). Given a choice between competing alternatives, normal animals will tend to choose their preferred reinforcer, even at the cost of a little extra work. In contrast, dopamine-depleted animals are still perfectly willing to eat a preferred food if it is placed in front of them, but they are unwilling to work hard to earn it (Salamone, Arizzi, Sandoval, Cervone, & Aberman, 2002).

A good example of this is seen in experiments where rats can choose to work for food. For example, most healthy rats prefer sugar pellets to rat chow, and they will work for the pellets by lever pressing, even if chow is freely available (Figure 5.11, green bars). Rats given a dopamine antagonist also prefer sugar to rat chow, if both are freely available. But, as shown in Figure 5.11 (red bars), if they have to work for the sugar pellets by lever pressing, they mostly settle for the free chow instead (Salamone et al., 2002). Whereas animals with normal dopamine levels prefer to work to obtain their preferred food; animals with reduced dopamine prefer not to work, even if this results in inferior food.

In an even more extreme case, mice that have been genetically engineered to be completely unable to produce dopamine will not seek food, and they generally starve to death by about 20 to 30 days of age, even if pellets are placed

incentive salience hypothesis. The hypothesis that dopamine helps provide organisms with the motivation to work for reinforcement.

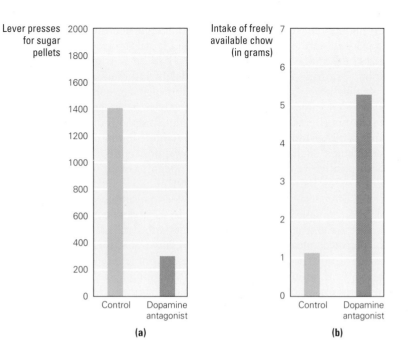

Figure 5.11 Dopamine and incentive salience If rat chow is freely available, but sugar pellets (which rats prefer) have to be "earned" by pressing a lever, control rats (green) will spend most of their time working for sugar pellets and eating relatively little free chow. Rats given a dopamine antagonist (red) are less willing to work for the sugar pellets, and instead settle for eating more of the freely available chow.
Information from Salamone et al., 2002.

directly in front of them (Palmiter, 2008). However, if the food is placed in their mouths, these animals will chew and swallow and even exhibit "yum" responses, indicating that they still "like" food and can consume it, they just lack the motivation to obtain it. These mice can be "rescued" by infecting cells in the striatum with a recombinant virus that allows the cells to produce and release dopamine; afterward, the mice eat enough normal chow to maintain body weight without further interventions.

Dopamine seems to affect incentive salience in humans, too. For example, the drug amphetamine can produce pleasurable feelings in humans, and these pleasurable feelings are not altered if the human is also given the dopamine-blocker pimozide (Brauer & de Wit, 1996, 1997). But the pimozide does suppress cravings for the amphetamine high. In other words, interfering with the dopamine system reduces "wanting" but not "liking" of amphetamine.

Conversely, increasing brain dopamine levels can increase craving. For example, in one study, humans addicted to cocaine were given the drug pergolide, which increases brain dopamine levels; the participants reported an increased craving for cocaine, but no increase in the self-reported "high" from cocaine (Haney, Foltin, & Fischman, 1998). Thus, stimulating the dopamine system increases "wanting" but not "liking" of cocaine.

The dopamine system can also be stimulated naturally by exposure to a stimulus that has previously been associated with reinforcement, increasing the "temptation power" of that stimulus (Berridge, 2012). For example, the sight of chocolate can stimulate intense desire in a chocolate-lover, even if she's not particularly hungry, while a cigarette smoker who is sincerely trying to quit may experience an overwhelming craving if he enters a room where he can see and smell others smoking. For this reason, many smokers and drug addicts who wish to quit try to stay away from environments where they are likely to encounter people using the addictive substance. Remember the concept of precommitment, discussed earlier in this chapter? Precommitment strategies can help counteract a strong $S^D \rightarrow R$ association not only by making it difficult to execute the response but also by reducing exposure to the S^D, thus reducing the release of dopamine, which in turn helps reduce craving.

In addition to evidence that dopamine signals "wanting," there is also considerable evidence that dopamine helps strengthen learning of $S^D \rightarrow R$ associations during operant conditioning (Wickens, 2009). Although dopamine isn't required for new learning, studies show that increases in brain dopamine levels (through drug administration or by presenting a reward) do tend to enhance new $S^D \rightarrow R$ learning (Wise, 2004). Dopamine generally promotes synaptic plasticity, possibly by increasing the ability of the presynaptic neuron to activate the target neuron, and since (as you read in Chapter 2) neurons that fire together wire together, this tends in turn to strengthen the synaptic connection between those neurons (Jay, 2003). However, the effects of dopamine on neurons are notoriously variable and complicated, and a great deal remains to be clarified about this neurotransmitter and its role in learning.

Endogenous Opioids: How the Brain Signals "Liking"?

If dopamine signals "wanting," then what signals "liking" in the brain? Probably the best-studied candidate is the opioid system. Opiate receptors in the brain were discovered quite by accident in the 1970s, by researchers trying to figure out how heroin and morphine work. Heroin and morphine belong to a class of drugs called *opiates*, which bind to a class of neuronal receptors called *opiate receptors*. Rather than assume that the brain evolved special receptors to respond to heroin and morphine, researchers suspected there might be naturally occurring brain chemicals that also activate the opiate receptors. They found a class of brain chemicals, named the **endogenous opioids**, that are naturally occurring neurotransmitter-like substances (peptides) with many of the same effects as opiate drugs. (The word *endogenous* means "originating on the inside"; *opioid* means "opiate-like.") Endogenous opioids are distributed throughout the central nervous system, and when released into the body they have a wide range of effects, including lessening the normal perception of pain and producing feelings of euphoria.

Although there is still a great deal to be learned about the endogenous opioids, many researchers believe these substances may mediate hedonic value, or "liking." If so, the reason that heroin and morphine are so intensely pleasurable could be that they happen to activate the same brain receptors as the endogenous opioids do.

For example, morphine makes sweet food taste sweeter and bitter food taste less bitter (Rideout & Parker, 1996). It can also make pain feel less painful; morphine is used medically for patients who are enduring extreme, long-term pain (in cases where the benefits of relieving suffering outweigh the risks of morphine addiction). These patients usually report that they still feel the pain but that it doesn't trouble them as much as it did before.

Endogenous opioids are released in response to primary reinforcers, such as food, water, and sex, and they may be released in response to secondary reinforcers and pleasurable behaviors, too (Le Merrer, Becker, Befort, & Kieffer, 2009). Differences in the amount of endogenous opioid released, and in the specific opiate receptors they activate, may help determine an organism's preference for one reinforcer over another (Le Merrer et al., 2009), contributing to effects such as you saw back in Figure 5.3, where infants sucked harder to obtain sweetened water, even though plain water satisfies thirst just as effectively. Just like infants, rats normally prefer sweetened to plain water, but rats given the opioid antagonist naloxone choose the sweetened water much less often than control rats (Hayward, Schaich-Borg, Pintar, & Low, 2006).

endogenous opioid. Any of a group of naturally occurring neurotransmitter-like substances that have many of the same effects as opiate drugs such as heroine and morphine; may help signal hedonic value of reinforcers in the brain.

How do "Wanting" and "Liking" Interact?

Given that "wanting" seems to be signaled by dopamine, and "liking" by the endogenous opioids, and that both contribute to driving behavior, how do these two brain systems interact? The answer is not yet clear. One possibility is that some endogenous opioids may modulate dopamine release. For example, some neurons in the VTA have opiate receptors on their dendrites that, when activated, could affect those neurons' normal tendency to release dopamine. In this model, the endogenous opioids would signal "liking," which in turn would affect the VTA's ability to signal information about "wanting." But other studies have suggested that different subpopulations of dopamine neurons might exist, conveying salience ("wanting") and valence ("liking") separately (Matsumoto & Hikosaka, 2009). The picture is complicated because some drugs, such as heroin, may manipulate both pathways: activating the "liking" system to produce a pleasurable high, while also activating the "wanting" system to produce a craving for more of the drug and the high.

Punishment Signaling in the Brain

As described above, neurons in the orbitofrontal cortex code expected outcomes—including specific anticipated reinforcers and punishers—and the dopamine and opioid systems may help code "liking" (hedonic value) and "wanting" (motivational value) of reinforcers. So what codes the aversive value of punishers? So far, there doesn't appear to be just one, singular "pain center" in the brain. Rather, both physical and emotional pain can activate multiple pathways and systems in the brain.

Physical pain often begins in the skin or musculature, where specific receptors called *nociceptors* respond to intense pressure, heat, or other stimulation that can cause damage. Messages from these receptors pass through the brainstem and thalamus to reach somatosensory areas in the cortex, such as primary somatosensory cortex (S1), which you read about back in Chapter 2 (and saw in Figure 2.7). Brain imaging studies have shown that the more intense the pain, the more activity in S1. When you shower, for example, as the water gets hotter, the more activity you'll have in S1. But although S1 encodes the physical location and intensity of pain, it does not encode how bad it "feels"—the affective component of pain. If you have spent all day freezing outside in the snow, standing under that same very hot shower may actually feel good, rather than painful. Similarly, a man swallowing wasabi-flavored snacks may gasp for breath and wipe away tears—and then reach for another handful to do it again. Clearly, not all intense stimuli are aversive. And not all aversive stimuli cause physical pain: disgusting smells, loud dischordant sounds, and social rejection can all be highly aversive, even though no physical pain occurs.

So, how does the brain decide whether a particular stimulation is aversive? Several brain areas have been implicated, including the **insular cortex**, or **insula**, shown in Figure 5.12. The insular cortex is located in the deep fold that separates the temporal lobe from the parietal and frontal lobes, and is important for our conscious awareness of our own bodies and emotional states. One subregion of the insular cortex, the *dorsal posterior insula*, plays a role in perception of physical pain, as well as other negative emotional states such as hunger, anger, and disgust (Naqvi & Bechara, 2009; Chang, 2013). For example, the dorsal posterior insula is active when participants experience painful heat or cold (for review, see Craig, 2003), and also when they experience social rejection, such as being excluded by the other players in an online video game (Eisenberger et al., 2003) or when viewing pictures of an ex-partner after an unwanted breakup (Kross et al., 2011). The degree of activation appears to be roughly proportional to the to the magnitude of the punisher. So, for example, in a study where errors could be punished by loss of 50 cents or of 5 cents, the insula showed more activity after a larger loss (Hester et al., 2010).

insular cortex (insula). A region of cortex lying in the fold between parietal and temporal lobes that is involved in conscious awareness of bodily and emotional states and may play a role in signaling the aversive value of stimuli.

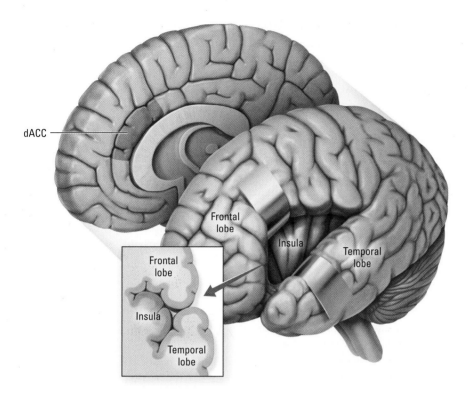

Figure 5.12 The insular cortex (insula) and dorsal anterior cingulate cortex (dACC) The insula, which lies buried in the fold separating the temporal lobe from the parietal and frontal lobes, is implicated in conscious awareness, and also plays a role in signaling the aversive value of stimuli. The dACC, which lies on the inner, or medial, surface of the prefrontal cortex, may play a role in the motivational value of punishers, helping select the actions we take in response.

Thus, just as the opioid system may signal pleasantness or "liking," the insula may be one way in which the brain determines degree of unpleasantness or "disliking." In fact, when the insula is damaged, learning to avoid unpleasant outcomes is impaired. One study found that patients with brain lesions that damaged the insula were as good as healthy controls at learning to obtain reward (point gain) but impaired at learning to avoid punishment (point loss), compared with patients whose brain damage spared the insula (Palminteri et al, 2012).

Once we've established that a stimulus is subjectively painful, the next step is to decide whether to do something about it. The **dorsal anterior cingulate cortex** (abbreviated **dACC**), which lies on the inner, or medial, surface of the prefrontal cortex, has been implicated in the motivational value of pain—the degree to which it can drive changes in behavior (Craig, 2003). Some current theories suggest that the dACC detects unexpected events (including pain) and suggests an appropriate response (Bush et al., 2002). For example, in one study, participants played a game in which they could win and lose money; during the game, neurons in the dACC responded both to errors that resulted in outright punishment and also to errors that merely resulted in no reward—but there was more activity in the former case (Simões-Franklin et al., 2010). Presumably, the worse the consequences of the error, the more motivation to change behavior.

On the other hand, dACC also shows increased activation when participants unexpectedly receive a reduced reward (Bush et al., 2002; Williams et al., 2004), and the activity level is predictive of whether participants actually change their response (Williams et al., 2004). Remember the phenomenon of negative contrast, in which monkeys and children refuse to work for a reward that is smaller than the one they've been trained to expect? In effect, the smaller-than-expected reward is functioning as a punisher, leading to decreased responding. It's possible that the dACC is recognizing this negative contrast, and signaling reduced motivation to work for the disappointing reward.

dorsal anterior cingulate cortex (dACC). A subregion of prefrontal cortex that may play a role in the motivational value of pain.

Thus, just as the brain has multiple systems for signaling the hedonic value and motivational value of reinforcers—"liking" via the opioid system and "wanting" via the dopamine system—the brain may also have multiple systems to signal the aversive value and motivational value of punishers, via brain areas such as the insula and dACC. However, much still remains to be understood about how we process and respond to punishers in the brain.

Interim Summary

- The dorsal striatum is an important brain substrate for storing stimulus–response ($S^D \rightarrow R$) associations; striatal-mediated $S^D \rightarrow R$ associations may be relatively automatic and habitual.

- The orbitofrontal cortex may be an important brain substrate for storing response–outcome ($R \rightarrow O$) associations, and in helping organisms to choose particular responses based on the expected outcomes of those actions.

- Reinforcers and punishers may activate neurons in the ventral tegmental area (VTA) and substantia nigra pars compacta (SNc), which project dopamine to the dorsal striatum, frontal cortex, and elsewhere. Interrupting these pathways, by lesions or drugs, disrupts operant conditioning.

- The incentive salience hypothesis suggests that dopamine modulates "wanting" rather than "liking," determining how hard an organism is willing to work for a reinforcement. Dopamine also affects plasticity, possibly helping to create or strengthen $S^D \rightarrow R$ associations in the dorsal striatum and elsewhere.

- The endogenous opioids, which are mimicked by many highly addictive drugs, may signal the hedonic value ("liking") of reinforcers.

- The dorsal posterior insula is a brain region that helps us determine subjective "disliking" of painful physiological and psychological stimuli. The dorsal anterior cingulate cortex (dACC) may help determine the motivational value of punishers, which is used to guide changes in behavioral responding.

5.3 Clinical Perspectives

Through the brain's reinforcement system, animals are hardwired to seek and obtain the things they need for survival (food, water, sleep, etc.) and to avoid those things that threaten survival (pain, sickness, predators, etc.). Unfortunately, this powerful reinforcement system can go awry. As an example, consider the pleasure we feel when we eat fatty food, which ensures that we are sufficiently motivated to repeat the experience. The human brain evolved millennia ago, when our ancestors had to forage for food and could never be sure when they'd find their next meal. Fat could be stored in the body and used for energy later, when food was scarce. Under these conditions, seeking out fatty foods was a good strategy for survival. In 21st-century America, however, food is easier for most of us to obtain, but our biological drives have not changed, and many of us—still driven to obtain the taste of fatty foods—have become dangerously overweight.

Drug addiction represents another way in which the reinforcement system can malfunction (or, rather, function only too well). You read in Chapter 4 how classical conditioning can contribute to drug addiction. Another large piece of the addiction puzzle is operant conditioning: learned responding to obtain a particular kind of reinforcement. Insights from operant conditioning theory may deepen our understanding of addiction and lead to more effective treatments.

Drug Addiction

We all know people who are "addicted" to their morning cup of coffee, their afternoon chocolate bar, or even their favorite television show. Such people may experience intense cravings for the addictive substance between uses and even experience withdrawal symptoms if the addictive substance is taken away. Someone who is addicted to her morning coffee may show signs of withdrawal (crankiness, sleepiness, headaches, difficulty paying attention) if she goes without. However, in most cases, such everyday addictions are not serious enough to interfere with our lives or our health.

Medically, **pathological addiction** is defined as a strong habit (or compulsion) that is maintained despite known harmful consequences (Berke, 2003; Leshner, 1999; McLellan, Lewis, O'Brien, & Kleber, 2000). The difference between pathological addiction and simple habit is largely one of degree. A coffee drinker may be sleepy or cranky until she gets her morning caffeine, and she may have trouble kicking the habit, but this would not usually be considered a pathological addiction unless she drank enough coffee to cause harmful medical consequences or to interfere with her normal life (for example, if she failed to pay the rent because she's spending all her income at Starbucks).

By contrast, a person is diagnosed as pathologically addicted to cocaine if he is unable to quit, suffers withdrawal symptoms between highs, and is obsessed with obtaining his next hit of the drug, to the point where he starts neglecting other aspects of his life—such as his family and his job—because nothing else is as important to him as cocaine. Alcohol can drive pathological addiction in the same way: an alcoholic may be unable to give up drinking, even though it has cost him his job, his health, and his family. Similarly, a rat that starves rather than cease performing the response that brings it electrical brain stimulation could be considered pathologically addicted to the stimulation.

Remember the college student Jamie who had to choose how to allocate his resources between eating out and buying DVDs (Figure 5.6)? We can think of a person with addiction as having similar choices for allocating resources (time, money, effort) and increasingly choosing the addictive substance at the expense of all other options.

Many individuals with pathological addictions want to quit, and try very hard to overcome their addictions. Unfortunately, there are several processes working against them. Addiction may involve not only seeking the "high" but also avoiding the adverse effects of withdrawal from the drug. In a sense, the high provides a positive reinforcement, and the avoidance of withdrawal symptoms provides a negative reinforcement—and both processes reinforce the drug-taking responses.

Many highly addictive drugs are opiates, meaning that they target opiate receptors in the brain. Heroin and morphine are two examples of opiate drugs. Other commonly abused drugs, including amphetamines and cocaine, work by increasing brain dopamine levels. Recall from Chapter 2 that neurons communicate when the presynaptic neuron releases molecules of a neurotransmitter into the synapse, and these neurotransmitter molecules activate receptors on the postsynaptic neuron (Figure 5.13a). Amphetamine causes dopaminergic neurons to release higher levels of dopamine. Cocaine works by blocking dopamine reuptake, so that dopamine remains in the synapse longer before being reabsorbed. In both cases, the effect is to increase the amount of dopamine available to activate the postsynaptic neuron (Figure 5.13b). Both amphetamine and cocaine can be used as reinforcers. Thus, for example, rats and mice will learn to lever-press vigorously for injections of amphetamine or cocaine (McBride, Murphy, & Ikemoto, 1999).

One interesting aspect of cocaine and amphetamine use is that, although "liking" seems to be critical in the early stages of drug use, people with long-term

pathological addiction. A strong habit that is maintained despite harmful consequences.

Figure 5.13 The effects of amphetamine and cocaine on dopaminergic neurons (a) A presynaptic dopamine-producing neuron releases dopamine into the synapse (1). These molecules activate dopamine receptors on the postsynaptic neuron (2). Unused molecules are broken down (3) and taken back into the presynaptic neuron, a process called reuptake (4). (b) Amphetamine works by causing dopaminergic neurons to make and release more dopamine (1). Cocaine works by blocking the reuptake of unused dopamine molecules (4). Both drugs thus increase the amount of dopamine in the synapse, increasing the chance that dopamine molecules will activate receptors on the postsynaptic neuron (2).

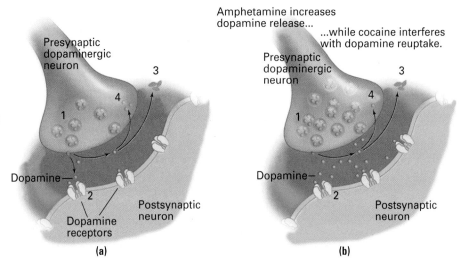

addictions often report that they no longer experience an appreciable high from the drug but crave it anyway—as if their "wanting" system has disconnected from their "liking" system and has run amok. In fact, individuals who have taken a dose of cocaine or amphetamine don't typically report feeling happy or pleasured—they feel aroused or excited. These facts fit nicely with the incentive salience hypothesis, which proposes that dopamine is involved in "wanting" but not necessarily in "liking."

A number of studies have shown that the insula is activated when drug abusers experience cravings; this has been shown for cocaine, alcohol, opiates, and nicotine. On the other hand, several intriguing studies have shown that cigarette smokers who happened to suffer strokes damaging the insula had their addiction to cigarettes practically eliminated (Naqvi et al., 2007; Suñer-Soler et al., 2012; Gaznick et al., 2014). Similarly, animals that have been addicted to amphetamine and then are administered drugs to temporarily inactivate the insula show disruption of their drug-seeking behavior (Contreras et al., 2007). These studies and others like them suggest that the representation of negative feelings (cravings and withdrawal) by the insula helps maintain the addiction.

In summary, drug addiction is currently thought to result from several factors (Robinson & Berridge, 2000), including positive reinforcement (the pleasurable high), negative reinforcement (avoiding withdrawal), and malfunction of the dopaminergic "wanting" system (the craving). As you read in Chapter 4, long-term drug use can also cause physiological changes in the synapse, so that ever-larger doses of drug are needed to get the same effect. Of course, the relative role of each of these factors varies among individuals, as a function of genetics, personality, and experience. Some people become strongly addicted to drugs after a single use, some become addicted over time, and a very few individuals can use drugs over a long period without developing pathological addictions. As yet there is no way to predict whether a particular individual who starts using a particular drug will become addicted, or how difficult it will be for that individual to break free of addiction.

behavioral addiction. Addiction to a behavior that produces reinforcement, as well as cravings and withdrawal symptoms when the behavior is prevented.

Behavioral Addiction

For some people, behaviors such as skydiving or winning at gambling can provide highs that are just as reinforcing as drugs—and just as addicting. **Behavioral addictions** are addictions to behaviors, rather than drugs, that produce reinforcements or highs, as well as cravings and withdrawal symptoms when the behavior is prevented.

Perhaps the most widely agreed-upon example of a behavioral addiction is compulsive gambling. Many people gamble occasionally, buying a weekly lottery ticket, playing online poker once in a while, or spending their vacations in Las Vegas or Atlantic City. These people pay their money, have their fun, and then walk away. But other people get hooked: they start to gamble more and more often, risking progressively larger sums of money, until nothing is as important as the chance to gamble. Up to about 1.6% of the general population may suffer from compulsive gambling at some point in their lifetime, and the problem may be even more widespread in particular groups, such as African Americans and college students (Potenza, Kosten, & Rounsaville, 2001).

For some, gambling is an occasional, harmless pastime. How might you determine whether a friend's gambling habit had developed into a pathological addiction?

Skinner suggested that one reason gambling is so seductive is that it is often reinforced on a VR schedule, as you read earlier: you can never be sure when the next big payoff will come, which makes it easy to talk yourself into playing just one more time, then just one more time . . . (Skinner, 1953). Each big win provides a powerful reinforcement of the gambling behavior.

Gambling is not the only behavior that can affect the brain's reinforcement system and become addictive. Examples of other behavioral addictions are compulsive eating, sex addiction, compulsive exercising, kleptomania, compulsive shopping—the list goes on and on. In each of these cases, the addicted person experiences a high from the behavior, followed by craving for another high, and withdrawal symptoms if the behavior is prevented. Some researchers even class romantic infatuation as a type of behavioral addiction, in which lovers devote large amounts of time and attention to their beloved, often at the expense of other activities and responsibilities—and suffer withdrawal when separated or rejected (see "Learning and Memory in Everyday Life: Addicted to Love?" on page 206 for more discussion of the addictive properties of romantic love).

It increasingly seems that behavioral addictions may reflect dysfunction in the same brain substrates affected by drug addictions. Modern research using fMRI has documented that gambling activates the brain in much the same pattern as seen when people with cocaine addiction receive an infusion of the drug (Breiter, Aharon, Kahneman, Dale, & Shizgal, 2001). Similarly, mice selectively bred for excessive exercise show greater concentrations of dopamine in the dorsal striatum, as do mice selectively bred for overeating (Mathes et al., 2010).

Other evidence for the similarity between drug addiction and behavioral addiction comes from Parkinson's disease, which results from the progressive death of dopamine-producing neurons that project to the dorsal striatum (and elsewhere). Parkinson's disease can be treated with a number of drugs, including dopamine agonists that "mimic" dopamine by activating dopamine receptors in the brain, and many patients benefit from this treatment. But, curiously, a small percentage of patients treated with high doses of dopamine agonists suddenly develop serious gambling problems (Santangelo, Barone, Trojano & Vitale, 2013). Apparently, in these individuals, the dopamine agonists disrupt the brain's "wanting" system in much the same way as shown in Figure 5.13 for amphetamine and cocaine, reinforcing the problem behavior. Often, the gambling problem can be cured simply by switching the patient to a different type of medication.

LEARNING AND MEMORY IN EVERYDAY LIFE

Addicted to Love?

Thinking about the object of his desire, Sam's heart starts to pound, his palms get sweaty, and he feels excitement and anticipation. Denied access, he becomes irritable, has trouble sleeping, and develops an overwhelming obsession that swamps all other interests.

Based on the above description, Sam might be a cocaine addict. Or he might just be passionately in love. Humans viewing pictures of their beloved show increased brain activity in areas including the dorsal striatum, the VTA/SNc, and the orbitofrontal cortex (Aron et al., 2005; Xu et al., 2011). These are some of the same brain areas activated by addictive drugs such as cocaine and amphetamine, and they are different from the brain areas activated by sexual arousal, indicating that romantic love is more than just a drive to obtain sex (Fisher, Aron & Brown, 2005). Viewing pictures of a romantic partner can even produce pain relief, apparently by activating reward centers in the brain that overrule the simultaneous processing of pain (Younger, Aron, Parke, Chatterjee, & Makey, 2010).

If romantic love activates the same reward circuits as cocaine, can it be just as addictive? Individuals experiencing intense romantic infatuation can display behaviors reminiscent of drug-seeking: pursuit of the beloved to the exclusion of other activities, obsessive and intrusive thoughts, and even impulsiveness and poor decision-making—leading, for example, to crimes of passion (Frascella, Potenza, Brown, & Childress, 2010). On the other hand, just because romantic love shares some brain circuitry with cocaine and can lead to some of the same behaviors doesn't necessarily justify calling love an "addictive substance." Not everything that evokes reward-seeking behavior or that provokes withdrawal symptoms qualifies for that label. (You seek out water when you're thirsty, and you experience distress if you go too long without; yet would you consider yourself "addicted" to water?) Many experts believe that the depression and grief that accompany a breakup are a normal part of life—not evidence of an addictive disorder.

Nonetheless, some individuals do display excessive devotion to their beloved, and upon romantic rejection experience severe withdrawal symptoms, including clinical depression and (in rare cases) suicide or homicide. It is possible that, just as some individuals can try cocaine and walk away while others become pathologically addicted, so too some individuals can survive a painful breakup while others remain trapped in a state of loss. Debate continues regarding whether such individuals should be diagnosed with a pathological addiction (Reynaud, Karila, Blecha, & Benyamina, 2010).

As research elucidates the brain substrates of drug addiction and suggests therapies (including medication) to reduce the cravings associated with drug withdrawal, should we consider using the same medications to help reduce cravings following romantic rejection? If you've ever had your heart broken by a failed romance, would you have taken advantage of such a treatment, if it existed?

Together, these results suggest there is a general reinforcement system in the brain, activated in similar ways for different categories of reinforcers, including primary reinforcers (food), secondary reinforcers (money), and drugs (cocaine) (Breiter et al., 2001). If so, a better understanding of the biochemical and behavioral principles underlying drug addiction may also help in the treatment of individuals suffering from behavioral addictions.

Treatments for Addiction

Until fairly recently, addiction was generally considered to be a character flaw. It was assumed that all a person had to do was display enough willpower to stay away from the addictive substance (whether a crack pipe, a gambling table, or a pack of cigarettes). Nowadays, it's more widely appreciated that the intensity of the cravings experienced in addiction, not to mention the often excruciating physical pain of withdrawal, make it impossible for many people to break free of addiction without outside help.

Currently, in the United States, the vast majority of treatment plans for addiction include cognitive therapy, often centered on self-help sessions with a support group (such as Alcoholics Anonymous and its many spin-off organizations— Gamblers Anonymous, Narcotics Anonymous, Overeaters Anonymous, and so on). Medical treatment may also help. For example, naltrexone is a drug that blocks opiate receptors, presumably decreasing the ability of heroin to bind to those receptors and cause a hedonic reaction. In some studies, people with heroin addiction who had undergone detoxification were able to stay off heroin longer if they received continuing treatment that included naltrexone (Kirchmayer et al., 2002; Rawson & Tennant, 1984), and compulsive gamblers have also reported reductions in gambling urges following naltrexone treatment (Grant, Kim & Hartman, 2008). But there are problems, too, including the fact that naltrexone must be taken daily and the fact that it doesn't reduce the patient's craving ("wanting") for heroin. As a result, a recent review of treatments for people addicted to heroin or other opiate drugs concluded that oral naltrexone treatment was not statistically superior to placebo in preventing relapse (Minozzi, Amato, Vecchi et al., 2011).

The behavioral principles of operant conditioning suggest some other therapies to help fight addiction. Addiction could be considered as a strong $S^D \rightarrow R \rightarrow O$ association, with sets of environmental stimuli (S^D) that trigger the addictive behavior (R), resulting in the reinforcing outcome (O) of a "high" or a reduced craving or both. When we look at addiction this way, the challenge for treatment is to break or reduce the strength of the conditioned association. Perhaps the most obvious approach is simple *extinction:* if response R stops producing outcome O, the frequency of R should decline. This is one way of interpreting the effectiveness of naltrexone: once the brain's reinforcement system is blocked, subsequent heroin (or gambling) doesn't produce the outcome that it used to, so the response (drug taking or gambling) should decline.

Another conditioning-based method for combating addictions and habits is *distancing:* avoiding the stimuli that trigger the unwanted response. For example, a cigarette smoker who is struggling to quit and who gets the urge to light up whenever she hangs out with friends who are heavy smokers should try to avoid those situations. If the S^D is never present, the R may never be triggered.

A third method is *differential reinforcement of alternate behaviors (DRA),* which you read about earlier in this chapter. If the smoker makes it through a whole week without a cigarette, she can reinforce her own abstinent behavior by treating herself to a favorite food or activity. Friends can also help by praising the nonsmoking behavior (one aspect of Alcoholics Anonymous is the social reinforcement provided by the group for each week the alcoholic stays sober). Some programs for heroin addicts reinforce abstinence with actual monetary vouchers, providing yet another form of reinforcement for the alternative behavior of not using the drug (Preston, Umbricht, & Epstein, 2000).

A final conditioning-inspired technique is *delayed reinforcement:* whenever the smoker gets the urge to light up, she can impose a fixed delay (e.g., an hour) before giving in to it. Recall that increasing the delay between response and outcome weakens learning (Figure 5.4). Imposing long delays between cravings and cigarettes may similarly weaken the association and will also, by default, reduce the total number of cigarettes smoked per day.

These and other behavioral approaches can be used in combination, increasing the chances of success. But even with all these behavioral therapies, addicted cigarette smokers (and alcoholics and drug users and gamblers) can still have a very hard time kicking their habits. Currently, the most successful approaches appear to be those that combine cognitive therapy (including counseling and support groups) with behavioral therapy based on conditioning principles—and medication for the most extreme cases (Grant, Potenza, Weinstein, & Gorelick, 2010).

Interim Summary

- Addictive drugs may hijack the brain's reinforcement system and can produce psychological as well as physiological addiction.

- Opiates such as heroin and morphine mimic the endogenous opioids that form the brain's "liking" system, while drugs such as amphetamine and cocaine affect the dopamine system that signals "wanting" or craving.

- In addition, addiction is driven by the desire to avoid the aversive symptoms of withdrawal; these aversive symptoms may be signaled by the insula.

- Behavioral addictions may reflect the same brain processes as drug addictions.

- Among the treatments for people with addictions are cognitive therapies, medications, and behavioral therapies, including principles learned from operant conditioning.

Synthesis

Remember Priscilla the Fastidious Pig? Her trainers taught her to turn on the radio, eat breakfast at a table, put away dirty clothes, and run a vacuum cleaner. They did this using the basic principles of operant conditioning: shaping one element of the routine, reinforcing the response with a bit of food each time the animal approximated a desired behavior, and then chaining the various elements of the routine together. The same general principles applied to Annie the toilet-trained toddler: her parents shaped the desired response (use of the potty seat), reinforcing this behavior by verbal praise and punishing alternate responses with scolding.

Operant conditioning is a powerful form of learning that can be applied to adult humans as well as infants and pets. You can even use it on yourself, if you want to break a bad habit or reinforce good study habits. And the applications have been implicitly appreciated at least since the time of the ancient Greeks; in Aristophanes's play *Lysistrata*, the women of Athens agree to withhold sexual favors from their men until the men call off a frivolous war with Sparta—a clear example of negative punishment.

Many brain areas participate in operant conditioning. $S^D \rightarrow R$ associations may be stored in connections between sensory and motor cortex and in the dorsal striatum; predictions about the outcome O that will follow R depend on frontal areas, including the orbitofrontal cortex. The brain also seems to have a general-purpose reinforcement system—including the VTA/SNc dopaminergic system—that helps strengthen the $S^D \rightarrow R$ connection and also allows the organism to choose between competing responses that result in different predicted outcomes. Meanwhile, the insula helps us evaluate the punishment value of stimuli, and may provide this information to the striatum to help us learn which actions will result in avoiding or mitigating that punishment.

Many kinds of addiction, including drug addictions and behavioral addictions, result when chemicals or behaviors interfere with the brain's reinforcement system; behavioral therapy for addiction is a clear application of operant conditioning procedures to help improve people's lives. Operant conditioning

In what ways can human employment resemble operant conditioning? In what ways might it be different?

"Oh, not bad. The light comes on, I press the bar, they write me a check. How about you?"

also forms the basis for behavioral economics, the study of how individuals allocate their time and energy among different available responses.

The bottom line: operant conditioning isn't just for circus animals. People use many operant conditioning techniques in daily life without even realizing it. By understanding the underlying principles, you can use them much more effectively.

KNOW YOUR KEY TERMS

basal ganglia, *p. 193*

behavioral addictions, *p. 204*

behavioral economics, *p. 189*

bliss point, *p. 189*

chaining, *p. 174*

concurrent reinforcement schedules, *p. 188*

continuous reinforcement schedules, *p. 184*

cumulative recorder, *p. 172*

differential reinforcement of alternative behaviors (DRA), *p.179*

discrete trials paradigm, *p. 170*

discriminative stimulus, *p. 169*

dorsal anterior cingulate cortex (dACC), *p. 201*

dorsal striatum, *p. 193*

drive reduction theory, *p. 175*

endogenous opioids, *p. 199*

fixed-interval (FI) schedule, *p. 186*

fixed-ratio (FR) schedule, *p. 185*

free-operant paradigm, *p. 170*

hedonic value, *p. 196*

incentive salience hypothesis, *p. 197*

insular cortex (insula), *p. 200*

matching law of choice behavior, *p. 189*

motivational value of a stimulus, *p. 196*

negative contrast, *p. 177*

negative punishment, *p. 182*

negative reinforcement, *p. 182*

operant conditioning, *p. 167*

orbitofrontal cortex, *p. 194*

partial reinforcement schedules, *p. 184*

pathological addiction, *p. 203*

positive punishment, *p. 182*

positive reinforcement, *p. 182*

postreinforcement pause, *p. 185*

Premack principle, *p. 191*

primary reinforcers, *p. 175*

punishers, *p. 177*

punishment, *p. 177*

reinforcement, *p. 169*

reinforcement schedules, *p. 180*

reinforcer, *p. 175*

response deprivation hypothesis, *p. 191*

secondary reinforcers, *p. 176*

self-control, *p. 181*

shaping, *p. 173*

Skinner box, *p. 171*

substantia nigra pars compacta (SNc), *p. 196*

token economies, *p. 176*

variable-interval (VI) schedule, *p. 187*

variable-ratio (VR) schedule, *p. 186*

ventral tegmental area (VTA), *p. 196*

QUIZ YOURSELF

1. In operant conditioning, _____ signal whether a particular response will lead to a particular outcome. (p. 169)

2. The _____ states that the opportunity to perform a highly frequent behavior can reinforce a less frequent behavior. A later refinement, called the _____ hypothesis, suggested that the opportunity to perform any behavior can be reinforcing if access to that behavior is restricted. (p. 191)

3. The _____ is a part of the brain that helps determine subjective values of punishers, such as whether the intense heat of a chili pepper on the tongue is perceived as pleasurable or painful. The _____ is a part of the brain that helps determine motivational value of punishment—what we do about it. (p. 200–201)

4. A _____ is a strong habit that is maintained despite harmful consequences; if the habit is a behavior, it is called a _____. (p. 203–204)

5. The part of the brain called the _____ contains dopamine-producing neurons that project to the _____, which is important for stimulus–response learning. Both these brain areas are part of the _____, which lies at the base of the forebrain. A different area called the _____

contains dopamine-producing neurons that project to the frontal cortex and other brain areas. (p. 193, 196)

6. The _____ theory states that learning is driven by organisms' biological need to reduce innate drives to obtain primary reinforcers. (p. 175)

7. In operant conditioning, _____ is the process of providing outcomes for a behavior that increase the probability of that behavior occurring again in future, while _____ is the process of providing outcomes that decrease the probability. (p. 169, 177)

8. _____ is the study of how organisms allocate their time and resources among possible options. (p. 189)

9. In the operant conditioning technique of _____, organisms are gradually trained to execute complicated sequences of discrete responses. In the operant conditioning technique of _____, successive approximations to a desired response are reinforced. (p. 173–174)

10. _____ are stimuli such as food and sleep that can function as reinforcers due to their innate biological value to the organism; if these stimuli are paired with other stimuli that have no biological value, those other stimuli can become _____. (p. 175–176)

11. In a _____ schedule, every instance of the response is followed by the consequence; in a _____ schedule, only some responses are reinforced. (p. 184)

12. An area of the prefrontal cortex, called the _____, is important for learning to predict which outcomes follow particular responses. (p. 194)

13. If an organism expects its favorite reinforcer, but receives a less-preferred reinforcer, the phenomenon of _____ predicts that the organism may respond less than if it had received that less-preferred reinforcer. (p. 177)

14. _____ are naturally occurring neurotransmitter-like substances that may help signal hedonic value ("liking") of reinforcers in the brain. (p. 199)

15. In a _____ reinforcement schedule, where an organism has a choice between multiple possible responses that may each lead to different outcomes, the _____ predicts that the organism will make each response at a rate proportional to how often that response is reinforced relative to the other choices. (p. 188–189)

16. In the process of _____, organisms learn to make responses in order to obtain or avoid certain outcomes. (p. 167)

17. Training paradigms that can cause responses to become less frequent over time include _____, in which the reinforcer is taken away after a response, and _____, in which a punisher is provided after a response. (p. 182)

18. In a fixed-ratio schedule of reinforcement, organisms typically give bursts of responding leading up to each reinforcement, followed by a _____ before the next burst begins. (p. 185)

19. _____ refers to the subjective "goodness" of a stimulus. The amount of work an organism will be willing to do to obtain that stimulus depends on the _____ of that stimulus. (p. 196)

20. Training paradigms that can cause responses to become more frequent over time include _____, in which the punisher is taken away after a response, and _____, in which a reinforcer is provided after a response. (p. 182)

Answers appear in the back of the book.

CONCEPT CHECK

1. A new kindergarten teacher wants to train her pupils to put away toys after playtime. Suggest three conditioning techniques she could use to train this behavior.

2. An employer wants to start testing her employees for drugs. She hopes that the threat of such tests will encourage employees to avoid drug use. According to the principles of conditioning, what would be the best way to schedule these drug tests?

3. Imagine that the police raid a house party and find the crowd taking an unfamiliar kind of drug. The users are sitting in front of a TV enthusiastically munching on stale bread and laughing hysterically at an old sitcom. Even without submitting samples of the drug to a laboratory, what might we hypothesize about the mechanisms by which this drug works?

4. After the 9/11 terrorist attacks on the World Trade Center in New York City, sniffer dogs were used to search for survivors among the rubble. As the days went by and no survivors were found, handlers reported that the dogs showed signs of "depression," or "not wanting to go to work in the morning." To combat this, at the end of a long day of failure, handlers would arrange for the dogs to find a "survivor" (really, a confederate hiding in the rubble) so that the dogs would end the day on a high note. Without invoking cognitive or emotional concepts, how could the utility of these arranged finds be explained using the principles of operant conditioning?

Answers appear in the back of the book.

CHAPTER 6

Generalization, Discrimination Learning, and Concept Formation

SITTING IN HER HIGH CHAIR, two-year-old Sabrina picks up a small piece of green broccoli from her plate and puts it in her mouth. Then, scrunching up her nose in disgust, she spits the broccoli out onto the floor and begins to pick through her plate for something else to try. Soon she comes upon another vegetable. In shape and size it resembles the broccoli, but it is white, not green. If the white cauliflower tastes anything like the green broccoli, Sabrina would certainly want to avoid it. But she is hungry, and if the white cauliflower tastes good to her (in contrast to the green broccoli), she'd love to eat it. Sabrina faces what philosophers and psychologists have long understood to be a fundamental challenge for learning: how and when to generalize. **Generalization** is the transfer of past learning to new situations and problems.

If, after tasting (and spitting out) the green broccoli, Sabrina assumes that all vegetables taste terrible, she might find herself missing out on lots of wonderful foods to enjoy. On the other hand, if she assumes that only vegetables that look exactly like the green broccoli are distasteful, she may suffer over and over again from eating related but not quite identical vegetables whose flavors are similar. Sabrina is faced with the core issue of generalization: the need to find an appropriate balance between *specificity*, deciding how narrowly a rule applies (for example, deciding that only green-broccoli-like vegetables are nasty tasting), and *generality*, deciding how broadly a rule applies (for example, assuming all vegetables will taste nasty).

As her palate matures and her experience with different foods expands, Sabrina learns to recognize the similarities and differences between vegetables—to treat some of them the same (generalization) while discriminating between those she considers

Behavioral Processes

Generalization: When Similar Stimuli Predict Similar Outcomes

Learning and Memory in Everyday Life: How Does Amazon.com Know What You Want to Buy Next?

Discrimination Learning and Stimulus Control: When Similar Stimuli Predict Different Outcomes

Learning and Memory in Everyday Life: Sleep Better Through Stimulus Control

Beyond Similarity: When Dissimilar Stimuli Predict the Same Outcome

Concept Formation, Category Learning, and Prototypes

Brain Substrates

Cortical Representations in Generalization

Generalization in the Hippocampal Region

Clinical Perspectives

Generalization Deficits in Schizophrenia

Stereotypes, Discrimination, and Racism in Generalizations About Other People

Jag_cz/Shutterstock

213

discrimination learning. The process by which animals or people learn to respond differently to different stimuli.

delicious and those she finds unappetizing. **Discrimination learning** is the process by which animals or people learn to respond differently to different stimuli. Generalization is seen in all the forms of learning and memory presented in this book. In classical Pavlovian conditioning, such as the rabbit eyeblink conditioning described in Chapter 4, rabbits that are trained to blink to a 1,000-Hz tone will generalize this learning, to some degree, to a 900-Hz tone and other tones of similar frequency. In operant conditioning, described in Chapter 5, a pigeon that has been trained to peck a yellow light for food will generalize this learning, to some degree, from yellow to orange lights.

This chapter considers the behavioral and biological principles of generalization and discrimination and how they allow us to apply past learning to novel future situations. It also presents basic principles of **concept formation,** the process by which we learn about new categories of entities in the world, usually based on common features. Vegetables, for example, are a concept, and a category of objects. Our ability to function in a complex world and deal with novel challenges depends on our ability to form categories, recognize similarities between events or objects, make generalizations, and discriminate between members of different categories.

formation. The process by which we learn about new categories of entities in the world, usually based on common features.

Life never replays exactly the same events, with exactly the same objects or circumstances that you have experienced before. To adapt—to survive and prosper—you need to apply what you have learned in the past to new situations that may be similar, but not identical, to what you have previously experienced.

6.1 Behavioral Processes

Two scenarios are possible given Sabrina's dilemma of whether or not to eat the white cauliflower, with its similarity in shape to the green broccoli she dislikes. Either eating the two vegetables will have the same outcome—and the cauliflower will taste bad to her—or eating the two vegetables will lead to different outcomes, and she'll find the white cauliflower, unlike the green broccoli, to be yummy. These are special cases of the more general problem of generalization, schematized in Table 6.1. The discussion in the next few pages is organized around this table, addressing in turn each of the four situations it describes.

Table 6.1 **Alternatives for generalization about and discrimination between two stimuli**

Sports *Dancing/cheerleading*

	Same outcome	Different outcomes
Similar stimuli	Similar stimuli → same outcome *Broccoli and cauliflower → nasty*	Similar stimuli → different outcomes *Broccoli → nasty* *Cauliflower → yummy*
Dissimilar stimuli	Dissimilar stimuli → same outcome *Broccoli and red peppers → nasty*	Dissimilar stimuli → different outcomes *Broccoli → nasty* *Red pepper → yummy*

As we examine each of these facets of generalization, we will see how the efforts of psychologists to understand them led to models that accomplished two things. First, the models allowed psychologists to formulate general principles of behavior and predict, often with quantitative detail, the behaviors to be expected in a wide range of learning and memory experiments. Second, the models—originally posited as abstract theories about networks of associations—identified the basic mechanisms brains use to accomplish these processes (which are described in Section 6.2), and did so years before science was able to verify their existence.

Our first discussion concerns the learning that occurs when similar stimuli predict similar outcomes or consequences, such as when a child decides that both the broccoli and the cauliflower are nasty tasting, corresponding to the top-left quadrant of Table 6.1. The key questions that psychologists have asked about these situations are (1) how do people mentally represent the fact that two entities, such as broccoli and cauliflower, are similar, and (2) when we know two things are similar, what are our expectations for how likely they are to lead to the same outcome?

Generalization: When Similar Stimuli Predict Similar Outcomes

Using a situation comparable in structure to the problem of Sabrina and her vegetables, Harry Guttman and Norman Kalish trained pigeons to peck at a yellow light for food reinforcement (Guttman & Kalish, 1956). They then tested what the pigeons had learned by showing them, in each of a succession of test trials, a single colored light that was either green, yellow, orange, or one of the in-between colors yellow-green or yellow-orange. By counting how often the pigeons pecked at each color, the investigators were able to measure how the similarity of the color to the yellow training stimulus affected the amount of pecking. Because the sensation of color results from physically different wavelengths of light—for example, yellow light has a wavelength of 580 nanometers (nm)—researchers can compare colors in terms of wavelengths. In this case, the colors ranged along a physical continuum from green (520 nm) to orange (620 nm).

Figure 6.1 shows how the pigeons responded. Not surprisingly, the pigeons pecked most at the stimulus on which they were trained: the yellow light, with its wavelength of 580 nm. However, the pigeons also responded to lights of other colors. Lights most similar to yellow (as measured by wavelength) produced the next-highest levels of responding. As the colors grew increasingly different from the original training stimulus (yellow), responding decreased rapidly.

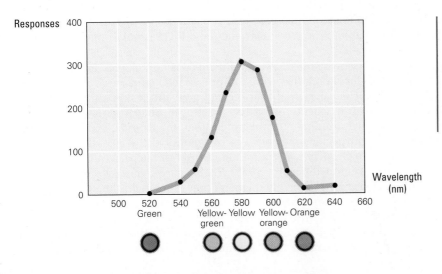

Figure 6.1 Stimulus-generalization gradients in pigeons Pigeons were trained to peck at a yellow light, having a wavelength of about 580 nm. When the pigeons were tested with other colors of light, their response rates decreased as the colors (wavelengths) departed farther from the trained color.

Data from Guttman & Kalish, 1956, pp. 79–88.

generalization gradient. A graph showing how physical changes in stimuli (plotted on the horizontal axis) correspond to changes in behavioral responses (plotted on the vertical axis).

The curve seen in Figure 6.1 is a **generalization gradient,** a curve showing how changes in the physical properties of stimuli (plotted on the horizontal axis) correspond to changes in responding (plotted on the vertical axis). The curve is called a "gradient" because it generally shows that an animal's response changes in a graded fashion that depends on the degree of similarity between a test stimulus and the original training stimulus. After training in which a single stimulus (such as a light of a particular color) has been reinforced repeatedly, generalization gradients around that trained stimulus show a peak, or point of maximal responding, corresponding to the original stimulus on which the animal was trained. This responding drops off rapidly as the test stimuli become less and less similar to the training stimulus.

From looking at a generalization gradient, you can deduce to what degree animals (including people) expect similar outcomes for stimuli that vary in some physical property, such as light wavelength. Thus, a generalization gradient is often taken to be a measure of the animal's or person's perception of similarity, in that if two stimuli are perceived as being highly similar (or identical) there will be significant generalization between them.

Generalization gradients have been studied for stimuli that vary in height, angle, size, or tone frequency. The generalization gradient in Figure 6.1 represents typical behavior for many different stimuli and across a broad range of generalization experiments. The fundamental characteristic of these generalization gradients is that they decline rapidly on either side of the peak. Roger Shepard, an influential American cognitive psychologist, described this feature of generalization gradients as one of the most constant basic laws of psychology (Shepard, 1987).

Generalization as a Search for Similar Consequences

Why should a pigeon that has been trained to peck at a yellow light respond to an orange light at all? Could the pigeon be making a mistake—confusing the orange light and the yellow light or failing to tell them apart? Probably not. Pigeons can easily be trained to discriminate yellow from orange. One explanation for generalized responding is that pigeons (and all animals, including humans) are savvy estimators of the probability of future events.

Imagine you are prospecting for gold and you find a mountain stream that yields bountiful quantities of ore. After you've taken all the gold from that one stream, you wonder where you might find more. If you are optimistic, you imagine that you have stumbled onto a fabulous mother lode and that all the streams in the entire valley are filled with gold. At your most pessimistic, you realize that there may only be gold in this one particular stream. Alternatively, the truth lies between these two extremes, and there is gold in just a few more streams in the valley.

Your initial discovery of gold in one stream does not tell you the size or shape of the gold-producing region or the location of its boundaries. All you know is that this one particular stream that yielded gold lies inside a gold-producing region of unknown extent. According to Roger Shepard, the fundamental challenge of generalization—for the gold miner, for Sabrina, and for Guttman and Kalish's light-pecking pigeons—is to identify the set of all stimuli that have the same consequence as the training stimulus. Shepard called this set the **consequential region** (Shepard, 1987). In Shepard's view, the generalization gradient in Figure 6.1 reflects the pigeon's best estimate of the probability that novel stimuli will have the same consequence as a training stimulus. The pigeon, Shepard argues, is not *confusing* a yellow-orange 600-nm light with the original yellow 580-nm light; rather, the pigeon, by responding at about 50% of its original rate to the yellow-orange light, is implicitly showing that it *expects*, based on

consequential region. A set of stimuli in the world that share the same consequence as a stimulus whose consequence is already known.

what it learned from pecking the yellow light (which always resulted in food), that there is an even chance that pecking the yellow-orange light will yield the same food delivery. The shape of generalization gradients, Shepard argued, suggests that animals (including people) consistently expect that the chance that two stimuli will have the same consequence drops off sharply as the stimuli become more distinct. This implies that you can view generalization gradients as an attempt to predict, based on past experience, the likelihood that the consequences of one stimulus will also be the same as that of other, similar stimuli.

The Challenge of Incorporating Similarity into Learning Models

Chapter 4 described formal models of classical conditioning, such as the Rescorla–Wagner model, in which networks of associations (each with an associative weight) link stimuli (lights and tones) to outcomes (airpuffs or shocks). In the studies that led to these models, the stimuli were highly distinct, with little perceptual similarity between them. When two stimuli were employed, they were usually from two different modalities, such as a light and a tone. But what if the stimuli in a conditioning experiment are two tones of similar frequency or two lights of similar wavelength? The application of Rescorla and Wagner's associative learning model from Chapter 4 to Guttman and Kalish's pigeon experiment (which used similarly colored lights) provides a good illustration of how easily the Rescorla–Wagner model falls apart and makes erroneous predictions unless you incorporate an additional assumption about how to represent the physical similarity of different stimuli.

Recall from Chapter 4 that when learning involves multiple cues in compound cue training, the Rescorla–Wagner model can be visualized as a simple one-layer network with links from the various cues to the possible outcomes, as was illustrated in Figure 4.12 (Gluck & Bower, 1988a). Each presentation of a trial was modeled by activating the corresponding input node for each stimulus cue (such as a tone), which then caused activation to travel through links (modulated by the association weights) to an output node (e.g., the prediction of the airpuff). When activation from a given input node reaches an output node, it is added to the incoming activations of all the other active stimulus cues on that trial. Learning resulted when the associative weights on the links were modified at the end of each trial so as to reduce the likelihood of a future mismatch (or "error") between the network's prediction for an outcome (the activation in the output nodes) and the actual outcome that was presented as feedback on that trial by the experimenter. Thus, as described in Chapter 4, the Rescorla–Wagner model details a process whereby an animal or person learns to minimize the difference between what actually happens (the airpuff) and the animal or person's expectation of that outcome. It is that expectation of the airpuff outcome that generates an anticipatory conditioned response, such as an eyeblink.

In our earlier applications of this model to classical conditioning, you saw how a tone and a light were identified as two distinct stimuli, each with an associative weight communicated from a corresponding input node to an output node that produced the conditioned response. To apply the same idea to Guttman and Kalish's operant pigeon paradigm, we'd need five input nodes, one for each of the five discrete colors that might be presented.

Figure 6.2a shows how one might model stimulus generalization using a simple network that has a single input node for each possible color of light (five are shown). This is an example of **stimulus representation,** the form in which stimuli are encoded in a theory or model. Figure 6.2a shows a particular type of stimulus representation called a **discrete-component representation,** meaning that each possible stimulus is represented by its own unique node in the model.

stimulus representation. The form in which information about stimuli is encoded within a model or brain.

discrete-component representation. A representation in which each individual stimulus (or stimulus feature) corresponds to one element (node) in the model.

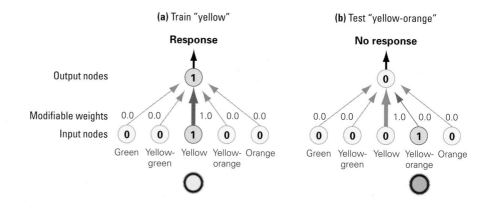

Figure 6.2 A model of stimulus generalization, using discrete-component representations A first attempt to model stimulus generalization would have one input node for each possible color of light, making this a discrete-component representation. Active nodes and weights are shown in red. (a) The network is first trained to respond to a yellow light, which activates the "yellow" input node. At the end of training, the weight from the "yellow" input node to the output node is strong (illustrated by a thick red line). (b) When a novel yellow-orange light is presented to the network, the yellow-orange light activates a different input node. This input node has never had its weight strengthened, and so it does not cause activation in the output node. Thus, the discrete-component network does not produce any response to the yellow-orange light despite the similarity to the trained yellow light. This model does *not* account for the generalization gradient seen in pigeons that is shown in Figure 6.1.

The network also contains a single output node for the response and has weights from the input nodes to the output node that are modifiable by learning, according to a learning algorithm such as the Rescorla–Wagner rule. Each of the input nodes in Figure 6.2a represents a different color of light (for example, green, yellow, or orange). Depending on the pattern of inputs, activity may be evoked in the output node; strong activity in this output node will cause the model to generate a response.

Before training, the weights from all the input nodes to the output node are set to 0.0, meaning that there are no prior associations between any of the lights and the response. Each training trial is modeled by activating the yellow-light input node, letting the activation from that node be regulated by the yellow-response associative weight and then updating this weight based on the difference between the actual output activation and the ideal output activation (1 in this case, because it should respond on every trial with the light cue). If the model is given repeated training trials of this sort over and over, in which the yellow light is presented followed by a reward, then the weight of the association connecting the yellow node to the response node will increase until it has a value of close to 1.0. Figure 6.2a displays the weight from the yellow node as being thicker than the others, to represent this greater weight.

Figure 6.2b shows what happens when this model is now tested with presentation of a novel yellow-orange light. There is still a strong 1.0 weight from the yellow node to the output node (because of the previous training), but that weight is not active (because a pure yellow light is not presented during this new test trial). Instead, only the yellow-orange input node is active, and it causes no activity in the output node because the weight from this input node is still 0.0. Thus, the model will produce no response to the yellow-orange light, even though that stimulus is very similar to the trained yellow light. In fact, this model will produce no response to any stimulus other than the original yellow training stimulus and so shows no generalization. The result would be a generalization gradient as shown in Figure 6.3: the model produces strong (about 80%)

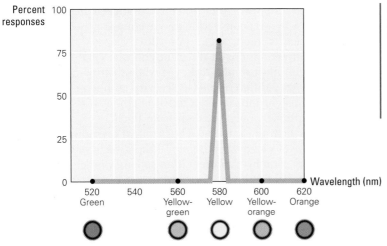

Figure 6.3 The generalization gradient produced by the discrete-component network of Figure 6.2 The discrete-component network gives no response to the yellow-orange light despite the similarity in color to the previously trained yellow light. It only responds to the trained "yellow" stimulus. In other words, this simple network fails to show a smooth generalization gradient like that shown by the pigeons in Figure 6.1.

responding to the yellow test stimulus but no (0%) responding to any other color. This does not look like the more gently sloping generalization gradient obtained from Guttman and Kalish's pigeons, seen in Figure 6.1. Clearly, the model in Figure 6.2 is wrong: it predicts a generalization gradient that is totally at odds with what Guttman and Kalish actually found.

This analysis suggests that the simple models that use one discrete node for each different stimulus feature are limited in scope. Such discrete models are useful for describing, understanding, and predicting how organisms learn about highly dissimilar stimuli, such as a tone and a light, but they don't work as well with stimuli that have some inherent similarity, such as lights of different colors. Do we throw out the old models when we run into a problem like this and simply assume that the Rescorla–Wagner rule is wrong? Not necessarily. Instead, given the otherwise wide range of success of this learning model, researchers have tried to extend it to account for generalization gradients. In this way, simple models can be considered to be preliminary steps toward a more complete understanding of learning and memory that builds, cumulatively, on past progress.

The learning model shown in Figure 6.2 uses the simplest-possible scheme for representing stimuli: a discrete-component representation in which each distinct stimulus is represented by a single input node that is then connected, by a modifiable weight to an output node. Discrete-component representations are applicable to situations in which the similarity between cues is small enough that there is negligible transfer of response from one to another. This was the case in the experiments discussed previously in Chapters 4 and 5, many of which used just a single tone or light. However, discrete-component representations fail in cases where stimuli have a high degree of physical similarity, since the models then produce unrealistic generalization gradients like the one shown in Figure 6.3.

Before moving on, let's consider how different kinds of representations can have different degrees of usefulness depending on the task, whether in our models, in our mental activities, or in the actual physical workings of our brain. Let's compare some of the different kinds of representations you use in everyday life. The letters in these words on the page, for example, are representations of sounds, and the words themselves represent ideas and concepts. To represent Rachel, a student at Rutgers University, the government may use her nine-digit Social Security number, 015-88-6999; the university uses her student ID number; and the phone company her mobile phone number.

Each of these representations was chosen to suit a particular need. However, what is appropriate for use as a representation in one context may not be appropriate in others. Of particular importance to our discussions in this chapter is the fact that different representations in different contexts yield different patterns of similarity: Rachel is most similar to Reyna when their names are spoken aloud (even if they have very different Social Security numbers). However, to the government, Rachel may be more similar to Elizabeth, whose social security number, 016-88-6999, differs by only one digit from Rachel's.

With this deeper appreciation for the effect of context on similarity between representations, we next explore how psychological theorists have grappled with the limitations of various stimulus representation schemes in learning models and how their solutions changed modern approaches to understanding the interplay between similarity, representation, and generalization. Meanwhile, the "Learning and Memory in Everyday Life" box below describes how companies such as Amazon.com have learned to use similarity to generalize for much the same adaptive purpose.

Shared Elements and Distributed Representations

distributed representation. A representation in which information is coded as a pattern of activation distributed across many different nodes.

Recall from Chapters 1 and 5 the work of Edward Thorndike, whose *law of effect* states that the probability of a response will increase or decrease depending on the outcomes that follow. Thorndike was well aware back in the 1920s of the limitations of discrete-component representations of stimulus features. He proposed that stimulus generalization occurs because of the elements shared by similar stimuli (Thorndike, 1923). For example, in Thorndike's view, yellow and yellow-orange are not two totally separate stimuli. Rather, he argued, they are each composed of many distinct elements, some shared and others not shared. As you read back in Chapter 1, ideas much like this were embraced by W. K. Estes in his *stimulus sampling theory* and by David Rumelhart and colleagues in their *connectionist models*. All these approaches embraced the basic idea of **distributed representations,** in which stimuli are represented by overlapping

---

LEARNING AND MEMORY IN EVERYDAY LIFE

How Does Amazon.com Know What You Want to Buy Next?

Have you ever had the pleasure of meeting someone and discovering you have many interests and tastes in common? You both like the same obscure music, enjoy the same French films, and read many of the same books. Finding someone like this is like finding your doppelganger (your phantom twin or double), and once you have found such a person and confirmed that you like the same 10 of the books that you discussed, you would take very seriously his recommendation of a book that is unfamiliar to you.

Amazon.com and other websites attempt to achieve much the same thing when they use a form of generalization to predict what books you might want to buy from them. They do it by trying to find as many of your doppelgangers as possible among their other customers. The process they use, called *collaborative filtering,* is an automatic filtering (or making of predictions) based on information from a large number of other people's past behaviors. In essence, collaborative filtering works by creating a very detailed stereotype of what kind of reader you are.

Once Amazon.com has found a sufficiently large number of like-minded individuals among its customers, it collates their purchasing histories to find books they have not yet purchased but that were purchased by one or more other individuals like them. Thus, by profiling you and creating a mini-category of individuals similar to you, Amazon.com seeks to generalize from your past behaviors to what you might do in the future. In this way, Amazon.com and other websites not only increase their ability to sell large numbers of books but also help you discover the hidden gems you might miss if you never met your own personal doppelganger.

sets of nodes or stimulus elements. Similarity emerges naturally from the fact that two similar stimuli (such as yellow and orange lights, or golden retrievers and cocker spaniels) activate elements belonging to both sets. Thus, what is learned about one stimulus will tend to transfer or generalize to other stimuli that activate some of the same nodes.

Figure 6.4a shows how distributed representations might be used in a network model that is only slightly more complicated than the model of Figure 6.2. This network has three layers of nodes and two layers of weights; by convention we refer to it as a two-layer network, counting the number of layers of weights. In the network model in Figure 6.4a, each stimulus activates an *input node* that is connected, by a layer of fixed (nonmodifiable) weights, to several nodes in an *internal representation*. These fixed weights, which do not change during learning, are drawn in light blue to help distinguish them from the modifiable weights, which are shown in gray. (Later, we'll consider more complicated models where the lower weights can be trained, but for now let's stick to this simpler case.) The internal representation nodes are then connected, via modifiable weights (in gray), which will change during learning, to a final *output* node. Thus, the presentation of a yellow light would activate the corresponding "yellow" node in the input layer, which in turn would activate three nodes at the internal representation (nodes 3, 4, and 5); but notice that two of these internal representation nodes (3 and 4) could also be activated by a yellow-green light, and nodes 4 and 5 could also be activated by yellow-orange light. In this manner, yellow-green, yellow, and yellow-orange all activate overlapping sets of internal representation nodes.

The nodes in Figure 6.4a are laid out as a topographic representation, meaning that nodes responding to physically similar stimuli, such as yellow and yellow-orange light, are placed next to each other in the model (this concept was introduced in Chapter 3). However, the physical layout itself is not what's important. What is important to a topographic representation is that the degree of overlap between the representations of two stimuli reflects their physical similarity. Thus, in Figure 6.4a, there is more overlap between the representations for yellow and yellow-orange than between those for yellow and orange. There is no overlap between the representations of very different colors, such as green and orange.

Now suppose this network model is trained to respond to a yellow light, which activates the three internal representation nodes as shown in Figure 6.4b. Note that this network transforms a representation of yellow light on the input to a different representation in the middle. If you were to view the input nodes as a string of ones and zeros where 1 means a node is on (colored red in Figure 6.4b) and 0 means a node is off (outlined in gray in Figure 6.4b), then this network transforms the representation 00100 at the input nodes to 0011100 at the middle nodes. Both of these strings of numbers represent the yellow light but in different ways at different places in the model (much the way Rachel, in the earlier example, can be represented by both her Social Security number and her phone number, in different contexts and for different purposes).

Note that the representation of yellow at the input nodes (00100) is a discrete-component representation because each light has one and only one node that is activated (and no other colors activate this node). In contrast, the representation at the middle nodes (0011100) is a distributed representation because the yellow color's representation is distributed over three nodes (3, 4, and 5). So this network can be viewed as one that converts a discrete representation at the input nodes to a distributed representation at the middle nodes. As you will see next, this distributed representation allows the model to account for similarity and generalization.

One way of determining how much the active weights should be increased is to use the Rescorla–Wagner learning rule. As you read in Chapter 4, this rule states that weights should be changed in proportion to the error on each trial

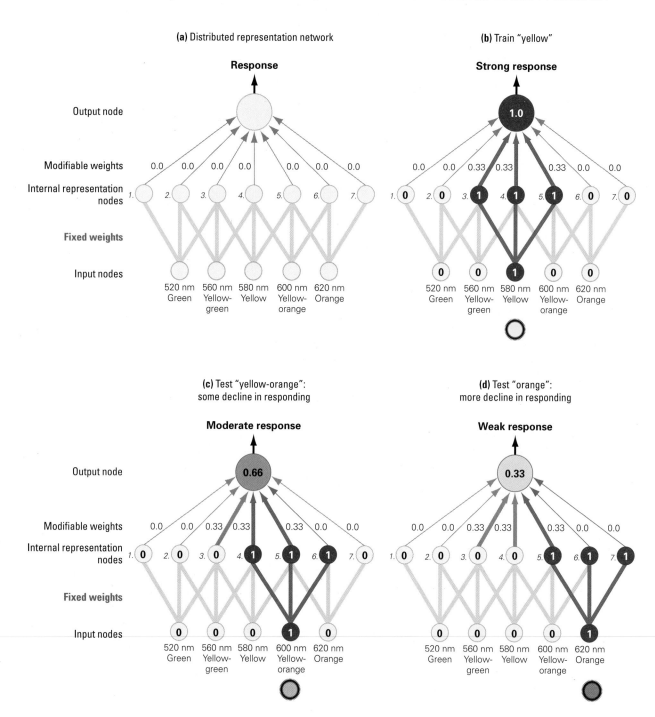

Figure 6.4 A network model using distributed representations (a) Presentation of a colored light activates a unique node in the input layer of the network. Each input layer node is connected, through fixed (nonmodifiable) weights—shown in light blue—to several nodes in the internal representation. The seven (numbered 1 to 7) nodes in the internal representation are then connected, by modifiable weights, shown in gray, to a single output node. (b) First, the network is trained to respond to yellow light. Presentation of the stimulus activates the corresponding input node, which activates three nodes in the internal representation (3, 4, 5), which connect to the output node. If the yellow light is repeatedly paired with a reward, weights from these three active internal-representation nodes to the output node are strengthened. (c) Next, the network is tested with a similar stimulus (a yellow-orange light) that activates internal nodes 4, 5, and 6. Because yellow-orange and yellow share two overlapping internal representation nodes (4 and 5), some response activation is produced at the output node. (d) An even more different color, orange, evokes even less overlap in the internal representation nodes because it shares only one common internal node (5), and thus orange evokes only weak response activation.

(with error defined as the mismatch between the outcome that occurred and the actual response activation, which is equivalent to the outcome that was predicted). Following many trials of training in which yellow is paired with reward, the weights from the three active nodes would each come to equal 0.33, as shown in Figure 6.4b, illustrated by the thickened lines connecting internal representation nodes 3, 4, and 5 to the output node. Presentation of a yellow light now activates nodes 3, 4, and 5, which in turn results in a net response activation of 1.0 in the output node, that being the sum of these three weights. (Note that the weights from internal representation nodes that have never been activated or associated with reward remain at their initial value of 0.)

Compare the distributed network in Figure 6.4b, which was trained to respond to a yellow light, with the discrete-component network in Figure 6.2, which was trained with the very same stimulus and outcome pairings. In the distributed network of Figure 6.4b, the learning is distributed over weights from three internal representation nodes, each with a trained weight of 0.33; in contrast, the discrete-component network in Figure 6.2 localizes this same respond-to-yellow rule into a single weight of 1.0 from one input node. Both network models give a response of 1.0 when the original yellow light is presented.

The difference between the distributed network of Figure 6.4 and the discrete-component network of Figure 6.2 becomes apparent only on presentation of stimuli that are similar—but not identical—to the trained stimulus. The distributed network is able to generalize. This generalization behavior can be assessed by testing a yellow-orange light, as shown in Figure 6.4c. Here, yellow-orange activates an internal representation that has considerable overlap with the representation activated by the trained yellow light. Specifically, both nodes 4 and 5 are also activated by the yellow-orange light, and each of these internal representation nodes will contribute to partially activate the output node. As a result, a reasonably strong output node activation of 0.66 results, proportional to the two-thirds degree of overlap between the representations for yellow and yellow-orange light. If the same network was tested with orange light, there would be less overlap with the representation of yellow light and a consequently weaker response of 0.33 (as shown in Figure 6.4d).

Figure 6.5 shows that when this model is used to generate responses to a series of novel lights, it produces a stimulus-generalization gradient that decreases smoothly for stimuli of increasing distance from the trained stimulus, similar to the pigeons' generalization gradient shown in Figure 6.1. This ability

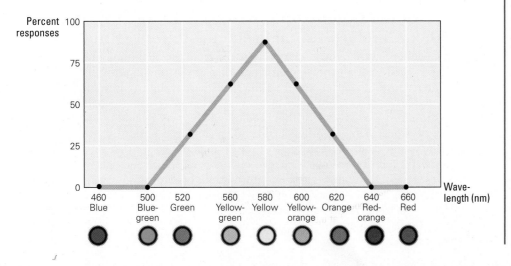

Figure 6.5 Stimulus-generalization gradient produced by the distributed representation model of Figure 6.4 The trained network in Figure 6.4 generates this stimulus-generalization gradient, which shows peak responding to the trained stimulus, yellow, and decreased responses for stimuli that are increasingly different from the trained stimulus. This smooth gradient is similar in shape to the ones seen in animals (including humans), such as that obtained from pigeons, shown in Figure 6.1.

to capture animals' and humans' natural tendency to generalize—that is, to treat similar stimuli similarly—contrasts markedly with the (lack of a) generalization gradient in Figure 6.3, which was produced using the network that had only discrete-component representation. Thus, even though the two models can learn the same initial task (respond to yellow light), they differ considerably in their generalization performance.

The generalization gradients in Figures 6.5 and 6.1 are not identical. The network model responds more strongly to orange light than the pigeons do. The exact width and shape of the generalization gradient produced by a model can, however, be manipulated by varying the number and amount of overlap of nodes in the model. Nevertheless, the overall shape makes the necessary point. Distributed-representation systems capture a fundamental property of learning: humans and other organisms tend, all other things being equal, to treat similar events similarly and to expect similar stimuli to have similar consequences. As you will read in Section 6.2, these early theoretical notions of shared elements and distributed representations within psychological models presciently anticipated later findings by neuroscientists demonstrating that, indeed, there are overlapping neural networks in our brains for similar stimuli.

Test Your Knowledge

Discrete or Distributed Representation Models?

Which of the following learning experiments can be understood and modeled using a discrete-component representation of the stimuli? Which require a distributed representation with overlapping patterns of elements? (Answers appear in the back of the book.)

1. A low-frequency tone predicts a shock and a high-frequency tone predicts a shock, but a light predicts food. What does a medium-frequency tone predict?

2. Patients in a hospital that has the walls painted blue take 2 days, on average, to recover and be discharged, while patients in a hospital that has red walls take 4 days to recover and be discharged. How many days would you expect it to take for patients in a hospital with green walls to recover? Why?

Discrimination Learning and Stimulus Control: When Similar Stimuli Predict Different Outcomes

Remember Sabrina, the fussy two-year-old from the beginning of this chapter? She is faced with a problem similar to that of Guttman and Kalish's pigeons. If green broccoli tastes awful to her, she may assume that a similar-shaped vegetable, such as cauliflower, has a good chance of being equally unappealing to her. On the basis of this prediction, she may decide it isn't worth the risk of experiencing another icky taste to eat the cauliflower. . . *unless* she is really hungry and there are few other options for her at that meal. If hunger motivates Sabrina to take a chance on the cauliflower and she finds that she loves the taste, she now has new information: broccoli tastes nasty to her, but cauliflower tastes yummy. From this experience, Sabrina has learned that it is important to *discriminate* between broccoli and cauliflower even though they have similar shapes (but different colors) because they lead to different outcomes when eaten.

One way of thinking about what has happened when Sabrina discriminates between the nasty tasting broccoli (which she avoids) and the yummy cauliflower (which she eats) is that Sabrina's eating behavior has come under the control of external stimuli. Psychologists would say that her behavior has come under **stimulus control** in that her choice of what she does or does not eat is now under the influence of the broccoli and cauliflower. Stimulus control is seen in all facets of life. If you drive through an intersection when you see a yellow light but brake to a stop when you see a red light, your own driving behavior can be considered to be controlled, or at least influenced, by these visual stimuli.

Through experience and discrimination learning, people can master many fine distinctions, as was introduced previously in Chapter 3's discussion of perceptual learning. Some can discriminate the tastes of Pepsi and Coca-Cola or can tell the French fries at McDonald's from those at Burger King. Similarly, gem cutters may learn to distinguish diamonds of subtly different color or quality, and parents of identical twins learn to tell their children apart. A dog fancier can identify many different breeds of terriers, all of whom may appear virtually identical in the eyes of a cat fancier who couldn't care less. Two objects or substances that initially seem very similar, or even indistinguishable, eventually come to be distinguishable when each is repeatedly paired with a different label, name, or outcome.

What determines whether two stimuli are to be treated as similar (generalization) or different (discrimination)? This is a fundamental problem in psychology, and the ensuing discussion reviews some of what psychologists have learned about it from years of careful studies of generalization in animals and humans. For a look at how stimulus control and discrimination learning can be applied to help you sleep better, see the "Learning and Memory in Everyday Life: Sleep Better Through Stimulus Control," below.

stimulus control. The mediation of behavior through responses to cues in the world.

Discrimination Learning and Learned Specificity

We turn now to look more closely at discrimination learning and what it tells us about mechanisms for learning and generalization. One important study in this area, conducted by Herbert Jenkins, a Canadian psychologist, was based on the behavior of two groups of pigeons. One group received standard training in which a

---

Sleep Better Through Stimulus Control

Have trouble falling asleep at night? Wake up tired and then find yourself unable to keep awake during the psychology exam review session? Maybe what you need is better control of the stimulus cues in your bedroom. The reason many people have trouble sleeping at night is that their bed and bedroom are filled with many conflicting stimulus cues that have been associated with wakeful activities, not with sleeping. Do you watch TV in your bedroom? If so, then the sight of the TV (even off) may control your desire to want to watch TV. Do you lie in bed for hours trying to fall asleep, worrying about your exam (or the guy who did not return your last seven email messages)? If so, then the bed and the room are becoming associated with—and hence controlling—the initiation of your worrying behaviors, not your sleep behaviors.

Sleep experts routinely advise good sleep hygiene—which mostly boils down to limiting your bedroom to stimulus cues associated with sleep and only sleep (and perhaps sex, as well; some flexibility needed here). As you saw in this chapter, discrimination training rarely happens in one trial (other than for fear associations), so it may take many days or weeks to train up better sleep habits. The first step, however, is to take all the stimulus cues that lead to (and hence, control) wakeful behaviors—the laptop, tablet, smartphone, and TV—and move them into another room.

1,000-hertz (Hz) tone signaled that pecking a key would result in food delivery (Jenkins & Harrison, 1962). Because the birds only received the food after pecking the key, the food reinforcement was contingent on the birds' behavior. Recall from Chapter 5 that this operant conditioning can be described as

S (1,000-Hz tone) → R (key peck) → O (food)

The second group of pigeons received discrimination training, in which one of two different (but similar) stimuli was presented on each trial. For these pigeons, the 1,000-Hz tone signaled that a key peck would result in food reinforcement, but another, very similar tone of 950 Hz signaled that a key peck would *not* result in food reinforcement:

S (1,000-Hz tone) → R (key peck) → O (food)

S (950-Hz tone) → R (key peck) → O (no food)

Because the two stimuli in this experiment differ within a single dimension, tone frequency, the paradigm is referred to as an *intradimensional discrimination*. In contrast, many of the paradigms presented in earlier chapters, where animals learned to discriminate between stimuli that differ across multiple dimensions (such as tones and lights), are known as *extradimensional discriminations*.

Following this training, both groups of pigeons were given test trials with new tones, ranging from very low frequency (300 Hz) tones to very high frequency (3,500 Hz) tones. The experimenters measured how frequently the birds pecked in response to each test tone. As shown in Figure 6.6a, the group receiving training with a single tone showed a broad, bell-shaped generalization gradient similar to what Guttman and Kalish found for light stimuli (see Figure 6.1).

In contrast, the pigeons given discrimination training showed a different pattern of generalization. Their generalization gradient was much steeper, centered immediately around the 1,000-Hz tone and dropping off much more rapidly—so that they were not responding at all to the nearby 950-Hz tone or to any other tones higher or lower than 1,000 Hz. The difference in shape of the two generalization gradients in Figure 6.6a shows that with discrimination training,

Figure 6.6 Generalization gradients following discrimination training (a) Data from a study in which one group of pigeons learned that a 1,000-Hz tone signaled that key pecks would be reinforced; these birds showed a typical generalization gradient when tested with novel tones. A second group of pigeons learned that the 1,000-Hz tone signaled that pecks would be rewarded but that the (very similar) 950-Hz tone signaled no reward ("discrimination training"); these birds showed a much steeper generalization gradient. (b) Examples of the prototypical category A and category B exemplars used in the Wills and McLaren (1997) categorization study, and a graph showing generalization gradients following discrimination versus A-only training.

(a) Data from Jenkins and Harrison, 1962.
(b) Research from Wills & McLaren, 1997.

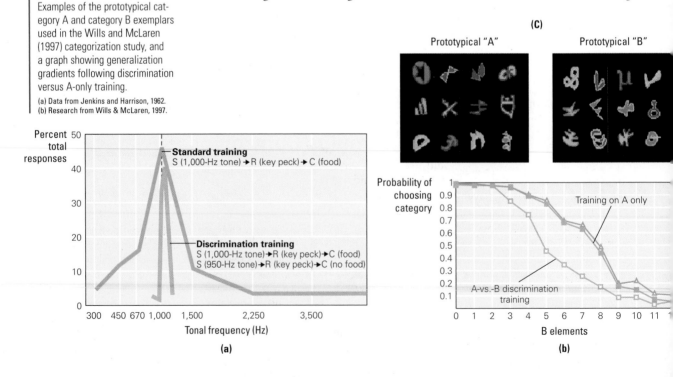

the generalization gradient can change to reflect more specific (more narrowly focused) responding to the reinforcing stimulus. In fact, the generalization gradient following discrimination training in Figure 6.6a looks very much like the gradient in Figure 6.3, which illustrated what a component-representation model predicts when there is no overlap in stimulus representations. This suggests that Figure 6.3 wasn't wrong; it was just an illustration of what happens after discrimination training when the stimuli do not have overlapping representations.

A similar difference between the generalization gradients that emerge from training with a single stimulus as compared to discrimination training can also be seen in studies of human category learning in which people are shown visual stimuli consisting of sets of abstract geometric elements (Wills & McLaren, 1997). Each subject was presented with two 12-member sets of abstract geometric elements. One of the sets was presented as a prototypical exemplar of category A, and a distinct set of 12 was presented as prototypical of category B (Figure 6.6b). Other, potential exemplars were then presented, constructed with different mixtures of the elements from the prototypical A and the prototypical B exemplars. An exemplar was considered to be a member of category A if it possessed at least 8 out of the 12 elements from the category A prototype.

Participants in this study were assigned to one of two types of training. Participants who received discrimination training were shown many examples of category A and many examples of category B, with each example labeled according to its correct category assignment. Other participants did not receive discrimination training but instead were only shown exemplars from category A. After receiving one or the other form of training, participants were given a subsequent generalization test in which they were asked to judge whether unlabeled exemplars were members of category A. As you can see from the generalization gradients in Figure 6.6b, people who were trained only with the category A stimulus showed broader generalization gradients than those who received A-versus-B discrimination training, endorsing more of the ambiguous exemplars as being members of category A. This pattern of data echoes the pattern seen in Herbert Jenkins's pigeon study (Figure 6.6a): broad generalization gradients after standard acquisition training and narrower, more focused generalization gradients after discrimination training.

Peak Shifts in Generalization

To understand another very important phenomenon in generalization, let's meet Lisa and consider a conundrum she faces. She decides it is time to get married, and so she goes online to look for prospective husbands at an Internet dating site. Of the first four bachelors she meets, the two whom she likes, Ian and Jim, are both 5'10" tall; the other two, Bart and Mauricio, are 5'11", and she does not fancy either of them. What do you think will happen when she comes upon the profile of Marcus, who is 5'9"? Would you expect her to like Marcus as much as Ian or Jim (both 5'10"), whom she previously found to be acceptable, or will she be disposed to like Marcus even more than any of the others?

One study (Hanson, 1959) looked at this very issue, albeit using pigeons and colored lights, not marital prospects. Pigeons were trained to peck at a 550-nm light (for which they received food reward) until they were responding reliably and consistently to this stimulus (a form of operant conditioning). Some of these pigeons (the control group, also called the S+ group) received only this training, while another group (the experimental group, or S−) were given additional discrimination trials with a very similar light, at 555 nm, that was not reinforced. Both groups of pigeons were later tested with probe trials using a full range of different-colored lights, measuring from 480 to 620 nm. The results are shown in Figure 6.7.

Figure 6.7 Peak shift following discrimination training along a physical continuum Pigeons were reinforced for pecking in the presence of a 550-nm light and then were divided into two groups. One group received only this training (the control, or S+, group), while the other received discrimination training in which the 550-nm lights were positively reinforced while a similar 555-nm light was negatively reinforced (the S− group).

Data from Hanson, 1959, *Journal of Experimental Psychology, 58*, pp. 321–333.

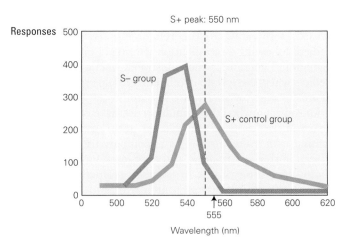

As you can see, the peak responding of the experimental animals shifted away from the nonreinforced stimulus, an effect that is therefore called peak shift. It has been observed in many different discrimination paradigms in which stimuli vary along some physical continuum, such as color, brightness, tone, pitch, tilt, or numerosity. Experimental studies of peak shifts in learning are not limited to pigeons pecking, either. Peak shift effects have been observed in bees (Lynn, Cnaani, & Papaj, 2005), horses (Dougherty & Lewis, 1991), rats, goldfish, guinea pigs, chickens, pigeons, and humans (Purtle, 1973). Studies in humans have found evidence of peak shift effects in discriminating complex categories (McLaren & Mackintosh, 2002; Wills & Mackintosh, 1998), pictures of faces that morph along a complex visuospatial dimension (Spetch, Cheng, & Clifford, 2004), and complex acoustic sounds that vary in time (Wisniewski, Church, & Mercado, 2009).

Why does peak shift occur so ubiquitously in animal and human discrimination learning? Kenneth Spence (1937), building on the earlier physiologically inspired theories of Pavlov (1927), suggested an interpretation of the peak shift phenomenon that demonstrates how it might arise from the summation of both excitatory and inhibitory cue–outcome associations.

As schematized in Figure 6.8, Spence proposed that a positive (excitatory) generalization gradient develops around S+ and that an inhibitory gradient develops around S−, each emerging as a result of the fact that each of the two stimuli activates a range of elements shared with stimuli above and below it, as hypothesized in Figure 6.4. If the net associative strength for any test stimulus

Figure 6.8 Spence's theory of peak shifts Spence argued that the peak shift arises through the combination of excitatory and inhibitory stimulus-generalization gradients that are established around S+ and S−, respectively. The net association is presumed to be the sum of these gradients, calculated by subtracting the level of inhibition from the level of excitation at each point along the stimulus domain. The peak shift is the movement between the previous maximal responding to S+ at the right vertical line to the new point of maximal responding at the left vertical line.

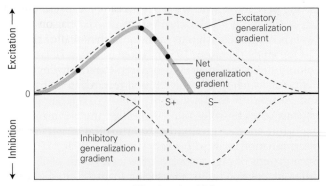

is the difference between the excitatory gradient formed around S+ and the inhibitory gradient formed around S− and if these two gradients overlap considerably, then the greatest net positive strength will be to the left of S+ because this region is both close to S+ (550) and farther away from S− (555). The peak shift is the movement from the previous maximal responding to S+ at the red vertical line to the new point of maximal responding at the blue vertical line shown in Figure 6.8. This is analogous to arguing that Lisa will like 5'9" Marcus the most because he is very similar to the 5'10" men she liked (Ian and Jim) and very dissimilar from the 5'11" Mauricio and Bart, whom she rejected.

Pavlov (1927) and Spence (1937), and also Shepard (1987), viewed the interactions between excitatory and inhibitory generalization as being fundamentally hardwired, in line with the historical tradition of seeking biologically oriented, "nature" explanations for learning phenomena, discussed in Chapter 1. Other researchers, however, suggested that some of what seemed like a nature-driven, biological determinant of generalization could, alternatively, emerge from learned, or "nurture," explanations. In particular, the Lashley–Wade theory (1946), building on Pavlov's earlier proposals, argued that the generalization gradients seen in the peak-shift and other paradigms depend on an animal's prior experience with these cues. Testing such a theory is challenging, however, because it often requires raising animals in artificial environments, where they are deprived of prior exposure to such cues. Nevertheless, there is some evidence to suggest that prior experience, or familiarity, with cues can influence the steepness of the generalization gradients they engender in subsequent discrimination training (see, for example, the discussion in Chapter 3 on learning from mere exposure versus explicit training).

Errorless Discrimination Learning and Easy-to-Hard Transfer

Recall from Chapter 4 the principles of error-correction learning, where learning in the Rescorla–Wagner model is driven by prediction errors—that is, by the mistakes in prediction that an animal makes when it does or does not anticipate a US. Later, the chapter revealed that errors need not be the key to all forms of learning. In fact, as we will now see, it is possible to develop training regimens that all but avoid errors—and in doing so, allow animals (including people) to learn very difficult discriminations with little or none of the frustration and emotional angst that come from making mistakes (emotions you might have experienced yourself on the last test or quiz you took).

Herbert Terrace developed a training procedure he called **errorless discrimination learning,** in which training begins with a discrimination task that is readily learned and then transitions to a similar but different discrimination task that is harder to learn, so as to eliminate, or drastically reduce, the errors made during the harder task.

In one study of errorless discrimination learning, Terrace trained pigeons to discriminate between a red disk (S+) and a green disk (S−), pecking only to the red disks (Terrace, 1963a). Normally this would take many trials and produce many errors, much as in the classical and operant conditioning curves shown in the last two chapters. Terrace got the pigeons to learn this discrimination quickly, and with almost no errors, by giving them a hint—like of a set of "training wheels" for learning—to keep them from making the wrong

errorless discrimination learning.
A training procedure in which a difficult discrimination is learned by starting with an easy version of the task and proceeding to incrementally harder versions as the easier ones are mastered.

Falling off a two-wheeler can hurt, so this child's parents adopted a variation of what learning procedure?

Ariel Skelley/Getty Images

choices. Early in training he made the red disks very bright and bold (which naturally attracts pigeons' attention) and kept them available for three full minutes. In contrast, the green disks were presented as dark or dimly lit and were only available for a few seconds. Since pigeons generally don't peck at dark objects, especially if they have limited time to do so, the pigeons rarely pecked the wrong green S− keys. Gradually, over many trials, Terrace increased the brightness and duration of the green S− keys until they were as bright and were lasting as long as the red S+ keys. Terrace's pigeons were now able to discriminate the two colors without the extra hint and guidance of the modified duration or brightness of the keys.

Terrace's errorless learning procedure has had many applications in education but has seen its greatest success in training people with learning disabilities. By means of a procedure similar to the one in the Terrace study, children with Down syndrome were taught to identify basic shapes such as ovals and rectangles (Duffy & Wishart, 1987). Flash cards were used that initially contained only the correct shape for the name given (so no errors were possible). Then the children were shown cards containing two choices, one being the correct shape in a large format and the other being the incorrect shape very small. Making the incorrect choice very small guides the child to ignore it, akin to the dim lights in the Terrace study, and thus the child is naturally inclined to choose the larger option. Over time, the sizes of the two alternative choices were made increasingly similar until they were the same (much as Terrace gradually made the lights for the pigeons the same brightness and duration), and the children with Down syndrome ultimately learned to identify shapes correctly—avoiding the errors and frustration that would have resulted had they been given the final test at the very start.

Errorless discrimination learning does have significant drawbacks. While it produces rapid and strong (and painless) learning of the discriminations being trained, many later studies showed that this learning is very rigid and inflexible, adhering to the details of the original training procedure rather than generalizing to new situations and stimuli not trained in this fashion (Jones & Eayrs, 1992; Clare et al., 2002). Nevertheless, in the learning-disabled children described above, the errorless discrimination learning, by preventing errors, also prevented the frustration, trauma, and self-doubt the children might have suffered from making many errors at the start. Like a parent who doesn't want to see a child fall and hurt himself trying to ride a two-wheeler before he is ready, the errorless learning procedure offers a gradual form of learning that begins with an easy task and then incrementally moves to the harder version when the person is ready and able.

Beyond Similarity: When Dissimilar Stimuli Predict the Same Outcome

So far in this chapter, we have discussed the process of learning in three of the kinds of cases schematized in Table 6.1: (1) those in which similar stimuli lead to similar consequences; (2) those in which dissimilar stimuli lead to different consequences; and (3) those in which similar stimuli lead to different consequences. But there's a fourth possibility: what happens when two dissimilar stimuli predict the same outcome? As you will see next, generalization can occur even when physical similarities between the stimuli are absent.

One way in which generalization can extend to dissimilar stimuli is through frequent pairing, or co-occurrence. William James (1890) argued that if all cold objects were wet and all wet objects were cold, the two characteristics would be viewed as a single concept; the presence of one (for example, wet) would imply the presence of the other (that is, cold). James concluded that organisms would tend to cluster, or treat equivalently, stimulus features that tend to co-occur. More recently, in his historical novel *The Alienist*, author Caleb Carr told the story of a nineteenth-century forensic psychologist, a former student of William James at Harvard, who uses this very example from James's Introductory Psychology lectures to hunt for a serial murderer who is terrorizing New York City. The criminal had a childhood history of being beaten by the people he loved, and as a consequence he came to view violence and love as so intertwined that when one was present, he expected or exhibited the other, beating to death any woman he loved and loving any woman whom he beat.

Much common wisdom is based on examples of this kind of clustering, such as "where there's smoke, there's fire." The same kind of clustering of stimuli based on common outcomes or consequences can be demonstrated in the learning laboratory, as seen in the following discussions of sensory preconditioning and acquired equivalence.

Sensory Preconditioning: Co-occurrence and Stimulus Generalization

One way in which co-occurrence of two stimuli can lead to generalization is through a training procedure known as **sensory preconditioning,** in which the prior presentation of two stimuli together, as a compound, results in a later tendency for any learning about one of these stimuli to generalize to the other.

In the laboratory, sensory preconditioning is usually tested in three phases, as summarized in Table 6.2. In phase 1, animals in the compound-exposure group (that is, the experimental group) are first exposed to a compound of two stimuli, such as a tone and a light presented simultaneously. In phase 2, the animals learn that one of the stimuli by itself (such as a light) predicts an important consequence (such as a blink-evoking airpuff), and they eventually give a blink response to the light. In phase 3, the animals are then exposed to the tone only.

If you take a look at the training of the compound exposure group in sensory preconditioning in Table 6.2, you might find that it reminds you of the blocking procedure from Table 4.5 in Chapter 4—only backwards! As you will see below, reversing the order of training—by training the compound stimulus tone + light first (as in sensory preconditioning) rather than last (as in blocking)—has a big impact on what is or isn't learned. This reminds us that a key aspect of the error-correction nature of learning is that the order of presentation matters.

Most of the compound exposure group will show at least some response to the tone. In contrast, a second (control) group of animals are given exposure to the tone and light separately in phase 1. They are then given phase 2 training identical to the phase 2 training given the other group: they learn that the light by itself predicts the airpuff. But when tested with the tone alone in phase 3, these animals show little or no response (Thompson, 1972).

sensory preconditioning. Training in which presentation of two stimuli together as a compound results in a later tendency to generalize what is known about one of these stimuli to the other.

Table 6.2 **Sensory preconditioning**

Group	Phase 1	Phase 2	Phase 3: Test
Compound exposure	Tone + light (together)	Light → Airpuff ⇒ Blink!	Tone ⇒ Blink!
Separate exposure (control group)	Tone, light (separately)	Light → Airpuff ⇒ Blink!	Tone ⇒ No blink

It seems that the compound exposure in phase 1 establishes an association between the tone and light. In phase 2, the light becomes associated with the airpuff, and this learning is indirectly transferred to the tone too. This transfer can be interpreted as a *meaning-based generalization*, because the tone and light are assumed to have the same meaning (that is, they both predict the airpuff) even though they do not have any relevant physical similarity. A meaning-based generalization can be contrasted with a *similarity-based generalization*, which arises naturally between two stimuli that are physically similar. Sensory pre-conditioning shows that co-occurrence of two stimuli is sufficient to produce meaning-based generalization from one stimulus to the other.

As suggested above, the order of phase1 and phase 2 is very important. If we reversed the order, we would have a blocking procedure (Table 4.5 from Chapter 4), and this leads to the opposite effect—little or no conditioning to the tone even when it is repeatedly presented in training.

Acquired Equivalence: Novel Similar Predictions Based on Prior Similar Consequences

Another form of meaning-based generalization can occur when two non-combined stimuli share the same consequence, that is, predict the same outcome. In this case, it is possible for generalization to occur between two very dissimilar stimuli even if they never co-occur. Consider two girls, Mandy and Kamila, who look nothing alike but who both love hamsters. Later you learn that Mandy's favorite fish is a guppy. Given that Mandy and Kamila have similar taste in pet rodents, you might expect that Kamila will also like Mandy's favorite pet fish.

Geoffrey Hall and colleagues have found a similar form of generalization in their studies with pigeons (Bonardi, Rey, Richmond, & Hall, 1993; Hall, Ray, & Bonardi, 1993). In one study, they trained pigeons to peck at a light that changed between six different colors, identified as A1, A2, B1, B2, X1, Y1. The researchers then trained the animals to associate the four two-color sequences A1–X1, A2–X1, B1–Y1, and B2–Y1 with the arrival of a food reward (Table 6.3, left column).

In effect, the colors A1 and A2 were "equivalent" because they were both paired with X1. Likewise, colors B1 and B2 were equivalent in their pairing with Y1. Next, the pigeons learned that pecking to A1 alone resulted in food; in contrast, no food followed pecks to B1 alone (Table 6.3, middle column). In phase 3, the pigeons were tested for response to A2 and B2. The birds responded strongly to A2 but not to B2 (Table 6.3, right column), suggesting that the birds had learned equivalencies in phase 1 between A1 and A2 and between B1 and B2. After phase 1 training that A2 was "equivalent" to A1 and phase 2 training that responses to A1 resulted in food, the birds expected that responses to A2

Table 6.3 **Acquired equivalence**		
Phase 1 Training	**Phase 2 Training**	**Phase 3: Test**
A1 → X1 → food A2 → X1 → food	A1 → food	A2: strong pecking response
B1 → Y1 → food B2 → Y1 → food	B1 → no food	B2: no strong response

would also result in food. Hall and colleagues called this behavior **acquired equivalence** because prior training that two stimuli were equivalent increased the amount of generalization between them—even if those stimuli were superficially dissimilar. Similar effects have been shown in humans (Spiker, 1956) and rats (Honey & Hall, 1991; Hall & Honey, 1989). In summary, although physical similarity is a frequent cause of generalization, generalization may also have other causes. Animals and people can learn to generalize from one stimulus to another that is superficially dissimilar if the stimuli have a history of co-occurring or of predicting the same consequence.

acquired equivalence. A learning and generalization paradigm in which prior training in stimulus equivalence increases the amount of generalization between two stimuli even if those stimuli are superficially dissimilar.

Negative Patterning: When the Whole Means Something Different than the Parts

In another complication of generalization from compounds composed of stimuli with different attributes, consider what happens when Sabrina starts playing with other children. She might learn from experience on the playground that freckle-faced children are usually bratty and that red-haired children are also bratty. Given these two associations, you might expect her to be especially wary of a girl she meets one day who is both red haired and freckle faced. Based on her past experiences, she expects the girl to be really horrid because she has both of the attributes Sabrina associates with brattiness. All other things being equal, we, like Sabrina, tend to assume that combinations of cues will have consequences that combine, and possibly summate, what is known about the individual cues.

But is this always the case? What if a certain combination of cues implies something totally different from what the individual cues mean? For example, you know what the letter "c" sounds like and you know what the letter "h" sounds like, but when you see these two letters together as "ch," they represent quite a different sound. Thus, readers of English learn that certain combinations of letters can sound very different than their component letters. Consider another example, from driving a car. While waiting at an intersection, you notice that the antique Citroën car in front of you has its *left* rear red taillight flashing, signaling the car is about to turn left (Figure 6.9a). If its *right* rear red taillight were flashing, you would assume the driver intends to turn right (Figure 6.9b).

But what if both taillights were flashing, as in Figure 6.9c? Although either the left or the right turn signal flashing indicates an imminent turn, both taillights flashing together certainly does not indicate a combination of two turns. Instead, twin flashing taillights signal a hazard; the car is proceeding slowly or is disabled. Although our tendency may be to assume that what is true of

Figure 6.9 The challenge of interpreting combined cues (a) Left blinking light means left turn, (b) right blinking light means right turn, (c) both lights blinking means that the driver has turned on the hazard lights.

(a)

(b)

(c)

Mark Gluck

component features presented individually is also true of their combination, clearly it is possible to override this tendency to generalize from components to compounds, as do automobile drivers who learn that the combination of both left and right lights flashing means something quite different from either of them flashing alone.

This kind of situation, where cue combinations have radically different meanings than their components, has been extensively studied with both animal and human learning tasks. Suppose, for example, that a rabbit in a classical conditioning study is trained to expect that either a tone or a light, presented alone, predicts an airpuff US to the eye but that there will be *no* airpuff US if the tone and light appear together. To respond appropriately, the animal must learn to respond with a blink to the individual tone cue or light cue but to withhold responding to the compound tone-and-light cue. This task, schematized as

Tone → Airpuff US

Light → Airpuff US

Tone + Light → No US

negative patterning. A behavioral paradigm in which the response to the individual cues should be positive while the response to the pattern is negative (no response).

is known as **negative patterning** because the response to the individual cues is positive while the response to the compound (i.e., the "pattern") is negative (no response).

Because both the tone and the light cues are part of the tone-and-light compound, there is a natural tendency for the animal to generalize from the component cues to the compound cue and vice versa. However, this natural tendency to generalize from component features to compounds doesn't work in this case because the components and the compound are associated with very different outcomes. Negative patterning is difficult to learn because it requires suppressing the natural tendency to generalize about similar stimuli.

With training, the negative-patterning task can be mastered by many animals, including humans. Figure 6.10 shows an example of negative patterning in rabbit eyeblink conditioning (Kehoe, 1988). After only a few blocks of training, the animals learn to give strong responses both to the tone alone and to the light alone. In addition, during this early phase of training, the rabbits make the mistake of overgeneralizing from the components to the compound, giving incorrect strong responses to the compound tone-and-light stimulus. Only with extensive further training do the rabbits begin to suppress responding to the tone-and-light compound.

Can associative-network learning models such as those illustrated in Figure 6.2 (with discrete-component representation) or Figure 6.4 (with distributed

Figure 6.10 Negative patterning in rabbit eyeblink conditioning Negative patterning requires learning to respond to two cues (a tone and light) when each is presented separately but to withhold the response when the two cues are presented together.
Data from Kehoe, 1988.

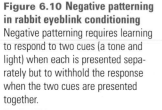

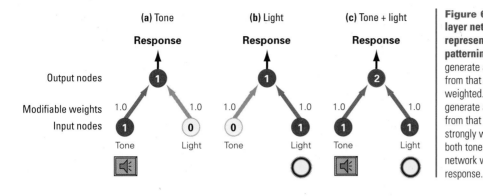

(a) Tone **(b)** Light **(c)** Tone + light

Figure 6.11 Failure of a single-layer network with discrete-component representations to learn negative patterning (a) For the tone cue to correctly generate a strong response, the connection from that input to the output must be strongly weighted. (b) For the light cue to correctly generate a strong response, the connection from that input to the output must also be strongly weighted. (c) Consequently, when both tone and light cues are present, the network will incorrectly give a strong response.

representations to indicate stimulus similarity) provide an explanation of how rabbits and other animals learn negative patterning? Figure 6.11 illustrates why single-layer network models, like those in Figure 6.2, using discrete-component representations cannot learn the negative-patterning problem. To produce correct responding to the tone alone, the weight from the input unit encoding tone must be strengthened to 1.0 (Figure 6.11a). To produce correct responding to the light alone, the weight from the input unit encoding light must also be strengthened to 1.0 (Figure 6.11b). But this means that if the tone and light are presented together, activation will flow through both those modifiable weighted connections and produce strong responding to the compound—stronger responding, in fact, than to either component alone (Figure 6.11c).

All the weights could be decreased, of course, to reduce the level of response to the compound in Figure 6.11c, but this would also, incorrectly, reduce responding to the individual components. In fact, there is no way to assign association weights in the network of Figure 6.11 that would make the network respond correctly to all three different types of training trials.

One way to resolve this dilemma is to use a two-layer network, as shown in Figure 6.12. This network has two layers of weights (but three layers of nodes); the critical additions are the three nodes in its internal representation layer. One of these nodes (designated "Tone only") becomes active whenever the tone is present, and another ("Light only") becomes active whenever the light is present. To solve negative patterning (and other similar tasks), the internal layer of nodes of this model also contains a new type of node, called a **configural node**. This node (labeled "Tone + light") acts as a detector for the unique configuration (or combination) of two cues. It will fire only if *all* of the inputs are active, that is, when *both* tone and light are present.

Configural nodes are equivalent to what engineers call an "AND" gate, because they respond only when all the inputs are active. For example, a configural node might fire when tone *and* light are present but not when only one or the other of these two cues is present. Note that these configural ("AND") nodes are very different from the nodes in Figure 6.4, which capture similarity through overlapping representations. The reason the shared nodes in Figure 6.4 are able to capture the fact that orange and yellow are similar is that these shared nodes are active when either orange or yellow is present. As such, the nodes in Figure 6.4 are equivalent to what engineers call an "OR" gate, because they fire if one *or* the other input is present. Just as engineers have long appreciated that they need both "AND" and "OR" gates to build a broad range of complex circuits in hardware, evolution appears to have similarly constructed neural systems capable of encoding both types of logical operations.

configural node. A detector for a unique configuration of two cues, such as a certain tone and light.

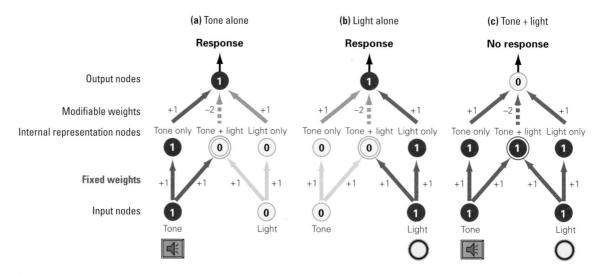

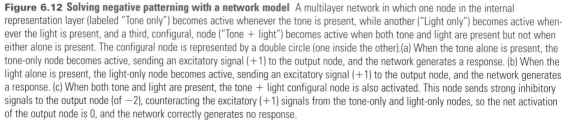

Figure 6.12 Solving negative patterning with a network model A multilayer network in which one node in the internal representation layer (labeled "Tone only") becomes active whenever the tone is present, while another ("Light only") becomes active whenever the light is present, and a third, configural, node ("Tone + light") becomes active when both tone and light are present but not when either alone is present. The configural node is represented by a double circle (one inside the other).(a) When the tone alone is present, the tone-only node becomes active, sending an excitatory signal (+1) to the output node, and the network generates a response. (b) When the light alone is present, the light-only node becomes active, sending an excitatory signal (+1) to the output node, and the network generates a response. (c) When both tone and light are present, the tone + light configural node is also activated. This node sends strong inhibitory signals to the output node (of −2), counteracting the excitatory (+1) signals from the tone-only and light-only nodes, so the net activation of the output node is 0, and the network correctly generates no response.

Configural "AND" nodes, which require all their inputs to be on in order to fire, are indicated in Figure 6.12 by a double circle to distinguish them from the shared nodes in Figure 6.4 that represent the "OR" function (that of firing when any of the inputs are present). Figure 6.12 shows how such a network might look after it has been trained to solve the negative-patterning problem. Figure 6.12a shows that when the tone (alone) is present, the tone-only node in the internal representation layer becomes active and in turn activates the output node. Similarly, in Figure 6.12b, the light by itself activates the light-only node, which subsequently activates the output node. However, when both tone and light are present (Figure 6.12c), all three internal representation layer nodes are activated. The tone-only and light-only internal nodes each have a linkage weight of +1 to the output node, so their activation together would tend to cause—contrary to the rules—an output activation of 2 (their sum). However, the connection of the tone-and-light compound node to the output node is given a *negative* weight of −2. Therefore, when the configural node is activated, it cancels out the effects of the tone-only and light-only nodes, for a net output activation of (+1) + (+1) + (−2), or 0, as shown in Figure 6.12c. Thus, the network correctly responds to either cue alone, but (equally correctly) not to the compound, solving the negative-patterning problem. This shows how and why it is important to have the ability to respond to, and represent, the presence of unique configuration stimuli.

Negative patterning is just one example of a larger class of learning phenomena that involve configurations of stimuli and that cannot be explained using single-layer networks or networks whose internal nodes are "OR" nodes only. To master configural learning tasks, an animal must be sensitive to the unique configurations (or combinations) of the stimulus cues, above and beyond what it knows about the individual stimulus components.

Test Your Knowledge

Discriminating between Generalization Paradigms

To be sure that you have learned to discriminate between the various behavioral paradigms of generalization, see if you can assign each of the following four paradigms to the real-world example that best exemplifies it in the numbered list below. (Answers appear in the Answers section in the back of the book.)

   a. Discrimination training

   b. Sensory preconditioning

   c. Acquired equivalence

   d. Negative patterning

1. Elizabeth is quite impressed by men who, on a first date, bring her either candy or flowers. However, if a man shows up with both, she is turned off, feeling he is coming on too strong.

2. As a child, Samson learned that people who have deep voices also tend to have beards. He later became convinced that men with beards are strong, and he inferred that a deep voice was also likely a sign of strength.

3. By playing snippets of music by Brahms, then Schubert, and then Brahms again, a music teacher is able to teach his class how to recognize the style of each.

4. Mark and Kaori enjoy many of the same foods and people. Based on this observation, Mark guesses that Kaori will also like a particular song of which he is fond.

Concept Formation, Category Learning, and Prototypes

Before we can delve further into the topic of concepts and categories, it is important to clarify the distinction between the two. **Concepts** are psychological, or mental, entities; they are ideas we construct on the basis of our experiences with the world. In contrast, **categories** are of the world—classes or divisions of people or things that have some shared characteristics (Smith, 1989). Part of the confusion between concepts and categories is that we often use the same word to refer to both. The category of "dog" is a subdivision of mammals and refers to all entities in the real world that can be described as dogs. The concept of "dog," however, is the mental representation through which we represent, understand, and think about the category of dogs.

The formation of concepts is a basic cognitive process through which people organize, describe, and generalize about the world. It is the means by which we learn about categories in the world. In turn, categories help us make inferences about objects and events and guide us in predicting the future. The study of how people learn categories, especially in cases where there is only a fuzzy or probabilistic relationship between the features and categories in question, has been a rich domain for applying principles of animal learning to understand human cognition.

Forming concepts requires both generalization and discrimination. We generalize within a class but discriminate between members of different classes. To understand the concept of dogs, we must recognize a wide variety of dogs, be able to generalize the concept of dog to new dogs that we have never seen before, and be able to discriminate between dogs and other similar entities, such as wolves and coyotes.

How and why do psychologists differentiate between concept formation and discrimination learning? The distinctions between the two are subtle, and many learning paradigms can be accurately described as either one. In general, however, discrimination learning refers to paradigms where there are a relatively

concept. A psychological representation of a category of objects, events, or people in the world.

category. A division or class of entities in the world.

small number of stimuli (sometimes only two), the stimuli are simple idealized and often unnatural images or sounds produced in a laboratory, and the distinction between positive and negative examples is usually well defined. In contrast, concept formation often involves many (often countless) stimuli, which may be naturalistic and highly varying and complex, and the distinction between positive and negative instances of a concept may be ill defined or very difficult to make. Although concept formation was originally viewed as belonging exclusively to the domain of human learning, while discrimination learning was predominantly the purview of animal learning, this distinction no longer holds, as you will see in the material to follow.

In the remainder of Section 6.1, we will discuss how concepts can emerge from discrimination training, relate our past discussion of configural cues to models of how people learn complex categories, introduce the concept of prototypes in understanding and reasoning about natural categories, and finally note some of the generalization errors that can result from faulty reasoning about concepts.

Emergence of Concepts Through Discrimination Learning

Animals have remarkable abilities of discrimination learning. Pigeons can be trained to discriminate between the Baroque classical music of Bach and the modern twentieth-century neoclassical music of Stravinsky (Porter & Neuringer, 1984). Not only were the pigeons able to learn this discrimination well, they were able to generalize this learning to novel music from other composers who worked in related stylistic genres. For example, to the music of Telemann, another Baroque composer, the birds pecked the Bach response disk; in contrast, to the mid-twentieth-century neoclassical music of Eliott Carter, they pecked the Stravinsky disk. It seems from these studies that pigeons are able to form and distinguish the abstract concepts of Baroque and neoclassical music styles.

Pigeons can also learn to discriminate between the abstract paintings of Picasso and the impressionist paintings of Monet, and then to generalize this learning to other paintings by these and other artists they have never seen before (Watanabe et al., 1995). After being trained on only Picasso and Monet paintings, pigeons identified the paintings of other impressionists like Renoir and Cezanne as being "like" the Monets, while paintings by other abstract painters, such as Matisse and Braque, were treated like Picasso paintings. Much as the pigeons in the music study appeared to infer the concepts of Baroque and neoclassical styles, these pigeons appear to have induced the distinction between impressionist and abstract painting styles. Interestingly, the birds in the painting study were successful at recognizing the novel abstract paintings of Picasso even when they were shown upside down. However, the pigeons did much less well when the more realistic and representational paintings of Monet were presented to them upside down.

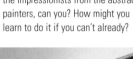

If a pigeon can learn to differentiate the impressionists from the abstract painters, can you? How might you learn to do it if you can't already?

Nano Calvo/age fotostock

category learning. The process by which animals and humans learn to classify stimuli into categories.

Configural Learning in Categorization

Earlier in this chapter, in our discussion of negative patterning, we noted the importance of being sensitive to configural cues—the unique combination of two or more elementary cues. Configural learning is especially important in **category learning,** the process by which animals and humans learn to classify stimuli into different categories. Chapter 4 reviewed work by Mark Gluck and Gordon Bower that utilized simple networks based on the Rescorla–Wagner model to capture some aspects of how people learn to categorize multidimensional stimuli (Gluck & Bower, 1988a). As you will recall, these studies showed that people acquire feature–category associations in much the same way that animals acquire CS → US associations in classical conditioning, using the same error-correcting learning rule described by the Rescorla–Wagner model of classical conditioning.

One of Gluck and Bower's studies tested people's ability to learn to diagnose fictitious medical patients. On each trial, participants were given the description of a patient who had one or more symptoms. The participants were then asked to determine, based on that pattern of symptoms, whether the patient had a particular disease. Gluck and Bower's original model for this task (shown in Figure 4.15) looked much like the associative network in Figure 6.2, with discrete-component representations for each input symptom and one layer of modifiable associative weights connecting those inputs to an output node. However, just like the network in Figure 6.2, this category-learning model could only capture learning for tasks in which there were no important configural relationships among the cues. To ensure that their model could solve complex multi-cue tasks such as negative patterning, Gluck and Bower later added configural nodes to their category-learning model (Gluck & Bower, 1988b; Gluck, Bower, & Hee, 1989).

As an example of how such a model could work, Figure 6.13a shows a network that can learn to diagnose hypothetical patients based on three symptoms: fever, ache, and soreness. Each symptom has its own input node that is active

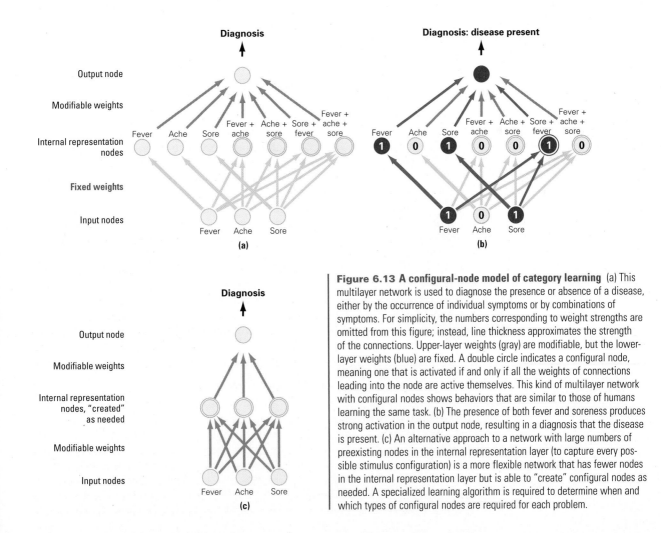

Figure 6.13 A configural-node model of category learning (a) This multilayer network is used to diagnose the presence or absence of a disease, either by the occurrence of individual symptoms or by combinations of symptoms. For simplicity, the numbers corresponding to weight strengths are omitted from this figure; instead, line thickness approximates the strength of the connections. Upper-layer weights (gray) are modifiable, but the lower-layer weights (blue) are fixed. A double circle indicates a configural node, meaning one that is activated if and only if all the weights of connections leading into the node are active themselves. This kind of multilayer network with configural nodes shows behaviors that are similar to those of humans learning the same task. (b) The presence of both fever and soreness produces strong activation in the output node, resulting in a diagnosis that the disease is present. (c) An alternative approach to a network with large numbers of preexisting nodes in the internal representation layer (to capture every possible stimulus configuration) is a more flexible network that has fewer nodes in the internal representation layer but is able to "create" configural nodes as needed. A specialized learning algorithm is required to determine when and which types of configural nodes are required for each problem.

whenever the symptom is present. This network also has one internal representation node for each individual symptom as well as internal representation nodes for each possible combination of two or more symptoms. A double circle indicates a configural node, meaning one that is activated if and only if all the weights of connections leading into the node are active themselves. The output node is used to make a prediction of disease: when the output node is highly active, the diagnosis is that the disease is present; otherwise, the diagnosis is that the disease is absent. For instance, if a patient reports fever and soreness, the internal-layer nodes corresponding to these individual symptoms are activated as are nodes corresponding to the configuration of fever and soreness combined, as shown in Figure 6.13b. This leads to strong activation of the output node, resulting in a diagnosis that the disease is present.

There is, however, a critical drawback to this configural representation. Note that the disease-diagnosis network of Figure 6.13a and Figure 6.13b has one internal-layer node for each symptom and another for each possible combination of symptoms. When there are only three symptoms, the model need only keep track of the weights of eight nodes. If the patient exhibited 10 symptoms, however, more than one thousand internal-layer nodes would be required to encode every possible combination of symptoms. Unfortunately, the problems that confront us in the real world consist of numerous stimuli occurring alone or in combination. The number of nodes needed in a network to encode all possible combinations of all possible stimuli would be vast—too many for even a powerful computer to handle. And yet only a small fraction of these combinations will ever actually occur. This dilemma, called **combinatorial explosion**, stems from the rapid expansion of resources required to encode configurations as their number of component features increases.

An alternative to the configural-node network model of Figure 6.13a would be a network like the one shown in Figure 6.13c. This alternative has a smaller number of nodes in the internal representation layer, but those nodes can be assigned the role of configural nodes when needed. The problem of how a network might designate new configural nodes as needed puzzled researchers for many years. However, in the mid-1980s, David Rumelhart and his colleagues, about whom you read in Chapter 1, developed sophisticated new learning algorithms to show how the problem might be solved (Rumelhart & McClelland, 1986). In Figure 6.13c, for example, the network has two layers of modifiable weights—one layer going from the input nodes to the internal nodes and another layer going from the internal nodes to the output node. When experience shows a particular combination of stimuli (for example, fever + ache) to be useful for the purposes of solving a problem, changes in the values of the lower-layer weights can cause the network to adapt so that in the future, a particular internal node will become active only when that specific combination of inputs is present. This advance in learning theory created an explosion of research in network models for learning, memory, and other aspects of cognition.

combinatorial explosion. The rapid expansion of resources required to encode configurations as the number of component features increases.

Test Your Knowledge

Configural Representation of Cues

If we construct an associative network model that uses pair-wise configural cues to discriminate among the eight different objects that can be formed from three binary dimensions—*small/large, black/white,* and *circle/square* (i.e., small black circle, small black square, small white circle, etc.)—what are all the possible pair-wise configural cues that would be needed in the model? (Answers appear in the back of the book.)

Prototypes and the Structure of Natural Categories

The discussions above about categories and concepts have mostly involved situations, often contrived in a laboratory experiment, where membership in a category is all or none: either an entity does, or does not, belong to a category. In real life, however, natural categories can be very different. Are robins and penguins both equally good examples of birds? Most people would say no. Is an olive a fruit? Well, technically, maybe, but that's not what we usually mean by a fruit, and relatively few people would classify an olive as a fruit. In a series of seminal papers, Eleanor Rosch (1973, 1975) showed that natural categories often have ill-defined boundaries, with some members of categories being viewed as better, more central, and more typical examples of the category than others. Robins, for example, are generally viewed as typical members of the class of birds, while penguins are not.

If I ask you to imagine a typical bird, the creature you think of might not look like any particular breed of bird, but it probably has the physical features typically associated with birds—wings, feathers, a beak, and two legs—and the functional attributes of singing, flying, and perching in trees. This kind of abstract representation of the idealized or typical member of a category is called the category's **prototype.** Rosch argued that the most commonly used concepts are organized around prototypes that are based on family resemblances, sets of features shared by most members of a category. Thus, a robin would be judged a very typical bird because it has many features in common with most other birds, while a penguin has relatively few features shared with other birds (Rosch & Mervis, 1975).

Categories with a high degree of family resemblance (and hence many shared clusters of common features) are especially useful because they permit **inductive inference,** the making of logical inferences that are probably (but not necessarily) true and are usually based on attempts to draw a general rule from one or more specific instances or premises (Goldstone et al., 2012). If we know something is a dog, then it probably barks, has four legs, eats dog food, and likes to mark its territory, using trees, fire hydrants, and occasionally people's legs. Of course, there are exceptions to all of these inferences, such as the Basenji dog of Africa, which does not bark, and the rare dog that has had the misfortune to lose a limb. While it is true that very few dogs will pee on your leg if no tree is available, it is still a prudent person who moves out of the way when any dog lifts its leg.

Inductive inferences are about what is likely (but not necessarily) true; based on those inductive inferences, we make choices about how we want to respond. From this perspective, concepts are tools for helping us recognize meaningful relationships between features in the world. Concepts facilitate our making choices that advance our own interests (e.g., keeping our shoes free of dog urine). But even as we form useful concepts about categories in the world, we may find that the inductive inferences we make from them can sometimes lead us astray.

Generalization Errors Based on Faulty Reasoning about Categories

We turn next to some of the ways in which generalization can fail us. One of the most common generalization errors is the use of faulty inverse reasoning about categories. For example, it is trivially obvious that all criminals have mothers. However, the inverse (that all people who have mothers are criminals) is clearly not true. As absurd as it might seem to confuse these two inferences, there is compelling evidence that, in a broad range of situations, people routinely misinterpret probabilities and statistics in just this way (Bar-Hillel, 1984).

Are these both birds? Are they equally typical birds? If not, what does that tell us about our concept of birds?

prototype. The central tendency or idealized version of a concept or category.

inductive inference. A logical inference that is probably (but not necessarily) true and is usually based on attempts to draw a general rule from one or more specific instances or premises.

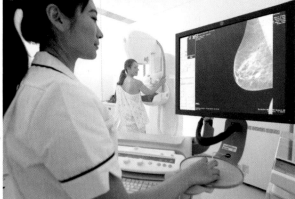

Her mammogram may look similar to those seen in women with breast cancer. But given the low frequency of breast cancer in the general population (12% of women in the United States will develop it in their lifetime), is the doctor able to make an accurate diagnosis from it? If not, why not?

The problem of faulty inverse reasoning is especially prevalent in medical diagnoses. For example, a woman with breast cancer is very likely to have a positive reading on a mammogram test. But the inverse assumption is false: a woman with a positive reading on her mammogram does not necessarily have a high probability of having breast cancer; this is because the test has a tendency to produce a high rate of false positives. Thus, many women who test positive actually do not have cancer. Unfortunately, people often mistakenly confuse the probability that a member of a category has a particular feature (an inductive inference about features) with the inverse relationship, the probability that a particular feature is predictive of category membership (an inductive inference about category membership). Statistics tells us that these two types of inference—inferring features from categories and inferring categories from features—diverge considerably in predictive value when the category in question (e.g., women with breast cancer) is relatively rare in the world at large.

Education and expertise do not make a person immune to faulty inverse reasoning from otherwise valid generalizations. By confusing the two relationships, physicians often assume that a woman who has a positive mammogram probably has breast cancer, a mistake in logical inference that can result in women undergoing needless biopsies and surgery (Eddy, 1982). Few of us, in fact, are immune to erroneous decision making of this type. Later in this chapter, in the section on Clinical Perspectives, we will discuss the origins and consequences of faulty inferences based on categories of people, especially when those categories are based on people's race or ethnicity.

Interim Summary

- Generalization enables us to apply prior experience to new situations. However, it requires finding an appropriate balance between specificity (knowing how narrowly a rule applies) and generality (knowing how broadly the rule applies).

- The problem of generalization is really four different subproblems: what happens when similar stimuli (or events) have the same outcome (or consequences), what happens when they have different outcomes, what happens when dissimilar stimuli have the same outcomes, and what happens when the outcomes are dissimilar.

- Generalization gradients show the strength of an organism's expectation that the consequences of one stimulus will follow other, similar stimuli. Through discrimination training, the generalization gradient can be modified to allow an organism to distinguish (and respond differently to) highly similar stimuli.

- Different models of generalization represent stimuli in different ways. A discrete-component representation depicts each stimulus (or stimulus feature) as one node (or network component). Such representations only apply to situations in which the similarity between the stimuli is small enough that learning about one stimulus should not transfer appreciably to the others. In contrast, distributed representations, in which stimuli are represented by sets of nodes (that overlap when the stimuli share some of the same features or elements), provide a framework for modeling stimulus similarity and generalization.

Ian Lishman/Juice Images/Corbis

- Categories enable us to make inferences—that is, generalizations—about members of categories and guide us in predicting the future (to the extent possible), leading us to formulate expectations about new experiences, events, or people.

- One of the most common misuses of generalization is faulty inverse reasoning about categories. Even fundamentally accurate generalizations based on categories of events or people can be misapplied to draw inaccurate conclusions.

6.2 Brain Substrates

Why devote a whole chapter to generalization and discrimination learning? As was noted in the introduction, generalization is the payoff for learning. A medical student may be exposed to many rules and examples during her years of training, but there is no way she can study every possible kind of patient that she might ever meet. Rather, as she approaches each new and novel patient in her practice, she will have to decide when and in what ways their particular symptoms and case histories are like and unlike the examples and principles she studied in medical school.

The psychological theories described in the previous section were developed to explain the four kinds of generalization we explored there. These theories were, for many years, just abstractions—tools that psychologists used to help organize, understand, and predict behavioral phenomena. As you read in that section, many of the theories were developed as simple models of how relationships between stimuli and outcomes might be represented—that is "encoded"—in patterns of mental activity or the structure of associative networks. In recent years, however, the associative network theories from psychology have become increasingly useful to neuroscientists as a blueprint for how the brain may actually accomplish certain mental processes. These developments are the focus of our inquiries in this section.

One of the ideas we'll be considering is represented by artist Saul Steinberg's most famous cover for the *New Yorker* magazine (Figure 6.14), caricaturing his view of a typical New York City dweller's mental map of the world. Within this depiction of New York City, Ninth and Tenth Avenues are drawn in such fine detail that they take up half the map. The rest of the country, the area between New Jersey and California, is represented as a largely barren desert marked by a few scattered rocks and hills.

This painting satirizes the belief of many New Yorkers that they are living in the most important place in the world. It also illustrates an important psychological principle. Fine distinctions that are meaningful to New Yorkers, such as the differences between fashionable street addresses, are emphasized and highly elaborated in their mental maps; these places are physically spread out and detailed within this drawing. At the same time, distinctions that may be irrelevant to the typical New Yorker, such as the difference between Illinois and Indiana, are de-emphasized and compressed into less space on the map.

Figure 6.14 Caricature of a New York City resident's mental map of the United States Regions that are important to a New Yorker, such as Ninth and Tenth Avenues, are exaggerated in this representation, while other regions, such as the entire Midwest, are disproportionately small.

The idea of representations of important places being elaborated with fine details and taking up lots of space, while representations of less important places lack definition, may sound familiar to you. In Chapter 2, you read about motor and sensory maps in the cortex and how the area in the cortex devoted to each body part relates in extent to the levels of sensitivity and fine motor control of that body part (a topic that will be revisited in Chapter 8 where you read about cortical maps and how they expand with extensive practice, as seen in violin players). The basic principle explored in those discussions was that regions of the cerebral cortex that mediate a highly practiced skill can expand with practice, while regions that are less used may even shrink.

What does this have to do with generalization? As described by the models in Section 6.1, representations directly influence generalization behaviors. If the drawing in Figure 6.14 were, indeed, an accurate representation of a New Yorker's mental map of the world, what would that imply? Based on this representation, you might expect a New Yorker to make very few generalizations grouping one neighborhood with a nearby one in New York despite their proximity. A New Yorker can discriminate between real estate prices on Central Park West (expensive) and those on Columbus Avenue (much cheaper), even though these two streets are actually only a few hundred yards apart (and even though a midwesterner would consider both of them expensive to live on). In other words, a New Yorker is unlikely to generalize from one to the other and make the mistake of expecting that an apartment for sale on Central Park West would cost the same as an identical apartment one block over on Columbus Avenue (but if you find one that does, grab it!).

The preceding example might suggest that New Yorkers are pretty knowledgeable people (and, indeed, they like to think so). However, everything changes when they are tested on their knowledge of the Midwest. For a New Yorker with a mental map like Figure 6.14, all the midwestern states are functionally equivalent. If you tell this New Yorker that Kansas has lots of corn farms, he will probably assume the same must surely be true of Iowa and Illinois. In other words, a New Yorker who has identical (or very similar) mental representations of these states will automatically generalize from one midwestern state to another and have great difficulty telling them apart.

Are New Yorkers unusual in having such a warped view of the world, with extreme generalization in some areas and extreme discrimination in others? To some extent, we all create similarly idiosyncratic worldviews, with uniquely distorted representations; distinctions important to us are enhanced, while less relevant ones are de-emphasized. For example, students asked to sketch a map of the world tend to draw their home region disproportionately large—and in the center of the map. Figure 6.15 is an actual map drawn by a student from Illinois, who overemphasized Illinois relative to the rest of the country, omitted most other states (including New York!), and enlarged North America relative to the other continents. Many American students have this tendency. In contrast, European students tend to draw Eurocentric maps, while students from Australia are naturally more likely to place Australia and Asia in the center.

These kinds of representational distortions, although sometimes comic in their egocentricity, are actually very useful. A similar process allows a violinist to devote more of her cerebral cortex to the fine control of her left hand, which must perform the demanding work of holding down different combinations of strings on the proper frets of the instrument, as compared with her right hand, which is only used for the less intricate movements of drawing the bow back and forth across the strings. With only a finite number of neurons available to control all our behaviors, it makes sense to allocate them efficiently according to which distinctions are, and are not, most needed.

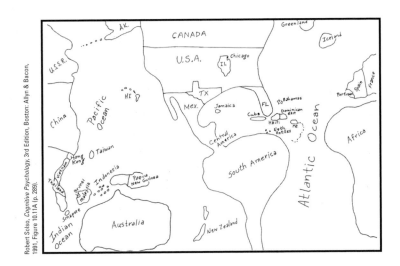

Robert Solso, *Cognitive Psychology*, 3rd Edition, Boston: Allyn & Bacon, 1991, Figure 10.11A (p. 289).

Figure 6.15 Representational distortion: the Midwest version A student from Chicago, when asked to sketch a map of the world, drew his home state disproportionately large and omitted most of the other states. He also drew North America larger than the other continents.

The studies reviewed in the first part of this Brain Substrates section will relate the plasticity of the sensory cortices to behavioral properties of stimulus generalization and discrimination learning. The section concludes with a look at the special role of the hippocampal region in stimulus generalization.

Cortical Representations and Generalization

Chapter 3 discussed three main findings about perceptual learning and cortical plasticity. First, when perceptual learning occurs in humans, cortical changes accompany the enhanced discrimination abilities. Second, the selectivity of individual cortical neurons in responding to specific stimulus features can be modified through experience. Third, learning can change the spatial organization of interconnected neurons in the sensory cortex. Each of these principles of perceptual learning and cortical plasticity has a bearing on the generalization and discrimination behaviors described above in the Behavioral Processes section of this chapter, especially with regard to what happens to mapping in the brain when similar stimuli are associated with similar outcomes and what happens when these mappings are altered through discrimination training so that similar stimuli come to be associated with different outcomes. The overlapping and distributed representations for similar stimuli that you saw modeled in Figure 6.4 return in the discussion below, to model the cortical representations of tones of different frequencies in the auditory cortex.

Cortical Representations of Sensory Stimuli

Let's begin our discussion of cortical representations by reviewing some basic features of cortical anatomy. Recall that initial cortical processing of sensory information occurs in a region dedicated to the sensory modality in question: primary visual cortex (or V1) for vision, primary auditory cortex (or A1) for sounds, primary somatosensory cortex (S1) for touch, and so on. From these initial-processing regions, sensory information progresses to higher sensory areas that integrate it with other information, first within and then across sensory modalities. Many primary sensory cortical areas are organized topographically (as described in Chapters 2 and 3). This means that each region of the cortex responds preferentially to a particular type of stimulus and neighboring cortical regions respond to similar stimuli. It is therefore possible to draw various "maps" on the cortical surface by studying the responses of different cortical regions.

For example, as described in Chapters 2 and 3, S1 is a thin strip of cortex running down each side of the human brain (see Figure 3.15). Some neurons respond primarily to stimulation on a particular finger, some primarily to touch on a certain region of the face, and so on. If this procedure is followed for a large number of S1 neurons, it is possible to draw a "map" of the body on S1, with each body part lying over the cortical region that shows the greatest response when touched, as was illustrated previously in Figure 3.15

To some extent, adjacent areas within S1 contain neurons that respond to neighboring areas of the body (albeit with some discontinuities; for example, Figure 3.15 shows that the parts of S1 that respond to sensations on the fingers lie near those that respond to sensations on the forehead). Parts of the body that are especially sensitive to touch, such as fingers and lips, activate larger areas of S1. The result is a *homunculus*, a distorted neural representation of the human figure with exaggerated hands and lips but a greatly shrunken torso, as shown in Figure 3.15. This figure of a human is distorted in much the same way as the *New Yorker* cover in Figure 6.14: regions where fine discriminations are important (such as sensations on the fingertips) are disproportionately large and detailed.

The primary somatosensory cortex in other animals shows similar organization, with the homunculus replaced by a distorted figure of the species in question, altered to reflect body areas important to that animal. For instance, primates receive a great deal of touch information through their fingers and lips, which are disproportionately elaborated in their cortical map. Rats receive a great deal of information from the displacement of their whiskers, meaning that a rat's whisker area is disproportionately represented on its cortical map.

The primary auditory cortex (A1) lies near the top of the temporal lobe in humans, and it too is organized as a topographic map, as shown in Figure 6.16. In A1, however, neurons respond to sound instead of touch stimulation. Areas of A1 that are adjacent to each other respond to similar frequencies. Each neuron in the auditory cortex responds most to one particular tone, as was discussed in Chapter 3.

We know what these auditory maps look like because of studies that recorded how often a single neuron fires in response to tones of different frequencies. Figure 3.14 presented data collected from such an electrophysiology experiment. This information represents the receptive field for a neuron, meaning the range (or "field") of physical stimuli that activate it. The wider a neuron's receptive field is, the broader the range of physical stimuli that will activate the neuron.

Figure 6.16 A topographic map of the primary auditory cortex In the primary auditory cortex, neurons respond to auditory stimuli of different frequencies. Areas lying adjacent to each other respond to similar frequencies.

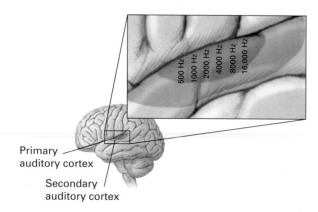

Primary auditory cortex

Secondary auditory cortex

Shared-Elements Models of Receptive Fields

How well does the functioning of receptive fields of neurons match the theories of generalization described in the section on behavioral processes? If the brain is organized to use distributed representations, then physically similar stimuli, such as two tones with similar frequencies, will activate common nodes, or neurons. In other words, two similar tones—of 550 Hz and 560 Hz, for example—should cause overlapping sets of neurons to fire.

Figure 6.17a shows how brain organization might resemble the distributed-component representation (or "shared elements") model from the Behavioral

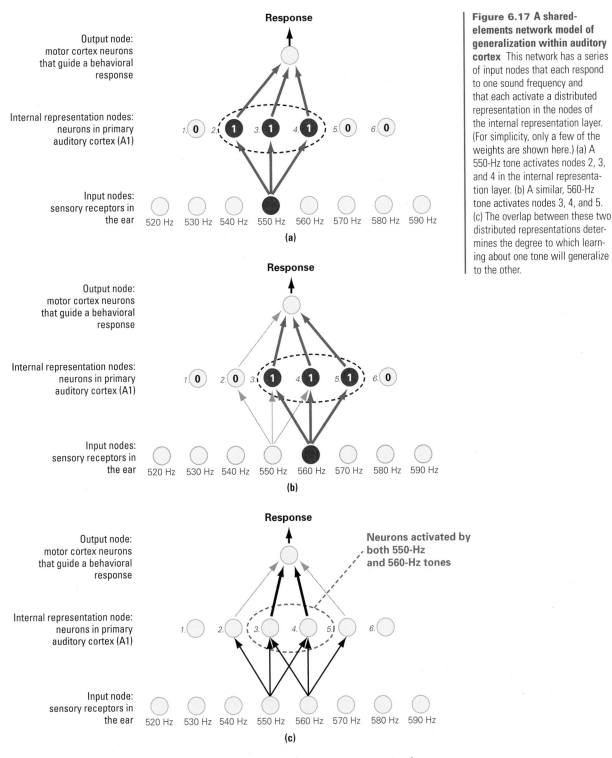

Figure 6.17 A shared-elements network model of generalization within auditory cortex This network has a series of input nodes that each respond to one sound frequency and that each activate a distributed representation in the nodes of the internal representation layer. (For simplicity, only a few of the weights are shown here.) (a) A 550-Hz tone activates nodes 2, 3, and 4 in the internal representation layer. (b) A similar, 560-Hz tone activates nodes 3, 4, and 5. (c) The overlap between these two distributed representations determines the degree to which learning about one tone will generalize to the other.

Processes section. A 550-Hz tone might activate sensory receptors in the ear that travel to primary auditory cortex (A1) and there activate three nodes—numbers 2, 3, and 4 in Figure 6.17a. Activation from A1 neurons might then travel (through one or more way stations in the brain) to activate other neurons (possibly in the motor cortex) that can execute a learned behavioral response.

A 560-Hz tone activates a different subset of A1 neurons—numbers 3, 4, and 5 in Figure 6.17b. These subsets overlap, in that both of them contain neurons 3 and 4, as shown in Figure 6.17c. Thus, learning about the 550-Hz tone is highly likely to generalize to the 560-Hz tone. This diagram is much the same as the illustration used in the Behavioral Processes section (see Figure 6.4) to show how a shared-elements representation of yellow and orange explains pigeons' generalization between these two physically similar stimuli.

This simplified network may explain why cortical neurons display receptive fields. For each tone in a continuum, you can ask how a particular A1 neuron, such as neuron 3, will respond. The curve in Figure 6.18 shows the results we'd expect. The neuron's best frequency is 550 Hz; similar tones also activate this neuron, although not as strongly as a tone of 550 Hz. The result is a generalization gradient that looks very like the actual receptive fields obtained during cortical mapping studies, like the one shown earlier in Figure 3.14.

Topographic Organization in Generalization

The idea of topographic organization was a central part of Pavlov's theories of learning in the early 1920s, but it remained only a theoretical conjecture until nearly a half a century later. In the 1960s, Richard Thompson established a direct relationship between behavioral properties of auditory generalization and certain anatomical and physical properties of the auditory cortex (Thompson, 1962).

A common experimental finding was that cats trained to respond to a tone of a particular frequency would show a generalization gradient to tones of other frequencies, much like the sloping gradient seen in Figure 6.1. However, after

Figure 6.18 A simulated electrophysiology study The activity of node or neuron 3 is recorded for each of the tones between 520 Hz and 580 Hz; the frequency leading to the strongest response is 550 Hz.

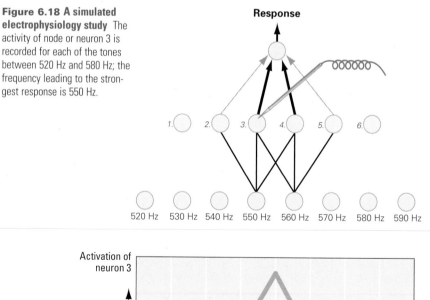

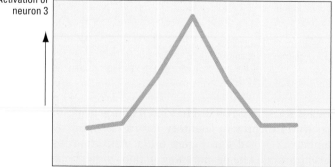

Thompson removed the primary auditory cortex (A1) of some of the cats, they responded equivalently to all tones, even those separated by 5 octaves or more! This experiment demonstrated that A1 was necessary for the production of appropriate generalization gradients to auditory stimuli (Thompson, 1965). The indiscriminate behavior of the lesioned cats reflected massive overgeneralization resulting in a flat generalization gradient. As a control study, Thompson also tested cats who had undergone removal of primary somatosensory cortex (area S1) instead. These animals showed normal generalization behavior with regard to tones, indicating that the auditory overgeneralization occurred specifically in animals with A1 lesions. Similar overgeneralization of visual stimuli has been reported in monkeys with damage to V1, the primary visual cortex (Thompson, 1965).

These studies suggest that, although it is possible for an animal to learn to respond to stimuli while lacking the corresponding areas of sensory cortex, an intact sensory cortex for that stimulus type is essential for normal generalization. Thus, without A1, animals can learn to respond to the presence of a tone but cannot respond precisely to a *specific* tone. In other words, without the primary sensory cortex, animals overgeneralize and have difficulty discriminating stimuli in the corresponding sensory modality. What these studies do not show is whether the receptive sets of neurons in the brain can be changed as a result of learning and experience. This question is addressed in more recent research, as we see below.

Plasticity of Cortical Representations

We saw in earlier chapters that if a particular part of the body receives frequent stimulation, the corresponding parts of the somatosensory map will grow and expand (at the expense of adjacent cortical areas, which compensate by contracting). Lack of stimulation or use can cause change of a different kind in cortical representations, with disused cortical areas shrinking. For example, when a limb is amputated, the part of S1 representing the lost limb will no longer be receiving sensory input. Rather than allowing that region of cortex to remain idle, nearby areas of the homunculus may "spread" into the vacated space. As a result, those areas acquire increased cortical representation and consequent increased sensitivity to stimulation and touch.

In seminal studies on the neural bases of learning and cortical plasticity, Norman Weinberger and his colleagues recorded responses from individual neurons in the primary auditory cortex of guinea pigs before and after the animals were trained to respond to auditory cues (Weinberger, 1993). In one study, Weinberger and colleagues recorded the activity of neurons in A1 before and after the animals experienced presentations of a 2500-Hz tone paired with a shock. Through training, many neurons changed their receptive field to become most responsive to tones near the training frequency of 2,500 Hz. One such neuron is shown in Figure 6.19. This neuron, which had originally responded most strongly to tones of about 1,000 Hz, now responded most strongly to tones of the trained frequency. If enough neurons were to show this type of change, the overall result could amount to cortical remapping that allows a larger area of A1 to respond to the trained frequency. These cortical changes occurred quickly, after as few as five pairings of the tone and shock.

In another study, Weinberger showed that if a tone is repeatedly presented alone (as in habituation, described in Chapter 3), then the opposite effect occurs: there is a decrease in neuronal responding to this frequency (Condon & Weinberger, 1991). Moreover, if the tone and shock are both presented but not paired (that is, if they are presented separately), then no significant changes are observed in the neurons' responses to tones (Bakin & Weinberger, 1990). This result indicates that the cortical plasticity is a result of the tone–shock pairing. It implies that stimulus presentation alone doesn't drive cortical plasticity; the stimulus has to be meaningfully related to ensuing consequences, such as a shock.

Figure 6.19 Plasticity of representation in the primary auditory cortex After training in which a 2,500-Hz tone predicted a shock, the response of an A1 neuron changed from previously being most responsive to a 1,000-Hz tone to being most responsive to tones nearer to the training frequency.
Data from Weinberger, 1977, Figure 2.

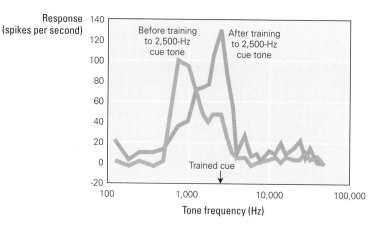

nucleus basalis. A small group of neurons located in the basal forebrain. These neurons deliver acetylcholine to the cortex, enabling cortical plasticity.

acetylcholine (ACh). A neuromodulator that strongly influences hippocampal function.

Figure 6.20 The role of the nucleus basalis in cortical plasticity This medial view of the human brain shows the nucleus basalis within the basal forebrain. Neurons in the nucleus basalis transmit the neurotransmitter acetylcholine throughout the cerebral cortex.

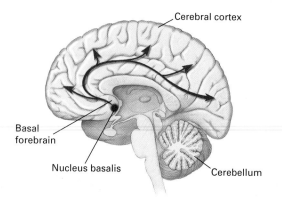

If cortical change occurs because a stimulus in one sensory modality is meaningfully related to—or in other words, is predictive of—a salient consequence (such as food or shock) in a different sensory modality, how did information about that consequence reach the primary sensory cortex of the first modality in order to produce the change there? After all, A1 is specialized to process information about sounds, but food is a gustatory (taste) stimulus and shocks are somatosensory, not auditory, stimuli, and yet, the findings in Figure 6.19 clearly indicate that pairing a tone with a shock *does* bring about a change in auditory cortex.

Weinberger has argued that A1 does not receive specific information about somatosensory or gustatory stimuli but instead only receives information that some sort of salient event has occurred (Weinberger, 2004). This information is enough to instigate cortical remapping and expand the representation of the cue stimulus. The primary sensory cortices (A1, V1, S1, and so on) only determine which stimuli deserve expanded representation within that primary cortex and which do not.

How does the brain determine whether a stimulus merits cortical remapping, without necessarily specifying exactly why? It turns out that several brain regions may serve this function. The basal forebrain is a group of nuclei important for learning and memory; damage to it can produce *anterograde amnesia*, which is a severe impairment in forming new fact and event memories (more on this in Chapter 7). Many cortical mapping researchers have focused on a small group of neurons located in an area of the basal forebrain called the **nucleus basalis** (Figure 6.20). The nucleus basalis projects to all areas of the cortex and to the amygdala. When nucleus basalis neurons are activated, they release **acetylcholine (ACh)**, a neurotransmitter that has many functions in the brain, including the promotion of neuronal plasticity. In summary, the nucleus basalis functions to enable cortical plasticity: when a CS is paired with a US, the nucleus basalis becomes active and delivers acetylcholine to the cortex, enabling cortical remapping to enlarge the representation of that CS (Weinberger, 2003).

But how does the nucleus basalis "know" when to become active? It receives the information through connections from areas such as the *amygdala*, which codes emotional information such as discomfort and pain (for example, from an electric shock) and pleasure (from food). (The function of the amygdala is discussed further in Chapter 10.) Several studies have confirmed that the nucleus basalis can play a role in mediating cortical plasticity. Most important, experiments show that if a tone is paired with nucleus basalis stimulation—rather than with a "real" consequence, such as food or shock—cortical remapping occurs to enhance response to that tone (Bakin & Weinberger, 1990; Kilgard & Merzenich, 1998).

These findings are very exciting because of their implications for rehabilitation after cortical damage. It may eventually be possible to use judicious stimulation of the nucleus basalis to encourage cortical remapping in individuals who have lost the use of one of their cortical areas. Although that is still far in the future, Michael Merzenich and colleagues have shown that strategic application of behavioral training procedures that encourage cortical remapping can be used to remediate certain types of brain disorders in people.

Test Your Knowledge

Cholinergic Neurons and Learning

In an experiment to test the function of specific cholinergic (acetylcholine-releasing) neurons in learning and memory, Jackie lesions cholinergic neurons in the nucleus basalis of the rat brain. How will this lesion affect discrimination learning the rats acquired before the surgery? How will it affect discrimination learning after the surgery? (Answers appear in the back of the book.)

Generalization and the Hippocampal Region

Recall the configural representations modeled in Figures 6.12 and 6.13; these represent an essential form of learning in which a unique combination of two (or more) cues acquires a meaning distinct from that of the component cues. You can view this as a form of learning that requires sensitivity to the relationship between two sensory cues. Other forms of learning and generalization that involve relationships between sensory cues are the sensory preconditioning and acquired-equivalence processes also discussed in Section 6.1. Learning about relationships among stimuli in the environment is part of the special role in learning and conditioning served by the hippocampus and related structures, referred to as the **hippocampal region** in rats and other small animals and as the **medial temporal lobe** in humans (Figure 6.21).

Effect of Damage to the Hippocampal Region

To examine the role of the hippocampal region in generalization, we must return to the procedure for sensory preconditioning summarized in Table 6.2. In the first phase of sensory preconditioning experiments, animals in the compound exposure group are exposed to a combination of two stimuli, such as a tone and a light, presented together. Control group animals are exposed to each stimulus separately. In phase 2, presentation of one of the stimuli by itself—say, the light—predicts a salient event, such as a blink-evoking airpuff; control animals

hippocampal region. The hippocampus and associated brain regions, including the entorhinal cortex and dentate gyrus. In humans, also referred to as the medial temporal lobe.

medial temporal lobe. The medial (or inner) surface of the temporal lobe that contains the hippocampus, the amygdala, and other structures important for memory.

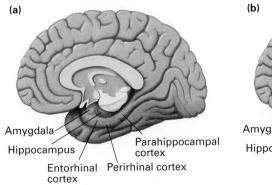

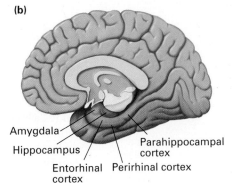

(a)

Amygdala
Hippocampus
Entorhinal cortex
Perirhinal cortex
Parahippocampal cortex

(b)

Amygdala
Hippocampus
Entorhinal cortex
Perirhinal cortex
Parahippocampal cortex

Figure 6.21 The hippocampal region in rats and the analogous medial temporal lobe in humans (a) The hippocampus and broader hippocampal region in rats. (b) The hippocampus and broader medial temporal lobe in humans.

Figure 6.22 The hippocampal region and sensory preconditioning In rabbit eyeblink conditioning, hippocampal damage abolishes the sensory preconditioning effect, so that lesioned rabbits given compound exposure to tone and light in phase 1 show no more response to the tone in phase 3 than do rabbits given separate exposure.

Data from Port & Patterson, 1984.

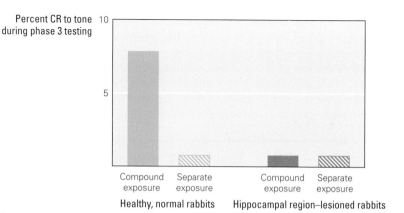

Percent CR to tone during phase 3 testing

Healthy, normal rabbits — Compound exposure, Separate exposure
Hippocampal region–lesioned rabbits — Compound exposure, Separate exposure

Figure 6.23 Latent inhibition in rabbit eyeblink conditioning Latent inhibition in rabbit eyeblink conditioning is eliminated by hippocampal region damage, specifically a lesion of the entorhinal cortex. When control rabbits did not receive any pre-exposure to the tones ("sit exposure condition, solid green bar), they produced many more eyeblink CRs during subsequent tone–airpuff training than control rabbits that had been previously exposed to the tone (green-striped bar). In contrast, animals with entorhinal cortex (EC) lesions (shown in red) showed no such effect. In fact, the rabbits with EC lesions in the "CS exposure" group (red-striped bar) learned better than control rabbits in the equivalent CS exposure group (green-striped bar). Brain damage actually helped these rabbits learn faster.

Date from Shohamy, Allen, & Gluck, 2000.

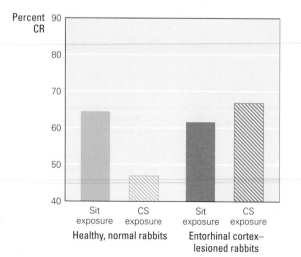

Percent CR

Healthy, normal rabbits — Sit exposure, CS exposure
Entorhinal cortex–lesioned rabbits — Sit exposure, CS exposure

and compound exposure animals learn to respond to the light with an eyeblink. Finally, in phase 3, the two groups of animals are tested with the other stimulus (in this case, the tone) alone. Normal animals of the compound exposure group will give a significant eyeblink response to the tone in phase 3, indicating that they have generalized the training from the tone to the light based on the prior co-occurrence of tone and light (Figure 6.22). By contrast, normal animals of the control group, given separate exposure to the tone and light in phase 1, show little or no responding to the tone in phase 3.

The results are different, however, for animals with damage to their hippocampal region. Rabbits with surgically created lesions in the fornix (part of the hippocampal region) display no sensory preconditioning (Figure 6.22; Port & Patterson, 1984). That is, lesioned animals in the compound exposure group show no more transfer in phase 3 than animals in the separate exposure group. It seems that an intact and functioning hippocampal region is needed for generalizing between stimuli that have co-occurred in the past.

Similarly, in a study of acquired equivalence using rats (see Table 6.3 on page 232), researchers found that rats with hippocampal region damage—specifically lesions of the entorhinal cortex, which lies next to the hippocampus—show impaired acquired equivalence: they can learn the associations in phases 1 and 2 but show no generalization in phase 3 (Coutureau et al., 2002). Here again, animal lesion studies show that the hippocampal region is critical for meaning-based generalization.

Other evidence supporting a key role for the hippocampal region in generalization comes from studies of latent inhibition, a classical conditioning paradigm in which learning a CS–US association is slower in animals given prior exposure to the CS (*CS exposure* condition) compared with animals given equivalent prior exposure to the context alone (*sit exposure* condition). This is essentially a generalization task in which the CS-exposed animals are tricked into overgeneralizing from phase 1 (where there is no US) to phase 2 (where the CS now does predict a US).

One such finding is shown in Figure 6.23, from a study which demonstrated that latent inhibition in rabbit eyeblink conditioning is eliminated by hippocampal region damage—specifically, a lesion of the entorhinal cortex (Shohamy, Allen, & Gluck, 2000). One interpretation of latent inhibition is that the experimental procedure manipulates the relationship between the stimulus cue and the context during pre-exposure. According to this view, in the CS-exposed group, the CS is generalized to the context during phase 1 and therefore is harder to discriminate from the context in phase 2, when the animal has to learn to respond to the CS in the context but not to the CS alone. Consistent with this idea, other studies have shown that latent inhibition is highly context sensitive and requires that the animal be exposed (phase 1) and trained (phase 2) in the same context (Lubow, 1989).

In summary, studies of hippocampal region lesions in animals, using three different experimental paradigms—sensory preconditioning, acquired equivalence, and latent inhibition—all converge to suggest that this brain region is critical for stimulus generalization, especially when that generalization involves learning relationships between different stimuli.

Modeling the Role of the Hippocampus in Adaptive Representations

The data described above suggest that the hippocampal region is involved in even the most elementary forms of associative learning, including classical conditioning. (Chapter 7 shows how the hippocampus and related structures in the medial temporal lobe are critical for learning about facts and events, too.) This does not mean that the hippocampal region is necessary for learning a stimulus–response association. Instead, the hippocampal region appears to be critically involved in developing new representations. Mark Gluck and Catherine Myers proposed a model in which the hippocampal region operates as an "information gateway" during associative learning, storing new representations of events that are experienced (Gluck & Myers, 1993, 2001). In their model, illustrated in Figure 6.24, the hippocampal region selects what information is allowed to enter memory and how it is to be encoded by other brain regions. Specifically, Gluck and Myers proposed that the representation of unimportant or redundant information undergoes shrinkage (or compression) by the hippocampal region, while the representation of useful information is expanded (or differentiated), creating a new, efficient, optimized representation that encodes only the key aspects of incoming information.

Remember Figure 6.14, caricaturing a typical New Yorker's mental map of the world? This image captures just the kind of compression (for example, of the entire Midwest into a small, barren strip) and expansion (for example, the exaggerated detail of Ninth and Tenth Avenues) that Gluck and Myers propose are dependent on the hippocampal region. In their model, these representational changes are computed in the hippocampal region and then used by other brain regions, such as the cerebral cortex and the cerebellum, where the stimulus–response associations that control motor outputs are actually stored.

Gluck and Myers applied their model of the hippocampal region's role in conditioning to a broad range of experimental findings, including the studies of sensory preconditioning and latent inhibition summarized above. In both cases, they showed that the learning displayed by healthy, normal animals was similar to how the model behaved when the representational compression and differentiation processes were turned on. In contrast, when these hippocampal-dependent changes in representation were turned off, the resulting "lesioned" model provided a good description of the altered learning seen in animals with lesions to their hippocampal region, as in the studies of sensory preconditioning, acquired equivalence, and latent inhibition (Gluck & Myers, 2001).

Figure 6.24 Gluck and Myers's model of hippocampal region function in learning The hippocampal region (on right) compresses or differentiates representations of new events into optimized representations for transmission (indicated by red arrow) to other brain regions, such as the cerebellum and cortex (on the left).

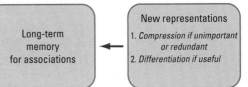

Cerebellum and cortex	Hippocampal region
Long-term memory for associations	New representations 1. *Compression if unimportant or redundant* 2. *Differentiation if useful*

Further evidence implicating hippocampal region function in the modification of stimulus representations comes from functional brain imaging. The model predicts that the hippocampal region should be very active early in training, when subjects are learning about stimulus–stimulus regularities and developing new stimulus representations, but should be less active later in training, when other brain regions (such as the cerebellum and cerebral cortex) are using these representations to perform the behavioral response. As predicted, a functional magnetic resonance imaging (fMRI) study of normal humans learning a probabilistic categorization task (similar to Gluck and Bower's study of medical diagnoses, described earlier) found that activity in the hippocampal region was high early in training and then tapered off as the task was learned (Poldrack et al., 2001).

Interim Summary

- Although animals can learn to respond to auditory stimuli without the primary auditory cortex, an intact A1 is essential for normal auditory learning and generalization. Without A1, animals can learn to respond to the presence of a tone but cannot respond precisely to a specific tone.

- Cortical plasticity is driven by the correlations between stimuli and salient events, with the nucleus basalis mediating between the amygdala (which decides what stimuli are salient) and the cortex.

- The hippocampal region plays a key role in forms of learning that depend on stimulus generalization, including the classical conditioning paradigms of sensory preconditioning and latent inhibition.

- Modeling suggests that one role of the hippocampal region is to bring about compression or differentiation of stimulus representations as appropriate.

6.3 Clinical Perspectives

In the final section of the chapter, we consider some of the consequences when generalization breaks down and leads to incorrect beliefs and inferences about the world around us. The first part of Section 6.3, on generalization in schizophrenia, continues our pattern from earlier chapters of exploring the clinical impact of medical and psychological disorders on fundamental properties of learning and memory. The second and final part presents something quite different from what we cover in other chapters. Here we consider how naturally occurring variants and errors of generalization can contribute to inappropriate beliefs about other people, leading to stereotypes, prejudice, and racism. This topic brings us into the realm of social disorders and considers how we, as a society, are affected by inappropriate generalizations about our fellow humans.

Generalization Deficits in Schizophrenia

Given what animal studies have shown about the importance of the hippocampal region in generalization, it will not surprise you to learn that damage or dysfunction in the hippocampal region in humans can also have deleterious consequences for learning and generalization. We discuss here evidence that hippocampal dysfunction in the mental disorder schizophrenia leads to significant changes in how patients with this disorder learn and generalize, impairing their interaction with the world, especially in novel situations. Other disorders that disrupt the hippocampal region include amnesia (discussed in Chapter 7) and Alzheimer's disease (discussed in Chapter 12). The hippocampus is not, however, the only brain region affected in schizophrenia; schizophrenia is a complex and heterogeneous disorder that involves many brain areas. Chapter 9 addresses some of the ways in which frontal lobe dysfunction impairs other aspects of learning, memory, and attention that are pertinent to schizophrenia.

Schizophrenia is a severe mental disorder with symptoms of hallucinations, delusions, flattened affect, and social impairment. Functional brain imaging studies have shown reduced hippocampal activity in patients diagnosed with schizophrenia (Heckers et al., 1998), while a wide range of structural and functional brain imaging studies have identified abnormalities in the hippocampus as a core feature of the illness, present from the onset and, to a lesser degree, also seen in first-degree relatives of people diagnosed with schizophrenia (Heckers, 2001). In particular, people diagnosed with schizophrenia show hippocampal shape abnormalities, most notably an overall smaller volume, as illustrated in the three-dimensional renderings of hippocampi in controls and patients shown in Figure 6.25.

More recently, studies of associative learning and generalization have shown that most patients diagnosed with schizophrenia are able to learn simple associations but are markedly impaired when these associations must be transferred to a new context (Polgár et al., 2007) or flexibly modified in some other way (Waltz & Gold, 2007). We turn next to several studies that help us understand how some of the cognitive impairments in schizophrenia may be related to dysfunction in the hippocampus.

Acquired Equivalence in Schizophrenia

Catherine Myers and colleagues have adapted the acquired-equivalence procedure from animal conditioning for use with humans (Myers et al., 2003). In consideration of the data that the hippocampal region in rats is essential for acquired equivalence (Coutureau et al., 2002), Myers and colleagues applied their human version of the task to the study of generalization impairments in people with schizophrenia.

On each of several trials in the Myers et al. human acquired-equivalence tasks, participants see a cartoon face and two colored fish and are asked to learn which fish each person prefers, as shown in Figure 6.26. In phase 1, for example, the

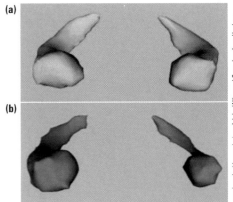

Reproduced with permission of John Wiley and Sons, Inc. from Heckers, S., "Neuroimaging studies of the hippocampus in schizophrenia," Hippocampus 5 (2001): 520–528; permission conveyed through. Copyright Clearance Center, Inc. Image reconstruction and figure

Figure 6.25 The shape of the hippocampus in schizophrenia Three-dimensional volume rendering of hippocampi (with the amygdala at the front) as seen from the front of the brain in both a normal subject (a) and an age-matched patient diagnosed with schizophrenia (b). Note the smaller hippocampi and amygdalae in the patient, especially on the left (right side of image, as is the convention for clinical scans used by radiologists).

Image reconstruction and figure courtesy of Martha Shenton and Robert McCarley. As reproduced in Heckers, 2001.

Phase 1: equivalence training   Phase 2: train new outcome   Phase 3: transfer

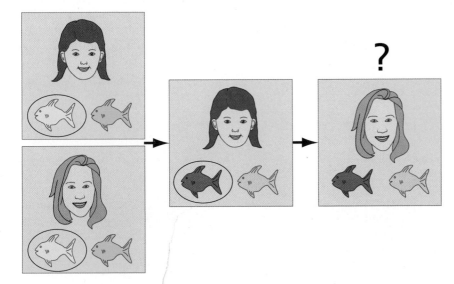

Figure 6.26 An acquired equivalence task for humans The figure shows a schematic diagram of the task's three phases. On each trial of the task, participants must choose which of two fish they think the person will prefer.

Research from Myers et al., 2003.

participants might be asked to learn that a certain brown-haired girl prefers blue fish over green fish and that a certain other person (a blond-haired woman) also prefers blue fish over green fish (Figure 6.26, left). Participants should gradually learn that these two people are equivalent in the sense that they are to be paired with the same fish. In phase 2, participants learn some new information: the brown-haired girl also prefers red fish over yellow fish (Figure 6.26, center). Finally, phase 3 is a testing phase, in which participants are quizzed on all the pairings they've learned so far. Intermixed with this testing are some critical pairings that the participants have never seen before. For example, they are shown the blond-haired woman and asked if she is likely to prefer a red or a yellow fish (Figure 6.26, right).

Healthy adults reliably judge that the blond-haired woman prefers red fish over yellow fish, even though they've never specifically been taught this (Myers et al., 2003). In essence, they are showing acquired equivalence: when they learn that two people show an equivalent pattern of past preferences (as in phase 1) and one of the two prefers the red fish over the yellow fish (in phase 2), then they judge that the other person will probably prefer the red fish over the yellow as well.

How do people with schizophrenia perform on this task? Szabolcs Kéri and colleagues in Hungary have conducted several studies using the task from Figure 6.26, comparing patients with schizophrenia with control subjects (Kéri et al., 2005; Farkas et al., 2008). The deficit observed in the transfer generalization phase in patients with schizophrenia (Figure 6.27) suggests that hippocampal region–dependent functions are indeed impaired in schizophrenia. More recently, antipsychotic medications have been shown to partially remediate the acquired-equivalence deficits in people diagnosed with schizophrenia, suggesting that these medications either enhance hippocampal region function directly or else indirectly enhance the ability of the hippocampal region to cooperate with other brain regions (Shohamy et al., 2010).

To further clarify the role of the hippocampal region in generalization, Daphna Shohamy and Anthony Wagner studied brain activity in healthy undergraduates with fMRI while using a variant on the Myers et al. acquired-equivalence procedure illustrated in Figure 6.26. As shown in Figure 6.28, they found that the magnitude of activation increase in the hippocampus (as well as in the midbrain) during phase 1 training correlated with subsequent accuracy on the generalization trials in phase 3. Interestingly, they found no such correlation between hippocampal activation during the generalization trials and the accuracy on those trials. Their finding that the critical hippocampal activity occurred during learning, not activation, confirms Gluck and Myers's prediction that the hippocampal role in acquired equivalence is to lay down an appropriate stimulus representation during learning that permits subsequent use of this learning in a broader, more flexible range of future transfer situations.

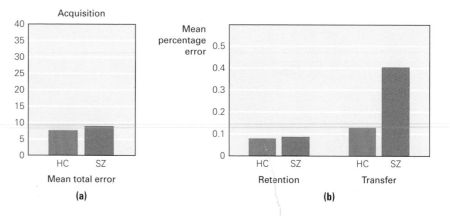

Figure 6.27 Acquired equivalence data from people diagnosed with schizophrenia When tested on the acquired-equivalence task from Figure 6.26, patients diagnosed with schizophrenia (SZ) are normal at learning and retention of associations but are impaired at transfer generalization as compared with matched healthy controls (HC).

Data from Kéri et al., 2005.

Other Studies of Transfer Generalization in Schizophrenia

Acquired equivalence is not the only task that has been used to study the role of the hippocampal region in generalization in people with schizophrenia. Other studies of people diagnosed with schizophrenia have shown that they are impaired at transitive inference, a form of hippocampal-region–dependent reasoning in which learned information is used to guide later inferences. If you learn that Liz is smarter than Alice and Alice is smarter than Isabel, then by transitive inference, you would infer that Liz is smarter than Isabel. Using ">" to represent "is smarter than," we would write this inference as "if Liz > Alice and Alice > Isabel, then Liz > Isabel."

In a study of this kind of learning and transitive inference, patients and controls were trained on a series of learned discriminations that were hierarchically organized according to the pattern A > B, B > C, C > D, and D > E (Titone, Ditman, Holzman, Eichenbaum, & Levy, 2004). They were then tested on each of these four training pairs as well as on two novel "inference" pairs. The novel pairs, consisting of stimuli the participants had seen before but that had not previously been paired, were AE, which can be evaluated without consideration of hierarchical relations (because A and E only appear in one type of relationship, superior or inferior to another cue), and BD, which can only be evaluated by hierarchical relations because both B and D have previously been shown in superior and inferior relationships to other cues.

Patients and controls successfully learned the training pairs and correctly responded to the nonrelational AE pair. However, the patients were less accurate than controls in responding to the relational BD pair, consistent with the hypothesis that higher-level memory processes associated with relational memory organization, and with its role in supporting generalization from training to transfer tasks, are impaired in schizophrenia.

Kéri and colleagues have also studied transfer generalization in schizophrenia using a task in which participants navigate a cartoon character, Kilroy, through a

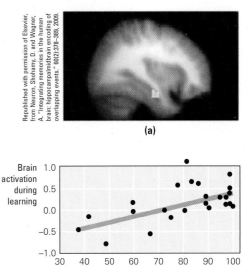

Republished with permission of Elsevier, from Neuron, Shohamy, D. and Wagner, A. "Integrating memories in the human brain: hippocampalmidbrain encoding of overlapping events." 60(2):378–389, 2009.

(a)

Brain activation during learning / % Correct on transfer generalization

(b)

Figure 6.28 Individual differences in acquired equivalence learning in healthy subjects (a) Brain image showing the hippocampus activation that was correlated with transfer generalization performance. (b) Brain activation signal during learning correlated with accuracy in tests of transfer generalization across all subjects in the Shohamy and Wagner study.

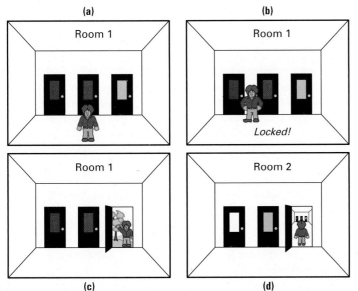

(a) Room 1 / **(b)** Room 1 — Locked! / **(c)** Room 1 / **(d)** Room 2

Figure 6.29 The chaining task used to study learning and generalization in schizophrenia Upper row, left panel: At the start of the experiment, participants choose among the closed doors in room 1. Upper row, right panel: Choosing the purple door is incorrect and results in no exit. Lower row, left panel: Choosing the yellow door in room 1 is correct, and Kilroy goes outside. Lower row, right panel: In room 2, the participant chose the correct yellow door (on right), allowing Kilroy to enter into room 1.

sequence of four rooms by learning to choose the unlocked door from three colored doors in each room. In the training phase, each stimulus leading to reward (the unlocked door in each room) is trained via feedback until the complete sequence is learned (Figure 6.29). Note that on each run through the experiment, the location of each of the colored doors moves around, and it is color, not location, that is the cue to be learned. In the transfer generalization phase, the decision-making context is manipulated so that in a given room, a door whose color was correct in another room is not the same color in the new room, and therefore is not the correct door in the new room. Compared with controls, patients diagnosed with schizophrenia were markedly impaired at the transfer generalization of the previously learned rules to rooms with different alternative options, even when they had successfully learned the initial training phase (Polgár et al., 2009).

Stereotypes, Discrimination, and Racism in Generalizations About Other People

When our behavior toward another person is based on his or her membership in a category defined by race, ethnicity, national origin, gender, religion, or age, we are implicitly making a generalization on the basis of a stereotype, a set of beliefs about the attributes of the members of a group (Ashmore & Del Boca, 1981). Unfortunately, many familiar stereotypes based on categories of humans are exaggerated and somewhat unkind images of what a typical member of the group is like: the dim-witted blonde, the aloof Englishman, the punctual German, the amorous Frenchman.

Stereotypes have a long history of being associated with a broad range of social evils: they can foment intergroup hostilities, encourage racial and other forms of prejudice, bolster exploitive hierarchies of power, rationalize social abuses, corrupt interpersonal relationships, undermine the self-confidence of those who are the objects of stereotyping, and be used to promote many harmful and illegal forms of discrimination (Jussim, 2012; Steele, 1995). In the context of neuroscience and the study of learning, the term "discrimination" usually refers to the ability to tell apart two or more stimuli and generate different responses to each. In everyday social contexts, however, *discrimination* is more often used to mean the unfair differential treatment of individuals on the basis of the group to which they belong. A critical question for this discussion is, when does *appropriate* psychological discrimination become *inappropriate* social discrimination against an individual?

As you read earlier in this chapter, categorization is a basic cognitive process through which we form concepts to organize, describe, and understand the world around us. Forming conceptual categories allows people, as well as all other animals, to recognize statistical patterns in our world that help predict future events. The ability to generalize is the natural (and rational) extension of these processes. Unfortunately, when generalizations are about a group of people, there is a fine, and hotly debated, line between what constitutes a rational generalization and what is an offensive misrepresentation inviting prejudicial behavior towards members of that group.

In this section, we discuss four key questions about stereotypes. First, how do we learn stereotypes about categories of people? Second, how should we evaluate the accuracy of a stereotype? Third, how do we distinguish between appropriate and inappropriate uses of stereotypes when making inductive inferences about other people? Fourth, how can we balance the value and risks associated with using stereotypes? For each of these four questions, we will ask if the scientific insights in this chapter can help provide answers and also help us understand why generalizations about groups of people can be so fraught with controversy and conflict.

1. How do we learn stereotypes about other people?

Although some of our stereotypes are based on personal encounters with members of another group, many stereotypes are socially communicated through our parent, friends, and secondhand reports in books, movies, TV, and the Internet, all of which vary greatly in their accuracy (for more on social learning, see Chapter 11). For instance, if the only Colombians a person ever hears about are those portrayed on TV as drug dealers, it might not be surprising for the person to assume that many, if not most, Colombians are dangerous criminals. Stereotypes can also be transmitted through news media, which tend to oversimplify and focus primarily on salient negative events. One African American man being arrested for robbery may make the 6 p.m. news, whereas 10 African American men working late on Wall Street will not. Thus, even when presenting true events, media in their various forms can contribute to the development of stereotypes through a bias toward presenting bad news. As they used to say in the newspaper business, "If it bleeds, it leads."

In the process of acquiring stereotypes, people filter what they attend to through the personal lens of their own needs and self-interest. We tend to believe good things about the groups we belong to and view groups that are different from ours with varying degrees of skepticism. Once we have formed a negative stereotype about members of another group, we are more likely to pay attention to examples that confirm this stereotype. If we believe that Arabs are prone to be terrorists, then every time we hear about an Arab involved in a bombing or other attack, we will pay extra attention and remember the incident. On the other hand, when we meet an Arab doctor or scientist, or read about Arab entrepreneurs and philanthropists, we may try to explain away these disconfirming examples as being due to some extraneous factor not related to their being Arab. This process is known as **confirmation bias** (Pettigrew, 1979).

confirmation bias. A tendency to ignore information that conflicts with a prior belief and focus on information that is consistent with that belief.

As you saw in Chapter 5's discussion of operant conditioning, one limit to learning is that organisms often learn only about the outcomes of the actions they choose to perform; they do not learn about the outcomes of actions that they do not perform. For example, a pigeon that pecks a green key and is reinforced with a food pellet for every third peck may never peck the red key, which might in fact have a higher rate of reinforcement. In a similar fashion, a business owner might continue for years to do fine in business by hiring only people who have a Harvard degree, never realizing that he would have done better if he had hired the brilliant *summa cum laude* from the local state university whom he didn't bother to interview.

2. How should we evaluate the accuracy of a stereotype?

Before we can discuss whether or not a given stereotype is accurate, we need to have a consensus on how a stereotype's accuracy should be judged. Law professor Frederick Schaeur (2003) offers an example based on a commonly held stereotype about a particular category of dogs. In the aftermath of attacks on several people by pit bulls, many communities enacted laws that ban pit bulls, arguing that such laws are justified because *pit bulls are dangerous dogs*. Others objected to these laws, calling them a form of "speciesism," because, they claimed, these laws were unfairly biased against the many pit bulls that have never harmed anyone at all (Schauer, 2003). Is the stereotype of pit bulls as dangerous dogs accurate or not?

Are laws banning pit bulls a form of inappropriate stereotyping or sensible public policy?

Yvonne Hemsey/Liaison/Getty Images

Although seemingly clear in meaning, this generalization about pit bulls is actually ambiguous, in that logically it has three potential interpretations. Do we mean that (1) all pit bulls are dangerous, (2) most pit bulls are dangerous, or (3) pit bulls are more dangerous than most other breeds of dog? According to the first interpretation, the existence of even a single non-dangerous pit bull would imply the stereotype is inaccurate. According to the second interpretation, a randomly chosen pit bull is more likely to be dangerous than not because half or more of all pit bulls are dangerous. Although either of these interpretations of "pit bulls are dangerous" is logically plausible, neither corresponds to what is generally believed by people who hold a stereotype about a category of people (or dogs).

In fact, the interpretation most in line with psychological research about generalizations is the third: *pit bulls are more dangerous than other breeds of dog*. Under this interpretation, a generalization about pit bulls as dangerous could be accurate even if only 10% of pit bulls are dangerous, so long as this is higher than the percent of dogs of other breeds that are dangerous (which, for example, might be only 2% of dogs overall). "Pit bulls are dangerous dogs" could be a useful stereotype if knowing that a dog is a pit bull increases—by five times, in this hypothetical example—our expectation that the dog will be dangerous.

This discussion demonstrates that our concept of pit bulls is, like most natural categories, fuzzy and ill-defined. The relationships between the category (pit bull) and some of the key features or attributes ascribed to its members (e.g., being dangerous) are only partial or probabilistic. In other words, certain features may be common to many of the members but not to all of them, much as seen in Rosch's work on natural categories, reviewed earlier in this chapter.

Rosch described the most useful natural categories as those organized around a central prototype that embodies features common to most typical members of the category. The concepts of prototype (introduced earlier in this chapter) and stereotype are very close in meaning and definition, but with subtle differences worth noting. A prototype is usually defined *externally* based on the central or common tendency of exemplars of the category, while a stereotype is a *psychological concept* that may or may not closely correspond to an accurate prototype for the category of people (or dogs) to which it refers. Rosch argued that natural categories are adopted when they provide us with value in improving our ability to make inductive inferences (Rosch et al., 1976).

The idea that a category or generalization's value is based on its ability to help us make inductive inferences is, in fact, the same analysis that Robert Rescorla applied to his study of contingency learning in rats (Rescorla, 1968), described in Chapter 4. Rescorla showed that rats will learn a tone   shock association so long as the frequency of shocks following the tone is higher than the frequency of shocks experienced otherwise. Thus, a rat may respond with fear to a tone even though this is the wrong response most of the time, so long as the cost of these errors (in terms of wasted fear) is less than the cost of being unexpectedly shocked. Many prejudicial behaviors toward individuals—or dogs—might also be understood as resulting from a similar cost–benefit comparison: the natural mechanisms operating in the brain may decide that the cost of finding out about an individual person or dog is too high relative to the ease of making a choice informed by only an inductive inference based on category membership.

The ability of rats to sense the informational value of cues is a fundamental feature of associative learning found in all species. Humans are also sensitive to the informational value of cues for organizing and interpreting the world around us, using them as the basis for the formation of new categories

(Gluck & Bower, 1988a; Corter & Gluck, 1992). This sensitivity suggests that people are more likely to develop categories when features they can easily perceive (as is the case with race, ethnicity, and gender) are predictive of other variables of interest to us, such as the person's income level, crime rate, or amount of education.

3. How do we distinguish between appropriate and inappropriate uses of stereotypes?

Stereotypes, like all generalizations, enable us to apply prior experience to new situations, especially when we have little or no specific information available. However, using stereotypes appropriately requires finding a balance between specificity (knowing how narrowly a given stereotype applies) and generality (knowing how broadly it applies). Many commonly held assumptions about specific groups of people do accurately reflect statistical realities (Jussim, 2012). There are, however, two common ways in which a statistically accurate generalization about other people can be misused.

The first type of error is to assume that all members of a category must inflexibly conform to the generalization. For example, it is a fact of life in the United States today that different racial groups have statistically different crime rates, medical maladies, educational achievements, and incomes. According to normative statistics, it would be irrational—actuarially unsound—to ignore these differences when generating expectations (Pinker, 2002). What is important to remember, however, is that these categorical generalizations apply only to groups or to expectations for individuals about whom we know nothing other than their group membership. There are large numbers of individuals in every group who do not fit the statistical profile, and these statitics are not static and can evolve and change with time. Even if a stereotype was once accurate, it may no longer be so.

The second way in which generalizations are commonly misused is by faulty inverse reasoning, much as described earlier in this chapter. While it true that most zebras have four legs and hooves, relatively few of the four-legged hooved animals you will encounter while traveling across America will be zebras; most, if not all, will be horses. The mathematics of statistical (or probabilistic) inference tells that to equate an attribute inference based on category membership (zebras are likely to have four legs) with a categorical inference based on attributes (four-legged animals are zebras) is clearly erroneous, especially when the category in question is a rare one like zebras (or in the parlance of ethnic and racial categories, a minority group). This effect of rarity is routinely underestimated by people (Kahneman & Tversky, 1973). It is the reason that doctors are often prone to misdiagnose rare diseases from symptoms that are also associated with much more common maladies. A high temperature may be typical of someone with malaria, but most students reading this book who have experienced fever were probably suffering from the flu or common cold, not malaria. Nevertheless, as described earlier in this chapter, people routinely make these kinds of inductive errors in a broad range of situations (Bar-Hillel, 1984).

Thus, even a fundamentally accurate generalization—a stereotype that reflects some statistical reality in the world—can form the basis of inaccurate conclusions if it is misused. Accurate generalizations, including stereotypes about people, can be put to beneficial use, as long as they are interpreted correctly as descriptors of statistical characteristics of a large group, and not confused with features that are diagnostic or predictive for group membership, especially when the group is infrequent or rare in the general population.

Granger Wootz/Blend Images/Corbis

Should taxi drivers be allowed to pick up whoever they think will lead to the highest fares? Why or why not?

4. How can we balance the value and risks associated with using stereotypes?

From time to time, we may be faced with situations in which the choice that seems best for us may not be best for society. Consider for example a taxi driver who sees two potential fares on a midtown street: a black man right in front of him and a white woman a block further along. The driver may worry that a black man will ask him for a ride to a poor area of town far from the city center, where the driver would be less likely to find a paying fare back to the center of town. Or, he may believe that most robberies in taxi cabs are committed by black men. The frustrated black man trying to hail a cab may be a corporate CEO of a Fortune 500 company (or the well known black actor, Danny Glover, who filed a complaint against the New York City Taxi commission for being passed by five cab drivers who refused to pick him up). The taxi driver may, however, simply reckon that the probability of being robbed or taken to a remote area of town is higher if he picks up a black man than if he picks up a young white woman. In his own self-interest, it may, indeed, be optimal for him to drive past the black man and pick up the white woman on the next block.

If the taxi driver's behavior is, indeed, optimal for his own well-being (there being little cost to him for passing up one fare for another), why do we frown on it as a form of racial prejudice? We do so because as a society, we have decided that it is in our collective best interest if everyone has equal access to all forms of public transportation and that, indeed, everyone has a right to such access. We have moral principles that we have collectively decided are more important than an individual's interests (Pinker, 2002).

Our laws alter the taxi driver's reward contingencies by imposing severe financial penalties for discriminatory actions (in the rare cases, of course, when they can be proven and prosecuted). As discussed in Chapters 1 and 8, B. F. Skinner believed that society should be organized on the basis of instrumental conditioning principles, with positive and negative consequences so arranged to shape each individual toward actions that maximize societal aims.

Theories and data from the learning laboratory offer no easy solutions to the social problems caused by stereotypes and prejudice, but they do help us understand that the underlying behavior of generalizing to individuals from category membership is not, in and of itself, a bad thing. The trouble with stereotypes arises principally when people use generalizations about a group to justify discrimination against individuals, denying the possibility that the generalization may not pertain to everyone in the group. In cognitive terms, it is neither prejudiced nor irrational to note actual differences in statistical frequencies in the characteristics of different groups; what is prejudicial, and irrational, is when a statistical generalization is applied over-rigidly to an individual or otherwise misused.

All species, including sea slugs, rats, and humans, are hardwired to infer contingencies between cues and outcomes, obtaining information about the structure of the world that increases their ability to predict the future. Although some forms of stereotyping have negative consequences for individuals and society, it would be overgeneralizing about generalizing to conclude that all forms of pre-judging about groups of other people are inappropriate. Generalization and categorization, including about other people, are fundamental tools for our survival.

Interim Summary

- People with schizophrenia show deficits in generalization, consistent with their impaired medial temporal lobe function.

- Generalization deficits in acquired equivalence are probably linked to impaired hippocampal function during learning, as shown by functional brain-imaging studies

- When our behavior toward another person is based on his or her membership in a category defined by race, ethnicity, national origin, gender, religion, or age, we are implicitly making a generalization based on a **stereotype.** The trouble with stereotypes arises principally when people use stereotypes to justify discrimination against individual people, denying the possibility that the generalization may not pertain to every individual in the group.

stereotype. A set of beliefs about the attributes of the members of a group.

Synthesis

Since we last saw her, two-year-old Sabrina has wiggled out of her high chair, walked across the kitchen, and sneaked out the back door. While exploring the backyard, she came across a small brown dog blocking her path. It turns to Sabrina and begins to growl. Sabrina has never seen this dog before. He looks something like her own friendly dog, Max, of whom she is quite fond, but this dog is new to her. Should Sabrina approach the dog or flee?

Sabrina's visual cortex registered the visual information about the animal's brown fur, and her auditory cortex picked up the growling sound. Because her dog, Max, is brown, the brown-detecting regions of Sabrina's visual cortex are highly sensitive and enlarged and can quickly detect and recognize Max when he comes into the room. On the basis of this dog's similar color to Max, she is disposed to generalize her positive feelings toward Max to this new dog and view him as friendly. At the same time, Sabrina's auditory cortex is highly attuned to Max's unique bark, and this dog sounds less like Max and more like the snarling and scary dogs she sometimes sees in Central Park. Discriminating on the basis of bark, she is inclined to view this dog as being different from Max and potentially dangerous. In sum, the information from her visual cortex and auditory cortex are suggesting conflicting tendencies: one suggests generalization and the other discrimination.

However, as her primary sensory cortices are processing the sights and sounds associated with this new dog, Sabrina's hippocampal region is combining the information with other information about the overall context in which this event is occurring: the backyard of her home in New Rochelle, on a warm summer day. The combination of this contextual information along with the visual and auditory cues about the animal allows Sabrina's hippocampus to detect an important pattern: her father's friends often visit during the summer with their dogs so that all can enjoy the lovely frontage on Long Island Sound. Based on this configuration of local contextual information (the place and the season) and the sight and sound of the animal, Sabrina infers that this particular dog is more likely to be friendly than aggressive. She reaches out and pets him, and he rolls over to let her scratch his belly. Like Sabrina, your ability to discriminate and generalize, to recognize friend from foe, will govern your choices—and determine what you learn from each experience.

KNOW YOUR KEY TERMS

acetylcholine (ACh), *p. 250*
acquired equivalence, *p. 233*
category, *p. 237*
category learning, *p. 238*
combinatorial explosion, *p. 240*
concept, *p. 237*
concept formation, *p. 214*
configural node, *p. 236*
confirmation bias, *p. 259*

consequential region, *p. 216*
discrimination learning, *p. 214*
discrete-component representation, *p. 217*
distributed representation, *p. 220*
errorless discrimination learning, *p. 229*
generalization gradient, *p. 216*
hippocampal region, *p. 251*

inductive inference. *p. 241*
medial temporal lobe, *p. 251*
negative patterning, *p. 234*
nucleus basalis, *p. 250*
prototype, *p. 241*
sensory preconditioning, *p. 231*
stereotype, *p. 263*
stimulus control, *p. 225*
stimulus representation, *p. 217*

QUIZ YOURSELF

1. After training in which a single stimulus (such as a light of a particular color) has been reinforced repeatedly, _____ around that trained stimulus show a peak, or point of maximal responding, corresponding to the original stimulus on which the animal was trained. (p. 216)

2. Discrete-representation learning models are useful for describing how organisms learn about highly _____ stimuli, such as a tone and a light, but they don't work as well with stimuli that have some inherent _____, such as lights of different colors. (p. 217)

3. In Thorndike's view, yellow and yellow-orange are not two totally separate stimuli. Rather, he argued, they are each composed of many distinct elements, some shared and others not shared, much like W. K. Estes and his _____ theory and by David Rumelhart and colleagues in their _____ models. (p. 220)

4. Two objects or substances that initially seem very similar, or even indistinguishable, eventually come to be distinguishable when each is repeatedly paired with a different label, name, or outcome. This is an example of _____. (p. 214)

5. A transition from easy to hard discrimination learning so as to all but eliminate errors is called _____. (p. 229)

6. The _____ procedure shows that co-occurrence of two stimuli is sufficient to produce meaning-based generalization from one stimulus to the other. (p. 231)

7. Negative patterning is just one example of a larger class of learning phenomena that involve configurations of stimuli and that cannot be explained using _____. (p. 236)

8. _____ are psychological, or mental, entities constructed on the basis of our experiences with the world. In contrast, _____ are of the world, a class or division of people or things that have some shared characteristics. (p. 237)

9. Many primary sensory cortical areas are organized _____ in that each region responds preferentially to a particular type of stimulus and neighboring regions respond to similar stimuli. (p. 245)

10. One key brain region that determines whether a stimulus merits cortical remapping is the _____. (p. 250)

11. Animals with hippocampal damage are impaired at tasks that require sensitivity to stimulus–stimulus relationships such as _____ and _____. (p. 251–252)

12. People with schizophrenia show abnormalities in the shape of the _____, most notably an overall smaller volume. (p. 251)

13. Although some of our stereotypes are based on personal encounters with members of another group, many stereotypes are acquired through _____. (p. 259)

14. Rosch argued that natural categories are adopted when they provide us with value in improving our ability to make _____ inferences. (p. 241)

15. Confirming Gluck and Myer's prediction of the hippocampal role in acquired equivalence, Shohamy and Anthony Wagner found that critical hippocampal activity occurs during _____, rather than _____. (p. 256)

16. Lesions of the entorhinal cortex (within the hippocampal region), eliminated _____ in rabbit eye blink conditioning. (p. 252)

17. Upon activation, the nucleus basalis neurons release _____, a neurotransmitter that promotes neuronal plasticity. (p. 250)

18. Richard Thompson's experiments in the 1960's suggested that animals _____ and have difficulty discriminating various stimuli when their primary sensory cortex is damaged. (p. 249)

19. If you are asked to think about a typical cat, you can think of a creature with four legs that would enjoy eating meat. This abstract representation of the idealized or typical member of a category is called the category's _____. (p. 241)

Answers appear in the back of the book.

CONCEPT CHECK

Consider the following experiment, conducted by Robert Rescorla in 1976: In phase 1, he trained rats to associate a yellow light (the CS) with a US (Rescorla, 1976). After all the rats were fully trained and giving reliable CRs to the yellow light, he divided the animals into two groups. Rats in the experimental group received a second phase of training with an orange light as the CS until they learned to give reliable CRs. The control rats, however, continued to be trained with the yellow-light CS. Finally, in the third test phase of the experiment, all animals were exposed to a yellow light as the possible CS.

1. What do you predict occurred in phase 3: did the rats in the experimental group give a larger or smaller response to the yellow light compared with the rats in the control group?

2. Why? And what does this suggest about the best way for you to prepare for your tennis tournament?

Hint: In keeping with the shared-elements approach of Thorndike and Estes, designate X as a shared element common to both yellow lights and orange lights (capturing the similarity of these two cues) and designate Y and O as the elements unique to yellow and orange lights, respectively. Thus, the yellow light can be viewed as a compound cue YX, and the orange light can be viewed as a compound cue OX. Using this shared-elements representation for these two similar stimuli, apply the Rescorla–Wagner model to each of the three phases of the experiment and predict which group should give a stronger response to the yellow light in phase 3.

Answers appear in the back of the book.

CHAPTER 7

Episodic and Semantic Memory

Memory for Facts and Events

FOR OVER 50 YEARS, THE IDENTITY OF THE MAN KNOWN ONLY BY THE INITIALS H.M. was one of the most closely guarded secrets in psychology. Before H.M., many scientists held to Karl Lashley's view, described in Chapter 2, that memory is encoded in a distributed fashion across the brain. But H.M. participated in experiments that revolutionized scientific thinking by documenting that the formation of new fact and event memories depends on distinct brain regions, separate from the brain regions that mediate other cognitive functions and other kinds of memory.

H.M.'s troubles began in childhood. By the age of 10, he was having epileptic seizures, during which the neurons in his brain fired wildly and uncontrollably. By age 16, the seizures were frequent and debilitating. Severe attacks, during which he might convulse and lose consciousness, occurred weekly; minor attacks occurred up to 10 times a day. H.M. struggled to complete high school, finally graduating at age 21, but the seizures were so frequent and so severe that he had difficulty holding a simple job. His doctors put him on a near-toxic diet of anticonvulsant drugs, but still the seizures continued.

In 1953, in desperation, H.M. and his family agreed to try brain surgery. At the time, doctors knew that, in many epileptic patients, seizures start in either the left or right hemisphere, usually in the **medial temporal lobes**, the inner (or medial) surfaces of the temporal lobes. Doctors had found that surgical removal of the medial temporal lobe from the hemisphere where the seizures originated could eliminate the source of the problem and cure the epilepsy in these patients. Because H.M.'s seizures were so severe, and because their precise origin could not be determined, the doctors decided to remove his medial temporal lobes bilaterally (Corkin, Amaral, Gonzalez, Johnson, & Hyman, 1997).

Medically, the operation was a success: H.M.'s seizures declined drastically in frequency and severity. But there was a terrible cost.

Behavioral Processes

Features of Episodic and Semantic Memories

Encoding New Memories

Retrieving Existing Memories

Learning and Memory in Everyday Life: Total Recall! The Truth about Extraordinary Memorizers

When Memory Fails

Learning and Memory in Everyday Life: Remembering Computer Passwords

Memory Consolidation and Reconsolidation

Metamemory

Brain Substrates

Neuronal Networks for Semantic Memory

The Medial Temporal Lobes in Memory Storage

The Frontal Cortex in Memory Storage and Retrieval

Subcortical Structures Involved in Episodic and Semantic Memory

Clinical Perspectives

Learning and Memory in Everyday Life: The Cost of Concussion

Transient Global Amnesia

Functional Amnesia

Mr Elliott Neep/Getty Images

Photograph by Jenni Ogden, first published in "Trouble In Mind: Stories from a Neuropsychologist's Casebook" OUP, New York, 2012; Scribe Publications, Melbourne, 2013."©Jenni Ogden Jenni Ogden jenniogden@farmside.co.nz

Henry Molaison, known to brain researchers everywhere as H.M. This photo was taken in 1986, at age 60, in the neuropsychology test laboratory at Massachusetts Institute of Technology, Cambridge, Massachusetts.

medial temporal lobes. The medial (or inner) surface of the temporal lobes that contains the hippocampus, the amygdala, and other structures important for memory.

amnesia. Memory loss.

H.M. developed **amnesia**, or memory loss. Specifically, he lost the ability to form new memories for facts and events (Scoville & Milner, 1957). He could no longer remember what he had eaten for breakfast or why he was in the hospital. He could spend all morning working intensively with a psychologist and then take a break for lunch; an hour later he would not recognize the psychologist at all (Haglund & Collett, 1996). When H.M. found out that a favorite uncle had died, he experienced intense grief—then forgot. Again and again, he asked after the uncle and reacted with surprise and fresh grief every time he was told of the death (Milner, 1966). H.M. himself was painfully aware of his poor memory and described his life as constantly waking from a dream he couldn't remember (Milner, Corkin, & Teuber, 1968).

Despite his devastated memory, H.M.'s personality was basically unchanged, and after the operation his IQ actually went up—probably because, without constant seizures, he could now concentrate better on whatever he was doing. He could no longer follow the plot of a television show, because the commercials would interrupt his memory of the story line, but he could still amuse himself solving crossword puzzles. As long as H.M. paid attention to a task, he could perform well; as soon as he turned his attention to something else, the information vanished. H.M. was living proof that the ability to form new fact and event memories depends on the medial temporal lobes but that many other kinds of memory (and cognitive function) do not.

On December 2, 2008, H.M. passed away, and—by prior agreement—the details of his identity were finally released to the public. Scientists and students of the brain finally learned the name—Henry Gustav Molaison (pronounced "Mollisson")—and saw the face of the man who has taught us so much about memory and the brain. Even in death, H.M. continues to contribute. His brain was donated to science, and a team of researchers at the University of California–San Diego digitized images of the preserved tissue to create a "virtual" map for others to study.

Fortunately, amnesia as severe as H.M.'s is extraordinarily rare. But amnesia does occur, sometimes as the result of a brain injury and sometimes as the result of disease or extreme stress. Some patients, like H.M., lose the ability to form new memories. In other cases, patients lose memories of a specific past event or—rarer still—lose all memories of their identity and personal history. Cases such as these remind us that our memories—the facts we know and the events we remember—define us.

7.1 Behavioral Processes

Think back to the day of your high school graduation. Where was the ceremony held? Who sat near you? What were you wearing? Did a local celebrity speak? Did the school band perform? What were your feelings—pride, excitement, or perhaps impatience for the ceremony to end so you could celebrate with your friends?

These details of your graduation constitute an **episodic memory**: a memory for a specific event in your life (Tulving, 1972, 1983, 2002). An episodic memory includes information about the spatial and temporal context: where and when the event occurred.

Related to, though distinct from, episodic memories are **semantic memories**: memories for facts and general knowledge about the world, as well as for personal information such as your own name and your favorite food. Unlike episodic memory, semantic memory is *not* tagged in time and space. For example, if asked to name the first president of the United States, or to state your mother's maiden name, you probably know the answers. But you may not remember the specific event—the when and where—in which you first learned either piece of information. Whereas episodic memory is what we "remember," semantic memory is what we "know" (Tulving, 1985).

Features of Episodic and Semantic Memories

Episodic and semantic memories share two key features (Table 7.1). First, both episodic and semantic memories can be communicated flexibly, in formats different from the way they were originally acquired. When you remember an episodic memory—say, the memory of your graduation—you can describe the details you recall, even if you've never tried putting them into words before. Similarly, if someone were to show you a photo of the graduation taken from a different vantage point (perhaps taken from the stage rather than from where you and your classmates were seated), you would probably be able to recognize the scene, even though you had never seen it in quite this way.

As for semantic memory, if someone asks you how to get from the library to the cafeteria, you can answer by giving verbal directions or by drawing a map, even though you may never have attempted to put the information into these specific formats before. Similarly, after memorizing a list of historical facts, you can communicate that knowledge on an exam whether the format is true/false, multiple-choice, or essay questions.

The issue of flexibility may seem trivial, but some memories are hard to communicate in ways other than how they were originally learned. For example, in Chapter 8, you'll read about perceptual-motor skills, like tying your shoes.

episodic memory. Memory for specific autobiographical events; it includes information about the spatial and temporal contexts in which the event occurred.

semantic memory. Memory for facts or general knowledge about the world, including general personal information.

Table 7.1 Comparing and contrasting episodic and semantic memory

Episodic memory event-related: "I remember"	Semantic memory factual: "I know"	Same (✓) or Different (✗)
Can be communicated flexibly—in a format other than that in which it was acquired	Can be communicated flexibly—in a format other than that in which it was acquired	✓
Consciously accessible (you know that you know)	Consciously accessible (you know that you know)	✓
Tagged with spatial and temporal context	**Not necessarily** tagged with spatial or temporal context	✗
You must have experienced the event personally	Can be **personal or general** information	✗
Learned in a **single exposure**; can be weakened by exposure to similar events	Can be learned in a single exposure, but can also be **strengthened by repetition**	✗

declarative memory. A broad class of memories, both semantic and episodic, that can typically be verbalized ("declared") or explicitly communicated in some other way.

nondeclarative memory. A broad class of memory that includes skill memory and other types of learning that do not fall under the heading of episodic or semantic memory and that are not always consciously accessible or easy to verbalize.

explicit memory. A category of memory that includes semantic memory and episodic memory and consists of memories of which the person is aware: you know that you know the information.

implicit memory. Memory that occurs without the learner's awareness.

You can probably tie a shoe easily, but imagine if someone asked you for a short description of how to do it. Odds are you'd find it difficult to comply—you might even have to go through the hand movements to remind yourself what comes next. Skill memories are generally not easy to communicate flexibly in the same way that episodic and semantic memories are.

The second key commonality between episodic and semantic memories is that both are consciously accessible. When someone asks you about a specific fact or event, you know whether you know the answer or recall the event.

Because of these similarities between episodic and semantic memory, some researchers use the term **declarative memory** as a broader term that includes both episodic and semantic memory, reflecting the fact that it is easy to verbalize ("declare") or otherwise communicate your knowledge (J. Anderson, 1976; Cohen & Squire, 1980; Squire, Knowlton, & Musen, 1993). Other kinds of memory—grouped under the heading **nondeclarative memory**—are not always easy to communicate verbally (Squire & Knowlton, 1995). Skill learning is one kind of nondeclarative memory, as are classical and operant conditioning.

Other researchers use the term **explicit memory** (Graf & Schacter, 1985; Schacter, 1987), to reflect the fact that episodic and semantic information is consciously accessible or "explicit" (you know that you know); by comparison, **implicit memory** is memory that you may not be aware you've acquired. For example, H.M. (who couldn't acquire new episodic or semantic memories) could learn new skills such as reading mirror-reversed text (Gabrieli, Corkin, Mickel, & Crowden, 1993). Just like healthy controls, H.M.'s performance slowly improved with practice. But when asked about these new skills, H.M. reported having no conscious memories of the training sessions and no knowledge of his new skill. Thus, this learning was implicit.

H.M. is a special case, of course; most of us, while practicing new skills, will also form consciously available episodic and semantic memories of what we're learning. In fact, it's proven extraordinarily difficult to disentangle explicit and implicit learning in healthy adults (Shanks, 2010). What H.M.'s case demonstrates is that conscious awareness is not absolutely *necessary* for implicit memories to form.

What Distinguishes Episodic from Semantic Memory?

Despite their similarities, episodic and semantic memory have several contrasting properties (Table 7.1). First, episodic memories concern specific events that occurred at a particular place and time: you must remember when and where those events occurred. Semantic memories involve factual information: you need not remember where and when you learned this information—only the fact itself.

Second, episodic memory is always autobiographical, in the sense that the event must have happened to you. In contrast, semantic memory can be personal (remembering your mother's maiden name or your favorite flavor of ice cream), but it can also be general factual information (remembering the atomic weight of boron or the name of the first U.S. president); you need not remember where or how you acquired the information.

Some memories straddle the line. Suppose you participate in a laboratory experiment that takes place over three days. On day 1, you're asked to memorize a list of familiar words (DOG, CHAIR, CLOUD, etc.). On day 2, you're given a second list to memorize (CAT, TABLE, STAR, etc.). Finally, on day 3, the experimenter asks you whether a specific word (CHAIR) was on the first or second list. Here, you have to remember the specific event in which you saw that word—in the testing lab, on the first day of the experiment—as distinct from all the other times in your life when you saw that word. Thus, your memory of learning the word CHAIR on study day 1 is an episodic memory, tagged in time and place. On the other hand, suppose the experimenter sends you home to study the two lists. Every night before bed, you take the lists out and memorize the words. A week later you return to the lab for your memory test. Now, you may have acquired a semantic memory of which words were on which list, but you may not distinctly remember all the individual study sessions that helped you acquire the information. In this case, your memory of the list items would be semantic memory.

This leads to a third important difference between episodic and semantic memory. Episodic memory is acquired in a single exposure: the event itself. In principle, semantic memories can be acquired in a single exposure too, particularly if the information is sufficiently interesting or important. For example, it might take you several exposures to memorize the Latin word for "arch"—*fornix*—unless you are also told that, in ancient Rome, prostitutes used to ply their trade under arches, which is where we get the modern word "fornicate." Such extra information, which relates the vocabulary item to other information you know, may help you remember the word after only a single exposure.

But ordinary semantic information generally needs a few additional exposures before being fully acquired. So, for example, you may have to study a Latin vocabulary list several times before you have all the items memorized. In general, repeated exposures to a single fact *strengthen* semantic memory for that fact (Linton, 1982); by contrast, repeated exposure to very similar events may *weaken* episodic memory for any one of those events (Figure 7.1). If you park your car in the same large parking lot every day, you may confuse the episodic memories of all the prior, highly similar parking events, making it hard to remember exactly where you parked the car today. This is one reason why any large parking lot contains a number of people walking around with panicked expressions on their faces. ✂

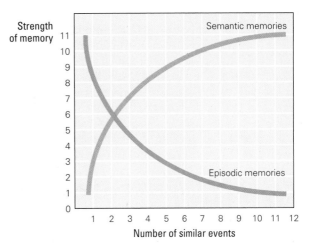

Figure 7.1 Episodic and semantic memory In general, semantic memory is strengthened by repetition, but episodic memory can be weakened by repeated exposure to similar events.

Which Comes First, Episodic or Semantic Memory?

The exact relationship between episodic and semantic memory is a matter of intense debate. The distinction between episodic memory and semantic memory was first made by psychologist Endel Tulving, who argued that episodic memory grows out of semantic memory (Tulving, 2002). According to this view, an organism has to have a certain amount of semantic information before episodic memories can be built on that framework. If you don't know what a graduation is, you can hardly have an episodic memory for any specific graduation—even your own.

An alternative possibility is that semantic memory represents information we have encountered repeatedly—so often that the actual learning episodes are blurred and only the semantic "fact" content remains (Conway, 2009). For example, if you remember the very first time you learned about George Washington, then you have an episodic memory for that event—perhaps it was a history class. But if you have heard about George Washington in many different classes and have also read about him in books and seen television portrayals, then you have accumulated a general store of knowledge about the first U.S. president, whether or not you remember the individual episodes.

A third possibility is that episodic and semantic memory are fundamentally interdependent: each can affect the other (Greenberg & Verfaellie, 2010). On the one hand, episodic memories will be formed more strongly, and last longer, when there is a rich background of semantic information to help us recognize and encode aspects of the event; on the other hand, semantic memories will be formed more strongly, and last longer, when we have a distinct episodic memory of the context in which we encountered the information (Neath, 2010). Under this view, it may be most useful not to classify memories as being either strictly episodic or strictly semantic but to acknowledge that many of our memories include both episodic and semantic content.

Can Nonhumans Have Episodic and Semantic Memory?

The easiest way to assess semantic memory in humans is by question-and-answer. If an experimenter asks you the name of the first U.S. president and you reply "George Washington," then the experimenter can safely conclude that you have a semantic memory of that fact. Things get a little more problematic with nonhuman animals; we can't ask a rat to name the president. But we can assess semantic memory in other ways. For example, Figure 7.2 shows a *radial arm maze*: a maze with a central area from which several arms branch off like the spokes of a wheel. The top of the maze is open so that a rat placed in the maze can see out and use landmarks in the room, such as the placement of windows or posters, to help navigate.

A radial arm maze can be used to assess many kinds of learning and memory. In one version, researchers put food at the end of one arm (the "goal arm") and place the rat at the end of a different arm (the "start arm"). The rat is then allowed to roam the maze until it finds and consumes the food. Over many such trials, the rat learns where the food is located, and when it is placed in the start arm, it will run directly to the goal arm. If a well-trained rat is placed in a new start arm and still runs to the food—via a route it has never used before—then researchers conclude that the rat "knows" where the food is and can use this information flexibly in new ways (such as using a new route to get there). Thus, most researchers would agree that this is an example of semantic memory in rats.

Episodic memory is harder to assess in animals. In fact, some researchers have explicitly argued that animals cannot maintain episodic memories, at least not in the way that humans do (Roberts & Feeney, 2009; Tulving, 2002). Endel Tulving, in particular, has argued that episodic memory requires "mental time travel," a re-experiencing of the event in memory; this in turn requires a conscious sense of self, as well as a subjective sense of time passing, which—Tulving argued—have not been demonstrated in nonhumans (Tulving, 2002). But other researchers argue that there is mounting evidence that animals can indeed form "episodic-like" memories for specific events, including information about the spatial and temporal context in which those events occurred (Clayton, Yu, & Dickinson, 2001; Crystal, 2010).

For example, gorillas seem to remember specific autobiographical events, and they can communicate this information flexibly to human testers. One gorilla, King, was taught to "name" various fruits and humans by using cards with drawings that represented the fruits and humans (Schwartz, Colon, Sanchez, Rodriguez, & Evans, 2002). This general knowledge about how to use the cards qualifies as semantic memory. Researchers then attempted to assess whether King could remember distinct autobiographical episodes. During the day, King received various pieces of fruit from different human handlers. Twenty-four hours later, when asked (via the cards) who had given him a particular fruit the day before, King could use the cards to name the

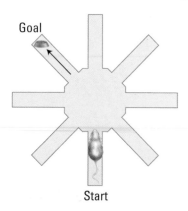

Figure 7.2 The radial arm maze After many trials in which the rat is allowed to explore the maze until it finds food located at the end of the "goal arm," it will eventually learn to run straight to the goal arm, indicating it has semantic memory for where the food is located in the maze.

Goal

Start

(a)

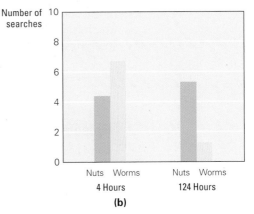

Dr. Nicola S. Clayton, University of Cambridge

(b)

Figure 7.3 Episodic-like memory in birds (a) Scrub jays were permitted to cache worms and nuts in the compartments of sand-filled ice cube trays. (b) Four hours later, the birds tended to dig in the compartments where they had buried worms (their preferred food). But after a delay of 124 hours, during which time the worms would have rotted, the birds went after the nuts instead. This suggests that the birds remembered what they had buried where and how long ago—an "episodic-like" memory.

(b) Information from Roberts, 2002.

correct human. Because King had eaten several fruits and interacted with other humans during the course of the day, his performance seems to demonstrate that he had episodic-like memory for the events of the prior day—remembering not just that he ate fruit but the specific type of fruit, who gave it to him, and approximately when this happened. And he could communicate this behavior to the experimenters, using abstract symbols on cards. This behavior seems to satisfy the criteria for an episodic memory (Schwartz & Evans, 2001).

Birds may also be able to remember specific events and how long ago they happened. Scrub jays, for example, bury extra food in caches so they can retrieve it later. These birds accurately remember their cache locations and will return to those locations later even if an experimenter has secretly removed the food in the meantime to ensure that the birds can't use scent to locate the buried food. To test episodic-like memory, Nicola Clayton and her colleagues allowed scrub jays to cache worms and nuts in sand-filled compartments of an ice cube tray (Figure 7.3a). The birds were then allowed to recover food either 4 hours or 124 hours (about 5 days) later. Normally, scrub jays prefer worms to nuts, and when tested after a 4-hour interval, they chose to recover the worms more often than the nuts (Figure 7.3b). But worms decay over a 124-hour interval, and nuts do not. And, indeed, when tested at a 124-hour interval, the birds typically preferred to recover the nuts (Clayton & Dickinson, 1999). These results suggest that scrub jays can remember not only where they have stored food but what type of food was stored and how long ago (Clayton, Yu, & Dickinson, 2001; Griffiths, Dickinson, & Clayton, 1999). Rats, dolphins, and pigeons may have similar abilities to remember specific events, including when and where those events took place (Kart-Teke, De Souza Silva, Huston, & Dere, 2006; Mercado, Murray, Uyeyama, Pack, & Herman, 1998; Zentall, Singer, & Stagner, 2008; Zhou & Crystal, 2011).

Some researchers go even farther, arguing that some nonhuman animals (rats, dolphins, nonhuman primates, and some birds) do have a subjective sense of self and of time, and that their behavior demonstrates they can indeed mentally re-create autobiographical events from their own past and imagine their own future (Dere, Kart-Tecke, Huston, & De Souza Silva, 2006; Zentall, 2006).

For the rest of this chapter, we'll adopt the convention of referring to "episodic-like" memories in nonhuman animals if those memories include what-where-when information about the spatial and temporal context in which the episode occurred (Crystal, 2010; Eacott & Easton, 2010; Wang & Morris, 2010). Use of the term "episodic-like" (rather than just "episodic") acknowledges that we cannot directly ask non-verbal animals about their subjective sense of self or their ability to perform "mental time travel."

In the absence of direct evidence on these points, controversy continues over whether nonhuman animals can form true episodic memories or whether this ability is uniquely human.

Test Your Knowledge

Episodic versus Semantic Memory

Episodic memories are memories for autobiographical events, set in a particular time and spatial location; semantic memories are memories for fact or general knowledge about the world, independent of when and how this information was acquired. Sometimes, though, the line between the two is blurred. A single behavior can contain components of both semantic and episodic information. Read the following scenarios to check whether you understand the difference. (Answers appear in the back of the book.)

1. A college senior takes his Latin vocabulary exam. The first phrase to be translated is *carpe diem*. This is an easy one; he knows the answer is "seize the day," even though he can't remember exactly where he first heard this expression. Is this student using semantic or episodic memory?

2. The second phrase to be translated is *ne tentes, aut perfice*. This is harder; the student can remember studying the phrase, and he even recalls that the phrase was printed in black ink on the lower left of a page in his textbook, but he can't recall the translation. Is the student using semantic or episodic memory?

3. Later in the day, the senior is helping a new student learn her way around campus. When the tour finishes, the newcomer asks where she can buy a cup of coffee. The senior thinks for a moment, then says that the coffee is better at a nearby Starbucks than at the student center. How might the senior be using both semantic and episodic memory?

Encoding New Memories

Much of the time, the formation of new episodic and semantic memories seems automatic and effortless. For example, you probably remember a great deal of information about your high school graduation even if you did not spend the day consciously trying to memorize the details so you could recall them later. On the other hand, every student who's ever studied for a test knows that some types of information are easier to learn than others. Here are three basic principles that govern how successfully a new episodic or semantic memory is *encoded*, or stored in memory.

Mere Exposure to Information Does Not Guarantee Memory

On the principle that practice makes perfect, you might think that the best way to learn new information is to study, study, study. But the truth is a little more complicated. Mere repeated exposure to information is not enough to guarantee memory. One telling example of this occurred when BBC Radio in the United Kingdom was planning to change its broadcast frequency. The BBC saturated the airwaves with announcements informing listeners about the new station call numbers. A survey of radio listeners who had heard the announcement at least 25 times a day for many weeks found that less than a quarter of these individuals had learned the new call numbers (Bekerian & Baddeley, 1980). Just presenting the information again and again wasn't enough to guarantee that listeners would remember.

Memory for visual details can be just as bad. Here's a quick test: try to remember what a U.S. penny looks like. You probably remember that Lincoln's face appears on the front, but can you remember whether he's facing to the left or the right? If you're not sure, you're not alone. Few U.S. students can accurately draw a penny; in fact, few can even pick out an accurate drawing from among a set of fakes (Nickerson & Adams, 1979). Residents of other countries are just as poor at remembering details of their own national currency (Jones, 1990; Martin & Jones, 1995). Most of us handle money every day and are quite capable of recognizing coins when we see them. Yet most of us have remarkably poor memory for the details of what these familiar objects actually look like.

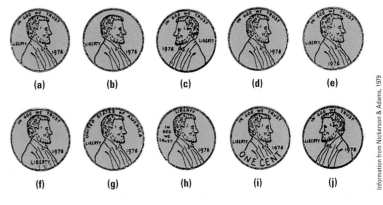

(a) (b) (c) (d) (e)

(f) (g) (h) (i) (j)

Information from Nickerson & Adams, 1979

Can you pick out the correct drawing of a penny? Most people have very poor ability to recognize the details of a coin face, though they see and handle the coin every day. What principle of memory does this illustrate?

In short, sheer repetition of either verbal or visual information isn't enough to ensure its being remembered. So what does determine whether information gets encoded and retained?

Memory Is Better for Information That Relates to Prior Knowledge

Earlier in the chapter, you read that the Latin word for "arc" or "arch" is *fornix*. To help make this information memorable, we presented the tidbit about Roman prostitutes. The idea was to provide a link between *fornix* and "fornication" (a word you already know), which should help you remember better than if you were just trying to memorize an otherwise meaningless Latin word.

A basic principle of memory is that new information is easier to remember if you can relate it to things you already know. In a classic study, John Bransford and Marcia Johnson read participants a paragraph such as the following:

> *The procedure is actually quite simple. First, you arrange things into different groups. Of course, one pile may be sufficient depending on how much there is to do. If you have to go somewhere else due to lack of facilities that is the next step, otherwise you are pretty well set. It is important not to overdo things. That is, it is better to do too few things at once than too many.....After the procedure is completed one arranges the materials into different groups again. Then they can be put into their appropriate places. Eventually they will be used once more and the whole cycle will then have to be repeated. However, that is part of life.*

Presented in this way, the paragraph makes little sense. Not surprisingly, most participants could recall very little of it later (Bransford & Johnson, 1972). However, a second group of participants were first told the topic of the paragraph: doing laundry. If you read the paragraph again in the light of this background information, you will find that it makes much more sense. Indeed, participants who knew the topic before hearing the paragraph were able to recall twice as much about the paragraph (Figure 7.4). Importantly, the effect of background information on memory is limited to the process of encoding; it does not help with recall. Thus, people who learned the topic only after they heard the paragraph did not recall the information any better than people who were never told the topic at all. Only people who knew the background information ahead of time remembered the paragraph well.

This principle has clear implications for optimizing study habits. In general, you will remember textbook material better if you take the time to scan a chapter first to get a sense of the major points before reading the details. This is also the reason that

Figure 7.4 The effects of prior knowledge on memory An experimenter read a paragraph aloud to participants. Participants who heard the paragraph by itself ("No topic") recalled few items, but participants who were first informed of the topic and then heard the paragraph ("Topic before") recalled significantly more items. Participants who learned the topic only after hearing the paragraph ("Topic after") performed no better than those who had never heard the topic at all.
Data from Bransford and Johnson, 1972, Table 2.

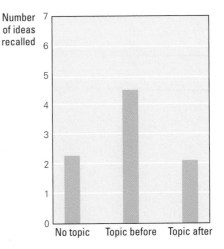

Number of ideas recalled

No topic   Topic before   Topic after

many professors encourage students to complete assigned readings before each lecture. With this preparation, the students' minds are better able to encode the information presented in the lecture.

Deeper Processing at Encoding Improves Recognition Later

A third important principle is that the more deeply you analyze information, the more likely you are to successfully encode it in memory. Specifically, in the **levels-of-processing effect**, the more deeply you process new information during encoding, the more likely you are to remember the information later (Craik & Lockhart, 1972; Craik & Tulving, 1975). If you think about the word *fornix* and its relationship to "fornication," you're processing the word more deeply than if you just tried to memorize the fact that *fornix* = "arch." Many experiments have shown that people recall words better if they're forced to think about the semantic content (meaning) of the words (Galli, 2014).

In one such study, subjects were shown a list of words, presented one at a time. For some of the words, participants were told to decide whether the word described something animate or inanimate. For other words, participants were asked to decide whether the first and the last letters of the word were in alphabetical order. Presumably, the "animate/inanimate" decision required thinking deeply about the meaning of the word, but the "alphabetic/nonalphabetic" decision required only superficial thinking about how the letters were arranged. Later, the participants were shown another list, and were asked to identify which words they had studied earlier (Figure 7.5). Just as you'd expect, the deeply processed "animate/inanimate" words were better recognized than the superficially processed "alphabetic/nonalphabetic" words (Otten, Henson & Rugg, 2001).

One criticism of the levels-of-processing idea is that it is vague. How, exactly, can we be sure whether individuals are processing information "deeply" or "superficially"? Just because an experimenter asks participants to think about the spelling of a word, how can we know they are not thinking about the meaning of the word too? And, for that matter, how can we be sure that thinking about word meanings requires deeper processing than comparing the first and last letters of a word?

It is hard to answer these questions by using purely behavioral measures, but functional neuroimaging provides some clues. Researchers have used functional magnetic resonance imaging (fMRI) to look at brain activity while participants encode words either "deeply" or "superficially," and have shown that participants' brains are much more active during deep-processing than superficial-processing trials (Otten et al., 2001; Davachi et al., 2003). This suggests that the brain is indeed working harder during deep processing of information. Later in this chapter, we'll talk more about specific brain areas that play roles in episodic and semantic memory; for now, though, simply note that the psychological concepts of deep versus superficial processing seem to correspond to physiological measures of how hard the brain is working to encode new information.

Retrieving Existing Memories

Of course, successfully encoding a new memory is only half the battle; the other half is successfully accessing, or retrieving, that memory when we want it. You've probably experienced the "tip-of-the-tongue" phenomenon, when you were trying to summon a word or a name from memory that you were sure you knew but simply couldn't retrieve at the moment. In these cases, the information is not permanently lost, only temporarily inaccessible. You may succeed in recalling the information later, often after you've turned your attention to something else.

levels-of-processing effect. The finding that, in general, deeper processing (such as thinking about the semantic meaning of a word) leads to better recall of the information than shallow processing (such as thinking about the spelling or pronunciation of the word).

Figure 7.5 Levels-of-processing effect Participants were shown words and asked either to decide whether the word described something animate or inanimate (the "animate/inanimate" condition) or to decide whether the first and last letters of the word were in alphabetical order (the "alphabetic/nonalphabetic" condition). Later, when shown a second list and asked whether or not each word had been previously viewed, participants recognized many more words from the deeply processed "animate/inanimate" condition than from the superficially processed "alphabetic/nonalphabetic" condition.
Data from Otten et al., 2001.

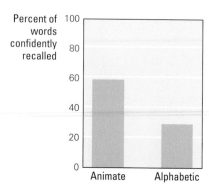

Why can we retrieve stored memories at some times, yet at other times they elude us? Like encoding, successful retrieving is governed by several basic principles. We'll present three key principles below.

Memory Retrieval Is Better When Study and Test Conditions Match

One factor in our ability to retrieve a memory is the degree to which the current context resembles the context in which the information was originally acquired. The **transfer-appropriate processing effect** refers to the finding that retrieval is more likely to be successful if the cues available at recall are similar to those that were available at encoding. (This is also sometimes called the *encoding specificity effect*.) For example, suppose you are initially shown a series of pictures of objects (a dog, a house, and so on) and then later are given a recognition test in which some of the objects are presented as pictures and some as words. Which objects do you think you'd remember best? Most people show better recognition if the format is the same at encoding as at testing: if objects presented as words are tested as words, and objects presented as pictures are tested as pictures (Köhler, Moscovitch, Winocur, & McIntosh, 2000). Performance is worse when the encoding and testing formats differ.

Some researchers have argued that the levels-of-processing effect, in which "deeper" processing leads to better memory than "superficial" processing, is really a transfer-appropriate processing effect in disguise. People who process a word "deeply," thinking about its meaning and visualizing it, may indeed be better at a standard visual recognition test (as you saw in Figure 7.5). But people asked to merely rhyme a word—a "superficial" processing task that doesn't involve thinking about the word's semantic meaning—actually perform better if the later memory test involves rhyming recognition (Morris, Bransford, & Franks, 1977). In short, perhaps deep processing during encoding will help only if the test also requires deep processing. If the test instead involves the physical attributes or sounds of a word, superficial processing may be preferable!

Transfer-appropriate processing involves not only the physical appearance of the stimuli but also the physical context in which memory is stored and retrieved. Have you ever been at the gym or the supermarket and run into someone you know from school and been temporarily unable to recognize that person in the unusual setting? You may even have struggled to chat for a while (without admitting you couldn't remember exactly who this person was) before something "clicked" and the memory fell into place. If you've ever had this type of experience, then you already know the powerful effect of physical context on memory retrieval.

In a famous demonstration of this principle, researchers tested memory in members of a diving club (Godden & Baddeley, 1975). Some of the divers were asked to learn a list of 40 words while on dry land; the remainder learned the list underwater. The divers were then tested on their recall of the words. Divers who were tested in the same environment where they had studied the list (either on land or underwater) could remember more words than those who were trained in one environment and tested in the other. Similarly, students who learn a list either standing up or sitting down will later recall a few more words if they are in the same position during testing (Godden & Baddely, 1975). A list learned while classical or jazz music plays will be remembered better if the same music plays during recall (S. Smith, 1985). In each case, recall is slightly better if the retrieval conditions are similar to the encoding conditions.

So, does this mean that studying in the same room where you will take a test will improve your performance? Not necessarily. A large study of 5,000 college students found no effect on performance when final exams were administered

transfer-appropriate processing effect. The finding that, in general, memory retrieval is best when the cues available at testing are similar to those available at encoding.

"THEN, AS YOU CAN SEE, WE GIVE THEM SOME MULTIPLE CHOICE TESTS."

Sidney Harris/ScienceCartoonsPlus.com

Even if rats could take multiple-choice tests, they would probably perform very poorly on this one. What principle of strong memory retrieval does this multiple-choice test violate?

free recall. A memory test that involves simply generating requested information from memory.

cued recall. A memory test that involves some kind of prompt or cue to aid recall.

recognition. A memory test that involves picking out (or recognizing) a studied item from a set of options.

in the same room where the course had been taught or in a novel classroom (Saufley, Otaka, & Bavaresco, 1985). (This may be because most classrooms are pretty much alike; taking the exam in a novel classroom may be much less disruptive to retrieval than taking the exam underwater.) But there are other ways to use the principles of transfer-appropriate processing to your advantage. For example, suppose you can study for an exam either by taking online multiple-choice tests or by recruiting a friend to ask you open-ended questions from your class notes. If you know that the professor usually gives essay exams, which study method should you use? The best way to prepare for a test is by processing the material in a way that is similar to how you expect to be tested on it, making the study and recall formats as similar as possible (Butler & Roediger, 2007).

More Cues Mean Better Recall

Of course, many formats are available for testing memory. The first and most obvious is **free recall**, in which you are simply asked an open-ended question and you supply the answer from memory (What is the Latin word for "arch"?). A second possibility is **cued recall**, in which you are given some kind of a prompt or clue to the correct answer (What is the Latin word for "arch"? F_____). A third possibility is **recognition**, in which you pick out the correct answer from a list of possible options (What is the Latin word for "arch"? A = *fenestra*, B = *fornix*, or C = *fundus*).

In general, free recall is harder than cued recall, which in turn is harder than recognition. This ranking directly reflects the number of cues available to jog the memory. In free recall, the tester provides no (or minimal) explicit cues; in cued recall, the tester provides at least some kind of cue; and in recognition, the entire item is provided. In one study, when asked to recall the names of their high school classmates, recent graduates could, on average, produce about 50% of the names; individuals who had graduated several decades earlier could produce only about 20 to 30% of the names. But when shown a list of names and asked to recognize which people had been classmates, recent graduates could get about 90% correct, and even long-ago graduates got about 85% correct (Bahrick, Bahrick, & Wittlinger, 1975).

Most people instinctively understand that free recall is harder than recognition. This is one reason why many students prefer exams containing multiple-choice rather than essay questions (recognition as opposed to free recall). Of course, professors understand this too, and they usually compensate by designing multiple-choice questions to include choices that can easily be mistaken for the correct response if a student hasn't studied the material closely. (Have you ever wished you were better at memorization? See "Learning and Memory in Everyday Life" on the next page.)

Struggling (and Even Failing) to Remember Can Improve Memory

Students and teachers usually think of studying (encoding) as distinct from testing (retrieval), with the latter mainly serving to assess whether learning was successful. But in fact, the mere act of taking a test can serve as a powerful

Total Recall! The Truth about Extraordinary Memorizers

We have all heard stories about people who have phenomenal memory abilities. Probably the most famous expert memorizer was a Russian journalist named Solomon Shereshevskii (more commonly known as S.). Russian neuropsychologist Aleksandr Luria could read S. a list of 70 words, which S. could then repeat accurately from memory; 15 years later, Luria wrote, "S would sit with his eyes closed, pause, then comment: 'Yes, yes . . . This was a series you gave me once in your apartment. You were sitting at the table and I in the rocking chair . . . You were wearing a gray suit . . .' And with that he would reel off the series precisely as I had given it to him at the earlier session" (Luria, 1982 [1968], p. 384). Other famous memorizers include basketball great Jerry Lucas, who amazed his teammates by memorizing portions of the New York City phone book.

How could such feats be possible? S. visualized stimuli mentally, in great detail, and these images helped him recall information later. Jerry Lucas also formed unusual visual images of the to-be-remembered information, making it more memorable

and easier to recall. Such strategies are examples of *mnemonics* (pronounced "nee-MON-ics"), which are techniques that make information easier to memorize. You yourself may have used simple mnemonic devices such as the acronym ROY G. BIV (to remember the colors of the spectrum: red, orange, yellow, green, blue, indigo, violet) or the rhyme "Thirty days hath September . . ." (to remember the number of days in each month).

Most world-class memory performers use mnemonics of one sort or another. A recent neuroimaging study of exceptional memorizers found no differences in brain anatomy between exceptional memory performers and people with average memories (Maguire, Valentine, Wilding, & Kapur, 2003). The implication is that almost anyone could attain a "world-class memory" by mastering the right mnemonic system (Ericsson, 2003). Unfortunately, there is no evidence that such memory masters are any better than the rest of us at memory challenges in the real world, such as remembering where we parked the car or when someone's birthday is.

---

enhancer of later memory for the information tested. This "testing effect" on memory has been observed numerous times in many conditions (for review, see Roediger & Butler, 2011). In fact, a difficult test—one that forces you to struggle to retrieve the information—may be most helpful of all. The benefits of testing on memory can occur even if you fail to remember the material during the test, and even if you don't receive feedback on whether your answers were correct.

In one study, students were asked to study two short paragraphs. Later, they were asked to re-read one of the paragraphs (Reading Condition); for the other paragraph, they were given a blank sheet with the title printed at the top, and asked to write down all the material they could remember (Testing Condition). A week later, students only recalled about 40% of the ideas from the paragraph they'd re-read—but they successfully recalled about 55% of the ideas from the paragraph they'd previously been tested on (Roediger & Karpicke, 2006). Thus, prior testing improved later recall—even though no feedback had been provided during the test.

There are probably several mechanisms behind the testing effect on memory. First, as you saw earlier, mere passive exposure to information (the Reading Condition) does not necessarily promote strong memory encoding. Second, as you also know, the phenomenon of transfer-appropriate processing predicts better performance when prior exposure to information occurs in the same format as later testing (as in the Testing Condition, where both sessions involved free recall tests). But a third possible mechanism has been dubbed the *desirable difficulties* phenomenon (Soderstrom & Bjork, 2015). This is roughly the idea that "difficult" learning conditions—ones that challenge your ability to recall—promote better long-term retention of the information being recalled.

So the next time you have to study for a test, remember these principles: instead of just re-reading the chapter, consider taking an online quiz (if you think the exam will include multiple-choice questions), using flashcards (short answer), or taking a blank piece of paper and writing down everything you can remember about the topic (if you think the exam will include essay questions). Chances are, the effort you put into remembering the information during your practice test will pay off later, when it comes time to perform on the actual exam. In fact, several studies suggest that if instructors periodically interrupt lectures to give short quizzes, perhaps polling students via electronic "clicker" devices, students perform better on subsequent exams—even when the exams contain material that wasn't explicitly included in the quizzes (for review, see Glass & Sinha, 2013).

When Memory Fails

You've just read about some basic principles affecting encoding and retrieval of episodic and semantic memories. At each stage, various conditions (format, context, etc.) can help or hinder the process. When you consider all the opportunities for failure, it is amazing how often our memories serve us well.

But there are many situations in which episodic and event memory do fail us. The tip-of-the-tongue phenomenon, mentioned above, is an example of a temporary failure: the memory is inaccessible at the moment but may resurface later. In other cases, though, memories are truly lost or corrupted. Many failures of memory reflect one of four basic phenomena: simple forgetting; interference from other memories; false memory; and source monitoring errors. We'll discuss these in more detail next.

Forgetting

It's probably obvious that you are more likely to remember things that happened recently than things that happened long ago. For example, you probably remember most of the events that have happened to you today, but not what happened to you on, say, July 16, 2013. However, if someone had questioned you on July 17, 2013, you probably could have reported the prior day's events in great detail. Somehow, that information has trickled away as the months passed. What governs how fast we forget?

As you read back in Chapter 1, Hermann Ebbinghaus conducted a series of early studies to quantify human learning and forgetting. Ebbinghaus memorized lists of nonsense words and then tested his own memory for the items. He concluded that most forgetting occurs in the first few hours or days after learning (Ebbinghaus, 1885/1964). Information that survives the critical first few days might last in memory indefinitely.

Ebbinghaus's basic finding has since been replicated in a variety of studies. For example, in the 1980s, memory researcher Larry Squire developed a test in which people were queried about television shows that had aired for a single season from 1 to 15 years earlier (Squire, 1989). (In those days, there were still a relatively small number of television networks, and most people were familiar with most programs that aired.) On average, people did quite well at this test of semantic memory. Most people could correctly recognize the names of more than 75% of TV shows that had aired in the prior year, although they recognized progressively fewer shows from earlier years (Figure 7.6a). Most forgetting occurred within the first decade, so people remembered almost as many TV shows from 15 years ago as from 10 years ago.

We normally think of forgetting as a passive process, in which old memories—particularly those we haven't accessed in a while—just quietly fade away. But we may have more power over what we remember (and forget) than we realize. **Directed forgetting** occurs when information is forgotten on demand. For example, Michael Anderson and colleagues trained participants

directed forgetting. A procedure in which subjects are first asked to learn information and later asked to remember or forget specific items; typically, memory is worse for items a subject was directed to forget.

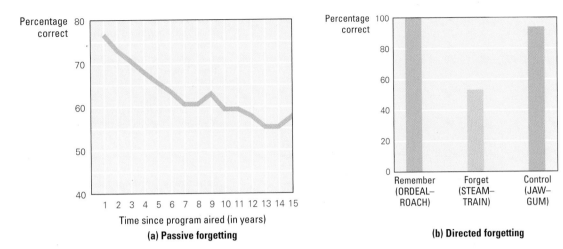

(a) Passive forgetting

(b) Directed forgetting

on a series of word pairs: ORDEAL–ROACH, STEAM–TRAIN, JAW–GUM, and so on (M. Anderson et al., 2004). Next, the researchers showed participants some of the studied words. For some words (ORDEAL), people were now asked to *remember* the associate (ROACH). For others (STEAM), they were asked to try to *forget* the associate (TRAIN). Later, Anderson tested memory for all the studied words (Figure 7.6b). People were less able to remember the words they'd tried to forget than those they'd tried to remember or those they hadn't seen since original training (GUM). Note that in the Forget condition of Figure 7.6b, people still remembered about 50% of the items on average. Thus, directed forgetting isn't perfect. But these results suggest that we have some control over what we do and don't forget. Other studies have even shown that intentional forgetting can extend to autobiographical events: participants who kept a daily diary and were then instructed to forget the previous week's events subsequently recalled fewer events than participants who kept a diary but did not receive instructions to forget (Joslyn & Oakes, 2005).

Obviously, intentional forgetting in the laboratory may be very different from forgetting in real life. Nevertheless, the fact that it is theoretically possible to intentionally forget unwanted information may help explain some real-world cases of memory suppression in which individuals forget highly traumatic and unpleasant events such as war, rape, or natural disasters. And it may be possible to exploit this ability in developing therapy for psychiatric disorders in which people suffer from intrusive and unwanted thoughts, such as posttraumatic stress disorder and obsessive compulsive disorder. In this way, the "memory failure" of forgetting may actually have some psychological benefits.

Interference

Remember the parking lot example, in which memories of prior days' parking locations disrupt your ability to recall where you parked the car today? This is an example of **interference**: when two memories overlap in content, the strength of either or both memories may be reduced.

Suppose you're participating in a memory experiment and the experimenter asks you to learn a list of word pairs—say, List 1 in Figure 7.7. You might practice this list, repeating it aloud, until you have it memorized. Then, after some delay, the experimenter gives you a test of cued recall: given the stems (e.g., DOG-____), fill in the appropriate associate (CHAIR) for each stem.

Now suppose the experimenter asks you to memorize a second list, List 2 in Figure 7.7. Note that some of the items (DOG, SHIRT) appear in both lists.

Figure 7.6 Two kinds of forgetting (a) Passive forgetting occurs as a function of time: older information is more likely to be forgotten than more recently acquired information. Here, people tested in the 1980s could correctly recognize the names of more TV shows that had aired in the prior year than of shows that had aired a decade previously. (b) Directed forgetting occurs when we intentionally try to suppress memory. Here, participants' memory was worse for studied word pairs they had been instructed to forget than for pairs they'd been instructed to remember or control pairs they hadn't seen since the original study phase.

(a) Information from Squire, 1989, Figure 1.
(b) Information from M. Anderson et al., 2004, Figure 1B.

interference. Reduction in the strength of a memory due to overlap with the content of other memories.

Figure 7.7 Two kinds of interference Imagine you are asked to learn the word pairs in List 1 and then the word pairs in List 2. After that, if you are asked to recall List 2, older items from List 1 may interfere (proactive interference). Conversely, if you are asked to recall List 1, newer items from List 2 may interfere (retroactive interference).

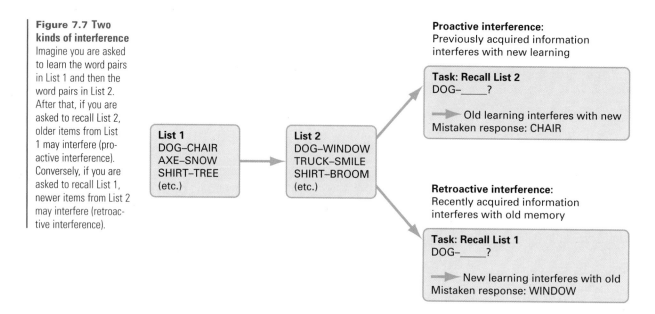

Proactive interference: Previously acquired information interferes with new learning

List 1
DOG–CHAIR
AXE–SNOW
SHIRT–TREE
(etc.)

List 2
DOG–WINDOW
TRUCK–SMILE
SHIRT–BROOM
(etc.)

Task: Recall List 2
DOG–_____?

Old learning interferes with new
Mistaken response: CHAIR

Retroactive interference: Recently acquired information interferes with old memory

Task: Recall List 1
DOG–_____?

New learning interferes with old
Mistaken response: WINDOW

proactive interference. Disruption of new learning by previously stored information.

retroactive interference. Disruption of old (previously stored) information by new learning.

source monitoring error. Remembering information but being mistaken about the specific episode that is the source of that memory.

As you attempt to learn the new pair DOG–WINDOW, the stem (DOG) will stimulate recall of the old associate (CHAIR). This may interfere with your learning of List 2, and when it comes time to test your memory for List 2, you may mistakenly respond with the old associate (CHAIR) instead of the new one (WINDOW). This process, whereby old information can disrupt new learning, is called **proactive interference** (J. Anderson, 1981; Wickelgren, 1966).

The opposite process also occurs: suppose that, after heavy practice with List 2, you try to go back and recall List 1. Now, when the experimenter prompts DOG———, you might recall WINDOW from List 2 instead of CHAIR from List 1. This process, whereby new information can disrupt old learning, is called **retroactive interference**. A simple mnemonic to help you remember the difference between proactive interference and retroactive interference is that *PRoactive* interference means *PReviously acquired* information is at fault; *REtroactive* interference means *REcently acquired* information is at fault.

Proactive and retroactive interference occur in many real-life contexts. For example, the last time you changed a frequently used computer password, you probably went through a phase during which you sometimes typed the old password by mistake. This is an example of *proactive* interference, as memory of the *previous* password interfered with your ability to retrieve memory for the new one. On the other hand, once you had successfully mastered the new password, you might have had some trouble remembering the password you used to use. This is an example of *retroactive* interference, as memory of the *recently* acquired password interfered with your ability to remember the old one. (For help creating memorable passwords that at the same time are hard to crack, see "Learning and Memory in Everyday Life" on the next page.)

Source Monitoring

Some memory failures are **source monitoring errors**, which occur when we remember information but are mistaken about the specific episode that is the source of that memory. For example, we may read some gossip in a trashy tabloid, and even though we know better than to take such reading material seriously, we may later remember the gossip but forget the dubious source—and thus give the rumor more credence than it deserves. In effect, the semantic

Remembering Computer Passwords

Almost everyone who has Internet access has to remember multiple passwords—for email accounts, bank and credit card accounts, household wireless server . . . the list goes on and on. Each online system may have its own set of rules for choosing an acceptable password—a minimum or maximum number of characters, required inclusion (or exclusion) of numbers, capital letters, and punctuation marks—so that a password accepted by one system may be rejected by another. On top of all this, some systems require that passwords be changed every few months.

Survey after survey reports that trying to remember all those passwords is the number-one frustration for users of online services. Many people, overwhelmed at the task, wind up writing their passwords down—creating just the kind of security risk that passwords are intended to avoid. Other people settle for memorable but hackable passwords; in early 2010, the *New York Times* reported that the most popular account password was "123456," closely followed by "abc123" and "password" (Vance, 2010).

You probably know that you're supposed to avoid easy-to-guess passwords that include your name, date of birth, or other personal information that can be gleaned from your Facebook profile (favorite band or pets' names). But the more complicated the password you choose, the harder it is to remember, right?

Not necessarily. And what you know about memory can help. Here are three tips for creating memorable computer passwords that are still hard for others to crack.

1. Remember that memory is better for information that you can link to items you already know. So, don't choose random, hard-to-remember passwords ("6ws@ij444"). Choose passwords that have some meaning for you—such as a favorite song lyric or movie quote: "Toto, I've got a feeling we're not in Kansas anymore!" Meaningful phrases are easier to remember than random strings of characters.

2. Choose long passwords. The truth is that it's the length, not the oddness, of a password that makes it harder for hackers to crack. Longer passwords are also easier to remember because they have more semantic content. If the account requires shorter passwords, try just the first letters of each word: "T,IgafwniKa!"—complete with capitals and punctuation.

3. Use cued recall. If you must write a note to help you remember your passwords, use a clue, not the whole password ("Clue: Wizard of Oz"). The cue will help jog your memory while still making it hard for anyone who finds the note to pin down exactly what your password is.

content of the memory is preserved, but the episodic details (the time and place in which we encountered the information) are distorted.

In one widely studied paradigm, called the Deese–Roediger–McDermott (DRM) paradigm, researchers ask people to learn lists of words. In each list, the words all share a particular implicit theme (Deese, 1959; Roediger & McDermott, 1995). For example, a word list based on the theme "sweet" might contain words such as CANDY, SUGAR, HONEY, and TASTE but not the word SWEET itself. Figure 7.8 shows data from one such study. In general, when participants are given a second list and asked to recognize the studied words, they correctly identify the studied words and correctly reject (fail to recognize) novel, unrelated words (e.g., DOG, HOUSE, or TOMATO). But participants also often claim to recognize the theme word (SWEET) even though that wasn't on the original list.

One explanation of this effect invokes source monitoring. Specifically, while learning such a list, people encode the semantic meaning of the words—the theme—and form a memory of thinking about that theme word; later, they mistakenly remember having encountered the word on the list, rather than in their own thoughts. A more dramatic example of this phenomenon could underlie some of the delusions experienced by patients with schizophrenia, who may self-generate ideas but mistakenly think that an external source—such as God, or a voice in the television—suggested the idea (Keefe, Arnold, Bayen & Harvey, 1999).

Figure 7.8 False memory for studied words People were first asked to learn lists of words organized around an unstated theme (such as "sweet"). Later, participants were generally accurate at recognizing the studied words and at rejecting (failing to recognize) novel, unrelated words. But they would also claim to recognize the unstudied theme words.
Data from Cabeza et al., 2001.

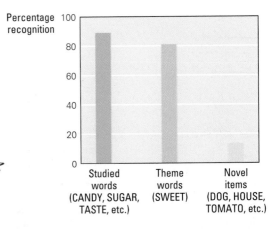

Why might someone mistakenly think he had attended a highly publicized event?

A famous real-world example of an apparent source monitoring error occurred in the early 1970s, when ex-Beatle George Harrison released the hit single "My Sweet Lord" and was sued for copyright infringement because the tune was so similar to an earlier song, the Chiffons' "He's So Fine." Harrison argued that "My Sweet Lord" was his own creation and denied any plagiarism, although he admitted to having heard the Chiffons' song. A judge ruled that Harrison had indeed been influenced by his memories of the earlier song, although the judge was convinced that Harrison's plagiarism was unintentional. Apparently, the ex-Beatle had suffered a type of source monitoring error: remembering the melody and mistakenly thinking he had composed it himself.

Similar source monitoring errors can occur when a student reads a sentence in a textbook and remembers it; later, when the sentence pops to mind, it "feels" new and gets included in a term paper. The student may honestly think this is an original idea—but if the instructor has read the same textbook, accusations of plagiarism will follow.

False Memory

false memory. Memory of an event that never actually happened.

Related to the phenomenon of source monitoring errors is **false memory**, or memory for events that never actually happened. Elizabeth Loftus and her colleagues have conducted several studies in which they intentionally "implanted" false memories of childhood events in ordinary people. For example, in one study the researchers invented several fictitious events, such as getting lost in a shopping mall or surviving a vicious animal attack, and then told research participants that these events had happened to them as children (Loftus & Pickrell, 1995). Family members (who had agreed to collaborate) also spoke about the events as if they had really happened. Sure enough, a few days later, about 25% of the participants seemed to believe the events were real—and even "remembered" additional details that had not been present in the original story.

In another study, Kimberley Wade and her colleagues pasted childhood photos of their adult research participants into a photograph of a hot-air-balloon ride. The researchers then showed participants the doctored photos and asked them to describe everything they could remember about the fictitious ride. After three such sessions, about half the people in the study claimed to remember having taken the ride—even though none had ever been in a hot-air balloon (Wade, Garry, Read, & Lindsay, 2002).

(a)   (b)

False memories are particularly likely to occur when people are prompted to imagine missing details; later, they may mistakenly remember those details as the truth. The more that people imagine an event, the more likely they are to subsequently believe it really happened (Goff & Roediger, 1998; Thomas & Loftus, 2002).

Outside the lab, false memory may be just as common. The online political magazine *Slate* conducted a mass experiment in altering readers' memories. *Slate* showed readers photos of several highly controversial political events, such as Florida Secretary of State Katharine Harris presiding over the disputed 2000 presidential election recount. Intermixed with these pictures were photos of events that never actually happened, such as President Obama shaking hands with Iranian President Ahmadinejad, or President G. W. Bush relaxing at his ranch while Hurricane Katrina was devastating New Orleans. The fake photos had been constructed by altering real pictures, as in Figure 7.9, which shows how an existing photo of Obama was doctored to include Ahmadinejad. Readers visiting the *Slate* website were asked whether they remembered each picture. More than five thousand readers responded. While most people reported remembering the real photos, almost half said they also "remembered" the fictitious events, and many provided comments describing how they'd first heard the news (Frenda, Knowles, Saletan, & Loftus, 2013). These results are particularly striking because visitors to the *Slate* website are presumably interested in and well informed about political events. Yet even they fell victim to the false memory manipulation.

The apparent pervasiveness of false memories should be a matter of public concern, particularly in criminal court cases where the strongest evidence against a suspect is eyewitness testimony. Elizabeth Loftus and other false-memory researchers have been vocal in warning that the types of procedures that induce false memory in the lab must be scrupulously avoided in the justice system (Loftus, 1996, 2003; Radelet, 2002; Wells, Memon, & Penrod, 2006). For example, if an eyewitness is shown the photo of a suspect, the witness's memory of the photo may become confused with the actual memory of the crime, leading the witness to "recognize" the suspect as the perpetrator even though the suspect is innocent. Such a recognition error occurred when a woman who had been raped identified psychologist Donald Thompson as her attacker (Thompson, 1988). Fortunately for Thompson, he had an iron-clad alibi: he was appearing on live TV at the time the rape occurred. Apparently, the woman had been watching TV just before the assault and mistakenly associated her memory of Thompson's face with the event of the rape.

Figure 7.9 Creating false memories in the real world The online political magazine *Slate* displayed photos of controversial political events, and asked readers if they remembered each. In reality, several of the pictures represented events that never occurred; for example, the image here of President Obama shaking hands (left) was doctored to include the president of Iran (right). Approximately half of *Slate*'s politically savvy respondents "remembered" the fictitious events.

Although, in this case, the faulty eyewitness testimony did not lead to conviction of an innocent man, other examples abound to suggest that mistakes are all too frequent. One study reviewed 62 cases in which people were convicted of crimes and later exonerated based on DNA evidence (Neufield & Dwyer, 2000). In more than 80% of these cases, the crucial evidence leading to conviction was eyewitness testimony, where witnesses had mistakenly identified people later proven to be innocent.

Even first-hand confessions may sometimes be unreliable. Laboratory studies suggest that, with appropriate prompting, a majority of research participants can be led to develop false memories of committing a crime, and to volunteer a detailed false account of that incident (Shaw & Porter, 2015). This creates concerns about real-world convictions based on confession evidence, particularly if the confession was obtained via interrogation tactics that can encourage creation of false memories. In fact, the Innocence Project (2012) claims that false confessions play a role in about 25% of wrongful convictions later overturned by DNA evidence. Some of these individuals pled guilty to avoid a harsher sentence, but some may have been misled by their own false memories of having participated in the crime.

Memory Consolidation and Reconsolidation

Passive-forgetting curves, such as the one shown in Figure 7.6a, suggest that, if you can still remember a fact or event after a few months, then the odds are good that you'll remember it permanently (or at least for a very long time). One implication of this finding is that semantic and episodic memories have a **consolidation period**: a time window during which new memories are vulnerable and easily lost (Dudai, 2004; McGaugh, 2000; Ribot, 1882).

In an early demonstration of this principle, Carl Duncan trained rats to make a simple conditioned response. He then gave the rats **electroconvulsive shock**, a brief pulse of electricity passed through the brain via electrodes on each side of the head. If the shock was given 20 seconds after the end of training, the rats' memory of the conditioned response was severely disrupted. However, if the shock was given an hour or more after training, there was little disruption. Intermediate delays produced intermediate levels of disruption (Duncan, 1949). Thus, the consolidation period for this type of learning in rats appears to extend for a few minutes; older memories (from several hours ago) are relatively stable and difficult to disrupt; more recent memories (from less than a minute ago) are highly vulnerable to disruption.

Electroconvulsive shock is sometimes administered to humans to provide temporary relief from certain kinds of mental illness, particularly severe depression. Patients are given general anesthesia and a muscle relaxant beforehand. No one knows exactly why the procedure, called *electroconvulsive therapy*, or *ECT*, relieves depression, but patients often experience relief for weeks or even months afterward (Glass, 2001; National Institutes of Health Consensus Conference, 1985).

By studying patients who are undergoing ECT, researchers have been able to investigate the effects of electroconvulsive shock on human memory. For example, Larry Squire and his colleagues administered the TV-show test to patients with severe depression (Squire, Slater, & Chace, 1975; Squire, Slater, & Miller, 1981). Before an ECT session, the patients remembered recent shows (from 2 to 3 years earlier) very well and older shows (from 8 to 15 years earlier) less well (Figure 7.10a). This is similar to the performance of healthy adults, which you saw in Figure 7.6a. A week after ECT, the patients retook the TV-show test. Almost invariably, they had forgotten some of the information

consolidation period. A length of time during which new episodic and semantic memories are vulnerable and easily lost or altered; each time a memory is recalled, it may become vulnerable again until it is "reconsolidated."

electroconvulsive shock. A brief pulse of electricity that is passed through the brain and can severely disrupt newly formed memories; electroconvulsive therapy is sometimes used to alleviate severe depression.

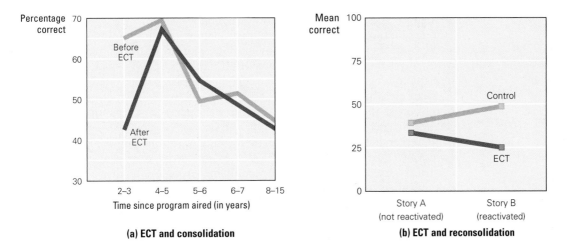

Figure 7.10 Effects of ECT on memory (a) Before electroconvulsive shock therapy (ECT), patients with depression show a forgetting curve (purple line) similar to that of nondepressed adults (compare Figure 7.6a). After the patients undergo ECT (red line), retrieval of recent memories is impaired. This suggests that there is a consolidation period for new memories, during which they are vulnerable to disruption such as ECT. (b) ECT also affects reconsolidation. In one study, subjects in the control group (purple line) heard two stories (A and B); a week later, they were given a pre-test on story B. The next day, their memory for story B was better than for story A, indicating that reactivation of the memory for story B improved later recall. A second group of subjects received ECT right after reactivation of story B (red line); the next day, their memory for story B was much worse than the control group's, indicating that reactivating the memory of story B right before ECT made it vulnerable to disruption. Recall of story A, which had not been reactivated, was not affected by the ECT.

(a) Information from Squire et al., 1975. (b) Data from Kroes et al., 2014.

they'd reported earlier, especially memories for shows that had aired within the last few years; older memories (>3 years) were generally unaffected. A similar pattern was seen for autobiographical memories. Other kinds of memory, such as newly acquired motor skills, seem to be spared by ECT (Squire, Cohen, & Zousounis, 1984; Vakil et al., 2000). For many patients who undergo ECT, this limited memory loss is a small price to pay for relief from the debilitation of severe depression.

The idea of a consolidation period, during which new memories are vulnerable to disruption, is attractive because it accounts for a great deal of data from animals and humans. Recently, though, new data is resurrecting an old idea that no memory, however ancient, is really permanent and immutable (Nadel & Land, 2000; Nader & Hardt, 2009; Nader, Schafe, & LeDoux, 2000a). For example, it has long been known that, if an old memory is recalled just before electroconvulsive shock is administered, it can be disrupted too (e.g., Misanin, Miller, & Lewis, 1968). Apparently, each time an old (presumably consolidated) memory is recalled or reactivated, it may become vulnerable again, a process termed **reconsolidation**.

In one study of reconsolidation (Kroes et al., 2014), two groups of patients undergoing ECT to treat depression were told two stories (A and B), each accompanied by a slide show. A week later, some patients (the "control" group) were given a short pre-test on story B. As you read above, the mere act of testing can improve memory, and so you shouldn't be surprised to learn that, when given a final multiple-choice test on both stories the next day, the control group remembered more of story B than story A (Figure 7.10b, purple line). As a matter of fact, the testing effect itself may be an example of reconsolidation—reactivating story B allowed the memory of it to become modifiable, which in this case strengthened the memory. But a second group of patients (the "ECT" group)

reconsolidation. The process whereby each time an old memory is recalled or reactivated, it may become vulnerable to modification.

were given the same pre-test on story B, followed immediately by ECT. The next day, on the multiple-choice test, their memory for story A was about as good as the control group's—but their memory for story B was much worse. In other words, reactivating the memory for story B right before ECT made it vulnerable to disruption by the ECT. Story A, which had not been reactivated, was safe.

Memories can also be disrupted if they are reactivated just before administration of drugs that block the formation or maintenance of synaptic connections (Nader, Schafe, & LeDoux, 2000b; Przybyslawsky & Sara, 1997). On the other hand, researchers can use noninvasive techniques to stimulate the brain, such as *transcranial direct current stimulation (tDCS)*, in which experimenters apply weak electrical current to the scalp, temporarily increasing excitability of the neurons below. When tDCS is applied during memory reactivation, later recall of that information is often stronger (Javadi & Cheng, 2013).

These and other reconsolidation studies illustrate that memory is not static, like a printed record, but dynamic. Each time we retrieve an old memory, we can modify it by integrating new information into it (Dudai, 2004; Sara, 2000; Wang & Morris, 2010). This opens the door to potential disruption—but it also allows existing memories to be continually updated, refined, and elaborated based on new experiences (Tronson & Taylor, 2007; McKenzie & Eichenbaum, 2011).

And this, in fact, may be a key mechanism underlying the creation of false memories. Each time a person remembers or re-imagines an event, that memory may be subject to modification, allowing minor distortions to creep in that, over time, become indistinguishable from the real facts of the case.

Metamemory

metamemory. Knowledge of, and ability to think about, our own memories, including both feeling of knowing and judgment of learning.

Suppose you were given a pop quiz, right now, on the material in this chapter so far. How well do you think you'd do? **Metamemory** refers to knowledge or belief about one's own memory, and it applies to both episodic and semantic memory.

You've already read about one familiar example illustrating metamemory: the *tip-of-the-tongue* (TOT) phenomenon, in which we're challenged to retrieve a bit of information (such as the name of a film star, or the answer on a test question), and feel sure that we know the answer, even though we can't retrieve it at the moment ("It's on the tip of my tongue!"). Often, once we hear the answer, we "recognize" it—because, at some level, we already knew. On the other hand, sometimes we are asked a question and we know that we *don't* know the answer; for example, if someone asks you the atomic number of the chemical element boron, you may automatically know that you don't know the answer, no matter how long you're given to try to recall the information.

A formal name for such phenomena is *feeling of knowing (FOK)*, which refers to our ability to predict whether or not we can retrieve a specific piece of information if asked. FOK judgments are not always accurate. Usually FOK errors reflect overconfidence: a person may report feeling that he knows the answer to a question even when he does not (e.g., Nelson, Gerler, & Narens, 1984). One factor contributing to FOK errors is familiarity with the cue: the feeling that one "should" know the answer may lead to an illusion that one actually does know the answer. Thus, someone who recently completed a chemistry course may be more subject to a FOK error regarding the atomic number of boron than someone who never studied the topic and has no reason to believe he "should" know the answer.

A related metamemory phenomenon is *judgment of learning (JOL)*, which is a judgment during learning of whether the information has been successfully acquired. For example, a student studying for an exam has to decide when he can stop studying because the material to be tested is securely in memory. Like FOKs, JOLs can be extremely inaccurate—again, usually in the direction of overconfidence. One factor is that people tend to assume that they will always remember information as well as they remember it right now. In one particularly striking study, participants studied lists of word pairs, and were asked to predict how well they would remember the pairs if tested immediately, if not tested until 1 day after, or if not tested until 1 week after (Koriat, Bjork, Sheffer, & Bar, 2004). Most participants predicted that they would recall the information equally well in each case; in fact, as you should predict after viewing Figure 7.6a, subjects' recall fell sharply as the delay between learning and testing increased.

One factor contributing to JOL errors is that people are relatively poor at judging the most effective ways to learn new information (for review, see Bjork, Dunlosky & Kornell, 2013). For example, as you read earlier, self-testing typically strengthens memory much more than mere re-reading does. But in one poll of college students, only 11% reported using self-tests while studying. Even among those students who did self-test, only 18% said that they did it because they learned more when they self-test than when they re-read; the rest said that they used self-testing to assess how well they had learned the information (Kornell & Bjork, 2007). JOL errors can lead students to feel overconfident in their familiarity with course material, which is why students can sometimes be honestly surprised at poor performance on the exam, when they feel they studied hard to prepare.

Jupiterimages, Brand X Pictures/Getty Images

What kinds of metamemory errors might lead this student to stop studying before he has really mastered the information? What study strategies might he try instead of simply reading and re-reading the textbook?

Interim Summary

- Episodic memory is our memory for specific events that we experienced in a unique spatial and temporal context; it is information we "remember."

- Semantic memory is memory for facts about the world and personal information about ourselves. It does not necessarily include information about where or when the memory was originally acquired; it is information we "know."

- Both episodic and semantic memories can be flexibly communicated in ways other than those in which they were originally acquired, and both are available to conscious recollection.

- Researchers still debate whether nonhuman animals can have true episodic memories; some believe this faculty belongs to humans alone, but others cite mounting evidence for "episodic-like" memory in nonhuman species.

- Several principles govern the encoding of new memories: (1) Mere exposure to information does not guarantee memory. (2) Memory for new information is stronger if it can be related to existing knowledge. (3) Memory is also affected by how deeply the information is processed during encoding.

- Successful retrieval of existing memories is more likely if (1) encoding and retrieval conditions match (transfer-appropriate processing) and (2) if more cues are available to prompt recall.

- Struggling to retrieve material (such as during a test) often promotes longer-lasting memories than simply studying the material again.

- Memory can also "fail" in many ways due to simple forgetting, interference, and creation of false memories. Source amnesia is a related phenomenon in which we remember information but are mistaken about where or how we learned it.

- Semantic and episodic memories appear to have a time window (the consolidation period) during which they are vulnerable and easily lost. Newer research suggests that each time a memory is accessed, it may become vulnerable again and need to be reconsolidated.

- Metamemory refers to knowledge or belief about one's own memory, and includes feeling-of-knowing (illustrated by the tip-of-the-tongue phenomenon) and judgment-of-learning (such as when a student decides he's mastered the material well enough to stop studying). People are not always very accurate at evaluating or predicting their own memory.

sensory cortex. Areas of cerebral cortex involved in processing sensory information such as sight and sounds.

association cortex. Areas of cerebral cortex involved in associating information within and across sensory modalities.

Figure 7.11 Semantic memory and the cerebral cortex Some areas of the cerebral cortex specialize in processing specific kinds of sensory information; these include areas in the parietal lobe (somatosensory cortex), the occipital lobe (visual cortex), and the superior temporal lobe (auditory cortex). Many of the remaining cortical areas are association areas that link information within and across modalities, forming a basic substrate for semantic information.

7.2 Brain Substrates

Functions as complex as semantic and episodic memory depend on many interacting brain systems, and scientists are still a long way from fully understanding them all. At present, most researchers agree that semantic memories are stored in the cerebral cortex. Similarly, most researchers agree that the encoding of new episodic memories depends on structures in the medial temporal lobes, but there's ongoing debate about whether the same structures encode semantic and episodic memories, and whether their role is limited to encoding or is required throughout the life of an episodic memory. Finally, many other brain structures, including the frontal lobes, the basal forebrain, and the diencephalon, have roles in modulating the storage, maintenance, and retrieval of semantic and episodic memories, but the exact nature of these roles is still under study.

Neuronal Networks for Semantic Memory

As you've read in earlier chapters, the cerebral cortex can be divided into different regions, some of which are specialized to process particular kinds of sensory information. These include the somatosensory cortex in the parietal lobe, the visual cortex in the occipital lobe, and the auditory cortex in the superior temporal lobe. Cortical areas that specialize in one kind of sensory information are often grouped under the heading of **sensory cortex**. Some research suggests that specific types of semantic knowledge are stored in cortical areas devoted to processing that kind of information, with visual information stored in the occipital lobe, auditory information in the superior temporal lobe, and so on.

Other cortical areas (e.g., many of the areas shown in pale pink in Figure 7.11) are called **association cortex**, meaning they are involved in associating information within and across modalities. Association cortex helps us link the word "dog" with the visual image of a dog and with semantic information about what dogs are like, as well as with linguistic information about how to pronounce and recognize the spoken word itself. Some studies suggest that specific categories of semantic information are encoded by specific

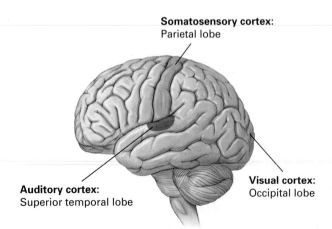

Somatosensory cortex: Parietal lobe

Auditory cortex: Superior temporal lobe

Visual cortex: Occipital lobe

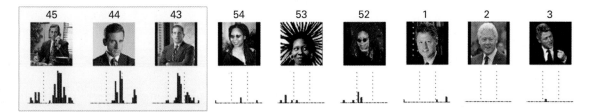

Figure 7.12 Category-sensitive neurons in the human brain Patients with electrodes implanted in the medial temporal lobes were shown photos of famous celebrities and landmarks, including the nine photos shown here (Quiroga et al., 2005). Multiple neurons were recorded from each patient; this figure shows the response of one such neuron to several photos. For each photo, the neuron's response is plotted below, with the height of the red bars indicating the strength of the neuron's response; the x-axis represents time, with the dashed vertical lines on each graph indicating the start and end of that photo's presentation. This neuron responded strongly to pictures of actor Steve Carell (pictures 43–45) but not to photos of other celebrities such as Whoopi Goldberg (pictures 52–54) or Bill Clinton (pictures 1–3).

Republished with permission of Elsevier, from Quian Quiroga, R. and Kreiman, G. and Koch, C. and Fried, I. (2008) Sparse but not 'Grandmother-cell' coding in the medial temporal lobe. *Trends in Cognitive Sciences*, 12 (3). pp. 87–91.

groups of neurons. For example, in one study, Edmund Rolls and colleagues (Thorpe, Rolls, & Maddison, 1983) recorded neurons in the orbitofrontal cortex of rhesus monkeys. (This is a small area located at the base of the frontal lobes.) Out of 494 neurons analyzed, Rolls and colleagues found 26 neurons that responded selectively to visual stimuli representing food; even more striking, four neurons responded most strongly to oranges, four responded to peanuts, two responded to bananas, and one responded to raisins.

Similar specificity can be observed in humans. Sometimes patients who need brain surgery have intracranial electrodes implanted in preparation for the surgery, and some of these patients are willing to undergo memory testing while the electrodes are in place. In certain studies, the patients are shown pictures, and the responses of individual neurons to each picture can be recorded. Some neurons respond to many pictures; others respond to none. But some neurons respond to pictures of particular categories of objects, such as animals, faces, or houses (Krieman, Koch, & Fried, 2000). Some neurons respond to sad faces but not to happy, angry, or neutral faces (Fried, MacDonald, & Wilson, 1997). And some neurons even respond to pictures of one person but not others (Quiroga, Reddy, Kreiman, Koch, & Fried, 2005).

For example, Figure 7.12 shows some sample responses of a single neuron from one patient. This neuron fired strongly in response to photos of actor Steve Carell but was nearly silent in response to photos of other celebrities such as Whoopie Goldberg or Bill Clinton. Another patient had a neuron that responded to photos of Jennifer Aniston and Lisa Kudrow, both actresses in the TV series *Friends*; a different neuron in the same patient responded to pictures of the Eiffel Tower and the Tower of Pisa but not to other famous landmarks (Quiroga et al., 2005).

Remarkable as these results are, the fact that the neuron from Figure 7.12 responded "only" to Steve Carell in the experiment doesn't mean that we have individual neurons each specialized to detect images of a single person (one neuron for Steve Carell, one for Jennifer Aniston, one for your grandmother, and so on). In fact, there might be many other people or objects—not explicitly tested in the experiment—that would also elicit a response from that neuron. Most researchers believe it is more likely that we have networks of neurons that respond primarily to information representing simple, familiar categories, such as TV-sitcom actors, large pointy landmarks, or bananas. This way, loss of a single brain cell wouldn't erase all memories of the category, as long as some of the network survives.

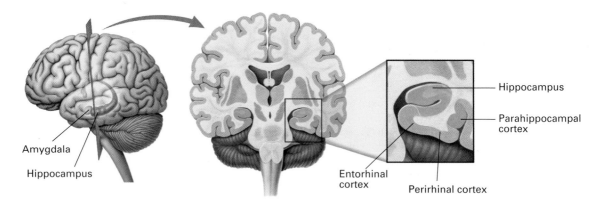

Figure 7.13 The medial temporal lobe in humans The medial (inner) portion of the temporal lobes contains the hippocampus, the amygdala, and several other cortical areas, including the entorhinal cortex, perirhinal cortex, and parahippocampal cortex.

hippocampus. A brain structure located in the medial temporal lobe that is important for new memory formation.

anterograde amnesia. A severe loss of the ability to form new episodic and semantic memories.

The Medial Temporal Lobes in Memory Storage

The medial temporal lobes in humans contain the **hippocampus**, the amygdala, and nearby cortical areas, including the entorhinal cortex, the perirhinal cortex, and the parahippocampal cortex (Figure 7.13). Chapter 3 described the role of the hippocampus in spatial learning, and Chapter 4 described the role of the hippocampus in certain forms of classical conditioning. But in fact, the most widely studied role of the human hippocampus is in the storage of new episodic and semantic memories, and the most obvious impairment in humans with damage to the medial temporal lobe is the loss of this function. At the start of this chapter, you read about H.M., the man who became amnesic after bilateral surgical removal of his medial temporal lobes (Scoville & Milner, 1957). Before H.M., other neurologists in the late 1800s and early 1900s had noted the role of the medial temporal lobes in memory. But H.M.'s case provided especially strong, widely accepted evidence for this idea—partly because of the severity of his impairment and partly because of H.M.'s decades-long willingness to participate in all kinds of memory tests that carefully documented exactly what he could and couldn't learn and remember.

Obviously, after H.M., no more surgeries were performed to remove the medial temporal lobes bilaterally in humans (although unilateral surgeries, which don't cause severe amnesia, are still sometimes performed for patients with intractable epilepsy). Unfortunately, bilateral medial temporal lobe damage does occur in humans as a result of various other kinds of injury and disease, and these patients often show a pattern of memory impairment very similar to that exhibited by H.M.

By studying memory in such patients, as well as in nonhuman animals with medial temporal lobe lesion or dysfunction, neuroscientists are building up a picture of the role this brain area plays in memory.

The Hippocampus Is Critical for Forming New Episodic Memory

The most profound and noticeable memory impairment observed in patients such as H.M. is **anterograde amnesia**, a severe loss of the ability to form new episodic and semantic memories. For example, Larry Squire and colleagues studied one patient, known by his initials E.P., who suffered bilateral medial temporal damage as a result of viral encephalitis (Stefanacci, Buffalo, Schnolck, & Squire, 2000). Viewed on structural MRI, E.P.'s brain damage looked rather similar to H.M.'s, and he also showed a similar pattern of memory impairment. When questioned about autobiographical events, E.P. could remember his

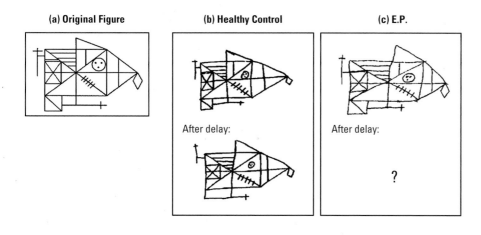

(a) Original Figure **(b) Healthy Control** **(c) E.P.**

After delay: After delay:

?

Figure 7.14 Anterograde amnesia in patient E.P. Given a complex figure (a), healthy controls can usually copy it accurately (b, top); 15 minutes later, they can still produce a reasonably accurate drawing from memory (b, bottom). Patient E.P. could copy the drawing about as well as healthy controls (c, top). However, when asked to draw the figure from memory 15 minutes later, E.P. did not recall making the copy and declined to try and draw it from memory.

Insausti, R., Annese, J., Amaral, D. G., & Squire, L. G. (2013). Human amnesia and the medial temporal lobe illuminated by neuropsychological and neurohistological findings for patient E. P. (2013). *Proceedings of the National Academy of Sciences USA*, 11, E1953–1962.

childhood, his marriage, and his travels during World War II. But he could not recall what he had done yesterday or almost anything that had happened to him since the onset of his amnesia in 1992. Within a one-hour session, he might repeat the same anecdotes over and over as many as 10 times, unaware that he had told the stories before (Stefanacci et al., 2000).

Like H.M., E.P. participated in a large number of memory tests. A standard test of visual memory uses the complex figure shown in Figure 7.14a. Participants are first asked to copy the figure and then to draw it from memory 10 to 15 minutes later. Healthy adults can usually copy the figure quite accurately and manage to reproduce the figure from memory reasonably well after the delay (Figure 7.14b). E.P. could copy the drawing without difficulty, but after the delay, he had no memory of the picture at all (Figure 7.14c; Insausti et al., 2013). His memory for verbal information was similarly poor: immediately after listening to a short story, he could only recall about 10% of the words or concepts; 15 minutes later, he could remember nothing about it.

Like H.M., animals with broad lesions of the hippocampal region have difficulty learning new information (Mishkin, 1978; Squire, 1992). They are especially impaired at episodic-like learning that involves memory of unique events set in a particular context (Gaffan & Hornak, 1997; Gaffan & Parker, 1996). For example, the radial maze shown in Figure 7.2 can be used for a task in which researchers place a piece of food at the end of every arm and then place a hungry rat in the center of the maze. The rat has a few minutes in which to obtain all the food it can. Notice that once a rat has entered a given arm and eaten the food there, subsequent entries into the same arm are a waste of time. Therefore, the rat can solve this task most efficiently by visiting each arm exactly once. This requires that the rat remember where it's already been. But if the task is given on several successive days, the rat will have to remember which arms it's already visited so far today, distinct from the memories of prior days on which the rat entered those arms and found food there. Proactive interference affects rats in a radial arm maze, just as it affects humans in a parking lot!

The only way out of this dilemma is to remember the spatial and temporal context of visits—namely, whether a specific arm was visited yet *today*, as distinct from all other visits on all other days. In other words, this task requires "episodic-like" memory, a memory of not just what happened but where and when. After several days of training, healthy rats learn to navigate the radial arm maze very efficiently: they collect all eight rewards, and in the process, they make very few erroneous reentries into previously visited arms. In contrast, rats with hippocampal lesions make many more errors: they repeatedly reenter previously visited arms, apparently aware that there is food to be found but unable to remember which specific arms they've already visited on this particular day (Cassel et al., 1998; Jarrard, Okaichi, Steward, & Goldschmidt, 1984; Olton, 1983).

In birds, hippocampal-region damage also disrupts episodic-like learning. Remember the scrub jays, who bury food in caches and then return to the caches later? When the birds' hippocampal region is lesioned, they lose the ability to locate their caches (Capaldi, Robinson, & Fahrback, 1999). They continue to store new food, but they quickly forget where they've put it; they search almost at random—much like the lesioned rat running around the radial maze.

Is the Hippocampus Critical for Forming New Semantic Memory?

While most researchers agree that the hippocampus is critical for the acquisition of new episodic memories, which are "tagged" in space and time, there is more controversy about the acquisition of new semantic memories. Many studies now suggest that acquisition of new semantic memories depends less on the hippocampus than on other medial temporal lobe structures, such as the perirhinal cortex or parahippocampal cortex (Figure 7.13), or even on the temporal lobe (Eichenbaum et al., 2007; Diana, Yonelinas, and Ranganath, 2007). Thus, although patient H.M. had profound anterograde amnesia, he could learn new semantic information after laborious study. For example, when asked about John F. Kennedy and Michael Gorbachov, who each became famous after the onset of H.M.'s amnesia, H.M. could correctly respond that Kennedy had been president and that someone had shot him, and that Gorbachov had been head of the Russian parliament (O'Kane et al., 2004).

In contrast, patient E.P. (whose damage extended further into the medial temporal lobe than H.M.'s did) was largely unable to acquire new semantic information. Thus, in 1993, a year after the onset of E.P.'s amnesia, he and his family moved to a new home in California, but after seven years of living there, E.P. could not draw a floor plan of the new home, describe how to get to the grocery store, or even point in the direction of the Pacific Ocean, which was less than two miles from his home (Stefanacci et al., 2000). Other patients with even more extensive damage to the temporal lobes perform even worse on tests of semantic memory, while patients with damage limited to the hippocampus itself tend to have much more modest semantic memory impairments (Insausti et al., 2014).

Thus, it currently appears that encoding of new semantic memories may depend primarily on cortical areas in the medial temporal lobes, including parahippocampal and perirhinal cortex, rather than on the hippocampus itself. In addition, parahippocampal cortex may aid the hippocampus during episodic learning, by providing background knowledge about the context, including the spatial location where the event occurs (Aminoff, Kveraga & Bar, 2013; Eichenbaum, Yonelinas & Ranganath, 2007).

Functional Neuroimaging of the Healthy Hippocampal Region

Our knowledge of the role of the hippocampal region in new memory formation is not limited to studies of humans and other animals with brain damage. Functional neuroimaging studies allow us to see the hippocampus in action in brains with normal memory function. For example, in the *subsequent memory* paradigm, developed by Anthony Wagner and his colleagues (e.g., Wagner et al., 1998), participants first view a list of words and are asked to categorize each word as abstract or concrete; fMRI is used to take images of brain activity during this initial phase. This phase is called an "incidental encoding" phase because any learning about the words is incidental to the task at hand. Next, the researchers administer a surprise recognition test, showing the participants a new list of words and asking them to identify which words were on the previous list. As you might expect, people correctly recognize some of the words but not all of them. The important finding is that fMRI activity during the incidental encoding phase differs for words that will be successfully recognized later compared to words that will not. For example, remember the task from Figure 7.5, where subjects had to judge whether words represented animate objects or not? Later, subjects correctly remembered some of the words but forgot others. Figure 7.15a shows that the left hippocampus was more active during initial encoding of words that would be subsequently remembered than of words that would be subsequently forgotten (Otten et al., 2001). (There is a similar effect in the left prefrontal cortex, shown in Figure 7.15b; we'll return to this later in the chapter.)

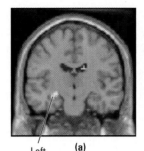

Left **(a)**
hippocampus

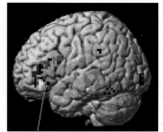

Left prefrontal **(b)**
cortex

Figure 7.15 The "subsequent memory" paradigm Brain imaging (fMRI) records activity while participants make categorization judgments on a series of words. Later, participants are given a recognition test; typically, they correctly recognize some but not all of the previously viewed words. Some areas of the brain, including the left hippocampus (a) and left prefrontal cortex (b), are more active during initial viewing of words that will subsequently be remembered compared to initial viewing of words that will subsequently be forgotten.

(a, b) Research from Otten et al., 2001.

The medial temporal lobe is also more active during incidental encoding of pictures that will be remembered than pictures that will be forgotten—but whereas words tend to activate only the left medial temporal lobe, pictures tend to activate the medial temporal lobe bilaterally (Brewer, Zhao, Desmond, Glover, & Gabrieli, 1998). The bottom line from all these studies is that researchers viewing the fMRI of a participant's brain during learning can predict with reasonable accuracy whether the information will be recalled or forgotten later (Wagner et al., 1998).

These studies suggest that pictures and words that are processed more elaborately in the medial temporal lobes (visible as increased temporal lobe activity on fMRI during encoding) are more likely to be remembered later. This may underlie the levels-of-processing effect. For example, the study in Figure 7.5 showed that thinking about the meaning of a word, such as whether it represents an animate or inanimate object (deep processing), produces better recall than merely thinking about how the word is spelled (superficial processing). The same brain areas are active during both tasks, but there is more activity during deep processing than during superficial processing (Otten et al., 2001), which may lead to better memory later.

Other functional neuroimaging studies have considered false memory, the "remembering" of events that never actually occurred. In the false-memory test described earlier, in which people study a list of words related to an unnamed theme word (Figure 7.8), fMRI during the recognition phase shows a striking pattern. Several brain areas are more active for studied list words than for novel words, but the (unstudied) theme words evoke high activity too (Cabeza & Nyberg, 2000). This could explain why people are prone to falsely recognize the theme words.

The hippocampus is one of the brain areas that is "fooled" into responding as strongly to the theme words as to the studied list words. But a small area in the parahippocampal cortex also responds more strongly to studied words than to novel words, and yet does not respond strongly to the (unstudied) theme words. Apparently, this small brain region is able to correctly distinguish true episodic memories from false ones (Cabeza et al., 2001; Okado & Stark, 2003)—at least in the lab. If this finding extends to false memories outside the lab, it may have real-world application, particularly for court cases in which a witness claims to remember details of a crime and the defense charges that the memory is a false

retrograde amnesia. Loss of memories for events dating from before a brain injury or disruption; memory loss generally occurs in a time-graded manner so that more recent memories are devastated but older ones may be spared.

Ribot gradient. A pattern of retrograde memory loss in which recently acquired memories are more prone to disruption than older memories.

standard consolidation theory. The theory that the hippocampus and related medial temporal lobe structures are required for storage and retrieval of recent episodic memories but not older ones.

Figure 7.16 Retrograde and anterograde amnesia A healthy adult (green line) may be able to recall most of what happened today and will recall progressively less about events that happened weeks, months, and years ago. In contrast, a person with bilateral medial temporal lobe damage (red line) may suffer anterograde amnesia, a loss of the ability to form new episodic and semantic memories since the injury, as well as retrograde amnesia for events that occurred days or weeks before the injury. If the brain damage extends beyond the hippocampus into nearby cortical areas, retrograde amnesia may be much more severe and may extend back for decades or longer.

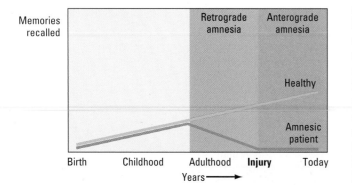

one. Maybe someday the defense will be able to present an fMRI of a witness's brain as evidence that the witness may not have experienced the event the way she or he is recalling it. For now, though, nobody has developed a foolproof brain-mapping procedure for distinguishing a true from a false memory.

The Hippocampus and Cortex Interact during Memory Consolidation

In the late 1800s, French philosopher Theodore Ribot noticed that individuals with head injury often developed **retrograde amnesia**, loss of memories for events that occurred before the injury (Ribot, 1882). This is in contrast to anterograde amnesia, in which patients lose the ability to form memories for events that occur after the injury. Typically, retrograde amnesia follows a pattern called the **Ribot gradient**: retrograde memory loss is worse for events that occurred shortly before the injury than for events that occurred in the distant past. For example, a man who hit his head during a car accident might lose all memories of the accident itself and might also have some disruption of memories from the minutes or hours before the accident, but he would have relatively little disruption of memories for events that occurred months or years earlier (Figure 7.16). The Ribot gradient also describes the effects of electroconvulsive shock, which preferentially disrupts recently formed memories (see Figure 7.10a).

People with bilateral medial temporal lobe damage generally show some retrograde amnesia along with their anterograde amnesia. These patients don't forget their own identity—H.M. could remember his name and his childhood—but they often lose memories for events that happened days or months before the brain damage, and this retrograde amnesia can affect information acquired decades earlier (Manns et al., 2003). For example, as you read above, patient E.P. suffered bilateral medial temporal lobe damage that left him with dense anterograde amnesia, meaning that he could recall almost nothing that had happened to him since 1992. In addition, E.P. displayed retrograde amnesia. His memory for childhood events was excellent—as good as that of healthy controls of the same age. But when asked about adulthood events that had occurred decades before his encephalitis, E.P. remembered significantly less than the controls (Reed & Squire, 1998; Stefanacci et al., 2000).

You've already read about the consolidation period, during which new memories are especially vulnerable to disruption. E.P.'s case suggests that the consolidation period may last for decades, because he lost memories of at least some decades-old events. So just how long is the consolidation period in humans? How long before a new memory becomes independent of the medial temporal lobes and is "safely" stored in sensory and association cortex?

An early and influential idea, sometimes called **standard consolidation theory**, holds that the hippocampus and related medial temporal lobe structures are required for the initial storage and retrieval of an episodic memory but that their contribution diminishes over time until the cortex is capable of retrieving the memory without hippocampal help (Dudai, 2004; McGaugh, 2000; Squire & Alvarez, 1995). This view conceptualizes an episodic memory as consisting of many components (sight, sound, texture, context, etc.) that are stored in different areas of the cortex (Figure 7.17a). Initially, all of these components are linked together

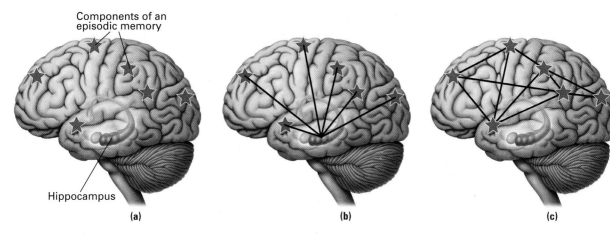

Components of an episodic memory

Hippocampus

(a)   (b)   (c)

Figure 7.17 Standard consolidation theory (a) An episodic memory consists of many components, such as sight, sound, texture, and other features, stored in sensory and association cortex. (b) Initially, the hippocampal region helps link these components into a single episodic memory. (c) Standard consolidation theory states that, over time, the components become linked to each other directly, and hippocampal involvement is no longer required. In contrast, multiple memory theory holds that the stage depicted in part (c) never occurs, and that all episodic memories remain at least partially dependent on the hippocampus.

via the hippocampus into a unified episodic memory (Figure 7.17b). Over time, through the process of consolidation, the components can form direct connections with each other and no longer need hippocampal mediation (Figure 7.17c). If the hippocampus is damaged, older memories would be more likely to have such connections, and thus be more likely to survive, than new memories. This would explain the temporal gradient of retrograde amnesia observed in many amnesic patients with medial temporal lobe damage, such as H.M. and E.P.

But other researchers noted that some patients' amnesia does not fit this profile; for example, some patients have severe retrograde memory loss that extends as far back as childhood and is not temporally graded (Nadel & Moscovitch, 1997; Cipolotti et al., 2001). To account for such extensive retrograde amnesia, Morris Moscovitch and Lynn Nadel developed the **multiple trace theory**. According to this theory, when an event is experienced, it can be stored as an episodic memory by an ensemble of neurons in the hippocampus and in neocortex. Each time that memory is retrieved, the retrieval itself becomes a new episodic memory. (This is similar to the process of reconsolidation, which you read about earlier in the chapter.) Thus, an old and often-recalled event can have multiple "memory traces" in the brain. Over time, the general content or gist of these memories can become a semantic memory, which can be stored in the cortex, independent of the hippocampus. But the initial episodic memory, with the specific details of the spatial and temporal context in which it occurred, remains dependent on the hippocampus (Moscovitch & Nadel, 1998; Nadel & Moscovitch, 2001; Rosenbaum et al., 2014).

According to this view, individuals with hippocampal damage effectively lose all their episodic memories (Nadel, Samsonovich, Ryan, & Moscovitch, 2000). Such individuals might be able to rehearse a piece of autobiographical information so many times that it becomes a semantic memory. But this is a far cry from how people normally recall episodic memories. It would be equivalent to a person "remembering" the day she was born because she's heard the family stories so often. She has semantic information about the event and knows it happened to her, but that isn't the same thing as remembering the episode firsthand. In short, according to multiple trace theory, individuals with medial temporal lobe damage lose the capacity for "mental time travel" and with it the capacity for true episodic memory (Steinvorth, Levine, & Corkin, 2005).

Various studies have attempted to test the predictions of standard consolidation theory against those of multiple trace theory. For example, standard consolidation theory predicts that hippocampal activity during memory retrieval should be greatest for recently acquired episodic memories (which are still dependent on the hippocampus) and lowest for very old memories (which

multiple trace theory. The theory that episodic (and possibly semantic) memories are encoded by an ensemble of hippocampal and cortical neurons and that both hippocampus and cortex are normally involved in storing and retrieving even very old memories.

should be fully consolidated and independent of the hippocampus). Multiple trace theory predicts the opposite: the medial temporal lobes should be equally active during recall of autobiographical memory, whether the event occurred recently or long ago, because they are always involved in episodic memory retrieval (Winocur et al., 2010). In fact, several studies have now found equal hippocampal activation for recent and remote memories (Bernard et al., 2004; Kapur, Friston, Young, Frith, & Frackowiak, 1995; Maguire, 2001), which is evidence in favor of multiple trace theory. But other studies have shown that hippocampal activity during retrieval of semantic information decreases as the memories get older (Smith & Squire, 2009), consistent with the idea that semantic—unlike episodic—memories can eventually become independent of the hippocampus as the specific autobiographical details fade.

The debate continues.

The Frontal Cortex in Memory Storage and Retrieval

frontal cortex. Those regions of cortex that lie within the frontal lobes and that may play a role in determining which memories are stored and in producing metamemory for that information.

The **frontal cortex**, those regions of cortex that lie within the frontal lobes, may help determine what information we store (and remember) and what information we don't store (and therefore forget). Recall that subsequent memory studies typically find heightened medial temporal lobe activity during the incidental encoding of words that will subsequently be remembered (Figure 7.15a). As Figure 7.15b showed, an area of the left prefrontal cortex is also more active during incidental encoding of subsequently remembered information (Otten et al., 2001; Wagner et al., 1998). This suggests that some areas in prefrontal cortex promote memory storage.

In contrast, other areas in the prefrontal cortex may *suppress* hippocampal activity, *inhibiting* storage and retrieval of "unwanted" memories. For example, in the directed forgetting task of Figure 7.6b, participants studied words and then were asked to explicitly try to remember or forget each one. Later, participants' memory was worse for items they'd been instructed to forget than for items they'd been instructed to remember (or items they hadn't seen since the original study phase).

What could underlie this effect? Michael Anderson and colleagues collected fMRI data comparing brain activity while participants were trying to remember words, and while they were trying to forget words. As Figure 7.18 shows, the hippocampus was more active while participants were trying to remember than when they were trying to forget; this is not particularly surprising given the role of the hippocampus in memory (M. Anderson et al., 2004). But several areas in the prefrontal cortex were more active while the subjects were intentionally trying to forget than when they were trying to remember. One possible explanation is that certain areas of prefrontal cortex inhibit the hippocampus, and so their heightened activity during intentional forgetting suppresses hippocampal memory encoding. And indeed, the greater the prefrontal activation in a participant, the more likely the participant was to forget on the final test. The specific prefrontal areas activated during intentional forgetting are slightly different than those that are active during intentional remembering (Wylie, Foxe, & Taylor, 2008).

These and similar experiments strongly suggest that the frontal lobes contribute to determining what new information gets

Figure 7.18 Directed forgetting fMRI images show the hippocampus to be less active (blue) while people were actively trying to forget than while they were actively trying to remember. Several prefrontal areas, however, were more active (yellow) while participants were trying to forget.

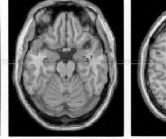
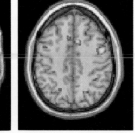

More active during "forget" than "remember"

More active during "remember" than "forget"

encoded as episodic and semantic memories and what gets forgotten. The frontal lobes may also help us bind contextual information to event memory, allowing us to form episodic memories that encode not only what happened but also where and when the episode took place (Schacter & Curran, 1995).

In keeping with these ideas, you might expect that people with frontal-lobe damage would be especially prone to source monitoring errors—an inability to remember where and when an event occurred. And this seems to be the case: individuals with frontal-lobe damage may be able to remember a story but not whether it occurred in their own past, or on television, or in their imagination (Kapur & Coughlan, 1980). Such source monitoring errors are generally not as devastating as the all-out memory failure of anterograde amnesia or retrograde amnesia, but it can still be a serious problem if a person can't reliably tell the difference between a fictional story and a real-life experience.

The frontal cortex also plays an important role in metamemory, helping us keep track of what we know and don't know. People with frontal lobe lesions do poorly on tests of metamemory (Pannu & Kaszniak, 2005), while the right medial frontal cortex is active in healthy young adults who experience tip-of-the-tongue events in which they try and fail to retrieve information that they think they should remember (Maril, Wagner & Schacter, 2001).

In sum, whereas the hippocampus and medial temporal lobes are key players in the actual storage of new information, the frontal cortex appears to be involved at a higher level, helping to determine what gets stored as episodic and semantic memory and what gets forgotten—and then helping us keep track of it all through metamemory.

Test Your Knowledge

Going Retro

The wordstem "retro-" is used in two ways in this chapter. First, you read about retroactive interference, when new information interferes with old memories. Later, you read about retrograde amnesia, when an event such as brain injury disrupts old memories. In each case, "retro-" means reaching back in time (think of "retro" fashions or "retroactive pay"). In contrast, proactive interference and anterograde amnesia both involve reaching forward in time: proactive interference occurs when old information reaches forward in time to disrupt future learning, and anterograde amnesia occurs when an event such as brain injury reaches forward in time to disrupt future formation of new memories. Can you correctly identify retroactive versus proactive interference, and retrograde versus anterograde amnesia in the examples below? (Answers appear in the back of the book.)

1. Scott took two years of Latin in college, then spent a semester abroad in Spain, and learned some Spanish while he was there. The next year, he enrolled in another Latin course, but on his first test he mistakenly used some Spanish words instead.

2. Marina recently broke up with her long-time boyfriend Carl; last month, she started dating Lance. One night while she was tired and distracted, she called him Carl by mistake.

3. Ten years ago, John was involved in a motorcycle accident that caused damage to his medial temporal lobes, including his hippocampus. He spent two weeks in the hospital recovering before being released to the care of his wife at home. Now, John has no memory of the time he spent in hospital.

4. John also has no memory of events that occurred in the months before his accident, although he remembers his childhood in Minnesota.

Subcortical Structures Involved in Episodic and Semantic Memory

Two other brain structures deserve special mention in the context of episodic and semantic memory: the basal forebrain and the diencephalon (Figure 7.19). The **basal forebrain** is a collection of structures that lie—as the name suggests—at the base of the forebrain. Structures of the basal forebrain include the *nucleus basalis* and the *medial septal nuclei*, which contain neurons that produce the neuromodulator *acetylcholine* and distribute it throughout the brain. The **diencephalon** is an area near the core of the brain, just above the brainstem, that includes the *thalamus*, the *hypothalamus*, and the *mammillary bodies* (which are sometimes considered to be part of the hypothalamus). The thalamus consists of several nuclei, many of which help relay sensory information from sensory receptors to the appropriate areas of sensory cortex; the hypothalamus plays an important role in regulating involuntary functions such as heartbeat, appetite, temperature control, and the wake/sleep cycle. (The function of the mammillary bodies isn't clear, although, as you'll read below, they play a role in memory.) Parts of the basal forebrain and diencephalon connect with the hippocampus via an arch-like fiber bundle called (you guessed it) the **fornix**. Damage to the basal forebrain, the diencephalon, or the fornix can result in amnesia.

The Basal Forebrain May Help Determine What the Hippocampus Stores

The basal forebrain receives blood and oxygen from a small artery, the anterior communicating artery (ACoA). The ACoA is a common site of *aneurysm*, a type of stroke in which an artery wall balloons out under pressure and may even rupture. ACoA aneurysm rupture may cause damage to the basal forebrain, and survivors often have anterograde amnesia very similar to that caused by medial temporal lobe damage (DeLuca & Diamond, 1995).

Why should basal forebrain damage cause amnesia? As you read in Chapter 2, neurotransmitters such as GABA and neuromodulators such as acetylcholine are critical for proper brain function. The medial septum, a group of cells in the basal forebrain, sends acetylcholine and GABA via the fornix to the hippocampus. These projections affect the activity and synaptic plasticity of hippocampal neurons, and may help determine whether and when the hippocampus will process and store information (Buzsaki & Gage, 1989; Damasio, Graff-Radford, Eslinger, Damasio, & Kassell, 1985; Hasselmo, 1999; Myers, Ermita, Hasselmo, & Gluck, 1998). This could explain why basal forebrain damage leads to amnesia: although the hippocampus is undamaged, it can't work effectively without neuromodulation from the basal forebrain telling it when to store new information.

When questioned about past events, many individuals with basal forebrain damage will respond with highly detailed but false memories, a phenomenon called **confabulation**. For example, asked what he did yesterday, a patient may say that he went into the office for a few hours, met an old friend for lunch, and then did some grocery shopping on the way home; the story may sound perfectly convincing except for the fact that the patient has been in the hospital

basal forebrain. A collection of structures that lie at the base of the forebrain and are important in the production of acetylcholine that is distributed throughout the brain.

diencephalon. A brain area that lies near the core of the brain, just above the brainstem, and includes the thalamus, the hypothalamus, and the mammillary bodies.

fornix. A fiber bundle that connects portions of the diencephalon and basal forebrain to the hippocampus.

confabulation. A behavior associated with some forms of amnesia in which individuals, when asked to remember past events, respond with highly detailed but false memories.

Figure 7.19 The basal forebrain and diencephalon
Structures in the basal forebrain and diencephalon connect with the hippocampus via a fiber bundle called the fornix. Damage to the diencephalon, the basal forebrain, or the fornix can cause anterograde amnesia that resembles the effects of direct hippocampal damage.

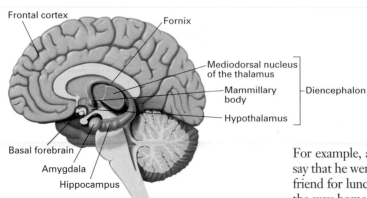

for the past two weeks! Individuals who confabulate are not lying. Rather, they seem to believe the stories they've made up and are often sincerely confused when confronted with proof that the stories are false.

Confabulation typically appears in patients in whom the damage from the aneurysm rupture extends beyond the basal forebrain and into the frontal cortex. And, consistent with what we know about the role of the frontal cortex in memory, some examples of confabulation seem to be no more than a kind of source monitoring error. In the above example, the patient can't remember what he did yesterday because of the amnesia produced by his basal forebrain damage. But he can retrieve a plausible answer from old memory. His frontal cortex is damaged, impairing metamemory, and leaving him unable to determine whether the retrieved memory is old or new (DeLuca, 2000).

In many patients, confabulation is most severe immediately after the aneurysm but tends to decrease as time passes, possibly due to some recovery of function in prefrontal cortex; the amnesia, however, is generally permanent.

The Diencephalon May Help Guide Consolidation

Over a century ago, doctors noted memory problems in individuals with **Korsakoff's disease**, a condition caused by a deficiency in thiamine (a B vitamin) that sometimes accompanies chronic alcohol abuse (Kopelman, Thompson, Guerrini, & Marshall, 2009). Korsakoff's disease consistently damages two areas of the diencephalon: the mammillary bodies and the mediodorsal nucleus of the thalamus (shown in Figure 7.19), although other brain regions may be damaged too. In many cases of Korsakoff's, patients develop anterograde amnesia and time-graded retrograde amnesia broadly similar to that observed in H.M. and other individuals with medial temporal lobe damage—even though patients with Korsakoff's have no direct damage to their medial temporal lobes. Some people with damage to the thalamus due to other causes also show anterograde amnesia with time-graded retrograde amnesia (Collinson, Meyyappan, & Rosenfeld, 2009; Hampstead & Koffler, 2009; Kapur, Thompson, Cook, Lang, & Brice, 1996), as do rats given conjoint lesions to the mammillary bodies and the mediodorsal nucleus of the thalamus (Aggleton & Mishkin, 1983; Mair, Knoth, Rabchenuk, & Langlais, 1991).

It is still unclear why diencephalic damage causes amnesia. Because the mammillary bodies and thalamic nuclei are anatomically connected to both the cerebral cortex and the medial temporal lobes, one possibility is that the diencephalic structures help mediate the interaction between the frontal cortex and the hippocampus during memory storage and consolidation, so that diencephalic damage disrupts this interaction (Collinson et al., 2009). Consistent with this idea, patients with Korsakoff's disease may also confabulate, providing detailed and fictitious stories when questioned about events they've forgotten—again suggesting a failure to distinguish between old and new memories.

Many questions remain unanswered about these subcortical structures and their role in memory. But the fact that amnesia can result from so many different types of brain damage provides compelling evidence that memory is a function of the whole brain. Many structures—including the hippocampus, cortex, diencephalon, and basal forebrain—must all be working well and working together for episodic and semantic memory to function properly. Lashley would feel at least partially vindicated.

Interim Summary

- Semantic memories seem to be stored in the cortex; to some extent, specific kinds of semantic information are stored in the cortical areas devoted to processing that kind of information (visual, auditory, etc.).

Korsakoff's disease. A condition caused by a deficiency in thiamine (a B vitamin) that sometimes accompanies chronic alcohol abuse; patients often show severe anterograde amnesia and engage in confabulation.

- Some research suggests that specific categories of semantic information are stored in specific groups or networks of neurons.

- The hippocampal region (which lies in the medial temporal lobe in humans and other primates) is important for new episodic memory formation; patients with bilateral hippocampal-region damage show anterograde amnesia (loss of ability to encode new episodic and semantic memories); they may also show retrograde amnesia (disruption of old memories acquired before the damage).

- In healthy humans, functional neuroimaging shows that the hippocampal region is especially active during encoding of information that will be successfully remembered later.

- Some researchers believe that while the hippocampus is required for new episodic memory formation, other areas of the medial temporal lobes are sufficient to store new semantic memories; other researchers believe that the hippocampus is necessary for both episodic and semantic memory formation.

- Standard consolidation theory states that older memories are stored in cortex and eventually become independent of the hippocampus, but multiple trace theory argues that episodic memories always require both the cortex and hippocampus.

- The frontal cortex is important for determining which new memories are stored or forgotten, as well as for metamemory and remembering the source of information.

- Other brain areas involved in episodic and semantic memory include the basal forebrain (which may help guide how the hippocampus stores new information), and the diencephalon (which may mediate communication between the hippocampus and the frontal cortex).

7.3 Clinical Perspectives

Patients such as H.M. and E.P. have permanent memory loss caused by identifiable brain damage. E.P.'s amnesia, for example, can be traced directly to medial temporal lobe damage dating to his bout with encephalitis, and H.M.'s amnesia stems from his brain surgery. Once the medial temporal lobes are damaged or destroyed, the lost memories cannot be recovered.

In other cases, however, the memory dysfunction may not be permanent. You've already learned about one kind of "temporary amnesia" in patients who undergo electroconvulsive shock therapy. These patients typically experience anterograde amnesia for the events of the ECT session and retrograde amnesia for events that happened a short time before the session. But their memory machinery is not permanently damaged. After a few hours, their brains are again able to encode new memories and retrieve old ones. (The "Learning and Memory in Everyday Life" box, on the next page, reviews post-concussive amnesia, which may also be temporary or may have longer-lasting effects.) The following pages review two more kinds of amnesia that do not involve permanent disruption of the ability to store memories: transient global amnesia (TGA) and functional amnesia.

Transient Global Amnesia

As its name suggests, **transient global amnesia (TGA)** is a transient, or temporary, disruption of memory not due to known causes such as head injury or

transient global amnesia (TGA). A transient, or temporary, disruption of memory typically including elements of both anterograde and retrograde amnesia.

The Cost of Concussion

Mild traumatic brain injury (mTBI), also known as concussion, may affect over 1.7 million people per year in the United States alone (Cassidy et al., 2004). Typical causes of mTBI are falls, car or bike accidents, and sports injury; military personnel are at high risk due to exposure to blast waves from nearby explosions (Langlois, Rutland-Brown, & Wald, 2006).

One of the defining symptoms of mTBI is amnesia, which can include both retrograde and anterograde memory loss. For example, a football player who sustains a concussion may not remember the details of his on-field collision, or what team he's playing, or the score; in addition, he may experience confusion and disorientation. One study of young patients (aged 10–18 years) with sports-related concussion found that about a quarter reported amnesia for the events surrounding the injury (Register-Mihalik, De Maio, Tibbo-Valeriote, & Wooten, 2014). Until fairly recently, it was assumed that the memory loss, like that following ECT, was temporary: that in the days after the injury, as the other symptoms of concussion (such as headache and blurred vision) resolve, so too does the amnesia, with only the memories for the hours immediately preceding and after the injury permanently lost—forming a temporal "hole" in the patient's memory.

But newer research has shown that memory effects may linger much longer. One study examined retired athletes who had sustained a sports-related concussion more than 30 years previously, compared to same-aged former athletes who had never sustained a concussion (De Beaumont et al., 2009). Both groups were given the picture memory task shown in Figure 7.14a. The non-concussed group performed normally for their age group (similar to the healthy controls in Figure 7.14b). The concussed group performed normally on the copying portion of the task, but were impaired in their ability to draw the figure from memory. This pattern is similar to, although much less severe than, that shown by amnesic patient E.P. in Figure 7.14c.

Worse, individuals who have suffered one concussion are vulnerable to poorer outcomes if they suffer a second concussion, particularly if the second injury occurs before the symptoms from the first one have completely resolved (Ling, Hardy & Zetterberg, 2015). Individuals who sustain repeated mTBI, like some athletes who play contact sports, are also at increased risk for cognitive decline and dementia late in life (Danshevar et al., 2011). American football is one such sport that has come under intense scrutiny in recent years following the deaths of several high school football players—including three in one week in October 2014 (Carver, 2014)—and a lawsuit against the National Football League (NFL) by former players who claimed the league did not adequately disclose the risks of concussion (Martin, 2013).

As a result, many school athletic programs now require sophisticated protective gear, have strict rules governing return to play for athletes who do sustain a concussion, and even prohibit game maneuvers such as head hits in hockey, headers in soccer, and head-down tackling in football (Ling et al., 2015). Meanwhile, in 2013, the NFL settled its lawsuit, agreeing to pay $675 million to retired players suffering from long-term effects of concussion, and $10 million to fund brain injury research and educational programs (Martin, 2013).

epilepsy (Brand & Markowitsch, 2004; Kritchevsky et al., 1988; Shekhar, 2008). Underlying causes are enigmatic, but about a third of patients have an apparent precipitating event such as vigorous exercise, swimming in cold water, or emotional stress (Hodges, 1990). Typically, TGA starts suddenly, persists for several hours, and then gradually dissipates over the course of a day or so. During the amnesic episode, the patient shows severe anterograde amnesia. There is usually also some degree of retrograde amnesia for events that occurred within the preceding decade or so (Kritchevsky & Squire, 1989; Kritchevsky et al., 1988).

Transient global amnesia is one of the more common forms of amnesia; annual incidence has been estimated at about 5 cases per 100,000 people per year in the United States (Miller, Petersen, Metter, Millikan, & Yanagihara, 1987). Despite the prevalence, TGA is difficult to study because it doesn't usually last long. But there are a few well-documented cases in the literature. One such case involves a 38-year-old man, S.G., who underwent brain surgery (Kapur, Millar, Abbott, & Carter, 1998). The surgery seemed to go smoothly, but there may have been some complication that temporarily reduced blood flow to his brain. When S.G. woke up, he knew his own name but did not remember his occupation, the month, or how long he had been in the hospital.

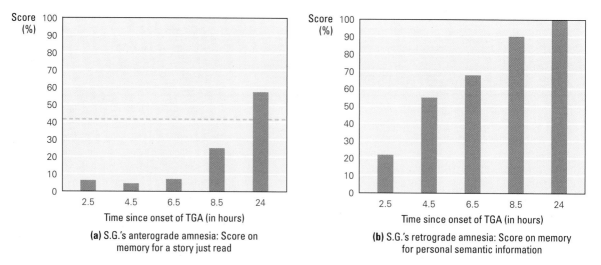

(a) S.G.'s anterograde amnesia: Score on memory for a story just read

(b) S.G.'s retrograde amnesia: Score on memory for personal semantic information

Figure 7.20 Transient global amnesia (TGA) (a) Patient S.G., 2.5 hours after the onset of amnesia, could remember almost nothing from a story he'd heard a few minutes ago. By 24 hours after onset, however, his performance improved, and he scored even better than the average expected from a same-age healthy control on this task (dotted line). (b) Similarly, 2.5 hours after the onset of his amnesia, S.G. showed severe retrograde amnesia for autobiographical information; his memories returned to normal 24 hours later with only a short "blackout" window for events that had occurred slightly before the surgery.
Information from Kapur et al., 1998.

The onset of S.G.'s amnesia occurred around 12:30 p.m. Memory researchers rushed to the scene, and S.G. agreed to an extensive battery of testing. At about 3 p.m., S.G. showed profound anterograde amnesia: he could listen to a short story, but a few minutes later he would recall only a few words of it (Figure 7.20a). S.G. also showed retrograde amnesia. Given a questionnaire about jobs he had held, places he had lived, and other personal semantic information, he could provide only a few answers (Figure 7.20b). (The correct answers were verified by S.G.'s fiancée.) S.G.'s memory was similarly poor for recent public events, although it was better for events that had happened at least a few decades before.

Researchers continued to test S.G. every few hours through the afternoon and evening; gradually, his anterograde and retrograde amnesia lessened. By noon of the next day, 24 hours after the onset of amnesia, S.G.'s memory had returned to normal, except for a slight retrograde amnesia for events that had occurred shortly before the surgery. The TGA was over; S.G.'s brain seemed to be back in working order.

Why might TGA occur? Like S.G., many individuals with TGA probably experience a temporary interruption of blood flow to the brain from a head injury, a hypoglycemic episode (low blood sugar), or a heart attack or stroke. (In a few cases, migraine headaches are implicated.) As in ECT, the temporary disruption in neuronal activity might completely erase unconsolidated memories of recent events but only temporarily limit access to fully consolidated older memories. When the blood flow resumes, so does the brain function.

Studies using neuroimaging methods such as positron emission tomography (PET) and magnetic resonance imaging (MRI) suggest that some individuals with TGA show small abnormalities in the hippocampus (Gonzalez-Martinez, Comte, de Verbizier, & Carlander, 2010; Yang, Kim, Kim, Kwak, & Han, 2009); in some cases, these abnormalities are no longer detectable on follow-up imaging two months after the TGA (Alberici et al., 2008; Della Marca et al., 2010). While this may not explain all cases of TGA, it suggests that the temporary disruption of memory storage and recall may reflect temporary disruption of the hippocampus.

Functional Amnesia

In the 2002 film *The Bourne Identity*, Jason Bourne (played by Matt Damon) awakes on a fishing boat with no memory of his own name, his past, or why he has the number of a Swiss bank account implanted in his hip. Throughout the movie, Bourne struggles to regain his memories while staying one step ahead of the CIA agents who are trying to kill him. Such memory loss has formed the basis of countless books, movies, and plays, from Alfred Hitchcock's 1945 classic *Spellbound*, to 2014's *The Maze Runner*, based on James Dashner's novel in which a sixteen-year-old hero wakes up trapped in a maze with no memory of his prior life, to an episode of *The Simpsons* in which Marge develops amnesia and forgets all about her dysfunctional animated family.

Such memory loss can also happen in real life, although it is far rarer than Hollywood might lead you to believe. **Functional amnesia** (sometimes called *psychogenic amnesia*) is a sudden, massive retrograde memory loss that seems to result from psychological causes, in contrast to *organic amnesia*, which arises from obvious physical causes, such as brain injury (Kritchevsky, Chang, & Squire, 2004; Schacter & Kihlstrom, 1989). One type of functional amnesia is *dissociative amnesia*, in which patients lose memory of a specific, traumatic event; an even more dramatic type is *dissociative fugue*, in which patients lose all memory of their identity. Dissociative fugue is extraordinarily rare. Moreover, some individuals who claim to have lost their memory will later admit to faking functional amnesia in order to avoid dealing with a difficult situation such as a crime or a relationship problem (Jenkins, Kapur, & Kopelman, 2009). Some cases, however, do seem to involve genuine memory loss.

Daniel Schacter records one case of functional amnesia involving a 21-year-old man, P.N., who was admitted to the hospital complaining of back pains (Schacter, Wang, Tulving, & Freedman, 1982). When questioned about his identity, P.N. could not remember his name or anything about his past except that he had once been given the nickname "Lumberjack." Schacter later concluded that P.N. had developed functional amnesia following the death of his grandfather, to whom P.N. had been close. P.N.'s extreme grief was the psychological trauma that triggered the memory loss.

In contrast to P.N.'s severe retrograde amnesia for autobiographical events, his semantic memories were intact: both his language functions and his knowledge about the world seemed normal. However, P.N. also showed anterograde amnesia, having difficulty remembering new information for more than a few minutes at a time. The functional amnesia persisted for about a week until P.N. happened to watch a television show that included a funeral scene; as if by magic, lost memories came flooding back, and P.N. recalled his own identity and history. Only the memories of events that occurred during the previous week were permanently lost, possibly because his anterograde amnesia had prevented those memories from being successfully stored in the first place.

Not all cases of functional amnesia resolve so well. Mark Kritchevsky and his colleagues studied 10 individuals with functional amnesia; all were unable to report their names or personal histories (Kritchevsky et al., 2004). One of these patients later admitted to feigning his amnesia, and Kritchevsky and colleagues suspected a second may have been feigning too. But of the eight patients whose amnesia seemed genuine, only one fully recovered all the lost memories, and a few patients never recovered any memories at all, even 2 or more years after the onset of their amnesia. Another case study involving a woman who lost the memories of her identity and the past 33 years of her life reported that her memories had not returned even after 11 years (Helmes, Brown & Elliott, 2015). Currently, there is no way to predict when or whether particular patients will recover their memory.

Given that patients with functional amnesia have no known brain damage, what could cause this syndrome? Functional imaging may provide some clues. In one study using PET, an individual with functional amnesia had abnormal activity patterns in areas of the medial temporal lobes and the diencephalon;

functional amnesia. A sudden massive retrograde memory loss that seems to result from psychological causes rather than physical causes such as brain injury; also called *psychogenic amnesia*.

these abnormalities disappeared when the amnesia resolved (Markowitsch et al., 1998). This suggests that functional amnesia may result from a (possibly temporary) malfunction of the brain areas normally involved in episodic memory storage and retrieval. Another study using functional magnetic resonance imaging (fMRI) showed that when two people with functional amnesia "failed to recognize" individuals with whom they were actually acquainted, there was increased activity in the prefrontal cortex and decreased activity in the hippocampus (Kikuchi et al., 2010). This is the same basic pattern observed during directed forgetting in healthy adults (see Figure 7.18) and suggests that—consciously or unconsciously—the patients may have been suppressing recall. Interestingly, when one patient's amnesia resolved, the abnormal pattern of prefrontal activation disappeared.

Together, these imaging results suggest that functional amnesia may reflect dysfunction of the same brain regions that are damaged in organic amnesia (Oullet, Rouleau, Labrecque, Bernier, & Scherzer, 2008). The major differences would be that, whereas organic amnesia is brought on by a physiological injury, functional amnesia is brought on by a psychological trauma, and so—because there is no permanent injury to the brain—it may be possible for patients with functional amnesia to recover both their brain function and their memories in a way that would be impossible for patients such as H.M. and E.P.

Interim Summary

- Transient global amnesia (TGA) is a temporary disruption of memory that occurs without evidence of head injury or epilepsy; however, there may be precipitating events such as vigorous exercise or stress.

- During a TGA episode, patients typically show severe anterograde amnesia and usually some degree of retrograde amnesia.

- TGA may reflect a temporary disruption of brain function due to interruption of blood (and nutrients) to the brain; typically, as the brain recovers, memory returns to normal.

- Functional amnesia is a very rare form of amnesia in which patients lose memory for specific episodes in their lives or even forget their entire identity.

- Functional amnesia seems to result from psychological trauma rather than any physical cause.

Test Your Knowledge

Don't Forget Your Amnesias

"Amnesia" is a general term for memory loss. For each specific type of amnesia listed below, can you remember what kind of information is lost or disrupted, as well as what kind of brain damage might be responsible? (Answers appear in the back of the book.)

1. Anterograde amnesia

2. Functional amnesia

3. Retrograde amnesia

4. Source amnesia

5. Transient global amnesia (TGA)

Synthesis

In the Clinical Perspectives section of this chapter, we mentioned a few examples of the many movie and television characters who have been depicted as developing amnesia. Knowing what you now know about memory and amnesia, you should be able to assess the plausibility of these characters—as well as of amnesia portrayals in other movies, TV shows, and books.

The vast majority of these, like Jason Bourne in *The Bourne Identity*, are afflicted with functional amnesia—usually a complete loss of identity caused by psychological trauma rather than physical brain damage. These characters typically maintain their semantic memory, as well as their skills. This profile is roughly similar to that observed in real-world patients such as P.N., whose functional amnesia stripped him of his personal history, though his general knowledge about the world seemed intact. Jason Bourne (like the protagonists of many other amnesia stories) spends much of the movie trying to solve the mystery of what triggered his amnesia, as well as trying to recover his lost identity. In this sense, *The Bourne Identity* and other "lost identity" stories share many features with real-world cases of functional amnesia. Where these stories depart from reality is mainly in their resolution: in many a TV drama, the heroine who has lost her memory following a blow to the head needs nothing more than a second blow to bring the memories flooding back. In the real world, head injuries don't cure functional amnesia. Some patients recover spontaneously, but others recover slowly or not at all.

Organic amnesia is a much less common plot device than functional amnesia. Exceptions include the 2000 film *Memento*, a psychological thriller featuring a protagonist who suffers from anterograde amnesia, and Pixar's 2003 *Finding Nemo*, featuring an animated fish (voiced by Ellen DeGeneres) with the same disorder. In both these cases, the characters are intelligent and motivated individuals who are unable to acquire new episodic or semantic memory; anything they learn or do is forgotten within a few minutes. While *Finding Nemo* doesn't explore the medical causes underlying amnesia, *Memento*'s protagonist explains that he developed his condition following a head injury that damaged his hippocampus. These fictional characters share many characteristics with real-world amnesic patients such as H.M. and E.P., who developed anterograde amnesia following medial temporal lobe damage. However, real-world patients such as H.M. and E.P. usually have at least some retrograde amnesia as well—loss of some (and often quite a lot) of their memories from before the brain damage.

Yet another class of memory-related plots revolves around false memories. For example, the 1990 sci-fi classic *Total Recall* (Lion's Gate) stars Arnold Schwarzenegger as a construction worker who pays to have memories of an expensive trip to Mars implanted in his brain—at a fraction of the time and cost that it would take to actually vacation on another planet. In *The Manchurian Candidate* (1962, Metro-Goldwyn-Mayer, starring Frank Sinatra; remade in 2004 by Universal Studios, starring Denzel Washington), an evil corporation uses brainwashing and hypnotism to implant false memories. These stories are obviously science fiction, but the phenomenon of false memories is science fact: researchers can implant false memories that feel as rich and real as true memories—so real that research participants will often argue when researchers attempt to explain the hoax. False memories lead to exciting adventures in the movies, but they can lead to serious real-world problems too, as when eyewitnesses confuse memories of a crime scene with pictures of a suspect aired on the nightly news.

In all of these plots, the drama springs from a universal sense that our episodic and semantic memories—the facts we know and the events we've experienced—make us who we are. It is easy to empathize with a character whose memories have been stripped away, because we can imagine the devastating impact.

On a more mundane level, everyone experiences occasional failures of episodic and semantic memory. Some of these failures, such as forgetting where we parked the car or blanking on the name of someone we meet unexpectedly at the gym, are just a normal part of everyday life. Some of us have experienced an episode of TGA following a sports injury, have fallen prey to source monitoring errors while writing a term paper, or have experienced judgment-of-learning errors while studying for an exam. Most of the time, our access to episodic and semantic memory is effortless, and our memories are long lasting and largely accurate—but at the same time, our memory processes may fail more often than we like. Understanding these processes may help us improve their function while giving us—like Jason Bourne and his fellows—a better appreciation of the episodic and semantic memories we do possess.

KNOW YOUR KEY TERMS

amnesia, *p. 268*
anterograde amnesia, *p. 292*
association cortex, *p. 290*
basal forebrain, *p. 300*
confabulation, *p. 300*
consolidation period, *p. 286*
cued recall, *p. 278*
declarative memory, *p. 270*
diencephalon, *p. 300*
directed forgetting, *p. 280*
electroconvulsive shock, *p. 286*
episodic memory, *p. 269*
explicit memory, *p. 270*
false memory, *p. 284*

fornix, *p. 300*
free recall, *p. 278*
frontal cortex, *p. 298*
functional amnesia, *p. 305*
hippocampus, *p. 292*
implicit memory, *p. 270*
interference, *p. 281*
Korsakoff's disease, *p. 301*
levels-of-processing effect, *p. 276*
medial temporal lobes, *p. 267*
metamemory, *p. 288*
multiple trace theory, *p. 297*
nondeclarative memory, *p. 270*
proactive interference, *p. 282*

recognition, *p. 278*
reconsolidation, *p. 287*
retroactive interference, *p. 282*
retrograde amnesia, *p. 296*
Ribot gradient, *p. 296*
semantic memory, *p. 269*
sensory cortex, *p. 290*
source monitoring error, *p. 282*
standard consolidation
    theory, *p. 296*
transfer-appropriate processing
    effect, *p. 277*
transient global amnesia
    (TGA), *p. 302*

QUIZ YOURSELF

1. The general term for conditions involving severe memory loss is _____. _____ involves loss of the ability to form new episodic and semantic memories, while _____ involves loss of previously acquired information. (p. 268, 292, 296)

2. Three ways in which memory can be tested are free recall, which entails _____; cued recall, which entails _____; and recognition, which entails _____. Of the three, _____ usually produces the best performance. (p. 278)

3. The _____ effect refers to the finding that, in general, deeper processing leads to better recall than shallow processing. A related principle, _____, states that memory is usually best when the cues available at testing are similar to those at encoding. (p. 277)

4. In the _____ paradigm, subjects typically show worse memory for items that they have been specifically instructed to forget. (p. 280)

5. Newly acquired episodic and semantic memories are particularly vulnerable during the _____. However, each time a memory is reactivated or recalled, it may again become vulnerable to modification, a process termed _____. (p. 286–287)

6. _____ occurs in some forms of amnesia when patients, asked to remember past events, respond with highly detailed but false memories. This behavior is often observed in _____, a disorder that sometimes accompanies chronic alcohol abuse. (p. 300–301)

7. _____ is memory for facts and information about the world (including personal information); _____ is memory for specific events that occurred at a particular time and place. (p. 269)

8. The _____ is located in the medial temporal lobe of the brain, and is connected to the diencephalon and the basal forebrain by a fiber bundle called the _____. (p. 300)

9. A false memory is _____. (p. 284)

10. Areas of cerebral cortex involved in processing specific types of information, such as sights and sounds, are called _____; other areas of cortex, called _____, process information both within and across sensory modalities. (p. 290)

11. The Ribot gradient describes a pattern of memory loss in which _____ memories are more prone to disruption than _____ memories. (p. 296)

12. _____ is a sudden memory loss that does not seem to result from physical causes such as brain injury. (p. 305)

13. The frontal cortex may play a role in memory by _____ and also in _____. (p. 288)

14. Therapy involving _____ is sometimes used to treat severe depression, but can severely disrupt newly formed memories. (p. 286)

15. Whereas _____ memory includes information we are aware that we know, _____ memory can exist without the learner's awareness. (p. 270)

16. Severe and permanent amnesia can be caused by brain damage that includes the _____, the _____, or the _____. (p. 300–301)

17. _____ refers to a disruption of memory due to overlap with the content of other memories. In _____, new learning disrupts old (previously stored) information. In _____, old learning interferes with the ability to recall newly learned information. (p. 281–282)

18. Metamemory involves _____. (p. 288)

19. Episodic and semantic memory are sometimes grouped together under the heading of _____, whereas other types of memory such as skill memory that are not always consciously accessible or easy to verbalize are sometimes grouped under the heading of _____. (p. 270)

20. _____ is a transient or temporary disruption of memory that typically includes both anterograde and retrograde amnesia. (p. 302)

21. Standard consolidation theory states that brain structures including the _____ are required for storage and retrieval of _____ memories but not _____ memories. In contrast, multiple trace theory suggests that _____. (p. 296)

22. Remembering a fact, but thinking you learned it in school when you actually only saw it in a movie, is an example of a _____. (p. 282)

Answers appear in the back of the book.

CONCEPT CHECK

1. Suppose you join a club with six members, and you want to remember each member's name for the next meeting. What are three ways, based on the principles described in this chapter, that you can improve your likelihood of remembering the names?

2. A semantic memory is a memory for a fact without memory of the spatial and temporal context in which that fact was learned. How does this differ from source amnesia?

3. Failures of episodic and semantic memory can be annoying, but they serve a purpose. Why might it be desirable for an organism to be able to forget some information?

4. In adult humans with normal memory function, fMRI shows that the hippocampus is active even for retrieval of very old autobiographical information (Ryan et al., 2001). Does this prove that autobiographical memories always remain at least partially dependent on the hippocampus?

5. Suppose you are working in an emergency room when a man comes in who claims to have forgotten his entire identity. What questions would you ask the friend who drove him to the hospital? What tests might you conduct to find out what's going on?

Answers appear in the back of the book.

Skill Memory

Learning by Doing

"When starting a kiss, the rule of thumb is to start slow. This just makes sense, and it lets everyone get used to the dynamics of that particular kiss. A slow start is a good introduction . . . and sometimes the kiss should just stay slow. Jumping into rapid tongue maneuvers can scare your partner, and is rude to boot. Athletes always warm up before moving onto serious play . . . why should kissing be any different?"

("Kiss Tempo," Hays, Allen, & Hanish, 2015, Reprinted with permission from virtualkiss.com.)

D O YOU REMEMBER YOUR FIRST KISS? For some, it is a magical memory. For others, it was an awkward experience in which a single thought kept recurring: "Am I doing this right?" Kissing is simple enough in concept. Take your lips and press them against someone else's lips. What could be easier? After just a few experiences with bad kissers, however, a person realizes that simple as kissing appears, it is not an ability humans are born with. By the same token, a single encounter with an especially good kisser is enough to make you appreciate that kissing well requires some skill.

The success of a first kiss may depend in part on the setting and the partner, but most young people are savvy enough to know that they need to practice if they want their first real kiss to be a good one. Practice might consist of kissing one's own hand or arm, a pillow, or a stuffed animal. The hope is that these practice sessions will provide an edge when a real opportunity comes along. Practicing by kissing your hand or arm is a good strategy because that way you get feedback about what your lips feel like. Taking a class might also help, but you will not become an adept kisser by memorizing lists of rules about how to kiss. To become an **expert**, someone who performs a skill better than most, you need to get in there and kiss (a lot), you need to get feedback about your kissing, and most important, your brain has to store memories of your kissing successes and failures. Some of what

Behavioral Processes
Features of Skill Memories
Encoding New Memories
Learning and Memory in Everyday Life: Are Some Cognitive Skills Easier for Men Than Women?
Retrieving Existing Memories
When Memory Fails

Brain Substrates
The Basal Ganglia and Skill Learning
Learning and Memory in Everyday Life: Are Video Games Good for the Brain?
Cortical Representations of Skills
The Cerebellum and Timing

Clinical Perspectives
Parkinson's Disease
Human–Machine Interfaces: Learning to Consciously Control Artificial Limbs

expert. A person who performs a skill better than most.

T. Nakamura Volvox Inc./Getty Images

you learn about kissing can be shared verbally, but a lot of what you learn will be easier to demonstrate than to explain. You might not think of making out as "practicing a skill," but your kissing experiences can change your abilities whether you are aware of it or not. And, with enough practice, you might even become an expert.

This chapter describes how repeated experiences can incrementally enhance the performance of a skill by gradually modifying memories of how the skill can best be executed. As you will discover, repeated experiences not only can change how a person performs a skill, they also can change the structure of the brain circuits that are used to perform that skill. Skill memories are formed and processed by several brain regions, including the basal ganglia, the cerebral cortex, and the cerebellum. People with damage in one or more of these brain regions have trouble learning new skills as well as performing skills already learned.

8.1 Behavioral Processes

The previous chapter dealt with memories for events and facts—in other words, information an individual remembers and knows about. Skill memories, in contrast, relate to what one knows how to do.

A **skill** is an ability to perform a task that has been honed through experience. The kinds of skills you are probably most familiar with are those that athletes demonstrate when they compete or that musicians reveal when they perform. More mundane skills include driving a car, dancing, drinking out of a glass, and recognizing when a band is playing out of tune. These are all examples of **perceptual-motor skills**: learned movement patterns and perceptual abilities.

The kinds of abilities that you can improve through practice go far beyond fancy limb movements and subtle sensory distinctions. How about playing cards, budgeting your money, taking tests, or managing your time? These are all **cognitive skills**, which require you to solve problems or apply strategies rather than to execute physical maneuvers or to sharpen your senses (Ackerman, 2007; Rosenbaum, Carlson, & Gilmore, 2001; van Lehn, 1996). By reading this sentence, you are exercising a cognitive skill that you learned a long time ago. Reading may now seem so effortless that you can hardly recall the challenge of acquiring this complex ability. When you turn a page, highlight a sentence, take notes, or study the contents of this chapter, you are making use of skill memories.

Features of Skill Memories

As you will soon discover, skill memories are similar in many respects to episodic and semantic memories. But, they also possess some unique qualities (Table 8.1). Like memories for facts, skill memories are long lasting and improved by repeated experiences. Unlike memories for events and facts, however, skill memories can't always be verbalized. As you'll recall from Chapter 7, psychologists sometimes classify memories that are not easily put into words, including skill memories, as *nondeclarative* memories. Skill memories may be acquired and retrieved without the feelings of remembering associated with recalling episodic memories—they are thus often *implicit memories*. It was H.M.'s ability to acquire new skill memories, despite his inability to recall recent episodes, that initially

skill. An ability that can improve over time through practice.

perceptual-motor skill. Learned movement patterns guided by sensory inputs.

cognitive skill. A skill that requires problem solving or the application of strategies.

Table 8.1 Comparison of memories for skills, events, and facts	
Skill memories	**Memories for events and facts**
1. Are difficult to convey except by direct demonstration	1. Can be communicated flexibly, in different formats
2. May be acquired without awareness	2. Have content that is consciously accessible
3. Require several repetitions	3. Can be acquired in a single exposure

led researchers to classify a subset of memories (declarative memories) as being consciously accessible (see Table 7.1).

Skills can be learned in many ways, but the most common methods involve practice, instruction, and the observation of others performing the skills. Chapter 5 describes one technique, *operant conditioning*, that is commonly used to train animals to perform skills. Pressing a lever, pecking a key, or rolling over on command might seem like easy abilities for an animal to learn to perform, but that does not disqualify them as skills (skills need not be difficult to learn or impressive to watch). Neither does the fact that the training was done using automated techniques. What distinguishes these abilities as skills is not so much how they were acquired or how difficult they were to learn as that they improve with practice. This section looks at different kinds of skill memories, exploring how performance of skills (recall of skill memories) varies and what factors determine how performance varies.

How Different Are Cognitive from Perceptual-Motor Skill Memories?

Historically, philosophers and psychologists have distinguished perceptual-motor skills from cognitive skills. However, recent evidence suggests there are many more similarities in how humans learn and remember both types of skills than was previously thought (Rosenbaum, Carlson, & Gilmore, 2001), and many skills involve both cognitive and perceptual-motor components. For instance, professional athletes in team sports have to make split-second decisions about which of several possible actions they will take and keep in mind the idiosyncratic strengths and weaknesses of individual competitors. Olympic gymnasts must maintain mental focus and poise while under tremendous emotional pressure to perform specific movement sequences.

Psychologists classify skills such as gymnastics, which consist of performing a predefined sequence of movements, as **closed skills**. On the other hand, skills that require the individual to respond based on predictions about the changing demands of the environment are classified as **open skills**. Just as many activities require both perceptual-motor and cognitive skills, they also may demand both open and closed skills. Passing a basketball involves particular movement patterns, but in addition requires the players to vary the way they move their arms and legs based on the length of the pass and the positions of defenders. The success of a pass depends on the players' predicting (or directing) their teammate's next move. Most perceptual-motor skills contain aspects of both closed and open skills, and so it is better to think of any particular skill as lying somewhere along a continuum from open to closed (Magill, 1993).

closed skill. A skill that involves performing predefined movements that, ideally, never vary.

open skill. A skill in which movements are made on the basis of predictions about changing demands of the environment.

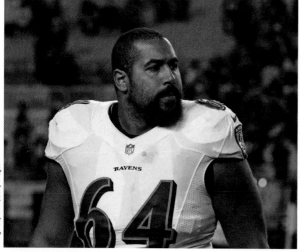

What memory mechanisms helped John Urschel to become both a professional football player and an expert mathematician?

Psychologists usually associate cognitive skills with the ability to reason and solve problems or to perform tasks that require sorting through large amounts of knowledge (such as writing a textbook). Traditionally, cognitive skills are portrayed as depending more on intellectual prowess, whereas perceptual-motor skills are thought to depend more on physical dexterity, speed, and strength—the classic nerds-versus-jocks split. While solving math problems does clearly differ in many respects from playing football, the memory mechanisms that enable people to gradually improve at both skills are quite similar, as we will discover throughout this chapter.

Research on perceptual-motor skills typically focuses on much less complex skills than those needed to do backflips or play basketball. Skills studied in the laboratory might consist of pressing buttons quickly or tracking the position of a moving object (Doyon, Penhune, & Ungerleider, 2003). Likewise, psychologists studying cognitive skills often use tasks that participants can learn relatively quickly, such as simple puzzles like the Tower of Hanoi (Figure 8.1). In this puzzle, the objective is to move different-size disks from one peg to another, one disk at a time (we discuss this task in greater detail in Chapter 9). The puzzle would be trivially easy except that the rules forbid you to put a larger disk on top of a smaller one. The numbered sequence in Figure 8.1 shows one solution to the puzzle. Normally, people get better at solving this puzzle with practice. This is not because they are getting better at physically moving the disks from one peg to another (a perceptual-motor skill), but because they are learning new strategies for moving the disks so that they end up in the desired position (J. R. Anderson, 1982). Researchers studying both perceptual-motor and cognitive skills want to keep things as simple as possible so they can control the relevant variables more precisely. This gives them a better chance of understanding how experience affects an individual's ability to perform a particular skill.

Test Your Knowledge

Open and Closed Skills

Psychologists classify skills in many ways. One conventional scheme for classifying perceptual-motor skills is the extent to which skills are open or closed. Open skills involve movements that are modified based on predictions about environmental demands, and closed skills depend on performing predefined movements that, ideally, never vary. Try to label each of the following perceptual-motor skills as either an open or a closed skill, considering all the possible contexts in which the skills might be performed. (Answers appear in the back of the book.)

1. A sea lion balancing a ball
2. A girl swimming
3. A young man kissing
4. A bear catching a fish
5. A fish catching insects
6. A boy playing a piano
7. A young woman throwing darts

Which Comes First, Cognitive or Perceptual-Motor Skill Memory?

The learning of new skills often begins with a set of instructions. Let's say that you've just started college and that you hand your new roommate a bag of ramen to make for lunch. If your roommate has never seen ramen before, she might start scanning the bag for clues about what to do next. The makers of ramen predicted that your roommate might not possess memories of how to cook ramen, and so they provided written instructions about how to do it. A few weeks later, when your roommate decides to treat you to lunch, she may simply try to recall the ramen-making steps from memory. Because she will depend on her memories for events and facts to cook the lunch, you could say that her skill memories are her memories of the instructions or of a past episode. In other words, skill memories can be memories for events and facts!

Following a written recipe for how to prepare food requires the ability to read, which is a cognitive skill. Correctly following the instructions to make ramen also requires the ability to perform various perceptual-motor skills, such as opening the bag and boiling water. Both kinds of memories can contribute to learning new skills. Nevertheless, several lines of evidence suggest that perceptual-motor skill memories provide the foundation for learning cognitive skills.

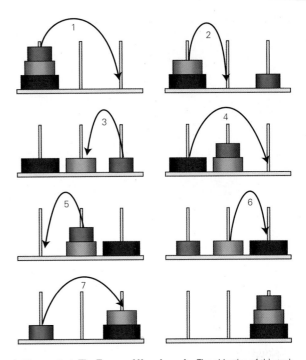

Figure 8.1 The Tower of Hanoi puzzle The objective of this task is to move all the disks from the leftmost peg to the rightmost peg, one disk at a time, without placing a larger disk on a smaller disk. The numbered sequence shows one way of doing this. The ability to solve such puzzles is a cognitive skill. The ability to move a disk from peg to peg is a perceptual-motor skill.

First, humans learn perceptual-motor skills at younger ages than they learn cognitive skills. How various memory abilities develop after birth is discussed in detail in Chapter 12. Second, many cognitive skills, including reading and writing, are difficult or impossible to acquire without first learning basic perceptual-motor skills such as producing speech or drawing lines. Finally, many different species can learn to perform a wide range of perceptual-motor skills, as described in Chapter 5, but only a few seem to be able to learn cognitive skills. In fact, many researchers and philosophers have argued that humans are the only organisms that can learn cognitive skills, and that this ability is what makes humans special.

Can Nonhumans Have Cognitive Skill Memories?

Descartes (Chapter 1) proposed that the ability to reason is what distinguishes humans from other animals. Descartes would probably have been willing to accept that dogs can store memories for how to perform perceptual-motor skills such as how to catch a Frisbee, but he would have considered it impossible for a dog or any other nonhuman animal to learn a cognitive skill. Following Descartes's lead, many psychologists assume that only humans can reason or perform complex cognitive tasks. Consequently, most of what is currently known about cognitive skill memories comes from studies of humans.

Humans are not the only animals that can learn cognitive skills, however. For instance, it was once thought that only humans used tools and that this particular problem-solving ability played a key role in the evolution of the human mind. But in the past two decades, psychologists and animal behavior researchers have described tool use in many animals, including

Lars Bedjer

Figure 8.2 Dolphins using tools Some dolphins in Australia have taken to carrying around sponges when they are foraging. Researchers suspect that the dolphins use the sponges as tools to protect themselves against injuries from sea urchins and other spiny sea creatures as they probe the seafloor for food.

elephants, apes, octopuses, birds, otters, and dolphins (Beck, 1980; Hart, 2001; Hunt, Corballis, & Gray, 2001; Krutzen et al., 2005; Whiten et al., 1999). In the lab, experimenters have taught primates and other animals to use various tools. There is also recent evidence that animals in the wild can teach themselves to use tools—for example, dolphins have learned to use a sponge while foraging (Krutzen et al., 2005), as shown in Figure 8.2. Researchers have also observed chimpanzees in the wild that learn how to use stones to crack nuts (Whiten & Boesch, 2001). Tool use is an ability that often involves both perceptual-motor and cognitive skills. Movement patterns required for using a tool improve with practice as does the recognition that a particular tool (or strategy) can be useful in solving various problems.

Clearer evidence of cognitive skills in nonhumans comes from laboratory studies showing that various species can learn to perform cognitive tasks on command. In one study, mentioned briefly in Chapter 7, dolphins learned to repeat whatever action they had performed most recently when instructed to do so by a trainer (Mercado, Murray, Uyeyama, Pack, & Herman, 1998). Most of the "tricks" that you may have seen dolphins performing on TV or in oceanariums are perceptual-motor skills. The trainer gives a signal, and in response the dolphin performs a particular movement sequence. When a dolphin is instructed to repeat an action, however, the signal to do so is not associated with one particular motor response. Almost any action a dolphin can perform could be a correct response to such an instruction, depending on what the dolphin was doing before the instruction was given. To successfully follow a "repeat" instruction, the dolphin must actively recall its recent actions. Recall and reenactment of past episodes is a cognitive skill—it can be improved through practice (Brehmer, Li, Muller, von Oertzen, & Lindenberger, 2007). By successfully learning to repeat actions on command, dolphins have demonstrated that they can perform the cognitive skill of recalling past events.

Not all animals are equally capable of learning complex cognitive and perceptual-motor skills. By comparing different animals' abilities to learn skills and by exploring which neural systems they use when forming and retrieving memories of different skills, scientists are beginning to gain a clearer understanding of what skill memories are like and how they are formed (Mercado, 2008).

Encoding New Memories

Now that you know how researchers classify different kinds of skills, let's consider the question of what allows some individuals to excel at a particular skill. You won't be surprised to hear that practice is an important factor. We'll examine how different kinds of practice affect performance and retention of skill memories and why individuals who are great at one skill are not necessarily as good at other, similar skills.

More Repetition Does not Guarantee Improvement

In the 2010 movie *The Karate Kid*, a young boy asks a kung fu master to give him a crash course in martial arts. The master reluctantly agrees and begins by making the student repeatedly drop his coat on the floor, pick it up, put it on, take it off, and hang it up on a peg. This goes on for several days. The student does as he is told and later discovers that the movements he has been laboriously repeating are the kung fu movements that he needs to perform to defend himself. Because he has repeated these movements thousands of times, he is able to reproduce them rapidly and effortlessly. He (supposedly) has learned the skills of kung fu without even knowing it!

The portrayal of the relationship between practice and skill memories in this movie is similar to several early psychological theories of skill learning. The basic idea is that the more times you perform a skill, the faster or better you'll be able to perform it in the future. Is this how practice works? Or is there more to practice than just repetition? To address this issue, Edward Thorndike conducted experiments in which he repeatedly asked blindfolded individuals to draw a line exactly 3 inches long (Thorndike, 1927). Half of the participants were told when their line was within one eighth of an inch of the target length, and the other half were not given any feedback about their lines. Both groups drew the same number of lines during the experiment, but only the participants who received feedback improved in accuracy as the experiment progressed. This simple study suggests that repeatedly hanging up a coat is probably not a good way to learn kung fu moves. Feedback about performance, what researchers in the field usually call **knowledge of results**, is critical to the effectiveness of practice (Butki & Hoffman, 2003; Ferrari, 1999; Liu & Wrisberg, 1997; Schmidt & Lee, 2005; A. P. Turner & Martinek, 1999; Weeks & Kordus, 1998). Coaches, professors, and kung fu instructors all provide learners with knowledge of the results of practice (including studying), which can play a major role in how an individual's skills improve.

The earliest detailed studies of how practice affects performance were conducted by military researchers who were interested in the high-speed, high-precision performance of perceptual-motor skills such as tracking and reacting to targets (these studies are reviewed by Holding, 1981). One of the basic findings from this early research was that the extent to which practice can lead to further improvements decreases as the amount of practice increases. For example, Figure 8.3a shows that as participants practiced a reading task, the amount of time they required to read each page decreased (A. Newell & Rosenbaum, 1981). Early in training, participants showed large gains in reading speed, but after this initial improvement, additional training led to much smaller

knowledge of results. Feedback about performance of a skill; critical to the effectiveness of practice.

Figure 8.3 Effects of practice and feedback on skill performance (a) As training on a reading task progressed, improvements in reading speed became smaller. (b) After improvement slows, new sources of feedback can lead to a new burst of rapid improvement. In this graph, after his initial rate of improvement in speed of kicking had begun to slow, a participant was shown a film of optimum kicking. The film helped him improve his own kicking speed.

(a) Data from Singley and Anderson, 1989; (b) Data from Hatze, 1976.

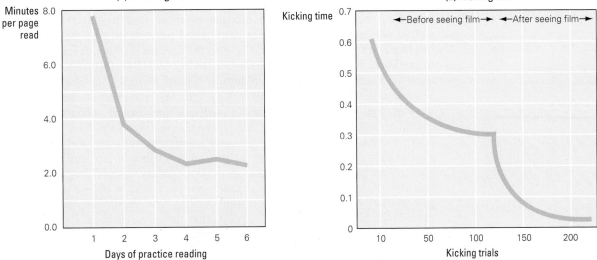

(a) Reading task

Minutes per page read

Days of practice reading

(b) Kicking task

Kicking time

◄—Before seeing film—► ◄—After seeing film—►

Kicking trials

power law of practice. A law stating that the degree to which a practice trial improves performance diminishes after a certain point, so that additional trials are needed to further improve the skill; learning occurs quickly at first, then slows.

increases in speed. This pattern is known as the **power law of practice**. It holds for a wide range of cognitive and perceptual-motor skills, both in humans and in other species.

When you first learned to use a computer keyboard, you had to search for keys, and the number of words you could type per minute was probably low. After your first year of using a keyboard, you probably had doubled or tripled the number of words you could type per minute. If your typing speed doubled after every year of practice, you would be typing incredibly fast by now! The power law of practice, however, predicts that this won't happen. According to the power law, each additional year of practice after the first produces smaller increases in typing speed; learning occurs quickly at first, but then gets slower.

It may seem obvious that as you become more proficient at a skill, there is less room for improvement. What is surprising about the power law of practice is that the rate at which practice loses its ability to improve performance does not depend on either the skill being practiced or the type of animal learning the skill. In many cases, psychologists can use a simple mathematical function (called a power function) to describe how rapidly individuals will acquire a skill; the number of additional practice trials necessary to improve a skill almost inevitably increases dramatically as the number of completed practice trials increases.

The power law of practice provides a useful description of how practice generally affects performance. It is possible to overcome this law, however, and enhance the effects of practice. For example, in one experiment, researchers asked a participant to kick a target as rapidly as possible. With visual feedback about his kicking speed, the participant was able to increase that speed, and his pattern of improvement was exactly what the power law of practice would predict (Hatze, 1976). When the man stopped improving, the researchers showed him a film comparing his movements with movements known to minimize kicking time. After seeing the film, the man improved his kicking speed considerably (Figure 8.3b). This is an example of *observational learning*, a topic we discuss in detail in Chapter 11. The participant observing the film formed memories of the observed performance techniques that he later used to improve his own performance. These memories can be viewed as an additional source of feedback about how successfully he was performing the kicking skill relative to what is physically possible.

All feedback is not equally helpful, and the kinds of feedback provided can strongly determine how practice affects performance. The secret to improvement is to discover what kinds of feedback will maximize the benefits of practicing a particular skill. Experiments show that frequent feedback in simple perceptual-motor tasks leads to good performance in the short term but mediocre performance in the long term, whereas infrequent feedback leads to mediocre performance in the short term but better performance in the long term (Schmidt & Wulf, 1997; Schmidt, Young, Swinnen, & Shapiro, 1989). For the most part, however, instructors, coaches, and their students discover through trial and error what types of feedback work best in each situation. For example, dance instructors have discovered that the visual feedback provided by mirrors enhances the effects of practicing dance movements, and most dance studios now have mirrors on the walls. Can you think of any similar advances that college professors have made in the last century in providing feedback to improve students' cognitive skills? One example might be online tutorials that provide immediate feedback about the accuracy of students' responses to intermittent quizzes; some research suggests that these can produce faster learning and greater achievement levels than classroom instruction (J. R. Anderson, Corbett, Koedinger, & Pelletier, 1995).

Timing and Sequencing of Practice Matters

Feedback is critical to the acquisition of skill memories because it affects how individuals perform the skills during practice. Certain forms of information that precede practice, such as instructional videos, can have similar effects. Skill memories do not depend only on the way skills are taught and practiced, however. They also depend on how practice time is apportioned. Concentrated, continuous practice, or **massed practice**, generally produces better performance in the short term, but **spaced practice**, spread out over several sessions, often leads to better retention in the long run (Arthur et al., 2010).

Consider the following classic experiment. Three groups of post office workers were trained to use a keyboard to control a letter-sorting machine. One group practiced 1 hour a day for 60 days. The other two groups practiced either 2 hours a day for 40 days or 4 hours a day for 20 days (Baddeley & Longman, 1978). Contrary to what you might guess, the group that practiced for only 1 hour a day (spaced practice) required fewer total hours of training than any other group to become proficient at using the keyboard (Figure 8.4). The downside was that this group had to be trained over a longer period—2 months instead of 1. Interestingly, when participants were surveyed about their satisfaction with their training schedule, those trained for 1 hour a day were the least satisfied, while those trained for 4 hours a day were the most satisfied, suggesting that satisfaction with a training program (or course) may not be a very good measure of the learning achieved in that program. Although researchers have conducted many studies to determine what kinds of practice schedules lead to optimal learning and performance, there is still no consensus about how to identify the best schedule for any given individual attempting to learn any particular skill.

Researchers also observe differences in the outcomes after equal amounts of practice when they compare different kinds of practice (as opposed to different schedules of practice). In this case, the comparison is between practice with a very limited set of materials and skills, a process called **constant practice**, and practice with more varied materials and skills, a process called **variable practice**. Constant practice consists of repeatedly practicing the same skill—for example, repeatedly attempting to throw a dart at the bull's-eye of a dartboard under fixed lighting conditions or attempting to master a single trick shot in pool. Variable practice consists of practicing a skill in a wider variety of conditions, such as attempting to hit each number on a dartboard under various levels of lighting or trying to improve one's performance at interviews by applying for a diverse range of jobs. Several studies have shown that variable practice leads to better performance in later tests. In one such study, individuals tracked targets that were moving along various paths. People who used variable practice to learn this task performed better, both in training sessions and in later tests, than individuals who trained with constant practice (Wulf & Schmidt, 1997). Variable practice is not always more effective than constant practice, however (van Rossum, 1990); researchers have not discovered how to reliably predict when variable practice will lead to better learning and performance.

Variable practice can sometimes lead to slower progress than constant practice. Even in these cases, however, later performance usually is superior (Schmidt & Bjork, 1992). Just as the benefits of

massed practice. Concentrated, continuous practice of a skill.

spaced practice. Practice of a skill that is spread out over several sessions.

constant practice. Practice involving a constrained set of materials and skills.

variable practice. Practice involving the performance of skills in a wide variety of contexts.

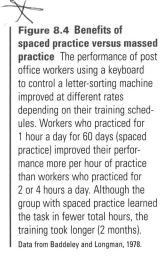

Figure 8.4 Benefits of spaced practice versus massed practice The performance of post office workers using a keyboard to control a letter-sorting machine improved at different rates depending on their training schedules. Workers who practiced for 1 hour a day for 60 days (spaced practice) improved their performance more per hour of practice than workers who practiced for 2 or 4 hours a day. Although the group with spaced practice learned the task in fewer total hours, the training took longer (2 months). Data from Baddeley and Longman, 1978.

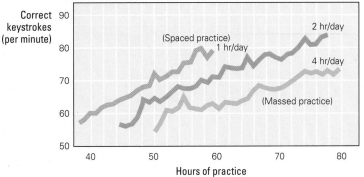

spaced training were not obvious to participants learning keyboard skills in the study depicted in Figure 8.4, the benefits of variable training are not always apparent during variable practice. One type of variable practice that has been shown to be particularly effective involves gradually increasing the difficulty of trials during training (Kagerer, Contreras-Vidal, & Stelmach, 1997; Sawers, Kelly, & Hahn, 2013). During gradual training, performance is initially easy and then is made incrementally more difficult as training progresses. Intuitively, you might think that spending several hours practicing a difficult task would lead to more improvement on that task than spending most of those hours practicing easier versions of the task followed by only a few hours practicing the actual task you need to perform. For many tasks, however, the opposite is true. Gradual training often leads to better overall performance, despite the fact that the practice trials require less effort overall. Musicians take advantage of this effect by initially practicing musical pieces at slower rates than they will ultimately be required to play them, and by practicing various musical scales. The timing, variability, and ordering of training trials can be as important as the quality of feedback and amount of practice. Surprisingly, making less effort (gradual training) spread out over longer periods (spaced practice) can enhance skill acquisition more than grueling, nonstop practice.

Skill Memories are Often Formed Unconsciously

When you acquire a skill, it is usually because you have made an effort to learn the skill over time. If you learn a skill and are able to verbalize how it is done, the process is called **explicit learning** (which creates *explicit memories*, described in Chapter 7). In many cases, however, it is possible to learn to perform certain skills without ever being aware that learning has occurred. You probably wouldn't be able to master kung fu without knowing that you're learning the moves, but you might be able to learn to be a better kisser without being aware that you're improving. Learning of the second sort, called **implicit learning**, probably happens to you more often than you think. Implicit learning produces implicit memories, which were defined in Chapter 7 (and mentioned above with reference to H.M.) as memories that are acquired without conscious awareness. Given this lack of conscious awareness, you'd be hard pressed to estimate how many skills you've acquired in this way. For all you know, you're implicitly learning right now!

Implicit skill learning has been studied in individuals with anterograde amnesia (like H.M.) and also in people without brain damage (Knowlton et al., 1996; Pohl, McDowd, Filion, Richards, & Stiers, 2001; Willingham, 1999; Wulf & Schmidt, 1997). We described in Chapter 7 the problems that H.M. and other individuals with anterograde amnesia have with learning and remembering events and facts. However, such individuals can acquire skills relatively normally, showing improvement from one session to the next even if they show no awareness that they have practiced or observed the skill in the past (Cohen, Poldrack, & Eichenbaum, 1997; Seger, 1994; Sun, Slusarz, & Terry, 2005). Individuals with anterograde amnesia make an effort to learn the skill during each session but always think they are trying it for the first time. The fact that their performance improves with each session demonstrates that they are forming skill memories even though they can't verbally describe prior practice sessions. H.M. was able to learn new perceptual-motor skills, but he did not know that he had learned them (Corkin, 2002; Gabrieli, Corkin, Mickel, & Growdon, 1993; Tranel, Damasio, Damasio, & Brandt, 1994).

One need not be amnesic, however, to learn skills implicitly. You may perform some task, such as washing windows, and incidentally learn an underlying skill that facilitates performance of that task; maybe you learn that circular rubbing movements shine the window brighter and faster than random rubbing. You may

explicit learning. A learning process that includes the ability to verbalize about the actions or events being learned.

implicit learning. Learning that occurs without the learner's awareness of improvements in performance or, in the case of people with amnesia, awareness that practice has occurred.

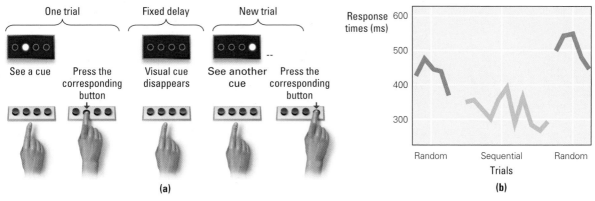

(a)
(b)

Figure 8.5 Serial reaction time task in the study of implicit learning (a) In a serial reaction time task, participants learn to press keys as rapidly as possible in response to visual cues provided on a computer screen. (b) Participants' reaction times are slower when the cues are presented in random order than when they are presented in a fixed sequence. Quicker reaction times for the sequential cues indicate that the participants implicitly learned to anticipate which key they needed to press next even though their verbal reports reveal no awareness that there was a fixed sequence.
Research from Robertson, 2007.

or may not realize that you have discovered a faster, better manner of execution. A task that psychologists commonly use to study implicit skill learning in people without brain damage is the **serial reaction time task**. In this task participants learn to press one of four keys as soon as a visual cue (a light) indicates which key to press (Figure 8.5a). The computer presents the visual cues in long sequences that are either unpredictably ordered (the so-called random condition) or ordered in a fixed sequence of about 12 cues (called the sequential or implicit learning condition). For example, if we designate the four keys from right to left as A through D, then the fixed sequence might be ABADBCDACBDC. Participants eventually begin to get a feel for the repeating sequential patterns and anticipate which key to press next, as reflected by faster reaction times for implicitly learned sequences relative to random sequences (Figure 8.5b). When researchers interview participants after training, however, they typically show no awareness that any of the sequences were repeating patterns (Exner, Koschack, & Irle, 2002). In other words, they have learned the sequences without knowing that they learned them, making their learning implicit.

As mentioned earlier in this chapter and in Chapter 7, people often have difficulty verbalizing what they have learned after mastering a perceptual-motor skill. This might seem to suggest that perceptual-motor skills are more likely than cognitive skills to be learned implicitly. But people can also acquire many components of cognitive skills through implicit learning. No one becomes a chess grand master simply by reading the rules of chess and listening to other players explaining why they made particular moves. Mathematical whizzes do not become experts by simply hearing about mathematical axioms and proofs (Lewis, 1981). Development of both of these skills requires extensive practice during which implicit learning undoubtedly occurs. In the case of cognitive skill acquisition, it is difficult to assess which abilities are improving independent of awareness, because the changes in thinking produced by practice are not easy to observe. Moreover, the learner would, by definition, be unaware of these changes and therefore unable to report them. Consequently, there is currently no way to assess whether implicit learning is more likely to occur during the learning of perceptual-motor or cognitive skills.

The distinction between implicit and explicit learning—one being unconscious, the other requiring conscious awareness—suggests they may be two quite different modes of forming skill memories. This distinction may not be as sharp as it seems, however (Robertson, 2007; Song, 2009). Because there are no definitive methods for showing that someone is unaware during learning (Hannula, Simons, & Cohen, 2005), it is difficult to identify any threshold point at which an

serial reaction time task. An experimental task that requires individuals to press keys in specific sequences on the basis of cues provided by a computer; used to study implicit learning.

It takes two (the combo)

unaware learner is transformed into an aware learner, but perhaps a continuum of awareness exists throughout the learning process. For example, you might become aware that you are improving at a skill before realizing what it is that you are doing differently, or you might be aware that your attempts at improving a skill (say, the skill of getting a date) are not working without recognizing what you are doing wrong. In this case, implicit and explicit learning would correspond to points along a continuum of awareness rather than to two different kinds of learning. Despite such ambiguities, there is evidence suggesting that conscious awareness may be a prerequisite for acquiring skills to certain levels of expertise. For example, elite athletes may consent to endure grueling practice sessions not because they enjoy such activities or because they are more talented and therefore have greater endurance than other athletes but because they are more aware of the necessity of such practice regimens for achieving the highest levels of performance (Yarrow, Brown, & Krakauer, 2009). So, although you may be able to learn many skills without making a conscious effort to do so, you're unlikely to accidently become a professional athlete, rock star, or kung fu master.

Expertise Requires Extensive Practice

When you practice a skill, you typically do so because you want to become better at performing that skill. To most people, "becoming better" means that their performance becomes more controlled and effortless. Say the skill you are practicing is juggling. The goal is to keep the objects moving in the air and in and out of your hands. Ideally, you'd like to be able to juggle while casually talking to a friend. In this case, your friend would know you are an expert juggler because you don't need to pay attention to what you are doing. The skill has become automatic. Some might even say that your juggling actions have become reflexive. Reflexes, however, are inborn, involuntary responses to stimuli, distinct from highly learned responses. Sequences of movements that an organism can perform virtually automatically (with minimal attention) are called **motor programs**—they are also sometimes referred to as *habits* (James, 1890; Graybiel, 2008). Unlike reflexes, motor programs can be either inborn or learned. Releasing an arrow from a bow is not an inborn reflex, but for the expert archer it has become as automatic and precise as a reflex. More complex action sequences such as juggling can also become motor programs.

motor program. A sequence of movements that an organism can perform automatically (with minimal attention).

What stage of skill acquisition has this juggler achieved?

Brooke Slezak/Getty Images

One way to determine whether a skill has become a motor program is to interrupt the action sequence and observe the results. For example, if someone grabs one of the balls in mid-air as you are juggling, does your arm still "catch and throw" the nonexistent ball? If so, it suggests that your juggling skill has become a motor program. In Chapter 5, we described rats that had learned to run down an alley to receive food and became so accustomed to doing this that they actually would run over a pile of food to reach the end of the alley; in this case, running down the alley had become a motor program.

Classifying highly learned perceptual-motor skills as motor programs is straightforward, but what about highly learned cognitive skills? Might they also, with extended practice, become motor programs? The surprising answer is yes. Think back to when you learned the multiplication tables. This probably required some practice, but now if someone asks you, "What is two times three?" you will respond promptly: "Six." You no longer need to think about quantities at all. You perceive the spoken words, and your brain automatically generates the motor sequence to produce the appropriate spoken word in response. Similarly, in the laboratory, once a person has solved the Tower of Hanoi problem many times, she has learned that particular movement sequences always lead to the solution. Eventually, practicing enables her to perform these motor sequences rapidly, without thinking about which disk goes where. In both cases, a cognitive skill has become a motor program.

Paul Fitts, a psychologist who focused on human movement, proposed that skill learning usually includes an initial period when an individual must exert some effort to encode a skill, acquiring information through observation, instruction, trial and error, or some combination of these methods (Fitts, 1964). This period is followed by stages in which performance of the skill becomes more "automatic," or habitual. Fitts called the first stage of skill learning the **cognitive stage**, to emphasize the active thinking required to encode the skill. When your roommate is making ramen based on written instructions or memories of the steps that were previously successful, she is in the cognitive stage of skill acquisition. During this stage, she bases her performance on what she knows, as well as on her ability to control her movements and thoughts so as to accomplish specific goals. If you're learning to juggle for the first time, then you will initially have to find out what the steps are and keep them constantly in mind. This, too, corresponds to the cognitive stage of skill learning.

Fitts called the second stage in his model of skill acquisition the **associative stage**. During this stage, learners begin using stereotyped actions when performing the skill and rely less on actively recalled memories of steps that can be verbalized. The first few times you play a video game, for example, you may need to keep reminding yourself about the combinations of controller button presses that are necessary to produce certain outcomes. Eventually, you no longer need to think about these combinations. When you decide that you want a particular action to occur on the screen, your hands do what is necessary to make that action happen. What began as a process of understanding and following instructions has become a process of remembering and reenacting previously performed actions.

Of course, mastering the skills needed to succeed when playing a video game requires far more than simply memorizing hand movements. You must be able to produce very rapid sequences of precisely timed combinations of those movements to achieve specific outcomes. To reach high levels of performance, your movement patterns must become quick and effortless. Fitts described this third level of skill learning as the **autonomous stage**—the stage at which the skill or subcomponents of the skill have become motor programs. At this stage it may be impossible to verbalize in any detail the specific movements being performed, and performance may have become much less dependent on memories for events and facts that can be verbalized. In fact, at this stage, thinking too much about what you are doing when you perform a skill can actually impair performance—a phenomenon related to "choking" under pressure. If you can juggle while having a casual conversation, you have reached the autonomous stage. You can perform the skill without paying much attention to what you're doing, and if someone unexpectedly snatches a ball, your arms will continue to move as if the missing ball were still there.

cognitive stage. The first stage in Fitts's model of skill learning; in this stage, an individual must exert some effort to encode the skill on the basis of information gained through observation, instruction, and trial and error.

associative stage. The second stage in Fitts's model of skill learning; in this stage, learners begin using stereotyped actions when performing a skill and rely less on actively recalled memories of rules.

autonomous stage. The third stage in Fitts's model of skill learning; in this stage, a skill or subcomponents of the skill become motor programs.

Simon had mastered clicking his mouse while he slept, but he would soon learn this was useless without the correct posture.

Patrick Hickey/cartoonstock.com

Table 8.2 Fitts's three-stage model of skill learning

Stage	Characteristics	Example
1. Cognitive stage	Performance is based on rules that can be verbalized.	Using written instructions to set up a tent
2. Associative stage	Actions become stereotyped.	Setting up a tent in a fixed sequence, without instructions
3. Autonomous stage	Movements seem automatic.	Setting up a tent while carrying on a discussion about politics

The model of skill acquisition developed by Fitts (summarized in Table 8.2) provides a useful framework for relating skill performance and expertise to practice. Although psychologists have developed this model extensively over the past 50 years, many recent versions retain the same basic progression of stages (Ackerman, 2007). The "three stages" are, of course, abstractions. There is generally no single performance that can be identified as the last performance belonging to, say, stage one. Additionally, the three-stage model of skill acquisition is primarily descriptive. It won't help you predict how much practice you need to convert your skill memories into motor programs or give you pointers about how and when you should practice. The model does suggest, however, that skill memories may rely on different memory processes as practice progresses.

Some psychologists argue that practice alone determines who will become an expert (Ericsson, Krampe, & Tesch-Romer, 1993; Ericsson & Lehman, 1996). In particular, it has been argued that the amount of deliberate practice is the main determinant of skill level and that a minimum of 10,000 hours of practice is what is required for an individual to become an expert at a particular skill. This viewpoint has been challenged by studies showing that mastery of skills at an early age (for example, playing chess or a musical instrument) is predictive of which individuals will reach the highest levels of performance (Howard, 2009), even among individuals that have experienced similar amounts of practice. Until more is known about how practice affects skill memories, it will be difficult to reliably predict either an individual's maximum level of skill performance or the amount of practice someone needs to reach peak performance. In any case, scientists investigating skill memory in experts suggest that, for all individuals, the total amount of practice is critical in predicting whether a person will be an expert at performing a particular skill.

Researchers studying expertise have occasionally examined the abilities of athletes, chess masters, or other professional game players. There are several reasons for this. First, people who learn to play games outside a research lab serve as good examples of "real world" skill learning. Second, it is relatively easy to find people with widely varying levels of expertise in sports or games such as chess, and individual variations in ability often can be quantitatively assessed based on performance in competitions. Finally, sports and games require a variety of perceptual-motor and cognitive skills, making them useful for investigating many different psychological phenomena.

For example, a person must practice thousands of hours to become a master chess player, learning more than 50,000 "rules" for playing chess in the process (Simon & Gilmartin, 1973). Researchers studying expert chess players found that experts and less experienced players scan the game board (a visual-motor skill) differently (Charness, Reingold, Pomplun, & Stampe, 2001). When chess masters look at chess pieces, their eyes move rapidly to focus on a small number of locations on the board, whereas amateur chess players typically scan larger numbers of locations and do so more slowly. When experts stop moving their eyes, they are more likely than non-experts to focus on empty squares or on strategically relevant chess pieces. Succeeding at chess clearly requires cognitive skills in terms of implementing strategies and recognizing threats, but it also seems to depend on implicitly learned visual scanning patterns.

Differences in visual processing are also seen in expert athletes. Inexperienced soccer players tend to watch the ball and the player who is passing it, whereas expert players focus more on the movements of players who do not have the ball (Williams, Davids, Burwitz, & Williams, 1992). A recent study of basketball players found that experts were better able to predict the outcome of a shot based on viewing a player's movements before the ball was released than were amateur players or professional spectators (Aglioti, Cesari, Romani, & Urgesi, 2008). These studies suggest that *perceptual learning* (discussed in Chapter 3) may contribute to the superior abilities of experts.

Talent Takes Time to Blossom

Different individuals start with different capabilities, and the extent to which practice can improve their performance levels also varies from one person to the next. People who seem to master a skill with little effort (the way Mozart mastered anything related to music) are often described as having a **talent** or "gift" for that skill. The people who start off performing a skill well are often those who end up becoming experts (Howard, 2009), but someone who initially has little ability to perform a skill may, with practice, become better at that skill than someone who seemed destined to become a star. So, if your significant other is currently lacking in the kissing department, don't lose hope! Additional practice (or guidance) may yet unleash his or her full potential.

What role does talent play in achieving expertise in cognitive or perceptual-motor skills? Even child prodigies are not born able to perform the skills that make them famous. Like everyone else, they learn to perform these skills. Mozart's father, a professional musician, trained Mozart extensively from a young age. So it's difficult to determine to what extent Mozart's musical abilities were a result of his musical talents versus his father's teaching abilities and persistence. Most modern research equates talent with genetic predispositions that positively affect an individual's acquired abilities.

Psychologists have attempted to gauge the role of genetics in skill learning and performance by conducting studies with twins—some identical (sharing 100% of their genes) and some fraternal (sharing, like other siblings, 50% of their genes)—who were raised in different homes. Other twin studies look at the differences between twins reared together. In one large study of twins reared apart, researchers at the University of Minnesota trained participants to perform a skill in which they had to keep the end of a pointed stick, called a stylus, above a target drawn on the edge of a rotating disk, as shown in Figure 8.6a (Fox, Hershberger, & Bouchard, 1996). Researchers frequently use this task, known as the **rotary pursuit task**, to study perceptual-motor skill learning. The task requires precise hand-eye coordination. When individuals first attempt the rotary pursuit task, they generally show some ability to keep the stylus over the target but often have to adjust the speed and trajectory of their arm movements to correct for errors (such as lagging behind the target). With additional practice, most individuals rapidly improve their accuracy, increasing the amount of time they can keep the stylus tip over the target (Figure 8.6b).

The researchers found that when they trained twins to perform the rotary pursuit task, identical twins' abilities to keep the stylus on the target became

talent. A person's genetically endowed ability to perform a skill better than most.

rotary pursuit task. An experimental task that requires individuals to keep the end of a pointed stick (stylus) above a fixed point on a rotating disk; used to study perceptual-motor skill learning.

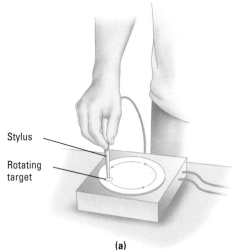

(a)

Stylus

Rotating target

Time on target (s)

Trial

(b)

Degree of correlation

Identical Twins

Fraternal Twins

Trial block

(c)

Figure 8.6 Effects of practice on performance of the rotary pursuit task (a) In the rotary pursuit task, a person gradually learns to keep a stylus above a particular point on a rotating disk. (b) With repeated trials, individuals become better at keeping the stylus over the target. (c) In studies of how twins perform on this task, correlations between the performances of identical twins increased slightly as training progressed, indicating that, after training, the accuracy at tracking a rotating target is similar for each twin. In contrast, correlations between the performances of fraternal twins decreased with training, indicating that their capacity to track the rotating target becomes less similar with practice. These findings suggest that practice decreases the effects of previous experience (i.e., nurture) on motor performance and increases the effects of genetic influences (nature).

(b, c) Data from Fox et al., 1996.

more similar as training progressed, whereas fraternal twins' abilities became more dissimilar. That is, during training, the performance of one twin became more correlated with the performance of the second twin when the two twins shared 100% of their genes (Figure 8.6c). Put another way, if you were to view videos of the participants' hands after training as they attempted to keep the stylus above the rotating target, you would judge the movements of identical twins' hands to be the most similar. Their movements might remind you of synchronized swimming. In the case of fraternal twins, however, you would probably judge their movements after training to be dissimilar. For example, one twin might keep the stylus over the target continuously, while the other twin might have to increase her speed a bit every few seconds to catch up with the target.

One interpretation of these data is that, during the experiment, practice decreases the effects of participants' prior experiences on the accuracy of their tracking movements and increases the effects of genetic influences. In other words, the more practice people have, the more their performance differences are due to genetic differences. Identical twins have the same genes, so when practice increases the contributions of genes to their perceptual-motor skills, their performances become more similar. Because fraternal twins have different genes, increasing the role of their genes in behavior makes their behavior more different. Researchers have tested for such effects only in tasks, such as

Are Some Cognitive Skills Easier for Men Than Women?

In 2005, the president of Harvard University, Larry Summers, provoked a national uproar when he suggested that one reason why there are more men than women in top-tier science and engineering positions is because of "different availability of aptitude at the high end." Essentially, he was suggesting that among the most scientifically or technologically talented people that are born, there are more men than women. If this claim had been made in relation to athletic skills, then it probably would not have made a ripple, because one need only consult the record books (or rosters of professional sports leagues) to see that the fastest sprints, highest jumps, and longest shot puts were all performed by men. This does not mean that men are able to learn to perform all (or even most) perceptual-motor skills at levels beyond what is possible for women, but it certainly supports the idea that there are some biological qualities (e.g., strength and height) that give men an edge when it comes to reaching the upper echelons of athletic performance. Might something similar be true for cognitive skill learning by males?

If one examines the historical record of scientific and technological achievements, then it is clear that men have received more accolades and high-level positions than women. Unlike the findings in modern sports, however, this pattern could easily reflect sociocultural constraints rather than intrinsic differences in capacities. Stronger evidence of sex differences in cognitive performance comes from standardized high school achievement exams such as the Advanced Placement (AP) tests. In these tests, substantially more men receive high scores in Calculus, Chemistry, and Physics despite the fact that more women take the tests (Ackerman, 2006). But these data do not show that men are better able to learn about scientific topics; they show that men currently are acquiring more cognitive skills related to retrieving and applying scientific knowledge during their early education. The resulting greater facility with scientific knowledge would make the learning of related cognitive skills in college courses easier, and in this sense, scientific and technological skills would be easier for the most capable male undergraduates to learn than they would be for the most capable females. However, there is currently no way to assess whether these differences in performance reflect differences in the intellectual talents of men versus women or whether they reflect differences in the interests, motivation, instruction, or practice of men versus women when learning about science and technology. Until more is known about how neural mechanisms constrain learning capacity, it may be impossible to assess which features of male or female brains might enhance (or depress) learning of different cognitive skills.

---

the rotary pursuit task, that require individuals to learn simple perceptual-motor skills. It is possible, however, that practice has similar effects on more complex perceptual-motor and cognitive skills. For example, perhaps you possess hidden talents that you're unaware of because you have never practiced the skills that would reveal those talents or have not practiced them enough. Perhaps future genetic analyses will discover biological correlates of specific talents, thus permitting identification of individuals who have inherited propensities to perform certain skills exceptionally well. (See "Learning and Memory in Everyday Life" above for a brief look at whether men and women are born with different innate abilities in what they can learn.)

Retrieving Existing Memories

Skill memories are often highly restricted in terms of how they can be used (Brady, 2008; Goodwin, Eckerson, & Voll, 2001; Goodwin & Meeuwsen, 1995; Ma, Trombly, & Robinson-Podolski, 1999). You may have mastered the culinary skills needed to make great Italian food, but this will not make you a great sushi chef. In some cases, skill memories are so specific that the introduction of additional informative cues can disrupt retrieval. For example, after individuals were trained to touch a target with a stylus without visual feedback about their arm movements, their performance was *worse* when researchers allowed them to see their arm moving as they carried out the task (Proteau, Marteniuk, & Levesque, 1992). Most people normally use visual feedback when learning to aim at a target, so it is surprising that providing such feedback can interfere with the skill memory.

In other cases, skills seem to transfer to novel situations relatively easily. For example, you learned to write with your right or left hand, and you may even have practiced with each hand, but have you ever written with your mouth or feet? If you try, you will discover that you can write semi-legible text using these and other body parts. You are able to transfer what you have learned about writing with one hand to other body parts despite large differences in the specific movements you must perform to do so. In sports, teams spend much of their time practicing in scrimmages, with the hope that these experiences will transfer positively to similar situations in real games. If skills learned during practice did not transfer to real games, it is unlikely that so many coaches in so many different sports would train their teams in this way.

The restricted applicability of some learned skills to specific situations is known as **transfer specificity**. This phenomenon led Thorndike to propose that the transfer of learned abilities to novel situations depends on the number of elements in the new situation that are identical to those in the situation in which the skills were encoded (Thorndike & Woodworth, 1901). Thorndike's proposal, called the **identical elements theory**, provides one possible account of why transfer specificity occurs. It predicts that a tennis player who trained on hard courts might suffer a bit the first time she attempted to play on a clay court and would do progressively worse as the game was changed from tennis to badminton or table tennis. Conceptually, transfer specificity is closely related to transfer-appropriate processing, which was described in Chapter 7. The main differences between the two stem from whether the memories being recalled are memories of skills or memories of facts and events.

When you perform a skill that you have learned in the past, you are generalizing from a past experience to the present (generalization is discussed in detail in Chapter 6). From this perspective, every performance of a skill involves transfer of training. For example, each time you open a door, you are making use of skill memories you acquired by opening doors in the past. Opening a door can require combinations of complex actions: key grasping, inserting, and turning; handle grasping, pushing, pulling, or sliding; knob turning, latch unhooking, and so on. At this point in your life, you probably have encountered so many different doors that you are easily able to open almost any door you encounter.

Acquiring the ability to learn novel tasks rapidly based on frequent experiences with similar tasks is called **learning set formation** (Harlow, 1949), or learning-to-learn. Learning set formation occurs in infants learning basic perceptual-motor skills (Adolph & Joh, 2009), as well as in adults learning more complex motor skills (Ranganathan et al., 2014; Braun, Mehring, & Wolpert, 2010). Learning set formation can also play an important role in the development and application of cognitive skills. For example, after years of practice, professional actors acquire the ability to quickly adopt the personas of fictional characters and to memorize detailed scripts and action sequences in a relatively short period. Actors implicitly use many of the strategies that are known to benefit memory encoding, such as elaboration during encoding (discussed in Chapter 7) and chunking (discussed in Chapter 9), suggesting that at least one of the skills that

transfer specificity. The restricted applicability of learned skills to specific situations.

identical elements theory. Thorndike's proposal that learned abilities transfer to novel situations to an extent that depends on the number of elements in the new situation that are identical to those in the situation in which the skills were encoded.

learning set formation. Acquisition of the ability to learn novel tasks rapidly based on frequent experiences with similar tasks.

Janet Kimber/Getty Images

| Will practicing the "Guitar Hero" video game help this man improve his skill at playing a real guitar?

actors acquire and transfer flexibly throughout their careers is the ability to rapidly encode and recall dialogue (Noice & Noice, 2006).

Test Your Knowledge

Tasks That Test Skill Memory

Several tasks are commonly used to investigate different phenomena related to skill memory, including the Tower of Hanoi, the serial reaction time task, and the rotary pursuit task. Identify which aspects of skill memories each of these three tasks has been useful for testing. (Answers appear in the back of the book.)

When Memory Fails

Like the strength of memories for facts and events, the memorability of a skill—how well the skill, after being acquired, is performed on a later occasion—depends on the complexity of the skill, how well the skill memory was encoded in the first place, how often the skill has subsequently been performed, and the conditions in which recall is attempted (Arthur, Bennett, Stanush, & McNelly, 1998). The common wisdom that you never forget how to ride a bicycle once you learn to do it is not accurate. Although skill memories can last a lifetime, they do deteriorate with non-use. Generally, retention of perceptual-motor skills is better than retention of cognitive skills, but unless you actively maintain your bike-riding skills, the skill memories you created when you first learned to ride will gradually deteriorate.

Researchers have studied the forgetting of events and facts much more than they have studied the forgetting of skills. Perhaps this is because if someone loses the ability to do something, it is hard to judge whether he has forgotten how to do it, or forgotten that he knows how to do it, or lost the physical control or strength necessary to perform what he recalls. Loss of motor control does not imply that a skill memory is forgotten. To the outside observer, however, it may be impossible to distinguish whether someone knows how to perform a skill but has impaired movement abilities or whether the person has forgotten how to perform the skill.

Psychologists call loss of a skill through non-use **skill decay**. Most of the data collected so far indicate that skill decay follows patterns similar to those seen in the forgetting of memories for events and facts. Motor deficits and injuries (including brain damage) can clearly affect skill decay because they are likely to lead to non-use of learned skills.

In some ways, forgetting a skill is like learning it in reverse. Not performing the skill is almost the opposite of practice: if you don't use it, you lose it. Most forgetting occurs soon after the last performance of the skill; as time goes by, less and less forgetting occurs. Thus, forgetting curves are similar to learning curves. Forgetting occurs quickly at first, then gets slower (as is seen with memories for lists of nonsense words in Figure 1.5 and for passive forgetting of television shows in Figure 7.6).

Does the mere passage of time cause a skill to be "unlearned"? It often may seem this way, but forgetting can also result when new memories interfere with the recollection of old memories. As time passes, you perform more new skills, creating more memories that potentially interfere with the recollection of earlier skill memories. (Recall from Chapter 7 that interference and decay are also involved in the forgetting of memories for events and facts.) Much of this interference can occur without any awareness on the part of the person attempting to

skill decay. Loss of a skill because of non-use.

Mom dancing: retrieval interference, skill decay, or lack of good judgment?

recall a skill. For example, you might have difficulty recalling some of the dances you learned when you were younger but easily recall dance steps you learned recently. Rather than thinking this recent learning is hampering your ability to perform the old dances, you'd probably assume that you can't remember an older dance simply because it has been so long since you last did it. However, there is no subjective way for you to distinguish whether your forgetting is due to the passage of time or due to interference.

Interference of skill memories during recall can occur even within a single day. Students trained to perform a finger-tapping task, similar to the serial reaction time task discussed above, demonstrated more rapid and accurate pressing times after a period of sleep (Walker, Brakefield, Hobson, & Stickgold, 2003; Walker, Brakefield, Morgan, Hobson, & Stickgold, 2002; Walker, Brakefield, Seidman, et al., 2003). This simple task qualifies as a perceptual-motor skill because the students' ability to perform it improved with practice. If students learned to press keys in two different sequences on the same day, sleep-dependent enhancement of their performance was seen only for the *second* sequence learned. However, if participants learned the second sequence one day after the first sequence, sleep enhanced the performance of both sequences. Interestingly, if on the second day the students reviewed the first day's sequence immediately before learning the new sequence, then on the third day sleep enhanced their accuracy on only the second sequence. Thus, not only can practicing two skills on the same day interfere with retention of memories for the first skill, but reviewing a recently learned skill before beginning to practice a new one can interfere with subsequent recall of the skill that was reviewed! These findings highlight the intimate relationship between skill acquisition and skill recall and the fragile nature of newly acquired skill memories. Note, however, that athletes and musicians commonly practice multiple skills in parallel with no obvious evidence of interference, and variable practice generally leads to better long-term performance than constant practice. Thus, skills more complex or more distinctive than learning sequences of finger movements may be less susceptible to interference effects.

Interim Summary

- Memories for perceptual-motor skills are memories for sensory-guided movement patterns; they enable us to flexibly perform most physical actions.

- Memories for cognitive skills are memories for how to solve problems, apply strategies, and manipulate information: they enable us to think.

- Skill memories differ from memories for facts and events in that they are more difficult to verbalize and depend more on practice.

- Feedback about performance, or knowledge of results, is critical to the effectiveness of practice.

- The power law of practice, which holds for a wide range of cognitive and perceptual-motor skills, states that the extent to which practice can lead to further improvements decreases with extended practice.

- Several principles determine how new skill memories are formed and generalize: (1) Massed practice produces better performance in the short term, but spaced practice leads to faster learning and better retention. (2) Constant practice often does not improve performance as much as variable practice. (3) Gradual training can enhance skill learning despite requiring less effort overall.

- Practice can decrease the effects of past learning on performance and increase the effects of genetic influences.

- Generalization of skill learning depends on the similarity between the conditions during retrieval and the conditions experienced while learning the skill.

- Learning set formation occurs when the learning of several similar actions leads to more rapid acquisition of related actions.

8.2 Brain Substrates

What neural systems do humans and other animals need to acquire memories of perceptual-motor and cognitive skills? Is there something special about the human brain that makes acquisition of new skills easier for humans than it is for other animals? Or do humans use the same neural systems to learn skills as other animals do, but in slightly different ways? How might we judge whether the skill memories that underlie a dolphin's ability to use a sponge differ from the skill memories a human uses to juggle?

Neuroscientists have used neuroimaging and neurophysiological recordings to monitor brain activity in humans and other animals during the acquisition and performance of skills. These techniques have enabled researchers to identify several brain regions involved in the formation and recall of skill memories. Scientists have also compared brain activity in experts and amateurs performing various skills, as well as in individuals before and after they have learned a particular skill. Neuropsychological studies of skill learning by patients with brain damage are also an important source of information. Through these kinds of research, scientists hope to associate stages of skill acquisition with changes in brain structure and activity.

All movements and postures require coordinated muscle activity. As you saw in Chapter 2, a major function of the nervous system is to initiate and control patterns of muscle activity. The spinal cord and brainstem play a critical role in the performance of perceptual-motor skills by controlling and coordinating movements. Brain regions dedicated to sensation and perception, including the sensory cortices, are also involved, processing information that contributes to the guidance of movements. Of these, the somatosensory and visual systems (described in Chapter 2) are particularly important for learning perceptual-motor skills. Remember the experiment described earlier in this chapter in which researchers instructed the participant to kick a target as quickly as possible? He improved at the task by processing visual feedback about how effectively he was coordinating the muscles in his leg.

In this section, we describe how practicing skills can change neural circuits. Although you can form skill memories in ways other than practice (such as studying videos of expert athletes or kissers), neuroscientists have focused much of their effort on understanding the incremental effects of practice on brain

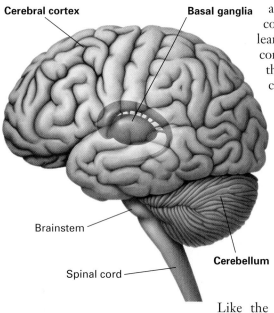

Cerebral cortex

Basal ganglia

Brainstem

Spinal cord

Cerebellum

Figure 8.7 Brain regions that contribute to skill learning Skill-memory systems in the brain include the basal ganglia, cerebral cortex, and cerebellum. These three regions modulate the control of movements by circuits in the brainstem and spinal cord.

activity during skill learning. Sensory processing and motor control by circuits in the spinal cord are clearly necessary for learning and performing perceptual-motor skills. However, the core elements of skill learning seem to depend in particular on three other areas of the brain (introduced in Chapter 2 and discussed in Chapters 3 through 7): the basal ganglia, the cerebral cortex, and the cerebellum (Figure 8.7). When any of these brain regions becomes dysfunctional, the performance and learning of both cognitive and perceptual-motor skills become seriously impaired.

The Basal Ganglia and Skill Learning

Basal ganglia is one of the few names for a brain structure that literally describe the region (or in this case regions) to which they refer. You may recall from Chapter 5 that the basal ganglia are a collection of ganglia (clusters of neurons) that lie at the base of the forebrain (the most prominent part of the human brain). The basal ganglia are positioned close to the hippocampus (see Figure 2.3). Like the hippocampus, the basal ganglia receive large numbers of inputs from cortical neurons. In fact, most cortical areas send inputs to the basal ganglia. These inputs provide the basal ganglia with information about what is happening in the world—in particular, about the sensory stimuli the person is experiencing. Many of these cortical inputs are initially processed by the *dorsal striatum*, a subregion of the basal ganglia that we describe in greater detail in Chapter 5, as it is known to play an important role in operant conditioning. The basal ganglia send output signals mainly to the thalamus (affecting interactions between neurons in the thalamus and motor cortex) and to the brainstem (influencing signals sent to the spinal cord). By modulating these motor control circuits, the basal ganglia play a role in initiating and maintaining movement.

The basal ganglia are particularly important for controlling the velocity, direction, and amplitude of movements, as well as for preparing to move (Desmurget, Grafton, Vindras, Grea, & Turner, 2003; Graybiel, 1995; R. S. Turner, Grafton, Votaw, Delong, & Hoffman, 1998). For example, suppose you are performing the rotary pursuit task. You need to move your arm in a circle at a velocity matching that of the rotating target. In this task, your basal ganglia will use information from your visual system about the movements of the target, the stylus, and your arm, as well as information from your somatosensory system about the position of your arm, to help control the direction and velocity of your arm movements. Similarly, if you dive into a pool to retrieve a coin, your basal ganglia will help you avoid colliding with the bottom of the pool.

Given all the interconnections between the basal ganglia and motor systems, it's not surprising that disruption of activity in the basal ganglia impairs skill learning. Such disruption does not, however, seem to affect the formation and recall of memories for events and facts. Consider the case of Muhammad Ali. Ali was one of the most agile and skilled boxers of his era, but his career was ended by a gradual loss of motor control and coordination. Doctors identified these deficits as resulting from Parkinson's disease, a disorder that disables basal ganglia circuits (we discuss this disease in more detail later in the chapter). Over time, the loss of basal ganglia function resulting from Parkinson's disease affects even the most basic of skills, such as walking. Whereas H.M.'s hippocampal damage (described in Chapter 7) prevented him from reporting on his past experiences, Muhammad Ali's basal ganglia dysfunction hinders his use of skill memories and his ability to learn new skills; it has not affected his memory for facts or events.

Many researchers suspect that processing in the basal ganglia is a key step in forming skill memories, although how it contributes is still debated (Barnes, Kubota, Hu, Jin, & Graybiel, 2005; Graybiel, 2005, 2008). Most researchers agree, however, that practicing a skill can change how basal ganglia circuits participate in the performance of that skill and that synaptic plasticity is a basic neural mechanism enabling such changes (Conn, Battaglia, Marino, & Nicoletti, 2005; Graybiel, 2008). We describe here experimental results that show the importance of the basal ganglia not only for performing skills but also for forming and accessing skill memories.

Learning Deficits After Lesions

Much of what is known about the role of basal ganglia in skill learning comes from studies of rats learning to navigate mazes, such as the radial maze shown in Figure 7.2. In the standard radial maze task, rats learn to search the arms in the maze for food without repeating visits to the arms they have already searched. This task simulates some features of natural foraging (because food does not magically reappear at locations where a rat has just eaten) and has often been used to test rats' memories for events and locations (discussed in Chapter 7). However, the entrances to the arms of the maze are all very similar, so unless the rat remembers specifically which arms it has visited, it is likely to go to the same arm more than once. In early sessions, this is just what rats do. They often go to the same arm multiple times and consequently waste a lot of time running back and forth along arms that contain no food. With practice, the rats learn that they can get more food for their effort by keeping track of where they have been, and they make fewer repeat visits to the same arm—their performance improves incrementally with practice, and so their ability to navigate through the maze is a skill. Food acts as a kind of feedback in the radial maze task, in that correct performance leads to food.

To learn to navigate the radial maze efficiently, rats must remember certain aspects of past events. Not surprisingly, rats with hippocampal damage have major problems with this task (Figure 8.8a). Even after many sessions, they continue to visit arms they have visited before. In contrast, rats with basal ganglia damage learn this task as easily as rats with no brain damage. This shows

Figure 8.8 Effects of brain damage on rats' learning in a radial maze (a) When placed in a maze with food at the end of each arm, intact control rats learn, over repeated trials, to avoid revisiting arms they have already visited. Rats with basal ganglia damage can also learn this, but rats with a dysfunctional hippocampus cannot. (b) Intact rats can also learn to enter only the illuminated arms in a radial maze. Rats with hippocampal damage can learn this, too, but rats with basal ganglia damage cannot. This result shows that basal ganglia damage can disrupt perceptual-motor skill learning.

Data from Packard et al., 1989.

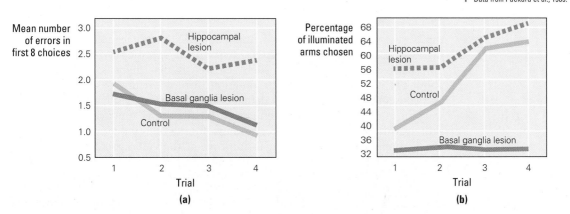

(a)

(b)

that basal ganglia damage does not disrupt rats' memories for events, nor does it prevent them from performing the skills necessary to find food in a radial maze.

Researchers can modify the radial maze task slightly to make it less dependent on memories of past events. If instead of putting food in all the arms, the experimenter places food only in arms that are illuminated, rats quickly learn to avoid the nonilluminated arms (Figure 8.8b). Rats with hippocampal damage can learn this version of the task because they only need to associate light with food, which does not require keeping track of arms they've visited. Surprisingly, rats with basal ganglia damage have difficulty learning this "simpler" version of the task. They continue to search nonilluminated arms even though they never find food in those arms (Packard, Hirsh, & White, 1989). Basal ganglia damage seems to prevent rats from learning the perceptual-motor skill of avoiding dark arms and entering illuminated arms.

Rats with brain damage show similar learning deficits in another task: the Morris water maze. In the standard version of this maze, experimenters fill a circular tank with murky water. They then place rats in the tank, and the rats must swim around until they discover a platform hidden just beneath the water surface. Once a rat finds the platform, it no longer has to swim, and the trial is over. Researchers measure the time it takes a rat to find the platform and use this as a measure of learning. Intact rats gradually learn the location of the hidden platform after repeated trials in the tank. In this case, the skill the rats have learned is to direct their swimming movements based on visual cues present around the tank. With practice, rats become better at selecting which directions to swim given their observations of which cues are currently visible. Rats with hippocampal damage have severe difficulties learning this standard task but have no problem learning the task if the platform is visible at the surface of the water. Rats with basal ganglia damage can learn to swim to the location of the platform whether it is visible or not. This seems to suggest that basal ganglia damage does not affect a rat's ability to learn this task.

Tests of transfer of training, however, tell a different story. If experimenters move a visible platform in the Morris water maze to a new location during testing, rats with hippocampal damage (or no damage) swim directly to the platform to escape the water. Rats with basal ganglia damage, however, swim to where the platform used to be and only afterward do they find the platform in its new location (McDonald & White, 1994). One interpretation of this finding is that rats with basal ganglia damage have difficulty learning to swim toward a platform to escape the water (even when the platform is clearly visible) and instead learn to swim to a particular location in the tank to escape the water. This study illustrates that just because two animals may seem to be performing a skill in the same way doesn't mean that their skill memories and their ability to use those memories in novel situations are equivalent.

These and other experiments with rats have led researchers to conclude that the basal ganglia are particularly important in perceptual-motor learning that involves generating motor responses based on specific environmental cues. The basic assumption behind such research is that there is nothing unique about the way the basal ganglia function in rats learning to navigate mazes, and consequently basal ganglia damage should disrupt skill learning in similar ways in humans. Conversely, enhanced basal ganglia function may facilitate skill learning. For example, researchers found that individuals with larger basal ganglia were the quickest to improve at the video game Space Fortress (Erickson et al., 2010). (See "Learning and Memory in Everyday Life" on the next page for more insight into how video game playing might in turn affect brain function.)

Are Video Games Good for the Brain?

Since the advent of television, people have been spending much of their lives staring at the glow of a rectangular screen. Video games have transformed passive viewing into an interactive process, and today's video games are as complex as any sport, card game, or board game. Video games are quickly replacing other recreational activities as the preferred pastime of children around the world. Many parents are concerned that this new pastime is turning children's brains into mush and that the skills acquired by playing such games are worthless. What is actually going on? Does video game playing have a negative impact on a person's mental capacities?

Video games have some advantages over traditional games. They offer a wide variety of experiences and options, they build expertise without requiring instruction from an expert, they present minimal risk of injury, and they can be played in any weather at any time. On the other hand, video games are blamed for provoking teen violence, contributing to obesity and a general lack of physical fitness, reducing literacy, decreasing opportunities for face-to-face interactions with family members and peers, and occupying children's minds with useless information (see C. A. Anderson & Bushman, 2001, for a review of the scientific literature on this topic).

The question of whether video games are good or bad for your brain has received little scientific study. One series of experiments found that college students who played high-action video games such as Grand Theft Auto 3, Crazy Taxi, Counter-Strike, and Spider-Man at least 1 hour a day, at least 4 days a week, for at least 6 months had increased visual attention abilities compared with students who did not play video games (Green & Bavelier, 2003). The reported benefits of playing fast-action games included increased visual capacity and enhanced spatial attention, with an increased ability to apprehend and count sets of visual stimuli. Interestingly, a control group that spent the same amount of time playing a non-action video game, Tetris, showed no enhancement in visual attention. However, critics suggest that the apparent benefits in these studies are a statistical artifact rather than an effect of video game playing (Unsworth et al., 2015).

There is increasing interest in using video games as educational aids (Howard-Jones et al., 2014), and as a way of slowing down cognitive decline in the elderly (Mishra & Gazzaley, 2014). Extensive playing of video games undoubtedly can change the structure and function of a player's brain, otherwise players would never improve. Do such brain changes have benefits (or costs) for any skills other than video-game playing? As with transfer of other skills, the answer likely depends on how much overlap there is between the skills learned in the games and skills used in other non-gaming situations.

Neural Activity During Perceptual-Motor Skill Learning

Measures of neural activity in the basal ganglia during learning provide further clues about the role of the basal ganglia in the formation of skill memories. Experimenters can train rats to turn right or left in a T-shaped maze in response to a sound cue that the rats hear just before reaching the intersection where they must turn (Figure 8.9). For example, an experimenter releases a rat in the maze, and then a computer plays a specific sound instructing the rat to make a right turn. If the rat turns to the right, the experimenter gives the rat food (as discussed in Chapter 5, this is a particularly effective form of feedback). With practice, rats learn to perform this simple perceptual-motor skill accurately. Researchers can use electrodes implanted in rats before training to record how neurons in the basal ganglia fire as rats learn the T maze task (Jog, Kubota, Connolly, Hillegaart, & Graybiel, 1999).

Such recordings revealed four basic patterns of neural activity in the basal ganglia when rats were in the T maze: (1) some neurons fired most at the start of a trial, when the rat was first released into the maze; (2) some fired most when the instructional sound was broadcast; (3) some responded strongly when the rat turned right or left; and (4) some fired at the end of a trial, when the rat received food. During the early stages of learning, about half of the recorded basal ganglia neurons showed one of these four patterns of activity. Most of these neurons fired

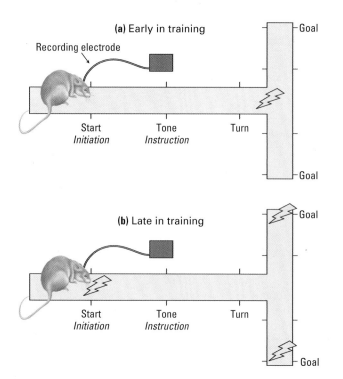

Figure 8.9 Changes in basal ganglia firing patterns during skill learning (a) Researchers implanted electrodes in rats' basal ganglia, then trained the rats to turn right or left in a T maze after hearing a tone instruction. Early in training, 50% of basal ganglia neurons fired strongly (indicated by the lightning bolt) when the rats chose which direction to turn. (b) As training progressed, basal ganglia neurons began to fire mainly at the beginning and end of the rats' movements through the maze; finally, more than 90% of neurons fired almost exclusively when rats were at these positions.

Research from Jog et al., 1999.

only when a rat turned right or left in the maze (Figure 8.9a). The other half of the recorded neurons fired in ways that were not clearly related to the rats' movements or experiences in the maze. As the rats' performance improved with practice, the percentage of neurons that showed task-related activity patterns increased to about 90%, with most neurons firing strongly at the beginning and at the end of the task rather than during turning (Figure 8.9b). These measurements show that neural activity in the basal ganglia changes during the learning of a perceptual-motor skill, suggesting that encoding or control of skills by the basal ganglia changes as learning progresses.

The increased neural activity seen in the beginning and end states during the maze task suggests that the basal ganglia developed (or monitored) a motor plan that was initiated at the beginning of each trial. The motor plan then directed the rat's movements until the trial ended (Graybiel, 2008). This hypothetical process is consistent with Fitts's model of skill learning, in which automatically engaged motor programs gradually replace active control of movements (Fitts, 1964). Someone learning to juggle might show similar changes in basal ganglia activity—that is, if we could record signals from her neurons, which is not yet possible. In a novice juggler, still in the cognitive stage of skill acquisition, basal ganglia neurons might fire most strongly when the balls are in the air (when an action must be chosen based on visual information). In an expert juggler, who has reached the autonomous stage of skill learning, basal ganglia neurons might fire most strongly when she is catching and tossing the balls.

The data presented above show that the basal ganglia contribute to learning of perceptual-motor skills. Do they also contribute to cognitive skill learning?

Brain Activity During Cognitive Skill Learning

Neuroimaging studies of the human brain reveal that the basal ganglia are indeed active when participants learn cognitive skills (Poldrack, Prabhakaran, Seger, & Gabrieli, 1999; Poldrack et al., 2001; Seger & Cincotta, 2006). In one series of experiments, participants learned to perform a classification task in which a computer presented them with sets of cards and then instructed them to guess what the weather would be, based on the patterns displayed on the cards (Figure 8.10a). Each card showed a unique pattern of colored shapes. Some patterns appeared when rain was likely, and others appeared when the weather was likely to be sunny. As each card was presented on-screen, participants predicted either good or bad (sunny or rainy) weather by pressing one of two keys. The computer then determined and reported the actual weather outcome based on the patterns on the cards. Participants had to learn through trial and error which patterns predicted which kind of weather (Gluck, Shohamy, & Myers, 2002; Knowlton, Squire, & Gluck, 1994). The task mimics real-world weather prediction in that no combination of "patterns" (that is, of cloud cover, temperature, wind, and so on) is 100% predictive of the weather that will follow; meteorologists must develop a wide range of cognitive skills to accurately forecast the weather. For participants in this study, the task may have seemed

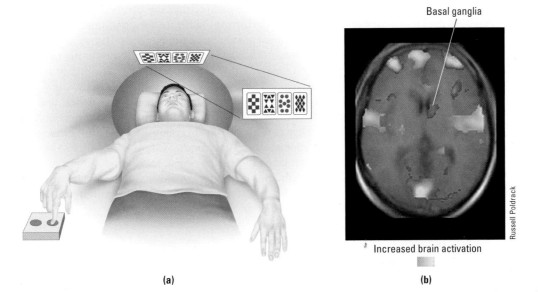

Figure 8.10 Neuroimaging during learning of the weather prediction task (a) A participant, lying with his head in the MRI scanner, is shown a set of cards on-screen that he must use to judge what weather conditions are likely to occur. Different patterns correspond to different predictions; for example, the pattern of squares on the leftmost card shown here predicts a 60% chance of rain. The participant is not given this information but must figure out through trial and error which patterns indicate a high chance of rain. (b) During the weather prediction task in a well-trained subject, fMRI difference images show increased activation (orange) in the basal ganglia.

(b) Information from Poldrack et al., 2001.

more like reading tarot cards than learning a cognitive skill, but the participants usually did improve at this task with practice.

Although each card was associated with the likelihood that a particular kind of weather would occur, there was no simple rule that participants could use to make accurate predictions. Instead, to improve at the task, participants gradually had to learn which cards *tended* to predict certain types of weather. Brain-imaging data showed increased activity in the basal ganglia as individuals learned to make these judgments (Figure 8.10b). This and similar imaging studies suggest that the basal ganglia contribute to both cognitive and perceptual-motor-skill learning. But how do they contribute?

Despite considerable evidence that the basal ganglia enable skill learning, their specific function in this process is still debated. Because the basal ganglia are involved in the control and planning of movements, it is possible that damage to the basal ganglia leads to changes in performance that impair learning processes in other brain regions: if you can't control how your arms are moving, you will have difficulty learning how to juggle. Consequently, changes in skill learning caused by lesions to the basal ganglia, as seen in rats learning the radial maze task, do not definitively prove that this region is critical for encoding or retrieving skill memories. Similarly, learning-dependent changes in the activity of basal ganglia neurons, as seen in rats learning to follow instructions in a T maze, could reflect changes in the information coming from the sensory cortex rather than changes generated by the basal ganglia.

Are basal ganglia neurons doing most of whatever is required to form memories of skills, or are other brain regions such as the cortex and cerebellum doing the bulk of the encoding and retrieval? Is it possible that the basal ganglia contribute no more to skill-memory formation than do other brain regions but that they (the basal ganglia) are specialized for specific aspects of the learning process? We need to take a closer look at different cortical regions during and after practice sessions to shed light on these issues.

Cortical Representations of Skills

How important is the cerebral cortex for the learning and performance of skills? Given that most animals don't have a cerebral cortex and that animals born with a cortex can continue to perform many actions after surgical removal of all their cortical neurons, you might conclude that the cerebral cortex isn't very important for either learning or performing skills. In fact, mammals are the only animals that make extensive use of cortical circuits for any purpose, so whatever the role of the cerebral cortex in skill memory, it probably plays this role most extensively in mammals. Coincidentally (or not), mammals are highly flexible, relative to most other species, when it comes to learning new skills.

Neural circuits in your cerebral cortex that become active when you run, jump, or sing are continuously changing over time in ways that may enhance your ability to perform these actions. From this perspective, skill memories are the neural outcomes of repeated performances. A simple analogy is the way your muscles and performance change in response to a bodybuilding regimen. Just as increasing the strength and flexibility of your leg muscles can affect how well you jump, changing patterns of activity in your cortex through practice and performance may also influence your jumping ability.

Cortical Expansion

If cortical networks are like brain "muscles," then you'd expect that practicing different skills should affect different cortical regions, just as different physical exercises affect different muscle groups. This seems to be true. Regions of the cerebral cortex involved in performing a particular skill often expand in area with practice, while regions that are less relevant to the skill show fewer changes. Neuroimaging techniques such as fMRI reveal this expansion by showing increased blood flow to particular regions. For example, brain-imaging studies of professional violinists showed that the cortical activation evoked in the somatosensory cortex during use of the fingers that control note sequences was more extensive than in nonviolinists (Elbert, Pantev, Wienbruch, Rockstroh, & Taub, 1995). Interestingly, the cortical maps of violinists' bow hands (on which the fingers always move together) showed no such elaborations: the cortical changes were specific to the hand that moves the fingers separately. Similar differences in cortical activation have also been observed in the motor cortices of expert racquetball players when they use their playing hand versus their non-playing hand (Pearce, Thickbroom, Byrnes, & Mastaglia, 2000).

Although expansion of cortical regions is usually associated with superior performance, there is some evidence that too much expansion can cause problems. In a disorder called *musician's dystonia*, extensive practice playing an instrument can lead to a reduction or loss of motor control. Experimental work indicates that this loss of control reflects excessive reorganization of the motor cortex (Rosenkranz, Butler, Williamon, & Rothwell, 2009).

Measures of blood flow reveal larger areas of activation in sensory and motor cortices after extensive practice, which implies that experience is affecting cortical circuits. These measures do not reveal what physical changes occur, however. Studies using structural MRI techniques indicate that practice can actually change the amount of cortical gray matter, which is where the cell bodies of neurons are found. For example, after about 3 months of training, people who learned to juggle three balls continuously for at least 1 minute showed a 3% increase in gray matter in areas of the visual cortex that respond to motion (Draganski et al., 2004). In fact, changes in gray matter can be observed as early as 7 days after training begins (Driemeyer, Boyke, Gaser, Buchel, & May, 2008). No comparable structural changes were observed in the motor cortex, basal ganglia, or cerebellum. It is not

Anatoli Styf/Shutterstock

Why might a professional violinist who practices daily suddenly start to lose the ability to correctly finger the strings when playing a familiar piece?

known whether this expansion of gray matter reflected changes in the number or size of synapses, changes in the number of glia (the cells providing functional and structural support to neurons), or changes in the size of cortical neurons.

Like neuroimaging studies in humans, electrophysiological studies in monkeys show that practice can expand cortical representations. In one such study, researchers trained monkeys to perform a tactile discrimination task (Recanzone, Merzenich, Jenkins, Grajski, & Dinse, 1992). The task required the monkey to release a handgrip whenever it felt a stimulus on its fingertip that differed from a standard stimulus. During each trial, the monkey initially felt a vibration having a certain fixed speed for about half a second on one of its fingers. This initial tactile stimulus, always the same, provided a standard for comparison. The initial stimulus was followed by a half-second interval of no stimulation and then a series of one to four additional vibrating stimuli, each vibrating either at the same rate as the standard or faster. The monkey was given fruit juice if it released the handgrip when vibrations were faster than the standard. This task is similar to the T maze task described earlier, in which researchers recorded the activity of basal ganglia neurons in a rat as it learned to turn right or left in response to acoustic cues. Both the T maze and the tactile discrimination task require the animal to perform one of two responses (in one task, turn right or turn left; in the other, grip or release) based on specific cues provided to a single sensory modality (sound in one task, touch in the other). These two tasks might not seem to require much skill compared with the musical performances of professional violinists or the physical feats of professional athletes, but it is important to keep in mind that the animals would never perform these trained actions in the wild. The criterion for whether an ability is a skill is not how hard it would be for a human to perform the action but whether the ability can be improved through experience.

When a monkey learned to respond to a vibrating tactile stimulus that predicted the delivery of juice, the area of the somatosensory cortex that processed the cue increased. As a result, monkeys that learned the tactile discrimination task had enlarged cortical representations for the finger they used to inspect tactile stimuli. Studies such as this show that perceptual-motor skill learning is often associated with expansion of representations within the sensory cortex involved in performing the skill. Similarly, practicing a perceptual-motor skill can cause representations within the motor cortex to expand. For example, electrical stimulation of the motor cortex (a technique introduced in Chapter 2) in monkeys trained to retrieve a small object showed that the area of the cortex that controlled movements of the fingers expanded (Nudo, Milliken, Jenkins, & Merzenich, 1996). In monkeys that learned to turn a key with their forearm, cortical representation of the forearm expanded. Researchers don't know how many different cortical regions are modified during learning of a particular skill, but the current assumption is that any cortical networks that contribute to performance of the skill are likely to be modified as training improves (or degrades) performance. Researchers also have yet to determine exactly how the expansion of cortical representations occurs, but most neuroscientists believe that representational expansion reflects the strengthening and weakening of connections within the cortex resulting from synaptic plasticity (basic mechanisms of synaptic plasticity are described in Chapter 2).

Are Skill Memories Stored in the Cerebral Cortex?

Many experiments have shown that cortical networks change as skill learning progresses, but this tells us only that the two phenomena are correlated, not that changes in the cerebral cortex actually cause the improved performance. Such studies also do not establish that skill memories are stored in cortical networks. As you saw earlier, changes in neural activity in the basal ganglia also take place during skill learning. The cerebral cortex clearly contributes to skill learning and performance, but knowing this is not the same as knowing what cortical circuits do during skill learning.

One way to get closer to understanding the cortical contribution to skill learning is to measure cortical activity during training. Much of what is known about skill learning pertains to how different practice regimens relate to differences in skill acquisition and forgetting. If it were possible to show that cortical changes parallel known behavioral patterns or that improvements in performance can be predicted from cortical changes, we could be more certain that skill levels and cortical activity are closely related. Initial investigations in this direction suggest that the behavioral stages of skill acquisition are indeed paralleled by changes in cortical activity.

Data from brain-imaging studies show that when people begin learning a motor skill that requires sequential finger movements, the part of the motor cortex activated during performance of the task expands rapidly during the first training session and more gradually in later sessions. Avi Karni and colleagues required participants to touch each of their fingers to their thumb in a fixed sequence as rapidly and accurately as possible (Karni et al., 1998). In parallel with the changes seen in the motor cortex during training, participants' performance of this task improved rapidly in early sessions and more gradually in later sessions (Figure 8.11a), consistent with the power law of practice. Imaging data collected over 6 weeks of training suggested that practice beyond the third week of training (after performance had stabilized) resulted in additional increases in the representation of learned movements in the motor cortex.

Overall, the region of motor cortex activated during performance of the practiced sequence expanded relative to the area activated by different, untrained

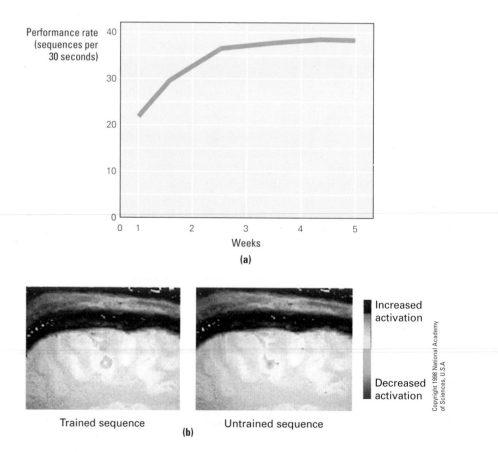

Figure 8.11 Changes in skill performance and associated motor cortex during training (a) Participants who practiced performing a sequence of finger movements gradually increased the rate and accuracy with which they could perform this skill. The plot shows average scores for the group of participants. (b) After training, fMRI scans revealed that the area of motor cortex activated when participants performed the practiced sequence expanded (left panel) relative to the region activated when they performed an untrained sequence of identical finger movements (right panel).

Information from Karni et al., 1998.

sequences of finger movements (Figure 8.11b). Karni and colleagues hypothesized that the period of "fast learning" involves processes that select and establish the optimal plans for performing a particular task, whereas the subsequent slower stages of learning reflect long-term structural changes of basic motor control circuits in the cortex. Recent data from studies of perceptual-motor skill learning in rats are consistent with this interpretation. Rats trained in a reaching task showed significant differences in their motor map only after practicing the task for at least 10 days (Kleim et al., 2004). This finding suggests that structural changes in the cortex reflect the enhancement of skill memories during later stages of training.

A wide variety of sensory and motor events activate circuits in the cerebral cortex, so it is not surprising that these brain regions contribute to skill learning and performance. However, the respective roles of the cortex and basal ganglia in forming and recalling skill memories remain to be assessed and will require studying the interactions between the cerebral cortex and the basal ganglia while individuals are learning various perceptual-motor and cognitive skills.

Test Your Knowledge

Which Cortical Regions Change during Skill Learning?

As skill learning progresses, cortical regions change in ways that mimic patterns of skill acquisition. Based on what is known from neurophysiological experiments with monkeys and from behavioral experiments with humans, what cortical regions do you think might show different activation levels in a chess grand master compared with a beginner? (Answers appear in the back of the book.)

The Cerebellum and Timing

What about skill learning in animals such as birds and fish that don't have much cortex? Researchers can train pigeons to perform a wide range of perceptual-motor skills, and fish can rapidly learn to navigate mazes. Animals without much cortex must rely on evolutionarily older parts of the brain to learn skills. One region that seems to be particularly important in this process is the cerebellum. You may recall from Chapter 4 that the cerebellum plays a key role in learning to predict important events, especially in the formation, execution, and timing of conditioned responses. These functions also are important for skill learning.

The cerebellum is probably one of the most basic neural systems involved in encoding and retrieving skill memories. Even animals as lowly as fish and frogs, which may seem to have little potential for skill learning, have a cerebellum. And although you aren't likely to see a fish or a frog performing in a circus, this doesn't mean these animals cannot learn perceptual-motor skills; for example, with practice, fish can learn to press little levers for food. You are more likely to have seen parrots riding tricycles or heard them producing intelligible sentences. Birds, too, have a cerebellum, which may facilitate their ability to learn such tricks. In fact, most animals that have a spine also have a cerebellum, yet there are relatively few studies of cerebellar function in nonmammals. Consequently, much less is known about how the cerebellum contributes to skill-memory formation in animals possessing little cortex than is known about cerebellar function in mammals with lots of cortex.

Most of the inputs to the cerebellum are from the spinal cord, sensory systems, or cerebral cortex, and most of the output signals from the cerebellum go to the spinal cord or to motor systems in the cerebral cortex. Experiments conducted in the early 1800s showed that cerebellar lesions impair the performance of motor sequences. People with cerebellar damage, for example, have difficulty playing a musical instrument or writing. Collectively, these anatomical and neuropsychological data indicate that the cerebellum contributes to the performance of perceptual-motor skills in mammals. Because the structure of the cerebellum is organized similarly across different species, it is presumed to serve similar functions in both mammals and nonmammals (Lalonde & Botez, 1990).

Other evidence suggests that, in addition to facilitating the performance of skills, the cerebellum is involved in forming memories for skills. The cerebellum appears to be especially important for learning movement sequences that require precise timing, such as acrobatics, dancing, or competitive team sports. A person with cerebellar damage might be able to learn new dance moves but would probably have trouble learning to synchronize those moves to musical rhythms. For example, early brain-imaging studies of systems involved in motor learning showed that there is a sudden increase in cerebellar activity when humans begin learning to perform sequences of finger movements (Friston, Frith, Passingham, Liddle, & Frackowiak, 1992). Similarly, rats that learn complex motor skills to navigate an obstacle course (for example, balancing on tightropes and seesaws) develop predictable physiological changes in cerebellar neural circuitry, such as increased numbers of synapses (Kleim et al., 1997). Cerebellar changes in acrobatic rats seem to depend on skill learning rather than on activity levels because rats that run in an exercise wheel for the same amount of time do not show such changes. Furthermore, studies have found that rats depended on cerebellar processing even when they learned to perform a task by simply watching other rats perform the task (Leggio et al., 2000). Rats that received cerebellar lesions after observing other rats navigate a maze benefited from those observations when they were later trained in the maze, whereas rats that received lesions before observing other rats traverse the maze did not benefit from their observations. Studies in humans similarly found cerebellar involvement during observational learning of a perceptual-motor skill (Torriero et al., 2011), further suggesting that memories of skills either performed or witnessed depend at least in part on cerebellar processing.

The cerebellum is also important for tasks that involve aiming at or tracking a target. A task that psychologists commonly use to assess such abilities is **mirror tracing**. In this task, individuals learn to trace drawings by looking in a mirror to observe their hand and the figure to be traced, which are otherwise hidden from view (Figure 8.12a). It's hard to draw well under these conditions, but if the

mirror tracing. An experimental task that requires individuals to trace drawings by watching a mirror image of their hand and the figure to be traced, with the hand and figure concealed; used to test perceptual-motor skill learning.

Figure 8.12 The mirror-tracing task (a) In this task, participants learn to trace a figure using only a mirror reflection of their hand and the figure for guidance. (b) Cerebellar lesions disrupt performance of the mirror-tracing task. Note, however, that the rate of learning is the same for individuals with and without cerebellar lesions.

(b) Data from Laforce and Doyon, 2001.

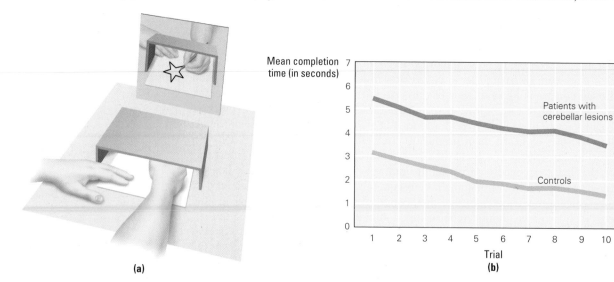

(a)

(b)

cerebellum is working properly, the participant can eventually learn to perform this task well. In contrast, a person with cerebellar damage would find this task to be quite difficult. It took patients with cerebellar damage twice as long to trace images shown in a mirror as individuals without damage (Figure 8.12b), even after several sessions of training (Laforce & Doyon, 2001).

It is interesting to note in Figure 8.12b that the *rate* of learning for patients with cerebellar damage was comparable to that of the control group. This seems to suggest that learning in the patients with cerebellar damage was similar to that of the control group and that the patients simply performed more poorly. However, subsequent transfer tests in which both groups traced more complex figures revealed that the individuals in the control group benefited more from their training experiences than did the individuals with cerebellar damage. Thus, although both groups were learning at a similar rate, they were not transferring the mirror-tracing skill in the same way. This finding is similar to that in the study described earlier in which rats with basal ganglia lesions seemed to have learned to find a visible platform in the Morris water maze in the same way as intact rats but then performed differently when the platform was moved to a new location.

So far, we have discussed how the cerebellum contributes to perceptual-motor-skill learning. Recent brain-imaging studies show that activity in the cerebellum also changes when individuals learn certain cognitive skills, such as **mirror reading.** In the mirror-reading task, individuals learn to read mirror-reversed text. Researchers found that cerebellar changes that occur during learning of the mirror-reading task are *lateralized*—that is, are different in each hemisphere (Figure 8.13), with the left cerebellum showing decreased activity and the right cerebellum showing increased activity with training (Poldrack & Gabrieli, 2001). Were you assuming that both sides of your brain are doing the same thing while you're reading this chapter? Think again. How such hemisphere-specific differences in cerebellar processing contribute to skill learning or performance is not yet known.

Keep in mind that almost all cognitive skills require the performance of some perceptually guided movements, if only eye movements. For example, we learned earlier in this chapter that chess masters move their eyes more efficiently to scan a chessboard than do less experienced players. Similar perceptual-motor skills may also be important for tasks such as mirror reading. So, it is possible that changes in cerebellar activity during the learning of cognitive skills might partially reflect the learning of motor sequences required for performing the cognitive activity.

In summary, then, the cerebellum, cerebral cortex, and basal ganglia are each critical, in different ways, to skill learning. If you're having trouble learning a skill, which part of your brain should you blame? There is no

mirror reading. An experimental task that requires individuals to read mirror-reversed text; used to test cognitive skill learning.

Figure 8.13 Cerebellar activation during cognitive skill learning fMRI imaging studies shows that after the learning of a mirror-reading task, activation in the right cerebellum increased and activation in the left cerebellum decreased.

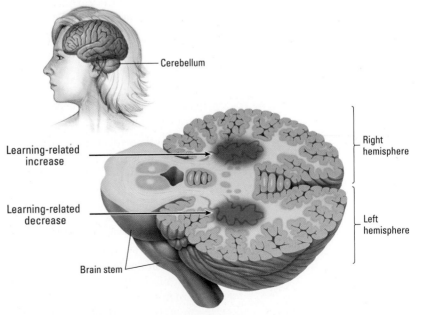

Cerebellum

Learning-related increase

Learning-related decrease

Brain stem

Right hemisphere

Left hemisphere

cut-and-dried division of labor between these three brain regions that would allow you to identify the culprit. The importance of each for encoding or performing any given skill probably depends on the particular skill and your level of expertise. Nevertheless, the cerebellum seems most critical for timing; the cerebral cortex, most critical for controlling complex action sequences; and the basal ganglia, most critical for linking sensory events to responses. Knowing this, which brain region do you think would be most important for learning to run down stairs? The answer is probably all three, at different points in the learning process (Hubert et al., 2007; Steele & Penhune, 2010; Yin et al., 2009). Early on, the cerebellum, visual cortex, and motor cortex may work together to coordinate the timing and sequencing of leg movements. After extensive practice, the basal ganglia may begin to initiate and control more-automatic sequences of leg movements. How these three brain regions work together during the acquisition and retention of skill memories is a question that researchers are still attempting to answer.

One feature that all three systems have in common is that skill learning is associated with gradual changes in the firing of neurons in these areas during performance of the skill. This finding means that practice can change the structure of neural circuits to make the control and coordination of movements (or thoughts, in the case of cognitive skills) more accurate and efficient. The most likely mechanism for such changes is synaptic plasticity. Understanding how and when the brain is able to adjust specific synapses within and between the cerebellum, basal ganglia, and cortex will clarify how humans and other animals learn skills.

Interim Summary

- Skill learning depends on three brain areas: the basal ganglia, the cerebral cortex, and the cerebellum.

- Studies of how rats with basal ganglia damage learn to navigate mazes suggest that the basal ganglia are critical for learning to generate motor responses based on environmental cues.

- Neural response patterns in the basal ganglia change during the learning of a perceptual-motor skill, suggesting that representations of that skill are dynamically modified as learning proceeds. The basal ganglia are also activated when people learn cognitive skills such as the weather predic-tion task.

- Regions of the somatosensory cortex and motor cortex needed to perform a particular skill expand with practice, but regions that are less relevant show fewer, if any, changes.

- The cerebellum is especially critical for learning and performing movement sequences that require precise timing, such as dancing, and tasks that involve tracking a target, as in mirror tracing.

- The cerebral cortex is mainly involved in controlling complex actions, and the basal ganglia link sensory events to responses.

8.3 Clinical Perspectives

In Chapter 7 you learned how damage to the hippocampus and surrounding brain regions can disrupt memories for events and facts. Although there are no reports of brain damage that leads to a similarly dramatic loss of the ability to form skill memories, dysfunctions of the basal ganglia resulting from injury or disease can interfere with the formation and use of skill memories. Additionally, injuries to the brain, spinal cord, and limbs can severely impair a person's ability to perform skills. Patients often must make use of their ability to learn new skills to compensate. In this section, we explore some deficits caused by dysfunction in the basal ganglia, as well as new technologies that can help patients to counteract disease- and injury-related impairments in skill performance.

Parkinson's Disease

Parkinson's disease is a nervous system disease involving disruptions in the normal functions of the basal ganglia and progressive deterioration of motor control (Delong & Wichmann, 2007; Redgrave et al., 2010). The main brain damage associated with Parkinson's disease is a reduction in the number of dopaminergic neurons in the substantia nigra pars compacta (SNc) that control activity in the basal ganglia (see discussion of the dorsal striatum in Chapter 5). Neurons in the SNc normally determine the levels of dopamine in the basal ganglia, and when these neurons are gone, dopamine levels are greatly reduced.

Patients with Parkinson's disease show increasing muscular rigidity and muscle tremors and are generally impaired at initiating movements. Symptoms of the disease usually do not appear until after the age of 50 but can arise much earlier. People with Parkinson's find it harder to learn certain perceptual-motor tasks, such as the serial reaction time task and tracking tasks (including the rotary pursuit task). Parkinson's disease may selectively disrupt circuits in the basal ganglia that contribute to the learning and performance of closed skills, especially those that have reached the autonomous stage of learning, where movements normally would be automatic (Redgrave et al., 2010).

Currently, the main treatments for Parkinson's disease are drug therapies to counteract the reduced levels of dopamine, and surgical procedures to counteract the disruption caused by lack of dopamine in the basal ganglia. One surgical technique, **deep brain stimulation**, has become the most effective neurosurgical technique for treating Parkinson's, but scientists are still not sure why it works (Benabid, 2003; Naskar, Sood, Goyal, & Dhara, 2010). In deep brain stimulation, an electrical current is delivered through one or more electrodes permanently implanted deep in the patient's brain. Neurosurgeons place the ends of the electrodes near neurons that connect basal ganglia neurons with cortical circuits (for example, in the thalamus or basal ganglia), as shown in Figure 8.14. When electrical current from an implanted stimulator passes through these electrodes, many of the motor symptoms associated with Parkinson's disease, such as tremors, disappear within seconds, although they eventually return. One theory of how this technique works is that without proper levels of dopamine, interactions between neurons in the cerebral cortex and the basal ganglia become locked into fixed patterns (Dowsey-Limousin & Pollak, 2001). This creates a situation similar to the endless back and forth of young children arguing (Child 1: "No, you be quiet!" Child 2: "No, you be quiet!" Child 1: "No, you . . ."— ad infinitum) and disrupts the control of movements. Stimulation from the electrode is thought to quiet both brain regions, allowing normal brain activity to resume. Another

Parkinson's disease. A disorder resulting from disruptions in the normal functioning of the basal ganglia and progressive deterioration of motor control and perceptual-motor skill learning.

deep brain stimulation. A procedure that delivers an electrical current into a patient's brain through one or more implanted electrodes; used to alleviate tremors and other motor symptoms associated with Parkinson's disease.

Figure 8.14 Deep brain stimulation for treatment of Parkinson's disease Neurosurgeons position the tip of an electrode in a brain location (such as the thalamus) that, on stimulation, will affect neural activity in the basal ganglia and cerebral cortex. An implanted stimulator periodically passes current through this electrode to temporarily relieve symptoms of Parkinson's disease.

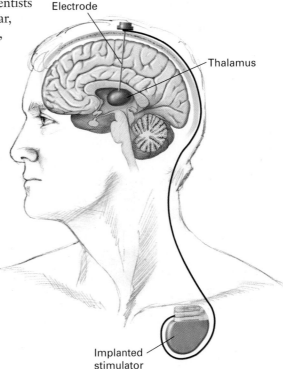

Electrode

Thalamus

Implanted stimulator

possibility is that deep brain stimulation replaces disruptive activity in the basal ganglia and cerebral cortex with a new pattern of activity that is less disruptive (Naskar et al., 2010). Using electrical stimulation to treat Parkinson's disease illustrates how increased knowledge of the brain systems underlying skill memories can help doctors repair these systems when things go awry.

Human–Machine Interfaces: Learning to Consciously Control Artificial Limbs

New electronic technologies are enabling people who are limited in the ability to see or hear to partially regain function in these sensory modalities (discussed in Chapter 3). Just as such *sensory prostheses* can help people to overcome deficits in perceptual abilities, electromechanical devices called **motor prostheses** can help people to recover lost abilities to learn and perform perceptual-motor skills. Unlike sensory prostheses, which automatically respond to environmental inputs (lights and sounds), motor prostheses must be consciously controlled by their users.

motor prosthesis. An electromechanical device that can help people recover lost abilities to learn and perform perceptual-motor skills.

Like deep brain stimulation, use of motor prostheses requires a surgical procedure to implant electrodes in a person's nervous system. Instead of delivering electricity to neurons, however, these electrodes collect electrical signals from neurons and transmit those signals to a computer for processing. The computer then uses the signals to determine how to control the movements of a robotic limb. Generally, these limbs are artificial arms or hands, but they could be almost any appendage. Essentially, the computer transforms neural signals into robotic movements in real time.

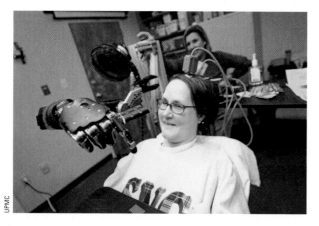

In what brain region would electrodes likely be implanted to enable a person to consciously control a robotic hand or arm to feed herself chocolate?

Much of the research on motor prostheses has been conducted on nonhumans, specifically monkeys and rats (Borton et al., 2013; Carmena et al., 2003; Koralek et al., 2012; Velliste et al., 2008). This is because animals can be trained to control robotic limbs even if all of their motor abilities are intact. Researchers can first develop programs that translate neural activity into signals that make a robotic arm move in ways that match how a monkey is actually moving its arm, after which they can restrain the monkey's arm and train the monkey to use the robotic arm to perform tasks that it originally learned to perform with its own arm (Carmena, 2013). This involves transfer of training in that the monkey must retrieve its memories of the skills used in the task, even though its own arm is no longer performing the actions it normally would. By reinforcing the monkey for performing the task with the robot arm, researchers are able to facilitate transfer such that the monkey can eventually learn to control robot arms even when they are not anywhere near the monkey (Lebedev & Nicolelis, 2006).

The few humans that have had the necessary electrodes implanted in their brains are patients who have lost the ability to move any of their limbs. Recordings from multiple electrodes positioned within the motor cortex have made it possible for tetraplegic patients to control the movements of a mouse pointer on a computer screen, a motorized wheelchair, and a robotic arm with the capability of grasping objects (Collinger et al., 2013; Hochberg e t al., 2012).

Motor prosthetics also are currently being tested for use in people who are missing an arm or hand. In these cases, the electrodes are typically attached to nerves of the person's peripheral nervous system rather than implanted in their brain. In some cases, separate electrodes have been connected to incoming sensory pathways and outgoing motor pathways (see Figure 2.8 for a reminder of how these different pathways control movements), making it possible for amputees to both control the movements of an artificial hand and to feel the consequences of those movements (Talbot, 2014).

It might seem that a person who still possesses memories of how to perform basic perceptual-motor skills should be able to immediately use those memories to control similar movements with an artificial limb. Remember, however, that millions of neurons in multiple brain regions contribute to the performance of such skills. The electrodes that control the movements of robotic arms or prosthetic limbs are usually connected to relatively few neurons in a single part of the nervous system. Patients have to learn to generate neural activity that will enable the computer to determine what actions to initiate, much as Jedi in the Star Wars movies learned to use "the Force" to move objects with their thoughts. Like those who receive sensory prosthetics, humans and nonhumans with motor prosthetics gradually improve their ability to control them with practice (Ganguly & Carmena, 2010; Koralek et al., 2012; Shenoy & Carmena, 2013). How much of an expert a human can become at mentally controlling artificial limbs or electronic devices remains to be seen. What is certain is that a better understanding of the mechanisms that enable humans to master new skills will be critical to maximizing people's ability to flexibly use such technologies.

Interim Summary

- Parkinson's disease involves both disruptions in the normal functioning of the basal ganglia and progressive deterioration of motor control and skill-learning abilities.

- Deep brain stimulation can decrease the negative consequences of Parkinson's disease for skill performance by changing activity in the basal ganglia and cerebral cortex.

- Motor prostheses enable individuals with lost motor function or missing limbs to learn new ways of performing perceptual-motor skills.

Synthesis

Kissing requires both perceptual-motor and cognitive skills, acquired and improved through observation and practice. Differentiating the cognitive aspects from the perceptual-motor ones can be difficult, as this chapter shows. Cognitive skills often depend on perceptual-motor skills (and vice versa) and may even become transformed into perceptual-motor skills over time.

Certainly, one cognitive aspect of kissing is the use of social skills to motivate someone to want to kiss you or be kissed by you. Once you solve this problem—which in some cases may be as strategically challenging as a chess game—you face the perceptual-motor challenge of coordinating your own kissing movements with those of your partner, based on what you perceive of your partner's maneuvers. Your skills at this point will depend on how much and how often you have practiced, as well as on the types of feedback you have received from past partners. Perhaps you are in the cognitive stage of learning to kiss, still thinking carefully about each move you make, or perhaps in the associative stage, feeling comfortable with your performance but knowing there is room for improvement and still having to keep in mind things to avoid. Possibly you are at the autonomous stage of skill acquisition, having become an expert—your kissing makes use of various motor programs that you perform without thinking in response to sensory stimuli. If you are an experienced kisser, the skill memories you rely on are dependent on the coordination of several brain regions, including the basal ganglia, the cerebral cortex, and the cerebellum.

In short, there is more to kissing than simply recalling and executing a fixed series of movements. Kissing is an open skill in which the recent actions and reactions of your partner provide important feedback that you can use to guide your own actions. Keeping track of what has happened in the recent past is thus a key component of skillful kissing. The ability to maintain and flexibly use memories of the recent past requires input from brain regions other than those we have focused on thus far in our discussion of skill learning and performance. You will learn more about these kinds of memories and their neural substrates in the next chapter, on working memory.

KNOW YOUR KEY TERMS

associative stage, *p. 323*
autonomous stage, *p. 323*
closed skill, *p. 313*
cognitive skill, *p. 312*
cognitive stage, *p. 323*
constant practice, *p. 319*
deep brain stimulation, *p. 345*
explicit learning, *p. 320*
expert, *p. 311*
identical elements theory, *p. 328*
implicit learning, *p. 320*

knowledge of results, *p. 317*
learning set formation, *p. 328*
massed practice, *p. 319*
mirror reading, *p. 343*
mirror tracing, *p. 342*
motor program, *p. 322*
motor prosthesis, *p. 346*
open skill, *p. 313*
Parkinson's disease, *p. 345*
perceptual-motor skill, *p. 312*
power law of practice, *p. 318*

rotary pursuit task, *p. 325*
serial reaction time
   task, *p. 321*
skill, *p. 312*
skill decay, *p. 329*
spaced practice, *p. 319*
talent, *p. 325*
transfer specificity, *p. 328*
variable practice, *p. 319*

QUIZ YOURSELF

1. Surfing is an example of a(n) _____ skill because surfers have to adapt to variations in the qualities of each wave. (p. 313)

2. Updating a website is an example of a(n) _____ skill because it requires using computer programming knowledge to solve a problem. (p. 312)

3. Skiing is an example of a(n) _____ skill because it requires coordinating movements based on sensory information. (p. 312)

4. Historically, researchers have questioned whether it is possible for animals other than humans to learn _____ skills. (p. 312)

5. According to _____, performance during learning improves rapidly at first, and then slows down. (p. 318)

6. People improve at the serial reaction time task without realizing that some sequences are being repeatedly presented or that their performance is improving, which suggests that their learning is _____. (p. 320)

7. If a baby is able to eat Grape Nuts using a spoon, but shows no ability to eat them using a spork, then this may be a case of _____. (p. 328)

8. Historically, researchers have questioned whether it is possible for animals other than humans to learn _____ skills. (p. 312)

9. A teenager who is learning to make macaroni and cheese for the first time is likely to be in the _____ stage of skill acquisition. (p. 323)

10. Getting drunk will impair processing in your _____, which will make it harder to perform skills such as walking in a straight line. (p. 341)

11. Cramming the night before an exam is an example of _____. (p. 319)

12. Practicing the piano once a week for several months is an example of _____. (p. 319)

13. Practicing a single dance routine that is synchronized to a specific piece of music is an example of _____ practice. (p. 319)

14. Practicing catching a baseball thrown at various heights, speeds, and distances is an example of _____ practice. (p. 319)

15. The fact that professional athletes generally are not exceptional at all sports can be viewed as a case of _____. (p. 328)

16. Thorndike proposed the _____ to explain why skills transfer best when they are used in situations that are highly similar to the one in which they were originally learned. (p. 328)

17. Being able to type a text message without looking at the phone is an example of the _____ stage of skill acquisition. (p. 323)

18. Neurons in the _____ change their firing patterns as rats learn to perform a perceptual-motor skill. (p. 312)

19. In _____ extensive practicing of an instrument leads to loss of motor control. (p. 338)

20. An age-related disorder involving a reduction in the number of dopaminergic neurons that affect basal ganglia activity is _____. (p. 345)

Answers appear in the back of the book

CONCEPT CHECK

1. A teenage boy wants to improve his kissing skills. What are some strategies he might try for learning these skills?

2. A graduate student who believes her pet tarantula is exceptionally bright wants to prove to the world that spiders can reason and solve problems. How might she convince others that she is correct?

3. Some researchers believe that the right kinds and amounts of practice can make anyone an expert. What sort of experimental evidence might convince these researchers that there is such a thing as talent?

4. According to Fitts's model of skill learning, individuals must go through an initial cognitive stage before they can master a skill. Does this imply that for a fish to learn to press a lever, it must first think about what is required to perform the task?

5. Neuroscience research has shown that regions in the somatosensory cortex and motor cortex expand in parallel with learning of perceptual-motor skills. Does this mean that practicing a skill causes regions of cortex not involved in performing that skill to shrink?

Answers appear in the back of the book

Working Memory and Cognitive Control

I
T IS TUESDAY AT 8:10 A.M., AND KAMILA, a high school senior, must rush if she is going to run several errands on the way to her first class—an 8:30 a.m. business class— and still arrive on time. She has only 20 minutes to get cash from the bank machine, sign up for the cheerleading tryouts, and drop off her biology homework, which is due by 10:00 a.m. Before heading out the door, Kamila grabs the various things she will need for the rest of the day, including her cheerleader pompoms and iPad (for last-minute cramming for this afternoon's quiz). The sign-up sheet for the tryouts is in the cafeteria, which is near the biology building and close to where her business class is being held. It is quicker, she figures, to go to the bank machine first, as that requires just a short detour from her homeroom. After signing up for cheerleading tryouts, she starts to walk to business class across campus when, *darn*, she realizes she forgot one of her errands. She doubles back quickly to the biology department, drops off her homework there, and then heads on to business class.

As she walks toward the classroom, Kamila remembers that today's lecture has been moved from the usual third-floor location to the large auditorium in the basement, where they will have a guest speaker. She is so used to running up the stairs every Tuesday and Thursday that she has to struggle to remember that today she needs to bypass those stairs and take the elevator to the basement instead.

Slipping into the back of the auditorium, Kamila listens with half an ear to the speaker. Some of the material he is presenting is new, but when he covers topics that are familiar from her own past reading, she switches her attention to her biology textbook (she needs to prepare for next week's quiz) and also to her iPhone, lying discreetly in her lap; she is uploading photos from last night's awesome party to Instagram while checking to see how

David Gee 3/Alamy Stock Photo

Marcio Eugenio/Shutterstock

"How many different tasks is Kamila trying to do at once? What are the costs of multitasking?"

working memory. The active maintenance and manipulation of short-term memory.

cognitive control. The manipulation and application of working memory for planning, task switching, attention, stimulus selection, and the inhibition of inappropriate reflexive behaviors.

sensory memory. Brief, transient sensations of what has just been perceived when someone sees, hears, or tastes something.

short-term memory. A temporary memory that is maintained through active rehearsal.

long-term memory. Permanent or near-permanent storage of memory that lasts beyond a period of conscious attention.

many "likes" her photos from last week's B'Nai Brith leadership retreat have been getting. This isn't the perfect situation for learning about business, studying biology, *or* keeping up with her busy social life, but by switching back and forth between the three activities, she manages to make some progress on all of them.

A day in the life of a high school senior is taxing indeed. To keep track of all her activities and commitments and deal efficiently with emergencies and last-minute changes, Kamila needs something like a mental blackboard. In fact, that is a good description of her **working memory**, the active and temporary representation of information that is maintained for the short term in Kamila's mind to help her think and allow her to decide what to do next. As she attends to her various responsibilities during the day, Kamila's ability to control the flow of information into and out of her working memory is critical to the multi-tasking and planning she has to do to thrive in high school. **Cognitive control** is the manipulation and application of working memory for planning, task switching, attention, stimulus selection, and the inhibition of inappropriate reflexive behaviors. Thus this chapter is about both working memory itself and the broader range of cognitive control tasks in which working memory plays a crucial role.

9.1 Behavioral Processes

Most psychologists would agree that there are three main distinctions among different types of memory: *sensory memory*, where information automatically and rapidly decays; **short-term memory (STM)**, where information can be maintained as long as it is rehearsed or consciously attended to; and **long-term memory (LTM)**, where memories can be retained for long periods, possibly permanently, without requiring ongoing maintenance or conscious attention. This view was laid out in an influential model by Richard Atkinson and Richard Shiffrin and is diagrammed in Figure 9.1 (Atkinson & Shiffrin, 1968). In this conceptualization of the stages of memory, short-term memory is the part of the memory system used as a temporary storage area and as the site of working memory (WM) operations.

The episodic and semantic memories discussed in Chapter 7 are long-term memories, which may last for hours, days, or even years. (They are represented in Figure 9.1 by the panel at the far right.). Skill memories, as discussed in Chapter 8, can also be very long-lasting parts of LTM. In contrast, the memories that are the main focus of this chapter—short-term memories—are transient, existing briefly for seconds or minutes at most. These temporary memories are crucial for performing many high-level cognitive control functions, such as planning, organization, and task management.

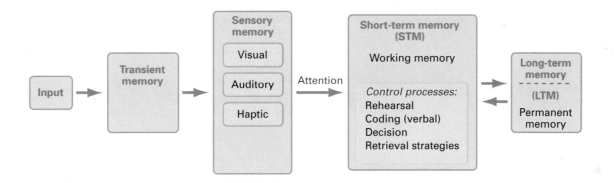

Figure 9.1 The Atkinson–Shiffrin model of memory
Richard Atkinson and Richard Shiffrin's model depicted incoming information as flowing first into sensory memory (shown as having distinct visual, auditory, and haptic, i.e., touch, registers). Elements of sensory information that are attended to are then transitioned to short-term memory (STM). From there they go through various control processes and in some cases are transferred into long-term memory (LTM).

Transient Memories

Transient memories are short-lasting mental representations, sometimes persisting for only a few seconds. The Atkinson–Shiffrin model describes two types of transient memory—sensory memory and short-term memory—and sees them as corresponding to the first two stages through which information from the world enters our consciousness and potentially becomes part of our long-term memory.

Sensory Memory

Sensory memories are brief, transient sensations of what you have just perceived when you have seen, heard, touched, smelled, or tasted something. Considerable research has been devoted to understanding how sensory memories are held in the mind so that they are accessible for further processing. Take a quick look at the table of letters in Figure 9.2; just glance at it for a second, no more. Now, without looking back at the figure, try to remember as many of the letters as you can. You probably only recalled four or five letters, or about 30–40% of the total array.

Based on this exercise, you might imagine that four or five items are the limit of your **visual sensory memory**, the temporary storage in sensory memory for information perceived by your visual system. Perhaps, however, you felt as if your eyes saw more than four or five letters, but you just couldn't recall more of them. In a seminal 1960 paper, George Sperling conducted a study confirming that you probably did, very briefly, register more than just the few items you were able to recall. Sperling presented people with a three-by-four visual array

transient memory. Nonpermanent memory that lasts seconds or minutes. The Atkinson–Shiffrin model describes two types: sensory and short-term.

visual sensory memory. The initial temporary storage for information perceived by the visual system.

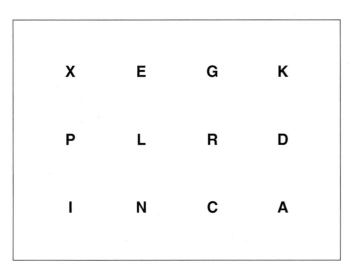

Figure 9.2 The Sperling task These three rows of four letters each are similar to the array George Sperling used in his studies of visual sensory memory (Sperling, 1960). How many of the letters did you remember after glancing at them for a second?

much like that shown in Figure 9.2. He then played one of three tones after the array was removed. A high tone indicated that participants were to report the first row of letters, a medium tone corresponded to the middle row, and a low tone corresponded to the bottom row.

When this partial report procedure was used, participants were able to report about 75% of the letters. Note that this is about double the number of letters recalled when people are simply asked to report as many letters as they can after the array is removed. What accounts for this doubled recall in Sperling's partial report procedure? Sperling interpreted it as meaning that people have a visual memory that persists for a very short time—less than a second—but includes *all* the items recently seen.

If there is rapidly decaying sensory memory for visual information, you might imagine that there would also be an analogous rapidly decaying sensory memory for other sensory modalities, such as touch, smell, and hearing. Indeed, there have been studies showing similar phenomena with auditory memory (Moray, Bates, & Barnett, 1965). As illustrated in Figure 9.1, there is a form of sensory memory for each sensory modality (auditory, visual, haptic, i.e., touch, etc.), which lasts very briefly and captures raw incoming sensory stimuli so that they can be processed and passed on to the short-term memory store, from which they may later be entered into long-term memory.

Short-Term Memory

Consider the common experience of looking up a phone number and then repeating it over and over to yourself as you prepare to press the buttons on your phone. The phone number has already been recognized and registered by sensory memory, but now it is the job of your short-term memory to maintain this information temporarily through active rehearsal. William James, whom you read about in Chapter 1, described short-term memory as being of limited capacity, effortlessly available, and fleeting in contrast to long-term memory, which holds permanent memories of the past, retrieved with effort, and which has potentially unlimited capacity (James, 1890). Short-term memory was, in James's view, the essence of our active conscious awareness. As summarized in Table 9.1, short-term memory and long-term memory can be distinguished in several ways.

Your ability to hold on to the information in short-term memory has certain limitations. First, as James noted, your memory is limited in capacity; a 10-digit phone number is a lot of information to keep in mind, even more so if you also have to remember a 4-digit extension. In Chapter 1, you read about the classic studies of George Miller, who in the early 1950s suggested that the capacity of short-term memory is about 7 items, a number he described as "the magic number 7" because it recurred so frequently in studies of memory capacity (Miller, 1956). Actually, Miller argued that there is a range of short-term memory capacities centered on 5 items but ranging from about 5 to 9 in most people (with the lower limits being more common).

Table 9.1 **Behavioral distinctions between short-term memory (STM) and long-term memory (LTM)**	
STM	**LTM**
Active contents of consciousness	Not currently in consciousness
Access is rapid	Access is slower
Capacity is limited	Capacity is unlimited
Forgotten quickly	Forgotten more slowly

Short-term memory is also limited to what you can pay attention to. If you get distracted by something else, you are likely to forget all or some of the phone number as you walk across the room to get your phone: that's why you rehearse it over and over in your head. By continuing to rehearse the number, you could potentially remember it indefinitely, as long as you do nothing else. Of course, there are plenty of things that could distract you and interrupt this rehearsal. If your roommate asks you a question—such as, "When is the chemistry exam?"—your rehearsal might be interrupted just long enough for you to forget some or all of the phone number. If you do forget it, you have to go back to look up the number again.

The capacity of short-term memory is also determined by how we encode the information we try to retain. As noted above, most people can only keep about half a dozen random numbers in short-term memory. Given this limited capacity for short-term memory, you might think it impossible to keep the following 11 digits in mind without memorizing them: 91117761492. Actually, it is quite easy, because you really only need to remember three historic dates: the month–day reference to the attack on the World Trade Center (9-11), the signing of the U.S. Declaration of Independence (1776), and Columbus's discovery of America (1492). Miller argued that the limit to short-term memory was not an absolute amount of information (or digits) but rather a limit in the number of unique concepts or links to long-term memory that could be held active. Miller argued that recoding of information is key to optimizing the amount of information that can be maintained in short-term memory.

(a)

(b)

(c)

What 11 digits do these three images convey?

" These drugs will affect your short-term memory so you better pay me now."

Paul Taylor/CartoonResource.com

It is no accident that 10-digit American phone numbers are broken into three chunks of three, three, and four digits, respectively. Chunking is an essential tool for controlling our short-term memory and using it effectively to store, temporarily, as much information as possible. Note that in the case of storing three historically significant dates to increase capacity to 11 digits, you must utilize your long-term memory to retrieve the dates from your knowledge of American history. As you will read later, these interactions between short-term memory and long-term memory are critically important.

Working Memory

Rehearsal is an important part of how we keep information active and accessible within short-term memory. As you walk across the room from your computer—where you found the phone number—to the phone, you rehearse the number to keep from forgetting it. Your goal isn't necessarily to store the phone number in your long-term memory (although that might be useful for future reference); rather, your immediate aim is to remember the number just long enough to get to your phone and make the call.

Short-term memory used in this way serves as a buffer, or temporary holding station, maintaining information for a brief period before it is manipulated or otherwise used to affect behavior. It is when short-term memory is employed in this fashion that it is referred to as our working memory. Thus, working memory involves the temporary retention of information just experienced or just retrieved from long-term memory. When information is maintained in working memory, it can be manipulated in ways that make it useful for goal-directed behavior, such as making decisions and retrieving other information from long-term memory. These processes will be described in more detail below.

Baddeley's Working-Memory Model

Alan Baddeley, an English psychologist, proposed an influential model of working memory illustrated in Figure 9.3 (Baddeley & Hitch, 1974). It can be viewed as an alternate (and more detailed) version of what goes on inside

Figure 9.3 Baddeley's working-memory model This model consists of two material-specific temporary stores for short-term maintenance of information—a visuospatial sketchpad for object and location information and a phonological loop for verbal material—that are controlled by a central executive. Baddeley's model can be viewed as depicting what goes on inside the STM box in Figure 9.1.

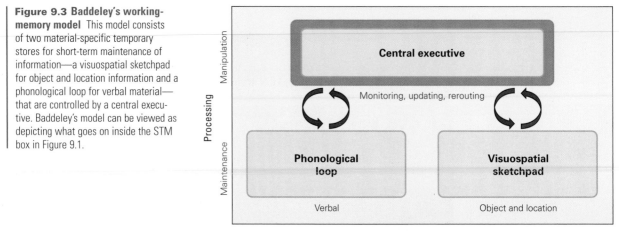

the STM/working-memory box in Figure 9.1. Baddeley's model includes two independent short-term memory buffers: the visuospatial sketchpad and the phonological loop. The **visuospatial sketchpad** holds visual and spatial images for manipulation. The **phonological loop** does the same for auditory memories, maintaining them by means of internal (subvocal) speech rehearsal (much like a "loop" of a tape recording that goes around and around, playing the same song over and over). A key feature of Baddeley's theory was that visuospatial information and verbal–phonological information are stored separately in working memory.

A third component of Baddeley's model is the **central executive**, which monitors and manipulates both of these working-memory buffers, providing cognitive control of working memory. The central executive's manipulations include adding to and deleting from the items in the buffers, selecting among the items in order to guide behavior, retrieving information from long-term memory, and transferring information from the visuospatial sketchpad and phonological loop to long-term memory. In these ways, the central executive manages the work that takes place in short-term memory and the traffic of information back and forth between short-term and long-term memory.

Figure 9.3 highlights two important distinctions made by Baddeley's model. First, it distinguishes between two general processes of working memory: manipulation (which depends on the central executive) and maintenance (which requires only rehearsal of information in the two memory buffers). Second, it identifies the memory buffers as being material specific: one stores verbal material and the other stores object and location material. We will proceed now with a discussion of the two memory buffers: the phonological loop and the visuospatial sketchpad. Later, in the Brain Substrates section, we will discuss recent data from neuroscience suggesting how both the material-specific and process-specific dichotomies in Baddeley's model of working memory have guided research on the brain mechanisms of working memory and cognitive control.

The idea of material-specific buffers in short-term memory received support from a series of studies of selective interference. These studies posited that if two tasks are using the same processing mechanism, they should interfere with each other if performed at the same time. Indeed, a wide range of studies show that verbal tasks interfere with verbal short-term memory but not visual short-term memory, and visual tasks interfere with visual short-term memory but not verbal short-term memory, lending support to the notion that working memory contains independent, material-specific systems for verbal and visual memories. The following paragraphs review some of this data.

The Phonological Loop

Read this list of seven numbers: 5 6 2 8 1 7 3. Now look away for 5 seconds and then repeat the list out loud. How did you solve the problem of remembering the numbers in this digit-span test? Most likely, you rehearsed them silently in your mind during the interval. In fact, if you didn't rehearse the numbers, you probably would have been unable to remember them. Without rehearsal, most people retain about 2 seconds' worth of information in their phonological memory, which gives most people enough time to remember about 5 to 7 items, Miller's magic number 7. Because of this time limit, people with slow rates of speech but normal intelligence do worse on short-term verbal memory tasks than people of normal intelligence who speak at a normal rate (Raine et al., 1991). (A person's internal speech proceeds at about the same rate as the person's speech spoken aloud.) This internal, unspoken speech used during rehearsal is key to the phonological loop and verbal working memory.

visuospatial sketchpad. The component of Baddeley's model of working memory that holds visual and spatial images for manipulation.

phonological loop. An auditory memory maintained by internal (subvocal) speech rehearsal.

central executive. The component of Baddeley's model of working memory that monitors and manipulates the two working memory buffers.

In fact, if this internal rehearsal is disrupted or eliminated, phonological storage cannot occur. For instance, if you were to say out loud, "good morning, good morning . . ." during the delay period while you were trying to remember the list of numbers in the digit-span test, your ability to internally rehearse would be greatly disrupted, impairing your ability to recall the seven numbers. On the other hand, tapping your fingers (a motor task) does not interfere with internal vocal rehearsal because it requires different modalities of processing, speech versus motor.

Additional insights into the processes for internal rehearsal in short-term memory come from studies where people are asked to remember lists of words. For example, which list do you think would be easier to remember?

List 1: bat, hit, top, cat, door

List 2: university, expedition, conversation, destination, auditorium

Most people would say the first is easier. As the length of the words increases, the number of words you can remember declines; this is known as the **word-length effect**. Short, one-syllable words like "bat" and "hit" are easier to rehearse in working memory than longer, multisyllable words like "university" and "auditorium." Longer words take longer to rehearse (Baddeley, Thomson, & Buchanan, 1975).

word-length effect. The tendency for a person to remember fewer words from a list as the length of the words increases.

The Visuospatial Sketchpad

The visuospatial sketchpad in Baddeley's model of working memory (see Figure 9.3) is a mental workspace for storing and manipulating visual and spatial information. Here is an example of it in use: without writing anything down, picture a four-by-four grid (16 squares) in your mind and imagine a "1" in the square that is the second column of the second row. Then place a 2 to the right of that. Next, in the square above the 2, put a 3, and to the right of that put a 4. Below the 4, put a 5 and below that, a 6, and then to the left of that, a 7. Now, what number is just above the 7? To correctly answer this question ("2"), you had to use your visuospatial sketchpad.

Just as the phonological loop has a 2-second time limit, the visuospatial sketchpad also has a limited capacity. The two capacities, however, are independent: filling up one does not much affect the capacity of the other. Dual-task experiments, in which subjects are asked to maintain information in the visuospatial sketchpad while simultaneously carrying out a secondary task using the other modality—such as retaining an auditory list of words in the phonological loop—provide evidence for the independence of these two memory buffers.

For example, Lee Brooks used a dual-task paradigm in which people were shown a block-capital letter "F" and were then asked to visualize this letter (from memory) and imagine an asterisk traveling around the edge of it (Figure 9.4a; Brooks, 1968). When the imaginary asterisk reaches a corner, it turns left or right to continue following the outline of the letter F. At each such turning point, the people were asked to indicate whether or not the asterisk was at a corner at the extreme top or bottom of the F (for example, the point at the F's upper right) or at one of the in-between corners. The crucial manipulation was that the participants were divided into three groups, and each group was assigned a different way of signaling. The *vocal group* signaled their answer to each question with a verbal "yes" or "no," the *tapping group* signaled with one tap for yes and two taps for no, and the *pointing group* pointed to a visual array of Y's and N's on a screen. Of the three groups, the pointing group performed most slowly, suggesting that the visuospatial demands of pointing at the appropriate symbol interfered with the visuospatial memory task (Figure 9.4b).

Because visual memory can be easily studied in a wide range of species, it has become the modality of choice for many carefully controlled laboratory experiments on working memory in animals. For example, in an early study of spatial working memory, Carlyle Jacobsen trained monkeys on a delayed

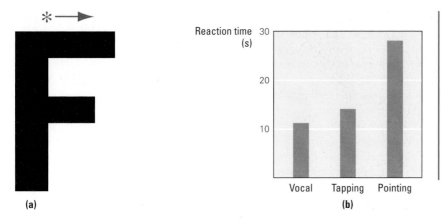

(a)

(b)

Figure 9.4 A dual-task experiment
(a) Participants were asked to imagine an asterisk traveling along the periphery of a letter "F." Whenever the asterisk was turning a corner, they were to signal whether it was turning at a corner on the extreme top or bottom of the letter or at some point in between. (b) Reaction times varied depending on whether subjects signaled vocally (fastest times), by tapping (intermediate times), or by pointing at symbols on a screen (slowest times).
Research from Brooks, 1968.

spatial-response task (Jacobsen, 1936). Each monkey watched food being placed in either the left or the right of two bins. Next, an opaque screen came down and blocked the monkey's view of the bins for several seconds or minutes. When the screen was removed, the bins now had lids hiding the food. To be marked correct, the monkey first had to remember in which bin the food had been stored and then displace the lid of just that bin to retrieve the reward.

The **delayed nonmatch-to-sample (DNMS) task** is another test of visual memory. Each trial involves remembering some novel object. Figure 9.5a shows Pygmalion, a rhesus monkey in Mortimer Mishkin's laboratory at the National Institute of Mental Health. He is shown a novel "sample" object, a blue ring, under which he finds a food reward, such as a peanut or a banana pellet. Afterward, an opaque black screen obscures Pygmalion's view (Figure 9.5b) for a delay period ranging from seconds to minutes, depending on the experiment

delayed nonmatch-to-sample task. A test of visual memory in which a subject must indicate which of two novel objects is not the same as one that was recently seen.

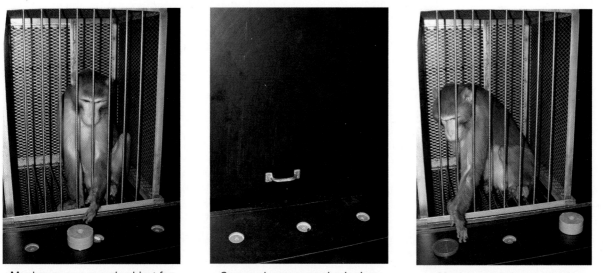

Monkey moves sample object for reward.

(a)

Screen obscures monkey's view during delay.

(b)

Monkey must choose novel nonmatch object for next reward.

(c)

Figure 9.5 Delayed nonmatch-to-sample task (a) A monkey is shown a sample object, here a blue ring, and finds a reward under it. (b) During the delay period, an opaque black screen blocks the monkey's view of any test objects. (c) The monkey is shown two objects, the blue ring from before (the sample) and a new object, a red disk. Through training, the monkey has learned that a food reward will be hidden under whichever object is the new one, the nonmatch to the original sample. The monkey chooses the nonmatch.
Courtesy of David Yu, Mortimer Mishkm, and Janita Turchi, Laboratory of Neuropsychology, NIMH/NIH/DHHS.

design. During this delay period, the experimenters introduce a new object, a red disk. When the screen is raised, Pygmalion sees both objects, one on the right and the other on the left. As shown in Figure 9.5c, Pygmalion has learned that a reward will now be found under the red disk because this is the novel object, a "nonmatch" to the sample object he saw previously. Training on this delayed nonmatch-to-sample task continues for several trials, each of which involves two objects not used in previous trials. Thus, the next trial might involve a yellow box as the sample and a green disk as the novel object. Over many such trials, the correct answer is sometimes on the left and sometimes on the right so that spatial location will not be a useful cue.

Because each trial uses a new set of objects, the monkeys must learn to remember which unique sample they saw previously and hold this memory in their visuospatial memory buffer until presented with the choice of that previous sample and the new novel object. With short delays, the DNMS task can be used to assess working memory; with longer delays, however, the same task has also been used to study long-term memory.

Is Working Memory a Place or a State?

Working memory is often conceptualized as the mind's active workspace—something akin to the top of your desk, where you bring files that have been stored elsewhere, physically moving them to where you can work with them all in one place. This idea of two different places, a long-term memory (LTM) and an active working memory, originated in the pre-computer days, when LTM was described using the metaphor of file cabinets filled with manila folders that had to be retrieved from storage in order to be used.

This metaphor of a place for working memory was further ingrained when computer systems came into use. Computer hardware distinguishes between a large hard drive and a smaller set of random-access memory (RAM) chips. The RAM chips in a computer define how many programs and how much data you can work on at any one time (like the limits on working memory), while the hard drive, with far more storage capacity, defines the total limits on memory storage for all your files and information, even those you have not looked at or thought about in a long time (like emails to your high school boyfriend, or last year's chemistry homework).

The idea of working memory and LTM as being two concrete, physical places in the mind dominated the first several decades of research on working memory. The Atkinson–Shiffrin Model in Figure 9.1, where information is diagrammed as flowing from STM/WM to LTM and back, seems naturally to suggest that memories move back and forth between these places. There is, however, another way of thinking about these transitions that has come to the forefront of working memory research in recent years. "Working memory" may not, in fact, describe a separate *place* for memories to be moved; rather, "working memory" may describe an active *state* for memories otherwise resident in LTM but not accessible to conscious reflection and manipulation until they are activated.

Consider an art museum that has a vast collection of paintings, far more than can be viewed at any one time. One way to focus on a small subset of the paintings might be to bring them out, a few at a time, to a special viewing workroom. This is akin to the place model of working memory. If the workroom were small (far smaller than the museum), you might only be able to bring a few of the paintings in there at a time. Alternatively, you could leave all the paintings where they are stored on the walls of the vast halls of the museum, and bring in several high intensity lights to shine on the few paintings you want to observe. The paintings stay where they always are, but the state of the paintings changes: they go from being obscure and unseen to being illuminated and visible.

As appealing and as useful as it has been for researchers in psychology to think of working memory as a place in the mind or brain, a growing body of research has shifted the field toward thinking about working memory as being more like an illuminated state and less like a physical place. Does this mean the Baddeley model is wrong? Not entirely. However, the state model of working memory does suggest that the central executive and phonological and visuospatial sketchpads of Figure 9.3 might be better thought of as states of activity and processing, rather than as physically distinct places within memory. The phonological loop and the visuospatial sketchpad could then be re-interpreted as the active states of phonological and visuospatial memories rather than as physically distinct places or components of memory.

Nelson Cowan (1995) has described a model of short-term memory in which several chunks of information in LTM can be activated as the focus of current attention. Recently activated items in LTM that are no longer the focus of attention can, for some limited period of time, remain partially activated and thus more easily brought back into focal attention. This would imply that STM is characterized by at least two different types of activated states, one directly accessible to attention and the other somewhat removed from the current attentional focus but easily brought back into focus. A number of variants on this state-based model of short-term and working memory have been proposed (Oberaauer, 2002, 2013; Awh & Jonides, 1998; Luck & Vogel, 2013).

Place models of memory are known as "multi-store" models of memory, because they imply the existence of two or more different places for memories to be stored; similarly, state-based models of memory have been referred to as "unitary-store" models of memory, because they imply there is only one place for memory, although the memories can be in various states.

A key question for all researchers in this subject area has been how much information can be stored in STM (Jonides et al., 2008). As we reviewed above, George Miller argued that STM has a capacity of "seven plus or minus two" (Miller, 1956). Place models of memory view these capacity limits as being governed by the rate at which information is rehearsed, forgotten, and transferred from one store to another (Baddeley, 1986). In contrast, state-based models of STM view capacity limits as arising from the bandwidth of attention that can be focused on activated areas of LTM (D'Esposito & Postle, 2015).

Overall, state-based models of working memory are able to account for much of the same data as the place-based models of working memory. The principal reason they have gained prominence in recent years is that they are better able to account for new brain-imaging data from cognitive neuroscience studies of the brain substrates of working memory. We will discuss these studies in more detail later in the Brain Substrates section of this chapter.

Cognitive Control

Most of the tasks described in the preceding section require the person or animal simply to maintain some word, digit, object, sound, or location in working memory during a delay period. But there is much more to working memory than just the maintenance of phonological or visuospatial memories: there is the far more complex and involved process of *manipulating* working memory. This is **cognitive control** (also known as **executive control** or **executive function**): the manipulation of working memory that allows for the exercise of various aspects of higher-order cognition, including reasoning, task flexibility, problem solving, and planning.

We saw earlier, for example, that Kamila has to keep several of her day's goals in mind: get cash, prepare for cheerleading, study for biology, and listen to a

executive control. The manipulation of working memory through the updating of stored information to facilitate goals, planning, task switching, stimulus selection, and response inhibition.

Test Your Knowledge

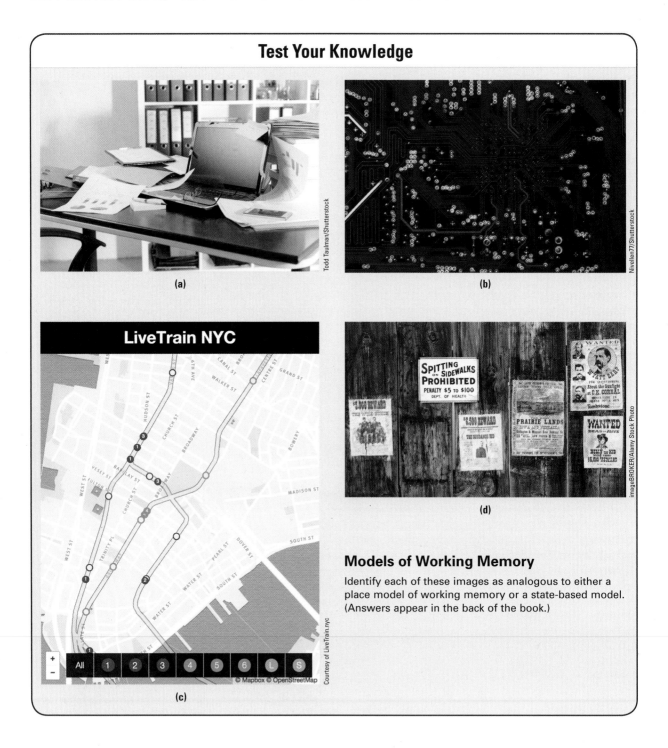

(a)

(b)

LiveTrain NYC

(c)

(d)

Models of Working Memory

Identify each of these images as analogous to either a place model of working memory or a state-based model. (Answers appear in the back of the book.)

business lecture. Balancing these multiple goals requires her to switch her attention back and forth between activities as the situation requires. Her working memory is constantly being updated and reorganized to accomplish different and competing tasks. New tasks are constantly added. All of these tasks require the cognitive-control function of her working memory's central executive.

Table 9.2 Cognitive control through the manipulation of working memory

Behaviors	Tasks used to explore these behaviors
Controlled updating of short-term memory	*N*-back task, self-ordered search
Setting goals and planning	Tower of Hanoi
Task switching	Wisconsin Card Sorting Test
Stimulus attention and response inhibition	Stroop task

Of the three components of Baddeley's model, the central executive is the most important, the most complex, and the least well understood. What is common to all the functions of the central executive is that they involve the *manipulation* of information in short-term memory, including adding or removing items, reordering items, and using working memory to guide other behaviors. Through this manipulation of information held in short-term memory, the central executive goes beyond simple rehearsal to become, in effect, the *working* component of working memory. Researchers have found evidence of cognitive control in many behaviors, including, but not limited to, (1) controlled updating of short-term memory buffers, (2) setting goals and planning, (3) task switching, and (4) stimulus attention and response inhibition. We will discuss each of these in turn in the following pages, and they are summarized in Table 9.2. This list of behaviors may seem, at first glance, like a random selection of activities, but they all depend on the controlled manipulation of working memory. The list is by no means exhaustive—there are many other behaviors that involve working-memory manipulation—but these four examples serve to illustrate the breadth and diversity of mental activities that involve working memory and cognitive control.

Controlled Updating of Short-Term Memory Buffers

The central executive component of working memory functions much like a manager at a large corporation who is responsible for assigning specific people to certain jobs at particular times. On Monday, he might tell Mike to work the front desk and Stephanie to work on the sales floor. Come Tuesday, however, he might fire Mike, promote Stephanie to the front desk, and then hire Kristy to work on the sales floor. In an analogous fashion, the central executive in Baddeley's model is responsible for updating working memory by receiving and evaluating sensory information, moving items into and retrieving them from long-term memory, and deciding which memories are needed for which tasks.

To study the controlled updating of working memory, researchers often use what is called a 2-back test. In a 2-back test, a participant is read a seemingly random list of items, usually numbers. A certain item—let's say the number 7— is designated as the "target." Whenever the target number 7 is read, the participant is to respond with the number that was read *two numbers previously* (hence the name 2-back). Sound tough? Try it. If the numbers read aloud are 4 8 3 7 8 2 5 6 7 8 0 2 4 6 7 3 9 . . . , what would the correct responses be? (Answer: "8" to the first 7, "5" to the second 7, and "4" to the third 7.)

To succeed at this task, the participant must constantly keep track of the last two numbers that were read: the 1-back and 2-back numbers. As each new number is read, a new 1-back number must be stored and the old 1-back number must be shifted to the 2-back slot, replacing the previous 2-back number in working memory. In addition, each number must be checked as it is read to see if it is the target number. If it *is* the target number, the participant has to respond with the 2-back number; if it isn't the target number, the participant says nothing. Not easy!

Performing the 2-back task requires active maintenance of many kinds of items in working memory. First are the target number and the rules for performing the task, both of which stay constant throughout the experiment. Second, the last two numbers that were read must always be remembered in case the next number is the target number. These two items change in identity, priority, or both with each new number that is read and must be regularly updated in working memory.

What might happen to your performance on this type of task if you were asked to repeat the 3-back or 4-back number instead of the 2-back number? Although the 2-back task is the most commonly used variation, this class of tasks is generally called *N*-back because *N* can be any number. The larger *N* is, the greater the challenge. The *N*-back task taps into many aspects of the central executive's manipulation of working memory, including online storage of recent information, selective attention, remembering task demands, and updating and reorganizing stored items. For this reason, it is considered an excellent tool for assessing the functioning of working memory's central executive. We will discuss several experimental studies of the *N*-back task in the Brain Substrates section.

A more common situation faced by your own central executive functioning is the need to keep track of the various everyday tasks you need to perform: What have you done already? What remains to be accomplished? For example, if you have lost your eyeglasses *somewhere* in your home, you might search every room for them. While it may not matter which rooms you search first, you do want to keep track of the rooms so as not to waste time searching where you have already been. Self-ordered tasks that ask people to keep track of their previous responses (analogous to keeping track of the rooms they already searched) are another tool that can be used to assess the central executive's manipulation of working memory.

Michael Petrides, at McGill University in Canada, developed self-ordered memory tasks in studying the behavioral and neural bases of working memory (Petrides & Milner, 1982; Petrides, 2000). In the human version of this task, people are shown a stack of cards, each containing the same set of items but in a different order. In the example shown in Figure 9.6, there are six items on each card. In card 1, the drawing of a rose (to which the subject is pointing) appears in the lower right corner, while in card 2 the rose is in the upper left corner, and in card 3 it is in the upper right corner.

The experiment proceeds as follows: On trial 1 a participant is shown the first card and is asked to choose any of the six items on it. The participant in Figure 9.6 has chosen the rose. This card is then flipped over. Next, on trial 2, the participant is shown the second card (with the same six items in a different order) and is asked to choose any of the five items not yet selected. In Figure 9.6, the participant has chosen the goat. This second card is then flipped over. Then the participant is shown the third card and must pick any of the four remaining items that were not chosen on the previous two cards, that is, any image except the rose or the goat. This self-ordered task continues until the participant has pointed to all six different items without repeating any. Note that this task requires the participants to monitor (keep track of) the information being held in short-term memory and decide what to keep there given the current task.

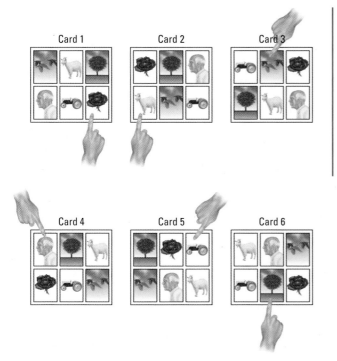

Figure 9.6 A self-ordered memory task for humans
Sample cards from a self-ordered search task for humans (Petrides & Milner, 1982). Participants are presented with a stack of cards, each containing all the items in the target set but in different random order. Participants must point to a different item on each card without repeating any of the items.
Information from Petrides, 2000.

This task is appealing to researchers who want to understand working memory in both human and nonhuman primates because it can also be studied in monkeys, as shown in Figure 9.7 (Petrides & Milner, 1982). On the first trial, a monkey sees a row of three nonmatching containers, each of which contains a reward, and selects the reward from one of them. Following this step, an opaque screen is placed between the monkey and the containers for 10 seconds, and the containers are shuffled so that on the second trial the monkey sees the same containers in a new order. Now the monkey must choose one of the other containers in order to get a reward. Like the human self-ordered task described above, this task requires the monkey to remember the items chosen previously. On the third trial, the monkey has to choose again, with only one remaining container still baited with a reward. Because this kind of working-memory task can be performed by both monkeys and humans, it is useful for comparative studies of the neural substrates of working memory, as will be described later in the Brain Substrates section.

Setting Goals and Planning

As Kamila prepared for the school day ahead of her, she had to be aware of her immediate goals (getting to business class on time in the morning) as well as her goals for later that afternoon (cheerleading tryouts). To make sure she could participate in the tryouts and get to them on time after her afternoon class, she had to (1) search through her closet to find her cheerleading pom-poms and (2) stop by the cafeteria to sign up for the tryouts. Only then would she go to business class. Kamila's busy schedule requires her to keep track of many goals at once and to juggle them in her mind as the day passes, noting which tasks have been accomplished and which are left to be done, and of those left to be done, which should be done next. Keeping track of goals, planning how to achieve them, and determining priorities all draw heavily on the central executive of working memory.

Figure 9.7 A self-ordered memory task for monkeys The monkey sees three distinct containers and selects a reward from one of them. Their order is shuffled on each trial, and the monkey must remember which containers have had rewards removed so that on subsequent trials the monkey does not pick a previously chosen (and hence empty) container.

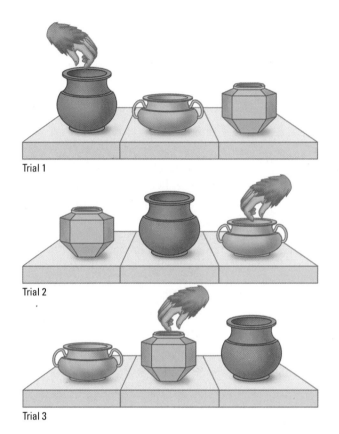

Trial 1

Trial 2

Trial 3

The French mathematician Edouard Lucas invented a game back in 1883 that requires many of these same planning and goal-setting abilities. The game is based on an ancient legend about a temple in India where a certain puzzle was used to develop mental discipline in young priests. A stack of 64 gold disks, each slightly smaller than the one beneath, were all stacked on a large pole. The young priest's assignment was to transfer all 64 disks from the first pole to a second and, finally, to a third pole by moving one disk at a time and only placing smaller disks on top of larger disks. According to the legend, if any priest ever solved the problem, the temple would crumble into dust, and the world would vanish. Perhaps one reason the world still exists today, thousands of years later, is that even if a very smart and quick priest were to move one disk per second, solving this task with 64 disks would take him 580 billion years.

Lucas called his simplified version, which was marketed as a board game, the Tower of Hanoi. You were briefly introduced to it in Chapter 8. At the game's start, the disks are placed on the left-most of three pegs, arranged by increasing size from bottom to top, as in Figure 8.1, which shows a small blue disk on top of a medium yellow disk on top of a large red disk (see p. 315). In order to move the disks properly and solve the puzzle, it helps to establish subgoals, such as getting the large red disk over to the right-most peg, a maneuver that takes four moves.

Solving the Tower of Hanoi requires a great deal of manipulation of working memory because you must remember at least three things at all times: (1) what subgoals have been accomplished, (2) what subgoals remain, and (3) what the next subgoal is to be addressed. After each move, some of these will be updated and changed, while others will stay the same. This kind of goal-directed controlled updating of short-term memory is exactly the kind of task that places a

Test Your Knowledge

Varieties of Working Memory and Cognitive Control

For each of the following scenarios (1 through 4), indicate which facet of working memory (A through D, below) is in evidence. (Answers appear in the back of the book.)

1. Texting while driving

2. Remembering not to wake up in the middle of night and call out the name of your old girlfriend while you are sleeping with your new girlfriend

3. Remembering to pick up donuts, toilet paper, and seltzer water at the convenience store while you make your way up and down the aisles

4. Preparing dinner for your friends with an entrée, salad, and two side dishes—and having all of them ready to serve at the same time

CHOICES:

   A. *Controlled updating of short-term memory buffers*

   B. *Setting goals and planning*

   C. *Task switching*

   D. *Stimulus selection and response inhibition*

Are Working Memory and Cognitive Control the Keys to Intelligence?

"Intelligence," defined as the capacity for learning, reasoning, and understanding, is a familiar enough term, but the concept itself is often poorly understood. Intelligent people are frequently described as "quick," but a growing body of research suggests that intelligence has less to do with the brain's processing speed and more to do with executive control of working memory.

Assessing students' working memory using a delayed recall task, Meredyth Daneman and Patricia Carpenter found a strong correlation between working-memory scores and verbal SAT tests of reading comprehension, often viewed as an approximate indication of intelligence (Daneman & Carpenter, 1980), although others have argued they are is simply an indicator of expected performance in college.

However, the relationship between working memory and intelligence does not depend only on verbal intelligence. Carpenter and her colleagues used puzzles based on standard non-verbal tests of intelligence, the Raven Progressive Matrices. These employ two-dimensional visual analogy problems in which the participant is directed to select the design that completes each pattern. The illustrative example shown in Figure 9.10 is a 3-by-3 array of geometric figures with one in the lower-right-hand corner missing. Participants must pick which of the six alternatives at the bottom best fits the pattern. What is the pattern? Note that each figure varies on two dimensions: the color (black, gray, or white) and the number of triangles (1, 2, or 3). Moreover, no row or column has two figures with the same number of triangles or the same color. To complete this pattern, the figure in the lower right would have to be white (there is no white figure in the third row or third column) and contain two triangles (there is no figure with two triangles in the third row or third column). Thus, the correct answer is #5, two white triangles.

Figure 9.10 Raven Progressive Matrix Test of Nonverbal Intelligence In this example, subjects are shown a three-by-three array of eight geometric figures and a space, in the lower-right-hand corner, where the ninth figure belongs. They must pick which of the six alternatives shown at the bottom best fits the pattern. (The correct answer is #5.)

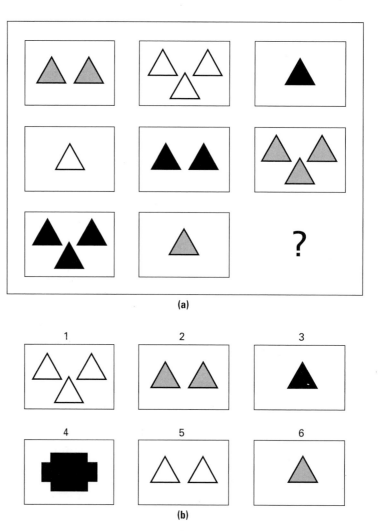

An enormous range of difficulty can be introduced into this kind of task simply by increasing the complexity of the patterns or the number of components. Carpenter and colleagues showed that being able to juggle many rules in one's head is correlated with scoring high on non-verbal tests of intelligence. These kinds of evidence suggest that general intelligence, as detected by intelligence tests, is not just a matter of thinking or responding quickly. Rather, general intelligence appears to be associated with a strong working memory, especially the control and manipulation of larger numbers of rules, concepts, goals, and ideas.

Interim Summary

- Transient memories are temporary representations of information. They are found in the first two stages—sensory memory and short-term, or working, memory—of the Atkinson–Shiffrin model of the stages of memory storage. Short-term memories can be maintained by active rehearsal but are easily displaced by new information or distractions.

- Alan Baddeley characterized working memory as consisting of two independent short-term memory buffers—the visuospatial sketchpad, which holds visual and spatial images, and the phonological loop, an auditory memory that uses internal speech rehearsal—along with a central executive.

- In Baddeley's model, the central executive is responsible for manipulating memories in the two buffers by, for example, adding and deleting items, selecting items to guide behavior, and retrieving information from and storing it in long-term memory.

- The manipulation and use of working memory for cognitive control can be measured through neuropsychological tests that assess such functions as controlled updating of short-term memory, setting goals and planning, task switching, and stimulus attention and response inhibition.

- Earlier conceptions that viewed working memory (and short-term memory) as being in a different place from long-term memory have now evolved to a more nuanced "single unitary-storage" view of memory, which sees these different facets of memory as being different states of memory rather than in different places.

9.2 Brain Substrates

Could the frontal lobes contain the brain's chief executive, in charge of working memory, reasoning, and other cognitive functions? There is a growing consensus that the prefrontal cortex, with its extensive connections to more posterior regions of the brain, is critical for initiating executive functions and cognitive control and does so by integrating external and internal information needed to guide complex behaviors (Miller & Wallis, 2008). If this is the case, how do the frontal lobes mediate working memory and cognitive control? How does working memory work in the brain? These questions drive current research as scientists seek to understand to what extent psychological theories, such as Baddeley's model, correspond to how working memory is organized in the brain. Does the brain in fact possess a distinct, recognizable working memory system, or is working memory simply the transient and current activity of the brain's memory system in general? What about the hippocampus and medial temporal lobes: are they relevant to working memory, or are they only involved in storing new facts and events in long-term memory as described in Chapter 7?

The Frontal Lobes and Consequences of Frontal-Lobe Damage

Studies of animals and humans implicate the frontal lobes—especially the **prefrontal cortex (PFC)**, the most anterior (farthest forward) section of the frontal lobes—as being critical for working memory and executive control. Since the beginning of modern brain research in the mid-1800s, the intellectual functions of planning, foresight, decision making, and related behaviors have been associated with this brain region (Markowitsch, 1992).

In humans, the prefrontal cortex encompasses approximately one-third of the cerebral cortex (Goldman-Rakic, 1987). Cats and many other mammals, on the other hand, get by with frontal lobes that occupy less than 4% of their cerebral cortex. Figure 9.11 compares the relative sizes of the prefrontal cortex in several mammalian species, showing how much larger, proportionally, our prefrontal cortex is compared with the prefrontal cortex in the cat, rhesus monkey, and chimpanzee. Because the prefrontal cortex occupies a markedly larger proportion of the cerebral cortex in humans than in many other mammals, many people have assumed that it is what makes us human. More recent studies, however, have shown that human frontal cortices are not disproportionally larger than those seen in great apes such as gorillas and orangutans. This suggests that the special human cognitive abilities

prefrontal cortex (PFC). The frontmost (anterior) part of the frontal-lobe cortex, essential for working memory and executive control.

Figure 9.11 Comparative frontal-lobe anatomy These drawings show the relative sizes of the prefrontal cortex in different mammals.

Information from Fuster, 1995.

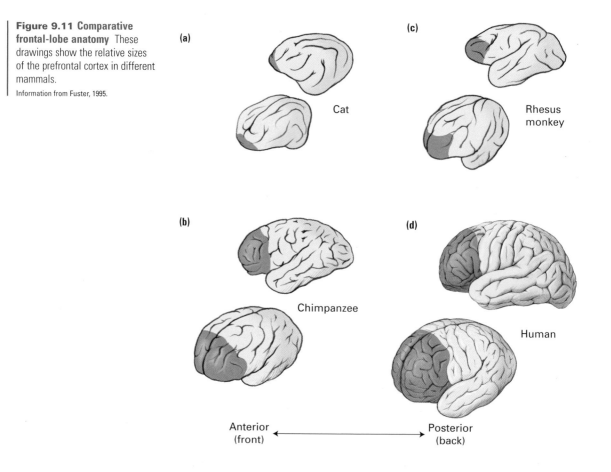

(a) Cat

(c) Rhesus monkey

(b) Chimpanzee

(d) Human

Anterior (front) ←——————→ Posterior (back)

attributed to large frontal lobes may also reflect characteristics other than size, such as more complex interconnections or specialized subregions found within the frontal cortex of humans (Semendeferi, Lu, Schenker, & Damasio, 2002).

Behavior Changes Following Frontal-Lobe Damage

Other insights into the role of the prefrontal cortex came from observing the behaviors of people with frontal-lobe damage. During World War I, for example, the many soldiers returning from battle with head wounds provided evidence of links between frontal lobes and intellect. A study of 300 veterans returning from World War I with head wounds showed that those veterans with frontal-lobe damage were the most impaired in higher intellectual abilities (Pfeifer, 1922).

One noted characteristic of frontal-lobe damage is a loss of ability to plan and to organize. Wilder Penfield, a famous neurosurgeon from the mid-twentieth century who did pioneering work on brain mapping, described the changes in his own sister after she had a large tumor removed from her frontal regions. She had been an accomplished cook, but after the surgery she lost all ability to organize her cooking; she would move haphazardly from dish to dish, leaving some dishes uncooked while others burned (Miller & Wallis, 2003).

Consider Elliot, a successful and happily married accountant, who had always been viewed by others as reliable and responsible. In his late thirties he developed a large tumor in his frontal lobes. Surgeons were able to remove the tumor and save his life. However, the operation severely damaged his frontal lobes (Eslinger & Damasio, 1985; Damasio, 1994; Miller & Wallis, 2008). Soon after the surgery, he divorced his wife, remarried and divorced again, lost touch with most of his friends and family, got involved in corrupt business deals, and was soon bankrupt. The formerly responsible and cautious Elliot had become impulsive and easily swayed by momentary whims, retaining little of his previous ability to organize and plan.

Penfield's sister and Elliot were both behaving as we might expect in the absence of a cognitive-control system. They were no longer guided by long-term goals or task-specific constraints. Rather, they appeared to be ruled by their reflexive and automatic impulses and to have little capacity for foresight and planning. For this reason, people like Penfield's sister and Elliot are described as having **dysexecutive syndrome**, a disrupted ability to think and plan (Duncan, Emslie, Williams, Johnson, & Freer, 1996). As you will read below, patients with frontal-lobe damage routinely exhibit deficits in both executive function and working memory despite normal long-term memory and skill-learning abilities.

In addition to tumors and surgery, frontal lobes can be damaged by strokes or blunt trauma to the front of the head—or, as often happens, from a rapid deceleration (as in a car crash) in which the frontal lobes compress against the front of the skull. Professional (and even some high school) football players, who routinely head-butt other players and experience rapid deceleration, also show a pattern of frontal-lobe damage and associated cognitive problems (Amen et al., 2011).

Deficits in Working Memory Following Frontal-Lobe Damage

People with damage to the frontal lobes show deficits on all of the working-memory and cognitive-control tasks described in Section 9.1. For example, they have great difficulty updating working memory in the *N*-back task as well as performing self-ordered tasks that require frequent updating to recollect items that have been previously chosen (Petrides, 2000). Patients with frontal-lobe damage are also often impaired at tasks that tap short-term memory span, including digit-span tasks, in which they may fail to recall even a short series of numbers (Janowsky, Shimamura, Kritchevsky, & Squire, 1989). Other studies of these patients have shown similar impairments in short-term memory for colors, shapes, and object locations (Baldo & Shimamura, 2000; Ptito, Crane, Leonard, Amsel, & Caramanos, 1995). Additionally, as you might expect, patients with frontal-lobe damage show deficits in neuropsychological tests such as the Tower of Hanoi, which assesses planning abilities and requires maintaining and linking multiple subgoals to achieve the final desired goal. On the Tower of Hanoi task, patients like Elliot or Penfield's sister move the disks around aimlessly, without a clear plan for getting the disks from the first peg to the last.

The ability to shift appropriately from one task to another is a central feature of executive control. Thus, task-switching test procedures such as that described in Section 9.1 provide another means of assessing frontal-lobe function. One study had participants monitor two streams of simultaneously presented stimuli, a series of letters on the left and a stream of digits on the right (Duncan, Emslie, Williams, Johnson, & Freer, 1996). At the beginning of the experiment, the participant was to read aloud the letters on the left. Later, when a signal cue was sounded, the person was supposed to switch to the other stream and begin reporting the digits. Later still, the signal would sound again as a sign that the participant should switch back to the letters. Although patients with frontal lesions had no trouble complying with the first part of the experiment, they had great difficulty switching between the left and right streams on cue.

The Wisconsin Card Sort Test (see Figure 9.8) is frequently used in clinical settings for assessment of frontal-lobe function. Frontal-lobe patients have no problem learning an initial sorting rule, such as to sort by color. Later, however, when the person must learn a new rule for sorting—say, by shape—frontal-lobe patients are severely impaired at making the transition. They show **perseveration**, which means they fail to learn a new rule and, instead, persist

dysexecutive syndrome. A disrupted ability to think and plan.

perseveration. A failure to learn a new response, especially as demonstrated by continued adherence to an old, no longer valid response rule.

in using an old rule despite repeated feedback indicating that the old rule is no longer correct. The severe deficits in task shifting associated with frontal-lobe damage suggest that purposeful shifts in processing may be especially demanding of executive-control processes mediated by the frontal lobes (Delis, Squire, Bihrle, & Massman, 1992; Owen et al., 1993).

Carlyle Jacobsen, an early and important researcher in this area, conducted animal studies in the early 1930s that implicated the frontal cortex in working memory (Jacobsen, 1936). Specifically, he looked at the effects of lesions in different parts of the brain on delayed spatial-response learning in monkeys. In these studies, monkeys were permitted to observe food being placed either in a location on the left or on the right of a surface outside their cages. After a delay during which the monkeys were not able to see the food, the monkeys were required to point to where the food had been placed. Jacobsen demonstrated that only monkeys with prefrontal lesions were impaired at responding correctly, exhibiting a selective and delay-dependent deficit in the tasks. Based on these results, he argued that an animal's frontal lobes are critical for maintaining an internal representation of information in working memory over a delay prior to making some response.

One limitation of this early work was the relative crudity of Jacobsen's surgical techniques by modern standards: he removed a rather large part of the prefrontal cortex that likely included many specialized subregions. More recent research has shown that different subregions of the prefrontal cortex participate in different aspects of working-memory function.

Divisions of the Prefrontal Cortex (PFC)

The primate prefrontal cortex can be divided into three main regions: the *orbital prefrontal cortex*, the *medial prefrontal cortex*, and the *lateral prefrontal cortex*. The lateral prefrontal cortex can be further subdivided into two components: the **dorsolateral prefrontal cortex (DLPFC)** on the top and the **ventrolateral prefrontal cortex (VLPFC)** below it, as shown in Figure 9.12. (The orbital frontal cortex is not visible in these drawings because it lies ventral to—that is, below—the regions shown; and the medial prefrontal cortex is not visible because it is inside the regions shown, tucked away above and behind the orbital region; see, however, Figure 5.8 in Chapter 5.) Both the orbital and medial prefrontal cortexes are implicated in many memory and cognitive-control functions,

dorsolateral prefrontal cortex. The left and right sides of the topmost part of the prefrontal cortex (PFC), often abbreviated DLPFC.

ventrolateral prefrontal cortex. The lower left and right sides of the PFC.

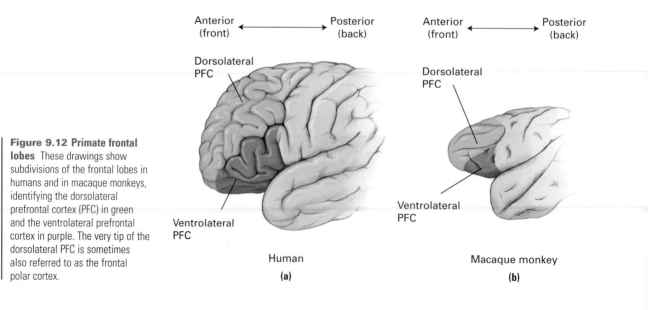

Figure 9.12 Primate frontal lobes These drawings show subdivisions of the frontal lobes in humans and in macaque monkeys, identifying the dorsolateral prefrontal cortex (PFC) in green and the ventrolateral prefrontal cortex in purple. The very tip of the dorsolateral PFC is sometimes also referred to as the frontal polar cortex.

Anterior (front) ⟷ Posterior (back)

Dorsolateral PFC

Ventrolateral PFC

Human
(a)

Anterior (front) ⟷ Posterior (back)

Dorsolateral PFC

Ventrolateral PFC

Macaque monkey
(b)

especially goal-driven behavior and planning, but they are less involved in working memory than the lateral regions of the prefrontal cortex and so will not be discussed further in this chapter. Much of what we know about the role of the DLPFC and VLPFC in working memory comes from recordings of brain activity in humans and monkeys. Data from such studies will be discussed next.

Frontal Brain Activity During Working-Memory Tasks

Guided by lesion studies suggesting that the prefrontal cortex plays a role in working memory, researchers in the early 1970s began to record prefrontal-cortex neural activity during working-memory tasks (Fuster & Alexander, 1971; Kubota & Niki, 1971). In a study by Joaquin Fuster, using a delayed-response task similar to the one used in the Jacobsen studies described above, rhesus macaque monkeys were required to remember either where they had seen a target object or what object they had previously seen (Fuster & Alexander, 1971). The researchers found that some prefrontal-cortex neurons fired only during a delay period and only when the animals were required to maintain information about a spatial location of a particular object. This suggested to them that the prefrontal cortex might be "holding in mind" information needed to make a later response. If so, then the neural activity in the prefrontal cortex was acting as a temporal bridge between stimulus cues and a contingent response concerning object location, so as to facilitate linking events across time. Such activity appears to be a key component of sensorimotor behaviors that span delays (Fuster, 2001, 2003). Persistent activity of this type in the DLPFC during blank memory intervals (delays, when no external stimulation is present) is a strong argument implicating the DLPFC as a critical brain region supporting the maintenance of items in working memory (Curtis & D'Esposito, 2006).

Instead of requiring an animal to pick up an object or point to a location, some experiments simply track the animal's gaze. Eye-tracking technology offers well-controlled methods for testing spatial and object working memory in animals. Patricia Goldman-Rakic of Yale University Medical School, one of the pioneers in working-memory research, used this technology in a series of highly influential studies of primate working memory.

In her studies, Goldman-Rakic trained monkeys to fixate on a central spot on a display as shown in Figure 9.13a (top row). The monkeys maintained their fixation on the central spot while a square cue was presented at one of eight locations around the edge of the display (e.g., the upper-right corner, as in Figure 9.13a). After the cue was removed, the monkeys waited during a delay period of several seconds (Figure 9.13b), as they were trained to do, and then, at a certain signal, responded by moving their gaze to the cue's former location (Figure 9.13c). Moving the gaze to the correct location resulted in a reward.

In electrophysiological recordings of these tasks, Goldman-Rakic and colleagues found that some of the neurons in the dorsolateral prefrontal cortex fired only while the animal was remembering the stimulus location (Funahashi, Bruce, & Goldman-Rakic, 1989). As shown in the electrical recordings in the middle row of Figure 9.13, certain neurons in the prefrontal cortex fire during presentation of the cue itself (Figure 9.13a; note the increase in firing during presentation of the cue in the area between the two red lines on the left), others fire only during the delay period (Figure 9.13b; note the increase in firing during the delay period), while others fire during the response (Figure 9.13c; note the increase in firing to the right of the right-most red line). Each of these three recordings in Figure 9.13 shows a different neuron.

Figure 9.13 The spatial delayed-response eye-gaze task (a) The monkey fixates on a central spot on the screen while a cue flashes in the upper-right corner. (b) During a delay period, the cue disappears and the monkey remains fixated on the central point. (c) Finally, when the central spot turns off, the monkey looks where the cue previously appeared. (For clarity, the monkey is shown in mirror image in the figure so we can see it gaze in the direction of the stimulus shown above).

Data from Funahashi, Bruce, & Goldman-Rakic, 1989.

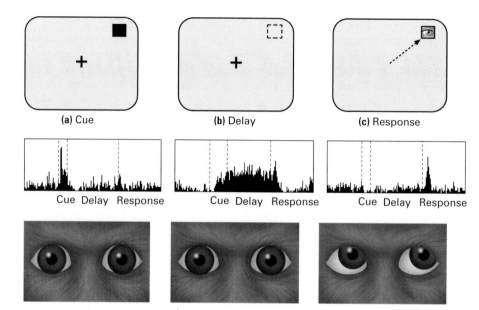

Most interesting of all is that the "delay" neurons were individually tuned to different directional movements. For example, one neuron might code for a movement to the right, while another neuron might code for a downward movement, and so on. Figure 9.14 shows the strong response of a particular neuron when the cue was located at the bottom center of the screen (bottom-center graph), compared with the inhibition of its electrical activity when the cue was in the opposite location (top-center) and to the moderate activity when the cue was at other locations.

The strong firing seen in Figure 9.14 during the delay for the trial in which the cue was at bottom center could represent one of two things: it could be a memory for where the cue had appeared or it could be an anticipatory coding for the later movement of the eye gaze to that location. To distinguish between these alternatives, the researchers conducted an experiment in which the monkeys were trained to move their eyes to the location opposite to the cue. In that study, about 80% of the delay cells seemed to encode where the target had been (regardless of the eye-gaze response), while the other 20% seemed to encode the intended movement. These results suggest that the neurons of the dorsolateral prefrontal cortex that fire during the delay are encoding a combination of sensory and movement-response information.

The monkeys did quite well at this delayed-response task, but they never performed it with 100% accuracy. Occasionally, they would make an error and move their eyes to the wrong position. Was it just a motor mistake, or was the prefrontal cortex itself confused as to the correct answer? The researchers found the latter to be true: the electrophysiological recordings predicted when a monkey was going to make an error, because the "wrong" neurons fired in the dorsolateral prefrontal cortex.

Sustained neuronal activity during the delay period is not limited, however, to the dorsolateral prefrontal cortex. Similar sustained activity can also be seen in the relevant primary and secondary sensory and motor regions in the temporal and parietal lobes located in the more posterior regions of the brain. These regions are reciprocally connected to the prefrontal cortex.

If the sensory and motor cortexes can sustain activity during a delay, assuming that sustained activity is indeed critical for working memory, why should

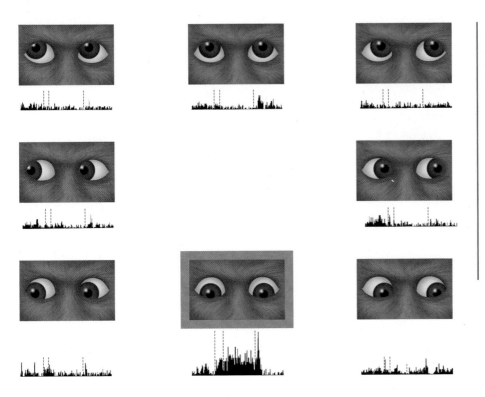

Figure 9.14 Response of one prefrontal cortex neuron during the delayed-response eye-gaze task Electrophysiological activity of the neuron during the cue, delay, and response periods of the task when the cue was presented at different locations. Note the strong response when the cue was at the bottom location (indicated by the blue outline) compared with the inhibited activity when the cue was presented at the top-center location. (For clarity, the monkey is shown in mirror image in the figure so that we see it gaze in the same direction as the stimulus being shown to it.)

Data from Funahashi, Bruce, & Goldman-Rakic, 1989.

the prefrontal cortex be necessary for working memory to function? Earl Miller argued that the key "cognitive" contribution of the prefrontal cortex to working memory is the ability of the prefrontal cortex to sustain activity *despite distractions* (Miller, 2000). To test his hypothesis, Miller and colleagues trained monkeys to maintain the visual memory of an object throughout a delay period filled with visually distracting events (Miller, Erickson, & Desimone, 1996). They found that activity in the posterior visual cortical areas was easily disrupted by the distractors. In contrast, the corresponding dorsolateral prefrontal-cortex activity remained robust despite distractions. The ability of the prefrontal cortex to provide focused control over working memory is consistent with lesion data demonstrating that one salient consequence of prefrontal-cortex damage, both in humans and in monkeys, is a high degree of distractibility. Studies in humans, too, have shown persistent activity in the DLPFC during the retention interval of delayed-response tasks. Event-related fMRI studies of humans have recorded persistent activity in the DLPFC during retention intervals of delayed-response tasks. This is illustrated in Figure 9.15, which shows similar patterns of activity from both monkey and human DLPFC during the delay period in a task in which subjects were required to withhold responding to a cue, as in the studies of Goldman-Rakic and others described above.

Why is this persistent activity in the DLPFC critical for executive-control processes? One view is that top-down signals from the DLPFC have a diverse range of roles in controlling behavior, depending on which brain region is the recipient of the signal (Curtis & D'Esposito, 2003). That is, the DLPFC may always be performing the same general function: control. However, when DLPFC control is exerted over different brain regions, the effects on behavior may be quite varied. Thus, top-down signals from the DLPFC might enhance and maintain internal representations of relevant sensory stimuli in different posterior sensory and motor centers until those representations are required for subsequent actions and decisions.

Figure 9.15 Activity in monkey and human DLPFC during the retention interval of a delayed-response task
(a) Average of single-unit recordings of neurons with delay-period activity from monkey DLPFC.
(b) Significant maintenance-related activity (left) and average fMRI signal (right) from right DLPFC in a human performing a delayed-response task. The green bar represents the length of the delay interval. In both examples, the level of DLPFC activity persists throughout the delay, seconds after the stimulus cue has disappeared.

(a) Data from Funahashi et al., 1989.
(b) Research from C. E. Curtis & M. D'Esposito, 2003 with permission from Elsevier.

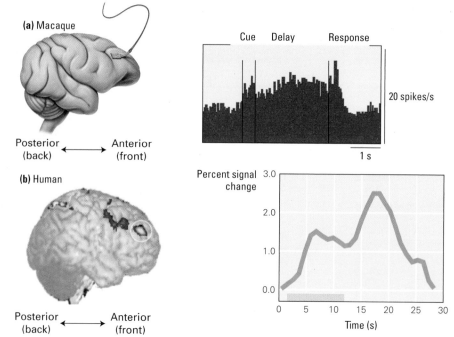

Mapping Executive Processing and Working Memory onto PFC Anatomy

The lesion, electrophysiological, and imaging studies reviewed above leave two critical questions unanswered: (1) how are the frontal lobes organized, and (2) how does working memory actually work? In particular, are there different physical systems (or anatomical regions) in the brain for executive processes (memory manipulation) and rehearsal processes (memory maintenance), as suggested by Baddeley's model? That is, does the *functional* distinction between manipulation and rehearsal proposed by Baddeley correspond to an actual *anatomical* distinction between distinguishable brain regions? Also, are there anatomical distinctions associated with the two material-specific rehearsal stores, namely, the visuospatial sketchpad and the phonological loop? These questions concerning organization and function have dominated research in the neurobiology of working memory, and we turn next to discussing them in more detail.

Maintenance (Rehearsal) versus Manipulation (Cognitive Control)

The manipulation-versus-maintenance distinction suggested by Baddeley's model has been explored extensively by Michael Petrides and colleagues, who have concluded that the dorsal and ventral regions of the prefrontal cortex perform qualitatively different processes (Owen, Evans, & Petrides, 1996; Petrides, 1994, 1996). Their findings, summarized in Figure 9.16, indicate that the ventrolateral prefrontal cortex supports the active controlled encoding and retrieval of information. This ventrolateral prefrontal region, in interaction with posterior cortical regions, may be contributing to the roles of the visuospatial sketchpad and phonological rehearsal loop (more recently described as two separate loops, as we observe at the end of the

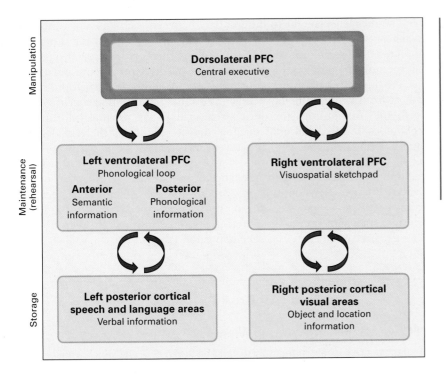

Figure 9.16 Brain substrates of working memory The dorsolateral prefrontal cortex supports higher-order cognitive-control functions, such as monitoring and manipulating of stored information, and acts much like Baddeley's central executive. The ventrolateral prefrontal cortex supports encoding and retrieval of information, performing the functions of the visuospatial sketchpad (right) and phonological rehearsal loops (left). Other brain regions named at bottom are connected to the VLPFC for maintenance of verbal and object and location information.

Brain Substrates section) proposed by Baddeley. In contrast, the dorsolateral prefrontal cortex supports higher-order cognitive-control functions, such as monitoring and manipulation of stored information, functioning much like Baddeley's central executive.

To test this mapping of processes to brain regions, as portrayed in Figure 9.16, Petrides and colleagues developed the self-ordered delayed-response tasks described in Section 9.1. You'll recall that in the monkey version of this task (see Figure 9.7), the monkey obtains the most treats by remembering which of three containers it has already chosen. A 10-second delay, during which the containers are hidden, occurs between each opportunity to choose. Monkeys with lesions to parts of the DLPFC were severely impaired at this task and could not determine which containers had already been emptied and which still contained a reward. The spatial component of the information was made irrelevant in this task because the containers were moved randomly during the delays. In contrast, in another condition of the study, these same DLPFC-lesioned monkeys were able to *maintain* object memories over varying delays (as opposed to manipulating those memories) and showed no problems solving basic delayed-*recognition* tasks (Petrides, 1995). Later, Petrides (2000) showed that increasing the number of items to be monitored in these tasks exacerbated the impairments due to DLPFC lesions, whereas simply extending the delay time did not. Again, this finding implicates the DLPFC in monitoring but not in the maintenance of information in working memory. Thus, basic mnemonic judgments about recently seen objects, which require only maintenance of information during a delay, are not affected by DLPFC lesions. These maintenance functions are instead thought to be controlled by loops between the frontal lobes and more posterior regions of the brain, such as the posterior cortical speech and language areas (for verbal information) and the posterior cortical visual areas (for object and location information), as shown in Figure 9.16.

Several studies have sought to differentiate between the brain substrates for passive rehearsal of information in working memory and those for the more active process of updating information in working memory. Rehearsal supports working memory by reactivating or refreshing briefly stored representations, whereas the updating of information consists of adding information to or removing it from working memory. Imaging studies indicate that there is brain activity in the premotor cortex during rehearsal of visuospatial information (Awh & Jonides, 1998). Additional imaging studies suggest that the ventrolateral prefrontal cortex is activated by simple rehearsal, especially internal rehearsal (Awh et al., 1996). In contrast, more posterior regions of the brain appear to be involved only in the temporary maintenance of spatial working memory, not in its rehearsal. Many other neuroimaging studies have also confirmed a general distinction between storage mechanisms in the posterior regions of the brain and rehearsal mechanisms in the anterior regions (Smith & Jonides, 2004), including the prefrontal cortex, as schematized in Figure 9.16.

Test Your Knowledge

DLPFC vs. VLPFC in Working Memory

Which of these tasks would more likely depend on the DLPFC, and which would depend more on the VLPFC?

1. Scanning the people gathered in the student lounge, looking for the cute guy you saw there last week.
2. As captain of the baseball team, figuring out the optimal order for your top players to come to bat.
3. Rehearsing your acceptance speech as you wait for the name of this year's class president to be announced.

Visuospatial and Phonological–Verbal Working Memory

As you learned in the Behavioral Processes section, Baddeley's model of working memory assumed the existence of two main memory buffers, one for visuospatial memory and the other for phonological–verbal memory. Studies of working memory in monkeys have, of course, been limited to studies of visuospatial memory because of the lack of verbal language in these nonhuman primates. All studies of phonological and verbal working memory have thus relied on the use of human participants. In spite of such limitations, there is evidence to support the idea that these two forms of working memory are produced in different parts of the brain. Studies of patients with selective brain damage to different parts of their frontal lobe suggest that the neural substrates of verbal working memory are localized more on the left side of the brain, while spatial working memory is more dependent on the right side of the brain.

Consistent with this finding of right-side dominance in spatial working memory from patient studies, Petrides and colleagues (Petrides, Alivisatos, Evans, & Meyer, 1993a, 1993b) have conducted functional brain imaging studies of healthy individuals performing self-ordered tasks and found that when the items to be monitored were abstract designs, the self-ordered tasks produced significant activity in the DLPFC, predominantly in the right hemisphere (Figure 9.17a). When the items consisted of verbal material, the activity was more intense in the left hemisphere, although strong activity occurred in both the left and right sides of the DLPFC (Figure 9.17b). From these results, the researchers concluded that while the right DLPFC has a dominant role in all monitoring processes, the left DLPFC is specialized for verbal materials.

Behavioral studies reviewed earlier in this chapter have indicated that verbal working memory retains items in a phonological code based on the sounds of the words and that these items are retained through a rehearsal process similar to internally rehearsed speech (Baddeley, 1986). Consistent with the general tendency for language to be left-lateralized in the brain, frontal-lobe patients with damage to the left side are most likely to show specialized deficits in verbal (as opposed to visuospatial) working memory (Shallice, 1988).

Given how critical an optimally functioning working memory is to our daily lives, many people wish they could make better use of theirs. For tips on how this might be possible, see the "Learning and Memory in Everyday Life" box on the next page.

The Neural Bases of State-Based Accounts of Working Memory

Previously, we discussed early work by Fuster and Goldman-Rakic that demonstrated the importance of the frontal cortex for working memory (Funahashi et al., 1989; Fuster, 1973). The sustained activity seen in the frontal cortex during delay periods in working memory tasks was originally interpreted as suggesting that this region is the site of temporary storage of items in working memory—in essence, a place-model interpretation. However, increasing evidence suggests that the frontal-cortex activations reflect not the *storage* of information in working memory but rather the executive *processes* that are needed to maintain the representations of memory items in posterior areas of cortex, where they are permanently stored (Postle, 2006). More generally, computational modeling and lesion data alike have argued that both working memory and long-term memory representations are stored in the same posterior cortical regions involved in the initial perception, encoding, and long-term storage of memories (Jonides et al., 2008). Data from human brain imaging studies have also argued in favor of a common storage for both LTM and working memory in posterior brain regions (Nee & Jonides, 2013). For example, the patterns of activity seen in the posterior cortices when participants are making judgments about information recalled from LTM (e.g., the likability of famous people or the desirability of visiting famous locations) is similar to the patterns seen when the same participants use the same items in a working memory task that involves delayed recognition of pairs of items (Lewis-Peacock & Postle, 2008).

It is well established that posterior cortices are specialized for different sensory modalities (i.e., visual cortex, auditory cortex, etc.). In fact, this specialization of different regions, with their modality-specific resource limits, suggests a way of integrating Baddeley's distinct visuospatial and phonological loops (see Figure 9.3) into the state-based unitary model of memory.

The newer state-based approach to theories of working memory views working memory as a property of many different brain systems, including those that underlie semantic and episodic memory, sensory systems, and motor control (D'Esposito & Postle, 2015). How is working memory created in the brain through the operation of these various systems? One way is through persistent neural activity—much as seen earlier in studies of the frontal cortex. Other studies have shown that changes in synaptic properties in posterior cortical systems may also contribute to altering their state so as to produce the active attention that is the nature of working memory (Erickson et al, 2010). By these means, networks of neurons located anywhere in the brain—from primary sensory cortices to multimodal association cortices—can activate stored information

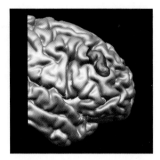

Posterior ←——→ Anterior
(back)   (front)

(a)

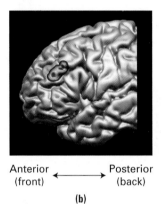

Anterior ←——→ Posterior
(front)   (back)

(b)

Figure 9.17 Brain imaging during self-ordered tasks (a) Imaging data from a self-ordered task in which subjects had to remember previous selections made from a set of abstract designs show predominantly right-hemisphere activity in the prefrontal cortex. (b) Imaging data from a self-ordered task in which the items to be remembered were a set of verbal stimuli show both left- and right-hemisphere activity in the prefrontal cortex (although only the left activity is shown here).

Data from Petrides, 2000, *Brain Mapping*, with permission from Elsevier.

Give Your Working Memory a Break

Because working memory and executive control are fundamental to our higher cognitive abilities, it is natural to ask, what can I do to improve mine? A key finding from research on working memory is that our visuospatial and verbal working memories are independent, each with a limited capacity. You can probably keep only about 3 to 5 items in either store at any one time, which makes remembering a 10-digit phone number a bit tricky. One possible solution when you need to remember a long list of items is to make the independence of visuospatial and verbal memory stores work *for* you rather than against you. For example, if you need to remember several words at once, such as people's names, consider converting some of the words into pictures so that both memory buffers can share the daunting task.

The biggest drain on our working memory comes from multi-tasking, or attempting to accomplish several goals at once. How often do you talk on the phone, listen to music, and surf the Internet all at the same time? You can bet that your dorsolateral PFC is working overtime when you do. Of more concern is multi-tasking during dangerous tasks, such as driving in traffic. Have you ever seen someone try to read the news-paper, apply nail polish, or talk on a cell phone while behind the wheel? Unfortunately, traffic accidents often result from people's attempts to multi-task while driving their cars. For this reason, many states have banned cell-phone use while driving, especially the use of handheld phones.

An overloaded working memory impairs the ability to accurately monitor and evaluate our cognitive functioning. You may think your driving is just fine or that you can absorb the main ideas in your professor's lecture while you work on other projects (like Kamila, who studies biology during business class), but research has shown that you are probably not operating at as high a level as you think. Focusing on one task at a time greatly improves the ability to use working memory effectively. In contrast, high levels of stress reduce the working-memory span and the ability to concentrate and focus cognitive control. Some research has suggested that stress elevates dopamine levels in the prefrontal cortex, impairing its ability to efficiently monitor and update information.

Why tax your working memory if you don't need to? Maybe it's time to shut off that cell phone, grab a pad of paper (think of it as a third working-memory buffer), and start writing things down.

---

in a temporary fashion, allowing it to be used as working memory to support a variety of goal-directed behaviors (D'Esposito & Postle, 2015).

What about the frontal cortices? What role do they play if they are not the "place" where working memory buffers are to be found? The state-based approach to working memory suggests that the frontal cortex maintains high-level representations of goals and plans that guide the flow, activation, and distinctiveness of representations across posterior regions of the cortex (Postle, 2015).

In summary, this view of working memory sees working memory as emerging from a network of brain regions, all of which send and receive controlling information to and from the prefrontal cortex. Together these networks accomplish the active maintenance of internal representations necessary for goal-directed behavior (D'Esposito, 2007; Postle, 2006), as illustrated in Figure 9.18.

Goal Abstraction and Frontal-Lobe Organization

"What are you doing?" asks your roommate. Any of several answers would be equally correct: "Making a sandwich," "Spreading peanut butter on bread," or "Moving this knife from left to right." These three answers all accurately describe what you are doing at the moment, but they do so at different levels of abstraction. "Making a sandwich" is the most abstract description of your current activity, and it also describes your ultimate goal. There are of course many different ways to make a sandwich, as well as a wide variety of ingredients. "Spreading peanut butter on bread" is thus a more specific description of what you are doing and also defines a more specific goal (it begins to identify what type of sandwich you are making). To spread the peanut butter on the bread, however, requires a specific action, the movement of the knife across the bread from left to right (and afterward, back from right to left).

Keeping goals of various degrees of abstraction in working memory as you proceed with a task has long been known to involve the frontal lobes. This is why people like Penfield's sister, with frontal-lobe damage, have so much trouble cooking (including, most likely, preparing peanut butter sandwiches). The Tower of Hanoi, introduced in Chapter 8 (see Figure 8.1), also requires keeping a wide range of goals in mind, from the most abstract ("Move all disks to the right-hand peg") to the most specific level ("Move the yellow disk to the middle peg"). Impairments in solving the Tower of Hanoi puzzle have long been recognized as a sign of frontal-lobe dysfunction.

Although neuroscientists have long known that keeping goals in working memory while working on complex tasks depends heavily on the frontal lobes, recent research has suggested that the gradient of abstraction from general plans and goals to more specific action plans follows a physical gradient beginning at the front of the frontal lobes and moving back (Badre, 2008; Badre & D'Esposito, 2007). As illustrated in Figure 9.19, the most abstract plans (make sandwich, move all disks to right peg) depend on the most anterior (front) part of the frontal lobes. If the goals and plans to be maintained in working memory are specific and concrete (such as spreading peanut butter on the sandwich), they are likely to be localized in the more posterior regions of the frontal lobes.

Some of the evidence for this gradient of abstraction comes from people with brain damage due to stroke: people with damage toward the front of their frontal lobes are most impaired at tasks requiring cognitive control at a high level of abstraction. Converging data comes from lesion studies in monkeys that show a double dissociation between the effects of posterior frontal-lobe lesions and the effects of mid-frontal-lobe lesions. Lesions to the more posterior regions of the

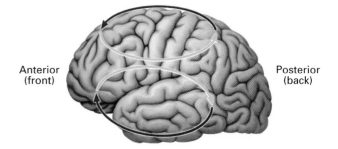

Anterior (front)   Posterior (back)

Figure 9.18 Maintenance in working memory through frontal–posterior circuits This schematic representation of frontal–posterior connections illustrates two sample loops, one dorsal and the other ventral. For each, the frontal activity projects back to the posterior areas (along green arrows), which in turn project back to the frontal lobes (along blue arrows). The net result is that frontal activity induces sustained activation of posterior regions.

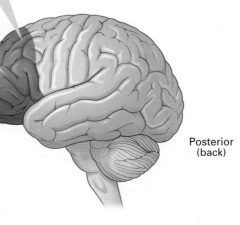

Move knife from left to right
Move yellow disk to middle peg

Spread peanut butter on bread
Get red disk to bottom of right peg

Make sandwich
Move all disks to right peg

Anterior (front)   Posterior (back)

Figure 9.19 The anterior–posterior gradient of goal abstraction within the frontal cortex Three levels of abstraction of goals are shown for two examples—the making of a sandwich (top text in each balloon) and the Tower of Hanoi task (lower text)—illustrating approximate locations in the frontal cortex for control of each level of abstraction.

frontal lobes disrupt performance in domain-specific motor learning tasks but not in domain-general monitoring; in contrast, lesions to the middle part of the DLPFC impair performance in general monitoring tasks but not in domain-specific tasks (Fuster, 2004; Petrides, 2006).

Human functional imaging studies provide converging evidence for this abstraction-specific gradient: tasks that require maintaining more abstract, high-level goals activate a wider part of the frontal lobes, including the more anterior regions toward the frontal pole of the brain (Koechlin, Ody, & Kouneiher, 2003; Badre & D'Esposito, 2007). Imaging studies have also suggested that the flow of control within the frontal cortex goes from the most anterior regions (for the highest levels of abstract goals) toward the back of the frontal lobes (for the more specific subgoals), consistent with the idea that it is the desire to make a sandwich that drives you to butter the bread, not vice versa (Koechlin et al., 2003).

What if it was not your roommate who asked what you were doing but your kid brother? And what if he wanted to help? If your kid brother is 15, you might point him to the cabinets and say, "Make a sandwich for yourself." But if he were only 6, you might hand him a piece of bread with peanut butter on it along with a (plastic) knife and instruct him to spread it back and forth. In other words, the older the child, the more likely you are to assign him a higher-level abstract goal. Younger children need more specific, concrete goals and plans. Might the difference in their abilities be due to differences in the maturity of the circuits in the more anterior parts of their frontal lobes? Indeed, longitudinal data show that maturation of the circuit wiring in the frontal lobes progresses throughout childhood from the more posterior regions that support concrete plans toward the anterior regions that support more abstract planning, with the latter not becoming fully mature until late adolescence (Shaw et al., 2008). Chapter 12 provides more information about critical periods in brain maturation and their impact on cognition across the lifespan.

Prefrontal Control of Long-Term Declarative Memory

What was the last movie you saw? To answer this question, you may have to perform a number of mental operations making use of your long-term memory. For example, you might search your memory by calling to mind every movie that you know to be currently playing, noting which ones you have seen and then trying to recall which of them you saw most recently. Alternatively, you could search your memory by thinking back over your recent activities in reverse chronological order. Knowing that you go out to movies on the weekends, you might first think back to last weekend. Did you see a movie? If not, think back to the previous weekend. However you choose to set about answering this question, the process of searching your memory requires considerable strategic manipulation and control of memory processes as well as maintaining, throughout this search, an awareness of your ultimate goal: the name of the last movie you saw. This is exactly the kind of task that uses the prefrontal cortex in multiple capacities. Some patients with prefrontal-cortex damage exhibit significant deficits in retrieval of long-term memories (Shimamura et al., 1995; Mangels, Gershberg, Shimamura, & Knight, 1996).

In the beginning of this chapter, we defined short-term memory as an active, temporary representation of information that either was just perceived or was just retrieved from long-term memory. Most of this chapter has focused on the former class of information—information that was recently experienced. In this section, we briefly discuss how working memory (and hence short-term memory) interacts with long-term memory. We focus especially on long-term memories of previously stored episodes or facts.

Neuroimaging has been particularly useful in furthering our understanding of how the frontal lobes and working memory guide the controlled search of long-term memory. Recall that Petrides and colleagues argued that the ventrolateral prefrontal cortex supports active rehearsal and maintenance functions, while the dorsolateral prefrontal cortex supports higher-order executive-control functions, such as monitoring and manipulation of stored information (Petrides, 2002). Thus, the kinds of executive control and manipulation of memory needed for retrieval of specific episodic memories, such as the last movie you saw, should be subserved by the dorsolateral prefrontal cortex. In fact, this is exactly what functional neuroimaging has shown: the dorsolateral prefrontal cortex is activated during people's attempts to remember past events (Nyberg, Cabeza, & Tulving, 1996; Wagner, Desmond, Glover, & Gabrieli, 1998).

Have you ever met someone at a party who seems familiar and yet you can't remember how you know her? (Is she an elementary school classmate or did you meet on that summer trip to Israel?) You just can't recall, but you do know you met before. On the other hand, very often you will see a person and not only realize that he is familiar but immediately remember how and where you met. (The former phenomenon, known as the tip-of-the-tongue phenomenon, is introduced in Chapter 7, where it is identified as the feeling of trying to recall information that is not forgotten but only temporarily inaccessible.) According to a study by Anthony Wagner, Daniel Schacter, and colleagues, you probably used your dorsolateral prefrontal cortex in the latter situation, in which you recollected the source of your memory, but not in the former situation, in which you knew that the person was familiar but could not remember why (Dobbins, Foley, Schacter, & Wagner, 2002). In their study, people were shown various words and asked one of two questions: "Is it abstract or concrete?" or "Is it pleasant or unpleasant?" Later, they were shown the words again and were asked either if they remembered seeing the word during the first part of the experiment (that is, did they recall whether the word was considered at all) or if they remembered which task the word appeared in (did they recall whether they judged it on the concrete/abstract dimension or on the pleasant/unpleasant dimension). As shown in Figure 9.20, the dorsolateral prefrontal cortex was more active when people were asked to recall the source of the word (that is, which task it was used in) than when they were asked whether or not the word had appeared at all (regardless of task).

If, as Petrides argued, the ventrolateral prefrontal cortex supports active rehearsal and maintenance functions, then we might expect to see more VLPFC

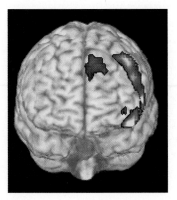

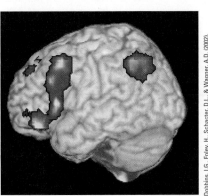

Anterior ←——————→ Posterior
(front)   (back)

(a)   (b)

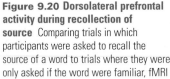

Dobbins, I.G., Foley, H., Schacter, D.L., & Wagner, A.D. (2002). Executive control during episodic retrieval: Multiple prefrontal processes subserve source memory. *Neuron*, 35, 989–996, with permission from Elsevier.

Figure 9.20 Dorsolateral prefrontal activity during recollection of source Comparing trials in which participants were asked to recall the source of a word to trials where they were only asked if the word were familiar, fMRI studies show that multiple left prefrontal, as well as lateral and medial parietal, regions were more active during source recollection than during mere familiarity judgments. (a) The view from the front of the brain; (b) the brain's left side.

activity during intentional active encoding when participants are explicitly told to remember something, in contrast to the DLPFC activity seen in retrieval (Petrides, 2002). Functional imaging studies using fMRI and PET have indeed reliably shown that intentional encoding of new memories activates the ventrolateral prefrontal cortex. Because most of these studies used meaningful stimuli, such as images of nameable real-word objects, the *left* VLPFC is primarily activated, consistent with the general tendency of the left prefrontal cortex to be specialized for verbal processing (Nyberg et al., 1996).

The functional role of the left ventrolateral prefrontal cortex during encoding of new semantic information can be further subdivided into the contributions of its anterior (front) and posterior (back) regions, as illustrated in Figure 9.16. Anterior regions are activated during tasks that involve semantic processing (Thompson-Schill, D'Esposito, Aquirre, & Farah, 1997), while posterior regions are activated during phonological processing (Buckner, Raichle, Miezin, & Petersen, 1996). Thus, remembering the name of a wealthy new acquaintance, Bill, by noting that he probably has lots of bills in his wallet (a *semantic* elaboration of a meaning of the word "bill") would likely involve processing by your *anterior* ventrolateral prefrontal cortex. In contrast, rehearsing a complex foreign-sounding name over and over likely involves *phonological* processing in the *posterior* ventrolateral prefrontal cortex.

Further support for this anterior–posterior differentiation comes from a study that compared brain activity of people making either a semantic analysis of words ("Is it abstract or concrete?") or a phonological analysis ("How many syllables does it contain?"). Although the posterior region of the left ventrolateral prefrontal cortex was activated during both tasks—reflecting a common phonological component—only the semantic task resulted in activation of the anterior left ventrolateral prefrontal cortex (Poldrack et al., 1999). In contrast, other researchers subsequently demonstrated that nonsemantic tasks that involved only phonological processing activated the posterior, but not the anterior, regions of the left ventrolateral prefrontal cortex (Wagner, Koutstaal, Maril, Schachter, & Buckner, 2000). Refer again to Figure 9.16 for a schematic map of which type of working memory tasks involve which brain regions.

Overall, there are numerous parallels between the role of the prefrontal cortex in working memory (along with the precise location of its activity) and its role in episodic memory. Thus, the control processes and rehearsal mechanisms implicated in working memory appear to also play crucial roles in the encoding and retrieval of long-term memories for episodic and semantic information (Wagner, 2002).

Test Your Knowledge

Functional Neuroanatomy of the Prefrontal Cortex

Identify the region of the prefrontal cortex whose activity is most critical for each of the following four activities. (Answers appear in the back of the book.)

1. Deciding who should sit where around a dinner table set for eight to avoid seating ex-spouses and feuding ex-business partners next to each other

2. Rehearsing the toast you will make at your brother's wedding

3. Learning the definitions of "distributor," "ignition coil," and "carburetor" by reading a car-repair manual

4. Remembering how to pronounce the name of the French exchange student you just met

5. Remembering where you parked and deciding which way to walk to your parking spot as you exit the department store at the mall

Interim Summary

- Studies with both animals and humans implicate the frontal lobes of the brain—especially the prefrontal cortex (PFC), the most anterior section of the frontal lobes—as critical for working memory and cognitive control.

- The ventrolateral prefrontal cortex supports encoding and retrieval of information (including rehearsal for maintenance), performing as the visuospatial sketchpad and phonological rehearsal loop proposed by Baddeley, while the dorsolateral prefrontal cortex supports higher-order executive-control functions such as monitoring and manipulating of stored information, thus doing the job of Baddeley's central executive.

- Working memory is now believed to result from functional interactions between the prefrontal cortex and the rest of the brain.

- The more concrete and specific the goals or plans that must be maintained in working memory, the more posterior the localization of their function within the frontal lobes, forming an anterior-to-posterior gradient that follows the functional gradient from abstract to specific.

- During encoding of new verbal information, the *anterior* prefrontal cortex is activated for tasks that involve *semantic* processing, while the *posterior* prefrontal cortex is activated for *phonological* processing.

9.3 Clinical Perspectives

Research on the role of the prefrontal cortex in working memory and cognitive control has provided clues for improving the diagnosis and treatment of several common neurological and psychiatric disorders. Two of the most common disorders involving dysfunctional prefrontal circuits are schizophrenia and attention deficit/hyperactivity disorder (ADHD).

The Prefrontal Cortex in Schizophrenia

Chapter 6 describes some of the memory deficits associated with hippocampal dysfunction in schizophrenia. In the current chapter, our discussion of schizophrenia focuses instead on the ways in which frontal lobe dysfunction contributes to symptoms of the disorder. People diagnosed with schizophrenia display disturbances in both cognition and memory, especially in working memory and executive control (Forbes, Carrick, McIntosh, & Lawrie, 2009). This finding is consistent with a wide range of other data suggesting that the dorsolateral prefrontal cortex is dysfunctional in schizophrenia. In contrast, functions attributed to the ventrolateral prefrontal cortex seem relatively unimpaired in patients with schizophrenia. For example, people with schizophrenia have close to normal performance on phonological or visuospatial memory tasks (Barch, Csernansky, Conturo, Snyder, & Ollinger, 2002) and on memory tasks involving only minimal delays or few items to keep track of (Park & Holzman, 1992). However, patients with schizophrenia are especially impaired at visuospatial working-memory tasks when these tasks involve the manipulation or updating of information in working memory (Park & Holzman, 1992). Similar cognitive-control deficits are also seen in close relatives of schizophrenia patients (Park, Holzman, & Goldman-Rakic, 1992).

Neuroimaging provides further insights into prefrontal-cortex dysfunction in schizophrenia. Daniel Weinberger and colleagues presented the first neuroimaging evidence for dorsolateral prefrontal-cortex dysfunction in schizophrenia by measuring blood flow in different cerebral regions (Weinberger, Berman, & Zec, 1986).

They found that when patients with schizophrenia tried to solve the Wisconsin Card Sorting Test (see Figure 9.8), their dorsolateral prefrontal cortex showed no evidence of increased blood flow as it would in control individuals. Moreover, there was a correlation among the schizophrenia subjects between the amount of blood flow in this region and performance: the greater the blood flow in the dorsolateral prefrontal cortex, the better the patients performed on the Wisconsin Card Sorting Test.

More recent studies provide further evidence for localization of a cognitive-control deficit in schizophrenia within the dorsolateral prefrontal cortex. For example, researchers found that schizophrenia correlates with depressed dorsolateral prefrontal-cortex activity during the *N*-back task, which, as you learned in Section 9.1, is a standard test of the manipulation of working memory. Ventral and posterior prefrontal-cortex activity, however, is normal in these patients, suggesting that rehearsal mechanisms, associated with these ventral and posterior areas, are less affected by schizophrenia (Barch et al., 2002). These neuroimaging results are consistent with postmortem studies of schizophrenia patients that reveal neural pathologies in the dorsolateral prefrontal cortex but not in more ventral regions.

Inefficient Prefrontal Cortical Systems in Schizophrenia

Recent functional brain imaging studies of patients diagnosed with schizophrenia suggest that their reduced capacity for executive aspects of working memory is accompanied by engagement of a larger network of other cortical regions, consistent with the idea that they are recruiting compensatory networks that utilize other, less impaired brain regions (Tan et al., 2007). Even when patients are able to keep up with the processing demands of tasks that require cognitive control and do exhibit normal working-memory behaviors, brain imaging shows that these patients are meeting the demands less efficiently by employing greater posterior cerebral metabolic brain activity with less focused cortical activity. Recall from earlier in this chapter the data indicating that higher-order processes in the dorsolateral prefrontal cortex exert control over more ventrolateral regions responsible for less complex processes, such as rehearsal of information within working memory (D'Esposito et al., 1995; Koechlin et al., 2003). In comparison, brain imaging in schizophrenia patients shows increased patterns of activity in their ventrolateral prefrontal cortex, even during tasks where the patients show near-normal working-memory performance (Tan, Choo, Fones, & Chee, 2005, 2006). Evidently, while control subjects use the dorsolateral prefrontal cortex in executive working-memory tasks, schizophrenia patients are often unable to do so; rather, they engage greater ventrolateral prefrontal cortex involvement, possibly as a form of compensation for the dysfunctional dorsolateral prefrontal response.

Dopamine and the Genetics of Schizophrenia

What is wrong with the dorsolateral prefrontal cortex in schizophrenia patients? One view is that the deficits in working memory and executive control found in schizophrenia may be linked to deficiencies in cortical dopamine processing. **Dopamine** is a neuromodulator that alters neuron-to-neuron communication, and most pharmacological treatments for schizophrenia work by altering the transmission of dopamine.

Genetic research into the causes of schizophrenia includes a search for genes that convey a heightened susceptibility for the disease. For example, Daniel Weinberger and colleagues have shown that mutation in the *COMT* gene affects dopamine metabolism in the frontal lobes (Egan et al., 2001). COMT is one of several enzymes that are critical for degrading dopamine (and other related neuromodulators). Several pharmaceutical treatments target the COMT enzyme to alter its activity, thereby affecting the availability of dopamine and related neuromodulators. For example, COMT inhibitors prevent the breakdown of dopamine and are used as a treatment in Parkinson's disease to increase levels of dopamine in the brain.

dopamine. A neuromodulator that alters neuron-to-neuron communication.

In control subjects, the status of the *COMT* gene was seen to predict 4% of the variance in performance on the Wisconsin Card Sorting Test. As shown in Figure 9.21, having 2, 1, or 0 copies of the less effective allele for the *COMT* gene predicted the number of perseverative errors a person would make on the Wisconsin Card Sorting Test. Patients diagnosed with schizophrenia who had two copies of the less effective allele showed worse performance (which is seen on the graph as a higher line indicating more perseverative errors) on this task than patients with none or one— and the same was true for non-symptomatic siblings of schizophrenia patients and for non-symptomatic controls drawn from the general population. This finding suggests that a mutation in one kind of gene causes only a small change in cognitive performance but that a combination of mutations in many different genes could push a person past a tipping point into a high-risk category for schizophrenia.

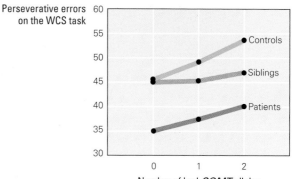

Figure 9.21 Effect of a gene mutation on frontal-lobe function The number of copies of a less effective *COMT* allele correlates with the relative numbers of perseverative errors (higher number of errors being indicative of worse performance) on the Wisconsin Card Sorting Test in schizophrenia patients, their siblings, and controls. Data from Egan et al., 2001.

Weinberger and colleagues also used the 2-back task, with its heavy dependence on working memory and executive control, to do brain imaging studies of the effects of the *COMT* gene. They looked at the brains of non-symptomatic individuals with 0, 1, or 2 copies of the less effective *COMT* allele to see which brain regions showed activity during the 2-back task. The region that was most highly correlated with this allele was the prefrontal cortex. The more copies of the less effective *COMT* allele (and hence the worse the dopamine functioning), the less prefrontal-cortex activity was seen during the 2-back task. This suggests that having 1 or 2 copies of the less effective allele (as is most common in those with schizophrenia) impairs activation of the prefrontal cortex during working-memory and executive-function tasks. These studies provide evidence that genetic mutations affecting dopamine activity in the prefrontal cortex are related to the emergence of the cognitive deficits seen in schizophrenia.

As noted earlier, increased prefrontal activation is thought to reflect inefficient function in the prefrontal areas because the increased activity is necessary to support a given level of performance. Several groups have now shown that this prefrontal inefficiency is also present in certain unaffected siblings of schizophrenia patients. The siblings show greater activation than controls even though their task performance does not differ from that of matched controls (Figure 9.22). These results suggest that physiological indices derived from neuroimaging may provide a more direct reflection of the effects of genes (e.g., on level of dopamine metabolism) than do behavioral changes.

Attention Deficit/Hyperactivity Disorder

Attention deficit/hyperactivity disorder (ADHD) is one of the most commonly diagnosed psychiatric problems in children. About 5% of children are diagnosed with ADHD, although its true prevalence is hard to estimate given that the diagnostic definition of ADHD is under constant refinement. Children and adults with this disorder have great difficulty with cognitive-control processes such as planning, organizing their time, keeping attention focused on a task, and inhibiting responses to distracting stimuli. ADHD symptoms are especially evident in settings that require the exercise of self-control. For example, children diagnosed with ADHD can sit still for hours when they are actively engaged in playing interactive video games, but they have trouble paying attention in school, where they must sit for long periods and pay attention to less captivating information. Given these problems, it is not surprising that students with ADHD are at elevated risk for academic underachievement (Martinussen & Major, 2011).

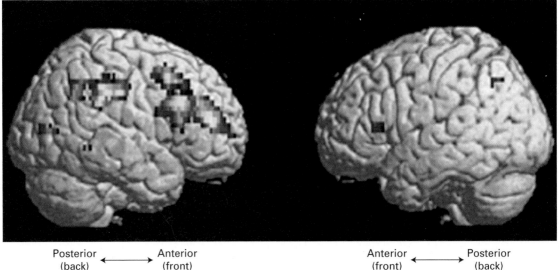

Posterior (back) ←→ Anterior (front)

(a)

Anterior (front) ←→ Posterior (back)

(b)

Figure 9.22 Regions of increased, inefficient fMRI activation in unaffected siblings of schizophrenia patients relative to demographically matched control participants during performance of a working-memory paradigm These brain images show the differences between two groups of subjects: healthy siblings of people diagnosed with schizophrenia and healthy matched controls. Regions of increased activation in the siblings as compared with the controls include right-dorsolateral and ventrolateral prefrontal cortices. In contrast, behavioral performance did not discriminate between the groups.

Adapted from Figure 2 of Callicott et al. "Abnormal fMRI Response of the Dorsolateral Prefrontal Cortex in Cognitively Intact Siblings of Patients With Schizophrenia." *Am J Psychiatry* 160 (2003): 709–719. Reprinted with permission from the American Journal of Psychiatry, (Copyright ©2003). American Psychiatric Association.

Most researchers and clinicians believe that ADHD involves dysfunction in the prefrontal cortex and its cortical and subcortical connections (Solanto, Arnsten, & Castellanos, 2000), including connections to the cerebellum and the basal ganglia. The fact that ADHD patients have difficulty sustaining a behavior or thought over a delay is consistent with the data reviewed earlier showing that prefrontal cortical cells play a critical role in regulating thought and behavioral output through their sustained firing over delays, in the absence of external input. Structural neuroimaging of children with ADHD shows that they have a smaller right prefrontal cortex, the region associated with spatial attention and working memory. Functional brain imaging studies have shown evidence of decreased prefrontal activity in ADHD, while diffusion tensor imaging has indicated weaker prefrontal white matter connections (Arnsten, 2006; Castellanos & Tannock, 2002).

Behavioral research suggests that working memory in particular is impaired in patients with ADHD. People with ADHD show marked deficits in mental calculations that require use of working memory (Schweitzer et al., 2000). As with schizophrenia, current medications for ADHD act in part by altering dopamine function in the cortex. The most common treatments for ADHD, such as Ritalin (also known as methylphenidate), are stimulants that either increase dopamine release or block its reuptake at synapses. Unfortunately, the effects of these medications are temporary, and the behavioral problems often reappear after 3 or 4 hours.

There is strong evidence for frontal dysfunction in ADHD, but is the frontal cortex the *origin* of the attentional and cognitive control problems of ADHD? Some investigators have suggested that frontal-cortex dysfunction, and the associated working-memory and attentional problems, are actually the consequence of deficits in other subcortical structures, especially the basal ganglia (Volkow, Wang, Fowler, & Ding, 2005, 2007). The basal ganglia, as described in Chapters 5 and 8, are critically involved in skill learning and action selection. If the origins of ADHD are in the basal ganglia, not the frontal lobes, why do stimulants improve working memory and reduce symptoms of ADHD? One view is that people with ADHD have "noisy" basal ganglia that sometimes send inappropriate signals to the prefrontal cortex, resulting in distractible behavior, while at other times the basal ganglia do not signal the prefrontal cortex when appropriate, resulting in perseveration or inattention (Volkow et al., 2005).

How and why do stimulant medications remediate the attentional problems in people with ADHD? One possibility is that stimulant medications increase the saliency of the basal ganglia signal to the prefrontal cortex by increasing extracellular dopamine in the striatal region of the basal ganglia (Volkow et al., 2004, 2005). This hypothesis is consistent with studies (reviewed in Chapter 5) describing a key role for dopamine in the basal ganglia (as well as in the frontal lobes). Recent brain imaging studies have argued that increased but inefficient activity in the prefrontal cortex, found during certain task conditions in children with ADHD, may serve a compensatory function for dealing with noisy input from the basal ganglia (Sheridan, Hinshaw, & D'Esposito, 2010).

Medications are not the only treatment for ADHD. Behavioral training methods may also offer some relief. Several studies have shown that training children with ADHD to learn to better manage their cognitive control and to use their working memory more effectively can, over the course of several weeks, lead to improvements in their working memory on certain tasks as well as reduce some of the core symptoms of inattention and hyperactivity (Klingberg et al. 2005; Beck, Hanson, Puffenberger, Benninger, & Benninger, 2010). Thus, working-memory training appears promising as an intervention for improving cognitive functioning and ADHD symptoms.

Like schizophrenia, ADHD is a heritable psychiatric disorder (which therefore tends to run in families), and scientists are hot on the trail of the genetic bases for this heritability. Recent research has identified some of the genes believed to be linked to ADHD. Like some of the genes associated with schizophrenia, these ADHD genes regulate the function of dopamine in the brain (Durston, 2010). Future research will hopefully identify the genes more clearly, discover how they relate to the behavioral problems of ADHD, and thus provide us with clues for developing more effective treatments. Advances in diagnosis are also sorely needed: studying mental illnesses like schizophrenia and ADHD is difficult because of the lack of clear disease markers, lack of uniformly applied diagnostic criteria, and the growing realization that these disorders are highly heterogeneous, with each patient sharing some but not all symptoms with other patients in the same diagnostic category.

Interim Summary

- Working-memory impairments become apparent in people with schizophrenia during attempts to maintain a large number of items in the mind over a temporal delay, an activity that requires functions associated with the dorsolateral prefrontal cortex. In contrast, functions attributed to the ventrolateral prefrontal cortex seem relatively unimpaired; thus, performance on phonological or visuospatial memory tasks, and on memory tasks involving only minimal delays or few items, appears normal.

- People with ADHD show deficits in mental calculations that require use of working memory.

- Neuroimaging of people with ADHD indicates that they have a smaller prefrontal cortex as well as noisy input signals from the basal ganglia that prevent the basal ganglia from accurately indicating what is or is not important to attend to.

| Synthesis

Let's return for the last time to Kamila, to see what insights we have gained into the cognitive and other brain processes that she calls on throughout the day. Early that morning, a Tuesday, Kamila checks her class schedule. Her dorsolateral prefrontal cortex is heavily activated while she sorts through her list of courses, paying most attention to the classes she has on Tuesday. This attention helps her plan and organize for that particular day, triggering her memory to recall the items she will need to bring along with her. As she considers them, the various objects are briefly represented in her ventrolateral prefrontal cortex. As she then arranges the items in her backpack, the order and location of each activate the spatial working-memory capabilities of her dorsolateral prefrontal cortex.

When she stops at the bank to get some cash, Kamila relies on her DLPFC to help retrieve her PIN from long-term memory, after which she rehearses it through her phonological loop, activating her VLPFC. With cash in hand, she dashes straight to class, or would have done so had not her DLPFC been maintaining a reminder that tells her she has to switch from her normal routine, suppress her automatic tendency to go directly to business class, and instead make a side trip to the biology department to drop off her homework.

Finally, Kamila arrives at business class. While she listens to the lecture, she also discretely reads bits and pieces of biology, relying on activity in her DLPFC to alert her whenever the speaker is discussing something especially new or important, at which times she tries to pay more attention to the lecture. What really grabs her attention, however, is his announcement of a surprise quiz. If Kamila had not been playing the piano and singing her own compositions at the Cheerleading Fundraiser party until 2 a.m., she might have had the time to review her reading in case of just such a quiz. Unfortunately, she didn't do any reviewing (although she had certainly been exercising her VLPFC recalling song lyrics). During the pop quiz, Kamila realizes she has far less knowledge in her long-term memory to draw on than she needs. She engages her DLPFC as she desperately tries to recall the answers to the quiz questions, but alas, she never learned the material in the first place.

All in all, a busy morning for Kamila as her prefrontal cortex, working closely with long-term memory storage areas in the posterior parts of her brain, assists her in controlling her memory, mind, and life.

KNOW YOUR KEY TERMS

central executive, *p. 357*

cognitive control, *p. 352*

delayed nonmatch-to-sample (DNMS) task, *p. 359*

dopamine, *p. 388*

dorsolateral prefrontal cortex (DLPFC), *p. 374*

dysexecutive syndrome, *p. 373*

executive control, *p. 361*

long-term memory, *p. 352*

perseveration, *p. 373*

phonological loop, *p. 357*

prefrontal cortex (PFC), *p. 371*

sensory memory, *p. 353*

short-term memory, *p. 352*

transient memory, *p. 353*

ventrolateral prefrontal cortex (VLPFC), *p. 374*

visual sensory memory, *p. 353*

visuospatial sketchpad, *p. 357*

word-length effect, *p. 358*

working memory, *p. 352*

QUIZ YOURSELF

1. In the Tower of Hanoi puzzle, moving all the disks to the right is an abstract plan that depends on the _____ part of the frontal lobes, whereas specific plans for completing individual steps to solve the puzzle (moving the yellow disk to the middle peg, for example) depend on a more _____ part of the frontal lobes. (p. 383)

2. In the Wisconsin Card Sort Test, frequently used in clinical settings, patients with frontal-lobe lesions show _____ —that is, they fail to learn a new rule despite feedback indicating that the old rule is incorrect. (p. 373)

3. It is hypothesized that in ADHD, projections to the frontal cortex from _____-containing neurons in the _____ are hypoactive or underdeveloped. (p. 390)

4. Carol sustained frontal-lobe damage when she was hit by a car last year. Now she is unable to hold down a job, as she never cares to show up on time. Given her brain damage and behavior, it is likely that Carol has _____ syndrome. (p. 373)

5. Jamie forgets the color of Carrie's shirt as soon as they exchange good-byes. The fleeting visual sensation that Jamie had before she forgot the color is called a _____. (p. 353)

6. Jim can remember a long (seven- or eight-item) list of colors without much thought, but when asked to remember a list of full names, he can only remember four or five. From what we know about short-term memory storage, this is likely due to _____. (p. 358)

7. Schizophrenia patients with two less-effective alleles of the *COMT* gene—a gene that functions in _____metabolism—are more likely to perform _____ on the Wisconsin Card Sorting Task compared to patients with zero or one abnormal copy. (p. 389)

8. _____ is the active and temporary representation of information that is maintained for the short-term in the mind, assisting the individual to think and decide what to do next. (p. 352)

9. The _____ in Baddeleys' model monitors and manipulates both of the working-memory buffers, providing cognitive control of working memory. (p. 357)

10. Many studies suggest that _____ is dysfunctional in patients with schizophrenia. (p. 387)

11. Most pharmacological treatments for schizophrenia work by altering the transmission of _____, a neuromodulator that alters neuron-to-neuron communication. (p. 388)

12. Short delays are used in the _____ task for the purpose of assessing working memory; longer delays are used in the same task for the purpose of studying long-term memory. (p. 360)

13. Place-based models of memory are also known as _____ models of memory because they imply the existence of two or more different places for memories to be stored; similarly, state-based models of memory have been referred to as _____ models of memory because they imply that there is only one place for memory, although these memories can be in various states. (p. 361)

14. The _____ task consists of a series of names of colors, each printed in a color that is *different* from the color being named. (p. 368)

15. General _____, the capacity for learning, reasoning, and understanding, appears to be associated with a strong _____memory, especially for manipulating larger numbers of rules, concepts, goals, and ideas. (p. 370)

16. In humans, the prefrontal cortex encompasses approximately _____ of the cerebral cortex. (p. 371)

17. Earl Miller argued that the key "cognitive" contribution of the prefrontal cortex to working memory is the ability to sustain activity despite _____. (p. 377)

18. Frontal-lobe patients with damage to the _____ side are most likely to show specialized deficits in verbal (as opposed to visuospatial) working memory. (p. 381)

19. _____ is one of several enzymes that are critical for degrading dopamine. (p. 388)

Answers appear in the back of the book.

CONCEPT CHECK

1. Juan chats with a pretty girl at a party. She tells him her phone number is (617) 555-1812, extension 2001, but he has no way to write it down. How can Juan remember the 14 numbers of her phone number until he can find a pencil and paper?

2. Describe two aspects of executive control that are used both in driving a car and in talking on a cell phone.

3. If you could see an image of someone's frontal lobes while they were rehearsing a list of words, would you see more activity on the left side or the right side? What if they were rehearsing visual images?

4. Tanya is trying to concentrate during a neuroanatomy lecture because she really wants to get into medical school, but she keeps noticing Peter's adorable dimples. Which part of her brain is showing sustained attention to the neuroanatomy images and which part is being distracted by Peter's dimples?

5. Jerry is trying to remember the name of a woman he met, but all he can recall is that her name is similar to the word for a part of a woman's anatomy. As Jerry struggles to recall her name, is he more likely to be activating his anterior or his posterior left ventrolateral prefrontal cortex?

6. Would a person with ADHD be more likely to take up soccer or duck hunting?

Answers appear in the back of the book.

CHAPTER 10

Emotional Influences on Learning and Memory

O N THE MORNING OF SEPTEMBER 11, 2001, terrorists hijacked four commercial airplanes and crashed
them into the Twin Towers in New York City, the
Pentagon in Washington, and a field in Pennsylvania.
It was the worst terrorist attack in U.S. history, killing more than
2000 people. Most Americans who are old enough to remember
that morning report that they still recall exactly where and when
they heard the news. To this day, the events of 9/11 are etched into
their memory in crisp detail, even if they lived far from the sites
and even if they did not personally know anyone who died in the
attacks. Some remember hearing the news on TV or radio or from a
friend; some remember what they were doing at that moment, what
emotions they felt, and how they spent the rest of the day.

But few Americans would remember where they were on, say,
the morning of September 10, 2001. The reason for this contrast
is emotion: the events of September 11 aroused intense emotions,
while for most Americans, September 10 was just another ordinary
day. Memories laid down during times of heightened emotion are
more likely to be remembered longer, and in greater detail, than
memories that are not connected with strong emotions.

Andrey Nekrasov/Getty Images

©2001 Peter C. Brandt

Highly emotional events such as the 9/11 terrorist attacks can produce exceptionally vivid and long-lasting memories.

This chapter explores the relationship between memory and emotion. Most of the time, this is a positive relationship, with emotion promoting faster learning and more enduring memories. But the darker side is that too much emotion can *interfere* with memory and even cause or contribute to clinical disorders—such as depression, stress disorders, and phobias. One of the chief reasons for studying emotion is to understand these linkages—and to help those who suffer from emotions gone awry.

10.1 Behavioral Processes

Suppose a young man, Sammy, is walking home alone late at night and takes a shortcut through a dark alley. He is aware that he's not in the safest of neighborhoods, and he is feeling a little nervous. Suddenly he hears a noise behind him—possibly an attacker—and jumps out of his skin. His heart skips a beat, his hands grow clammy, and his face pales. Breathing heavily, he turns to look behind him for the source of the threat. All of these responses are part of the emotional experience of fear. Some emotional responses—like the reaction to a loud noise in a dark alley—are innate, and others—like Sammy's general anxiety as he walks through what he knows is a dangerous neighborhood—are learned through experience or cultural transmission.

What Is Emotion?

We all know an emotion when we feel one, yet emotion, like attention and consciousness, is one of those psychological concepts that are maddeningly difficult to define. In scientific terms, **emotion** is a cluster of three distinct but interrelated phenomena: physiological responses, overt behaviors, and conscious feelings. Physiological responses associated with emotion may include changes in heart rate, perspiration levels, respiration, and other body functions. Overt (or observable) behaviors associated with emotion include facial expression, vocal tone, and posture. Conscious feelings associated with emotion are the subjective experiences of sadness, happiness, and so on.

Sammy's physiological responses to walking in the dark alley include an increase in heart rate, an increase in perspiration, and a diversion of blood away from the capillaries in his face (making him appear pale). His overt behaviors include jumping and looking around. The conscious feeling is the fear that accompanies his understanding that he is potentially in danger. This cluster of physiological, motor, and conscious reactions constitutes a **fear response**. Other emotions produce different combinations of physiology, behavior, and conscious feelings. For example, a 6-year-old, asked to eat broccoli, may experience a conscious feeling of disgust; her overt behaviors may include sticking out her tongue and poking at her food, and her physiological responses may include a decrease in heart rate.

Emotion researcher Paul Ekman suggests there is a small set of universal emotions, hardwired in humans from birth. This set includes happiness, sadness, anger, fear, disgust, and surprise (Figure 10.1; Ekman & Friesen, 1984;

emotion. A cluster of three distinct but interrelated sets of phenomena—physiological responses, overt behaviors, and conscious feelings—produced in response to an affecting situation.

fear response. A cluster of physiological, motor, and conscious reactions that accompany the emotion of fear. In the laboratory, these physiological changes and motor behaviors are often taken to imply presence of fear whether or not the accompanying conscious experience of fear can be documented.

McNally, Bryant, & Ehlers, 2003). (Other researchers would enlarge the basic set slightly to include other emotions, such as interest and shame.) All humans, from all cultures, feel these emotions and can recognize the markers of these emotions in others. For example, Ekman and his colleague Wallace Friesen showed pictures like those in Figure 10.1 to people of an isolated tribe in New Guinea. Although these New Guineans lived in a culture very different from that of industrialized North America, they had no difficulty in recognizing the emotions connoted by the facial expressions of North American college students—and the New Guineans' facial expressions were equally well understood by North Americans (Ekman & Friesen, 1971).

This is not to say that all humans manifest emotion identically. Different cultures may teach their members different rules about the appropriate ways to display emotions in various social contexts. For example, traditional Japanese culture (which places a premium on respect and orderly behavior) encourages suppression of emotional display to a greater degree than American culture (which tends to value individualism more than social order). Thus, while watching a film containing unpleasant scenes, both American and Japanese students display similar overt behaviors (such as grimacing at the nastiest parts), but if an authority figure, such as an experimenter, is present, the Japanese students tend to mask their negative expressions more than American students do (Ekman, 1992).

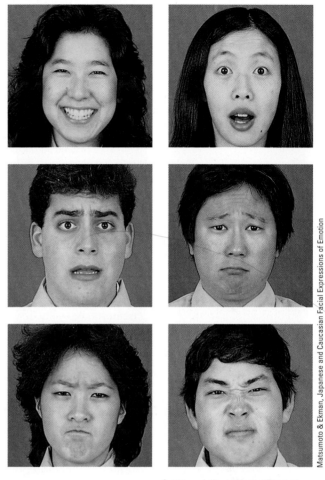

Matsumoto & Ekman, Japanese and Caucasian Facial Expressions of Emotion

Figure 10.1 Faces illustrating "universal" human emotions Humans of every race and culture seem to experience happiness, surprise, fear, sadness, anger, and disgust and can recognize the expression of these emotions in others.

Similarly, in many cultures around the world, men and women show more or less the same physiological measures of emotion, but women are much more likely to express happiness and sadness overtly, perhaps because of cultural rules dictating that "men don't cry" (Eisenberg & Lennon, 1983; Kring & Gordon, 1998). In short, human emotion seems to be innate and universal, but its outward expression may be modified by cultural learning.

Autonomic Arousal and the Fight-or-Flight Response

Imagine you are walking through the forest, and you come face-to-face with a bear. First, you probably freeze (an overt behavior). But what physiological responses do you experience? Most likely, your heartbeat speeds up, and your respiration rate increases. Fine hairs on your arms and neck may stand on end, and your hands may sweat. Hormones flood your body, causing you to feel a "rush" of energy and excitement. Other bodily responses may be less noticeable to you: digestion halts, your pupils dilate, and extra blood is directed to the muscles in your legs in case you have to run away.

This collection of bodily responses, called **arousal** or (more colorfully) the **fight-or-flight response**, is the body's way of preparing you to face a challenge or threat: either by fighting or by running away. Blood pressure and heart rate increase, and blood flow—with its cargo of glucose that provides energy—is

arousal. A collection of bodily responses (including increased blood flow to muscles, increased respiration, and depressed digestion and immune function) that prepare the body to face a threat; also known as the *fight-or-flight response*.

fight-or-flight response. A collection of bodily responses (including increased blood flow to muscles, increased respiration, and depressed digestion and immune function) that prepare the body to face a threat; also known as *arousal*.

Table 10.1 **Some Components of the Fight-or-Flight Response**	
Increases in	**Decreases in**
Blood pressure and heart rate	Digestion
Respiration	Immune system function
Blood glucose level	Sexual arousal
Pain suppression	Touch sensitivity
Perception and awareness	Peripheral vision
Blood flow to large muscles in legs and arms	Growth

autonomic nervous system (ANS). A collection of nerves and structures that control internal organs and glands.

stress hormone. A hormone that is released in response to signals from the *autonomic nervous system (ANS)* and helps mediate the *fight-or-flight response*; examples include norepinephrine and the *glucocorticoids*.

stress. Any stimulus or event that causes bodily arousal and release of stress hormones.

epinephrine. A stress hormone that helps to mediate the *fight-or-flight response*; also known as *adrenaline*.

glucocorticoid. Any of a class of *stress hormones* (including *cortisol* in humans) that help to mediate the *fight-or-flight response*.

cortisol. The chief *glucocorticoid* in humans.

James–Lange theory of emotion. The theory that conscious feelings of emotion occur when the mind senses the physiological responses associated with fear or some other kind of arousal.

diverted toward the body systems that are most likely to help you in this effort, including your brain, your lungs, and the muscles in your legs (Table 10.1). Other systems such as digestion and the immune system are temporarily deprived of energy. These latter systems are important for proper functioning under normal circumstances—but if you don't survive the immediate threat, it doesn't really matter whether you digested that last meal or fought off that cold.

These body changes are mediated by the **autonomic nervous system (ANS)**, the collection of nerves and structures that control internal organs and glands. The word "autonomic" is related to "autonomous," meaning that the ANS can operate autonomously, without conscious control. When the brain senses a challenge or threat, the ANS sends a signal to the adrenal glands, which release **stress hormones**, hormones that act throughout the body to turn the fight-or-flight response on and off. One formal definition of **stress** is any event or stimulus that causes bodily arousal and the release of stress hormones. Major stress hormones include **epinephrine** (also called *adrenaline*) and **glucocorticoids**. The chief glucocorticoid in humans is **cortisol**. In the short term, our reactions to stress through arousal and release of stress hormones prepare us to deal with the challenge before us; normally, once the challenge is past, the ANS turns off the fight-or-flight response, and stress hormone levels drop back to normal.

Strong, pleasant emotions, such as happiness and surprise, can cause physiological arousal that is very similar to the components of the fight-or-flight response. Thus, a young man in the throes of sexual arousal may experience many of the same physiological responses (dilated pupils, increased heart rate and blood pressure, sweating, and so on) as one who is suddenly attacked by a masked gunman. Many of the same features of arousal occur in a range of emotions, although there are differences. For example, heart rate increases during many emotions but falls during disgust (Levenson, 1992). So, why do we experience increased heart rate and blood pressure as components of a pleasant emotion in one situation and as part of a negative emotion in another? Several theories have been proposed.

Theories of Emotion

An early and influential theory of emotion was independently proposed by William James and by the Danish physiologist Carl Lange and so is often called the **James–Lange theory of emotion** (LaBar & LeDoux, 2003). The James–Lange theory states that conscious feelings of emotion occur when the mind senses the physiological responses associated with fear or some other kind of arousal. Figure 10.2a illustrates this idea: first, our bodies respond to an

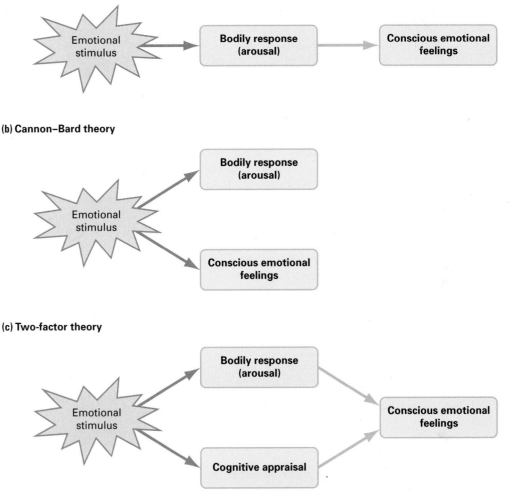

(a) James–Lange theory

Emotional stimulus → **Bodily response (arousal)** → **Conscious emotional feelings**

(b) Cannon–Bard theory

Emotional stimulus → **Bodily response (arousal)**
Emotional stimulus → **Conscious emotional feelings**

(c) Two-factor theory

Emotional stimulus → **Bodily response (arousal)** → **Conscious emotional feelings**
Emotional stimulus → **Cognitive appraisal** → **Conscious emotional feelings**

Figure 10.2 Theories of emotion (a) The James–Lange theory posits that physiological responses come first and cause our conscious feelings of emotion; this is an example of a somatic theory of emotion. (b) The Cannon–Bard theory posits that stimuli simultaneously evoke both emotions and physiological responses. (c) The two-factor theory of emotion posits that emotions are produced through interaction between our cognitive appraisal of the situation and our physiological responses.

emotional situation with physiological changes; conscious feelings follow as our mind interprets this physiological response. Several modern researchers have developed related theories, often called **somatic theories of emotion**, all based on this central premise that physiological responses to stimuli come first, and these determine or induce emotions (Damasio, 1996, 1999; Zajonc, 1980, 1984).

One prediction of somatic theories of emotion is that researchers should be able to evoke a given emotion in a person just by inducing the corresponding bodily responses. For example, experimenters can often produce moods in volunteers just by asking the volunteers to move various facial muscles (without telling them what mood this is intended to produce). For example, one instruction went as follows: "Pull your eyebrows down and together; raise your upper eyelids and tighten your lower eyelids; narrow your lips and press them together." How do you feel when you make this expression and hold it for a few seconds? In case you couldn't guess, these facial contortions were meant to simulate anger. Volunteers who made such a face generally showed physiological responses corresponding to the emotion of anger, including increased heart rate and blood pressure. Most of them also reported feelings of mild anger or annoyance (Ekman, 1992).

somatic theories of emotion.
Theories of emotion based on the central premise that physiological responses to stimuli come first, and these determine or induce emotions.

This process works for positive emotions too. When volunteers were told to turn up the corners of their mouths and crinkle their eyes, they reported a mild overall increase in feelings of happiness (Ekman, 1992). Another way to "induce" happiness is by holding a chopstick between your teeth without letting your lips touch the wood; the muscles involved are the same ones that are active during a natural smile. Participants engaging in such "smile-inducing" manipulations judge cartoons to be funnier (Strack, Martin, & Stepper, 1988) and exhibit faster physiological recovery from stress (Kraft & Pressman, 2012).

In short, there seems to be some truth behind the old notion of "put on a happy face"—the simple act of smiling can actually make you feel happier. More generally, these results support somatic theories of emotion, which posit that our conscious feelings of emotion depend on what our body is telling us; biological responses come first, conscious feelings second.

But Walter Cannon, a former student of William James, thought that somatic theories had it backwards. People, he argued, can experience arousal without necessarily experiencing emotion. For example, after running, a person may experience a racing heart, but this doesn't mean she will feel afraid. In addition, as you read above, many emotion-provoking stimuli give rise to similar sets of biological responses: fight (anger), flight (fear), and sexual excitement can all cause increases in heart rate, perspiration, and hormone release. How, then, does your conscious mind determine which emotion is being signaled by the increased heart rate and other biological responses?

Cannon's proposal, which was later extended by Philip Bard and became known as the **Cannon–Bard theory of emotion**, was that stimuli simultaneously evoke both emotions and arousal, with neither causing the other (Cannon, 1927). Figure 10.2b illustrates this idea.

A few decades later, Stanley Schachter and Jerome Singer came up with another theory of emotion that incorporated aspects of both the James–Lange and the Cannon–Bard theories. Schachter and Singer claimed James was partly correct that arousal is an important determinant of emotion, but they said Cannon and Bard were also partly correct to note that arousal alone isn't sufficient to determine what we feel.

In a famous experiment, Schachter and Singer injected volunteers with epinephrine, one of the stress hormones that help produce physiological arousal (increased heart rate, increased blood pressure, and so on). They then put each volunteer in a room with a person who (unbeknownst to the volunteer) had been instructed to act in a certain way. The volunteers began to catch the mood of their companions. Some volunteers were paired with companions who were acting joyful, and they began to act happy too, whereas volunteers who had been paired with companions who were acting angry began to act annoyed themselves. In other words, epinephrine injections caused bodily arousal, which each volunteer's brain interpreted according to the context in which that individual had been placed (Schachter & Singer, 1962). This suggests that the same ambiguous bodily responses can occur in different emotions, and the label we apply to the responses (e.g., "joy" or "anger") depends on the situation we are in.

This result led Schachter and Singer to propose a **two-factor theory of emotion**, which posits that a combination of cognitive appraisal and perception of biological changes together determine our experience of emotion (Figure 10.2c). In other words, if we are alone in the woods and see a bear, cognitive appraisal warns us of the danger, and this appraisal interacts with our experience of a fight-or-flight response to produce the emotional experience of fear. In contrast, a young man meeting his girlfriend after a long absence may have

Cannon–Bard theory of emotion.
The theory that conscious emotions stimulate appropriate behaviors and physiological responses.

two-factor theory of emotion.
The theory that a combination of cognitive appraisal and perception of biological changes together determines our experience of emotion.

The moviegoers on the left appear to be enjoying the experience of biological responses normally associated with fear and excitement; in contrast, the New Yorkers on the right, fleeing the scene of the World Trade Center attacks, do not appear to be enjoying the fear and excitement. How would the two-factor theory of emotion explain the difference?

a similar pattern of physiological arousal, but his cognitive appraisal of the situation will lead to a very different emotional experience. On the one hand, as James proposed, the particular pattern of physiological responses contributes to our conscious feelings of emotion; on the other hand, our cognitive awareness helps us to interpret that arousal in accordance with our current context. In sum, emotion is a complex phenomenon arising from the interplay of conscious feelings, cognitive assessments, and bodily responses.

A famous experiment supporting the two-factor theory of emotion was the "High Bridge" study (Dutton & Aron, 1974). In this study, an attractive female researcher, stationed on a footbridge, asked male passersby to complete a brief survey. In some cases the footbridge was a low, safe-looking structure; in others it was a swaying cable bridge that spanned a deep ravine (the Capilano Suspension Bridge in Vancouver). After each participant completed the survey, the researcher would give him her phone number "in case you have further questions." The researchers predicted that men on the dangerous-looking bridge would be highly aroused, likely to misinterpret this feeling as sexual arousal, and therefore more likely to call the woman back looking for a date compared with men who took the survey while on the safe-looking bridge. The results? A few of the men who'd been tested on the low bridge called the experimenter back, but fully 50% of the men tested on the high bridge phoned. In contrast, when the study was repeated with a male survey taker, there were hardly any follow-up phone calls from males tested on either bridge, allowing the researchers to rule out the possibility that participants tested on the high bridge were simply more interested in the scientific details of the experiment.

The two-factor theory may also help explain the popularity of horror movies, at which viewers expect to be made to scream in terror. Given that fear is a "negative" emotion, why would otherwise rational people stand in line and pay good money to experience it? Part of the answer is that the strong biological responses caused by a terrifying movie are not so different from the strong biological responses caused by intense joy or sexual pleasure. Viewers know they are relatively safe in the context of the movie theater, and this cognitive assessment allows them to interpret the strong arousal as pleasurable rather than threatening.

Test Your Knowledge

Theories of Emotion

Janet is at a music concert featuring her favorite band. As the lights dim and the band walks onstage to a crashing opening chord, she jumps to her feet and cheers along with the rest of the crowd, her heart racing with excitement. How would each of the following theories of emotion describe this situation? (Answers appear in the back of the book)

1. James–Lange theory
2. Cannon–Bard theory
3. Two-factor (cognitive appraisal) theory

Assessing Emotion in Nonhuman Animals

So far, we've discussed emotions as defined in and by humans. What about other animals? Can nonhuman animals experience emotion? Many researchers believe that they can.

The literature on animal behavior is rich with examples that seem to describe animal emotions. Poachers shoot an elephant nicknamed Tina; the other elephants in her tribe try to revive her by propping her up and sticking grass in her mouth. When Tina dies despite their efforts, they sprinkle earth and branches over the body; Tina's daughter returns to the site periodically thereafter and strokes the bones with her trunk (Moss, 1988). A female chimpanzee gives birth; as the baby is delivered, the chimpanzee who is the mother's best friend shrieks and embraces nearby chimpanzees, then spends the next few days caring for mother and baby (de Waal, 1996). A killer whale grows sick; his podmates flank him and protect him, helping him stay near the surface, where he can breathe, even guiding him into shallow waters at the risk of beaching themselves, refusing to abandon him until he finally dies (Porter, 1977).

Can elephants feel sadness, monkeys feel empathy, and killer whales feel sympathy? Or are the animals described above simply acting on blind instinct, without any of the emotional overtones we would attribute to humans? Although these animals often *seem* to behave as if they feel emotions, the fact is that we may never know if they experience subjective feelings or, if they do, what those feelings are like. But remember that subjective feelings are only one component of emotions. The other two components, biological responses and overt behaviors, are certainly apparent and can be studied in nonhuman animals.

Fear Responses Across Species

As early as the mid-nineteenth century, Charles Darwin noted that many species of animals react to arousing stimuli in similar ways (Darwin, 1872). For example, when a gorilla encounters a frightening stimulus, its first reactions may include a sudden jump ("startle") followed by a period of alert immobility ("freezing"). It may display **piloerection**, meaning that its body hair stands on end; this makes the animal look bigger and more threatening. In extreme situations, the gorilla may defecate or urinate. These responses are remarkably similar to Sammy's physiological reactions in the dark alley: hearing a suspicious noise makes him "jump out of his skin" and then freeze (his heart skipping a beat) while he assesses the situation. Tiny hairs on the back of Sammy's neck and arms may stand on end, and he may develop goose bumps, which Darwin suggested are the remnants of our hairy ancestors' piloerection response. In extreme circumstances, Sammy may even be terrified enough to lose bladder or sphincter control. All of these fear reactions in humans seem to have direct analogues in other primates.

piloerection. A fear response in mammals in which body hair stands on end, making the animal look bigger and more threatening than it is.

Iudex/Getty Images

Nick Stubbs/Shutterstock

Eliot Lyons/Nature Picture Library

Bele Olmez/Getty Images

To some degree, we can see the same reactions in other mammals. A startled rat shows changes in blood pressure, heart rate, and hormonal release that are broadly similar to the changes seen in cats, rabbits, monkeys, and humans. Even fish, reptiles, and birds show some of these responses. For example, many birds fluff their feathers when alarmed, and some fish spread their fins wide or puff up their bodies, which makes them look larger, in a defensive adaptation analogous to piloerection in mammals. When such reactions appear, researchers report that the animal is expressing physiological and behavioral components of a fear response even if we can't be sure whether the animal is actually feeling emotion.

It's important to keep in mind that physiological responses don't automatically equate with emotions in humans either. Remember the woman whose heart races after running but who doesn't feel fear. Another example comes from research in which human learning is tested by training participants to predict or avoid an unpleasant event, such as electrical stimulation (shock). Here, ethical concerns typically dictate that participants be allowed to self-select the intensity of the shock to be "unpleasant but not painful." Under these conditions, humans may produce physiological responses to the shock, but they typically don't report conscious feelings of fear while anticipating upcoming shock (LaBar, 2009). So in humans, just as in rats and other animals, researchers evoking and studying emotional responses need to be clear that physiological responses are consistent with—but not necessarily proof of—emotions.

Emotional displays in animals often have striking similarities to displays of human emotion. For example, when startled, many animals including fish, birds, and other mammals will puff themselves up, fluff their feathers, or bristle their fur, in an apparent attempt to make themselves look bigger (and scare off predators). Darwin suggested that goosebumps in humans are a remnant of our ancestors' piloerectino response. Human emotions have three components. Which of these three components can (and can't) we identify in other animals?

Beyond Fear

Because fear responses are relatively easy to induce, detect, and record, the vast majority of animal studies on emotion and its effects on learning and memory have focused on the learning of fear responses. But in recent years, there has been increasing attention paid to the other emotions as well. Back in Chapter 5, you read about "yum" and "ugh" responses (Berridge & Robinson, 1998). In particular, rats given a taste of sweetness show rhythmic movements of the mouth and protrusion of the tongue—just like humans tasting something pleasant ("yum!"); rats given a bitter taste show mouth gapes, shakes of the head, and wiping of the face with the paws—just like humans shuddering at a disgusting taste ("ugh!"). Again, while we can't be sure that the rat is experiencing conscious feelings of pleasure or disgust, these physiological responses seem consistent across mammalian species.

One way that humans express the emotion of joy, particularly within a social context, is through laughter. There is now accumulating evidence of laughter-like responses in other mammals too. For instance, tickling is rewarding to young rats, in the sense that they will perform behaviors such as running mazes and pressing levers in order to obtain tickle reinforcement (Burgdorf & Panskepp, 2001). During tickle, rats tend to emit ultrasonic vocalizations that share many acoustic features with the sounds of human laughter (Panksepp & Burgdorf, 2003). Tickle-induced vocalizations can also be elicited in chimpanzees and gorillas (Davila-Ross, Owren, & Zimmerman, 2009). Even dogs emit a characteristic "laugh" vocalization during play, and one study has suggested that dogs in a kennel experience reduced stress if exposed to recordings of dog-laugh vocalizations (Simonet, Versteeg, & Storie, 2005).

The presence of laughter-like vocalizations in rats, dogs, and apes doesn't necessarily mean that these animals have a sense of humor; rather, it appears to be a social expression of joy. Thus, young rats emit laughter-like vocalizations during play behavior, and they prefer to spend time with older animals that "laugh" frequently (Panksepp & Burgdorf, 2003). Although the study of nonhuman laughter is still relatively young, there is already some evidence that the same brain regions that are active during social laughter in humans are also active in these other animals during laughter-like responses (Meyer, Baumann, Wildgruber, & Alter, 2007). Thus, recording laughter-like vocalizations may be one way researchers can measure joy responses in nonhuman animals. Again, we can't be sure that "laughing" animals are experiencing the emotion of joy, only that their physiological and behavioral responses are similar to those exhibited by happy humans.

Learning Emotional Responses: Focus on Fear

Further research into joy responses in animals may produce insights into how nonhuman animals learn joy responses and whether this differs from how they learn fear responses. In the meantime, however, as stated above, the vast majority of studies on emotional learning in nonhuman animals have focused on learning responses consisting of negative emotions, particularly fear. This is not because fear is inherently more important or interesting than the other emotions but simply because a long tradition exists of how to elicit and recognize fear responses in nonhuman animals. The learning of these emotional responses, including both overt behavior and physiological changes, can be particularly fast, strong, and long lasting.

Conditioned Emotional Responses: Learning to Predict Danger

When a rat is given an unpleasant surprising stimulus, such as an unexpected electric shock, it typically displays a short period of alert immobility: the freezing response that was described above as also occurring in humans and gorillas.

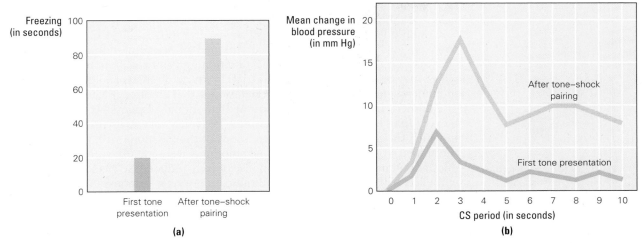

Figure 10.3 Two types of conditioned emotional responding in rats (a) On first presentation, a tone CS may cause a brief freezing response, but after the CS has been paired with a foot-shock US, it evokes a strong freezing response (the fear CR). (b) Similarly, the first CS presentation evokes only a mild and transient increase in blood pressure, but after CS–US pairing, there is a strong increase in blood pressure that persists through the CS period. Blood pressure changes and freezing are conditioned emotional responses, indicating that the rat has learned the CS–US association.
Research from LeDoux, 1993.

Responding to a potential threat by staying very still may help a small animal avoid predators, which often have visual systems tuned to detect movement. It may also allow an animal of any size to allocate full attention to sensory inputs to help it determine what and where the threat is. After a moment, if nothing further happens, the animal typically relaxes and goes back to what it was doing before.

The freezing response is not learned; rather, it is an innate fear response to a threatening situation. In this example, the freezing behavior is an unconditioned response (UR) evoked by the shock US. (See Chapter 4 if you need to review classical conditioning and the concepts of CS, US, CR, and UR.) In addition to freezing behavior, the shock US also evokes autonomic unconditioned responses (URs), such as increases in blood pressure and heart rate. However, if the shock US is repeatedly preceded by a neutral conditioned stimulus (CS)—say, a tone or a light—the animal will learn the CS–US association and may then produce conditioned responses (CRs) to the CS. Such CRs are *conditioned emotional responses*, which you read about in Chapter 4. Figure 10.3 shows an example of conditioned emotional responding in rats. In this example, researchers play a 10-second tone CS, and the rats respond with a brief freezing response (Figure 10.3a). Next, the tone is paired with a foot-shock US. Later, the tone is presented alone; now the rat expects the foot shock and manifests this learning through a behavioral CR: increased freezing in anticipation of the upcoming shock (Figure 10.3a).

At the same time as the animal learns a freezing CR, other fear responses are conditioned too. Thus, the first time the tone is presented, it evokes a mild, temporary increase in blood pressure (Figure 10.3b); after tone–shock pairing, the tone evokes a sharp rise in blood pressure that persists through the duration of the tone. If the experimenters had chosen to measure other variables indicative of a fight-or-flight response—such as increased heart rate, stress hormone release, or defecation—they would probably have found that the tone elicited many of these responses as well, as further proof of the conditioned emotional response. These learned fear responses are similar to the behaviors a rat would exhibit on being confronted with a natural fear-provoking stimulus, such as a cat (Fendt & Fanselow, 1999).

The same basic rules of conditioned emotional responding apply in other species too. For example, recall from Chapter 4 that the sea snail *Aplysia* can learn to withdraw its gill (CR) in response to a gentle touch (CS) that predicts a tail shock (US). Is the sea snail "feeling" fear in the same way as a rat huddling in a corner of its cage or as a New Yorker trying to flee the scene of the terrorist attacks on 9/11? We can't be sure. All we can know is that the overt behavior of *Aplysia* is a conditioned emotional response not so different from the overt behavior shown by a freezing rat or a fleeing human.

Conditioned freezing in rats may occur after only a single CS–US pairing, and even lowly *Aplysia* can learn a conditioned gill withdrawal in about four trials. Compare that with the eyeblink conditioning you read about in Chapter 4—which may require several hundred trials in rats and rabbits and dozens of trials in humans—and the inescapable conclusion is that emotional learning is fast.

Another characteristic of conditioned emotional responses is that they can be very long lasting and hard to extinguish. It may take many extinction trials, in which the animal receives presentations of the CS alone with no US, before the animal stops giving a conditioned emotional response. Even then, extinction does not eliminate the learned response; it only reduces the chance that the CS will elicit it. For this reason, conditioned emotional responses are very easily reinstated after extinction: sometimes, merely placing the animal back in the experimental chamber where it experienced the US is enough to restore conditioned emotional responding (Bouton & Peck, 1989).

Conditioned Escape: Learning to Get Away from Danger

conditioned escape. An experimental design in which animals learn to make particular responses in order to escape from or terminate an aversive stimulus.

Learning to recognize which stimuli signal upcoming danger is a good thing, but getting away from the danger is even better. In **conditioned escape**, animals learn to make particular responses in order to escape from or terminate an aversive stimulus. For example, a rat might receive a series of foot shocks that are terminated if the rat presses a lever, or a rat might be placed in a pool of water and learn to locate and climb onto a submerged platform in order to escape from the water. (Rats are quite competent swimmers, but just like humans at the beach, if the water is chilly, they prefer to get out of it.)

Escape learning is a form of operant conditioning. Remember from Chapter 5 that in operant conditioning, a discriminative stimulus S^D evokes a behavioral response R, leading to an outcome O:

$$\text{Discriminative stimulus } S^D \rightarrow \text{Response R} \rightarrow \text{Outcome O}$$

In the shock example, the discriminative stimulus S^D is the initiation of shock, the response R is lever pressing, and the outcome O is escape from shock. Since the shock is aversive, this is an example of negative reinforcement: the response causes something aversive (shock) to be subtracted from the environment, and so the frequency of the response increases. Similarly, in the pool example, S^D is the water, R is locating and climbing onto the platform, and O is escape from the water.

Conditioned escape learning can be very fast; the first time the rat is placed in the pool, it may swim around randomly until it locates the submerged platform, but once it has learned the location of the platform, a rat placed back in the pool will typically swim straight to the platform and climb out of the water.

Conditioned Avoidance: Learning to Avoid Danger Altogether

conditioned avoidance. An experimental design in which animals learn to make particular responses to avoid or prevent exposure to an aversive stimulus.

Even better than escaping from danger is learning to avoid it altogether. In **conditioned avoidance**, animals learn to make particular responses to avoid or prevent arrival of an aversive stimulus. For example, a rat may be placed in a chamber with a response lever. From time to time, a series of foot shocks is delivered, and if the rat presses the lever during this time, it can terminate (escape from) the shock. In addition, a warning signal, such as a tone, is played just before the foot shock starts; if the rat presses the lever before the tone is finished, the foot shock is avoided altogether. Typically, a rat first learns to escape the shock and eventually learns to avoid it altogether by pressing the lever when the warning signal plays.

At first glance, it may appear that avoidance learning also is simple operant conditioning: the warning signal (S^D) triggers the response (R), which causes avoidance of the shock (O). Since shock is aversive, avoidance of the shock reinforces the response, making the organism more likely to repeat the response in future.

But this simple explanation doesn't quite hold up. As the animal learns the avoidance response, the shock no longer occurs. Therefore, there is no explicit reinforcement for making the avoidance response (since the shock is not presented in the first place, it cannot be subtracted from the environment!). Therefore, the response should extinguish. But it does not. In fact, avoidance behaviors can be incredibly persistent: animals may keep making the avoidance response long after the US is no longer delivered. This is a paradox that requires further explanation.

Some researchers have proposed a *two-factor theory of avoidance learning*, which states that avoidance learning involves an interaction between classical and operant conditioning (Dinsmoor, 1954; Mowrer, 1960). According to this view, the first stage of avoidance learning is actually classical conditioning: as the tone is paired with the shock, it comes to function as a warning signal and becomes a conditioned stimulus (CS) that evokes a conditioned emotional response (fear CR) in anticipation of the upcoming shock (US). Then operant conditioning occurs: the avoidance response (lever pressing) is reinforced because it causes cessation of the warning signal and therefore a reduction in fear (Figure 10.4a). In effect, animals don't learn to lever press in order to avoid the shock; rather, they learn to lever press in order to escape from the warning signal (or, more specifically, from the fear response it produces).

But there are several problems with two-factor theories of avoidance learning (Dymond & Roche, 2009). One major difficulty is that these theories assume that avoidance learning is based on conditioned fear of the warning signal. But, in fact, as the avoidance response is learned, the organism's fear response to the warning signal decreases. In this case, the avoidance response should extinguish, just like any other operant response, once the outcome is no longer presented. Yet avoidance learning is often extremely resistant to extinction.

Figure 10.4 Theories of avoidance learning (a) In the two-factor theory of avoidance learning, (1) rats learn a classically conditioned fear response to a warning signal (CS) paired with shock (US); (2) then rats learn an operant response to terminate the warning signal and the fear it evokes. (b) In the cognitive expectancy theory of avoidance learning, rats learn that different responses predict different outcomes and use this cognitive expectancy to guide their decision of which response to make.

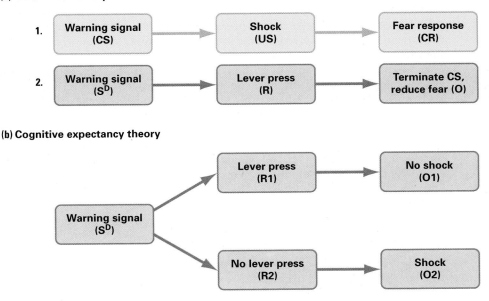

(a) Two-factor theory

1. Warning signal (CS) → Shock (US) → Fear response (CR)

2. Warning signal (S^D) → Lever press (R) → Terminate CS, reduce fear (O)

(b) Cognitive expectancy theory

Warning signal (S^D) → Lever press (R1) → No shock (O1)

Warning signal (S^D) → No lever press (R2) → Shock (O2)

Various researchers have proposed modifications to the basic two-factor theory, to address this and other limitations (B. A. Williams, 2001). For example, cognitive theorists have proposed that animals form *cognitive expectancies* and decide between competing possible behaviors based on those expectancies. According to this view, animals learn the expected outcomes of responding and of not responding and then make a decision to respond or not based on a comparison between the two expected outcomes (Figure 10.4b; Dickinson & Balleine, 2000; Seligman & Johnston, 1973).

More recently, some have argued for integrated theories that combine aspects both of two-factor theory and of cognitive expectancy (Lovibond, Saunders, Weidemann, & Mitchell, 2008). Avoidance learning may therefore be a useful test bed for studying the potentially complex interactions between classical conditioning, operant conditioning, and cognitive processing—and a reminder that many seemingly "simple" behaviors may actually reflect more than one type of learning.

Learned Helplessness

Back in the 1960s, psychologist Martin Seligman and his colleagues studied an avoidance task involving a large box with a low wall that divided the box into two chambers (Overmier & Seligman, 1967; Seligman & Maier, 1967). They placed a dog in one chamber, called the "avoidance" chamber, where the dog periodically received an electric shock. At first, dogs reacted to the shock by running around the chamber; eventually, they learned that they could jump over the wall into the "safe" chamber to escape the shock. If the shock was always preceded by a warning signal, such as a tone, the dogs also learned to jump over the wall as soon as the tone sounded, thus avoiding the shock altogether.

Seligman and his colleagues wondered what would happen if, before a dog was first put in the avoidance chamber, the tone stimulus had already been explicitly paired with a shock in a classical fear-conditioning paradigm:

CS (tone) → US (shock)

If the dog had already learned this CS–US association and knew that the tone signaled shock, would the dog be able to transfer this learning to the avoidance learning paradigm? Might the dog jump over the wall the very first time it heard the tone in the avoidance chamber to avoid being shocked?

What the dogs actually did surprised everyone. The first time they heard the tone in the avoidance chamber, the dogs ran around for a few seconds—and then they lay down in the corner and whined. Even after repeated trials, the dogs never learned to jump over the wall and escape the shock. Intrigued, the experimenters tried to encourage the animals to escape: removing the barrier wall, baiting the safe chamber with food, even climbing into the safe chamber themselves and calling to the dogs to cross over. Still, the dogs continued to lie in the corner, miserably enduring the shock.

Seligman concluded that the prior exposure to an inescapable shock (during the classical-conditioning phase) had taught the animals that they were helpless to escape *any* shock—even in the operant-learning phase. Seligman named this phenomenon **learned helplessness**, meaning that exposure to an uncontrollable punisher teaches an expectation that responses are ineffectual, which in turn reduces the motivation to attempt new avoidance responses. Learned helplessness has since been demonstrated in a variety of species, from cockroaches (G. Brown & Stroup, 1988) to rats (Besson, Privat, Eschalier, & Fialip, 1999) to humans (Hiroto, 1974; Hiroto & Seligman, 1974).

Understanding this phenomenon may provide clues for how to promote resilience or resistance to negative emotions and even to **depression**, a

learned helplessness. A phenomenon in which exposure to an uncontrollable punisher teaches an expectation that responses are ineffectual, which in turn reduces the motivation to attempt new avoidance responses.

depression. A psychiatric condition that involves sadness as well as a general loss of initiative and activity.

psychiatric condition characterized by sadness and a general loss of initiative and activity (see "Learning and Memory in Everyday Life" below). Seligman himself went on to study what he calls "positive psychology," arguing that just as negative emotional responses such as fear and unhappiness can be learned, so can positive emotional responses such as happiness and hope for the future (Seligman, 1991; Seligman, Steen, Park, & Peterson, 2005).

Effect of Emotions on Memory Storage and Retrieval

The previous section described the learning of emotional responses to stimuli that predict upcoming emotion-evoking events (such as conditioned learning of fear in response to a stimulus that predicts incipient shock) and also described how animals can learn to escape or avoid such events. But there is another important way emotion interacts with learning and memory: strong emotions can affect the storage and retrieval of episodic memories.

For example, let's turn again to the morning of September 11, 2001. Most Americans who were old enough to understand what was happening felt strong emotional responses that day, ranging from sadness at the deaths, to anger at the terrorists, to fear that further attacks would follow. And most report that they still have vivid, detailed memories of that day. This phenomenon isn't limited to negative emotions; think back to the happiest day of your life. You can probably describe that day in a comparable level of detail.

One reason we usually have strong memories for episodes of intense emotion (fear and anger, but also happiness and surprise) is that these tend to be memories that we rehearse frequently, reviewing them mentally and talking

---

"Immunizing" against Learned Helplessness

Although learned helplessness was originally discovered, and studied, under highly controlled laboratory conditions, there is evidence that it also occurs in natural environments—and the consequences can be devastating. For example, Martin Seligman suggested that learned helplessness might be an important component of human depression (Seligman, 1975). People suffering from depression spend a lot of time sitting around or sleeping, sometimes skipping work or school because they lack the energy to leave home. Some depression appears to be triggered by external problems, but affected individuals often feel unable to do anything to change the conditions that are making them feel depressed. Like Seligman's dogs, they seem to sit and endure their pain rather than explore ways to escape or avoid it. The idea that learned helplessness may at least partially underlie human depression is supported by the finding that antidepressant drugs, which alleviate depression in humans, can also eliminate learned helplessness in rats previously exposed to inescapable shock (Besson, Privat, Eschalier, & Fialip, 1999).

If learned helplessness does play a role in human depression, then perhaps the same behavioral techniques that help animals overcome learned helplessness could also benefit depressed patients. For example, Seligman found that if he first trained his animals to escape the shock, then exposed them to inescapable shock, and then tested them again, the animals continued to make escape responses (Seligman Rosellini, & Kozak, 1975). Apparently, the earlier learning that they could escape shocks "immunized" the animals against learned helplessness when they were later exposed to inescapable shock. Perhaps some humans could be "immunized" against depression in the same way: if humans are exposed early in life to adversities that they can overcome, perhaps this early training could protect them against learned helplessness when confronted with more difficult challenges later in life.

The same insight could apply to educational methods. Some children attribute their academic failures to inescapable conditions: "I'm bad at math" or "I'm not as smart as the other children." Confronted with a new math problem, such a child might not bother to try—just like Seligman's helpless dogs. Maybe this attitude could be reversed or lessened by a training procedure that mixes hard problems with problems the child can solve, gradually teaching the child a way to "escape" from the cycle of failure by exposure to challenges that he can master (Dweck, 1975).

about them with others (Heuer & Reisberg, 1992). So, for example, in the days following the 9/11 attacks, people discussed the situation with friends and families and watched intensive TV coverage—and each time, their memories for the original event were retrieved, rehearsed, and strengthened. And, as you read in Chapter 7, rehearsal strengthens memory. However, the effect of emotion goes beyond rehearsal: strong emotions can actually affect the probability that an episodic memory is encoded in the first place.

Emotion and Encoding of Memories

Researchers can study the effect of emotional content on memory by "creating" emotional experiences in the laboratory and then testing for memories of those events. In a classic set of experiments, one group of participants saw a slide show accompanied by a highly emotional story. The beginning of the story described a boy who went on an outing with his mother; in the dramatic middle part, the boy was involved in a traumatic accident, and was rushed to surgery; finally, at the end of the story, his mother arranged to take him home (Cahill, Babinsky, Markowitsch, & McGaugh, 1995; Cahill & McGaugh, 1995; Heuer & Reisberg, 1990). A second group of participants saw the same slide show, with the same narrative accompanying the beginning of the story (boy accompanies his mother) and end of the story (mother takes boy home). But for this second group, the middle part of the narrative was changed: these participants saw the same surgery-related photos, but they were told that the boy was observing the hospital's disaster drill, during which hospital workers were practicing their skills on volunteers made up to look like trauma victims.

Two weeks later, participants were shown the pictures again and asked to recall the accompanying narrative. Those who had heard the emotional accident story remembered the dramatic middle events very well; their memories for the comparatively unemotional beginning and end parts were somewhat worse (Figure 10.5). In contrast, participants who had heard the less exciting story about a disaster drill recalled fewer events, particularly from the middle (Cahill, Uncapher, Kilpatrick, Alkire, & Turner, 2004). Apparently, even though both groups of participants saw the same pictures, those for whom the story was emotionally arousing were better able to encode the details and remember them later (Cahill, Babinsky, Markowitsch, & McGaugh, 1995).

The strong encoding and persistence of emotionally charged memories is one reason why advertisers often attempt to use arousing images in their commercials. If they can evoke pleasurable emotion such as excitement, sexual interest, or humor, there is a better chance you'll remember the commercial and, perhaps, buy the product later. (Some advertisers take this attempt at emotional manipulation a step further, using overtly sexual or provocative images, even to pitch comparatively non-erotic items such as deodorant or hamburgers. The hope is that viewers will experience sexual arousal while viewing the ad, and misinterpret this arousal as an attraction to the product—just like the participants in the "High Bridge" study who misinterpreted their arousal as an attraction to the researcher.)

Emotion and Retrieval of Memories

Emotion not only affects how memories are stored; it also affects how they are recalled. In Chapter 7 you read about the concept of

Figure 10.5 Memory for emotionally arousing material Participants who heard the emotional story (in which the boy was injured) were later able to recall more details of the middle part than participants who saw the same pictures accompanied by the emotionally neutral story (in which the boy merely observed a hospital drill). The beginning and ending parts of the story were identical for both groups of participants. Research from Cahill et al., 1995.

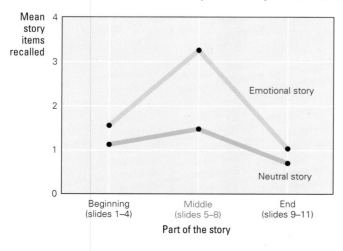

transfer-appropriate processing, in which chances of recall are increased if the cues available at retrieval are similar to the cues available at testing. It is likewise easier to retrieve memories that match our current mood or emotional state; this effect is termed **mood congruency of memory**. For example, in one study, students first listened to music and reported whether it made them feel happy or sad. They then saw a list of words (SHIP, STREET, etc.) and were asked to recall an autobiographical memory associated with each word. Students who had reported being in a happy mood tended to generate mostly positive memories, and relatively few neutral or negative memories, as shown in Figure 10.6 (Eich, Macaulay, & Ryan, 1994). Students in a sad mood recalled fewer positive and more negative memories. Few students in either mood generated many neutral memories—consistent with the general principle that our strongest memories tend to be associated with strong emotions, whether those emotions are positive or negative.

Mood-congruent memory effects occur in real-life contexts too. For example, patients suffering with clinical depression are more likely to recall sad or unpleasant events than pleasant memories (Clark & Teasdale, 1982; Fogarty & Hemsley, 1983). This can lead to a vicious cycle in which the recollection of sad memories makes the patient feel even more depressed and hopeless.

Why might mood influence recall? A strong mood or emotion causes biological responses and subjective feelings, and these can be incorporated into the memory just like other contextual cues. As you learned in Chapter 7, one of the factors influencing our ability to retrieve a memory is the number of cues available to guide retrieval. From this perspective, a strong mood or emotion is simply one kind of memory cue, and as the number of cues available at the time of recall increases, the more likely we are to successfully retrieve the original information.

Flashbulb Memories You've just read how our everyday emotional highs and lows can strengthen memories. Extreme emotions can result in memories that appear to have exceptional strength and durability. Such memories are called **flashbulb memories** because they form quickly, as if the brain were taking "flash photographs" to preserve the incident forever in vivid detail, while other, less arousing memories fade with time (R. Brown & Kulik, 1977). Some of us have flashbulb memories for important personal events, like the death of a parent, a car accident, or a first kiss. We may remember these events vividly, recollecting not just the place and time of day where, say, that first kiss occurred but even things like the smell of the room, the sound of a clock ticking in the background, and the color and texture of the clothes we were wearing.

Every so often an event (usually a tragedy) occurs that causes an entire society to form flashbulb memories. September 11 is one example. Other examples include the assassination of public figures—such as President John F. Kennedy or Martin Luther King, Jr.—and disasters such as hurricanes, earthquakes, floods, or spaceship explosions. The assassination of President Kennedy is perhaps the best studied such event. Five decades later, many older Americans still maintain vivid memories of when and how they heard that the president had been shot. For example, 10 years after the event, one man recalled,

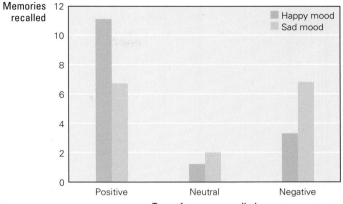

Figure 10.6 Mood congruency of memory People in a happy mood tend to recall more positive than negative or neutral autobiographical memories; by contrast, people in a sad mood recall significantly fewer positive and more negative memories. Data from Eich & Macaulay, 2002.

mood congruency of memory. The principle that it is easier to retrieve memories that match our current mood or emotional state.

flashbulb memory. A memory formed under conditions of extreme emotions that seems especially vivid and long lasting.

"I was seated in a sixth-grade music class, and over the intercom I was told that the president had been shot. At first, everyone just looked at each other. Then the class started yelling, and the music teacher tried to calm everyone down. About ten minutes later I heard over the intercom that Kennedy had died and that everyone should return to their homeroom. I remember that when I got to my homeroom my teacher was crying and everyone was standing in a state of shock. They told us to go home." (R. Brown & Kulik, 1977)

Other Americans recalled the moment in similar detail:

"... I was having dinner in a French restaurant ..."
"... talking to a woman friend on the telephone ..."
"The weather was cloudy and gray ..."
"... I was carrying a carton of Viceroy cigarettes which I dropped ..."
(R. Brown & Kulik, 1977)

Flashbulb memories for the events of September 11, 2001, seem to be similarly vivid. Several years after the event, many people can still remember where they were, what they were doing, and whom they were with when they heard the news. By contrast, memory for other, ordinary days (such as September 10, 2001) is generally much less detailed (Paradis, Solomon, Florer, & Thompson, 2004).

Can Flashbulb Memories Be Trusted? People generally report being very confident of the accuracy of their flashbulb memories. In fact, however, it appears that what distinguishes flashbulb memories from other episodic memories is not that they are more objectively accurate than other memories but rather that we strongly "feel" that they are accurate (Phelps & Sharot, 2008). Viewed this way, flashbulb memories are merely episodic memories that are experienced with great vividness and confidence (Sharot, Martorella, Delgado, & Phelps, 2007). Ulrich Neisser, one of the foremost memory researchers of the twentieth century, recounted a memory of his boyhood as follows:

For many years I have remembered how I heard the news of the Japanese attack on Pearl Harbor, which occurred on [December 7, 1941,] the day before my thirteenth birthday. I recall sitting in the living room of our house ... listening to a baseball game on the radio. The game was interrupted by an announcement of the attack, and I rushed upstairs to tell my mother. This memory has been so clear for so long that I never confronted its inherent absurdity until last year: no one broadcasts baseball games in December! (Neisser, 1982, p. 45)

> What features of an event make it likely to produce flashbulb memories?

Some details of Neisser's flashbulb memory are obviously inconsistent with common sense, and so we (like he) can conclude that his memory is almost certainly wrong in some of its details. However, although baseball is not played in December, football is: the New York Dodgers and Giants (two football teams with the same names as New York baseball teams of the day) were in fact playing on December 7, 1941, when the radio broadcast was interrupted with news of the Pearl Harbor bombing. Neisser's flashbulb memory was probably reasonably accurate—except for the minor detail

" Sure I remember our 20th wedding anniversary - that was the year Denver beat Atlanta, 31-19 in the Super Bowl ! "

Roy Delgado/www.CartoonStock.com

that he misremembered the type of game he'd been listening to on the radio (Thompson & Cowan, 1986).

Unfortunately, it is not always so easy to determine whether the details of a flashbulb memory are correct or not. For example, when someone remembers dropping a carton of Viceroy cigarettes after hearing of the Kennedy assassination, how can we tell whether that detail is correct? In general, unless the detail is obviously inconsistent with known facts, we cannot be sure of its accuracy.

Several studies have attempted to address this issue by judging flashbulb memories immediately after the arousing event and again sometime later. For example, on September 12, 2001, researchers Jennifer Talarico and David Rubin contacted 54 Duke University students and asked a series of open-ended questions about how the students had heard of the terrorist attacks (Talarico & Rubin, 2003). On average, students remembered about 12 details, such as where they heard the news, who was with them at the time, and so on. The researchers then contacted the same students again later. Talarico and Rubin found that the memories decayed over time, with students remembering fewer details as the weeks and months passed. Students contacted a week after the event might remember only about 10 of the details they'd previously reported, and students contacted 8 months after the event might remember only about 7 details. At the same time, inconsistent details crept into the reports. For example, on September 12, a student might have reported hearing the news from a friend; by May 2002, that same student might "remember" hearing the news on television.

A similar pattern of distortion over time has been demonstrated for memories of other notable events (Neisser & Harsch, 1992; Schmolck, Buffalo, & Squire, 2000). The bottom line on all these studies is that flashbulb memories are long lasting, vivid, and largely accurate—but they are not perfect photographic records of the event: they can be incomplete and can contain inaccurate details.

Why should such errors creep into our memories? One cause is source monitoring errors, which you read about in Chapter 7, such as forgetting that a friend told you the news and instead "remembering" that you first heard it on the television or radio (Greenberg, 2004). This is perhaps an understandable mistake, given our cultural tendency to become glued to the TV following a national tragedy; the repetition and visual impact of news coverage may swamp our memories of how we really heard the news. Another possibility is that memories of particularly important events are continuously pondered, rehearsed, and discussed. Each time, we are liable, quite unconsciously, to fill any little gaps in our memory with details that seem to fit the context. Later, we remember those inserted details as part of the original event. As you read in Chapter 7, this is one way that false memories can form. The result is that although many remembered details may be quite correct, others—that seem equally vivid—may be entirely wrong.

In fact, numerous studies have now documented that, while emotion often enhances memory for key events, this benefit does not always extend to background details (e.g., Kensinger, Piguet, Krendl & Corkin, 2005; Kim, Vossel & Gamer, 2013; Waring & Kensinger, 2011). For example, in one study, subjects saw photos in which emotional stimuli (such as a snake) or neutral stimuli (such as a chipmunk) were placed in the context of a neutral background scene (such as a riverbank). Later, participants were given a recognition test in which stimuli and scenes were presented separately. Unsurprisingly, memory was typically better for the emotional stimuli (snake) than for the neutral stimuli (chipmunk)— but memory was worse for background scenes that had been presented with an emotional stimulus than for scenes presented with a neutral stimulus (Waring & Kensinger, 2009). In effect, there is a "trade-off" in which the strong memory for the central emotional content comes at the cost of weaker memory for surrounding details.

So, think back to the morning of September 11, 2001—or another occasion on which you heard important, emotionally arousing news, such as the death of a family member. Where were you when you got the news? What were you doing at the time? Who was with you? It may be instructive to ask those people what they remember about the day and to see whether their memories match yours. Chances are, you will be right about many of the important facts—after all, strong emotions do encourage strong memories—but at least some of the smaller details that you remember quite vividly may indeed turn out to be false memories (see "Learning and Memory in Everyday Life" below).

Interim Summary

- Emotions have three components: physiological responses, overt behavioral responses, and conscious feelings. Each component influences the others.
- The major emotions, such as happiness, fear, and anger, seem to be universal, although the overt display of these emotions may be influenced by culture.
- Arousal, also called the fight-or-flight response, is the body's way of preparing to face or run away from a threat. Energy is diverted toward the brain, lungs, and legs, and away from other systems such as digestion and the immune system.

LEARNING AND MEMORY IN EVERYDAY LIFE

Truth or Consequences

In February 2015, Brian Williams, the anchorman of NBC's *Nightly News*, became the center of controversy related to his descriptions of being in a helicopter forced down by enemy fire in Iraq in 2003. In fact, what appears to have happened is that the helicopter ahead of him was hit and made an emergency landing; Williams himself was on another helicopter following some distance behind (Somaiya, 2015). In the wake of the controversy, NBC suspended Williams, who stated in a public apology that he had misremembered the event.

How could someone possibly misremember such an important event? In his initial on-air report of the incident in 2003, Williams said that the helicopter he was flying in was ordered to land quickly, and that the helicopter ahead had been "almost blown out of the sky." By 2007, Williams was telling a version of the story in which his own helicopter had come under fire, and in a 2013 TV interview, Williams described how his helicopter had been shot down.

Some accused Williams of exaggerating or misrepresenting the incident to embellish his public image. Memory researchers, in general, were kinder, noting that, while it's possible Williams simply lied, it's also quite plausible that, in telling and re-telling the story over the years, distortions crept in and details became confused (Bello, 2015). In this case, the terror of hearing that the lead helicopter had been hit, and the subsequent confusion of an unscheduled landing in dangerous territory, may have gradually coalesced into a memory that it was Williams's own helicopter that had been fired upon. The more Williams talked about it, on TV and in his personal life, the stronger the false memory may have become.

In 2008, Hillary Clinton came under similar scrutiny for her repeated description of running off a plane under sniper fire during a 1996 trip to Bosnia; in fact, news footage of the event shows no evidence of sniper fire while Clinton and the other passengers emerge smiling from the plane (Harnden, 2008). As with Williams, it's possible that Clinton's episodic memory may have become confused with another, similar incident where there was actual gunfire, or might simply reflect that, at the time, she was sincerely worried about the possibility of sniper fire. Repeated re-imagining and re-telling of the story may have led to distortion and confusion of details until she really believed she had been exposed to enemy fire that day.

For a political figure, the cost of being caught in a misstatement is a chance for the opposition to level accusations of dishonesty. For a journalist, the cost can be a loss of credibility as an unbiased presenter of the news. For the rest of us, episodes like these serve as reminders that memory is malleable and fallible, and that eyewitness description is no substitute for checking the facts.

- The James–Lange theory of emotion proposes that physiological responses cause our conscious feelings of emotion. The Cannon–Bard theory proposes that stimuli simultaneously evoke physiological responses and conscious emotions. The two-factor theory of emotion posits that emotions are produced by an interaction between physiological responses and our cognitive appraisal of the situation.

- While we cannot be sure whether nonhuman animals have conscious emotional feelings, their physiological and behavioral responses to emotional stimuli are often very similar to those in humans.

- Conditioned emotional learning is a form of classical conditioning in which a CS (such as a tone) that has been paired with an emotion-evoking US (such as an electric shock) evokes a CR (such as a freezing response or an increased heartbeat). Conditioned escape learning involves operant conditioning: a stimulus S^D (such as an electric shock) can evoke a motor response R to produce an outcome O (escape from shock).

- Avoidance learning, learning that a particular response results in avoidance of an aversive event, may involve both classical and operant conditioning; in addition, cognitive expectancies may allow the organism to choose between various possible responses.

- Learned helplessness occurs when exposure to an inescapable punisher impairs learning to escape or avoid future punishment.

- Emotions can increase the strength and duration of memory storage. Emotion can also affect retrieval: we are more likely to retrieve memories that fit our current mood.

- Flashbulb memories are vivid and long lasting, but they are not always completely accurate.

10.2 Brain Substrates

From the earliest days of brain science, scientists have tried to understand how the brain gives rise to emotion. One of the most influential attempts to locate the brain substrates of emotion was made by Cornell University anatomist James Papez in 1937. (Papez is pronounced "papes," to rhyme with "grapes.") Based on the information available to him at the time from patients with different types of brain damage, Papez concluded that the hippocampus and cingulate cortex play major roles in emotions—along with other regions such as the thalamus, by which sensory information enters the brain, and the hypothalamus, which helps regulate the body's response to emotion. Papez proposed that these brain regions operate in a loop, later named the *Papez circuit*, that he described as the central processing pathway for emotion.

The Papez circuit is important historically because it represents one of the first systematic attempts to understand the brain substrates of emotion by combining information about lesion studies with what was then known about anatomical structures. Remarkably, many of the presumed pathways connecting the structures in the Papez circuit were not yet known to exist; Papez merely deduced they must be there. Almost all of them have since been discovered in the brain.

But we now know that there is no specialized "emotion circuit." Each emotion activates many different brain regions. One report combined data across 55 functional neuroimaging (fMRI and PET) studies of emotion, to determine which brain areas are activated by the emotions of happiness, sadness, disgust,

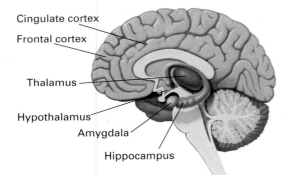

Cingulate cortex
Frontal cortex
Thalamus
Hypothalamus
Amygdala
Hippocampus

Figure 10.7 Key brain structures involved in processing emotion Brain structures that have special roles in emotional learning include the amygdala, hippocampus, thalamus, hypothalamus, and cingulate cortex. The frontal cortex also plays a key role in interpreting the context and monitoring the display of emotion.

amygdala. A collection of brain nuclei lying at the anterior tip of each *hippocampus*, critical for learning and expressing emotional responses as well as mediating the emotional modulation of memory formation.

fear, and anger (Phan, Wagner, Taylor, & Liberzon, 2002). The report concluded that (1) each emotion activated many different brain regions, and (2) no single brain region was activated by all the different emotions. Thus, emotion appears to be a function of the brain as a whole rather than arising from special circuits dedicated to individual emotions. All the same, some parts of the brain appear to be particularly important for emotion. First and foremost among these is the amygdala.

The Amygdala: A Central Processing Station for Emotions

As shown in Figure 10.7, the **amygdala** is a small almond-shaped structure that lies at the anterior tip of the hippocampus. (The word *amygdala* is taken from the Greek word for "almond.") Just as the brain has one hippocampus in each hemisphere, it also has one amygdala in each hemisphere, at the tip of each hippocampus, but for convenience, most researchers refer to "the amygdala," just as they refer to "the hippocampus."

The amygdala is a collection of more than 10 separate subregions, or *nuclei*, all of which have different input and output pathways. Figure 10.8 depicts some key nuclei and connections within the amygdala. (Many other nuclei and pathways exist but are not shown in Figure 10.8 for simplicity.) The *lateral nucleus* is a primary entry point for sensory information into the amygdala; this sensory information arrives directly from the thalamus and also indirectly from the thalamus by way of the cortex. The *central nucleus* receives inputs from other amygdala nuclei and projects out of the amygdala to the autonomic nervous system (ANS), driving expression of physiological responses such as arousal and release of stress hormones, and also to motor centers, driving expression of behavioral responses such as freezing and startle. The *basolateral nucleus* receives input from the lateral nucleus and projects to the cerebral cortex, basal ganglia, and hippocampus, providing a pathway by which the amygdala can modulate memory storage and retrieval in those structures. The amygdala is thus critical both in learned emotional responses and in the emotional modulation of memory storage and retrieval.

The Central Nucleus: Expressing Emotional Responses

In the research lab, electrical stimulation of the amygdala can produce dramatic emotional displays. For example, stimulating the amygdala of a predator, such as a cat, can cause a species-typical defensive reaction, including lowering of the head, flattening of the ears, piloerection, and growling or hissing (Roldan, Alvarez-Pelaez, & Fernandez de Molina, 1974). In a prey animal, such as a rabbit, stimulation of the amygdala causes a different species-typical defensive reaction, including freezing and a lowered heart rate (Kapp, Gallagher, Underwood, McNall, & Whitehorn, 1981). Stimulating the amygdala in humans doesn't produce such dramatic results. Humans given amygdala stimulation may report subjective feelings of mild positive or negative emotion, but they are not likely to exhibit an all-out emotional response such as occurs in cats and rabbits (Bancaud, Brunet-Bourgin, Chauvel, & Halgren, 1994; Halgren, 1982).

Why might stimulation of the amygdala cause such a dramatic fear response in some animals but only mild feelings of foreboding in humans? According to a two-factor theory of emotion (see Figure 10.2c), our conscious emotional feelings depend not only on our biological responses but also on how we interpret

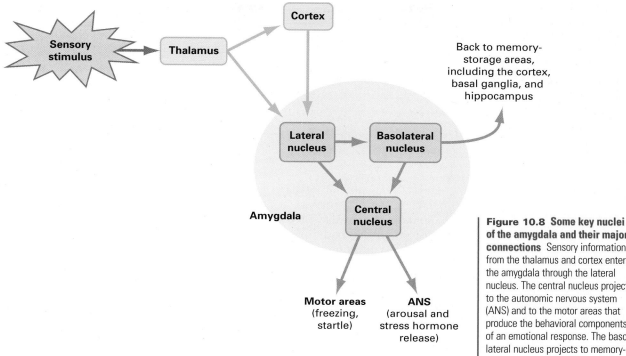

Figure 10.8 Some key nuclei of the amygdala and their major connections Sensory information from the thalamus and cortex enters the amygdala through the lateral nucleus. The central nucleus projects to the autonomic nervous system (ANS) and to the motor areas that produce the behavioral components of an emotional response. The basolateral nucleus projects to memory-storage areas such as the cortex and the hippocampus, where emotional information can influence memory storage and retrieval (LeDoux, 1998, 2000; McGaugh, 2002).

the situation. In the relatively "safe" context of a lab environment, human participants receiving amygdala stimulation know they are in a controlled situation and that a full panic response is not warranted. On the other hand, in a truly menacing situation—such as a walk through a dark alley at night—outputs from the amygdala would initiate a biological fear response—a speeded heart rate, sweaty palms, and other components of the fight-or-flight response.

Given that the amygdala helps initiate the body's emotional responses, it is not too surprising that lesions of the central nucleus of the amygdala disrupt the ability to learn, as well as display, new emotional responses. Bilateral damage limited to the amygdala is rare in humans (Markowitsch et al., 1994), although a few such cases have been identified and studied. These patients often show deficits in learning emotional responses. For example, Chapter 3 introduced the *skin conductance response* (SCR), a tiny but measurable change in the electrical conductivity of the human skin that occurs when people feel arousal. In healthy people, a loud sound, such as a 100-decibel boat horn (the US), produces a sharp increase in skin conductance (the UR). If this US is always preceded by a neutral stimulus, such as the appearance of a colored shape, healthy participants learn that the visual CS predicts the US, and they therefore produce an SCR to the CS alone (Figure 10.9a). This is an example of classical conditioning.

The SCR is mediated by outputs from the central amygdala to the ANS that cause the skin conductance to change. As a result, conditioning of the SCR can be disrupted by damage to the amygdala. Figure 10.9a shows the responses of a patient with bilateral amygdala damage. Although the US evoked a strong SCR in this patient, the CS did not. This patient could exhibit arousal when startled but could not learn a conditioned emotional response (Bechara et al., 1995). In contrast, a different patient with damage that included the nearby hippocampus (but not the amygdala) could learn a conditioned emotional response as well as

Figure 10.9 Conditioned emotional responses (a) In humans, a loud boat horn (US) produces a skin conductance response (SCR). If a colored shape (CS) is paired with the US, then healthy humans (controls) produce a strong SCR to the CS. A patient with selective lesion of the amygdala (AL) does not show this conditioned emotional response, although a patient with lesion of the nearby hippocampus (HL) does. (b) In rats, conditioned emotional responding (freezing) is similarly abolished by AL but not HL.

(a) Research from Bechara et al., 1995.
(b) Research from Phillips & LeDoux, 1992.

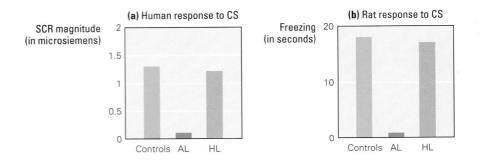

controls. Thus, the amygdala is important for learning and expressing conditioned emotional responses.

Nonhuman animals with lesions of the amygdala central nucleus show similar disruptions in conditioned emotional responding. For example, after three days of CS–US training with a shock US, a normal rat will give an emotional response to the CS that can include physiological changes (such as increased blood pressure) and overt behavioral responses (such as freezing, shown in Figure 10.9b). Lesions that damage the central nucleus of the amygdala abolish this learned fear response, so there is no freezing to the CS alone; just like in humans, damage to the nearby hippocampus that spares the amygdala does not affect the learned freezing response (Phillips & LeDoux, 1992).

These disruptions in conditioned emotional responses occur because the central nucleus provides the major outputs from the amygdala to the ANS and to motor centers that drive the freezing response. (These pathways are shown in Figure 10.8.) Lesion of the central nucleus therefore disrupts the ability to express a learned fear response. Some researchers believe that the conditioned emotional response is learned and stored in the lateral nucleus, with the central nucleus behaving more like a simple way station that signals other brain stations to turn on the fear responses (Cahill, Weinberger, Roozendaal, & McGaugh, 1999; Fanselow & LeDoux, 1999; Maren, 1999; McGaugh & Cahill, 2003). Thus, animals with lesions of the central nucleus might still be able to learn about a fear-evoking CS; they would simply be unable to express this learning by freezing or by activating the ANS. Other researchers suggest that the central nucleus is not just a passive way station but encodes other aspects of emotional learning, particularly when appetitive, or pleasant, rather than aversive, or unpleasant, stimuli are involved (Balleine & Kilcross, 2006; Everitt, Cardinal, Parkinson, & Robbins, 2003).

Two Pathways for Emotional Learning in the Amygdala

As you saw in Figure 10.8, the amygdala receives sensory input from two separate pathways. The thalamus is the first site in the brain where most kinds of sensory input converge and are processed; for this reason, the thalamus is sometimes called the "sensory gateway to the brain." From the thalamus, stimulus information travels directly to the amygdala and also up to the cortex. As you read in Chapter 3, the cortex processes sensory information more fully, discriminating fine details and so on. Information from the cortex also travels down to the amygdala. Emotion researcher Joseph LeDoux proposes that each of these pathways—the direct path from the thalamus to the amygdala and the indirect path from the thalamus to the cortex to the amygdala—plays an important role in responding to fear-evoking stimuli (LeDoux, 1993, 1994). The direct path is faster—carrying information from the thalamus to the amygdala in about 12 milliseconds in rats—but it also conveys less detail, just the bare outlines of stimulus information. The indirect pathway is slower—taking about 19 milliseconds for information from the thalamus to reach the amygdala in rats—but the involvement of the cortex allows much finer discrimination of stimulus details. In LeDoux's terms, the direct path is "fast and rough" and the indirect path is "slow but accurate." The faster, direct path allows us to react quickly in a life-and-death situation, activating the fight-or-flight response; the slower, more accurate path then provides extra information, allowing us to terminate the fear response if the stimulus is not dangerous after all.

Here's a simple example of how this dual pathway might work. Suppose you're walking home alone at night, feeling a little nervous. A big, dark shape approaches. This visual stimulus activates your thalamus, which shoots this information directly to the amygdala. The amygdala interprets this stimulus as possibly signaling danger and activates an immediate fear response ("yikes!"), preparing you to fight or run away. A few milliseconds later, the signals from the thalamus reach your visual cortex, which processes the stimulus more fully and allows you to recognize the stimulus as nonthreatening: it's only a friend walking toward you. The cortex sends this information ("no danger here") down to the amygdala, shutting off the fear response. (It may take a few moments for stress hormone levels to decline enough so that your heart rate returns to normal and your goose bumps fade away.)

The cost of using the "fast-and-rough" pathway from thalamus to amygdala is that you have gotten yourself all worked up over nothing. On the other hand, the cost of overreacting to a harmless stimulus is much less, in general, than the cost of failing to respond to a truly dangerous stimulus (LeDoux, 2000; LeDoux, Iwata, Cicchetti, & Reiss, 1988). If the approaching shape really had been a threat, the cost of waiting for your cortex to make a definitive identification could have been the difference between escape and injury. From an evolutionary perspective, animals with a genetic predisposition to freeze or dart for cover when they see movement in the bush ("Was that rustling in the bushes caused by a predator or just the wind? Better to play it safe and survive another day …") are more likely to live long enough to produce offspring that share the same cautious instincts.

Once having survived a brush with danger, the next challenge is to learn from it. Some of this learning probably takes place in the lateral nucleus of the amygdala, where neural connections change as a result of experiencing a neutral CS paired with a fear-evoking US. For example, in one study, researchers implanted recording electrodes into the lateral amygdala of rats so as to simultaneously monitor the activity of about 100 neurons (Rosenkranz & Grace, 2002). When the rats were presented with various odors—say, almond and anise—the neurons showed a low baseline level of response to each (Figure 10.10). The researchers then trained the rats that one odor—say, almond—always preceded a tail-shock US. Not surprisingly, the rats quickly learned to freeze in anticipation of a shock whenever they encountered almond odor, although they showed no such fear response to the anise odor, which had not been paired with shock. Figure 10.10 shows that, after training, neurons in the lateral amygdala responded strongly to the almond odor that had been paired with the US.

This is exactly the pattern you would expect to see if *long-term potentiation* (LTP) were occurring in the lateral amygdala. (To review LTP, see

Figure 10.10 The lateral amygdala and conditioning Baseline responding of lateral amygdala neurons of a rat is similar for two odors. If one of the odors (almond) is subsequently paired with a tail shock, the response to that odor increases strongly from the baseline value. This is exactly the pattern of responding that would be expected if the lateral amygdala neurons were encoding the associations between odor CS and shock US.
Data from Rosenkranz and Grace, 2002.

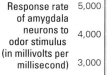
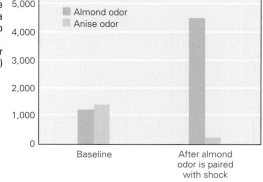

Chapter 2.) Assume that the almond odor activates sensory neurons in the rat's nose, and these in turn project (directly and by way of sensory cortex) to neurons in the lateral nucleus of the amygdala. Initially, presentation of either odor causes little activity in these neurons (the baseline condition in Figure 10.10), but a shock stimulus strongly activates them. If the almond odor is paired with the shock, the almond odor arrives just as the neurons are activated by shock, and since "neurons that fire together, wire together," the synapse between them is strengthened. The end result of these events is that when the almond odor is presented again, it will cause more activity in the lateral amygdala (the "after" condition shown in Figure 10.10). No such strengthening occurs in pathways carrying information about anise or other odors because they have not been paired with shock.

Further evidence of the role of the amygdala in fear conditioning comes from the new technique of **optogenetics**, in which researchers inject living animals with a virus that will insert new genes into specific cells, causing those cells to become sensitive to light (Deisseroth, 2010). If the infected cells are neurons, researchers can then precisely target light stimulation to specific areas of the brain, and selectively turn these infected neurons on and off, rather like turning on and off an electrical appliance. Researchers can use this technique to examine whether activity in some neurons actually causes changes in other parts of the brain. In one study, researchers first conditioned rats that a tone CS predicted a foot-shock US; the animals quickly learned the CS–US association and would display freezing responses when they heard the CS (Nabavi et al., 2014). Then, the researchers replaced the tone CS with optogenetic stimulation of the pathway from auditory cortex to the lateral amygdala. When the light was turned on, there was initially no effect. But when the light stimulation was paired with a foot shock, the animals quickly learned the freezing response—just as they had done with the tone CS. In other words, a "real" stimulus such as a tone isn't required; as long as the lateral amygdala is active when the US arrives, conditioning occurs.

The amygdala's job isn't limited to learning CS–US associations. It also plays a role in modulating memory storage elsewhere that represents other aspects of the experience—such as the episodic memory of an emotional event. So, let's turn next to consider the ways in which emotion can modulate storage and recall of episodic memory.

The Amygdala and Episodic Memory Storage

Recall the experiment in which a slide show accompanied narration of either an emotionally arousing story or a neutral story. Healthy people remembered more details of the emotionally arousing story, particularly from the dramatic middle part, than of the neutral story (Figure 10.5). By contrast, a patient with amygdala damage recalled the beginning and end of the story about as well as did healthy controls but showed no physiological arousal during the emotional middle section and no tendency, later, to recall that material better (Cahill, Babinsky, Markowitsch, & McGaugh, 1995). It wasn't that the patient couldn't remember the story but that the memory of the middle part didn't get an emotional "boost." This finding implies that the amygdala may provide a signal to strengthen the storage of information in declarative memory.

Even in healthy brains, the degree of amygdala activation may reflect how effectively information is processed and stored in memory. If healthy people are shown emotionally arousing short films while their brain activity is recorded using PET, those individuals with the highest level of amygdala activation during viewing tend to remember more details later than individuals with lower

optogenetics. A technique for causing specific cells (particularly *neurons*) to become sensitive to light, after which researchers can use light stimulation to turn those specific neurons "on" and "off" at will.

levels of amygdala activity (Cahill et al., 1996). Other studies have documented that the amygdala is also activated while participants view pleasant pictures, and greater amygdala activity during encoding of specific pictures is correlated with better recognition of those pictures later (Canli, Zhao, Brewer, Gabrieli, & Cahill, 2000; Hamann, Ely, Grafton, & Kilts, 1999).

Degree of amygdala activity may therefore help determine whether new information gets stored as an episodic or a semantic memory. Recall from Chapter 7 that episodic memory is information we "remember" and semantic memory is information we "know." The key difference is that episodic memory has supporting contextual information—we remember the time and place where the event that produced the memory happened to us. Healthy adults, shown a series of emotional photographs and asked to recognize them later, can be asked whether they "remember" previously studying that picture or merely "know" that the picture is familiar (but don't actually remember the study episode). Amygdala activity is higher both at encoding (Dolcos, LaBar, & Cabeza, 2004) and recognition (Sharot, Delgado, & Phelps, 2004) of emotionally arousing photographs that are subsequently judged as "remembered" than for those that are merely "known." Thus, emotional arousal (and amygdala activation) may promote encoding of contextual details, creating a subjective sense of "remembering" and causing the information to be stored as an episodic rather than semantic memory (LaBar, 2007). This in turn could be why we often have such a vivid sense of recollection for highly emotional events—flashbulb memories are formed when episodic memories are tagged with a particularly strong feeling of "remembering."

There are also intriguing sex differences in amygdala responses during memory formation: in women, left amygdala activation during encoding predicts better memory later; in men, right amygdala activation predicts better memory later (Cahill et al., 2001; Cahill et al., 2004; Canli, Desmond, Zhao, & Gabrieli, 2002). No one is quite sure yet why these left–right sex differences occur or how they might relate to observed sex differences in memory and behavior (Haman 2005).

The Role of Stress Hormones

Given the association between amygdala activation and the strength of episodic memory, the next question is, exactly how might the amygdala influence memory storage? One possible pathway is schematized in Figure 10.11. Outputs from the central nucleus of the amygdala travel to the ANS, which in turn signals the adrenal glands to release the stress hormone epinephrine. Epinephrine, along with other stress hormones, helps mediate the various components of the fight-or-flight response, including increased heart rate and dilation of blood vessels, to facilitate blood flow to brain and muscles.

But epinephrine can't affect the brain directly. The brain has a defense called the *blood-brain barrier*, a membrane that controls passage of substances from the blood into the central nervous system, including the brain. This protects the brain from many chemicals that might otherwise enter and harm it. Epinephrine cannot cross the blood-brain barrier, but it can activate brainstem nuclei that produce the chemically related neurotransmitter norepinephrine, and these nuclei project to the basolateral amygdala, as shown in Figure 10.11 (McGaugh, 2002, 2003). From there, outputs from the basolateral amygdala travel to brain regions including the hippocampus and cortex. Emotional stimuli such as foot shocks do indeed cause increased levels of norepinephrine in the basolateral amygdala—and the precise amount of norepinephrine in an individual rat's amygdala is a good predictor of how well that rat will remember the learning experience (McIntyre, Hatfield, & McGaugh, 2000).

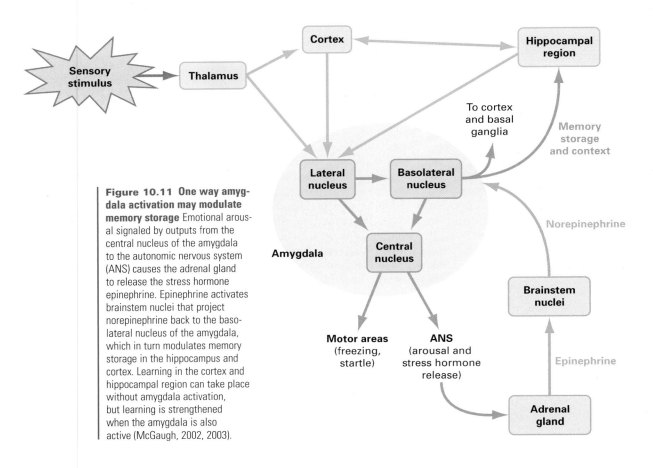

Figure 10.11 One way amygdala activation may modulate memory storage Emotional arousal signaled by outputs from the central nucleus of the amygdala to the autonomic nervous system (ANS) causes the adrenal gland to release the stress hormone epinephrine. Epinephrine activates brainstem nuclei that project norepinephrine back to the basolateral nucleus of the amygdala, which in turn modulates memory storage in the hippocampus and cortex. Learning in the cortex and hippocampal region can take place without amygdala activation, but learning is strengthened when the amygdala is also active (McGaugh, 2002, 2003).

Back in Chapter 7, you read that the cerebral cortex is the primary storage site of episodic memories, with this storage mediated by the hippocampus and other medial temporal lobe structures. So how might release of norepinephrine into the basolateral amygdala affect episodic memory storage in these other brain areas? Let's assume that a rat (or human) experiences an emotional event that causes norepinephrine to activate the basolateral amygdala. The neurons of the basolateral amygdala tend to fire in rhythmic waves (Paré, 2003), and they project out to the cortex, hippocampal region, and other memory-storage sites, where they may cause similarly rhythmic activation in large groups of neurons. Such rhythmic activation of many neurons facilitates LTP between the coactive neurons (again, "neurons that fire together, wire together"). In this way, the basolateral amygdala may facilitate learning in the cortex and hippocampal region.

Just as increasing the levels of norepinephrine in the basolateral amygdala can improve emotional memory, disruptions in norepinephrine transmission can impair emotional memory. Once again, let's consider the study in which Larry Cahill and colleagues showed participants a series of slides accompanied by an emotional story. In one variant, before starting the slides and story, Cahill gave some volunteers the drug propranolol, which blocks norepinephrine; the control group received an inactive placebo (Cahill, Prins, Weber, & McGaugh, 1994). Later, those people who'd received the placebo showed the normal pattern of remembering the emotionally charged middle part best (just like the participants in Figure 10.5). In contrast, people who had been given propranolol remembered the middle part no better (and no worse) than the emotionally neutral beginning and end parts. In general, blocking stress hormones (by administering drugs that interfere with epinephrine, norepinephrine, or glucocorticoids) reduces the ability of emotions to enhance memory.

These results help explain why the patient with amygdala damage had poor memory for the emotional middle part of the story. Without input from the amygdala, the other memory-storage areas may not be encouraged to form a strong memory of the emotionally arousing material, so the material is stored no more (or less) strongly than any other information. On the other hand, increasing stress hormones (by injecting epinephrine, norepinephrine, or glucocorticoids) can improve memory for emotional material (Buchanan & Lovallo, 2001; Cahill & Alkire, 2003)—to a point (see "Learning and Memory in Everyday Life" below).

Retrieval and Reconsolidation

The influence of the amygdala isn't limited to the initial learning experience. As you learned in Chapter 7, memories are not formed instantaneously but remain malleable throughout a *consolidation period*, during which time they are vulnerable to such interventions as electroconvulsive shock or head injury. You also read about *reconsolidation*, in which—under some circumstances—reactivation

---

LEARNING AND MEMORY IN EVERYDAY LIFE

A Little Stress Is a Good Thing

Three high school students, Larry, Moe, and Curly, are facing a stressful experience: taking their SATs. But they are reacting in different ways. Larry has gained early acceptance to Princeton, so he is relatively relaxed about the exam. Moe is nervous; he needs strong SAT scores to get into the college of his choice. Curly dreads tests of all sorts, and he's downright panicked now. On the (admittedly fictitious) assumption that all three students have equal knowledge going into the exam, who is likely to perform best?

Of course, Curly is at a disadvantage; he is so stressed out that he may well forget everything he ever knew as soon as he looks at the first question. But Larry may also be at a disadvantage if he's too relaxed. A little stress is good for memory, and this applies to recall (taking a test) as well as encoding (initial learning). Mild stress causes release of stress hormones, including glucocorticoids. The hippocampus has a particularly high concentration of glucocorticoid receptors (McEwen & Sapolsky, 1995), and low levels of stress hormones facilitate LTP and encourage dendritic growth, improving memory formation and recall (McEwen, 1999). Thus, Moe may actually benefit from his mild anxiety during the SATs.

Unfortunately, although low levels of stress can improve recall, chronic high levels of stress often impair recall (de Quervain, Roozendaal, & McGaugh, 1998; de Quervain, Roozendaal, Nitsch, McGaugh, & Hock, 2000). This may be because, although

low levels of stress hormones facilitate hippocampal learning, higher levels can overexcite the hippocampus, interfering with both learning and recall (Benjamin, McKeachie, Lin, & Holinger, 1981). Long-term exposure to high levels of stress may even cause neuronal death in the hippocampus (McEwen, 1997; Sapolsky, 1996).

How much stress is too much? Unfortunately, there is no easy answer: each individual seems to have a different breaking point (Kemeny, 2003). Furthermore, an individual's response to stress depends partly on whether he or she feels helpless to control it (see "Learning and Memory in Everyday Life" on page 409). If you are constantly feeling stressed, try making a list of the things that bother you and then look for ways of changing (controlling) one or two of them. You can also try methods of reducing stress, such as meditation, yoga, prayer, or exercise, that may help you calm down and may help get your hippocampus back into its normal operating range (Davidson et al., 2003).

As for Curly ... the best thing he can do is try to calm himself during the test—perhaps by taking deep breaths and thinking positive thoughts (Naveh-Benjamin, 1991). Once his stress hormones drop back to normal levels, his hippocampus can again function normally. This is one reason why, after the SATs are over, Curly will probably remember all those answers that he "forgot" under pressure during the test.

of an old memory makes it vulnerable all over again (Nader, 2003). The reactivation of a memory for an emotional event provides a window of opportunity during which a fresh dose of stress hormones could strengthen the neural circuits encoding that memory. Thus, while the principles of reconsolidation may apply to all types of memory, emotional memories may be particularly susceptible. This in turn suggests one way in which small distortions could creep into flashbulb memories: the memory might initially be accurate, but each time it is recalled, tiny details might be forgotten or altered, and over time, the memory could become quite different from its original form.

Reconsolidation can be demonstrated in rats using a conditioned avoidance procedure. Control rats, after having received a shock in a dark chamber, will hesitate about 60 seconds before daring to enter the dark chamber again (Figure 10.12a). But if the rats are given injections of epinephrine immediately (0 minutes) after the foot shock, this delay skyrockets, so that the rats now hesitate for more than 200 seconds before reentering the dark chamber (Figure 10.12b). As you saw in Figure 10.11, epinephrine stimulates norepinephrine release to the basolateral amygdala, which in turn stimulates learning in the cortex and hippocampus—making the rats remember more strongly that the dark chamber is a dangerous place. The effects of epinephrine are greatest if injection occurs immediately after the foot shock, but epinephrine can still boost memory if administered 10 or 30 minutes after the training session (Gold & van Buskirk, 1975). By 120 minutes, though, the memory seems to have stabilized, and epinephrine injections have no effect.

Emotion researcher James McGaugh has suggested that there is an important reason why animals might have evolved so as to allow the emotional system to modulate memory after the fact. In many cases, the importance of a particular event might not be immediately apparent. If a pigeon drinks colored water that contains a nausea-inducing agent, the symptoms of sickness may not appear for some time—but once those symptoms do appear, it is very important for the sick pigeon to be able to encode a strong memory of the colored water. Similarly, a child who scribbles on the wall but isn't punished until hours later, when Mother finds out, must be able to reach back in time and strongly associate the earlier action with the

Figure 10.12 Stress hormones can increase memory (a) If control rats are given a shock the first time they enter a dark chamber, they will delay an average of about a minute before reentering that chamber. (b) Rats given an injection of epinephrine after the training session will delay much longer, indicating that the post-training epinephrine increased their memory for the episode. The effects are time sensitive, so an injection given immediately (0 minutes) after training has more effect than one given after a longer delay (Gold and van Buskirk, 1975). Information from McGaugh, 2003.

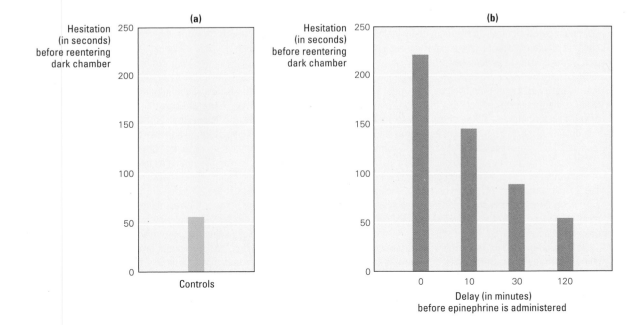

later consequence. In such cases, the ability of stress hormones to affect previously acquired memories allows the amygdala to tinker with the strength of the memory later, when the delayed consequences become apparent (McGaugh, 2003).

Encoding Emotional Contexts in the Hippocampus

In discussing how the amygdala might modulate learning about emotional events, we have already mentioned the hippocampal region, which is critical for new episodic (event) memory formation. But the hippocampal region also plays a role in many other kinds of memory, especially those that require learning about context and other stimulus–stimulus relationships (see Chapter 6). Remember that simple association of a conditioned stimulus (CS) and unconditioned stimulus (US) is not dependent on the hippocampus. For example, consider the conditioned-emotional-learning experiments described earlier in which a rat learns that a tone CS is associated with a fear-evoking shock US. Figure 10.9b showed that such CS–US learning is not disrupted in rats with hippocampal lesions, but it is devastated in rats with amygdala lesions (LeDoux, 1994).

During conditioning, a normal rat learns not only about the CS and the US but also about the context in which the US is presented. Thus, after CS–US training in a particular chamber, the rat may show a conditioned emotional response (freezing) as soon as it is placed back into that chamber—before any CS (or US) is presented. In fact, a healthy animal's response to the context may be almost as strong as its response to the CS! This contextual freezing response is greatly reduced in animals with hippocampal lesions (Figure 10.13a). Amygdala lesions also abolish the contextual fear response, possibly because the lesion damages the output pathway from the central nucleus to the motor areas that produce the freezing response (Phillips & LeDoux, 1992).

A similar interplay occurs between hippocampus and amygdala in humans monitored for the skin conductance response. Figure 10.9a showed that healthy humans give an SCR to a CS that has been paired with a US (loud boat horn). A patient with bilateral amygdala damage could not learn this conditioned response, but one with bilateral hippocampal damage could (Bechara et al., 1995). After conditioning, participants were asked what they remembered about the experiment. Healthy individuals could report that the CS predicted that the US was coming (Figure 10.13b). The patient with hippocampal damage, who had learned to produce the SCR, could not report any details of the conditioning experiment. This is consistent with the general expectation that a hippocampal lesion abolishes the ability to form new episodic memories but does not prevent simple classical conditioning. The patient with amygdala damage showed the opposite pattern: she could report the details of the conditioning experiment quite well—specifically, that the CS predicted the US—even though she did not generate an SCR to the CS. Thus, amygdala damage in humans seems to spare hippocampal-dependent context learning but to disrupt the learning and expression of an emotional response.

Figure 10.13 Conditioned contextual learning (a) During conditioning of an emotional response such as freezing in response to a CS that signals shock, control rats also learn a response (freezing) to the context where shock was experienced; this contextual learning is impaired by both amygdala lesion (AL) and hippocampal lesion (HL). (b) Healthy humans can also report contextual information during a skin conductance conditioning experiment; AL spares this contextual memory, but HL greatly impairs it. These data suggest a dissociation between conditioned emotional responding (which depends on the amygdala) and contextual or episodic learning (which depends on the hippocampus).

(a) Research from Phillips and LeDoux, 1992; (b) Research from Bechara et al., 1995.

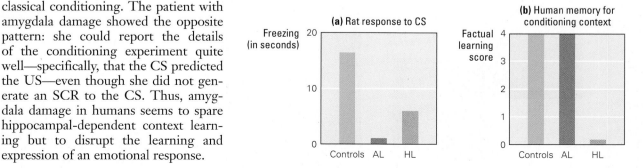

How might the hippocampal region mediate the effect of context on fear learning in the amygdala? The path from amygdala to hippocampal region is a two-way street, as illustrated in Figure 10.11. Signals from the amygdala travel to the hippocampal region. But signals from the hippocampal region containing information about the learning context also travel back to the amygdala, where they can be incorporated into ongoing emotional processing. This is part of the reason why returning to the place (or context) where an emotional experience occurred is often enough to evoke arousal. For example, when individuals return to a place where they experienced intense sadness or fear, they are sometimes struck with a fresh wave of grief or terror. Similarly (and more happily), couples celebrating an anniversary sometimes choose the restaurant where they had their first date because returning to the context where they once experienced strong feelings of romance can help evoke those same emotions again.

Feelings and the Frontal Lobes

The amygdala interacts with the hippocampus during emotional learning and memory, and it also interacts with the cortex. As you read in Chapter 9, the *frontal lobes* of the cortex are often considered the seat of executive function, where we do most of our planning and decision making. The frontal lobes are also intensively involved in social behavior, and appropriate social behavior demands the ability to express emotion and to read it in others.

Patients with damage to the frontal lobes often exhibit fewer and less intense facial expressions (Kolb & Taylor, 1981) and are impaired in their ability to recognize negative facial expressions (such as fear and disgust) in others (Kolb & Taylor, 2000). These patients may show a general disruption of emotion and mood, which can be manifested as social withdrawal and loss of normal emotional display. (The old medical procedure of prefrontal lobotomy was a way of making chronically agitated people "calmer" by destroying parts of the frontal lobes so as to reduce emotional expression.) Other patients with frontal lesions experience the opposite extreme, of heightened emotionality, and exhibit inappropriate social behavior (profanity, public masturbation, and so on) and rapid mood swings, including violent bouts of anger and aggression for no discernible reason. Apparently, the frontal lobes help people maintain a balance between too little emotion and too much.

The prefrontal cortex also plays a role in helping people "read" the expression of emotion in others. In a recent study, volunteers were shown pictures of fearful or emotionally neutral human faces (Figure 10.14a) while researchers measured skin conductance responses and observed brain activation with

Figure 10.14 The prefrontal cortex and emotional processing (a) Volunteers were shown pictures of fearful and emotionally neutral faces while brain activity was recorded by fMRI. (b, c) Difference images show that the amygdala was more active during the viewing of fearful faces—and so was the medial prefrontal cortex. The prefrontal cortex may help individuals to interpret the emotional displays they see in others.

(a) Reprinted by permission from Macmillan Publishers Ltd: NATURE Phillips, M.L., et al. "A specific neural substrate for perceiving facial expressions of disgust," 89, 495–498. Copyright 1997.
(b) and (c) Williams, L., Phillips, M. et al, Arousal dissociates amygdala & hippocampal fear reponse; Evidence from silutaneous fMRI and skin conductance recording, *NeuroImage* 14 (2001) 1070-1079. Copyright Elsevier 2001.

(a) Fearful face

Neutral face

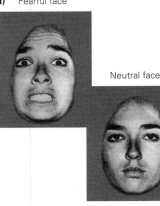

(b) Amygdala

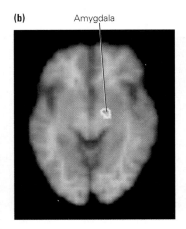

(c) Medial prefrontal cortex

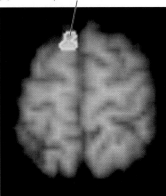

fMRI (L. Williams et al., 2001). By now, you should be completely unsurprised to hear that amygdala activation was greater while participants viewed the fearful faces than while they viewed the emotionally neutral faces (Figure 10.14b). The novel finding was that fearful faces also caused more activity than emotionally neutral faces in the medial prefrontal cortex (Figure 10.14c). These data are consistent with the idea that this area of the prefrontal cortex is active during emotional processing, helping to interpret the meaning of emotional stimuli, such as other people's facial displays of emotion.

Several researchers have further proposed that the medial prefrontal cortex allows us to process emotional stimuli in a manner appropriate to the context in which the stimuli occur (Hornak et al., 2003; Kolb & Taylor, 1990; Rolls, 1999). For example, your emotional reaction to seeing a bear should be very different depending on whether you encounter the bear as you walk through the woods or through the zoo. The prefrontal cortex may be the brain region that exerts this control on our emotional reactions, modulating the degree to which amygdala outputs produce emotional responses in different contexts. Remember the finding—described at the start of this chapter—that Japanese students tended to mask their emotional reactions in the presence of an authority figure? Most likely, the students were successfully using their frontal cortex to inhibit facial expressions. Similarly, if the big, dark shape you see approaching really is a bear and yet you are not really in danger because you are viewing the bear in the zoo, the amygdala will attempt to turn on the emotional response at the sight of the bear, but the medial prefrontal cortex will dampen this response. In effect, the medial prefrontal cortex tells the amygdala not to bother because the bear *in this particular context* is no threat. Consistent with this idea, experiments show that stimulating the medial prefrontal cortex in rats "turns off" or inhibits the normal emotional response provoked by amygdala stimulation (al Maskati & Zbrozyna, 1989; Quirk, Likhtik, Pelletier, & Paré, 2003).

Test Your Knowledge

Brain Substrates of Emotion

Emotional responses depend on a complex interplay between many brain areas, including the amygdala, hippocampus, and prefrontal cortex. Read the story below and identify some ways these brain areas could be contributing at each step identified by a number in parentheses. (Answers appear in the back of the book.)

Jared is afraid of heights. However, on a visit to Washington, DC, his friends say he should go to the top of the Washington Monument for the best view of the city. On the elevator up, Jared feels the beginnings of a nervous reaction (1): his heart beats faster, his mouth feels dry, and his stomach tightens. He remembers when he was similarly terrified standing on the high diving board at school (2).

When he arrives at the observation area, Jared's first impulse is to flatten himself against the wall and stay as far away from the edge as possible. But having come this far, he takes a few deep breaths, walks up to the window, and looks out over the city (3). In spite of everything, he is able to appreciate the beautiful view (4).

Interim Summary

- Emotion depends on many brain areas, and each brain area may contribute to more than one emotion.
- Part of the body's response to strong emotion comes from activation of the amygdala; outputs from the central nucleus of the amygdala drive

many of the behavioral and physiological components of emotional responses. Animals (including people) with amygdala damage show reduced emotionality and a reduced ability to learn conditioned emotional responses.

- The amygdala also modulates storage of emotional memories by means of outputs from the basolateral nucleus projecting to the cortex and the hippocampal region. Memories can be formed in the cortex and hippocampus without amygdala input, but if the emotional system is triggered, then memory formation will be stronger.

- If stress hormones (such as epinephrine, norepinephrine, or glucocorticoids) are blocked during learning, the strength of an emotional memory is reduced.

- The hippocampal region can, in turn, influence emotional learning by providing information about the context in which the learning occurs. Animals and people with hippocampal damage can still learn an emotional response to a stimulus, but they will fail to learn about the context in which they encountered the stimulus.

- The frontal lobes seem to play an important role in humans' ability to display emotions appropriately and to read emotional expressions in others and also in the ability to process emotional stimuli in a manner appropriate to the context in which they are experienced.

10.3 Clinical Perspectives

Much of the research covered in this chapter has focused on negative emotions—particularly fear—in part because negative emotions have a tremendous impact on our health and well-being. The stress associated with long-term unremitting fear and anger can lead to physiological problems such as high blood pressure and immune system suppression. Negative emotions can also cause psychological problems. Two of these in particular—phobias and posttraumatic stress disorder—may involve learning and memory processes in their development and in their successful treatment.

Phobias

A **phobia** is an excessive and irrational fear of an object, place, or situation that leads to anxiety and panic attacks. Currently, most phobias are classified into two categories, *specific phobias* and *agoraphobia*.

Specific phobias are fears of particular objects or social situations. Examples include fear of closed spaces (claustrophobia), fear of heights (acrophobia), fear of snakes (ophidiophobia), and fear of spiders (arachnophobia). In many (not all) cases, the phobia centers on an object or situation in which a fear reaction might be justified. For example, it is appropriate to be alarmed by the sight of a snake since snake venom can be deadly. Similarly, a healthy fear of heights may keep you from falling off cliffs. But when a fear has reached a point where it interferes with daily life, it is classified as a phobia. For example, if a person were so afraid of heights that she was unable to ride the elevator at work, or so afraid of snakes that

phobia. An excessive and irrational fear of an object, place, or situation.

Common specific phobias include fear of snakes, fear of spiders, fear of heights, and fear of closed spaces. What determines whether a person's fear is a normal, healthy response to danger or a phobia?

ChinaFotoPress via Getty Images

she avoided sitting outside in her own backyard, these fears would be classified as phobias.

Whereas specific phobias center on particular objects or situations, *agoraphobia* involves a generalized fear of leaving home or familiar "safe" areas, usually because of fear of having a panic attack in public. During a panic attack, epinephrine is released in large amounts, triggering the fight-or-flight response, with symptoms that include rapid heartbeat, trembling, nausea, and dizziness. Fear of experiencing a panic attack, and of the social embarrassment associated with having a panic attack in public, can lead individuals with agoraphobia to go to great lengths to avoid open, public places. In the most severe cases, individuals with agoraphobia become completely housebound, some unable to leave home for years on end.

What Causes Phobias?

One theory about the formation of phobias is that they arise through classical conditioning. Back in Chapter 1, you read about John Watson, the "father" of behaviorism. In one famous series of studies, Watson and his research assistant Rosalie Rayner studied fear conditioning in an 11-month-old boy known as Little Albert (possibly a pseudonym). Two months before the experiment began, they'd exposed Albert briefly to a white rat, a rabbit, a bearded Santa Claus mask, a burning newspaper, and various other items. Albert had showed no fear responses when presented with any of these objects although he did react with fear to a loud clanging noise. To study fear conditioning, Watson and Rayner placed a white rat near Albert, allowing him to reach out toward it. As he did, Watson and Rayner startled Albert with the loud clanging noise, and he began to cry. After several pairings of the rat and the noise, the researchers presented Albert with the rat (and no noise); Albert cried at the sight of the rat and tried to crawl away. The researchers concluded that Little Albert had been classically conditioned to associate the rat (a CS) with a fear-provoking loud noise (the US) (Watson & Rayner, 2000 [1920]). This learning appeared to generalize to other, similar objects: Albert now reacted with fear and avoidance to other objects, including white, furry objects such as the rabbit and the Santa Claus mask, but not to wooden blocks.

Shortly after, Little Albert and his mother moved away. There is no record of how severe Albert's fear of rats was, how long it persisted, or whether it generalized to rats encountered outside of Watson's lab (Beck, Levinson, & Irons, 2009; Harris, 1979). Today, of course, ethical guidelines would preclude experiments like the one conducted on Little Albert. (At a bare minimum, Watson and Rayner should have made an effort to extinguish Albert's conditioned fear before he left the study.) But the experiment did raise some interesting questions about classical conditioning and phobias. Maybe some naturally arising phobias also reflect classical conditioning; perhaps some people develop claustrophobia after a traumatic experience such as being locked in a closet and others develop a fear of dogs after being attacked by an out-of-control pet.

While Little Albert was playing with a pet rat, John Watson and Rosalie Rayner paired the rat with a loud, frightening noise. Albert developed a conditioned fear response to the rat. Watson and Rayner (visible in the photo) claimed that they had induced a phobia in Albert and that such classical conditioning could underlie the formation of real-world phobias. Assuming that Albert had indeed developed a phobia based on classical conditioning, how might Watson and Raynor have attempted to "cure" Little Albert before sending him home?

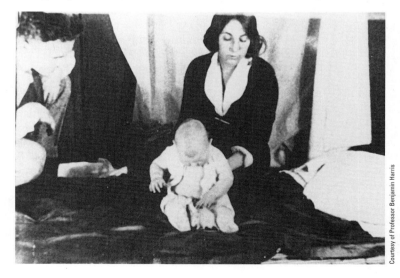

Courtesy of Professor Benjamin Harris

On the other hand, not everyone who has a fear-evoking experience develops a phobia. One study reported that two-thirds of people with a dog-related phobia can recall a dog-related trauma (such as being bitten), but so can the same percentage of people with no fear of dogs (DiNardo, Guzy, & Bak, 1988). Conversely, some people have a terror of snakes despite never having come into contact with a living snake, and others are morbidly afraid of flying without ever having been in an airplane.

One possible explanation is that some phobias may be conditioned through social transmission. For example, a person can develop a fear of flying after seeing televised reports of an airplane crash or a fear of snakes after seeing other people panic at the sight of snakes. Monkeys show socially transmitted fear too. A monkey raised in the lab will not react with fear the first time it sees a snake. But if the lab-reared monkey is caged next to another monkey and if that neighboring monkey reacts with fear at the sight of a snake, the lab-reared monkey will begin to show the same fear response (Mineka & Cook, 1988). Possibly, the sight of a frightened neighbor is itself a fear-evoking US, and the object that evokes that fear becomes a CS in the observer monkey.

Treating Phobias

If some phobias arise through conditioning, can they be extinguished in the same way as ordinary conditioned responses—by repeated exposure to the CS with no US? In many cases they can. In **systematic desensitization** therapy for phobias, successive approximations of the CS are presented while the patient learns to remain relaxed; eventually, even the CS itself does not elicit a fear response (Kazdin & Wilcoxon, 1976; Linden, 1981). For example, a person who is afraid of snakes may first be presented with some snake-shaped item (like a hose or rope) different enough from a real snake that no fear reaction is evoked. In successive sessions, the patient is progressively exposed to, say, a toy rubber snake, then a photograph of a real snake, then a person holding a live snake; the steps are taken so gradually that they don't evoke a fear reaction. Eventually, the patient may be asked to touch a live snake, then to hold it himself. As you might imagine, systematic desensitization therapy can be a slow and painstaking process, but it is often successful and long lasting.

Sometimes it is dangerous, inconvenient, or very expensive to expose the patient (and the therapist!) to the object of the phobia. For example, if the patient is afraid of flying over the ocean, systematic desensitization would require her to practice approaching an airport, then practice sitting on a grounded plane, then start taking short overland trips, and finally work up to longer transatlantic flights. This would be prohibitively expensive for most people. Instead, the therapist may recommend virtual-reality therapy using computer-generated virtual environments. The patient can "experience" sitting in an airplane seat, gradually getting used to the sights and sounds of an aircraft and even taking simulated flights before spending the energy and money to board a real plane. Virtual-reality therapy, particularly in combination with other relaxation training and cognitive therapy, can be very effective in treating phobias (Emmelkamp et al., 2002; Muhlberger, Herrmann, Wiedeman, Ellgring, & Pauli, 2001).

As you might expect, some studies have reported hyperactive amygdala in individuals with a phobia; there have also been reports of abnormalities in the anterior cingulate cortex and insula—which, as you read in Chapter 5, are important for helping us determine what is aversive and what we are motivated to avoid. It's not too surprising that these same brain areas might be overactive in individuals with a phobia. Interestingly, several studies have now reported that, when patients undergo therapy to treat their phobias, these same fear-related brain structures show reduced activity (Galvao-de Almeida et al.,

systematic desensitization. Therapy for *phobias* in which successive approximations of the fear-evoking stimulus are presented while the patient learns to remain relaxed; eventually, even presentation of the stimulus itself does not elicit a fear reaction.

2013; Lipka, Hoffmann, Miltner & Straube, 2014). These findings suggest that successful treatment of phobias helps patients' brains recalibrate, so that the previously feared object or situation is no longer interpreted as quite so threatening.

Test Your Knowledge

Classical Conditioning and Phobias

At least some phobias appear to arise through classical conditioning, when a previously neutral stimulus is paired with a strongly aversive or fear-evoking event. Read the scenario below, and see if you can identify the CS, US, and CR. (Answers appear in the back of the book.)

> Nancy has recently lost her job and is worried that she will not be able to provide for her children. This worry is exacerbated when she goes to the grocery store and sees the high prices. While at the store, Nancy has a panic attack, a sudden and overwhelming feeling of intense fear. She feels like the room is spinning; her heart pounds and she can't seem to get enough air. After a few minutes, the episode passes, but she is deeply shaken by the experience. In the days that follow, she is terrified of having another panic attack, especially in public. She finds herself dreading the thought of returning to the grocery store, and reassigns the household chores so that her teenaged children take care of the grocery shopping.

Posttraumatic Stress Disorder

Following the terrorist attacks on the World Trade Center on September 11, 2001, thousands of counselors traveled to New York City to offer their services to survivors, families, and rescue workers. In addition to these volunteers, $23 million in federal funds was allocated to Project Liberty, a program that provided free counseling to New Yorkers.

The rationale for this convergence of mental health professionals and funding was the expectation that in the wake of the attacks, many New Yorkers would develop **posttraumatic stress disorder (PTSD)**. PTSD is a psychological disorder that can develop after a traumatic event (such as combat, rape, or natural disaster); the symptoms include re-experiencing the event (through intrusive recollections, flashbacks, or nightmares), avoidance of reminders of the trauma, emotional numbing, and heightened anxiety (McNally, Bryant, & Ehlers, 2003). Such fear reactions are a perfectly normal human response to distressing events, but for most people exposed to trauma, the fear reactions subside with time (Figure 10.15). For individuals with PTSD, the fear reactions may persist for months or years. One report combined data collected from almost 5 million veterans of the war in Iraq and Afghanistan, and estimated that about 23% of these veterans had PTSD (Fulton et al., 2015); another report estimated that, of 3271 workers who evacuated the World Trade Center towers during the 9/11 attacks, about 15% had PTSD 2 to 3 years later (Perlman et al., 2011).

Causes and Treatment of PTSD

Why might PTSD occur? One prominent theory assigns a role to classical conditioning. By definition, PTSD involves an experience that causes a strong fear response, including feelings of helplessness or terror. This event may function as a US, and it may be such a strong and effective US that any other co-occurring stimuli become strongly associated with that US. Thus, sights, sounds, and smells may all become conditioned stimuli. When any such CS is experienced again, it may evoke the memory of the US—and a conditioned fear response. This is one way in which PTSD is hypothesized to differ from specific phobias:

posttraumatic stress disorder (PTSD). A psychological syndrome that can develop after exposure to a horrific event (such as combat, rape, or natural disaster); symptoms include re-experiencing the event (through intrusive recollections, flashbacks, or nightmares), avoidance of reminders of the trauma, emotional numbing, and heightened anxiety.

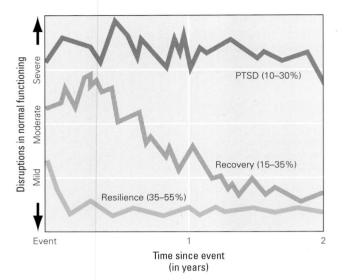

Figure 10.15 Patterns of psychological recovery after a traumatic event Immediately after experiencing a traumatic event, such as rape, combat exposure, or a terrorist attack, most people show a disruption in normal functioning due to fear reactions; these may include heightened anxiety, nightmares, flashbacks, and avoidance of reminders of the trauma. As time passes, most people either bounce back quickly (a pattern described as "resilience") or show initial fear reactions that dissipate with time ("recovery"). But some individuals develop posttraumatic stress disorder ("PTSD"), with symptoms that persist for months or years after the event.

Hypothetical data; information from Bonanno, 2005.

in specific phobias, a fear reaction is triggered by a particular stimulus (such as a snake or a spider); in PTSD, fear reactions can be triggered by a wide variety of stimuli reminiscent of the original trauma. These fear reactions are not necessarily abnormal, but for most people, re-experiencing these CSs without recurrence of the traumatic US should gradually lead to extinction of the fear response in the weeks and months after the trauma. Individuals with PTSD may simply fail to extinguish the normal fear response to stimuli associated with the traumatic event (Rothbaum & Davis, 2003). In fact, in the laboratory, individuals with PTSD do typically show faster learning but impaired extinction of conditioned emotional responses (Orr et al., 2000; Peri, Ben-Shakhar, Orr & Shalev, 2000).

Why can't those with PTSD simply forget their unwanted memories? Back in Chapter 7, you read about the phenomenon of *directed forgetting*: people who are explicitly instructed to forget information do, indeed, show worse recall of that information later. Functional imaging (fMRI) has shown that the prefrontal cortex plays a key role in controlling directed forgetting, by suppressing the hippocampus, which in turn impairs retention of the information. Perhaps PTSD reflects reduced ability to use prefrontal cortex to inhibit hippocampal function and control the recall of unwanted memories (Anderson & Levy, 2009). And, in fact, in the lab, individuals with PTSD who are given a directed forgetting task involving emotional pictures are indeed less successful at intentionally forgetting the images than control participants with no PTSD (Catarino et al., 2015). This could be why those with PTSD experience intrusive memories, nightmares, and flashbacks—a wide variety of stimuli start to trigger recall, and the patients cannot use prefrontal cortex to stop the traumatic memories in their tracks.

Consistent with the theory that PTSD involves a failure of extinction, some of the most widely used treatments for PTSD include exposing the patient to cues that trigger his anxiety but doing so in the absence of danger. The purpose is to encourage extinction of the abnormally strong fear response (Rothbaum & Davis, 2003). Such *extinction therapy* for PTSD may require the patient to repeatedly imagine and describe the feared situations under the guidance of a therapist. Virtual-reality techniques also prove useful—for example, allowing veterans to navigate through a simulated version of the region where they had their most stressful combat-related experiences, undergoing repeated exposure to the fear-evoking stimuli within the safe context of a therapist's office. Under these conditions, many individuals experience gradual reduction of PTSD symptoms.

Vulnerability to PTSD

As illustrated in Figure 10.15, PTSD is the exception, not the rule, in individuals exposed to traumatic events. Apparently, there are some preexisting vulnerability factors that help determine an individual's risk to develop PTSD, which is why one person will develop the disorder but another will prove resilient when exposed to the same traumatic event. Understanding these vulnerability factors is of critical importance because there is some evidence that widespread intervention to prevent PTSD among individuals exposed to traumatic events can actually increase rates of the disorder—presumably by inducing symptoms in individuals who would most likely have been resilient if simply left alone to deal with the trauma in their own way (Bonanno, 2004).

A better approach might be to give the preventive therapy only to those individuals who are most likely to develop PTSD. But how can we identify such individuals in advance? Structural MRI suggests some answers. Individuals with PTSD typically have hippocampal volumes that are somewhat smaller than those of individuals who experienced similar trauma but did not develop PTSD (Smith, 2005). For example, a study by Mark Gilbertson and colleagues examined the brains of a group of combat veterans who had fought in the Vietnam War (Gilbertson et al., 2002). Even though the war officially ended in the 1970s, many veterans of that war still have trouble with combat-related PTSD symptoms. Using MRI, Gilbertson and colleagues showed that those veterans with PTSD typically had a smaller hippocampal volume than veterans who had not developed PTSD (Figure 10.16a, b). One interpretation of these findings would be that PTSD might cause the hippocampus to shrink, since we know that long-term exposure to chronic stress can damage the hippocampus (McEwen, 1997; Sapolsky, 1996). But another possibility was that the veterans who developed PTSD had a smaller hippocampus to start with—and that made them more vulnerable to PTSD.

Gilbertson and colleagues found a clever way to determine the answer: each of the veterans included in the study had an identical twin brother who had not fought in Vietnam and who had never developed PTSD. If the veterans who did develop PTSD (Figure 10.16a) experienced a reduction in hippocampal volume as a result of their trauma, then their unexposed brothers should have a normal hippocampal volume. But if these veterans had a smaller hippocampal volume to start with, then their twins should also have smaller-than-average hippocampal volumes. In fact, the twins of the veterans with PTSD did have smaller-than-average hippocampal volumes too (Figure 10.16c). This suggests that PTSD doesn't *cause* hippocampal shrinkage; instead, it seems that some individuals have a smaller-than-average hippocampal volume, and this may *predispose* them to develop PTSD later (Gilbertson et al., 2002). For example, connections from the hippocampus to the prefrontal cortex are important in extinguishing learned associations; individuals with a slightly smaller hippocampus might be less able to extinguish fear responses than their peers. If an individual leads a relatively quiet life (like the brothers who weren't sent to Vietnam), this may not be a problem, but if that same individual is exposed to trauma (like the brothers who did serve in the war), there could be heightened risk for PTSD.

Another key brain area, unsurprisingly, appears to be the amygdala. It has been known for years that individuals with PTSD often show increased amygdala responses to negative emotional stimuli, but—as with the hippocampus—it was harder to tell whether the abnormality was a preexisting condition or only developed as a symptom of PTSD. In 2011–2012, researchers in the Boston area were

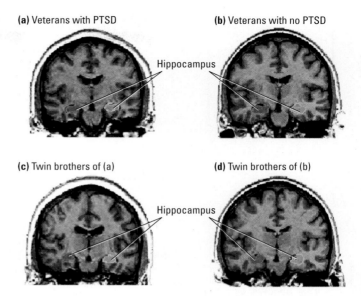

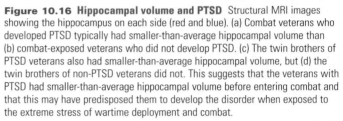

Figure 10.16 Hippocampal volume and PTSD Structural MRI images showing the hippocampus on each side (red and blue). (a) Combat veterans who developed PTSD typically had smaller-than-average hippocampal volume than (b) combat-exposed veterans who did not develop PTSD. (c) The twin brothers of PTSD veterans also had smaller-than-average hippocampal volume, but (d) the twin brothers of non-PTSD veterans did not. This suggests that the veterans with PTSD had smaller-than-average hippocampal volume before entering combat and that this may have predisposed them to develop the disorder when exposed to the extreme stress of wartime deployment and combat.

Studies suggest that about 30% of combat veterans in Iraq will develop PTSD, which means that one or two of the soldiers in this picture are statistically likely to develop the disorder. What factors help determine which individuals are, and are not, vulnerable to PTSD?

performing a study using fMRI to study amygdala reactions in adolescents. Then, on April 15, 2013, two bombs went off near the finish line of the Boston Marathon. Three people were killed, over 200 were injured, and thousands of Boston-area residents were told to "shelter in place" for several days during the subsequent manhunt for one of the bombers. A month later, the researchers sent online surveys to the teenagers who had previously participated in the fMRI study, asking them about PTSD symptoms related to the attack. It turned out that those specific teenagers who had shown heightened amygdala reactions to negative emotional stimuli during the test were at higher risk of developing PTSD in the wake of the bombing (McLaughlin, Sheridan, Duys, Busso, Alves, & Green, 2015). Thus, again, it appears that amygdala abnormality may precede, and confer risk for, PTSD in individuals later exposed to trauma.

In addition to decreased hippocampal volume and heightened amygdala activity, other factors that make individuals vulnerable to PTSD may include genetic factors (Norrholm & Ressler, 2009); increased startle responses to sudden, loud noises (Orr et al., 2003; Pitman et al., 2006); and personality traits such as neuroticism, harm avoidance, and a tendency to withdraw from or avoid novel situations (Aidman & Kollaras-Mitsinikos, 2006; Gil & Caspi, 2006; Hatcher, Whitaker, & Karl, 2009). On the other hand, individuals with strong social support from family and friends are somewhat *less* likely to develop PTSD after a traumatic event (Pietrzak, Johnson, Goldstein, Malley, & Southwick, 2009; Polusny et al., 2010). Understanding the factors that make an individual vulnerable to, or resilient against, PTSD could be very useful in screening people for wartime service as well as for jobs such as firefighting, disaster recovery, and foreign aid work, where traumatic situations are especially likely to occur. Not all trauma is avoidable, of course; in fact, most people experience at least one traumatic event during the course of a lifetime. But if we knew in advance which individuals are most vulnerable to PTSD, there would be the opportunity to provide those individuals with aggressive care and counseling if and when exposure to trauma occurs.

Interim Summary

- Certain psychological problems may be fear responses gone awry.
- Phobias are excessive fears that interfere with daily life. Specific phobias are phobias that are related to objects or situations such as snakes, spiders, heights, or enclosed spaces. In agoraphobia, patients have a generalized fear of leaving home or a "safe" environment for fear of having a panic attack in public.
- On the basis that some phobias may arise through classical conditioning, the therapy of systematic desensitization uses the concept of extinction to reduce the ability of the phobic stimulus to elicit a fear response. Other phobias may arise through social transmission.
- In posttraumatic stress disorder (PTSD), a natural fear reaction does not subside with time, possibly reflecting a failure of extinction.
- Some research suggests that certain individuals have preexisting characteristics, such as reduced hippocampal volume or heightened amygdala response to emotional stimuli, that could increase the risk for PTSD following exposure to a traumatic event.

Synthesis

If you've ever tried to list the similarities between yourself and a rat, chances are that emotions did not top the list. But humans, chimpanzees, elephants, dogs, rats, and even the lowly *Aplysia* all show emotional responses in the form of overt behaviors and physiological changes. Confronted with the prospect of an electric shock, a rat may freeze and defecate, a sea snail may retract its siphon, and a dog may whine and put its tail between its legs. Each animal is demonstrating a learned fear response, and these responses can be induced and measured by experimenters. The same goes for physiological variables, such as heart rate, respiration, and other components of the fight-or-flight response. Additionally, emotional learning depends on similar brain substrates in many species, especially mammals, including the amygdala, the hippocampus, and the frontal cortex. This commonality allows the use of insights gained in rats, and even *Aplysia*, to help elucidate the neural bases of human emotional responses.

As you saw in this chapter, the vast majority of research on emotions and learning has focused on a single emotion, fear. One reason is that the critical brain substrates for fear are at least partially understood, whereas the brain substrates for happiness and other positive emotions are only now being discovered. And while we can reasonably assume that anticipating shock leads to fear in animals because we can observe and measure fear responses, it has been less clear whether animals feel "happiness" and, if so, how we could induce and measure this emotion. But newer research is focusing on animal models of emotions such as joy and disgust and may lead to new breakthroughs in understanding the human versions of these emotions too.

Another reason for the historical emphasis on fear is its association with clinical syndromes such as phobias, PTSD, and depression. This link to real-world medicine drives many researchers to study fear in the hope that their findings will have clinical relevance. And indeed, existing clinical treatments such as systematic desensitization and virtual-reality therapy were developed based on our understanding of how emotional memories are acquired and maintained.

Given what we know about the brain substrates of emotion and how stress hormones such as epinephrine help strengthen emotional memories, some researchers have even wondered whether it's possible to reduce the risk of an individual developing PTSD by administering drugs such as propranolol that interfere with epinephrine. The idea is that injections given after the trauma would not cause patients to forget the traumatic episode but would reduce the damaging emotional reactions to the memory. To date, existing studies don't show a reliable benefit of propranolol injections in reducing rates of PTSD (Argolo, Cavalcanti-Ribeiro, Netto & Quarantini, 2015). But even if the treatment worked reliably, this would open serious ethical questions: should such prophylactic treatment be routinely administered to individuals who experience a trauma, given that the majority of such individuals will never develop PTSD if simply left alone?

More generally, if emotion-modifying drugs were available, would people routinely want to lose the emotional content of their "negative" episodic memories? Would the result be happier lives for all or a kind of gray existence in which nothing really matters because nothing causes lasting emotional scars? And without lasting emotional scars, would humans lose some of the ability to learn from mistakes—the very reason emotions may have evolved in the first place?

KNOW YOUR KEY TERMS

amygdala, *p. 416*
arousal, *p. 397*
autonomic nervous system,
  (ANS) *p. 398*
Cannon–Bard theory of
  emotion, *p. 400*
conditioned avoidance, *p. 406*
conditioned escape, *p. 406*
cortisol, *p. 398*
depression, *p. 408*

emotion, *p. 396*
epinephrine, *p. 398*
fear response, *p. 396*
fight-or-flight response, *p. 397*
flashbulb memory, *p. 411*
glucocorticoid, *p. 398*
James–Lange theory of
  emotion, *p. 398*
learned helplessness, *p. 408*
mood congruency of memory, *p. 411*

optogenetics, *p. 420*
phobia, *p. 428*
piloerection, *p. 402*
posttraumatic stress disorder
  (PTSD), *p. 431*
somatic theories of emotion, *p. 399*
stress, *p. 398*
stress hormone, *p. 398*
systematic desensitization, *p. 430*
two-factor theory of emotion, *p. 400*

QUIZ YOURSELF

1. Emotion involves three distinct but interrelated phenomena—_____, _____, and _____—that are produced in response to an affecting situation. (p. 396)

2. The _____ theory of emotion states that conscious emotions stimulate appropriate behaviors and physiological responses. The _____ theory of emotion states that conscious feelings of emotions occur when the mind senses the physiological responses associated with arousal. The _____ theory of emotion states that a combination of cognitive appraisal and perception of biological changes together determine our experience of emotion. (p. 398–400)

3. The _____ is a collection of nerves and structures that control internal organs and glands and help mediate the physiological components of emotion. (p. 398)

4. A _____ is an excessive and irrational fear of an object, place, or situation. One type of therapy includes _____, in which successive approximations of the fear-evoking stimulus are presented while the patient learns to remain relaxed. (p. 428–430)

5. The _____ response (which is also known as _____) is a collection of bodily responses, including increased blood flow to the muscles, increased respiration, and depressed digestion and immune functions, that prepare the body to face a threat, either by facing it down or by running away. (p. 397)

6. The principle that it is easier to retrieve memories that match our current mood or emotional state is known as _____. (p. 411)

7. The _____ is a collection of brain nuclei lying at the anterior tip of each hippocampus and which are critical for learning and expressing emotional responses as well as for mediating the emotional modulation of memory formation. (p. 416)

8. Whereas _____ is an experimental design in which animals learn to make particular responses in order to terminate an aversive stimulus, _____ is a design in which animals learn to make particular responses in order to prevent exposure to that aversive stimulus. (p. 406)

9. When we experience emotions such as fear or anger, the ANS releases _____ that help to mediate the fight-or-flight response. Two examples are _____ and _____. (p. 398)

10. _____ is a psychiatric condition that involves feelings of sadness as well as a general loss of initiative and activity. (p. 408)

11. A memory formed under conditions of extreme emotion and that seems especially vivid and long-lasting is called a _____. (p. 411)

12. _____ theories of emotion are theories based on the central premise that physiological responses to stimuli come first, and these determine or induce emotions. (p. 399)

13. The _____ is a cluster of physiological, motor, and conscious reactions that accompany the emotion of fear. An example of a physiological reaction is _____, where mammals' hair stands on end, making the animal look bigger and more threatening than it is. (p. 402)

14. Any stimulus or event that causes bodily arousal is a form of _____. (p. 398)

15. _____ is a psychological disorder that can develop after exposure to a horrific event, with symptoms including _____, _____, _____, and _____. (p. 431)

16. _____ is a phenomenon in which exposure to an uncontrollable punisher teaches an organism that responses are ineffectual, which in turn reduces the motivation to attempt new avoidance responses. (p. 408)

Answers appear in the back of the book.

CONCEPT CHECK

1. In earlier chapters, you read about habituation (decreased responding to a repeatedly presented stimulus). Do you think habituation is an example of emotional learning? Why or why not?

2. After losing a game by a lopsided score, professional football teams are statistically more likely to perform worse than usual in their next game, and this tendency is particularly pronounced if the upcoming opponent is considered hard to beat (Reisel & Kopelman, 1995). How might this phenomenon be explained in terms of the principles of emotional learning?

3. Decorticate animals (animals with their cortex surgically removed) often show "sham rage," overreacting to seemingly trivial stimuli as though they were being seriously threatened. Why might this happen?

4. Suppose you have a roommate who is terrified of spiders, to the point of being unable to take a shower if there is a spider in the bathtub unless you're there to kill the spider or remove it. Based on what you read in this chapter, speculate about why your roommate has this fear.

5. Continuing the example in question 4, what might you suggest to help your roommate overcome this fear?

Answers appear in the back of the book.

CHAPTER 11

Social Learning and Memory

Observing, Interacting, and Reenacting

D OLPHINS ARE THE ONLY KNOWN animals other than humans that can imitate both actions and sounds on request. Specifically, scientists have trained dolphins to imitate human actors and computer-generated sounds when instructed to do so. Chimpanzees and orangutans can imitate other animals' actions when humans ask them, but they seem to be unable to imitate sounds. Parrots can imitate sounds, but they typically must have lots of experience hearing the sound first; unlike humans and dolphins, they have not shown the flexibility to imitate a novel sound the first time they hear it. Most other animals show no ability to imitate actions or sounds when instructed to do so by humans. This could be because they don't know how to imitate, or don't have the right vocal control mechanisms, or have not been properly trained to imitate, or possibly because, unlike dolphins and apes, they don't understand human instructions.

Yes, you read that last paragraph correctly. Scientists can communicate with dolphins and apes, and these newly discovered communication channels have revealed unsuspected learning and memory abilities in those animals. One dolphin named Akeakamai (pronounced "uh-KAY-uh–ka-MY," Hawaiian for "lover of wisdom") learned to interpret hand signals asking her to imitate the actions of dolphins and humans. She learned this through one-on-one interactions with her human instructors. She would watch intently as a hairless ape stood in front of her, gesticulating rapidly with its oddly shaped "flippers." Over time, she learned that one of those gestures meant she was supposed to imitate a recently demonstrated action, such as a human spinning around or a dolphin shooting a basketball through a hoop. When Akeakamai interpreted this gesture correctly, the instructor rewarded her with shouts of approval. Occasionally, the instructor's vocal accolades proved

Behavioral Processes
Copying What Is Seen
Copying What Is Heard
  Learning and Memory in Everyday Life: Karaoke
Social Transmission of Information
  Learning and Memory in Everyday Life: Learning What to Like from Super Bowl Ads

Brain Substrates
Mirror Neurons
Song Learning in Bird Brains
Hippocampal Encoding of Socially Transmitted Food Preferences

Clinical Perspectives
Autism Spectrum Disorder
Imitative Deficits after Stroke

Synthesis

Barcroft Media via Getty Images

439

infectious, and Akeakamai joined in the celebration with her own loud vocalizations. Akeakamai observed the actions of those around her and reacted based on her past training, her recent experiences, and her emotional state.

Observations and interactions can contribute to learning and memory in many ways. You can watch television to learn about exotic vacation destinations, listen to the radio to learn about an approaching storm, or read a textbook to learn about how your brain enables you to learn and remember. People generally assume that humans learn much of what they know by *interacting* socially with others, *observing* how things work in society, and then *reenacting* what they have observed. Elementary school teachers, for example, often demonstrate how tasks should be performed (say, how to multiply two numbers) and then encourage students to repeat the demonstrated steps in class. Many believe that the abilities this requires make human learning and memory different from that of all other animals. However, this view is based more on presupposition than on experimental evidence. Here we explore what psychologists have discovered about how humans and other animals learn through social observations and interactions.

11.1 Behavioral Processes

social learning. Learning from others; often used as a synonym for observational learning.

observational learning. A process in which the learner actively monitors events and then chooses later actions based on those observations.

Psychologists use the term **social learning** to identify situations in which the learner actively monitors events involving other individuals and then chooses later actions based on those observations. Often called **observational learning**, it is one of the many means by which an individual may learn, and is much broader than just learning how to behave in social situations. (In other words, social learning is not to be confused with learning to socialize.) You are currently observing (reading) the words in a textbook describing learning and memory and may use your observations to guide your later actions when you are studying for and taking tests on the subject. If your test includes short-answer questions, you might even answer those questions with sentences very similar to the ones you are reading in these chapters. In fact, the more precisely you replicate what you have read (or heard during lectures) when answering such questions, the more likely it is that your professor will judge your answers to be correct. Successful performance on tests depends heavily on social learning.

Social learning differs from classical and operant conditioning in that researchers cannot reliably predict what an organism will learn from observing the actions of others. One reason it is difficult to predict how observations will affect future behavior is that there is no way for one observer (the researcher) to detect what another observer (the research subject) actually perceives while observing. An organism can observe a wide variety of events without showing any obvious changes in behavior or giving any other indication of what they have observed. If you watch your fellow students during a lecture, do you think you would be able to tell if one of them is daydreaming about being on the beach?

Psychologists are frequently faced with this ambiguity. Edward Thorndike, for example, concluded that cats could not imitate other cats that had learned to escape from a puzzle box (Thorndike, 1898). However, there is no way to know what Thorndike's observer cats were focusing on in those experiments. Perhaps the food outside the box or the identity of the cat trapped in the box was more interesting to the feline observer than the specific actions the cat inside the box was performing.

Another reason it is difficult to predict how observations will affect future behavior is that nothing compels an observer to copy any given model. Furthermore, even if the observer does copy a particular model, there is more than one way to copy, as we now discuss.

Copying What Is Seen

Social learning differs from most other forms of learning discussed in this book in that not all species can learn by reproducing what they observe. In fact, many psychologists believe that only humans learn extensively by copying. **Copying** consists of replicating what one observes another doing. Children *can* learn a great deal by copying the actions of adults and other children. However, there is very little experimental data showing what children *do* learn through imitation in everyday life.

Much of what we know about the role of imitation in learning stems from influential experimental studies conducted in the early 1960s by Albert Bandura. Bandura (b.1925) grew up in Canada before heading to the University of Iowa for graduate school. Soon after starting his academic career at Stanford University, he became interested in how parents' aggressive behavior might affect the actions of their children. Bandura and his colleagues wanted to see whether preschool children would become more aggressive after observing aggressive adults (Bandura, Ross, & Ross, 1961). They had one group of children observe adults beating up a "Bobo doll" (an inflatable clown doll), while other groups of children (control groups) simply played in an empty room or observed adults playing quietly with toys. Afterward, Bandura used a one-way mirror to spy on the children as they played in a room containing the Bobo doll (Figure 11.1). Children who had observed an adult pummeling the Bobo doll were more likely than children in the control groups to pound on the doll themselves, and, most important, their attack styles were often similar to those used by the adults. Bandura and colleagues concluded that the children had learned new aggressive actions by observing the actions of an adult.

Studies like Bandura's Bobo doll experiment seem to suggest that children will copy aggressive acts they have observed. However, the children were tested in a context similar to the one in which they observed the aggression occurring, soon after they viewed the aggressive acts. It is unclear whether they would have behaved similarly if they had encountered a Bobo doll at their neighbor's house. Additionally, the children in Bandura's experiment who showed significant imitation of aggressive acts had first been provoked by being deprived of an attractive toy immediately before the test (Bandura, Ross, & Ross, 1961).

copying. The act of doing what one observes another organism doing.

Figure 11.1 Scenes from a Bobo doll experiment After viewing an adult acting aggressively toward a Bobo doll, some children imitated what they had seen (Bandura, Ross, & Ross, 1961). The pictures have been paired to emphasize similar actions.

Courtesy Albert Bandura, Stanford University

Specifically, the experimenter told the provoked children that some attractive toys in the room were there for them to play with, but as soon as a child began playing with a toy, she told the child that these were her very best toys and that she had decided to reserve them for some other children. Children who had viewed an aggressive model but who had not been provoked were actually less likely to behave aggressively during the test than children who did not observe any aggressive acts. This finding suggests that viewing aggressive acts can in some cases inhibit aggressive behavior rather than increase it.

One of the main findings from the Bobo doll experiments was that viewing an adult acting aggressively toward an inflatable toy strongly influenced the later behavior of children presented with that same toy, despite the fact that the children were neither reinforced nor punished for their behavior. The absence of direct reinforcement or punishment would appear to exclude the possibility that the children were learning through operant conditioning, which requires that the learners' actions be either reinforced or punished. Bandura proposed that children observed the actions of the adult, formed ideas about what actions could be performed using the doll, and later used memories of those ideas to reproduce the adult's actions (Bandura, 1969). Note that by this account, the formation of memories that changed behavior occurred while the children were observing the adult, *not* when they were imitating the behavior. In other words, what is encoded is information about a specific episode, and the act of imitating is simply a way of recalling the episodic memory. The children's imitative acts simply revealed what they had learned from watching someone demonstrate an action; Bandura called these demonstrations **modeling**. Modeling is a prerequisite for all kinds of copying.

modeling. Demonstration of actions.

Social Learning Theory

To account for cases of social learning such as the imitative walloping revealed in Bandura's Bobo doll experiment, psychologists developed a broad theory of human behavioral development called **social learning theory**. A key feature of social learning theory was (and for some adherents, still is) the idea that the kinds of reinforcements an individual has observed or experienced in the past will determine how that individual will act in any given situation. Early social learning theorists proposed that reinforcement determines personality traits (Rotter, 1954) and that social learning is a special case of operant conditioning in which actions that replicate observed acts are either directly or indirectly reinforced (Miller & Dollard, 1941).

social learning theory. A theory of human behavior prominent from the 1940s through the 1960s that proposed that the kinds of reinforcements an individual has experienced in past social contexts will determine how that individual will act in any given situation.

According to Bandura (1969), observers can gain information about whether a particular action will be rewarded or punished by witnessing the outcomes of a model's actions. A person who imitates actions that have been seen to lead to positive outcomes may in turn experience positive outcomes. If so, the person has a greater likelihood of again copying such actions in the future (consistent with Thorndike's law of effect).

Modern social learning theory places less emphasis on conditioning and instead explains behavior in terms of more cognitive processes, such as thinking, evaluating possible future outcomes, and learning about how people interact. A basic premise of contemporary social learning theory is that any behavior can be learned without direct reinforcement or punishment (Bandura, 1986; Ladd & Mize, 1983). Expectations of reinforcers and punishments will influence the likelihood that a learned action will be performed, but the learning itself (the knowledge gained about an action and its outcome) is taken to be the result of observation rather than the result of conditioning. In other words, a relationship between an action and an outcome only needs to be observed, not performed, in order to be learned. Within this framework, an imitated action is simply a performance that reveals what has been learned.

Bandura cited four basic processes to explain people copying what they see. First, the *presence of a model* is thought to increase an observer's attention to the situation. The actions of others can be especially salient cues that act as a magnet for attention (Bandura, 1986). Second, memories for the observed situation must be stored in an *accessible format* so that they can guide later actions. If the observer forgets how an action was performed, it will be difficult for that person to imitate the action. Third, the observer must have the *ability to reproduce the action*. You might remember quite well what it looks like when someone dunks a basketball, but unless you can jump quite high, you won't be able to imitate this action. Finally, the observer must have some *motivation for reproducing* the observed actions. You probably wouldn't burn your money just because you saw someone else doing it, even though it would be easy to do.

In some cases, the status or identity of the model can provide the motivation for an observer to imitate an action. For example, individuals are more likely to imitate the actions of someone they admire. Similarity between a model and the observer also increases the likelihood of copying, especially if the outcome is desirable. In other cases, the desirability of the observed outcome in itself is enough to provide motivation for an imitative act. For example, you might be more likely to burn your money if you observe that other people who burn their money are invited to parties with celebrities.

Copying can involve either the replication of actions that have been observed or the performance of novel actions that lead to the observed outcome of a modeler's actions (Morgan, 1896). For example, when Leti was still in elementary school, she happened to see her parents picking berries and putting them in a bucket. She then copied her parents' berry-picking technique but put the berries in her pockets rather than in a bucket. The movements Leti made while picking berries replicated those of her parents. Copying in which motor acts are replicated is called **true imitation**. The movements Leti performed to store the berries that had been picked, however, differed from those of her parents. But Leti and her parents' actions led to a similar outcome—berries were collected in a container. Copying that replicates an outcome without replicating specific motor acts is called **emulation**. We'll discuss both kinds of copying and provide more examples of each in the following sections. We'll also describe several other social learning mechanisms that look like true imitation but that do not involve copying.

Studies of True Imitation: Copying Actions

Scientists use the term "true imitation" because they often disagree about what behaviors really count as imitation, as well as about which organisms possess the ability to imitate (Thorndike, 1898; Thorpe, 1963; Whiten, Horner, Litchfield, & Marshall-Pescini, 2004). One technique that has been developed to investigate imitation abilities is called the **two-action test**. In preparation for this test, two individuals are each trained to perform a different action, but the two actions have the same outcome. For instance, one individual might be trained to dislodge an object that is stuck by hitting at it with a stick, and the other might be trained to pry the object free with a stick. Next, one group of naive observers is allowed to watch a demonstration of one of the techniques, and a second equally naive group is allowed to observe the other technique. If the naive observers later perform the operation in a way that matches the technique they observed, then their behavior is accepted as evidence of true imitation.

JGI/Jamie Grill/Getty Images

Is this an instance of true imitation?

true imitation. Copying that involves reproducing motor acts.

emulation. Copying that involves replicating an outcome without replicating specific motor acts.

two-action test. A technique developed to investigate imitation abilities that involves exposing naive animals to demonstrators trained to achieve the same goal using different actions.

Figure 11.2 Two-action test of true imitation in children and chimpanzees (a) Children and chimpanzees observed an adult human use one of two techniques (poke or twist) to open a plastic box containing a reward. (b) Later, both children and chimpanzees were more likely to use the box-opening technique they had observed than the one they did not observe. This means that both chimps and children can truly imitate.
Research from Whiten et al., 1996.

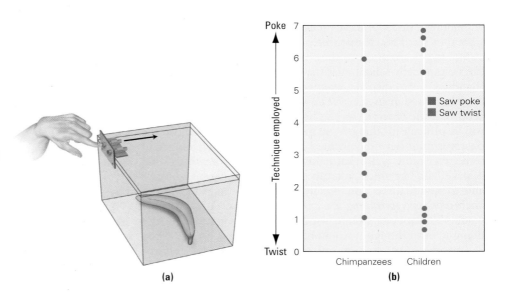

The two-action test has enabled researchers to compare imitative capacities across species. For example, one experiment compared the imitative tendency of young children (ages 2–4) with that of juvenile chimpanzees (ages 4–5) (Whiten, Custance, Gomez, Teixidor, & Bard, 1996). In this study, children and chimpanzees were shown how to open a plastic box to obtain a food reward (Figure 11.2a). Half of the participants saw an adult human open the box by poking pins out of its latch before lifting the lid. The other half saw an adult human open the box by twisting and pulling the pins out of the latch. After observing their respective models, the participants were given a chance to open the box themselves. Nothing about this task requires precise copying because the box can be opened in many ways that are equally effective. Nevertheless, both children and chimpanzees usually copied the opening technique that they had observed (Figure 11.2b). Children were more likely than chimpanzees to copy the details of the observed actions, including details that were not essential to getting the box open. Two-action tests have been used to study imitation in several species, including birds (Akins & Zentall, 1996; Dawson & Foss, 1965), rodents (Heyes & Dawson, 1990), and primates (Whiten et al., 1996), and in most of these studies, some copying of actions occurred.

Humans can imitate a wide variety of actions, including novel, nonfunctional actions. To assess whether any other animals share the ability to imitate arbitrary actions requires methods that are more flexible than the two-action test or the technique used by Bandura and colleagues. One approach involves teaching animals to imitate on command (often referred to as the "do-as-I-do" task). For example, researchers trained a chimpanzee to imitate a person's actions when the person gave the command "Do this!" (Hayes & Hayes, 1952). The researchers would perform an action, such as clapping hands, while telling the chimpanzee to "Do this!" and then would record whether or not the chimpanzee performed the same action. Initially, the chimpanzee was unlikely to imitate the actions the first time they were demonstrated. However, after learning to "Do this!" for about 12 actions, the chimpanzee was able to replicate certain new actions the first time she was asked. In a replication of this experiment, two other chimpanzees showed they could replicate 30 actions the first time they saw them (Custance, Whiten, & Bard, 1995). This is the same type of instruction that the dolphin Akeakamai learned to use to imitate actions on request except that she learned to respond to gestures rather than to speech.

One reason psychologists have gone to such great lengths to precisely define true imitation and to develop definitive methods for revealing imitative abilities is because some researchers claim that imitation requires high-level cognitive processes that are unique to humans (Bandura, 1986; Piaget, 1962). For example, imitation by humans is often taken to imply some awareness on the observer's part that he or she is voluntarily copying actions. **Perspective taking**, or imagining oneself in the place of another, is another cognitive ability that some researchers have suggested is a prerequisite for the voluntary imitation of actions. It is an ability that few species other than humans may possess. Perspective taking is thought to facilitate imitation because it enables people (or animals) to imitate others without watching themselves doing so. For example, you can imitate someone's facial expressions without watching yourself make faces.

Your ability to imagine an outside observer's perspective provides feedback that may help you to perform such a feat, but that doesn't mean that imitation requires perspective taking or vice versa. In fact, consideration of the perspective of the individual performing the action may lead you to adopt a totally different strategy that is more effective than imitating what you observed.

perspective taking. Imagining oneself in the place of another.

Studies of Emulation: Copying Goals

As noted earlier, emulation involves replicating an observed outcome without reproducing the actions the model used to achieve that outcome. Chimpanzees and adult humans often perform actions that replicate the outcome of another's actions rather than copying the specific motor acts observed. For example, chimpanzees that saw people using a rake to collect food outside their cage were more likely to use a rake for this purpose than other chimpanzees, but they did not reliably copy the specific raking actions they observed (Nagell, Olguin, & Tomasello, 1993). A chimpanzee might hold the metal end of the rake and use the wooden end to knock the food closer to the cage. This type of copying has been distinguished from more exact copying, with some theorists claiming that when specific actions are not replicated, the copying does not qualify as true imitation (Tomasello, Davis-Dasilva, Carnak, & Bard, 1987; Wood, 1989).

Most evidence of emulation in chimpanzees and adult humans comes from studies intended to show true imitation. For example, in the plastic-box study described on the previous page, the human children were more likely to truly imitate the precise box-opening actions of the model (such as poking the pegs with an index finger), whereas the chimpanzees were more likely to emulate the behavior of the model while using their own methods for opening the plastic box (for example, pushing the pegs with their palms). One interpretation of this difference is that the chimpanzees learned some features of the task by observing the model's behavior but then chose actions different from the ones they had observed in order to perform the task. Matching the outcomes of a set of motor actions by performing somewhat different actions is one kind of emulation. Interestingly, when adult humans were tested on the plastic-box task, their matching behavior was more similar to that of the chimpanzees than to that of the children, in that adults were more likely to emulate than to imitate the model's actions (Horowitz, 2003).

Reproducing Actions Without Copying

Although much of social learning research has focused on organisms imitating the actions of others, there are a number of ways that humans and other animals can replicate the actions of others without employing imitation or emulation. Carefully executed experiments must be conducted to determine which instances of similar behavior involve true imitation, because many of

"You've just been copying things from my sex diary into your sex diary."

True imitation? Emulation? Both?

emotional contagion. An inborn tendency to react emotionally to visual or acoustic stimuli that indicate an emotional response by other members of one's species, typically in ways that replicate the observed response.

observational conditioning. A process in which an individual learns an emotional response after observing similar responses in others.

these other phenomena look just like imitation to the casual observer. Below, we describe three phenomena that closely resemble imitation: emotional contagion, observational conditioning, and stimulus enhancement. Each of these processes can contribute to social learning, but are thought to involve less sophisticated mechanisms than true imitation.

When you hear laughter, you too may feel the urge to laugh (which is why laugh tracks are a common feature of sitcoms). When you see someone yawn, you are more likely to yawn. When one baby starts crying on a plane, the other babies who are there will likely join in. The inborn tendency to react emotionally to sights or sounds of emotion in other members of one's species is called **emotional contagion** (Byrne, 1994; Kramer, Guillory, & Hancock, 2014). Emotional contagion is a relatively common phenomenon in which the observation of a given response increases the likelihood that the observer will produce a similar response. Typically, the kinds of motor acts that lead to emotional contagion are not actions that an animal or person has learned. Babies yawn and cry in utero. Actions that result from emotional contagion usually match the observed actions, but *not* as a result of imitation; the matching reaction is instead often an unconditioned response (like those described in Chapter 4).

We described a situation in Chapter 10 in which naive lab monkeys learned to fear snakes after watching wild monkeys react fearfully to them (Mineka & Cook, 1988). In this case, observer monkeys experienced emotional contagion when they saw the fearful responses of wild monkeys. They associated their unconditioned fear (sparked by the wild monkeys) with the snake (a conditioned stimulus). Recall from Chapter 4 that this is exactly the sort of association that is learned during classical conditioning. Instances such as this, in which an individual learns an emotional response after observing it in others, have been described as **observational conditioning** (Heyes, 1994). This is one way that phobias can develop. Observational conditioning need not always lead to panic, however. Observing individuals who respond fearlessly to "dangerous" situations can help a person to learn to overcome a fear of those situations. For instance, watching videotapes of sexual activity can reduce sexual anxiety and increase sexual activity in people with sexual dysfunctions (Nemetz, Craig, & Reith, 1978).

Some instances of observational conditioning are almost indistinguishable from situations that have been described as learning through imitation. In fact, psychologists once used this similarity to argue that all social learning experiments involve nothing more than classical or operant conditioning. Consider the following example. In the wild, blackbirds automatically attack predators when they observe other blackbirds attacking those predators. Once a blackbird has learned from other birds that a particular object is worthy of attack, it will continue to attack this object on sight for quite a while. In lab studies of this phenomenon, one blackbird can "teach" a second bird to attack something as harmless as a plastic bottle (Curio, Ernst, & Vieth, 1978). Researchers get the birds to do this by showing the "model" bird a stuffed owl, a predator that blackbirds naturally attack. Meanwhile, the second bird observes the model's attacks, but a clever optical illusion causes the second bird to think the model is attacking a bottle rather than an owl (Figure 11.3). Consequently, the second blackbird learns to attack bottles.

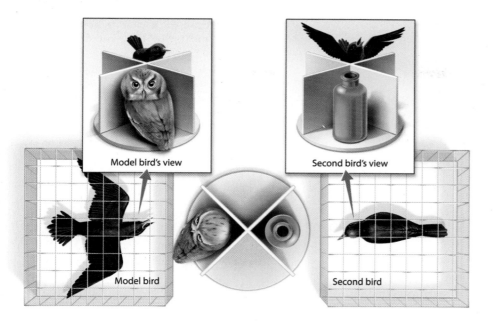

Model bird's view

Second bird's view

Model bird

Second bird

Figure 11.3 Observational conditioning in blackbirds Blackbirds can learn to attack harmless objects such as bottles if they observe other blackbirds doing so—or are tricked into thinking that is what they are observing, as is shown here. Information from Shettleworth, 1998.

This might seem like a clear case of imitation: one bird sees another bird attacking a bottle and then does the same thing. Moreover, this experiment is a lot like the Bobo doll experiment described above, which is considered to be a definitive demonstration of imitation by children. The key difference is that in the case of the blackbirds, attacking possible predators is a species-specific behavior (an unconditioned response) that almost always occurs when a blackbird detects either a predator or sees a blackbird attacking something. A simpler explanation of this example of social learning is thus that the observing blackbird is being classically conditioned: the "model" is an unconditioned stimulus, the initial attacks lead to an unconditioned attack response, and the bottle is the conditioned stimulus. This example doesn't show that birds are incapable of social learning or imitation. In fact, researchers have conducted numerous studies demonstrating social learning in ravens and crows (Bugnyar & Kotrschal, 2002; Holzhaider, Hunt, & Gray, 2010). This study simply illustrates the difficulties associated with identifying the mechanisms that contribute to social learning and imitation in natural situations.

Observational conditioning and emotional contagion are two phenomena in which an observer seems to be imitating the actions of others but is not. A third phenomenon that bears a deceptive resemblance to imitation is when an observer's attention is drawn to stimuli by the actions of others. Redirecting an individual's attention can lead to matching actions that may be mistaken for imitation (Roberts, 1941; Thorpe, 1963). For example, you may have seen a group of people (typically younger people) collectively directing their attention to try and trick other people into looking up at the sky. The way this trick generally works is that the group will start looking up at the sky and pointing as if there were something interesting (or frightening) happening up there. Inevitably, a passerby will look up to where the group is looking to see what all the excitement is about. The passerby then experiences confusion because there is nothing to see.

Because the passerby replicates the looking actions of the tricksters, one might think that the passerby is imitating them. In this case, however, the similarity in actions is a by-product of a similar focus of attention. Just because people watching

Getty Images/Imageworks

Pointing to produce stimulus enhancement Stimulus enhancement consists of directing attention to a particular part of the environment; this can lead to actions that appear similar to imitation. In this case, do you think the stimulus being enhanced is an object or a particular location?

stimulus enhancement. A process in which observation of other individuals causes an organism's attention to be directed toward specific objects or events within an environment.

a movie in a movie theater behave similarly does not mean that they are all imitating one another. Direction of one organism's attention toward specific objects, events, or locations within an environment as a result of another organism's action is called **stimulus enhancement** (Spence, 1937).

Stimulus enhancement can powerfully affect what an individual learns (Heyes, 1994). Essentially, the individual's focus is drawn to a subset of features of the environment that might provide more useful information than other features present. In general, stimulus enhancement increases the likelihood that an animal will be exposed to particular stimuli and their associated consequences. The animal may learn things after being attracted to locations and objects that other animals have been near, but it does so without ever needing to replicate any actions that it may have observed.

Given the many ways that individuals can learn from others without copying their actions or goals, you might wonder how often social learning involves imitation or emulation. There are no definitive studies showing how frequently individuals learn by emulating or imitating. However, one case in which imitation plays a dominant role is during early language learning by children. In the following section, we see how vocal imitation differs from visually based imitation, as well as some ways that vocal imitation contributes to social learning of communicative skills. In Chapter 12, we explore details of how early language learning depends on vocal imitation.

Test Your Knowledge

What Is Imitation?

Much of what people describe as imitation may not be what scientists consider to be true imitation and in fact might not even involve copying. Below are some scenarios that may seem to, and possibly do, involve imitation. Your job is to try to provide alternative explanations for what is happening. (Answers appear in the back of the book.)

1. You smile at your friend's baby. The baby smiles back. Is your friend's baby imitating you?

2. You discover that almost anything you do makes the baby smile (apparently, you are a talented clown). But when you stick out your tongue at the baby, the baby sticks out her tongue at you. Is she imitating you?

3. Leti sees her father make a face when he is eating asparagus, and his expression seems to indicate that he thinks asparagus is disgusting. Later in the week, Leti's grandmother serves asparagus and notices that Leti is making a similar face while eating. Is Leti imitating her father?

4. While watching *America's Funniest Home Videos*, you see a video of a cat jumping up to turn a doorknob so that it can open the door and go outside. Is the cat imitating people?

5. Leti has stumbled into one of the oldest conundrums of childhood. She tells her friend, "Stop repeating whatever I say!" Her friend replies, "Stop repeating whatever I say!" Leti counters, "I mean it, you better stop!" To which her friend replies, "I mean it, you better stop!" And so on. Is Leti's friend imitating her?

Copying What Is Heard

Early psychologists considered the fact that some birds seemed to mimic the sounds of other animals to be the strongest evidence that animals other than humans had the ability to remember and reenact events in the same way as humans (Morgan, 1896; Romanes, 1898). Thorndike (1911) argued, however, that birds were not really imitating sounds, but were instead learning through trial-and-error to make sounds similar to ones they heard, a special case of instrumental conditioning. Modern researchers tend to agree with Thorndike, rejecting the idea that acts of vocal imitation are examples of true imitation (Byrne & Russon, 1998; Heyes, 1994). As illustrated in the previous section, it can be quite tricky to tell when an animal is really imitating. Of course, Thorndike never had the opportunity to watch home videos of parrots swearing on YouTube. You really only have to see one parrot telling someone to "f*** off" to suspect that perhaps birds *can* flexibly reproduce human speech.

Vocal Imitation

When infants are learning to talk, they sometimes imitate speech produced by others around them (Kuhl & Meltzoff, 1996). For example, hearing infants raised in different locales produce speech sounds similar to the ones they hear, whereas deaf infants do not. Infants 12 to 20 weeks old who listened to an adult making vowel sounds immediately produced sounds similar to those they heard (Kuhl & Meltzoff, 1996). This implies that speech imitation abilities are present very early in development.

Speech imitation is a type of **vocal imitation**, imitation that involves pushing air through membranes to re-create some properties of a previously experienced sound. This action may be either voluntary (as is seen in professional impersonators) or involuntary (as occurs when a catchy song gets stuck in your head). In many ways, it is like imitating an action you've never seen. For example, when you imitate someone's speech, you don't need to see the motor actions the person used to produce that speech. You only need to hear the outcomes of those actions. Nevertheless, to reproduce features of the speech you heard, you need to produce motor acts similar to the ones the model used when speaking.

Surprisingly, no mammals other than humans are able to imitate speech sounds as well as birds can. In fact, most mammals, including our closest ape relatives, show little or no ability to imitate sounds and rarely learn to produce vocalizations through experience. Dolphins are the only mammals other than humans that are known to be able to flexibly imitate sounds (Janik & Slater, 1997; Mercado, Mantell, & Pfordresher, 2014). Some dolphins, like Akeakamai, have been trained to imitate computer-generated sounds on command (Richards, Wolz, & Herman, 1984) and may also spontaneously imitate sounds (Reiss & McCowan, 1993; Hooper et al., 2006). Sometimes when Akeakamai was instructed to imitate a sound that she could not easily reproduce, she would produce a transposed copy of the sound (Richards et al., 1984), much as a singer might transpose a song to a higher- or lower-pitch range to make it easier to sing (see "Learning and Memory in Everyday Life" on the next page for a brief discussion of how vocal imitation abilities contribute to people's prowess at karaoke). Several other marine mammal species also show some ability to imitate vocally,

vocal imitation. Copying that involves reproducing sounds.

"That's not *my* political opinion. That's just stuff I hear on the radio."

Leo Cullum The New Yorker Collection/The Cartoon Bank

Karaoke

Karaoke is a relatively recent form of musical entertainment in which amateurs attempt to sing popular songs while being accompanied by instrumental music. Such performances have been compared with singing in the shower, but with an audience and less soap. Unlike sing-alongs, in which singing is typically led by someone with at least moderate musical talent, karaoke is pretty much a free-for-all in which singing ability is optional. Some participants in karaoke produce sounds so awful and out of tune that it is hard to believe they actually think their performance counts as singing.

Surprisingly, little is known about what it takes for someone to produce a good karaoke performance. Obviously, you have to be familiar with the song you are attempting to sing, so memory for the tune and the way the words correspond to the notes is a crucial ingredient. This alone is not sufficient, though, because plenty of people are familiar with songs such as "Happy Birthday" and yet still sound like a broken robot when they attempt to sing them. Recent experiments suggest that the secret ingredient to singing pop songs like a star may be good vocal imitation abilities (Pfordersher & Brown, 2007). A person might have a near-perfect memory of what the original song sounds like, but without the ability to translate that memory into vocal actions that re-create those sounds, this memory will be of little help.

The good news is that people tend to underestimate their ability to vocally imitate songs. Only about 15% of college students are actually hopeless at karaoke, even though many college students (around 60%) believe their ability to sing melodies familiar to them is quite poor (Pfordresher & Brown, 2007). Perhaps as more is learned about how vocal imitation works, even those who sound like dying cows can be transformed into songbirds.

---

including humpback whales and belugas (Ridgway, Carder, Jeffries, & Todd, 2012). In contrast to mammals, numerous species of birds have the ability to vocally imitate. Some, such as the superb lyrebird, can precisely replicate a wide variety of man-made sounds (including car alarms and chainsaws) with astonishing precision.

The ability to imitate vocalizations of adults may help an infant or young bird to learn new communication skills. But to a certain extent the imitating is separate from the learning. For instance, it is relatively easy to construct an electronic toy parrot that can imitate sounds or a robot that can imitate actions (Breazeal & Scassellati, 2002), yet such mimicking machines show little if any capacity to learn to communicate. It is only when imitation guides communicative skill learning that the advantages of the imitative ability are revealed.

Animals that do not naturally imitate vocalizations appear to be unable to learn this skill. Early in the twentieth century, researchers made great efforts to teach chimpanzees to imitate speech, without much progress. Catherine Hayes described the most successful effort of the time, in which a chimpanzee named Viki learned to garble "cup," "mama," and "papa." (Hayes, 1951). This achievement provides no evidence of vocal imitation abilities because Viki was explicitly trained to produce words through operant conditioning and physical molding of her lip positions. You have probably seen videos of dogs and cats that seem to say "I love you" or "I want my mama." Many animals can be trained to produce speech-like sounds, but this again is an example of operant conditioning, not vocal imitation. In the following section, we describe situations in which individuals learn to communicate in ways that seem a lot like vocal imitation, but that do not always involve imitation (much like the cases of emotional contagion, observational conditioning, and stimulus enhancement discussed earlier).

Learning to Vocalize Without Imitating

As noted above, Thorndike (1911) claimed that vocal imitation by birds was not true imitation (reenactment of previously observed actions) but a specialized form of instrumental conditioning in which birds gradually adjust the sounds they make based on how their performance differs from sounds they have previously heard. Differences between produced sounds and remembered sounds provide feedback that in principle could help a bird to gradually make sounds more similar to ones it has heard. Learning to vocalize by adjusting one's own sound production based on sounds one has heard is called **vocal learning**. Some researchers suggest that vocal imitation is a type of vocal learning. However, adult humans imitate sounds in situations where they are not really learning anything new, such as in weddings when the bride and groom are instructed to repeat specific vows, or when a beatboxer imitates the sound of a drum machine at the couple's reception. Vocal imitation can contribute to vocal learning, as it does in young children learning language, but these two phenomena are not identical. All animals that can vocalize are to some extent capable of vocal learning, but only a few learn through vocal imitation.

The most extensively studied form of vocal learning in any species (including humans) is song learning by birds. Birdsongs typically consist of sounds lasting from 1 to 10 seconds, separated by regular silent intervals. The timing, order, and qualities of individual sounds in the songs are all components that can be controlled by vocal actions of the singer. Birds that learn their songs do so in part by listening to other birds. Young songbirds in the wild use their memories of the songs produced by mature birds to guide their own song production. Young birds can form memories of adult songs that can last the rest of their lives. Scientists can tell that songbirds learn songs socially by isolating the animals at a very young age (even prior to birth) so that they never hear another bird singing. Singing insects, frogs, and monkeys that are isolated early in life will develop relatively normal songs even if they never come into contact with another member of their species (Bradbury & Vehrencamp, 1998). In contrast, many songbirds never produce normal songs if they are isolated during early stages of development (Hinde, 1969). Behavioral experiments show that in order to learn to produce normal adult songs, birds must have heard the songs when they were young and must be able to hear themselves sing.

Like human speech, the songs that birds sing may show differences in dialect, the locale-specific idiosyncrasies of a given language (Baptista & King, 1980; Marler, 1970; Thorpe, 1958). Just as your accent can reveal to others where you grew up and learned to speak, a bird's "accent" can reveal where the bird grew up and learned to sing. Baby birds raised by an adult of another species can sometimes even learn the foreigner's song (Immelman, 1969). This would be the equivalent of an infant being raised by chimpanzees and learning how to produce chimpanzee vocalizations (à la Tarzan). Interestingly, learning to sing foreign songs seems to require that the adult interact with the young bird. If young birds are simply exposed to recordings of foreign songs, they do not learn to sing them (Pepperberg, 1994). By analogy, you would probably be more likely to learn a foreign language spoken by neighbors if you regularly interacted with them than if you simply heard them speaking to one another from a distance.

Song learning seems to occur in three basic phases. To begin with, most songbirds seem to be born with a crude inherited "template" that biases their brain toward storing certain sound patterns. In the first phase of song learning, young birds memorize the songs they hear that best fit their template, and these memorized songs provide a model against which later performance is judged. The second phase ensues when the young bird begins attempting to sing songs. While the bird is singing, it hears itself singing and can compare its own song with memories of songs it has heard in the past. With practice, the young bird increases the match between its own performance and the songs it remembers hearing. In the third stage of song learning, the bird learns when to sing. For example, a territorial songbird might sing primarily when it hears a song it has never heard before or when it hears a familiar song sung by an unfamiliar bird. The actions and reactions of a nearby female may influence a male songbird's singing. These three phases of song learning are described in, and collectively

vocal learning. Modifying vocal output using memories of previously experienced sounds.

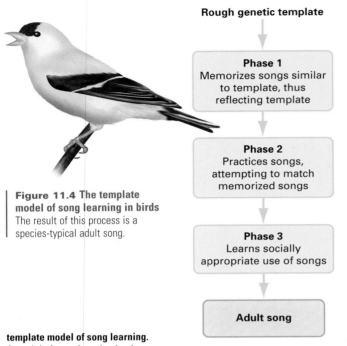

Rough genetic template

Phase 1
Memorizes songs similar to template, thus reflecting template

Phase 2
Practices songs, attempting to match memorized songs

Phase 3
Learns socially appropriate use of songs

Adult song

Figure 11.4 The template model of song learning in birds The result of this process is a species-typical adult song.

template model of song learning. A model of song learning having three basic phases: song memorization, song practice, and song utilization.

make up, the **template model of song learning** (Figure 11.4). The process of song learning can potentially involve vocal imitation, but, as noted by Thorndike, gradually modifying sound production does not require reenacting any previously experienced event. The fact that an adult bird's songs are similar to ones it heard when it was young does not provide strong evidence that imitation contributed to learning.

Certain species-specific features of bird songs are genetically controlled, constraining what a learning bird is likely to copy. For example, young birds exposed to both the songs of their own species and the songs of other species will typically learn the song associated with their species (Marler, 1997). Similar constraints seem to operate in human infants as well. Infants are exposed to a wide range of sounds, possibly including the sounds of birds, dogs, and musical instruments, yet the sounds they learn to produce themselves are invariably the spoken sounds produced by their own species. This could be because sounds produced by members of the same species are inherently the easiest to produce (because they were made using similar vocal organs), or perhaps it is because individuals are genetically predisposed to recognize species-specific sounds.

As noted earlier, most mammals do not imitate vocalizations, and even fewer learn to sing through imitation. In fact, the only mammals other than humans known to do this naturally are some of the larger whales. For instance, humpback whales learn to sing new songs throughout their lives by listening to other whales' songs (Guinee, Chu, & Dorsey, 1983). Intriguingly, they continuously change the properties of their songs throughout their lives (Payne & Payne, 1985), so that in any given year, whales are singing a song that no humpback whale has ever sung before (there are no "golden oldies" in the world of humpback whales). Researchers can tell that whales are learning their songs because when a whale introduces a new song into a particular region, many other whales will then begin to sing that song (Noad, Cato, Bryden, Jenner, & Jenner, 2000). Identifying the mechanisms that endow humans or humpback whales with such flexible vocal-learning capacities is difficult. As discussed in Section 11.2, studies of vocal learning by other species (especially birds) are currently the best hope for understanding the relationship between vocal learning, vocal imitation, and imitation more generally.

Learning to speak or sing like your parents and peers may not only make it easier for you to communicate with them, it may also increase your ability to "fit in" and participate in social activities, which in turn may increase opportunities for learning new things from others. The next section examines how such interactions can contribute to social learning.

Social Transmission of Information

social transmission of information. A process seen in all human cultures in which an observer learns something new through experiences with others.

Imagine you are waiting to purchase a soda from a vending machine, and you notice that the person ahead of you just lost money in the machine. On the basis of observing the person's misfortune, you might decide not to put your money into that particular machine. This is an example of **social transmission**

of information, a process in which an observer learns something new through experiences involving other agents. Social transmission of information is seen in all human cultures. It is historically evident in the development of spoken and written language, and more recently in the development of libraries, television, telephones, and the Internet. Through these various channels, information can be transmitted rapidly to vast numbers of individuals.

The many ways in which humans are able to transmit information enables them to learn more rapidly than all other animals in an almost unlimited range of contexts. Unfortunately, this phenomenon has seldom been studied in the laboratory, except in relation to skill learning. You may recall from Chapter 8 the experiment in which a person was asked to kick a target as rapidly as possible. His performance changed incrementally in keeping with the power law of learning: improving quickly at first and then more slowly. However, when he was shown a film of someone kicking the target in a more effective way, his performance improved dramatically. In this particular example, information about better ways to kick was socially transferred by means of a film. (The person in this experiment probably improved by imitating the model he visually observed, but because the experiment focused on skill learning rather than imitation, the exact mechanism of learning was not closely assessed.)

Because so much transfer of information between humans occurs in highly sophisticated ways, it is easy to overlook examples of socially transferred information in other species. However, the very complexity of social transmission of information in humans causes difficulty for researchers when they try to isolate the basic mechanisms through which it occurs. As a result, studies of the simpler forms of information transfer that can be measured in other species are important for understanding the processes underlying this ability.

Singing humpback whale
Humpbacks are the only mammals other than humans that naturally learn to sing songs by hearing them—a unique case of vocal learning. Or, is it a case of vocal imitation?

Learning Through Social Conformity

If you've ever looked through your parents' or grandparents' photo albums, you've probably come across one or more pictures that made you wonder how they could have ever gotten it into their heads to wear clothes that were so ugly or uncomfortable. You may have even found a picture of the younger you wearing clothes and a hairstyle that you would be humiliated to be seen in today. In contrast, if you've seen photos of tigers taken in the 1920s, you would be hard-pressed to tell them apart from photos of tigers that were taken yesterday. Why is it that humans do things to collectively change their appearance over time? Why do you even cut your hair or shave at all? A major reason you do any of these things is because you've learned to do them.

Here's how you can know when learning, and not some other force of nature, is guiding your actions and preferences. If you go to a city in China or Africa that has a climate similar to the one you are used to and compare your hair, clothes, and speech to those of the native inhabitants, you will find that most of the inhabitants are more similar to one another in how they dress and speak than they are to you. This would not be the case if you yourself had lived in that city your whole life. If you were raised in the foreign city, you would probably dress and speak like everyone else there. Cultural differences in dress and language are easily apparent. What is not so apparent is how you learn to choose jeans over a kilt.

Studies of the social transmission of food preferences in rats may shed some light on such questions (Galef & Wigmore, 1983). Infant rats begin life preferring foods their mother has eaten because they can taste those foods in her milk. However, rats naturally pay attention to the food consumption of other rats and can learn to eat novel foods after observing that another rat has eaten them. In studies of this phenomenon, rats are typically housed together in pairs for a few days, during which they are fed rat chow (Figure 11.5a). One rat from each pair—chosen to be the "demonstrator" rat—is moved to another cage. *Both* rats are deprived of food for one day, and then *the demonstrator rat* is fed cinnamon- or cocoa-flavored food (half of the demonstrator rats are given one flavor and half the other), after which the demonstrator rats are returned to their original cages and allowed to interact with the "observer" rat for 15 minutes. On the subsequent day, the observer rat is given access to two food bowls, one containing cocoa-flavored food and the other cinnamon-flavored food. Observer rats typically eat more food of the flavor they smelled on the demonstrator's breath (Figure 11.5b). This shows that the observer rats acquired information about foods from the demonstrator rat and later used this information when choosing food.

Observer rats need to smell food in the context of another rat's breath to acquire a new food preference (Galef, 1996). Once a food becomes preferred,

Figure 11.5 Social transmission of food preferences by rats Given a choice of two novel foods, observer rats are more likely to eat the food they smelled on a demonstrator rat's breath. This means that information about food has been transmitted between the rats.

Information from Shettleworth, 1998.

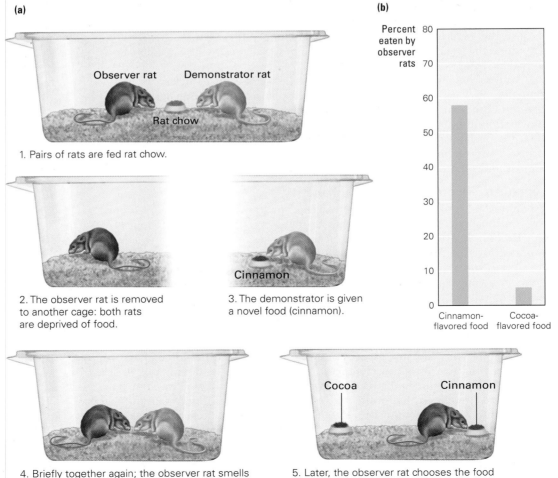

(a)

1. Pairs of rats are fed rat chow.

2. The observer rat is removed to another cage: both rats are deprived of food.

3. The demonstrator is given a novel food (cinnamon).

4. Briefly together again; the observer rat smells the novel food on the demonstrator rat's breath.

5. Later, the observer rat chooses the food that the demonstrator rat ate.

(b)

that preference may be transmitted to successive generations. Several factors affect how easily food preferences are transmitted to others (Galef & Whiskin, 1997). For example, larger numbers of demonstrations and demonstrating rats increase the likelihood of transfer. Isolated (one-time) observations produce only a short-term effect, but repeated exposures lead to long-term retention.

Rats tend to follow what the majority of colony members do; this tendency to adopt the behavior of the group is called **social conformity**. Social conformity has many protective functions, but it can also hinder the development of novel behavior patterns that might be advantageous. In one experiment, guppies (a kind of fish) were trained to follow specific escape paths in order to evade an artificial predator (Brown & Laland, 2002). The artificial predator consisted of a net being moved across a tank to trap the guppies, and the escape paths were holes at different positions in the net (Figure 11.6). One of two holes was closed during training, and demonstrator guppies quickly learned where the one open hole in the net was located. After training, the demonstrator fish continued to use only the escape path they had learned even after the second hole was opened. When naive fish were introduced into this situation, with both holes open, they typically chose to escape through the hole that they observed the trained fish using. If the demonstrator guppies were then removed from the tank, the observer guppies continued to use the hole they had seen the demonstrator guppies using, even when the alternate path led to a quicker escape. These results from rats and fish suggest that social conformity may be driven in part by stimulus enhancement—odors, locations, or actions that are relevant to one individual become more salient to others.

social conformity. The tendency to adopt the behavior of the group.

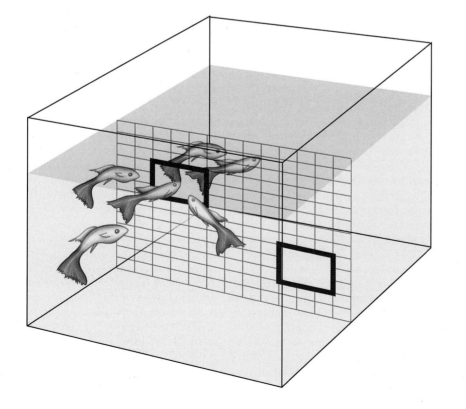

Figure 11.6 Social transmission of escape routes by guppies After demonstrator guppies were trained to escape from a net by swimming through a particular hole (with a second escape hole closed), observer guppies tended to use the same escape path as the demonstrator guppies when both holes were open.
Research from Brown & Laland, 2002.

Social conformity allows rapid acquisition of information that may be adaptive for a particular situation, but it can lead to traditions that may provide no general benefit. Interestingly, a reduction in the number of trained guppies (that is, a decrease in the number of demonstrators during training) increased the likelihood that new escape solutions would emerge (Brown & Laland, 2002). Apparently, even guppies can be affected by peer pressure.

Effects of Media on Behavior

When Leti entered elementary school, her parents (like most) began worrying about how much time she spent watching television and about what she would learn if she watched programs they considered inappropriate. She didn't watch any more TV than the average child (about 24 hours per week), but this still seemed like a lot to Leti's parents. In particular, they worried that commercials might be making their daughter overly materialistic and that trailers for action movies glamorized violent behavior. Their worries intensified when Leti reached adolescence and began copying what they considered to be the "bizarre" behaviors of her YouTube idols (such as twerking). Like most parents, Leti's parents worried about what Leti would learn from observing and copying behaviors she encountered through the mass media.

Much public transfer of information in the United States occurs through the mass distribution of moving images and audio signals in the form of television, movies, the Internet, and recorded music. Most of the content transmitted by these media outlets is designed to entertain paying customers. Even news programs focus on the news stories that will attract the most viewers. Over the last few decades, however, there has been increasing concern that the entertaining images and words broadcast by the media are having negative effects on the population. In particular, numerous organizations have concluded that excessive depiction of violence in the mass media is a public health risk because it stimulates violent behavior (Anderson et al., 2003). The basic assumption driving this concern is "monkey see, monkey do"—that people will imitate what they see.

Researchers have collected strong evidence of a general association between violent behavior and increased exposure to violent media (Anderson et al., 2003). For example, the amount of violent TV watched by children in elementary school is correlated with their aggressiveness as teenagers and with their criminal behavior as adults (Anderson et al., 2003). Similarly, statistics show the rate of homicides to have increased dramatically soon after television was introduced in the United States, whereas no such increases were observed in regions where television was banned during the same time period (Centerwall, 1992; see Figure 11.7). Given that such correlations exist, the main questions relevant to this discussion are (1) do violent media increase aggressive behavior or do aggressive individuals find violent media more entertaining, and (2) does exposure to violent media lead to social learning and the performance of imitative actions?

Most research addressing these questions has focused on the effects of viewing violent images. In the typical experiment, researchers randomly assign young participants to watch either a short violent film or a short nonviolent film. Later, the researchers observe the participants' behavior. Usually these observations are made a few minutes or days after the participants view the film, in contexts where aggression might normally occur. Such experiments show that children exposed to the violent film are more likely to behave aggressively in play sessions immediately after viewing the film (Cornstock, 1980; Geen, 1990). For example, 7- to 9-year-old boys who scored high on measures of aggressiveness were more likely to physically assault other boys in a hockey game after watching a violent

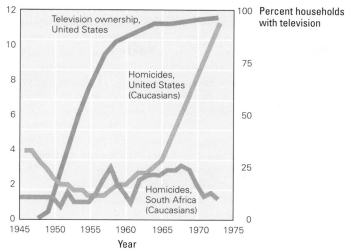

Figure 11.7 Correlation between television and homicides in the United States The rate of homicides increased dramatically among Caucasians in the United States soon after television was introduced, whereas no such increases were observed among Caucasians in South Africa, where television was banned during the same time period.

Data from Centerwall, 1992.

video (Josephson, 1987). As was seen in the Bobo doll experiment, aroused participants are generally more likely than nonaroused participants to behave aggressively after viewing violent images. Researchers produced the arousal by some kind of provocation. Thus, college men who viewed a violent sex film were more willing to deliver electric shocks to a woman who had previously provoked them (by giving them a mild electrical shock in a laboratory experiment) than were men who viewed a violent film containing no sex (Donnerstein & Berkowitz, 1981).

Such short-term experiments generally do not prove that children have learned to be aggressive from watching the violent performances, because a general increase in arousal levels (brought on by watching violent behavior) might be what is leading to the children's increased aggressiveness rather than anything they specifically learned from watching the videos (Anderson et al., 2003). In addition, this research does not provide evidence that exposure to violence in movies and songs increases aggressive behavior any more than violence depicted in other sources of entertainment such as books, plays, and puppet shows. Lastly, researchers have seldom studied the possibility that exposure to violent television shows might be correlated with positive outcomes, such as an increased likelihood that a person will pursue a career as a medical professional, firefighter, soldier, or police officer. Many violent shows depict both heroes and villains, and nothing about watching a video compels children to choose the villains as their models.

Interactive media such as video games and the Internet have been the subjects of similar research. Part of this interest stems from the fact that students who gunned down other students in certain school shootings were avid video game players (Anderson, 2004). Experiments designed to test the negative effects of violent video games compare aggressive behavior in children who have recently played a violent video game with aggressive behavior in children who recently played a nonviolent video game. As in studies of more passive media, children who played the violent video game generally were more likely to behave aggressively (Anderson et al., 2010; Irwin & Gross, 1995).

Such correlations do not prove that observing violence increases violent behavior, and the effects of media on aggression are still intensely debated (Ferguson & Kilburn, 2010). Another explanation, suggested above, could be that children who are predisposed to violence are also more likely to enjoy watching violence on television. This would mean that watching violent TV doesn't cause the violence but is merely another way in which the predisposition is manifested. Nevertheless, a report issued by the National Institute of Mental Health in the 1980s concluded that children who are repeatedly exposed to violent television may become less sensitive to the suffering of others, more fearful of the world around them, and more likely to behave in aggressive ways toward others (APA Online, 2004). Consequently, governmental agencies have introduced regulatory measures to reduce the possible negative effects of mass media on children, including requiring warnings to be displayed on CDs, placing ratings and age restrictions on movie viewing and video games, and requiring televisions for U.S. sale to contain V-chips (V for "violence") that enable parents to restrict what their children watch.

Although researchers have proposed that social learning involving imitation underlies the association between exposure to violent media and aggressive behavior (Anderson et al., 2003), most studies of exposure to violent media do not report instances of emulation or true imitation after exposure. In general, it remains unclear what it is that individuals learn from watching movies or listening to songs.

In addition to the mere presence or absence of violence in mass media, researchers and public officials have voiced concern about the total amount of violence being depicted. Their fear is that greater exposure to violent scenes leads to a higher incidence of aggressive behavior. This may be true, but there are no experiments showing that children who are repeatedly exposed either to the same violent movie or to multiple violent movies are more likely to behave more aggressively than children who have seen such a movie only once. Just as it is difficult to identify the effects of a single entertaining event on future behavior, it is also difficult to predict the effects of multiple exposures to depictions of violence. That being said, the general consensus is that massive amounts of viewing or listening to violence is more likely to do harm than good, whether or not social learning plays a role. (For speculation about the effect of other aspects of television viewing on behavior, see "Learning and Memory in Everyday Life," on the next page.)

Recently, there has been an explosion of interest in modeling social learning processes (Galef & Laland, 2005; Kendal, Galef, & von Schaik, 2010). Some of this work continues to focus on children's social development (Crick & Dodge, 1994; Dodge, 2011), but much of it is now concerned with understanding social learning in animals (Laland & Galef, 2009; Margoliash, 2002). Also, emphasis has shifted from describing the mechanisms of social learning within individuals to exploring the social dynamics that determine when an individual will copy others (Jones et al., 2007; Laland, 2004; Rendell et al., 2010). Studies of social learning in animals have also opened up new opportunities for identifying the neural mechanisms of imitation and of the social transmission of information, as described in the next section.

Interim Summary

- Psychologists use the term *social learning* to identify situations in which a learner actively monitors the acts of others and later chooses actions based on those observations.

- Social learning theorists sometimes describe imitative learning as a special case of operant conditioning in which the act of copying is either directly or indirectly reinforced.

Learning What to Like from Super Bowl Ads

Breweries spend billions of dollars each year on producing and distributing commercials and other marketing materials intended to increase the probability that consumers will choose their product when deciding which alcoholic beverage to consume. Many of these advertisements are designed to change people's behavior not by making them more informed about a product (social transmission) but by associating the product with attractive situations and rewards. In particular, commercials often provide models of drinking behavior that are designed to encourage imitation or emulation by viewers (Anderson et al., 2009). Presumably, companies would not be spending such large sums on advertisements if they were not effective. Ads convert watchers into brand-biased consumers through a variety of learning mechanisms, some of which can change a viewer's preferences without the person's knowing this is happening.

Controlled experiments that show how long-term exposure to beer commercials affect consumption have not been conducted, for ethical reasons. Correlational studies generally look for associations between familiarity with the content of commercials and drinking behavior, but usually do not look at details about brand preferences. Such studies have shown that greater exposure to alcohol advertising is correlated with a greater likelihood of binge drinking in young adults (Hanewinkel & Sargent, 2008).

By portraying episodes of attractive people having fun while drinking, commercials not only promote social conformity by viewers but may also associate positive emotional responses with a particular brand. Repeatedly pairing the image and name of a specific company with observations of happy people drinking may lead to observational conditioning. Likewise, repeatedly pairing a brand with humorous situations may lead to classical conditioning of emotional responses.

Super Bowl ads have become famous as a medium through which companies can influence viewers' preferences on a massive scale. The emotional excitement associated with such annual traditions and big sporting events more generally can amplify the memories formed during exposure to advertisements (as discussed in Chapter 10), suggesting that the alcoholic preferences of football fans are especially likely to be a result of ad-driven conditioning disguised as entertainment.

- Copying that involves reproducing motor acts is called true imitation. Copying that involves replicating an outcome without replicating specific motor acts is called emulation.

- In emotional contagion, the observation of a response reflexively evokes that same response. Stimulus enhancement increases the likelihood that an animal will be exposed to particular stimuli and their associated consequences.

- The ability to either imitate or emulate ultimately depends on the availability of memories for facts or events.

- Many bird species learn songs, but among mammals, only humans and a few species of whales and dolphins show the ability to vocally imitate sounds.

- Social transmission of information provides a way for individuals to take advantage of the lessons learned by others.

- Observing others behaving in specific ways can influence the likelihood that an individual will behave in similar ways.

11.2 Brain Substrates

The Behavioral Processes section discussed how social learning often seems to depend both on memories for facts and events (such as memories of actions or their outcomes only experienced once) and on skill memories (learning how to perform an action observed in the past). So, you might expect that the neural substrates of social learning would be similar to those previously described in the chapters on memories for facts, events, and skills. But the fact that only a few species seem to be capable of certain kinds of social learning suggests that something beyond these basic neural systems is needed. In the following discussion, we describe neuroscience research on social learning in mammals and birds that provides some clues about how brains make either imitation or the social transmission of information possible.

The basic problem faced by the brain of an imitating animal is how to map observed events onto the motor commands that are needed to generate those same events. In visually based imitation, the model's observed actions are the events to be replicated. In vocal imitation, the outcomes of the model's actions (the produced sounds) are the events to be replicated.

One proposed explanation for how cortical networks store memories of actions is the **direct-matching hypothesis**. The direct-matching hypothesis proposes that memories for actions are stored in specialized cortical regions that map observed actions onto the motor representations of the acts (Buccino, Binkofski, & Riggio, 2004). In other words, visually observing an action automatically activates the same neural systems required to perform the action, and memories for the action are stored as part of this process. The following section describes recently identified cortical networks that appear to link visual inputs to motor outputs in exactly this way.

Mirror Neurons

The fact that humans can imitate actions implies that the human brain can translate visual inputs into corresponding motor patterns. Neurons that fire both during performance of an action and during visual observations of that same action were first identified in a monkey's cortex (di Pellegrino, Fadiga, Fogassi, Gallese, & Rizzolatti, 1992; Gallese, Fadiga, Fogassi, & Rizzolatti, 1996). Such neurons are called **mirror neurons** because they fire the same way when the monkey performs an action as they do when the monkey sees another monkey or person performing that action (Rizzolatti & Craighero, 2004). Mirror neurons that respond to actions of the hands or the mouth are the most prevalent (Ferrari, Gallese, Rizzolatti, & Fogassi, 2003). For example, some mirror neurons fire most strongly when a monkey either grasps an object or observes a monkey grasping an object. Mirror neurons provide a neural link between seeing an action and doing that action. A monkey could potentially use this link to imitate an observed action, because all the monkey would need to do is reactivate neural circuits that had recently been activated. However, there is no direct evidence that mirror neurons are necessary for imitative abilities, and monkeys generally have shown little ability to imitate observed actions.

Some mirror neurons seem to fire most strongly during observation of the outcome of an action rather than in response to observations of the action itself (Gallese et al., 1996). This means that the neurons fire the same way when a monkey is seeing a particular outcome (which could be the result of various actions) as when the monkey is achieving that same outcome. So, mirror neurons provide the kinds of neural links necessary for emulation (copying a goal) as well as imitation (copying an action).

It is difficult to directly observe mirror neurons in humans because invasive surgery is necessary to record from individual neurons. However, indirect measures of cortical activity, such as electroencephalographs (EEGs) (Raymaekers, Wiersema, & Roeyers, 2009), transcranial magnetic stimulation (Gangitano, Mottaghy, & Pascual-Leone, 2001), and cerebral blood flow (Martineau

direct-matching hypothesis. The proposal that memories for actions are stored in specialized cortical regions that map observed actions onto the motor representations of the acts.

mirror neurons. Neurons that respond during performance of an action and during visual observations of that same action.

et al., 2010) indicate that regions of the human cortex behave as if they contain mirror neurons. The basic procedure for such studies in humans generally involves an "observation-only" condition, an "imitation" condition, and an "instructed action" condition. For example, researchers might ask participants to (1) observe an image of someone moving a certain finger, (2) imitate someone moving a certain finger, and (3) move a certain finger in response to a specific command (Figure 11.8). Neuroimaging experiments of this kind show overlap between cortical regions that are activated by the performance of an action and cortical regions that are activated by observing that action being performed (Iacoboni et al., 1999; Rizzolatti & Craighero, 2004). The areas of the human brain that become active during both the observation and performance of actions are located in cortical regions similar to those examined in monkeys. This suggests that monkeys and humans may use similar circuits to match observations to actions.

Researchers hypothesize that mirror neurons provide a basic mechanism for simple imitation (Rizzolatti & Sinigaglia, 2010). In fact, some researchers suggest that deficits in mirror neurons may contribute to developmental disorders (we discuss this idea in more detail later, in the Clinical Perspectives section). This idea is significant because in the past, researchers assumed that imitation involved higher-level cognitive processes that would be difficult to trace to specific brain activity in humans and impossible to trace to specific brain activity in other animals. If mirror neurons are involved in imitation, then researchers should be able to directly examine the mechanisms of imitation in animal models.

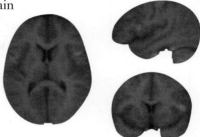

Execution   Observation

Frontal cortex
activity

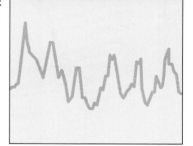

Republished with permission of AAAS, from Cortical mechanisms of human imitation, Iacoboni, M., Woods, R. P., Brass, M., Bekkering, H., Mazziotta, J. C., & Rizzolati, G., 286, 1999.

Figure 11.8 Mirror neurons in a human cortex? The red areas indicate regions in the cortex that became more active when humans either watched a video of someone moving their finger or when they performed the same finger movements either by imitating the video or following instructions. The line graph on the bottom shows changes in cortical activation over time when participants were executing movements or observing them.

Data from Iacoboni et al., 1999.

Test Your Knowledge

Who Has Mirror Neurons and What Do They Do?

Mirror neurons in monkeys respond the same to observed actions and performed actions. On the basis of the preceding discussion, which of the following statements are also true of mirror neurons? (Answers appear in the back of the book.)

1. Mirror neurons are important for imitative abilities.

2. Mirror neurons in humans respond like those in monkeys.

3. Only primates have mirror neurons.

4. Many mirror neurons in monkeys often respond to actions of the hands or mouth.

Song Learning in Bird Brains

You might suppose that the neural mechanisms you use to imitate actions would be very different from the brain circuits used by young birds learning to sing. However, they are actually quite similar.

The neural circuits that birds use for learning and producing songs are complex (Figure 11.9). Birds use specific brain regions to store memories of songs and use other regions to learn the perceptual-motor skills for singing. Lesion studies and electrophysiological recordings have identified two main neural regions that birds use for producing songs: the high vocal center (HVC) and the robust nucleus of the archistriatum (RA). The HVC controls the timing of

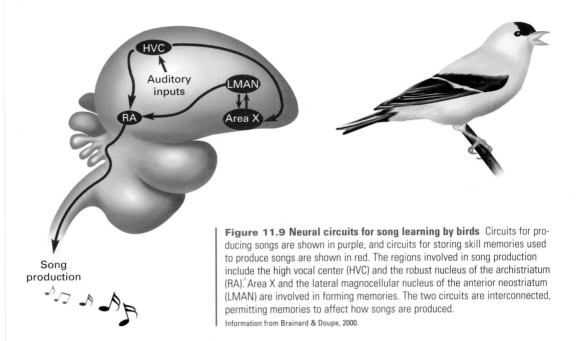

Figure 11.9 Neural circuits for song learning by birds Circuits for producing songs are shown in purple, and circuits for storing skill memories used to produce songs are shown in red. The regions involved in song production include the high vocal center (HVC) and the robust nucleus of the archistriatum (RA). Area X and the lateral magnocellular nucleus of the anterior neostriatum (LMAN) are involved in forming memories. The two circuits are interconnected, permitting memories to affect how songs are produced.
Information from Brainard & Doupe, 2000.

song production—for example, when a bird will start or stop singing and the rate at which notes are produced. The RA controls more detailed features of the individual sounds within a song (Mooney, 2009). Neurons in the RA that fire strongly when a bird hears a song are also seen to become active just before the bird begins to sing. This means that the RA neurons fire similarly when the bird hears particular songs and when the bird sings those same songs. This description should sound familiar to you because it is very similar to the depiction of mirror neuron activity presented above. Neurons in HVC also respond both when birds sing and when they are listening to their own song (Prather et al., 2008). These findings suggest that bird brains contain neurons that map observed events onto vocal acts in a manner comparable with that of the mirror neurons seen in primates.

Birds also possess a neural region called Area X that is thought to be analogous to the mammalian basal ganglia. Lesions to Area X disrupt song learning just as lesions to the basal ganglia of mammals impair perceptual-motor learning (as you may recall from the discussion in Chapter 8 on skill memories). Area X receives inputs from a region called the lateral magnocellular nucleus of the anterior neostriatum (LMAN). The LMAN is thought to function like the frontal cortex in mammals. Disrupting activity in LMAN neurons when a songbird is first hearing other birds' songs impairs, but does not prevent, song learning (Basham, Nordeen, & Nordeen, 1996). Similarly, frontal damage in humans can interfere with a person's ability to learn from social interactions, a topic we discuss in greater detail in the Clinical Perspectives section of this chapter.

Imitation invariably requires a circuit that maps sensory representations onto motor systems, so different species are likely to exhibit similar neural solutions to this problem. Future clarification of the neural processes underlying vocal learning by birds will enable scientists to meaningfully compare the mechanisms underlying social learning of both sounds and sights in the brains of many organisms.

Hippocampal Encoding of Socially Transmitted Food Preferences

When rats learn a food preference from smelling the odor of the food on another rat's breath, they create memories of the experience that can influence their behavior for a lifetime. As little as 10 minutes of exposure to a novel food odor on another rat's breath, with no repetition of exposure, can influence eating behavior at least 3 months later (Clark, Broadbent, Zola, & Squire, 2002).

You may recall from Chapter 7, on memories for facts and events, that when humans experience a unique event and are then able to remember it several months later, an episodic memory has been created. Could it be that rats form episodic memories of experiences involving unique odors coming from another rat's mouth? Based on the studies of human episodic memory described in Chapter 7, you might expect that if a rat were forming memories for such events, then damage to the rat's hippocampus should disrupt its ability to acquire preferences for specific foods from interactions with other rats. Specifically, you might expect that hippocampal damage could disrupt the rat's old memories for past interactions (retrograde amnesia) or disrupt its ability to acquire new memories (anterograde amnesia).

This prediction has received some experimental support. Observer rats were exposed to a food odor on a demonstrator rat's breath and then were given hippocampal lesions 1, 10, or 30 days later. In each case, the lesions reduced the observer rat's preference for the food, but the disruption was worst when the lesion was produced right after the observation period (Bunsey & Eichenbaum, 1995; Clark et al., 2002). In other words, the rats appeared to show retrograde amnesia following hippocampal damage, and the "amnesia" was worse for newly acquired memories than for older ones. This effect is consistent with the results of human studies showing that hippocampal-region damage affected newer episodic memories more than older ones. In short, hippocampal damage disrupts the ability of animals to learn from social interactions in ways that parallel episodic memory deficits in humans suffering from amnesia.

Chapter 7 also described how lesions of the basal forebrain in human patients can lead to amnesia similar to the amnesia caused by hippocampal damage. Recall that this deficit resulted from the loss of neuromodulatory neurons in the basal forebrain that modulated activity in the hippocampus. It turns out that basal forebrain circuits that modulate activity in a rat's hippocampus are similarly critical for social transmission of food preferences. If a rat's basal forebrain is damaged, its memories of previously acquired food preferences will be drastically impaired. Its future ability to learn about novel foods from other rats will not be affected, however—a case of retrograde amnesia without anterograde amnesia (Berger-Sweeney, Stearns, Frick, Beard, & Baxter, 2000; Vale-Martinez, Baxter, & Eichenbaum, 2002). Just as in humans with amnesia, basal forebrain lesions in rats produce patterns of memory loss for socially transmitted information that are comparable with, but distinguishable from, those associated with hippocampal damage.

It seems that in rats, memory for socially transmitted information depends on the hippocampus and basal forebrain. This doesn't necessarily mean that food preferences are based on episodic memories, but it does mean that hippocampal processing is relevant to the mechanisms that enable both rats and humans to learn from socially transmitted information. Memories for facts and events are rarely described by psychologists as resulting from social learning—more often, these memories are described as outcomes of an unspecified process of "storage" or "encoding"—but the similarities between memory loss in humans and impaired social transmission of information in rats suggest that researchers may be using different terminology to describe comparable phenomena.

Interim Summary

- In both visually based imitation and vocal imitation, sensory representations are translated into the motor acts necessary to replicate the observed events.
- Before any action can be imitated, it must be recognized. Mirror neurons fire in the same way when the monkey performs an action as they do when the monkey sees another monkey performing that action.
- Neuroimaging studies of humans have correlated activation in cortical areas where mirror neurons are likely to be found with the performance or observation of particular actions.
- The song-learning circuits of birds share many features in common with mammalian brain circuits for learning perceptual-motor skills.
- The memories that rats form based on socially transmitted information about foods depend on the hippocampus and basal forebrain.

11.3 Clinical Perspectives

Most of the disorders known to affect social learning have an impact on imitation, often in two seemingly paradoxical ways. Patients with imitative deficits cannot seem to prevent themselves from involuntarily imitating the actions of individuals with whom they are interacting, and yet they have difficulties imitating specific actions when asked to do so. This pattern, which is seen both in individuals with autism spectrum disorder and in some stroke patients, is consistent with current theories about the cortical substrates of imitation.

Autism Spectrum Disorder

autism spectrum disorder. A set of disorders associated with deficits in social interactions and social learning.

Individuals who have difficulties interacting socially, require highly consistent routines, are susceptible to sensory overload, use language abnormally when communicating with others, and repeatedly produce certain stereotyped movement patterns are described clinically as having an **autism spectrum disorder** (more generally referred to as *autism*). For centuries, children who would today be diagnosed as having autism spectrum disorder were grouped with the insane or mentally retarded. Because these children often did not learn to speak, they sometimes were misdiagnosed as being deaf! It was only in the last century that researchers began to identify this disorder with a distinctive pattern of symptoms (Kanner, 1943). Studies of autism spectrum disorders provide insight into how social learning contributes to much of what humans learn throughout their lives and into the neural systems that make social learning possible.

echolalia. The automatic repetition of words or phrases immediately after hearing them spoken.

In addition to engaging in repetitive and stereotyped actions, individuals with autism may repeat words or phrases immediately after hearing them spoken, a phenomenon called **echolalia**. Echolalia requires vocal imitation abilities, which might seem to suggest that individuals with autism would be good imitators.

However, these children actually turn out to be worse at imitating actions than other children.

Some of the earliest evidence that children with autism spectrum disorder are impaired at imitating actions came from the reports of mothers. For example, one mother reported that she was unable to teach her child to play the "patty-cake" game until she physically moved the child's arms in the correct patterns (Ritvo & Provence, 1953). The fact that the child did eventually learn to play this game shows that the earlier learning deficit was not the result of impaired visual–motor coordination abilities. Instead, the child's impaired ability to imitate most probably prevented him from successfully copying his mother. Another possible explanation for this difficulty, however, is that copying adults may be less reinforcing for children with autism than for other children, and so they may be less motivated to do it, whatever their imitative ability. A popular theory of autism spectrum disorder called the *mind-blindness theory* suggests that children with this disorder have problems with perspective taking that prevent them from imagining themselves in someone else's shoes (Baron-Cohen, 2009). This theory would explain the boy's deficits in imitation as a side effect of a more general deficit in understanding his mother's intentions.

If children with autism spectrum disorder suffer from impaired imitation abilities early on, perhaps this deficit is actually a source of their other behavioral and social impairments (Rogers & Pennington, 1991). Different studies have reported different levels of imitative deficits, however, so it remains unclear exactly which aspects of imitative abilities are affected by autism (Beadle-Brown & Whiten, 2004; Hamilton, 2008). People with autism can recognize when they are being imitated, but they do not reliably imitate the actions of others (Smith & Bryson, 1994; Leighton et al., 2008; Vanvuchelen et al., 2013). Children with autism tested in a do-as-I-do task could imitate simple actions, like drinking, but had problems imitating sequences of actions (Beadle-Brown & Whiten, 2004). When tested in the two-action task portrayed in Figure 11.2 (the task with a plastic box containing a food reward), older children with autism imitated the model's actions normally, but younger children with autism did not (Smith & Bryson, 1998; Whiten & Brown, 1999). Interestingly, imitations of meaningless gestures (like those used in the patty-cake game) and of "nonsense" actions performed with a common object seem more likely to be impaired than meaningful actions (DeMeyer et al., 1972; Smith & Bryson, 1994; Williams, Whiten, & Singh, 2004). These findings suggest that there is not an overarching imitative capacity that is "broken" in individuals with autism, but that certain tasks requiring imitation are difficult for them.

As mentioned earlier, spontaneous inappropriate copying of observed speech and actions is actually typical of autism, so why might children with autism have difficulty voluntarily imitating meaningless actions? Neural abnormalities associated with autism provide some clues. Several areas in the brains of individuals with autism are anatomically abnormal, including the sensory cortex, prefrontal cortex, hippocampus, cerebellum, amygdala, and basal ganglia (Brambilla et al., 2003; Minshew & Williams, 2007; Waterhouse et al., 1996). Structural MRI studies show that the cerebellum, temporal lobes (including the hippocampus), amygdala, and corpus callosum of individuals with autism are often abnormal in

Kim Gunkel/Getty Images

Teaching through demonstration Children with autism spectrum disorder often show atypical imitation abilities. Given that adults often try to teach children how to perform tasks by providing demonstrations, how might this affect what children with autism spectrum disorder learn during their early years?

size. In addition, functional MRI experiments show less overall activity-related circulation of blood within the temporal lobes as well as abnormal patterns of cortical activation. Many of these differences in brain structure and function seem to result from abnormal development early in life. One or more of these affected brain regions may contribute to the imitative abnormalities associated with autism.

Researchers have explored whether the mirror neuron system might be contributing to the imitation deficits seen in individuals with autism spectrum disorder (Ramachandran & Oberman, 2006; Rizzolatti & Fabbri-Destro, 2010; Southgate & Hamilton, 2008; Williams, Whiten, Suddendorf, & Perrett, 2001). Neuroimaging studies show that circuits within and around the regions where mirror neurons are thought to be located in these individuals, and patterns of activation within these circuits, differ systematically from those in typical brains (Martineau et al., 2010; Nishitani, Avikainen, & Hari, 2004; Waiter et al., 2004). For example, individuals with autism spectrum disorder showed slower activation of cortical regions when asked to imitate facial expressions. In these studies, measures of cortical activity were recorded using a magnetoencephalograph (MEG) while participants were imitating facial expressions. MEGs are similar to EEGs except that instead of recording changes in electrical activity in a person's brain over time, MEGs record changes in magnetic fields generated by the brain, which are measured with highly sensitive magnetometers. Imitations started later and took longer to complete in individuals with autism spectrum disorder. Measurements using MEG showed that when all participants were imitating the expressions, different cortical regions became active at different times, in the following sequence: (1) visual cortex, (2) auditory cortex, (3) parietal cortex, (4) frontal cortex, and (5) motor cortex. Each of these regions was slower to become active in individuals with autism spectrum disorder, suggesting that in those individuals, the cortical processes contributing to imitation were impaired.

In monkeys, mirror neurons vary in their responsiveness to specific observed and performed actions (Rizzolatti & Sinigaglia, 2010). Some respond only to observed actions, whereas others respond to a wider range of stimuli. If some networks of mirror neurons in a person's brain are dysfunctional, the person could suffer deficits in particular imitative abilities, such as the ability to imitate nonfunctional actions (Williams et al., 2001; Ramachandran & Oberman, 2006). Because individuals with autism spectrum disorder have difficulty imitating only certain actions, their deficit could be related to abnormal function in a subset of mirror neurons rather than to a general dysfunction of cortical neural circuits involved in imitation. Alternatively, their deficit might reflect weaknesses in several interacting neural systems, with mirror neurons playing a less critical role (Leighton et al., 2008; Southgate & Hamilton, 2008).

At the moment, it is not clear whether the deficit seen in individuals with autism spectrum disorder is truly an imitative deficit or whether it might instead be a deficit in mechanisms underlying stimulus enhancement, emulation, reinforcement mechanisms, emotional processes, or generalization from past experience. Just as many nonimitative actions can look like imitation, many apparent deficits in imitative abilities may actually be deficits in mechanisms other than those directly involved in imitation. As our understanding of social learning processes increases, so will our understanding of the roles different brain regions and learning mechanisms play in autism spectrum disorder.

Test Your Knowledge

Imitative Deficits in Individuals with Autism Spectrum Disorder

Individuals with autism spectrum disorder show several abnormalities in their ability to imitate actions. Try to identify which of the below are consistent with imitative deficits observed in these individuals. (Answers appear in the back of the book.)

1. A loud sound leads to a panic response.
2. One specific cartoon is repeatedly watched.
3. The individual has problems when trying to keep up with a fitness video.
4. On the phone, the individual often repeats the last phrase she heard.

Imitative Deficits after Stroke

Individuals with autism spectrum disorder have atypical imitative capacities because of abnormal brain development. Similar deficits can also occur, however, after brain injuries. As noted in Chapter 8, a common source of brain damage is stroke, which causes neurons in the affected region to die, effectively creating a brain lesion. Stroke-related damage in any of several brain regions is known to disrupt imitative abilities.

Frontal-lobe damage in particular can affect imitation abilities. Alexander Luria discovered that patients with frontal-lobe damage tend to produce involuntary imitative responses (Luria, 1966). This tendency included echolalia, which you may recall is also common in individuals with autism spectrum disorder. Luria examined unintentional imitative responses in his patients by having them perform an action at the same time that he performed a related but incompatible action. For example, Luria might show his fist immediately after asking a patient to hold up his palm. Often, seeing Luria make a fist would interfere with a frontal-lobe patient's ability to show his palm when instructed to do so. The patient would tend instead to involuntarily imitate Luria. Patients with reduced activity in the frontal lobes (such as occurs during major depressive episodes) also show this tendency to automatically imitate observed actions (Archibald, Mateer, & Kerns, 2001). Luria's finding suggests that activity in frontal-lobe circuits normally inhibits such imitation.

To further explore this tendency, a group of researchers measured the degree to which observations of finger movements interfered with the ability of patients with brain damage to move their fingers in response to commands (Brass, Derrfuss, Matthes-von Cramon, & von Cramon, 2003). Patients were asked to lift their index finger from a key when they saw the numeral 1 and to lift their middle finger when they saw the numeral 2. While they performed this task, they watched either a video image of a stationary hand, a video image of a hand producing finger movements consistent with the presented numeral, or a video of a hand producing movements inconsistent with the presented numeral (Figure 11.10a). Frontal-lobe patients made more mistakes than patients with nonfrontal lesions when the movement on the video was inconsistent with the instruction (Figure 11.10b), because they were less able to stop themselves from imitating observed finger movements.

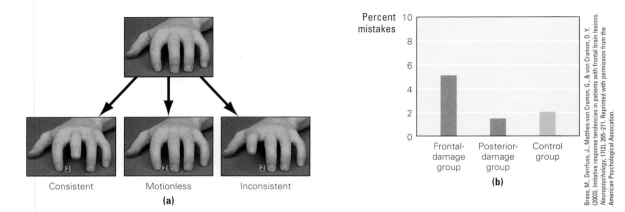

Brass, M., Derrfuss, J., Matthes-von Cramon, G., & von Cramon, D. Y. (2003). Imitative response tendencies in patients with frontal brain lesions. *Neuropsychology,* 17(2), 265–271. Reprinted with permission from the American Psychological Association.

Figure 11.10 Spontaneous imitation induced by frontal-lobe damage Patients with lesions in the frontal cortex or posterior cortex and control participants with no lesions were asked to perform specific finger movements in response to numerals displayed on a screen while ignoring the movements of a hand shown on the screen. (a) The finger movements shown on the screen were either consistent with the instructions or inconsistent with the instructions. (b) Patients with frontal-lobe lesions were more likely (5% versus 2%) to make a mistake when the finger movement shown was inconsistent with the movement corresponding to the displayed numeral.

Research from Brass, Derrfuss, Matthes-von Cramon, & von Cramon, 2003.

As in autism spectrum disorder, increases in automatic imitation after a stroke are often correlated with deficits in the ability to voluntarily imitate actions. Note that both conditions suggest a loss of autonomy, specifically a lost ability to decide or control which observed acts to copy. Cortical circuits in the frontal and parietal lobes may enable people to control when observations (or memories of observations) guide their actions.

Interim Summary

- Individuals with autism spectrum disorder may repeat words or phrases immediately after hearing them spoken. This phenomenon, called echolalia, requires vocal imitation abilities. However, children with autism spectrum disorder actually seem less able to learn from imitation than typically developing children.

- Patients with frontal-lobe lesions tend to imitate observed actions automatically, but have difficulty imitating actions when instructed to do so, like children with autism spectrum disorder.

Synthesis

Sticking out your tongue at people to indicate you dislike them is probably not an innate response (although as noted in Chapter 10 on emotional learning and memory, tongue protrusion is an unconditioned response to bad tastes). When Leti's mother sees Leti sticking out her tongue at a neighbor's child, she is likely to conclude that Leti learned this gesture by imitating someone else. Perhaps Leti did learn to stick out her tongue through imitation, as her mother suspects, but many other mechanisms could also account for her learning to do this that do not require copying. Imitation, observational conditioning, stimulus enhancement, and social transmission of information are some of the mechanisms that make social learning—learning through the observation of others—possible in humans and certain other animals. Determining which social learning mechanisms contribute to specific changes in an individual's behavior is a major challenge that psychologists are still grappling with.

Perhaps Leti's older sister told her to go stick out her tongue at the neighbor. This kind of active instruction through social transmission of information seems to be limited to humans and is closely tied to language abilities. You're receiving socially transmitted information at this very moment. Social transmission of information through lectures and textbooks forms the basis for learning in many courses taught in universities and colleges.

College instructors rely on social learning What sorts of social learning are professors trying to promote by giving lectures?

Learning theorists have traditionally assumed that learning results from the conditioning of passive reflexive reactions (classical conditioning) or from the reinforcement of voluntary responses (operant conditioning). Is social learning anything more than a mixture of classical and operant conditioning? Research into how different cortical and subcortical brain regions mediate social learning is already providing some insights into this issue. As you might expect, some social learning processes, such as observational conditioning, can be explained as a special case of classical conditioning. Other abilities—as when humans, apes, and dolphins imitate actions on command—are more difficult to account for in terms of incremental-learning models and instead seem to require unique cortical-processing mechanisms.

Understanding what happens when social learning mechanisms go awry can also lead to new ideas about how social learning works. Correlating the imitative deficits in individuals with autism spectrum disorder with those of stroke patients may provide clues about the relationship between automatic imitation and voluntary imitation. The fact that in both conditions echolalia tends to co-occur with involuntary imitation of actions and with an inability to imitate certain actions on command suggests that vocal and visually based imitation may rely on overlapping neural systems. At the same time, many current psychological models of imitation assume that visually based imitation of actions requires processes that are fundamentally different from those involved in vocal imitation.

Albert Bandura has suggested that social learning is a process that permits the rapid, errorless acquisition of cognitive and perceptual–motor skills and that humans who take full advantage of this process have "learned to learn." From this perspective, social learning is itself a cognitive skill of the sort described in Chapter 8 (involving learning-set formation), and understanding how individuals learn to learn from others is simply an extension of understanding how organisms form learning sets when acquiring cognitive skills. With luck, future behavioral and physiological studies of social learning processes will one day help scientists to reveal the mechanisms that enable students to learn to learn.

KNOW YOUR KEY TERMS

autism spectrum disorder, *p. 464*
copying, *p. 441*
direct-matching hypothesis, *p. 460*
echolalia, *p. 464*
emotional contagion, *p. 446*
emulation, *p. 443*
mirror neuron, *p. 460*
modeling, *p. 442*

observational conditioning, *p. 446*
observational learning, *p. 440*
perspective taking, *p. 445*
social conformity, *p. 455*
social learning, *p. 440*
social learning theory, *p. 442*
social transmission of
    information, *p. 452*

stimulus enhancement, *p. 448*
template model of song
    learning, *p. 452*
true imitation, *p. 443*
two-action test, *p. 443*
vocal imitation, *p. 449*
vocal learning, *p. 451*

QUIZ YOURSELF

1. A child that copies adults who crazily beat on inflatable dolls provides evidence of _____ learning because his observations have produced a change in his behavior. (p. 440)

2. A toddler who makes a stuffed animal pretend to talk after observing her sibling do this may be _____ her sibling. (p. 441)

3. A chimpanzee that learns to open doors by banging them with its feet from seeing humans open doors with their hands is likely showing evidence of _____. (p. 443)

4. The two-action test requires training _____ to serve as models performing a task that observers will be allowed to watch. (p. 443)

5. The two-action test has been used by researchers to test whether animals are capable of _____. (p. 443)

6. The ability to imagine what it would be like to be in a commercial requires _____. (p. 445)

7. The reason that laugh tracks are used so often in sitcoms is because hearing laughter leads to _____. (p. 446)

8. If crows learn to attack all clowns after seeing other crows attacking clowns, then this is likely a case of _____. (p. 446)

9. In observational conditioning, observation of a model produces a(n) _____. (p. 446)

10. If one crying baby on an airplane triggers a flurry of crying infants, then this is likely due to _____. (p. 446)

11. When a model on a game show waves her arms in front of a prize contestants may win, this may lead to _____. (p. 448)

12. True imitation differs from _____ in that true imitation requires replicating the actions of a model. (p. 443)

13. Stimulus enhancement may be mistaken for _____ because the actions of the observer match the actions of the "model." (p. 448–452)

14. Birds are important subjects in studies of neural and behavioral social learning because of their _____ ability. (p. 451)

15. One form of imitation that is rare among mammals is _____. (p. 449)

16. A(n) _____ has the ability to imitate both sounds and actions. (p. 449)

17. Speech imitation in humans is an example of _____. (p. 449)

18. The fact that some songbirds raised alone never sing normally is evidence that _____ is important for their song development. (p. 451)

19. The _____ suggests that songbirds memorize the songs of adults before learning to sing them. (p. 452)

20. When observer rats learn to prefer certain foods from exposure to other rats, this is a case of _____. (p. 452)

21. If you take notes in class because other students do, but never actually look at them, then this could be an instance of _____. (p. 455)

22. The _____ states that observations are directly mapped onto motor representations. (p. 460)

23. Cells that respond when a monkey grabs a stick or sees someone grab a stick are called _____ . (p. 460)

24. Brain regions in humans that respond similarly when a person performs finger movements or observes finger movements are found in the _____. (p. 467)

25. Song learning by birds involves activity in a brain region known as _____. (p. 462)

26. For social transmission of food preferences to occur normally in rats, their _____ must be intact. (p. 463)

27. Children with autism spectrum disorder often repeat sounds or sentences they have recently

heard, a phenomenon known as _____. (p. 464)

28. Because individuals with autism show difficulties performing certain imitation tasks, it has been theorized that they have dysfunctional _____. (p. 466)

29. Patients with _____ show a tendency to imitate actions involuntarily. (p. 467)

30. Findings from Bandura's_____ study have been used to argue that children exposed to violence are more likely to behave violently. (p. 457)

Answers appear in the back of the book.

CONCEPT CHECK

1. Some researchers have suggested that the only way you can be sure that you are observing imitation is if the actions or sounds being copied are so bizarre that there is no other plausible explanation for why they might occur (Thorpe, 1963). What are some other ways researchers can tell when an animal is truly imitating?

2. Edward Thorndike (1898) defined imitation as learning to do an act from seeing it done, but visual observations are not the only way to get the information needed to imitate or emulate. What are some examples of imitative actions described in this chapter that would not count as imitation under Thorndike's definition?

3. In the wild, animals may gain an advantage from spending more effort investigating areas that have been occupied by other members of the same species. Such behavior could increase the chances of finding food, mates, or a safe place to hide. What forms of social learning might provide animals with these advantages?

4. Children may (a) be born with an ability to copy that depends on specialized mechanisms for matching visual perceptions to motor responses (Meltzoff, 1996; Piaget, 1955), (b) learn to copy through experience, and (c) consciously consider the perspective or social status of other individuals when they copy (Guillaume, 1971). For which of these types of learning have neural substrates been identified?

5. Albert Bandura argued that operant conditioning without imitation is an inefficient way of learning new actions and that only humans learn by copying because learning from models requires abstracting rules and forming memories based on verbal codes and imagery (Bandura, 1986). List information from this chapter that either supports or refutes these ideas.

Answers appear in the back of the book.

CHAPTER 12

Development and Aging

Learning and Memory across the Lifespan

TWENTY-YEAR-OLD DENISE IS ENTERING THE PRIME OF HER LIFE. As a state champion on the basketball court, she understands that her body is at the peak of its physical strength and stamina. As a college student, she challenges her brain every day to learn new skills, organize and retrieve information for exams, and integrate new knowledge—including what she's studied in her learning and memory course—into her broadening understanding of the adult world.

At Thanksgiving, Denise goes home to visit her family and plays with her young nieces and nephews. The youngest, Kelly, is a 10-month-old, busily soaking up information about the world. Kelly is just beginning to stand and start walking, to recognize and respond to spoken words, and to produce babbling sounds that will someday lead to fluent language.

Denise's grandparents are the oldest family members gathered for the holiday. Her grandmother, a wise, funny woman, is a walking library of family history and special recipes. But Denise's grandfather has gone downhill since last Thanksgiving. He repeats the same stories over and over again and has trouble remembering Kelly's name. The family worries that this is not just normal old age but a sign of something more serious, such as Alzheimer's disease. The specter of this worry hangs over the family's holiday celebration.

In this chapter, we'll trace the development of learning and memory abilities across the lifespan, starting with infants like Kelly and culminating with elderly individuals like Denise's grandparents. You'll recognize many types of memory that were introduced in earlier chapters, but here we'll view them from the standpoint of how a person's memory changes over the lifespan and how this reflects underlying age-related changes in the brain. You'll also encounter topics that may be new to you, such as the ability of adult brains to grow new neurons, the effects of sex hormones

Behavioral Processes

The Developing Memory: Infancy through Childhood

Sensitive Periods for Early Learning

Learning and Memory in Everyday Life: Teaching Babies Signs before Speech

Adolescence: Crossing from Childhood into Adulthood

The Aging Memory: Adulthood through Old Age

Brain Substrates

The Genetic Basis of Learning and Memory

Learning and Memory in Everyday Life: Can Exposure to Classical Music Make Babies Smarter?

Neurons and Synapses in the Developing Brain

Brain Changes in Adolescence

The Brain from Adulthood to Old Age

Clinical Perspectives

Down Syndrome

Alzheimer's Disease

A Connection between Down Syndrome and Alzheimer's Disease

Learning and Memory in Everyday Life: Can Mental Exercise Protect against Alzheimer's Disease?

Kurt Stricker/Getty Images

on developing and mature memories, and the concept of sensitive periods—"windows of opportunity"—for specific kinds of learning, after which such learning may never again be so easy or effective.

12.1 Behavioral Processes

One reason to study learning and memory across the lifespan is to understand the different capabilities of children compared to young adults and of young adults compared to older adults. Understanding the kinds of learning and memory that are comparatively strong or weak at each age can help us make the most of our potential at every stage of life and can also help educators tailor their teaching methods to different age groups.

As you read, though, be sure to keep in mind that we're talking about the *average* learning and memory abilities of groups at various ages. Within any age group, there is wide variation in the abilities of individuals. For one thing, certain kinds of memory can mature at different rates, so that there are always some youngsters who show a different pattern of development, acquiring new abilities faster or slower than their peers. Similarly, at the other end of the lifespan, certain kinds of learning and memory tend to decline, but others keep going strong—while in some unfortunate individuals, cognitive abilities decline at an accelerated rate, due to injury or disease such as Alzheimer's disease.

With these thoughts in mind, let's begin at the beginning: with the learning and memory of individuals at the earliest stages of life.

The Developing Memory: Infancy through Childhood

If you've spent any time with a young child, you've witnessed the immense surge of learning that takes place in the first few years of life. In those years, a child acquires abilities ranging from the motor skills needed to grasp and walk, to the ability to produce and understand language, to a fund of semantic knowledge about the world. Learning continues across the lifespan, of course, but its progress is especially dramatic in young children. More recently, it's become apparent that some learning occurs even before birth.

Learning before Birth

The human uterus is a surprisingly noisy place. A human fetus is exposed to the sounds of maternal speech and heartbeats as well as noises from the outside world. By about 25 weeks of **gestational age**, or time since conception, a fetus's brain and sense organs are sufficiently developed for the fetus to start perceiving and learning about these sounds.

For example, remember from Chapter 3 that *habituation* is the phenomenon of reduced responding to a repeated stimulus. Habituation can be used to test fetal learning about sounds. Researchers place a speaker against the mother's abdomen and play sounds that the fetus can hear. The first time a sound plays, most human fetuses with gestational ages of 34 to 36 weeks will respond by moving (Figure 12.1). If the same sound is played several times, the fetuses gradually stop responding (Hepper & Shahidullah, 1992). When a different sound is played, the responses reappear—indicating that the loss of response to the first stimulus was due to habituation, not fatigue. Eventually, responses to the second stimulus habituate too. When the first sound is played again, the fetuses respond but habituate almost immediately, indicating that they "remember" having experienced that sound before. Fetal habituation can be observed in nonhuman species too, including rats (Smotherman & Robinson, 1992).

gestational age. Time since conception.

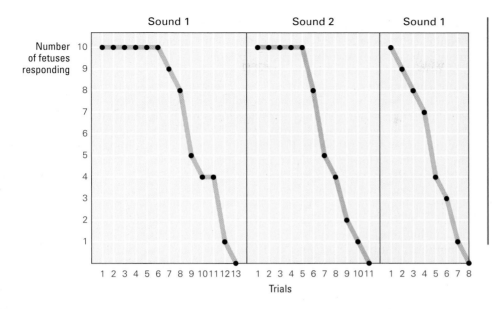

Number of fetuses responding

Trials

Figure 12.1 Habituation to sound in 10 human fetuses
When sound 1 is presented, all 10 human fetuses initially respond with movement; as the sound is repeated, the number of fetuses responding decreases. By trial 13, all have habituated. When a new stimulus (sound 2) is presented, all the fetuses again respond; this response also habituates over about a dozen trials. Finally, the original stimulus (sound 1) is presented again. The fetuses show spontaneous recovery of responding followed by fast habituation (only 8 trials).

Information from Hepper & Shahidullah, 1992.

Such prenatal learning can persist after birth. Researchers Anthony DeCasper and Melanie Spence constructed a set of short stories with strong, simple rhyming patterns, such as excerpts from Dr. Seuss's *The Cat in the Hat* (DeCasper & Spence, 1986). The researchers then asked mothers in the last six weeks of pregnancy to read one of these stories aloud to their unborn babies, twice a day. Two or three days after birth, each newborn was placed in a crib with an artificial nipple positioned where the infant could suck at it. Under these conditions, infants usually suck in bursts: giving a series of brisk individual sucks, pausing a few seconds, and then giving another burst of sucks. For this experiment, the nipple was rigged so that each burst of sucking caused a tape recorder to turn on and play a story recorded in the mother's voice. But it wasn't always the same story. For one set of babies, if a sucking burst followed a longer-than-average pause, then the familiar story played, but if a sucking burst followed a shorter-than-average pause, then an unfamiliar story played:

S^D (artificial nipple) → R (long pause before sucking burst) → O (familiar story)

S^D (artificial nipple) → R (short pause before sucking burst) → O (novel story)

For other babies, the contingencies were reversed so that short pauses triggered the familiar story and long pauses triggered the novel story. Over a period of 20 minutes, the infants changed their sucking behavior, timing their pauses in such a way as to result in the familiar story being played more often. In short, the familiar story reinforced a particular pattern of sucking behavior. This learning is an example of *operant conditioning*, which you read about in Chapter 5. Obviously, the babies did not understand the meaning of the words in either story; the difference in their responses probably reflected an ability to discriminate the cadence and rhythm of the two stories. Still, the study demonstrates that prenatal infants are capable of learning and that the learned information persists and can affect behavior after birth. DeCasper and colleagues suggest that fetal exposure to the mother's language patterns may help the brain start to encode language-relevant speech sounds, giving the babies a head start on acquiring language after birth (DeCasper, Lecanuet, Busnel, Granier-Deferre, & Maugeais, 1994). Studies such as this show that newborns come into the world not as blank slates, but having already experienced stimuli and begun to learn about them.

Conditioning and Skill Learning in Young Children

Despite evidence for fetal learning, the really impressive learning machines are infants. An explosion in learning marks the first few years of life in humans and analogous periods in other species. Just about every kind of learning that is present in adults is present in infants, at least in a rudimentary form. On the other hand, some of an infant's perceptual and motor systems are immature. Until these input and output systems develop more fully, an infant cannot begin to learn about certain stimuli or to express her learning using motor responses (Gerhardstein & West, 2003). For example, cats are born with their eyes sealed shut, so they obviously can't learn much about visual stimuli that are presented to them in the first few hours of life.

For humans, acquisition of *complex motor skills* comes gradually, as physical development produces gradual improvements in muscle strength and perceptual-motor coordination. Newborn humans cannot even hold their heads up unsupported, but most babies can roll over by the time they are 5.5 months old; by 7 months, most can sit up; by a year, most have learned to stand alone or even walk. As coordination improves, babies develop the fine motor skills needed for accurate eye tracking, babbling, and reaching to pick up objects. Skill acquisition is not limited to motor skills either; between 1 and 2 years of age, children begin to master the rudiments of language, and complex grammar and reading are usually evident by 4 to 5 years.

You read above that infants can show operant conditioning, learning particular sucking responses that produce outcomes such as tape recordings turning on and off. In another operant conditioning procedure, researchers hang a mobile over an infant's crib, then tie one end of a ribbon to the baby's leg and the other end to the mobile. When the baby kicks her leg, the mobile moves:

$$S^D \text{ (crib with mobile)} \rightarrow O \text{ (kick)} \rightarrow C \text{ (mobile moves)}$$

Just like a rat in a Skinner box, the baby makes her first response by chance. The resulting movement of the mobile, which babies find highly entertaining, reinforces this kicking response. Babies as young as 2 months of age quickly learn to kick vigorously to produce mobile movement (Rovee-Collier, 1993, 1997, 1999). The babies can maintain memory of this learned response for a few days with no reminders—or for up to 21 weeks if they receive periodic reminders in which they see the mobile move when an out-of-sight experimenter pulls the ribbon (Hayne, 1996).

One of the most interesting features of this operant learning in babies is that it is context-dependent, just like the adult learning you read about in Chapter 6. For example, in one variant of the mobile experiment, learning takes place in a crib with a striped crib liner. If this liner is replaced with one having a different pattern, the babies gape passively at the mobile—but don't kick (Borovsky & Rovee-Collier, 1990). Apparently, the change in crib liners represents a new context in which the old rules might not continue to hold. Infants, just like adults, incorporate details of the context during ongoing learning.

Classical conditioning takes place in infants, too. In Chapter 4, you read about eyeblink conditioning, in which a human or rabbit learns that a tone or light (the conditioned stimulus, or CS) predicts an airpuff (the unconditioned stimulus, or US). In the *delay-conditioning* paradigm, the CS and US overlap and co-terminate. With repeated CS–US pairings, the human or rabbit learns to respond to the CS by producing an eyeblink (the conditioned response, or CR) so that the eye is protected when the US arrives (see Figure 4.8).

Operant learning in infants
Movement of the mobile reinforces kicks. After the infant has learned this association, what do you think would happen if the ribbon connecting the infant's ankle to the mobile were removed?

Courtesy of Carolyn Rovee-Collier/George H. Collier Estate.

Infant humans can learn eyeblink CRs in the delay-conditioning paradigm, and so can infant rats, although in both species the infants learn more slowly than adults do (Ivkovich, Collins, Eckerman, Krasnegor, & Stanton, 1999; Ivkovich, Paczkowski, & Stanton, 2000; Little, Lipsett, & Rovee-Collier, 1984). By contrast, in the more difficult *trace-conditioning* paradigm, where there is a gap between the end of the CS and the arrival of the US, 2-month-old infant humans can't learn the eyeblink CR. By 4 years of age, children can learn the CR, but they learn it much more slowly than in the delay-conditioning paradigm; in contrast, young adult humans learn both paradigms about equally quickly (Herbert, Eckerman, & Stanton, 2003). In summary, the basic components of classical conditioning are available in very young individuals, but the capacity continues to develop as the organism matures, allowing the organism to learn more efficiently and under increasingly difficult conditions.

You read in Chapter 6 that an important aspect of conditioning (and all learning) is *generalization*, the ability to transfer past learning to new situations. One way to assess generalization is via *acquired equivalence*, in which learning about one stimulus generalizes to other stimuli that have been equivalent in the past (see Figure 6.26). For example, a child raised in a bilingual home may observe her English-speaking grandparents using one set of labels to refer to objects ("cat," "bottle"), while her Spanish-speaking grandparents use different labels for the same objects ("gato," "botella"). If she hears her Spanish-speaking grandmother refer to a new object as "perro," she should infer that her other Spanish-speaking relatives, but not the English-speaking ones, will use that same word. In the laboratory, 8-month-old infants show surprise when such rules are violated, indicating that this form of generalization is present even at a very young age (Werchan, Collins, Frank, & Amso, 2015). In fact, accumulating evidence suggests that even seemingly passive infants are active learners, who can develop fairly sophisticated hypotheses about how the environment behaves, use generalization to make predictions based on these hypotheses, and notice (and react with surprise) when these predictions are violated (Xu & Kushnir, 2013).

Development of Episodic and Semantic Memory

As you read back in Chapter 7, *semantic memory* involves factual knowledge, whereas *episodic memory* is memory for specific autobiographical events, including the spatial and temporal context in which the events occurred. Both episodic and semantic memory are most often tested through recall and recognition tests, but this is obviously not possible with pre-verbal infants. Researchers have been resourceful in devising creative techniques that allow infants to express their knowledge even if they can't yet speak about it.

One such technique for assessing memories in preverbal infants is **elicited imitation**, in which infants are shown an action and tested for their ability to mimic this action later (Bauer, 1996). For example, researchers showed a group of 10-month-old children how to operate a toy puppet. Four months later, they presented the children with the same toy puppet. These children showed more interest and ability in operating the puppet than did a second group of same-age children who had never seen the puppet used (N. Myers, Perris, & Speaker, 1994). This difference suggests that the very young children had at least some memory of the puppet, even if they couldn't verbalize it (Rovee-Collier, 1999).

elicited imitation. A technique for assessing memory in infants by observing their ability to mimic actions they have seen earlier.

Once children grow a little older and start to acquire language, it becomes much easier to investigate semantic memory. During the first few months of age, children begin to imitate the speech sounds they hear around them, and by about 1 to 2 years of age, babies learn and use individual words, usually acquiring a vocabulary of several hundred words (mostly nouns and verbs). Over the next few years, vocabulary continues to develop and children also begin to acquire a knowledge of *syntax*, or the rules governing how words are arranged into sentences. In addition, children learn about physical objects and events; a toddler's incessant "Why?" questions reflect how she is soaking up semantic information about the world. Much of this information, acquired in early childhood, remains with us for life.

Episodic memory matures more slowly than semantic memory. One factor may be that parts of the brain, such as the hippocampus and prefrontal cortex, which are critical for encoding and recall of episodic memories, are immature in humans at birth and continue to develop during the first few years of life (Durston et al., 2001; Serres 2001). Another factor may be that very young children do not show evidence of a "cognitive self." One widely used test of whether a child has a sense of self is whether she can recognize herself in the mirror. If a researcher surreptitiously marks a child's face with rouge and the child sees herself in the mirror and touches the marked spot, then we may conclude that the child recognizes the image as her own ("Hey, that's me—and what's that red dot doing on my nose?"). Infants younger than 16 months don't show mirror-recognition behavior, but children older than 24 months do (Lewis & Brooks-Gunn, 1979). This implies that 2-year-olds, but not 1-year-olds, have a sense of themselves as individuals. This cognitive milestone is probably a prerequisite for forming autobiographical memories (Howe & Courage, 1993). You can't remember that a particular event happened to you unless you have a sense of yourself and how you exist in time (Fivush & Nelson, 2004).

On the other hand, some infancy researchers, notably Carolyn Rovee-Collier and colleagues, argue that even very young children can and do form episodic memories—they just may not be able to communicate these verbally the way older children can (Rovee-Collier & Cuevas, 2009). In this sense, the "failure" of young children to display episodic memory is really a failure of the researchers' experimental design.

You may recall the experiment from Chapter 7 in which researchers assessed "episodic-like" memory by observing scrub jays digging for worms and nuts in an ice cube tray (Figure 7.3); the birds displayed evidence of remembering what, where, and when the items were buried, causing many researchers to conclude that the birds had a memory for the specific episode, including the spatial and temporal context, in which the burying occurred. Harlene Hayne and Kana Imuta developed an analogous task for young children, based on the game of hide-and-seek (Hayne & Imuta, 2011). Children may not be motivated to dig for worms and nuts, but they do like toys and are highly motivated to retrieve them. In the task, children hid three different stuffed toys in three separate locations around their own homes. Later, experimenters asked the children to verbally recall what (e.g., "the Eeyore toy") was hidden, where ("the bedroom"), and when ("the last room we entered"). Unsurprisingly, 4-year-old children recalled more information than 3-year-old children (Figure 12.2). But then the experimenters gave a behavioral test, asking the children

A test of self-awareness A red dot is placed on a child's face and the child is placed in front of the mirror. If the child tries to wipe the dot off her face, researchers conclude the child recognizes her own reflection, providing evidence of self-awareness and a sense of self. Why might a sense of self be considered a prerequisite for episodic memory?

Angela Georges/Getty Images

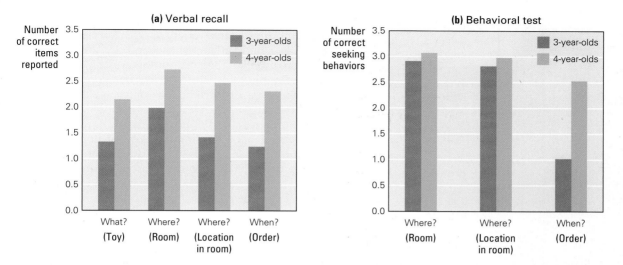

Figure 12.2 Episodic-like memory in children Just like in non-verbal animals, very young children can display memory for what happened where and when, even if they cannot yet verbalize those memories well. (a) 3- and 4-year-old children were asked to hide three stuffed toys around their homes. Later, the 3-year-olds were worse than the 4-year-olds at verbally reporting the what, where, and when of these events. (b) But when allowed to demonstrate their knowledge through behavior ("Can you show me the toy we hid first?"), the 3-year-olds performed as well as the 4-year-olds at remembering what was hidden where (which room and what specific location within the room), though they were still impaired at remembering the temporal order in which objects were hidden ("when"). Information from Hayne & Imuta, 2011.

questions such as: "Can you show me the room we went into first, and find who is hiding there?" Now 3-year-olds were just as good as 4-year-olds at remembering what was hidden where, although they were still not quite as good as the older children at remembering the temporal order of events. This study makes two important points: the first is that even children as young as 3 years old can display episodic-like memory, even if they cannot always report those memories verbally. Second, the 4-year-olds performed better, indicating that memory for temporal context, at least, continues to grow and mature over this period, along with the ability to express that information verbally.

Sensitive Periods for Early Learning

As you've just read, many kinds of learning are functional early in life but become more efficient as the organism matures. Sometimes, the opposite is true. In some species, certain kinds of learning are most effective early in life, during a specific time window known as a **sensitive period**.

Imprinting

One example of a sensitive period is **imprinting**, which refers to the fact that animals of many species, including birds, are especially likely to form an attachment to the first individual they see after birth (Insel & Fernald, 2004; Lorenz, 1935). Normally, the first individual a baby bird sees is its mother or a sibling in the nest, and so the chick appropriately imprints on a member of its own species. But, in a classic series of experiments, researcher Konrad Lorenz found that if he removed a newly hatched goose chick from an incubator, the chick would imprint on him—and would follow him about as if he were its mother. If the gosling were later placed among a brood of goose chicks following a goose mother, it would ignore the members of its own species in preference for following its human "parent." Researchers have since shown that chicks can be induced to imprint not only on individuals of the wrong species but even on rotating cylinders and

sensitive period. A time window, usually early in life, during which a certain kind of learning is most effective.

imprinting. The tendency of young animals of some species to form an attachment to the first individual they see after birth.

Thomas D. McAvoy/*Time Magazine*

Researcher Konrad Lorenz being followed by goslings that imprinted on him because he was the first moving object they saw after hatching. Thereafter, they responded to him as if he were their mother. Why might imprinting normally serve a useful function for young geese?

stuffed chickens (Johnson, 1992). Since Lorenz's time, imprinting has been demonstrated in a variety of other species, including turkeys, sheep, deer, and buffalo (Michel & Tyler, 2005).

It used to be thought that imprinting was an example of learning that had not just a sensitive period, but a *critical period*—meaning that this type of learning was only possible during a limited time window, and after the window closed, no further learning could ever occur. But it's now known that, at least under some circumstances, the time window for imprinting can be extended, and imprinting can sometimes even be unlearned (Thomas & Johnson, 2008). For this reason, most researchers use the term *sensitive period* to refer to time windows when learning is particularly fast or effective, without necessarily claiming that learning at other times will be downright impossible.

Sensitive Periods for Vision and Birdsong

Many other types of learning show sensitive periods. You already read about one example back in Chapter 3: tuning of neurons in the visual cortex. David Hubel and Torsten Wiesel conducted a classic series of studies in which they sewed shut one eye of newborn cats or monkeys and then after several weeks reopened the eye (Hubel & Wiesel, 1977, 1998). The result? The animals were "blind" in that eye even though they had no physical damage to the visual system. For cats, the period from about 3 weeks to 60 days after birth is a sensitive period for the development of the visual system; for monkeys, the period may last for about the first 6 months of life. Similar effects are seen in human infants who are born with cataracts that block vision in one eye. If corrective surgery is performed within a few months of birth, vision will develop normally (Maurer & Lewis, 1999), but if surgery is delayed for a few years, normal vision never develops (Vaegan, 1979).

Another example is song learning in birds. You read in Chapter 11 how some species of birds learn by listening to and imitating adults of their species. Adult white-crowned sparrows have a repertoire of about seven different sounds that serve various functions, including territory defense and courtship. Six of these sounds are more or less the same in all white-crowned sparrows, but one—the male song—differs by geographical location. In effect, male sparrows from different regions have different "dialects," just as people in different regions may speak the same language but have different accents. Normally, a male white-crowned sparrow spends his first 10 days or so in the nest and then moves out to live independently from, but close to, his parents. During the next few months, he will hear his father and other male neighbors sing, and eventually, he himself will begin to sing, using the same "dialect" as they do.

Male sparrows raised in isolation, with no opportunity to hear other adults, begin to sing too, but their songs are abnormal (Marler, 1970). Males raised in isolation but allowed to hear tape recordings of male song can learn normally as long as they hear the song during days 30 through 100 of their life (Marler, 1970). Earlier or later exposure is of no use: once the sensitive period has passed, the males will not learn normal song.

Language Learning

Some researchers have suggested that human language learning also has a sensitive period, which ends by about age 12 (or earlier). Early evidence for this idea came from the famous and tragic case of "Genie," a girl whose psychotic father kept her locked in an isolated room, chained to a potty chair, punishing her if she made any noise (Curtiss, 1977). The California authorities took Genie away from her parents in 1970, when she was 13 years old. At the time, Genie weighed only 59 pounds and could not straighten her arms or legs nor control her bladder or bowels. She could not speak at all.

Over the next several years, physicians, psychologists, and social workers worked hard to undo the damage that had been done to Genie. Her health improved greatly, and her IQ appeared to be in the low-normal range. But her language never developed beyond that of a 3- to 4-year-old. She could utter simple sentences ("want food"), but not much more. Apparently, Genie's lack of exposure to language during the first decade of life left her unable to acquire the complex grammar and vocabulary that characterizes normal adult speech (Curtiss, 1977; Rymer, 1994). Similarly, her lack of social interactions during development greatly reduced her opportunities to observe and imitate how people use language. As of 2008, Genie, then age 51, was living in California as a ward of the state and—according to an anonymous report—had once again reverted to speechlessness.

We don't have to look at cases as extreme as Genie to see evidence of a sensitive period in human language learning. In general, children can learn a second language more easily, and approximate a native accent more closely, than adults can (Newport, 1990). This is partly due to a sensitive period for the perceptual learning that allows phonetic discrimination.

Human languages have about 25 to 40 speech sounds (called *phonemes*), but not all languages have the same sounds. Adults who speak one language can distinguish between sounds from their own language but often cannot distinguish between pairs of sounds from non-native languages. For example, the phonemes /l/ and /r/ are distinct in English (so that "ray" and "lay" are different words) but not in Japanese; monolingual Japanese adults often cannot distinguish these two phonemes. On the other hand, monolingual English speakers can't hear the difference between a soft "p" and a sharp "p"—two speech sounds that are meaningfully separate in the Thai language. In effect, the phonemes /r/ and /l/ are part of the same sound category for Japanese speakers, while soft "p" and sharp "p" are part of the same sound category for English speakers.

Infants younger than 6 to 8 months can distinguish all these sounds, even when the distinction does not exist in their native language. Infants can express this learning by turning their head for reinforcement to one sound but not the other. Infants get better at distinguishing speech sounds from their own language as they age but become less able to tell non-native sounds apart (Kuhl, 2000). Thus, a 6-month-old "Japanese-speaking" baby will be able to distinguish "lay" and "ray," but an 11-month-old one will not. Similarly, a 6-month-old "English-speaking" infant can distinguish syllables from Hindi that sound alike to adult English speakers (Figure 12.3), but this ability is lost by about 10 to 12 months

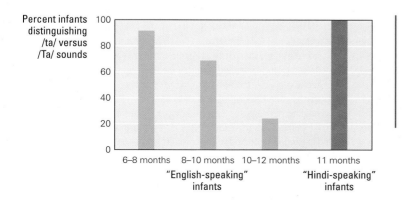

Percent infants distinguishing /ta/ versus /Ta/ sounds

"English-speaking" infants — 6–8 months, 8–10 months, 10–12 months

"Hindi-speaking" infants — 11 months

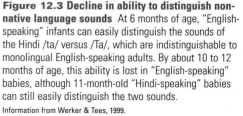

Figure 12.3 Decline in ability to distinguish non-native language sounds At 6 months of age, "English-speaking" infants can easily distinguish the sounds of the Hindi /ta/ versus /Ta/, which are indistinguishable to monolingual English-speaking adults. By about 10 to 12 months of age, this ability is lost in "English-speaking" babies, although 11-month-old "Hindi-speaking" babies can still easily distinguish the two sounds.
Information from Werker & Tees, 1999.

(Werker & Tees, 1999). Apparently, humans acquiring language—like birds acquiring birdsong—have a window of opportunity to learn to distinguish language sounds; beyond that period, learning is possible, but much less effective. Children who are fortunate enough to live in a bilingual home and be exposed to the sounds of multiple languages during this sensitive period are much more likely to grow up to be fluent speakers of those languages than children who must try to learn the sounds later. The same principle that early exposure facilitates fluency holds for gestural languages, such as American Sign Language (ASL), as well as for spoken languages. (For more on the possible relationship between learning spoken and gestural languages, see "Learning and Memory in Everyday Life" below).

On the other hand, not everyone agrees with the idea of a sensitive period for language learning. Adults obviously can master second languages, and they often do so more quickly than children, even if their final level of attainment is not as high (Thomas & Johnson, 2008). Apparently, learning a new language is different in children than in adults. In children, the dominant process is social imitation: children learn to mimic the speech around them. By contrast, in adults the dominant process is semantic memory—adopting explicit strategies such as memorization of new vocabulary (Hudsom Kam & Newport, 2005), although adults also use perceptual-motor and cognitive skills to produce and understand novel sentences. As a result, given an equivalent amount of time to learn a second language, adults and older children often make much faster progress than younger children (Snow & Hoefnagel-Höhle, 1978).

LEARNING AND MEMORY IN EVERYDAY LIFE

Teaching Babies Signs before Speech

In the 2004 movie *Meet the Fockers*, the toddler Little Jack uses sign language to inform his grandfather that he'd like a snack and then a nap, after which he'll probably need a diaper change. Just a Hollywood joke about overambitious parenting, right? Well, maybe not. Based on parents' reports, children as young as 6 to 9 months, who haven't yet mastered spoken language, can use gestures to communicate a desire for more food or for a bottle of milk (Acredolo & Goodwyn, 2002). At about 10 to 12 months, children can reach toward an object to indicate that it is wanted or hold an object upward to direct an adult's attention to it (Goodwyn, Acredolo, & Brown, 2000). A few months later, children master representational gestures, such as flapping their arms to represent "bird" or "flight" or spreading and unspreading the index and middle fingers to connote "scissors" or "cutting." Many studies show a positive correlation between gesturing and verbal development: the more gestures children learn between 1 and 2 years of age, the larger their verbal vocabularies at age 2 or 3 (Capone & McGregor, 2004; Goodwyn et al., 2000).

Why might communicating with gestures facilitate the development of verbal language? Susan Goodwyn and colleagues have suggested several possible reasons (Goodwyn et al., 2000). One is simply that infants learn verbal language more quickly if they are exposed to more vocalizations from their parents. A child who points at a bird in a tree can elicit a parental response ("Yes! That's a birdie!"); a child using 20 such gestures may be able to elicit such responses 10 times more often than a child with only two gestures. A second possibility is that babies (like all creatures) learn best about the things they're interested in. Communicating with gestures may allow the child to show the parent what the *child* is interested in, which then cues the parent to introduce language related to that interest. A third possibility is that communicating with gestures provides a "scaffolding" for the development of verbal language. The child learns an "easy" gesture that in turn provides insight into how useful communication can be, which motivates the child to explore other ways to communicate, including spoken language.

In the meantime, gestural language is a way for toddlers to communicate their needs when they do not have the ability to express themselves verbally. Goodwyn and her colleagues report an example in which a 14-month-old boy was able to use his "hot" gesture (blowing hard) to let his mother know when his bathwater was too hot, while another toddler signaled "gentle" (petting the back of one hand) to complain that her parent was holding her legs too tightly during a diaper change (Goodwyn, Acredolo, & Brown, 2000). This isn't quite the sophistication of Hollywood's Little Jack, but it's still impressive for an infant who would otherwise be reduced to frustrated squalling to get her point across.

Adolescence: Crossing from Childhood into Adulthood

Puberty, the process of physical change during which the body transitions to sexual maturity, occurs at different ages in different species. In the United States, girls typically begin the process of puberty around age 10 and have their first menstrual bleeding (this onset is called *menarche*) about two years later; first ovulation may occur a year or two after that, at which point girls are capable of sexual reproduction. Boys typically begin puberty around age 12, and full fertility is gained a few years after that. By contrast, elephants reach sexual maturity at about 9 to 12 years of age, and rats reach sexual maturity by the time they're about 14 months old. In some species, puberty does not occur at a predetermined age. For example, a fully grown female prairie vole remains sexually immature until exposed to scent signals from a male outside her kin group; within 24 hours of this exposure, she will become sexually receptive, mate, and form an enduring pair bond with her chosen partner.

Adolescence is defined as the transitional stage between the onset of puberty and entry into adulthood; in humans, this corresponds roughly to the teenage years (ages 13 through 19), although there are wide differences in each individual's physical and social development. Cultural rules also help determine the time frame, and there may be social or religious rites to mark the passage into adulthood. For example, in Western societies, adulthood is associated with the advent of new privileges such as the right to drive, purchase alcohol, and vote; new responsibilities such as leaving school and seeking full-time employment; and new social roles, such as marriage and parenthood.

Thus, while puberty is a strictly physical process, adolescence is a period of psychological and social change. Adolescence and puberty overlap, but whereas puberty has a defined end point (sexual maturity), the boundaries of adolescence are much less precisely defined.

Maturation of Working Memory

Some of the most profound changes during adolescence concern learning and memory abilities. Most prominently, working memory and executive function, which are among the latest learning and memory abilities to mature, continue to develop through adolescence and even early adulthood.

Recall from Chapter 9 that *working memory* is a short-term storage system where information can be held for active processing. In humans, we often measure working memory capacity in terms of *digit span*, the number of digits that a person can hold in memory at the same time. Figure 12.4a shows that young children have a relatively short digit span. On average, they can only remember and repeat three or four digits at a time. But digit span increases through

puberty. The process of physical change during which the body transitions to sexual maturity, usually beginning around age 10 in human females and age 12 in human males.

adolescence. The transitional stage between puberty and adulthood, corresponding roughly to the teenage years in humans (ages 13 to 19).

Figure 12.4 Working memory in adolescence (a) Digit span, the number of digits a person can hear and then repeat from memory, increases through childhood, reaching normal adult levels (about 7 digits) in late adolescence. (b) Performance on a spatial version of the "2-back" test; dots represent individual participant performance, and green line illustrates the trend for accuracy on this working memory task to continue to improve through adolescence and into young adulthood.

(a) Data from Gardner, 1981; (b) Information from Kwon et al., 2002.

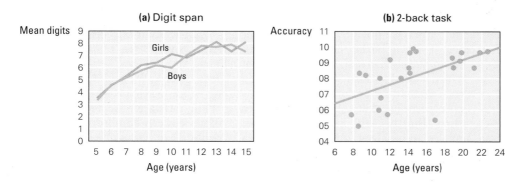

adolescence, so that by age 14 or 15, adolescents can remember approximately seven digits—the same as adults (Engle & Marshall, 1983). Similar results are obtained if the items to be remembered are visual patterns (Gathercole, 1998).

One reason very young children remember fewer numbers and pictures than adults is simply that the children have had less exposure to such things. By adolescence, individuals have accumulated much more experience with numbers, words, and patterns, and this knowledge may give them an advantage at encoding those items into working memory. Consistent with this idea is the finding that, if we use material the children are highly familiar with, their performance improves. In one clever study, adults and children were asked to remember the locations of chess pieces on a chessboard. Ten-year-old chess experts could remember more pieces than non-chess-playing adults, even though the children's digit spans were lower (Chi, 1978). This suggests that the age-related improvement in working memory capacity at least partially reflects exposure to and familiarity with the material to be remembered.

More complex working-memory abilities mature even later. For example, in Chapter 9, you read about the "2-back" task, in which participants are presented with a stream of items; as each new item is presented, participants decide whether it is the same as the one that appeared two items previously. The task can be altered to assess spatial working memory. For example, on each trial, the participant sees an object (such as an "O") at one of several locations on a computer screen; the participant's job is to press a button whenever the location on the current trial is the same as the location two trials back. The 2-back task requires a great deal of concentration, and even adults don't usually manage to get 100% correct. In one study, the task was administered to children ages 7 to 10 years, adolescents ages 13 to 17 years, and young adults ages 18 to 22 years. Figure 12.4b shows that performance continued to improve through adolescence and into adulthood (Kwon, Reiss, & Menon, 2002). Other complex working-memory tasks show similar increases throughout adolescence before leveling off, in late adolescence, at adult levels.

Male—Female Differences in Learning and Memory

Given the dramatic physical changes that occur during adolescence and the fact that most of them are associated with sexual maturation, it's not surprising that many differences between males and females in learning and memory arise during adolescence. For example, young adult women often outperform same-age men on tests of language and verbal memory, such as recalling a list or a story, and on some kinds of spatial learning, such as remembering the locations of objects (Barnfield, 1999). On the other hand, men generally outperform women on other kinds of spatial learning, such as learning the way around a maze (Astur, Ortiz, & Sutherland, 1998). In one study, men and women were asked to study a map of a fictitious town (Galea & Kimura, 1993). On average, men were quicker to learn a route within the town, whereas women were better at remembering the position of landmarks in the town. But these differences don't emerge until puberty. Thus, although adult women outperformed adult men at remembering landmarks in the fictitious town, 8- to 13-year-old girls did no better than same-age boys (Silverman & Eals, 1992).

What could cause such differences between girls and boys? One possible cause is cultural influences, such as cultural stereotypes in which boys are expected to excel at some kinds of learning while girls are expected to excel at others. But this can't be the whole story. Differences can be observed between females and males in nonhuman species, and these can't easily be attributed to cultural stereotyping. For example, in a radial arm maze, adult male rats are usually better than females at remembering which maze arms never contain any food, and adult female rats are usually better than males at remembering which arms have already been visited on the current day (Bimonte, Hyde, Hoplight, & Denenberg, 2000; Hyde, Sherman, & Denenberg, 2000). And just as in humans, male–female differences in spatial learning appear in sexually mature rats but not in immature ones (Kanit et al., 2000).

Given that male and female rats are unlikely to be subject to cultural stereotypes, some differences in learning and memory are more likely to reflect different levels of sex hormones in males and females. Starting in puberty, there is a dramatic increase in the release of sex hormones, primarily **estrogens** in mature females and **androgens**, particularly **testosterone**, in adult males. The increase in sex hormones occurs at about the same time that many differences between males and females in learning and memory appear, suggesting that the hormones are responsible for many of the behavioral effects. In the Brain Substrates section below, you'll read more about the specific ways these sex hormones influence male and female brains.

The Aging Memory: Adulthood through Old Age

Most of the studies of learning and memory that you've read about in earlier chapters were based on data collected from healthy young adults—whether those adults were humans, rats, chimpanzees, or sea slugs. This custom in research is partly because the brain is mature in young adults, so there is less variation among individuals as a result of minor differences in age than is seen earlier in life (the difference in performance due to age between a 6-month-old and an 18-month-old human is huge, but the difference due to age between a 20-year-old and a 21-year-old is usually minimal). In fact, most people (barring injury or disease) show relatively stable learning and memory—and other types of cognitive function—throughout adulthood. For example, the Seattle Longitudinal Study has tested over 6,000 individuals of different ages (Schaie, 2005). Participants are given tests to evaluate several types of cognitive ability and then re-evaluated at 7-year intervals. As shown in Figure 12.5, the study finds relatively little change in most kinds of cognitive ability—including verbal memory—as participants age from their twenties to their fifties.

Unfortunately, as Figure 12.5 also shows, many cognitive abilities start to decline as humans reach their sixties and beyond. In this and any discussion of age-related decline, it's important to remember that there are large individual differences in the rates of change, meaning that some people "age well" while

estrogen. Any member of the principal class of sex hormones present in adult females.

androgen. Any member of the principal class of sex hormones present in adult males.

testosterone. The most important *androgen* and hence the principal male sex hormone.

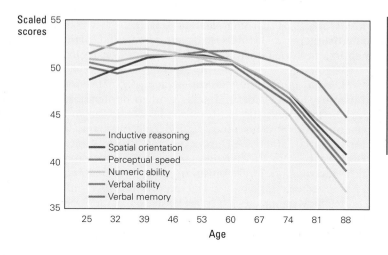

Figure 12.5 Human cognition across the lifespan In the Seattle Longitudinal Study, individuals of different ages were tested at 7-year intervals on several types of cognitive ability. Scores have been scaled so that 50 represents the median score observed for the 53-year-old age group in this study; this allows comparisons of data collected from different types of cognitive tests. Most cognitive abilities—including verbal memory—showed little change as subjects aged from 25 to 60 years but began to decline thereafter.

Information from Schaie, 2005, Figure 4.

others develop more severe deficits (Wilson et al., 2002). However, some general patterns exist. While some forms of memory, such as working memory, start to decline in humans as young as the mid-thirties, others, such as semantic knowledge and verbal ability, tend to remain strong well into old age.

Working Memory in Aging Adults

Working memory, one of the last memory systems to fully mature in humans and other animals, is also one of the first to show deficits in the course of healthy aging. For example, as you saw above, healthy young adults have a digit span that averages about 7 digits. However, in elderly adults, the average drops to about 6 to 6.5 digits. This small but significant drop could mean the difference between remembering or forgetting a seven-digit phone number. If the task is made more complicated, such as by presenting different digits simultaneously to each ear, reductions in digit span can be observed as early as age 30 or 40 (Barr, 1980). Why this should be so is not yet entirely clear; but one theory suggests that older adults are more susceptible to proactive interference. As you read back in Chapter 7, proactive interference occurs when previously stored information (such as a prior address or a computer password) interferes with the ability to remember newer information (see Figure 7.7). Possibly, older adults are less able to inhibit irrelevant, older information from entering working memory, where it crowds out the information that is relevant now (Bowles & Salthouse, 2003).

Conditioning and Skill Learning in Aging Adults

In general, learning by conditioning declines with age: older adults are less able than younger adults to adapt their behavior in response to reinforcement. For example, classical conditioning of the eyeblink response starts declining at about age 40 or 50 in humans. Older adults take about twice as long to learn an eyeblink response as younger ones do (Solomon, Pomerleau, Bennett, James, & Morse, 1989; Woodruff-Pak & Thompson, 1988). There are similar age-related declines in eyeblink conditioning in rabbits (Solomon & Groccia-Ellison, 1996), rats (Freeman & Nicholson, 2001), and cats (Harrison & Buchwald, 1983). Old age does not prevent such learning, but it makes such learning slower.

Skill learning also declines in old age. In Chapter 8, you read about the *rotary pursuit task*, which requires keeping a stylus positioned over a point on a disk that rotates rapidly (see Figure 8.6). Middle-aged adults can learn this task about as well as young adults, but elderly adults (over age 60) show a precipitous drop-off in performance (Ruch, 1934). Real-world skill learning shows the same age-related decline. For example, one study found that elderly individuals can master the mental and physical skills needed to use computers, but their rate of acquisition is slower than in younger learners, and they make more errors during learning than younger learners do (Czaja, Hammond, Blascovich, & Swede, 1993). In short, you *can* teach an old dog new tricks; it just takes a while longer.

On the other hand, even though the learning of new associations and skills is slowed in healthy aging, highly practiced skills tend to be maintained well. Famous examples are Spanish cellist Pablo Casals, who continued to compose music and conduct orchestras into his nineties, and Jack Nicklaus, who continued to win major golf tournaments in his forties and fifties—besting many younger players. Expert typists in their sixties and seventies can often execute their skill as quickly and accurately as typists in their twenties and thirties (Salthouse, 1984). Many expert chess and bridge players improve, rather than decline, with age, and airline pilots ages 40 to 60 actually have fewer accidents than younger pilots (Birren, 1964), all in support of the axiom that age and experience can often defeat youth and speed.

Episodic and Semantic Memory: Old Memories Fare Better Than New Learning

Existing episodic and semantic memories tend to survive very well, even into extreme old age. Remember from Chapter 7 that semantic memory is normally strengthened by repeated exposure. By the time a person reaches old age, semantic information such as vocabulary and general knowledge about the world has been encoded, retrieved, and re-encoded many times. Healthy elderly adults generally experience little or no drop-off in the ability to retain and retrieve such semantic memories (Light, 1991). Older individuals also tend to show only a modest drop-off in their ability to recall episodic memories from their distant past (Piolino, Desgranges, Benali, & Eustache, 2002).

But although well-formed memories may survive, elderly adults are generally less effective at forming new episodic and semantic memories. This is reflected in Figure 12.5 by participants' decline in "verbal memory," measured via free-recall tests for a short story and for a list of words. Elderly adults are also much worse than young adults on *paired associate learning*, in which participants first study a list of word pairs and are then given the first word of each pair and asked to recall the second member of the pair (Canestrari, 1963). The deficit in elderly adults appears to be due to encoding difficulties rather than retrieval difficulties. Thus, for example, elderly adults' performance at paired associate learning is much improved if items are presented at a slower pace during study, presumably because the elderly adults now have more time to encode the information (Canestrari, 1963). Elderly adults' performance improves too if the studied items have some meaning (Graf, 1990). For example, in one study, college-age adults outperformed elderly adults on memorizing a list of names of current rock stars, but the elderly adults outperformed the students on memorizing a list of musicians who had been popular with the earlier generation (Hanley-Dunn & McIntosh, 1984).

Aging also affects directed forgetting. As you read back in Chapter 7, directed-forgetting tasks ask participants to study information and then to intentionally forget some of the items (see Figure 7.6b). When participants are given a surprise memory test, they tend to recall fewer of the items they were specifically instructed to forget than items they were supposed to remember (or items for which they received no forgetting instructions). Under these conditions, younger adults can intentionally forget *more* items than elderly adults (Titz & Verhaeghen, 2010). In short, as we age, we seem to have less control over what gets encoded—becoming less able to store the items we do want to keep and simultaneously less able to discard those items we wish to forget. In support of this idea that aging compromises our control over memory retrieval, a recent study found that older adults could greatly improve their success on a directed forgetting task if they received focused instructions about how to inhibit unwanted retrieval (Murray, Anderson, & Kensinger, 2015).

Emotion may also affect memory differently as we age. In Chapter 10, you read that the emotional content of information can affect how strongly that information gets encoded in memory. Some studies suggest that older adults are more likely than young adults to remember positive information. In one such study, participants viewed a series of 16 positive images, such as smiling children and flowers, and 16 negative images, such as snakes and injured bodies (Charles, Mather, & Carstensen, 2003). Unsurprisingly, on a subsequent free-recall test, young adults recalled significantly more images than elderly adults did. But the nature of the recalled images differed. Whereas the young adults remembered about equal numbers of positive and negative images, the older adults remembered many more positive than negative images. One possible explanation is that younger participants process the negative images more deeply than older participants do—either by conscious choice, or due to age-related changes in the brain structures (such as the amygdala) that mediate emotional processing, or both—and, as you learned in Chapter 7, the *levels of processing* principle states that deeper encoding during learning tends to improve memory at recall.

Metamemory and Aging

Given the above findings, you may be surprised to learn that the most common memory-related complaints among healthy elderly are not about failure to learn new information but about failure to retrieve old information on demand. Back in Chapter 7, you read about "tip-of-the-tongue" (TOT) experiences, which occur when people feel sure that they know the information but cannot retrieve it at the present time. TOT events are among the most frequently reported and frustrating memory problems of healthy adults aged 64 to 75 years (Sunderland, Watts, Baddeley, & Harris, 1986).

The defining feature of tip-of-the-tongue events is the strong *feeling of knowing* (FOK), which in turn is a feature of *metamemory*, our knowledge and beliefs about our own memory. Some studies suggest that metamemory declines with age, and the age-associated increase in TOT events may not represent failures of memory retrieval so much as failures to accurately assess what information is available (Salthouse & Mandell, 2013).

Consistent with this idea, one study asked older and younger adults to predict how well they would remember information on a later test. Whereas the younger adults were fairly accurate in predicting how well they'd perform, the older adults were highly overconfident, predicting they'd remember much more than they actually did (Soderstrom, McCabe, & Rhodes, 2012). In summary, then, the age-related decline in acquiring new episodic and semantic memory appears to be accompanied by an age-related decline in the ability to accurately assess what we already know.

Test Your Knowledge

Learning and Memory in Old Age

Learning and memory abilities generally peak in young adulthood and may decline thereafter. Some kinds of learning and memory may begin to decline in middle age, while others may remain relatively robust through healthy old age. See if you can identify the learning and memory processes involved in each of the tasks described below and predict whether or not healthy older people should be able to perform them as well (or nearly as well) as when they were young adults. (Answers appear in the back of the book.)

1. Recalling one's wedding day
2. Remembering the items on this week's shopping list (without writing them down)
3. Remembering how to make coffee
4. Learning the name of a new friend
5. Learning how to take photos with a new phone

Interim Summary

- An individual's learning and memory abilities vary across the lifespan.
- Some simple learning, such as habituation and recognition, can occur even before birth.

- Most kinds of learning and memory ability are present in at least a rudimentary form from a very early age although they may become more efficient as the individual grows toward adulthood.

- Even before young children are able to verbalize their episodic memories, they show behavioral evidence of episodic-like memory, similar to the what-where-when memories that can be demonstrated in non-human animals.

- Sensitive periods are windows of time, usually early in life, when particular kinds of learning are easiest or most effective. In humans, there are sensitive periods for language learning as well as for sensory systems, such as vision.

- Puberty is the process of physical change during which the body transitions to sexual maturity. Adolescence is the transitional stage between puberty and adulthood.

- During puberty, there is a dramatic increase in release of sex hormones (primarily estrogens in females and androgens, particularly testosterone, in males), which may contribute to differences in learning and memory abilities between males and females.

- Working memory is one of the last systems to fully mature in humans, and may not be fully developed until early adulthood.

- Learning and memory abilities peak in young adulthood but generally decline in healthy aging. A rule of thumb is that old memories may survive well but new learning may be slowed in aging individuals.

- There may also be age-related declines in metamemory, contributing to frequent and frustrating tip-of-the-tongue (TOT) events.

12.2 Brain Substrates

Unsurprisingly, the age-related wax and wane of learning and memory abilities in an individual reflect underlying changes in the brain across the lifespan. In this section, you'll read about those changes. Again, we'll proceed chronologically: starting with the genetic biases laid down before birth, continuing with development in infancy and childhood, looking at the profound changes associated with adolescence and puberty, and finally exploring the changes that occur through adulthood and into old age.

The Genetic Basis of Learning and Memory

Starting at the moment of conception, aspects of an organism's learning and memory abilities are encoded in its genetic structure and begin to guide its future development. The influence of genes on brain function is a relatively new area of study, but researchers are beginning to understand some of the ways genes affect learning and memory.

Genetic Variation and Individual Differences in Learning Abilities

The *BDNF* gene on human chromosome 11 helps regulate production of brain-derived neurotrophic factor (BDNF), a protein that is vital for the health of neurons. Among other functions, BDNF appears to affect learning and memory by enhancing *long-term potentiation*, or LTP (Lu & Gottschalk, 2000; Poo, 2001). Like many genes, the *BDNF* gene comes in several naturally occurring variants, or **alleles**. The most common version of the *BDNF* gene is called the *Val allele*. However, about one-third of people inherit at least one copy of a different

allele. Naturally occurring variant of a gene.

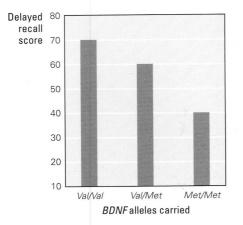

Figure 12.6 Genetic influences on learning and memory in humans BDNF (brain-derived neurotrophic factor) is a protein needed for neuron health and function. People carrying two copies of the *Met* allele (*Met/Met*) of the *BDNF* gene show worse performance on a test of memory recall than people carrying two copies of the *Val* allele (*Val/Val*). People carrying one copy of each allele (*Val/Met*) perform at intermediate levels.

Information from Egan et al., 2003.

version, the *Met allele*, which produces a slightly less effective form of BDNF. People carrying one or two copies of the *Met* allele are slightly worse at learning and memory tasks than people carrying two copies of the *Val* allele. Figure 12.6 shows performance on a test that requires participants to listen to short paragraphs and then repeat them from memory 20 minutes later. People with two copies of the *Val* allele (*Val/Val*) perform better than those with two copies of the *Met* allele (*Met/Met*); people with one copy of each allele (*Val/Met*) are intermediate in performance (Egan et al., 2003).

The *BDNF* gene is only one of many that appear to influence learning and memory behavior. Others include the *5-HT2AR* gene, which encodes the instructions for building a particular kind of receptor for the neurotransmitter serotonin and therefore may help determine the effectiveness of neural transmission (de Quervain et al., 2003); the *WWC1* (or "*KIBRA*") gene, which appears to help modify synaptic plasticity and may be associated with the rate at which we forget new information (Schneider et al., 2010); and the *SNC1A* gene, which appears to govern how action potentials propagate down the axon, determining whether the message gets passed on to the next neuron (Papassotiropoulos et al., 2009). Like the *BDNF* gene, each of these has several naturally occurring variants, and humans who carry different alleles of these genes have slight but significant differences in their ability to learn and recall new information.

To date, scientists have identified only a small number of genes that affect memory. There are doubtless many more—and they probably interact with each other and with the environment in complicated ways, a theme we return to more than once in the discussions that follow.

Selective Breeding and Twin Studies

Even without understanding the function of every gene, humans can manipulate genes through selective breeding for agricultural and other purposes. Since ancient times, humans have bred animals to obtain particular characteristics: winning racehorses bred together to produce ever-faster offspring, purebred dogs bred together to produce ever-better examples of the breed, and sheep bred together to produce thicker or finer wool. In each case, the idea is that the parent's "desirable" genes may be passed on to its offspring; by mating two animals with desirable characteristics, the breeder maximizes the possibility that the offspring will inherit those characteristics.

An early experiment in the genetics of learning and memory considered whether animals could be bred for learning ability (Tryon, 1940). Psychologist Robert Tryon trained a large group of rats in a complex maze; due to individual differences, some rats (which he called "maze-bright") learned quickly and others ("maze-dull") learned slowly (Figure 12.7a). Tryon then paired off the maze-bright rats and allowed them to breed; he also bred together the maze-dull rats and then trained the resulting offspring in the maze. Again, some offspring from each group learned better than their peers and some learned worse than average (Figure 12.7b).

Tryon repeated the process over and over, breeding together the best of the maze-bright offspring and also breeding together the worst of the maze-dull offspring. By the seventh generation of offspring, there was almost no overlap: the rats from the "maze-bright" line routinely outperformed the rats bred from the "maze-dull" line (Figure 12.7c). Later experiments have shown that many different species, including rats, mice, and fruit flies, can similarly be bred for ability on a variety of learning tasks (Tully, 1996).

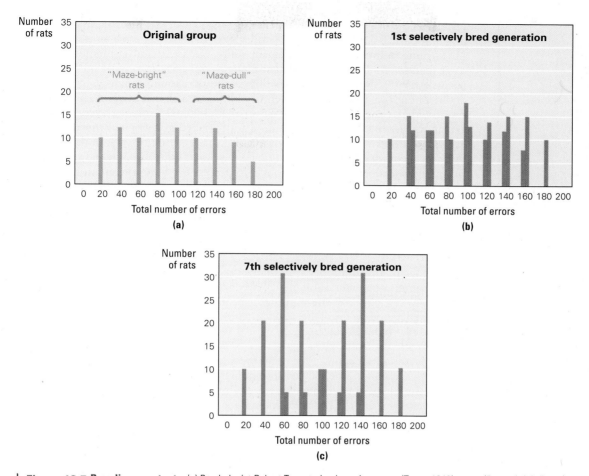

Figure 12.7 Breeding smart rats (a) Psychologist Robert Tryon trained rats in a maze (Tryon, 1940); some ("maze-bright" rats) made few errors before mastering the task, while others ("maze-dull" rats) made many errors. (b) Tryon bred the "maze-bright" rats together and trained their offspring in the maze (blue bars); he did the same with the offspring of "maze-dull" rats (purple bars). In this generation, there was considerable overlap between the two strains in terms of performance in the maze, but the "maze-bright" offspring tended to make somewhat fewer errors than the "maze-dull" offspring. (c) Tryon continued breeding the best of the "maze-bright" rats together and the worst of the "maze-dull" rats together; by the seventh generation, rats born into the "maze-bright" strain routinely outperformed rats from the "maze-dull" strain.

Data shown are hypothetical.

Presumably, "maze-bright" and "maze-dull" rats inherited a package of genes from their parents that contributed multiple characteristics that, all together, resulted in good or poor performance in a maze. These genes might be modifying learning indirectly rather than directly. For example, "maze-bright" rats may be less emotional, or more prone to explore, or more active overall—and any of these characteristics could translate into better performance in a maze. In fact, learning ability, like all facets of intelligence, appears to be determined by multiple genes interacting rather than by any single gene.

And what about inherited learning abilities in humans? Ethical concerns obviously preclude experiments in which pairs of "smart" or "dumb" people are made to breed with each other to see what kinds of offspring result. However, we can get some clues from twin studies. In these studies, researchers compare the mental abilities of identical twins (who have identical genetic makeup) and fraternal twins (who share 50% of their genes on average, just like any other siblings). Identical twins show more similarity than fraternal twins on several kinds of learning and memory measures, including tests of working memory (such as digit span) and memory for verbal and picture information (Finkel, Pedersen, & McGue, 1995; Swan et al., 1999). This suggests that genes play a strong role in determining our learning and memory abilities. Some studies of human twins suggest that over half of the variation in individuals' memory scores may be accounted for by differences in those individuals' genetic makeup (McClearn et al., 1997; Swan et al., 1999). However, this means that the rest of the variation must be accounted for by nongenetic factors, such as health, stress, living conditions, and social interactions. Genes set up the basic blueprint of an individual's learning and memory abilities, but the final outcome reflects an interaction of heredity and environment. (For more on one way environmental conditions may—or may not—influence cognitive abilities, see "Learning and Memory in Everyday Life" on the next page.)

Epigenetics

It's important to remember that genes are only the "recipes" for building and maintaining organisms. You may have a great recipe for birthday cake, but it's only when you buy the ingredients, mix the batter, and bake the cake that you actually get to taste the results. Similarly, a gene has to be activated, or "expressed," before it takes effect.

Continuing the analogy, an experienced cook may have a large recipe file from which she can select appropriate items for tonight's menu. If she is planning a Cinco de Mayo celebration, she may wish to prepare the recipes for tacos and enchiladas, but not the Thanksgiving-themed recipes for turkey and mashed potatoes. Similarly, our genes represent the entire recipe file for our bodies, and (almost) every cell in our bodies contains this file. So there must be mechanisms ("chefs") that determine which specific genes ("recipes") are activated in which cells and at which times, so that cells in the liver, heart, skin, brain, and elsewhere each develop into the appropriate types of cell and perform the appropriate types of function.

epigenetics. The study of mechanisms by which gene expression can be modified (without modifying the genes themselves).

The emerging field of **epigenetics** is the study of mechanisms by which gene activation can be modified (without modifying the genes themselves). One such mechanism is *methylation*, which occurs when a certain group of atoms (specifically, a methyl group) attaches to a gene, "tagging" that gene and altering (usually, inhibiting) its activity.

Whereas our genes are inherited at the moment of conception, and effectively fixed for life, epigenetic mechanisms are more flexible. They react to outside factors such as diet, environmental chemicals, and stress. For example, many forms of cancer are caused by genes that are normally suppressed by methylation; if methylation is decreased, these genes may be released from inhibition, triggering cancer. An important area of modern cancer research involves drugs that target epigenetic processes such as methylation, to restore proper balance of inhibited and activated genes.

Epigenetic mechanisms also play a key role in learning and memory (Day & Sweatt, 2010; Lockett, Wilkes & Maleszka, 2010). For example, you already read in Chapter 4 that memories can be encoded by long-term structural changes in neurons, as when the creation of new synapses is triggered by the activation and inactivation of genes such as *CREB-1* and *CREB-2*; this is an example of epigenetic modulation. The *BDNF* gene, which you met earlier in this section and which appears to enhance LTP, is also subject to epigenetic influence; specifically, both acute and chronic stress can lead to reduced *BDNF* activation, which in turn may be one way that stress can impair memory (Mitchelmore & Gede, 2014). In all, thousands of genes are subject to epigenetic influence, at specific times and in specific neurons, triggering processes such as synaptic changes that stabilize memory (Lockett et al., 2010).

Can Exposure to Classical Music Make Babies Smarter?

Walk through any children's store and you're likely to find shelves of music, books, and videos representing an entire industry dedicated to the premise that children exposed to classical music will reap intellectual benefits. It all started in 1993, when physicist Gordon Shaw and developmental psychologist (and concert cellist) Francis Rauscher reported that college students who had listened to 10 minutes of a Mozart sonata before taking an intelligence test scored about 8 or 9 points better than students who had sat quietly during the same interval (Rauscher, Shaw, & Ky, 1993).

The media quickly picked up the story of the "Mozart effect." Entrepreneurs rushed to produce intelligence-enhancing music products for babies, and well-intentioned parents rushed to buy them. Pregnant mothers spent afternoons playing sonatas to their unborn children, the governor of Georgia recommended that the state provide recordings of classical music to the parents of every newborn citizen, and Florida passed a law requiring all state-funded educational programs to play classical music every day for children under 6. All this effort derived from public perception of the scientific evidence that music could make babies smarter.

But, in fact, scientific evidence for the Mozart effect is mixed at best. Although some studies replicated the original findings (Rideout, Dougherty, & Wernert, 1998; Wilson & Brown, 1997), others did not (Bridgett & Cuevas, 2000; McCutcheon, 2000; McKelvie & Low, 2002; Steele, Bass, & Crook, 1999). Most researchers now conclude that any general claim of intellectual improvement following mere exposure to classical music is unwarranted (Chabris, 1999; Fudin & Lembeissis, 2004; Steele et al., 1999). Rauscher and Shaw themselves stress that their original paper only found an effect of classical music on very specific tasks involving abstract reasoning and mental imagery, such as imagining how a piece of paper will look when unfolded after several steps of folding and cutting (Rauscher & Shaw, 1998). And there is no evidence that this effect lasts more than 10 to 15 minutes.

It is true that listening to complex music activates the same brain regions that are used in abstract spatial reasoning. The music may "prime" or prepare those brain regions so that they are more efficient on subsequent spatial-reasoning tasks (Rauscher & Shaw, 1998; Rauscher, Shaw, & Ky, 1993). Listening to music can produce changes in mood and arousal that might also affect performance (Chabris, 1999; Steele, 2003; Thompson, Schellenberg, & Husain, 2001). However, such short-term effects would not cause long-term improvements in intelligence or memory ability.

And what about those parents who want a quick way to make their children smarter? Spending large amounts of money on Mozart-for-babies products may not be the answer. At best, such exposure results in a small, temporary increase in a specific kind of spatial ability. On the other hand, listening to Mozart doesn't cause babies any harm, and if early exposure helps foster a lifelong love of music, that may be a worthwhile benefit in and of itself.

One of the most striking features about epigenetic changes is that in some cases they, like genes, can be passed from parent to offspring. Thus, a mouse that experiences early-life stress will show epigenetic changes—and its own offspring may have the same epigenetic pattern, even if the offspring never even meet their biological parents (for review, see Dias, Maddox, Klengel & Ressler, 2015). In humans also, epigenetic changes can sometimes be inherited, so that individuals subjected to extreme stress (as were survivors of the Holocaust or the Rwandan genocide) resulting in epigenetic changes may pass those changes along to their children (for review, see Dias et al., 2015).

Some provocative studies suggest that epigenetics may even provide a mechanism for passing specific learning across generations. For example, in one study, male mice were classically conditioned to associate a particular odor with footshock; these mice developed a fear response to that odor and also showed cortical remapping that resulted in an increased number of olfactory neurons responding to that odor. The offspring of these mice also showed enlargement of these cortical regions, along with enhanced ability to learn about that specific odor (Dias & Ressler, 2014). Studies like this raise the intriguing possibility that the "smart offspring" of "smart rats," like those in Figure 12.7, might have inherited not only genetics but also epigenetics that contribute to the descendants' success in the maze their ancestors learned to run.

Neurons and Synapses in the Developing Brain

As you read above, our genetic inheritance lays down the blueprint for brain function before we're born. From this beginning, the developing brain, in interaction with our surroundings and in response to our experiences, produces the neurons and synapses that then shape our abilities. This process begins before birth and continues throughout childhood and into adolescence.

Early Overproduction of Neurons

Before birth, the brain develops with amazing speed; at certain points in human gestation, up to 250,000 new neurons are added *each minute* (Bornstein & Lamb, 1992). This process of neuronal birth is called **neurogenesis**. By about 25 weeks after conception, the majority of the human fetus's neurons are in place. At this point, the lower-brain centers responsible for such functions as breathing, digestion, and reflexes are almost fully developed.

neurogenesis. Creation of new neurons in the brain.

The process of neurogenesis is not uniform throughout the brain. For example, Purkinje cells in the cerebellum are one class of neuron that form relatively early in gestation (Sidman & Rakic, 1973). This helps explain why classical eyeblink conditioning, which depends on the cerebellum, is already possible in very young infants. But the cerebellum continues to develop after birth too, which may be why conditioning can occur faster, and under more complicated circumstances, in older children and adults than in infants (Herbert, Eckerman, & Stanton, 2003).

Surprisingly, after the prenatal flurry of neurogenesis, the infant brain undergoes a period of reduction in the number of neurons. Normally, neurons require compounds called *neurotrophic factors* that help them grow and thrive. BDNF, described above, is one example of a neurotrophic factor. Neurons obtain neurotrophic factors from their neighbors. When a neuron is deprived of neurotrophic factors, genes become active that cause the neuron to die. Such natural cell death is called **apoptosis**, to distinguish it from cell death caused by accident or disease. In a sense, apoptosis implements the brain's version of Darwinian natural selection: if many neurons are competing for a limited amount of neurotrophic factor, only some can survive. Those neurons that are densely connected to their neighbors, and thus probably play vital roles in brain function, may be more likely to obtain neurotrophic factors and win the competition. Those neurons that have less contact with their neighbors—and thus probably contribute less to overall brain function—may be more likely to die through apoptosis.

apoptosis. Natural cell death, as opposed to cell death caused by accident or disease.

During childhood, apoptosis may cull as many as one-third of all the neurons produced prenatally. This may seem like a roundabout way to build a brain: creating billions of neurons and then destroying a large number of them soon after. But the process allows for a great deal of fine-tuning after birth. The brain starts off with plenty of resources, in the form of neurons, and experience determines which of those resources are critical and which are not so necessary.

Pruning of Synapses

In the same way that the brain starts life with an oversupply of neurons, it also begins with a surplus of synapses. The creation of new synapses, called **synaptogenesis**, begins in the human brain as early as 5 months after conception. But after birth, synaptogenesis really gets going, with as many as 40,000 synapses being created *per second* in the infant macaque monkey! Like neurogenesis,

synaptogenesis. Creation of new synapses.

synaptogenesis occurs at different rates in different brain areas. For example, in humans, the bulk of synaptogenesis in the visual cortex is completed by about 3 or 4 months of age, but in the prefrontal cortex high rates of synaptogenesis continue until about 6 years of age (Huttenlocher & Dabholkar, 1997).

After this peak in synaptogenesis, the number of synapses begins to decline as the brain begins to prune unnecessary or incorrect connections. Just like neurons, synapses are subjected to a kind of Darwinian natural selection. Those synapses that are frequently used (and therefore presumably important to the neuron's function) are strengthened; those that are seldom used (and therefore presumably less important) may be weakened and may die away altogether. In humans, up to 42% of all synapses in the cortex may be pruned during childhood and adolescence (Bourgeois, 2001). Despite this pruning, there are still plenty of synapses available: the adult human brain, for example, has a staggering 10^{14} synapses. That's about 1,000 times as many synapses as there are stars in the Milky Way galaxy.

Synaptogenesis continues throughout life, although not at the same furious rate as during infancy. The vast majority of synapses on cortical neurons occur on **spines**, tiny protrusions from dendrites (Figure 12.8; Ottersen & Helm, 2002). There may be about 100,000 spines per neuron. Throughout life, new spines periodically appear at various locations on the dendrite. If the spines are contacted by another neuron, synapses can be formed and strengthened; otherwise, the unneeded spines disappear to be replaced in due course by new spines elsewhere on the dendrite that may prove more useful (Trachtenberg et al., 2002). Although individual spines come and go, as shown in Figure 12.8, the overall number of spines on a dendrite remains approximately constant; experience and learning determine which individual spines survive.

spine. A tiny protrusion on a dendrite where synapses may form.

Sensitive Periods for Neuronal Wiring

Earlier you read about the concept of sensitive periods, time windows during which certain types of learning are particularly efficient or effective. Sensitive periods in learning may reflect sensitive periods in neuronal development, when environmental inputs (such as visual stimulation) can easily alter brain organization by changing local cortical connectivity.

For example, you read above that infant cats and monkeys who have one eye sewn shut during a sensitive period in infancy will be "blind" in that eye when it is opened (Hubel & Wiesel, 1977). Normally, visual stimulation activates sensory neurons in the retina of the eye that project (through several way stations) to neurons in the primary visual cortex (V1). During the first few weeks of life, this visual pathway is very active, and since "neurons that fire together, wire together," connections between neurons in this pathway are strengthened. But if one eye is deprived of sight, there is no activity along the pathway from that eye to V1. The inactive synapses will be weakened or eliminated. At the same time, synapses in the active pathway from the open eye will be strengthened. By the time the deprived eye is reopened, visual activity in that eye will no longer elicit much activity in V1, and this weak activity will not be able to compete for synapses with the strong pathways from the never-closed eye (Majewska & Sur, 2003).

Figure 12.8 Most synapses occur on dendritic spines This figure shows a segment of one dendrite, photographed over several consecutive days. Spines (visible as protrusions) appear and disappear; over eight sequential days, this dendritic segment showed some spines that survived through the entire experiment (yellow arrowhead), some that lasted a few days then disappeared (red arrowhead), and some that lasted less than a single day (blue arrowhead; Reprinted by permission from Macmillan Publishers Ltd: NATURE Trachtenberg, J.T., et al. "Long-term *in vivo* imaging of experience-dependent synaptic plasticity in adult cortex," 420, 788–794. Copyright 2002.

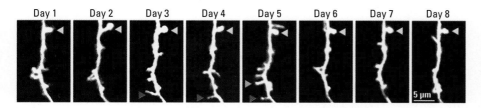

| Day 1 | Day 2 | Day 3 | Day 4 | Day 5 | Day 6 | Day 7 | Day 8 |

5 µm

Although sensitive periods restrict our later learning, they are actually beneficial to the developing brain. Early in life, the brain *should* be maximally open to new experiences and be able to change accordingly. But once its basic system is set up, the brain must not change dramatically with each new experience or it would risk overwriting critical older information. Of course the brain remains plastic throughout life, and reorganization can occur (such as the gradual changes in cortical maps that occur with extensive practice of a new motor skill, which you read about in Chapter 8), but the basic organization must remain relatively stable from day to day. Think of your brain as a canvas on which an artist's early broad strokes define the picture being painted; later, small details can be added or changed, but the overall layout of the picture is fixed.

Brain Changes in Adolescence

As you read above in the Behavioral Processes section, adolescence is a time of profound physical and psychological changes as the child transitions into an adult. The psychological changes, and particularly the changes in learning and memory abilities, reflect changes in the adolescent brain.

Profound Changes in Prefrontal Cortex

Although adolescence causes changes throughout the brain, some of the most profound and obvious changes in the adolescent brain occur in the prefrontal cortex, which appears not to become fully mature until after the teenage years. As you read in Chapter 9, the prefrontal cortex is a seat of many types of cognitive function, including working memory and also judgment and planning. During childhood, the prefrontal cortex undergoes robust synaptogenesis; but during adolescence, large numbers of these synapses are pruned until the number of synapses plateaus at the adult level (Glantz, Gilmore, Hamer, Lieberman, & Jarskog, 2007). At the same time, neurons in prefrontal cortex begin to show much more complicated branching patterns that probably allow more complex patterns of information flow (Lambe, Krimer, & Goldman-Rakic, 2000).

Another important change during development is that neuronal axons develop *myelin sheaths*, wrappings of a fatty substance called myelin that insulate the electrical signals traveling down the axon, speeding neuronal transmission. The myelin sheaths are produced by *glia*, cells in the brain that provide various support functions to neurons and that are as critical to proper brain function as the neurons themselves. Myelination of neurons in the human cortex doesn't start until after birth, and it continues throughout the first 18 years of life. Some brain areas, such as motor cortex and sensory cortex, are fully myelinated early, but the frontal cortex isn't fully myelinated until late adolescence or early adulthood. Neurons can function before myelination is complete, but transmission will be slow and weak. This could be part of the reason working memory is among the last types of learning and memory to fully mature.

"Young man, go to your room and stay there until your cerebral cortex matures."

If this young man's cerebral cortex is not yet fully mature, what learning and memory abilities may not be fully developed?

Yet another change in the prefrontal cortex of adolescents is a dramatic increase in the neurotransmitter *dopamine* (Lambe, Krimer, & Goldman-Rakic, 2000). As you read in Chapter 5, dopamine is important for learning about reward, and particularly about rewards that will happen in the future. This is probably one reason why teenagers tend to be impulsive and risk-taking, and why adolescent humans (and adolescent rats and monkeys) become easily attracted to drugs (Galván, 2013). The peak in reward sensitivity starts to drop off after about age 18 or 19 (Galván, 2013), as teenagers begin to mature into adults who show more impulse control and more ability to act based on judgments about the long-term consequences of their behavior.

Effects of Sex Hormones on Brain Organization

In the Behavioral Processes section above, you read about several kinds of learning and memory that are different, on average, in males and females. Since many of these differences in learning and memory don't emerge until puberty, a likely explanation is that these kinds of learning and memory are strongly affected by circulating estrogen and testosterone in sexually mature adults.

Not all sex hormone effects occur at puberty, though. In mammals and birds, there is a surge in testosterone near birth. This surge occurs in both sexes, although it is greater in males. Testosterone levels decline during the first year of life in both male and female humans and then remain low until puberty (Overman, Bachevalier, Schuhmann, & Ryan, 1996). But during that critical first year of life, testosterone strongly influences brain development. Curiously, in the brain, "male" hormones such as testosterone are converted to estradiol (a form of the "female" hormone estrogen), and so it may be the high level of estradiol in young males that actually makes their brains develop differently from female brains (Cohen-Bendahan, van de Beck, & Berenbaum, 2005).

And develop differently they do. By adulthood, men's brains are about 100 grams heavier, and contain about 4 billion more neurons, than women's brains (Pakkenberg & Gundersen, 1997). Aside from this difference in overall volume, some brain areas are proportionately larger in one sex than in the other (Goldstein et al., 2001, 2002; Jacobs, Schall, & Schiebel, 1993). Figure 12.9 shows some of these areas. One is the lateral frontal cortex, which is important for working memory; this area is usually larger in women than in men, perhaps helping to explain why women often outperform men on working-memory tasks. Other areas that are usually larger in women are the hippocampus and some language areas (such as the area labeled "supramarginal gyrus" in Figure 12.9). Again, this may help explain why women often outperform men on list learning, which requires both hippocampal-dependent episodic memory and language skill. Conversely, men are often better than women at navigating through space (Astur, Ortiz, & Sutherland, 1998). Such spatial navigation may depend on brain areas that process visual and spatial information, and some of these areas tend to be larger in men than in women, such as the ones labeled "angular gyrus" and "visual cortex" in Figure 12.9. In sum, many differences in learning and memory may reflect the fact that male and female brains are simply wired differently.

By the time an individual reaches sexual maturity, learning and memory abilities reflect both underlying brain organization and the effects of circulating sex hormones. These effects are not always simple to dissect.

Figure 12.9 Differences in brain volume in men and women Several brain areas (red) are proportionately larger in women than in men, including brain areas important for working memory and language processing, at which women often outperform men. Other brain areas (blue) are proportionately larger in men than women, including cortical regions important for visual and spatial processing, at which men often outperform women. Information from Goldstein et al., 2002.

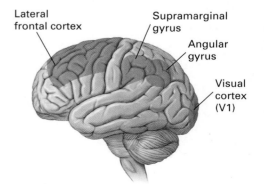

Lateral frontal cortex

Supramarginal gyrus

Angular gyrus

Visual cortex (V1)

For example, estrogen reliably stimulates neuronal growth and synaptic plasticity (LTP) in rats (Foy et al., 1999; Woolley, Weiland, McEwen, & Schwartzkroin, 1997). As a result, you'd expect that women should learn better at times in their menstrual cycle when circulating estrogen levels are highest than at other points when estrogen levels are lower. Unfortunately, such a clear pattern has not always been found. For example, although women normally outperform men at learning word pairs, women tested at points in their menstrual cycle when estrogen is high don't outperform women tested when estrogen is low (Phillips & Sherwin, 1992). One reason for this confusing result may be that the fluctuations in women's estrogen levels at different points in the menstrual cycle are very small compared to the difference in estrogen levels between women and men. On the other hand, women taking oral contraceptives (many of which work by raising levels of estrogen and progesterone) show faster classical conditioning than women not taking oral contraceptives (Figure 12.10; Beck et al., 2008)—and both groups learn faster than males (Holloway, Beck, & Servatius, 2011). Estrogen also affects emotional memory: naturally cycling women tend to remember more details of an emotional story than women using hormonal contraception (Nielsen, Ertman, Lakhani & Cahill, 2011). Because the women in these studies were not randomly assigned to pill versus placebo groups, the studies can't rule out the possibility that other, preexisting differences between the groups account for the different levels of performance. Still, the data are consistent with the premise that estrogen (and maybe progesterone) affects learning.

Another way to evaluate the effects of estrogen on learning and memory is to compare learning in transsexuals before and after they have begun hormone therapy. In one study, male-to-female transsexuals on estrogen therapy scored higher on a paired associate task than a similar group who had not yet started estrogen therapy (Miles, Green, Sanders, & Hines, 1998). Similarly, on a list-learning task, control females recalled the most words, control males recalled the fewest, and male-to-female transsexuals on estrogen scored intermediately—better than control males, though not quite as well as control females (Cohen-Kettenis, van Goozen, Doorn, & Gooren, 1998).

Whereas estrogen may improve verbal learning, there is some evidence that testosterone can improve spatial learning. For example, adult male rats normally outperform females on learning to swim to an escape platform hidden just below the surface in a pool filled with cloudy water. In one study, adult males given additional testosterone performed better than ordinary males (Naghdi, Majlessi, & Bozorgmehr, 2005). But other studies have found that testosterone causes no improvement or even impairs spatial memory (Goudsmit, Van de Poll, & Swaab, 1990). The results are complicated by the fact that testosterone exerts its influence on the brain mainly by affecting estrogen levels: on the one hand, testosterone inhibits estrogen function; on the other hand, when testosterone levels are high, some testosterone may be converted to estrogen, actually increasing estrogen levels in the brain. Perhaps as researchers come to better understand the complicated relationship between estrogen and learning, this will also shed light on the relationship between testosterone and learning.

Figure 12.10 Effects of sex hormones on classical conditioning Women taking oral contraceptives showed faster acquisition of a conditioned eyeblink response than women not taking oral contraceptives. This was true both for monophasic contraceptives, which deliver the same dose of estrogen and progesterone every day, and for triphasic contraceptives, which vary the dosages throughout a monthly cycle.

Information from Beck et al., 2008.

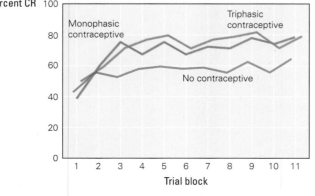

Test Your Knowledge

Everything Grows Together . . . at Different Rates

All forms of learning and memory available to adults tend to be present in infants, at least in rudimentary form, but some kinds of learning mature faster than others, apparently reflecting different rates of maturation for the brain substrates on which those types of learning and memory depend. See if you can reorder the types of learning and memory in the middle column below to produce an accurate, if rough, timetable for reaching maturity. Then reorganize the third column to match each type of learning and memory with the corresponding brain area. Bear in mind that this is a rough timetable only, with lots of room for individual differences as well as continued fine-tuning of abilities as the organism reaches adulthood, and that most kinds of learning and memory depend on more than one brain area. (Answers appear in the back of the book.)

(Rough) Timetable for Development	Types of Learning and Memory	Critical Brain Area(s)
Present before birth (in at least some forms)	Conditioning and skill learning	Frontal cortex
Infancy to early childhood (in at least some forms)	Episodic and semantic memory	Hippocampus
Childhood	Sensory processing and habituation	Sensory cortex
Late childhood to early adolescence	Social learning and imitation	Mirror neurons in motor cortex
Late adolescence to young adulthood	Working memory and executive function	Cerebellum and basal ganglia

The Brain from Adulthood to Old Age

Just as the brain grows in volume during development, so does it shrink in old age. This shrinkage begins in adolescence and continues thereafter, so that by age 80, the average human brain has lost about 5% of its weight. Some of this loss may reflect the early stages of degenerative disorders such as Alzheimer's disease. Some may reflect injury; a large-scale MRI study of 3,600 "healthy" individuals ages 65 to 97 years found that over one-third had brain lesions consistent with small strokes, which had presumably gone unnoticed by the individuals themselves (Bryan et al., 1997). But even in healthy aging, where there is no known disease or injury, some brain shrinkage appears to occur.

Localized Neuron and Synapse Loss

What causes brains to shrink with age? In some areas of the mammalian brain, neurons die off during the course of normal aging. For example, you know that the prefrontal cortex is important for working memory. In a young adult monkey (11 years old) the prefrontal cortex contains numerous, densely packed neurons (Smith, Rapp, McKay, Roberts, & Tuszynski, 2004). In an elderly monkey (25 years old), the same area of prefrontal cortex shows nearly a third fewer neurons. Similar changes occur in humans. Figure 12.11a shows that older adults tend to have smaller volume in the prefrontal cortex. This is not true for all cortical regions; thus, for example, primary visual cortex tends to shrink very little with age (Raz et al.,

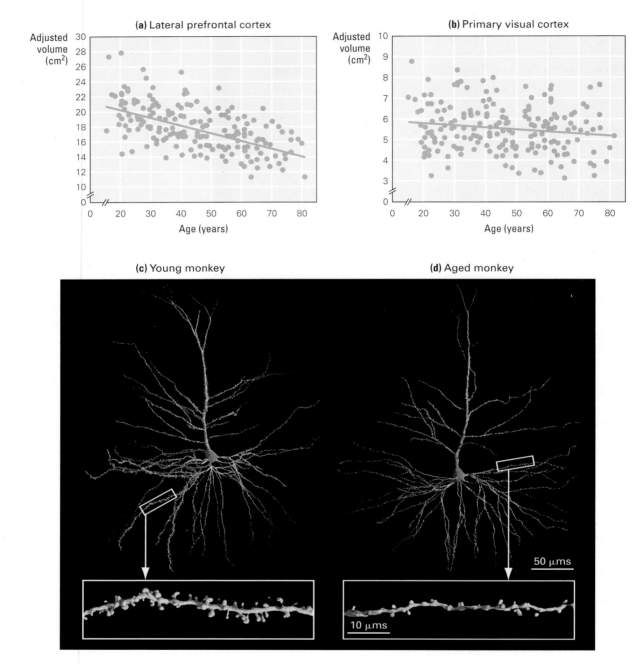

Figure 12.11 Aging in prefrontal cortex (a) Volume in several areas of the prefrontal cortex, including lateral prefrontal cortex, typically declines with age, shown here for humans ranging from about 20 to about 80 years in age. (b) Other cortical areas, such as primary visual cortex, shown here, do not typically show volume reductions in the course of healthy aging. (c) A representative prefrontal neuron from a young monkey; the inset shows a closeup of a segment of dendrite from this neuron, covered in spines, the tiny protrusions where synapses can form. (d) In the aged brain, the number of spines is greatly reduced.

(a, b) Research from Raz et al., 2004.

(c, d) Research from Morrison & Baxter, 2012. Image credit: John H. Morrison, Ph.D.

2004). The age-related shrinkage of prefrontal cortex is consistent with the fact that working memory declines sharply with age. Tellingly, the degree of impairment shown by an individual aged monkey on working-memory tasks correlates with that individual's degree of neuron loss in the prefrontal cortex (Smith et al., 2004). Another brain region where neurons are lost with age is the cerebellum (Hall, Miller, & Corsellia, 1975; Woodruff-Pak & Sheffield, 1987). This cell loss is consistent with the finding that classical eyeblink conditioning, which depends on the cerebellum, declines with age (Woodruff-Pak, Logan, & Thompson, 1990).

There may also be age-related decreases in the connectivity between existing neurons. For example, neurons in the cerebral cortex of aged monkeys tend to show fewer dendrites and less complex branching than neurons of young monkeys (Hof & Morrison, 2004). Such reductions in dendritic branching imply a reduction in the ability to receive signals from other neurons (Gallagher & Rapp, 1997). Neurons with fewer dendrites will also take up less space, which could be another reason why some cortical areas shrink with age.

The prefrontal cortex is an area where synapse loss may be particularly marked in aging. Figure 12.8 showed dendritic spines, tiny protrusions on dendrites where the majority of synapses are formed. The number of spines on prefrontal neurons decreases by about 33% overall in aged monkeys (Figure 12.11c,d; Dumitriu et al., 2010; Morrison & Baxter, 2012). But the loss is not universal. There are two kinds of spines: the majority (about 60 to 75%) are small, thin spines that are capable of growing and retracting and are believed to play a role in encoding new information; the minority are large, mushroom-shaped spines that tend to stay in place and are believed to be the locus of long-term memories. While aged monkeys have about 45% fewer thin spines than young monkeys, the number of mushroom spines remains approximately constant (Dumitriu et al., 2010). The age-related reduction in thin spines could be one reason aged individuals—as you read above—often show impairments in their ability to learn new information but little loss of old, well-established memories.

But some brain regions don't appear to lose appreciable numbers of neurons or synapses in old age. One such area is the primary visual cortex (Figure 12.11b). Another is the hippocampus, which may shrink in overall volume but doesn't appear to show much age-related neuron loss in humans (West, 1993), monkeys (Peters et al., 1996; Small, Chawla, Buonocore, Rapp, & Barnes, 2004), or rats (Rapp & Gallagher, 1996; Rasmussen, Schilemann, Sorensen, Zimmer, & West, 1996). In fact, many researchers now believe that significant reductions in the number of hippocampal neurons are warning signs of age-related disease, such as early Alzheimer's disease (Gallagher & Rapp, 1997). Similarly, it appears that the aging hippocampus doesn't normally show a decrease in number of synapses (Rosenzweig & Barnes, 2003). Yet, as you read in the Behavioral Processes section, age does cause decline in hippocampal-dependent episodic and semantic memory formation. If not loss of hippocampal neurons, what could cause this decline?

Loss of Synaptic Stability

Carol Barnes and colleagues have suggested that the *total number* of hippocampal neurons and synapses doesn't decline appreciably with aging; what does change is the ability to *maintain changes in synapse strength* (Barnes, Suster, Shen, & McNaughton, 1997; Rosenzweig & Barnes, 2003). Remember that synapse strength is increased by long-term potentiation (LTP), the process whereby conjoint activity in two neurons strengthens the synaptic connection between them. This is one way that neurons encode new learning. If LTP occurs but then fades away, the new learning will be lost.

To investigate this issue, Barnes and colleagues placed rats in a maze that, viewed from above, had the shape of a squared-off 8. As you read back in Chapter 3, the hippocampus contains *place cells* that fire whenever a rat wanders into a particular location in a maze. Figure 12.12a shows activity recorded from several such place cells in the hippocampus of a young rat during its first session in this maze (Barnes, 1979). In this figure, each neuron is encoded as a different color and each dot represents a location where the neuron fired. One neuron (coded as blue in Figure 12.12a) fired when the rat was near the left end of the center arm. If the rat turned the corner to the right, that neuron would stop firing and another neuron (coded green in Figure 12.12a) would start firing. In this way, just by knowing which neuron was firing at a given moment, the experimenters (and presumably the rat) could deduce the rat's location in the maze.

When this same young rat was returned to the maze later, for a second session, the same hippocampal neurons tended to fire in the same spatial locations as before (Figure 12.12b). For example, the same neuron (coded blue) that had fired when the rat was in the left end of the center arm during session 1 also fired when the rat was in that location during session 2. This consistency of spatial encoding across sessions helps the rat form a reliable mental map of its environment. Obviously, the ability to learn and recognize the environment is a key part of learning and remembering how to navigate around that environment.

Figure 12.12c shows a similar mental map generated by the hippocampal neurons of an older rat on its first session in the 8-shaped maze. It looks a bit different from the session 1 map of the young rat since each individual rat has its own way of encoding space. But when the older rat was returned to the maze for session 2 (Figure 12.12d), the neurons didn't always fire in the same place as before. For example, the neuron (coded blue) that originally fired when the aged rat was in the middle of the maze now fired when the rat was in the top half of the left-hand arm. This differs from the results for the young rat, whose neurons tended to fire in the same places in both sessions. Apparently, both the young rat and the old rat learned about the environment during session 1, but the old rat lost this information much faster than the young rat. One reason this could happen is that LTP in the old rat's hippocampal neurons was unstable and didn't last over the interval between session 1 and session 2. This instability of hippocampal LTP could contribute to age-related deficits in spatial learning as well as in other kinds of learning and memory that depend on the hippocampus, such as episodic memory, which requires remembering the context in which an event occurred.

Why should LTP become less stable with age? One possible factor involves epigenetics. As you read earlier in the chapter, epigenetic processes activate and inactivate genes that trigger synaptic changes and other processes to stabilize new memory. Major mechanisms of epigenetic control, such as methylation, change with age, although the reasons are not yet clear (Apuza & Eaton, 2015). This would also possibly explain the wide individual differences in healthy aging: because no two individuals experience precisely the same life events, epigenetic changes vary widely—resulting in different rates of cognitive decline.

It's not yet known whether the same instability of hippocampal LTP occurs in aged humans. But there is some evidence that in us, too, age-related declines in episodic and semantic memory may be due to reduction in the ability of the hippocampus to encode new information. For example, as you read back in Chapter 7, in the subsequent memory paradigm,

Figure 12.12 Hippocampal neurons encoding location in old and young rats (a) While a young rat explored a maze shaped like a figure 8, researchers noted where the rat was when each of several hippocampal neurons (coded as different colors) fired. (b) When the same rat returned to the maze the next day, the pattern of place-dependent neuronal firing was similar. (c) When an aged rat was placed in the maze, hippocampal neurons also fired when the rat was in specific spatial locations. (d) But on the next day, the aged rat's firing pattern changed dramatically. This suggests that spatial learning from the first day did not persist in the aged rat.

(a) Young rat session 1   **(b)** Young rat session 2

(c) Aged rat session 1   **(d)** Aged rat session 2

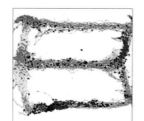

researchers record fMRI activity while subjects study new information such as words or pictures; later, subjects are tested with a second set of items and asked whether each is new or familiar. Typically, young adults show more activity in the medial temporal lobe and frontal lobe while studying items that will later be successfully recalled than while studying items that will later be forgotten (see Figure 7.15). Older adults show the same basic pattern, but the degree of difference in hippocampal and prefrontal activation for subsequently remembered versus subsequently forgotten items is much reduced (Daselaar, Fleck, Dobbins, Madden, & Cabeza, 2006; Dennis & Cabeza, 2011; Dennis et al., 2008).

Together, the results from animals and humans are generally consistent with the idea that age-related declines in new learning result from a general reduction in the ability to encode new information in the hippocampus and prefrontal cortex.

Adult Neurogenesis: New Neurons for Old Brains?

The news isn't all bad. Yes, the aging brain may lose neurons and synapses, and LTP may become unstable. But the brain itself may contain some mechanisms to fight this decline, including the ability to grow new neurons. Once it was thought that animals, particularly humans, were born with all the neurons they'd ever have. But we now know that neurogenesis occurs throughout life, although much less prolifically in the adult brain than in the developing brain.

Adult neurogenesis was first reliably observed in birds. Earlier in this chapter, you read how male white-crowned sparrows learn their song during a sensitive period early in life. In contrast, canaries are "lifelong" learners who can alter their song from year to year. Canary song is especially important during the spring, when males sing to defend their territory and to attract mates. This seasonal variation in singing is mirrored in the canaries' brains. For example, back in Chapter 11, you read about the high vocal center (HVC), which is a brain area important for song production (Figure 11.9). In canaries, the HVC doubles in volume during the spring relative to its size in the fall (Ball & Hulse, 1998).

To investigate this seasonal variation, Fernando Nottebohm and his colleagues injected radioactive *thymidine* into adult canaries. Thymidine is a compound that is taken up by cells undergoing mitotic division; it therefore can be used as a marker for newly born cells. The researchers found traces of thymidine in the birds' HVC as well as in the forebrain (Goldman & Nottebohm, 1983), suggesting that new neurons were either being born in these brain areas in the adult bird or migrating there soon after being formed. Nottebohm and his colleagues demonstrated that these newly generated cells developed into functional neurons, making connections with existing neurons and generally appearing anatomically and physiologically indistinguishable from older cells (Burd & Nottebohm, 1985; Paton & Nottebohm, 1984). Similar adult neurogenesis has since also been confirmed in fish, amphibians, and reptiles (Zupanc, 2001).

Neurogenesis in the brain of an adult monkey This radiograph shows a cell labeled with BrdU (arrow) in the dentate gyrus, a subregion of the hippocampus. The cell appears to be in anaphase, the phase of cell division in which the nucleus of the cell has begun to separate but the cell body itself is not yet divided in two (Gould & Gross, 2000).
From Nowakowski, R.S. and Hayes, N. L. (2000). New neurons: Extraordinary evidence or extraordinary conclusion?—Authors' response. *Science*, 288, 771a. Reprinted with permission from AAAS.

But what about mammals? In the 1990s, Elizabeth Gould and colleagues injected adult monkeys with a synthetic form of thymidine called *BrdU* (short for "bromodeoxyuridine"). One to three weeks later, the researchers found traces of BrdU in prefrontal, inferior temporal, and parietal cortex, suggesting that these areas contained neurons that had been born in the last few weeks (Gould, Reeves, Graziano, & Gross, 1999). Around the same time, Swedish neuroscientist Peter Eriksson gave BrdU to human cancer patients in an attempt to quantify the progress of their disease by tagging proliferating cancer cells (Eriksson et al., 1998). Unexpectedly, the BrdU labeled not only cancer cells but also neurons in the basal ganglia and in the hippocampus. Neurogenesis has also been observed in the hippocampus of adult rats (Kuhn, Dickinson-Anson, & Gage, 1996) and monkeys (Kornak & Rakic, 1999).

Estimates of birthrates vary widely, but one estimate suggested that in the adult macaque monkey, a few thousand new neurons might be born daily in the hippocampus alone (Gould & Gross, 2000). At least some of the new neurons in the hippocampus become functional in the sense of forming viable connections with other neurons (Toni et al., 2008; Vivar et al., 2012).

No one is quite sure what purpose new neurons serve in the adult brain, but one possibility is that they create a constantly renewed pool of "fresh" neurons available to encode new information (Becker, 2005; Kempermann, Wiskott, & Gage, 2004; Wiskott, Rasch, & Kempermann, 2006). If so, then at least some kinds of learning and memory should be improved or impaired by increasing or decreasing the rate of neurogenesis. But so far, there's only indirect evidence for this hypothesis (Aimone, Deng, & Gage, 2010; Shetty, 2010). For example, rats treated with low-dose radiation, which inhibits neurogenesis in the hippocampus, are impaired at new hippocampal-dependent learning (Winocur, Wojtowicz, Sekeres, Snyder, & Wang, 2006). On the other hand, rats undergoing new hippocampal-dependent learning tend to show higher rates of neurogenesis—suggesting that new neurons might be created on demand to encode the new information (Epp, Spritzer, & Galea, 2007). Further, both physical exercise and environmental enrichment increase neurogenesis, which may be why, as you read in Chapter 2, physical exercise and environmental enrichment can improve learning and memory.

Aside from their possible role in normal learning and memory, it would be nice to think that adult-born neurons can be generated to replace old ones that die off during aging or even as a result of injury. But it is a long leap from the existing evidence to that conclusion. To date, neurogenesis in the adult primate brain has only been documented unambiguously in a few brain regions, including the hippocampus and the basal ganglia (Eriksson, 2003; Lie, Song, Colamarino, Ming, & Gage, 2004). A few studies have reported evidence of large-scale neurogenesis in the cerebral cortex of adult monkeys (Gould et al., 1999) and human children (Shankle et al., 1998), but other researchers have challenged the methodology of those studies (Korr & Schmitz, 1999; Nowakowski & Hayes, 2000; Rakic, 2002).

Worse, the vast majority of newly born neurons appear to die off within a few weeks after formation (Gould & Gross, 2000). In one study, researchers damaged the basal ganglia in rats and then watched for neurogenesis. The number of newly born neurons that survived longer than two weeks was less than 1% of the number of neurons that had died—meaning there probably weren't enough new cells to make up for the ones that had been damaged (Lie et al., 2004).

In sum, so far there's little evidence that adult neurogenesis in mammals is widespread enough—or that the new neurons last long enough—for neurogenesis to serve as a general way to repair brains. The fact that adult mammals generally can't "regrow" cortical tissue following brain damage suggests that widespread replacement of dead neurons does not normally occur in mammalian brains (Eriksson, 2003). Neurogenesis in adult mammals may be limited to a few cells in a few brain regions (Kempermann et al., 2004). Apparently, in most regions of the human brain, the benefits of new neurons are outweighed by the difficulties of integrating new neurons into old networks without disrupting existing memories.

Interim Summary

- Genes strongly influence learning and memory abilities. Epigenetic processes determine whether and when specific genes are activated, and play an important role in activating and inactivating genes to cause changes to neurons and synapses during memory encoding and consolidation.

- In the developing brain, neurons and synapses are first overproduced, then weeded out in a process similar to Darwinian natural selection: those that make functional connections (and presumably encode important information) survive, while others die off. Growth and pruning occur at different rates in different brain areas, perhaps helping to explain why some learning and memory abilities mature faster than others.

- Sensitive periods in learning reflect sensitive periods in neuronal development, when specific kinds of environmental input can quickly and easily alter brain organization.

- Differences between males and females in learning and memory may reflect the effects of sex hormones on the developing brain and also on the activity of the adult brain.

- In the aging brain, some brain areas may lose appreciable numbers of neurons and synapses; changes due to neuronal plasticity (LTP) may also become less stable, meaning that new learning may not survive for long.

- Adult brains can grow new neurons, but many of these new neurons may die off before becoming functional.

12.3 Clinical Perspectives

Finally, let's consider two of the many ways learning and memory can be impaired at different points in the lifespan. Down syndrome strikes individuals at the beginning of their life and causes a lifelong impairment in learning ability and other aspects of intellectual function. At the other end of the lifespan, Alzheimer's disease afflicts mainly elderly individuals, resulting in a gradual loss of memory and an intellectual decline. As different as these two syndromes may appear, it turns out that there is an intriguing connection between them.

Down Syndrome

Down syndrome is a congenital disorder that causes mild-to-moderate intellectual disability. (Although "Down syndrome" is the term currently preferred by medical professionals in the United States and Canada, the older term "Down's syndrome" is still commonly used in the United Kingdom and some other countries.) Down syndrome occurs in about 1 of 700 live births (National Down Syndrome Society, 2015). It affects males and females equally and occurs in all ethnic groups—and an apparently analogous syndrome has been observed in our close primate relatives, the chimpanzees (McClure, Belden, Pieper, & Jacobson, 1969).

Children with Down syndrome show slowed development of speech and language, and even as adults they may score as low as 25–55 on IQ tests, although a few score in the "normal" range from 80–120 (Pennington, Moon, Edgin, Stedron, & Nadel, 2003). In addition, individuals with Down syndrome have physical growth delays and a characteristic facial profile, including a flattened nose and folds of skin over the inner corners of the eyes. Often, there are also severe medical complications; for example, almost half of all babies born with Down syndrome have congenital heart defects. As recently as 1980, the average life expectancy for individuals with Down syndrome was about 25 years, but, largely due to better medical care and treatment, the average lifespan has now risen to about 60 years (National Down Syndrome Society, 2015). This can create new challenges as individuals with Down syndrome balance the desire for adult independence, possibly including marriage and employment, with what is in many cases an ongoing need for support and care from family and community.

Down syndrome. A congenital disorder that causes mild-to-moderate intellectual disability, due to trisomy 21.

Individuals with Down syndrome have a characteristic facial profile, as well as delayed physical growth and mild-to-moderate intellectual disability. The life expectancy for those with Down syndrome, which was once only about 25 years, has greatly increased in the last few decades.

trisomy 21. A condition in which the embryo inherits three (rather than two) copies of chromosome 21, resulting in Down syndrome.

Down syndrome was first described by English physician John Langton Down in the mid-1800s (Down, 1866), but its genetic basis wasn't discovered until a century later (LeJeune, Gautier, & Turpin, 1959). Healthy human beings carry 23 pairs of chromosomes in almost every cell of the body, with one member of each pair contributed by each parent. Down syndrome is usually caused when an individual carries a third copy of the genes on chromosome 21. Usually, this happens when the baby inherits an extra copy of chromosome 21, a condition called **trisomy 21**. In 5 to 10% of such cases, the extra copy comes from the father, but in most of the remaining cases, the extra copy comes from the mother, a risk that rises dramatically with maternal age. The likelihood of giving birth to a child with Down syndrome is approximately 1 in 2,000 for a 20-year-old mother but 1 in 1,000 for a 30-year-old and 1 in 10 for a 49-year-old.

Brain Abnormalities and Memory Impairments in Down Syndrome

Chromosome 21 contains several hundred genes (Wiseman, Alford, Tybulewicz, & Fisher, 2009). At present, researchers don't know exactly which of those genes cause the intellectual disability in Down syndrome; currently, a half-dozen candidate genes have been identified, and any or all of these may contribute (Crnic & Pennington, 2000). We do know that the brains of individuals with Down syndrome appear normal at birth, but by 6 months of age, the brains are visibly smaller than those of other same-age children (Nadel, 2003).

By adolescence, several key brain areas are particularly small in individuals with Down syndrome; these include the hippocampus, frontal cortex, and cerebellum (Wiseman et al., 2009). As a result, we might expect to see particularly severe impairments in memory tasks that depend on these brain areas. To some extent, this seems to be the case. For example, one study considered a group of young adults with Down syndrome (mean age 21 years). On standard intelligence tests, these individuals were found to have an intelligence level slightly above that of 5-year-old children with normal mental abilities (Figure 12.13a; Vicari, Bellucci, & Carlisimo, 2000), but on a hippocampal-dependent task—recalling words

Figure 12.13 Impairments in Down syndrome may be particularly severe for hippocampal-dependent learning (a) A group of young adults (average age 21 years) with Down syndrome had an intelligence level comparable to that of 5-year-olds with normal mental abilities. (b) However, on hippocampal-dependent tests, such as recalling words from a studied list, the adults with Down syndrome performed much worse than the 5-year-olds.
Data from Vicari et al., 2000.

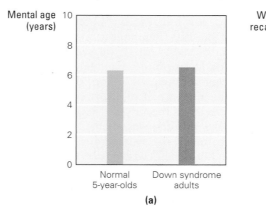

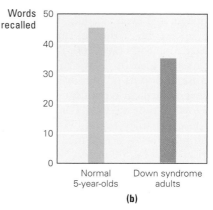

from a studied list—the adults with Down syndrome performed significantly worse than the 5-year-olds (Figure 12.13b). By the same token, children with Down syndrome are greatly impaired at recalling recent episodic events, such as what they had for breakfast or what time they went to bed last night (Pennington et al., 2003). In other words, although Down syndrome involves general intellectual disability, the impairments in Down syndrome are particularly profound for memory abilities that depend on the hippocampus (Nadel, 1999, 2003).

Animal Models of Down Syndrome

Since we know that trisomy 21 causes Down syndrome in humans, researchers have worked to develop animal models with the same genetic abnormality. In mice, for instance, a large region of chromosome 16 appears to serve the same functions as a region on human chromosome 21. Mice born with trisomy 16 (a third copy of their 16th chromosome) generally do not survive birth. (Down syndrome is also a common cause of miscarriage in humans.) So, researchers have bred mice with trisomy of only a segment of chromosome 16 (a condition called *segmental trisomy*). A widely studied example of these mouse strains is called the Ts65Dn mouse (Davisson et al., 1993).

Ts65Dn mice can be contrasted with littermates who share most of the same genes and environment but who do not have the trisomy. Compared to the control littermates, Ts65Dn mice have irregularities in the hippocampus and cortex, just like humans with Down syndrome (Belichenko et al., 2004). The Ts65Dn mice also show memory deficits reminiscent of the memory deficits in humans with Down syndrome. For example, Ts65Dn mice show impairments on hippocampal-dependent tasks, such as remembering the goal location in a maze (Escorihuela et al., 1995).

Ts65Dn mice also have excessive inhibition in the hippocampus and cortex, and this may contribute to their learning and memory deficits. Two genes that have a role in the balance between excitation and inhibition in the brain are the *Olig1* and *Olig2* genes on chromosome 21; three rather than two copies of these genes are present in individuals with Down syndrome and also in Ts65Dn mice, perhaps causing over-inhibition in the hippocampus. When given drugs that reduce neuronal inhibition (by interfering with the inhibitory neurotransmitter GABA), Ts65Dn mice show significant improvement of hippocampal-dependent learning and memory (Fernandez et al., 2007). When the number of gene copies is re-normalized (by breeding Ts65Dn females with males that only have one copy of the *Olig1* and *Olig2* genes), hippocampal inhibition is restored to normal levels in the offspring (Chakrabarti et al., 2010). Thus, the mouse models suggest that these two genes may play a key role in the learning and memory deficits in humans with Down syndrome.

Mouse models have also been used to study how behavioral therapy can improve cognitive function in Down syndrome. One intriguing study has shown that being housed in an enriched environment improves spatial memory in Ts65Dn females (though they never do quite as well as control mice). But environmental enrichment actually *exacerbates* the spatial memory impairment in Ts65Dn males (Martínez-Cué et al., 2002). This difference is curious, but the overall result is encouraging because it suggests that appropriately enriched postnatal experiences might help remediate the memory deficits associated with Down syndrome in humans.

Alzheimer's Disease

In 1901, German neuropathologist Alois Alzheimer examined a 51-year-old woman named Auguste Deter who could no longer remember her own last name or her husband's name. Auguste was experiencing a type of **dementia**,

dementia. Progressive cognitive decline usually due to accumulating brain pathology.

Alzheimer's disease. A form of dementia due to accumulating brain pathology (specifically, amyloid plaques and neurofibrillary tangles).

a progressive cognitive decline usually due to accumulating brain pathology. When Auguste died five years later, Alzheimer examined her brain and found curious abnormalities, including neurons that were bunched up like knotted ropes. Thinking Auguste was a unique case study, Alzheimer published a report on his findings (Alzheimer, 1987 [1907]). The condition became known as **Alzheimer's disease**, a form of dementia characterized by accumulation of abnormalities known as "plaques" and "tangles" in the brain (more about these later). Initially, Alzheimer's report raised little interest; at a time when life expectancy was about 50 years, conditions that selectively affected older people appeared to be rare. Now we know that Alzheimer's disease is not rare at all.

As of 2015, an estimated 5.3 million Americans have the disease, including about one-third of people aged 85 or over (Alzheimer's Association, 2015). The disease appears to have similar incidence throughout the world, although it appears to affect women more often than men (Alzheimer's Association, 2015). Famous victims include film star Charlton Heston, civil rights activist Rosa Parks, country music legend Glen Campbell, and Ronald Reagan, who at age 89 no longer remembered having once been president of the United States.

Progressive Memory Loss and Cognitive Deterioration

For many patients, the earliest symptoms of Alzheimer's disease are episodic memory disruptions, such as failures to remember recent conversations or visitors (Collie & Maruff, 2000). As the disease progresses, patients show marked declines in semantic memory, forgetting the names of acquaintances or the layout of familiar locations such as the local supermarket. Patients may ask the same question over and over again, forgetting not only the answer but also the fact that they've asked the question before.

Among the memory processes that survive the longest in Alzheimer's patients are conditioning and skill memory. For example, many patients can execute well-learned skills such as making tea (Rusted, Ratner, & Sheppard, 1995), and can acquire new motor skills such as mirror tracing (Gabrieli, Corkin, Mickel, & Crowden, 1993) and rotary pursuit (Heindel, Salmon, Shults, Walicke, & Butters, 1980), even when they cannot remember verbal information for more than a few minutes. But by the late stages of the disease, memory fails completely, and other cognitive systems begin to fail too. Patients with late-stage Alzheimer's may display personality changes, disorientation, loss of judgment, confusion, loss of speech, and eventually an inability to perform daily activities such as bathing, dressing, and eating. At this point, patients may require round-the-clock supervision and professional care.

Plaques and Tangles in the Brain

Technically, Alzheimer's disease is defined not by its behavioral symptoms, such as memory loss, but rather by the presence of two kinds of pathology in the brain: amyloid plaques and neurofibrillary tangles. **Amyloid plaques** are deposits of *beta-amyloid*, which is an abnormal by-product of a common protein called amyloid precursor protein, or APP (Figure 12.14a). Amyloid plaques accumulate in the brain of a patient with Alzheimer's disease, and some researchers believe they are toxic to nearby neurons. In 2000, an experimental vaccine was developed that could clear out amyloid plaques in human brains, but it did not have any significant effect on the cognitive symptoms in Alzheimer's patients, and so it was never approved for use as a treatment (Holmes et al., 2008). More recently, some researchers have suggested that the amyloid plaques are not the true culprit in Alzheimer's disease but rather an innocent by-product or even evidence of the brain's attempt to isolate and protect against damaging types of beta-amyloid (Gandy et al., 2010; Nikolaev, McLaughlin, O'Leary, & Tessier-Lavigne, 2009).

amyloid plaque. A deposit of beta-amyloid protein; these deposits accumulate in the brains of patients with Alzheimer's disease.

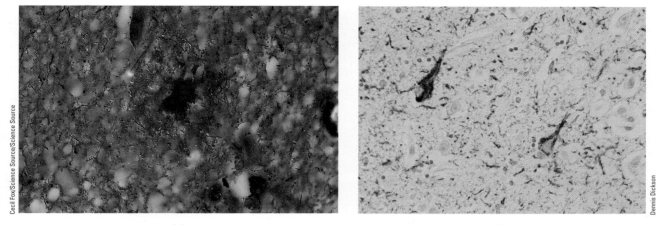

Cecil Fox/Science Source/Science Source

(a)

Dennis Dickson

(b)

The second hallmark of Alzheimer's disease in the brain is the presence of **neurofibrillary tangles**, the "knotted ropes" Alois Alzheimer described in his original report. Neurofibrillary tangles are the collapsed wreckage of abnormal tau proteins that normally function as scaffolding to hold a neuron in place and that help ferry nutrients around the cell (Figure 12.14b). In Alzheimer's, tau molecules undergo changes, and begin to clump together, forming tangles and causing the neuron to disintegrate. Some researchers believe that tau, rather than the amyloid, holds the real key to understanding Alzheimer's disease (Johnson & Bailey, 2002).

As plaques and tangles accumulate in the brain, synapse loss and neuron death occur on a large scale. Amyloid plaques tend to be fairly evenly distributed throughout the cerebral cortex, with the hippocampus relatively spared. In contrast, neurofibrillary tangles accumulate first in the hippocampus and nearby areas. The hippocampus and nearby brain areas of patients with early Alzheimer's disease are smaller than normal, as can be seen on structural MRI (Figure 12.15a; de Leon, George, Stylopoulos, Smith, & Miller, 1989; Risacher et al., 2009). This pattern of hippocampal damage with relative sparing of frontal lobes in early Alzheimer's is the opposite of "healthy" aging, which, as you read earlier, tends to involve shrinkage of the cerebral cortex with relatively little loss of neurons or synapses in the hippocampus (Braak & Braak, 1997; Price & Morris, 1999).

Currently, it is believed that brain changes, such as accumulation of amyloid plaques and neurofibrillary tangles, and shrinkage of brain areas such as the hippocampus begin during an early, "presymptomatic" phase of Alzheimer's (Jack, Knopman et al., 2010). The idea is that the underlying pathology is a slow process that occurs over decades, and only when the pathology accumulates to a tipping point do cognitive and clinical symptoms appear. The presymptomatic phase is followed by a second phase, sometimes called *mild cognitive impairment (MCI)*, in which there are mild cognitive symptoms, usually deficits in episodic memory, that don't yet meet criteria for dementia. All the while, pathology continues to accumulate beneath the surface. Some people will never go beyond these phases (or they will die before reaching the tipping point). But in principle, if these individuals live long enough, the pathology will eventually be so severe that cognitive impairments will emerge that are serious enough to be classified as dementia.

This is a fairly new view of Alzheimer's disease, and it's potentially important because of the idea of a long presymptomatic phase—during which the disease

Figure 12.14 The hallmarks of Alzheimer's disease in the brain (a) An amyloid plaque (the dark spot in the center of the image), surrounded by a residue of degenerating cells. (b) Neurofibrillary tangles (seen as dark brown areas) within neurons.

neurofibrillary tangle. An aggregation of collapsed remains of the tau proteins that normally hold a neuron in place and help to transport nutrients around the cell; such tangles occur in the brains of patients with Alzheimer's disease.

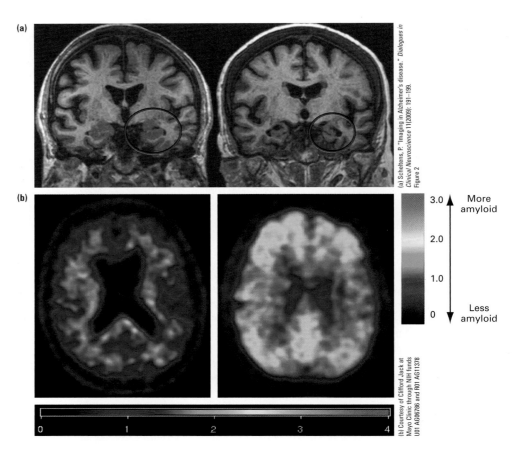

(a)

(b)

(a) Scheltens, P. "Imaging in Alzheimer's disease." *Dialogues in Clinical Neuroscience* 11(2009): 191–199. Figure 2

More amyloid

3.0

2.0

1.0

0

Less amyloid

(b) Courtesy of Clifford Jack at Mayo Clinic through NIH funds U01 AG06786 and R01 AG11378

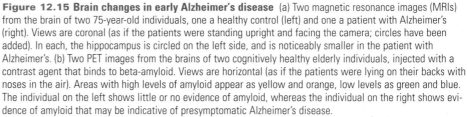

0   1   2   3   4

Figure 12.15 Brain changes in early Alzheimer's disease (a) Two magnetic resonance images (MRIs) from the brain of two 75-year-old individuals, one a healthy control (left) and one a patient with Alzheimer's (right). Views are coronal (as if the patients were standing upright and facing the camera; circles have been added). In each, the hippocampus is circled on the left side, and is noticeably smaller in the patient with Alzheimer's. (b) Two PET images from the brains of two cognitively healthy elderly individuals, injected with a contrast agent that binds to beta-amyloid. Views are horizontal (as if the patients were lying on their backs with noses in the air). Areas with high levels of amyloid appear as yellow and orange, low levels as green and blue. The individual on the left shows little or no evidence of amyloid, whereas the individual on the right shows evidence of amyloid that may be indicative of presymptomatic Alzheimer's disease.

could theoretically be recognized and even treated—before serious clinical symptoms emerge. An important new research area is the effort to develop reliable, inexpensive, and safe methods to detect these underlying brain changes. Some approaches center on measuring levels of beta-amyloid—for instance, by injecting a radioactive compound that binds to amyloid plaques, allowing the plaques to be visualized on PET scans. Figure 12.15b shows example PET scans of the brains of two elderly individuals who both appeared to be cognitively normal; yet one brain shows high levels of beta-amyloid, suggesting that the pathology of Alzheimer's may have started and will, over the next few years, begin to produce cognitive impairments in that individual (Jack et al., 2010). Similar methods are available to detect evidence of abnormal tau protein.

Such methods for detecting evidence of abnormal levels of amyloid and tau provide measures that correlate well with degree of Alzheimer's symptoms, and can help predict risk for future cognitive decline in elderly individuals who do not yet show symptoms. One limitation of these methods is that, currently, the available tests are invasive and expensive: requiring methods such as PET scans (where patients must be injected with a radioactive agent) or spinal taps to withdraw cerebrospinal fluid, each of which can carry their own risks.

Another approach has been to look for evidence of structural changes, using conventional MRI. In fact, among cognitively normal elderly, volume reductions in the hippocampus and nearby medial temporal structures (such as the entorhinal cortex) predict that cognitive decline and Alzheimer's will develop over the next few years (Apostolova et al., 2010; Duara et al., 2008; Risacher et al., 2009).

This finding leads in turn to the intriguing possibility of cheaper, behavioral methods to detect early Alzheimer's. Back in Chapter 6, you read about the role of the hippocampus and associated hippocampal region structures in such tasks as acquired equivalence that require the ability to generalize when familiar information is presented in a new way. Consequently, you might expect that individuals with atrophy of the hippocampus might be selectively impaired at such generalization, experiencing subtle deficits that might appear well before the onset of clinical symptoms of Alzheimer's disease. Some early evidence suggests this is so. Catherine Myers and colleagues gave a test of acquired equivalence to a group of elderly individuals who had each also received MRI to assess hippocampal volume. Those individuals with normal hippocampal volume performed well, but those with mild-to-moderate hippocampal atrophy (equivalent to a volume reduction of about 10 to 15%) were severely impaired at generalization (Myers, Kluger, Golomb, Gluck, & Ferris, 2008). Further, those participants who showed poor performance on the acquired equivalence task were more likely to show symptoms of cognitive decline two years later. While preliminary, these data suggest that poor performance on acquired equivalence tasks and similar tests of hippocampal-dependent generalization might provide very sensitive early-warning signals to help diagnose which elderly individuals are at highest risk of developing Alzheimer's disease within the next few years.

Diagnosing and Treating Alzheimer's Disease

Currently, a diagnosis of Alzheimer's disease is only confirmed if plaques and tangles are seen in the patient's brain at autopsy, when a portion of the brain is removed and examined. For this reason, living patients with Alzheimer's symptoms are only diagnosed as having "probable Alzheimer's." In making this diagnosis, clinicians may also use MRI scans of brain structure, PET scans to image beta-amyloid deposits, and tests of cerebrospinal fluid to check for unusual levels of circulating beta-amyloid and abnormalities. At present, a diagnosis of Alzheimer's based on a combination of these tests, as well as the individual's symptoms and genetic history, can be made with about 90% accuracy. In the remaining 10% of cases, patients have some other form of dementia that produces symptoms similar to Alzheimer's.

As of 2015, five medications are approved in the United States to treat patients with Alzheimer's disease. Four of these—donepezil, galantamine, rivastigmine, and tacrine—are *cholinesterase inhibitors*, which work by reducing the breakdown of unused acetylcholine in synapses between neurons. A fifth drug, memantine, blocks certain receptors for the excitatory neurotransmitter glutamate, which is produced in overly large amounts in the brains of patients with Alzheimer's. These five drugs aren't effective in all patients, and they only treat symptoms temporarily rather than stopping or reversing the underlying brain damage. Clearly, more effective treatments are needed. As of this writing, over 500 candidate drugs have been tested, and at least 100 more are currently in various stages of research; however, since 2003, no additional drugs have yet proven both safe enough and effective enough to be approved to treat the cognitive symptoms in Alzheimer's disease.

Genetic Basis of Alzheimer's Disease

To date, several genes have been implicated in Alzheimer's disease. Most progress has been made in understanding the genetic basis of a rare early-onset form of Alzheimer's. Early-onset Alzheimer's represents less than 1% of all cases of the disease, but it is especially heartbreaking because it can strike people as young as 35 to 50 years old. Mutations on three genes are associated with early-onset Alzheimer's: the *APP* gene on chromosome 21, the *presenilin-1* (*PS1*) gene on chromosome 14, and the *presenilin-2* (*PS2*) gene on chromosome 1. A child who inherits just one of these mutated genes from either parent will inevitably develop Alzheimer's (unless she dies of something else first).

Another gene, *APOE* on chromosome 19, has been associated with the more common, late-onset form of Alzheimer's, which appears in individuals age 60 or older. *APOE* comes in several alleles, three of which—called *E2*, *E3*, and *E4*—occur frequently in the general population. The *E3* allele is the most common and is considered the "normal" allele; many people carry two copies of *E3* (one inherited from each parent). People who carry one copy of the *E4* allele are at three times higher risk of developing Alzheimer's, and people carrying two copies of *E4* are at 15 times higher risk (Blennow, de Leon, & Zetterberg, 2006). On the other hand, having one or two copies of the *E2* allele reduces the risk of developing Alzheimer's.

At present, it's unclear why these alleles have such effects. Some studies suggest that *E4* carriers have fewer dendritic spines in the hippocampus than *E3* carriers do, but we don't know whether this is a cause or an effect of developing Alzheimer's disease (Teter & Finch, 2004). Another possibility is that the *APOE* gene may help control how the brain clears out beta-amyloid; some alleles (such as *E2*) may perform this function well, but other alleles (such as *E4*) may be less effective and allow plaques to build up, contributing to the brain pathology in Alzheimer's patients.

A number of other genes have been identified as conferring risk for late-onset Alzheimer's disease, including the *TREM2*, *CLU*, *PICALM*, and *CR1* genes (Jonsson et al., 2013; Jun et al., 2010; Seshadri et al., 2010). But genes alone don't tell the whole story. For example, some individuals carrying two "good" copies of the *APOE E2* allele still develop late-onset Alzheimer's, and some individuals carrying two "bad" copies of the *APOE E4* allele never do. It seems likely that these genes only predispose a person to develop Alzheimer's, meaning that additional environmental factors (such as exposure to toxins, poor vascular health, or brain inflammation) may be needed to actually trigger the disease.

The good news is that if environmental factors help trigger the disease, then changing these factors might prevent the disease from developing (or slow it down so that cognitive symptoms never emerge within the patient's lifetime). Right now, evidence suggests that physical exercise—even light physical activity once or twice per week—can improve cardiovascular health, increasing blood flow with its cargo of oxygen and nutrients throughout the body and brain, thus helping to protect against cognitive decline (Radak, Hart, Sarga, Koltai, Atalay, Ohno & Boldogh, 2010; Schlosser Covell et al., 2015). Physical exercise may also improve function in people already diagnosed with probable Alzheimer's (Rao, Chou, Bursley, Smulofsky & Jezequel, 2014). Although many studies have searched for a similar protective effect of mental exercise, the evidence to date is not as strong (see "Learning and Memory in Everyday Life: Can Mental Exercise Protect against Alzheimer's Disease?" on the next page).

Can Mental Exercise Protect against Alzheimer's Disease?

Many researchers have argued that high levels of cognitive activity ("mental exercise") can help protect against Alzheimer's disease. There is accumulating evidence that older individuals who participate in mentally challenging pastimes—reading, playing chess, or doing crossword puzzles—are less likely to experience cognitive decline than those who stick to more passive pursuits such as watching television (Bennett et al., 2003; Wilson & Bennett, 2003). Individuals with a high educational level or a wide social support network are also at lower risk of Alzheimer's, and when such individuals do develop the disease, they can often tolerate a greater degree of brain pathology before they begin to show clinical symptoms (Scarmeas & Stern, 2004). In all these cases, the common theme is that mental activity protects against Alzheimer's disease—leading to the common exhortation to "use it or lose it."

One possible interpretation of these findings is the idea of *cognitive reserve*. On average, individuals who have been cognitively active throughout life enter old age at a high level of cognitive function. If Alzheimer's disease strikes, these individuals have further to decline before showing sufficient loss of function to interfere with daily life (Scarmeas & Stern, 2004; Stern, Albert, Tang, & Tsai, 1999).

A second, not mutually exclusive, possibility is that cognitive activity actually combats Alzheimer's disease. You read in Chapter 2 that *environmental enrichment* can lead to changes in the brains of adult animals, including growth of new neurons and connections. Similar changes in the brains of physically and cognitively active people might help them compensate for the loss of neurons and connections that occur in early Alzheimer's (Nithianantharajah & Hannan, 2009; Wilson & Bennett, 2003).

So far, the studies linking cognitive activity with reduced Alzheimer's risk are only observational, meaning that they don't prove a cause–effect relationship. On the one hand, it is indeed possible that mental exercise helps prevent Alzheimer's and that people who choose to spend their time on mentally challenging pursuits, such as crossword puzzles, are in fact protecting themselves against the risk of developing Alzheimer's. But it is also possible that an individual in the earliest (pre-symptomatic) stages of Alzheimer's is simply less competent at such mentally challenging pursuits, and so he is unlikely to choose to engage in them—just as someone with chronic joint pain might be unlikely to choose to engage in extreme physical sports. Viewed this way, cognitive inactivity would not be a *cause* of Alzheimer's but rather a *symptom*. In 2010, an independent government panel of experts concluded that there simply isn't enough evidence to conclude that mental exercise actually protects against Alzheimer's disease (Daviglus et al., 2010).

One reason for this disappointing finding may be that no *single* lifestyle choice determines whether we will or won't get Alzheimer's disease. Rather, it may be that a number of seemingly minor lifestyle choices—including healthy diet, regular low-level exercise, and mental and social stimulation—all work together to help prevent or at least postpone the onset of cognitive decline in individuals at risk for Alzheimer's.

A Connection between Down Syndrome and Alzheimer's Disease

Did you notice a connection between the genes implicated in Down syndrome and Alzheimer's disease? Chromosome 21, the chromosome that is tripled in Down syndrome, also contains the *APP* gene, which is implicated in one form of Alzheimer's disease. This intriguing fact has led researchers to look for connections between Down syndrome and Alzheimer's. In fact, almost all people with Down syndrome who survive beyond age 40 develop plaques and tangles in their brains—just like Alzheimer's patients (Moncaster et al., 2010). And about 50% of adults with Down syndrome show memory decline and other symptoms similar to the cognitive impairments in Alzheimer's disease (Brugge et al., 1994; Cutler, Hesten, Davies, Haxby, & Schapiro, 1985). You read above about Ts65Dn mice as an animal model of Down syndrome. In Ts65Dn mice, learning and memory can be improved by drugs that reduce beta-amyloid (Netzer et al., 2010) as well as by the Alzheimer's drug memantine (Rueda et al., 2010), and so there is some hope that these drugs may also improve cognition in humans with Down syndrome.

But the other 50% of adults with Down syndrome do not show age-related cognitive decline—even though they have the same brain pathology! As yet, it's not clear why this should be so. But the explanation might add to our understanding of both Alzheimer's disease and Down syndrome and suggest some possible therapies to help prevent such brain pathology from causing memory decline.

Test Your Knowledge

Alzheimer's Fact Sheet

See how well you remember some of the key facts about Alzheimer's disease. Identify each statement below as true or false. Answers appear at the back of the book.

1. Dementia is the most common form of Alzheimer's in the United States.
2. Over 50% of Americans over age 65 have Alzheimer's.
3. Alzheimer's is usually only formally diagnosed at autopsy (after death).
4. Current Alzheimer's drugs work by modifying neuronal activity, not reducing plaques or tangles.
5. Tangles are formed from a toxic protein called beta-amyloid.
6. In Alzheimer's, tau molecules begin to clump together, causing neurons to collapse.
7. Whereas plaques tend to accumulate in the cerebral cortex, tangles appear first in the hippocampus and nearby brain areas.
8. It's currently believed that Alzheimer's pathology starts accumulating in the brain long before behavioral symptoms start to appear.
9. Although genes have been identified that cause the rare early-onset form of the disease, no genes have yet been implicated in the common, late-onset form.
10. Current evidence suggests regular physical exercise is the best way to help protect against Alzheimer's disease.

Interim Summary

- Down syndrome is a condition in which babies are born with an extra copy of chromosome 21.
- Children with Down syndrome have cognitive impairments, including memory impairments, and certain brain areas, including the hippocampus, frontal cortex, and cerebellum, tend to be abnormally small.
- Alzheimer's disease is a form of dementia in which amyloid plaques and neurofibrillary tangles accumulate in the brain. It's now thought that pathology accumulates slowly, over decades, before cognitive and clinical symptoms emerge.
- Memory symptoms prominent early in Alzheimer's disease are consistent with the finding that the hippocampus and nearby medial temporal areas suffer pathology early in the disease.
- Genes have been identified that cause rare, early-onset forms of Alzheimer's disease; other identified genes may contribute to an individual's risk for the common, late-onset form of the disease.
- There may be a connection between Down syndrome and Alzheimer's disease, because chromosome 21 (which is tripled in Down syndrome) also contains one of the genes implicated in an early-onset form of Alzheimer's disease, and almost all people with Down syndrome who live long enough develop Alzheimer's-like plaques and tangles in their brains.

Synthesis

At the beginning of this chapter, you met Denise, the quintessential "healthy young adult," at the peak of physical health and also of memory ability. Aside from appreciating her own memory abilities, how might Denise apply the lessons of this chapter next time she's home for the holidays?

First, let's think about Denise's young niece Kelly. At 10 months of age, many areas of Kelly's brain are still undergoing intensive neurogenesis, synaptogenesis, and myelination. Yet Kelly is already quite capable of habituation, conditioning, skill learning, and observational learning, and she can express this learning by action and imitation, if not yet by words. On the other hand, her episodic memories may not yet have the same richness of information about spatial and temporal context as adult memories. In addition, Kelly's frontal lobes are also not yet fully operational, which means she may have trouble juggling several pieces of information in memory at the same time. This works to the family's advantage when Kelly cries in frustration: it's still fairly easy to distract her attention from whatever upsets her, by waving a shiny, brightly colored toy.

Denise may also be able to apply learning and memory principles to her interactions with her grandparents. Although her grandmother seems to be handling old age well, Denise can expect there will be some deficiencies in the older woman's working memory and in her ability to form new episodic memories, and she can be understanding and supportive when her grandmother misplaces something or tells a favorite story for the tenth time. But Denise should take advantage of her grandmother's fund of semantic and episodic knowledge while it's still available, perhaps encouraging the older woman to create a family cookbook or written history to preserve these memories for future generations.

Denise's grandfather is a more difficult case. Instead of chalking his memory deficits up to old age, Denise should encourage the family to take him for a thorough neuropsychological exam to determine whether his memory lapses probably reflect early Alzheimer's disease or whether they stem from some other type of dementia that might be treatable. If the diagnosis is "probable Alzheimer's," then the sad fact is that Denise's family is in for a long struggle as they watch her grandfather slowly decline and become more dependent on a caregiver's assistance. Although there is currently no way to reverse or prevent the cognitive decline in Alzheimer's disease, the younger members of the family can hope that by the time they become grandparents themselves, better treatments will be available, increasing their chances of facing old age with their brains and memories intact.

KNOW YOUR KEY TERMS

adolescence, *p. 483*	Down syndrome, *p. 505*	neurogenesis, *p. 494*
allele, *p. 489*	elicited imitation, *p. 477*	puberty, *p. 483*
Alzheimer's disease, *p. 508*	epigenetics, *p. 492*	sensitive period, *p. 479*
amyloid plaque, *p. 508*	estrogen, *p. 485*	spine, *p. 495*
androgen, *p. 485*	gestational age, *p. 474*	synaptogenesis, *p. 494*
apoptosis, *p. 494*	imprinting, *p. 479*	testosterone, *p. 485*
dementia, *p. 507*	neurofibrillary tangle, *p. 509*	trisomy 21, *p. 506*

QUIZ YOURSELF

1. _____ refers to the process of physical change during which the body transitions to sexual maturity. (p. 483)

2. A spine is a protrusion on a _____ where a _____ may form. (p. 495)

3. Down syndrome is a form of _____, caused by a genetic condition called _____, in which the embryo inherits three (rather than two) copies of a specific chromosome. (p. 505–506)

4. The _____ are the principal sex hormones present in adult females. The _____ are the principal sex hormones present in adult males, and the most important of these is _____. (p. 485)

5. _____ is a technique for assessing memory in infants, by observing their ability to mimic actions they have seen earlier. (p. 477)

6. _____ is the most common form of dementia. (p. 508)

7. A naturally occuring variant of a gene is called an _____. (p. 489)

8. The _____ age of an embryo or fetus is the age in terms of time since conception. (p. 474)

9. Whereas _____ encode the instructions for building and maintaining an organism, _____ mechanisms determine how and when those instructions are executed, by turning gene activity on and off. (p. 492)

10. The brains of patients with Alzheimer's disease accumulate brain pathology in the form of _____, which are deposits of beta-amyloid protein, and _____, which are collapsed remains of the proteins that normally hold a neuron in place. (p. 508–509)

11. _____ is the transitional stage between puberty and adulthood, corresponding roughly to the _____ years in humans. (p. 483)

12. Natural cell death, not caused by accident or disease, is called _____. (p. 494)

13. The tendency of youngsters in some species to form an attachment to the first individual they see after birth is called _____. (p. 479)

14. _____ refers to the creation of new neurons in the brain. _____ refers to the creation of new synapses on neurons. (p. 494)

15. A time window, usually early in life, during which a certain kind of learning is most effective, is known as a _____ for that learning. (p. 479)

16. _____ refers to progressive cognitive decline, usually due to accumulating brain pathology. (p. 507)

Answers appear in the back of the book.

CONCEPT CHECK

1. Kelly's older brother, Kyle, didn't speak until he was nearly 20 months old. What factors might have contributed to such a difference between these children, assuming no diseases or disabilities?

2. A healthy 80-year-old businessman wants to continue working at his job although he admits his memory isn't quite what it used to be. What are some habits he could develop that might help him minimize memory lapses?

3. Among tree lizards, some males are dominant and defend territories; others are nomadic foragers. Males given testosterone injections during the first 30 days of life are more likely to grow up to be dominant territory holders, but similar injections have no effect on adult non-dominant males. Why might this be?

4. "Antagonistic pleiotropy" is a formal name for the idea that a gene may be beneficial early in life (while an organism is still capable of reproducing) and yet have adverse consequences later in life. As long as the organism carrying the gene survives long enough to produce offspring, the gene can propagate through the population. Restate this general idea, using Alzheimer's disease as an example. Can you think of specific examples from this chapter where processes that are beneficial early in life would be maladaptive if they continued into later life?

Answers appear in the back of the book.

ANSWERS TO TEST YOUR KNOWLEDGE SECTIONS

CHAPTER 1

Who's Who in the History of Learning and Memory?

1. Aristotle; Descartes
2. Locke
3. James
4. Ebbinghaus; Pavlov; Thorndike

Borrowing from the Physical and Natural Sciences to Explain the Mind

1. How the body could function like a machine with input and output control pathways.
2. How complex ideas could be formed from combinations of simpler and more elementary components.
3. How psychology of memory could be a rigorous natural science, defined by precise mathematical laws.
4. The distinction between a direct fixed connection and a modifiable indirect connection as when a switchboard operator makes the call.
5. That of all possible behavioral responses, the ones that are more successful and adaptive are more likely to be retained (i.e., learned).
6. The search for simple, powerful equations that unify many disparate observations.
7. The ability to measure the amount of information in a message or stored memory, independent of the content.

Answers to Quiz Yourself

1. reasoned thought, logical arguments, scientific experimentation
2. frequency
3. nativism, empiricism
4. dualism, Descartes, reflex arc
5. natural selection, makes an individual more fit to survive or procreate
6. experimental psychology
7. Hermann Ebbinghaus
8. forgetting, retention curve
9. instrumental conditioning, operant conditioning
10. conditioned stimulius, CS; unconditioned stimulus, US; conditioned response, CR
11. behaviorism
12. Clark Hull
13. Thorndike, effect, more
14. cognitive maps
15. latent learning
16. cognitive, behaviorist
17. stimulus sampling theory, Estes
18. George Miller
19. Gordon Bower, insight learning
20. connectionist, distributed

Sample Answers to Concept Checks

1. NATIVISM: Plato, Descartes, Leibniz, Darwin. EMPIRICISM: Aristotle, Locke, James, Pavlov, Thorndike. Refer to Table 1 to see the historical progression.
2. Teasing apart nature from nurture is only possible if children are reared by someone other than their parents. Parents with high memory ability may be more prone to challenge their children's memory and speak to them in more complex, rich sentences, giving them more opportunities to expand and train their memory.
3. Rats in Tolman's studies learned during a latent period, when there was no reinforcement; strictly reward/punishment views of learning would not expect this to happen. A variation on behaviorism would need to suggest that there was some implicit form of reward that comes from exploring the maze that was not otherwise evident or manipulated by the experimenter.
4. Describing someone as a "large white male" (if we assume that people can be simply characterized as large/small, white/non-white, male/female). The most basic form of information would be a signal like 101, which has three binary bits.

CHAPTER 2

Synaptic Transmission

All of the statements correctly describe a process of synaptic transmission.

Equipotentiality versus Phrenology

Gall proposed that particular mental abilities were associated with specific cortical regions. Lashley proposed that mental abilities were not associated with specific cortical regions but instead could be performed by any sufficiently large region of cortex. Gall used correlations between skull features and individual variations in humans to support his ideas. Lashley used differences in the capacity of rats to learn mazes after undergoing cortical lesion to support his theory.

Synaptic Plasticity

1. True. This is what happened in the original LTP studies: the researchers stimulated one neuron and observed LTP in the postsynaptic neuron, indicating that the synapse had been strengthened.
2. False. A neuron changes its firing pattern when its inputs change, whether or not any synaptic change takes place.

3. True.

4. False. fMRI does not measure neural activity and cannot detect synapses; it measures changes in blood flow, which is an indirect measure of neural activity.

5. False. LTP has only occasionally been observed in animals that are learning. It is commonly measured independent of any observable behavior.

Answers to Quiz Yourself

1. central nervous system
2. peripheral nervous system
3. cerebral cortex/hemispheres
4. cerebellum
5. receptors/dendrites/postsynaptic neurons/presynaptic neurons
6. glia, blood cells
7. MRI/magnetic resonance imaging
8. reflex/diving reflex
9. M1/primary motor cortex/cerebellum/basal ganglia
10. axons/dendrites
11. engram/memory trace
12. difference images
13. EEG/electroencephalographic
14. transcranial magnetic stimulation/slap to the head
15. drugs
16. synaptic plasticity/Hebbian learning/long-term potentiation

Sample Answers to Concept Checks

1. Activity of neurons in primary visual cortex would likely overlap with activity in the neurons that respond to the presence of food (leading to salivation). Because the visual neurons activated by sights of Pavlov were repeatedly paired with presentation of food, Hebbian learning predicts that the neurons would "wire together" such that ultimately, seeing Pavlov would make dogs slobber. This would imply that neurons in the dog's visual cortex were changing their connections with cortical regions involved in detecting food (such as primary somatosensory cortex).

2. Differences in activity would be consistent with the brains of individuals functioning differently. However, the theory of equipotentiality suggests that different cortical regions can achieve the same functionality. To the extent that this theory is true, two individuals' brains might function identically using different regions of cerebral cortex.

3. There is not a simple one-to-one mapping between the presence/absence of LTP and the presence/absence of learning. Put another way, LTP and learning are not the same thing.

4. One example would be to test sensory deficits in each modality to determine whether primary sensory cortices have sustained damage.

5. It implies that the cerebral cortex is not the only part of nervous systems that makes learning possible.

CHAPTER 3
Maximizing Habituation

1. The weaker the stimulus, the faster the habituation. So, one option is to try to make the stimulus—in this case the itch—less intense, perhaps by using lotion or washing the shirt with fabric softener.

2. Sensitization is associated with increased arousal. If you decrease your arousal while wearing the shirt—say, by going to sleep—you will decrease the likelihood of sensitization. Sleeping, or just meditating, will also make the stimulus weaker, further increasing the rate of habituation.

3. Assuming that you've slathered on the lotion so that the itching is not too intense, wear the shirt all the time. The more you wear it, the more your responses will become habituated to its itchiness.

Perceptual Learning versus Habituation

1. This dog show judge has learned to perceptually discriminate a dog's quality based in part on its teeth or other features of its mouth. She probably also has habituated to having a gaping mouth full of sharp teeth up near her face. The dog's response has become habituated to strangers sticking their hands and face near its mouth and holding it open.

2. This man has probably learned to perceive differences among wines based on odors—an example of perceptual learning. Perhaps he has also habituated to the feel of dressing formally in a jacket and tie.

3. Repeated experiences have habituated the homeless man to being ignored by the general public and have habituated the pedestrians to seeing destitute people on the street.

Synaptic Mechanisms of Learning in *Aplysia*

1. The reduction in synaptic connections indicates habituation; less glutamate is being released in the stimulus-response pathway.

2. The increase in glutamate release indicates sensitization; stimulus-response pathways are more likely to become active.

3. The increased number of connections suggests sensitization; the increase in connections should increase the amount of glutamate released in stimulus-response pathways.

4. The number of action potentials generated usually reflects the amount of glutamate released; if this number is reduced, glutamate release is probably reduced, suggesting habituation.

Answers to Quiz Yourself

1. sensitized
2. habituated

3. dishabituate
4. orienting response
5. weaker
6. spaced, massed
7. SCR/skin conductance response
8. dual process theory
9. latent learning
10. novel object recognition
11. serotonin, interneurons
12. cortical plasticity
13. multimodal/somatosensory/auditory
14. place cells
15. sensitization
16. sensory prostheses, perceptual learning

Sample Answers to Concept Checks

1. You cannot determine whether this is habituation or not from the evidence given, because all you know is that his responses decreased. A likely alternative explanation is fatigue. However, these two possibilities cannot be distinguished without additional tests. An arousing stimulus, such as an angry look from a coach might dishabituate the lifter, leading to renewed responding.

2. Haunted houses at amusement parks use a variety of acoustic and lighting stimuli to sensitize visitors as they walk through the creepy corridors. Sporting events use light displays and loud musical introductions to rile up fans at the start of a game.

3. Yes. A better question is, what learning processes are involved, and the answer to that question is pretty much all of the processes described in the chapter. You will be habituating to the style of the text and figure captions; primed by familiar words; possibly sensitized to the amount of time you spend reading that you could have spent on more entertaining activities; perceptually learning about squiggles; becoming familiar with novel images of brains, methods, and data; and spatially learning about where the Concept Check question answers are located.

4. Taxi driving taxes spatial memory abilities, which depend on spatial learning. Given that place cells in the hippocampus are known to be important for spatial learning, it is likely that extensive use of place cells is in some way contributing to the increased size of hippocampal structures in experienced taxi drivers.

CHAPTER 4

Pavlov's Experiment

CS = dog drool, CR = write in book.

Classical Conditioning in Everyday Life

1. US, female model; UR, sexual arousal (most likely in men, who are the targeted customers); CS, the car; CR, arousal of pleasurable feelings at the thought and sight of the sports car.

2. US, hot pizza for dinner; UR, anticipation of dinner and salivation; CS, smell of cardboard burning; CR, hunger pangs and salivation.

3. US = ice cream, CS = bell, CR = running to truck, UR = salivate/anticipate ice cream

Contrasting the Rescorla-Wagner and Mackintosh Models

1. US, CS
2. (a) Mackintosh; (b) Rescorla–Wagner

The Cerebellum in Motor Reflex Conditioning

1. The Purkinje cells are involved in response timing. The evidence includes findings that lesions of the cerebellar cortex lead to smaller and poorly timed CRs, and that mice with degeneration of Purkinje cells are slow to learn eyeblink conditioning.

2. Cerebellar cortex containing Purkinje cells and the cerebellar deep nuclei. The CS input pathway and the US input pathway. The two sites of convergence are the Purkinje cells and the interpositus nucleus.

3. Researchers recording unpaired CS- or US-alone trials in naive rabbits found that where there is no CR, there is no activity in the interpositus nucleus. Despite a strong UR (eyeblink) during the US-alone trials, there was a lack of substantial interpositus activity.

Answers to Quiz Yourself

1. does not
2. preparatory
3. CR/UR, timing
4. faster
5. compensatory, homeostasis
6. context or timing
7. first
8. summed
9. context
10. prediction error
11. Purkinje, interpositus
12. mossy fibers
13. inferior olive
14. inhibit
15. poorly timed
16. hippocampus
17. glutamate
18. activity-dependent enhancement, synaptic plasticity
19. initiate, inhibits
20. conditioned tolerance
21. Rescorla–Wagner
22. aversive conditioning
23. absence, contingency

Sample Answers to Concept Checks

1. Try diagramming it as if Doris and Herman were CSs and predicting the market was the US.

$$Doris \rightarrow Prediction\ (1)$$
$$Doris + Herman \rightarrow No\ prediction\ (0)$$

The association weight for Doris (W_{Doris}) will rise on the Doris-alone trials, but both W_{Doris} and W_{Herman} will decline on the compound trials until the weights stabilize at $W_{Doris} = +1$ and $W_{Herman} = -1$, indicating that Herman is a conditioned inhibitor.

2. One reason might be that as extinction learning is context-specific, exposure therapy will not be as effective in the therapy center as it would be at home.

CHAPTER 5

Is It Classical or Operant?

1. Whistling is the discriminative stimulus, birds arriving is the learned response, eating crumbs is the outcome. The birds don't get the crumbs (O) unless they arrive (R), so this is operant conditioning.

2. Thunder always follows lightning. This occurs whether or not Snoopy hides. Therefore this is classical conditioning (CS = lightning, US = thunder, CR = hiding).

3. Presence of clouds is the discriminative stimulus, carrying the umbrella is the learned response, and staying dry is the outcome. The outcome (O) doesn't occur unless Miguel carries the umbrella (R), so this is operant conditioning.

4. Scalding water always follows flushing. This occurs whether or not Carlos flinches. Therefore, this is classical conditioning (CS = noise, US = hot water, CR = flinching).

Reinforcement vs. Punishment

1. (a) Lucy; (b) R is tantrum; (c) O is obtaining candy; (d) S^D is seeing candy at the store, because tantrums at other times won't cause mother to buy candy; (e) candy is added—so this is "positive"; (f) response increases—so this is a reinforcement paradigm. *Conclusion:* Lucy learns to throw tantrums to obtain candy. This is positive reinforcement.

2. (a) Susan; (b) R is giving candy; (c) O is the tantrum stops (or is avoided altogether); (d) S^D is her child's tantrum, because candy won't terminate the tantrum unless there is already a tantrum present; (e) the tantrum is taken away—so this is "negative"; (f) response increases—so this is a reinforcement paradigm. *Conclusion:* Susan learns to give her child candy to stop (or avoid) tantrums. This is negative reinforcement.

3. (a) Snoopy; (b) R is crossing the boundary; (c) O is the noise; (d) S^D is wearing the collar while in the yard, because straying at other times won't produce the noise; (e) the noise is added—so this is "positive"; (f) response decreases—so this is a punishment paradigm. *Conclusion:* Snoopy learns to stay inside the yard. This is positive punishment.

4. (a) Miguel; (b) R is drinking alcohol; (c) O is revocation of playing privileges by the coach; (d) S^D is football season, because Miguel won't be punished by the coach for drinking alcohol at other times; (e) playing privileges are taken away—so this is "negative"; (f) response decreases—so this is a punishment paradigm. *Conclusion:* Miguel learns not to drink alcohol during football season. This is negative punishment.

5. (a) Rachel; (b) R is getting a stomach ache (and telling the nurse about it); (c) O is avoiding gym; (b) S^D is school lunch , or possibly coming to school on gym days, because getting sick at other times doesn't affect gym class; (e) gym class is taken away—so this is "negative"; (f) the response increases—so this is a reinforcement paradigm. *Conclusion:* Rachel learns to feel (or report) sickness in order to avoid gym. This is negative reinforcement.

Reinforcement Schedules

1. FR (5 homeworks = 1 toy); note that the stars are actually secondary reinforcers (on an FR 1 schedule).

2. VR (20 phone calls = 2 sales on average, but he can't be sure exactly when the next sale will come; it might be immediately after a previous call resulted in a sale).

3. VI (can't be sure exactly when the table will be ready, so check back periodically; only the last response will be reinforced). We'd expect the couple to check more frequently near the end of the expected 30-minute interval.

4. FI (money can be obtained for the first donation after a 2-week interval).

5. VI (can't be sure exactly when the next big wave will arrive, so the best policy is to hang around in anticipation, even immediately after catching the previous wave).

6. FR (one stick of gum = one negative reinforcement, which is removal of bad breath); this is also an example of CR (continuous reinforcement), since each R elicits O.

7. FI (address occurs after a fixed 1-week interval). We'd expect revisions to be most frantic right before the speech is delivered, resulting in the scalloped cumulative response curve characteristic of FI schedules.

8. VR (100 cards = 1 winner on average, but the very next card after a winner might also be a winner).

Answers to Quiz Yourself

1. discriminative stimuli

2. Premack principle, response deprivation

3. insula/insular cortex, dorsal anterior cingulate cortex/ dACC

4. pathological addiction, behavioral addiction
5. substantia nigra, dorsal striatum, basal ganglia, ventral tegmental area
6. drive reduction theory
7. reinforcement, punishment
8. behavioral economics
9. shaping, chaining
10. primary reinforcers, secondary reinforcers
11. continuous reinforcement, partial reinforcement
12. orbitofrontal cortex
13. negative contrast
14. endogenous opioids
15. concurrent, matching law
16. operant conditioning
17. negative punishment, positive punishment
18. postreinforcement pause
19. hedonic value, motivational value
20. negative reinforcement, positive reinforcement

Sample Answers to Concept Checks

1. She could reinforce good behavior through *positive reinforcement*, giving each child a gold sticker for helping clean up; if the stickers themselves are not sufficiently reinforcing, she could institute a "token economy" in which ten stickers can be exchanged for a toy. She can use *positive punishment*, scolding children who fail to help clean up. (Although she must make sure that such extra attention from the teacher is not an inadvertent form of reinforcement for the bad behavior.) She can use *negative punishment*, a timeout from a reinforcing activity (such as playtime). She could use the *Premack principle*: children must engage in a certain amount of cleaning up before they are allowed to spend time doing something else they like.

2. According to the principles of conditioning, the best would be a variable interval (VI) schedule. This way, employees never know exactly when the next test is coming—and it might come immediately after the last test. Therefore, there is never a "safe" time to take drugs (no postreinforcement pause in abstinence).

3. Apparently, this drug is affecting hedonic impact—making stale food taste "good" and stale jokes seem "funny." Possibly, this drug is an opiate.

4. During training, the sniffer dogs were presumably initially reinforced with primary reinforcers such as food whenever they searched for and correctly identified a human scent; later, they may have been trained to exhibit these behaviors in response to secondary reinforcement such as praise from their handlers. During the 9/11 search, lack of reinforcement (because no survivors were located) would have led to extinction of the learned response, making the animals less willing to exhibit searching behavior. Occasional reinforcement (perhaps on a VI schedule, approximately once per day) would have helped to maintain the learned response, keeping the dogs motivated to work.

CHAPTER 6

Discrete or Distributed Representation Models?

1. A discrete-component model is sufficient because all the tones are predictive of shock and there is no need to discriminate among them.

2. A distributed representation, because the model needs to have a way to capture the degree to which green is more or less similar to blue and red.

Discriminating between Generalization Paradigms

1. d (negative patterning), candy → good, flowers → good, candy + flowers → bad.

2. b (sensory preconditioning). Phase 1: deep voice + beard. Phase 2: beards → strong. Phase 3: infer deep voice → strong.

3. a (discrimination training). music1 → Brahms, music2 → Shubert.

4. c (acquired equivalence). Mark → food1, Kaori → food1; Mark → music1, infer Kaori → music1.

Configural Representation of Cues

There are six different elemental cues in this example: small, large, black, white, circle, and square. Six cues can be combined into 15 different pairs. However, three of these pairs are not possible because both members describe the same feature (size, color, or shape), and something cannot be both big and small (or black and white, or circle and square). So this leaves a total of 12 possible configural cues (note that order within a configural cue is not relevant): small–black, small–white, small–circle, small–square, large–black, large–white, large–circle, large–square, black–circle, black–square, white–circle, white–square.

Cholinergic Neurons and Learning

Since the nucleus basalis promotes discrimination learning by altering cortical mapping, discrimination memories that were acquired before the lesion will be unaffected. However, any attempts to teach discrimination learning after surgery will not be effective, as cortical plasticity is no longer possible.

Answers to Quiz Yourself

1. generalization gradients
2. dissimilar/similarity
3. stimulus sampling, connectionist
4. discrimination training
5. errorless discrimination learning
6. sensory preconditioning
7. single-layer networks
8. Concepts/categories
9. topographically
10. nucleus basalis or the amygdala

11. latent inhibition, sensory preconditioning
12. hippocampal region
13. social communication
14. inductive
15. learning, activation
16. latent inhibition
17. acetylcholine
18. overgeneralize
19. prototype

Sample Answers to Concept Checks

Yx = Orange light
Ox = Orange Light

Phase 1: All

Yx-US

Assuming the common cue is less salient than the distinctive cue, let's assume the weights in the R-W model wind up being W(Y) = .75, W(x) = .25

Phase 2: Exp

Ox-US

Because O is new color W(O) = 0 at beginning so that there is an error of .75 because W(O)+ W(x) = .25 at start of this phase. Thus with acquisition training the weights will increase, perhaps to something like W(O) = .5 and W(x) = .5 (again assuming the salient color has higher learning rate).

Phase 2: Control

Yx-US

There will be no change in weights as there is no error so the weights remain as W(Y) = .75 and W(x) = .25

PHASE 3: TEST

Experimental Group: Response to yellow will be W(Y) + W(x) = .75+.5 = 1.25
Control Group: Will be .75+.25 = 1.0

So experimental group will show higher responding. This suggests that it may be better to "cross train" with similar stimuli to build better responding rather than with just the same stimulus all along. When preparing for a tennis match, you might try to play a variety of sports that involve similar skills in a broad range of environments with different balls and on different courts.

CHAPTER 7

Episodic versus Semantic Memory

1. The student remembers the meaning of *carpe diem* using semantic memory, and he has no episodic memory of acquiring this information.

2. Here, the student does have an episodic memory, tagged in space and time, of studying the phrase *ne tentes, aut perfice*, but no semantic memory for what the phrase means in English (roughly, "either succeed, or don't bother trying").

3. Knowing that coffee is better at Starbucks than at the student center is an example of general knowledge about the world, so it counts as semantic memory. (Knowing how to get to Starbucks from the present location counts as semantic memory too.) But why does the college senior think that the coffee is better at Starbucks? If he can remember a specific episode in which he went to the student center and had terrible coffee and if this is why he believes Starbucks is superior, then that is an episodic memory.

Going Retro

1. This is *retroactive interference*: Scott's new learning (Spanish) reaches backward in time to disrupt old learning (Latin).

2. This is *proactive interference*: the old name (Carl) is reaching forward in time to disrupt the new name (Lance).

3. This is *anterograde amnesia*: even though the event (his hospitalization) happened a long time ago, it happened *after* John's brain injury, and the hippocampal damage prevented him from forming a new memory of it.

4. This is *retrograde amnesia*: John's injury reaches back in time to disrupt memory for events that occurred *before* his injury.

Don't Forget Your Amnesias

1. *What is lost or disrupted*: the ability to form new episodic and semantic memories. *Common causes*: damage to the medial temporal lobes (or the diencephalon or basal forebrain).

2. *What is lost or disrupted*: all personal (episodic and semantic) memories. *Common causes*: strong psychological trauma but no obvious physiological injury.

3. *What is lost or disrupted*: the ability to retrieve existing episodic (and possibly semantic) memories. *Common causes*: broad damage to the medial temporal lobes and beyond.

4. *What is lost or disrupted*: the context describing where or when an episodic memory was acquired. *Common causes*: possibly, damage to the frontal cortex; can also occur intermittently in healthy people.

5. *What is lost or disrupted*: anterograde (and possibly retrograde) memory, usually for a day or less. *Common causes*: unknown, but possibly, a brief interruption of blood flow to the brain.

Answers to Quiz Yourself

1. amnesia, anterograde amnesia, retrograde amnesia
2. generating requested information from memory, some kind of a prompt or cue to aid recall, picking out/recognizing the correct item, recognition
3. levels-of-processing, transfer-appropriate processing
4. directed forgetting
5. consolidation period, reconsolidation
6. confabulation, Korsakoff's disease
7. Semantic memory, episodic memory
8. hippocampus, fornix
9. a memory of an event that never actually happened
10. sensory cortex, association cortex
11. recently acquired, older
12. functional amnesia
13. helping to determine which memories are stored, metamemory
14. electroconvulsive shock
15. explicit, implicit
16. medial temporal lobe, diencephalon, basal forebrain
17. interference, retroactive interference, proactive interference
18. knowledge of, and ability to think about, our own memories
19. declarative memory, nondeclarative memory
20. transient global amnesia (TGA)
21. hippocampus/medial temporal lobes, new episodic, old episodic, these brain structures are involved in storing and retrieving both old and new memories
22. source monitoring error

Sample Answers to Concept Checks

1. You could strengthen the semantic memories by repetition. You could relate the information to items you already know—by linking the new faces to old friends with similar names. You could process the names "deeply" by thinking about the meaning of each name. You could transform the task from a free recall test to a recognition test by writing down the six names on a slip of paper and using it as a crib sheet at the next meeting.
2. A semantic memory has no attached context information. In source amnesia, the learning context is "remembered" incorrectly.
3. Forgetting could help reduce proactive interference: imagine trying to remember where you parked the car today if you remembered every previous episode just as clearly.
4. No. Another possible hypothesis to explain the activity of the hippocampus during retrieval of very old autobiographical memories is that the hippocampus is normally involved but not always necessary. Or perhaps the hippocampus is active during recall, not because

it is helping to recall the old memory but because it is storing a new episodic memory for the current test situation! We can't exclude these possibilities based simply on seeing hippocampal activity during a retrieval task.

5. Questioning the friend could help establish what brought on the amnesic episode: Did the patient suffer from a head trauma, for example during a sports match or a car crash? Could it be a "blackout" related to alcohol or drugs? In any of these cases, the patient may have TGA. On the other hand, if the patient experienced a traumatic episode just before developing amnesia, he may have functional amnesia. If the friend can provide details about the patient's prior life, you could test the patient's episodic memory (similar to how P.N.'s fiancée provided answers for his questionnaire). A structural MRI might show evidence of brain damage, particularly in the hippocampus, frontal cortex, diencephalon, and basal forebrain. You could also order functional imaging (fMRI or PET) to look for abnormal activity patterns in these brain areas.

CHAPTER 8

Open and Closed Skills

1. Mostly open: balancing a ball on one's nose requires continuous feedback.
2. Mostly closed: swimming movements are predefined, and inputs are stable.
3. Mostly open if skilled: kissing requires continuous feedback.
4. Mostly open: fishing requires accurate prediction of changing inputs.
5. Depends on the fish and the insect. Mostly closed if the insect falls into the water; mostly open if the insect lives underwater.
6. Depends on the type of music. Mostly closed if classical; mostly open if jazz.
7. Mostly closed: dart-throwing movements are predefined, and inputs are stable.

Tasks That Test Skill Memory

- The Tower of Hanoi is a classic task for studying cognitive skill learning. It involves moving disks from one peg to another until all are stacked on a new peg.
- The serial reaction time task is a perceptual-motor learning task that requires participants to press a key in response to a light as quickly as possible. It is used to test for unconscious (implicit) skill learning.
- The rotary pursuit task is a standard perceptual-motor skill learning task that measures how quickly individuals learn to coordinate their movements with a spinning disk. It has also been used to measure similarities in how twins perform before and after learning.

Which Cortical Regions Change during Skill Learning?

Behavioral studies (described in the Behavioral Processes section of this chapter) show that chess experts visually scan the chessboard in ways that differ from those of amateur chess players. Experiments with monkeys show that learning to distinguish tactile stimulation leads to changes in somatosensory cortex, the cortical region involved in processing tactile inputs. In combination, these findings suggest that one cortical region where you might see differences between novices and grand masters is in the visual cortex because it is a major source of the information that chess players use to select moves.

Answers to Quiz Yourself

1. open
2. cognitive
3. perceptual-motor
4. cognitive
5. the power law of practice
6. implicit
7. transfer specificity
8. cognitive
9. cognitive
10. cerebellum
11. massed practice, procrastination
12. spaced practice
13. constant
14. variable
15. transfer specificity
16. identical elements theory
17. autonomous
18. basal ganglia, cerebellum, motor cortex
19. musician's dystonia
20. Parkinson's disease

Sample Answers to Concept Checks

1. He could practice with a small group of volunteers repeatedly trying out various techniques over periods of several weeks, getting feedback afterward about what "worked" and what did not. Repetition combined with knowledge of results generally increases performance. Practicing with multiple partners can potentially provide benefits associated with variable practice. Practicing in different contexts (movie theaters, backseat of a car, in a closet), can also increase the chances that his skills will transfer in future kissing situations.

2. The student needs to find or develop a task that can potentially provide evidence that her spider has learned a cognitive skill. Possibly a digital version of the Tower of Hanoi task could be developed using a highly sensitive touch screen that would enable a spider to move disks by walking over them. A similar setup might be used to attempt to train the spider to classify pairs of shapes as being either the same or different.

3. Studies with identical twins separated at birth who, with different levels of training, both become chess grandmasters, would be consistent with genetic predispositions for chess playing abilities. Similarly, if two grandmasters had a baby that they anonymously put up for adoption, and later the child also became a grandmaster, this outcome would support the idea that talent at chess playing can be inherited. Most experiments that would show this in humans are unethical to perform since they would require controlling participants' genetics or lifelong experiences. Experiments showing that animals can be bred or genetically engineered to perform certain skills at expert levels with minimal training would provide strong evidence that talent for those skills can be genetically determined.

4. Fitts's model was developed mainly to describe skill learning by adult humans. If applied to fish, this model would require that fish know what pressing a lever entails before they start trying to learn how to do it. However, studies of implicit learning show that even humans can learn skills without being aware that they have learned anything, so it is likely that fish might also be able to learn to press levers implicitly. This example suggests that Fitts's model describes stages that occur during the learning of some skills, but not all skills.

5. Observations of cortical expansion resulting from skill learning are correlational; changes in activation are associated with changes in performance. These findings say nothing about changes in other regions of cortex. It is not safe to assume that skill learning has any effect on cortical regions that are not involved in performing the skill. This might be true, but the fact that cortical regions contributing to skill performance expand during learning does not imply that other regions must shrink to make room for this expansion.

CHAPTER 9
Models of Working Memory
Place: 1 & 4
State: 2 & 3

Varieties of Working Memory and Cognitive Control
1. C; 2. D; 3. A; 4. B

DLPFC vs. VLPFC in Working Memory
1. VLPFC
2. DLPFC
3. VLPFC

Functional Neuroanatomy of the Prefrontal Cortex
1. Monitoring and manipulating information requires the DLPFC.

2. Verbal rehearsal requires the left VLPFC.

3. Semantic encoding is done by the anterior left VLPFC.

4. Phonological encoding is a specialty of the posterior left VLPFC.

5. Visuospatial rehearsal requires the right VLPFC.

Answers to Quiz Yourself

1. anterior, posterior
2. perseveration
3. dopamine, basal ganglia
4. dysexecutive
5. visual sensory memory
6. the word-length effect
7. dopamine, poorly
8. Working memory
9. central executive
10. dorsolateral prefrontal cortex
11. dopamine
12. delayed nonmatch to sample (DNMS)
13. multi-store, unitary-store
14. Stroop
15. intelligence, working
16. one-third
17. distractions
18. left
19. COMT

Sample Answers to Concept Checks

1. In the early 1950s, it was suggested that we have a short-term memory capacity of seven items. Eventually, George Miller posited the range of this capacity to be 5 to 9 items in most people. In order for Juan to remember ten digits plus a four-digit extension, he must make use of uninterrupted rehearsal, chunking, and associating the information he wants to remember with unique concepts. This will allow Juan to retain the information in his long-term memory. For example, Juan can remember the last four digits, 1812, as the War of 1812, the armed conflict between the United States and England. Furthermore, Juan can remember the extension 2001 as the year of the attack on the World Trade Center.

2. There is more to working memory than just the maintenance of phonological or visuospatial memories. The far more complex process of cognitive control (executive control) that manipulates working memory to achieve higher order cognition includes task flexibility, planning, and problem solving. Let's take task flexibility and planning as the two aspects to compare. A person talking on a cellphone is very likely to *switch tasks* from auditory stimuli to visual in order to make progress with other work while on the phone, or perhaps to locate a pen and paper for taking notes.

Furthermore, the person would have to be *planning* what to say next on the phone while retaining the incoming auditory information. While driving a car, a person would definitely be *task switching*—integrating numerous stimuli and switching from analysis of visual input to exercise of motor skills in order to regulate the speed, direction, and course of the car. *Planning* is also involved in driving a car: for example, planning one's route while simultaneously receiving and accounting for stimuli from the environment.

3. The brain would treat a list of words as verbal information. We would therefore see more activity on the brain's left side (left ventrolateral prefrontal context). During rehearsal of visual images, however, we would find more activity on the right side (right ventrolateral prefrontal cortex), the location of the visuospatial sketchpad.

4. Earl Miller proposed that a key contribution of the prefrontal cortex to cognition and working memory is its ability to sustain activity despite distractions. In this case, we would see activity in the dorsolateral prefrontal cortex reflecting Tanya's effort to keep her mind on the neuroanatomy images, and we would see activity in the posterior visual cortex reflecting her awareness of Peter's dimples.

5. Jerry is making use of a semantic elaboration and an association to the name of the mystery woman. This would likely involve processing of his anterior ventrolateral prefrontal cortex.

6. ADHD is a disorder that involves dysfunction in the activity of the prefrontal circuits. With impairment of the cognitive-control processes needed for planning, focus of attention on a task, and inhibition of distracting stimuli, it makes sense that a person with ADHD would likely take up soccer over duck hunting. A person with ADHD would probably not enjoy sitting still long enough to lure a duck close enough to shoot, might have difficulty acquiring the skills needed to shoot accurately, and so would be unlikely to bag a duck. In contrast, playing soccer would involve constant motion and stimulation and be more suitable.

CHAPTER 10
Theories of Emotion

1. James–Lange: Janet sees and hears the band; her body experiences arousal, including increased heart rate and pupil dilation; as a result of this arousal, she feels joy and excitement.

2. Cannon–Bard: Janet sees and hears the band. In response to these stimuli, she feels joy and excitement, and at the same time, her body experiences arousal.

3. Two-factor theory: Janet sees and hears the band, which causes arousal; in the context of a music concert, Janet interprets this arousal as signaling joy and excitement.

Brain Substrates of Emotion

1. The elevator ride may be a CS that activates Jared's amygdala; outputs from the central nucleus travel to the ANS and turn on the fight-or-flight response.

2. Jared's current fear response acts as a contextual stimulus and helps the hippocampus and/or cortex trigger memories of earlier events that caused a fear response. If the diving incident was traumatic enough, Jared may even have a flashbulb memory for the event.

3. Rationally, Jared knows he won't fall off the Washington Monument. His prefrontal cortex, the site of higher decision making, helps to overrule the impulse to flee.

4. Appreciation of the beautiful view is itself an emotional response. If Jared is lucky, his amygdala will help process this emotional response and send signals to the prefrontal cortex and elsewhere. Maybe the next time he's at the top of a tall building, Jared will remember his pleasure at the view from the top of the Washington Monument, and this will help counteract some of his fear.

Classical Conditioning and Phobias

In this example, the US is the panic attack. Because Nancy previously experienced a panic attack at the grocery store, the grocery store becomes a CS which can itself evoke a CR—her fear of another panic attack.

Answers to Quiz Yourself

1. physiological responses, overt behaviors, conscious feelings
2. Cannon–Bard, James–Lange, two-factor
3. autonomic nervous system (ANS)
4. phobia, systematic desensitization
5. fight-or-flight, arousal
6. mood congruency of memory
7. amygdala
8. conditioned escape, conditioned avoidance
9. stress hormones, epinephrine, glucocorticoids/cortisol
10. depression
11. flashbulb memory
12. somatic
13. fear response, piloerection
14. stress
15. posttraumatic stress disorder (PTSD), re-experiencing the event, avoidance, emotional numbing, heightened anxiety
16. learned helplessness

Sample Answers to Concept Checks

1. Habituation starts with a stimulus (such as a loud noise) that has the ability to produce a response. Often, this is an innate fear response. For example, a rat that hears a loud sound may respond with startle, freezing, and/or changes in heart rate and respiration. When the loud sound is played over and over again, the fear response extinguishes. In such cases, it is probably reasonable to say that habituation is equivalent to extinguishing of an emotional response—the animal learns not to "fear" the sound – and is thus a form of emotional learning. It is important to note, however, that not all habituation necessarily involves emotion. For example, when an infant is presented with a recording of an adult's voice, the infant will respond by turning her head in the direction of the sound, but if the recording is played over and over, the infant's response habituates. In this case, it probably isn't accurate to say that the infant has learned not to "fear" the sound—just that she's learned to stop responding to it.

2. Learned helplessness could account for this pattern. After a heavy defeat, the players might experience feelings of helplessness related to the failure of their own efforts to produce the desired outcome (a victory for the team). This could make the upcoming game seem like an insurmountable challenge, particularly if the opponent is known to be tough.

3. The cortex (particularly frontal cortex) plays a role in modulating emotions according to context and in damping down emotional responses when the context doesn't call for them. For example, when you see a snake in the zoo, the context is such that an emotional response to the snake isn't justified. Animals with cortical damage may be less able to damp down inappropriate emotional responses.

4. Your roommate might have developed a fear of spiders because of a traumatic episode with a spider, such as being bitten (or seeing someone bitten) by a poisonous spider or even seeing a particularly vivid film in which people are attacked by spiders. A person might also learn this fear observationally if he observed other people reacting with fear to spiders—for example, if his mother always screamed when she saw spiders. He might have been conditioned to fear spiders if he were in highly frightening situations where spiders were present (in which case the spiders would be a CS associated with a fear-evoking US).

5. You could suggest your friend try systematic desensitization, in which a person starts by looking at photos of spiders until they no longer evoke a fear response and gradually works up to exposure to real ones. If the fear is serious enough to be a phobia (if, say, your roommate has gone for days without showering rather than face the spider in the bathtub), you could suggest that your roommate consider therapy and/or medications that block stress hormones.

CHAPTER 11

What Is Imitation?

1. Perhaps the baby is imitating you. However, another possibility is that smiling faces are a reinforcing stimulus for the baby. Reinforced babies are more likely to smile, and thus the baby may be responding to you in the same way that she would if you had handed her a cookie (another reinforcing stimulus). No copying is required.

2. This could just be a case of contagion. If a few pigeons in a group start to fly, there is a good chance that you will see other pigeons start to fly, not because they are copying each other but as a reflexive response—the same as when schooling fish move in synchrony. To assess this possibility, you need to know more about what causes babies to stick out their tongues.

3. This could be a case of observational conditioning. Perhaps Leti has seen her father eating asparagus several times. Seeing her father express disgust might induce similar negative emotions in Leti. The asparagus could become a conditioned stimulus that leads to a conditioned response of disgust. Alternatively, maybe this is the first time Leti has tried asparagus and she simply does not like it.

4. Darwin thought so. However, the cat might have been trained to perform these actions through shaping. (Remember the waterskiing squirrels in Chapter 5, on instrumental conditioning?) Alternatively, this could be a case of stimulus enhancement. Humans approaching the door always focus their actions on the doorknob, which might direct the cat's attention to the doorknob as well. Cats often hit the objects of their attention with their paws. A few instances of accidental door opening would likely increase the cat's tendency to swat at the doorknob.

5. Yes. Leti's friend is replicating Leti's actions in a way that cannot be explained as anything other than imitation (unless they are both reading from scripts).

Who Has Mirror Neurons and What Do They Do?

1. There is no direct evidence in monkeys or humans that mirror neurons are necessary for imitative abilities, so whether they are important or not is not yet known.

2. There are currently no measures of recordings from mirror neurons in humans that are directly comparable to those from monkeys, and so this is currently unknown.

3. Primates are the only species in which mirror neurons related to visual observations of actions have been observed, but this does not provide evidence that other animals do not also have mirror neurons.

4. This is true.

Imitative Deficits in Individuals with ASD

1. This is a symptom seen in some individuals with ASD but has nothing to do with imitation or social learning.

2. Narrow interests are a symptom of ASD, but do not depend on imitative abilities.

3. Fitness videos often require viewers to imitate arbitrary actions, so this difficulty could reflect an imitative deficit.

4. This is an example of echolalia, which is an imitative deficit often seen in individuals with ASD.

Answers to Quiz Yourself

1. social/observational
2. copying/imitating
3. emulation
4. two individuals
5. true imitation
6. perspective taking
7. emotional contagion
8. observational conditioning
9. unconditioned emotional response
10. emotional contagion
11. stimulus enhancement
12. emulation
13. true imitation
14. vocal learning/song learning
15. vocal imitation
16. human/dolphin
17. vocal imitation
18. vocal learning/social learning
19. template model of song learning
20. social transmission of information
21. social conformity
22. direct-matching hypothesis
23. mirror neurons
24. frontal lobe
25. Area X, LMAN, HVC, RA
26. hippocampus/basal forebrain
27. echolalia
28. mirror neurons
29. frontal lobe damage
30. Bobo doll

Sample Answers to Concept Checks

1. One method that has been developed to establish true imitation abilities in animals is the two-action test. Another is the "Do-what-I-do" task.

2. All examples of vocal imitation (including karaoke) would not count as imitation under Thorndike's definition.

3. Stimulus enhancement is one mechanism that would enable animals to focus their efforts on areas frequented by other members of their species. Imitation and social conformity would also enable animals to focus on areas favored by others. In humans, social transfer of information would serve to make this possible (for

example, asking one's friends where to find the best beaches).

4. (a) Evidence of mirror neurons suggests specialized mechanisms for matching visual percepts to motor responses. (b) Studies in which children learn the "Do-what-I-do" task show that they can learn to copy through experience, but the neural mechanisms that make this possible are not known. (c) The neural bases of consciousness are still debated.

5. All of the experiments showing that animals can truly imitate actions refute the claim that verbal codes are a prerequisite for learning actions through imitation. Studies on learning set formation show that operant conditioning can be an efficient way of learning new actions.

CHAPTER 12

Learning and Memory in Old Age

1. This involves recalling an old episodic memory; recall of old, well-formed episodic memories tends *not* to decline much in healthy old age.

2. This involves working memory, which *does* tend to decline with old age.

3. This involves performance of a well-learned skill, which tends *not* to decline with healthy aging.

4. This involves acquiring new semantic information, an ability that *does* tend to decline with old age.

5. This involves learning a new skill, an ability that *does* tend to decline with old age.

5. False: Amyloid plaques are formed from clumps of beta-amyloid. Tangles are formed from clumps of the tau protein.

6. True.

7. True.

8. True.

9. False: Although no genes have been identified that *cause* late-onset Alzheimer's, several genes have been identified that increase *risk* for late-onset Alzheimer's.

10. True.

Answers to Quiz Yourself

1. puberty
2. dendrite, synapse
3. intellectual disability, trisomy 21
4. estrogens, androgens, testosterone
5. elicited imitation
6. Alzheimer's disease
7. allele
8. gestational age
9. genes, epigenetic
10. amyloid plaques, neurofibrillary tangles
11. adolescence, teenage (ages 13–19)
12. apoptosis
13. imprinting
14. Neurogenesis, Synaptogenesis
15. sensitive period
16. dementia

Everything Grows Together...at Different Rates

Timetable for Development	Types of Learning and Memory	Critical Brain Area(s)
Present before birth (in at least some forms)	Sensory processing and habituation	Sensory cortex
Infancy to early childhood (in at least some forms)	Conditioning and skill learning	Cerebellum and basal ganglia
Childhood	Social learning and imitation	Mirror neurons in the motor cortex
Late childhood to early adolescence	Episodic and semantic memory	Hippocampus
Late adolescence to young adulthood	Working memory and executive function	Frontal cortex

Alzheimer's Fact Sheet

1. False: Alzheimer's is the most common form of dementia.

2. False: Only about one-third of people aged 85+ are thought to have Alzheimer's.

3. True.

4. True.

Sample Answers to Concept Checks

1. Different children have different genetic profiles (nature) as well as different environments (nurture). Even if the parents provide similarly "enriched" environments for all their children, the oldest child spent the first few years of life as an only child, while the youngest has always had siblings—which produces differences in environment that could

affect learning (by forcing younger children to work harder to compete for parental attention, by providing younger children with older siblings to watch and imitate, and so on). In addition, different abilities tend to mature at different rates in girls and boys. Kyle may lag behind his sister on language, but he might outstrip her in other areas, such as the motor coordination needed to play catch.

2. Usually, healthy older individuals have the most trouble with working memory and new episodic and semantic learning. The businessman could help himself by relying less on these abilities. For example, he could use memory aids such as notes and schedules to jot down information instead of relying on working memory. He could also use mnemonics (see Chapter 7) to help encode new information in declarative memory.

3. Sex hormones affect early brain development. Apparently, tree lizards have a sensitive period in the first month of life. During this period, sex hormones (testosterone) affect development of aggressiveness, that is, of whether the animal is willing and able to fight to defend a territory. After this sensitive period, the wiring is fixed, so that giving additional testosterone to a non-dominant male (or, presumably, to a female) does not change the basic wiring (Hews et al., 1994; Hews & Moore, 1996).

4. Possibly, the genes associated with Alzheimer's cause some evolutionary benefit early in life that caused them to spread through the population even though they are detrimental late in life (after reproductive age). Examples from this chapter of processes that may be adaptive early in life but maladaptive late in life are widespread neurogenesis (dramatic changes to the neural networks in an old brain might overwrite a life's learning) and imprinting (a young animal may be well served by quickly learning to recognize its mother but would be poorly served by imprinting on every individual thereafter).

acetylcholine (ACh) A neuromodulator that strongly influences hippocampal function.

acoustic startle reflex A defensive response (such as jumping or freezing) to a startling stimulus (such as a loud noise).

acquired equivalence A learning and generalization paradigm in which prior training in stimulus equivalence increases the amount of generalization between two stimuli even if those stimuli are superficially dissimilar.

activity-dependent enhancement Paired training of CS and US that produces an increase in the glutamate vesicles released from sensory to motor neurons.

adolescence The transitional stage between puberty and adulthood, corresponding roughly to the teenage years in humans (ages 13 to 19).

allele Naturally occurring variant of a gene.

Alzheimer's disease A form of dementia due to accumulating brain pathology (specifically, *amyloid plaques* and *neurofibrillary tangles*).

amnesia Memory loss.

amygdala A collection of brain nuclei lying at the anterior tip of each *hippocampus*, critical for learning and expressing emotional responses as well as mediating the emotional modulation of memory formation.

amyloid plaque A deposit of beta-amyloid protein; these deposits accumulate in the brains of patients with *Alzheimer's disease*.

androgen Any member of the principal class of sex hormones present in adult males.

anterograde amnesia A severe loss of the ability to form new episodic and semantic memories.

apoptosis Natural cell death, as opposed to cell death caused by accident or disease.

appetitive conditioning Conditioning in which the US is a positive event (such as food delivery).

arousal A collection of bodily responses (including increased blood flow to muscles, increased respiration, and depressed digestion and immune function) that prepare the body to face a threat; also known as the *fight-or-flight response*.

association cortex Areas of cerebral cortex involved in associating information within and across sensory modalities.

associationism The principle that memory depends on the formation of linkages ("associations") between pairs of events, sensations, and ideas, such that recalling or experiencing one member of the pair elicits a memory or anticipation of the other.

associative stage The second stage in Fitts's model of skill learning; in this stage, learners begin using stereotyped actions when performing a skill and rely less on actively recalled memories of rules.

associative weight In the Rescorla–Wagner model of conditioning, a value representing the strength of association between a conditioned stimulus (CS) and an unconditioned stimulus (US).

autism spectrum disorder A set of disorders associated with deficits in social interactions and social learning.

autonomic nervous system (ANS) A collection of nerves and structures that control internal organs and glands.

autonomous stage The third stage in Fitts's model of skill learning; in this stage, a skill or subcomponents of the skill become motor programs.

aversive conditioning Conditioning in which the US is a negative event (such as a shock or an airpuff to the eye).

axon The output extension of a neuron, specialized for transmitting information to other neurons or to muscles.

basal forebrain A collection of structures that lie at the base of the forebrain and are important in the production of acetylcholine that is distributed throughout the brain.

basal ganglia A brain region that lies at the base of the forebrain and includes the dorsal striatum.

basal ganglia A group of brain structures, including the dorsal striatum and nucleus accumbens, that are important in learning voluntary responses.

behavioral addiction Addiction to a behavior that produces reinforcement, as well as cravings and withdrawal symptoms when the behavior is prevented.

behavioral economics The study of how organisms allocate their time and resources among possible options.

behaviorism A school of thought that argues that psychology should restrict itself to the study of observable behaviors (such as lever presses, salivation, and other measurable actions) and not seek to infer unobservable mental processes.

blind design An experimental design in which the participants do not know the hypothesis being tested or whether they are part of the experimental group or the control group. See also *double-blind design*.

bliss point In behavioral economics, the allocation of resources that maximizes subjective value or satisfaction.

blocking A two-phase training paradigm in which prior training to one cue (CS1 US) blocks later learning of a second cue when the two are paired together in the second phase of the training (CS1 + CS2 US).

brainstem A group of structures that connects the rest of the brain to the spinal cord and plays key roles in regulating automatic functions such as breathing and body temperature.

Cannon–Bard theory of emotion The theory that conscious emotions stimulate appropriate behaviors and physiological responses.

category A division or class of entities in the world.

category learning The process by which animals and humans learn to classify stimuli into categories.

cell body The central part of the neuron that contains the nucleus and integrates signals from all the dendrites; also known as the soma.

central executive The component of Baddeley's model of working memory that monitors and manipulates the two working memory buffers.

central nervous system (CNS) The part of the vertebrate nervous system consisting of the brain and spinal cord.

cerebellum A brain region lying below the cerebral cortex in the back of the head. It is responsible for the regulation and coordination of complex voluntary muscular movement, including classical conditioning of motor-reflex responses.

cerebral cortex The brain tissue covering the top and sides of the brain in most vertebrates; involved in storage and processing of sensory inputs and motor outputs.

chaining An operant conditioning technique in which organisms are gradually trained to execute complicated sequences of discrete responses.

classical conditioning A type of learning in which the organism learns to respond with a conditioned response (CR) to a previously neutral stimulus (the CS) that has been repeatedly presented along with an unconditioned stimulus (US); also called Pavlovian conditioning.

closed skill A skill that involves performing predefined movements that, ideally, never vary.

cochlear implant A sensory prosthesis that directly stimulates auditory nerves to produce hearing sensations in deaf individuals.

cognitive control The manipulation and application of working memory for planning, task switching, attention, stimulus selection, and the inhibition of inappropriate reflexive behaviors; also known as *executive control* or *executive function*.

cognitive map An internal psychological representation of the spatial layout of the external world.

cognitive psychology A subfield of psychology that focuses on human abilities—such as thinking, language, and reasoning—that are not easily explained by a strictly behaviorist approach.

cognitive science The interdisciplinary study of thought, reasoning, and other higher mental functions.

cognitive skill A skill that requires problem solving or the application of strategies.

cognitive stage The first stage in Fitts's model of skill learning; in this stage, an individual must exert some effort to encode the skill on the basis of information gained through observation, instruction, and trial and error.

combinatorial explosion The rapid expansion of resources required to encode configurations as the number of component features increases.

combinatorial explosion compound conditioning The simultaneous conditioning of two cues, usually presented at the same time.

concept A psychological representation of a category of objects, events, or people in the world.

concurrent reinforcement schedule A reinforcement schedule in which the organism can make any of several possible responses, each of which may lead to a different outcome reinforced according to a different reinforcement schedule.

conditioned avoidance An experimental design in which animals learn to make particular responses to avoid or prevent exposure to an aversive stimulus.

conditioned escape An experimental design in which animals learn to make particular responses in order to escape from or terminate an aversive stimulus.

conditioned response (CR) The trained response to a conditioned stimulus (CS) in anticipation of the unconditioned stimulus (US) that it predicts.

conditioned stimulus (CS) A cue that is paired with an unconditioned stimulus (US) and comes to elicit a conditioned response (CR).

conditioned taste aversion A conditioning preparation in which a subject learns to avoid a taste that has been paired with an aversive outcome, usually nausea.

confabulation A behavior associated with some forms of amnesia in which individuals, when asked to remember past events, respond with highly detailed but false memories.

configural node A detector for a unique configuration of two cues, such as a certain tone and light.

confirmation bias A tendency to ignore information that conflicts with a prior belief and focus on information that is consistent with that belief.

connectionist models Networks of uniform and unlabeled connections between simple processing units called nodes.

consequential region A set of stimuli in the world that share the same consequence as a stimulus whose consequence is already known.

consolidation period A length of time during which new episodic and semantic memories are vulnerable and easily lost or altered; each time a memory is recalled, it may become vulnerable again until it is "reconsolidated."

constant practice Practice involving a constrained set of materials and skills.

constraint-induced movement therapy A motor rehabilitation technique in which unaffected limbs are restrained to increase usage of dysfunctional limbs.

contiguity Nearness in time (temporal contiguity) or space (spatial contiguity).

continuous reinforcement schedule A reinforcement schedule in which every instance of the response is followed by the consequence.

copying The act of doing what one observes another organism doing.

cortical plasticity The capacity to change cortical organization as a result of experience.

cortisol The chief *glucocorticoid* in humans.

CS modulation theory Any of the theories of conditioning holding that the stimulus that enters into an association is determined by a change in how the CS is processed.

cued recall A memory test that involves some kind of prompt or cue to aid recall.

cumulative recorder A device that records behavioral responses; the height of the line drawn represents the number of responses that have been made (cumulatively) up to the present time.

data Facts and figures from which conclusions can be inferred.

declarative memory A broad class of memories, both semantic and episodic, that can typically be verbalized ("declared") or explicitly communicated in some other way (contrast *nondeclarative memory*).

deep brain stimulation A procedure that delivers an electrical current into a patient's brain through one or more implanted electrodes; used to alleviate tremors and other motor symptoms associated with Parkinson's disease.

delay conditioning A conditioning procedure in which there is no temporal gap between the end of the CS and the beginning of the US, and in which the CS co-terminates with the US.

delayed nonmatch-to-sample task A test of visual memory in which a subject must indicate which of two novel objects is not the same as one that was recently seen.

dementia Progressive cognitive decline usually due to accumulating brain pathology.

dendrite Extension of a neuron that is specialized to receive signals from other neurons.

dependent variable In an experiment, the factor whose change is measured as an effect of changes in the independent variable.

depression A psychiatric condition that involves sadness as well as a general loss of initiative and activity.

diencephalon A brain area that lies near the core of the brain, just above the brainstem, and includes the thalamus, the hypothalamus, and the mammillary bodies.

difference image An image of differences in brain activity obtained by taking an fMRI or PET image of a person performing a particular task, then subtracting the image of the same individual at baseline (not performing a task).

differential reinforcement of alternative behaviors (DRA) A method to decrease frequency of unwanted behaviors by instead reinforcing preferred alternate behaviors.

diffusion tensor imaging (DTI) A type of MRI that measures the diffusion of water in brain tissue, permitting bundles of axons throughout the brain to be imaged.

direct-matching hypothesis The proposal that memories for actions are stored in specialized cortical regions that map observed actions onto the motor representations of the acts.

directed forgetting A procedure in which subjects are first asked to learn information and later asked to remember or forget specific items; typically, memory is worse for items a subject was directed to forget.

discrete trial paradigm An operant conditioning paradigm in which the experimenter defines the beginning and end points.

discrete-component representation A representation in which each individual stimulus (or stimulus feature) corresponds to one element (node) in the model.

discrimination learning The process by which animals or people learn to respond differently to different stimuli.

discriminative stimulus (S^D) In operant conditioning, a stimulus that signals whether a particular response will lead to a particular outcome.

dishabituation A renewal of a response, previously habituated, that occurs when the organism is presented with a novel stimulus; compare *habituation*.

distributed representation A representation in which information is coded as a pattern of activation distributed across many different nodes.

dopamine A neuromodulator that alters neuron-to-neuron communication.

dorsal anterior cingulate cortex (dACC) A subregion of prefrontal cortex that may play a role in the motivational value of pain.

dorsal striatum A region of the basal ganglia that is important for stimulus–response learning.

dorsolateral prefrontal cortex The left and right sides of the topmost part of the prefrontal cortex (PFC), often abbreviated DLPFC.

double-blind design An experimental design in which neither the experimenters nor the subjects know group assignment.

Down syndrome A congenital disorder that causes mild-to-moderate intellectual disability, due to *trisomy 21*.

drive reduction theory The theory that organisms have innate drives to obtain primary reinforcers and that learning is driven by the biological need to reduce those drives.

drug A chemical substance that alters the biochemical functioning of the body and in many cases affects the brain.

dual process theory The theory that habituation and sensitization are independent of each other but operate in parallel.

dualism The principle that the mind and body exist as separate entities.

dysexecutive syndrome A disrupted ability to think and plan.

echolalia The automatic repetition of words or phrases immediately after hearing them spoken.

electroconvulsive shock A brief pulse of electricity that is passed through the brain and can severely disrupt newly formed memories; electroconvulsive therapy is sometimes used to alleviate severe depression.

electroencephalography (EEG) A method for measuring electrical activity in the brain by means of electrodes placed on the scalp; the resulting image is an electroencephalogram (also EEG).

elicited imitation A technique for assessing memory in infants by observing their ability to mimic actions they have seen earlier.

emotion A cluster of three distinct but interrelated sets of phenomena—physiological responses, overt behaviors, and conscious feelings—produced in response to an affecting situation.

emotional contagion An inborn tendency to react emotionally to visual or acoustic stimuli that indicate an emotional response by other members of one's species, typically in ways that replicate the observed response.

empiricism A philosophical school of thought that holds that all the ideas we have are the result of experience; contrast *nativism*.

emulation Copying that involves replicating an outcome without replicating specific motor acts.

endogenous opioid Any of a group of naturally occurring neurotransmitter-like substances that have many of the same effects as opiate drugs such as heroine and morphine; may help signal hedonic value of reinforcers in the brain.

engram A physical change in the brain that forms the basis of a memory.

enriched environment An environment that provides sensory stimulation and opportunities to explore and learn; for a rat, this may mean housing in a large cage with many toys to play with and other rats to socialize with.

epigenetics The study of mechanisms by which gene expression can be modified (without modifying the genes themselves).

epinephrine A stress hormone that helps to mediate the *fight-or-flight response*; also known as *adrenaline*.

episodic memory Memory for specific autobiographical events; it includes information about the spatial and temporal contexts in which the event occurred.

error-correction learning A mathematical specification of the conditions for learning that holds that the degree

to which an outcome is surprising modulates the amount of learning that takes place.

errorless discrimination learning A training procedure in which a difficult discrimination is learned by starting with an easy version of the task and proceeding to incrementally harder versions as the easier ones are mastered.

estrogen Any member of the principal class of sex hormones present in adult females.

event-related potential (ERP) Electroencephalograms (EEGs) from a single individual averaged over multiple repetitions of an event (such as a repeated stimulus presentation).

evolution The theory that species change over time, with new traits or characteristics passed from one generation to the next; natural selection is one mechanism by which evolution occurs.

evolutionary psychology A branch of psychology that studies how behavior evolves through natural selection.

executive control The manipulation of working memory through the updating of stored information to facilitate goals, planning, task switching, stimulus selection, and response inhibition; also known as *cognitive control* or *executive function*.

experiment A test made to examine the validity of a hypothesis, usually by actively manipulating the variable(s) being investigated and measuring the effect on a behavior.

experimenter bias The degree to which an experimenter's prior knowledge or expectations can (consciously or unconsciously) influence the outcome of an experiment.

expert A person who performs a skill better than most.

explicit learning A learning process that includes the ability to verbalize about the actions or events being learned.

explicit memory A category of memory that includes semantic memory and episodic memory and consists of memories of which the person is aware: you know that you know the information (contrast *implicit memory*).

extinction The process of reducing a learned response to a stimulus by ceasing to pair that stimulus with a reward or punishment.

eyeblink conditioning A classical conditioning procedure in which the US is an airpuff to the eye and the conditioned and unconditioned responses are eyeblinks.

false memory Memory of an event that never actually happened.

familiarity The perception of similarity that occurs when an event is repeated.

fear response A cluster of physiological, motor, and conscious reactions that accompany the emotion of fear. In the laboratory, these physiological changes and motor behaviors are often taken to imply presence of fear whether or not the accompanying conscious experience of fear can be documented.

fight-or-flight response A collection of bodily responses (including increased blood flow to muscles, increased respiration, and depressed digestion and immune function) that prepare the body to face a threat; also known as *arousal*.

fixed-interval (FI) schedule In operant conditioning, a reinforcement schedule in which the first response after a fixed amount of time is reinforced; thus, FI 1-m means that reinforcement arrives for the first response made after a one-minute interval since the last reinforcement.

fixed-ratio (FR) schedule In operant conditioning, a reinforcement schedule in which a specific number of responses are required before a reinforcer is delivered; for example, FR 5 means that reinforcement arrives after every fifth response.

flashbulb memory A memory formed under conditions of extreme emotions that seems especially vivid and long lasting.

forgetting The loss or deterioration of memory over time.

formation The process by which we learn about new categories of entities in the world, usually based on common features.

fornix A fiber bundle that connects portions of the diencephalon and basal forebrain to the hippocampus.

free recall A memory test that involves simply generating requested information from memory.

free-operant paradigm An operant conditioning paradigm in which the animal can operate the experimental apparatus "freely," responding to obtain reinforcement (or avoid punishment) when it chooses.

frontal cortex Those regions of cortex that lie within the frontal lobes and that may play a role in determining which memories are stored and in producing metamemory for that information.

frontal lobe The part of the cerebral cortex lying at the front of the human brain; enables a person to plan and perform actions.

functional amnesia A sudden massive retrograde memory loss that seems to result from psychological causes rather than physical causes such as brain injury; also called *psychogenic amnesia*.

functional magnetic resonance imaging (fMRI) A method of functional neuroimaging based on comparing an MRI of the brain during performance of a task with an MRI of the brain at rest.

functional neuroimaging Techniques (such as fMRI or PET) for observing the activity or function of a living brain.

generalization The transfer of past learning to novel events and problems.

generalization gradient A graph showing how physical changes in stimuli (plotted on the horizontal axis) correspond to changes in behavioral responses (plotted on the vertical axis).

gestational age Time since conception.

glia A type of cell that provides functional or structural support to neurons.

glucocorticoid Any of a class of *stress hormones* (including *cortisol* in humans) that help to mediate the *fight-or-flight response*.

habituation A decrease in the strength or occurrence of a behavior after repeated exposure to the stimulus

that produces that behavior; compare *dishabituation*.

Hebbian learning The principle that learning involves strengthening the connections of coactive neurons; often stated as, "Neurons that fire together, wire together."

hedonic value of a stimulus The subjective "goodness" or value of that stimulus.

heterosynaptic Occurring in several nearby synapses simultaneously.

hippocampal region The hippocampus and associated brain regions, including the entorhinal cortex and dentate gyrus. In humans, also referred to as the medial temporal lobe.

hippocampus A brain structure located in the medial temporal lobe that is important for new memory formation.

homeostasis The tendency of the body (including the brain) to gravitate toward a state of equilibrium or balance.

homosynaptic Occurring in one synapse without affecting nearby synapses.

identical elements theory Thorndike's proposal that learned abilities transfer to novel situations to an extent that depends on the number of elements in the new situation that are identical to those in the situation in which the skills were encoded.

implicit learning Learning that occurs without the learner's awareness of improvements in performance or, in the case of people with amnesia, awareness that practice has occurred.

implicit memory Memory that occurs without the learner's awareness (contrast *explicit memory*).

imprinting The tendency of young animals of some species to form an attachment to the first individual they see after birth.

incentive salience hypothesis The theory that dopamine helps provide organisms with the motivation to work for reinforcement.

independent variable The factor that is manipulated in an experiment, such as the factor that differentiates

the control group and experimental group; contrast *dependent variable*.

inductive inference A logical inference that is probably (but not necessarily) true and is usually based on attempts to draw a general rule from one or more specific instances or premises.

inferior olive A nucleus of cells with connections to the thalamus, cerebellum, and spinal cord.

instrumental conditioning The process whereby organisms learn to make responses in order to obtain or avoid important consequences; compare *classical conditioning*.

insular cortex (insula) A region of cortex lying in the fold between parietal and temporal lobes that is involved in conscious awareness of bodily and emotional states and may play a role in signaling the aversive value of stimuli.

interference Reduction in the strength of a memory due to overlap with the content of other memories.

interpositus nucleus One of the cerebellar deep nuclei.

interstimulus interval (ISI) The temporal gap between the onset of the CS and the onset of the US.

James–Lange theory of emotion The theory that conscious feelings of emotion occur when the mind senses the physiological responses associated with fear or some other kind of arousal.

knowledge of results Feedback about performance of a skill; critical to the effectiveness of practice.

Korsakoff's disease A condition caused by a deficiency in thiamine (a B vitamin) that sometimes accompanies chronic alcohol abuse; patients often show severe anterograde amnesia and engage in confabulation.

latent inhibition A conditioning paradigm in which prior exposure to a CS retards later learning of the CS–US association during acquisition training.

latent learning Learning that is undetected (latent) until explicitly demonstrated at a later stage.

law of effect The observation, made by Thorndike, that the probability of a particular behavioral response increases or decreases depending on the consequences that have followed that response in the past.

learned helplessness A phenomenon in which exposure to an uncontrollable punisher teaches an expectation that responses are ineffectual, which in turn reduces the motivation to attempt new avoidance responses.

learning curve A graph showing learning performance (the dependent variable, usually plotted along the vertical axis) as a function of training time (the independent variable, usually plotted along the horizontal axis).

learning set formation Acquisition of the ability to learn novel tasks rapidly based on frequent experiences with similar tasks.

learning The process by which changes in behavior arise as a result of experiences interacting with the world.

lesion Damage caused by injury or illness.

levels-of-processing effect The finding that, in general, deeper processing (such as thinking about the semantic meaning of a word) leads to better recall of the information than shallow processing (such as thinking about the spelling or pronunciation of the word).

long-term depression (LTD) A process in which synaptic transmission becomes less effective as a result of recent activity; with long-term potentiation, widely believed to represent a form of synaptic plasticity that could be the neural mechanism for learning.

long-term memory Permanent or near-permanent storage of memory that lasts beyond a period of conscious attention.

long-term potentiation (LTP) A process in which synaptic transmission becomes more effective as a result of recent activity; with long-term depression, widely believed to represent a form of synaptic plasticity that could be the neural mechanism for learning.

magnetic resonance imaging (MRI) A method of structural neuroimaging based on recording changes in magnetic fields.

massed practice Concentrated, continuous practice of a skill.

matching law of choice behavior The principle that an organism, given a choice between multiple responses, will make a particular response at a rate proportional to how often that response is reinforced relative to the other choices.

mathematical psychology A subfield of psychology that uses mathematical equations to describe the laws of learning and memory.

medial temporal lobe The medial (or inner) surface of the temporal lobe that contains the hippocampus, the amygdala, and other structures important for memory.

medial temporal lobes The medial (or inner) surface of the temporal lobes that contains the hippocampus, the amygdala, and other structures important for memory.

memory The record of past experiences acquired through learning.

mere exposure learning Learning through mere exposure to stimuli, without any explicit prompting and without any outward responding.

metamemory Knowledge of, and ability to think about, our own memories, including both feeling of knowing and judgment of learning.

mirror neurons Neurons that respond during performance of an action and during visual observations of that same action.

mirror reading An experimental task that requires individuals to read mirror-reversed text; used to test cognitive skill learning.

mirror tracing An experimental task that requires individuals to trace drawings by watching a mirror image of their hand and the figure to be traced, with the hand and figure concealed; used to test perceptual-motor-skill learning.

modeling Demonstration of actions.

mood congruency of memory The principle that it is easier to retrieve memories that match our current mood or emotional state.

motivational value of a stimulus The degree to which an organism is willing to work to obtain access to that stimulus.

motor program A sequence of movements that an organism can perform automatically (with minimal attention).

motor prosthesis An electromechanical device that can help people recover lost abilities to learn and perform perceptual-motor skills.

multiple trace theory The theory that episodic (and possibly semantic) memories are encoded by an ensemble of hippocampal and cortical neurons and that both hippocampus and cortex are normally involved in storing and retrieving even very old memories (contrast *standard consolidation theory*).

nativism A philosophical school of thought that holds that the bulk of knowledge is inborn (or native); contrast *empiricism*.

natural selection A proposed mechanism for evolution, also known as "survival of the fittest," which holds that species evolve when there is some trait that varies naturally across individuals, is inheritable, and increases an individual's "fitness," or chance of survival and reproductive success.

negative contrast Situation in which an organism will respond less strongly to a less-preferred reinforcer that is provided in place of an expected preferred reinforcer than it would have if the less-preferred reinforcer had been provided all along.

negative patterning A behavioral paradigm in which the response to the individual cues should be positive while the response to the pattern is negative (no response).

negative punishment A type of operant conditioning in which the response causes a reinforcer to be taken away, or "subtracted from," the environment; over time, the response becomes less frequent.

negative reinforcement A type of operant conditioning in which the response causes a punisher to be taken away, or "subtracted from," the environment; over time, the response becomes more frequent.

nervous system An organism's system of tissues specialized for distributing and processing information.

neurofibrillary tangle An aggregation of collapsed remains of the tau proteins that normally hold a neuron in place and help to transport nutrients around the cell; such tangles occur in the brains of patients with *Alzheimer's disease*.

neurogenesis Creation of new *neurons* in the brain.

neuromodulator A neurotransmitter that acts to modulate activity in a large number of neurons rather than in a single synapse.

neuron A type of cell that is specialized for information processing.

neurophysiology The study of the activity and function of neurons.

neuropsychology The branch of psychology that deals with the relation between brain function and behavior.

neuroscience The study of the brain and the rest of the nervous system.

neurotransmitter One of several classes of molecule released by neurons to carry chemical messages to other neurons.

nondeclarative memory A broad class of memory that includes skill memory and other types of learning that do not fall under the heading of episodic or semantic memory and that are not always consciously accessible or easy to verbalize (contrast *nondeclarative memory*).

novel object recognition An organism's detection of and response to unfamiliar objects during exploratory behavior.

nucleus basalis A small group of neurons located in the basal forebrain. These neurons deliver acetylcholine to the cortex, enabling cortical plasticity.

observational conditioning A process in which an individual learns an emotional response after observing similar responses in others.

observational learning A process in which the learner actively monitors events and then chooses later actions based on those observations.

occipital lobe The part of the cerebral cortex lying at the rear of the human brain; important for visual processing.

open skill A skill in which movements are made on the basis of predictions about changing demands of the environment.

operant conditioning The process whereby organisms learn to make responses in order to obtain or avoid important consequences; compare *classical conditioning*.

operant conditioning The process whereby organisms learn to make responses in order to obtain or avoid certain outcomes; compare *classical conditioning*.

optogenetics A technique for causing specific cells (particularly *neurons*) to become sensitive to light, after which researchers can use light stimulation to turn those specific neurons "on" and "off" at will.

orbitofrontal cortex An area of the prefrontal cortex that is important for learning to predict the outcomes of particular responses.

orienting response An organism's innate reaction to a novel stimulus.

overshadowing A effect seen in compound conditioning when a more salient cue within a compound acquires more association strength, and is thus more strongly conditioned, than does the less salient cue.

parietal lobe The part of the cerebral cortex lying at the top of the human brain; important for processing somatosensory (touch) information.

Parkinson's disease A disorder resulting from disruptions in the normal functioning of the basal ganglia and progressive deterioration of motor control and perceptual-motor-skill learning.

partial reinforcement schedule A reinforcement schedule in which only some responses are reinforced.

pathological addiction A strong habit that is maintained despite harmful consequences.

perceptual learning Learning in which experience with a set of stimuli makes it easier to distinguish those stimuli.

perceptual-motor skill Learned movement patterns guided by sensory inputs.

peripheral nervous system (PNS) The part of the nervous system that carries information from sensory receptors to the central nervous system and carries commands from the CNS to muscles.

perseveration A failure to learn a new response, especially as demonstrated by continued adherence to an old, no longer valid response rule.

perspective taking Imagining oneself in the place of another.

phobia An excessive and irrational fear of an object, place, or situation.

phonological loop An auditory memory maintained by internal (subvocal) speech rehearsal.

phrenology A field of study that attempted to determine mental abilities by measuring head shape and size.

piloerection A fear response in mammals in which body hair stands on end, making the animal look bigger and more threatening than it is.

place cell A neuron that fires maximally when the organism enters a particular location within an environment.

placebo An inactive substance, such as a sugar pill, that is administered to the control subjects in an experiment to compare against the effects of an active substance, such as a drug.

positive punishment A type of operant conditioning in which the response causes a punisher to be "added" to the environment; over time, the response becomes less frequent.

positive reinforcement A type of operant conditioning in which the response causes a reinforcer to be "added" to the environment; over time, the response becomes more frequent.

positron emission tomography (PET) A method of functional neuroimaging based on detecting radiation from the emission of subatomic particles called positrons, associated with the brain's use of glucose from the blood.

postreinforcement pause In operant conditioning with a fixed-ratio (FR) schedule of reinforcement, a brief pause following a period of fast responding leading to reinforcement.

postsynaptic On the receiving side of a synapse.

posttraumatic stress disorder (PTSD) A psychological syndrome that can develop after exposure to a horrific event (such as combat, rape, or natural disaster); symptoms include re-experiencing the event (through intrusive recollections, flashbacks, or nightmares), avoidance of reminders of the trauma, emotional numbing, and heightened anxiety.

power law of practice A law stating that the degree to which a practice trial improves performance diminishes after a certain point, so that additional trials are needed to further improve the skill; learning occurs quickly at first, then slows.

prediction error The difference between what was predicted and what actually occurred.

prefrontal cortex (PFC) The frontmost (anterior) part of the frontal-lobe cortex, essential for working memory and executive control.

Premack principle The theory that the opportunity to perform a highly frequent behavior can reinforce a less frequent behavior; later refined as the *response deprivation hypothesis.*

presynaptic On the sending side of a synapse.

primary reinforcer A stimulus, such as food, water, sex, or sleep, that has innate biological value to the organism and can function as a reinforcer.

priming A phenomenon in which prior exposure to a stimulus can improve the ability to recognize that stimulus later.

proactive interference Disruption of new learning by previously stored information.

prototype The central tendency or idealized version of a concept or category.

psychology The study of mind and behavior.

puberty The process of physical change during which the body transitions to sexual maturity, usually beginning around age 10 in human females and age 12 in human males.

punisher A consequence of behavior that leads to decreased likelihood of that behavior occurring again in the future.

punishment In operant conditioning, the process of providing outcomes for a behavior that decrease the probability of that behavior occurring again in the future.

Purkinje cell A type of large, drop-shaped, and densely branching neuron in the cerebellar cortex.

radical behaviorism An extreme form of behaviorism, championed by B. F. Skinner, holding that consciousness and free will are illusions and that even so-called higher cognitive functions (e.g., human language) are merely complex sets of stimulus response associations.

receptive field The range (or "field") of physical stimuli that activates a single neuron.

receptor A specialized molecule, located on the surface of a neuron, to which one or more particular neurotransmitters can bind; when a neurotransmitter activates a receptor, effects may be initiated in the neuron.

recognition A memory test that involves picking out (or recognizing) a studied item from a set of options.

reconsolidation The process whereby each time an old memory is recalled or reactivated, it may become vulnerable to modification.

reflex An involuntary and automatic (unlearned) response.

reflex arc An automatic pathway from a sensory stimulus to a motor response.

reinforcement In operant conditioning, the process of providing outcomes for a behavior that increase the probability of that behavior occurring again in the future.

reinforcement schedule A schedule determining how often reinforcement is delivered in an operant conditioning

paradigm. See also *continuous reinforcement schedule, partial reinforcement schedule, fixed-ratio (FR) schedule, fixed-interval (FI) schedule, variable-ratio (VR) schedule, variable-interval (VI) schedule, concurrent reinforcement schedule.*

reinforcer A consequence of behavior that leads to increased likelihood of that behavior occurring again in future.

response deprivation hypothesis A refinement of the Premack principle stating that the opportunity to perform any behavior can be reinforcing if access to that behavior is restricted.

response The behavioral consequence of perception of a stimulus.

retention curve A graph showing forgetting or relearning as a function of time since initial learning.

retroactive interference Disruption of old (previously stored) information by new learning.

retrograde amnesia Loss of memories for events dating from before a brain injury or disruption; memory loss generally occurs in a time-graded manner so that more recent memories are devastated but older ones may be spared.

Ribot gradient A pattern of retrograde memory loss in which recently acquired memories are more prone to disruption than older memories.

rotary pursuit task An experimental task that requires individuals to keep the end of a pointed stick (stylus) above a fixed point on a rotating disk; used to study perceptual-motor-skill learning.

secondary reinforcer A stimulus (such as money or tokens) that has no intrinsic biological value but that has been paired with primary reinforcers or that provides access to primary reinforcers.

self-control An organism's willingness to forego a small immediate reinforcement in favor of a large future reinforcement.

semantic memory Memory for facts or general knowledge about the world, including general personal information.

sensitive period A time window, usually early in life, during which a certain kind of learning is most effective.

sensitization A phenomenon in which a salient stimulus (such as an electric shock) temporarily increases the strength of responses to other stimuli.

sensory preconditioning Training in which presentation of two stimuli together as a compound results in a later tendency to generalize what is known about one of these stimuli to the other.

sensory cortex Areas of cerebral cortex involved in processing sensory information such as sight and sounds.

sensory memory Brief, transient sensations of what has just been perceived when someone sees, hears, or tastes something.

sensory prosthesis A mechanical device designed to supplement or substitute for a faulty sensory modality such as vision or hearing; the device's sensory detectors interface with brain areas that normally process those sensory inputs.

serial reaction time task An experimental task that requires individuals to press keys in specific sequences on the basis of cues provided by a computer; used to study implicit learning.

shaping An operant conditioning technique in which successive approximations to a desired response are reinforced.

short-term memory A temporary memory that is maintained through active rehearsal.

single-cell recording Use of an implanted electrode to detect electrical activity (spiking) in a single cell (such as a neuron).

skill An ability that can improve over time through practice.

skill decay Loss of a skill because of non-use.

skin conductance response (SCR) A change in the skin's electrical conductivity associated with emotions such as anxiety, fear, or surprise.

Skinner box A conditioning chamber in which reinforcement or punishment is delivered automatically whenever an animal makes (or ceases making) a particular response (such as pressing a lever).

social conformity The tendency to adopt the behavior of the group.

social learning Learning from others; often used as a synonym for observational learning.

social learning theory A theory of human behavior prominent from the 1940s through the 1960s that proposed that the kinds of reinforcements an individual has experienced in past social contexts will determine how that individual will act in any given situation.

social transmission of information A process seen in all human cultures in which an observer learns something new through experiences with others.

soma The central part of the neuron that contains the nucleus and integrates signals from all the dendrites; also known as the cell body.

somatic theories of emotion Theories of emotion based on the central premise that physiological responses to stimuli come first, and these determine or induce emotions.

source monitoring error Remembering information but being mistaken about the specific episode that is the source of that memory.

spaced practice Practice of a skill that is spread out over several sessions.

spatial learning The acquisition of information about one's surroundings.

spine A tiny protrusion on a *dendrite* where *synapses* may form.

spontaneous recovery Reappearance (or increase in strength) of a previously habituated response after a short period of no stimulus presentation.

standard consolidation theory The theory that the hippocampus and related medial temporal lobe structures are required for storage and retrieval of recent episodic memories but not older ones (contrast *multiple trace theory*).

stereotype A set of beliefs about the attributes of the members of a group.

stimulus A sensory event that provides information about the outside world.

stimulus control The mediation of behavior through responses to cues in the world.

stimulus enhancement A process in which observation of other individuals causes an organism's attention to be directed toward specific objects or events within an environment.

stimulus representation The form in which information about stimuli is encoded within a model or brain.

stress Any stimulus or event that causes bodily arousal and release of stress hormones.

stress hormone A hormone that is released in response to signals from the *autonomic nervous system* (*ANS*) and helps mediate the *fight-or-flight response*; examples include norepinephrine and the *glucocorticoids*.

stroke When blood flow to some region of the brain stops or when an artery ruptures, causing neurons in the affected region to die.

structural neuroimaging Techniques (such as MRI) for creating images of anatomical structures within the living brain.

subject bias The degree to which a subject's prior knowledge or expectations concerning an experiment can (consciously or unconsciously) influence the outcome.

substantia nigra pars compacta (SNc) A part of the basal ganglia that contains dopamine-producing neurons which project to the striatum.

synapse A narrow gap between two neurons across which chemical messages can be transmitted.

synaptic depression A reduction in synaptic transmission; a possible neural mechanism underlying habituation.

synaptic plasticity The ability of synapses to change as a result of experience.

synaptogenesis Creation of new *synapses*.

systematic desensitization Therapy for *phobias* in which successive approximations of the fear-evoking stimulus are presented while the patient learns to remain relaxed; eventually, even presentation of the stimulus itself does not elicit a fear reaction.

talent A person's genetically endowed ability to perform a skill better than most.

template model of song learning A model of song learning having three basic phases: song memorization, song practice, and song utilization.

temporal lobe The part of the cerebral cortex lying at the sides of the human brain; important for language and auditory processing and for learning new facts and forming new memories of events.

testosterone The most important *androgen* and hence the principal male sex hormone.

theory A set of statements devised to explain a group of facts.

theory of equipotentiality The theory that memories are stored globally, by the brain as a whole, rather than in one particular brain area.

token economy An environment (such as a prison or schoolroom) in which tokens function the same way as money does in the outside world.

tolerance A decrease in reaction to a drug so that larger doses are required to achieve the same effect.

trace conditioning A conditioning procedure in which there is a temporal gap between the end of the CS and the beginning of the US.

transfer specificity The restricted applicability of learned skills to specific situations.

transfer-appropriate processing effect The finding that, in general, memory retrieval is best when the cues available at testing are similar to those available at encoding.

transient global amnesia (TGA) A transient, or temporary, disruption of memory typically including elements of both anterograde and retrograde amnesia.

transient memory Nonpermanent memory that lasts seconds or minutes. The Atkinson–Shiffrin model describes two types: sensory and short-term.

trial-level model A theory of learning in which all of the cues that occur during a trial and all of the changes that result are considered a single event.

trisomy 21 A condition in which the embryo inherits three (rather than two) copies of chromosome 21, resulting in *Down syndrome*.

true imitation Copying that involves reproducing motor acts.

two-action test A technique developed to investigate imitation abilities that involves exposing naive animals to demonstrators trained to achieve the same goal using different actions.

two-factor theory of emotion The theory that a combination of cognitive appraisal and perception of biological changes together determines our experience of emotion.

unconditioned response (UR) The naturally occurring response to an unconditioned stimulus (US).

unconditioned stimulus (US) A cue that has some biological significance and in the absence of prior training naturally evokes a response.

US modulation theory Any of the theories of conditioning that say the stimulus that enters into an association is determined by a change in how the US is processed.

variable practice Practice involving the performance of skills in a wide variety of contexts.

variable-interval (VI) schedule In operant conditioning, a reinforcement schedule in which the first response after a fixed amount of time, on average, is reinforced; thus, VI 1-m means that the first response after one minute, on average, is reinforced.

variable-ratio (VR) schedule In operant conditioning, a reinforcement schedule in which a certain number of responses, on average, are required before a reinforcer is delivered; thus, VR 5 means that, on average, every fifth response is reinforced.

ventral tegmental area (VTA) A region in the midbrain that contains dopamine-producing neurons which project to the frontal cortex and other brain areas.

ventrolateral prefrontal cortex The lower left and right sides of the PFC.

visual sensory memory The initial temporary storage for information perceived by the visual system.

visuospatial sketchpad The component of Baddeley's model of working memory that holds visual and spatial images for manipulation.

vocal imitation Copying that involves reproducing sounds.

vocal learning Modifying vocal output using memories of previously experienced sounds.

word-length effect The tendency for a person to remember fewer words from a list as the length of the words increases.

word-stem completion task A task in which participants are asked to fill in the blanks in a list of word stems (e.g., MOT___) to produce the first word that comes to mind; in a priming experiment, participants are more likely to produce a particular word (e.g., MOTEL) if they have been exposed to that word previously.

working memory The active maintenance and manipulation of short-term memory.

Abi-Dargham, A, Mawlawi, O., Lombardo, I., Gil, R., Martinez, D., Huang, U., Hwang, Dr, Keiop, J., Kochan, L., VanHeertum, R., Gorman, J., & Laruelle, M. (2002). Prefrontal dopamine D1 receptors and working memory in schizophrenia. *Journal of Neuroscience, 22*(9), 3708–3719.

Ackerman, P. L. (2006). Cognitive sex differences and mathematics and science achievement. *American Psychologist, 61*, 722–723.

Ackerman, P. L. (2007). New developments in understanding skilled performance. *Current Directions in Psychological Science, 16*, 235–239.

Acredolo, L., & Goodwyn, S. (2002). *Baby signs*. Chicago: Contemporary Books.

Addis, D. R., Moscovitch, M., Crawley, A. P., & McAndrews, M. P. (2004). Recollective qualities modulate hippocampal activation during autobiographical memory retrieval. *Hippocampus, 14*, 752–762.

Adolph, K. E., & Joh, A. S. (2009). Multiple learning mechanisms in the development of action. In A. Woodward & A. Needham (Eds.), *Learning and the infant mind* (pp. 172–207). New York, NY: Oxford University Press.

Aggleton, J., & Mishkin, M. (1983). Visual recognition impairment following medial thalamic lesion in monkeys. *Neuropsychologia, 21*, 189–197.

Aglioti, S. M., Cesari, P., Romani, M., & Urgesi, C. (2008). Action anticipation and motor resonance in elite basketball players. *Nature Neuroscience, 11*, 1109–1116.

Aidman, E. V., & Kollaras-Mitsinikos, L. (2006). Personality dispositions in the prediction of posttraumatic stress reactions. *Psychological Reports, 99*(2), 569–580.

Aimone, J. B., Deng, W., & Gage, F. H. (2010). Adult neurogenesis: integrating theories and separating functions. *Trends in Cognitive Science, 14*(7), 325–337.

Akins, C. K., & Zentall, T. R. (1996). Imitative learning in male Japanese quail (*Coturnix japonica*) using the two-action method. *Journal of Comparative Psychology, 110*(3), 316–320.

al Maskati, H., & Zbrozyna, A. (1989). Cardiovascular and motor components of the defence reaction elicited in rats by electrical and chemical stimulation in amygdala. *Journal of the Autonomic Nervous System, 28*(2), 127–131.

Alberici, E., Pichiecchio, A., Caverzasi, E., Farina, L. M., Persico, A., Cavallini, A., et al. (2008). Transient global amnesia: hippocampal magnetic resonance imaging abnormalities. *Functional Neurology, 23*(3), 149–152.

Allen, M. T., Chelius, L., & Gluck, M. A. (2002). Selective entorhinal lesions and non-selective cortical-hippocampal region lesions, but not selective hippocampal lesions, disrupt learned irrelevance in rabbit eyeblink conditioning. *Cognitive Affective and Behavioral Neuroscience, 2*, 214–226.

Allen, M. T., Chelius, L., & Gluck, M. A. (2002). Selective entorhinal lesions and non-selective cortical-hippocampal region lesions, but not selective hippocampal lesions, disrupt learned irrelevance in rabbit eyeblink conditioning. *Cognitive Affective and Behavioral Neuroscience, 2*, 214–226.

Allen, M. T., Padilla, Y., Myers, C. E., & Gluck, M. A. (2002). Blocking in rabbit eyeblink conditioning is not due to learned inattention. *Integrative Physiological and Behavioral Science, 37*(4), 254–264.

Allison, J. (1993). Response deprivation, reinforcement, and economics. *Journal of the Experimental Analysis of Behavior, 60*, 129–140.

Allport, G. and Postman, L. (1947). *The psychology of rumor*. New York: Henry Holt and Co

Allport, G. W. (1954). *The nature of prejudice*. Reading: MA: Addison-Wesley.

Alzheimer, A. (1987 [1907]). Über eine eigenartige Erkrankung der Hirnrinde [About a peculiar disease of the cerebral cortex]. Translated by L. Jarvik and H. Greenson. *Alzheimer's Disease and Associated Disorders, 1*, 3–8.

Alzheimer's Association (2015). 2015 Alzheimer's disease facts and figures. Downloaded from www.alz.org, 25 May 2015.

Amen, D. G., Newberg, W., Thatcher, R., Jin, Y., Wu, J., Keater, D., & Willeumier, K. (2011). Impact of playing American professional football on long-term brain function. *The Journal of Neuropsychiatry and Clinical Neurosciences, 23*, 98–106.

Aminoff, E. M., Kveraga, K., & Bar, M. (2013). The role of the parahippocampal cortex in cognition. *Trends in Cognitive Science, 17*, 379–390.

Anderson, C. A. (2004). An update on the effects of playing violent video games. *Journal of Adolescence, 27*(1), 113–122.

Anderson, C. A., & Bushman, B. J. (2001). Effects of violent video games on aggressive behavior, aggressive cognition, aggressive affect, physiological arousal, and prosocial behavior: a meta-analytic review of the scientific literature. *Psychological Science, 12*, 353–359.

Anderson, C. A., Berkowitz, L., Donnerstein, E., Huesmann, L. R., Johnson, J. D., Linz, D., et al. (2003). The influence of media violence on youth. *Psychological Science in the Public Interest, 4*, 82–110.

Anderson, C. A., Shibuya, A., Ihori, N., Swing, E. L., Bushman, E. J., Sakamoto, A., et al. (2010). Violent video game effects on aggression, empathy, and prosocial behavior in eastern and western countries: a metanalytic review. *Psychological Bulletin, 136*(2), 151–173.

Anderson, J. (1976). *Language, memory, and thought.* Hillsdale, NJ: Erlbaum.

Anderson, J. (1981). Interference: the relationship between response latency and response accuracy. *Journal of Experimental Psychology: Human Learning and Memory, 7,* 311–325.

Anderson, J. R. (1982). Acquisition of cognitive skill. *Psychological Review, 89,* 369–406.

Anderson, J. R., Corbett, A. T., Koedinger, K. R., & Pelletier, R. (1995). Cognitive tutors: lessons learned. *Journal of the Learning Sciences, 4,* 167–207.

Anderson, M. C. & Levy, B. J. (2009). Suppressing unwanted memories. *Current Directions in Psychological Science, 18,* 189–194.

Anderson, M., Ochsner, K., Kuhl, B., Cooper, J., Robertson, E., Gabrieli, S., et al. (2004). Neural systems underlying the suppression of unwanted memories. *Science, 303*(5655), 232–235.

Anderson, P., de Bruijn, A., Angus, K., Gordon, R., & Hastings, G. (2009). Impact of alcohol advertising and media exposure on adolescent alcohol use: a systematic review of longitudinal studies. *Alcohol & Alcoholism, 44,* 229–243.

Annese, J., Schenker-Ahmed, N., Bartsch, H., Maechler, P., Sheh, C. et al. (2014). Postmortem examination of patient H.M.'s brain based on histological sectioning and digital 3D reconstruction. *Nature Communications, 5,* 3122.

APA Online. (2004). Violence in the media—psychologists help protect children from harmful effects. Retrieved from http://www.psychologymatters.org/mediaviolence.html

Apostolova, L. G., Mosconi, L., Thompson, P. M., Green, A. E., Hwang, K. S., Ramirez, A., Mistur, R., Tsui, W. H. & de Leon, M. J. (2010). Subregional hippocampal atrophy predicts Alzheimer's dementia in the cognitively normal. *Neurobiology of Aging, 31,* 1077–1088.

Apostolova, L., Dutton, R., Dinov, I., Hayashi, K., Toga, A., Cummings, J., & Thompson, P. (2006). Conversion of mild cognitive impairment to Alzheimer disease predicted by hippocampal atrophy maps. *Archives of Neurology, 63,* 693–699.

Archibald, S. J., Mateer, C. A., & Kerns, K. A. (2001). Utilization behavior: clinical manifestations and neurological mechanisms. *Neuropsychology Review, 11*(3), 117–130.

Argolo, F. C., Cavalcanti-Ribeiro, P., Netto, L. R., & Quarantini, L. C. (2015). Prevention of posttraumatic stress disorder with propranolol: A meta-analytic review. *Journal of Psychosomatic Research, 79*(2), 89–93.

Arkes, H. R., & Tetlock, P. E. (2004). Attributions of implicit prejudice, or "Would Jesse Jackson 'fail' the implicit association test?". *Psychological Inquiry, 15(4),* 257–278.

Arnsten, A.F. (2006). Fundamentals of attention-deficit/hyperactivity disorder: Circuits and pathways. *Journal of Clinical Psychiatry, 67*(suppl 8), 7–12.

Aron, A., Fisher, H., Mashek, D., Strong, G., Li, H., & Brown, L. L. (2005). Reward, motivation, and emotion systems associated with early-stage intense romantic love. *Journal of Neurophysiology, 94,* 327–337.

Arthur, W., Bennett, W., Stanush, P. L., & McNelly, T. L. (1998). Factors that influence skill decay and retention: a quantitative review and analysis. *Human Performance, 11*(1), 57–101.

Arthur, W., Day, E. A., Villado, A. J., Boatman, P. R., Kowollik, V., Bennett, W., & Bhupatkar, A. (2010). The effect of distributed practice on immediate posttraining and long-term performance on a complex command-and-control simulation task. *Human Performance, 23,* 428–445.

Ashby, F. G., & Waldron, E. (2000). The neuropsychological bases of category learning. *Current Directions in Psychological Science, 9*(1), 10–14.

Ashmore, R. D., & Del Boca, F. K. (1981). Conceptual approaches to stereotypes and stereotyping. In D. L. Hamilton (Ed.), *Cognitive processes in stereotyping and intergroup behavior* (pp.1–35). Hillsdale, NJ: Erlbaum.

Astur, R., Ortiz, M., & Sutherland, R. (1998). A characterization of performance by men and women in a virtual Morris water task: a large and reliable sex difference. *Behavioural Brain Research, 93,* 185–190.

Awh, E., & Jonides J. (2001). Overlapping mechanisms of attention and spatial working memory. *Trends in Cognitive Science, 5,* 119–26.

Awh, E., and Jonides, J. Spatial selective attention and spatial working memory. (1998). In R. Parasuraman (Ed.), The attentive brain. Cambridge, MA: MIT Press,.

Awh, E., Jonides, J., Smith, E.E., Schumacher, E.H., Koeppe, R.A., & Katz, S. (1996). Dissociation of storage and rehearsal in verbal working memory: Evidence from PET. *Psychological Science, 7,* 25–31.

Azpurua, J. & Eaton, B. A. (2015). Neuronal epigenetics and the aging synapse. *Frontiers in Cellular Neuroscience, 9,* 208.

Baddeley, A. D. (1986). Working memory. Oxford: Oxford University Press, New York.

Baddeley, A. D., & Longman, D. (1978). The influence of length and frequency of training session on the rate of learning to type. *Ergonomics, 21,* 627–635.

Baddeley, A., & Hitch, G. (1974). Working memory. In G. H. Bower (Ed.), The psychology of learning and motivation (pp. 47–89). New York: Academic Press.

Baddeley, A.D., & Logie, R.H. (1992). Auditory imagery and working memory. In D. Reisberg (Ed.), Auditory imagery (pp. 179–197). Hillsdale, NJ: Erlbaum.

Baddeley, A.D., Thomson, N., & Buchanan, M. (1975). Word length and the structure of short-term memory. *Journal of Verbal Learning and Verbal Behavior, 14,* 375–589.

Badre, D. (2008). Cognitive control, hierarchy, and the rostro-caudal organization of the frontal lobes. *Trends in Cognitive Sciences, 12*,193–200.

Badre, D. and D'Esposito, M. (2007) Functional magnetic resonance imaging evidence for a hierarchical organization of the prefrontal cortex. *Journal of Cognitive Neuroscience, 19,* 2082–2099

Badre, D., & D'Esposito, M. (2009). Is the rostro-caudal axis of the frontal lobe hierarchical? *Nature Reviews Neuroscience, 10*(9), 659–69.

Badre, D., Hoffman, J., Cooney, J. W. & D'Esposito, M. (**2009**). **Hierarchical cognitive control deficits following damage to the human frontal lobe. Nature Neuroscience, 12, 515–522** (2009).

Bahrick, H., Bahrick, P., & Wittlinger, R. (1975). Fifty years of memory for names and faces: a cross-sectional approach. *Journal of Experimental Psychology: General, 104,* 54–75.

Bakin, J. S., & Weinberger, N. M. (1990). Classical conditioning induces CS-specific receptive field plasticity in the auditory cortex of the guinea pig. *Brain Research, 536, 271–286.*

Bakin, J., & Weinberger, N. (1996). Induction of a physiological memory in the cerebral cortex by stimulation of the nucleus basalis. *Proceedings of the National Academy of Sciences, 93,* 11219–11224.

Baldo, J.V., & Shimamura, A.P. (2000).Spatial and color working memory in patients with lateral prefrontal cortex lesions. *Psychobiology, 28,* 156–167.

Ball, G., & Hulse, S. (1998). Birdsong. *American Psychologist, 53,* 37–58.

Balleine, B. W., & Kilcross, S. (2006). Parallel incentive processing: an integrated view of amygdala function. *Trends in Neuroscience, 29*(5), 272–279.

Balleine, B., Daw, N., & O'Doherty, J. (2008). Multiple forms of value learning and the function of dopamine. In P. W. Glimcher, C. Camerer, E. Fehr & R. A. Poldrack (Eds.), *Neuroeconomics: Decision Making and the Brain* (pp. 367–387). London: Academic Press.

Bancaud, J., Brunet-Bourgin, F., Chauvel, P., & Halgren, E. (1994). Anatomical origin of déjà vu and vivid "memories" in human temporal lobe epilepsy. *Brain, 117* (Pt. 1), 71–90.

Bandura, A. (1969). *Principles of behavior modification.* New York: Holt, Reinhart, & Winston.

Bandura, A. (1986). *Social foundations of thought and action: a social cognitive theory.* Englewood Cliffs, NJ: Prentice-Hall.

Bandura, A., Ross, D., & Ross, S. A. (1961). Transmission of aggression through imitation of aggressive models. *Journal of Abnormal and Social Psychology, 63,* 575–582.

Bao, J. X., Kandel, E. R., & Hawkins, R. D. (1998). Involvement of presynaptic and postsynaptic mechanisms in a cellular analog of classical conditioning at *Aplysia* sensory-motor neuron synapses in isolated cell culture. *Journal of Neuroscience 18*(1), 458–466.

Bao, J. X., Kandel, E. R., & Hawkins, R. D. (1998). Involvement of presynaptic and postsynaptic mechanisms in a cellular analog of classical conditioning at *Aplysia* sensory-motor neuron synapses in isolated cell culture. *Journal of Neuroscience 18*(1), 458–466.

Baptista, L. F., & King, J. R. (1980). Geographical variation in song and song dialects of montane white-crowned sparrows. *Condor, 82,* 267–281.

Bar-Hillel. (1984). Representativeness and the fallacies of probability. *Acta Psychologica, 55,* 91–107.

Barch, D.M. (2003). Cognition in schizophrenia: Does working memory work? *Current Directions in Psychological Science, 12*(4) 146–150.

Barch, D.M., Carter, C. S., Braver, T.S., McDonald, A, Sabb, F.W., Noll, D.C., & Cohen, J.D. (2001). Selective deficits in prefrontal cortex regions in medication naïve schizophrenia patients. *Archives of General Psychiatry, 50,* 280–288.

Barch, D.M., Csernansky, J., Conturo, T., Snyder, A. Z., & Ollinger, J. (2002). Working and long-term memory deficits in schizophrenia: Is there a common underlying prefrontal mechanism? *Journal of Abnormal Psychology, 111,* 4778–494.

Barnes, C. A. (1979). Memory deficits associated with senescence: a neurophysiological and behavioral study in the rat. *Journal of Comparative and Physiological Psychology, 93*(1), 74–104.

Barnes, C., Suster, M., Shen, J., & McNaughton, B. (1997). Multistability of cognitive maps in the hippocampus of old rats. *Nature, 388,* 272–275.

Barnes, T. D., Kubota, Y., Hu, D., Jin, D. Z., & Graybiel, A. M. (2005). Activity of striatal neurons reflects dynamic encoding and recoding of procedural memories. *Nature, 437,* 1158–1161.

Barnfield, A. (1999). Development of sex differences in spatial memory. *Perceptual and Motor Skills, 89*(1), 339–350.

Baron-Cohen, S. (2009). Autism: the Empathizing-Synthesizing (E-S) theory. *Annals of the New York Academy of Sciences, 1156,* 68–80.

Barr, R. (1980). Some remarks on the time-course of aging. In L. Poon, J. Fozard, L. Cermak, D. Arenberg & L. Thompson (Eds.), *New directions in memory and aging* (pp. 143–149). Hillsdale, NJ: Erlbaum.

Bartolomei, F., Barbeau, E. J., Nguyen, T., McGonigal, A., Regis, J., Chauvel, & Wendling, F. (2012). Rhinal-hippocampal interactions during *déjà vu*. *Clinical Neurophysiology, 123,* 489–495.

Bartsch, D., Ghirardi, M., Skehel, P. A., Karl, K. A., Herder, S. P., Chen, M., Bailey, C. H., & Kandel, E. R. (1995). *Aplysia* CREB2 represses long-term facilitation: Relief of repression converts transient facilitation into long-term functional and structural change. *Cell, 83,* 979–992.

Bartsch, D., Ghirardi, M., Skehel, P. A., Karl, K. A., Herder, S. P., Chen, M., Bailey, C. H., & Kandel, E. R. (1995). *Aplysia* CREB2 represses long-term facilitation: Relief of repression converts transient facilitation into long-term functional and structural change. *Cell, 83*, 979–992.

Basham, M. E., Nordeen, E. J., & Nordeen, K. W. (1996). Blockade of NMDA receptors in the anterior forebrain impairs sensory acquisition in the zebra finch. *Neurobiology of Learning and Memory, 66*, 295–304.

Bauer, P. (1996). What do infants recall of their lives? Memory for specific events by one- to two-year-olds. *American Psychologist, 51*, 29–41.

Bauer, R.H. & Fuster, J. M. (1976). Delayedmatching and delayedresponse deficit from cooling dorsolateral prefrontal cortex in monkeys. *Journal of Comparative and Physiological Psychology, 90*, 293–302.

Baum, W. M. (2002). From molecular to molar: A paradigm shift in behavior analysis. *Journal of the Experimental Analysis of Behavior, 78*, 95–116.

Baum, W. M. (2004). Molar and molecular views of choice. *Behavioural Processes, 66*, 349–359.

Baumrind, D. (2002). Ordinary physical punishment: Is it harmful? Comment on Gershoff (2002). *Psychological Bulletin, 128*, 580–589.

Beadle-Brown, J. D., & Whiten, A. (2004). Elicited imitation in children and adults with autism: Is there a deficit? *Journal of Intellectual & Developmental Disability, 292*, 147–163.

Bechara, A., Tranel, D., Damasio, H., Adolphs, R., Rockland, C., & Damasio, A. (1995). Double dissociation of conditioning and declarative knowledge relative to the amygdala and hippocampus in humans. *Science, 269*, 1115–1118.

Beck, B. (1980). *Animal tool behavior: the use and manufacture of tools by animals.* New York: Garland STPM Press.

Beck, H. P., Levinson, S., & Irons, G. (2009). Finding Little Albert: a journey to John B. Watson's infant laboratory. *American Psychologist, 64*(7), 605–614.

Beck, K. D., McLaughlin, J., Bergen, M. T., Cominski, T. P., Moldow, R. L., & Servatius, R. J. (2008). Facilitated acquisition of the classically conditioned eyeblink response in women taking oral contraceptives. *Behavioural Pharmacology, 19*(8), 821–828.

Beck, S. J., Hanson, C. A., Puffenberger, S. s., Benninger, K. L., & Benninger, W. B. (2010). A controlled trial of working memory training for children and adolescents with ADHD. *Journal of Clinical Child & Adolescent Psychology, 39*(6). 825–836.

Becker, S. (2005). A computational principle for hippocampal learning and neurogenesis. *Hippocampus, 15*(6), 722–738.

Bee, M. A. (2001). Habituation and sensitization of aggression in bullfrogs (*Rana catesbeiana*): testing the dual-process theory of habituation. *Journal of Comparative Psychology, 115*, 307–316.

Beglinger, L. J., Gaydos, B. L., Kareken, D. A., Tangphao-Daniels, O., Siemers, E. R., & Mohs, R. C. (2004). Neuropsychological test performance in healthy volunteers before and after donepezil administration. *Journal of Psychopharmacology, 18*, 102–108.

Bekerian, D., & Baddeley, A. (1980). Saturation advertising and the repetition effect. *Journal of Verbal Learning and Verbal Behavior, 19*(1), 17–25.

Belichenko, P. V., Masliah, E., Kleschevnikov, A. M., Villar, A., Epstein, C. J., Salehi, A., et al. (2004). Synaptic structural abnormalities in the Ts65Dn mouse model of Down Syndrome. *Journal of Comparative Neurology, 480*(3), 281–298.

Bell, C. (1811). *An idea of a new anatomy of the brain.* London: Strahan and Preston.

Bello, M. (2015 February 6) Brian Williams not alone in having false memories. *USA Today* online. Retrieved May 5, 2015, from www.usatoday.com.

Benabid, A. L. (2003). Deep brain stimulation for Parkinson's disease. *Current Opinion in Neurobiology, 13*, 696–706.

Benjamin, M. McKeachie, W., Lin, Y.-G., & Holinger, D. (1981). Test anxiety: deficits in information processing. *Journal of Educational Psychology, 73*, 816–824.

Bennett, D., Wilson, R., Schneider, J., Evans, D., Mendes de Leon, C., Arnold, S., et al. (2003). Education modifies the relation of AD pathology to level of cognitive function in older persons. *Neurology, 60*(12), 1909–1915.

Berger-Sweeney, J., Stearns, N. A., Frick, K. M., Beard, B., & Baxter, M. G. (2000). Cholinergic basal forebrain is critical for social transmission of food preferences. *Hippocampus, 10*(6), 729–738.

Bergvall, U. A., Rautio, P., Luotola, T., & Leimar, O. (2007). A test of simultaneous and successive negative contrast in fallow deer foraging behaviour. *Animal Behaviour, 74*, 395–402.

Berke, J. (2003). Learning and memory mechanisms involved in compulsive drug use and relapse. In J. Wang (Ed.), *Methods in Molecular Medicine, vol. 79: Drugs of Abuse: Neurological Reviews and Protocols* (pp. 75–101). Totowa, NJ: Humana Press.

Bernard, F. A., Bullmore, E. T., Graham, K. S., Thompson, S. A., Hodges, J. R., & Fletcher, P. C. (2004). The hippocampal region is involved in successful recognition of both remote and recent famous faces. *Neuroimage, 22*, 1704–1714.

Berridge, K. (1996). Food reward: Brain substrates of wanting and liking. *Neuroscience and Biobehavioral Reviews, 20*(1), 1–25.

Berridge, K. C. (2007). The debate over dopamine's role in reward: The case for incentive salience. *Psychopharmacology, 191*(3), 391–431.

Berridge, K. C. (2012). From prediction error to incentive salience: mesolimbic computation of reward motivation. *European Journal of Neuroscience, 35,* 1124–1143.

Berridge, K. C., & Robinson, T. (1998). What is the role of dopamine in reward: Hedonic impact, reward learning, or incentive salience? *Brain Research Reviews, 28,* 309–369.

Berry, C. J., Shanks, D. R., Speekenbrink, M., & Henson, R. N. A. (2011). Models of recognition, repetition priming, and fluency: exploring a new framework. *Psychological Review, 119,* 40–79.

Berry, S. D., & Thompson, R. F. (1978). Neuronal plasticity in the limbic system during classical conditioning of the rabbit nictitating membrane response. I. The hippocampus. *Brain Research, 145,* 323–346.

Besson, A., Privat, A., Eschalier, A., & Fialip, J. (1999). Dopaminergic and opioidergic mediations of tricyclic antidepressants in the learned helplessness paradigm. *Pharmacology, Biochemistry and Behavior, 64,* 541–548.

Biederman, I., & Shiffrar, M. (1987). Sexing day-old chicks: a case study and expert systems analysis of a difficult perceptual learning task. *Journal of Experimental Psychology: Learning, Memory, and Cognition, 13,* 640–645.

Bimonte, H., Hyde, L., Hoplight, B., & Denenberg, V. (2000). In two species, females exhibit superior working memory and inferior reference memory on the water radial-arm maze. *Physiology and Behavior, 70(3–4),* 311–317.

Birren, J. (1964). *The psychology of aging.* Englewood Cliffs, NJ: Prentice Hall.

Bjork, R. A., Dunlosky, J., & Kornell, N. (2013). Self-regulated learning: beliefs, techniques, and illusions. *Annual Review of Psychology, 64,* 417–444.

Blennow, K., de Leon, M. J., & Zetterberg, H. (2006). Alzheimer's disease. *Lancet, 368(9533),* 387–403.

Bliss, T. V., & Gardner-Medwin, A. (1973). Long-lasting potentiation of synaptic transmission in the dentate area of the unanaesthetized rabbit following stimulation of the perforant path. *Journal of Physiology (London), 232,* 357–371.

Bliss, T. V., & Lømo, T. (1973). Long-lasting potentiation of synaptic transmission in the dentate area of the anaesthetized rabbit following stimulation of the perforant path. *Journal of Physiology, 232,* 331–356.

Blough, D. S. (1975). Steady-state data and a quantitative model of operant generalization and discrimination. *Journal of Experimental Psychology: Animal Behavior Processes, 104,* 3–21.

Blough, D. S. (1975). Steady state data and a quantitative model of operant generalization and discrimination. *Journal of Experimental Psychology: Animal Behavior Processes, 1,* 3–21.

Boedeker, E., Friedel, G., & Walles, T. (2012). Sniffer dogs as part of a bimodal bionic research approach to develop a lung cancer screening. *Interactive Cardiovascular and Thoracic Surgery, 1,* 511–515.

Bonanno, G. A. (2004). Loss, trauma, and human resilience: have we underestimated the human capacity to thrive after extremely aversive events? *American Psychologist, 59(1),* 20–28.

Bonanno, G. A. (2005). Resilience in the face of potential trauma. *Current Directions in Psychological Science, 14(3),* 135–138.

Bonardi, C., Rey, V., Richmond, M., & Hall, G. (1993). Acquired equivalence of cues in pigeon autoshaping: Effects of training with common consequences and common antecedents. *Animal Learning and Behavior, 21(4),* 369–376.

Bond, A. B., & Kamil, A. C. (1999). Searching image in blue jays: facilitation and interference in sequential priming. *Animal Learning and Behavior, 27,* 461–471.

Bornstein, M., & Lamb, M. (1992). **Development in infancy** (3rd ed.). New York: McGraw-Hill.

Borovsky, D., & Rovee-Collier, C. (1990). Contextual constraints on memory retrieval at six months. *Child Development, 61,* 1569–1583.

Borszcz, G., Cranney, J., & Leaton, R. (1989). Influence of long-term sensitization of the acoustic startle response in rats: central gray lesions, preexposure, and extinction. *Journal of Experimental Psychology: Animal Behavior Processes, 15,* 54–64.

Borton, D., Micera, S., Millan, J. R., & Courtine, G. (2013). Personalized neuroprosthetics. *Science Translational Medicine, 5,* 1–12.

Bourgeois, J.-P. (2001). Synaptogenesis in the neocortex of the newborn: the ultimate frontier for individuation? In C. Nelson & M. Luciana (Eds.), *Handbook of developmental cognitive neuroscience.* Cambridge, MA: MIT Press.

Bourtchuladze, R., Frenguelli, B., Blendy, J., Cioffi, D., Schutz, G., & Silva, A. J. (1994). Deficient long-term memory in mice with a targeted mutation of the CAMP-responsive element-binding protein. *Cell, 79,* 59–68.

Bouton, M & King, D (1983). Contextual control of the extinction of conditioned fear: Tests for the associative value of the context. *Journal of Experimental Psychology: Animal Behavior Processes, 9(3),* 248–265

Bouton, M. (1991). Context and retrieval in extinction and in other examples of interference in simple associative learning. In L. Dachowski & C. F. Flaherty (Eds). *Current Topics in Animal Learning: Brain, Emotion, and Cognition* (pp. 25–53). Hillsdale. NJ: Lawrence Erlbaum Associates.

Bouton, M. E. (2000). A learning theory perspective on lapse, relapse, and the maintenance of behavioral change. *Health Psychology, 19(1),* 57–63.

Bouton, M., & Peck, C. (1989). Context effects on conditioning, extinction and reinstatement in an appetitive conditioning paradigm. *Animal Learning and Behavior, 17,* 188–198.

Bower, G. H. (1961). Application of a model to paired-associate learning. *Psychometrika, 26,* 255–280.

Bower, G. H., & Trabasso, T. R. (1964). Concept identification. In R. C. Atkinson (Ed.), *Studies in Mathematical Psychology* (pp. 32–93). Stanford, CA: Stanford University Press.

Bower, G., & Trabasso, T. (1968). *Attention in learning: theory and research.* New York: Wiley.

Bowles, R. P., & Salthouse, T. A. (2003). Assessing the age-related effects of proactive interference on working memory tasks using the Rasch model. *Psychology and Aging, 18*(3), 608–615.

Braak, H., & Braak, E. (1997). Frequency of stages of Alzheimer-related lesions in different age categories. *Neurobiology of Aging, 18,* 351–357.

Bradbury, J. W., & Vehrencamp, S. L. (1998). *Principles of animal communication.* Sunderland, MA: Sinauer.

Brady, F. (2008). The contextual interference effect and sport skills. *Perceptual and Motor Skills, 106,* 461–472.

Braff, D. L., Geyer, M. A., & Swerdlow, N. R. (2001). Human studies of prepulse inhibition of startle: normal subjects, patient groups, and pharmacological studies. *Psychopharmacology, 156,* 234–258.

Brainard, M. S., & Doupe, A. J. (2000). Auditory feedback in learning and maintenance of vocal behavior. *Nature Reviews Neuroscience, 1,* 31–40.

Brambilla, P., Hardan, A., di Nemi, S. U., Perez, J., Soares, J. C., & Barale, F. (2003). Brain anatomy and development in autism: review of structural MRI studies. *Brain Research Bulletin, 61*(6), 557–569.

Brand, M., & Markowitsch, H. (2004). Amnesia: neuroanatomic and clinical issues. In T. Feinberg & M. Farah (Eds.), Behavioral neurology and neuropsychology (2nd ed., pp. 431–443). New York: McGraw-Hill.

Bransford, J., & Johnson, M. (1972). Contextual prerequisites for understanding: some investigations of comprehension and recall. *Journal of Verbal Learning and Verbal Behavior, 11,* 717–727.

Brass, M., Derrfuss, J., Matthes-von Cramon, G., & von Cramon, D. Y. (2003). Imitative response tendencies in patients with frontal brain lesions. *Neuropsychology, 17*(2), 265–271.

Brauer, L., & de Wit, H. (1996). Subjective responses to D-amphetamine alone and after pimozide pretreatment in normal, healthy volunteers. *Biological Psychiatry, 39,* 26–32.

Brauer, L., & de Wit, H. (1997). High dose pimozide does not block amphetamine-induced euphoria in normal volunteers. *Pharmacology, Biochemistry and Behavior, 56,* 265–272.

Braun, D. A., Mehring, C., & Wolpert, D. W. (2010). Structure learning in action. *Behavioural Brain Research, 206,* 157–165.

Breazeal, C., & Scassellati, B. (2002). Robots that imitate humans. *Trends in Cognitive Sciences, 6*(11), 481–487.

Brehmer, Y., Li, S. C., Muller, V., von Oertzen, T., & Lindenberger, U. (2007). Memory plasticity across the life span: uncovering children's latent potential. *Developmental Psychology, 43,* 465–478.

Breiter, H., Aharon, I., Kahneman, D., Dale, A., & Shizgal, P. (2001). Functional imaging of neural responses to expectancy and experience of monetary gains and losses. *Neuron, 30,* 619–639.

Breland, K., & Breland, M. (1951). A field of applied animal psychology. *American Psychologist, 6,* 202–204.

Brembs, B. (2003). Operant reward learning in *Aplysia. Current Directions in Psychological Science, 12*(6), 218–221.

Brewer, J., Zhao, Z., Desmond, J., Glover, G., & Gabrieli, J. (1998). Making memories: brain activity that predicts whether visual experiences will be remembered or forgotten. *Science, 281,* 1185–1187.

Brewer, J.B., Zhao, Z., Desmond, J.E., Glover, G.H., & Gabrieli, J.D.E. (1998). Making memories: Brain activity that predicts how well visual experience will be remembered. *Science, 281,* 1185–1187.

Bridgett, D., & Cuevas, J. (2000). Effects of listening to Mozart and Bach on the performance of a mathematical test. *Perceptual and Motor Skills, 90,* 1171–1175.

Bristol, A. S., Sutton, M. A., & Carew, T. J. (2004). Neural circuit of tail-elicited siphon withdrawal in *Aplysia.* I. Differential lateralization of sensitization and dishabituation. *Journal of Neurophysiology, 91,* 666–677.

Brooks, L. (1968). Spatial and verbal components of the act of recall. *Canadian Journal of Psychology, 22,* 349–368.

Brown, C., & Laland, K. N. (2002). Social learning of a novel avoidance task in the guppy: conformity and social release. *Animal Behaviour, 64,* 41–47.

Brown, G., & Stroup, K. (1988). Learned helplessness in the cockroach (Periplaneta Americana). *Behavioral and Neural Biology, 50,* 246–250.

Brown, J. (1969). Factors affecting self-punitive locomotive behaviors. In B. Campbell & R. Church (Eds.), *Punishment and Aversive Behavior* (pp. 467–514). New York: Appleton, Century, Crofts.

Brown, R., & Kulik, J. (1977). Flashbulb memories. *Cognition, 5,* 73–99.

Brozoski, T.J., Brown, R.M., Rosvold, H.E., & Goldman P.S. (1979). Cognitive deficit caused by regional depletion of dopamine in prefrontal cortex of rhesus monkey. *Science, 205,* 929–932.

Brugge, K., Nichols, S., Salmon, D., Hill, L., Delis, D., Aaron, L., et al. (1994). Cognitive impairments in adults with Down's syndrome: similarities to early cognitive changes in Alzheimer's disease. *Neurology, 44*(2), 232–238.

Brunelli, M., Castellucci, V., & Kandel, E. R. (1976). Synaptic facilitation and behavioral sensitization in *Aplysia*: possible role of serotonin and cyclic AMP. *Science, 194,* 1178–1181.

Bryan, R., Wells, S., Miller, T., Elster, A., Jungreis, C., Poirier, V., et al. (1997). Infarctlike lesions in the brain: prevalence and anatomic characteristics at MR imaging of the elderly—data from the Cardiovascular Health Study. *Radiology, 202,* 47–54.

Buccino, G., Binkofski, F., & Riggio, L. (2004). The mirror neuron system and action recognition. *Brain and Language, 89*(2), 370–376.

Buchanan, T., & Lovallo, W. (2001). Enhanced memory for emotional material following stress-level cortisol treatment in humans. *Psychoneuroendocrinology, 26,* 307–317.

Buckner, R.L., Koutstaal, W., Schacter, D. L., Wagner, A.D., & Rosen, B.R. (1998). Functional-anatomic study of episodic retrieval using fMRI: I. Retrieval effort versus retrieval success. *NeuroImage, 7,* 151–162.

Buckner, R.L., Raichle, M.E., Miezin, F.M., & Petersen, S.E. (1996). Functional anatomic studies of memory retrieval for auditory words and visual pictures. *The Journal of Neuroscience. 16(19),* 6219–6235.

Bugnyar, T., & Kotrschal, K. (2002). Observational learning and the raiding of food caches in ravens, *Corvus corax*: Is it "tactical" deception? *Animal Behaviour, 64,* 185–195.

Bunsey, M., & Eichenbaum, H. (1995). Selective damage to the hippocampal region blocks long-term retention of a natural and nonspatial stimulus-stimulus association. *Hippocampus, 5*(6), 546–556.

Burd, G., & Nottebohm, F. (1985). Ultrastructural characterization of synaptic terminals formed on newly generated neurons in a song control nucleus of the adult canary forebrain. *Journal of Comparative Neurology, 240,* 143–152.

Burgdorf, J., & Panksepp, J. (2001). Tickling induces reward in adolescent rats. *Physiology and Behavior, 72,* 167–173.

Bush, G., Vogt, B. A., Holmes, J., Dale, A. M., Greve, D., Jenike, M. A., & Rosen, B. R. (2002). Dorsal anterior cingulate cortex: a role in reward-based decision making. *Proceedings of the National Academy of Sciences, 99,* 523–528.

Bushman, B. J., & Bonacci, A. M. (2002). Violence and sex impair memory for television ads. *Journal of Applied Psychology, 87,* 557–564.

Butki, B. D., & Hoffman, S. J. (2003). Effects of reducing frequency of intrinsic knowledge of results on the learning of a motor skill. *Perceptual and Motor Skills, 97,* 569–580.

Butler, A. C., & Roediger, H. L. (2007). Testing improves long-term retention in a simulated classroom setting. *European Journal of Cognitive Psychology, 19*(4/5), 514–527.

Buzsáki, G. (1989). Two-stage model of memory trace formation: A role for "noisy" brain states. *Neuroscience, 31,* 551–557.

Buzsáki, G. (2002). Theta oscillations in the hippocampus. *Neuron, 33,* 324–340.

Buzsaki, G., & Gage, F. (1989). Absence of long-term potentiation in the subcortically deafferented dentate gyrus. *Brain Research, 484,* 94–101.

Byrne, R. W. (1994). The evolution of intelligence. In P. Slater & T. R. Halliday (Eds.), *Behavior and evolution* (pp. 223–264). London: Cambridge University Press.

Byrne, R. W., & Russon, A. E. (1998). Learning by imitation: a hierarchical approach. *Behavioral and Brain Sciences, 21,* 667–721.

Cabeza, R., & Nyberg, L. (2000). Imaging cognition II: an empirical review of 275 PET and fMRI studies. *Journal of Cognitive Neurology, 12,* 1–47.

Cabeza, R., Rao, S., Wagner, A., Mayer, A., & Schacter, D. (2001). Can medial temporal lobe regions distinguish true from false? An event-related functional MRI study of veridical and illusory recognition memory. *Proceedings of the National Academy of Sciences USA, 98*(8), 4805–4810.

Cahill, L. R., & Alkire, M. (2003). Epinephrine enhancement of human memory consolidation: interaction with arousal at encoding. *Neurobiology of Learning and Memory, 79,* 194–198.

Cahill, L. R., & McGaugh, J. (1995). A novel demonstration of enhanced memory associated with emotional arousal. *Consciousness and Cognition, 4*(4), 410–421.

Cahill, L. R., Babinsky, R., Markowitsch, H., & McGaugh, J. (1995). The amygdala and emotional memory. *Nature, 377,* 295–296.

Cahill, L. R., Haier, R., Fallon, J., Alkire, M., Tang, C., Keator, D., et al. (1996). Amygdala activity at encoding correlated with long-term, free recall of emotional information. *Proceedings of the National Academy of Sciences USA, 93*(15), 8016–8021.

Cahill, L. R., Haier, R., White, N., Fallon, J., Kilpatrick, L., Lawrence, C., et al. (2001). Sex-related difference in amygdala activity during emotionally influenced memory storage. *Neurobiology of Learning and Memory, 75,* 1–9.

Cahill, L. R., Prins, B., Weber, M., & McGaugh, J. (1994). Beta-adrenergic activation and memory for emotional events. *Nature, 371*(6499), 702–704.

Cahill, L. R., Uncapher, M., Kilpatrick, L., Alkire, M. T., & Turner, J. (2004). Sex-related hemispheric lateralization of amygdala function in emotionally-influenced memory: an FMRI investigation. *Learning & Memory, 11,* 261–266.

Cahill, L. R., Weinberger, N., Roozendaal, B., & McGaugh, J. (1999). Is the amygdala a locus of "conditioned fear"?: some questions and caveats. *Neuron, 23,* 227–228.

Callicott JH, Egan MF, Mattay VS, Bertolini, A, Bone, AD, Verchinski, B, & Weinbergers DR (2003). Abnormal fMRI response of the dorsolateral prefrontal cortex in cognitively intact siblings of patients with schizophrenia. *American Journal of Psychiatry, 160,* 709–719.

Canestrari, R., Jr. (1963). Paced and self-paced learning in young and elderly adults. *Journal of Gerontology, 18,* 165–168.

Canli, T., Desmond, J. E., Zhao, Z., & Gabrieli, J. D. E. (2002). Sex differences in the neural basis of emotional memories. *Proceedings of the National Academy of Science USA, 99,* 10789–10794.

Canli, T., Zhao, Z., Brewer, J., Gabrieli, J., & Cahill, L. (2000). Event-related activation in the human amygdala associates with later memory for individual emotional experience. *Journal of Neuroscience, 20,* RC99.

Cannon, W. B. (1927). The James-Lange theory of emotion: a critical examination and an alternative theory. *American Journal of Psychology, 39,* 10–124.

Capaldi, E., Robinson, G., & Fahrback, S. (1999). Neuroethology of spatial learning: the birds and the bees. *Annual Review of Psychology, 50,* 651–682.

Capone, N. C., & McGregor, K. K. (2004). Gesture development: a review for clinical and research practices. *Journal of Speech, Language, and Hearing Research, 47,* 173–186.

Carew, T. J., Hawkins, R. D., & Kandel, E. R. (1983). Differential classical conditioning of a defensive gill-withdrawal reflex in *Aplysia californica. Science, 219,* 397–400.

Carmena, J. M. (2013). Advances in neuroprosthetic learning and control. *PLoS Biology, 11,* e1001561.

Carmena, J. M., Lebedev, M. A., Crist, R., O'Doherty, J. E., Santucci, D. M. et al. (2003). Learning to control a brain-machine interface for reaching and grasping by primates. *PLoS Biology, 1,* e42.

Carpenter, P. A., Just, M.A., and Shell, P. (1990). What one intelligence test measures: A theoretical account of the processing in the Raven Progressive Matrices Test. *Psychological Review, 97,* 404–431.

Carroll, K. M. (1999). Behavioral and cognitive behavioral treatments. In B. McCrady & E. S. Epstein (Eds.), *Addictions: a comprehensive guidebook* (pp. 250–267). New York: Oxford University Press.

Carver, Marina (2014). Third high school football player dies in a week. CNN.com. Posted October 6, 2014; retrieved May 31, 2015.

Cassel, J., Cassel, S., Galani, R., Kelche, C., Will, B., & Jarrard, L. (1998). Fimbria-fornix vs. selective hippocampal lesions in rats: effects on locomotor activity and spatial learning and memory. *Neurobiology of Learning and Memory, 69*(1), 22–45.

Cassidy, J. D., Carroll, L. J., Peloso, P. M., Borg, J., von Holst, H., Holm, L., Kraus, J. & Coronado, V. G. (2004). Incidence, risk factors and prevention of mild traumatic brain injury: Results of the WHO Collaborating Centre Task Force on Mild Traumatic Brain Injury. *Journal of Rehabilitation Medicine, 36* (Supplement 43), 28–60.

Castellanos, F.X., & Tannock, R. (2002). Neuroscience of attention-deficit/hyperactivity disorder: the search for endophenotypes. *Nature Reviews Neuroscience, 3,* 617–628.

Castellucci, V. F., & Kandel, E. R. (1974). A quantal analysis of the synaptic depression underlying habituation of the gill-withdrawal reflex in *Aplysia. Proceedings of the National Academy of Sciences USA, 71,* 5004–5008.

Castellucci, V. F., & Kandel, E. R. (1976). Presynaptic facilitation as a mechanism for behavioral sensitization in *Aplysia. Science, 194,* 1176–1178.

Catarino, A., Küpper, C. S., Werner-Seidler, A., Dalgleish, T., & Anderson, M. C. (2015). Failing to forget: Inhibitory-control deficits compromise memory suppression in posttraumatic stress disorder. *Psychological Science, 26*(5), 604–616.

Centerwall, B. S. (1992). Television and violence: the scale of the problem and where to go from here. *Journal of the American Medical Association, 22,* 3059–3063.

Chabris, C. (1999). Prelude or requiem for the Mozart effect? *Nature, 400,* 826–827.

Chakrabarti, L., Best, T. K., Cramer, N. P., Carney, R. S., Isaac, J. T., Galdzicki, Z., et al. (2010). Olig1 and Olig2 triplication causes developmental brain defects in Down syndrome. *Nature Neuroscience, 13*(8), 927–934.

Chang, L. J., Yarkoni, T., Khaw, M. W., & Sanfey, A. G. (2013). Decoding the role of the insula in human cognition: Functional parcellation and large-scale reverse inference. *Cerebral Cortex, 23,* 739–749.

Charles, S., Mather, M., & Carstensen, L. (2003). Aging and emotional memory: the forgettable nature of negative images for older adults. *Journal of Experimental Psychology: General, 132*(2), 310–324.

Charness, N., Reingold, E. M., Pomplun, M., & Stampe, D. M. (2001). The perceptual aspect of skilled performance in chess: evidence from eye movements. *Memory and Cognition, 29,* 1146–1152.

Chen, L. Y., Rex, C. S., Casale, M. S., Gall, C. M., & Lynch, G. (2007). Changes in synaptic morphology accompany actin signaling during LTP. *Journal of Neuroscience, 27,* 5363–5372.

Chen, L., Bao, S., Lockard, J. M., Kim, J. K., & Thompson, R. F. (1996). Impaired classical eyeblink conditioning in cerebellar-lesioned and Purkinje cell degeneration (pcd) mutant mice. *Journal of Neuroscience, 16,* 2829–2838.

Chi, M. (1978). Knowledge structures and memory development. In R. Siegler (Ed.), *Children's thinking: what develops?* Hillsdale, NJ: Erlbaum.

Chomsky, N. (1959). A review of B. F. Skinner's verbal behavior. *Language, 35*(1), 26–58.

Cipolotti, L., Shallice, T., Chan, D., Fox, N., Scahill, R., Harrison, G., Stevens, J., & Rudge, P. (2001). Long-term retrograde amnesia…the crucial role of the hippocampus. *Neuropsychologia, 39,* 151–172.

Clare, L., Wilson, B. A., Carter, G., Roth, I., & Hodges, J. R. (2002). Relearning face-name associations in early Alzheimer's disease. *Neuropsychology, 16*, 538–547.

Clark, D., & Teasdale, J. (1982). Diurnal variation in clinical depression and accessibility of positive and negative experiences. *Journal of Abnormal Psychology, 91*, 87–95.

Clark, R. E., Broadbent, N. J., Zola, S. M., & Squire, L. R. (2002). Anterograde amnesia and temporally graded retrograde amnesia for a nonspatial memory task after lesions of hippocampus and subiculum. *Journal of Neuroscience, 22*(11), 4663–4669.

Clark, S., Allard, T., Jenkins, W., & Merzenich, M. (1986). Cortical map reorganization following neurovascular island skin transfers on the hands of adult owl monkeys. *Society for Neuroscience Abstracts, 12*, 391.

Clarke, G. (2002). Learning to understand speech with the cochlear implant. In M. Fahle & T. Poggio (Eds.), *Perceptual learning* (pp. 147–160). Cambridge, MA: MIT Press.

Clayton, N., & Dickinson, A. (1999). Scrub jays (*Aphelocoma coerulescens*) remember the relative time of caching as well as the location and content of their caches. *Journal of Comparative Psychology, 113*, 403–417.

Clayton, N., Yu, K., & Dickinson, A. (2001). Scrub jays (*Aphelocoma coerulescens*) form integrated memories of the multiple features of caching episodes. *Journal of Experimental Psychology: Animal Behavior Processes, 27*, 17–29.

Cohen-Bendahan, C., van de Beck, C., & Berenbaum, S. (2005). Prenatal sex hormone effects on child and adult sex-typed behavior. *Neuroscience and Biobehavioral Reviews, 29*(2), 353–384.

Cohen-Kettenis, P., van Goozen, S., Doorn, C., & Gooren, L. (1998). Cognitive ability and cerebral lateralisation in transsexuals. *Psychoneuroendocrinology, 23*(6), 631–641.

Cohen, J.D., Forman, S.D., Braver, T.S., Casey, B. J., Servan-Schreiber, D., & Noll, D.C. (1994).Activation of prefrontal cortex in a non-spatial working memory task with fMRI. *Human Brain Mapping, 1*, 293–304.

Cohen, N. J., Poldrack, R. A., & Eichenbaum, H. (1997). Memory for items and memory for relations in the procedural/ declarative memory framework. *Memory, 5*, 131–178.

Cohen, N., & Squire, L. (1980). Preserved learning and retention of pattern-analyzing skill in amnesia: dissociation of knowing how and knowing that. *Science, 210*, 207–210.

Cohen, T. E., Kaplan, S. W., Kandel, E. R., & Hawkins, R. D. (1997). A simplified preparation for relating cellular events to behavior: mechanisms contributing to habituation, dishabituation, and sensitization of the *Aplysia* gill-withdrawal reflex. *Journal of Neuroscience, 17*, 2886–2899.

Colle, H.A. and Welsh, A. (1976). Acoustic masking in primary memory. *Journal of Verbal Learning and Verbal Behavior, 15*, 17–32.

Collie, A., & Maruff, P. (2000). The neuropsychology of preclinical Alzheimer's disease and mild cognitive impairment. *Neuroscience and Biobehavioral Reviews, 24*, 365–374.

Collinger, J. L., Wodlinger, B., Downey, J. E., Wang, W., Tyler-Kabara, E. C., Weber, D. J. et al. (2013). High-performance neuroprosthetic control by an individual with tetraplegia. *Lancet, 381*, 16–22.

Collinson, S. L., Meyyappan, A., & Rosenfeld, J. V. (2009). Injury and recovery: severe amnestic syndrome following traumatic brain injury. *Brain Injury, 23*(1), 71–77.

Condon, C. D., & Weinberger, N. M. (1991). Habituation produces frequency-specific plasticity of receptive fields in the auditory cortex. *Behavioral Neuroscience, 105*(3), 416–430.

Conn, P., Battaglia, G., Marino, M., & Nicoletti, F. (2005). Metabotropic glutamate receptors in the basal ganglia motor circuit. *Nature Reviews Neuroscience, 6*, 787–798.

Contreras, M., Ceric, F. & Torrealba, F. (2007). Inactivation of the interoceptive insula disrupts drug craving and malaise induced by lithium. *Science, 318*, 655–658.

Convit, A., de Asis, J., de Leon, M., Tarshish, C., De Santi, S., & Rusinek, H. (2000). Atrophy of the medial occipitotemporal, inferior, and middle temporal gyri in nondemented elderly predict decline to Alzheimer's Disease. *Neurobiology of Aging, 21*, 19–26.

Conway, M. A. (2009). Episodic memories. *Neuropsychologia, 47*(11), 2305–2313.

Cooke, S. F., Komorowski, R. W., Kaplan, E. S., Gavornik, J. P., & Bear, M. F. (2015). Visual recognition memory, manifested as long-term habituation, requires synaptic plasticity in V1. *Nature Neuroscience, 18*, 262–271.

Cooper, B. G., & Mizumori, S. J. (2001). Temporary inactivation of the retrosplenial cortex causes a transient reorganization of spatial coding in the hippocampus. *Journal of Neuroscience, 21*, 3986–4001.

Corkin, S. (2002). What's new with the amnesic patient H.M.? *Nature Reviews Neuroscience, 3*, 153–160.

Corkin, S., Amaral, D., Gonzalez, A., Johnson, K., & Hyman, B. (1997). H. M.'s medial temporal lobe lesion: findings from magnetic resonance imaging. *Journal of Neuroscience, 17*, 3964–3979.

Cornstock, G. (1980). New emphases in research on the effects of television and film violence. In E. L. Palmer & A. Dorr (Eds.), *Children and the faces of television: teaching, violence, selling* (pp. 129–148). New York: Academic Press.

Cornu, J.-N., Cancel-Tassin, G., Ondet, V., Girardet, C., & Cussenot, O. (2011). Olfactory detection of prostate cancer by dogs sniffing urine: A step forward in early diagnosis. *European Urology, 59*, 197–201.

Corter, J. E., & Gluck, M. A. (1992). Explaining basic categories: Feature predictability and information. *Psychological Bulletin, 111*(2), 291–303.

Courtney, S.M., Ungerleider, L. G., Keil, K., & Haxby, J.V. (1997). Transient and sustained activity in a distributed neural system for human working memory. *Nature, 386*, 608–611.

Coutureau E, Killcross A. S., Good M, Marshall V. J., Ward-Robinson J, Honey R. C. (2002). Acquired equivalence and distinctiveness of cues: II. Neural manipulations and their implications. *Journal of Experimental Psychology: Animal Behavior Process, 28*(4), 388–96.

Cowan, N. (1995). Attention and memory: An integrated framework. New York: Oxford University Press.

Craig, A. D. (2003). Pain mechanisms: labeled lines versus convergence in central processing. *Annual Review of Neuroscience, 26*, 1–30.

Craik, F., & Lockhart, R. (1972). Levels of processing: a framework for memory research. *Journal of Verbal Learning and Verbal Behavior, 11*, 671–684.

Craik, F., & Tulving, E. (1975). Depth of processing and the retention of words in episodic memory. *Journal of Experimental Psychology: General, 104*(3), 268–294.

Crick, N. R., & Dodge, K. A. (1994). A review and reformulation of social information processing mechanisms in children's social adjustment. *Psychological Bulletin, 115*, 74–101.

Crnic, L., & Pennington, B. (2000). Down syndrome: neuropsychology and animal models. In C. Rovee-Collier, L. Lipsitt & H. Hayne (Eds.), *Progress in infancy research, Volume I* (pp. 69–111). Mahwah, NJ: Erlbaum.

Crystal, J. D. (2010). Episodic-like memory in animals. *Behavioural Brain Research, 215*(2), 235–243.

Curio, E., Ernst, U., & Vieth, W. (1978). The adaptive significance of avian mobbing. *Zeitschrift für Tierpsychologie, 48*, 184–202.

Curtis, C. E. & D'Esposito, M. (2004). The effects of prefrontal lesions on working memory performance and theory. *Cognitive, Affective, and Behavioral Neuroscience, 4*(4), 528–539.

Curtis, C. E. & D'Esposito, M. (2006). Working memory: Handbook of functional neuroimaging of Cognition, 2nd ed. R. Cabezza & A. Kingstone. MIT Press, Cambridge, Mass

Curtis, C.E., and D'Esposito M. (2003). Persistent activity in the prefrontal cortex during working memory. *Trends in Cognitive Science, 7*, 415–423.

Curtiss, S. (1977). *Genie: a psycholinguistic study of a modern-day "wild child."* New York: Academic Press.

Cusato, B., & Domjan, M. (1998). Special efficacy of sexual conditioned stimuli that include species typical cues: test with a CS pre-exposure design. *Learning and Motivation, 29*, 152–167.

Custance, D. M., Whiten, A., & Bard, K. A. (1995). Can young chimpanzees imitate arbitrary actions? Hayes and Hayes revisited. *Behaviour, 132*, 839–858.

Cutler, N., Hesten, L., Davies, P., Haxby, J., & Schapiro, M. (1985). Alzheimer's disease and Down's syndrome: new insights. *Annals of Internal Medicine, 103*, 566–578.

Czaja, S., Hammond, K., Blascovich, J., & Swede, H. (1993). Age-related differences in learning to use a text editing system. *Behavior and Information Technology, 8*, 309–319.

D'Esposito, M. & Postle B.R. (2015). The cognitive neuroscience of working memory. *Annual Review of Psychology, 66*, 115–142. doi:10.1146/annurev-psych-010814–015031.

D'Esposito, M. and Postle, B.R. (1999). The dependence of span and delayed-response performance on prefrontal cortex. *Neuropsychologia, 37*, 1303–1315.

D'Esposito, M., Detre, J.A., Alsop, D.C., Shin, R.K., Atlas, S., & Grossman, M. (1995). The neural basis of the central executive system of working memory. *Nature, 378*, 279–281.

Damasio, A. (1996). The somatic marker hypothesis and the possible functions of the prefrontal cortex. *Philosophical Transactions of the Royal Society of London, Series B, 351*, 1413–1420.

Damasio, A. (1999). *The feeling of what happens: body and emotion in the making of consciousness.* New York: Harcourt Brace.

Damasio, A. R. (1994). Descartes' error: emotion, reason, and the human brain. New York, Putman.

Damasio, A., Graff-Radford, N., Eslinger, P., Damasio, H., & Kassell, N. (1985). Amnesia following basal forebrain lesions. *Archives of Neurology, 42*, 263–271.

Daneman, M., and Carpenter, P.A. (1980). Individual differences in working memory and reading. *Journal of Verbal Learning and Verbal Behavior, 12*, 450–466.

Danshevar, D. H., Riley, D. O., Nowinski, C. J., McKee, A. C., Stern, R. A. & Cantu, R. C. (2011) Long-term consequences: Effects on normal development profile after concussion. *Physical Medicine and Rehabilitation Clinics of North America, 22*, 683–700

Darwin, C. (1845). *Journal of researches into the natural history and geology of the countries visited during the voyage of H.M.S. Beagle round the world: under the command of Capt. Fitz Roy.* London: John Murray.

Darwin, C. (1859). *On the origin of species by means of natural selection: or the preservation of favoured races in the struggle for life.* London: John Murray.

Darwin, C. (1872). The expression of emotions in man and animals. Chicago: Chicago University Press (1965).

Darwin, C. (1872). *The expression of the emotions in man and animals.* London: John Murray.

Darwin, C. (1883). *The descent of man and selection in relation to sex.* New York: Appleton-Century-Crofts.

Darwin, E. (1794). *Zoönomia, vol. I; or, the organic laws of life.* London.

Daselaar, S. M., Fleck, M. S., Dobbins, I. G., Madden, D. J., & Cabeza, R. (2006). Effects of healthy aging on hippocampal and rhinal memory functions: an event-related fMRI study. *Cerebral Cortex, 16*(12), 1771–1782.

Dash, P. K., Hochner, B., & Kandel, E. R. (1990). Injection of cAMP-responsive element into the nucleus of *Aplysia* sensory neuron blocks long-term facilitation. *Nature, 345,* 718–721.

Daum, I., Schugens, M. M., Ackermann, H., Lutzenberger, W., Dichgans, J., & Birbaumer, N. (1993). *Behavioral Neuroscience, 107*(5), 748–756.

Davachi, L., Mitchell, J., & Wagner, A. (2003). Multiple routes to memory: distinct medial temporal lobe processes build item and source memories. *Proceedings of the National Academy of Sciences USA, 100*(4), 2157–2162.

Davidson, R., Kabat-Zinn, J., Schumacher, J., Rosenkranz, M., Muller, D., Santorelli, S., et al. (2003). Alterations in brain and immune function produced by mindfulness meditation. *Psychosomatic Medicine, 65,* 564–570.

Daviglus, M. L., Bell, C. C., Berrettini, W., Bowen, P. E., Connolly, E. S., Jr., Cox, N. J., et al. (2010). National Institutes of Health State-of-the-Science Conference statement: preventing Alzheimer disease and cognitive decline. *Annals of Internal Medicine, 153*(3), 176–181.

Davila-Ross, M., Owren, M. J., & Zimmerman, E. (2009). Reconstructing the evolution of laughter in great apes and humans. *Current Biology, 19,* 1106–1111.

Davis, H. (1989). Theoretical note on the moral development of rats (*Rattus norvegicus*). *Journal of Comparative Psychology, 103,* 88–90.

Davis, M. (1972). Differential retention of sensitization and habituation of the startle response in the rat. *Journal of Comparative and Physiological Psychology, 78,* 260–267.

Davis, M. (1980). Habituation and sensitization of a startle-like response elicited by electrical stimulation at different points in the acoustic startle circuit. In E. Grastyan & P. Molnar (Eds.), *Advances in physiological science: Vol. 16. Sensory functions* (pp. 67–78). Elmsford, NY: Pergamon Press.

Davis, M. (1989). Sensitization of the acoustic startle reflex by footshock. *Behavioral Neuroscience, 103,* 495–503.

Davisson, M., Schmidt, C., Reeves, R., Irving, N., Akeson, E., Harris, B., et al. (1993). Segmental trisomy as a model for Down syndrome. In C. Epstein (Ed.), *Phenotypic mapping of Down syndrome and other aneuploid conditions* (pp. 117–133). New York: Wiley-Liss.

Dawson, B. V., & Foss, B. M. (1965). Observational learning in budgerigars. *Animal Behaviour, 13,* 470–474.

Day, J. J. & Sweatt, J. D. (2010). DNA methylation and memory formation. *Nature Neuroscience, 13,* 1319–1323.

De Beaumont, L., Theoret, H., Mongeon, D., Messier, J., Leclerc, S., Tremblay, S. et al. (2009). Brain function decline in healthy retired athletes who sustained their last sports concussion in early adulthood. *Brain, 132,* 695–708.

de Leon, M., George, A., Golomb, J., Tarshish, C., Convit, A., Kluger, A., de Santi, S., McRae, T., Ferris, S., Reisberg, B., Ince, C., Rusinek, H., Bobinski, M., Quinn, B., Miller, D., & Wisniewski, H. (1997). Frequency of hippocampal formation atrophy in normal aging and Alzheimer's disease. *Neurobiology of Aging, 18*(1), 1–11.

de Leon, M., George, A., Stylopoulos, L., Smith, G., & Miller, D. (1989). Early marker for Alzheimer's disease: the atrophic hippocampus. *The Lancet, 2*(8664), 672–673.

de Leon, M., Golomb, J., George, A., Convit, A., Tarshish, C., McRae, T., De Santi, S., Smith, G., Ferris, S., Noz, M., & Rusinek, H. (1993a). The radiologic prediction of Alzheimer Disease: The atrophic hippocampal formation. *American Journal of Neuroradiology, 14,* 897–906.

de Quervain, D., Henke, K., Aerni, A., Coluccia, D., Wollmer, M., Hock, C., et al. (2003). A functional genetic variation of the 5-HT2a receptor affects human memory. *Nature Neuroscience, 6*(11), 1141–1142.

de Quervain, D., Roozendaal, B., & McGaugh, J. (1998). Stress and glucocorticoids impair retrieval of long-term spatial memory. *Nature, 394,* 787–790.

de Quervain, D., Roozendaal, B., Nitsch, R., McGaugh, J., & Hock, C. (2000). Acute cortisone administration impairs retrieval of long-term declarative memory in humans. *Nature Neuroscience, 3,* 313–314.

de Waal, F. (1996). *Good natured: the origins of right and wrong in humans and other animals.* Cambridge, MA: Harvard University Press.

DeCasper, A., & Spence, M. (1986). Prenatal maternal speech influences newborns' perception of speech sounds. *Infant Behavior and Development, 9*(2), 133–150.

DeCasper, A., Lecanuet, J.-P., Busnel, M.-C., Granier-Deferre, C., & Maugeais, R. (1994). Fetal reactions to recurrent maternal speech. *Infant Behavior and Development, 17*(2), 159–164.

Deese, J. (1959). On the prediction of occurrence of particular verbal intrusions in immediate recall. *Journal of Experimental Psychology, 58,* 17–22.

Deisseroth, K. (2010). Controlling the brain with light. *Scientific American, 303*(5), 48–55.

Delis, D.C., Squire, L.R., Bihrle, A., & Massman, P. (1992). Componental analysis of problem-solving ability: Performance of patients with frontal lobe damage and amnesic patients with frontal lob damage and amnesic patients on a new sorting test. *Neuropsychologia, 30*(8), 683–697.

Della Marca, G., Broccolini, A., Vollono, C., Dittoni, S., Frisullo, G., Pilato, F., et al. (2010). The stolen memory: a case of transient global amnesia. *Biological Psychiatry, 67*(6), e31–e32.

Delong, M. R., & Wichmann, T. (2007). Circuits and circuit disorders of the basal ganglia. *Archives of Neurology, 64*, 20–24.

DeLuca, J. (2000). A cognitive neuroscience perspective on confabulation. *Neuro-Psychoanalysis, 2*, 119–132.

DeLuca, J., & Diamond, B. (1995). Aneurysm of the anterior communicating artery: a review of neuroanatomical and neurophysiological sequelae. *Journal of Clinical and Experimental Neuropsychology, 17*(1), 100–121.

DeMeyer, M. K., Alpern, G. D., Barton, S., DeMyer, W. E., Churchill, D. W., Hingtgen, J. N., et al. (1972). Imitation in autistic, early schizophrenic, and non-psychotic subnormal children. *Journal of Autism and Childhood Schizophrenia, 2*(3), 264–287.

Dennis, N. A., & Cabeza, R. (2011). Age-related dedifferentiation of learning systems: An fMRI study of implicit and explicit learning. *Neurobiol Aging, 32*(12), 2318.e2317–2318.e2330.

Dennis, N. A., Hayes, S. M., Prince, S. E., Madden, D. J., Huettel, S. A., & Cabeza, R. (2008). Effects of aging on the neural correlates of successful item and source memory encoding. *Journal of Experimental Psychology: Learming, Memory and Cognition, 34*(4), 791–808.

Dere, E., Kart-Tecke, E., Huston, J. P., & De Souza Silva, M. A. (2006). The case for episodic memory in animals. *Neuroscience and Biobehavioral Reviews, 30*(8), 1206–1224.

Descartes, R. (1662). *De homine.* Leyden (in Latin.)

Desmurget, M., Grafton, S. T., Vindras, P., Grea, H., & Turner, R. S. (2003). Basal ganglia network mediates the control of movement amplitude. *Experimental Brain Research, 153*, 197–209.

Dewsbury, D. A. (1981). Effects of novelty on copulatory behavior: the Coolidge effect and related phenomena. *Psychological Bulletin, 89*, 464–482.

Dewsbury, D. A. (1990). Early interactions between animal psychologists and animal activists and the founding of the APA committee on precautions in animal experimentation. *American Psychologist, 45*, 315–327.

di Pellegrino, G., Fadiga, L., Fogassi, L., Gallese, V., & Rizzolatti, G. (1992). Understanding motor events: a neurophysiological study. *Experimental Brain Research, 91*(1), 176–180.

Diana, R. A., Yonelinas, A. P., & Ranganath, C. (2007). Imaging recollection and familiarity in the medial temporal lobe; A three-component model. Trends in *Cognitive Science, 11*, 379–386.

Dias, B. G. & Ressler, K. J. (2010). Parental olfactory experience influences behavior and neural structure in subsequent generations. *Nature Neuroscience, 17*, 89–96.

Dias, B. G., Maddox, S. A., Klengel, T. & Ressler, K. J. (2015). Epigenetic mechanisms underlying learning and the inheritance of learned behaviors. *Trends in Neurosciences, 38*, 96–107.

Dias, R., Robbins, T.W., & Roberts, A.C. (1996). Dissociation in prefrontal cortex of affective and attentional shifts. *Nature, 380*(6569): 69–72.

Dickinson, A. (1980). *Contemporary Animal Learning Theory.* Cambridge, England: Cambridge University Press.

Dickinson, A., & Balleine, B. W. (2000). Causal cognition and goal-directed action. In C. Heyes & L. Huber (Eds.), *The evolution of cognition* (pp. 185–204). Cambridge, MA: MIT Press.

DiNardo, P., Guzy, L., & Bak, R. (1988). Anxiety response patterns and etiological factors in dog-fearful and non-fearful subjects. *Behaviour Research and Therapy, 26*, 245–252.

Dinse, H. R., & Merzenich, M. M. (2002). Adaptation of inputs in the somatosensory system. In M. Fahle & T. Poggio (Eds.), *Perceptual learning* (pp. 19–42). Cambridge, MA: MIT Press.

Dinse, H. R., Ragert, P., Pleger, B., Schwenkreis, P., & Tegenthoff, M. (2003). Pharmacological modulation of perceptual learning and associated cortical reorganization. *Science, 301*, 91–94.

Dinsmoor, J. A. (1954). Punishment. I. The avoidance hypothesis. *Psychological Review, 61*(1), 34–46.

Dodge, K. A. (2011). Social information processing models of aggressive behavior. In M. Mikulncer & P. R. Shaver (Eds.), *Understanding and reducing aggression, violence, and their consequences* (pp. 165–186). Washington, DC: American Psychological Association.

Dolcos, F., LaBar, K. S., & Cabeza, R. (2004). Interaction between the amygdala and the medial temporal lobe memory system predicts better memory for emotional events. *Neuron, 42*, 855–863.

Domjan, M. (1977). Selective suppression of drinking during a limited period following aversive drug treatment in rats. *Journal of Experimental Psychology: Animal Behavior Processes, 8*, 204–210.

Domjan, M., Lyons, R., North, N. C., & Bruell, J. (1986). Sexual Pavlovian conditioned approach behavior in male Japanese quail (*Coturnix coturnix japonica*). *Journal of Comparative Psychology, 100*, 413–421.

Donnerstein, E., & Berkowitz, L. (1981). Victim reactions in aggressive erotic films as a factor in violence against women. *Journal of Personality and Social Psychology, 41*(4), 710–724.

Dougherty, D. M., & Lewis, P. (1991). Stimulus generalization, discrimination learning, and peak shift in horses. *Journal of the Experimental Analysis of Behavior, 56*, 97–104.

Down, J. (1866). Observations on ethnic classification of idiots. *Mental Science, 13,* 121–128.

Dowsey-Limousin, P., & Pollak, P. (2001). Deep brain stimulation in the treatment of Parkinson's disease: a review and update. *Clinical Neuroscience Research, 1,* 521–526.

Doyon, J., Penhune, V., & Ungerleider, L. G. (2003). Distinct contribution of the cortico-striatal and cortico-cerebellar systems to motor skill learning. *Neuropsychologia, 41,* 252–262.

Draganski, B., Gaser, C., Busch, V., Schuierer, G., Bogdahn, U., & May, A. (2004). Neuroplasticity: changes in grey matter induced by training. *Nature, 427,* 311–312.

Driemeyer, J., Boyke, J., Gaser, C., Buchel, C., & May, A. (2008). Changes in gray matter induced by learning—revisited. *PLOS One, 3,* e2669.

Duara, R., Loewenstein, D. A., Potter, E., Appel, J., Greig, M. T., Urs, R. et al. (2008). Medial temporal lobe atrophy on MRI scans and the diagnosis of Alzheimer disease. *Neurology, 71,* 1986–1992.

Dudai, Y. (2004). The neurobiology of consolidations, or, How stable is the engram? *Annual Review of Psychology, 55,* 51–87.

Dudai, Y., Jan, Y. N., Byers, D., Quinn, W. G., & Benzer, S. (1976). Dunce, a mutant of *Drosophila* deficient in learning. *Proceedings of the National Academy of Science USA, 73*(5), 1684–1688.

Duffy, L., & Wishart, J. G. (1987). A comparison of two procedures for teaching discrimination skills to Down's syndrome and non-handicapped children. *British Journal of Educational Psychology, 57,* 265–278.

Dumitriu, D., Hao, J., Hara, Y., Kaufmann, J., Janssen, W. G. M., Lou, W., et al. (2010). Selective changes in thin spine density and morphology in monkey prefrontal cortex correlate with aging-related cognitive impairment. *Journal of Neuroscience, 30*(22), 7507–7515.

Duncan J, Emslie H, Williams P, Johnson R, & Freer C. (1996). Intelligence and the frontal lobe: the organization of goal-directed behavior. *Cognitive Psychology, 30,* 257–303.

Duncan, C. (1949). The retroactive effect of electro-shock on learning. *Journal of Comparative and Physiological Psychology, 42,* 32–44.

Dunwiddie, T., & Lynch, G. (1978). Long-term potentiation and depression of synaptic responses in the rat hippocampus: localization and frequency dependency. *Journal of Physiology, 276,* 353–367.

Durston, S. (2010). Imaging genetics in ADHD. *Neuroimage, 53,* 832–838.

Durston, S., Hulshoff, E., Hilleke, E., Casey, B., Giedd, J., Buitelaar, J., et al. (2001). Anatomical MRI of the developing human brain: what have we learned? *Journal of the American Academy of Child and Adolescent Psychiatry, 40,* 1012–1020.

Dutton, D. G., & Aron, A. P. (1974). Some evidence for heightened sexual attraction under conditions of high anxiety. *Journal of Personality and Social Psychology, 30*(4), 510–517.

Dweck, C. (1975). The role of expectations and attributions in the alleviation of learned helplessness. *Journal of Personality and Social Psychology, 31,* 674–685.

Dymond, S., & Roche, B. (2009). A contemporary behavioral analysis of anxiety and avoidance. *The Behavior Analyst, 32,* 7–28.

Eacott, M. J., & Easton, A. (2010). Episodic memory in animals: remembering which occasion. *Neuropsychologia, 48*(8), 2273–2280.

Ebbinghaus, H. (1885/1964). *Memory: a contribution to experimental psychology* (H. Ruger & C. Bussenius, Trans., 1964). New York: Dover.

Ebbinghaus, H. (1964). *Memory: a contribution to experimental psychology* (H. Ruger & C. Bussenius, Trans.). New York: Dover. (Original work published 1885.)

Eddy (1982). Probabilistic reasoning in clinical medicine: Problems and opportunities. In D. Kahneman, P. Slovic, & A. Tversky (Eds.). *Judgment under uncertainty: Heuristics and biases* (pp. 249–267). Cambridge, UK: Cambridge University Press.

Eddy, D. M. (1982) Clinical policies and the quality of clinical practice. *New England Journal of Medicine. 307*(6). 343–347.

Egan, M., Kojima, M., Callicott, J., Goldberg, T., Kolachana, B., Bertolino, A., et al. (2003). The BDNF val66met polymorphism affects activity-dependent secretion of BDNF and human memory and hippocampal function. *Cell, 112,* 257–269.

Egan, M.F., Goldberg, T.E., Kolachana, B.S., Callicot, J.H., Mazzanti, C.M., Straub, R.E., Goldman, D., & Weinberger, D. (2001). Effect of COMT Val 108/158 Met genotype on frontal lobe function and risk for schizophrenia. *Proceedings of the National Academy of Sciences, 98,* 6917–6922.

Eich, E., Macaulay, D., & Ryan, L. (1994). Mood dependent memory for events of the personal past. *Journal of Experimental Psychology: General, 123,* 201–215.

Eichenbaum, H. (2000). A cortical-hippocampal system for declarative memory. *Nature Reviews Neuroscience, 1,* 41–50.

Eichenbaum, H., Yonelinas, A. P., & Ranganath, C. (2007). The medial temporal lobe and recognition memory. *Annual Review of Neuroscience, 30,* 123–152.

Eisenberg, N., & Lennon, R. (1983). Sex differences in empathy and related capacities. *Psychological Bulletin, 94,* 100–131.

Eisenberger, N. I., Lieberman, M. D. & Williams, K. D. (2003). Does rejection hurt? *Science, 302,* 290–292.

Eisenstein, E. M., Eisenstein, D., & Bonheim, P. (1991). Initial habituation or sensitization of the GSR depends on magnitude of first response. *Physiology and Behavior, 49*, 211–215.

Ekman, P. (1992). Facial expressions of emotion: new findings, new questions. *Psychological Science, 3*, 34–38.

Ekman, P., & Friesen, W. (1971). Constants across cultures in the face and emotion. *Journal of Personality and Social Psychology, 17*, 124–129.

Ekman, P., & Friesen, W. (1984). *Unmasking the face*. Palo Alto, CA: Consulting Psychology Press.

Elbert, T., Pantev, C., Wienbruch, C., Rockstroh, B., & Taub, E. (1995). Increased cortical representation of the fingers of the left hand in string players. *Science, 270*, 305–307.

Elliot, M. H. (1928). The effect of change of reward on the maze performance of rats. *University of California Publications in Psychology, 4*, 19–30.

Emmelkamp, P., Krijn, M., Hulsbosch, A., de Vries, S., Schuemie, M., & van der Mast, C. (2002). Virtual reality treatment versus exposure in vivo: a comparative evaluation in acrophobia. *Behavior Research and Therapy, 40*(5), 509–516.

Engle, R., & Marshall, K. (1983). Do developmental changes in digit span result from acquisition strategies? *Journal of Experimental Child Psychology, 36*, 429–436.

Epp, J. R., Spritzer, M. D., & Galea, L. A. (2007). Hippocampus-dependent learning promotes survival of new neurons in the dentate gyrus at a specific time during cell maturation. *Neuroscience, 149*(2), 273–285.

Erickson, M.A., Maramara, L.A., Lisman, J. (2010). A single brief burst induces GluR1–dependent associative short-term potentiation: a potential mechanism for short-term memory. *Journal of Cognitive Neuroscience, 22*, 2530–40.

Ericsson, K. (2003). Exceptional memorizers: made, not born. *Trends in Cognitive Sciences, 7*(6), 233–235.

Ericsson, K. A., & Lehman, A. (1996). Expert and exceptional performance: evidence of maximal adaptation to task constraints. *Annual Review of Psychology, 47*, 273–305.

Ericsson, K. A., Krampe, R., & Tesch-Romer, C. (1993). The role of deliberate practice in the acquisition of expert performance. *Psychological Review, 100*, 363–406.

Eriksson, P. (2003). Neurogenesis and its implications for regeneration in the adult brain. *Journal of Rehabilitation Medicine, 41*(Supplement), 17–19.

Eriksson, P., Perfilieva, E., Björk-Eriksson, T., Alborn, A., Nordberg, C., Peterson, D., et al. (1998). Neurogenesis in the adult human hippocampus. *Nature Medicine, 4*, 1313–1317.

Escorihuela, R., Fernandez-Teruel, A., Vallina, I., Baamonde, C., Lumbreras, M., Dierssen, M., et al. (1995). A behavioral assessment of Ts65Dn mice: a putative Down syndrome model. *Neuroscience Letters, 199*(2), 143–146.

Eslinger, P.J. & Damasio, A.R. (1985). Severe disturbance of higher cognition after bilateral frontal lobe ablation: patient EVR. *Neurology, 35*(12): 1731–41.

Estes, W. K. (1950). Toward a statistical theory of learning. *Psychological Review, 57*, 94–107.

Estes, W. K., & Skinner, B. F. (1941). Some quantitative properties of anxiety. *Journal of Experimental Psychology, 29*, 390–400.

Estes, W. K., & Skinner, B. F. (1941). Some quantitative properties of anxiety. *Journal of Experimental Psychology, 29*, 390–400.

Evans, A. H., & Lees, A. J. (2004). Dopamine dysregulation syndrome in Parkinson's disease. *Current Opinion in Neurology, 17*, 393–398.

Everitt, B. J., Cardinal, R. N., Parkinson, J. A., & Robbins, T. W. (2003). Appetitive behavior: impact of amygdala-dependent mechanisms of emotional learning. *Annals of the New York Academy of Sciences, 985*, 233–250.

Exner, C., Koschack, J., & Irle, E. (2002). The differential role of premotor frontal cortex and basal ganglia in motor sequence learning: evidence from focal basal ganglia lesions. *Learning and Memory, 9*, 376–386.

Fanselow, M., & LeDoux, J. (1999). Why we think plasticity underlying Pavlovian fear conditioning occurs in the basolateral amygdala. *Neuron, 23*, 229–232.

Farkas, M., Polgar, P., Kelemen, O., Rethelyi, J., Bitter, I., Myers, C. E., Gluck, M. A., & Kéri, S. (2008). Associative learning in deficit and non-deficit schizophrenia. *Neuroreport, 19*(1), 55–58

Farmer, A., & Terrell, D. (2001). Crime versus justice: Is there a trade-off? Journal of Law and Economics. 44. 345–366.

Featherstone, R., & McDonald, R. (2004). Dorsal striatum and stimulus–response learning: lesions of the dorsolateral, but not dorsomedial, striatum impair acquisition of a simple discrimination task. *Behavioural Brain Research, 150*, 15–23.

Ferguson, C. J., & Kilburn, J. (2010). Much ado about nothing: the misestimation and overinterpretation of violent video game effects in eastern and western nations: comment on Anderson et al. (2010). *Psychological Bulletin, 136*(2), 174–178.

Fernandez, F., Morishita, W., Zuniga, E., Nguyen, J., Blank, M., Malenka, R. C., et al. (2007). Pharmacotherapy for cognitive impairment in a mouse model of Down syndrome. *Nature Neuroscience, 10*(4), 411–413.

Ferrari, M. (1999). Influence of expertise on the intentional transfer of motor skill. *Journal of Motor Behavior, 31*, 79–85.

Ferrari, P. F., Gallese, V., Rizzolatti, G., & Fogassi, L. (2003). Mirror neurons responding to the observation of ingestive and communicative mouth actions in the monkey ventral premotor cortex. *European Journal of Neuroscience, 17*(8), 1703–1714.

Ferrier, D. (1886). The functions of the brain (2nd. ed.). London: Smith, Elder, & Co.

Finkel, D., Pedersen, N., & McGue, M. (1995). Genetic influences on memory performance in adulthood: comparison of Minnesota and Swedish twin data. *Psychology and Aging, 10*(3), 437–446.

Fiorito, G., Agnisola, C., d'Addio, M., Valanzano, A., & Calamandrei, G. (1998). Scopolamine impairs memory recall in *Octopus vulgaris. Neuroscience Letters, 253,* 87–90.

Fisher, A. E. (1962). Effects of stimulus variation on sexual satiation in the male rat. *Journal of Comparative and Physiological Psychology, 55,* 614–620.

Fisher, H., Aron, A., & Brown, L. L. (2005). Romantic love: An fMRI study of a neural mechanism for mate choice. *Journal of Comparative Neurology, 493,* 58–62.

Fitts, P. (1964). Perceptual-motor skill learning. In A. Melton (Ed.), *Categories of human learning* (pp. 243–285). New York: Academic Press.

Fivush, R., & Nelson, K. (2004). Culture and language in the emergence of autobiographical memory. *Psychological Science, 15*(9), 573–577.

Flaherty, C. F. (1982). Incentive contrast: A review of behavioral changes following shifts in reward. *Animal Learning and Behavior, 10*(4), 409–440.

Floel, A. (2014). tDCS-enhanced motor and cognitive function in neurological diseases. *Neuroimage, 85,* 934–947.

Flourens, P. (1824). Investigations of the properties and the functions of the various parts which compose the cerebral mass. In *Some papers on the cerebral cortex* (G. von Bonin, Trans., pp. 3–21). Springfield, IL: Charles C Thomas.

Flynn, J. (1972). Patterning mechanisms, patterned reflexes, and attack behaviour in cats. In J. Cole & D. Jensen (Eds.), *Nebraska Symposium on Motivation* (pp. 125–153). Lincoln, Nebraska: University of Nebraska Press.

Fogarty, S., & Hemsley, D. (1983). Depression and the accessibility of memories—a longitudinal study. *British Journal of Psychiatry, 142,* 232–237.

Forbes, N. F., Carrick, L. A., McIntosh, A. M., & Lawrie, S. M. (2009). Working memory in schizophrenia: a meta-analysis. *Psychological Medicine, 39,* 889–905.

Fox, P. W., Hershberger, S. L., & Bouchard, T. J., Jr. (1996). Genetic and environmental contributions to the acquisition of a motor skill. *Nature, 384,* 356–358.

Foy, M., Xu, J., Xie, X., Brinton, R., Thompson, R., & Berger, T. (1999). 17ß-estradiol enhances NMDA receptor-mediated EPSPs and long-term potentiation. *Journal of Neurophysiology, 81,* 925–929.

Francis, P., Palmer, A., Snape, M., & Wilcock, G. (1999). The cholinergic hypothesis of Alzheimer's disease: a review of progress. *Journal of Neurology, Neurosurgery, and Psychiatry, 66,* 137–147.

Frascella, J., Potenza, M. N., Brown, L. L., & Childress, A. R. (2010). Shared brain vulnerabilities open the way for nonsubstance addictions: Carving addiction a new joint? *Annals of the New York Academy of Sciences, 1187,* 294–315.

Freeman, J., & Nicholson, D. (2001). Ontogenetic changes in the neural mechanisms of eyeblink conditioning. *Integrative Physiological and Behavioral Science, 36*(1), 15–25.

Frenda, S. J., Knowles, E. D., Saletan, W., & Loftus, E. F. (2013). False memories of fabricated political events. *Journal of Experimental Social Psychology, 49,* 280–286.

Fried, L., MacDonald, K., & Wilson, C. (1997). Single neuron activity in human hippocampus and amygdala during recognition of faces and objects. *Neuron, 18,* 753–765.

Friston, K. J., Frith, C. D., Passingham, R. E., Liddle, P. F., & Frackowiak, R. S. J. (1992). Motor practice and neurophysiological adaptation in the cerebellum: a positron emission tomography study. *Proceedings of the Royal Society London, 244,* 241–246.

Fudin, R., & Lembeissis, E. (2004). The Mozart effect: questions about the seminal findings of Rauscher, Shaw & colleagues. *Perceptual and Motor Skills, 98*(2), 389–405.

Fulton, J. J., Calhoun, P. S., Wagner, H. R., Schry, A. R., Hair, L. P., Feeling, N., Elbogen, E., & Beckham, J. C. (2015 9). The prevalence of posttraumatic stress disorder in Operation Enduring Freedom/Operation Iraqi Freedom (OEF/OIF) veterans: A meta-analysis. *Journal of Anxiety Disorders, 31,* 98–107.

Funahashi, S. et al. (1989) Mnemonic coding of visual space in the monkey's dorsolateral prefrontal cortex. *Journal of Neurophysiology, 61,* 331–349

Funahashi, S., Chafee M.V., & Goldman-Rakic, P.S. (1993). Prefrontal neuronal activity in rhesus monkeys performing a delayed anti-saccade task. *Nature, 365*(6448), 753–6.

Fuster, J. M. (1973). Unit activity in the prefrontal cortex during delayed response performance: neuronal correlates of transient memory. *Journal of Neurophysiology, 36,* 61–78.

Fuster, J. M. (1995). Memory in the cerebral cortex. Cambridge, MA: MIT Press.

Fuster, J. M. (2001). The prefrontal cortex—an update: time is of the essence. *Neuron, 30,* 319–333.

Fuster, J. M. (2003). Functional neuroanatomy of executive process. In P. Holligar (Ed.), Oxford handbook of clinical neuropsychology (pp. 753–765),. Oxford: Oxford University Press.

Fuster, J. M., & G. E. Alexander (1971). Neuron activity related to short-term memory. *Science, 173*(997), 652–4.

Gabrieli et al (2004) Neural deficits in children with dyslexia ameliorated by behavioral remediation: Evidence from functional MRI. Proceedings of the National Academy of Sciences.

Gabrieli, J. D., Corkin, S., Mickel, S. F., & Growdon, J. H. (1993). Intact acquisition and long-term retention of mirror-tracing skill in Alzheimer's disease and in global amnesia. *Behavioral Neuroscience, 107,* 899–910.

Gabrieli, J., Corkin, S., Mickel, S., & Crowden, J. (1993). Intact acquisition and long-term retention of mirror-tracing skill in Alzheimer's disease and in global amnesia. *Behavioral Neuroscience, 107*(6), 899–910.

Gadian, D. G., Aicardi, J., Watkins, K. E., Porter, D. A., Mishkin, M., & Vargha-Khadem, F. (2000). Developmental amnesia associated with early hypoxic-ischaemic injury. *Brain, 123*(Pt 3), 499–507.

Gaffan, D., & Hornak, J. (1997). Amnesia and neglect: beyond the Delay-Brion system and the Hebb synapse. *Philosophical Transactions of the Royal Society of London—Series B, 352*(1360), 1481–1488.

Gaffan, D., & Parker, A. (1996). Interaction of perirhinal cortex with the fornix-fimbria: memory for objects and "object-in-place" memory. *Journal of Neuroscience, 16*(18), 5864–5869.

Galbicka, G. (1994). Shaping in the 21st century: Moving percentile schedules into applied settings. *Journal of Applied Behavior Analysis, 27*(4), 739–760.

Galea, A., & Kimura, D. (1993). Sex differences in route-learning. *Personality and Individual Differences, 14*, 53–65.

Galef, B. G., Jr. (1996). Social enhancement of food preferences in Norway rats: a brief review. In C. M. Heyes & B. G. Galef, Jr. (Eds.), *Social learning in animals: the roots of culture* (pp. 49–64). New York: Academic Press.

Galef, B. G., Jr., & Laland, K. N. (2005). Social learning in animals: empirical studies and theoretical models. *Bioscience, 55*(6), 489–499.

Galef, B. G., Jr., & Whiskin, E. E. (1997). Effects of social and asocial learning on longevity of food-preference traditions. *Animal Behaviour, 53*(6), 1313–1322.

Galef, B. G., Jr., & Wigmore, S. W. (1983). Transfer of information concerning distant foods: a laboratory investigation of the "Information-centre" hypothesis. *Animal Behaviour, 31*, 748–758.

Gall, F., & Spurzheim, J. (1810). *Anatomie et physiologie du système nerveux en général, et du cerveau en particulier, avec des observations sur la possibilité de reconnaître plusieurs dispositions intellectuelles et morales de l'homme et des animaux, par la configuration de leur têtes.* Paris: F. Schoell.

Gallagher, M., & Rapp, P. (1997). The use of animal models to study the effects of aging on cognition. *Annual Review of Psychology, 48*, 339–370.

Gallese, V., Fadiga, L., Fogassi, L., & Rizzolatti, G. (1996). Action recognition in the premotor cortex. *Brain, 119*(Pt 2), 593–609.

Galli, G. (2014). What makes deeply encoded items memorable? Insights into the levels of processing framework from neuroimaging and neuromodulation. *Frontiers in Psychiatry, 5*, 61.

Gallistel, C. R., & Gibbon, J. (2000). Time, rate, and conditioning. *Psychological Review 107*(2), 289–344.

Gallistel, C. R., & Gibbon, J. (2000). Time, rate, and conditioning. *Psychological Review 107*(2), 289–344.

Galván, A. (2013). The teenage brain: sensitivity to rewards. *Current Directions in Psychological Science, 22*, 88–93.

Galvao-de Almeida, A., Araujo Filho, G. M., Berberian Ade, A., Trezniak, C., Nerv-Fernandes, F., Araujo Nego, C. A., Jackowski, A. P., Miranda-Scippa, A., & Oliveira, I. R. (2013). The impacts of cognitive-behavioral therapy on the treatment of phobic disorders measured by functional neuroimaging techniques: a systematic review. *Revista brasileira de psiquiatria, 35*, 279–283.

Gandy, S., Simon, A. J., Steele, J. W., Lublin, A. L., Lah, J. J., Walker, L. C., et al. (2010). Days to criterion as an indicator of toxicity associated with human Alzheimer amyloid-beta oligomers. *Annals of Neurology, 68*(2), 220–230.

Gangitano, M., Mottaghy, F. M., & Pascual-Leone, A. (2001). Phase-specific modulation of cortical motor output during movement observation. *Neuroreport, 12*(7), 1489–1492.

Ganguly, K. & Carmena, J. M. (2010). Neural correlates of skill acquisition with a cortical brain-machine interface. *Journal of Motor Behavior, 42*, 355–360.

Garcia, J., & Koelling, R. A. (1966). Relation of cue to consequence in avoidance learning. *Psychonomic Science, 4*, 123–124.

Gardner, R. (1981). Digits forward and digits backward as two separate tests: Normative data on 1567 school children. *Journal of Clinical Child Psychology, Summer 1981*, 131–135.

Garner, W. R. (1970). The stimulus in information processing. *American Psychologist. 25*, 350–358.

Gatchel, R. (1975). Effect of interstimulus interval length on short- and long-term habituation of autonomic components of the orienting response. *Physiological Psychology, 3*, 133–136.

Gathercole, S. (1998). The development of memory. *Journal of Child Psychology and Psychiatry, 39*(1), 3–27.

Gauthier, L. V., Taub, E., Perkins, C., Ortmann, M., Mark, V. W., & Uswatte, G. (2008). Remodeling the brain: plastic structural brain changes produced by different motor therapies after stroke. *Stroke, 39*, 1520–1525.

Gaznick, N., Tranel, D., McNutt, A. & Bechara, A. (2014). Basal ganglia plus insula damage yields stronger disruption of smoking addiction than basal ganglia damage alone. *Nicotine & Tobacco Research, 16*, 445–453.

Geen, R. G. (1990). *Human aggression.* Pacific Grove, CA: Brooks/Cole.

Georgopoulos, A. P., Taira, M., & Lukashin, A. (1993). Cognitive neurophysiology of the motor cortex. *Science, 260*, 47–52.

Gerhardstein, P., & West, R. (2003). The relation between perceptual input and infant memory. In H. Hayne & J. Fagen (Eds.), *Progress in infancy research Volume 3* (pp. 121–158). Mahwah, NJ: Erlbaum.

Gershoff, E. (2002). Child abuse and neglect and the brain: A review. *Journal of Child Psychiatry and Allied Disciplines, 41,* 97–116.

Giang DW, Goodman AD, Schiffer RB, Mattson DH, Petrie M, Cohen N, Ader R. J. (1996). Conditioning of cyclophosphamide-induced leukopenia in humans. *The Journal of Neuropsychiatry & Clinical Neurosciences, 8*(2), 194–201.

Gibson, E., & Walk, R. (1956). The effect of prolonged exposure to visual patterns on learning to discriminate them. *Journal of Comparative and Physiological Psychology, 49,* 239–242.

Gibson, J. J., & Gibson, E. J. (1955). Perceptual learning: differentiation or enrichment. *Psychological Review, 62,* 32–41.

Gil, S., & Caspi, Y. (2006). Personality traits, coping style, and perceived threat as predictors of posttraumatic stress disorder after exposure to a terrorist attack: a prospective study. *Psychosomatic Medicine, 68*(6), 904–909.

Gilbertson, M., Shenton, M., Ciszewski, A., Kasai, K., Lasko, N., Orr, S., et al. (2002). Smaller hippocampal volume predicts pathologic vulnerability to psychological trauma. *Nature Neuroscience, 5*(11), 1111–1113.

Glantz, L. A., Gilmore, J. H., Hamer, R. M., Lieberman, J. A., & Jarskog, L. F. (2007). Synaptophysin and PSD-95 in the human prefrontal cortex from mid-gestation into early adulthood. *Neuroscience, 149*(3), 582–591.

Glass, A. L. & Sinha, N. (2013) Multiple-choice questioning is an efficient instructional methodology that may be widely implemented in academic courses to improve exam performance. *Current Directions in Psychological Science, 22,* 471–477.

Glass, R. (2001). Electroconvulsive therapy: time to bring it out of the shadows. *Journal of the American Medical Association, 285,* 1346–1348.

Globus, A., Rosenzweig, R., Bennet, E., & Diamond, M. (1973). Effects of differential experience on dendritic spine counts in rat cerebral cortex. *Journal of Comparative and Physiological Psychology, 82,* 175–181.

Gluck, M. , Bower, G. , & Hee, M. (1989). A configural-cue network model of animal and human associative learning. In 11th Annual Conference of Cognitive Science Society (pp. 323–332). Ann Arbor, MI.

Gluck, M. A. & Bower, G. H. (1988). From conditioning to category learning: An adaptive network model. *Journal of Experimental Psychology: General, 117*(3), 227–247.

Gluck, M. A. & Myers, C. E. (2001). *Gateway to memory: An introduction to neural network models of the hippocampus and learning.* Cambridge, MA: MIT Press.

Gluck, M. A., & Bower, G. H. (1988). From conditioning to category learning: an adaptive network model. *Journal of Experimental Psychology: General, 117*(3), 227–247.

Gluck, M. A., Allen, M. T., Myers, C. E., & Thompson, R. F. (2001). Cerebellar substrates for error-correction in motor conditioning. *Neurobiology of Learning and Memory, 76,* 314–341.

Gluck, M. A., Reifsnider, E. S., & Thompson, R. F. (1990). Adaptive signal processing and the cerebellum: models of classical conditioning and VOR adaptation. In M. A. Gluck and D. E. Rumelhart (Eds.), *Neuroscience and Connectionist Theory* (pp. 131–185). Hillsdale, NJ: Lawrence Erlbaum.

Gluck, M. A., Shohamy, D., & Myers, C. (2002). How do people solve the "Weather Prediction" task? Individual variability in strategies for probabilistic category learning. *Learning & Memory, 9,* 408–418.

Gluck, M., & Bower, G. (1988a). From conditioning to category learning: An adaptive network model. *Journal of Experimental Psychology: General, 117*(3), 225–244.

Gluck, M., & Bower, G. (1988b). Evaluating an adaptive network model of human learning. *Journal of Memory and Language, 27,* 166–195.

Gluck, M., & Myers, C. (1993). Hippocampal mediation of stimulus representation: A computational theory. *Hippocampus, 3,* 491–516.

Godde, B., Ehrhardt, J., & Braun, C. (2003). Behavioral significance of input-dependent plasticity of human somatosensory cortex. *Neuroreport, 14,* 543–546.

Godden, D., & Baddely, A. (1975). Context-dependent memory in two natural environments: on land and under water. *British Journal of Psychology, 66,* 325–331.

Goff, L., & Roediger, H. (1998). Imagination inflation for action events: repeated imaginings lead to illusory recollections. *Memory and Cognition, 26,* 20–33.

Gold, P., & van Buskirk, R. (1975). Facilitation of time-dependent memory processes with posttrial epinephrine injections. *Behavioral Biology, 13,* 145–153.

Goldman-Rakic, P. S. (1987). Circuitry of primate prefrontal cortex and regulation of behavior by representational memory. In F Plum (Ed.), Handbook of physiology: The nervous system (pp. 373–417). Bethesda, MD: American Physiological Society.

Goldman-Rakic, P. S. (1996). Architecture of the prefrontal cortex and the central executive. *Annals of the New York Academy of Sciences, 769,* 71–83.

Goldman, P. S., and Rosvold, H.E. (1970). Localization of function within the dorsolateral prefrontal cortex of the rhesus monkey. *Experimental Neurology, 27,* 291–304.

Goldman, S., & Nottebohm, F. (1983). Neuronal production, migration, and differentiation in a vocal control nucleus of the adult female canary brain. *Proceedings of the National Academy of Sciences USA, 80,* 2390–2394.

Goldstein, J., Seidman, L., Horton, N., Makris, N., Kennedy, D., Caviness, V., et al. (2001). Normal sexual dimorphism of the adult human brain assessed by in vivo magnetic resonance imaging. *Cerebral Cortex, 11,* 490–497.

Goldstein, J., Seidman, L., O'Brien, L., Horton, N., Kennedy, D., Makris, N., et al. (2002). Impact of normal sexual dimorphisms on sex differences in structural brain abnormalities in schizophrenia assessed by magnetic resonance imaging. *Archives of General Psychiatry, 59*(2), 154–164.

Goldstone, R. L. (1994). Influences of categorization on perceptual discrimination. *Journal of Experimental Psychology: General, 123*, 178–200.

Goldstone, R. L., Kersten, A., & Cavalho, P. F. (2012). Concepts and Categorization. In A. F. Healy & R. W. Proctor (Eds.) *Comprehensive handbook of psychology, Volume 4: Experimental psychology.* (pp. 607–630). New Jersey: Wiley.

Goldstone, R. L., Steyvers, M., & Rogosky, B. J. (2003). Conceptual Interrelatedness and Caricatures. *Memory & Cognition, 31*, 169–180.

Golomb, J., de Leon, M., Kluger, A., George, A., Tarshish, C., & Ferris, S. (1993). Hippocampal atrophy in normal aging: An association with recent memory impairment. *Archives of Neurology, 50*(9), 967–973.

Gonzalez-Martinez, V., Comte, F., de Verbizier, D., & Carlander, B. (2010). Transient global amnesia: concordant hippocampal abnormalities on positron emission tomography and magnetic resonance imaging. *Archives of Neurology, 67*(4), 510.

Goodwin, J. E., & Meeuwsen, H. J. (1995). Using bandwidth knowledge of results to alter relative frequencies during motor skill acquisition. *Research Quarterly for Exercise and Sports, 66*, 99–104.

Goodwin, J. E., Eckerson, J. M., & Voll, C. A., Jr. (2001). Testing specificity and guidance hypotheses by manipulating relative frequency of KR scheduling in motor skill acquisition. *Perceptual and Motor Skills, 93*, 819–824.

Goodwyn, S. W., Acredolo, L. P., & Brown, C. A. (2000). Impact of symbolic gesturing on early language development. *Journal of Nonverbal Behavior, 24*, 81–103.

Gormezano, I., Kehoe, E. J., & Marshall, B. S. (1983). Twenty years of classical conditioning research with the rabbit. *Progress in Psychobiology and Physiological Psychology, 10*, 197–275.

Goudsmit, E., Van de Poll, N., & Swaab, D. (1990). Testosterone fails to reverse spatial memory decline in aged rats and impairs retention in young and middle-aged animals. *Behavioral and Neural Biology, 53*, 6–20.

Gould, E., & Gross, C. (2000). New neurons: extraordinary evidence or extraordinary conclusion?—authors' response. *Science, 288*, 771a.

Gould, E., Reeves, A., Graziano, M., & Gross, C. (1999). Neurogenesis in the neocortex of adult primates. *Science, 286*, 548–552.

Graf, P. (1990). Life-span changes in implicit and explicit memory. *Bulletin of the Psychonomic Society, 28*, 353–358.

Graf, P., & Schacter, D. (1985). Implicit and explicit memory for new associations in normal and amnesic subjects. *Journal of Experimental Psychology: Learning, Memory, and Cognition, 11*(3), 501–518.

Graf, P., Squire, L. R., & Mandler, G. (1984). The information that amnesic patients do not forget. *Journal of Experimental Psychology: Learning, Memory, and Cognition, 10*, 164–178.

Grant, J. E., Kim, S. W., & Hartman, B. K. (2008). A double-blind, placebo-controlled study of the opiate antagonist naltrexone in the treatment of pathological gambling urges. *Journal of Clinical Psychiatry, 69*(5), 783–389.

Grant, J. E., Potenza, M. N., Weinstein, A., Gorelick, D. A. (2010). Introduction to behavioral addictions. *American Journal of Drug and Alcohol Abuse, 36*, 233–241.

Graybiel, A. M. (1995). Building action repertoires: memory and learning functions of the basal ganglia. *Current Opinion in Neurobiology, 5*, 733–741.

Graybiel, A. M. (2005). The basal ganglia: learning new tricks and loving it. *Current Opinion in Neurobiology, 15*, 638–644.

Graybiel, A. M. (2008). Habits, rituals, and the evaluative brain. *Annual Review of Neuroscience, 31*, 359–387.

Green, C. S., & Bavelier, D. (2003). Action video game modifies visual selective attention. *Nature, 423*, 534–537.

Green, L., Fischer, E., Perlow, S., & Sherman, L. (1981). Preference reversal and self control: Choice as a function of reward amount and delay. *Behavior Analysis Letters, 1*, 43–51.

Green, L., Fry, A., & Myerson, J. (1994). Discounting of delayed rewards: A life-span comparison. *Psychological Science, 5*, 33–36.

Greenberg, D. (2004). President Bush's false "flashbulb" memory of 9/11/01. *Applied Cognitive Psychology, 18*, 363–370.

Greenberg, D. L. & Verfaellie, M. (2010). Interdependence of episodic and semantic memory: Evidence from neuropsychology. *Journal of the International Neuropsychological Society, 16*(5), 748–753.

Greenough, W., West, R., & DeVoogd, T. (1978). Subsynaptic plate perforations: changes with age and experience in the rat. *Science, 202*, 1096–1098.

Greenwald, A. G., McGhee, D. E., & Schwartz, J. L. K. (1998). Measuring individual differences in implicit cognition: the implicit association test. *Journal of Personality and Social Psychology, 74*, 1464–1480.

Griffiths, D., Dickinson, A., & Clayton, N. (1999). Episodic memory: what can animals remember about their past? *Trends in Cognitive Sciences, 3*, 74–80.

Groves, P. M., & Thompson, R. F. (1970). Habituation: a dual-process theory. *Psychological Review, 77*, 419–450.

Guillaume, P. (1971). *Imitation in children.* Chicago: University of Chicago Press.

Guinee, L. N., Chu, K., & Dorsey, E. M. (1983). Changes over time in the songs of known individual humpback whales (*Megaptera novaeangliae*). In R. Payne (Ed.), *Communication and behavior of whales.* Boulder, CO: Westview Press.

Gupta, K., Beer, N. J., Keller, L. A., & Hasselmo, M. E. (2014). Medial entorhinal grid cells and head direction cells rotate with a T-maze more often during less recently experienced rotations. *Cerebral Cortex, 24*, 1630–1644.

Guttman, N., & Kalish, H. (1956). Discriminability and stimulus generalization. *Journal of Experimental Psychology, 51*, 79–88.

Hackenberg, T. D. (2009). Token reinforcement: A review and analysis. *Journal of the Experimental Analysis of Behavior, 91*(2), 257–286.

Haglund, K., & Collett, C. (1996). Landmarks Interviews. *Journal of NIH Research, 8*, 42–51.

Haist, F., Bowden Gore, J. B. & Mao, H. (2001). Consolidation of human memory over decades revealed by functional magnetic resonance imaging. Nature Neuroscience, 4, 1139–1145.

Halgren, E. (1982). Mental phenomena induced by stimulation in the limbic system. *Human Neurobiology, 1*(4), 251–260.

Hall, G. (2009). Perceptual learning in human and nonhuman animals: A search for common ground. *Learning & Behavior, 37*, 133–140.

Hall, G., & Honey, R. (1989). Contextual effects in conditioning, latent inhibition, and habituation: Associative and retrieval functions of contextual cues. *Journal of Experimental Psychology: Animal Behavior Processes, 15*(3), 232–241.

Hall, G., Ray, E., & Bonardi, C. (1993). Acquired equivalence between cues trained with a common antecedent. *Journal of Experimental Psychology: Animal Behavior Processes, 19*, 391–399.

Hall, T., Miller, K., & Corsellia, J. (1975). Variations in the human Purkinje cell population according to age and sex. *Neuropathology and Applied Neurobiology, 1*, 267–292.

Hamann, S. (2005). Sex differences in the responses of the human amygdala. *Neuroscientist, 11*(4), 288–293.

Hamann, S., Ely, T., Grafton, S., & Kilts, C. (1999). Amygdala activity related to enhanced memory for pleasant and aversive stimuli. *Nature Neuroscience, 2*(3), 289–293.

Hamilton, A. F. D. C. (2008). Emulation and mimicry for social interaction: a theoretical approach to imitation in autism. *Quarterly Journal of Experimental Psychology, 61*(1), 101–115.

Hampstead, B. M., & Koffler, S. P. (2009). Thalamic contributions to anterograde, retrograde, and implicit memory: a case study. *Clinical Neuropsychology, 23*(7), 1232–1249.

Hanewinkel, R., & Sargent, J. D. (2009). Longitudinal study of exposure to entertainment media and alcohol use among German adolescents. *Pediatrics, 123*, 989–995.

Haney, M., Foltin, R., & Fischman, M. (1998). Effects of pergolide on intravenous cocaine self-administration in men and women. *Psychopharmacology, 137*, 15–24.

Hanley-Dunn, P., & McIntosh, J. (1984). Meaningfulness and recall of names by young and old adults. *Journal of Gerontology, 39*, 583–585.

Hannula, D. E., Simons, D. J., & Cohen, N. J. (2005). Imaging implicit perception: promise and pitfalls. *Nature Reviews Neuroscience, 6*, 247–255.

Hanson, H., M. (1959). Effects of discrimination training on stimulus generalization. *Journal of Experimental Psychology, 58*, 321–333

Hardt, O., Einarsson, E. O., & Nader, K. (2010). A bridge over troubled water: reconsolidation as a link between cognitive and neuroscientific memory traditions. *Annual Review of Psychology, 61*, 141–167.

Hardy, J., & Gwinn-Hardy, K. (1998). Classification of primary degenerative disease. *Science, 282*, 1075–1079.

Harkness, K. L., Hayden, E. P., & Lopez-Duran, N. L. (2015). Stress sensitivity and stress sensitization in psychopathology: An introduction to the special section. *Journal of Abnormal Psychology, 124*, 1–3.

Harlow, H. F. (1949). The formation of learning sets. *Psychological Review, 56*, 51–65.

Harnden, T. (2008 March 25) Hillary Clinton's Bosnia sniper story exposed. *The Daily Telegraph* online. Retrieved May 2, 2015, from www.telegraph.co.uk.

Harris, B. (1979). Whatever happened to Little Albert? *American Psychologist, 34*(2), 151–160.

Harrison, J., & Buchwald, J. (1983). Eyeblink conditioning deficits in the old cat. *Neurobiology of Aging, 4*, 45–51.

Hart, B. (2001). Cognitive behaviour in Asian elephants: use and modification of branches for fly switching. *Animal Behaviour, 62*, 839–847.

Hasselmo, M. (1999). Neuromodulation: acetylcholine and memory consolidation. *Trends in Cognitive Sciences, 3*(9), 351–359.

Hatcher, M. B., Whitaker, C., & Karl, A. (2009). What predicts post-traumatic stress following spinal cord injury? *British Journal of Health Psychology, 14*, 541–561.

Hatze, H. (1976). Biomechanical aspects of a successful motion optimization. In P. V. Komi (Ed.), *Biomechanics V-B* (pp. 5–12). Baltimore: University Park Press.

Hawkins, R. D., Abrams, T. W., Carew, T. J., & Kandel, E. R. (1983). A cellular mechanism of classical conditioning in *Aplysia*: activity-dependent amplification of presynaptic facilitation. *Science, 219*, 400–405.

Hayes, C. (1951). *The ape in our house.* New York: Harper & Bros.

Hayes, K. J., & Hayes, C. (1952). Imitation in a home-reared chimpanzee. *Journal of Comparative and Physiological Psychology, 45*, 450–459.

Hayne, H. (1996). Categorization in infancy. In C. Rovee-Collier & L. Lipsitt (Eds.), *Advances in infancy research, Volume 10* (pp. 79–120). Norwood, NJ: Ablex Publishing Corporation.

Hayne, H. & Imuta, K. (2011). Episodic memory in 3- and 4-year-old children. *Developmental Psychobiology, 53,* 317–322.

Hays, M., Allen, C., & Hanish, J. (2015). Kiss Tempo. Retrieved March 2015 from http://virtualkiss.com /kissingschool/101-tempo.php.

Hayward, M. D., Schaich-Borg, A., Pintar, J. E., & Low, M. J. (2006). Differential involvement of endogenous opioids in sucrose consumption and food reinforcement. *Pharmacology, Biochemistry, & Behavior, 85*(3), 601–611.

Hebb, D. (1949). *The organization of behavior.* New York: Wiley.

Heckers, S. (2002). Neuroimaging studies of the hippocampus in schizophrenia. *Hippocampus, 11,* 520–528.

Heckers, S., Rauch, S.L., Goff, D., et al. (1998). Impaired recruitment of the hippocampus during conscious recollection in schizophrenia. *Nat. Neurosci., 1,* 318–323.

Heindel, W., Salmon, D., Shults, C., Walicke, P., & Butters, N. (1989). Neuropsychological evidence for multiple implicit memory systems: a comparison of Alzheimer's, Huntington's and Parkinson's disease patients. *Journal of Neuroscience, 9*(2), 582–587.

Heinrichs, R. W., Zakzanis, K. K. (1998). Neurocognitive deficit in schizophrenia: a quantitative review of the evidence. *Neuropsychology, 12,* 426–445.

Helmes, E., Brown, J. M. & Elliott, L. (2015). A case of dissociative fugue and general amnesia with an 11-year follow-up. *Journal of Trauma and Dissociation, 16,* 100–113.

Hepper, P., & Shahidullah, S. (1992). Habituation in normal and Down's syndrome fetuses. *Quarterly Journal of Experimental Psychology B, 44B*(3–4), 305–317.

Herbert, J., Eckerman, C., & Stanton, M. (2003). The ontogeny of human learning in delay, long-delay, and trace eyeblink conditioning. *Behavioral Neuroscience, 117*(6), 1196–1210.

Herrnstein, R. (1961). Relative and absolute strength of a response as a function of frequency of reinforcement. *Journal of the Experimental Analysis of Behavior, 4,* 267–272.

Hester, R., Murphy, K., Brown, F. L., Skilleter, A. J. (2010). Punishing an error improves learning: The influence of punishment magnitude on error-related neural activity and subsequent learning. *Journal of Neuroscience, 30,* 15600–15607.

Heuer, F., & Reisberg, D. (1990). Vivid memories of emotional events: the accuracy of remembered minutiae. *Memory and Cognition, 18,* 496–506.

Heuer, F., & Reisberg, D. (1992). Emotion, arousal, and memory for detail. In S.-A. Christianson (Ed.), *The handbook of emotion and memory* (pp. 151–180). Hillsdale, NJ: Erlbaum.

Hews, D., & Moore, M. (1996). A critical period for the organization of alternative male phenotypes of tree lizards by exogenous testosterone? *Physiology and Behavior, 60*(2), 425–529.

Hews, D., Knapp, R., & Moore, M. (1994). Early exposure to androgens affects adult expression of alternative male types in tree lizards. *Hormones & Behavior, 28,* 96–115.

Heyes, C. M. (1994). Social learning in animals: categories and mechanisms. *Biological Reviews of the Cambridge Philosophical Society, 69*(2), 207–231.

Heyes, C. M., & Dawson, G. R. (1990). A demonstration of observational learning in rats using a bidirectional control. *Quarterly Journal of Experimental Psychology B, 42*(1), 59–71.

Hinde, R. A. (1969). *Bird vocalizations.* Cambridge, England: Cambridge University Press.

Hinkel, D. & Mahr, J. (6 January 2011). Tribune analysis: Drug-sniffing dogs in traffic stops often wrong. *Chicago Tribune Online.* Retrieved 5 July 2014.

Hiroto, D. (1974). Locus of control and learned helplessness. *Journal of Experimental Psychology, 102,* 187–193.

Hiroto, D., & Seligman, M. (1974). Generality of learned helplessness in man. *Journal of Personality and Social Psychology, 31,* 311–327.

Hitzig, E. (1874). Untersuchungen ̈uber das Gehirn [Investigations of the brain]. Berlin: A. Hirschwald.

Hochberg, L. R., Bacher, D., Jarosiewicz, B., Masse, N. Y., Simeral, J.D. et al. (2012). Reach and grasp by people with tetraplegia using a neutrally controlled robotic arm. *Nature, 485,* 372–375.

Hodges, J. R. & Warlow, C. P. (1990). Syndromes of transient amnesia: towards a classification. A study of 153 cases. *Journal of Neurology, Neurosurgery, and Psychiatry, 53,* 834–843.

Hodzic, A., Veit, R., Karim, A. A., Erb, M., & Godde, B. (2004). Improvement and decline in tactile discrimination behavior after cortical plasticity induced by passive tactile coactivation. *Journal of Neuroscience, 24,* 442–446.

Hof, P., & Morrison, J. (2004). The aging brain: morphomolecular senescence of cortical circuits. *Trends in Neurosciences, 27*(19), 607–613.

Hoffman, K. L., & Logothetis, N. K. (2009). Cortical mechanisms of sensory learning and object recognition. *Philosophical Transactions of the Royal Society B: Biological Sciences, 364,* 321–329.

Holding, D. H. (Ed.). (1981). *Human skills.* Chichester: John Wiley.

Holloway, J. L., Beck, K. D., & Servatius, R. J. (2011). Facilitated acquisition of the classically conditioned eyeblink response in females is augmented in those taking oral contraceptives. *Behavioural Brain Research, 216*(1), 302–407.

Holmes, C., Boche, D., Wilkinson, D., Yadegarfar, G., Hopkins, V., Bayer, A., et al. (2008). Long-term effects of Abeta42 immunisation in Alzheimer's disease: follow-up of a randomised, placebo-controlled phase I trial. *Lancet, 372*(9634), 216–223.

Holzhaider, J. C., Hunt, G. R., & Gray, R. D. (2010). Social learning in New Caledonian crows. *Learning & Behavior, 38,* 206–219.

Honey, R., & Hall, G. (1991). Acquired equivalence and distinctiveness of cues using a sensory-preconditioning procedure. *Quarterly Journal of Experimental Psychology, 43B,* 121–135.

Honey, R., Watt, A., & Good, M. (1998). Hippocampal lesions disrupt an associative mismatch process. *Journal of Neuroscience, 18*(6), 2226–2230.

Hooper, S., Reiss, D., Carter, M., & McCowan, B. (2006). Importance of contextual saliency on vocal imitation by bottlenose dolphins. *International Journal of Comparative Psychology, 19,* 116–128.

Hornak, J., Bramham, J., Rolls, E., Morris, R., O'Doherty, J., Bullock, P., et al. (2003). Changes in emotion after circumscribed surgical lesions of the orbitofrontal and cingulate cortices. *Brain, 126* (Pt. 7), 1691–1712.

Horowitz, A. C. (2003). Do humans ape? Or do apes human? Imitation and intention in humans (*Homo sapiens*) and other animals. *Journal of Comparative Psychology, 117*(3), 325–336.

Howard-Jones, P., Holmes, W., Demetriou, S., Jones, C., Tanimoto, E., Morgan, O., et al. (2014). Neuroeducational research in the design and use of a learning technology. *Learning, Media and Technology, 40,* 227–246.

Howard, R. W. (2009). Individual differences in expertise development over decades in a complex intellectual domain. *Memory & Cognition, 37,* 194–209.

Howe, M., & Courage, M. (1993). On resolving the enigma of childhood amnesia. *Psychological Bulletin, 113,* 305–326.

Hubel, D., & Wiesel, T. (1977). The Ferrier Lecture: functional architecture of macaque monkey visual cortex. *Proceedings of the Royal Academy of London: B198,* 1–59.

Hubel, D., & Wiesel, T. (1998). Early exploration of the visual cortex. *Neuron, 20*(3), 401–412.

Hubert, V., Beaunieux, H., Chetelat, G., Platel, H., Landeau, B. Danion, J. M., et al. (2007). The dynamic network subserving the three phases of cognitive procedural learning. *Human Brain Mapping, 28,* 1415–1429.

Hudson Kam, C. L., & Newport, E. L. (2005). Regularizing unpredictable variation: the roles of adult and child learners in language formation and change. *Language Learning and Development, 1,* 151–195.

Hull, C. (1943). *Principles of Behavior.* New York: Appleton-Century-Crofts.

Hull, C. (1952). *A Behavior System: An Introduction to Behavior Theory Concerning the Individual Organism.* New Haven: Yale University Press.

Hull, C. L. (1943). *Principles of behavior.* New York: Appleton-Century-Crofts.

Hulme. C., and Bradley. L. (1984). An experimental study of, sensory teaching with normal and retarded readers. In R. Malatesha and H. Whitaker (Eds), Dyslexia: A global issue (pp. 431–443). The Hague, The Netherlands: Martinus Nijhoff.

Hunt, G. R., Corballis, M. C., & Gray, R. D. (2001). Animal behaviour: laterality in tool manufacture by crows. *Nature, 414,* 707.

Huttenlocher, P., & Dabholkar, A. (1997). Regional differences in synaptogenesis in human cerebral cortex. *Journal of Comparative Neurology, 387,* 167–178.

Hyde, L., Sherman, G., & Denenberg, V. (2000). Nonspatial water radial-arm maze learning in mice. *Brain Research, 863*(1–2), 151–159.

Iacoboni, M., Woods, R. P., Brass, M., Bekkering, H., Mazziotta, J. C., & Rizzolatti, G. (1999). Cortical mechanisms of human imitation. *Science, 286*(5449), 2526–2528.

Immelman, K. (1969). Song development in the zebra finch and other estrildid finches. In R. A. Hinde (Ed.), *Bird vocalizations* (pp. 61–74). Cambridge: Cambridge University Press.

Innocence Project (2012) *False confessions.* Retrieved from www.innocenceproject.org/understand/False-Confessions.php

Insausti, R., Annese, J., Amaral, D. G., & Squire, L. G. (2013). Human amnesia and the medial temporal lobe illuminated by neuropsychological and neurohistological findings for patient E. P. (2013). *Proceedings of the National Academy of Sciences USA, 11,* E1953–1962.

Insel, T., & Fernald, R. (2004). How the brain processes social information: searching for the social brain. *Annual Review of Neuroscience, 27,* 697–722.

Irwin, A. R., & Gross, A. M. (1995). Cognitive tempo, violent video games, and aggressive behavior in young boys. *Journal of Family Violence, 10,* 337–350.

Ivkovich, D., Collins, K., Eckerman, C., Krasnegor, N., & Stanton, M. (1999). Classical delay eyeblink conditioning in 4- and 5-month-old human infants. *Psychological Science, 10*(1), 4–8.

Ivkovich, D., Paczkowski, C., & Stanton, M. (2000). Ontogeny of delay versus trace conditioning in the rat. *Developmental Psychobiology, 36*(2), 148–160.

Jack, C., Knopman, D. S., Jagust, W. J. Shaw, L. M., Aisen, P. S., et al. (2010). Hypothetical model of dynamic biomarkers of the Alzheimer's pathological cascade. *Lancet, 9,* 119–128,

Jack, C., Petersen, R., Xu, Y., O'Brien, P., Smith, G., Ivnik, R., et al. (1999). Prediction of AD with MRI-based hippocampal volume in mild cognitive impairment. *Neurology, 52,* 1397–1403.

Jack, C., Petersen, R., Xu, Y., O'Brien, P., Smith, G., Ivnik, R., et al. (1998). Rate of medial temporal atrophy in typical aging and Alzheimer's disease. *Neurology, 51,* 993–999.

Jacobs, B., Schall, M., & Schiebel, A. (1993). A quantitative dendritic analysis of Wernicke's area. II. Gender, hemispheric, and environmental factors. *Journal of Comparative Neurology, 237,* 97–111.

Jacobsen, C.F. (1936). Studies of cerebral function in primates. I. The functions of the frontal association areas in monkeys. *Comparative Psychololy Monographs, 13,* 1–60.

Jacobsen, C.F., Wolfe J.B., Jackson T.A. (1935): An experimental analysis of the functions of the frontal associations areas in primates. *The Journal of Nervous and Mental Disease, 82,* 1–14.

Jaeggi, S. M., Buschkuehl, M., Jonides, J., Perrig, W. J. (2008). Improving fluid intelligence with training on working memory. *Proceedings of the National Academy of Sciences, 105*(19).

Jaeggi, Susanne M.; Studer-Luethi, Barbara; Buschkuehl, Martin; Su, Yi-Fen; Jonides, John; Perrig, Walter J. (2010). The relationship between n-back performance and matrix reasoning—implications for training and transfer. *Intelligence, 38*(6), 625–635. doi:10.1016/j.intell.2010.09.001. ISSN 0160–2896.

James, W. (1890). *The principles of psychology.* Dover: New York.

James, W. (1890). *The principles of psychology.* New York: Henry Holt and Co, Inc.

James, W. (1890). *The principles of psychology.* New York: Henry Holt.

Janik, V., & Slater, P. (1997). Vocal learning in mammals. *Advances in the Study of Behavior, 26,* 59–99.

Janowsky, J.S., Shimamura, A.P., Kritchevsky, M., Squire, L.R., (1989). Cognitive impairment following frontal lobe damage and its relevance to human amnesia. *Behavioral Neuroscience, 103,* 548–60.

Jarrard, L., & Davidson, T. (1991). On the hippocampus and learned conditional responding: Effects of aspiration versus ibotenate lesions. *Hippocampus, 1,* 107–117.

Jarrard, L., Okaichi, H., Steward, O., & Goldschmidt, R. (1984). On the role of hippocampal connections in the performance of place and cue tasks: comparisons with damage to hippocampus. *Behavioral Neuroscience, 98*(6), 946–954.

Javadi, A. H. & Cheng, P. (2013). Transcranial direct current stimulation (tDCS) enhances reconsolidation of long-term memory. *Brain Stimulation, 6,* 668–674.

Jay, T. M. (2003). Dopamine: A potential substrate for synaptic plasticity and memory mechanisms. *Progress in Neurobiology, 69,* 375–390.

Jenkins, H. M. & Harrison, R. H. (1962). Generalization gradients of inhibition following auditory discrimination training. *Journal of the Experimental Analysis of Behavior, 5,* 435–441

Jenkins, K. G., Kapur, N., & Kopelman, M.D. (2009). Retrograde amnesia and malingering. *Current Opinion in Neurology, 22*(6), 601–605.

Jog, M. S., Kubota, Y., Connolly, C. I., Hillegaart, V., & Graybiel, A. M. (1999). Building neural representations of habits. *Science, 286,* 1745–1749.

Johnson, G., & Bailey, C. (2002). Tau, where are we now? *Journal of Alzheimer's Disease, 4,* 375–398.

Johnson, M. (1992). Imprinting and the development of face recognition: From chick to man. *Current Directions in Psychological Science, 1,* 52–55.

Johnston, R. B., Stark, R., Mellits, D. and Tallal, P. (1981). Neurological status of language impaired and normal children. *Annals of Neurology, 10,* 159–163.

Jones, B. C., DeBruine, L. M., Little, A. C., Burris, R. P., & Feinberg, D. R. (2007). Social transmission of face preferences among humans. *Proceedings of the Royal Society London: B, 274,* 899–903.

Jones, G. V. (1990). Misremembering a common object: when left is not right. *Memory and Cognition, 18*(2), 174–182.

Jones, R. S., & Eayrs, C. B. (1992). The use of errorless learning procedures in teaching people with a learning disability: A critical review. *Mental Handicap Research, 5,* 204–214.

Jonides et al., (2008). The mind and brain of short-term memory. *Annual Review of Psychology, 59,* 193–224. 10.1146/annurev.psych.59.103006.093615.

Jonsson, T., Stefanson, H., Steinberg, S., Jonsdottir, I., Jonsson, P. V., Snaedal, J. et al. (2013). Variant of TREM2 associated with the risk of Alzheimer's disease. *New England Journal of Medicine, 368,* 107–116.

Josephson, W. L. (1987). Television violence and children's aggression: testing the priming, social script, and disinhibition predictions. *Journal of Personality and Social Psychology, 53*(5), 882–890.

Joslyn, S. L., & Oakes, M. A. (2005). Directed forgetting of autobiographical events. *Memory and Cognition, 33*(4), 577–587.

Jun, G., Naj, A. C., Beecham, G. W., Wang, L. S., Buros, J., Gallins, P. J., et al. (2010). Meta-analysis confirms CR1, CLU, and PICALM as Alzheimer disease risk loci and reveals interactions with APOE genotypes. *Archives of Neurology.*

Jung, R. E., & Haier, R. J. (2007). The parieto-frontal integration theory of intelligence: converging neuroimaging evidence. *Behavioral and Brain Sciences, 30,* 135–154.

Jussim, L. (2012). *Social perception and social reality: Why accuracy dominates bias and self-fulfilling prophecy.* 2012 New York: Oxford University Press.

Jussim, L. (2005). Accuracy in social perception: criticisms, controversies, criteria, components, and cognitive processes. *Advances in Experimental Social Psychology, 37,* 1–93.

Jussim, L., Cain, T., Crawford, J., Harber, K., & Cohen, F. (2009). The unbearable accuracy of stereotypes. In T. Nelson (Ed.), *Handbook of prejudice, stereotyping, and discrimination* (pp. 199–227). Hillsdale, NJ: Erlbaum.

Kagerer, F. A., Contreras-Vidal, J. L., & Stelmach, G. E. (1997). Adaptation to gradual as compared with sudden visuo-motor distortions. *Experimental Brain Research, 115,* 557–561.

Kahn, D. M., & Krubitzer, L. (2002). Massive cross-modal cortical plasticity and the emergence of a new cortical area in developmentally blind mammals. *Proceedings of the National Academy of Sciences USA, 99,* 11429–11434.

Kamin, L. (1969). Predictability, surprise, attention and conditioning. In B. Campbell and R. Church (Eds.), *Punishment and aversive behavior* (pp. 279–296). New York: Appleton-Century-Crofts.

Kanit, L., Taskiran, D., Yilmaz, O., Balkan, B., Demiroeren, S., Furedy, J., et al. (2000). Sexually dimorphic cognitive style in rats emerges after puberty. *Brain Research Bulletin, 52*(4), 243–248.

Kanner, L. (1943). Autistic disturbances of affective contact. *Nervous Child, 2,* 217–250.

Kapp, B., Gallagher, M., Underwood, M., McNall, C., & Whitehorn, D. (1981). Cardiovascular responses elicited by electrical stimulation of the amygdala central nucleus in the rabbit. *Brain Research, 234,* 251–262.

Kapur, N., & Coughlan, A. (1980). Confabulation and frontal lobe dysfunction. *Journal of Neurology, Neurosurgery and Psychiatry, 43,* 461–463.

Kapur, N., Friston, K. J., Young, A., Frith, C. D., & Frackowiak, R. S. (1995). Activation of human hippocampal formation during memory for faces: a PET study. *Cortex, 31,* 99–108.

Kapur, N., Millar, J., Abbott, P., & Carter, M. (1998). Recovery of function processes in human amnesia: evidence from transient global amnesia. *Neuropsychologia, 36*(1), 99–107.

Kapur, N., Thompson, S., Cook, P., Lang, D., & Brice, J. (1996). Anterograde but not retrograde memory loss following combined mammillary body and medial thalamic lesions. *Neuropsychologia, 34*(1), 1–8.

Karlen, S. J., Kahn, D. M., & Krubitzer, L. (2006). Early blindness results in abnormal corticocortical and thalamocortical connections. *Neuroscience, 142,* 843–858.

Karni, A., Meyer, G., Rey-Hipolito, C., Jezzard, P., Adams, M. M., Turner, R., & Ungerleider, L. G. (1998). The acquisition of skilled motor performance: fast and slow experience-driven changes in primary motor cortex. *Proceedings of the National Academy of Sciences USA, 95,* 861–868.

Kart-Teke, E., De Souza Silva, M. A., Huston, J., & Dere, E. (2006). Wistar rats show episodic-like memory for unique experiences. *Neurobiology of Learning and Memory, 85*(2), 173–182.

Kazdin, A., & Benjet, C. (2003). Spanking children: Evidence and issues. *Current Directions in Psychological Science, 12*(3), 99–103.

Kazdin, A., & Wilcoxon, L. (1976). Systematic desensitization and nonspecific treatment effects: a methodological evaluation. *Psychological Bulletin, 83,* 729–758.

Keefe, R. S., Arnold, M. C., Bayen, U. J., & Harvey, P. D. (1999). Source monitoring deficits in patients with schizophrenia; a multinomial modelling analysis. *Psychological Medicine, 29,* 903–914.

Kehoe, E. J. (1988). A layered network model of associative learning. *Psychological Review, 95*(4), 411–433.

Kemeny, M. (2003). The psychobiology of stress. *Current Directions in Psychological Science, 12*(4), 124–129.

Kemler, D. G. & Smith, L. B. (1978). Is there a developmental trend from integrality to separability in perception? *Journal of Experimental Child Psychology. 26.* 498–507.

Kempermann, G., Wiskott, L., & Gage, F. (2004). Functional significance of adult neurogenesis. *Current Opinion in Neurobiology, 14*(2), 186–191.

Kendal, R. L., Galef, B. G., & van Schaik, C. P. (2010). Social learning research outside the laboratory: How and why? *Learning and Behavior, 38,* 187–194.

Kensinger, E. A., Piguet, O., Krendl, A. C., & Corkin, S. (2005). Memory for contextual details: effects of emotion and aging. *Psychology and Aging, 20,* 241–250.

Kikuchi, H., Fujii, T., Abe, N., Suzuki, M., Takagi, M., Mugikura, S., et al. (2010). Memory repression: brain mechanisms underlying dissociative amnesia. *Journal of Cognitive Neuroscience, 22*(3), 602–613.

Kilgard, M., & Merzenich, M. (1998). Cortical map reorganization enabled by nucleus basalis activity. *Science, 279,* 1714–1718.

Killiany, R., Hyman, B., Gomez-Isla, T., Moss, M., Kikinis, R., Jolesz, F., Tanzi, R., Jones, K. & Albert, M. (2002). MRI measures of entorhinal cortex vs. hippocampus in preclinical AD. *Neurology, 58,* 1188–1196.

Kim, J. S., Vossel, G. & Gamer, M. (2013). Effects of emotional context on memory for details: the role of attention. *PLOS ONE, 8,* e77405.

Kim, J., Krupa, D., & Thompson, R. F. (1998). Inhibitory cerebello-olivary projections and blocking effect in classical conditioning. *Science, 279,* 570–573.

Kirchmayer, U., Davoli, M., Verster, A., Amato, L., Ferri, A., & Perucci, C. (2002). A systematic review on the efficacy of naltrexone maintenance treatment in preventing relapse in opioid addicts after detoxification. *Addiction, 97*(10), 1241–1249.

Kleim, J. A., Hogg, T. M., VandenBerg, P. M., Cooper, N. R., Bruneau, R., & Remple, M. (2004). Cortical synaptogenesis and motor map reorganization occur during late, but not early, phase of motor skill learning. *Journal of Neuroscience*, 24, 628–633.

Kleim, J. A., Swain, R. A., Czerlanis, C. M., Kelly, J. L., Pipitone, M. A., & Greenough, W. T. (1997). -Learning-dependent dendritic hypertrophy of cerebellar stellate cells: plasticity of local circuit neurons. *Neurobiology of Learning and Memory*, 67, 29–33.

Klingberg, T. , Fernell, E., Oleson, P. J., Johnson, M., Gustafsson, P., Dahlstrom, K., Gilberg, C. G., Forssberg, H., & Westerberg, H. (2005). Computerized training of working memory in children with ADHAD: A randomized, controlled trial. *Journal of the American Academy of Child & Adolescent Psychiatry*. 44(2. 177–186.

Klinke, R., Kral, A., Heid, S., Tillein, J., & Hartmann, R. (1999). Recruitment of the auditory cortex in congenitally deaf cats by long-term cochlear electrostimulation. *Science*, 285, 1729–1733.

Knapp, H. D., Taub, E., & Berman, A. J. (1963). Movements in monkeys with deafferented forelimbs. *Experimental Neurology*, 7, 305–315.

Knowlton, B. J., Squire, L. R., & Gluck, M. A. (1994). Probabilistic classification learning in amnesia. *Learning & Memory*, 1, 106–120.

Knowlton, B. J., Squire, L. R., Paulsen, J. S., Swerdlow, N. R., Swenson, M., & Butters, N. (1996). Dissociations within nondeclarative memory in Huntington's disease. *Neuropsychology*, 10, 538–548.

Knutson, B., Fong, G., Adams, C., Varner, J., & Hommer, D. (2001). Dissociation of reward anticipation and outcome with event-related fMRI. *Neuroreport*, 21, 3683–3687.

Kobre, K., & Lipsitt, L. (1972). A negative contrast effect in newborns. *Journal of Experimental Child Psychology*, 14, 81–91.

Koechlin, E. Ody, C.& Kouneiher, F. (2003). The architecture of cognitive control in the human prefrontal cortex. *Science*, 302, 1181–1185

Köhler, S., Moscovitch, M., Winocur, G., & McIntosh, A. (2000). Episodic encoding and recognition of pictures and words: role of the human medial temporal lobes. *Acta Psychologica*, 105, 159–179.

Kolb, B., & Taylor, L. (1981). Affective behavior in patients with localized cortical excisions: role of lesion site and side. *Science*, 214, 89–91.

Kolb, B., & Taylor, L. (1990). Neocortical substrates of emotional behavior. In N. Stein, B. Leventhal & T. Trabasso (Eds.), *Psychological and biological approaches to emotion* (pp. 115–144). Hillsdale, NJ: Erlbaum.

Kolb, B., & Taylor, L. (2000). Facial expression, emotion, and hemispheric organization. In R. Lane & L. Nadel (Eds.), *Cognitive neuroscience of emotion* (pp. 62–83). New York: Oxford University Press.

Kolb, B., and Wishaw, I. (1996). **Fundamentals of Human Neuropsychology** (4th ed). New York: Freeman & Co.

Kopelman, M. D., Thomson, A. D., Guerrini, I., & Marshall, E. J. (2009). The Korsakoff syndrome: clinical aspects, psychology and treatment. *Alcohol*, 44(2), 148–154.

Koralek, A. C., Jin, X., Long, J. D., II, Costa, R. M., & Carmena, J. M. (2012). Cortiocstriatal plasticity is necessary for learning intentional neuroprosthetic skills. *Nature*, 483, 331–335.

Koriat, A., Bjork, R., Sheffer, L., & Bar, S. K. (2004). Predicting one's own forgetting: the role of experience-based and theory-based processes. *Journal of Experimental Psychology: General*, 133, 643–656.

Kornak, D., & Rakic, P. (1999). Continuation of neurogenesis in the hippocampus of the adult macaque monkey. *Proceedings of the National Academy of Sciences USA*, 96, 5768–5773.

Kornell, N. & Bjork, R. A. (2009). A stability bias in human memory: Overestimating remembering and underestimating learning. *Journal of Experimental Psychology: General*, 138, 449–468.

Korr, H., & Schmitz, C. (1999). Facts and fictions regarding post-natal neurogenesis in the developing human cerebral cortex. *Journal of Theoretical Biology*, 200, 291–297.

Kosslyn, S.M. and Shwartz, S.P. (1977). A simulation of visual imagery. *Cognitive Science*, 1, 265–295.

Koukounas, E., & Over, R. (2001). Habituation of male sexual arousal: effects of attentional focus. *Biological Psychology*, 58, 49–64.

Kraft, T. L. & Pressman, S. D. (2012). Grin and bear it: The influence of manipulated facial expression on the stress response. *Psychological Science*, 23, 1372–1378.

Kramer, A. D. I., Guillory, J. E., & Hancock, J. T. (2014). Experimental evidence of massive-scale emotional contagion through social networks. *Proceedings of the National Academy of Sciences, U.S.A.*, 111, 8788–8790.

Krank, M. D., & Wall, A. M. (1990). Cue exposure during a period of abstinence reduces the resumption of operant behavior for oral ethanol reinforcement. *Behavioral Neuroscience*, 104, 725–733.

Krank, M. D., & Wall, A. M. (1990). Cue exposure during a period of abstinence reduces the resumption of operant behavior for oral ethanol reinforcement. *Behavioral Neuroscience*, 104, 725–733.

Krieman, G., Koch, C., & Fried, I. (2000). Category-specific visual responses of single neurons in the human medial temporal lobe. *Nature Neuroscience*, 3(9), 946–953.

Kring, A., & Gordon, A. (1998). Sex differences in emotion: expression, experience, and physiology. *Journal of Personality and Social Psychology, 74*, 686–803.

Kritchevsky, M., & Squire, L. (1989). Transient global amnesia: evidence for extensive, temporally graded retrograde amnesia. *Neurology, 39*, 213–218.

Kritchevsky, M., Chang, J., & Squire, L. (2004). Functional amnesia: clinical description and neuropsychological profile of 10 cases. *Learning and Memory, 11*(2), 213–227.

Kritchevsky, M., Squire, L., & Zouzounis, J. (1988). Transient global amnesia: characterization of anterograde and retrograde amnesia. *Neurology, 38*, 213–219.

Kroes, M. C., Tendolkar, I., van Wingen, G. A., van Waarde, J. A., Strange, B. A. & Fernández, G. (2014). An electroconvulsive therapy procedure impairs reconsolidation of episodic memories in humans. *Nature Neuroscience, 17*, 204–206.

Kross, E., Berman, M. G., Mischel, W., Smith, E. E. & Wager, T. D. (2011). Social rejection shares somatosensory representations with physical pain. *Proceedings of the National Academy of Sciences, 108*, 6270–6275.

Kruschke, J. K., Kappenman, E. S., & Hetrick, W. P. (2005). Eye gaze and individual differences consistent with learned attention in associative blocking and highlighting. *Journal of Experimental Psychology: Learning, Memory, & Cognition, 31*(5), 830–845.

Krutzen, M., Mann, J., Heithaus, M. R., Connor, R. C., Bejder, L., & Sherwin, W. B. (2005). Cultural transmission of tool use in bottlenose dolphins. *Proceedings of the National Academy of Sciences USA, 102*, 8939–8943.

Kubota, K. and Nikin H. (1971). Prefrontal cortical unit activity and delayed alternation performance in monkeys. *Journal of Neurophysiology, 34*(3), 337–47.

Kuhl, P. K. (2000). A new view of language acquisition. *Proceedings of the National Academy of Sciences USA, 97*(22), 11850–11857.

Kuhl, P. K., & Meltzoff, A. N. (1996). Infant vocalizations in response to speech: vocal imitation and developmental change. *Journal of the Acoustical Society of America, 100*, 2425–2438.

Kuhn, H., Dickinson-Anson, H., & Gage, F. (1996). Neurogenesis in the dentate gyrus of the adult rat: age-related decrease of neurongal progenitor proliferation. *Journal of Neuroscience, 16*, 2027–2033.

Kujala, Y., & Naatanen, R. (2010). The adaptive brain: a neurophysiological perspective. *Progress in Neurobiology, 91*, 55–67.

Kwon, H., Reiss, A., & Menon, V. (2002). Neural basis of protracted developmental changes in visuo-spatial working memory. *Proceedings of the National Academy of Sciences USA, 99*(20), 13336–13341.

Laan, E., & Everaerd, W. (1995). Habituation of female sexual arousal to slides and film. *Archives of Sexual Behavior, 24*, 517–541.

LaBar, K. S. (2007). Beyond fear: emotional memory mechanisms in the human brain. *Current Directions in Psychological Science, 16*(4), 173–177.

LaBar, K. S. (2009). Imaging emotional influences on learning and memory. In F. Roesler, C. Ranganath, B. Roeder & R. H. Kluwe (Eds.), *Neuroimaging and psychological theories of human memory* (pp. 331–348). New York: Oxford University Press.

LaBar, K. S., & LeDoux, J. (2003). Emotion and the brain: an overview. In T. Feinberg & M. Farah (Eds.), *Behavioral Neurology and Neuropsychology* (2nd ed., pp. 711–724). New York: McGraw-Hill.

Ladd, G. W., & Mize, J. (1983). A cognitive social learning model of social skill training. *Psychological Review, 90*, 127–157.

Laforce, R., Jr., & Doyon, J. (2001). Distinct contribution of the striatum and cerebellum to motor learning. *Brain and Cognition, 45*, 189–211.

Laland, K. N. (2004). Social learning strategies. *Learning & Behavior, 32*, 4–14.

Laland, K. N., & Galef, B. G. (2009). *The question of animal culture.* Cambridge, MA: Harvard University Press.

Lalonde, R., & Botez, M. (1990). The cerebellum and learning processes in animals. *Brain Research Reviews, 15*, 325–332.

Lambe, E. K., Krimer, L. S., & Goldman-Rakic, P. (2000). Differential postnatal development of catecholamine and serotonin inputs to identified neurons in the prefrontal cortex of rhesus monkey. *Journal of Neuroscience, 20*(23), 8760–8787.

Lang, P. J., Davis, M., & Ohman, A. (2000). Fear and anxiety: animal models and human cognitive psychophysiology. *Journal of Affective Disorders, 61*, 137–159.

Langlois, J. A., Rutland-Brown, W., & Wald, M. M. (2006). The epidemiology and impact of traumatic brain injury: A brief overview. *Journal of Head Trauma Rehabilitation, 21*, 375–378.

Langston, R. F., & Wood, E. R. (2010). Associative recognition and the hippocampus: differential effects of hippocampal lesions on object-place, object-context, and object-place-context memory. *Hippocampus, 20*, 1139–1153.

Larzelere, R. (2000). Child outcomes of nonabusive and customary physical punishment by parents: An updated literature review. *Clinical Child and Family Psychology Review, 3*, 199–221.

Lashley, K. (1924). Studies of the cerebral function in learning: V. The retention of motor habits after destruction of the so-called motor areas in primates. *Archives of Neurology and Psychiatry, 12*, 249–276.

Lashley, K. S. (1929). *Brain mechanisms and intelligence: a quantitative study of injuries to the brain.* Chicago: University of Chicago Press.

Lashley, K. S., & Wade, M. (1946). The Pavlovian theory of generalization. *Psychological Review, 53*, 72–87.

Laurent, H. K., Gilliam, K. S., Wright, D. B., Fisher, P. A. (2015). Child anxiety symptoms related to longitudinal cortisol trajectories and acute stress responses: evidence of developmental stress sensitization. *Journal of Abnormal Psychology, 124*, 68–79.

Le Merrer, J., Becker, J. A. J., Befort, K., & Kieffer, B. L. (2009). Reward processing by the opioid system in the brain. *Physiological Reviews, 89*, 1379–1412.

Lebedev, M. A. & Nicolelis, M. A. L. (2006). Brain-machine interfaces: past, present and future. *Trends in Neurosciences, 29*, 536–545.

Lebrecht, S., Pierce, L. J., Tarr, M. J., Tanaka, J. W. (2009). Perceptual other-race training reduces implicit racial bias. *PLOS One, 4*, e4215.

LeDoux, J. (1993). Emotional memory systems in the brain. *Behavioural Brain Research, 58*, 69–79.

LeDoux, J. (1994). Emotion, memory and the brain. *Scientific American, 270*(6), 50–57.

LeDoux, J. (1998). *The emotional brain: the mysterious underpinnings of emotional life.* New York: Touchstone.

LeDoux, J. (2000). Emotion circuits in the brain. *Annual Review of Neuroscience, 23*, 155–184.

LeDoux, J., Iwata, J., Cicchetti, P., & Reis, D. (1988). Different projections of the central amygdaloid nucleus mediate autonomic and behavioral correlates of conditioned fear. *Journal of Neuroscience, 8*(7), 2517–2529.

Lee, Y. T., Jussim, L., & McCauley, C. R. (2013). Stereotypes as categories of knowledge: Complexity, validity, usefulness, and essence in perceptions of group differences. *Advances in Psychological Science, 21*, 1–21.

Leggio, M. G., Molinari, M., Neri, P., Graziano, A., Mandolesi, L., & Petrosini, L. (2000). Representation of actions in rats: the role of cerebellum in learning spatial performances by observation. *Proceedings of the National Academy of Sciences, 97*(5), 2320–2325.

Leibniz, G. W. (1704). *Nouveaux essais sur l'entendement humain* [New essays on human understanding].

Leighton, J., Bird, G., Charman, T., & Heyes, C. (2008). Weak imitative performance is not due to a functional "mirroring" deficit in adults with autism spectrum disorders. *Neuropsychologica, 46*, 1041–1049.

LeJeune, J., Gautier, M., & Turpin, R. (1959). Etudes des chromosomes somatiques de neuf enfants mongoliens. *Comptes Renus de l'Academic les Sciences, 48*, 1721.

Lenck-Santini, P. P., Save, E., & Poucet, B. (2001). Evidence for a relationship between place-cell spatial firing and spatial memory performance. *Hippocampus, 11*, 377–390.

Leshner, A. (1999). Science-based views of drug addiction and its treatment. *Journal of the American Medical Association, 282*, 1314–1316.

Levenson, R. (1992). Autonomic nervous system differences among emotions. *Psychological Science, 3*(1), 23–27.

Lever, C., Wills, T., Cacucci, F., Burgess, N., & O'Keefe, J. (2002). Long-term plasticity in hippocampal place-cell representation of environmental geometry. *Nature, 416*, 90–94.

Levy, R. and Goldman-Rakic, P.S. (2000). Segregation of working memory functions within the dorsolateral prefrontal cortex. *Experimental Brain Research, 133*, 23–32.

Lewis-Peacock, J.A., & Postle B.R. (2008). Temporary activation of long-term memory supports working memory. *Journal of Neuroscience, 28*, 8765–71.

Lewis, C. (1981). Skill in algebra. In J. R. Anderson (Ed.), *Cognitive skill learning* (pp. 85–110). Hillsdale, NJ: Lawrence Erlbaum.

Lewis, L. B., Saenz, M., & Fine, I. (2010). Mechanisms of cross-modal plasticity in early-blind subjects. *Journal of Neurophysiology, 104*, 2995–3008.

Lewis, M. C., & Brooks-Gunn, J. (1979). *Social cognition and the acquisition of self.* New York: Plenum.

Lie, C., Song, H., Colamarino, S., Ming, G.-l., & Gage, F. (2004). Neurogenesis in the adult brain: new strategies for central nervous system diseases. *Annual Review of Pharmacology and Toxicology, 44*, 399–421.

Light, L. (1991). Memory and aging: four hypotheses in search of data. *Annual Review of Psychology, 42*, 333–376.

Linden, W. (1981). Exposure treatments for focal phobias. *Archives of General Psychiatry, 38*, 769–775.

Ling, H., Hardy, J., & Zetterberg, H. (2015). Neurological consequences of traumatic brain injuries in sports. *Molecular and Cellular Neuroscience 66*(Part B), 114–122.

Linton, M. (1982). Transformations of memory in everyday life. In U. Neisser (Ed.), *Memory observed: remembering in natural contexts* (pp. 77–91). San Francisco: Freeman.

Lipka, J., Hoffmann, M., Miltner, W. H., & Straube, T. (2014). Effects of cognitive-behavioral therapy on brain responses to subliminal and supraliminal threat and their functional significance in specific phobia. *Biological Psychiatry, 76*, 869–877.

Lit, L., Schweitzer, J. B., & Oberbauer, A. M. (2011). Handler beliefs affect scent detection dog outcomes. *Animal Cognition, 14*, 387–394

Little, A., Lipsett, L., & Rovee-Collier, C. (1984). Classical conditioning and retention of the infant's eyelid response: effects of age and interstimulus interval. *Journal of Experimental Child Psychology, 37*, 512–524.

Liu, J., & Wrisberg, C. A. (1997). The effect of knowledge of results delay and the subjective estimation of movement form on the acquisition and retention of a motor skill. *Research Quarterly for Exercise and Sports, 68,* 145–151.

Liu, R. T. (2015). A developmentally informed perspective on the relation between stress and psychopathology: When the problem with stress is that there is not enough. *Journal of Abnormal Psychology, 124,* 80–92.

Locke, J. (1690). *An essay concerning human understanding.* London: T. Basset.

Locke, J. (1693). *Some thoughts concerning education.* London: Churchill.

Lockett, G. A., Wilkes, F. & Maleszka, R. (2010). Brain plasticity, memory and neurological disorders: An epigenetic perspective. *NeuroReport, 21*(14), 909–913.

Loftus, E. (1996). *Eyewitness testimony.* Cambridge, MA: Harvard University Press.

Loftus, E. (2003). Our changeable memories: legal and practical implications. *Nature Reviews Neuroscience, 4,* 231–234.

Loftus, E., & Pickrell, J. (1995). The formation of false memories. *Psychiatric Annals, 25*(12), 720–725.

Lømo, T. (1966). Frequency potentiation of excitatory synaptic activity in the dentate area of the hippocampal formation [abstract]. *Acta Physiologica Scandinavica, 68,* 128.

Lorenz, K. (1935). Der Kumpan in der Umwelt des Vogels [Companions as factors in the bird's environment]. *Journal of Ornithology, 83,* 137–215.

Lovaas, O. (1987). Behavioral treatment and normal educational and intellectual functioning in young autistic children. *Journal of Consulting and Clinical Psychology, 55*(3–9).

Lovibond, P. F., Saunders, J. C., Weidemann, G., & Mitchell, C. J. (2008). Evidence for expectancy as a mediator of avoidance and anxiety in a laboratory model of human avoidance learning. *Quarterly Journal of Experimental Psychology, 61*(8), 1199–1216.

Lu, B., & Gottschalk, W. (2000). Modulation of hippocampal synaptic transmission and plasticity by neurotrophins. *Progress in Brain Research, 128,* 231–241.

Lubow, R. (1989). *Latent inhibition and conditioned attention theory.* Cambridge, UK: Cambridge University Press.

Lubow, R. E. (1973). Latent inhibition. *Psychological Bulletin, 79,* 398–407.

Lubow, R. E., & Moore, A. U. (1959). Latent inhibition: the effect of nonreinforced preexposure to the conditioned stimulus. *Journal of Comparative and Physiological Psychology, 52,* 415–419.

Luck, S.J., & Vogel, E.K. (2013). Visual working memory capacity: From psychophysics and neurobiology to of STM capacity limits. *Trends in Cognitive Science, 17,* 391–400.

Luria, A. (1982 [1968]). *The Mind of a Mnemonist* (Lynn Solotaroff, Trans.)., New York, Basic Books. In U. Neisser (Ed.), *Memory observed: remembering in natural contexts* (pp. 382–389). New York: Freeman.

Luria, A. R. (1966). *Higher cortical functions in man.* New York: Basic Books.

Lynch, G., Palmer, L. C., & Gall, C. M. (2011). The likelihood of cognitive enhancement. *Pharmacology, Biochemistry, and Behavior, 99,* 116–129.

Lynn, S. K., Cnaani, J., & Papaj, D. R. (2005). Peak shift discrimination learning as a mechanism of signal evolution. *Evolution, 59,* 1300–1305.

Ma, H. I., Trombly, C. A., & Robinson-Podolski, C. (1999). The effect of context on skill acquisition and transfer. *American Journal of Occupational Therapy, 53,* 138–144.

Mackintosh, N. J. (1975). A theory of attention: variations in the associability of stimuli with reinforcement. *Psychological Review, 82*(4), 276–298.

Magendie, F. (1822). Expériences sur les fonctions des racines des nerfs rachidiens. *Journal de physiologie expérimentale et de pathologie, 2,* 366–371.

Magill, R. (1993). *Motor learning: concepts and applications.* Dubuque, IA: William C. Brown.

Maguire, E. A. (2001). Neuroimaging studies of autobiographical event memory. *Philosophical Transactions of the Royal Society B: Biological Sciences, 356,* 1441–1451.

Maguire, E. A., Gadian, D. G., Johnsrude, I. S., Good, C. D., Ashburner, J., Frackowiak, R. S., & Frith, C. D. (2000). Navigation-related structural change in the hippocampi of taxi drivers. *Proceedings of the National Academy of Science USA, 97,* 4398–4403.

Maguire, E., Valentine, E., Wilding, J., & Kapur, N. (2003). Routes to remembering: the brains behind superior memory. *Nature Neuroscience, 6,* 90–94.

Mair, R., Knoth, R., Rabchenuk, S., & Langlais, P. (1991). Impairment of olfactory, auditory, and spatial serial reversal learning in rats recovered from pyrithiamine-induced thiamine deficiency. *Behavioral Neuroscience, 105*(3), 360–374.

Majewska, A., & Sur, M. (2003). Motility of dendritic spines in visual cortex *in vivo*: changes during the critical period and effects of visual deprivation. *Proceedings of the National Academy of Sciences USA, 100*(26), 16024–16029.

Malcuit, G., Bastien, C., & Pomerleau, A. (1996). Habituation of the orienting response to stimuli of different functional values in 4-month-old infants. *Journal of Experimental Child Psychology, 62,* 272–291.

Malpass, R. S., & Kravitz, L. (1969). Recognition for faces of own and other race. *Journal of Personality and Social Psychology, 13,* 330–334.

Manns, J., Hopkins, R., & Squire, L. (2003). Semantic memory and the human hippocampus. *Neuron, 38,* 127–133.

Marcus, E. A., Nolen, T. G., Rankin, C. H., & Carew, T. J. (1988). Behavioral dissociation of dishabituation, sensitization, and inhibition in *Aplysia. Science, 241,* 210–213.

Maren, S. (1999). Long-term potentiation in the amygdala: a mechanism for emotional learning and memory. *Trends in Neurosciences, 22,* 561–567.

Margoliash, D. (2002). Evaluating theories of bird song learning: implications for future directions. *Journal of Comparative Physiology A—Neuroethology, Sensory, Neural and Behavioral Physiology, 188,* 851–866.

Maril, A., Wagner, A. & Schacter, D. L. (2001). On the tip of the tongue: An event-related fMRI study of semantic retrieval failure and cognitive conflict. *Neuron, 31,* 653–660.

Markowitsch, H. (1992). Intellectual functions and the brain—An historical perspective. Kirkland, WA: Hogrefe and Huber.

Markowitsch, H., Calabrese, P., Wurker, M., Durwen, H., Kessler, J., Babinsky, R., et al. (1994). The amygdala's contribution to memory—A study on two patients with Urbach-Wiethe disease. *Neuroreport, 5*(11), 1349–1352.

Markowitsch, H., Kessler, J., Van der Ven, C., Weber-Luxenburger, G., Albers, M., & Heiss, W. (1998). Psychic trauma causing grossly reduced brain metabolism and cognitive deterioration. *Neuropsychologia, 36,* 77–82.

Marler, P. (1970). A comparative approach to vocal song learning: song development in white-crowned sparrows. *Journal of Comparative and Physiological Psychology, 71,* 1–25.

Marler, P. (1997). Three models of song learning: evidence from behavior. *Journal of Neurobiology, 33*(5), 501–516.

Marsh, R., & Bower, G. (1993). Eliciting cryptomnesia: unconscious plagiarism in a puzzle task. *Journal of Experimental Psychology: Learning, 19*(3), 673–688.

Martin, J. P. (2013). NFL, ex-players reach $765 million deal in concussion case. Philly.com. Posted August 31, 2013; retrieved May 30, 2015.

Martin, M., & Jones, G. V. (1995). Danegeld remembered: taxing further the coin head illusion. *Memory 3*(1), 97–104.

Martineau, J., Andersson, F., Barthelemy, C., Cottier, J. P., & Destrieux, C. (2010). Atypical activation of the mirror neuron system during perception of hand motion in autism. *Brain Research, 1320,* 168–175.

Martínez-Cué, C., Baamonde, C., Lumbreras, M., Paz, J., Davisson, M., Schmidt, C., et al. (2002). Differential effects of environmental enrichment on behavior and learning of male and female Ts65Dn mice, a model for Down syndrome. *Behavioural Brain Research, 134,* 185–200.

Martinussen, R. & Major, A. (2011). Working memory weaknesses in students with ADHD: Implications for instruction. *Theory into Practice, 50*(1), 68–75.

Mathes, W. F., Nehrenberg, D. L., Gordon, R., Hua, K., Garland, T., & Pomp, D. (2010). Dopaminergic dysregulation in mice selectively bred for excessive exercise or obesity. *Behav Brain Res, 210*(2), 155–163.

Matson, J. L., & Boisjoli, J. A. (2009). The token economy for children with intellectual disability and/or autism: A review. *Research in Developmental Disabilities, 30*(2), 240–248.

Matsumoto, D., & Ekman, P. (1989). American-Japanese cultural differences in intensity ratings of facial expressions of emotion. *Motivation and Emotion, 13,* 143–157.

Matsumoto, M., & Hikosaka, O. (2009). Two types of dopamine neuron distinctly convey positive and negative motivational signals. *Nature, 459*(7248), 837–841.

Maurer, D., & Lewis, T. (1999). Rapid improvement in the acuity of infants after visual input. *Science, 286,* 108–110.

McAllister, W. R. (1953). Eyelid conditioning as a function of the CS-US interval. *Journal of Experimental Psychology, 45*(6), 417–422.

McBride, W. J., Murphy, J. M., & Ikemoto, S. (1999). Localization of brain reinforcement mechanisms: Intracranial self-administration and intracranial place-conditioning studies. *Behav Brain Res, 101*(2), 129–152.

McClearn, G., Johansson, B., Berg, S., Pedersen, N., Ahern, F., Petrill, S., et al. (1997). Substantial genetic influence on cognitive abilities in twins 80 or more years old. *Science, 276*(5318), 1560–1563.

McClure, H. M., Belden, K. H., Pieper, W. A., & Jacobson, C. B. (1969). Autosomal trisomy in a chimpanzee: resemblance to Down's syndrome. *Science, 165*(897), 1010–1012.

McCormick, D. A., & Thompson, R. F. (1984). Neuronal responses of the rabbit cerebellum during acquisition and performance of a classically conditioned nictitating membrane-eyelid response. *Journal of Neuroscience, 4*(11), 2811–2822.

McCutcheon, L. (2000). Another failure to generalize the Mozart effect. *Psychological Reports, 87*(1), 325–330.

McDonald, R., & White, N. (1994). Parallel information processing in the water maze: evidence for independent memory systems involving dorsal striatum and hippocampus. *Behavioral and Neural Biology, 61*(3), 260–270.

McEwen, B. (1997). Possible mechanism for atrophy of the human hippocampus. *Molecular Psychiatry, 2,* 255–262.

McEwen, B. (1999). Stress and hippocampal plasticity. *Annual Review of Neuroscience, 22,* 105–122.

McEwen, B., & Sapolsky, R. (1995). Stress and cognitive function. *Current Opinion in Neurobiology, 5,* 205–216.

McGaugh, J. (2000). Memory—a century of consolidation. *Science, 287*(5451), 248–251.

McGaugh, J. L. (2002). Memory consolidation and the amygdala: a systems perspective. *Trends in Neurosciences, 25*(9), 456–460.

McGaugh, J. L. (2003). *Memory and emotion: the making of lasting memories.* New York: Columbia University Press.

McGaugh, J. L., & Cahill, L. (2003). Emotion and memory: central and peripheral contributions. In R. Davidson,

K. Scherer & H. Goldsmith (Eds.), *Handbook of affective sciences* (pp. 93–116). New York: Oxford University Press.

McIntyre, C., Hatfield, T., & McGaugh, J. (2000). Amygdala norepinephrine levels after training predict inhibitory avoidance retention performance in rats. *European Journal of Neuroscience, 16*, 1223–1226.

McKelvie, P., & Low, J. (2002). Listening to Mozart does not improve children's spatial ability: final curtains for the Mozart effect. *British Journal of Developmental Psychology, 20*, 241–258.

McKenzie, S., and Eichenbaum, H. (2011). Consolidation and reconsolidation: two lives of memories? *Neuron 71*, 224–233.

McLaren, I. P. L., & Mackintosh, N. J. (2002). Associative learning and elemental representation: II. Generalization and discrimination. *Animal Learning & Behavior, 30*, 177–200.

McLaughlin, K. A., Busso, D. S., Duys, A., Green, J. G., Alves, S., Way, M., & Sheridan, M. A. (2014). Amygdala response to negative stimuli predicts PTSD symptom onset following a terrorist attack. *Depression and Anxiety, 31*, 834–842.

Mclaughlin, K. A., Conron, K. J., Koenen, K. C., & Gilman, S. E. (2010). Childhood adversity, adult stressful life events, and risk of past-year psychiatric disorder: a test of the stress sensitization hypothesis in a population-based sample of adults. *Psychological Medicine, 40*, 1647–1658.

McLellan, A., Lewis, D., O'Brien, C., & Kleber, H. (2000). Drug dependence, a chronic medical illness: implications for treatment, insurance, and outcomes evaluation. *Journal of the American Medical Association, 284*, 1689–1695.

McNally, R., Bryant, R., & Ehlers, A. (2003). Does early psychological intervention promote recovery from post-traumatic stress? *Psychological Science in the Public Interest, 4*(2), 45–79.

Mehta, M. A., Owen, A. M., Sahakian, B. J., Mavaddat, N., Pickard, J. D., & Robbins, T. W. (2000). Methylphenidate enhances working memory by modulating discrete frontal and parietal lobe regions in the human brain. *Journal of Neuroscience, 20*, RC65.

Mehta, M., Goodyer, I., and Sahakian, B. (2004). Methylphenidate improves working memory and set-shifting in AD/HD: relationships to baseline memory capacity. *Journal of Child Psychology and Psychiatry, 45*(2), 293.

Meissner, C. A., & Brigham, J. C. (2001). Thirty years of investigating the own-race bias in memory for faces—a meta-analytic review. *Psychology Public Policy and Law, 7*, 3–35.

Mengles, J.A., Gershberg, F.B., Shimanura, A.P., and Knight, R.T. (1996). Impaired retrieval from remote memory in patients with frontal lobe lesions, *Neuropsychology, 10*, 32–41.

Mercado, E., III (2008). Neural and cognitive plasticity: from maps to minds. *Psychological Bulletin, 134*, 109–137.

Mercado, E., III, Mantell, J. T., Pfordresher, P. Q. (2014). Imitating sounds: a cognitive approach to understanding vocal imitation. *Comparative Cognition & Behavior Reviews, 9*, 1–57.

Mercado, E., III, Murray, S., Uyeyama, R., Pack, A., & Herman, L. (1998). Memory for recent actions in the bottlenosed dolphin (*Tursiops truncates*): repetition of arbitrary behaviors using an abstract rule. *Animal Learning and Behavior, 26*(2), 210–218.

Merzenich, M. Jenkins, W., Johnston, P., S., Schreiner, C., Miller, S. L. & Tallal, P. (1996). Temporal Processing Deficits of Language-Learning Impaired Children Ameliorated by Training, *Science, 271*, 77–81.

Meyer, M., Baumann, S., Wildgruber, D., & Alter, K. (2007). How the brain laughs. comparative evidence from behavioral, electrophysiological and neuroimaging studies in human and monkey. *Behavioural Brain Research, 182*(2), 245–260.

Michel, G. F., & Tyler, A. N. (2005). Critical period: a history of the transition from questions of when, to what, to how. *Developmental Psychobiology, 46*, 209–221.

Michelmore, C. & Gede, L. (2014). Brain derived neurotrophic factor: Epigenetic regulation in psychiatric disorders. *Brain Research, 1586*, 162–172.

Miles, C., Green, R., Sanders, G., & Hines, M. (1998). Estrogen and memory in a transsexual population. *Hormones and Behavior, 34*(2), 199–208.

Miller, E.K. (2000). The prefrontal cortex and cognitive control. *Nature Reviews Neuroscience, 1*, 59–65.

Miller, E.K. and Cohen, J.D. (2001). An integrative theory of prefrontal cortex function. *Annual Review of Neuroscience, 24*, 167–202.

Miller, E.K. and Wallis, J.D. (2003). The prefrontal cortex and executive brain functions. In Squire, L.R., Bloom, F.E., Roberts, J.L., Zigmond, M.J., McConnell, S.K., Spitzer, N.C. (eds.), Fundamental Neuroscience (2nd ed., pp. 1353–1376). New York: Academic Press,.

Miller, E.K., Erickson, C.A., and Desimone, R. (1996). Neural mechanisms of visual working memory in prefrontal cortex of the macaque. Journal of Neuroscience 16, 5154–5167.

Miller, G. (1956). The magic number seven plus or minus two: some limits on our capacity for processing information. *Psychological Review, 63*, 81–97.

Miller, J. W., Petersen, R. C., Metter, E. J., Millikan, C. H., & Yanagihara, T. (1987). Transient global amnesia: clinical characteristics and prognosis. *Neurology, 37*(5), 733–737.

Miller, M.H. and Orbach J. (1972). Retention of spatial alternation following frontal lobe resections in stump-tailed macaques. *Neuropsychologia, 10*, 291–298.

Miller, N. E., & Dollard, J. (1941). *Social learning and imitation*. New Haven, CT: Yale University Press.

Milner, B. (1966). Amnesia following operation on the temporal lobes. In C. Whitty & O. Zangwill (Eds.), *Amnesia* (pp. 109–133). New York: Appleton-Century-Crofts.

Milner, B., Corkin, S., & Teuber, J. (1968). Further analysis of the hippocampal amnesic syndrome: a 14-year follow-up study of HM. *Neuropsychologia, 6,* 215–234.

Mineka, S., & Cook, M. (1988). Social learning and the acquisition of snake fear in monkeys. In T. Zentall & B. Galef (Eds.), *Social learning* (pp. 51–73). Hillsdale, NJ: Erlbaum.

Mineka, S., & Cook, M. (1988). Social learning and the acquisition of snake fear in monkeys. In T. R. Zentall & B. G. Galef (Eds.), *Social learning: psychological and biological perspectives* (pp. 51–73). Hillsdale, NJ: Erlbaum.

Minozzi S, Amato L, Vecchi S, Davoli M, Kirchmayer U, Verster A (2011). Oral naltrexone maintenance treatment for opioid dependence. *Cochrane Database of Systematic Reviews, 4,* CD001333 [online resource].

Minshew, N. J., & Williams, D. L. (2007). The new neurobiology of autism—cortex, connectivity, and neuronal organization. *Archives of Neurology, 64,* 945–950.

Misanin, J. R., Miller, R. R., & Lewis, D. J. (1968). Retrograde amnesia produced by electroconvulsive shock after reactivation of a memory trace. *Science, 160,* 554–555.

Mishkin, M. (1957). Effects of small frontal lesions on delayed alternation in monkeys. *Journal of Neurophysiology, 20,* 615–622.

Mishkin, M. (1964). Perseveration of central sets after frontal lesions in monkeys. In J. M. Warren, Akert, K.(Eds.), The frontal granular cortex and behavior (pp. 219–241). New York, McGraw-Hill.

Mishkin, M. (1978). Memory in monkeys severely disrupted by combined but not by separate removal of amygdala and hippocampus. *Nature, 273,* 297–299.

Mishkin, M. and Manning, F.J. (1978). Non-spatial memory after selective prefrontal lesions in monkeys. Brain Res 143:313–323.

Mishra, J, & Gazzaley, A. (2014). Harnessing the neuroplastic potential of the human brain & the future of cognitive rehabilitation. *Frontiers in Human Neuroscience, 8,* 218.

Mizumori, S. J., Miya, D. Y., & Ward, K. E. (1994). Reversible inactivation of the lateral dorsal thalamus disrupts hippocampal place representation and impairs spatial learning. *Brain Research, 644,* 168–174.

Mobbs, D., Greicius, M., Abdel-Azim, E., Menon, V., & Reiss, A. (2003). Humor modulates the mesolimbic reward centers. *Neuron, 40*(5), 1041–1048.

Moncaster, J. A., Pineda, R., Moir, R. D., Lu, S., Burton, M. A., Ghosh, J. G., et al. (2010). Alzheimer's disease amyloid-beta links lens and brain pathology in Down syndrome. *PLoS One, 5*(5), e10659.

Monti, B., & Contestabile, A. (2009). Memory-enhancing drugs: A molecular perspective. *Mini-Reviews in Medicinal Chemistry, 9,* 769–781.

Mooney, R. (2009). Neurobiology of song learning. *Current Opinion in Neurobiology, 19,* 654–660.

Moore, J. W., & Gormezano, I. (1961). Yoked comparisons of instrumental and classical eyelid conditioning. *Journal of Experimental Psychology, 62,* 552–559.

Morgan, C. L. (1896). *Habit and instinct*. London: Edward Arnold.

Morishita, H., & Hensch, T. K. (2008). Critical period revisited: impact on vision. *Current Opinion in Neurobiology, 18,* 101–107.

Morris, C., Bransford, J., & Franks, J. (1977). Levels of processing versus transfer appropriate processing. *Journal of Verbal Learning and Verbal Behavior, 16*(5), 519–533.

Morrison, J. H. & Baxter, M. G. (2012). The ageing cortical synapse: hallmarks and implications for cognitive decline. *Nature Reviews Neuroscience, 13,* 240–250.

Moscovitch, M., & Nadel, L. (1998). Consolidation and the hippocampal complex revisited: in defense of the multiple-trace model. *Current Opinion in Neurobiology, 8,* 297–300.

Moss, C. (1988). *Elephant memories: thirteen years in the life of an elephant family*. New York: Fawcett Columbine.

Mowrer, O. H. (1960). *Learning theory and behavior*. New York: Wiley.

Muhlberger, A., Herrmann, M., Wiedeman, G., Ellgring, H., & Pauli, P. (2001). Repeated exposure of flight phobics to flights in virtual reality. *Behavioral Research Therapy, 39*(9), 1033–1050.

Murray, B. D., Anderson, M. C., & Kensinger, E. A. (2015). Older adults can suppress unwanted memories when given an appropriate strategy. *Psychology and Aging, 30,* 9–25.

Myers, C., Ermita, B., Hasselmo, M., & Gluck, M. (1998). Further implications of a computational model of septohippocampal cholinergic modulation in eyeblink conditioning. *Psychobiology, 26*(1), 1–20.

Myers, C., Gluck, M., & Granger, R. (1995). Dissociation of hippocampal and entorhinal function in associative learning: A computational approach. *Psychobiology, 23*(2), 116–138.

Myers, C., Kluger, A., Golomb, J., Gluck, M., & Ferris, S. (2008). Learning and generalization tasks predict short-term outcome in non-demented elderly. *Journal of Geriatric Psychiatry and Neurology, 21,* 93–103.

Myers, C., Shohamy, D., Gluck, M., Grossman, S., Kluger, A., Ferris, S., Golomb, J., Schnirman, G., & Schwartz, R. (2003). Dissociating hippocampal versus basal ganglia contributions to learning and transfer. *Journal of Cognitive Neuroscience. 15*(2), 185–193.

Myers, N., Perris, E., & Speaker, C. (1994). Fifty months of memory: a longitudinal study in early childhood. *Memory, 2*, 383–415.

Nabavi, S., Fox, R., Proulx, C. D., Lin, J. Y., Tsien, R. Y., & Malinow, R. (2014). Engineering a memory with LTD and LTP. *Nature, 511*, 348–352.

Nadel, L. (1999). Down syndrome in cognitive neuroscience perspective. In H. Tager-Flusberg (Ed.), *Neurodevelopmental disorders* (pp. 197–221). Cambridge, MA: MIT Press.

Nadel, L. (2003). Down syndrome: a genetic disorder in biobehavioral perspective. *Genes, Brain, and Behavior, 2*(3), 156–166.

Nadel, L., & Land, D. (2000). Memory traces revisited. *Nature Reviews Neuroscience, 1*(3), 209–212.

Nadel, L., & Moscovitch, M. (1997). Memory consolidation, retrograde amnesia and the hippocampal complex. *Current Opinion in Neurobiology, 7*(2), 217–227.

Nadel, L., & Moscovitch, M. (2001). The hippocampal complex and long-term memory revisited. *Trends in Cognitive Science, 5*, 228–230.

Nadel, L., Samsonovich, A., Ryan, L., & Moscovitch, M. (2000). Multiple trace theory of human memory: computational, neuroimaging and neuropsychological results. *Hippocampus, 10*, 352–368.

Nader, K. (2003). Memory traces unbound. *Trends in Neurosciences, 26*(2), 65–72.

Nader, K., & Hardt, O. (2009). A single standard for memory: the case for reconsolidation. *Nature Reviews Neuroscience, 10*(3), 224–234.

Nader, K., Schafe, G. E., & LeDoux, J. E. (2000a). The labile nature of consolidation theory. *Nature Reviews Neuroscience, 1*(3), 216–219.

Nader, K., Schafe, G. E., & LeDoux, J. E. (2000b). Fear memories require protein synthesis in the amygdala for reconsolidation after retrieval. *Nature, 406*, 722–727.

Nagell, K., Olguin, R. S., & Tomasello, M. (1993). Processes of social learning in the tool use of chimpanzees (*Pan troglodytes*) and human children (*Homo sapiens*). *Journal of Comparative Psychology, 107*(2), 174–186.

Naghdi, N., Majlessi, N., & Bozorgmehr, T. (2005). The effect of intrahippocampal injection of testosterone enanthate (an androgen receptor agonist) and anisomycin (protein synthesis inhibitor) on spatial learning and memory in adult, male rats. *Behavioural Brain Research, 156*(2), 263–268.

Naqvi, N. H. & Bechara, A. (2009). The hidden island of addiction: the insula. *Trends in Neurosciences, 32*, 56–67.

Naqvi, N. H., Rudrauf, D., Damasio, H. & Bechara, A. (2007). Damage to the insula disrupts addiction to cigarette smoking. *Science 315*, 531–534.

Nargeot, R., Baxter, D., Patterson, G., & Byrne, J. (1999). Dopaminergic synapses mediate neuronal changes in an analogue of operant conditioning. *Journal of Neurophysiology, 81*, 1983–1987.

Naskar, S., Sood, S. K., Goyal, V., & Dhara, M. (2010). Mechanism(s) of deep brain stimulation and insights into cognitive outcomes of Parkinson's disease. *Brain Research Reviews, 65*, 1–13.

National Down Syndrome Society (2015). *Down syndrome fact sheet.* Retrieved from www.ndss.org , 25 May 2015.

National Institutes of Health Consensus Conference. (1985). Electroconvulsive therapy. *Journal of the American Medical Association, 254*, 2103–2108.

Naveh-Benjamin, M. (1991). A comparison of training programs intended for different types of test-anxious students: further support for an information processing model. *Journal of Educational Psychology, 83*, 134–139.

Neath, I. (2010). Evidence for similar principles in episodic and semantic memory: the presidential serial position function. *Memory and Cognition, 38*(5), 659–667.

Nee, D.E., & Jonides, J, (2013). Neural evidence for a 3-state model of visual short-term memory. *Neuroimage, 74*, 1–11.

Neisser, U. (1982). Snapshots or benchmarks? In U. Neisser (Ed.), *Memory observed: remembering in natural contexts* (pp. 43–49). San Francisco: Freeman.

Neisser, U., & Harsch, N. (1992). Phantom flashbulbs: false recollections of hearing the news about Challenger. In E. Winograd & U. Neisser (Eds.), *Affect and accuracy in recall: studies of "flashbulb" memories* (pp. 9–31). New York: Cambridge University Press.

Nelson, T. O., Gerler, D., & Narens, L. (1984). Accuracy of feeling-of-knowing judgments for predicting perceptual identification and relearning. *Journal of Experimental Psychology: General, 113*, 282–300.

Nemetz, G. H., Craig, K. D., & Reith, G. (1978). Treatment of sexual dysfunction through symbolic modeling. *Journal for Consulting and Clinical Psychology, 46*, 62–73.

Netzer, W. J., Powell, C., Nong, Y., Blundel, J., Wong, L., Duff, K., et al. (2010). Lowering ß-amyloid levels rescues learning and memory in a Down syndrome mouse model. *PLoS One5, 6*(e10943).

Neufield, P., & Dwyer, J. (2000). *Actual innocence: five days to execution and other dispatches from the wrongly convicted.* New York: Doubleday.

Newell, A., & Rosenbaum, P. S. (1981). Mechanism of skill acquisition and the law of practice. In J. R. Anderson (Ed.), *Cognitive skill acquisition* (pp. 1–56). Hillsdale, NJ: Lawrence Erlbaum.

Newport, E. (1990). Maturational constraints on language learning. *Cognitive Science, 14*, 11–28.

Nickerson, R. S., & Adams, M. J. (1979). Long-term memory for a common object. *Cognitive Psychology, 11*(3), 287–307.

Nielsen, S. E., Ertman, N., Lakhani, Y. S. & Cahill, L. (2011). Hormonal contraception usage is associated with altered memory for an emotional story. *Neurobiology of Learning and Memory, 96*, 378–384.

Nikolaev, A., McLaughlin, T., O'Leary, D. D., & Tessier-Lavigne, M. (2009). APP binds DR6 to trigger axon pruning and neuron death via distinct caspases. *Nature, 457*(7232), 981–989.

Nishitani, N., Avikainen, S., & Hari, R. (2004). Abnormal imitation-related cortical activation sequences in Asperger's syndrome. *Annals of Neurology, 55*(4), 558–562.

Nithianantharajah, J., & Hannan, A. J. (2009). The neurobiology of brain and cognitive reserve: mental and physical activity as modulators of brain disorders. *Progress in Neurobiology, 89*(4), 369–382.

Noad, M. J., Cato, D. H., Bryden, M. M., Jenner, M. N., & Jenner, K. C. S. (2000). Cultural revolution in whale songs. *Nature, 408*, 537.

Noice, H., & Noice, T. (2006). What studies of actors and acting tell us about memory and cognitive functioning. *Current Directions in Psychological Science, 15*, 14–18.

Norman, D. A., & Shallice, T. (1986). Attention to action. Willed and automatic control of behavior. In R.J. Davidoson, G.E. Schwartz, & D. Shapiro (Eds.), Consciousness and self regulation (pp. 1–17). New York: Plenum.

Norrholm, S. D., & Ressler, K. J. (2009). Genetics of anxiety and trauma-related disorders. *Neuroscience, 164*(1), 272–287.

Nowakowski, R., & Hayes, N. (2000). New neurons: extraordinary evidence or extraordinary conclusion? *Science, 288*, 771a.

Nudo, R. J., Milliken, G. W., Jenkins, W. M., & Merzenich, M. M. (1996). Use-dependent alterations of movement representations in primary motor cortex of adult squirrel monkeys. *Journal of Neuroscience, 16*, 785–807.

Nyberg, L., R. Cabeza, and E. Tulving. (1996). PET studies of encoding and retrieval: The HERA model. *Psychology Bulletin and Review, 3*, 135–148.

O'Doherty, J., Dayan, P., Schultz, J., Deichmann, R., Fristen, K., & Dolan, R. (2004). Dissociable roles of ventral and dorsal striatum in instrumental conditioning. *Science, 304*(5669), 452–455.

O'Kane, G., Kensinger, E. A., & Corkin, S. (2004). Evidence for semantic leanring in profound amnesia: An investigation with patient H.M. *Hippocampus, 14*, 417–425.

O'Keefe, J., & Dostrovsky, J. (1971). The hippocampus as a spatial map: preliminary evidence from unit activity in the freely-moving rat. *Brain Research, 34*, 171–175.

O'Scalaidhe, S. P., Wilson, F. A., Goldman-Rakic, P. S. (1997). Areal segregation of face-processing neurons in prefrontal cortex. *Science, 278*, 1135–38.

Oberauer, K. (2002). Access to information in working memory: Exploring the focus of attention. *Journal of Experimental Psychology: Learning, Memory and Cognition, 28*, 411–21.

Oberauer, K. (2013). The focus of attention in working memory—from metaphors to mechanisms. *Frontiers in Human Neuroscience, 7*, 673.

Okado, Y., & Stark, C. (2003). Neural processing associated with true and false memory retrieval. *Cognitive, Affective and Behavioral Neuroscience, 3*, 323–334.

Olds, J. (1955). "Reward" from brain stimulation in the rat. *Science, 122*, 878.

Olds, J. (1958). Self-stimulation of the brain. *Science, 127*, 315–323.

Olness, K., & Ader, R. (1992). Conditioning as an adjunct in the pharmacotheraphy of lupus erythematosus. *Journal of Developmental & Behavioral Pediatrics, 13*(2), 124–5.

Olton, D. (1983). Memory functions and the hippocampus. In W. Seifert (Ed.), *Neurobiology of the hippocampus* (pp. 335–373). London: Academic Press.

Orr, S. P., Metzger, L. J., Lasko, N. B., Macklin, M. L., Hu, F. B., Shalev, A. Y., et al. (2003). Physiologic responses to sudden, loud tones in monozygotic twins discordant for combat exposure. *Archives of General Psychiatry, 60*, 283–288.

Orr, S. P., Metzger, L. J., Lasko, N. B., Macklin, M. L., Peri, T., & Pitman, R. K. (2000). De novo conditioning in trauma-exposed individuals with and without posttraumatic stress disorder. *Journal of Abnormal Psychology, 109*(2), 290–298.

Otten, L. J., Henson, R. N. & Rugg, M. D. (2001). Depth of processing effects on neural correlates of memory encoding: Relationship between findings from across- and within-task comparisons. *Brain, 124*, 399–412.

Ottersen, O., & Helm, P. (2002). Neurobiology: how hardwired is the brain? *Nature, 420*, 751–752.

Otto, T. and Eichenbaum, H. (1992). Complementary roles of the orbitoal prefrontal cortex and the peririhanl-entorhinal cortices in an odor-guided delayed-nonmatching-to-sample task. Behavioral Neuroscience. 106. 762–775.

Ouellet, J., Rouleau, I., Labrecque, R., Bernier, G., & Scherzer, P. B. (2008). Two routes to losing one's past life: a brain trauma, an emotional trauma. *Behavioral Neurology, 20*(1–2), 27–38.

Overman, W., Bachevalier, J., Schuhmann, E., & Ryan, P. (1996). Cognitive gender differences in very young children parallel biologically based cognitive gender differences in monkeys. *Behavioral Neuroscience, 110*, 673–684.

Overmier, J., & Seligman, M. (1967). Effects of inescapable shock upon subsequent escape and avoidance learning. *Journal of Comparative and Physiological Psychology, 63*, 23–33.

Shohamy, D. & Wagner, A. D. 2008. Integrating memories in the human brain: hippocampal-midbrain encoding of overlapping events. *Neuron, 60*(2): 378–89.

Shohamy, D., Allen, M. T., & Gluck, M. A. (2000). Dissociating entorhinal and hippocampal involvement in latent inhibition. *Behavioral Neuroscience, 114*, 867–874.

Shohamy, D., Allen, M. T., & Gluck, M. A. (2000). Dissociating entorhinal and hippocampal involvement in latent inhibition. *Behavioral Neuroscience, 114*(5), 867–874.

Shohamy, D., Mihalakos, P., Chin, R., Thomas, B., Wagner, A.D., & Tamminga, C. (2010). Learning and generalization in Schizophrenia: Effects of disease and antipsychotic drug treatment. *Biological Psychiatry, 67*(10), 926–932.

Sidman, R., & Rakic, P. (1973). Neuronal migration, with special reference to developing human brain: a review. *Brain Research, 62*, 1–35.

Siegel, S. (1983). Classical conditioning, drug tolerance, and drug dependence. In Y. Israel, F. Glaser, H. Kalant, R. Popham, W. Schmidt, & R. Smart (Eds.), *Research advances in alcohol and drug problems. Vol. 7* (pp. 207–246). New York: Plenum Press.

Siegel, S. (1983). Classical conditioning, drug tolerance, and drug dependence. In Y. Israel, F. Glaser, H. Kalant, R. Popham, W. Schmidt, & R. Smart (Eds.), *Research advances in alcohol and drug problems. Vol. 7* (pp. 207–246). New York: Plenum Press.

Siegel, S. (2001). Pavlovian conditioning and drug overdose: when tolerance fails. *Addiction Research and Theory, 9*(5), 503–513.

Siegel, S., & Ellsworth, D. W. (1986). Pavlovian conditioning and death from apparent overdose of medically prescribed morphine: a case report. *Bulletin of the Psychonomic Society, 24*, 278–280.

Siegel, S., & Ramos, B. M. C. (2002). Applying laboratory research: drug anticipation and the treatment of drug addiction. *Experimental and Clinical Psychopharmacology, 10*(3), 162–183.

Siegel, S., Hinson, R. E., Krank, M. D., & McCully, J. (1982). Heroin "overdose" death: contribution of drug-associated environmental cues. *Science, 216 (4544)*, 436–437.

Silverman, I., & Eals, M. (1992). Sex differences in spatial abilities: evolutionary theory and data. In J. Barkow, L. Cosmides & J. Tooby (Eds.), *The adapted mind: evolutionary psychology and the generation of culture.* New York: Oxford University Press.

Simmons, R. (1924). The relative effectiveness of certain incentives in animal learning. *Comparative Psychology Monographs, No. 7.*

Simões-Franklin, C., Hester, R., Shpaner, M., Foxe, J. J., & Garavan, H. (2010). Executive function and error detection: The effect of motivation on cingulate and ventral striatum activity. *Human Brain Mapping, 31*, 458–469.

Simon, H., & Gilmartin, K. (1973). A simulation of memory for chess positions. *Cognitive Psychology, 5*, 29–46.

Simonet, P., Versteeg, D., & Storie, D. (2005). Dog-laughter: recorded playback reduces stress related behavior in shelter dogs. *Proceedings of the 7th International Conference on Environmental Enrichment*, July 31–August 5, 2005, 170–176.

Singley, M., & Anderson, J. (1989). *The transfer of cognitive skills.* Cambridge, MA: Harvard University Press.

Skinner, B. (1938). *The Behavior of Organisms: An Experimental Analysis.* New York: Appleton-Century-Crofts.

Skinner, B. (1951). How to teach animals. *Scientific American, 185*, 26–29.

Skinner, B. (1953). *Science and Human Behavior.* New York: Free Press.

Skinner, B. F. (1957). *Verbal bahavior.* New York: Appleton-Century-Crofts.

Skinner, B. F. (1958). Teaching machines. *Science, 128*, 969–977.

Skinner, B. F. (1979). *The shaping of a behaviorist: part two of an autobiography.* New York: Knopf.

Small, S., Chawla, M., Buonocore, M., Rapp, P., & Barnes, C. (2004). Imaging correlates of brain function in monkeys and rats isolates a hippocampal subregion differentially vulnerable to aging. *Proceedings of the National Academy of Sciences USA, 101*(18), 7181–7186.

Smith, C. N., & Squire, L. R. (2009). Medial temporal lobe activity during retrieval of semantic memory is related to the age of memory. *Journal of Neuroscience, 29*(4), 930–938.

Smith, D., Rapp, P., McKay, H., Roberts, J., & Tuszynski, M. (2004). Memory impairment in aged primates is associated with focal death of cortical neurons and atrophy of subcortical neurons. *Journal of Neuroscience, 24*(18), 4373–4381.

Smith, E. E. (1989). Concepts and induction. In M. I. Posner (Ed.), *Foundations of cognitive science* (pp. 501–526). Cambridge, MA: MIT Press.

Smith, E. E., & Jonides, J. (2003). Executive control and thought. *Fundamental neuroscience, 1377*–1394.

Smith, E.E. and Jonides, J. (1995). Working memory in humans: Neuropsychological evidence. In M. Gazzaniga (Ed.) *The cognitive neurosciences* (pp. 1009–1020). Cambridge, MA: MIT Press.

Smith, E.E. and Jonides, J. (1999). Storage and executive processes in the frontal lobes. *Science, 283*, 1657–1661.

Smith, E.E., & Jonides, J. (1997). Working memory: A view from neuroimaging. *Cognitive Psychology, 33*, 5–42.

Smith, I. M., & Bryson, S. E. (1994). Imitation and action in autism: a critical review. *Psychological Bulletin, 116*(2), 259–273.

Smith, I. M., & Bryson, S. E. (1998). Gesture imitation in autism I: nonsymbolic postures and sequences. *Cognitive Neuropsychology, 15*, 747–770.

Smith, M. (2005). Bilateral hippocampal volume reduction in adults with post-traumatic stress disorder: a meta-analysis of structural MRI studies. *Hippocampus, 15*, 798–807.

Smith, S. (1985). Background music and context-dependent memory. *American Journal of Psychology, 98,* 591–603.

Smotherman, W., & Robinson, S. (1992). Habituation in the rat fetus. *Quarterly Journal of Experimental Psychology B, 44B*(3–4), 215–230.

Snow, C. E., & Hoefnagel-Höhle, M. (1978). The critical period for language acquisition: evidence from second language learning. *Child Development, 49*(4), 1114–1128.

Soderstrom, N. C. & Bjork, R. A. (2015) Learning vs. performance: an integrative review. *Perspectives on Psychological Science, 10,* 176–199.

Soderstrom, N. C., McCabe, D. P., & Rhodes, M. G. (2012). Older adults predict more recollective experiences than younger adults. *Psychology and Aging, 27,* 1082–1088.

Sokolov, E. N. (1963). *Perception and the conditioned reflex.* Oxford, England: Pergamon Press.

Solanto, M., Arnsten., A, and Castellanos, F. (2000). The neuropharmacology of stimulant drugs: Implications for ADHD. New York: Oxford University Press.

Solomon, P., & Groccia-Ellison, M. (1996). Classic conditioning in aged rabbits: delay, trace and long-delay conditioning. *Behavioral Neuroscience, 110*(3), 427–435.

Solomon, P., & Moore, J. (1975). Latent inhibition and stimulus generalization of the classically conditioned nictitating membrane response in rabbits (Oryctolagus cuniculus) following dorsal hippocampal ablation. *Journal of Comparative and Physiological Psychology, 89,* 1192–1203.

Solomon, P., Pomerleau, D., Bennett, L., James, J., & Morse, D. (1989). Acquisition of the classically conditioned eyeblink response in humans over the life span. *Psychology and Aging, 4*(1), 34–41.

Somaiya, Ravi (2015) "Soldiers in Brian Williams's Group Give Account of 2003 Helicopter Attack." *New York Times,* February 8, 2015, page A17

Song, S. B. (2009). Consciousness and the consolidation of motor learning. *Behavioral Brain Research, 196,* 180–186.

Southgate, V., & Hamilton, A. F. D. (2008). Unbroken mirrors: challenging a theory of autism. *Trends in Cognitive Sciences, 12,* 225–229.

Spence, K. (1952). Clark Leonard Hull: 1884–1952. *American Journal of Psychology, 65,* 639–646.

Spence, K. W. (1937). The differential response in animals to stimuli varying within a single dimension. *Psychological Review, 44,* 430–444.

Spence, K. W. (1937). The differential response in animals to stimuli varying within a single dimension. *Psychological Review, 44,* 430–444.

Spetch, M. L., Cheng, K., & Clifford, C. W. G. (2004). Peak shift but not range effects in recognition of faces. *Learning & Motivation, 35,* 221–241.

Spiker, C. (1956). Experiments with children on the hypothesis of acquired distinctiveness and equivalence of cues. *Child Development, 27,* 253–263.

Squire, L. (1989). On the course of forgetting in very long-term memory. *Journal of Experimental Psychology: Learning, Memory and Cognition, 15*(2), 241–245.

Squire, L. (1992). Memory and the hippocampus: a synthesis from findings with rats, monkeys, and humans. *Psychological Review, 99*(2), 195–231.

Squire, L. & Alvarez, P. (1995). Retrograde amnesia and memory consolidation: An neurobiological perspective. *Current Opinion in Neurobiology, 5,* 169–177.

Squire, L. R., & Kandel, E. R. (2000). *Memory: from mind to molecules.* New York: Scientific American Library.

Squire, L. R., Wixted, J. T., & Clark, R. E. (2007). Recognition memory and the medial temporal lobe: a new perspective. *Nature Reviews Neuroscience, 8,* 872–883.

Squire, L., & Knowlton, B. (1995). Memory, hippocampus, and brain systems. In M. Gazzaniga (Ed.), *The cognitive neurosciences* (pp. 825–837). Cambridge, MA: MIT Press.

Squire, L., Cohen, N. J., & Zouzounis, J. A. (1984). Preserved memory in retrograde amnesia: sparing of a recently acquired skill. *Neuropsychologia, 22*(2), 145–152.

Squire, L., Knowlton, B., & Musen, G. (1993). The structure and organization of memory. *Annual Review of Psychology, 44,* 453–495.

Squire, L., Slater, P., & Chace, P. (1975). Retrograde amnesia: temporal gradient in very long term memory following electroconvulsive therapy. *Science, 1987,* 77–79.

Squire, L., Slater, P., & Miller, P. (1981). Retrograde amnesia and bilateral electroconvulsive therapy. *Archives of General Psychiatry, 38,* 89–95.

Staddon, J. (1995). On responsibility and punishment. *Atlantic Monthly, 275*(2), 88–94.

Stalnaker, T. A., Franz, T. M., Singh, T., & Schoenbaum, G. (2007). Basolateral amygdala lesions abolish orbitofrontal-dependent reversal impairments. *Neuron, 54*(1), 51–58.

Steele, C. & Aronson, J. (1995). Stereotype threat and the intellectual test performance of African Americans. *Journal of Personality and Social Psychology. 69*(5), 797–811

Steele, C. J., & Penhune, V. B. (2010). Specific increases within global decreases: a functional magnetic resonance imaging investigation of five days of motor sequence learning. *Journal of Neuroscience, 30,* 8332–8341.

Steele, K. (2003). Do rats show a Mozart effect? *Music Perception, 21*(2), 251–265.

Steele, K., Bass, K., & Crook, M. (1999). The mystery of the Mozart effect—failure to replicate. *Psychological Science, 10*(4), 366–369.

Stefanacci, L., Buffalo, E., Schmolck, H., & Squire, L. (2000). Profound amnesia after damage to the medial temporal lobe: a neuroanatomical and neuropsychological profile of patient EP. *Journal of Neuroscience, 20*(18), 7024–7037.

Steinmetz, J. E., Lavond, D. G., & Thompson, R. F. (1989). Classical conditioning in rabbits using pontine nucleus stimulation as a conditioned stimulus and inferior olive stimulation as an unconditioned stimulus. *Synapse, 3*, 225–233.

Steinvorth, S., Levine, B., & Corkin, S. (2005). Medial temporal lobe structures are needed to re-experience remote autobiographical memories: evidence from H.M. and W.R. *Neuropsychologia, 43*, 479–497.

Stephens, R. M., Metze, L. P., & Craig, J. R. (1975). The Protestant ethic effect in a multichoice environment. *Bulletin of the Psychonomic Society, 6*(2), 137–139.

Stern, S. A., & Alberini, C. M. (2013). Mechanisms of memory enhancement. *Wiley Interdisciplinary Reviews: Systems Biology and Medicine, 5*, 37–53.

Stern, Y., Albert, S., Tang, M., & Tsai, W. (1999). Rate of memory decline in AD is related to education and occupation: Cognitive reserve? *Neurology, 53*(9), 1942–1947.

Stoltz, S., & Lott, D. (1964). Establishment in rats of a persistent response producing a net loss of reinforcement. *Journal of Comparative and Physiological Psychology, 57*, 147–149.

Strack, F., Martin, L., & Stepper, S. (1988). Inhibiting and facilitating conditions of the human smile: a nonobtrusive test of the facial feedback hypothesis. *Journal of Personality and Social Psychology, 54*, 768–777.

Stroop. (1935) Studies of interference in serial verbal reactions. *Journal of Experimental Psychology, 18*, 643–662.

Subkov, A. A., & Zilov, G. N. (1937). The role of conditioned reflex adaptation in the origin of the hyperergic reactions. *Bulletin de Biologie et de Médecine Expérimentale, 4*, 294–296.

Sun, R., Slusarz, P., & Terry, C. (2005). The interaction of the explicit and the implicit in skill learning: a dual-process approach. *Psychological Review, 112*, 159–192.

Sunderland, A., Watts, K., Baddeley, A. D., & Harris, J. E. (1986). Subjective memory assessment and test performance in elderly adults. *Journal of Gerontology, 41*, 376–384.

Suñer-Soler, R., Grau, A., Gras, M. E., Font-Mayolas, S., Silva, Y., Dávalos, A., Cruz, V., Rodrigo, J. & Serena, J. (2012). *Stroke, 43*, 131–136.

Swan, G., Reed, T., Jack, L., Miller, B., Markee, T., Wolf, P., et al. (1999). Differential genetic influence for components of memory in aging adult twins. *Archives of Neurology, 56*, 1127–1132.

Tajudeen, B. A., Waltzman, S. B., Jethanamest, D., & Svirsky, M. A. (2010). Speech perception in congenitally deaf children receiving cochlear implants in the first year of life. *Otology & Neurotology, 31*, 1254–1260.

Takashima, A., Petersson, K. M., Rutters, F., Tendolkar, I., Jensen, O., Zwarts, M. J., et al. (2006). Declarative memory consolidation in humans: a prospective functional magnetic resonance imaging study. *Proceedings of the National Academy of Sciences USA, 103*, 756–761.

Talarico, J., & Rubin, D. (2003). Confidence, not consistency, characterizes flashbulb memories. *Psychological Science, 14*(5), 455–461.

Talbot, D. (2014). An artificial hand with real feeling. *MIT Technology Review, 117*, 49–53.

Tallal, P., Miller, S., Bedi, G., Byma, G., Wang, X., Nagarajan, S., Schreiner, C., Jenkins, W., & Merzenich, M. (1996). Language comprehension in language-learning impaired children improved with acoustically modified speech. *Science, 271*, 81–84.

Tallal, P., Stark, R. and Mellits, D. (1985). Identification of language-impaired children on the basis of rapid perception and production skills. *Brain and Language, 25*, 314–322.

Tamm, L., Menon, V., Reiss, A.L. (2006). Parietal attentional system aberrations during target detection in adolescents with attention deficit hyperactivity disorder: Event-related fMRI evidence. *American Journal of Psychiatry,163*(6), 1033–1043.

Tan, H. Y., Callicott, J. H., & Weinberger, D. R. (2007). Dysfunctional and compensatory prefrontal cortical systems, genes and the pathogenesis of schizophrenia. *Cerebral Cortex, 17*(suppl 1), i171-i181.

Tan, H.Y., Choo, W.C., Fones, C.S.L., & Chee, M.W.L. 2005. fMRI study of maintenance and manipulation processes within working memory in first-episode schizophrenia. *American Journal of Psychiatry, 162*,1849–1858.

Tan, H.Y., Sust, S, Buckholtz, J.W., Mattay, V.S., Meyer-Lindenberg, A.S., Egan, M.F., Weinberger, D.R., & Callicott, J.H. (2006). Dysfunctional prefrontal regional specialization and compensation in schizophrenia. *American Journal of Psychiatry, 163*, 1969–1977.

Tanaka, S. C., Balleine, B. W., & O'Doherty, J. P. (2008). Calculating consequences: Brain systems that encode the causal effects of actions. *Journal of Neuroscience, 28*(26), 6750–6755.

Taub, E., Uswatte, G., & Elbert, T. (2002). New treatments in neurorehabilitation founded on basic research. *Nature Reviews Neuroscience, 3*, 228–236.

Technau, G. (1984). Fiber number in the mushroom bodies of adult *Drosophila melanogaster* depends on age, sex and experience. *Journal of Neurogenetics, 1*, 13–26.

Temple E, Deutsch GK, Poldrack RA, Miller SL, Tallal P, Merzenich MM, Gabrieli JD. (2003). Neural deficits in children with dyslexia ameliorated by behavioral remediation: evidence from functional MRI. *Proceedings of the National Academy of Science, USA. 100*(5), 2860–5.

Terrace, H. S. (1963). Discrimination learning with and without "errors." *Journal of the Experimental Analysis of Behavior, 6*, 1–27.

Teter, B., & Finch, C. (2004). Caliban's heritance and the genetics of neuronal aging. *Trends in Neurosciences, 27*(10), 627–632.

Thomas, A. K., & Loftus, E. F. (2002). Creating bizarre false memories through imagination. *Memory and Cognition*, *30*(3), 423–431.

Thomas, M. S. C., & Johnson, M. H. (2008). New advances in understanding sensitive periods in brain development. *Current Directions in Psychological Science*, *17*(1), 1–5.

Thomas, R. (2002). *They cleared the lane: The NBA's black pioneers*. Lincoln, NE: University of Nebraska Press.

Thompson-Schill, S.L., D'Esposito, M., Aguirre, G.K., and Farah, M.J. (1997). Role of left inferior prefrontal cortex in retrieval of semantic knowledge: a reevaluation. *Proceedings of the National Academy of Sciences U.S.A.*, *94*, 14792–14797.

Thompson, C., & Cowan, T. (1986). Flashbulb memories: a nicer interpretation of a Neisser recollection. *Cognition*, *22*, 199–200.

Thompson, E. E., Carra, R., & Nicolelis, M. A. L. (2013). Perceiving invisible light through a somatosensory cortical prosthesis. *Nature Communications*, *4*, 1482.

Thompson, R. (1972). Sensory preconditioning. In R. Thompson & J. Voss (Eds.), *Topics in learning and performance* (pp. 105–129). New York: Academic Press.

Thompson, R. F. (1962). Role of cerebral cortex in stimulus generalization. *Journal of Comparative and Physiological Psychology. 55*, 279–287

Thompson, R. F. (1986). The neurobiology of learning and memory. *Science*, *233*, 941–947.

Thompson, R. F. (1986). The neurobiology of learning and memory. *Science*, *233*, 941–947.

Thompson, R. F. (2009). Habituation: a history. *Neurobiology of Learning and Memory*, *92*, 127–134.

Thompson, R. F., & Krupa, D. J. (1994). Organization of memory traces in the mammalian brain. *Annual Review of Neuroscience*, *17*, 519–549.

Thompson, R. F., & Krupa, D. J. (1994). Organization of memory traces in the mammalian brain. *Annual Review of Neuroscience*, *17*, 519–549.

Thompson, R. F., & Spencer, W. A. (1966). Habituation: a model phenomenon for the study of neuronal substrates of behavior. *Psychological Review*, *73*, 16–43.

Thompson, R. F., & Steinmetz, J. E. (2009). The role of the cerebellum in classical conditioning of discrete behavioral responses. *Neuroscience*, *162*, 732–755. doi:10.1016/j.neuroscience.2009.01.041

Thompson, R. F., & Steinmetz, J. E. (2009). The role of the cerebellum in classical conditioning of discrete behavioral responses. *Neuroscience*, *162*, 732–755. doi:10.1016/j.neuroscience.2009.01.041

Thompson, R.F. (1960). Function of auditory cortex of cat in frequency discrimination. *Journal of Neurophysiology*, *23*, 321–334.

Thompson, R.F. (1965). The neural basis of stimulus generalization. In D. Mostofsky (Ed.), *Stimulus generalization* (pp. 154–178). Stanford, CA: Stanford University Press.

Thompson, W. F., Schellenberg, E. G., & Husain, G. (2001). Arousal, mood, and the Mozart effect. *Psychological Science*, *12*, 248–251.

Thorndike, E. (1898). Animal intelligence: An experimental study of the associative processes in animals. *Psychological Review, Monograph 2, No. 8.*

Thorndike, E. (1911). *Animal intelligence*. New York: Macmillan.

Thorndike, E. (1932). *Fundamentals of Learning*. New York: Teachers College, Columbia University.

Thorndike, E. L. (1898). Animal intelligence: an experimental study of the associative processes in animals. *Psychological Review Monograph 2*(4), 1–8.

Thorndike, E. L. (1911). *Animal intelligence*. New York: Macmillan.

Thorndike, E. L. (1911). *Animal intelligence*. New York: Macmillan.

Thorndike, E. L. (1923). The variability of an individual in repetitions of the same task. *Journal of Experimental Psychology*, *6*, 161–167.

Thorndike, E. L. (1927). The law of effect. *American Journal of Psychology*, *39*, 212–222.

Thorndike, E. L. (1932). *The fundamentals of learning*. New York: Teachers College, Columbia University.

Thorndike, E. L. (1943). *Man and his works*. Cambridge: Harvard University Press.

Thorndike, E. L. (1949). *Selected writings from a connectionist's psychology*. New York: Appleton-Century-Crofts.

Thorndike, E. L., & Woodworth, R. (1901). The influence of improvement in one mental function upon the efficiency of other functions (I). *Psychological Review*, *8*, 247–261.

Thorpe, S. J., Rolls, E. T., & Maddison, S. (1983). The orbitofrontal cortex: neuronal activity in the behaving monkey. *Experimental Brain Research*, *49*(1), 93–115.

Thorpe, W. H. (1958). The learning of song patterns by birds with especial reference to the song of the chaffinch, *Fringilla coelebs. Ibis*, *100*, 535–570.

Thorpe, W. H. (1963). *Learning and instinct in animals*. Cambridge, MA: Harvard University Press.

Tijsseling, A. G. & Gluck, M. A. (2002). A connectionist approach to processing dimensional interaction. *Connection Science*, *14*, 1–48.

Timberlake, W. (1980). A molar equilibrium theory of learned performance. In G. Bower (Ed.), *The Psychology of Learning and Motivation* (Vol. 14, pp. 1–58). New York: Academic Press.

Timberlake, W., & Allison, J. (1974). Response deprivation: An empirical approach to instrumental performance. *Psychological Review, 81,* 146–164.

Tinbergen, N. (1951). *The Study of Instinct.* Oxford: Clarendon Press.

Tinbergen, N., & Kruyt, W. (1972). On the orientation of the digger wasp *Philanthus triangulum* Fabr. III. Selective learning of landmarks. In N. Tinbergen (Ed.), *The animal in its world.* Cambridge, MA: Harvard University Press. (Original work published 1938)

Titone D, Ditman T, Holzman, P. S., Eichenbaum H., Levy, D. L. (2004). Transitive inference in schizophrenia: Impairments in relational memory organization. *Schizophrenia Research, 68,* 235–247.

Titz, C., & Verhaeghen, P. (2010). Aging and directed forgetting in episodic memory: a meta-analysis. *Psychology and Aging, 25*(2), 405–411.

Tolman, E. C. (1932). *Purposive behavior in animals and men.* New York: Appleton-Century-Crofts.

Tolman, E. C. (1948). Cognitive maps in rats and men. *Psychological Review, 55,* 189–208.

Tolman, E. C., & Honzik, C. H. (1930). Introduction and removal of reward, and maze performance in rats. *University of California Publications in Psychology, 4,* 257–275.

Tomasello, M., Davis-Dasilva, M., Carnak, L., & Bard, K. A. (1987). Observational learning of tool-use by young chimpanzees. *Human Evolution, 2,* 175–183.

Toni, N., Laplagne, D. A., Zhao, C., Lombardi, G., Ribak, C. E. et al. (2008). Neurons born in the adult dentate gyrus form functional synapses with target cells. *Nature Neuroscience, 11,* 901–907.

Torriero, S., Oliveri, M., Koch, G., Lo Gerfo, E., Salerno, S., Ferlazzo, F., et al. (2011). Changes in cerebello-motor connectivity during procedural learning by actual execution and observation. *Journal of Cognitive Neuroscience, 23,* 338–348.

Trachtenberg, J., Chen, B., Knott, G., Feng, G., Sanes, J., Welker, E., et al. (2002). Long-term in vivo imaging of experience-dependent synaptic plasticity in adult cortex. *Nature, 420*(6917), 788–794.

Tranel, D., Damasio, A. R., Damasio, H., & Brandt, J. P. (1994). Sensorimotor skill learning in amnesia: additional evidence for the neural basis of nondeclarative memory. *Learning and Memory, 1,* 165–179.

Travers, J., Akey, L., Chen, S., Rosen, S., Paulson, G., & Travers, S. (1993). Taste preferences in Parkinson's disease patients. *Chemical Senses, 18,* 47–55.

Treffert, G. (2009). The savant syndrome: an extraordinary condition. A synopsis: past, present, future. *Philosophical Transactions of the Royal Society B: Biological Sciences, 364,* 1351–1357.

Tremblay, L., & Schultz, W. (1999). Relative reward preference in primate orbitofrontal cortex. *Nature, 398,* 704–708.

Tronson, N. C. & Taylor, J. R. (2007). Molecular mechanisms of memory reconsolidation. *Nature Reviews Neuroscience, 8,* 262–275.

Tryon, R. (1940). Genetic differences in maze learning in rats. *Yearbook of the National Society for the Study of Education, 39,* 111–119.

Tully, T. (1996). Discovery of genes involved with learning and memory: an experimental synthesis of Hirschian and Benzerian perspectives. *Proceedings of the National Academy of Sciences USA, 93,* 13460–13467.

Tulving, E. (1972). Episodic and semantic memory. In E. Tulving & W. Donaldson (Eds.), *Organization of memory* (pp. 381–403). New York: Academic Press.

Tulving, E. (1983). *Elements of episodic memory.* Oxford: Clarendon.

Tulving, E. (1985). Memory and consciousness. *Canadian Psychology, 26*(1), 1–12.

Tulving, E. (2002). Episodic memory: from mind to brain. *Annual Review of Psychology, 53,* 1–25.

Tulving, E., & Markowitsch, H. (1998). Episodic and declarative memory: role of the hippocampus. *Hippocampus, 8*(3), 198–204.

Tulving, E., & Schachter, D. L. (1990). Priming and human memory systems. *Science, 247,* 301–306.

Tulving, E., Schacter, D. L., & Stark, H. A. (1982). Priming effects in word-fragment completion are independent of recognition memory. Journal of Experimental Psychology: Learning, *Memory, and Cognition, 8,* 336–342.

Turner, A. P., & Martinek, T. J. (1999). An investigation into teaching games for understanding: effects on skill, knowledge, and game play. *Research Quarterly of Exercise and Sport, 70,* 286–296.

Turner, D. C., Robbins, T. W., Clark, L., Aron, A. R., Dowson, J., & Sahakian, B. J. (2003). Cognitive enhancing effects of modafinil in healthy volunteers. *Psychopharmocology, 165,* 260–269.

Turner, R. S., Grafton, S. T., Votaw, J. R., Delong, M. R., & Hoffman, J. M. (1998). Motor subcircuits mediating the control of movement velocity: a PET study. *Journal of Neurophysiology, 80,* 2162–2176.

Ungerleider, L.G., Courtney, S.M., & Haxby, J.V. (1998). A neural system for human visual working memory. *Proceedings of the National Academy of Sciences U.S.A., 95,* 883–890.

Unsworth, N., Redick, T. S., McMillan, B. D., Hambrick, D. Z., Kane, M. J., & Engle, R. W. (2015). Is playing video games related to cognitive abilities? *Psychological Science,* OnlineFirst.

Vaegan, T. (1979). Critical period for amblyopia in children. *Transactions of the Ophthalmological Societies of the United Kingdom, 99*(3), 432–439.

Vakil, E., Grunhaus, L., Nagar, I., Ben-Chaim, E., Dolberg, O. T., Dannon, P. N., et al. (2000). The effect of electroconvulsive therapy (ECT) on implicit memory: Skill learning and perceptual priming in patients with major depression. *Neuropsychologia, 38*(10), 1405–1414.

Vale-Martinez, A., Baxter, M. G., & Eichenbaum, H. (2002). Selective lesions of basal forebrain cholinergic neurons produce anterograde and retrograde deficits in a social transmission of food preference task in rats. *European Journal of Neuroscience, 16*(6), 983–998.

van Lehn, K. (1996). Cognitive skill acquisition. *Annual Review of Psychology, 47*, 513–539.

van Rossum, J. H. A. (1990). Schmidt's schema theory: the empirical base of the variability of practice hypothesis. *Human Movement Science, 9*, 387–435.

Vance, A. (2010 January 20). If your password is 123456, just make it HackMe. *New York Times*, p. A1.

Vanvuchelen, M., Schuerbeeck, L. V., Rpeyers, H., & De Weerdt, W. (2013). Understanding the mechanisms behind deficits in imitation: Do individuals with autism know 'what' to imitate and do they know 'how' to imitate? *Research in Developmental Disabilities, 34*, 538–545.

Vargha-Khadem, F., Gadian, D., Watkins, K., Connelly, A., Van Paesschen, W., & Mishkin, M. (1997). Differential effects of early hippocampal pathology on episodic and semantic memory. *Science, 277*, 376–380.

Velliste, M., Perel, S., Spalding, M. C, Whitford, A., & Schwartz, A. B. (2008). Cortical control of a prosthetic arm for self-feeding. *Nature, 453*, 1098–1101.

Vicari, S., Bellucci, S., & Carlesimo, G. (2000). Implicit and explicit memory: a functional dissociation in persons with Down syndrome. *Neuropsychologia, 38*, 240–251.

Vivar, C., Potter, M. C., Choi, J., Lee, J., Stringer, T. P., Callaway, E. M., et al. (2012). Monosynaptic inputs to new neurons in the dentate gyrus. *Nature Communications, 3*, 1107.

Volkow N, Wang G, Fowler J, Telang F, Maynard L, Logan J, et al. (2004). Evidence that methylphenidate enhances the saliency of a mathematical task by increasing dopamine in the human brain. *American Journal of Psychiatry, 161*(7), 1173–1180.

Volkow, N.D, Wang, G.J, Fowler, J.S., & Ding, Y.S. (2005). Imaging the effects of methylphenidate on brain dopamine: New model on its therapeutic actions for attention-deficit/hyperactivity disorder. *Biological Psychiatry, 57*(11), 1410–1415

Wade, K., Garry, M., Read, J., & Lindsay, S. (2002). A picture is worth a thousand words. *Psychonomic Bulletin and Review, 9*, 597–603.

Wagner, A. R. (1969). Stimulus validity and stimulus selection in associative learning. In N. J. Mackintosh & W. K. Honig (Eds.), *Fundamental issues in associative learning* (pp. 90–122). Halifax, Nova Scotia, Canada: Dalhousie University Press.

Wagner, A. R. (1981). SOP: a model of automatic memory processing in animal behavior. In N. Spear & G. Miller (Eds.), *Information processing in animals: memory mechanisms*. Hillsdale, NJ: Lawrence Erlbaum.

Wagner, A., Schacter, D., Rotte, M., Koutstaal, W., Maril, A., Dale, A., et al. (1998). Building memories: remembering and forgetting of verbal experiences as a function of brain activity. *Science, 281*, 1188–1191.

Wagner, A.D, Koutstaal, W. Maril, A., Schacter, D.L., and Buckner, R.L. (2000). Task- specific repetition priming in left inferior prefrontal cortex. *Cerebral Cortex, 10*, 1176–1184.

Wagner, A.D. (2002). Cognitive control and episodic memory. In L.R. Squire & D.L. Schacter (Eds.), Neuropsychology of Memory (third ed., pp. 174–192). New York: The Guilford Press.

Wagner, A.D., Desmond, J.E., Glover, G.H., Gabrieli, J.D. (1998). Prefrontal cortex and recognition memory. Functional-MRI evidence for context-dependent retrieval processes. *Brain, 121*(Pt 10): 1985–2002.

Wagner, A.D., Schacter, D.L., Rotte, M., Koutstaal, W., Maril, A., Dale, A.M., Rosen, B.R., & Buckner, R.L. (1998). Building memories: Remembering and forgetting of verbal experiences as predicted by brain activity. *Science, 281*, 1188–1191.

Waiter, G. D., Williams, J. H., Murray, A. D., Gilchrist, A., Perrett, D. I., & Whiten, A. (2004). A voxel-based investigation of brain structure in male adolescents with autistic spectrum disorder. *Neuroimage, 22*(2), 619–625.

Walker, M. P., Brakefield, T., Hobson, J. A., & Stickgold, R. (2003). Dissociable stages of human memory consolidation and reconsolidation. *Nature, 425*, 616–620.

Walker, M. P., Brakefield, T., Morgan, A., Hobson, J. A., & Stickgold, R. (2002). Practice with sleep makes perfect: sleep-dependent motor skill learning. *Neuron, 35*, 205–211.

Walker, M. P., Brakefield, T., Seidman, J., Morgan, A., Hobson, J. A., & Stickgold, R. (2003). Sleep and the time course of motor skill learning. *Learning and Memory, 10*, 275–284.

Walls, R., Zane, T., & Ellis, T. (1981). Forward and backward chaining, and whole task methods: Training assembly tasks in vocational rehabilitation. *Behavior Modification, 5*(61–74).

Waltz J. A., & Gold J. M. (2007). Probabilistic reversal learning impairments in schizophrenia: further evidence of orbitofrontal dysfunction. *Schizophrenia Research, 93*, 296–303.

Wang, S.-H., & Morris, R. G. M. (2010). Hippocampal-neocortical interactions in memory formation, consolidation, and reconsolidation. *Annual Review of Psychology, 61,* 49–79.

Waring, J. D. & Kensinger, E. A. (2009). Effects of emotional valence and arousal upon memory trade-offs with aging. *Psychology and Aging, 24,* 412–422.

Waring, J. D. & Kensinger, E. A. (2011). Howe emotion leads to selective memory: neuroimaging evidence. *Neuropsychologia, 49,* 1831–1842.

Warner, E. E. & Hall, D. J. (1974). Optimal foraging and the size selection of prey by the bluegill sunfish (*Lepornis Macrochirus*). *Ecology, 55,* 1042–1052.

Watanabe, S., Sakamoto, J., & Wakita, M. (1995). Pigeons' discrimination of paintings by Monet and Picasso. *Journal of the Experimental Analysis of Behavior, 63,* 165–174.

Waterhouse, L., Fein, D., & Modahl, C. (1996). Neurofunctional mechanisms in autism. *Psychological Review, 103,* 457–489.

Watson, J. B. (1907). Kinaesthetic and organic sensations: their role in the reactions of the white rat to the maze (monograph supplement). *Psychological Review, 4,* 211–212.

Watson, J. B. (1913). Psychology as the behaviorist sees it. *Psychological Review, 23,* 158–177.

Watson, J. B. (1924). *Behaviorism.* New York: Norton.

Watson, J., & Rayner, R. (2000 [1920]). Conditioned emotional reactions. Journal of *Experimental Psychology, 3,* 1–14 (reprinted 2000 in *American Psychologist, 2055*(2003), 2313–2317).

Weatherly, J. N., Plumm, K. M., Smith, J. R., & Roberts, W. A. (2002). On the determinants of induction in responding for sucrose when food pellet reinforcement is upcoming. *Animal Learning and Behavior, 30*(4), 315–329.

Weeks, D. L., & Kordus, R. N. (1998). Relative frequency of knowledge of performance and motor skill learning. *Research Quarterly for Exercise and Sports, 69,* 224–230.

Weiler, J. A., Bellebaum, C., Brune, M., Juckel, G., & Daum, I. (2009). Impairment of probabilistic reward-based learning in schizophrenia. *Neuropsychology, 23*(5), 571–580.

Weinberger, D. R., Berman, K. F., & Zec, R. F. (1986). Physiologic dysfunction of dorsolateral prefrontal cortex in schizophrenia: I. Regional cerebral blood flow evidence. *Archives of general psychiatry, 43*(2), 114–124.

Weinberger, N. (1977). Learning-induced receptive field plasticity in the primary auditory cortex. *Seminars in Neuroscience, 9,* 59–67.

Weinberger, N. (1993). Learning-induced changes of auditory receptive fields. *Current Opinion in Neurobiology, 3,* 570–577.

Weinberger, N. M. (2004). Specific long-term memory traces in primary auditory cortex. *Nature Reviews Neuroscience, 5*(4), 279–90.

Weinberger, N. M. (2003). The nucleus basalis and memory codes: auditory cortical plasticity and the induction of specific, associative behavioral memory. *Neurobiology of Learning and Memory. 80*(3), 268–84.

Weinberger, N. M. (2007). Auditory associative memory and representational plasticity in the primary auditory cortex. *Hearing Research, 229,* 54–68.

Wells, G. L., Memon, A., & Penrod, S. D. (2006). Eyewitness evidence: improving its probative value. *Psychological Science in the Public Interest, 7*(2), 45–75.

Werchan, D. M., Collins, A. G. E., Frank, M. J., & Amso, D. (2015). 8-month-old infants spontaneously learn and generalize hierarchical rules. *Psychological Science 26,* 805–815.

Werker, J. F., & Tees, R. C. (1984). Cross-language speech perception: evidence for perceptual reorganization during the 1st year of life. *Infant Behavior and Development, 7,* 49–63.

Werker, J., & Tees, R. (1999). Influences on infant speech processing: Toward a new synthesis. *Annual Review of Psychology, 50,* 509–535.

West, M. (1993). Regionally specific loss of neurons in the aging human hippocampus. *Neurobiology of Aging, 14*(4), 287–293.

Whitehead, A., Perdomo, C., Pratt, R. D., Birks, J., Wilcock, G. K., & Evans, J. G. (2004). Donepezil for the symptomatic treatment of patients with mild to moderate Alzheimer's disease: a meta-analysis of individual patient data from randomised controlled trials. *International Journal of Geriatric Psychiatry, 19,* 624–633.

Whiten, A., & Boesch, C. (2001). The cultures of chimpanzees. *Scientific American, 284*(1), 60–67.

Whiten, A., & Brown, J. (1999). Imitation and the reading of other minds: perspectives from the study of autism, normal children and non-human primates. In S. Braten (Ed.), *Intersubjective communication and emotion in early ontogeny* (pp. 260–280). Cambridge, England: Cambridge University Press.

Whiten, A., Custance, D. M., Gomez, J. C., Teixidor, P., & Bard, K. A. (1996). Imitative learning of artificial fruit processing in children (*Homo sapiens*) and chimpanzees (*Pan troglodytes*). *Journal of Comparative Psychology, 110*(1), 3–14.

Whiten, A., Goodall, J., McGrew, W. C., Nishida, T., Reynolds, V., Sugiyama, Y., et al. (1999). Cultures in chimpanzees. *Nature, 399,* 682–685.

Whiten, A., Horner, V., Litchfield, C. A., & Marshall-Pescini, S. (2004). How do apes ape? *Learning and Behavior, 32*(1), 36–52.

Wichers, M., Geschwind, N., Jacobs, N., Kenis, G., Peeters, F., Derom, C., Thiery, E., Delespaul, P., & van Os, J. (2009). Transition from stress sensitivity to depressive state: longitudinal twin study. *British Journal of Psychiatry, 195,* 498–503.

Wickelgren, W. (1966). Phonemic similarity and interference in short-term memory for single letters. *Journal of Experimental Psychology, 71*(3), 396–404.

Wickens, J. R. (2009). Synaptic plasticity in the basal ganglia. *Behav Brain Res, 199*(1), 119–128.

Wiesel, T. N. & Hubel, D. H. (1963). Single-cell responses in striate cortex of kittens deprived of vision in one eye. *Journal of Neurophysiology. 26,* 1003–17.

Wightman, D., & Sistrunk, F. (1987). Part-task training strategies in simulated carrier landing final-approach training. *Human Factors, 29,* 245–254.

Williams, A. M., Davids, K., Burwitz, L., & Williams, J. (1992). Perception and action in sport. *Journal of Human Movement Studies, 22,* 147–204.

Williams, B. A. (2001). Two-factor theory has strong empirical evidence of validity. *Journal of the Experimental Analysis of Behavior, 75*(3), 362–365.

Williams, G.V. and Goldman-Rakic, P.S. (1995). Modulation of memory fields by dopamine D1 receptors in prefrontal cortex. *Nature, 376*(6541), 572–5.

Williams, J. H., Whiten, A., & Singh, T. (2004). A systematic review of action imitation in autistic spectrum disorder. *Journal of Autism and Developmental Disorders, 34*(3), 285–299.

Williams, J. H., Whiten, A., Suddendorf, T., & Perrett, D. I. (2001). Imitation, mirror neurons and autism. *Neuroscience and Biobehavioral Review, 25,* 287–295.

Williams, L., Phillips, M., Brammer, M., Skerrett, D., Lagopoulos, J., Rennie, C., et al. (2001). Arousal dissociates amygdala and hippocampal fear responses: evidence from simultaneous fMRI and skin conductance recording. *Neuroimage, 14*(5), 1070–1079.

Williams, Z. M., Bush, G., Rauch, S. L., Cosgrove, G. R., & Eskandar, E. N. (2004). Human anterior cingulate neurons and the integration of monetary reward with motor responses. *Nature Neuroscience, 7,* 1370–1375.

Willingham, D. B. (1999). Implicit motor sequence learning is not purely perceptual. *Memory and Cognition, 27,* 561–572.

Wills, A. J., & McLaren, I. (1997). Generalization in human category learning: A connectionist account of differences in gradient after discriminative and non-discriminative training. *QJEP, 50A,* 607–630.

Wills, S., & Mackintosh, N. J. (1998). Peak shift on an artificial dimension. *Quarterly Journal of Experimental Psychology, 51B,* 1–31.

Wilson F.A., Scalaidhe, S.P., Goldman-Rakic, P.S. (1993). Dissociation of object and spatial processing domains in primate prefrontal cortex. *Science, 260,* 1955–1958.

Wilson, B., & Wearing, D. (1995). Prisoner of consciousness: a state of just awakening following herpes simplex encephalitis. In R. Campbell & M. Conway (Eds.), *Broken memories: case studies in memory impairments* (pp. 14–30). Cambridge, MA: Blackwell.

Wilson, R. S., Beckett, L. A., Barnes, L. L., Schneider, J. A., Bach, J., Evans, D. A. & Bennett, D. A. (2002). Individual differences in rates of change in cognitive abilities of older persons. *Psychology and Aging, 17,* 179–193.

Wilson, R., & Bennett, D. (2003). Cognitive activity and risk of Alzheimer's disease. *Current Directions in Psychological Science, 12*(3), 87–91.

Wilson, T., & Brown, T. (1997). Reexamination of the effect of Mozart's music on spatial-task performance. *Journal of Psychology 131,* 365–370.

Winek, C. L., Wahaba, W. W., & Rozin, L. (1999). Heroin fatality due to penile injection. *American Journal of Forensic Medicine and Pathology, 20,* 90–92.

Winocur, G., Moscovitch, M. & Bontempi, B. (2010). Memory formation and long-term retention in humans and animals: Convergence towards a transformation account of hippocampal-neocortical interactions. *Neuropsychologia, 48,* 2339–2356.

Winocur, G., Wojtowicz, J. M., Sekeres, M., Snyder, J. S., & Wang, S. (2006). Inhibition of neurogenesis interferes with hippocampus-dependent memory function. *Hippocampus, 16*(3), 296–304.

Wise, R. A. (2004). Dopamine, learning and motivation. *Nature Reviews Neuroscience, 5,* 483–494.

Wiseman, F. K., Alford, K. A., Tybulewicz, V. L. J., & Fisher, E. M. C. (2009). Down syndrome—recent progress and future prospects. *Human Molecular Genetics, 18*(Review Issue 1), R75–R83.

Wiskott, L., Rasch, M., & Kempermann, G. (2006). A functional hypothesis for adult hippocampal neurogenesis: avoidance of catastrophic interference in the dentate gyrus. *Hippocampus, 16*(3), 329–343.

Wisniewski, M. G, Church, B. A., & Mercado, Eduardo III. (**2009**). **Learning-related shifts in generalization gradients for complex sounds. Learning & Behavior. 37** (4). 325–335.

Wittenberg, G. F., & Schaechter, J. D. (2009). The neural basis of constraint-induced movement therapy. *Current Opinion in Neurology, 22,* 582–588.

Wolf, S. L., Thompson, P. A., Winstein, C. J., Miller, J. P., Blanton, S. R., Nichols-Larsen, D. S., et al. (2010). The EXCITE stroke trial comparing early and delayed constraint-induced movement therapy. *Stroke, 41,* 2309–2315.

Wood, D. (1989). Social interaction as tutoring. In M. H. Bornstein & J. S. Bruner (Eds.), *Interaction in human development.* Cambridge, MA: Harvard University Press.

Wood, E.R., Dudchenko, P.A., Eichenbaum, H. (1999). The global record of memory in hippocampal neuronal activity. *Nature, 397,* 613–616.

Woodruff-Pak, D. S., & Lemieux, S. K. (2001). The cerebellum and associative learning: parallels and contrasts in rabbits and humans. In J. E. Steinmetz, M. A. Gluck, & P. F. Solomon (Eds.), *Model systems of associative learning: a festschrift for Richard F. Thompson* (pp. 271–294). Mahwah, NJ: Lawrence Erlbaum.

Woodruff-Pak, D. S., & Lemieux, S. K. (2001). The cerebellum and associative learning: parallels and contrasts in rabbits and humans. In J. E. Steinmetz, M. A. Gluck, & P. F. Solomon (Eds.), *Model systems of associative learning: a festschrift for Richard F. Thompson* (pp. 271–294). Mahwah, NJ: Lawrence Erlbaum.

Woodruff-Pak, D., & Sheffield, J. (1987). Age differences in Purkinje cells and rate of classical conditioning in young and older rabbits. *Society for Neuroscience Abstracts, 13,* 41.

Woodruff-Pak, D., & Thompson, R. (1988). Classical conditioning of the eyeblink response in the delay paradigm in adults aged 18–83. *Psychology and Aging, 3,* 219–229.

Woodruff-Pak, D., Logan, C., & Thompson, R. (1990). Neurobiological substrates of classical conditioning across the life span. *Annals of the New York Academy of Sciences, 608,* 150–178.

Woolley, C., Weiland, N., McEwen, B., & Schwartzkroin, P. (1997). Estradiol increases the sensitivity of hippocampal CA1 pyramidal cells to NMDA receptor-mediated synaptic input: correlatin with spine density. *Journal of Neuroscience, 17,* 1848–1859.

Wulf, G., & Schmidt, R. A. (1997). Variability of practice and implicit motor learning. *Journal of Experimental Psychology: Learning, Memory and Cognition, 23,* 987–1006.

Wylie, G. R., Foxe, J. J., & Taylor, T. L. (2008). Forgetting as an active process: an fMRI investigation of item-method-directed forgetting. *Cerebral Cortex, 18*(3), 670–682.

Xiang, J.-Z., & Brown, M. W. (1998). Differential encoding of novelty, familiarity and recency in regions of the anterior temporal lobe. *Neuropharmacology, 37,* 657–676.

Xu, F. & Kushnir, T. (2013). Infants are rational constructivist learners. *Current Directions in Psychological Science, 22,* 28–32.

Xu, X., Aron, A., Brown, L., Cao, G., Feng, T., & Weng, X. (2011). Reward and motivation systems: A brain mapping study of early-stage intense romantic love in Chinese participants. *Human Brain Mapping, 32,* 249–257.

Yang, Y., Kim, J. S., Kim, Y. K., Kwak, Y. T., & Han, I. W. (2009). Cerebellar hypoperfusion during transient global amnesia: an MRI and oculographic study. *Journal of Clinical Neurology, 5*(2), 74–80.

Yarrow, K., Brown, P., & Krakauer, J. W. (2009). Inside the brain of an elite athlete: the neural processes that support high achievement in sports. *Nature Reviews Neuroscience, 10,* 585–596.

Yin, H. H., Mulcare, S. P., Hilario, M. R. F., Clouse, E., Holloway, T., Davis, M. I., et al. (2009). Dynamic reorganization of striatal circuits during the acquisition and consolidation of a skill. *Nature Neuroscience, 12,* 333–341.

Yin, J. C. P., Wallach, J. S., Del Vecchio, M., Wilder, E. L., Zhuo, H., Quinn, W. G., & Tully, T. (1994). Induction of dominant negative CREB transgene specifically blocks long-term memory in *Drosophila. Cell, 79,* 49–58.

Youn, G. (2006). Subjective sexual arousal in response to erotica: effects of gender, guided fantasy, erotic stimulus, and duration of exposure. *Archives of Sexual Behavior, 35,* 87–97.

Younger, J., Aron, A., Parke, S., Chatterjee, N., & Mackey, S. (2010). Viewing pictures of a romantic partner reduces experimental pain: Involvement of neural reward systems. *PLoS ONE, 5*(10), e13309.

Zajonc, R. (1980). Feeling and thinking: preferences need no inferences. *American Psychologist, 35,* 151–175.

Zajonc, R. (1984). On the primacy of affect. *American Psychologist, 39,* 117–123.

Zentall, T. R. (2006). Mental time travel in animals: a challenging question. *Behavioural Processes, 72*(2), 173–183.

Zentall, T. R., Singer, R. A., & Stagner, J. P. (2008). Episodic-like memory: pigeons can report location pecked when unexpectedly asked. *Behavioural Processes, 79*(2), 93–98.

Zhou, W. & Crystal, J. D. (2011) Validation of a rodent model of episodic memory. *Animal Cognition, 14,* 325–340.

Zola-Morgan, S., Squire, L., & Amaral, D. (1986). Human amnesia and the medial temporal region: enduring memory impairments following a bilateral lesion limited to field CA1 of the hippocampus. *Journal of Neuroscience, 6*(10), 2950–2967.

Zupanc, G. (2001). A comparative approach towards the understanding of adult neurogenesis. *Brain, Behavior and Evolution, 58,* 246–249.

SUBJECT INDEX

Acetylcholine (ACh), 250
Acoustic startle reflex, 73
Acquired equivalence, 232–233, 255–256
Activity-dependent enhancement, 156
Addictions
  behavioral, 204
  classical conditioning in tolerance to drugs, 159–161
  pathological, 203
Adolescence/adolescents, 483
  brain in, 496–499
  and crossing to adulthood, 483–485
  male-female differences in learning and memory, 484–485
  maturation of working memory, 483–484
  prefrontal cortex in, 496–497
  sex hormones, effects on brain organization, 497–499
Adulthood/adults
  adult neurogenesis and neurons for old brains, 503–504
  aging memory through, 485–488
  brain in, 499–504
  conditioning in aging, 486
  crossing from childhood to, 483–485
  localized neuron and synapse loss, 499–501
  loss of synaptic stability, 501–503
  skill learning in aging, 486
Adult neurogenesis, 503–504
Aging and metamemory, 488. *See also* Aging memory; Development and aging
Aging memory. *See also* Development and aging
  from adulthood through old age, 485–488
  conditioning in aging adults, 486
  episodic and semantic memory, 487–488
  metamemory and aging, 488
  old memories *vs.* new learning and, 487–488
  skill learning in aging adults, 486
  working memory in aging adults, 486
Allele, 489
Alzheimer's disease, 507–513
  defined, 508
  diagnosis of, 511
  Down syndrome and, connection between, 513–514
  genetic basis of, 512
  plaques and tangles in brain, 508–511
  progressive memory loss and cognitive deterioration, 508
  treatment of, 511
Amnesia, 268

anterograde, 292
  functional, 304–306
  retrograde, 296
  transient global, 302, 302–304
Amygdala, 416
  central nucleus for emotional response expression, 416–418
  as central processing station for emotions, 416–425
  emotional learning pathways in, 418–420
  episodic memory storage and, 420–421
  retrieval and reconsolidation of memories and, 423–425
  stress hormones and, 421–423
Amyloid plaque, 508
Androgen, 485
Animals
  hippocampus in, 101–102, 101f, 154f
  models of Down syndrome, 507
  nonhuman emotions in, 402–404
Anterograde amnesia, 292
Aplysia
  classical conditioning in, 111, 155t, 156–158, 156t
  habituation in, 155t
  sensitization in, 155t
  varieties of learning in, 155t
Apoptosis, 494
Appetitive conditioning, 119, 121, 124
Aristotle, 4–5. 5f, 6t
Arousal, 397
  autonomic, 397–398
Association, 4–6, 129
  extinguishing old, 127–128
  learned, 172–180
Association cortex, 290
Associationism, 4–5, 8–10
Associative bias, 145–146
Associative stage, 323
Associative weight, 134
Attention deficit/hyperactivity disorder (ADHD), 389–391
Autism spectrum disorder (autism), 464–467
  defined, 464
Autonomic arousal, 397–398
Autonomic nervous system (ANS), 398
Autonomous stage, 323
Aversive conditioning, 119–121, 124
Avoidance conditioning, 406
Avoidance learning, theories of, 407–408
Axon, 41, 41f

Bandura's Bobo doll experiment, 441–442, 457
Basal forebrain, 300–301

Basal ganglia, 209
  brain activity during cognitive skill learning, 336–337
  learning deficits after lesions, 333–335
  neural activity during perceptual-motor skill learning, 335–336
  and skill learning, 332–337
Behavior
  behavioral economics and bliss point, 189–190
  changes following frontal lobe damage, 372–373
  choice, 188–192
  differential reinforcement of alternative, 179
  media's impact on, 456–458
  Premack principle and reinforcement response, 190–192
  stimulation as substitute for training, 150–151
  variable-interval schedules and matching law, 188–189
Behavioral addictions, 204
Behavioral economics, 189–190
Behavioral processes
  classical conditioning and, 117–147
  cognitive control, 352–371
  concept formation, 214–243
  development and aging and, 474–489
  discrimination learning, 214–243
  emotional influences on learning and memory, 396–415
  episodic and semantic memory, 268–290
  familiarization, 72–91
  generalization, 214–243
  habituation, 72–91
  operant conditioning and, 168–192, 207
  semantic memory and, 268–290
  skill memory, 312–331
  social learning and memory, 440–459
  working memory, 352–371
Behaviorism, 18–23
  cognitive approach to, 24
  defined, 18
  Estes and, 24
  Hull and, 20
  John Watson and, 18–19
  mathematical models of learning and, 20
  neo-, 22–23
  radical, 21–22
  reign of, 18–23
  Skinner and, 21–22, 31
  Tolman and, 22–23
  Watson and, 18–19, 31, 36, 429